Lecture Notes in Artificial Intelligence   3339

Edited by J. G. Carbonell and J. Siekmann

Subseries of Lecture Notes in Computer Science

Geoffrey I. Webb Xinghuo Yu (Eds.)

AI 2004: Advances in Artificial Intelligence

17th Australian Joint Conference on Artificial Intelligence
Cairns, Australia, December 4-6, 2004
Proceedings

 Springer

Series Editors

Jaime G. Carbonell, Carnegie Mellon University, Pittsburgh, PA, USA
Jörg Siekmann, University of Saarland, Saarbrücken, Germany

Volume Editors

Geoffrey I. Webb
Monash University
School of Computer Science and Software Engineering
Clayton, Victoria, 3800, Australia
E-mail: webb@infotech.monash.edu.au

Xinghuo Yu
Royal Melbourne Institute of Technology
School of Electrical and Computer Engineering
City Campus, GPO Box 2476V, Melbourne, VIC 3001, Australia
E-mail: x.yu@rmit.edu.au

Library of Congress Control Number: 2004116040

CR Subject Classification (1998): I.2, F.4.1, H.3, H.2.8, F.1

ISSN 0302-9743
ISBN 3-540-24059-4 Springer Berlin Heidelberg New York

This work is subject to copyright. All rights are reserved, whether the whole or part of the material is concerned, specifically the rights of translation, reprinting, re-use of illustrations, recitation, broadcasting, reproduction on microfilms or in any other way, and storage in data banks. Duplication of this publication or parts thereof is permitted only under the provisions of the German Copyright Law of September 9, 1965, in its current version, and permission for use must always be obtained from Springer. Violations are liable to prosecution under the German Copyright Law.

Springer is a part of Springer Science+Business Media

springeronline.com

© Springer-Verlag Berlin Heidelberg 2004
Printed in Germany

Typesetting: Camera-ready by author, data conversion by Scientific Publishing Services, Chennai, India
Printed on acid-free paper   SPIN: 11365884   06/3142   5 4 3 2 1 0

Preface

AI 2004 was the seventeenth in the series of annual Australian artificial intelligence conferences. This conference is the major forum for artificial intelligence research in Australia. It has consistently attracted strong international participation. This year more than two thirds of the submissions were from outside Australia.

The current volume is based on the proceedings of AI 2004. A total of 340 papers were submitted, which we believe to be a substantial increase on previous submission numbers to this series. A national and international program committee refereed full-length versions of all submitted papers. Each accepted paper was reviewed by at least three reviewers. Of these 340 submissions, 78 were accepted for oral presentation and a further 62 for poster presentation. This volume contains a regular paper of up to 12 pages length for each oral presentation and a short paper of up to 6 pages length for each poster presentation.

In addition to the scientific track represented here, the conference featured an exciting program of tutorials and workshops, and plenary talks by four outstanding invited speakers: Mehran Sahami (Google Inc. and Stanford University, USA), Michael J. Pazzani (National Science Foundation and University of California, Irvine, USA), Paul Compton (University of New South Wales, Australia) and Ah Chung Tsoi (Australian Research Council, Australia). AI 2004 was collocated with Complex 2004, the 7th Asia-Pacific Conference on Complex Systems, with the aim of promoting cross-fertilization and collaboration in areas of complex and intelligent systems.

AI 2004 was hosted by the Central Queensland University, Australia, which provided generous financial and organizational support. Particular mention goes to the Conference General Chair, Russel Stonier, the Local Organizing Committee Secretary, Jeni Richardson, the Web Tech Chair, Jason Bell, the Publicity Chair, Dianhui Wang, the Tutorials Chair, Graham Williams, and the Workshops Chair, Andrew Jennings, whose selfless work was critical to the conference's success. We wish to thank Michelle Kinsman whose efficient organization kept the program committee's operations on track. We are also grateful for the support of John Debenham and the Australian Computer Society's National Committee for Artificial Intelligence and Expert Systems. Thanks also go to Alfred Hofmann and the team from Springer, who were responsible for the timely production and delivery of the conference proceedings. Finally, we thank the members of the Program Committee and the panel of reviewers who produced some 1,020 reviews under tight time constraints. The ongoing quality and success of this conference series is due to your efforts.

December 2004   Geoff Webb and Xinghuo Yu

Organization

AI 2004 was hosted by the Central Queensland University, Australia.

Executive Committee

Conference General Chair	Russel Stonier (Central Queensland University)
Advisory Co-chairs	Xinghuo Yu (RMIT University)
	John Debenham (University of Technology, Sydney)
	David Green (Monash University)
Program Chairs	Geoffrey I. Webb (Monash University)
	Xinghuo Yu (RMIT University)
Local Organizing Committee Secretary:	Jeni Richardson (Central Queensland University)
Tutorials Chair	Graham Williams (Australian Tax Office)
Workshops Chair	Andrew Jennings (RMIT University)
Publicity Chair	Dianhui Wang (La Trobe University)
Web Tech Chair	Jason Bell (Central Queensland University)

Program Committee

Abbass, Dr. Hussein A. ADFA, Australia
Alahakoon, Dr. Damminda, Monash, Australia
Albrecht, Dr. David, Monash, Australia
Alem, Dr. Leila, CSIRO, Australia
Bailey, Dr. James, Melbourne, Australia
Bain, Dr. Mike, UNSW, Australia
Barnes, Dr. Nick, NICTA, Australia
Barone, Dr. Luigi, UWA, Australia
Baxter, Dr. Rohan, ATO, Australia
Bennamoun, Assoc. Prof. Mohammed, UWA, Australia
Brain, Dr. Damien, Deakin, Australia
Brooks, Prof. Michael, Adelaide, Australia
Cameron-Jones, Dr. Mike, UTas, Australia
Cassidy, Dr. Steve, Macquarie, Australia
Corbett, Dr. Dan, SAIC, USA
Ciesielski, Assoc. Prof. Vic, RMIT, Australia
Dale, Prof. Robert, Macquarie, Australia
Dai, Dr. Honghua, Deakin, Australia

Debenham, Prof. John, UTS, Australia
Dowe, Assoc. Prof. David, Monash, Australia
Ford, Dr. Marilyn, Griffith, Australia
Fung, Assoc. Prof. Lance Chun Che, Murdoch, Australia
Gedeon, Prof. Tamas (Tom), ANU, Australia
Georgeff, Prof. Michael, Monash, Australia
Gopalan, Dr. Raj, Curtin, Australia
Goss, Dr. Simon, DSTO, Australia
Governatori, Dr. Guido, UQ, Australia
Hegland, Dr. Markus, ANU, Australia
Hendtlass, Prof. Tim, Swinburne, Australia
Hingston, Dr. Philip, ECU, Australia
Jarvis, Prof. Raymond A., Monash, Australia
Jennings, Prof. Andrew, RMIT, Australia
Kasabov, Prof. Nikola, KEDRI, New Zealand
Kendall, Dr. Graham, Nottingham, UK
Khan, Dr. Shamim, Murdoch, Australia
Kim, Prof. Jong-Hwan, KAIST, Korea
King, Assoc. Prof. Irwin, Chinese University, Hong Kong
Korb, Dr. Kevin, Monash, Australia
Leckie, Dr. Chris, Melbourne, Australia
Lee, Assoc. Prof. Vincent CS, Monash, Australia
Li, Dr. Wei, CQU, Australia
Li, Dr. Xiaodong, RMIT, Australia
Li, Dr. Yuefeng, QUT, Australia
MacNish, Dr. Cara, UWA, Australia
Maire, Dr. Frederic, QUT, Australia
Marriott, Prof. Kim, Monash, Australia
McKay, Dr. Bob, ADFA, Australia
Meyer, Dr. Thomas, NICTA, Australia
Mitchell, Dr. Matthew, Monash, Australia
Mohammadian, Dr. Masoud, UC, Australia
Nayak, Dr. Abhaya, Macquarie, Australia
Newlands, Dr. Douglas, Deakin, Australia
Nicholson, Dr. Ann, Monash, Australia
Ong Sing, Assoc. Prof. Goh, NTCU, Malaysia
Orgun, Assoc. Prof. Mehmet, Macquarie, Australia
Padgham, Assoc. Prof. Lin, RMIT, Australia
Pagnucco, Dr. Maurice, UNSW, Australia
Pearce, Dr. Adrian, Melbourne, Australia
Prokopenko, Dr. Mikhail, CSIRO, Australia
Roddick, Prof. John, Flinders, Australia
Rolfe, Dr. Bernard, Deakin, Australia
Sarker, Dr. Ruhul, ADFA, Australia
Sattar, Prof. Abdul, Griffth, Australia

Shi, Prof. Zhongzhi, Chinese Academy of Sciences, China
Simoff, Assoc. Prof. Simeon, UTS, Australia
Sitte, Assoc. Prof. Joaquin, QUT, Australia
Slaney, Dr. John, ANU, Australia
Sonenberg, Prof. Liz, Melbourne, Australia
Soubeiga, Dr. Eric, Nottingham, UK
Squire, Dr. David, Monash, Australia
Stumptner, Prof. Markus, Uni SA, Australia
Thornton, Dr. John, Griffith, Australia
Tsoi, Prof. Ah Chung, ARC, Australia
Wagner, Prof. Michael, University of Canberra, Australia
Walsh, Prof. Toby, UCC, Ireland
Wang, Assoc. Prof. Lipo, NTU, Singapore
Wang, Dr. Dianhui, LaTrobe, Australia
West, Prof. Geoff, Curtin, Australia
Wiles, Assoc. Prof. Janet, UQ, Australia
Williams, Dr. Graham, ATO, Australia
Williams, Prof. Mary-Anne, UTS, Australia
Wobcke, Assoc. Prof. Wayne, UNSW, Australia
Wong, Dr. Kok Wai Kevin, NTU, Singapore
Wu, Dr. Baolin, Swinburne, Australia
Xu, Dr. Yue, QUT, Australia
Zhang, Prof. Chenqi, UTS, Australia
Zhang, Assoc. Prof. Minjie, UOW, Australia
Zhang, Assoc. Prof. Yan, UWS, Australia
Zukerman, Assoc. Prof. Ingrid, Monash, Australia

Panel of Reviewers

Alsteris, Leigh
Anvar, Amir
Badham, Jennifer
Bain, Stuart
Bastian, John
Billlington, David
Blackburn, Terence
Blumenstein, Michael
Boyd, Sarah
Butler, Shane
Cao, Longbing
Chen, Jie
Chen, Wanli
Chojnacki, Wojtek
Choy, Faith

Collie, Greg
Collie, McGregor
Cregan, Anne
Dale, Michael
Dam, Helen
Davis, Anton
Di Pietro, Anthony
Dick, Anthony
Estivill Castro, Vladimir
Fan, Hongjian
Farr, Graham
Fenwick, Joel
French, Tim
Garcia de la Banda, Maria

Gawley, Darren
George, Martyn
George, Susan
Grundy, Ian
Hang, Xiaoshu
He, Hongxing
Hill, Rhys
Hope, Luke
Howard, Catherine
Huang, Faliang
Huband, Simon
Hu, Hong
Innes, Andrew
Iorio, Antony
Irlicht, Laurence

Jarvis, Bevan
Jauregui, Victor
Jiang, Qiang
Jin, Huidong
Jorgensen, Murray
Junor, Paul
Kadous, Waleed
Kant Kumar, Dinesh
Karim, Samin
Karol, Alankar
Kildea, Dan
Kirley, Michael
Koch, Fernando
Kopp, Carlo
Lagoon, Vitaly
Lam, Brian
Lazarescu, Mihai
Li, Chunsheng
Li, Gang
Li, Jiuyong
Li, Qingyong
Li, Yan
Li, Xiang
Lin, Weiqiang
Liu, Wei
Mayer, Wolfgang
McAullay, Damien
Misra, Avishkar
Mooney, Carl
Nasierding, Gulisong
Oxenham, Martin
Padmanabhan, Vineet
Peng, Tao
Pooley, Daniel
Prasad, Mithun
Qiu, Bin
Qiu, Lirong
Rahwan, Iyad
Rai, Shri
Rajaratnam, David
Rice, Sally
Riley, Jeff
Rock, Andrew
Rotolo, Antonino
Semonova, Tatiana
Shen, Chunhua
Sinna, Suku
So, Raymond
Song, Andy
Song, Insu
Stantic, Bela
Stuckey, Peter
Sucahyo, Yudho Giri
Sugianto, Lyfie
Tan, Peter
Thomas, Ian
Thu Bui, Lam
Tischer, Peter
Tu, Yiqing
Twardy, Charles
Unruh, Amy
Vahid, Farshid
Van den Hengel, Anton
Wallace, Mark
Wang, Jiaqi
Wang, Kewen
Wen, Peng
Wilkin, Tim
Woodberry, Owen
Wu, Sheng-Tang
Yan, Dr.
Yin, Yunfei
Zeleznikow, John
Zhang, Jilian
Zhang, Shichao
Zhang, Sulan
Zhao, Yanchang
Zheng, Fei
Zheng, Zheng
Zhuang, Ling

Table of Contents

Full Papers

Agents

Agent-Based Evolutionary Labor Market Model with Strategic Coalition
Seung-Ryong Yang, Jun-Ki Min, Sung-Bae Cho 1

A Multiagent Architecture for Privacy-Preserving ID-Based Service in Ubiquitous Computing Environment
Keon Myung Lee, Sang Ho Lee 14

Critical Damage Reporting in Intelligent Sensor Networks
Jiaming Li, Ying Guo, Geoff Poulton 26

Landscape Dynamics in Multi–agent Simulation Combat Systems
Ang Yang, Hussein A. Abbass, Ruhul Sarker 39

Safe Agents in Space: Lessons from the Autonomous Sciencecraft Experiment
Rob Sherwood, Steve Chien, Daniel Tran, Benjamin Cichy, Rebecca Castano, Ashley Davies, Gregg Rabideau 51

Biomedical Applications

Bio-discretization: Biometrics Authentication Featuring Face Data and Tokenised Random Number
Neo Han Foon, Andrew Teoh Beng Jin, David Ngo Chek Ling 64

Cochlea Modelling: Clinical Challenges and Tubular Extraction
Gavin Baker, Stephen O'Leary, Nick Barnes, Ed Kazmierczak 74

Combining Bayesian Networks, k Nearest Neighbours Algorithm and Attribute Selection for Gene Expression Data Analysis
B. Sierra, E. Lazkano, J.M. Martínez-Otzeta, A. Astigarraga 86

Medical Image Vector Quantizer Using Wavelet Transform and Enhanced SOM Algorithim
Kwang-Baek Kim, Gwang-Ha Kim, Sung-Kwan Je 98

SVM Classification for Discriminating Cardiovascular Disease Patients from Non-cardiovascular Disease Controls Using Pulse Waveform Variability Analysis
Kuanquan Wang, Lu Wang, Dianhui Wang, Lisheng Xu 109

Computer Vision, Imaging Processing and Pattern Recognition

Adaptive Enhancing of Fingerprint Image with Image Characteristics Analysis
Eun-Kyung Yun, Jin-Hyuk Hong, Sung-Bae Cho 120

Adaptive Image Classification for Aerial Photo Image Retrieval
Sung Wook Baik, Ran Baik 132

An Investigation into Applying Support Vector Machines to Pixel Classification in Image Processing
Douglas Clarke, David Albrecht, Peter Tischer 140

Applying Image Pre-processing Techniques for Appearance-Based Human Posture Recognition: An Experimental Analysis
M. Masudur Rahman, Seiji Ishikawa 152

A Stochastic Approach to Tracking Objects Across Multiple Cameras
Anthony R. Dick, Michael J. Brooks 160

Caption Detection and Removal in a TV Scene
JongBae Kim, KyoungKwan Ahn 171

Enhanced Importance Sampling: Unscented Auxiliary Particle Filtering for Visual Tracking
Chunhua Shen, Anton van den Hengel, Anthony R. Dick, Michael J. Brooks 180

Face Recognition Using Wavelet Transform and Non-negative Matrix Factorization
Neo Han Foon, Andrew Teoh Beng Jin, David Ngo Chek Ling 192

Modelling-Alignment for Non-random Sequences
David R. Powell, Lloyd Allison, Trevor I. Dix 203

Moments and Wavelets for Classification of Human Gestures Represented by Spatio-Temporal Templates
Arun Sharma, Dinesh K. Kumar 215

Personal Authenticator on the Basis of Two-Factors: Palmprint
Features and Tokenized Random Data
  Ying-Han Pang, Andrew Teoh Beng Jin, David Ngo Chek Ling 227

Practical Gaze Point Computing Method by 3D Position Estimation of
Facial and Eye Features
  Kang Ryoung Park 237

Ontologies

A Classification of Ontology Modification
  Kevin Lee, Thomas Meyer 248

Concept Type Hierarchy as Ontology: An Example Historical
Knowledge Base
  Dan Corbett, Wendy Mayer 259

Knowledge Discovery and Data Mining

A Dynamic Allocation Method of Basis Functions in Reinforcement
Learning
  *Shingo Iida, Kiyotake Kuwayama, Masayoshi Kanoh, Shohei Kato,
  Hidenori Itoh* 272

A Hybrid Classification Approach to Ultrasonic Shaft Signals
  Kyungmi Lee, Vladimir Estivill-Castro 284

A Landmarker Selection Algorithm Based on Correlation and Efficiency
Criteria
  Daren Ler, Irena Koprinska, Sanjay Chawla 296

A Learning-Based Algorithm Selection Meta-reasoner for the Real-Time
MPE Problem
  Haipeng Guo, William H. Hsu 307

A Novel Clustering Algorithm Based on Immune Network with Limited
Resource
  Li Jie, Gao Xinbo, Jiao Licheng 319

A Novel Modeling and Recognition Method for Underwater Sound
Based on HMT in Wavelet Domain
  Zhou Yue, Kong Wei, Xu Qing 332

BayesTH-MCRDR Algorithm for Automatic Classification of Web Document
  Woo-Chul Cho, Debbie Richards 344

Classification Rule Mining with an Improved Ant Colony Algorithm
  Ziqiang Wang, Boqin Feng 357

Clustering Large Datasets Using Cobweb and K-Means in Tandem
  Mi Li, Geoffrey Holmes, Bernhard Pfahringer 368

Cost-Sensitive Decision Trees with Multiple Cost Scales
  Zhenxing Qin, Shichao Zhang, Chengqi Zhang 380

Effective Sampling for Mining Association Rules
  Yanrong Li, Raj P. Gopalan 391

Improving the Centered CUSUMS Statistic for Structural Break Detection in Time Series
  Kwok Pan Pang, Kai Ming Ting 402

Investigating ID3-Induced Rules from Low-Dimensional Data Cleaned by Complete Case Analysis
  Jeanette Auer, Richard Hall 414

Investigating Learning Parameters in a Standard 2-D SOM Model to Select Good Maps and Avoid Poor Ones
  Hiong Sen Tan, Susan E. George 425

Key Element Summarisation: Extracting Information from Company Announcements
  Robert Dale, Rafael Calvo, Marc Tilbrook 438

Knowledge Discovery Using Concept-Class Taxonomies
  Venkateswarlu Kolluri, Foster Provost, Bruce Buchanan, Douglas Metzler 450

Learning the Grammar of Distant Change in the World-Wide Web
  Dirk Kukulenz 462

Mining Maximal Frequent ItemSets Using Combined FP-Tree
  Yuejin Yan, Zhoujun Li, Tao Wang, Yuexin Chen, Huowang Chen ... 475

Multinomial Naive Bayes for Text Categorization Revisited
  Ashraf M. Kibriya, Eibe Frank, Bernhard Pfahringer, Geoffrey Holmes 488

The Effect of Attribute Scaling on the Performance of Support Vector Machines
  Catherine Edwards, Bhavani Raskutti 500

Towards Efficient Imputation by Nearest-Neighbors: A Clustering-Based Approach
  *Eduardo R. Hruschka, Estevam R. Hruschka Jr.,
  Nelson F. F. Ebecken* 513

Univariate and Multivariate Linear Regression Methods to Predict Interval-Valued Features
  *Eufrasio de A. Lima Neto, Francisco A. T. de Carvalho,
  Camilo P. Tenorio* 526

Using Classification to Evaluate the Output of Confidence-Based Association Rule Mining
  Stefan Mutter, Mark Hall, Eibe Frank 538

Natural Language and Speech Processing

Analyzing the Effect of Query Class on Document Retrieval Performance
  Pawel Kowalczyk, Ingrid Zukerman, Michael Niemann 550

Combined Word-Spacing Method for Disambiguating Korean Texts
  Mi-young Kang, Aesun Yoon, Hyuk-chul Kwon 562

Extraction of Shallow Language Patterns: An Approximation of Data Oriented Parsing
  Samuel W.K. Chan 574

Improving the Presentation of Argument Interpretations Based on User Trials
  Ingrid Zukerman, Michael Niemann, Sarah George 587

Reliable Unseen Model Prediction for Vocabulary-Independent Speech Recognition
  Sungtak Kim, Hoirin Kim 599

Voice Code Verification Algorithm Using Competing Models for User Entrance Authentication
  Heungkyu Lee, Hanseok Ko 610

Problem Solving and Reasoning

A Logic Based Approach for Dynamic Access Control
  Vino Fernando Crescini, Yan Zhang 623

A New Neighborhood Based on Improvement Graph for Robust Graph Coloring Problem
  Songshan Guo, Ying Kong, Andrew Lim, Fan Wang 636

An Extension of the H-Search Algorithm for Artificial Hex Players
  Rune Rasmussen, Frederic Maire 646

Applying Constraint Satisfaction Techniques to 3D Camera Control
  Owen Bourne, Abdul Sattar 658

Constraints from STRIPS — Preliminary Report
  Norman Foo, Pavlos Peppas, Yan Zhang 670

Embedding Memoization to the Semantic Tree Search for Deciding QBFs
  Mohammad GhasemZadeh, Volker Klotz, Christoph Meinel 681

On Possibilistic Case-Based Reasoning for Selecting Partners in Multi-agent Negotiation
  Jakub Brzostowski, Ryszard Kowalczyk 694

Set Bounds and (Split) Set Domain Propagation Using ROBDDs
  Peter Hawkins, Vitaly Lagoon, Peter J. Stuckey 706

User Friendly Decision Support Techniques in a Case-Based Reasoning System
  Monica H. Ou, Geoff A.W. West, Mihai Lazarescu, Chris Clay 718

Robotics

Longer-Term Memory in Clause Weighting Local Search for SAT
  Valnir Ferreira Jr., John Thornton 730

Natural Landmark Based Navigation
  E. Lazkano, A. Astigarraga, B. Sierra, J.M. Martínez-Otzeta, I. Rañó 742

Soft Computing

A Novel Approach for Simplifying Neural Networks by Identifying Decoupling Inputs
  Sanggil Kang, Wonil Kim 754

Aggregation of Foraging Swarms
  Long Wang, Hong Shi, Tianguang Chu, Weicun Zhang, Lin Zhang ... 766

An ACO Algorithm for the Most Probable Explanation Problem
  Haipeng Guo, Prashanth R. Boddhireddy, William H. Hsu 778

Designing a Morphogenetic System for Evolvable Hardware
  Justin Lee, Joaquin Sitte 791

Evaluation of Evolutionary Algorithms for Multi-objective Train Schedule Optimization
  C.S. Chang, C.M Kwan 803

Fuzzy Modeling Incorporated with Fuzzy D-S Theory and Fuzzy Naive Bayes
  Jiacheng Zheng, Yongchuan Tang 816

Genetic Algorithm Based K-Means Fast Learning Artificial Neural Network
  Yin Xiang, Alex Tay Leng Phuan 828

Immune Clonal Selection Network
  Haifeng Du, Xiaoyi Jin, Jian Zhuang, Licheng Jiao, Sun'an Wang ... 840

Performance Improvement of RBF Network Using ART2 Algorithm and Fuzzy Logic System
  Kwang Baek Kim, Cheol Ki Kim 853

Solving Rotated Multi-objective Optimization Problems Using Differential Evolution
  Antony W. Iorio, Xiaodong Li 861

Sub-structural Niching in Non-stationary Environments
  Kumara Sastry, Hussein A. Abbass, David Goldberg 873

Suitability of Two Associative Memory Neural Networks to Character Recognition
  Orla McEnery, Alex Cronin, Tahar Kechadi, Franz Geiselbrechtinger 886

Using Loops in Genetic Programming for a Two Class Binary Image Classification Problem
Xiang Li, Vic Ciesielski 898

Short Papers

Agents

A Negotiation Agent
John Debenham 910

Agent Services-Driven Plug-and-Play in F-TRADE
Longbing Cao, Jiarui Ni, Jiaqi Wang, Chengqi Zhang 917

Applying Multi-medians Location and Steiner Tree Methods into Agents Distributed Blackboard Architecture Construction
Yi-Chuan Jiang, Shi-Yong Zhang 923

Meta-game Equilibrium for Multi-agent Reinforcement Learning
Yang Gao, Joshua Zhexue Huang, Hongqiang Rong, Zhi-Hua Zhou ... 930

Computer Vision, Image Processing and Pattern Recognition

A Fast Visual Search and Recognition Mechanism for Real-Time Robotics Applications
Quoc Vong Do, Peter Lozo, Lakhmi Jain 937

Adaptive Object Recognition with Image Feature Interpolation
Sung Wook Baik, Ran Baik 943

Effective Approach for Detecting Digital Image Watermarking via Independent Component Analysis
Lisha Sun, Weiling Xu, Zhancheng Li, M. Shen, Patch Beadle 949

Extended Locally Linear Embedding with Gabor Wavelets for Face Recognition
Zhonglong Zheng, Jie Yang, Xu Qing 955

Image Processing of Finite Size Rat Retinal Ganglion Cells Using Multifractal and Local Connected Fractal Analysis
H.F. Jelinek, D.J. Cornforth, A.J. Roberts, G. Landini, P. Bourke, A. Iorio 961

The DSC Algorithm for Edge Detection
Jonghoon Oh, Chang-Sung Jeong 967

Knowledge Based Systems

A Novel Statistical Method on Decision Table Analysis
Ling Wei, Wen-xiu Zhang 973

An Interaction Model for Affect Monitoring
Insu Song, Guido Governatori, Robert Colomb 979

Ontology Transformation in Multiple Domains
Longbing Cao, Dan Luo, Chao Luo, Li Liu 985

Knowledge Discovery and Data Mining

A Bayesian Metric for Evaluating Machine Learning Algorithms
Lucas R. Hope, Kevin B. Korb 991

A Comparison of Text-Categorization Methods Applied to N-Gram Frequency Statistics
Helmut Berger, Dieter Merkl 998

A Global Search Algorithm for Attributes Reduction
Songbo Tan 1004

A Symbolic Hybrid Approach to Face the New User Problem in Recommender Systems
Byron Bezerra, Francisco A.T. de Carvalho 1011

A Toolbox for Learning from Relational Data with Propositional and Multi-instance Learners
Peter Reutemann, Bernhard Pfahringer, Eibe Frank 1017

An Improvement to Unscented Transformation
Yuanxin Wu, Meiping Wu, Dewen Hu, Xiaoping Hu 1024

Automatic Wrapper Generation for Metasearch Using Ordered Tree Structured Patterns
Kazuhide Aikou, Yusuke Suzuki, Takayoshi Shoudai, Tetsuhiro Miyahara 1030

Building a More Accurate Classifier Based on Strong Frequent Patterns
Yudho Giri Sucahyo, Raj P. Gopalan 1036

Color Texture Analysis Using Wavelet-Based Hidden Markov Model
  Ding Siyi, Yang Jie, Xu Qing 1043

Contributions of Domain Knowledge and Stacked Generalization in
AI-Based Classification Models
  Weiping Wu, Vincent ChengSiong Lee, TingYean Tan 1049

Discovering Interesting Association Rules by Clustering
  Yanchang Zhao, Chengqi Zhang, Shichao Zhang 1055

Exploiting Maximal Emerging Patterns for Classification
  Zhou Wang, Hongjian Fan, Kotagiri Ramamohanarao 1062

Feature Extraction for Learning to Classify Questions
  *Zhalaing Cheung, Khanh Linh Phan, Ashesh Mahidadia,
  Achim Hoffmann* 1069

Mining Exceptions in Databases
  *Eduardo Corrêa Gonçalves, Ilza Maria B. Mendes,
  Alexandre Plastino* 1076

MML Inference of Oblique Decision Trees
  Peter J. Tan, David L. Dowe 1082

Naive Bayes Classifiers That Perform Well with Continuous Variables
  Remco R. Bouckaert 1089

On Enhancing the Performance of Spam Mail Filtering System Using
Semantic Enrichment
  Hyun-Jun Kim, Heung-Nam Kim, Jason J. Jung, Geun-Sik Jo 1095

Parameterising Bayesian Networks
  *Owen Woodberry, Ann E. Nicholson, Kevin B. Korb,
  Carmel Pollino* 1101

Radar Emitter Signal Recognition Based on Feature Selection Algorithm
  Gexiang Zhang, Laizhao Hu, Weidong Jin 1108

Selecting Subspace Dimensions for Kernel-Based Nonlinear Subspace
Classifiers Using Intelligent Search Methods
  Sang-Woon Kim, B. John Oommen 1115

Using Machine Learning Techniques to Combine Forecasting Methods
  Ricardo Prudêncio, Teresa Ludermir 1122

Web Data Mining and Reasoning Model
Yuefeng Li, Ning Zhong 1128

Natural Language and Speech Processing

A Framework for Disambiguation in Ambiguous Iconic Environments
Abhishek, Anupam Basu 1135

An Intelligent Grading System for Descriptive Examination Papers Based on Probabilistic Latent Semantic Analysis
Yu-Seop Kim, Jung-Seok Oh, Jae-Young Lee, Jeong-Ho Chang 1141

Domain-Adaptive Conversational Agent with Two-Stage Dialogue Management
Jin-Hyuk Hong, Sung-Bae Cho 1147

Feature Extraction Based on Wavelet Domain Hidden Markov Tree Model for Robust Speech Recognition
Sungyun Jung, Jongmok Son, Keunsung Bae 1154

Feature Unification and Constraint Satisfaction in Parsing Korean Case Phenomena
Jong-Bok Kim, Jaehyung Yang, Incheol Choi 1160

Problem Solving and Reasoning

A Comparison of BDI Based Real-Time Reasoning and HTN Based Planning
Lavindra de Silva, Lin Padgham 1167

A Formal Method Toward Reasoning About Continuous Change
Chunping Li 1174

A Time and Energy Optimal Controller for Mobile Robots
Sebastien Ancenay, Frederic Maire 1181

Inheritance of Multiple Identity Conditions in Order-Sorted Logic
Nwe Ni Tun, Satoshi Tojo 1187

Soft Computing

A Comparative Analysis of Fuzzy System Modelling Approaches: A Case in Mining Medical Diagnostic Rules
Kemal Kılıç, Özge Uncu, I.B. Türkşen 1194

A Parallel Learning Approach for Neural Network Ensemble
  Zheng-Qun Wang, Shi-Fu Chen, Zhao-Qian Chen, Jun-Yuan Xie 1200

An Intelligent Gas Concentration Estimation System Using Neural
Network Implemented Microcontroller
  Ali Gulbag, Fevzullah Temurtas 1206

Ant Colonies Discover Knight's Tours
  Philip Hingston, Graham Kendall 1213

Immune Clonal Selection Algorithm for Multiuser Detection in
DS-CDMA Systems
  Maoguo Gong, Haifeng Du, Licheng Jiao, Ling Wang 1219

Intrusion Detection Based on Immune Clonal Selection Algorithms
  Liu Fang, Qu Bo, Chen Rongsheng 1226

Mapping Dryland Salinity Using Neural Networks
  Matthew Spencer, Tim Whitfort, John McCullagh 1233

Normalized RBF Neural Network for Real-Time Detection of Signal in
the Noise
  *Minfen Shen, Yuzheng Zhang, Zhancheng Li, Jinyao Yang,
  Patch Beadle* 1239

Statistical Exploratory Analysis of Genetic Algorithms: The Influence
of Gray Codes upon the Difficulty of a Problem
  Andrew Czarn, Cara MacNish, Kaipillil Vijayan, Berwin Turlach 1246

The Semipublic Encryption for Visual Cryptography Using Q'tron
Neural Networks
  Tai-Wen Yue, Suchen Chiang 1253

The T-Detectors Maturation Algorithm Based on Genetic Algorithm
  Dongyong Yang, Jungan Chen 1262

Author Index 1269

Agent-Based Evolutionary Labor Market Model with Strategic Coalition

Seung-Ryong Yang, Jun-Ki Min, and Sung-Bae Cho

Department of Computer Science, Yonsei University,
134 Shinchon-dong, Sudaemoon-ku, Seoul 120-749, Korea
{saddo, loomlike, sbcho}@sclab.yonsei.ac.kr

Abstract. A real-world labor market has complex worksite interactions between a worker and an employer. This paper investigates the behavior patterns of workers and employers with a job capacity and a job concentration empirically considering a strategic coalition in an agent-based computational labor market. Here, the strategic coalition can be formed autonomously among workers and/or among employers. For each experimental treatment, the behavior patterns of agents are varied with a job capacity and a job concentration depending on whether a coalition is allowed. Experimental results show that a strategic coalition makes workers and employers aggressive in worksite interactions against their partners.

1 Introduction

A labor market is said simply to consist of workers and employers with complex worksite behaviors [1]. In a real-world labor market, the behavioral characteristics expressed by workers and employers, such as trustworthiness and diligence, depend on who is working for whom [2], [3]. Therefore, the behavioral patterns of the worksite interactions may affect heavily the flexibility of the labor market. Accordingly, there have been a great deal of studies on the analysis of the behavioral patterns of the agents and unemployment in the future labor market using agent-based computational models. However, they have focused principally on the analysis of the limited worksite interactions such as one to one mapping between a worker and an employer without considering the union of the agents.

Before the worksite interaction with a certain employer, a worker may want to form a strategic coalition with other workers to get more benefits from his/her worksite partner (i.e., employer) while so does an employer. Here, the strategic coalitions between workers and/or between employers may be spontaneously occurred without supervision. It is similar with the labor unions of workers and the federation of employers in a real-world labor market. In this paper, we model an agent-based evolutionary labor market with a strategic coalition using the prisoner's dilemma game. Furthermore, we investigate how the strategic coalition influences the behavioral patterns of the agents in an evolutionary labor market. For meaningful investigation, we adopt the asymmetric test environments reflecting real-world labor markets derived from the ratio of the number of workers and employers such as a job concentration and a job capacity.

This paper organizes as follows: Section 2 explains the related works such as the prisoner's dilemma game, and a labor market framework. Section 3 describes the definition of the strategic coalition between the agents and how they form a strategic coalition. In Section 4, we describe the experimental results of the strategic coalition in each test environment. Finally, we conclude this paper in Section 5 with a few remarks.

2 Backgrounds

2.1 Iterated Prisoner's Dilemma Game

In a real labor market, a worker and an employer compete to get more benefits from their worksite partner. Therefore, their actions appear in the form of cooperation and defection as if two prisoners do so. In the classical prisoner's dilemma game [4], [5], [6], two prisoners may cooperate with or defect from each other. If the game is played for one round only, the optimal action is definitely defection. However, if the game is played for many rounds, mutual defection may not be the optimal strategy. Instead, mutual cooperation will guarantee more payoffs for both of the prisoners [7]. In the same manner, mutual cooperation between a worker and an employer is helpful for the improvement of wage earning and the productivity in the real economy. Because it is non-zero sum game one player's gain may not be the same with the other player's loss. There is no communication between the two players.

2.2 Evolutionary Labor Market Framework

The labor market framework comprises NW workers who make work offers and NE employers who receive work offers, where NW and NE can be any positive integers. Each worker can have work offers outstanding to no more than wq employers at any given time, and each employer can accept work offers from no more than eq workers at any given time, where the work offer quota wq and the employer acceptance quota eq can be any positive integers [2], [3].

Each agent depicted in an evolutionary labor market framework has the internal social norms and behaviors with the same attributes represented in bit-string with a strategy table and a history table. They update their worksite strategies on the basis of the past own and opponent's actions. They also evolve with genetic operations such as selection, crossover, and mutation [5].

The interaction between a worker and an employer can be described as work offering and accepting. For example, a worker offers his work to a potential worksite partner who is randomly selected from the population of employers. Then the offered employer determines whether he/she will accept the worker's offer according to his/her past worksite interaction history. If the employer accepts the worker's offer they work together. On the other hand, if the employer refuses the worker's offer the worker receives the refusal payoff (F) which is regarded as a job searching cost in a negative form. At the time, the employer does not receive any penalty on the refusal. Instead, the employer receives the inactivity payoff (I). Being afraid of receiving the refusal payoff, a worker may do not submit work offer. In that case, the worker also receives the inactivity payoff.

If an employer accepts work offer from a worker, they are said to be matched as worksite partners and participate in the worksite interactions modeled as the prisoner's dilemma game. Then the worker can cooperate with or defect from the employer according to his/her worksite strategy while the employer does either one. For example, the worker may work hard in the worksite (Cooperation) or work lazily to exploit the employer's favor (Defection). The employer may make good working conditions for his/her worker (Cooperation) or decrease the worker's payment (Defection). Such worksite behaviors are determined by the last action of each worksite partner encoded in a history table.

In the worksite interaction between a worker and an employer, a cooperator whose worksite partner defects receives the sucker's payoff (S); a defector whose worksite partner also defects receives the mutual defection payoff (P); a cooperator whose worksite partner also cooperates receives the mutual cooperation payoff (R); and a defector whose worksite partner cooperates receives the temptation payoff (T). In this paper, we follow Tesfation's payoff values for labor market modeling described in [2] and the values also satisfy Axelrod's payoff function $(T+S) < 2R$ of the prisoner's dilemma game. The relation of each payoff value is as follows.

$$S < P < F < I(0) < R < T$$

Job Concentration. To model an evolutionary computational labor market, we initialize the population with the real number of workers (NW) and employers (NE). According to the ratio of the number of workers and employers, the behavioral patterns of workers and employers can be varied. To investigate the impact by the ratio of the number of workers and employers, three setting are tested such as a high job concentration ($NW/NE=2/1$), a balanced job concentration ($NW/NE=1$), and a low job concentration ($NW/NE=1/2$). Workers are more than employers when a job concentration is high, and the numbers of workers and employers are the same in a balanced job concentration, and workers are less than employers in a low job concentration.

Job Capacity. In worksite interactions, each worker has the same work offer quota wq, where wq is the maximum number of potential work offers that each worker can make. In the same manner, each employer has the same acceptance quota eq, where eq is the maximum number of job openings that each employer can provide. According to the ratio of the number of workers and employers with the quota, a job capacity can be divided into a tight job capacity $((NE*eq)/(NW*wq)=1/2)$, a balanced job capacity $((NE*eq)/(NW*wq)=1)$, and a excess job capacity $((NE*eq)/(NW*wq)=2/1)$. Particularly, jobs are less than demand in a tight job capacity, jobs are equal to demand when a job capacity is balanced, and jobs are in excess supply when a job capacity is excess.

Classification of Agents. There are many different types of behavioral patterns in a multi-agent environment. In an agent-based computational labor market, we analyze the behavioral patterns of the agents described as workers and employers with three classes: nice, aggressive, and inactive. A nice agent selects persistently cooperation in worksite interactions against his worksite partner in despite of defection. An aggressive agent selects at least one defection against his worksite partner that has not previously defected from him. An inactive agent plays like an observer so as not to lose the refusal payoff (F) against his potential opponent. The inactive worker becomes persistently unemployment and the inactive employer is persistently vacant.

3 Strategic Coalition in an Agent-Based Computational Labor Market

In this section, we suggest a strategic coalition which can model a labor market more dynamically. At first, we describe the definitions of a strategic coalition. Then we formulate the procedure of a coalition formation.

3.1 Strategic Coalition

To get more benefits in worksite interactions, workers and employers may consider a strategic coalition separately in each population. It is because the strategic coalition among autonomous agents may be mutually beneficial even if the agents are selfish and try to maximize their expected payoffs [8], [9], [10]. The coalition between two workers in a population is formed autonomously without any supervision. That is, if the conditions of coalition formation are satisfied they will form a coalition [11], [12].

For the definitions of a strategic coalition, let $W=\{w_1, w_2,\ldots, w_n\}$, $E=\{e_1, e_2,\ldots,e_n\}$ be the collection of workers and employers in each population, respectively. Let $C_w=\{w_i, w_j,\ldots, w_k\}$, $|C_w|\geq 2$ and $C_e=\{e_i, e_j,\ldots, e_k\}$, $|C_e|\geq 2$ be the strategic coalition that can be formed among workers and employers. The coalitions, C_w and C_e, are the elements of the individual group, $W: C_w \subseteq W$, $|C_w|\leq|W|$ and $E: C_e \subseteq E$, $|C_e|\leq|E|$. Every worker has his own payoff, p_w^i, and every employer has his own payoff, p_e^i, that earns from the prisoner's dilemma game against his opponent. Then the coalition has the vector, $C_w = \langle C_w^p, N_w^c, f_w^p, D_w \rangle$ for workers' coalition, $C_e = \langle C_e^p, N_e^c, f_e^p, D_e \rangle$ for employers' coalition. Here, C^p, N^c, f^p, and D of C_w and C_e, mean the average payoff of a strategic coalition, the number of agents in the coalition, payoff function, and a decision of the coalition, respectively. Now we can define the strategic coalition as follows.

Definition 1. Coalition Payoff: Let w_w^i and w_e^i be the weight vectors for a worker and an employer corresponding to each payoff. The coalition payoffs, C_w^p for workers' coalition and C_e^p for employers' coalition, are the average payoff by the corresponding weight of the agents that participate in each coalition.

$$C_w^p = \frac{\sum_{i=1}^{|C_w|} p_w^i w_w^i}{|C_w|}, \quad C_e^p = \frac{\sum_{i=1}^{|C_e|} p_e^i w_e^i}{|C_e|} \quad (1)$$

where $w_w^i = \dfrac{p_w^i}{\sum_{i=1}^{|C_w|} p_w^i}$ and $w_e^i = \dfrac{p_e^i}{\sum_{i=1}^{|C_e|} p_e^i}$

Definition 2. Payoff Function: Workers and employers belonging to each coalition get payoffs with a given function after worksite interactions. In this paper, we follow Tesfatsion's payoff values for each experiment [2].

Definition 3. Coalition Identification: Each coalition has its own identification number. This number is generated when the coalition is formed by given conditions, and it may be removed when the coalition exists no more. This procedure is made autonomously according to evolutionary process.

Definition 4. Decision Making of Coalition: A strategic coalition must have one decision (i.e., cooperation or defection) that combines the behaviors of all participants belonging to the coalition. We use the weighted voting method for decision making of the coalition in this experiment. Decision making of the coalition, D_w for workers' coalition and D_e for employers' coalition, are determined by the function including the coalition payoff and its weight.

$$D_w = \begin{cases} 0 = \text{Cooperation}, & \text{if } 1 < \frac{\sum_{i=1}^{|C_w|} p_i^C \cdot w_w^i}{\sum_{i=1}^{|C_w|} p_i^D \cdot w_w^i} \\ 1 = \text{Defection}, & \text{if } 0 < \frac{\sum_{i=1}^{|C_w|} p_i^C \cdot w_w^i}{\sum_{i=1}^{|C_w|} p_i^D \cdot w_w^i} \leq 1 \end{cases}, \quad D_e = \begin{cases} 0 = \text{Cooperation}, & \text{if } 1 < \frac{\sum_{i=1}^{|C_e|} p_i^C \cdot w_e^i}{\sum_{i=1}^{|C_e|} p_i^D \cdot w_e^i} \\ 1 = \text{Defection}, & \text{if } 0 < \frac{\sum_{i=1}^{|C_e|} p_i^C \cdot w_e^i}{\sum_{i=1}^{|C_e|} p_i^D \cdot w_e^i} \leq 1 \end{cases} \quad (2)$$

where p_i^C : an agent that selects cooperation for the next action

p_i^D : an agent that selects defection for the next action

3.2 Coalition Formation

To investigate other worker's intention for a coalition formation, the prisoner's dilemma game is played between two workers. A worker is selected at random in workers' population, and the other worker is orderly selected in the same population. Thus, the worker selected randomly in the population plays against all the other workers (single worker or coalition) in the population. After each game, each of the two agents considers making (or joining) a coalition to get more payoffs from his worksite partner. Table 1 shows three conditions in order to form a strategic coalition used in this paper. If all conditions are satisfied, they form a strategic coalition. Employers also follow the same procedure with workers.

Table 1. Three conditions for a coalition formation

Condition	Characteristics
condition 1	Each agent's payoff before the game between two agents must be higher than the average payoff of the population
condition 2	Each agent's payoff after the game between two agents must be less than the average payoff of the population.
condition 3	Each agent's payoff after a coalition must be higher than the average payoff of the population

As the game is played over and over again, there may be many coalitions in the population. Therefore a worker can play the game against a coalition. A coalition can also play the game against another coalition. In the case that a worker joins an existing coalition, the workers within the coalition (including a new one) play another prisoner's dilemma game in a round-robin way to update all participants' rank. For example, when there are k workers in a coalition, $k(k-1)/2$ games will be played totally. If the total number of workers (i.e., k) is greater than a pre-defined maximum coalition size, the weakest worker (in terms of the total payoff obtained in all round-robin games) will be removed from the coalition. All workers within the coalition are ranked (sorted) according to each payoff. Then each of the workers has weight corresponding to his rank in the coalition. The weight plays an important role in determining the worker's impact on the coalition's next move.

If workers form a strategic coalition they act as a single agent from the time. Therefore, there must be a decision making method to combine the behaviors of all participants in the coalition for the next action (refer to equation (2)). In this paper, we use the weighted voting method which determines the weight value according to each participant's payoff belonging to the coalition. In other words, a superior agent gets a higher weight value for decision making of the next action. Employers also follow the same procedure because a worker and an employer have the identical attributes and internal state.

4 Experimental Results

The experimental design focuses on the independent variation of three factors: job concentration as measured by JCON=(NW/NE); and job capacity as measured by JCAP=((NE*eq)/(NW*wq)); and coalition. Figure 1 describes the experimental design with three factors. For each experiment, the number of workers and employers are set as 24, respectively, when a job concentration is balanced (JCON=1). All remaining parameters are maintained at fixed values throughout all the experiments as shown in Table 2.

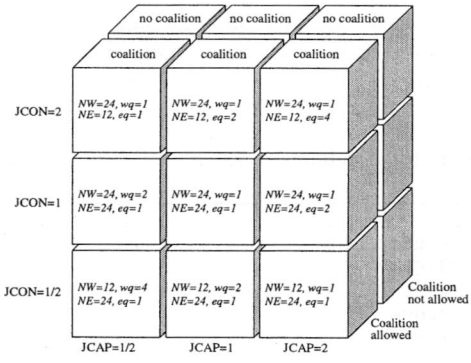

Table 2. Experimental parameters

Parameter	Value
population size	24
crossover rate	0.6
mutation rate	0.005
number of generations	50
number of iterations	100
initial payoff	1.4
refusal payoff	-0.5
inactivity payoff	0.0
sucker's payoff	-1.6
temptation payoff	3.4
mutual cooperation	1.4
mutual defection	-0.6
history size	2

Fig. 1. Experimental design with three factors

4.1 High Job Concentration

In a high job concentration (JCON=2), employers are beneficial when finding workers because the number of workers is more than that of employers. Such phenomena occur occasionally in a real-world labor market. Table 3 shows the experimental results of behavioral patterns of the agents in the high job concentration with each job capacity on average of 10 runs. In the table, when a coalition is not allowed and a job capacity is tight (JCAP=1/2), employers act more aggressively (employer 77%) and workers act principally inactively (worker 43%). The reason is that the tight job capacity causes the employers to exploit the workers who have weakness in job finding. The figure of percentage in the table describes the rate for each behavioral class of the agents in the final generation, and the sum of each class does not mean to equal 100% because some agents do not belong to the three classes or can be duplicated.

Table 3. The experimental results of a high job concentration considering a coalition

		Tight job capacity (JCAP=1/2)		Balanced job capacity (JCAP=1)		Excess job capacity (JCAP=2)	
		e	w	e	w	e	w
Coalition not allowed	Inact.	12%	56%	6%	9%	14%	5%
	Aggr.	77%	43%	37%	50%	52%	55%
	Nice	10%	13%	46%	36%	20%	16%
	Utility	0.98	0.04	0.95	0.81	0.60	1.14
Coalition allowed	Inact.	9%	54%	6%	14%	23%	15%
	Aggr.	62%	16%	46%	37%	61%	44%
	Nice	1%	3%	10%	0%	1%	6%
	Utility	0.96	0.16	0.92	0.53	0.94	0.48

Employers and workers act principally as a nice agent when a job capacity is balanced (employer 46%, worker 36%) when a coalition is not allowed. It means that employers and workers do not compete severely for job match because the labor market structure is stable in demand and supply. When a job capacity is excess, however, inactive employers appear more in worksite interaction (employer 14%), which means that the labor market structure is unfavorable to employers.

If a strategic coalition is allowed the experimental results are varied according to a job capacity. Employers and workers become non-cooperative when a coalition is not allowed in every job capacity. It explains that the coalition selects mainly defection from its worksite partners and then it makes the population more competitive. In other words, a coalition causes nice agents to decrease, which means the agents in the coalition select more defection as the next action. It is also shown in the rate of aggressive agents in each job capacity.

In terms of utility (i.e., payoff) as shown in Figure 2, the payoffs of employers and workers become less if a coalition is allowed because non-cooperative agents increase in a competitive labor market environment. In Figure 2(a), the payoff of employers in an excess job capacity is less than that in tight and balanced job capacity while that of workers in tight job capacity is less than that in an excess and a balanced job capacity in Figure 2(b). It means that an excess job capacity is unfavorable to employers while a tight job capacity is unfavorable to workers with the ratio of employers and workers.

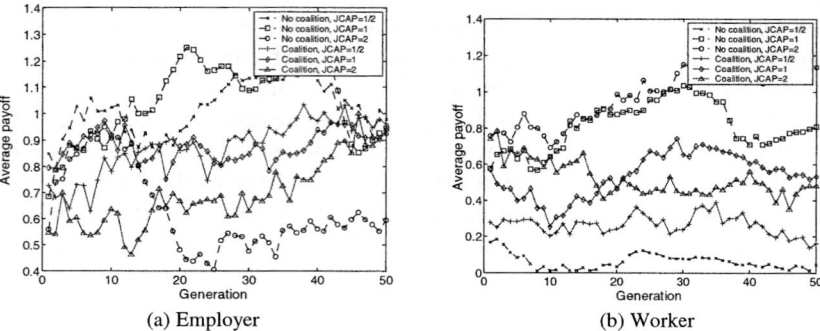

Fig. 2. Variation of average payoffs in a high job concentration. Employers get more payoffs than workers regardless of a coalition (Compare the average payoffs of two figures). It means that employers have more favorable position in finding worksite partners in a labor market as well as a real world

4.2 Balanced Job Concentration

Table 4 depicts the experimental results of a balanced job concentration with each job capacity. As shown in the table, although a job concentration is balanced the behavioral patterns of agents can be varied because work offer quota (wq) and work acceptance quota (eq) are different. When a job capacity is tight and a coalition is not allowed, workers act inactively in order not to lose the refusal payoff against employers (worker 38%). However, in a balanced job capacity, many employers and workers play nice strategy to cooperate with each worksite partner (employer 55%, worker 35%). That is, the behavior patterns of agents follow the labor market structure represented as a job capacity when a coalition is not allowed.

If coalition is allowed in a balanced job concentration, cooperative agents decrease in every job capacity. It is similar with the case of a high job concentration when a coalition allowed. Especially, 55% of nice employers and 35% of nice workers before a coalition decreases dramatically to 4% and 5%, respectively, after a coalition is allowed. It means that a coalition makes the population of employers and workers competitive extremely. Additionally, a coalition makes the increment of inactive agents from nice agents (employer 22%, worker 22%), which means that observers increase due to an unstable labor market structure.

The utility of agents are also varied on whether a coalition is allowed or not. Both of employer and worker get fewer payoffs when a coalition is allowed because the whole population becomes non-cooperative and each agent selects frequently defection in worksite interactions.

Table 4. The experimental results of a balanced job concentration considering a coalition

		Tight job capacity (JCAP=1/2)		Balanced job capacity (JCAP=1)		Excess job capacity (JCAP=2)	
		e	w	e	w	e	w
Coalition not allowed	Inact.	10%	38%	13%	13%	31%	3%
	Aggr.	65%	19%	34%	44%	57%	62%
	Nice	18%	18%	55%	35%	19%	19%
	Utility	1.33	-0.02	1.39	0.78	1.00	0.73
Coalition allowed	Inact.	8%	37%	22%	22%	40%	11%
	Aggr.	46%	19%	67%	20%	61%	31%
	Nice	2%	2%	4%	5%	1%	8%
	Utility	0.90	0.16	0.91	0.26	0.75	0.57

Figure 3 shows the payoff variation when a job concentration is balanced. Employers get more payoffs when a coalition is not allowed, which means that cooperative employers dominate the population and then the population converges to mutual cooperation. In the case of workers, they get the least payoff when a job capacity is tight and a coalition is not allowed, which means the labor market structure is disadvantageous to workers.

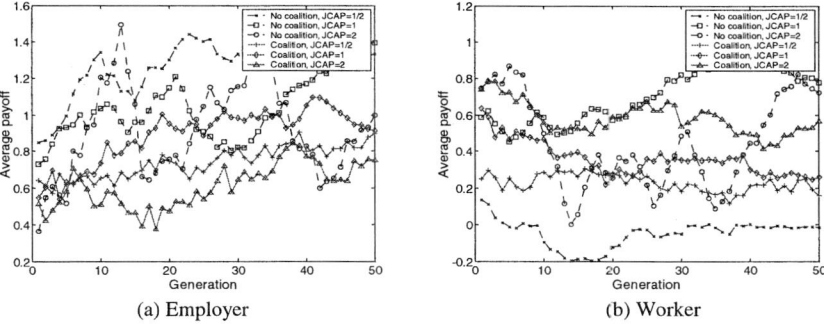

(a) Employer   (b) Worker

Fig. 3. Variation of average payoffs in a balanced job concentration. Notice Y axis value between two figures. Employers get more payoffs relatively when a coalition is not allowed (dashed lines in Fig. 3(a)). It is similar to the case of workers, but the difference is rather small

4.3 Low Job Concentration

In this section, we analyze the behavioral patterns of the agents when a job concentration is low (JCON=1/2) which means the number of employers is two times more than the number of workers (NW/NE=1/2). In this environment, workers have an advantage in finding his worksite partner. Table 5 shows the experimental results of a low job concentration with each job capacity. The rate of inactive agents is remarkably high in comparison with a high and a balanced job concentration regardless of a coalition. It describes that a low job concentration causes employers and workers to be a spectator by the low possibility of occupation. However, nice agents decrease when a coalition is allowed in the same manner of a high and a balanced job concentration (employer 6%, worker 5%). It results in the utility of employers and workers decreased when a coalition is allowed.

Table 5. The experimental results of a low job concentration considering a coalition

		Tight job capacity (JCAP=1/2)		Balanced job capacity (JCAP=1)		Excess job capacity (JCAP=2)	
		e	w	e	w	e	w
Coalition not allowed	Inact.	36%	47%	31%	24%	52%	5%
	Aggr.	63%	24%	58%	25%	48%	41%
	Nice	10%	18%	41%	52%	30%	21%
	Utility	1.47	-0.14	1.87	0.27	0.74	0.84
Coalition allowed	Inact.	16%	29%	28%	18%	58%	16%
	Aggr.	52%	24%	44%	38%	41%	37%
	Nice	8%	1%	6%	5%	2%	7%
	Utility	1.02	0.15	0.93	0.11	0.93	0.18

Figure 4 depicts the variation of average payoffs in a low job concentration along generations. Employers get near the mutual cooperation payoff (payoff value 1.4) when a job concentration is balanced and coalition is not allowed. It means that the labor market is stable and most of agents (i.e., employers and workers) are cooperative in worksite interactions. Workers get fewer payoffs relatively than employers in every job capacity, which describes that they are exploited by aggressive employers due to an unfavorable market structure. Needless to say, if a coalition is allowed the payoffs become less due to non-cooperative behaviors of the coalition as well as other job concentrations.

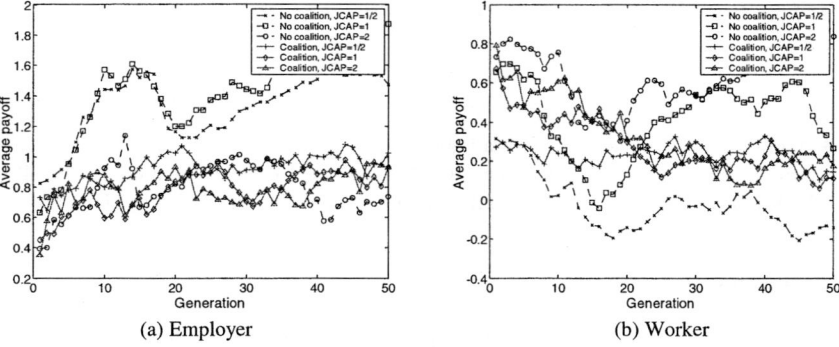

(a) Employer (b) Worker

Fig. 4. Variation of average payoffs in a low job concentration. Employers earn more payoffs rather than workers in every job capacity. Notice the values of Y axis in the figures. Most of payoff lines are lower when a coalition is allowed regardless of employers and workers

4.4 Number of Coalitions

Figure 2 shows how many coalitions are formed or dismissed along generations in each job concentration and a job capacity of 5 runs. Particularly, Figure 2(a), (b), (c)

describe the variation of the number of coalitions when a job concentration is high (Notice that the maximum number of coalitions is one third of a population). Here, the number of workers' coalition is more than that of employers' coalition. It is caused by that the total number of workers is more than that of employers in each generation.

Figure 2(d), (e), (f) describe the number of coalitions when a job concentration is balanced. In the figure, the number of coalitions is varied almost equivalently between an employer and a worker. The reason is that the balance of the number of employers and workers permits the equivalent possibility of coalition formation. Figure 2(g), (h), (i) depict the number of coalitions when a job concentration is low. Each of the figures shows that the number of employers' coalition is more than that of workers' coalition, which means the possibility of coalition formation for employers is higher than the workers.

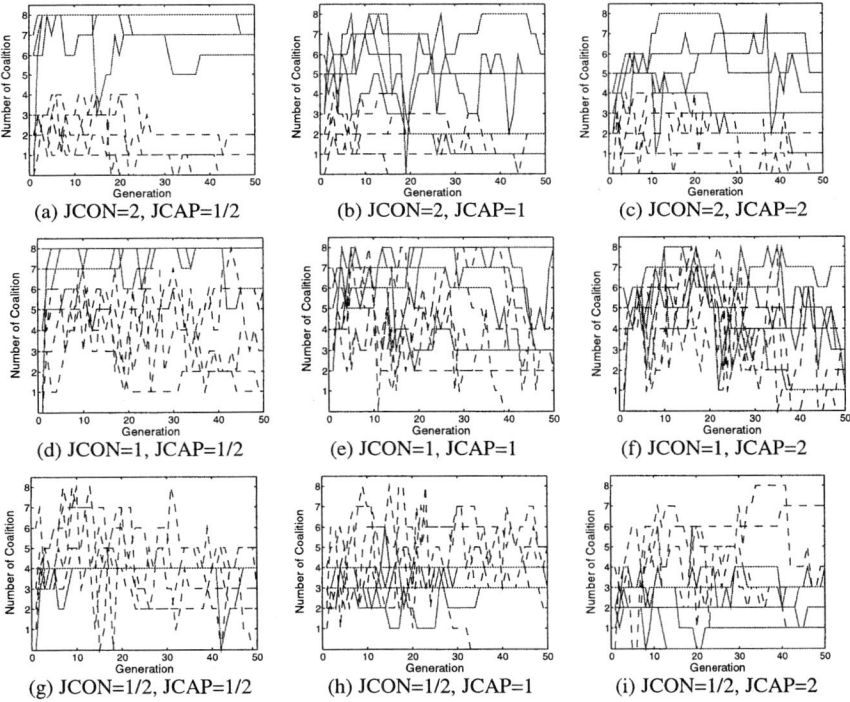

Fig. 5. The number of coalitions in each job concentration and a job capacity when a strategic coalition is allowed. Solid lines are for workers and dashed lines are for employers

5 Conclusions

A real-world labor market has complex worksite interactions among its constituents like workers and employers. Therefore, modeling the labor market and predicting the future market structure are an important study to help proper policies established and the policies adaptive to a changing environment. In this paper, we propose a strategic coalition to model complex interactions in an agent-based computational labor market. We also investigate how a strategic coalition affects the labor market structure and the behavior of workers and employers. Experimental results describe that a strategic coalition makes workers and employers more aggressive to their worksite partners. Specifically, employers and workers act cooperatively when a job capacity is balanced and a coalition is not allowed. However, they become non-cooperative players when a coalition is allowed. The number of coalitions varies according to a labor market structure which consists of the ratio of employers and workers. That is, employers form a coalition more actively when a job concentration is high. Conversely, workers form more coalitions when a job concentration is low. The utility level of employers and workers becomes less when a coalition is allowed. It means that labor market including a coalition between workers and/or between employers is changed to a competitive structure. This appears remarkably high when a labor market structure is in a tight and an excess job capacity.

Acknowledgements

This work was supported by Korea Research Foundation Grant(KRF-2002-005-H20002).

References

1. Tesfatsion, L.: Agent-based Computational Economics: Growing Economics from the Bottom Up, Artificial Life, Vol. 8 (2002) 55-82
2. Tesfatsion, L.: Structure, Behavior, and Market Power in an Evolutionary Labor Market with Adaptive Search, Journal of Economic Dynamics and Control, Vol. 25 (2001) 419-457
3. Tesfatsion, L.: Hysteresis in an Evolutionary Labor Market with Adaptive Search, S.-H. Chen (eds), Evolutionary Computation in Economics and Finance, Physics, Springer-Verlag, Heidelberg Germany (2002) 189-210
4. Axelrod, R.: The Evolution of Strategies in the Iterated Prisoner's Dilemma, Genetic Algorithms and Simulated Annealing, San Mateo, CA: Morgan Kaufmann, Ch. 3 (1987) 32-41
5. Colman, A. M.: Game Theory and Experimental Games, Pergamon Press, Oxford England (1982)
6. Darwen, P. J., Yao, X.: On Evolving Robust Strategies for Iterated Prisoner's Dilemma, Progress in Evolutionary Computation, Lecture Notes in Artificial Intelligence, Vol. 956. Springer-Verlag, Heidelberg Germany (1995) 276-292
7. Francisco, A.: A Computational Evolutionary Approach to Evolving Game Strategy and Cooperation, IEEE Transactions on Systems, Man and Cybernetics, Part B, Vol. 32, No. 5 (2002) 498-502
8. Shehory, O., Kraus, S.: Coalition Formation among Autonomous Agents: Strategies and Complexity, Fifth European Workshop on Modeling Autonomous Agents in a Multi-Agent World, Springer-Verlag, Heidelberg Germany (1993) 56-72

9. Shehory, O., Sycara, K., Jha, S.: Multi-agent Coordination through Coalition Formation, Proceedings of Agent Theories, Architectures, and Languages, Springer-Verlag, Heidelberg Germany (1997) 143-154
10. Garland, A., Alterman, R.: Autonomous Agents that Learn to Better Coordinate, Autonomous Agents and Multi-Agent Systems, Vol. 8, No. 3 (2004) 267-301
11. Tate, A., Bradshaw, M., Pechoucek, M.: Knowledge Systems for Coalition Operations, IEEE Intelligent Systems, Vol. 17 (2002) 14-16
12. Sandholm, T. W., Lesser, V. R.: Coalitions among Computationally Bounded Agents, Artificial Intelligence, Vol. 94 (1997) 99-137

A Multiagent Architecture for Privacy-Preserving ID-Based Service in Ubiquitous Computing Environment

Keon Myung Lee and Sang Ho Lee

School of Electric and Computer Engineering, Chungbuk National University,
and Advanced Information Technology Research Center(AITrc)*, Korea
kmlee@cbnu.ac.kr

Abstract. Privacy preservation is crucial in the ubiquitous computing because a lot of privacy-sensitive information can be collected and distributed in the ubiquitous computing environment. The anonymity-based approach is one of well-known ones for privacy preservation in ubiquitous computing. It allows users to use pseudonyms when they join in a service area of the ubiquitous computing environment. This approach can protect users' privacy by hiding the user's real IDs, but it makes it difficult to provide ID-based services like buddy service, safety alert service, and so on. This paper proposes a multiagent architecture to make it possible to provide ID-based services in the anonymity-based privacy awareness systems. The proposed architecture employs so-called the *white page agent* which maintains the current pseudonyms of users and allows users to get the pseudonyms of other users from the agent. Even though the white page agent contains the pseudonyms of users, it is enforced not to disclose the association of real user IDs with pseudonyms by adopting encryption techniques. This paper presents in detail the proposed architecture, its constituent components and their roles and how they provide ID-based services in the anonymity-based system. As an example, it also presents how buddy service can take place in the proposed architecture.

1 Introduction

Ubiquitous computing is an emerging field in computer systems research, which promises an environment in which users can use computing services without conscious thought at any time, at any place. To provide ubiquitous computing services, they need to use contextual information (e.g., the identity, location of user, service time, neighboring objects, and so on) about the user in order for her not to specify the details about how to operate the facilities. Lots of contextual information about users are collected through sensors embedded in the environment and stored somewhere in the environment. Some contextual information

---

* This work has been supported by Korea Science and Engineering Foundation through AITrc.

is privacy-sensitive, and thus if someone can access such information, he may figure out *when*, *where*, and *who* did *what*. Among the contextual information, the identity(ID) and location are most sensitive. If it is possible to completely hide real IDs of users, we are nearly free from privacy concerns. In practice users frequently confront with the situations their IDs are asked when they use some services. In the meanwhile, the locations of users may imply some aspects of privacy-sensitive information.

In the literature of ubiquitous computing, we can find several approaches to protecting users' privacy, especially, location privacy.[1-14] The policy-based approach and the anonymity-based approach are the representative ones for privacy protection. In the policy-based approach, a designated server takes charge of handling access control to privacy-sensitive information based on the privacy policies.[1] The server collects some privacy-related information about the users through the underlying sensor networks. Users register at the server their privacy preferences about who would be allowed to access their information. The server determines whether the requests from applications are accepted or not based on the users' privacy preference and the applications' privacy policy. An application's privacy policy is an assertion about which purposes the application uses the information about a user. In this scheme, the users should put their trust in the server. However, if the server conspires with an application against users, the users' privacy-sensitive information can be improperly disclosed. In the circumstances where there will be multiple servers, users would hesitate to trust those servers.

On the contrary, the anonymity-based approach does not demand users to trust any server.[2] In the approach, applications have their own spatial service area and take care of only users who enter into their service area. To protect their own privacy, users use pseudonyms when they join in a service area. Thanks to pseudonyms, attackers come to have difficulty in associating pseudonyms with real IDs. Even though the number of users in an service area affects the degree of privacy preservation and data mining techniques could reveal some association among pseudonyms, the anonymity-based approach has the advantage in that users do not have to unconditionally believe some server. However, this approach also has some restrictions in providing ID-based services like buddy service, safety alert service. The buddy service is one of popular services in cellular phone community, which informs a user of the presence of her buddy around her. The safety alert service is to help a user not to get into a dangerous place by tracking her location.

In this paper, we propose a multiagent architecture to enable ID-based services in the anonymity-based privacy awareness systems. The fundamental idea of the proposed architecture is to use a white page agent through which users and applications get other users' current pseudonyms. The white page agent is assumed to be not so much as secure and trustworthy as the users expect. To provide secure white page service, the proposed method employs encryption techniques and several interaction protocols. In the proposed architecture, the users register their pseudonyms to the white page agent each time they change their pseudonym. The users and applications having the friendship with a user can access the current pseudonym of the user stored in the white page agent. Even though the white agent stores the pseudonym data for users, it cannot figure out their contents because the pseudonyms are encrypted with the keys not known to the agent. By enabling to locate users by pseudonyms, the proposed method provides the ID-based services in the anonymity-based ubiquitous computing environment. In addition, by introducing a hierarchical naming scheme considering proximity among physical areas, the proposed architecture enables to easily provide location-based services.

This paper is organized as follows: Section 2 presents some related works to privacy preservation in ubiquitous computing. Section 3 introduces the proposed multiagent architecture for ID-based services in anonymity-based ubiquitous computing environment. Section 4 shows how to implement buddy service on the proposed architecture as an example. Finally, Section 5 draws conclusions.

2 Related Works

Privacy concerns have been addressed in various research works.[1-14] The policy-based privacy preservation method depends on a server which makes access control decision on privacy-sensitive information.[1] For the access control, the server refers to the applications' privacy policies and the users' privacy preferences. Users register to the server their privacy preferences about who can use which data of them. When an application requests data from the server, it also sends its privacy policy for the data along with the request. The server maintains a set of validators used to check the conformity of application's privacy policy against user's privacy preference. The privacy policy-based control method enables flexible access control based on various criteria such as time of the request, location, speed, and identities of the located objects. Despite this advantage, it is burdensome for average users to specify such complex policies. Privacy policies play the role of establishing a trust in the server. But, they cannot guarantee that the server adequately protects the collected data from various attacks. The users are also enforced to trust the server who controls the access to their privacy-sensitive data.

The anonymity-based privacy preservation method is an alternative of the policy-based method.[2] It tries to protect the individual's privacy by depersonalizing user data. In this scheme, when a user enters into a service area of an application, she uses a pseudonym instead of her real ID. The use of pseudonyms makes it difficult for malicious applications to identify and track individuals. There remain yet some vulnerabilities under the situations in which the only limited number of users move in and out the service areas, or the sensor network is owned by an untrusted party which can keep track of device-level IDs like MAC addresses. Due to the anonymity-based nature, it is not easy to incorporate detailed access control like privacy policies and to provide ID-based services like buddy services, safety alert service, callback service, etc. This method does not ask users to trust any application or server.

Grutester et al.[3] proposed a privacy preservation approach to use a distributed anonymity algorithm that is implemented at the sensor network level. In their architecture, the sensors can keep track of the number of users in an area and monitor changes in real-time, and a location server collects the sensor data and publishes it to applications. Their anonymity algorithm controls the resolution of users' IDs to guarantee users to be k-anonymous, which means that every user at the moment is indistinguishable from at least $k-1$ other users. To enable this, the approach takes the special naming scheme for locations in which names are encoded into a hierarchically organized bit stream. It reports only some upper part of the bit stream when it wants to increase the level of anonymity. This approach uses pseudonyms for locations instead of using pseudonyms for users. As the matter of fact, the pseudonyms for locations are the blurred IDs of the real location IDs.

In the Cricket location-support system[13], there are a set of beacons embedded in the environment and receiving devices that determine their location by listening to the radio and ultrasound beacons. The location information is initially only known to the devices, and then the owners of the devices decide to whom this information will be disclosed. Therefore, the users do not have to trust any embedded sensors or servers. To employ this approach, the sensor networks should be comprised of only the homogeneous types of sensors. The users should carry a device that is compatible with the beacons and powerful enough to process the tasks of location identification and communication.

3 The Proposed ID-Based Service System Architecture

We are interested in providing the ID-based services in the following situation: Two counterparts want to communicate with each other in an anonymity-based system despite they keep changing their pseudonyms. They do not disclose their real IDs to the sensor networks to preserve their privacy. While they communicate with each other, they use their pseudonyms. Therefore, they need some mechanism to keep track of their counterpart's pseudonyms. Their devices are assumed not to have unique IDs which the sensor networks could use to associate them with specific users. Therefore, it is assumed that there are no ways to directly bind user IDs with device IDs. There are special servers called *zone agents*, each of which takes care of a spatial service area, collects data from the sensors in their own area, communicates with user devices (i.e., user agents) placed in the area, and relays the communication messages between user devices and other users' devices or other applications outside the area. One of the most crucial capabilities for the ID-based services in the anonymity-based systems is to enable communicating partners to know their corresponding partners' pseudonyms in a secure way. This section describes the proposed ID-based service multiagent architecture in detail.

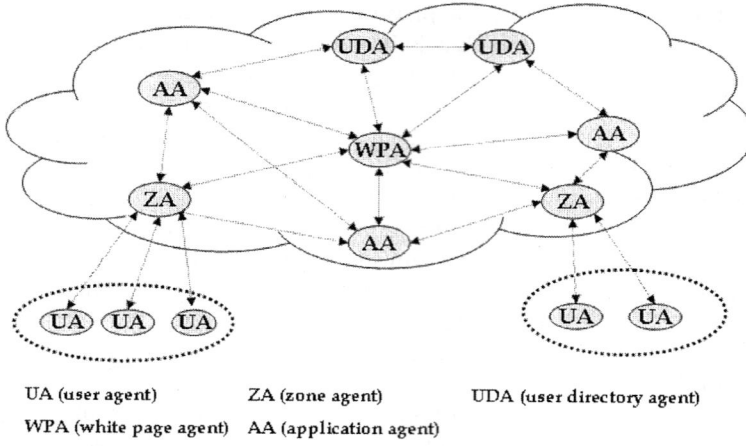

Fig. 1. Overview of the ID-based service multiagent architecture

3.1 System Architecture

Figure 1 shows the proposed multiagent architecture for the ID-based services in the anonymity-based systems. The architecture comprises of a white page agent, a set of zone agents, a set of user agents, a set of user directory agents, and a set of application agents. Each agent plays the following roles:

White Page Agent. It receives the users' pseudonym update request messages, delivers them to user directory agents, and updates the users' pseudonym records according to the requests from user directory agents. It also provides the white page service that enables users with proper keys to retrieve the current pseudonyms of their friends.

User Agents. Each user has her own agent which runs in the device carried with her. On behalf of users, the user agents communicate with other agents and applications in a privacy-preserving way.

Zone Agents. Each zone agent takes care of a designated physical zone. It monitors which user agents come in and go out its zone and assigns new pseudonyms to user agents (i.e., users) joining in its zone. It relays the communication messages between user agents in its zone and user agents or applications off the zone.

User Directory Agents. A user directory agent plays the role of updating the users' pseudonym records stored in the white page agent according to the requests from the users. In the considered architecture, there are multiple user directory agents, each of which can work for a set of users. A user makes a contract with a user directory agent and delegates to the user directory agent the task of maintaining her pseudonym. Each user directory agent creates friend keys which is used to encrypt the users' pseudonyms, and maintains the information whose and which keys are used for which user agents and which applications.

Application Agents. An application agent acts as an interface for an application. It receives requests from outside, transfers them to its corresponding application, and then sends back the results produced by the application. It also serves as the communication front-end of an application. Thus it can play the role of establishing initial set-up like acquiring the current pseudonym of a user when an application wants to communicate with the user.

3.2 Secure Registration of Pseudonyms

In the proposed architecture, users register their current pseudonyms to the white page agent, and both users and applications can get the pseudonyms of correspondents from the agent if they have proper encryption key information. Users would not feel easy for the white page agent to deal with pseudonym data in plain texts because they may think the white page agent is not so much secure and trustworthy as they expect. As a matter fact, the white page is a place which attackers would bombard to acquire useful information. In the proposed architecture, we store pseudonyms in an encrypted form. The database of the white page agent contains the records made of the pair (*real ID of user i, a list of user i's current pseudonyms encrypted with different friend keys*). The key issue here is how a user updates the encrypted pseudonym field of her record in the white page agent without revealing her identity.

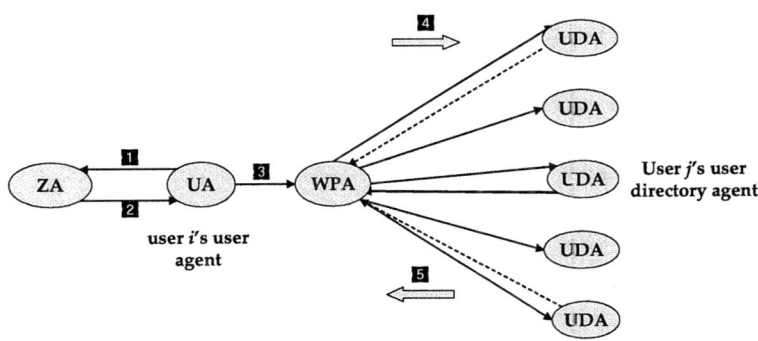

Fig. 2. Registration of new pseudonym to the white page agent

Figure 2 shows how new pseudonym is registered to the white page agent in the proposed architecture. The basic idea is to make the i's user directory agent register new pseudonym on behalf of user i. When the i's user agent joins in a zone (Step 1), the user agent is assigned a new pseudonym by the zone agent (Step 2). If a user agent directly updates its pseudonym record with its encrypted pseudonym, the attackers easily could infer which agent works for whom. To avoid this, we take the following strategy: The i's user agent encrypts the pseudonym update message with a key called *directory key* which is a secret key shared with its user directory agent, and then sends it to the white page agent.(Step 3) Due to the encryption, the white page agent cannot understand the contents of the message. It just delivers the copies of the message to all user directory agents.(Step 4) Once a user directory agent receives a pseudonym update message from the white page agent, it tries to decrypt the message with its own directory key. The user agents and their corresponding user directory agent share a unique directory key. Therefore, only the intended user directory agent can recovery a meaningful message from the received message. Now, the user directory agent encrypts the new pseudonym for user i with the so-called *friend keys*. A friend key is a secret key which is used to encrypt the current pseudonym of user i and is shared with some friends of user i. Therefore, the friends of user i can recover the pseudonym of user i from her encrypted pseudonym. The user directory agent asks the white page agent to update the pseudonym field for user i with the encrypted pseudonyms.(Step 5) At this moment, if an attacker could analyze the traffic over the network, he may bind the user agent initiating a pseudonym update request with the user's real ID since the user's pseudonym field in the white page agent, which can be accessible to any users including attackers, will be definitely changed after such a pseudonym update request. To avoid this kind of attacks, some portion of all user directory agents randomly request the white page agent to update some of their users' records regardless of whether they received the pseudonym update request from their user or not.(Step 5) When a user directory agent other than the i's user directory agent asks pseudonym update, it sends to the white page agent the already existing encrypted pseudonym with some meaningless modification. In Figure 2, the dotted lines indicate the message passing for such meaningless updates.

Now users should have trust in their own user directory agent. In this architecture, if all the user directory agents other than user i's would refuse to do the meaningless updates, some attacks could disclose the real ID of the i's user agent. However, all user directory agents have the same goal to protect their users' privacy. They have no choice but to cooperate each other for their common benefit. To strengthen the security, user directory agents come to ask the white page agent to update several users' pseudonyms at a time even though they need to update only one user's pseudonym.

3.3 Retrieval of a User's Pseudonym

When a user (or an application) i wants to communicate with a user j, i needs to know the current pseudonym of j. At the moment, user i is assumed to know the real ID of user j. The i's user agent asks the white page agent about the pseudonym of user j. After that, user i communicates with user j using the pseudonyms. Here the traffic analysis of their communication may reveal some information about their real IDs. Therefore, the pseudonym request message sent by the user agent is encrypted using the public key of the white page agent so that attackers cannot see whose pseudonym is requested. The request message contains a secret key as well as the counterpart's ID. The secret key is later used to encrypt the response message which consists of a collection of pairs (*real ID, a list of encrypted pseudonyms*). In the list, each encrypted pseudonym element is composed of the pair (*friend key f_k, pseudonym*) encrypted using the friend key f_k. If the user i is a friend of the user j, i must have a friend key for j's pseudonym. Therefore, the i's user agent can recover the pseudonym for user j from the response message.

3.4 Confirmation of a User's Pseudonym Update

After a user i asks the renewal of her pseudonym, i wants to make sure that the update request is properly treated. If the i's user directory agent informs the user i of the status of the request just after processing the update request, an attacker could catch the association relationship of user i with her user directory agent. Some data mining techniques could find privacy-sensitive information from the data collected by the traffic sniffing. Therefore, the i's user agent checks her pseudonym on a non-regular basis by asking the white page agent her pseudonym. In order to make confused for the attacker to analyze the traffic, the user agents may also ask arbitrary users' pseudonyms on a non-regular basis although they cannot decrypt them.

For each user i, the i's user directory agent has a special friend key for only i, encrypts the i's pseudonym with the friend key as well as other friend keys, and stores the encrypted pseudonyms in the database of the white page agent. The special friend keys are used when users check their pseudonyms stored in the white page agent.

3.5 Naming Scheme

In order to implement a white page, all users' real IDs must be unique because pseudonyms are retrieved based on the real IDs of users. In the meanwhile, users employ pseudonyms to hide their real IDs and use them as a temporary ID for the counterparts during communication. Therefore, pseudonyms should also be unique across the networks. In addition, in order to provide location-based services, it would be good for a naming scheme to associate pseudonyms with the locations at which the users with the pseudonyms are placed. The proposed architecture adopts the pseudonym naming scheme shown in Figure 3.

A pseudonym consists of several fields where all left side fields but the rightmost field represents the ID of a zone and the rightmost field contains a temporary user ID in the zone in which the user with the pseudonym is located. Each zone has a unique ID. Thus a pseudonym of a user is the combination of the zone ID of the user on the left side and a temporary user ID assigned by the zone agent. In the proposed architecture, zones are organized in a hierarchical manner according to their spatial proximity. Thus, the more the prefixes of two pseudonyms are the same, the more the corresponding zones are close.

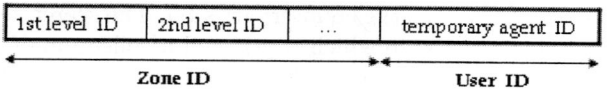

Fig. 3. Naming Scheme for pseudonyms

3.6 Friendship Agreement

Only friends of a user are allowed to get her pseudonym. When a user or an application i wants to communicate with user j or wants to use the location information of j, the proposed architecture uses the protocol shown in Figure 4.

At first the i's user agent asks the i's user directory agent to start the friendship establishment with user j.(Step 1) The i's user directory agent sends to the white page agent a friendship call message, which is made of the tuple (*the address of the i's user directory agent, the real ID of user j, an encryption key*) encrypted using the session key shared by the white page agent and all user directory agents.(Step 2) The white page agent broadcasts the copies of the message to all other user directory agents.(Step 3) On receiving the message, if a user directory agent takes care of the user j, it sends to the i's directory agent its address and a session key encrypted using the encryption key.(Step 4) At the moment, the user i does not know yet who made the friendship call. Now the i's user directory agent informs the j's user directory agent of the i's friendship call message encrypted using the session key.(Step 5) The friendship call message contains the ID of user i and the i's digital signature to be used to prove that user i is not spoofed. The j's user agent transfers the received friendship call to the j's user agent.(Step 6) Then the j's user agent asks whether she accepts the call or not.

If the user j declines the call, the decline message is sent back to the i's user agent from the j's user agent via the j's user directory agent and the i's user directory agent.(Steps 7, 9, 10) If the user j accepts the call, the j's user agent asks the j's user directory agent to prepare the friendship setup.(Step 7) Then, the j's user directory agent creates a friend key for i and registers the j's pseudonym encrypted using the friend key to the white page agent.(Step 8) Now, the j's user directory agent informs the i's user agent of the friend key using the encrypted message via the i's user directory agent.(Steps 9, 10)

A user may have multiple friend keys if she belongs to multiple friend groups. Each user agent has a repository which maintains the information about what friend keys are used for which friends. In terms of the same context, the white page agent comes to have multiple encrypted pseudonyms for a user ID.

3.7 Routing of Pseudonyms

In the proposed architecture, all agents but user agents running on users' mobile devices are connected to the Internet and thus they have corresponding IP(Internet Protocol) addresses. User devices are assumed not to be able to connect to the Internet directly. In the employed naming scheme, pseudonyms imply

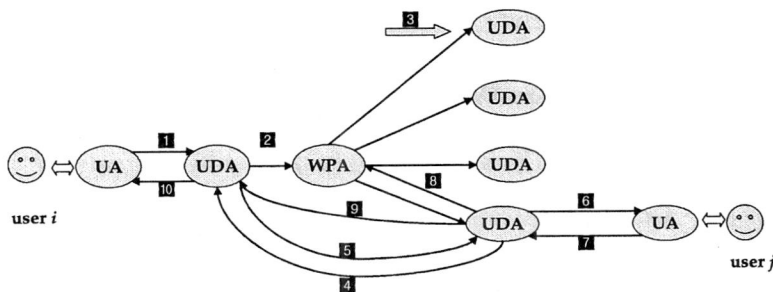

Fig. 4. Friendship Agreement

some proximity information among users, but have nothing to do with IP addresses. In order to provide the IP address resolution for pseudonyms, the white page agent maintains a database which keeps the mapping information between the pseudonyms (exactly to speak, zone IDs) and IP addresses, the proximity information among zone IDs, and addressing information for entities such as user directory agents, application agents, etc. When a user or an application wants to communicate with an entity on the Internet, she first gets the addressing information for the entity from the white page agent.

As a matter of fact, user agents do not have their own IP address. The zone agents to which they belongs have IP addresses and the user agents are distinguished by their temporary agent IDs within their zone. Therefore, a zone agent plays the role of a proxy which sends and receives messages on behalf of user agents. Therefore, the messages of user agents come to contain the fields of the IP address of a zone and an temporary agent ID of a user agent.

4 A Service Scenario: Buddy Service

Figure 5 shows how a buddy service can be provided in the proposed architecture. When user i wants to get a buddy service with user j, the following actions take place. It is assumed that i and j are already friends each other. Therefore, they can get counterpart's current pseudonym from the white page agent. Now suppose that i wants to get a buddy service with j. Then i should obtain the permission from j.

First, the i's user agent sends the ask-permission message to j's user agent. (Step 1) If j declines it, then the j's user agent informs the i's user agent of it.(Step 5) If j accepts the buddy service request with i, the j's user agent asks the j's user directory agent to create a friend key used for the buddy service.(Step 2) Then, the j's user directory agent creates a friend key for the buddy service, and registers to the white page agent the j's pseudonym encrypted using the friend key.(Step 3) After that, the j's user directory agent gives the friend key to the j's user agent.(Step 4) Now the j's user agent sends to the i's user agent the acceptance message with the friend key. Then the i's user agent asks its user

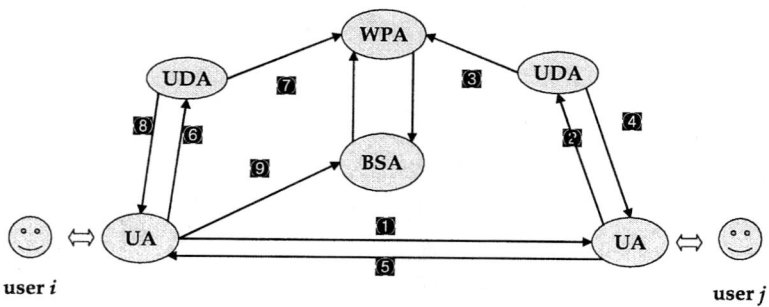

Fig. 5. Buddy Service

directory agent to register a new friend key for the buddy service.(Steps 6, 7) After registration, the i's user directory agent returns to the i's user agent the friend key.(Step 8) Finally, the i's user agent asks the buddy service agent(BSA) to start the buddy service for users i and j by sending the friend keys for i and j. The buddy service agent stores the buddy information about i and j such as their real IDs and their friend keys.

After all initial setup tasks, the buddy service agents periodically checks the locations of the users registered for the buddy service. If some pair of users happens to be located in the same or close zones, the buddy service agent informs them of the presence of their friends around them. When a user wants to cease the buddy service, she sends a service termination request message to the buddy service agent. Then the buddy service agent informs it to the user directory agents and performs some house-keeping tasks to remove the service for them. The informed user directory agents take steps like friend key removal and other house-keeping tasks.

5 Conclusions

Privacy preservation is vital in the ubiquitous computing environment. Without this, users feel uneasy to use and live in the environment. This paper proposed a multiagent architecture to provide ID-based services in the anonymity-based systems. The proposed architecture employs a white page agent to maintain the current pseudonyms of users by which ID-based services can be implemented. Through the encryption mechanism, the architecture hides the linkage between users' real IDs and their pseudonyms. Thanks to the pseudonym naming scheme, it is easy to get the proximity information among users and thus easy to provide location-based services such as buddy service. This architecture does not yet support delicate access control as in policy-based approach. As the further studies, there remain how to incorporate the delicate access control into this architecture and how to reduce communication overhead among agents.

References

[1] G. Myles, A. Friday and N. Davies. Preserving Privacy in Environments with Location-Based Applications. *IEEE Pervasive Computing* 2(1). (2003). 56-64.

[2] A. R. Beresford and F. Stajano. Location Privacy in Pervasive Computing. *IEEE Pervasive Computing* 2(1). (2002). 46-55.

[3] M. Gruteser, G. Schelle, A. Jain, R. Han and D. Grunwald. Privacy-Aware Location Sensor Networks. http://systems.cs.colorado.edu/Papers/Generated/2003PrivacyAwareSensors.html (2003).

[4] X. Jiang and J. Landay. Modeling Privacy Control in Context-aware Systems. *IEEE Pervasive* 1(3). (2002).

[5] M. Langheinrich. A Privacy Awareness System for Ubiquitous Computing Environments. In *Ubicomp 2002*. (2002).

[6] S. Lederer, A. K. Dey, J. Mankoff. Everyday Privacy in Uniquitous Computing Environment. In *Ubicomp 2002 Workshop on Socially-informed Design of Privacy-enhancing Solutions in Ubiquitous Computing*. (2002).

[7] A. Smailagic. D. P. Siewiorek, J. Anhalt, D. Kogan, Y. Wang. Location Sensing and Privacy in a Context Aware Computing Environment. In *Proc. Pervasive Computing, 2001*. (2001).

[8] J. Hightower, G. Borriello. Location Systems for Ubiquitous Computing. *IEEE Computer* 34(8). (2001). 57-66.

[9] A. R. Prasad, P. Schoo, H. Wang. An Evolutionary Approach towards Ubiquitous Communications: A Security Perspective. In *Proc. of SAINT 2004: The 2004 Symposium on Applications & Internet*. (2004).

[10] M. Hazas, A. Ward. A High Performance Privacy-Oriented Location System. In *Proc. of IEEE International Conference on Pervasive Computing and Communications*. (2003).

[11] P. Osbakk, N. Ryan. Expressing Privacy Preferences in terms of Invasiveness. In *Position Paper for the 2nd UK-UbiNet Workshop(University of Cambridge, UK)*. (2004).

[12] E. Snekkenes. Concepts for Personal Location Privacy Policies. In *Proc. of the 3rd ACM conference on Elctronic Commerce*. ACM Press. (2001). 48-57.

[13] N. B. Oriyantha, A. Chakraborty, H. Balakrishnan. The Cricket Location-Support System. In *Proc. of the Sixth Annual International Conference on Mobile Computing and Networking*. ACM Press. (2000). 32-43.

[14] U. Jendricke, M. Kreutzer, A. Zugenmaier. Pervasive Privacy with Identity Management. In *Ubicom2002*. (2002).

[15] W. Stallings. *Cryptography and Network Security*. Prentice Hall. (2003).

[16] M. J. Zaki. Parallel and Distributed Association Mining. *IEEE Conccurency*. (1999). 14-25.

Critical Damage Reporting in Intelligent Sensor Networks

Jiaming Li, Ying Guo, and Geoff Poulton

Intelligent Systems,
CSIRO Information and Communication Technology Centre,
Marsfield NSW 2122, Australia
{Jiaming.Li, Ying.Guo, Geoff.Poulton}@csiro.au

Abstract. In this paper, we present a Top-Down/Bottom-Up (TDBU) design approach for critical damage reporting in intelligent sensor networks. This approach is a minimal hierarchical decomposition of the problem, which seeks a balance between achievability and complexity. Our simulated environment models two-dimensional square cells as autonomous agents which sense their local environment, reporting critical damage as rapidly as possible to a report delivery site (portal) by using only the adjacent-cell communication links. The global goal is to design agent properties which will allow the multi-agent network to detect critical damage anywhere on the network and to communicate this information to a portal whose location is unknown to the agents. We apply a TDBU approach together with genetic algorithms (GA) to address the global goal. Simulations show that our system can successfully report critical damage much better than random methods.

1 Introduction

Intelligent sensor networks have been investigated recently for a number of applications including structural health monitoring, which is a critical factor for future aerospace vehicles. Such vehicles must operate in adverse environments where failure to recognise, assess and respond adequately to damage may prove disastrous. The advantage of intelligent sensor networks in such environments lies in the distributed nature of the intelligence which allows the monitoring process to continue even when considerable damage exists. This situation is far more robust than a more conventional centralised intelligence where damage to the central processor may disable the entire system [1].

The Ageless Aerospace Vehicle (AAV) project is being conducted jointly by CSIRO and NASA with the aim of investigating the use of intelligent sensor networks for structural health monitoring of future aerospace vehicles [2]. As part of this project a Concept Demonstrator (CD) system has been developed. Shown in Fig. 1, the CD is a hexagonal structure of approximately 1m. diameter and 1m. in length, covered by 48 1mm. thick aluminium panels behind which is a rectangular array of 192 sensor cells, each having four piezoelectric sensors and a microprocessor. Each cell also has the ability to communicate only with its four immediate neighbours. Since the cells have sensing and acting capabilities and are imbued with independent intelligence they may be regarded as "agents", and the sensor network itself is an example of a multi-agent system.

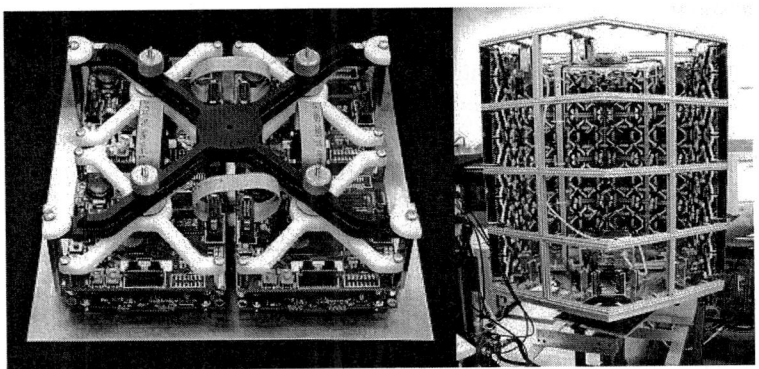

Fig. 1. Ageless Aerospace Vehicle Concept Demonstrator, showing an aluminium panel with four cells (left) and the demonstrator with four of the six sides populated (right)

This sensor network is intended to detect and assess impacts on the skin from fast-moving projectiles (which simulate micrometeoroids in a space environment). The degree of intelligence of the network can be varied by programming the microprocessors. A number of different detection, assessment and reporting tasks are possible, including determination of the location and severity of impacts together with an assessment of damage, both immediate and cumulative. Eventually prognosis of the effects of damage on the fitness of the vehicle and the ability to self-repair are envisaged. Although the network will have no control centre it will generally be the case that communication from a damage site to another part of the vehicle will be required, for example to initiate secondary inspections, repair or, in extreme cases, appropriate emergency action. Such communications will most likely be hierarchical and flexible, so that the report delivery site (portal) will vary with time as well as depending on where the damage occurred and its severity.

This paper examines the reporting of critical damage in such intelligent sensor networks. "Critical damage" means an impact severe enough to threaten the survival of the vehicle. In such situations time is of the essence, and the requirements on the network are to send an alarm as rapidly as possible to a (probably) unknown location using only the adjacent-cell communication links. In addition, there may exist barriers to communication due to the network configuration itself or to significant prior and continuing damage. Thus the communications environment is also unknown and changing.

The multi-agent sensor network described above is likely to be a complex system exhibiting emergent behaviour [3]. Such systems make life difficult for the designer, principally because of the essential unpredictability of emergence. On the other hand, emergence can offer a much richer solution space and lead to better solutions if the unpredictability can be controlled. Biological evolution offers many examples where this has been used to advantage [4]. A traditional approach to the design of complex systems is hierarchical decomposition [5], where the problem is broken down into a (sometimes large) number of layers which are more amenable to solution. Unfortunately this process, whilst often allowing a design to be achieved almost always suppresses emergent behaviour, thus denying the designer access to the rich solution space which complexity can provide. The authors have recently introduced an alternative to this approach which gives the advantages of hierarchical decomposition whilst retaining the possibility of emergent behaviour [6, 7]. Called Top-Down/Bottom-Up (TDBU) design, it is really a minimal decomposition of the problem which seeks to retain the complex nature of the original. The TDBU approach is described in more detail in the next section.

2 Top-Down/Bottom-Up (TDBU) Design

Our approach is to seek a balance between "top-down" (engineering) and "bottom-up" (scientific) processes. Engineering design starts with a system goal and employs a top-down approach to formulate more achievable intermediate goals. In contrast, the scientific method develops new knowledge of what is achievable by working from the bottom-up. Successful design is possible when the two processes can be matched, with intermediate "entities" (engineering goals) being capable of being achieved using existing scientific understanding. To access the rich space of potential solutions available from complex systems, it is important to preserve emergent behaviours that would be lost with a fully hierarchical design. A minimal hierarchical decomposition is a means of seeking a balance between achievability and complexity.

Of course, it is possible to bypass the TDBU process by using a genetic algorithm (GA) or similar to design directly for a specific goal. The disadvantages, however, are lack of generalisability and having to repeat time-consuming GAs for each design.

In contrast the TDBU approach can retain emergence in one (or both) parts, thus broadening the solution space. This is possible because, although the "intermediate entities" may result from an emergent process, they may be usable as generic building blocks to achieve a broader range of goals in the solution space, possibly leading to general design rules. Also, splitting the problem will lead to simpler optimization in most cases.

3 Application to the Sensor Network

3.1 Environment and Assumptions

A simplified version of a sensor network is a W x H array of squares, with each square representing a cell (agent) of the network. All agents are assumed to have identical properties which will be discussed in more detail below. One (or more) of the agents is designated as a "portal", the location to which, at any given time, critical damage must be reported. Any agent may become a portal and indeed the portal location may vary with time and circumstance. The rules for selecting the portal fall outside the scope of the present study, but may be due to decisions made outside the sensor network, or alternatively may be part of a self-organised hierarchical process which is an emergent property of the network itself [8]. The network may contain barriers to communication, across which communication cannot take place. Barriers may be inherent in the structure or due to prior damage. An example of such a network is shown in Figure 3.

3.1.1 Agent Properties
- Each agent may communicate directly with its four neighbours. For the purposes of this study two levels of communication will be defined: (a) Status query, a continuing process whereby each agent periodically makes and responds to status requests of its neighbours. Failure to respond (or a fault-indicating response) will set a flag which, after consistency checks, results in the initiation of a critical damage report. (b) Normal reporting, where an agent transmits a message to one or more of its neighbours.
- An agent has memory and can store data such as state, signals, IDs, logic, action lists, parameters, or programs.
- An agent has the ability to perform calculations.
- Each agent can become a portal, and the above resources must be sufficient to allow this.

3.2 Objective - Critical Damage Reporting

The objective is to design agent properties to allow detection of critical damage anywhere on the network and to communicate this information to a portal. The portal, which may be any agent in the network, is assumed to be capable of transferring the message to another part of the system which is capable of taking appropriate action. Critical damage is defined in this instance by the failure of an agent to respond to periodic status queries from a neighbour. Information about the location and severity of damage will not be reported in this initial trial, just the fact that critical damage has occurred. Time is of the essence for critical damage, so successful reporting in minimum time is the aim, over a wide variety of damage and environmental conditions. Minimising the use of resources (communications, etc.) is a subsidiary goal.

Agents have local knowledge only, so portal location and network status are unknown to them. Initial trials will assume a single portal only. A TDBU approach together with genetic algorithms will be used to design the required agent parameters.

3.3 TDBU Design for Critical Damage Reporting

This design problem can readily be made to match the TDBU framework by recognising that agents with portal status act differently to other agents. The problem may then be split into two parts, dealing with normal and portal agents respectively.

This method of splitting the problem has advantages since it is very likely that good solutions will involve communications from the portal as well as from the neighbours of a damaged cell. The value of this is that the portal may pass messages from cell to cell, storing the direction back to itself in each cell. This establishes a network of cells which know the portal direction and can guide incoming critical damage messages. Any such network must be able to operate effectively if portal positions change periodically by reconfiguring itself to accommodate such changes. One way of achieving this is to allow stored information about the portal to decay at a rate dependent on how much the portal moves.

This process has much in common with well known "ant" algorithms and the "pheromones" with which their tracks are marked [9]. However, we do not wish to restrict message-passing or the storage of information to single-track ant-like behaviour since there may be other types of behaviour which give better results. However, we will make use of the ant/pheromone terminology in the interests of brevity.

The top-down part of the design is thus provided by the variety of pheromone networks that may be generated by the portal. The intermediate entities may be identified with the pheromone networks themselves.

The corresponding bottom-up part of the design is to communicate critical damage to the portal with its pheromone network. In general this will be an easier task than locating the portal itself since use can be made of the information in the network about portal location.

The design space covers the reporting of critical damage over a wide range of conditions, including the existing prior damage/barrier environment, the rate of new damage and portal mobility.

3.4 Design Assumptions

The design is accomplished by finding sets of agent parameters which best provide time-critical reporting of damage for a wide range of environmental conditions, including variation of the rate of damage and the presence of boundaries. Having used the TDBU process to split the problem as described above we will proceed as follows:

(a) Agent behaviour when acting as a portal will be specified by the designer.
(b) A genetic algorithm (GA) will be used to design optimum agent parameters for a given fitness function, for agents in damage report mode.
(c) The overall solution will be tested on various environmental conditions and decisions made about the regions of applicability.
(d) The process will be repeated for other fitness functions and portal properties.

In each case the performance will be compared with benchmarks, including the case where agent properties provide random communications for damage reporting and no portal communications at all.

3.4.1 Examples of Portal Pheromone Networks

There are many choices for the type of networks of pheromones set up by portals, ranging from no network at all to a "flooding" broadcast. Figure 2 illustrates some of those used in the present simulations.

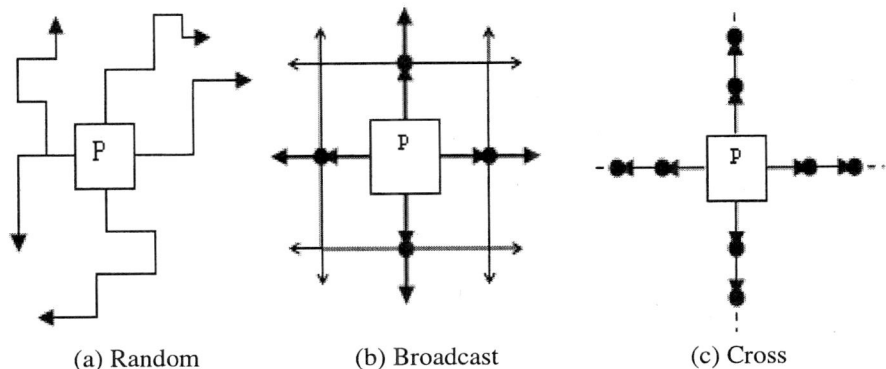

(a) Random   (b) Broadcast   (c) Cross

Fig. 2. Some examples of portal's information (pheromone) distribution

4 Simulation and Results

4.1 Simulation Environment and Agents' Properties

A simulation environment like that shown in Figure 3 was set up to test agent design in a TDBU framework. A "damage report" event has randomly located portal and damage sites, with both the portal and neighbours of the damaged agent being capable of sending messages. It is assumed that each event causes all four neighbours of a damaged cell to immediately initiate messages which are propagated through the network according to the agent properties. The aim is to find agent properties for maximum robustness of reporting to the portal and minimum reporting time, averaged over many events. Minimising communications cost is a subsidiary goal. Two key functions, G and G_p, determine how an agent responds to a message from a damage site or a portal respectively, telling it whether and in which direction to pass the message on. The parameters of G and G_p define the agent properties and are thus what must be found to optimise the performance of the network.

In these tests the portal-derived function G_p will be pre-chosen by the designer from a list of choices. The damage-derived function G, on the other hand, will be optimised using a genetic algorithm (GA).

The details of the simulation environment, agent properties and the genetic algorithm are as follows.

4.1.1 Simulation Environment

The simulation environment is a two-dimensional array as in Figure 3, with width $W = 10$ and height $H = 10$ cells. All agents are identical. For some tests a barrier to communications occupies the cells (5,1) to (5,5).

4.1.2 Agent Parameters and Properties

4.1.2.1 Data Storage
An agent stores the following data, if available:

- V_p: pheromone value (default zero);
- P: pheromone direction, where the portal-derived signal comes from;
- D: damage direction, where the damaged-derived signal comes from;
- g_{pr}: reporting direction from the last previous event (if it exists).
- r: a random direction generated by a reporting event.

V_p takes on integer values from zero to a maximum value V_{max}.
The domain of P, D and r is {UP, DOWN, LEFT, RIGHT, NONE}, ie. the four directions plus the option of not sending a message.

4.1.2.2 The Damage-Derived Function G
There are many choices for this function, which has the following form:

$$g = G(P, D, g_{pr}, r; \mathbf{w}),$$

where g is the direction of the outgoing message and $\mathbf{w} = [w_P, w_D, w_g, w_r]$ is a vector of weights associated with the four other parameters. Note that for these tests g depends on the direction, but not the value, of any pheromone present. The weights are real numbers in the domain [0, 1].

The choice of G for the present tests may be described as follows.

1. Define a vector $\mathbf{v} = [v_U\ v_D\ v_L\ v_R]$, where v_U, v_D, v_L, and v_R are the weights of the directions UP, DOWN, LEFT, RIGHT respectively. $\mathbf{v}$ is initially [0 0 0 0].
2. $\mathbf{v}$ is updated based on the values of the parameters P, D, g_{pr}, or r and their associated weights. For example, if P is "UP", v_U is updated by adding the weight of P, w_P: $v_U = v_U + w_P$. This process is carried out for all parameters.
3. Finally, the report direction g corresponds to the maximum element of $\mathbf{v}$.

A benchmark report-direction function G_{B1} was also used to test the efficacy of G. This is simply defined $g = r$, representing a fully random report direction.

4.1.2.3 The Portal-Derived Functions G_p and G_{pv}
The general form of the portal-derived function is similar to that for G, except that the pheromone value V_p needs to be considered. This requires an additional function to describe what pheromone value is passed. Thus,

$$g = G_p(V_p, P, D, g_{pr}, r; \mathbf{w}_p), \qquad V_{Pnew} = G_{pv}(V_p, P, D, g_{pr}, r; \mathbf{w}_p),$$

Again, g is the direction of the outgoing message and V_{Pnew} is the pheromone value passed to the next cell. The weight $\mathbf{w}_p$ has the same domain as $\mathbf{w}$.

As mentioned above, user-selected portal-derived functions will be in our tests. In all cases the pheromone value will decrease by one as it passes from agent to agent, ie. $V_{Pnew} = V_P - 1$.

Four examples of G_P are used and are described below. Because of their simplicity explicit functional representation is unnecessary.

- G_{P1} (Null): No portal-derived messages are passed on;
- G_{P2} (Ants): The signal direction depends only on the damage direction (75%) with a 25% random component;
- G_{P3} (Broadcast): The portal-derived signal is sent to all possible directions;
- G_{P4} (Cross): Signals maintain their original direction up to the edges of the environment.

4.1.2.4 Pheromone Decay and Portal Properties

Two other agent properties need mentioning. (i) Pheromone decay, where an agent's pheromone value decreases with time according to a specified rule. Only two situations are used in the current tests: (a) No decay, where pheromone values do not decrease, and (b) linear decrement, where the value decreases linearly.

The second is the behaviour of the portal which, although it is an agent like any other, has special properties, principally the initiation of messages. For simplicity the following assumptions have been made regarding a portal.

1. The portal issues messages from all four ports at once (or none at all).
2. When an agent becomes a portal it assumes the maximum pheromone vale V_{max}, which may decrease with time if pheromone decay operates.
3. When the pheromone value of a portal reaches a given threshold it issues new messages from all its ports.

4.2 Genetic Algorithm-Based Design

Genetic Algorithms (GA) are robust in complex search spaces and are appropriate for our current situation [10]. A colony of individuals (parameter sets) can be evolved for a number of generations, improving the performance of the colony. At the end of each generation, "parent" individuals are selected based on a fitness computation which must be strongly related to the desired outcome. After the two parents are selected, each is represented by a "chromosomal" string and are then combined, using one of several methods, to form two new chromosomes. Some old individuals are then replaced in the colony by the offspring (cf. [10, 11] for a detailed description of such algorithms).

In the current tests GA is used to optimise the parameters of the report-direction function G. In every generation each individual of the colony must be evaluated by calculating a value using an appropriate "fitness function", which is a well-behaved measure of relative fitness. For the current problem, obviously individuals that can robustly report damage to the portal in minimum time and with low communication costs will score highly. We define several such functions as follows.

$$f_1 = \sum_{i=1}^{N}\sum_{j=1}^{M} S_{i,j}, \quad S_{i,j} = \begin{cases} 1 & \text{if message reaches portal} \\ 0 & \text{otherwise} \end{cases} \quad (1)$$

Where f_1 is the fitness value, N is repeat time for each individual in the GA, M is the number of neighbours for each event. This fitness function only judges whether the damage report has arrived at the portal or not. Time and communications costs are ignored.

$$f_2 = \sum_{i=1}^{N}\sum_{j=1}^{M} \Psi_{i,j}, \quad \Psi_{i,j} = \begin{cases} -t_{i,j} & \text{if message reaches portal} \\ -2000 & \text{otherwise} \end{cases} \quad (2)$$

A large penalty is given for any signals not reaching the portal. Compared with equation (1), this fitness function includes the reporting efficiency, where t is the reporting time that the neighbour has taken.

$$f_3 = \sum_{i=1}^{N} \min_j C_{i,j}, \quad C_{i,j} = \begin{cases} -t_i & \text{at least one neighbour contacts portal} \\ -2000 & \text{otherwise} \end{cases} \quad (3)$$

f_3 differs from f_2 in that there is no penalty as long as at least one neighbour reports the damage to the portal.

$$f_4 = \sum_{i=1}^{N} \frac{C_i}{\tau_i}. \quad (4)$$

This fitness value is normalized by the minimum possible time for the neighbour to report to the portal, τ_i.

4.3 Experimental Results and Comparison

Two groups of experiments were conducted: (1) No barriers and no pheromone decay; (2) A single obstacle as in Figure 3 and pheromones decaying at constant rate.

Two functions help in judging aspects of the performance. The first is success rate,

$$S_R = \frac{S}{L}. \quad (5)$$

Where S is the number of successful reports and L the number of events. A report is successful if at least one message per event reaches the portal.

Secondly, the report efficiency is defined as follows.

$$E = \frac{1}{L}\sum_{k=1}^{L} \frac{\sum \tau_{k,i}}{\sum t_{k,i}}. \quad (6)$$

Where $\tau_{k,i}$ is the minimum possible time for a message to reach the portal, and $t_{k,i}$ the actual time for message i in event k.

4.3.1 No Obstacle and No Pheromone Decay

With no barriers, GA used to find the optimum damage-derived parameters. The highest pheromone value was $V_{max}=8$. GA training was very similar to that described in [2]. After training the performance of the best individuals was measured in terms of success rate and efficiency. Table 1 lists the test results using different strategies described in section 4.1. Each test result is the average over 1000 repeats.

Table 1. GA results comparison

	Portal-derived Function	Damage-derived Function	Fitness functions	Initial Generation Performance	Best Individual Performance	
				S_R	S_R	E
Test1	G_{P1}	G_{B1}	n.a.	n.a.	1%	2.3%
Test2	G_{P2}	G	Eq.(1)	27%	100%	18.40%
Test3	G_{P2}	G	Eq.(2)	27%	100%	46.92%
Test4	G_{P2}	G	Eq.(3)	27%	100%	47.12%
Test5	G_{P2}	G	Eq.(4)	27%	100%	47.55%

From Table 1 we can see that the damage-derived function is the main factor that affects the report efficiency. The benchmark results were far worse than any of the GA-designed results. Since fitness function f_1 did not consider time cost, Test2 is worse than Test3 to Test5 in report efficiency. f_2, f_3 and f_4 have little difference for either measure. We may conclude that the damage-derived function G, found by GA, is a good design for any of these fitness functions. From the Table 1 we can also see the initial generations' performances are much worse than the best individuals found by GA after the evolution process.

Table 2. Performance of best strategies for other portal rules

Strategy	Portal Rule	S_R	E
Test5	Broadcast	100%	75.24%
	Cross	100%	54.43%

Table 2 shows the results of using the strategy of Test5 with different portal rules. From the results we can see that this best damage-derived function can also achieve good results for different portal rules, thus vindicating the TDBU model.

4.3.2 With Barrier and Pheromone Decay

To further test the robustness of the design we implemented the best strategy found (Test5) under different environment and portal rule conditions, by adding a barrier to the environment as shown in Figure 3, and allowing pheromone values to decay as discussed previously. The maximum pheromone value was set to $V_{max} = 8$, and the pheromone value decays 0.4 every 60 time steps. The results of all three simulations are shown in Table 3.

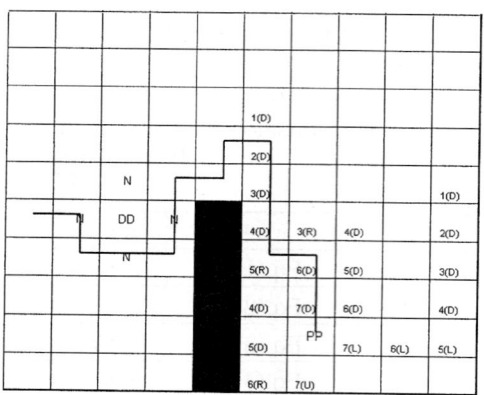

Fig. 3. The simulation environment with barrier

Table 3. Performance for different portal rules and environments

Environment	Portal Rules	S_R	E
Pheromone Decay, No Barrier	Ants	100%	40%
	Broadcast	100%	46%
	Cross	100%	41%
No Pheromone Decay, with Barrier	Ants	100%	39.69%
	Broadcast	100%	65.2%
	Cross	100%	43.7%
Pheromone Decay, with Barrier	Ants	95%	34%
	Broadcast	95.4%	35%
	Cross	95.6%	33.66%

As the results show, the original design is remarkably resilient, both to the addition of a barrier and to pheromone decay. Only when both properties are present does performance fall significantly, with success rates of less than 100%. Further work is necessary with a range of boundary configurations and pheromone decay rates, leading eventually to dynamic simulations when the new damage and portal shifts happen in real time.

5 Conclusions

We have demonstrated, for a simulated multi-agent sensor network, a design approach for the problem of robust and timely reporting of critical damage in the network, in a variety of environments including communications barriers and unknown (and time-varying) reporting sites (portals). A top-down/bottom-up (TDBU) approach, together with a genetic algorithm, has been successfully used to design properties of identical agents which are capable of reporting critical damage. From the simulations carried out we have seen that the design is far better than random searching method, and for the original design environment (no barriers, constant pheromones) gives average reporting times only twice that of the best possible when the portal location is known. We have also verified the robustness of the TDBU design for environments with barriers and with decaying pheromones. Remarkably, barriers or pheromone decay caused only a small decrease in reporting efficiency, and only when both were present did the robustness decrease significantly.

Further improvements can be expected with future research, for example by extending agent capabilities with more agent memory, defining new reporting functions with more parameters and adding pheromones to the report path. Significantly, thus far only the damage-derived agent parameters have been optimised. Joint optimisation of these and portal-derived parameters using co-evolution will maximise the usefulness of the TDBU approach.

References

1. Estrin, D., Govindan R., Heidemann J., Kumar S.: Next Century Challenges: Scalable Coordination in Sensor Networks. Proceedings of the Fifth Annual International Conference on Mobile Computing and Networks (MobiCOM '99), Seattle, August 1999.
2. Abbott, D., Doyle B., Dunlop J., Farmer T., Hedley M., Herrmann J., James G., Johnson M., Joshi B., Poulton G., Price D., Prokopenko M., Reda T., Rees D., Scott A., Valencia P., Ward D., and Winter J.: Development and Evaluation of Sensor Concepts for Ageless Aerospace Vehicles. Development of Concepts for an Intelligent Sensing System. NASA technical report NASA/CR-2002-211773, Langley Research Centre, Hampton, Virginia.
3. Vemuri, V.: Modeling of Complex Systems: an Introduction. New York (1978).
4. Mjolsness, E. and Tavormina A.: The Synergy of Biology, Intelligent Systems, and Space Exploration. IEEE Intelligent Systems - AI in Space, 3/4 2000.
5. Gadomski A. M., Balducelli C., Bologna S. and DiCostanzo G.: Integrated Parallel Bottom-up and Top-down Approach to the Development of Agent-based Intelligent DSSs for Emergency Management. The Fifth Annual Conference of The International Emergency Management Society, Washington, D.C. , May 19-22, 1998.
6. Guo, Y., Poulton P., Valencia P., and James, G.: Designing Self-Assembly for 2-Dimensional Building Blocks, ESOA'03, Melbourne, July 2003.
7. Poulton, G., Guo, Y., James, G., Valencia, P., Gerasimov, V., and Li, J.: Directed Self-Assembly of 2-Dimensional Mesoblocks using Top-down/Bottom-up Design. The Second International Workshop on Engineering Self-Organising Applications (ESOA'04), 20TH July 2004, New York, USA.

8. Kochhal M., Schwiebert L. and Gupta S.: Role-Based Hierarchical Self Organization for Wireless ad hoc Sensor Networks. Proceedings of the 2nd ACM International Conference on Wireless Sensor Networks and Applications, San Diego, CA, USA, 2003, pp: 98 – 107
9. Dorigo, M., Maniezzo V. and Colorni A.: The Ant System: An Autocatalytic Optimizing Process. Tech. Report No. 91-016 Revised, Politecnico di Milano, 1991.
10. Goldberg D.E.: Genetic Algorithms in Search, Optimisation, and Machine Learning. Addison-Wesley Publishing Company, Inc., Reading, Massachusetts, 1989.
11. Garis H.: Artificial Embryology: The Genetic Programming of an Artificial Embryo, Chapter 14 in book "Dynamic, Genetic, and Chaotic Programming", ed. Soucek B. and the IRIS Group, WILEY, 1992.

Landscape Dynamics in Multi–agent Simulation Combat Systems

Ang Yang, Hussein A. Abbass, and Ruhul Sarker

Artificial Life and Adaptive Robotics Laboratory (ALAR),
School of Information Technology and Electrical Engineering,
University of New South Wales, Australian Defence Force Academy,
Canberra, ACT 2600, Australia
{ang.yang, h.abbass, r.sarker}@adfa.edu.au

Abstract. Traditionally optimization of defence operations are based on the findings of human-based war gaming. However, this approach is extremely expensive and does not enable analysts to explore the problem space properly. Recent research shows that both computer simulations of multi-agent systems and evolutionary computation are valuable tools for optimizing defence operations. A potential maneuver strategy is generated by the evolutionary method then gets evaluated by calling the multi–agent simulation module to simulate the system behavior. The optimization problem in this context is known as a black box optimization problem, where the function that is being optimized is hidden and the only information we have access to is through the value(s) returned from the simulation for a given input set. However, to design efficient search algorithms, it is necessary to understand the properties of this search space; thus unfolding some characteristics of the black box. Without doing so, one cannot estimate how good the results are, neither can we design competent algorithms that are able to deal with the problem properly. In this paper, we provide a first attempt at understanding the characteristics and properties of the search space of complex adaptive combat systems.

1 Introduction

Traditionally, the Defence Capability Development Toolbox uses human-based warfare simulations, where a force is divided into two teams; one simulating the enemy (red team) while the other simulating friends (blue team), to optimize defence missions and also to make operational, tactical and strategic decisions. This approach is known as red teaming, scenario planning, or tiger teaming (mostly this term is used in Navy). However, this approach is extremely expensive and does not enable analysts to explore all aspects of the problem.

Recent research [1, 2] shows that warfare is characterized by non-linear behaviors and combat is a *complex adaptive system* (CAS). It opened a recent stream of research to use agent–based simulations to understand and gain insight of military operations. Meanwhile, as a combat enhancement technology

[1], evolutionary computation [3] plays a key role in helping defence analysts to develop strategies and tactics. It is undesirable to get a defence solution without proper quantification and/or qualification of how good this solution is and what opportunities have we missed out because of the computational cost involved. In order to shed light on these issues, this paper looks at the search space characteristics to provide insight to the significance of analyzing the landscape in warfare simulations.

The rest of the paper is organized as follows. In the following section, the information analysis approach for fitness landscape analysis will be covered. We will then highlight the characteristics of the warfare simulation system "WISDOM" that we use for the experiments in this paper followed by the fitness landscape analysis. Conclusions are then drawn.

2 Fitness Landscape Analysis

A fitness landscape is a representation of the structure of the search space, how solutions are spread, and what are the characteristics as defined by the fitness values of these solutions. A fitness landscape is defined by a fitness (or value) function, a solution's representation, and a neighborhood function which defines the local arrangements of solutions in the space. The concept of fitness landscape was first introduced by Wright (1932) [4] in biology to represent adaptive evolution as the population navigates on a mountainous surface where the height of a point specify how well the corresponding organism is adapted to its environment. The structure and properties of the fitness landscape play a major role in determining the success of the search method and the degree of problem difficulty [5–9]. Smith et. al. [10] and Teo and Abbass [8] used fitness landscape analysis to characterize problem difficulties in robotics and artificial organisms which in return helped them to develop efficient algorithms for their problems. When evolutionary computation methods are used to optimize problems where the objective is evaluated through multi-agent simulations, it is essential to understand the underlying nature of the search space and gain insight of the problem difficulties to help the analyst in designing better operators.

Two main approaches are used in the literature to analyze fitness landscapes: statistical analysis and information analysis. Vassilev [11] indicated that the statistical measures can only provide a vague notion of the structure of fitness landscape. Accordingly, he proposed a new approach inspired by classical information theory [12] and algorithmic information theory [13], where a fitness landscape is picturised as a set of basic objects each of which is represented by a point and the possible outcomes that may be produced by the corresponding evolutionary operators at that point. Four measures [11] were proposed for characterizing the structure of a fitness landscape $\mathcal{L}$ through analyzing the time series of fitness values $\{f_t\}_{t=1}^n$, which are real numbers taken from the interval $\mathcal{I}$ and obtained by a random walk on this fitness landscape : Information content $H(\varepsilon)$, Partial information content $M(\varepsilon)$, Information stability (ε^*) and density-basin information $h(\varepsilon)$.

Information content approximates the variety of shapes in the fitness landscape, thus it evaluates the ruggedness of the landscape path with respect to the flat area in the path. The modality encountered during a random walk on a fitness landscape can be characterized by **partial information content**. When the partial information content is zero, there is no slope in the path and the landscape is flat. If the partial information content is one, the landscape path is maximally multi-modal. The **information stability** is defined as the smallest value of ε for which the fitness landscape becomes flat. The higher the information stability is, the flatter the fitness landscape. The **density-basin information** evaluates the density and the isolation of the peaks in the landscape. Thus it is an indication of the variety of flat and smooth areas of the fitness landscape. Higher density-basin information means a number of peaks are within a small area while lower density-basin information means isolated optima. We refer the reader to [11] for a detailed explanation of the theory and calculations of these measures.

3 WISDOM - A Warfare Intelligent System for Dynamic Optimization of Missions

The Warfare Intelligent System for Dynamic Optimization of Missions (WISDOM) is a complex adaptive combat system which is developed at the Artificial Life and Adaptive Robotics Laboratory (ALAR), School of IT&EE, University of New South Wales at the Australian Defence Force Academy (UNSW@ADFA). This paper uses WISDOM as the simulation engine.

WISDOM employed a low-resolution abstract model that the detailed physics of combat are ignored while only characteristics of combatant, defense operation or behaviors are modeled. An agent in WISDOM consists of four components: sensors, capabilities, movements and communications. Each agent is driven by five types of personality weights: desire to move toward a healthy friend, injured friend, healthy opponent, injured opponent, and the flag (a target position in the environment) based on information gleaned from the sensors. The first four types of personality weights can be different for each sensor. In this paper, we only use a vision and a situation awareness communication sensor. At each simulation time step, an agent can either decide to move, fire, or communicate with other agents. Despite that in real-life systems, an agent can fire while moving, we assume that the time step is small that only one action can be performed. This assumption will help us in our future experiments to understand the trade-offs between these decisions. The movements of agents in WISDOM are determined by an attraction-repulsion weighting system based on agents' personalities. The weights are aggregated using a penalty function as in Equation 1. The movement equation is a variation of that implemented in ISAAC [1], EINSTein [14] and CROCACDILE [15] and simply selects the direction with maximum weights (minimum penalty) as the direction of an agent movement.

$$W_{new} = \sum_{i=1}^{n} \frac{P_i^v}{D_i^v} + \sum_{j=1}^{m} (\sigma_j \cdot \frac{P_j^c}{D_j^c}) + \frac{P^f}{D^f} \quad (1)$$

where:

W_{new} denotes the weight for a new location;
P_i^v denotes the personality of agent i in the vision range;
D_i^v denotes the distance between the new location to agent i in the vision range;
P_j^c denotes the corresponding personality of agent j based in the communication range;
D_i^c denotes the distance between the new location to agent j in the communication range;
σ_j denotes the probability to trust the message from agent j;
P^f denotes the desire to move toward the flag;
D^f denotes the distance between the new location to the flag;
n denotes the number of agents within the vision range;
m denotes the number of agents within the communication range.

Two run modes are supported in the current version of WISDOM. The first mode is the interactive mode, which enables users to interactively control the simulation. The second mode is the off–line batch mode, where search methods can call the simulation engine to evaluate potential configurations.

4 Experimental Objectives and Setup

The aim of these experiments is to characterize the fitness landscape for evolving personality characteristics for the blue team under different scenarios of fixed personality characteristics of the red team. The objective of a scenario is to maximize the differential advantage of blue's health over red's; that is, the larger the gap between the damage in the red team and the damage in the blue team, the more advantage the blue team would have over the red team. Formally, the objective is defined in Equation 2 as follows:

Let

HBE be the total number of health units associated with the blue team at the end of the simulation.

HRI be the initial total number of health units associated with the red team at the start of the simulation.

HRE be the total number of health units associated with the red team at the end of the simulation.

$$\textbf{maximize} \quad objective = HBE + (HRI - HRE) \quad (2)$$

To test the dynamics of the landscape, we used six different scenarios for the red team; these scenarios are listed in Table 1. In the *Balanced* scenario (BScenario), the team members tend to balance grouping together while having equal desire to follow the enemy and reach the goal (flag). In the *Goal Oriented* scenario (GScenario), team members are neutral about grouping together or following the enemy; however, they are determined to get to the flag. In the next four scenarios, the members are neutral about getting to the flag and the emphasis is more on their relationship with the enemy and themselves. In the *Very aggressive* scenario (VScenario), the team members tend not to cluster and being focused more on following the enemy. In the *aggressive* scenario (AScenario), the members tend to be more rational than those in the VScenario by being neutral about clustering together while running after the enemy. In the *Defensive* scenario (DScenario), the members tend to cluster together while being neutral about following the enemy. In the *Coward* scenario (CScenario), they are neutral about clustering together but they run away from the enemy. In all six experiments, the desire of the red team to fire at the blue team is fixed to the maximum of 1 and the same weights are used for information gleaned from the vision and communication sensors.

Table 1. Different setups for the red team used in the experiments

Scenario	Attraction to healthy friend	Attraction to injured friend	Attraction to healthy enemy	Attraction to injured enemy	Desire to get to the flag
Balanced	group	group	group	group	target
Goal Oriented	neutral	neutral	neutral	neutral	target
Very aggressive	avoid	avoid	group	group	neutral
Aggressive	neutral	neutral	group	group	neutral
Defensive	group	group	neutral	neutral	neutral
Coward	neutral	neutral	avoid	avoid	neutral

The evaluation of the game at any point of time involves running the simulation 100 times for 100 time steps each and repeating the run 10 different times. Two different fitness measures are used; the first is the average of the objective values over the 100 different simulation repeats, while the second is the normalized average which is the average fitness normalized by the standard deviation. The equation of the normalization is given as follows:

$$Fitness_2 = \frac{average}{1 + standard\ deviation} \quad (3)$$

We add 1 to the standard deviation to avoid division by 0 and to bound the fitness between the actual average fitness (when the standard deviation is 0) and 0 (when the standard deviation is very large). We used 20 agents in each team starting with 10 health units; therefore, both fitness values are in the range of 0 and 400 (when the current blue fitness $HBE = 20 \times 10$ and all red team members are dead; therefore $HRI - HRE = 20 \times 10 - 0 = 200$.

5 Results and Analysis

In order to understand the fitness landscape, we implemented three methods: random search, random walk, and hill climbing. The last two use a stochastic neighborhood defined by a bell shape with zero mean and 0.1 standard deviation to move to local solutions in the space. The runs for each method were undertaken for 10,000 solutions and were repeated 10 different times; therefore, we have 10^5 solutions being sampled in each experiment and the simulation engine was called 10^7 times. We will first look at the probability of generating a good solution at random using random search. The objective of this analysis is to find out if good solutions are common in this search space or they are simply rare to encounter.

Figure 1 presents the probability density function (pdf) and cumulative distribution function (cdf) of solutions generated by random search. The probability of generating an average fitness value of 200 or less is almost 1 in all scenarios. However, there is a slight probability of generating average fitness values more

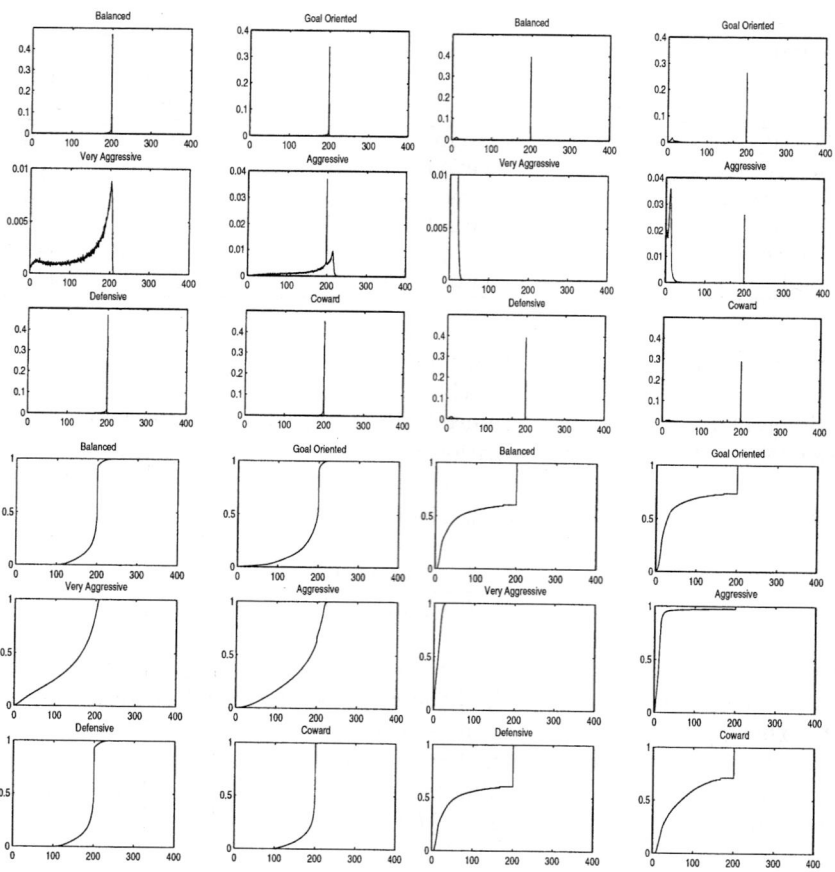

Fig. 1. Probability density function of solutions obtained for random search using average fitness (3x2 top left) normalized average fitness (3x2 top right), and cumulative distribution average fitness (3x2 bottom left) and normalized average fitness (3x2 bottom right)

than 200 and exactly 0 probability of generating normalized average fitness values greater than 200. This implies that the landscape is full of solutions with fitness value of 200. This fitness of 200 occurs only if the amount of damage in the blue is equal to the amount of damage in the red. This type of equilibrium seems to dominate the search space.

It is surprising to see the similarities between the balanced, goal oriented, defensive and coward strategies in terms of pdf and cdf. In the four strategies, the majority of solutions encountered have average and normalized fitness values of 200 and it is very unlikely to generate solutions with average fitness less than 100 or more than 200. However, when we look at the Very aggressive and aggressive strategies, the situation is different. In the very aggressive strategy, it seems that there are more solutions with lower fitness; that is, the blue team can face more troubles in finding better strategies under this strategy or even finding equilibrium. In the aggressive strategy, a similar situation occurs although there is a higher probability for encountering average fitness better than 200 as compared to all other strategies.

In terms of normalized average fitness, the probability of encountering solutions with normalized average fitness greater than 30 is almost 0. This implies that under this strategy, solutions are very unstable with large variance (almost 5% of the mean). When looking at the cdf, one can notice an almost sigmoid like shape for the balanced, goal oriented, defensive and coward strategies with average fitness and the half–truncated bell shape with normalized fitness.

After gleaning this insight from random search, we need to verify our findings through a more theoretically sound approach. In this experiment, we will generate random walks and look at the changes in the fitness. Random search is able to sample the search space but it does not tell us much about the local structure of the landscape. For example, it does not tell us if the fitness value of 200, which is commonly encountered in the experiment, causes the landscape to be flat or rugged.

Figures 2 and 3 depicts the time series being generated by random walk. Because every experiment was repeated 10 times, we only selected a representative run for each experiment. The figures reveal that the landscape is indeed rugged. However, the landscape for the balanced, goal oriented, defensive and coward strategies contains many flat areas.

We need to define the concept of the fitness signal in order to better analyze the data. The signal is usually defined in the literature as the difference between the fitness of the best solution and second best. We will call this signal as signal–best. A more generic definition that we will use for the purpose of our analysis in this paper is to define the signal as the difference between the best and worst fitness values encountered during the search. We will call this signal as signal–worst. The concept of signal–worst provides a simple mechanism to understand the range of fitness values in a landscape. Accordingly, one can see that the minimum signal–worst occurs with the balanced and coward strategies. Good solutions in both strategies seem to be more isolated and surrounded with low fitness values.

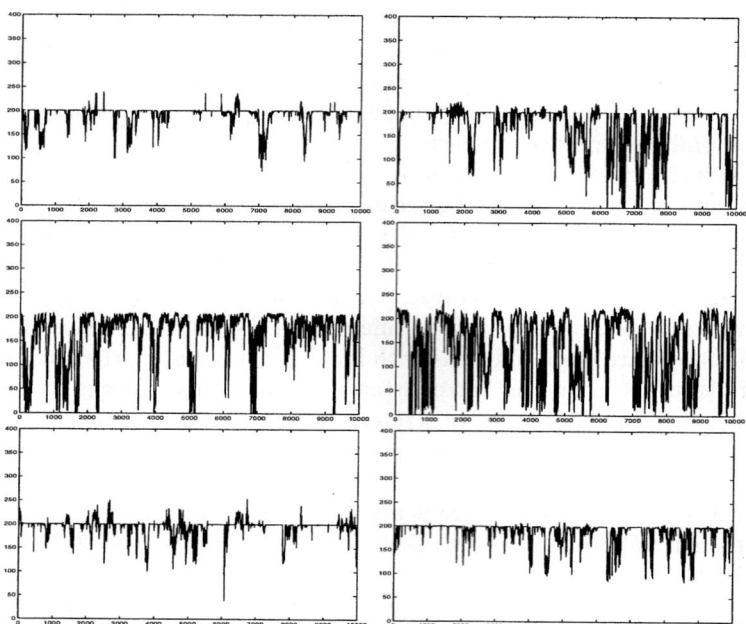

Fig. 2. The average fitness over time for random walk. The order is: Balanced(top left), Goal Oriented(top right), Very Aggressive(middle left), Aggressive(middle right), Defensive(bottom left), Coward(bottom right), respectively

However, the previous finding does not continue to hold when we look at the normalized fitness time series as depicted in Figure 3. Here, we can see that the minimum signal–worst occurs with the very aggressive and aggressive strategies while the balanced, goal oriented, defensive and coward strategies have almost the same value of signal–worst. It is also clear that using the normalized average as the fitness function creates a rugged landscape for the very aggressive and aggressive strategies, while for the other four, the landscape is full of flat regions.

To better understand the fitness landscape, we applied the information theoretic measures to quantify the characteristics of the landscape. Figures 4 lists some results of the fitness landscape analysis. It is clear that the findings between the two fitness values are consistent with each others. The highest number of peaks occurred in both cases with the very aggressive and aggressive scenarios. It is also interesting to see that all scenarios except the very aggressive scenario have similar or close–by information stability for both fitness functions. The very aggressive scenario seems to have much lower levels of fitness values than the other scenarios. What is intriguing here is that the fitness landscape for both fitness functions has very similar characteristics despite the differences in the range of possible actions embedded in these spaces.

In terms of information stability, we can see that it requires high value of ϵ except for the normalized fitness in the very aggressive scenario. The high value

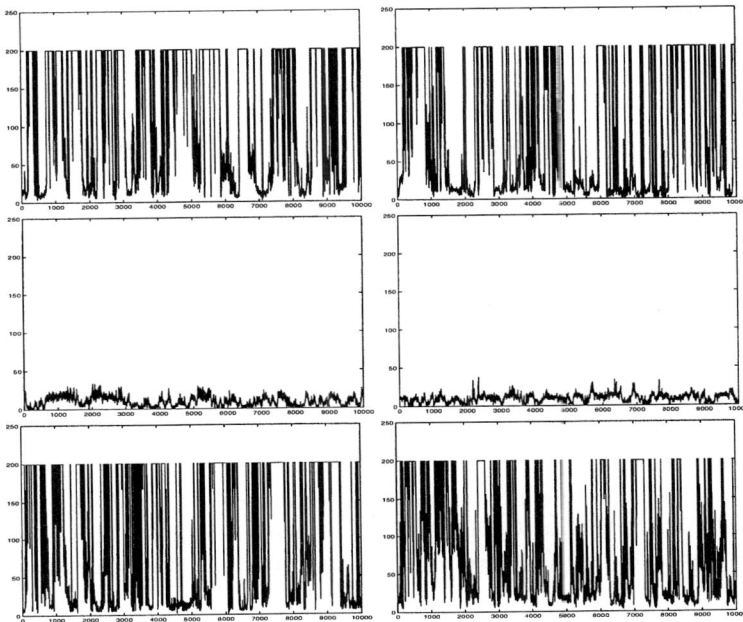

Fig. 3. The normalized fitness over time for random walk. The order is: Balanced(top left), Goal Oriented(top right), Very Aggressive(middle left), Aggressive(middle right), Defensive(bottom left), Coward(bottom right), respectively

of ϵ is almost 50% of the upper bound on the objective function. This entails that the highest difference between two neighbor solutions in the search space is less than or equal to 50% of the upper bound on the fitness value. Whether the results for the fitness landscape analysis will map well when using a hill-climbing like approach, is the issue we will investigate in the rest of this paper.

Figure 5 depicts the average fitness of the best solution found so far for hill climbing. By looking at the graphs, it is easy to see that hill climbing is much better than random search. Although the fitness value of 200 appear the most still, a number of fitness values is over 200 for all six scenarios, even in the Aggressive and Very Aggressive scenarios. The graphs of the average fitness of the best solution shows that the fitness is mostly improved at the initial stage of searching for all six scenarios. This is consistent with the fitness landscape analysis since the ruggedness in the fitness landscape will cause a quick improvement in the beginning then a harder to find good solutions later on.

Table 2 presents the best solution found over the ten repeats using the three methods. It is clear that Hill Climbing failed twice with normalized fitness in the aggressive and very aggressive scenarios. As predicted, these two cases had the smallest worst-signal and very rugged landscape. They also have the highest number of expected optima in the landscape.

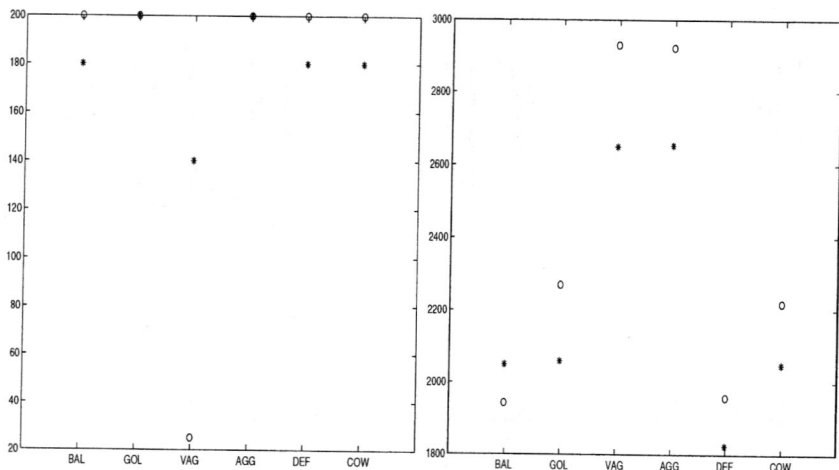

Fig. 4. The information stability (left) and expected optima (right) over six scenarios in order of Balanced, Goal Oriented, Very Aggressive, Aggressive, Defensive and Coward by using average (denoted by '*') and normalized fitness (denoted by 'o'), respectively

Table 2. The best average and normalized average fitness over the 10 runs in three experiments

	Random Search		Hill Climbing		Random Walk	
	AvgFit	NormFit	AvgFit	NormFit	AvgFit	NormFit
Balanced	264.98	200	267.34	200	258.44	200
Goal Oriented	226.32	200	231.22	200	228.92	200
Very Aggressive	210.46	41.78	213.30	25.55	210.58	41.68
Aggressive	240.68	200	246.38	17.54	239.32	200
Defensive	246.96	200	278.96	200	253.06	200
Coward	211.86	200	210.36	200	210.40	200

The previous findings are intriguing as they shed light on the design of efficient search algorithms for this problem. For example, with a very rugged landscape and almost no flat areas, a short memory is needed for Tabu search similar to the findings in job–shop scheduling problems. When the landscape is full of flat areas, one needs to allow for more neutral mutations to occur to be able to escape these flat areas. When the landscape is very rugged and the signal–worst value is small, amplifying the fitness function through scaling is essential to generate enough signal for an evolutionary computation methods to find good solutions.

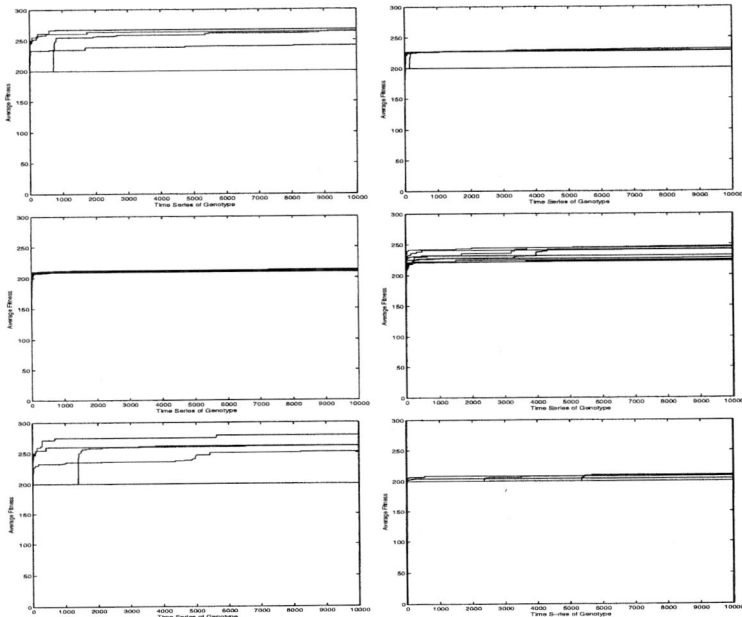

Fig. 5. The average fitness of the best solution found over time for hill climbing using average fitness. The order from top bottom left right is: Balanced, Goal Oriented, Very Aggressive, Aggressive, Defensive, Coward, respectively

6 Conclusion and Future Work

The fitness landscape was found to be rugged and multimodal under all scenarios. It was extremely difficult for random search, hill-climbing and random walk to find good fitness values. The level of difficulties in finding the right combination of weights for the blue team is largely dependent on the strategy of the red team as each strategy changes the fitness landscape of the problem. Being aggressive has the advantage of complicating the fitness landscape and making it difficult to find a defensive strategy, while being coward has the advantages of survival.

In this paper, we used homogenous model for each combat team which may limits our understanding the dynamics of the combat systems. In the future we would like to explore the dynamics by using inhomogeneous model.

Acknowledgment

This work is supported by the University of New South Wales grant PS04411 and the Australian Research Council (ARC) Centre on Complex Systems grant number CEO0348249. The authors also wish to thank Dr. Neville Curtis from Defence Science and Technology Organization (DSTO) for useful discussions.

References

1. Ilachinski, A.: Irreducible Semi-Autonomous Adaptive combat (ISAAC): An Artificial Life Approach to Land Combat. Research Memorandum CRM 97-61, Center for Naval Analyses, Alexandria (1997)
2. Lauren, M.K.: Modelling Combat Using Fractals and the Satistics of Scaling Ssystems. Military Operations Research **5** (2000) 47 – 58
3. Fogel, D.: Evolutionary Computation: towards a new philosophy of machine intelligence. IEEE Press, New York, NY (1995)
4. Wright, S.: The roles of mutation, inbreeding, crossbreeding, and selection in evolution. In Jones, D., ed.: Proceedings of the Sixth International Congress on Genetics. Volume 1., Brooklyn, NY (1932) 356–366
5. Horn, J., Goldberg, D.E.: Genetic algorithm difficulty and the modality of fitness landscapes. In Whitley, L.D., Vose, M.D., eds.: Foundations of Genetic Algorithms 3. Morgan Kaufmann, San Francisco, CA (1999) 243–269
6. Kallel, L., Naudts, B., Reeves, C.R.: Properties of fitness functions and search landscapes. In Kallel, L., Naudts, B., Rogers, A., eds.: Theoretical Aspects of Evolutionary Computing. Springer, Berlin (2001) 175–206
7. Mitchell, M., Forrest, S., Holland, J.H.: The royal road function for genetic algorithms: Fitness landscapes and ga performance. In Varela, F.J., Bourgine, P., eds.: Proceedings of the First European Conference on Artificial Life, Cambridge, MA, MIT Press (1992) 245–254
8. Teo, J., Abbass, H.A.: An information-theoretic landscape analysis of neurocontrolled embodied organisms. Neural Computing and Applications Journal **13** (2004)
9. Vassilev, V.K., Miller, J.F.: The advantages of landscape neutrality in digital circuit evolution. In: ICES. (2000) 252–263
10. Smith, T., Husbands, P., O'Shea, M.: Not measuring evolvability: Initial investigation of an evolutionary robotics search space. In: Proceedings of the 2001 Congress on Evolutionary Computation CEC2001, COEX, World Trade Center, 159 Samseong-dong, Gangnam-gu, Seoul, Korea, IEEE Press (2001) 9–16
11. Vassilev, V.K., Fogarty, T.C., Miller, J.F.: Information characteristics and the structure of landscapes. Evolutionary Computation **8** (2000) 31–60
12. Shannon, C.E.: A mathematical theory of communication. The Bell System Technical Journal **27** (1948) 379–423
13. Chaitin, G.J.: Information, randomness and incompleteness : papers on algorithmic information theory. World Scientific, Singapore (1987)
14. Ilachinski, A.: Enhanced ISAAC neural simulation toolkit (einstein), an artificial-life laboratory for exploring self-organized emergence in land combat. Beta-Test User's Guide CIM 610.10, Center for Naval Analyses (1999)
15. Barlow, M., Easton, A.: CROCADILE - an open, extensible agent-based distillation engine. Information & Security **8** (2002) 17–51

Safe Agents in Space: Lessons from the Autonomous Sciencecraft Experiment

Rob Sherwood, Steve Chien, Daniel Tran, Benjamin Cichy,
Rebecca Castano, Ashley Davies, and Gregg Rabideau

Jet Propulsion Laboratory, California Institute of Technology,
4800 Oak Grove Dr., Pasadena, CA 91109
{firstname.lastname@jpl.nasa.gov}

Abstract. An Autonomous Science Agent is currently flying onboard the Earth Observing One Spacecraft. This software enables the spacecraft to autonomously detect and respond to science events occurring on the Earth. The package includes software systems that perform science data analysis, deliberative planning, and run-time robust execution. Because of the deployment to a remote spacecraft, this Autonomous Science Agent has stringent constraints of autonomy and limited computing resources. We describe these constraints and how they are reflected in our agent architecture.

1 Introduction

The Autonomous Sciencecraft Experiment (ASE) has been flying autonomous agent software on the Earth Observing One (EO-1) spacecraft [5] since January 2004. This software demonstrates several integrated autonomy technologies to enable autonomous science. Several algorithms are used to analyze remote sensing imagery onboard in order to detect the occurrence of science events. These algorithms will be used to downlink science data only on change, and will detect features of scientific interest such as volcanic eruptions, flooding, ice breakup, and presence of cloud cover. The results of these onboard science algorithms are inputs to onboard planning software that then modify the spacecraft observation plan to capture high value science events. This new observation plan is then be executed by a robust goal and task oriented execution system, able to adjust the plan to succeed despite run-time anomalies and uncertainties. Together these technologies enable autonomous goal-directed exploration and data acquisition to maximize science return.

The ASE onboard flight software includes several autonomy software components:

- Onboard science algorithms that analyze the image data to detect trigger conditions such as science events, "interesting" features, changes relative to previous observations, and cloud detection for onboard image masking
- Robust execution management software using the Spacecraft Command Language (SCL) [6] package to enable event-driven processing and low-level autonomy

- The Continuous Activity Scheduling Planning Execution and Replanning (CASPER) [3] software that modifies the current spacecraft activity plan based on science observations in the previous orbit cycles

The onboard science algorithms analyze the images to extract static features and detect changes relative to previous observations. Several algorithms have already been demonstrated on EO-1 Hyperion data to automatically identify regions of interest including land, ice, snow, water, and thermally hot areas. Repeat imagery using these algorithms can detect regions of change (such as flooding and ice melt) as well as regions of activity (such as lava flows). We have been using these algorithms onboard to enable retargeting and search, e.g., retargeting the instrument on a subsequent orbit cycle to identify and capture the full extent of a flood. Although the ASE software is running on the Earth observing spacecraft EO-1, the long term goal is to use this software on future interplanetary space missions. For these missions, onboard science analysis will enable data be captured at the finest time-scales without overwhelming onboard memory or downlink capacities by varying the data collection rate on the fly.

The CASPER planning software generates a mission operations plan from goals provided by the onboard science analysis module. The model-based planning algorithms will enable rapid response to a wide range of operations scenarios based on a deep model of spacecraft constraints, including faster recovery from spacecraft anomalies. The onboard planner accepts as inputs the science and engineering goals and ensures high-level goal-oriented behavior.

The robust execution system (SCL) accepts the CASPER-derived plan as an input and expands the plan into low-level spacecraft commands. SCL monitors the execution of the plan and has the flexibility and knowledge to perform event-driven commanding to enable local improvements in execution as well as local responses to anomalies.

1.1 Typical ASE Scenario

A typical ASE scenario involves monitoring of active volcano regions such as Mt. Etna in Italy. (See Figure 1.) Scientists have used data from the Hyperion instrument onboard the EO-1 spacecraft for ground-based studies of this volcano. The ASE concept will be applied as follows:

1. Initially, ASE has a list of science targets to monitor that have been sent as high-level goals from the ground.
2. As part of normal operations, the CASPER planning software generates a plan to monitor the targets on this list by periodically imaging them with the Hyperion instrument. For volcanic studies, the infrared and near infrared bands are used.
3. During execution of this plan, the EO-1 spacecraft images Mt. Etna with the Hyperion instrument.
4. The onboard science algorithms analyze the image and detect a fresh lava flow. If new activity is detected, a science goal is generated to continue monitoring the volcanic site. If no activity is observed, the image is not downlinked.

5. Assuming a new goal is generated, CASPER plans to acquire a further image of the ongoing volcanic activity.
6. The SCL software executes the CASPER generated plan to re-image the site.
7. This cycle is then repeated on subsequent observations.

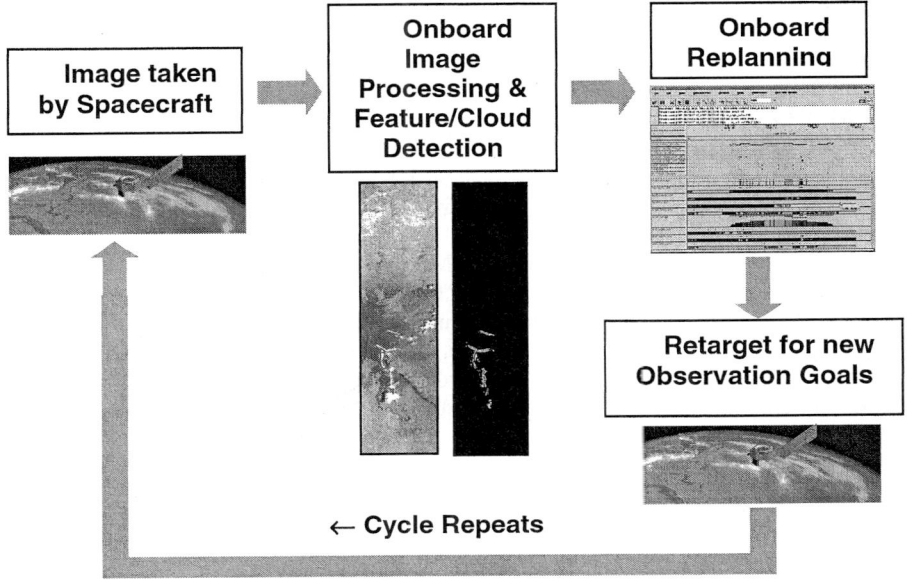

Fig. 1. Autonomous Science Scenario

1.2 Space-Based Autonomy Software Challenges

Building autonomy software for space missions has a number of key challenges; many of these issues increase the importance of building a reliable, safe, agent. Some examples include:

1. Limited, intermittent communications to the agent. A typical spacecraft may communicate several times a day (Earth orbiter) to once or twice per week (planetary spacecraft).
2. Spacecraft are very complex. A typical spacecraft has thousands of components, each of which must be carefully engineered to survive rigors of space (extreme temperature, radiation, physical stresses).
3. Limited observability. Because processing telemetry is expensive, onboard storage is limited, downlink bandwidth is limited, and engineering telemetry is limited. Thus onboard software must be able to make decisions based on limited information and ground operations teams must be able to operate the spacecraft with even more limited information.

4. Limited computing power. Because of limited power onboard, spacecraft computing resources are usually very constrained. On average, spacecraft CPUs offer 25 MIPS and 128 MB RAM – far less than a typical personal computer. Our CPU allocation for ASE on EO-1 spacecraft is 4 MIPS and 128MB RAM.

In the remainder of this paper we describe the ASE software architecture and components. We then discuss the issues of adapting the ASE software agent for space flight.

2 The EO-1 Mission

EO-1 was launched on November 21, 2000. EO-1 has 2 imaging instruments. Over 20-Gbits of data from the Advanced Land Imager (ALI) and Hyperion instruments are collected and stored for each image taken.

The EO-1 spacecraft has two Mongoose M5 processors. The first M5 CPU is used for the EO-1 spacecraft control functions. The secondary M5 CPU is a controller for the large mass storage device. Each M5 runs at 12 MHz (for ~8 MIPS) and has 256 MB RAM. Both M5's run the VxWorks operating system. The ASE software operates on the secondary CPU. This provides an added level of safety for the spacecraft since the ASE software does not run on the main spacecraft processor.

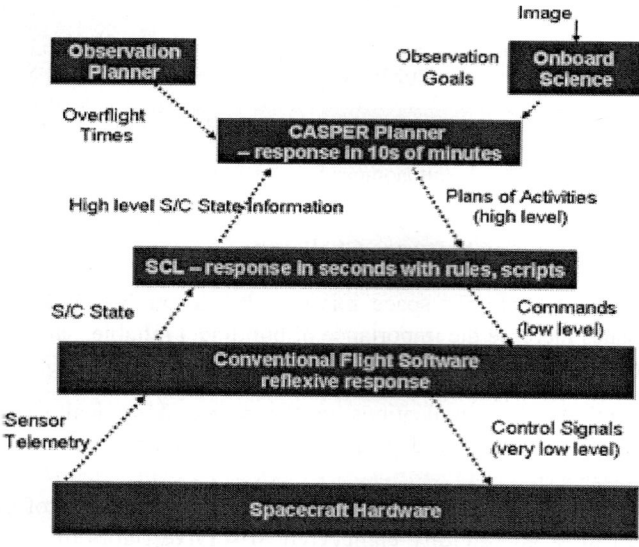

Fig. 2. Autonomy Software Architecture

3 Autonomy Software Architecture

The autonomy software on EO-1 is organized into a traditional three-layer architecture [4] (See Figure 2.). At the highest level of abstraction, the Continuous

Activity Scheduling Planning Execution and Replanning (CASPER) software is responsible for mission planning functions. CASPER schedules science activities while respecting spacecraft operations and resource constraints. The duration of the planning process is on the order of tens of minutes. CASPER scheduled activities are inputs to the Spacecraft Command Language (SCL) system, which generates the detailed sequence commands corresponding to CASPER scheduled activities. SCL operates on the several second timescale. Below SCL, the EO-1 flight software is responsible for lower level control of the spacecraft and also operates a full layer of independent fault protection. The interface from SCL to the EO-1 flight software is at the same level as ground generated command sequences. The science analysis software is scheduled by CASPER and executed by SCL in a batch mode. The results from the science analysis software result in new observation requests presented to the CASPER system for integration in the mission plan.

This layered architecture was chosen for two principal reasons:

1. The layered architecture enables separation of responses based on timescale and most appropriate representation. The flight software level must implement control loops and fault protection and respond very rapidly and is thus directly coded in C. SCL must respond quickly (in seconds) and perform many procedural actions. Hence SCL uses as its core representation scripts, rules, and database records. CASPER must reason about longer term operations, state, and resource constraints. Because of its time latency, it can afford to use a mostly declarative artificial intelligence planner/scheduler representation.
2. The layered architecture enables redundant implementation of critical functions – most notable spacecraft safety constraint checking. In the design of our spacecraft agent model, we implemented spacecraft safety constraints in all levels where feasible.

Each of the software modules operates at a separate VxWorks operating system priority. The tasks are shown below in Table 1 in decreasing priority. The ASE to flight software bridge is the task responsible for reading the real-time flight software telemetry stream, extracting pertinent data, and making it accessible to the remainder of the ASE software. The Band Stripping task reads the science data from the onboard solid state recorder and extracts a small portion of the science data (12 bands of Hyperion data) to RAM. The science analysis software then operates on the extracted data to detect science events.

Table 1. EO-1 Software Tasks in Decreasing Task Priority (e.g. upper tasks have highest priority for CPU)

Set of Tasks	Rationale for Priority
EO-1 Flight Software	Required for WARP hardware safety
ASE to FSW Bridge	Required to keep up with telemetry stream
Band Stripping	Utilizes WARP hardware while running
SCL	Lowest level autonomy, closes tightest loops
CASPER	Responds in tens of minutes timescale
Science Analysis	Batch process without hard deadlines

It is worth noting that our agent architecture is designed to scale to multiple agents. Agents communicate at either the planner level (via goals) or the execution level (to coordinate execution).

We now describe each of the architectural components of our architecture in further detail.

4 Onboard Mission Planning

In order for the spacecraft to respond autonomously to a science event, it must be able to independently perform the mission planning function. This requires software that can model all spacecraft and mission constraints. The CASPER [3] software performs this function for ASE. CASPER represents the operations constraints in a general modeling language and reasons about these constraints to generate new operations plans that respect spacecraft and mission constraints and resources. CASPER uses a local search approach [2] to develop operations plans.

Because onboard computing resources are scarce, CASPER must be very efficient in generating plans. While a typical desktop or laptop PC may have 2000-3000 MIPS performance, 5-20 MIPS is more typical onboard a spacecraft. In the case of EO-1, the Mongoose V CPU has approximately 8 MIPS. Of the three software packages, CASPER is by far the most computationally intensive. For that reason, our optimization efforts were focused on CASPER. Careful engineering and modeling were required to enable CASPER to build a plan in tens of minutes on the relatively slow CPU.

CASPER is responsible for long-term mission planning in response to both science goals derived onboard as well as anomalies. In this role, CASPER must plan and schedule activities to achieve science and engineering goals while respecting resource and other spacecraft operations constraints. For example, when acquiring an initial image, a volcanic event is detected. This event may warrant a high priority request for a subsequent image of the target to study the evolving phenomena. In this case, CASPER will modify the operations plan to include the necessary activities to re-image. This may include determining the next over flight opportunity, ensuring that the spacecraft is pointed appropriately, that sufficient power and data storage are available, that appropriate calibration images are acquired, and that the instrument is properly prepared for the data acquisition.

In the context of ASE, CASPER reasons about the majority of spacecraft operations constraints directly in its modeling language. However, there are a few notable exceptions. First, the over flight constraints are calculated using ground-based orbit analysis tools. The over flight opportunities and pointing required for all targets of interest are uploaded as a table and utilized by CASPER to plan. Second, the ground operations team will initially perform management of the momentum of the reaction wheels for the EO-1 spacecraft. This is because of the complexity of the momentum management process caused by the EO-1 configuration of three reaction wheels rather than four.

5 Onboard Robust Execution

ASE uses the Spacecraft Command Language (SCL) [6] to provide robust execution. SCL is a software package that integrates procedural programming with a real-time, forward-chaining, rule-based system. A publish/subscribe software bus allows the distribution of notification and request messages to integrate SCL with other onboard software. This design enables both loose or tight coupling between SCL and other flight software as appropriate.

The SCL "smart" executive supports the command and control function. Users can define scripts in an English-like manner. Compiled on the ground, those scripts can be dynamically loaded onboard and executed at an absolute or relative time. Ground-based absolute time script scheduling is equivalent to the traditional procedural approach to spacecraft operations based on time. SCL scripts are planned and scheduled by the CASPER onboard planner. The science analysis algorithms and SCL work in a cooperative manner to generate new goals for CASPER. These goals are sent as messages on the software bus.

Many aspects of autonomy are implemented in SCL. For example, SCL implements many constraint checks that are redundant with those in the EO-1 fault protection software. Before SCL sends each command to the EO-1 command processor, it undergoes a series of constraint checks to ensure that it is a valid command. Any pre-requisite states required by the command are checked (such as the communications system being in the correct mode to accept a command). SCL will also verify that there is sufficient power so that the command does not trigger a low bus voltage condition and that there is sufficient energy in the battery. Using SCL to check these constraints (while included in the CASPER model) provides an additional level of safety to the autonomy flight software.

6 Preparing the CASPER Planner for Space Flight

Given the many challenges to developing flight software, this section discusses several issues encountered in preparing the CASPER planner for flight. Specifically, we describe:

- *Reducing the CASPER Image Size* – With infrequent and short ground contacts and limited available memory, we needed to reduce the CASPER image size. We discuss our strategies to reduce the CASPER image size.
- *Approach to Long Term Planning* – CASPER must be able to autonomously plan for a week's worth of EO-1 activities, which includes over 100 science observations. We discuss how this is achieved within the available memory and CPU.
- *Speed Improvements to Meet Autonomy Requirements* – Several model and code optimizations were performed to increase the running speed of ASE.

In addition, we have performed several optimizations on the data collected relating to the state and actions of the planner. These optimizations are not described in this paper but can be referenced here [11].

6.1 Reducing the CASPER Image Size

CASPER's core planning engine is the Automated Scheduling and Planning Environment (ASPEN) [3] ground-based planner. ASPEN is a re-usable framework which is capable of supporting a wide variety of planning and scheduling applications. It provides a set of software components commonly found in most planning systems such as: an expressive modeling language, resource management, a temporal reasoning system, and support of a graphical user interface. Because of limited onboard computing memory, we had to reduce the image size. CASPER developers took two approaches to reducing the image size: removing unneeded components and reducing code image size inefficiencies. Prior to this work, the image size of CASPER was 12MB.

The CASPER development team went through the core software and removed each software component deemed unnecessary for flight. Several modules removed from the CASPER code include:

- *Backtracking Search* – The ASPEN framework provides several search algorithms that perform backtracking search. On ASE, we have decided to use the repair search algorithm, so these other algorithms were not needed.
- *Optimization* – CASPER provides the capability to optimize the schedule based on several preferences [10] defined by mission planners. However, we have decided not to use this functionality for ASE.
- *GUI Sockets* – Because ASPEN is a ground-based planner, it provides a GUI for visualizing the schedule and interacting with it. Communication with this GUI is done through the ASPEN socket interface. In flight, support for a GUI is not necessary.
- *General Heuristics* – The ASPEN core contains multiple sets of generic heuristics that have been found to be useful across multiple projects. CASPER for ASE requires a subset of these heuristics; therefore, the unused sets were removed.
- *Generalized Timelines* – Generalized timelines provides a general infrastructure to model complex state variables and resources. This infrastructure was not required for ASE and was removed.

Removing software components trimmed approximately 3MB from the CASPER image size.

CASPER also makes heavy use of the Standard Template Library (STL), specifically the containers provided. STL templates are widely known to increase code size in C++ because for each container defined in CASPER, the code may be duplicated several times. There exist various compiler techniques available that attempts to minimize the duplication. To minimize the impact of code bloat, we re-implemented the STL container and functions used in the CASPER code. This re-implementation, dubbed "lite STL", was developed to minimize the code generation, trading space for execution time. We were able to remove approximately 3MB from the CASPER image using this strategy.

Along with simple compiler optimization, removing unneeded software components, and reducing the impact of code duplication, the final size of the CASPER image was reduced to 5MB.

6.2 Approach to Long Term Planning

One of the scenarios planned for ASE is autonomous control of EO-1 for a week. This requires CASPER to support generation of a valid schedule for a week's worth of EO-1 operations. During a nominal week, EO-1 averages over 100 science observations and 50 S-Band/X-Band ground contacts. The size of this problem presents a challenge to CASPER, given the limited memory and CPU constraints.

While most desktop workstations have several GB's of memory available, CASPER on EO-1 is constrained with a 32MB heap. As result, we need to ensure that generation of a week's plan does not exhaust all available heap space. A science observation is the most complex activity within the CASPER model, consisting of over 78 activities. Planning a week's worth of operation would require scheduling over 7800 activities (not including downlink and momentum management activities) and exhaust our heap space.

Also, as the number of goals in the schedule increase, the computation time to schedule a goal will also increase, due to the interaction between goals. On EO-1, this problem is exacerbated with an 8 MIPS processor, of which 4 MIPS are shared by the SCL, CASPER, and science processing software.

To resolve the problems with CPU and memory consumption, CASPER utilizes a hierarchal planning approach with focused planning periods. CASPER performs abstract planning and scheduling of observations for the entire week, such as ensuring a constraint of one science observation per orbit. It also performs near-term planning for the next 24 hours by detailing the science observations to the low-level activities. This near-term planning window is continuously updated to include the next 24 hours of the schedule and as past observations exit the planning window, they are automatically removed from the plan. By reducing the number of science observations that need to be scheduled and detailed to a 24 hour period, we reduce memory and CPU consumption.

6.3 Speed Improvements to Meet Autonomy Requirements

The ASE experiment is constrained by the computing environment onboard EO-1. Because each of the EO-1 software builds is a single static image, all ASE components that dynamically allocate RAM require their own memory manager. SCL contains a memory manager previously used on the FUSE mission. CASPER uses a separate memory manager adapted from JPL's Deep Impact mission. However, performance from early flight tests indicated that the SCL memory manager was significantly hampering performance, so SCL was switched to use the same memory manager as CASPER (but with its own heap space). Note that these memory managers had to not only allocate and de-allocate memory quickly but also not suffer from longer term issues such as fragmentation.

The limited onboard computing power required changes to the SCL and CASPER models to meet operational timing constraints. For example, initially within SCL a much larger set of safety constraints was modeled and execution was designed to be much more closed loop. However, testbed runs and early flight tests indicated that telemetry delays and CPU bottlenecks meant that this design was delaying time-sensitive commands. Most importantly, instrument on-times were delayed (e.g. late) and too long (resulting in extra data acquired). The ASE team was forced to both streamline the code (including the memory manager modification) and streamline the model to speed execution.

The CASPER planner is a significant user of onboard CPU. When CASPER is planning future observations it utilizes all of the available CPU cycles and takes approximately 8 minutes to plan each observation. The CASPER model was designed to operate within a minimal CPU profile – and as a result observations are planned with less flexibility. By setting fixed values for temporal offsets between activities rather than retaining flexible offset times, search is reduced and response time improved at the cost of plan quality (in some cases). For example, an image take activity may require a camera heater warm up before the camera can operate. The heater may take 30-60 seconds to warm the camera up to its operational temperature. By setting the duration of the heater warm up activity to 60 seconds, the temporal offset between the heater warm up activity and the image data take activity is fixed at 60 seconds, rather than variable.

Other performance improvements for CASPER came from analysis of the running code. We found bottlenecks and made improvements in redundant calculations. In particular, this was critical for functions performed on every loop of CASPER (such as collecting conflicts). We made some simplifying assumptions to make some expensive calculations faster. For example, when initially scheduling activities, we ignore timeline constraints, assuming that temporal constraints are more critical than timelines (calculating valid start times for timelines can be expensive).

7 Flight Status

The ASE software has been flying onboard the EO-1 spacecraft since January 2004. We have steadily increased the level of autonomy during this period. In April 2004, we started the first closed-loop execution where ASE autonomously analyzes science data onboard and triggers subsequent observations. Since that time, we have run over 20 of these trigger experiments with over 100 autonomously planned image data takes. Our most recent focus has been to expand the duration of the tests until ASE is controlling the satellite for 7 days straight. This will involve over 100 image data takes and over 50 ground contacts.

8 Related Work and Summary

In 1999, the Remote Agent experiment (RAX) [8] executed for a few days onboard the NASA Deep Space One mission. RAX is an example of a classic three-tiered architecture [5], as is ASE. RAX demonstrated a batch onboard planning capability (as opposed to CASPER's continuous planning) and RAX did not demonstrate onboard science. PROBA [9] is a European Space Agency (ESA) mission demonstrates onboard autonomy and launched in 2001. However, ASE has more of a focus on model-based autonomy than PROBA.

The Three Corner Sat (3CS) University Nanosat mission will be using the CASPER onboard planning software integrated with the SCL ground and flight execution software [1]. The 3CS mission is scheduled for launch on a Delta IV rocket July 3, 2004. The 3CS autonomy software includes onboard science data validation, replanning, robust execution, and multiple model-based anomaly detection. The 3CS mission is considerably less complex than EO-1 but still represents an important step in the integration and flight of onboard autonomy software.

More recent work from NASA Ames Research Center is focused on building the IDEA planning and execution architecture [7]. In IDEA, the planner and execution software are combined into a "reactive planner" and operate using the same domain model. A single planning and execution model can simplify validation, which is a difficult problem for autonomous systems. For EO-1, the CASPER planner and SCL executive use separate models. While this has the advantage of the flexibility of both procedural and declarative representations, a single model would be easier to validate. We have designed the CASPER modeling language to be used by domain experts, thus not requiring planning experts. Our use of SCL is similar to the "plan runner" in IDEA but SCL encodes more intelligence. For example, the plan runner in IDEA does not perform safety checks or have knowledge about how long to retry execution in the event of a failure. The EO-1 science analysis software is defined as one of the "controlling systems" in IDEA. In the IDEA architecture, a communications wrapper is used to send messages between the agents, similar to the software bus in EO-1. In the description of IDEA there is no information about the deployment of IDEA to any domains, so a comparison of the performance or capabilities is not possible at this time. In many ways IDEA represents a more AI-centric architecture with declarative modeling at its core and ASE represents more of an evolutionary engineered solution.

Using ASE on longer-range interplanetary missions would require more autonomy to deal with the longer gaps between communications periods. This would require higher fidelity models and more computing power. The current generation of radiation hardened spacecraft computers such as the PowerPC 750 provides more than adequate power to run the ASE software.

We have outlined several constraints on spacecraft autonomy software involving limited CPU and memory resources, strict timing for spacecraft control, and spacecraft safety. We have also described how we addressed those constraints through several optimizations we have performed on the ASE. These have included removing unnecessary code within the planner, changing memory managers, performing planner and executive model optimizations, and optimizing the running code. We have also devised a strategy for long term planning using very limited memory and CPU. In addition, we described our use of a three-layer autonomy architecture to increase the safety and performance of the ASE software. Specifically, the three-layer architecture offers specific advantages for this application by allowing redundant safety checks at each layer, and allow the 3 layers to respond on appropriate time scales for spacecraft operations.

ASE on EO-1 demonstrates an integrated autonomous mission using onboard science analysis, planning, and robust execution. The ASE performs intelligent science data selection that will lead to a reduction in data downlink. In addition, the ASE will increase science return through autonomous retargeting. Demonstration of these capabilities onboard EO-1 will enable radically different missions with significant onboard decision-making leading to novel science opportunities. The paradigm shift toward highly autonomous spacecraft will enable future NASA missions to achieve significantly greater science returns with reduced risk and reduced operations cost.

Acknowledgement

Portions of this work were performed at the Jet Propulsion Laboratory, California Institute of Technology, under a contract with the National Aeronautics and Space Administration. We would like to acknowledge the important contributions of Nghia Tang and Michael Burl of JPL, Dan Mandl, Stuart Frye, Seth Shulman, and Stephen Ungar of GSFC, Jerry Hengemihle and Bruce Trout of Microtel LLC, Jeff D'Agostino of the Hammers Corp., Robert Bote of Honeywell Corp., Jim Van Gaasbeck and Darrell Boyer of ICS, Michael Griffin and Hsiao-hua Burke of MIT Lincoln Labs, Ronald Greeley, Thomas Doggett, and Kevin Williams of ASU, and Victor Baker and James Dohm of University of Arizona.

References

1. S. Chien, B. Engelhardt, R. Knight, G. Rabideau, R. Sherwood, E. Hansen, A. Ortiviz, C. Wilklow, S. Wichman, "Onboard Autonomy on the Three Corner Sat Mission," Proc i-SAIRAS 2001, Montreal, Canada, June 2001.
2. S. Chien, R. Knight, A. Stechert, R. Sherwood, and G. Rabideau, "Using Iterative Repair to Improve Responsiveness of Planning and Scheduling," Proceedings of the Fifth International Conference on Artificial Intelligence Planning and Scheduling, Breckenridge, CO, April 2000. (also casper.jpl.nasa.gov)
3. A.G. Davies, R. Greeley, K. Williams, V. Baker, J. Dohm, M. Burl, E. Mjolsness, R. Castano, T. Stough, J. Roden, S. Chien, R. Sherwood, "ASC Science Report," August 2001. (downloadable from ase.jpl.nasa.gov)
4. E. Gat et al., Three-Layer Architectures. in D. Kortenkamp et al. eds. AI and Mobile Robots. AAAI Press, 1998.
5. Goddard Space Flight Center, EO-1 Mission page: http://EO-1.gsfc.nasa.gov
6. Interface and Control Systems, SCL Home Page, sclrules.com
7. N. Muscettola, G. Dorais, C. Fry, R. Levinson, and C. Plaunt, "IDEA: Planning at the Core of Autonomous Reactive Agents," Proceedings of the Workshops at the AIPS-2002 Conference, Tolouse, France, April 2002.

8. NASA Ames, Remote Agent Experiment Home Page, http://ic.arc.nasa.gov/projects/remote-agent/. See also Remote Agent: To Boldly Go Where No AI System Has Gone Before. Nicola Muscettola, P. Pandurang Nayak, Barney Pell, and Brian Williams. *Artificial Intelligence* 103(1-2):5-48, August 1998
9. The PROBA Onboard Autonomy Platform, http://www.estec.esa.nl/proba/
10. G. Rabideau, R. Knight, S. Chien, A. Fukunaga, A. Govindjee, "Iterative Repair Planning for Spacecraft Operations in the ASPEN System," Intl Symp Artificial Int Robotics & Automation in Space, Noordwijk, The Netherlands, June 1999.
11. D. Tran, S. Chien, G. Rabideau, B. Cichy, Flight Software Issues in Onboard Automated Planning: Lessons Learned on EO-1, Proceedings of the International Workshop on Planning and Scheduling for Space (IWPSS 2004). Darmstadt, Germany. June 2004

Bio-Discretization: Biometrics Authentication Featuring Face Data and Tokenised Random Number

Neo Han Foon, Andrew Teoh Beng Jin, and David Ngo Chek Ling

Faculty of Information Science and Technology (FIST),
Multimedia University,
Jalan Ayer Keroh Lama,
Bukit Beruang,
75450 Melaka, Malaysia
{hfneo, bjteoh, david.ngo}@mmu.edu.my

Abstract. With the wonders of the Internet and the promises of the worldwide information infrastructure, a highly secure authentication system is desirable. Biometric has been deployed in this purpose as it is a unique identifier. However, it also suffers from inherent limitations and specific security threats such as biometric fabrication. To alleviate the liabilities of the biometric, a combination of token and biometric for user authentication and verification is introduced. All user data is kept in the token and human can get rid of the task of remembering passwords. The proposed framework is named as Bio-Discretization. Bio-Discretization is performed on the face image features, which is generated from Non-Negative Matrix Factorization (NMF) in the wavelet domain to produce a set of unique compact bitstring by iterated inner product between a set of pseudo random numbers and face images. Bio-Discretization possesses high data capture offset tolerance, with highly correlated bitstring for intraclass data. This approach is highly desirable in a secure environment and it outperforms the classic authentication scheme.

1 Introduction

Biometric has become the foundation of an extensive array of highly secure identification and verification solution. This is because the uniqueness of one person is in the dominant security defense which they are difficult to copy or forge. By utilizing biometric, a person does not need to remember a password or to carry a token. The former method is reliance on human cognitive ability to remember them and human tends to forget them easily whilst the latter is easy to be stolen or lost. On the other hand, biometric is convenient because it only requires the physical human presence at the point of identification and verification.

However, there exist some drawbacks or limitations in biometrics which we have to concern about [1]. The problem arises when the data associated with a biometric feature has been compromised. For authentication system based on physical token such as keys or badges, a compromised token can be easily cancelled and the user can be assigned a new token. Similarly, user ID and password can be changed as often as required. Yet, the user only has a limited number of biometric features. If the biometric data are compromised, the user may quickly run out of biometric features to be used for authentication and verification. These concerns are aggravated by the fact that a biometric cannot be changed, and yet, it is not replaceable.

In addition, biometric systems are vulnerable to attacks, which can decrease their security. If an attacker can intercept a person's biometric data, then the attacker might use it to masquerade as the person. The primary concern from the security viewpoint centers on protection of information during the representational transformations, and in particular whether (or how) these transformations can be inverted to recover the input information, ie. biometric fabrication.

In order to alleviate this problem, the framework of combination between token and biometric, namely Bio-Discretization is introduced. This novel personal authentication approach combined tokenized random number with face data to generate a unique compact bitstring per person is highlighted. The discretization is carried out by iterated inner product between tokenized random number and the Non-Negative Matrix Factorization face data in the wavelet domain, and finally deciding the sign of each bit based on the predefined threshold.

Incorporation of physical token, to the direct mixture of random and biometric data is, in fact, an extremely convenient mechanism. It protects against biometric fabrication without adversarial knowledge of the randomization, or equivalently possession of the corresponding token. Bio-Discretization enables straightforward revocation via token replacement, and furthermore, it has significant functional advantages over solely biometric ie. near zero EER point and eliminate the occurrence of FAR without overly imperil the FRR performance.

The outline of the paper is as follow. Section 2 describes the integrated framework of wavelet transform (WT) and the Non-Negative Matrix Factorization (NMF) for representing the face data as well as Bio-Discretization procedure. Section 3 presents the experimental results, and followed by conclusion in Section 4.

2 Bio-Discretization Formulation Overview

Bio-Discretization formulation consists of two stages as described below.

1. Transformation of a raw face image to a highly discriminative representative feature using WT and NMF.
2. Discretization of the data via an iterated inner-product of tokenized random and user data.

The details of the feature extraction and discretization components will be discussed as follow.

2.1 Feature Extraction

2.1.1 Wavelet Transform
Wavelet transform is an excellent scale analysis and interpreting tool [2]. It transforms image into multiresolution representation, which analyzes image variation

at different scales and provides good energy compaction (high image information contents) as well as adaptability to human visual system. Wavelet transform offers high temporal localization for high frequencies while offering good frequency resolution for low frequencies. Therefore, wavelet analysis has been utilized to extract the local characteristics from still images due to its local extent [3]. If an orthonormal wavelet basis, say Daubechies or Symmlets, was chosen, the coefficients computed are independent to each other, a set of distinct features of the original signal could be obtained. Besides, wavelet transform decomposes image into a lower dimension multiresolution representation, which grants a structural configuration for analyzing the image information and shorter computational time.

The basic idea is to represent any arbitrary function $f(x)$ as a superposition of a set of such wavelets or basis functions. The scaling and shifting variables are discretized so that wavelet coefficients can be described by two integers, m and n. Thus, the discrete wavelet transform is given in Equation 1,

$$(W_\psi f(x))(m,n) = \frac{1}{\sqrt{a_o^m}} \sum_k x[k]\psi[a_o^{-m}n-k] \qquad (1)$$

where $x[k]$ is a digital signal with sample index k, and $\psi(n)$ is the mother wavelet.

For two-dimensional signal such as images, there exist an algorithm similar to the one-dimensional case for two-dimensional wavelets and scaling functions obtained from one-dimensional ones by tensorial product. This kind of two-dimensional wavelet transform leads to a decomposition of approximation coefficients at level j-1 in four components: the approximations at level j, L_j and the details in three orientations (horizontal, vertical and diagonal), $D_{jvertical}, D_{jhorizontal}$ and $D_{jdiagonal}$ [3].

Discrete wavelet transform is used to decompose the face image onto a multiresolution representation in order to keep the least coefficients possible without losing useful image information. Fig. 1(a) demonstrates the decomposition process by applying two-dimensional wavelet transform of a face image in level 1 and Fig. 1(b) depicts three levels wavelet decomposition by applying wavelet transform on the low-frequency band sequentially.

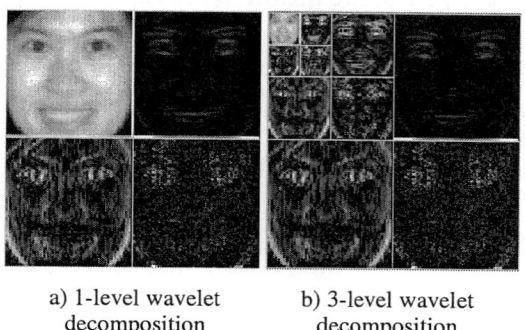

a) 1-level wavelet decomposition

b) 3-level wavelet decomposition

Fig. 1. Face image in wavelet subbands (a) 1-level wavelet decomposition (b) 3-level wavelet decomposition

In this paper, WT is used to decompose the face images onto wavelet decomposition of level two to reduce the computational load. Next, NMF is performed on the resultant face images which are now in wavelet domain. NMF ensured that all basis generated are non-negative.

2.1.2 Non Negative Matrix Factorization

NMF is a method to obtain a representation of data using non-negativity constraints. These constraints lead to a part-based representation in the image subface because they allow only additive, not subtractive, combinations of original data. Given an initial database expressed by a $n \times m$ matrix X, where each column is an n-dimensional non-negative vector of the original database (m vectors), it is possible to find two new matrices (W and H) in order to approximate the original matrix :

$$X \approx \tilde{X} \equiv WH, \text{where } W \in \Re^{nxr}, H \in \Re^{rxm} \qquad (2)$$

We can rewrite the factorization in terms of the columns of X and H as:

$$x_j \approx \tilde{x}_j = Wh_j, \text{where } x_j \in \Re^m, h_j \in \Re^r \text{ for } j = 1,...,n \qquad (3)$$

The dimensions of the factorized matrices W and H are $n \times r$ and $r \times m$, respectively. Assuming consistent precision, a reduction of storage is obtained whenever r, the number of basis vectors, satisfies $(n+m)r < nm$. Each column of matrix W contains basis vectors while each column of H contains the weights needed to approximate the corresponding column in V using the basis from W.

In order to estimate the factorization matrices, an objective function has to be defined. We have used the square of Euclidean distance between each column of X and its approximation of $X=WH$ subject to this objective function:

$$\Theta_{NMF}(W,H) = \sum_{j=1}^{n} \|x_j - Wh_j\|^2 = \|X - WH\|^2 \qquad (4)$$

This objective function can be related to the likelihood of generating the images in X from the basis W and encodings H. An iterative approach to reach a local minimum of this objective function is given by the following rules [4]:

$$W_{ia} \leftarrow W_{ia} \sum_{\mu} \frac{V_{i\mu}}{(WH)_{i\mu}} H_{a\mu}, \qquad (5)$$

$$W_{ia} \leftarrow \frac{W_{ia}}{\sum_j W_{ja}}, \qquad (6)$$

$$H_{a\mu} \leftarrow H_{a\mu} \sum_i W_{ia} \frac{V_{i\mu}}{(WH)_{i\mu}} \qquad (7)$$

Initialization is performed using positive random initial conditions for matrices W and H. Convergence of the process is also ensured. Fig. 2 demonstrates the NMF basis extracted from our database. These basis provide a sparse and part-based representation of face images.

In face recognition, NMF is performed where $W = (W^T W)^{-1} W^T$. In the feature extraction, each training facial images x_i is projected into the linear space as a feature vector $h_i = W x_i$. This is then used as a training feature point. A testing face image x_t to be classified is represented as $h_t = W x_t$. Next we classified them using nearest neighborhood classification scheme, Euclidean distance metric. The Euclidean distance between the testing image and each training image, $d(h_t, h_i)$ is calculated. The testing image is classified to the class to which the closest training image belong.

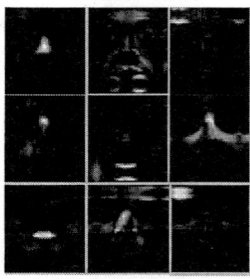

Fig. 2. NMF bases

2.2 Bio-Discretization

At this stage, the NMF projections, $w \in \mathbb{R}^r$, with r, the basis vector length of NMF is reducing down to a set of single bit, $b \in \{0,1\}^m$, with m the length of bit string via a tokenized pseudo random pattern, $\Re \in \mathbb{R}^m$, which distributed according to uniform distribution U[-1 1].

We can describe the procedure of Bio-Discretization as follow:

1. Raw intensity image representation, $I \in \mathbb{R}^N$, with N the image pixelisation dimension.
2. NMF in wavelet domain in a vector format, $w \in \mathbb{R}^r$, with r corresponding to the NMF length.
3. Discretization, $b \in \{0,1\}^m$, where $m=r$.

The above mentioned parameters are said to be zero knowledge representations of their inputs if the transformation is non-invertible. The transition between (a) and (b) is important as good feature location and extraction can reduce substantially the offset between two face images of the same person. Achieving (c) requires an offset-tolerant transformation by projected w onto each random pattern, and the choice of threshold, τ, to assign a single bit for each projection is described as :

1. Compute $x = <w, \Re>$, when $<\cdot, \cdot>$ denote their inner product process.
2. Assign $b(x) = \begin{cases} 0 : x < \tau \\ 1 : x \geq \tau \end{cases}$

Repetition of this procedure to obtain multiple bits renders the issue of inter-bit correlations, which is addressed via orthonormal set $\varsigma = \{r_k : k : 1, 2, ..., m\}$. Each bit $b(x)$ is hence rendered independent of all others, so that legitimate (and unavoidable) variations in w that inverts $b_{i+1}(x)$ would not necessarily have the same effect on $b_i(x)$. Inter-bit correlations and observations thereof are also important from the security viewpoint, the later of which is prevented via discretizing the concatenated bits.

Finally the images are classified using Hamming distance metric. Hamming distance calculate the number of bits which differ between two binary strings resultant from the thresholding process. The distance between two strings $b(x1)$ and $b(x2)$ is • | $x1_i - x2_i$ |.

The Bio-Discretization progression can be illustrated as in Fig. 3.

3 Experimental Results

The proposed methodology is tested on two standard databases, namely *Faces-93* Essex University Face Database [5] and Olivetti Research Laboratory (ORL) Database [6]. There are various aspects in the *Faces-93* Essex database which made it appropriate to this experiment. Data capture conditions are subject to photographed at fixed distance from camera, and individuals are asked to speak to produce images of the same individuals with different facial expressions. This database consists of 100 subjects with 10 images for each subject. The set of the 10 images for each subject is randomly partitioned into a training subset of 3 images and a test set of another 5 images. The image size is of 61 x 73 pixels, 256 – level grayscale. The face scale in the images is uniform and there are minor variations in turn, tilt and slant. On the other hand, ORL database contains 40 subjects with 10 images for each subject. The set of the 10 images for each subject is also randomly partitioned into a training subset of 3 images and a test set of another 5 images. The image size is of 92 x 112 pixels, 256 – level grayscale. There are major variations in turn, tilt and slant which we make use of the complexity of this database for our experiments.

The experimental notations are explained as follows:

1. *wNMF*: denoting NMF in wavelet domain verification scheme, through Euclidean distance metric.
2. *wNMFD-m*: denoting NMF in wavelet domain with Bio-Discretization scheme, through Hamming distance metric, where m is the bitlength, $\tau = 0$.

Generally speaking, all wavelet transforms with smooth, compactly support orthogonality can be in this approach. It is found that the selection of different wavelet does not seriously affect the performance of this testing [7]. An experiment was carried out to verify the performance rate when Symmlet 10 wavelet filter of level 2 is integrated with Non-Negative Factorization (NMF) as shown in Table 1. Two different databases were used to test the verification rate. From Table 1, multiple r were chosen to verify the best performance. $r=20, 40, 60, 80$ were used for verification rate calculation. The optimum verification rate for Essex Database is EER = 1.78% with FAR = 1.56%, FRR = 2% when $r = 20$. On the other hand, ORL database attains EER = 7.25% with FAR = 7%, FRR = 7.5% when $r = 40$. There is a significant difference in the verification rate of these two databases as ORL database contains more variations to Essex Database, therefore yield poorer verification rate. Nevertheless both are achieving relatively satisfying results.

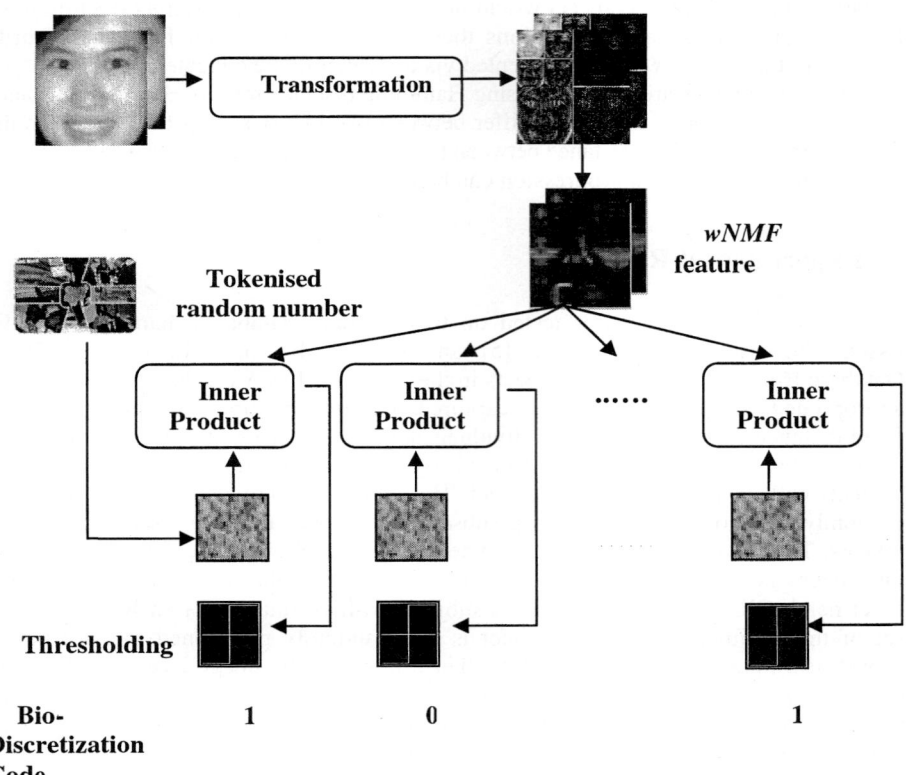

Fig. 3. Bio-Discretization Ilustration

Table 1. Comparison of Essex and ORL database with *wNMF*

Database	r	FAR(%)	FRR(%)	EER(%)
Essex	20	1.56	2.00	1.78
	40	2.90	3.00	2.95
	60	5.03	5.00	5.01
	80	5.10	5.00	5.05
ORL	20	7.40	7.50	7.45
	40	7.00	7.50	7.25
	60	7.30	7.50	7.40
	80	10.70	10.00	10.35

Another experiment was carried out by using a similar set of *r* to determine the optimum verification rate of *wNMFD-m*. We can clearly see from Table 2 that the EER = 0% when *r*=80 and EER = 0.0321% when *r*=80 in Essex and ORL database, respectively. Establishment of FRR (FAR=0%) and the Equal Error Rate (ERR) criteria, at which point FAR=FRR for a particular configuration requires analysis of FAR-FRR Receiver Operating Characteristics (ROC), which can be deployed by varying a range of normalized threshold values in between 0 to 1, as illustrated in Fig. 4 and 5.

Table 2. Comparison of Essex and ORL database with *wNMFD-m*

Database	r	FAR(%)	FRR(%)	ERR(%)
Essex	20	3.83	1.00	2.41
	40	0.75	1.00	0.87
	60	0.31	0.00	0.16
	80	0.00	0.00	0.00
ORL	20	4.17	10.00	7.08
	40	1.41	2.50	1.96
	60	1.67	5.00	3.33
	80	0.06	0.00	0.03

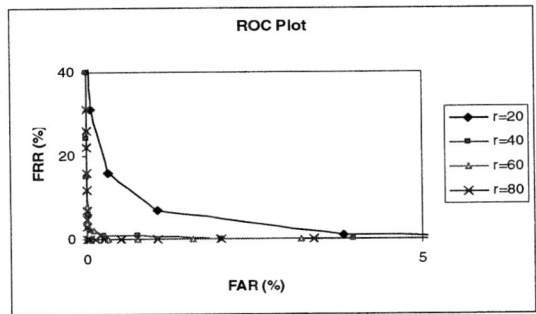

Fig. 4. ROC plot for *wNMFD-m* in Essex database

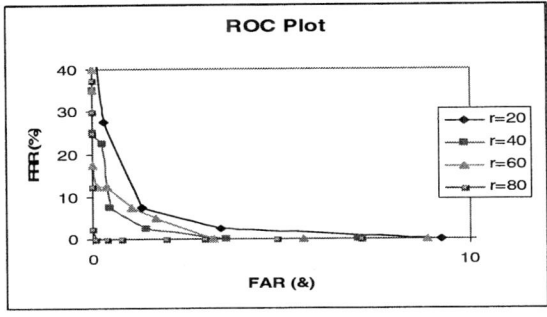

Fig. 5. ROC plot for wNMFD-m in ORL database

Fig. 6 and 7 illustrate the genuine and imposter population for *wNMF* and *wNMFD-m*, for Essex and ORL database, respectively. The results show the smaller overlapping in between genuine and imposter populations for *wNMF* in Essex database compared to ORL database. On the other hand, *wNMFD-m* in Essex database has clean separation compared to ORL database where minor overlapping occurs. The former minimize the distance between images from the same class, which can be observed from mean and variance values as shown in the Table 3, which make it more favor in the classification task.

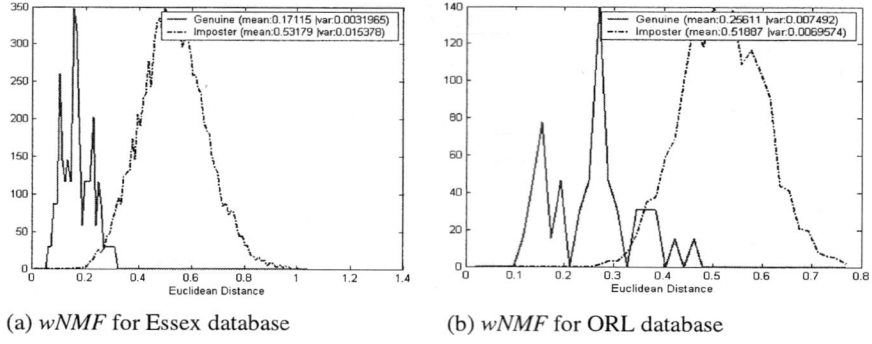

(a) *wNMF* for Essex database   (b) *wNMF* for ORL database

Fig. 6. Euclidean distance histograms for *wNMF*

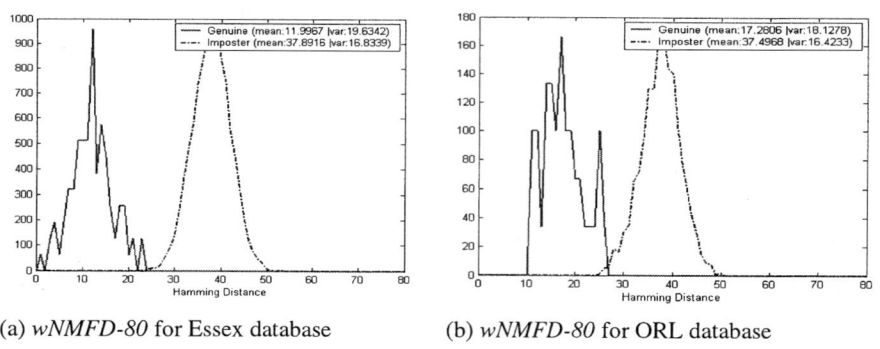

(a) *wNMFD-80* for Essex database   (b) *wNMFD-80* for ORL database

Fig. 7. Hamming distance histograms for *wNMFD-80*

Table 3. Statistic Data for the Genuine and the Imposter population

Database	Methods	Genuine Population		Imposter Population	
		Mean	Variance	Mean	Variance
Essex	*wNMF*	0.17	0.00	0.53	0.02
	wNMFD-m	11.99	19.63	37.89	16.83
ORL	*wNMF*	0.26	0.01	0.52	0.01
	wNMFD-m	17.28	18.13	37.50	16.42

4 Conclusion

A novel error-tolerant discretization methodology is described in this paper. This method has significant advantages over solely biometric or token usage, such as near zero EER level and clear separation between the genuine and imposter population, thereby mitigate the suffering from increased occurrence of FRR when eliminate the FAR. In order to produce a lower dimension multiresolution representation of the images that alleviates heavy computational load, wavelet transform is applied to the face images. NMF is chosen to be integrated with WT as the feature extractor because this subspace projection technique only allows non-negativity constraints which lead to a parts-based face image representation. This is consistent with the physiological fact that the firing rate is non-negative. Inner product between *wNMFD-m* and tokenized random number outcomes a string of compact binary code, which is highly desirable in a secure environment and outperforms the classic verification scheme. In addition, Bio-Discretization technique also addressed the invasion of privacy issue, such as biometric fabrication.

References

1. S.Wild, J.Curry, A.Dougherty, "Motivating Non-Negative Matrix Factorizations", 2003.
2. A. Laine. J. Fan, "Texture Classification by Wavelet Packet Signatures", IEEE Trans. Pattern Anal. Machine Intell., Vol. 15, pp. 1186-1191, 1993.
3. Mallat S., A Wavelet Tour of Signal Processing, San Diego: Academic Press, 1998.
4. D.D.Lee, H.S.Seung, "Algorithms for Non-Negative Matrix Factorization", Proceedings of Neural Information Processing Systems, vol. 13, pp. 556-562, 2001.
5. Vision Group of Essex University- Face Database http://cswww.-essex. ac. uk/mv/ allfaces/ index.html
6. Olivetti Research Laboratory (ORL) Database http://www.uk. research. att. com/ facedatabase.html
7. Andrew T.B.J., David N.C.L.,T.S.Ong, "An Efficient Fingerprint Verification System Using Integrated Wavelet and Fourier-Mellin Invariant Transform", Image and Vision Computing 22 (2004) 503-513

Cochlea Modelling: Clinical Challenges and Tubular Extraction

Gavin Baker[1], Stephen O'Leary[2], Nick Barnes[1,3], and Ed Kazmierczak[1]

[1] Department of Computer Science and Software Engineering,
The University of Melbourne, 3010 Australia
`gavinb@cs.mu.oz.au`
[2] Department of Otolaryngology,
The University of Melbourne, 3010 Australia
[3] National ICT Australia,
Locked Bag 8001, Canberra ACT 2601 Australia

Abstract. The cochlear ear implant has become a standard clinical intervention for the treatment of profound sensorineural hearing loss. After 20 years of research into implant design, there are still many unanswered clinical questions that could benefit from new analysis and modelling techniques. This research aims to develop techniques for extracting the cochlea from medical images to support clinical outcomes. We survey the challenges posed by some of these clinical questions and the problems of cochlea modeling. We present a novel algorithm for extracting tubular objects with non-circular cross-sections from medical images, including results from generated and clinical data. We also describe a cochlea model, driven by clinical knowledge and requirements, for representation and analysis. The 3-dimensional cochlea representation described herein is the first to explicitly integrate path and cross-sectional shape, specifically directed at addressing clinical outcomes. The tubular extraction algorithm described is one of very few approaches capable of handling non-circular cross-sections. The clinical results, taken from a human CT scan, show the first extracted centreline path and orthogonal cross-sections for the human cochlea.

1 Introduction

This paper describes a collaborative project being undertaken by the Departments of Computer Science and Software Engineering, and Otolaryngology at The University of Melbourne and National ICT Australia to model and analyse the shape of the human cochlea. In the first half of the paper, we describe the problems, challenges and clinical motivations for the research. In the second half of the paper, we present a novel algorithm for extracting tubular objects with non-circular cross-sections (such as the cochlea) from medical images. We present results from generated test data, and clinical results from human CT scans.

2 Clinical Background

Across the world, millions of people suffer from profound sensorineural hearing loss. This form of deafness affects many people; one in 1000 babies are born deaf with congenital hearing defects, while adults can develop profound hearing loss with age. Around 40% of people over the age of 75 and over 3 million children suffer from hearing loss. Until recent years, this type of hearing loss was incurable. Nerve-impaired deafness is not treatable with standard acoustic hearing aids, which only amplify the sound. It is characterised by damage to the nerve or hair cells in the inner ear, and has a variety of causes.

In normal human hearing, sound waves enter the outer ear via the *external auditory meatus* (ear canal) and strike the *tympanic membrane* (ear drum). This resonates the connected *auditory ossicles* (middle ear bones) which convert the sound waves into mechanical vibration that in turn resonates via the round window along the *scala* (internal channel) of the *cochlea* (shell-like hearing organ). The vibrations displace the *basilar membrane*, which runs the length of the cochlea. Hair cells attached to the membrane are displaced by the vibration and generate an electrochemical stimulus causing neurons in the local region to fire. The neuronal stimulus is transmitted via the *auditory nerve* to the cortex of the brain for processing. The sound frequency is a function of the distance along the cochlea, thus spatially encoding sound.

The cochlea is the organ of hearing, a tiny ($2cm^3$) shell-like spiral structure in the inner ear, embedded in the temporal bone of the skull. A normal cochlea revolves through $2\frac{1}{2}$ turns, from the *basal turn* (lower turn) up to the *helicotrema* (top of spiral). Three channels run the length of the cochlea: the *scala tympani*, *scala media* and *scala vestibuli*. The cochlear implant (described below) is inserted into the scala tympani. The path of the cochlea resembles a helical spiral, while the cross-sectional shape resembles a cardioid (rounded "B" shape). The *basilar membrane* resonates at different frequencies along its length; the distance along corresponds to the frequency perceived. The degree of neuronal stimulation determines the amplitude (volume) sensed.

The cochlear implant, also known as the bionic ear, was developed by Professor Graeme Clark at The University of Melbourne and later at The Bionic Ear Institute. The implant restores hearing to patients with sensorineural damage, and has become a standard clinical intervention for profound deafness. There have been over 50,000 recipients of the cochlear implant in 120 countries worldwide, since the first clinical trials in 1985 [2].

The cochlear ear implant consists of: an external microphone that picks up sound; a signal processing unit that converts the sound into electrical signals; and an electrode array that stimulates the nerve fibres inside the cochlea. This completely bypasses the outer and middle ear, and relies only on residual hearing in the form of viable neurons inside the cochlea. The signal processing unit performs spectrum analysis on the incoming sound, and determines the frequency and amplitude of the speech. The array consists of a series of electrodes that directly stimulate the auditory nerve with electrical current, thus recreating

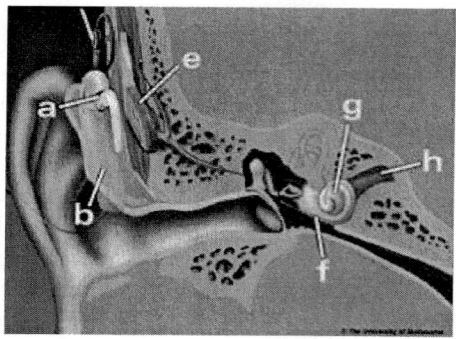

Fig. 1. Left: The middle and inner ear: a) external cochlea device, b) signal processor, f) basal turn, g) cochlea, h) auditory nerve

the sensation of hearing. The distance along the array encodes frequency, while current determines amplitude [3].

There are many clinical problems and questions that could benefit from new techniques for the analysis of the shape of the cochlea and implant, some of which are listed in Figure 2. In order to answer these questions, it is clear that

---

1. *Does the patient suffer from Mondini's syndrome [1]?*

   A normal cochlea revolves about $2\frac{1}{2}$ turns, whereas Mondini's syndrome is characterised by incomplete formation of turns. This needs a model of the cochlea path to determine number of turns of cochlea canal.

2. *Does the patient present surgical risks?*

   Pathologies such as ossification of the basal turn can complicate surgery. A model of cross-sectional shape could identify such an abnormality, given a statistical prior model of normal shape.

3. *Where are the electrodes with respect to the modiolus?*

   Calibration and tuning of the speech processor are affected by the distance to the modiolus and the position of each electrode. This requires a cochlea model and implant model to determine distances and path.

4. *How far has the electrode array been inserted?*

   Post-operative tuning of the signal processor depends on this information, to determine frequency correspondences with the electrodes. Requires a model of the cochlea and implant.

5. *Has the implant pierced the basilar membrane?*

   If this occurs during implant insertion, it may impair vestibular function or damage residual neurons. This information may also be used to improve electrode design, and have impact on surgical technique evaluation. Requires detailed cochlea model and implant model.

Fig. 2. Clinical questions, surgical outcomes and cochlea modelling requirements

we need a shape model of the cochlea that captures the path of the *otic capsule*, the cross-sectional shape (along with the position of the basilar membrane), and a model of the path of the implant with respect to the cochlea model.

Abnormalities in the shape of the cochlea may be associated with hearing impairment and deafness. Shape analysis of the cochlea also has implications for cochlear implant surgery in several areas: diagnosis, such as identifying Mondini's syndrome [1] and ossification of the basal turn; surgery planning, since vital structures may be found in unpredictable locations; and clinical management, as abnormal shape increases the risk of meningitis.

A variety of non-invasive imaging techniques are available to clinicians for diagnosis and surgery planning. Conventional 2D x-rays, or *radiographs*, have been in use for many years, and are still widely used. *Computed Tomography* (CT) is a form of 3-dimensional x-ray, which is particularly suited to imaging bone structures. *Magnetic Resonance Imaging* (MRI), also a 3-dimensional modality, images the subject in a magnetic field, and is best at discriminating different types of tissue. Since the implant is metallic, MRI cannot be used post-operatively, due to the risk of internal damage. X-rays and CT scans are currently the only practical means of post-operative evaluation *in vivo* for cochlear implant patients.

There are clearly many clinical motivations for imaging the cochlea. However, there are many significant challenges that remain before these questions can be answered. As the cochlea is only 2cm^3 (about the size of a marble), with current imaging resolutions, *in vivo* scans will resolve approximately 60x60x45 voxels at a 0.1mm anisotropic scale. The *scala tympani*, the part of the cochlea into which the electrode is inserted, is approximately 1mm in diameter. The electrode itself consists of 24×0.01mm wires with electrodes of 0.5mm in diameter.

Traditional 2D radiographs are currently used in clinical practice to post-operatively evaluate the position of the electrode. The individual wires and electrodes on the implant are visible, and the resolution is very good. However, it can be difficult to acquire an x-ray that is properly aligned with the basal turn. More significantly, since the radiograph is a planar projection, 3D information is lost. Current clinical practice relies on the surgeon's experience to make qualitative evaluations from this data. A CT scan can deliver a full 3D reconstruction of the cochlea and electrode array post-operatively. However, the metallic construction of the electrode (platinum) introduces significant blooming artifacts into the surrounding image, and distorts for more than 1mm. Individual electrodes are not detectable in CT [4]; only the path of the implant and wires. Since this distortion extends beyond the size of the cochlea affecting local structures, post-operative evaluation of the implant path is not ordinarily feasible. Clearly, neither CR nor CT is sufficient alone for these evaluations.

Surprisingly little attention has been paid to modelling the three-dimensional shape of the hearing organ itself, the cochlea. It is generally accepted that the cochlea resembles an Archemidean spiral [5, 6] or shell. The only models published have described the path, thus no model integrating path and cross-section exists.

Cohen's 2D Electrode Model. Cohen et al. present a 2-dimensional spiral template to model the path of the inserted electrode array [7], providing a model for frequency estimation and implant tuning. This can be seen as an approximation of the path of the *otic capsule* (defined by the walls of the bone structure containing the cochlea), however it is known that the implant does not always track the walls. Since the implant is inserted into the scala tympani, the electrode will not necessarily follow the precise centreline of the otic capsule itself. Thus this model is only an approximation to the cochlea tubular path.

Cohen's 2D spiral model is a piecewise logarithmic spiral based on a polar co-ordinate system (the second equation takes into account the curvature of the basal turn):

$$\begin{aligned} R &= ac^{-b\theta} & \theta \geq 100° \\ R &= c(1 - d\log(\theta - \theta_0)) & \theta < 100° \end{aligned} \quad (1)$$

for some constants a, b, c, d. The origin is centred at the modiolus.

Yoo's 3D Spiral Model. Cohen's 2D electrode path model was extended into 3D by Yoo et al. [5,8] in order to model the centreline path of the cochlea itself. This involved adding a Z-axis component to the existing polar coordinate system. First a linear function $z = e(\theta - \theta_1)$ was described [5], then an exponential function $h = ce^{d\theta}$ [8], where z and h both represent the height of the spiral curve, for some constants c, d, e and angle θ.

This model for the cochlea centreline is based on the electrode model, and assumes that the paths are coincident. It was evaluated on a single patient and validated against histological data, which is typically imprecise. The centreline is taken as the centroid of cross-section, which is extracted using Wang's unwrapping technique [9]. Ultimately this model is only an approximation to the path of the cochlea centreline; it does not address the shape of the cross-section of the cochlea along its path.

Ketten's Archimedean Spiral Model. Ketten et al. present an Archemidean spiral model, which is used to estimate cochlea length along the midcanal spiral path [6]. This model is aimed at predicting insertion depth and cochlea length, and thus does not directly address the 3D space-curve path that we seek. Yoo points out that this model does not take into account the basal turn [8], and thus is less faithful to cochlea morphometry than the models described above.

Models Summary. The most advanced model thus far is the 3D path model of Yoo et al.. It been derived from a single CT scan, is based on the assumption that the electrode path and centreline are equivalent, and does not address crosssection. These existing models are inadequate to respond to the clinical questions before us. This research aims to address this gap by producing a model that integrates both path and cross-sectional shape, developing an extraction algorithm capable of generating such a model, and one that will integrate with a model of the electrode.

3 Tubular Object Extraction

The cochlea is often described as an Archemidean spiral shell [5], which can be approximated by a logarithmic curve. However the cross-sectional shape of the cochlea is not elliptical; it resembles a cardioid (a rounded "B"). Both the shape and size of the cochlea vary along its length, posing some unique challenges for extraction and modeling. Most existing tubular extraction techniques are concerned with the vasculature, where a circular or elliptical cross-section is typically assumed. Since we cannot make this assumption, a new approach is required that explicitly treats complex cross-sectional shape. Our goal is therefore to develop techniques for extracting 3-dimensional tubular objects with non-circular cross-sections, and recover clinically relevant parameters that support medical outcomes.

The remainder of this paper is structured as follows: first we discuss related research in the area of tubular object extraction, and why these are unsuitable for our purposes. Then we describe the design of our algorithm, including parameter selection. We then present the results of processing synthetic data (a gold standard) based on Yoo's 3D model, and real CT dataset of a human cochlea.

A number of approaches exist for tubular object segmentation and extraction, however the majority of research has focused on segmenting vascular networks [10–14]. Since blood vessels are thin, long, have circular or elliptical cross-sections and form complex branching networks, most tubular research has focused on anatomy with these attributes. Consequently, larger tubular objects with non-trivial cross-sections such as the cochlea have received much less attention.

The intrinsic shape characteristics of a tube can be described by two related components: the *centerline path* and the *cross-sectional shape* along the path. Binford [15] first proposed the Generalised Cylinder (GC), a spatial curve defining the centerline path of the object, and a cross-section (typically circular or elliptical) that can vary as a function of the distance along the path. The Right Generalised Cylinder (RGC) [16] constrains the cross-section to be orthogonal to the tangent of the path. With some exceptions (eg. [13]), the majority of recent approaches to tubular models employ variations on the RGC. In the case of the cochlea, the centerline path is clinically significant (see Figure 2). Consequently, a tubular representation suitable for shape analysis would be highly desirable.

In scale space terms, the *gross-scale* shape of a tube is characterised by the path of its centerline (the tubular axis), and is typically modelled as a B-spline [11]. To extract the centreline of a tube, Principal Components Analysis (PCA) can be applied to a local image region directly to track the maximal eigenvector [9] and follow the principal axis. More common is to apply PCA to the local Hessian matrix, and track along the maximal eigenvectors [10, 11, 14].

Aylward *et al.* [10] use multi-scale intensity ridge traversal, driven by the eigenvalues of the local Hessian, to extract the centerline of blood vessels. This approach requires a near-circular cross-section, limiting its applicability to complex cross-sectional modeling. While Krissian [14] simply employs the local Hessian for orientation, Frangi [11] also employs a local discriminant function that identifies tubular structures locally to improve and guide tracking.

The Hessian is a 2nd-order directional derivative, which makes it more susceptible to noise than a 1st-order gradient operator (employed in our approach). Multi-scale blurring is typically used in conjunction with the local Hessian to mitigate noise. This also ensures the requisite Gaussian intensity profile to create the intensity ridge at the centre of the tube. However, this requires the cross-section to be nearly circular [10], thus limiting its generality. Bifurcations can also cause problems when using the local Hessian, due to filtered signal loss around the joint [11].

Yim et al. [13] employ a deformable curve (*snake*) in a novel tubular coordinate system, that deforms according to image and smoothing forces to model the wall as a mesh. It is assumed that the centerline has been manually specified as a sequence of points along the centre axis of the vessel, although Bitter [17] demonstrates how this can be error-prone.

Lorigo describes an approach based on Level Sets called CURVES [12], that uses an evolving curve driven by image intensity gradient to extract vasculature. However the result is still a segmentation, and thus further analysis would be required to produce a tubular model suitable for shape analysis.

The *fine-scale* detail of a tube is defined by the local shape of the orthogonal cross-section, which can vary along the length of the tube. This is difficult to extract and model explicitly. Most approaches either do not address cross-sectional shape [18], or assume a circular or elliptical [10] cross-section. These assumptions may generally be valid for vasculature, however in [11] Frangi points out that "*ex vivo* measurements have shown that this assumption is rather simplistic". Frangi describes a spline-based tubular model capable of representing non-circular cross-sections, and demonstrates the approach to model vessel stenosis.

3.1 Tubular Extraction Algorithm

The Tubular Extraction algorithm uses the *Principal Flow Filter* [19] to incrementally extract a tubular object by tracking along its path and taking cross-sectional slices. Since our approach is driven by the image gradient at the tube walls, there is no constraint imposed on the cross-sectional shape. In this paper, we do assume that the cross-sectional area does not vary significantly along the length, which is valid for the cochlea.

The Principal Flow Filter calculates the local orientation of flow along a tube. Given an input volume $I : \mathbb{R}^3 \mapsto \mathbb{R}$ containing a non-branching tubular object, we specify a point $\mathbf{p} = (x, y, z)$ inside the tube, and a vector $\boldsymbol{v}$ oriented approximately along the tube. We assume that the contrast along the tubular walls is strong (see Figure 3(a)). Thus the gradient intensity vectors along the walls will tend to be oriented approximately co-planar with the orthogonal cross-sectional plane. It follows that the cross-product of any two of these wall gradient vectors should produce a vector approximately oriented along the tubular axis. With a sufficiently robust analysis, a local region can be processed in this way to calculate a mean orientation from all the cross-products, yielding the principal flow vector $\boldsymbol{v}_f$.

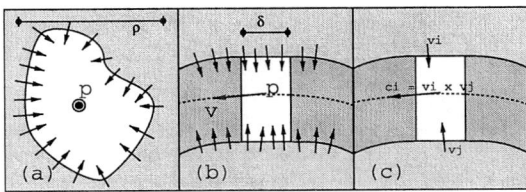

Fig. 3. (a) Cross-section of a tube, showing: centroid **p**, maximal diameter ρ, and gradient vectors around wall; (b) Side view of tube, showing: point **p**, flow vector v_f, longitudinal dimension δ and gradient vectors along the wall; (c) pairs of gradient vectors along the wall contribute to flow vector

Parameters are supplied for the expected maximum diameter of the tube ρ and the desired section depth δ (inversely proportional to the curvature). This specifies a Volume of Interest $\mathcal{V}$, centred at **p**, oriented such that v defines the new Z-axis, with size $\rho \times \rho \times \delta$. We size $\mathcal{V}$ such that it completely encloses a short and relatively uniform section of the tube; that is, the width and height ρ is slightly larger than the diameter of the tube, and the depth δ is small enough to minimise local curvature. Over the resampled VOI $I_\mathcal{V}$ we calculate the first-derivative image gradient:

$$G = \nabla I_\mathcal{V} \quad (2)$$

Thus G will yield strong gradient vectors normal to the walls. We randomly sample N vectors a from this vector field:

$$M = \{a_i : a_i = S(G), i \in [0, N], \|a_i\| > \epsilon\} \quad (3)$$

where S is a pseudo-random sampling function, and ϵ is the minimum gradient magnitude threshold. We then take the vector cross-product of all pairs from M:

$$\mathcal{C} = \{c_i : c_i = v_m \times v_n, \forall v_m, v_n \in M, m \neq n\} \quad (4)$$

We map the vectors from $\mathcal{C}$ into $(\phi, \psi) \in \mathbb{R}^2$, where ϕ is the angle of c_i in the XZ plane and ψ is the angle of in the YZ plane (see Figure 4(c)). This produces a cluster around the mean local orientation. To eliminate outliers and mitigate against sampling noise, we employ a robust random sampling approach based on the RANSAC algorithm [20]. A series of potential models is taken from the data set, and compared with all data points in the set using a Euclidean distance metric $d(a, b)$. The support for a model is increased by a data point falling within a given threshold of the model. After a sufficient number of iterations, the model with the greatest support is chosen. The new mean orientation is calculated from all points in this support set, which is transformed back into a vector in the original frame, and becomes the local flow vector v_f for that region oriented along the tube.

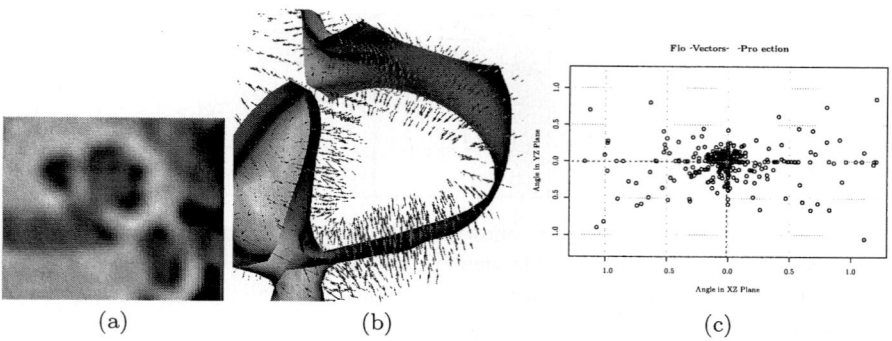

(a) (b) (c)

Fig. 4. (a) typical mid-saggital slice of human cochlea, showing upper and basal turns, and auditory nerve; (b) A VOI from the CT cochlea, showing wall with gradient vectors; (c) Flow vectors projected into a Euclidean space, with a cluster clearly showing consensus on orientation

The *Tubular Extraction* algorithm consists of the following steps:
1. Initialise with $\mathbf{p} = \mathbf{p}_0$ and $\mathbf{v} = \mathbf{v}_0$, and select ρ, δ
2. Resample the Volume Of Interest (VOI) centred at $\mathbf{p}$ oriented by $\mathbf{v}$, with dimensions $\rho \times \rho \times \delta$
3. Calculate the local flow direction $\mathbf{v}_f$ using the Principal Flow Filter
4. Extract the cross-sectional plane $\mathcal{P}$ given normal $\mathbf{v}_f$ centred about $\mathbf{p}$
5. Calculate the new centre $\mathbf{p}_c$ from centroid of $\mathcal{P}$
6. Calculate the new centre point with $\mathbf{p} = \mathbf{p}_c + \delta \mathbf{v}_f$
7. Repeat from step 2

3.2 Results

First the algorithm was evaluated against generated data, in order to have ground-truth for testing and validation. Yoo's 3D model of the cochlea [5] was used to generate a realistic test model (Figure 5i,ii). Two test volumes were rendered with different cross-sections: a circular shape with diameter 10mm, and a clover-leaf shape with diameter 12mm (resolution 1mm/voxel). The tracking results are shown in Figure 5 (iii,iv). The algorithm demonstrated excellent tracking in both cases, successfully extracting the entire length of the tubes automatically.

The algorithm has also been applied to a CT scan of a real human cochlea. The input data and tracking results are shown in Figure 5. The algorithm successfully tracked through the basal and mid-modiolar sections of the cochlea, for approximately $1\frac{1}{4}$ turns. The characteristic curve shape is clearly visible in the XZ plot of Figure 6(iv). At two points, anatomy adjoins the cochlea, creating a bifurcation that necessitated a manual restart. The tracking is not precisely on the centreline, mainly due to the low resolution available (limited by clinical considerations and x-ray dosage).

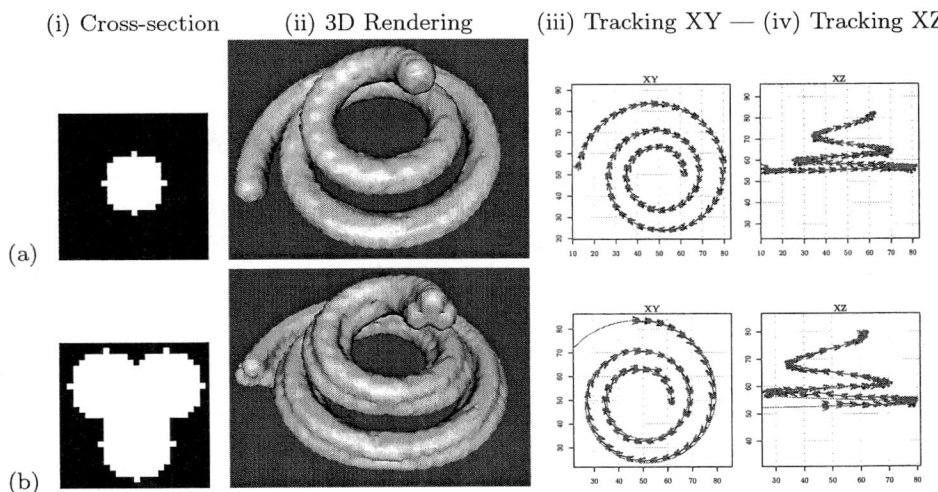

Fig. 5. Generated Data: Input data (i,ii) and tracking results (iii,iv) for (a) circular and (b) clover cross-section

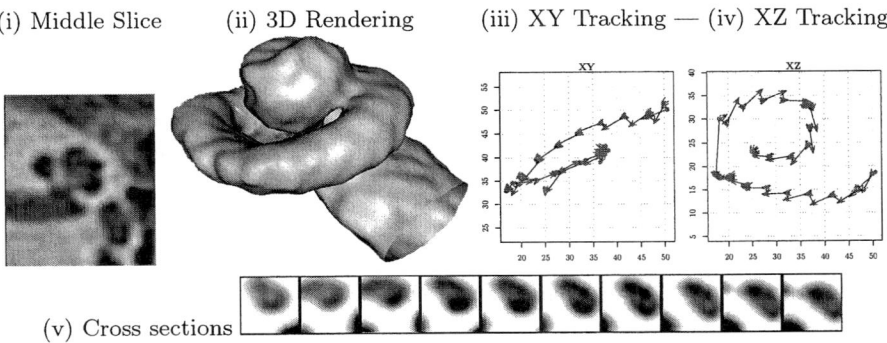

Fig. 6. Clinical Results: the input CT scan data showing a mid slice (i) and 3D view (ii), with tracking results (iii,iv) and the first 10 cross-sections (v). Note: the path in (iii) is not orthogonal to viewing plane

4 Conclusion

We have presented a survey of the clinical challenges of cochlea modelling. We have presented a novel tubular extraction algorithm that captures the path of tubular objects and their cross-sections. The algorithm explicitly handles non-circular cross-sections, which is relevant to numerous areas of anatomy. The output of the algorithm is model-centric, which has direct advantages for shape analysis, as the model directly captures clinically relevant parameters. The results demonstrated very accurate extraction of difficult generated test data. Significantly, the algorithm has been applied to CT and produced the first successful of the centreline and cross-sections of the human cochlea for $1\frac{1}{4}$ turns. This data will be validated, extended to analyse a small population, and form the basis of the first general cochlea shape model derived from clinical data. The challenge of bifurcations will need to be addressed to apply this technique to other anatomy.

Our thanks to the Royal Victorian Eye and Ear Hospital for supplying the CT scan data used in this study, to the reviewers for their helpful comments, and to the developers of the Insight Toolkit [21] imaging library, which was used to develop the analysis software for this project.

References

1. Mondini, C.: Anatomia surdi nati sectio: Bononiensi scientiarum et artium instituto atque academia commentarii. Bononiae **7** (1791) 419–431
2. The Bionic Ear Institute, Melbourne, Australia: About the bionic ear. http://www.bionicear.org/bei/AboutHistory.html (2004)
3. Loizou, P.: Introduction to cochlear implants. IEEE Engineering in Medicine and Biology (1999) 32–42
4. Whiting, B., Bae, K., Skinner, M.: Cochlear implants: Three-dimensional localisation by means of coregistration of CT and conventional radiographs. Radiology **221** (2001) 543–549
5. Yoo, S., Rubinstein, J., Vannier, M.: Three-dimensional geometric modeling of the cochlea using helico-spiral approximation. IEEE Transactions on Biomedical Engineering **47** (2000) 1392–1402
6. Ketten, D., Skinner, M., Wang, G., Vannier, M., Gates, G., Neely, G.: In vivo measures of cochlear length and insertion depth of nucleus cochlea implant electrode arrays. Ann. Otol., Rhinol. Laryngol. **107** (1989) 515–522
7. Cohen, L., Xu, J., Xu, S., Clark, G.: Improved and simplified methods for specifying positions of the electrode bands of a cochlear implant array. American Journal of Otology (1996)
8. Yoo, S., Wang, G., Rubenstein, J., Skinner, M., Vannier, M.: Three-dimensional modeling and visualisation of the cochlea on the internet. IEEE Transactions on Information Technology in Biomedicine **4** (2000) 144–151
9. Wang, G., Vannier, M., Skinner, M., Kalender, W., Polacin, A., Ketten, D.: Unwrapping cochlear implants by spiral CT. IEEE Transactions on Biomedical Engineering **43** (1996) 891–900
10. Aylward, S., Bullitt, E.: Initialization, noise, singularities, and scale in height ridge traversal for tubular object centerline extraction. IEEE Transactions on Medical Imaging **21** (2002) 61–75
11. Frangi, A., Niessen, W., Hoogeveen, R., van Walsum, T., Viergever, M.: Model-based quantitation of 3-D magnetic resonance angiographic images. IEEE Transactions on Medical Imaging **18** (1999) 946–956
12. Lorigo, L.M., Faugeras, O.D., Grimson, W.E.L., Keriven, R., Kikinis, R., Nabavi, A., Westin, C.F.: CURVES: Curve evolution for vessel segmentation. Medical Image Analysis **5** (2001) 195–206
13. Yim, P., Cebral, J., Mullick, R., Marcos, H., Choyke, P.: Vessel surface reconstruction with a tubular deformable model. IEEE Transactions on Medical Imaging **20** (2001) 1411–1421

14. Krissian, K., Vaillant, G.M.R., Trousset, Y., Ayache, N.: Model-based multiscale detection of 3D vessels. In: Computer Vision and Pattern Recognition, IEEE (1998) 722–727
15. Binford, T.: Visual perception by computer. In: IEEE Conference on Systems Science and Cybernetics. (1971)
16. Zerroug, M., Nevatia, R.: Three-dimensional descriptions based on the analysis of the invariant and quasi-invariant properties of some curved-axis generalized cylinders. IEEE Transactions on Pattern Analysis and Machine Intelligence **18** (1996) 237–253
17. Bitter, I., Sato, M., Bender, M., McDonnell, K.T., Kaufman, A., Wan, M.: CEASAR: a smooth, accurate and robust centerline extraction algorithm. In: Proceedings of the conference on Visualization '00, IEEE Computer Society Press (2000) 45–52
18. Flasque, N., Desvignes, M., Constans, J.M., Revenu, M.: Acquisition, segmentation and tracking of the cerebral vascular tree on 3D magnetic resonance angiography images. Medical Image Analysis **5** (2001) 173–183
19. Baker, G., Barnes, N.: Principal flow for tubular objects with non-circular cross-sections. In: Proceedings of the International Conference on Pattern Recognition, Cambridge, England (2004)
20. Fischler, M.A., Bolles, R.C.: Random sample consensus: a paradigm for model fitting with applications to image analysis and automated cartography. Communications of the ACM **24** (1981) 381–395
21. Ibáñez, L., Schroeder, W., Ng, L., Cates, J.: 1. In: The ITK Software Guide. Kitware Inc (2003)

Combining Bayesian Networks, k Nearest Neighbours Algorithm and Attribute Selection for Gene Expression Data Analysis*

B. Sierra, E. Lazkano, J.M. Martínez-Otzeta, and A. Astigarraga

Dept. of Computer Science and Artificial Intelligence,
University of the Basque Country,
P.O. Box 649, E-20080 San Sebastián, Spain
ccpsiarb@si.ehu.es
http://www.sc.ehu.es/ccwrobot

Abstract. In the last years, there has been a large growth in gene expression profiling technologies, which are expected to provide insight into cancer related cellular processes. Machine Learning algorithms, which are extensively applied in many areas of the real world, are not still popular in the Bioinformatics community. We report on the successful application of the combination of two supervised Machine Learning methods, Bayesian Networks and k Nearest Neighbours algorithms, to cancer class prediction problems in three DNA microarray datasets of huge dimensionality (*Colon, Leukemia* and *NCI-60*). The essential gene selection process in microarray domains is performed by a sequential search engine and after used for the Bayesian Network model learning. Once the genes are selected for the Bayesian Network paradigm, we combine this paradigm with the well known KNN algorithm in order to improve the classification accuracy.

1 Introduction

Development of high throughput data acquisition technologies in biological sciences, and specifically in genome sequencing, together with advances in digital storage and computing, have begun to transform biology, from a data–poor science to a data–rich science. In order to manage and deal with all this new biological data, the Bioinformatics discipline powerfully emerges.

These advances in the last decade in genome sequencing have lead to the spectacular development of a new technology, named DNA microarray, which can be included into the Bioinformatics discipline. DNA micro-array allows simultaneously monitoring and measurement of the expression levels of thousands

---

* This work was supported the University of the Basque Country under UPV 140.226-EA186/96 grant and by the Gipuzkoako Foru Aldundi Txit Gorena under OF761/2003 grant .

of genes in an organism. A systematic and computational analysis of these micro-array datasets is an interesting way to study and understand many aspects of the underlying biological processes.

There has been a significant recent interest in the development of new methods for functional interpretation of these micro-array gene expression datasets. The analysis frequently involves class prediction (supervised classification), regression, feature selection (in this case, gene selection), outliers detection, principal component analysis, discovering of gene relationships and cluster analysis (unsupervised classification). In this way, DNA micro-array datasets are an appropriate starting point to carry out the explained systematic and automatic cancer classification (Golub et al., [9]). Cancer classification is divided in two major issues: the discovery of previously unknown types of cancer (class discovery) and the assignment of tumor samples to already known cancer types (class prediction). While the class discovery is related with cluster analysis (or unsupervised classification), class prediction is related with the application of supervised classification techniques. Our work focuses on class prediction for cancer classification. In the last decade there has been a big growth in the accumulation of information in Economic, Marketing, Medicine, Finance, etc. databases. The larger size of these databases and the improvement of computer related technologies inspired the development of a set of techniques that are grouped under the Machine Learning (ML) (Mitchell [21]) term and that discover and extract knowledge in an automated way. Although ML techniques have successfully solved classification problems in many different areas of the real world, its application is nowadays emerging as a powerful tool to solve DNA micro-array problems (Li and Yang [19]; Xing et al. [30]; Ben-Dor et al. [1]; Inza et al. [11]; Blanco et al. [2]).

As micro-array datasets have a very large number of predictive genes (usually more than 1000) and a small number of samples (usually less than 100), a reduction in the number of genes to build a classifier is an essential part of any micro-array study. Moreover, for diagnostic purposes it is important to find small subsets of genes that are informative enough to distinguish between cells of different types [1]. All the studies also show that the main part of the genes measured in a DNA micro-array are not relevant for an accurate distinction between cancer classes (Golub et al., [9]). To this end we suggest a simple combinatorial, sequential, classic search mechanism, named Sequential Forward Selection (Kittler [13]), which performs the major part of its search near the empty subset of genes. Each found gene subset is evaluated by a wrapper (Kohavi and John [15]) scheme, which is very popular in ML applications and it is started to be used in DNA micro-array tasks (Inza et al. [11]; Blanco et al. [2]; Li et al. [18]; Xing et al. [30]).

In this paper, we present a new classifier combination technique that consists of combining the use of two well known paradigms: Bayesian Networks (BN) and K Nearest Neighbor (K-NN). We show the results obtained when using this new classifier in three micro-array datasets. Before running the classification process, Feature Subset Selection is applied using a wrapper technique in order to keep only the relevant features. The accuracy estimation is given using the Leaving One Out Cross Validation (LOOCV) technique because, due to its unbiased nature (Kohavi, [14]), it is the most suited estimation procedure for micro-array datasets.

The rest of the paper is organized as follows: section 2 focuses on the Feature Selection process; sections 3 and 4 present the Bayesian Networks and K-NN paradigms, respectively; section 5 is devoted to the new classifier proposed in this paper; obtained experimental results are shown in section 6, and in the final section 7 the conclusions are presented and the future work lines are pointed out.

2 Gene Selection Process: Feature Subset Selection

The basic problem of ML is concerned with the induction of a model that classifies a given object into one of several known classes. In order to induce the classification model, each object is described by a pattern of d features. Here, the ML community has formulated the following question: *are all of these d descriptive features useful for learning the 'classification rule'?* On trying to respond to this question, we come up with the Feature Subset Selection (FSS) [20] approach which can be reformulated as follows: *given a set of candidate features, select the 'best' subset in a classification problem.* In our case, the 'best' subset will be the one with the best predictive accuracy.

Most of the supervised learning algorithms perform rather poorly when faced with many irrelevant or redundant (depending on the specific characteristics of the classifier) features. In this way, the FSS proposes additional methods to reduce the number of features so as to improve the performance of the supervised classification algorithm.

FSS can be viewed as a search problem with each state in the search space specifying a subset of the possible features of the task. Exhaustive evaluation of possible feature subsets is usually infeasible in practice due to the large amount of computational effort required. In this way, any feature selection method must determine four basic issues that define the nature of the search process:

1. The starting point in the space. It determines the direction of the search. One might start with no features and successively add them, or one might start with all features and successively remove them.

2. The organization of the search. It determines the strategy of the search. Roughly speaking, the search strategies can be *complete* or *heuristic* (see [20] for a review of FSS algorithms). When we have more than 10-15 features the search space becomes huge and a *complete* search strategy is infeasible. As FSS is a classic NP-hard optimization problem, the use of search *heuristics* is justified. Classic deterministic heuristic FSS algorithms are sequential forward and backward selection (SFS and SBS [13]), floating selection methods (SFFS and SFBS [23]) and best-first search [15]. Two classic implementations of non-deterministic search engines are Genetic Algorithms [28], Estimation of Distribution Algorithms [10] and Simulated Annealing [6].

3. *Evaluation strategy of feature subsets.* The evaluation function identifies the promising areas of the search space. The objective of FSS algorithm is its maximization. The search algorithm uses the value returned by the evaluation function for helping to guide the search. Some evaluation functions carry out this objective looking only at the characteristics of the data, capturing the relevance of each feature or set of features to define the target concept: these type of evaluation functions are grouped below the *filter* strategy. However, Kohavi and John [15] report that when the goal of FSS is the maximization of the accuracy, the features selected should depend not only on the features and the target concept to be learned, but also on the learning algorithm. Thus, they proposed the *wrapper* concept: this implies that the FSS algorithm conducts a search for a good subset using the induction algorithm itself as a part of the evaluation function, the same algorithm that will be used to induce the final classification model. In this way, representational biases of the induction algorithm which are used to construct the final classifier are included in the FSS process. It is claimed by many authors [15, 20] that the wrapper approach obtains better predictive accuracy estimates than the filter approach. However, its computational cost must be taken into account.

4. *Criterion for halting the search.* An intuitive approach for stopping the search is the non-improvement of the evaluation function value of alternative subsets. Another classic criterion is to fix an amount of possible solutions to be visited along the search.

In our microarray problems, we propose to use Sequential Forward Selection (SFS) [13], a classic and well known hill-climbing, deterministic search algorithm which starts from an empty subset of genes. It sequentially selects genes until no improvement is achieved in the evaluation function value. As the totality of previous microarray studies note that very few genes are needed to discriminate between different cell classes, we consider that SFS could be an appropriate search engine because it performs the major part of its search near the empty gene subset.

To assess the goodness of each proposed gene subset for a specific classifier, a wrapper approach is applied. In the same way as supervised classifiers when no gene selection is applied, this wrapper approach estimates, by the LOOCV procedure, the goodness of the classifier using only the gene subset found by the search algorithm.

3 Bayesian Networks

Bayesian networks are probabilistic graphical models represented by directed acyclic graphs in which nodes are variables and arcs show the conditional (in) dependencies among the variables [12].

There are different ways of establishing the Bayesian network structure [8, 3]. It can be the human expert who designs the network taking advantage of his/her knowledge about the relations among the variables. It is also possible to learn the structure by means of an automatic learning algorithm. A combination of both

```
Input: ordering and database
Output: net structure
Begin:
    for i = 1 to n
        π_i = ∅
        p_old = g(i, π_i)
        ok_to_proceed = true
        while (ok_to_proceed) and (|π_i| < max_parents)
            z ∈ pred(i) where z = argmax_k g(i, π_i ⋃{k})
            p_new = g(i, π_i ⋃{k})
            if (p_new > p_old)
                p_old = p_new
                π_i = π_i ⋃{z}
            else
                ok_to_proceed = false
End
```

Fig. 1. Pseudo-code of the K2 structural learning algorithm

systems is a third alternative, mixing the expert knowledge and the learning mechanism. Within the context of microarray data it is beyond the knowledge of the authors the meaning and the inter-relations among the different genes (variables); this is the reason for not defining an expert made net structure for each of the databases.

Within the supervised classification area, learning is performed using a training datafile but there is always a special variable, namely the class, i.e. the one we want to deduce. Some structural learning approaches take into account the existence of that special variable [7, 28, 29, 17], but most of them do consider all the variables in the same manner and use an evaluation metric to measure the suitability of a net given the data. Hence, a structural learning method needs two components: the learning algorithm and the evaluation measure (score+search).

The search algorithm used in the experimentation here described is the K2 algorithm [4] (figure 1 shows its pseudo-code). This algorithm assumes an order has been established for the variables so that the search space is reduced. The fact that $X_1, X_2, \cdots, X_n$ is an ordering of the variables implies that only the predecessors of X_k in the list can be its parent nodes in the learned network. The algorithm also assumes that all the networks are equally probable, but because it is a greedy algorithm it can not ensure that the net resulting from the learning process is the most probable one given the data.

The original algorithm used the K2 Bayesian metric to evaluate the net while it is being constructed:

$$P(D|S) = \log_{10}\left(\prod_{i=1}^{n}\prod_{j=1}^{q_i}\left(\frac{(r_i-1)!}{(N_{ij}+r_i-1)!}\prod_{k=1}^{r_i}N_{ijk}!\right)\right) \qquad (1)$$

where: $P(D|S)$ is a measure of the goodness of the S Bayesian net defined over the D dataset; n is the number of variables; r_i represents the number of values or states that the i-th variable can take; q_i is the set of all possible configurations for the parents of variable i; N_{ijk} is the frequency with whom variable i takes the value k while its parent configuration is j; $N_{ik} = \sum_{j=1}^{q_i} N_{ijk}$; and N is the number of entries in the database

In addition to this metric, we have tried two more measures in combination with the algorithm.

The *Bayesian Information Criterion* [26] (BIC) includes a term that penalizes complex structures:

$$P(D|S) = \sum_{i=1}^{n}\sum_{j=1}^{q_i}\sum_{k=1}^{r_i} N_{ijk} \log \frac{N_{ijk}}{N_{ik}} - f(N)\sum_{i=1}^{n} q_i(r_i-1) \qquad (2)$$

where $f(N) = \frac{1}{2}\log N$ is the penalization term.

The well known entropy [27] metric measures the disorder of the given data:

$$P(D|S) = \sum_{i=1}^{n}\sum_{j=1}^{q_i} \frac{N_{ij}}{N}\left(-\sum_{k=1}^{r_i} \frac{N_{ijk}+1}{N_{ij}+r_i} \ln \frac{N_{ijk}+1}{N_{ij}+r_i}\right) \qquad (3)$$

Evidence propagation or probabilistic inference consists of, given an instantiation of some of the variables, obtaining the a posteriori probability of one ore more of the non-instantiated variables. It is known that this computation is a NP-hard problem, even for the case of a unique variable.

There are different alternatives to perform the propagation methods. Exact methods calculate the exact a posteriori probabilities of the variables and the resulting error is only due to the limitations of the computer where the calculation is performed. The computational cost can be reduced looking over the independence of the nodes in the net.

Approximated propagation methods are based on simulation techniques that obtain approximated values for the probabilities needed. [22] proposes a stochastic simulation method known as the *Markov Sampling Method*. In the case all the Markov Blanquet[1] of the variable of interest is instantiated there is no need of the simulation process to obtain the values of the non-evidential variables and thereby, $P(x|w_x)$ can be calculated using only the probability tables of the parents and children of the node, i.e. using the parameters saved in the model specification. The method becomes for that particular case an exact propagation method.

---

[1] The Markov Blanquet of a node is the set of nodes formed by its parents, its children and the parents of those children.

4 The k-NN Classification Method

A set of pairs $(x_1, \theta_1), (x_2, \theta_2), ..., (x_n, \theta_n)$ is given, where the x_i's take values in a metric space X upon which is defined a metric d and the θ_i's take values in the set $\{1, 2, ..., M\}$ of possible classes. Each θ_i is considered to be the index of the category to which the ith individual belongs, and each x_i is the outcome of the set of measurements made upon that individual. We use to say that "x_i belongs to θ_i" when we mean precisely that the ith individual, upon which measurements x_i have been observed, belongs to category θ_i.

A new pair (x, θ) is given, where only the measurement x is observable, and it is desired to estimate θ by using the information contained in the set of correctly classified points. We shall call:

$$x'_n \in x_1, x_2, ..., x_n$$

the nearest neighbor of x if:

$$min\ d(x_i, x) = d(x'_n, x) \qquad i = 1, 2, ..., n$$

The NN classification decision method gives to x the category θ'_n of its nearest neighbor x'_n. In case of tie for the nearest neighbor, the decision rule has to be modified in order to break it. A mistake is made if $\theta'_n \neq \theta$.

An immediate extension to this decision rule is the so called k-NN approach [5], which assigns to the candidate x the class which is most frequently represented in the k nearest neighbors to x.

5 Proposed Approach

We present a new classifier combination technique that could be seen either as a multi-classifier (or classifier combination technique) or as an hybrid classifier that uses the ideas of the two classifiers involved in the composition.

The new approach works as follows:

1. Select the genes by a wrapper Sequential Forward Selection with the Bayesian Network paradigm. Naive Bayes algorithm implemented in $\mathcal{MLC}$++ tool (Kohavi et al. [16]) has been used for this purpose.
2. Given a database containing the selected genes (and the variable corresponding to the class), learn the classification model (BN structure) to be used. The K2 algorithm has been used as a learning paradigm together with the three different metrics already explained. This algorithm treats all variables equally and does not consider the classifying task the net will be used for. In order to reduce the impact of the random order in the net structures learned, the experiments have been repeated 3000 times and the nets with the optimal values have been selected.
3. When a new case comes to the classifier, assign a class to the new case according to the following process:

- a) Look for its nearest neighbor case in the training database according to the 1-NN algorithm. The use of the nearest neighbor of the new case instead of the case itself allows us to avoid the negative effect that the Laplace correction could have when propagating instances in which almost all the probabilities to be calculated correspond to conditions not present in the database. Let K_i be this nearest case.
- b) Propagate the K_i case in the learned BN as if it was the new case,
- c) Give to the new case the class which a posteriori higher probability after the propagation is done.

6 Experimental Results

To test the performance of the presented approach the following three well known microarray class prediction datasets are used:

- *Colon* dataset, presented by Ben-Dor et al. (2000) [1]. This dataset is composed by 62 samples of colon ephitelial cells. Each sample is characterized by 2,000 genes.
- *Leukemia* dataset, presented by Golub et al. (1999) [9]. It contains 72 instances of leukemia patients involving 7,129 genes.
- *NCI-60* dataset, presented by Ross et al. (2000) [25]; it assesses the gene expression profiles in 60 human cancer cell lines that were characterized pharmacologically by treatment with more than 70,000 different drug agents, one at time and independently. Nine different cancers are considered.

We test the classification accuracy of the new proposed approach and compare the results with those obtained by K-NN and Naive Bayes with all the genes and by the BN models learned by the three metrics.

When learning Bayesian networks two subgoals can be identified. In one hand, the structure of the network must be fixed and in the other hand, the values of the probability tables for each node must be established. In this experimental work the probability tables are always estimated from the training database.

6.1 Structural Learning Using Different Quality Metrics

In this approximation, instead of using a fixed net structure the K2 algorithm has been used as a learning paradigm together with the three different metrics already explained.

Figure 2 shows some of the BN structures obtained by the K2 algorithms with the different metrics used in the three databases. As it can be seen, the structures obtained by the K2 metric are more complex, and those obtained by the BIC learning approach use to be disconnected due to the effect of the penalization. That is the reason, in our opinion, that makes the structures obtained by using the Entropy measure optimal for the classification task.

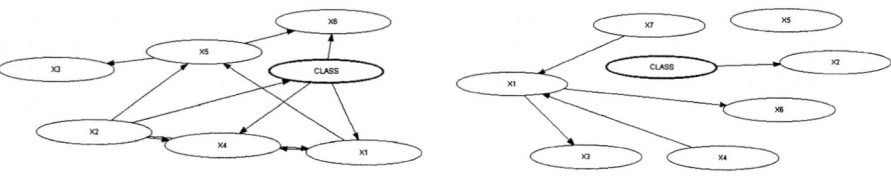

(a) Entropy metric for the Leukemia database

(b) BIC metric for the Colon database

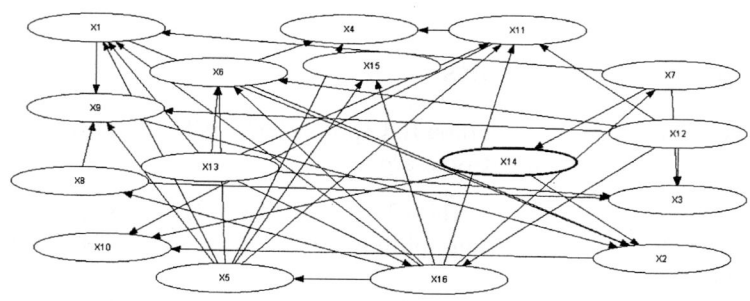

(c) K2 metric for the NCI-60 database

Fig. 2. The obtained Bayesian Network structures for different metrics in the three databases used in the experimental done

6.2 Classification Results

We present in this section the classification results obtained by each of the used paradigms.

Table 1 shows the LOOCV accuracy estimates for the K-NN algorithm and the Naive-Bayes approaches when all the genes of the databases are used as predictor variables in the microarray datasets, as well as the results obtained after the Feature Subset Selection has been performed for the BN, learned using the different metrics, and also for the K-NN paradigm. Naive-Bayes results are

Table 1. LOOCV accuracy percentage obtained for the three databases by using KNN and NB with all the genes, and by the BN and KNN algorithms after the gene selection process

Dataset	KNN-all	NB-all	K2-FSS	BIC-FSS	Entropy-FSS	KNN-FSS
Colon	32.26	53.23	82.29	80.65	83.87	82.26
Leukemia	65.28	84.72	88.88	93.05	91.66	91.66
NCI-60	73.33	48.33	55.00	25.00	66.66	61.66

Table 2. LOOCV accuracy percentage for obtained by the proposed classifier for each dataset after SFS is applied

Dataset	k2	bic	entropy
Colon	83.87	83.87	85.88
Leukemia	91.66	93.05	94.44
NCI-60	58.33	26.66	68.33

outperformed by the BN models when FSS is applied; notice that when considering the whle set of variables, we use the Naive-Bayes algorithm instead of the three learning approaches of the Bayesian Network paradigm due to the the complexity of the BN learning process when the number of variables is large.

After the FSS is done with the wrapper approach, we have 7 genes selected for the Colon database, 6 for the Leukemia and 15 for the NCI-60 when Naive Bayes is used as the classification method. The selected gene number, and the genes themselves, are different when K-NN paradigm is used in the FSS task (6 genes for the Colon database, 3 for the Leukemia and 14 for the NCI-60).

The results obtained by the new proposed approach are shown in Table 2. An accuracy increment is obtained in two of the databases (Colon and Leukemia) with respect to all the previous approaches. Nevertheless, the third dataset does not show the same behaviour, probably because this database is divided into 9 different classes, which makes difficult to the Bayesian Network paradigm to discriminate them using so few cases. For this third database, neither the new approach nor the FSS improves the results obtained by the K-NN when all the variables are considered.

7 Conclusions and Future Work

A new approach in the Machine Learning world is presented in this paper, and it is applied to the micro-array data expression analysis. We use a distance based classifier in combination with a BN, with the main idea of avoiding the *bad* effect of the application of the Laplace Correction in the a posteriori probability calculations due to the small number of cases of the used databases.

Obtained results indicate to the authors that the new approach can be used in order to outperform the well-classified case number obtained by a Bayesian Network when this paradigm is used as a classifier model, and also to obtain better results than the K-NN paradigm.

It must also be pointed out that the BN structure obtained gives us a view of the relations of conditional (in)dependences among the selected genes and the variable representing the class. This fact could be used by physicians in order to understand better the meaning of the existing relations.

As future work a more sophisticated searching approach should be used for the BN structure learning phase. Evolutionary computation based techniques are promising candidates for that job [24]. Filter measures should also be probed for the Gene Selection process instead of the wrapper approach here applied.

References

[1] A. Ben-Dor, L. Bruhn, N. Friedman, I. Nachman, M. Schummer, and Z. Yakhini. Tissue Classification with Gene Expression Profiles. *Journal of Computational Biology*, 7(3-4):559–584, 2000.

[2] R. Blanco, P. Larrañaga, I. Inza, and B. Sierra. Gene selection for cancer classification using wrapper approaches. *International Journal of Pattern Recognition and Artificial Intelligence*, 2004.

[3] D.M. Chickering. Optimal structure identification with greedy search. *Journal of Machine Learning Research*, 3:507–554, 2002.

[4] G. F. Cooper and E. Herskovits. A bayesian method for induction of probabilistic networks from data. *Machine Learning. Kluwer Academic PUBLISHERs, Boston*, 9:309–347, 1992.

[5] T. M. Cover and P. E. Hart. Nearest neighbor pattern classification. *IEEE Trans. IT-13*, 1:21–27, 1967.

[6] J. Doak. An evaluation of feature selection methods and their application to computer security. Technical Report CSE-92-18, University of California at Davis, 1992.

[7] N. Friedman and M. Goldszmidt. Building classifiers using bayesian networks. In *AAAI/IAAI, Vol. 2*, pages 1277–1284, 1996.

[8] N. Friedman and D. Koller. Being bayesian about network structure. a bayesian approach to structure discovery in bayesian networks. *Machine Learning*, 50:95–125, 2003.

[9] T.R. Golub, D.K. Slonim, P. Tamayo, C. Huard, M. Gaasenbeek, J.P. Mesirov, H. Coller, M.L. Loh, J.R. Downing, M.A. Caliguri, C.D. Bloomfield, and E.S. Lander. Molecular Classification of Cancer: Class Discovery and Class Prediction by Gene Expression Monitoring. *Science*, 286:531–537, 1999.

[10] I. Inza, P. Larrañaga, R. Etxeberria, and B. Sierra. Feature Subset Selection by Bayesian network-based optimization. *Artificial Intelligence*, 123(1-2):157–184, 2000.

[11] I. Inza, B. Sierra, R. Blanco, and P. Larra naga. Gene selection by sequential search wrapper approaches in microarray cancer class prediction. *JOURNAL of Intelligent and Fuzzy Systems*, 2002. accepted.

[12] F. V. Jensen. *Bayesian Networks and Decision Graphs (Statistics for Engineering and Information Science)*. Springer, 2001.

[13] J. Kittler. Feature set search algorithms. In C.H. Chen, editor, *Pattern Recognition and Signal Processing*, pages 41–60. Sithoff and Noordhoff, 1978.

[14] R. Kohavi. A study of cross-validation and bootstrap for accuracy estimation and model selection. In N. Lavrac and S. Wrobel, editors, *Proceedings of the International Joint Conference on Artificial Intelligence*, 1995.

[15] R. Kohavi and G. John. Wrappers for feature subset selection. *Artificial Intelligence*, 97(1-2):273–324, 1997.

[16] R. Kohavi, D. Sommerfield, and J. Dougherty. Data mining using MLC++, a Machine Learning library in C++. *International Journal of Artificial Intelligence Tools*, 6:537–566, 1997.

[17] E. Lazkano and B. Sierra. Bayes-nearest:a new hybrid classifier combining bayesian network and distance based algorithms. *Lecture Notes in Artificial Intelligence*, 2902:171–183, 2003.

[18] L. Li, L.G. Pedersen, T.A. Darden, and C. Weinberg. Computational Analysis of Leukemia Microarray Expression Data Using the GA/KNN Method. In *Proceedings of the First Conference on Critical Assessment of Microarray Data Analysis, CAMDA2000*, 2000.

[19] W. Li and Y. Yang. How many genes are needed for a discriminant microarray data analysis? In *Proceedings of the First Conference on Critical Assessment of Microarray Data Analysis, CAMDA2000*, 2000.

[20] H. Liu and H. Motoda. *Feature Selection for Knowledge Discovery and Data Mining*. Kluwer Academic Publishers, 1998.

[21] T.M. Mitchell. *Machine Learning*. McGraw Hill, 1997.

[22] J. Pearl. Evidential reasoning using stochastic simulation of causal models. *Artificial Intelligence*, 32 (2):247–257, 1987.

[23] P. Pudil, J. Novovicova, and J. Kittler. Floating search methods in feature selection. *Pattern Recognition Letters*, 15(1):1119–1125, 1994.

[24] D. Romero, P. Larrañaga, and B. Sierra. Learning bayesian networks on the space of orderings with estimation of distribution algorithms. *International Journal on Pattern Recognition and Artificial Intelligence*, 18 (4):45–60, 2004.

[25] D.T. Ross, U. Scherf, M.B. Eisen, C.M. Perou, C. Rees, P. Spellman, V. Iyer, S.S. Jeffrey, M. Van de Rijn, M. Waltham, A. Pergamenschikov, J.C.F. Lee, D. Lashkari, D. Shalon, T.G. Myers, J.N. Weinstein, D. Botstein, and P.O. Brown. Systematic variation in gene expression patterns in human cancer cell lines. *Nature Genetics*, 24(3):227–234, 2000.

[26] G. Schwarz. Estimating the dimension of a model. *Annals of Statistics*, 6(2):461–464, 1978.

[27] C.E. Shannon. A mathematical theory of communication. *The Bell System Technical Journal*, 27:379–423, 1948.

[28] B. Sierra and P. Larrañaga. Predicting survival in malignant skin melanoma using bayesian networks automatically induced by genetic algorithms. An empirical comparison between different approaches. *Artificial Intelligence in Medicine*, 14:215–230, 1998.

[29] B. Sierra, N. Serrano, P. Larrañaga, E. J. Plasencia, I. Inza, J. J. Jiménez, P. Revuelta, and M. L. Mora. Using bayesian networks in the construction of a bi-level multi-classifier. *Artificial Intelligence in Medicine*, 22:233–248, 2001.

[30] E.P. Xing, M.I. Jordan, and R.M. Karp. Feature Selection for High-Dimensional Genomic Microarray Data. In *Proceedings of the Eighteenth International Conference in Machine Learning, ICML2001*, pages 601–603, 2001.

Medical Image Vector Quantizer Using Wavelet Transform and Enhanced SOM Algorithm

Kwang-Baek Kim[1], Gwang-Ha Kim[2], and Sung-Kwan Je[3]

[1] Dept. of Computer Engineering, Silla University, Busan, Korea
[2] Dept. of Internal Medicine, Pusan National University College of Medicine, Busan, Korea
[3] Dept. of Computer Science, Pusan National University, Busan, Korea
gbkim@silla.ac.kr

Abstract. Vector quantizer takes care of special image features like edges also and hence belongs to the class of quantizers known as second generation coders. This paper proposes a vector quantization using wavelet transform and enhanced SOM algorithm for medical image compression. We propose the enhanced self-organizing algorithm to improve the defects of SOM algorithm, which, at first, reflects the error between the winner node and the input vector to the weight adaptation by using the frequency of the winner node. Secondly, it adjusts the weight in proportion to the present weight change and the previous weight change as well. To reduce the blocking effect and improve the resolution, we construct vectors by using wavelet transform and apply the enhanced SOM algorithm to them. Our experimental results show that the proposed method energizes the compression ratio and decompression ratio.

1 Introduction

Computer graphics and medical imaging applications have started to make inroads into our everyday lives due to the global spread of information technology. This has made image compression an essential tool in computing with workstations, personal computers and computer networks. Videoconferencing, desktop publishing and archiving of medical and remote sensing images all entail the use of image compression for storage and transmission of data [1]. Compression can also be viewed as a form of classification, since it assigns a template or codeword to a set of input vectors of pixels drawn from a large set in such a way as to provide a good approximation of representation. The vector quantization is the well-known method as a component algorithm for loss compression methods, and many loss compression methods are using LBG algorithm for the vector quantization, which was developed by Linde, Buzo, and Gray [2]. But, LBG algorithm is recursive and requires considerable times to get optimal code vectors [3]. The quantization method using the artificial neural network is well suitable to the application that the statistical distribution of original data is changing as time passes, since it supports the adaptive learning to data [4][5]. Also, the neural network has the huge parallel structure and has the possibility for high speed processing. The H/W implementation of vector quantizer using the neural network supports $O(1)$'s codebook search and doesn't require designing the extra structure for codebook.

The vector quantization for color image requires the analysis of image pixels for determinating the codebook previously not known, and the self-organizing map (SOM) algorithm, which is the self-learning model of neural network, is widely used for the vector quantization (VQ). However, the vector quantization using SOM shows the underutilization that only some code vectors generated are heavily used [6][7]. This defect is incurred because it is difficult to estimate correctly the center of data with no prior information of the distribution of data.

In this paper, we propose the enhanced SOM algorithm, which, at first, reflects the error between the winner node and the input vector to the weight adaptation by using the frequency of the winner node. Secondly, it adjusts the weight in proportion to the present weight change and the previous weight changes as well. By using the wavelet transform and the proposed SOM algorithm, we implement and evaluate the vector quantization. The evaluation result shows that the proposed VQ algorithm reduces the requirement of computation time and memory space, and improves the quality of the decompressed image decreasing the blocking effect.

2 Related Research

2.1 Definition of VQ

A minimum distortion data compression system or source coder can be modeled as a vector quantization (VQ), by mapping of input vectors into a finite collection of templates or reproduction code words called a codebook [3]. In VQ, the original image is first decomposed into n-dimensional image vectors. The process of mapping the decomposed image vector X into the template vector having a minimal error is called VQ. That is, VQ can be defined as a mapping Q of k-dimensional Euclidean space R^k into a finite subset Y of R^k. Thus,

$$Q: R^k \rightarrow Y, Y = (x_i': i = 1,....,N_c) \quad (1)$$

where $Y = (x_i': i = 1,....,N_c)$ is the set of reproduction vectors, the codebook. And N_c is the number of vectors in Y, the size of the codebook. It can be seen as a combination of two functions: an encoder, which views the input vector x and generates the address of the reproduction vector specified by $Q(x)$, and a decoder, which generates the reproduction vector x' using this address. To measure a degree of distortion of the reproduction vector x', a mean square (MSE) is generally used. For the color image, it is defined as follows and the dimension of image vector is an $n \times n$ blocks;

$$MSE = \frac{1}{n \times n} \sum_{k=1}^{RGB} \sum_{i=0}^{n-1}\sum_{j=0}^{n-1}(x_{ij} - x'_{ij}) \quad (2)$$

where x_{ij} is the input value of the original image, x'_{ij} is the value of reproduction vector, RGB has a value of 3.

2.2 LBG Algorithm

LBG algorithm, which was proposed by Linde, Buzo, and Gray, is most representative among the codebook generation algorithms. This algorithm generalizes the scalar quantizer designed by Lloyd and called GLA (Generalized Llyod Algorithm)[3]. LBG algorithm is mapped to representation vector with minimum distortion in all input vectors, and calculating the average distortion degree. LBG algorithm generates the optimal codebook according to the following steps: *Step 1.* all input vectors are mapped to code vectors with minimum error in the codebook. *Step 2.* the mean square of error between input vectors and code vector is calculated. *Step 3.* the error value is compared with the given allowance. If the error value is greater than the allowance, the current codebook is adjusted by recalculating the centers of code vectors. Otherwise, the current codebook is determined to be optimal. The selection of the initial codebook is important to generate the optimal codebook in LBG algorithm. The selection methods of the initial codebook are the random selection method, the separation method that divides all learning vectors to 2 groups, and the merging method that merges two adjacent vectors repeatedly from N clusters to the N_c's codebook. Without regard to the selection of the initialization method, LBG algorithm scans repeatedly all image vectors to generate the optimal codebook and requires the high computation time for images of large size.

2.3 Vector Quantization Using Neural Network

Self-Organizing Map (SOM) is widely applied in the vector quantization, which is the self-learning method among neural network algorithms [7][8]. The SOM algorithm, which is derived from an appropriate stochastic gradient decent scheme, results in a natural clustering process in which the network performs competitive learning to perceive pattern classes based on data similarity. Smoothing of vector elements does not take place in this unsupervised training scheme. At the same time, since it doses not assume an initial codebook, the probability of getting stranded in local minima is also small. The investigations for high quality reconstructed pictures have led us to the edge preserving self-organizing map. This greatly reduces the large computational costs involved in generating the codebook and finding the closest codeword for each image vector. The process adaptively adjusting the weight of the stored pattern in SOM algorithm is the same as the process generating dynamically a code vector in the codebook for the given input vector in the vector quantization. Therefore, the vector quantization using SOM algorithm generates the codebook dynamically for color images.

However, from practical experience, it is observed that additional refinements are necessary for the training algorithm to be efficient enough for practical applications [9]. And with no information of the distribution of training vectors, the vector quantization using SOM algorithm selects randomly the initial code vectors and progresses the adaptive learning. Therefore, this adaptive VQ algorithm generates code vectors never used after the initial codebook generation, incurring the underutilization of code vectors.

3 Medical Image Vector Quantizer Using Wavelet Transform and Enhanced SOM Algorithm

In this paper, we apply the wavelet transform and the enhanced SOM algorithm sequentially to images, generating the codebook for the compression of image as shown in Fig. 1. The vector quantization using the traditional SOM algorithm incurs the underutilization of code vectors. And, for the improvement of this defect, we propose the enhanced SOM algorithm that reflects the frequency of winner node for each class, the previous change of weight as well as the difference between input vector and winner node to the weight adaptation. The application of the enhanced SOM algorithm to the wavelet-transformed image reduces computation time and memory space for the codebook generation and lightens the blocking effect incurred by the insufficient size of codebook.

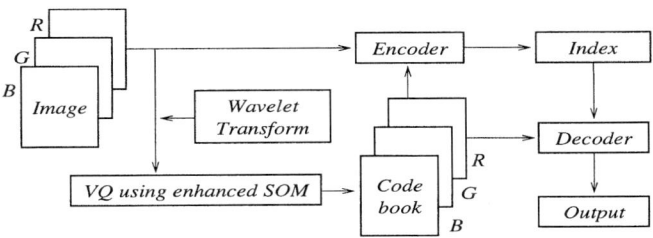

Fig. 1. The processing structure of the proposed vector quantizer

3.1 Enhanced SOM Algorithm

In this paper, we propose the enhanced SOM algorithm for the vector quantization that is able to generate the codebook in real-time and provide the high recovery quality. The generation procedure of codebook using enhanced SOM algorithm is showed in Fig. 2 and Fig. 3.

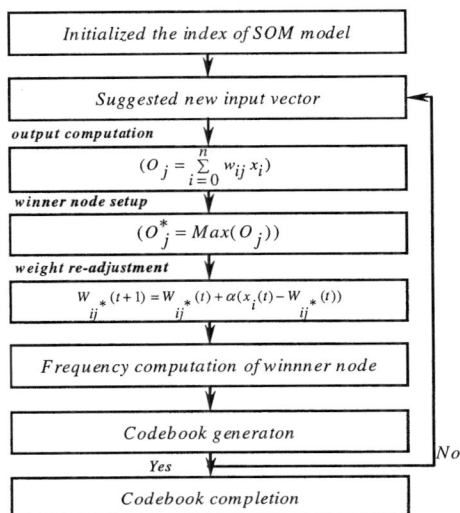

Fig. 2. The enhanced SOM algorithm for the generation of initial codebook

In this paper, we improved the SOM algorithm by employing three methods for the efficient generation of the codebook. First, the error between the winner node and the input vector and the frequency of the winner node are reflected in the weight adaptation. Second, the weight is adapted in proportion to the present weight change and the previous weight change as well. Third, in the weight adaptation for the generation of the initial codebook, the weight of the adjacent pixel of the winner node is adapted together.

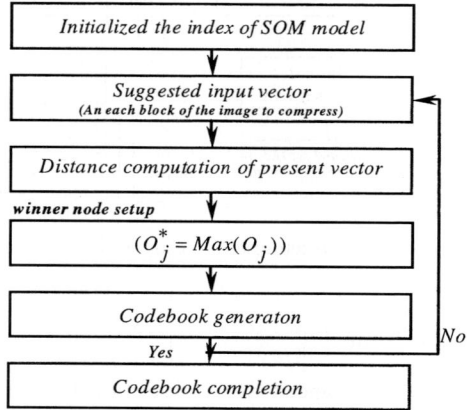

Fig. 3. The procedure of index determination and codebook generation for each block

In the proposed method, the codebook is generated by scanning the entire image only two times. In the first step, the initial codebook is generated to reflect the distribution of the given training vectors. The second step uses the initial codebook and regenerates the codebook by moving to the center within the decision region. To generate the precise codebook, it needs to select the winner node correctly and we have to consider the real distortion of the code vector and the input vector. For this management, the measure of frequency to be selected as winner node and the distortion for the selection of the winner node in the competitive learning algorithm are needed. We use the following equation in the weight adaptation.

$$w_{ij}(t+1) = w_{ij}(t) + \alpha(x_i - w_{ij}(t))$$
$$\alpha = f(e_j) + \frac{1}{f_j} \quad (3)$$

where α is the learning factor between 0 and 1 and is set between 0.25 and 0.75 in general. $(x_i - w_{ij}(t))$ is an error value and represents the difference between the input vector and the representative code vector. This means weights are adapted as much as the difference and it prefers to adapt the weight in proportion to the size of the difference. Therefore, we use the normalized value for the output error of the winner node that is converted to the value between 0 and 1 as a learning factor. The larger the output error is, the more the amount for the weight adaptation is. Therefore, the weight is adapted in proportion to the size of the output error. $f(e_j)$ is the normalization function that converts the value of e_j to the value between 0 and 1, e_j is the output error of the j-th neuron, and f_j is the frequency for the j-th neuron as the winner.

The above method considers only the present change of weight and does not consider the previous change. In the weight adaptation, we consider the previous weight change as well as the present one's. This concept corresponds to the momentum parameter of BP. We will also call this concept as a momentum factor. Based on the momentum factor, the equation for the weight adaptation is as follows:

$$w_{ij}(t+1) = w_{ij}(t) + \delta_{ij}(t+1) \tag{4}$$

$$\delta_{ij}(t+1) = \alpha(x_i - w_{ij}(t)) + \alpha\delta_{ij}(t) \tag{5}$$

In equation (5), the first term represents the effect of the present weight change and the second term is the momentum factor representing the previous change.
The algorithm is detailed below:

- *Step 1.* Initialize the network. i.e., initialize weights (w_{ij}) from the n inputs to the output nodes to small random values. Set the initial neighborhood, N_c to be large. Fix the convergence tolerance limit for the vectors to be a small quantity. Settle maximum number of iterations to be a large number. Divide the training set into vectors of size $n \times n$.
- *Step 2.* Compute the mean and variance of each training input vector.
- *Step 3.* Present the inputs $x_i(t)$.
- *Step 4.* Compute the Euclidean distance d_j between the input and each output node j, given by,

$$d_j = f_j \times d(x, w_{ij}(t)) \tag{6}$$

where f_j is the frequency of the jth neuron being a winner. Select the minimum distance. Designate the output node with minimum d_j to be j^*.

- *Step 5.* Update the weight for node j^* and its neighbors, defined by the neighborhood size N_c. The weights are updated:

if $i \in N_c(t)$

$$f_{j^*} = f_{j^*} + 1 \tag{7}$$

$$w_{ij^*}(t+1) = w_{ij^*}(t) + \delta_{ij^*}(t+1) \tag{8}$$

$$\delta_{ij^*}(t+1) = \alpha(t+1)(x_i - w_{ij^*}(t)) + \alpha(t+1)\delta_{ij^*}(t) \tag{9}$$

$$\alpha(t+1) = f(e_{j^*}) + \frac{1}{f_{j^*}} \tag{10}$$

$$e_{j^*} = \frac{1}{n}\sum_{i=0}^{n-1} |x_i(t) - w_{ij^*}(t)| \tag{11}$$

if $i \notin N_c(t)$

$$w_{ij}(t+1) = w_{ij}(t) \qquad (12)$$

The neighborhood $N_c(t)$ decreases in size as time goes on, thus localizing the area of maximum activity. And $f(e_j)$ is normalization function.

- *Step 6.* Repeat by going to step 2 for each input vector presented, till a satisfactory match is obtained between the input and the weight or till the maximum number of iterations are complete.

3.2 Application of Wavelet Transform

In this paper, for the proposed SOM algorithm, we apply a wavelet transform to reduce the block effect and to improve the decompression quality. After the wavelet transforms the color image, the color image is compressed by applying the vector quantization using the enhanced SOM algorithm to each separated RGB values. That is, by applying the wavelet transforms to the image, input vectors are generated, and the enhanced SOM algorithm are applied to the input vectors. If the index of the winner node corresponding to the input vector is found, the original image vector corresponding to the transformed input vector is stored in the codebook. Wavelet transform is applied to the original image in the vertical and horizontal direction of a low frequency prior to the codebook generation. Specially, the image information of the original resolution is maintained without the down sampling used in the existing wavelet transform. Using the low frequency pass filter of wavelet emphasizes the strong areas of image and attenuates weak areas, have an equalization effect and remove the noise. Fig. 4 shows the structure of wavelet transform [10]. Fig. 5 shows the example of the filters in high frequency and low frequency.

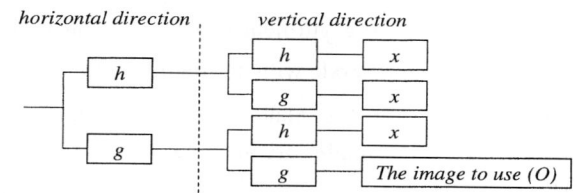

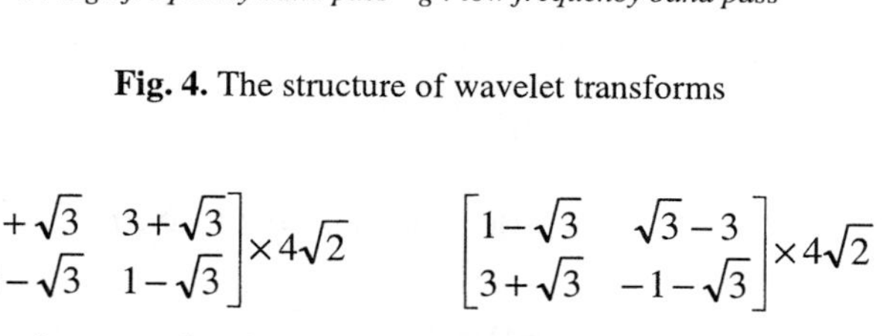

h : high frequency band pass   g : low frequency band pass

Fig. 4. The structure of wavelet transforms

$$\begin{bmatrix} 1+\sqrt{3} & 3+\sqrt{3} \\ 3-\sqrt{3} & 1-\sqrt{3} \end{bmatrix} \times 4\sqrt{2} \qquad \begin{bmatrix} 1-\sqrt{3} & \sqrt{3}-3 \\ 3+\sqrt{3} & -1-\sqrt{3} \end{bmatrix} \times 4\sqrt{2}$$

(a) Low-frequency band pass filter   (b) High-frequency band pass filter

Fig. 5. The filters used in wavelet transform

4 Simulation Results

An experiment environment was implemented on an IBM 586 Pentium III with C++ Builder. The image to be used experiment is a color bitmap images of 128×128 pixel size. The image is divided into blocks of 4×4 size and each block is represented by the vector of 16 bytes, which constitutes the codebook. In this paper, the proposed VQ algorithm and LBG algorithm are compared in performance. In the case of the codebook generation and image compression, the vector quantization using the enhanced SOM algorithm improves 5 times in the computation time than LBG algorithm and generates the codebook by scanning all image vectors only two times. This reduces the requirement of memory space. The application of the wavelet transform lightens the block effect and improves the recovery quality. Fig. 6 shows medical color images used in the experiment. Although the proposed algorithm can be applied to grayscale images, we selected various medical color images for this experiment because the proposed vector quantization algorithm is for the color medical image.

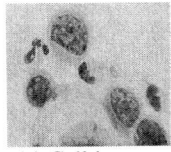

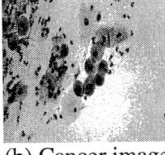
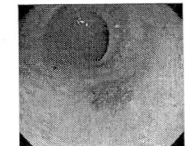
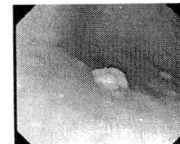

(a) Cell image   (b) Cancer image   (C) Endoscopic image 1   (d) Endoscopic image 2

Fig. 6. Medical image samples used for experiment

Table 1 shows the size of codebooks generated by LBG algorithm, SOM algorithm, enhanced SOM and the integration of wavelet transform and enhanced SOM for images in Fig. 6. In Table 1, the proposed integration of wavelet transform and enhanced SOM algorithm shows a more improved compression ratio than other methods. In the case of image 2 which the distribution of color is various, the compression ratio is low compared with different images. For the comparison of decompression quality, we measure the mean square error (MSE) between the original image and the recovered image, and presented in Table 2 the MSE of each image in the three algorithms.

Table 1. Size of codebook by VQ (unit: byte)

Algorithms Images	LBG	SOM	Enhanced SOM	Wavelet and Enhanced SOM
Cell Image	49376	52080	51648	27365
Cancer Cell Image	50357	53213	52347	30645
Endoscopic image 1	50232	54081	53649	28377
Endoscopic image 2	50125	54032	53591	28321

Table 2. Comparison of MSE (Mean Square Error) for compressed images

Algorithms Images	LBG	SOM	Enhanced SOM	Wavelet and Enhanced SOM
Cell Image	14.5	11.3	10.8	9.1
Cancer Cell Image	15.1	14.1	13.2	11.2
Endoscopic image 1	14.9	13.8	12.7	10.6
Endoscopic image 2	14.8	13.6	12.4	10.3

As shown in Table 2, the integration of wavelet transform and enhanced SOM algorithm shows the lowest MSE. Also, for images shown in Fig. 7, the decompression quality of LBG algorithm is worse than the above three algorithms.

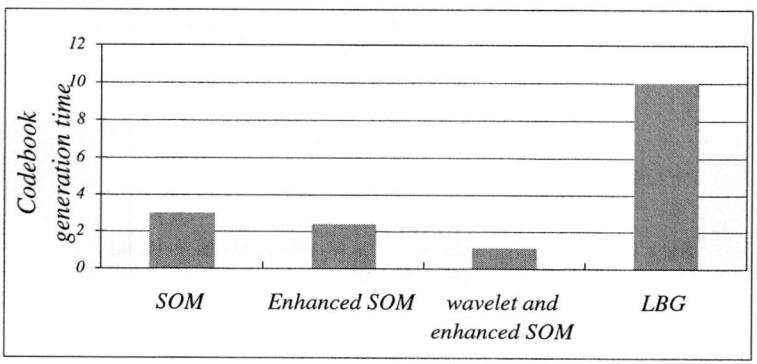

Fig. 7. Comparison of processing time for codebook generation

LBG algorithm generates 10's temporary codebooks until the creation of the optimal codebook and requires a high computation time for codebook generation. Oppositely, the proposed algorithm generates only one codebook in the overall processing and reduces greatly the computation time and the memory space required for the codebook generation. Fig.8, Fig.9, Fig.10 and Fig.11 show respectively recovered images for original images of Fig.6. The enhanced SOM algorithm improves the compression ratio and the recovery quality of images by the codebook dynamic allocation more than the conventional SOM algorithm.

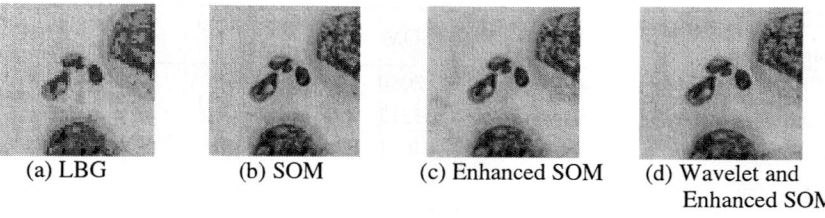

(a) LBG (b) SOM (c) Enhanced SOM (d) Wavelet and Enhanced SOM

Fig. 8. The recovered image for cell image

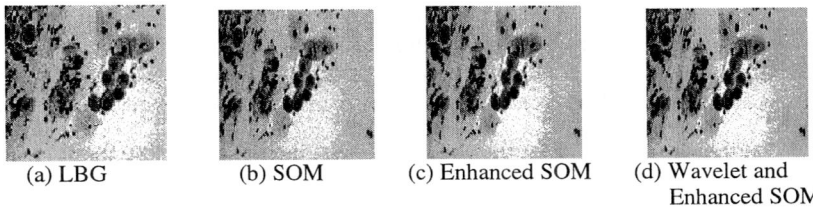

(a) LBG (b) SOM (c) Enhanced SOM (d) Wavelet and Enhanced SOM

Fig. 9. The recovered image for cancer cell image

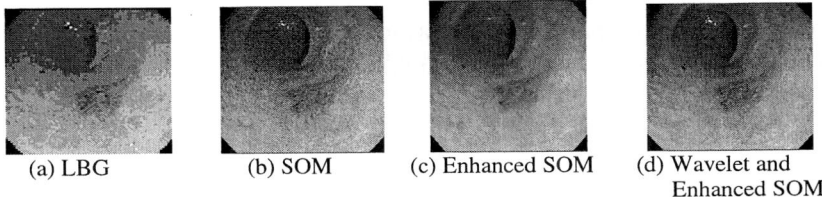

(a) LBG (b) SOM (c) Enhanced SOM (d) Wavelet and Enhanced SOM

Fig. 10. The recovered image for endoscopic image 1

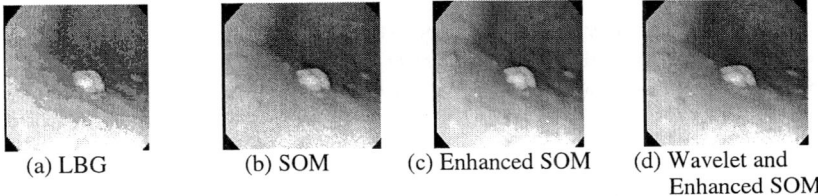

(a) LBG (b) SOM (c) Enhanced SOM (d) Wavelet and Enhanced SOM

Fig. 11. The recovered image for endoscopic image 2

5 Conclusion

The proposed method can be summarized as follows: using the enhanced SOM algorithm, the output error concept is introduced into the weight adaptation and the momentum factor is added. The simulation results show that the enhanced SOM algorithm for the medical color image compression produces a major improvement in both subjective and objective quality of the decompressed images. LBG algorithm is traditionally used for the codebook generation and requires considerable time especially for large size images, since the codebook is generated by repetitive scanning of the whole image. The proposed method is apt to real time application because the codebook is created by scanning the whole image only twice. The enhanced SOM algorithm performs the learning in two steps and total learning vectors are used only once in each step. In the first step, it produces the initial codebook by reflecting the distribution of learning vectors well. In the second step, it produces the optimal codebook by shifting to the current center of each code group based on the initial codebook. For reducing the memory space and the computation time for the codebook generation, we construct vectors by using wavelet transform and we apply the enhanced SOM algorithm to them. The simulation results showed that the integration of the wavelet transform and the enhanced SOM algorithm improves the defects of vector quantization such as the time and memory space caused by the complex computation and the block effect.

References

1. Rabbani M., and Jones P. W.: Digital Image Compression Technique. Spie Optical Engineering Press (1991) 144-169
2. Linde Y., Buzo A., and Gray R. M.: An Algorithm for Vector Quantizer Design. IEEE Trans. On Communications. **1(1)** (1980) 84-95
3. Gray R. M.: Vector Quantization. IEEE ASSP Magazine. (1984) 4-29
4. Kohonen T.: Improved versions of learning vector quantization. Proceedings of IJCNN. **(1)** (1990) 545-550
5. Godfrey K. R. L., and Attikiouzel, Y.: Self-Organized Color Image Quantization for Color Image Data Compression. Proc. of ICNN. **(3)** (1993) 1622-1626
6. Kim K. B., and Cha E. Y.: A Fuzzy Self-Organizing Vector Quantization for Image. Proceedings of IIZUKA. **(2)** (1996) 757-760
7. Madeiro F., Vilar R. M., Fechine J. M., and Aguiar Neto B. G.: A Self-Organizing Algorithm for Vector Quantizer Design Applied to Signal Processing. International Journal of Neural Systems. **9(3)** (1999) 219-226
8. Oehler K. L., and Gray R. M.: Combining Image Compression and Classification using Vector Quantization. IEEE Multimedia. (1997) 36-45
9. Seo S., Bode M., and Obermayer K.: Soft Nearest Prototype Classification. IEEE Trans. Neural Networks. **14(2)** (2003) 390-398
10. Strang G., and Nguyen T.: Wavelets and Filter Banks. Wellesley-Cambridge Press (1996)

SVM Classification for Discriminating Cardiovascular Disease Patients from Non-cardiovascular Disease Controls Using Pulse Waveform Variability Analysis*

Kuanquan Wang[1], Lu Wang[1], Dianhui Wang[2], and Lisheng Xu[1]

[1] Department of Computer Science and Engineering,
Harbin Institute of Technology (HIT), Harbin, 150001 China
{wangkq, wanglu, xulisheng}@hit.edu.cn
[2] Department of Computer Science and Computer Engineering,
La Trobe University, Melbourne, VIC 3086, Australia
csdhwang@ieee.org

Abstract. This paper analyzes the variability of pulse waveforms by means of approximate entropy (*ApEn*) and classifies three group objects using support vector machines (SVM). The subjects were divided into three groups according to their cardiovascular conditions. Firstly, we employed *ApEn* to analyze three groups' pulse morphology variability (PMV). The pulse waveform's *ApEn* of a patient with cardiovascular disease tends to have a smaller value and its variation's spectral contents differ greatly during different cardiovascular conditions. Then, we applied a SVM to discriminate cardiovascular disease patients from non-cardiovascular disease controls. The specificity and sensitivity for clinical diagnosis of cardiovascular system is 85% and 93% respectively. The proposed techniques in this paper, from a long-term PMV analysis viewpoint, can be applied to a further research on cardiovascular system.

1 Introduction

More and more noninvasive measurements of physiological signals, such as ECG, heart sound, wrist pulse waveform, can be acquired for the assessment of physical condition. Among these methods, the ECG provides information about the electrical activity of the heart [1], while the wrist pulse waveform affords the information on the pressure variation in the wrist vessel. Various civilizations in the past have used arterial pulse as a guide to diagnose and treat various diseases.

The Chinese art of pulse feeling, which is still being practiced, has more than 2,000 years of history. According to traditional Chinese pulse diagnosis, the pulse not only can deduce the positions and degree of pathological changes, but is also a convenient, inexpensive, painless, and noninvasive method promoteded by the U.N. [2, 3]. Recording and analyzing the pressure wave in the radial artery of the wrist provide a non-

---

* Supported by the National Natural Science Foundation of China under Grant No.90209020.

invasive measure of the arterial pressure wave in proximal aorta. The radial artery pulse wave can reveal central systolic, diastolic and mean arterial pressures, as well as supply an assessment of arterial wave reflection, which is closely related to cardiovascular condition and the degree of stiffness of arteries. Recently, increasingly numbers of western medicine researchers have begun to pay more attention to pulse diagnosis [4-5].

Pulse waveform is analyzed usually by traditional time and frequency domain methods. Having analyzed the pulse waveform with the conventional methods, we find that some dynamic characters of the pulse waveform are undiscovered [6, 7]. Few papers on pulse waveform's nonlinear analysis can be found [8]. Currently, a number of nonlinear methods have been recently developed to quantify the dynamics of physiological signals such as ECG, EEG and so on. These have achieved some meaningful results that the conventional statistics cannot achieve [9]. Consequently, we investigate the pulse's variability through nonlinear methods.

There are many methods that can disclose the dynamic characters of physiological signal, such as K-S entropy, the largest Lyapunov exponent, approximate entropy, coarse-grained entropy and so on. However, K-S entropy and largest Lyapunov exponent assume that the time series have enough length. It appears that ApEn has potential wide spread utility for practical data analysis and clinical application due to its five salient features [10]. Furthermore, the *ApEn* can be applied in both deterministic and stochastic processes. At present, whether pulse waveform's nature is deterministic chaos or not has not been proved yet. Therefore we employ the *ApEn* to disclose some clinical value of pulse variability [11].

This paper applies SVM to discriminate cardiovascular disease patients from non-cardiovascular controls. The technique of SVM, developed by Vapnik, was proposed essentially for classification problems of two classes. SVM use geometric properties to exactly calculate the optima separating hyper plane directly from the training data [12-14]. Based on structure risk minimum principal, SVM can efficiently solve the learning problem, with the strengths of good generalization and correct classification. It is important to emphasize that SVM have been employed in a number of applications [15]. However, few of them belong to the bioengineering field, and in particular to pulse waveform variability discrimination.

In Section 2, the long-term pulse data collection and preprocessing are stated firstly. Then the *ApEn*s analysis of long-term pulse and their corresponding experimental results are presented in Section 3. Having extracted 12 features on pulse variability, we apply a SVM classifier to discriminate cardiovascular disease patients from non-cardiovascular controls in this section. Section 4 draws our conclusions.

2 Material and Methods

This section describes the data collection and our analysis methodology.

2.1 Study Protocol and Data Collection

In this study, all the pulse data are acquired by our pulse monitoring and diagnosis system, illustrated in Fig. 1 [7].

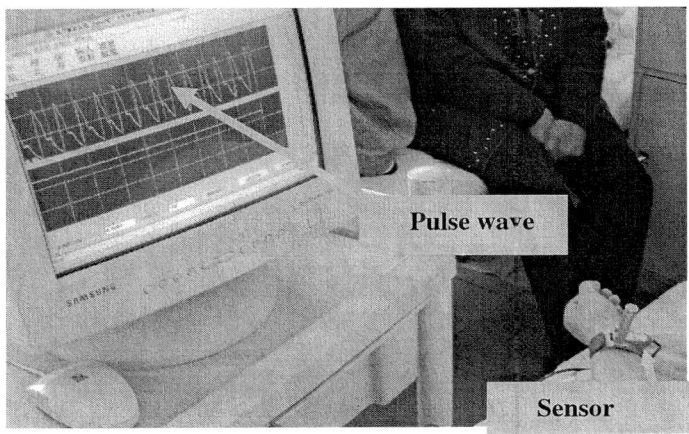

Fig. 1. Our pulse acquisition system

Pulse waveform recordings are acquired from 90 volunteers. Three groups are studied, each including 30 subjects, matched for age and gender. All of them are examined by ultrasonic test. They are confirmed to be without neural system problems.

- **Group1** is 30 patients with cardiovascular disease (15 females and 15 males, age 60±12 years);
- **Group2** is 30 patients hospitalized for non-cardiac cause (15 females and 15 males, age 55±12 years);
- **Group3** contains 30 healthy subjects who are selected as control subjects matched for sex and age (15 females and 15 males, age 55±12 years). Those selected control subjects have no documented history of cardiovascular diseases and disorders, and have been examined by ultrasonic, X-ray examination and so on.

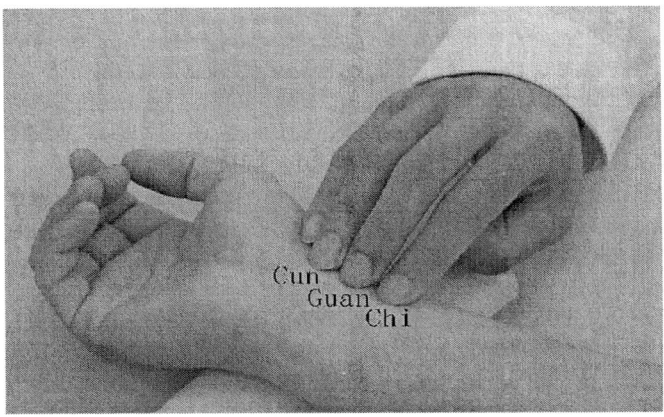

Fig. 2. The positions of *"Cun"*, *"Guan"*, *"Chi"*

The pulses of all subjects are acquired for 600 seconds long at the sampling rate of 100 Hz. Each subject was asked to relax for more than 5 minutes before pulse acquisition. According to the traditional Chinese pulse diagnosis, we can acquire pulse at the positions of *"Cun"*, *"Guan"*, *"Chi"*, which are demonstrated in Fig. 2. All of the subjects were lying on their backs during pulse acquisition. According to the theory of Traditional Chinese pulse diagnosis, the pulse in *"Cun"* position reflects the condition of the heart. As a result, we put our pulse sensor on the *"Cun"* positions of the subjects' left wrists to study the relationship between cardiovascular condition and pulse waveform variability.

2.2 Methods

We utilize an approximate entropy and SVM classifier techniques to analyze and classify wrist pulse waveform variability. The whole procedure is illustrated in Fig. 3. At first, we use the designed filter to remove the interference and baseline wander of pulse waveform. Then we segment the pulse waveform into 200 partitions and apply the approximate entropy to analyze the variability of pulse morphology. After that, we extract 12 features from the approximate entropies. Finally, we employ the SVM classifier to discriminate the cardiovascular disease patients from non-cardiovascular disease controls.

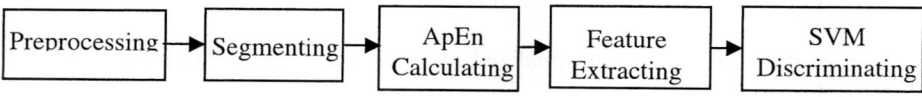

Fig. 3. The schematic figure on the procedure of pulse waveform

2.2.1 Pulse Waveform Preprocessing Based on Cascaded Adaptive Filter

The bandwidth of the acquiring system is with almost linear response from the 0.05Hz to 100Hz, causing no distortion of pulse waveform. However, distortion may arise from the subject's movement, respiration and so on. Thus, the baseline wander introduced in the acquisition process must be removed before computing the pulse waveform's *ApEn*. We apply the cascade adaptive filter as described in the paper [16] to remove this wander.

2.2.2 Waveform Variability Analysis Using ApEn

Over the past few decades, thanks to the advance of computer technology, the recording and storage of massive datasets of pulse waveform is possible. As a result, some nonlinear analysis methods can be used to extract useful clinical information from pulse data.

Nonlinear dynamical analysis is a powerful approach to understand biological system. Pincus introduced *ApEn* as a set of measures of system complexity, which has easily been applied to clinical cardiovascular and other time series. *ApEn* may contain the information that is neither visually apparent nor extractable with conventional methods of analysis.

ApEn is a measure of complexity and regularity. For instance, a small *ApEn* means a high degree of regularity. The approximate entropy, *ApEn(m, r, N)*, can be estimated as a function of the parameters m, r and N, where m is the dimension to which the signal will be expanded, r is the threshold and N is the length of the signal to be analyzed. Both theoretical analysis and clinical applications conclude that when $m=2$ or 3, and r is between 10% and 25% of the standard derivation of the data to be analyzed, the *ApEn(m,r,N)* produces good statistical validity. In this paper, we use $m=2$, $r=0.2$, $N=300$ (that means every segment includes 300 sampling points).

The procedure of pulse morphology variability (PMV) analysis is as follows:

- Dividing each 10 minutes pulse recording into 200 segments. Each segment contains data corresponding to a 3-second portion of the recording (300 sampling points);
- Calculating *ApEn* of every segment and obtaining 200 *ApEns* for each subject.

Having applied the *ApEn* for PMV analysis of three-groups, we illustrate the *ApEn* mean values of three groups in Fig. 4. The y-coordinate is the average of every subject's 200 *ApEns*. Each group contains 30 subjects and their *ApEn* Means all vary from 0.08 to 0.25. On average, the *ApEn* Means of **Group1** are smaller than **Group2** and **Group3**'s. But the *ApEn* Means of three groups don't have significant difference.

The *ApEn* averages of PMV don't have significant difference, but the fluctuation of their *ApEn* consequences differs notably. In Fig. 5, *ApEn1*, *ApEn2* and *ApEn3* is the typical *ApEns* of subject in **Group1**, **Group2** and **Group3** respectively. The y-axis is the value of *ApEn* and the x-axis is the segment's sequence number. From Fig. 5, we can find that the *ApEn1* fluctuates faster and more regularly than *ApEn2* and *ApEn3*. This means that the healthier the person's cardiovascular system is, the more complex his PMV is.

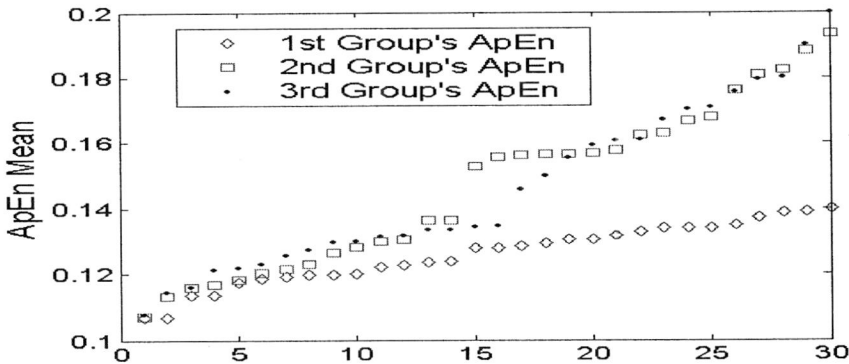

Fig. 4. The comparison of three groups' *ApEns* averages. Each group contains 30 persons. Each person's 10 minutes pulse waveform was portioned into 200 segments. Each point stands for the average of a person's 200 *ApEns*

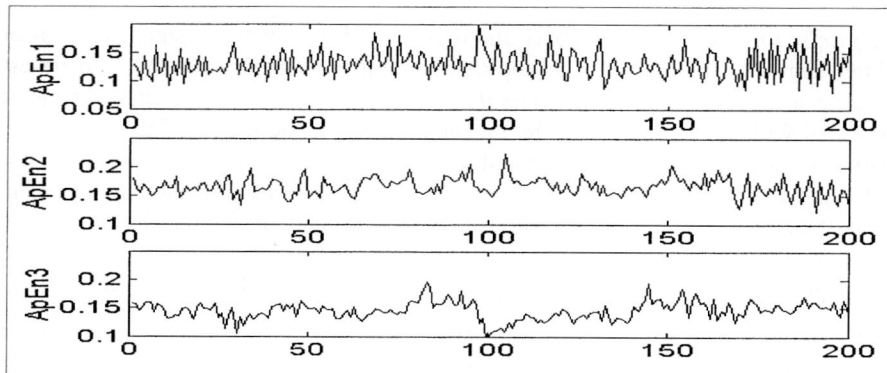

Fig. 5. The comparison of *ApEn*s

2.2.3 Pulse Morphology Variability Features Extraction

In the above part we analyze the PMV of the three groups and find that PMV has notable clinical value to differentiate cardiovascular conditions.

From the spectral point of view, we can discover some useful relationship between PMV and the cardiovascular system. Fig. 7 illustrates the power spectrum of PMV. All of them are computed from the 200 *ApEn*s of 10 minutes' pulse waveforms. The x-axis is the Nyquist frequency and the y-axis is the amplitude of its spectrum. The first row *PSD1* is the spectrum of one patient in **Group1**; the second *PSD2* is the spectrum of one patient in **Group2**; the third row *PSD3* is the spectrum of **Group3**'s. We can find that the healthy person's *ApEn* has more low frequency content as shown in *PSD3*. The *PSD1* has more high frequency content than *PSD2* and *PSD3*.

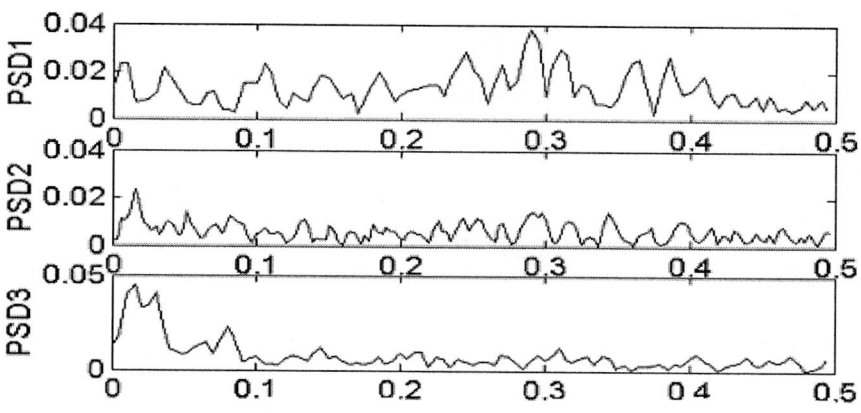

Fig. 6. The comparison on the spectral distribution of three groups' ApEn

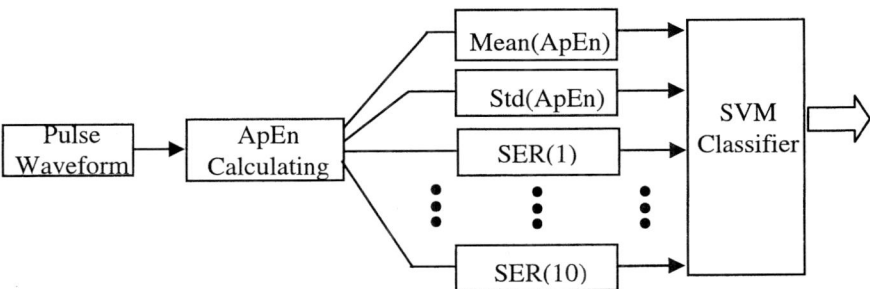

Fig. 7. The schematic figure of features extraction

In this part, we will extract some features from the PMV ApEns. Fig. 7 lists the features such as the mean, standard derivation of the ApEns and spectral energy ratio (*SER*) of ApEns. This paper partitions the power spectrum of the *ApEn* into 10 equidistant segments as $[0 \sim 0.05f_s, 0.05 \sim 0.1f_s, \cdots, 0.4 \sim 0.45f_s, 0.45 \sim 0.5f_s]$. Then we can get their spectral rates of those 10 segments. The PMV's *SER*s are computed as shown in Formula (1).

$$SER(i) = \sum_{f_i=(i-1)*0.05f_s}^{i*0.05f_s} A^2(f_i) \bigg/ \sum_{f_j=0f_s}^{0.5f_s} A^2(f_j) \text{, i=1,..., 10.} \quad (1)$$

where f_i is the spectral and $A(f_i)$ is its corresponding amplitude.

2.2.4 SVM Classifiers

Support Vector Machines were invented by Vapnik. They are learning machines that can create functions from a set of labeled training data. For classification, SVMs operate by finding a hypersurface in the space of possible inputs. This hypersurface will attempt to split the positive examples from the negative examples. The split will be chosen to have the largest distance from the hypersurface to the nearest of the positive and negative examples.

The discriminant equation of the SVM classifier is a function of kernel $k(x_i, x)$ and is given by:

$$D(x) = \text{sign}(\sum_{i=1}^{N_{sv}} \alpha_i y_i k(X_i, X) + b). \quad (2)$$

where X_i are the support vectors, N_{sv} is the number of support vectors, α_i is the weight parameters, b is the biased parameter, and $y \in \{-1,+1\}$ depending on the class. In the present study the two degree non-homogeneous polynomial function was used for the linear kernel, given by $K(x, y) = x^T \cdot y$, or Polynomial Kernel at the degree of two $K(x, y) = (x \cdot y + 1)^d$ with $d = 2$, resulting in the discriminant function of the SVM classifier.

3   PMV's SVM Classifier Discrimination Results

The SVM classifier has better generalization ability than neural network and other classifiers, especially for small training data sets. In this study, we apply a SVM to classify **Group1** with **Group2**, and **Group1** with **Group3**. As listed in Table1, we name the **Group1** as Cardiovascular Disease Group, **Group2** and **Group3** as Non-Cardiovascular Disease Group. We name the subjects who are classified into cardiovascular patients as positive and those subjects who are classified into non-cardiovascular person as negative. If a subject who was labeled as cardiovascular patient is indeed so afflicted, this situation is referred to as a true positive (TP); a non-cardiovascular disease subject erroneously labeled as cardiovascular patient is referred to as a false positive (FP). We define negative outcomes that are true (TN) and false (FN) in an analogous manner [17-18]. We calculate some characters according to Formulas (3) - (5).

$$specificit\ y = \frac{TN}{TN + FP}, \qquad (3)$$

$$sensitivity = \frac{TP}{TP + FN}, \qquad (4)$$

$$accuracy = \frac{TN + TP}{ALL}. \qquad (5)$$

The results list as Table2. The specificity, sensitivity, accuracy of **Group1/Group2** is 85%, 93%, and 89% respectively. They are slightly less than that of **Group1/Group3**.

Table 1. Definitions on this discrimination between these Groups

	Non-ardiovascular Disease	Cardiovascular Disease
"Non-Cardiovascular Disease"	TN	FN
"Cardiovascular Disease"	FP	TP

Table 2. The discrimination results of three Groups

	Specificity	Sensitivity	Accuracy
Group1/ Group2	85%	93%	89%
Group1/ Group3	90%	93%	92%

As the 12 dimensional features cannot be illustrated, of the 12 features, we demonstrate only two dimensional features: *mean(ApEn)* and *SER(1)* in Figs. 8, 9 and 10. Fig. 8 is SVM classifier's result to classify **Group1** and **Group2**. Fig. 9 is the linear kernel SVM classifier's result to classify **Group1** and **Group3**. We can find that during the two features, **Group1** can be discriminated from **Group2** and **Group3** with high accuracy. Fig. 10 is SVM classifier's result to classify **Group2** and **Group3**. In Fig. 10, **Group2** and **Group3** cannot be differentiated with each other: all the vectors are support vectors. These results demonstrate that the variability of pulse waveform morphology has a powerful ability in discriminating the cardiovascular disease patients from the non-cardiovascular controls.

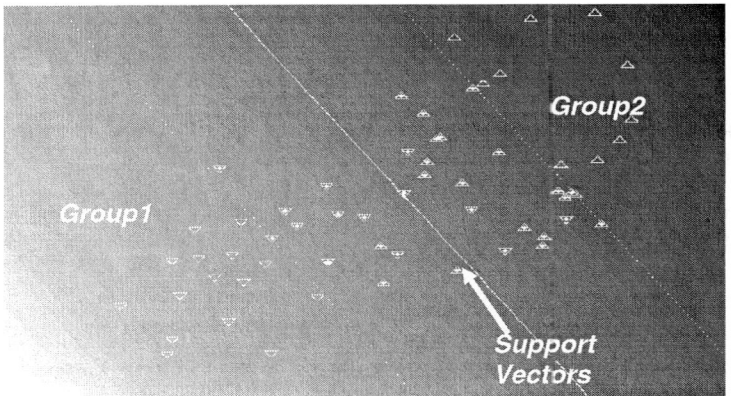

Fig. 8. The classification of **Group1/Group2** by SVM classifier

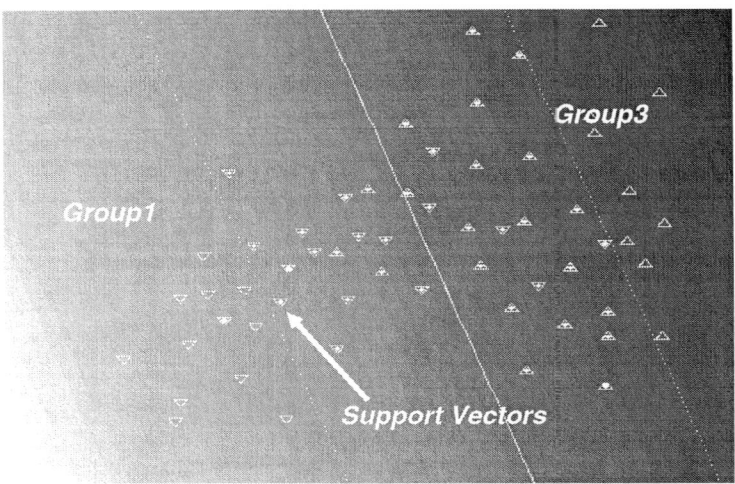

Fig. 9. The classification of **Group1/Group3** by SVM classifier

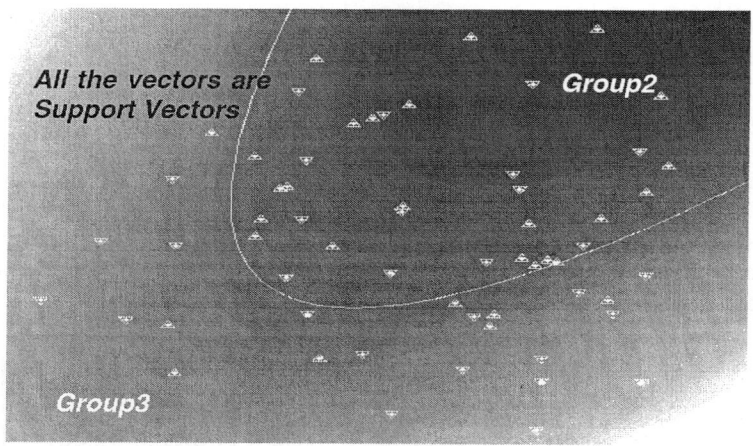

Fig. 10. The classification of **Group2/Group3** by SVM classifier (Polynomial Kernel at the degree of two)

4 Conclusions

This paper studies the variability of long-term pulse waveform and analyzes its clinical value for cardiovascular systems. Analysis of the dynamic behavior of pulse signal has opened up a new approach towards the assessment of normal and pathological cardiovascular behavior.

This paper also presents PMV's spectral energy ratio for differentiating person's cardiovascular condition. The results conform that the PMV can be used to differentiate the subjects in different cardiovascular condition. Using SVM to construct classifiers the accuracy of **Group1** to **Group2** is 89% and the accuracy of **Group1** to **Group3** is 92%. For the purpose of probing the mechanism of manifestations of the pulse, further work needs to be performed to quantitatively analyze cardiovascular system's behavior.

Acknowledgements

This study is supported by National Natural Science Foundation of China under Grant No.90209020. We thank all of the volunteers for providing us with the invaluable pulse data.

References

1. T.C. Joseph, Guide to ECG analysis, Lippincott Williams & Wilkins Press, (2002)
2. Y.Z. Feng, Chinese Journal of Biomedical Engineering, (1983)1(1)
3. W.A. Lu, Y.Y.Lin Wang, and W.K. Wang, "Pulse analysis of patients with sever liver problems," IEEE Engineering in Medicine and Biology, Jan/Feb, (1999) 73-75

4. Rourke, et al. "Pulse wave analysis", Br J Clin Pharmacol, Vol 51, (2001) 507-522
5. M. Aritomo, Y. Yonezawa, "A wrist-mounted activity and pulse recording system," Proceedings of the First Joint BMES/EMBS Conference Serving Humanity, Advancing Technology, (1999) 693
6. K.Q. Wang, L.S. Xu and D. Zhang, "TCPD based pulse monitoring and analyzing," ICMLC2002, Nov.3-7, Beijing, (2002)
7. L.S. Xu, K.Q. Wang and D. Zhang, "Modern researches on pulse waveform of TCPD," 2002 International Conference on Communications Circuits and Systems and West Sino Expositions Proceedings, Chengdu, China, (2002) 1073-1078
8. Yoshio Maniwa, Tadashi Iokibe, Masaya Koyama, Motoki Yamamoto, Shoichi Ohta, "The Application of Pulse Wave Chaos in Clinical Medicine", 17 Fuzzy System Symposium, Chiba, Sept. 5-7, (2001)
9. J.E. Naschitz, R. Itzhak, N. Shaviv and et al, "Assessment of cardiovascular reactivity by fractal and recurrence quantification analysis of heart rate and pulse transit time," J Hum Hypertension, Vol. 17, N. 2,(2 003)111-118
10. S. Pincus, "Approximate entropy (ApEn) as a complexity measure," Chaos 5, (1995) 110-117
11. K.Q. Wang, L.S. Xu and D. Zhang, "Approximate entropy based pulse variability analysis," Proceedings of the IEEE Symposium on Computer-Based Medical Systems, (2003) 236-241
12. Cristianini, N., Shawe-Taylor, J., An Introduction to Support Vector Machines, Cambridge University Press (2000)
13. S. Gunn. "Support vector machines for classification and regression", ISIS technical report, Image Speech & Intelligent Systems Group, University of Southampton (1997)
14. BE Boser, IM Guyon, and VN Vapnik. "A training algorithm for optimal margin classifiers", Proceedings of the 5th Annual ACM Workshop on Computational Learning Theory, ACM Press, (1992) 144–152
15. M. Z. Rahman, SML Kabir and J. Kamruzzaman, "Design and implementation of an SVM-based computer classification system for discriminating depressive patients from healthy controls using the P600 component of ERP signal", Comput Methods Programs Biomed, Jul; 75(1): (2004) 11-22
16. L.S. Xu, K.Q. Wang, D. Zhang, "Adaptive baseline wander removal in the pulse waveform", IEEE Proceeding of CBMS2002 International Conference, June, (2002) 143-148
17. M. Akay, Nonlinear Biomedical Signal Processing, New York, IEEE Press (2000)
18. X.H. Zhou, A.O. Nancy, and K.M. Donna, Statistical Methods in Diagnostic Medicine, Wiley-Interscience publication (2002)

Adaptive Enhancing of Fingerprint Image with Image Characteristics Analysis*

Eun-Kyung Yun, Jin-Hyuk Hong, and Sung-Bae Cho

Dept. of Computer Science, Yonsei University,
Biometrics Engineering Research Center,
134 Shinchon-dong, Sudaemoon-ku, Seoul 120-749, Korea
{ekfree, hjinh}@sclab.yonsei.ac.kr, sbcho@cs.yonsei.ac.kr

Abstract. The quality of the fingerprint images greatly affects the performance of the minutiae extraction. In order to improve the performance of the system, many researchers have been made efforts on the image enhancement algorithms. If the adaptive preprocessing according to the fingerprint image characteristics is applied in the image enhancement step, the system performance would be more robust. In this paper, we propose an adaptive preprocessing method, which extracts five features from the fingerprint images, analyzes image quality with Ward's clustering algorithm, and enhances the images according to their characteristics. Experimental results indicate that the proposed method improves both the quality index and block directional difference significantly in a reasonable time.

1 Introduction

Fingerprint identification is one of the most popular biometric technologies which is used in criminal investigations, commercial applications and so on. The performance of a fingerprint image matching algorithm depends heavily on the quality of the input fingerprint images [1]. Acquisition of good quality images is very important, but due to some environmental factors or user's body condition, a significant percentage of acquired images is of poor quality in practice [2]. From the poor quality images many spurious minutiae may be created and many genuine minutiae may be ignored. Therefore an image enhancement algorithm is necessary to increase the performance of the minutiae extraction algorithm.

Many researchers have been making efforts in the investigation of fingerprint image quality. Hong *et al.*, Ratha *et al.*, Shen *et al.*, and many researchers worked on this area with sine wave, wavelet scalar quantization, and Gabor filter. However, most of the quality checks have been used as a criterion, which determines image rejection, or a performance measurement of image enhancement algorithm. In this case, only

---

* This work was supported by the Korea Science and Engineering Foundation (KOSEF) through the Biometrics Engineering Research Center(BERC) at Yonsei University.

images are filtered uniformly without respect to the character of images. If the adaptive filtering is performed through appropriate analysis of image quality, images can be enhanced more effectively.

This paper proposes an adaptive preprocessing method to improve image quality appropriately. The preprocessing is performed after distinguishing the fingerprint image quality according to its characteristics. It is an adaptive filtering according to oily/dry/neutral images instead of uniform filtering. In the first stage, several features are extracted for image quality analysis and they go into the clustering module. Then, the adaptive preprocessing is applied to produce good quality images on two dataset: NIST DB 4 and private DB from Inha University.

2 Fingerprint Image Quality

In general, the fingerprint image quality relies on the clearness of separated ridges by valleys and the uniformity of the separation. Although the change in environmental conditions such as temperature and pressure might influence a fingerprint image in many ways, the humidity and condition of the skin dominate the overall quality of the fingerprint [2]. Dry skin tends to cause inconsistent contact of the finger ridges with the scanner's platen surface, causing broken ridges and many white pixels replacing ridge structure (see Fig. 1 (c)). To the contrary the valleys on the oily skin tend to fill up with moisture, causing them to appear black in the image similar to ridge structure (See Fig. 1 (a)). Fig. 1 shows the examples of the oily, neutral and dry images, respectively.

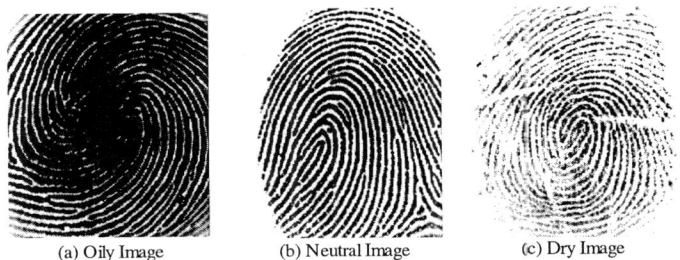

(a) Oily Image   (b) Neutral Image   (c) Dry Image

Fig. 1. Examples of fingerprint images

- Oily Image: Even though the separation of ridges and valleys is clear, some parts of valleys are filled up causing them to appear dark or adjacent ridges stand close to each other in many regions. Ridges tend to be very thick.
- Neutral Image: In general, it has no special properties such as oily and dry. It does not have to be filtered.
- Dry Image: The ridges are scratchy locally and there are many white pixels in the ridges.

In this paper, the preprocessing is applied differently to the three types of image characteristics (oily/dry/neutral): For the oily images, valleys are enhanced by dilating thin and disconnected ones (valley enhancement process). For the dry images, ridges are enhanced by extracting their center lines and removing white pixels (ridge enhancement process) [3]. Most of the fingerprint identification systems preprocess images without considering their characteristics. If the preprocessing suitable for their characteristics is performed, much better images can be obtained.

3 Adaptive Image Enhancement

Fig. 2 shows the overview of the proposed system in this paper. For fingerprint image quality analysis, it extracts several features in fingerprint images using orientation fields, at first. Clustering algorithm groups fingerprint images with the features, and the images in each cluster are analyzed and preprocessed adaptively.

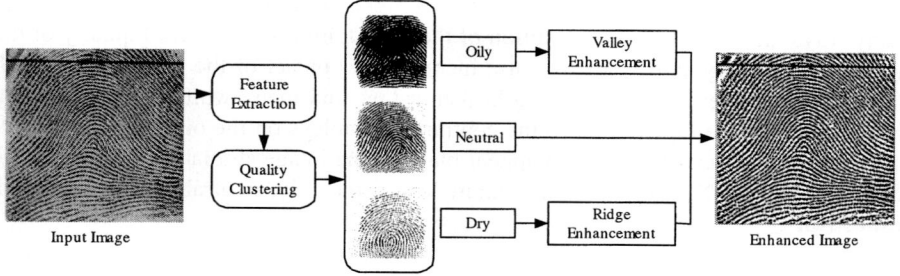

Fig. 2. Overview of the proposed system

3.1 Feature Extraction

In this paper, five features are used to measure the image quality. The mean and variance of a gray-level fingerprint image are defined as follows.

$$Mean = \frac{1}{NM} \sum_{i=0}^{N-1} \sum_{j=0}^{M-1} I(i,j)$$

$$Variance = \frac{1}{NM} \sum_{i=0}^{N-1} \sum_{j=0}^{M-1} (I(i,j) - Mean)^2$$

The mean of gray values indicates the overall gray level of the image and the variance shows the uniformity of the gray values. $I(i, j)$ represents the intensity of the pixel at the ith row and jth column and the image I is defined as an $N \times M$ matrix.

Fingerprint image can be divided into a number of non-overlapping blocks and block directional difference is computed [10]. Using the mask in Fig. 3, slit sum S_i, i = 1, ..., 8 is produced for center pixel C of the block.

P₅₁		P₄₁		P₃₁		P₂₁		P₁₁
P₆₁		P₅₂	P₄₂	P₃₂	P₂₂	P₁₂		P₈₄
		P₆₂				P₈₃		
P₇₁		P₇₂		C		P₇₃		P₇₄
		P₈₂				P₆₃		
P₈₁		P₁₃	P₂₃	P₃₃	P₄₃	P₅₃		P₆₄
P₁₄		P₂₄		P₃₄		P₄₄		P₅₄

Fig. 3. 9×9 Mask [10]

$$S_i = \sum_{i=1}^{8} P_{ij}$$

Block directional difference = $Sum(|S_{max} - S_{min}|)$

where $S_{max} = Max\{S_i, i = 1, ..., 8\}$ and $S_{min} = Min\{S_i, i = 1, ..., 8\}$.

P_{ij} denotes the gray-level value of the jth pixel in the direction i. S_{max} and S_{min} appear in each valley (white) pixel and in each ridge (black) pixel, respectively. Therefore, the directional difference of image block has a large value for good quality image blocks. In other words, ridge structures are characterized as well-separated. For bad quality image blocks, the directional difference of image block has a small value. Namely, ridge and valley are not distinguished in each other.

The ratio for ridge thickness to valley thickness is computed in each block [4]. Ridge thickness and valley thickness are obtained using gray level values for one image block in the direction normal to ridge flow. After that, the ratio of each block is computed and average value of the ratio is obtained over the whole image.

Orientation change is obtained by accumulating block orientation along each horizontal row and each vertical column of the image block. Orientation computation is as follows [5].

1) Divide I into blocks of size $w \times w$.
2) Compute the gradients $\partial_x(i, j)$ and $\partial_y(i, j)$ at each pixel (i, j) with the Sobel operator.
3) Estimate the local orientation of each block centered at pixel (i, j) using the following equations [6]:

$$V_x(i, j) = \sum_{u=i-\frac{w}{2}}^{i+\frac{w}{2}} \sum_{v=j-\frac{w}{2}}^{j+\frac{w}{2}} 2\partial_x(u,v)\partial_y(u,v)$$

$$V_y(i, j) = \sum_{u=i-\frac{w}{2}}^{i+\frac{w}{2}} \sum_{v=j-\frac{w}{2}}^{j+\frac{w}{2}} (\partial_x^2(u,v)\partial_y^2(u,v))$$

$$\theta(i, j) = \frac{1}{2} \tan^{-1}\left(\frac{V_y(i, j)}{V_x(i, j)}\right)$$

where $\theta(i, j)$ is the least square estimate of the local ridge orientation at the block centered at pixel (i, j). It represents the direction that is orthogonal to the direction of the Fourier spectrum of the $w \times w$ window. In this paper, we set $w=16$ and feature values are normalized between 0 and 1.

3.2 Image Quality Clustering

As mentioned before, fingerprint image quality is divided into 3 classes, dry/neutral /oily. In this paper, we cluster images according to their characteristics using 5 features defined before. Fingerprint images are clustered by Ward's clustering algorithm which is one of the hierarchical clustering methods [7].

In this paper, image quality clustering tests on NIST DB 4 using five features described before. A total 2000 (a half of NIST DB) 5-dimensional patterns are used as input vectors of clustering algorithm. To determine the proper number of clusters, Mojena's cut-off value is used [8].

$$Mojena's\ Value = h + \alpha s_h$$

where h is the average of dendrogram heights for all N-1 clusters and s_h is the unbiased standard deviation of the heights. α is a specified constant and according to Milligan and Cooper [9], the best overall performance of Mojena's rule occurs when the values of α is 1.25. For that reason, we set $\alpha = 1.25$ as the number of clusters.

3.3 Adaptive Preprocessing

Smoothing is one of the conventional filtering methods [10]. It can remove the white pixels of ridges in case of dry images; however, it also removes necessary ridges that are thinner than neighbor ridges. Similarly, in case of oily images, it removes necessary valleys that are very thin while it removes black noises of valleys. Therefore, adaptive filtering with classifying image characteristics is better than uniform filtering. Fig. 4 shows a preprocessing method appropriate to image quality characteristics [3]. That is, ridges are enhanced in dry images and valleys are enhanced in oily images.

1) Ridge enhancement of dry images: This extracts center lines of ridges and removes white pixels in ridges using this center-lined image. It also maintains the structure of the fingerprint.
    A. Smoothing: smoothing is applied to the original image to reduce noises.
    B. Thinning: a thinned image is obtained for extraction of ridge structures.
    C. Dilation: a thinned image is dilated.
    D. Extracting the union of black pixels in an original image and the image in C: white pixels in the ridges are removed. In this way, the ridge-enhanced image is obtained.
2) Valley enhancement of oily images: It is more complicated than ridge enhancement. It needs to detect regions where valleys are thin and disconnected. For this, thinning function extracts only the ridges thinner than a threshold. It means that the ridges wider than a threshold are eliminated.

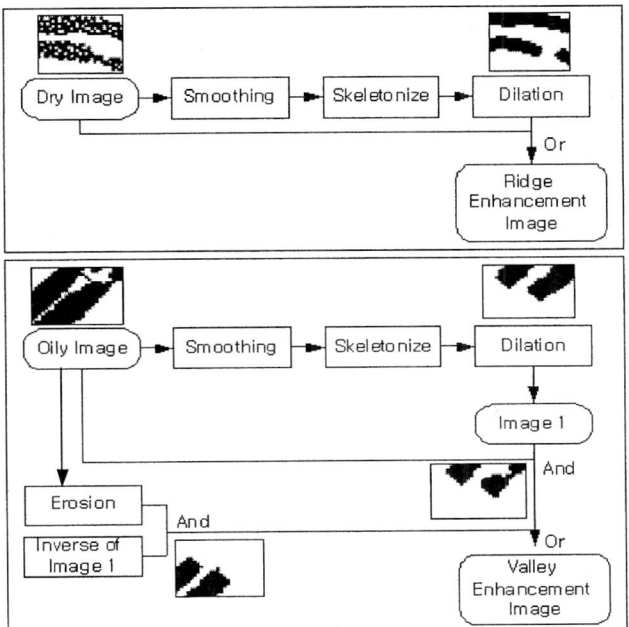

Fig. 4. Preprocessing appropriate to image characteristics

- A. Smoothing: it eliminates thin and disconnected valleys.
- B. Thinning: thinned image using the threshold is obtained for extraction of ridge structures.
- C. Dilation: dilated image is obtained and it contains the regions where ridges are sufficiently separated as black and the regions where ridges touch one another as white.
- D. Composition of black pixels in the original image and in the image obtained in C: it detects the ridges whose thickness is wider than a threshold.
- E. Composition of black pixels in the erosion of an original image and an inverse image of an image in C
- F. Extracting the union of black pixels of the images in D and E: in this way, the valley-enhanced image is obtained.

4 Experiments

The proposed method is verified with the NIST DB 4 (DB1) [11] and the highly controlled fingerprint DB at Inha University (DB2) [12]. DB1 consists of 4,000 fingerprint images (image size is 512×480) from 2,000 fingers. Each finger has two impressions. In DB2, the size of images is 248×292. Both of DB1 and DB2 are gray-level images. DB2 is used to check whether minutiae are extracted correctly or not.

We use the first 2,000 fingerprint images in DB1 for clustering and the remaining 2,000 images for adaptive filtering using the rules obtained from the clustering results. Fingerprint image characteristics are analyzed using the Ward's clustering results. 30 clusters in a high rank appear in the dendrogram and according to Mojena's rule the proper number of clusters is 5. Cluster 4 is assigned as dry, cluster 5 is oily and the remaining three clusters are neutral.

As a result, clustering made total 23 rules and Fig. 5 shows the essential rules. It indicates that in oily images ridges tend to be thicker than valleys and in dry images the ratio of ridge-valley thickness and mean are different from other clusters. In addition, the important factor of each feature is obtained by using the feature frequency in the rules. As shown in Table 1, the ridge-valley thickness ratio is the most important feature.

The image quality is measured in 2 different ways for quantitative analysis. First, block directional difference is used for quality check [11]. When the image quality is checked manually, we determine the image quality using the clearly separated ridges by valleys [4]. Hence, the block directional difference has a large value for good quality images. As shown in Fig. 6, the adaptive preprocessing is better than the uniform conventional filtering. The average values of the block directional difference with the adaptive enhancement are larger than those with the conventional filtering.

```
IF ((B < 0.041) and (R >= 2.17))
    THEN Oily Cluster
ELSE IF ((V <0.24) and (2.14 <= R < 2.17) and (B < 0.29))
    THEN Oily Cluster
ELSE IF ((V < 0.39) and (O >= 0.21) and (B < 0.33) and (R < 1.73))
    THEN Dry Cluster
ELSE IF ((M >= 0.54) and (B < 0.12) and (V >= 0.39) and (O >= 0.21) and (R < 1.73))
    THEN Dry Cluster
ELSE Neutral Cluster
```

Fig. 5. Rules obtained by clustering

Table 1. Important factor of each feature

Feature	Important factor
Mean (M)	0.67
Variance (V)	0.20
Block directional difference (B)	0.37
Orientation change (O)	0.36
Ridge-valley thickness ratio (R)	1.00

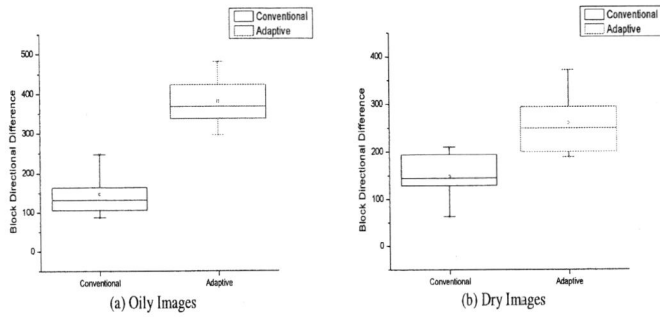

Fig. 6. Enhancement results with block directional difference

Second, the quality is measured with extracted minutiae. Image quality is assessed by comparing the minutiae set identified by human expert with that detected by minutiae extraction algorithm in an input fingerprint image. The larger the value of quality index, the better the minutiae extraction algorithm. Quality index is defined as follows:

$$quality\ index = \frac{c}{c+f+u}$$

where c is the number of correctly detected minutiae, f is the number of falsely detected minutiae, and u is the number of undetected minutiae.

We use the 50 typical poor fingerprint images from DB2 to measure the filtering performance using extracted minutiae. First, we compute the Quality Index of the extracted minutiae with the conventional filtering and then the Quality Index of the extracted minutiae is computed with the adaptive filtering. Table 2 shows the Quality Index values of 50 typical images and the mean and variance of Quality Index values for all images. The Quality Index values with the adaptive enhancement are larger than those with the conventional filtering. Thus, it means that the adaptive preprocessing method improves the quality of the fingerprint images, which improves the accuracy of the extracted minutiae. To determine if there is a reliable difference between two means, we conduct a paired t-test. The calculated t-value (5.49) and p-value (<0.0001) indicate that the difference between the two means is statistically very significant. That is, the quality difference between the conventional filtered images and adaptive filtered images is very significant in 99% confidence level.

On the other hand, Fig. 7 shows some examples of enhanced images through the adaptive preprocessing. As shown in the figure, adaptively filtered images have better quality than conventionally filtered images.

Fig. 8 and 9 show some examples of enhanced images through the adaptive preprocessing. Fig. 8 shows the minutiae extracted in dry images with conventional filtering and adaptive filtering: (a) and (c) are with conventional filtering, (b) and (d) are with ridge enhancement filtering. While (a) and (c) have some falsely detected

Table 2. The quality index values of fingerprint images: 50 typical images and the mean and variance

Image #	Conventional Filtering	Adaptive Filtering	Image #	Conventional Filtering	Adaptive Filtering
1	0.16	0.37	27	0.11	0.18
2	0.25	0.27	28	0.08	0.14
3	0.0	0.25	29	0.03	0.06
4	0.0	0.18	30	0.24	0.32
5	0.07	0.1	31	0.07	0.13
6	0.0	0.0	32	0.0	0.22
7	0.0	0.24	33	*0.34*	*0.32*
8	0.0	0.06	34	0.35	0.4
9	0.12	0.14	35	0.06	0.22
10	0.07	0.1	36	0.27	0.37
11	0.17	0.2	37	0.38	0.42
12	*0.09*	*0.07*	38	0.31	0.41
13	0.15	0.22	39	*0.33*	*0.22*
14	*0.16*	*0.14*	40	0.33	0.56
15	0.23	0.4	41	0.27	0.41
16	*0.21*	*0.2*	42	0.22	0.31
17	0.22	*0.16*	43	0.22	0.45
18	0.05	0.1	44	0.16	0.18
19	0.12	0.19	45	0.11	0.18
20	0.06	0.07	46	0.32	0.41
21	*0.22*	*0.1*	47	0.02	0.11
22	0.06	0.2	48	0.08	0.32
23	0.02	0.05	49	0.11	0.12
24	0.08	0.08	50	0.3	0.5
25	*0.28*	*0.25*	Mean	0.1512	0.2226
26	*0.06*	*0.03*	Variance	0.0130	0.0183

minutiae, endings, (b) and (d) have the correctly detected minutiae, bifurcations. Fig. 9 shows the minutiae extracted in oily images. While (a) and (c) with conventional filtering have falsely detected minutiae, bifurcations, or ridges connected, (b) and (d) with valley enhancement have correctly detected minutiae.

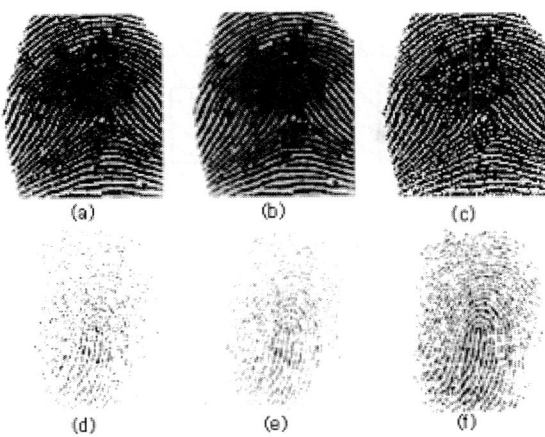

Fig. 7. Examples of enhancement results. (a) and (d) are original oily and dry images, respectively. (b) and (e) are results of general filtering and (c) and (f) are results of adaptive filtering for (a) and (d), respectively

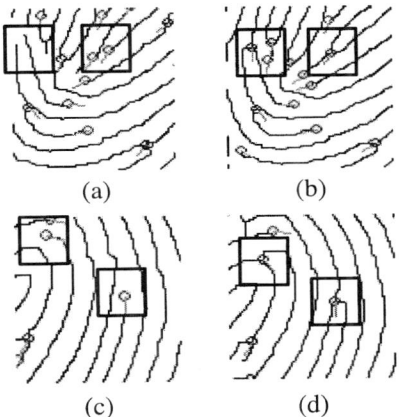

Fig. 8. Dry image examples of minutiae extraction with conventional/adaptive filtering: (a) and (c) show the extracted minutiae with the conventional filtering, (b) and (d) show the extracted minutiae with ridge enhancement

In order to incorporate the proposed preprocessing method into an online system, the whole process should be finished within a few seconds. Table 3 shows the time for each feature extraction and preprocessing.

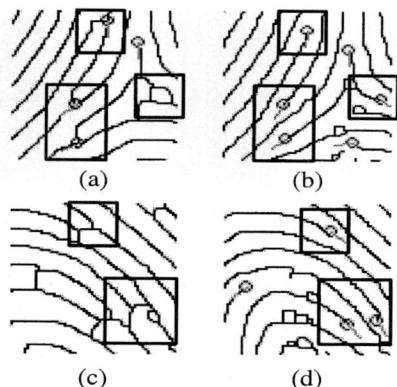

Fig. 9. Oily image examples of minutiae extraction with conventional/adaptive filtering: (a) and (c) show the extracted minutiae with the conventional filtering, (b) and (d) show the extracted minutiae with valley enhancement

Table 3. The time for the adaptive preprocessing (seconds) on Pentium 2GHz PC

M & V	B	O	R	Preprocessing	Total
0.001	0.141	0.063	0.047	0.301	0.553

5 Concluding Remarks

The performance of fingerprint identification system relies critically on the image quality. Hence, good quality image make the system performance more robust. However, it is very difficult to obtain good quality images in practical use. To overcome this problem, image enhancement step is required. But, most of the enhancement algorithms are applied equally to images without considering the image characteristics. Even though quality check is performed, it is not for quality analysis but for the performance evaluation of image enhancement algorithms or for checking whether an image is improved or not.

This paper has proposed an adaptive image enhancement method for fingerprint identification system. It is performed through the clustering of image quality characteristics. The performance of the proposed method was evaluated using the block directional difference and the Quality Index of the extracted minutiae. Experimental results show that the proposed method is able to improve both block directional difference and quality index, and the time required is in a reasonable range. Further works are going on to develop image characteristic factors for the identification system in real worlds.

References

1. N. K. Ratha, K. Karu, S. Chen, and A. K. Jain, "A Real-Time Matching System for Large Fingerprint Databases," *IEEE Transaction on Pattern Analysis and Machine Intelligence*, 18 (8), pp. 799-813, 1996.
2. L. C. Jain, U. Halici, I. Hayashi, S. B. Lee, and S. Tsutsui, *Intelligent Biometric Techniques in Fingerprint and Face Recognition*, CRC Press, 1999.
3. N. Ikeda, M. Nakanishi, K. Fujii, T. Hatano, S. Shigematsu, T. Adachi, Y. Okazaki and H. Kyuragi, "Fingerprint Image Enhancement by Pixel-Parallel Processing," *16th International Conference on Pattern Recognition*, pp. 752-755, 2002.
4. E. Lim, X. Jiang and W. Yau, "Fingerprint Quality and Validity Analysis," *IEEE International Conference on Image Processing*, 1, pp. 22-25, 2002.
5. K. Karu, and A. Jain, "Fingerprint Classification," *Pattern Recognition*, 29 (3), pp. 389-404, 1996.
6. A. Rao, *A Taxonomy for Texture Description and Identification*, New York, NY: Springer-Verlag, 1990.
7. J. H. Ward, "Hierarchical Grouping to Optimize an Objective Function," *Journal of the American Statistical Association*, 58 (301), pp. 236-244, 1963.
8. R. Mojena, "Hierarchical Grouping Methods and Stopping Rules: An Evaluation," *Computer Journal*, 20, pp. 353-363, 1977.
9. G. W. Milligan and K. C. Cooper, "An Examination of Procedures for Determining the Number of Clusters in a Data Set," *Psychometrika* 50, pp. 159-179, 1985.
10. F. Galton, *Finger Prints*, Macmillan, London, 1892.
11. C. I. Watson and C. L. Wilson, *NIST Special Database 4, Fingerprint Database*. U. S. Nat'l Inst. of Standards and Technology, 1992.
12. H. Kang, B. Lee, H. Kim, D. Shin, and J. Kim, "A Study on Performance Evaluation of Fingerprint Sensors," *The 4th International Conference Audio- and Video-based Biometric Person Authentication*, pp. 574-583, 2003.

Adaptive Image Classification for Aerial Photo Image Retrieval

Sung Wook Baik [1] and Ran Baik [2]

[1] College of Electronics and Information Engineering, Sejong University,
Seoul 143-747, KOREA
`sbaik@sejong.ac.kr`
[2] Department of Computer Engineering, Honam University,
Gwangju 506-090, KOREA
`baik@honam.ac.kr`

Abstract. The paper presents a content based image retrieval approach with adaptive and intelligent image classification through on-line model modification. It supports geographical image retrieval over digitized historical aerial photographs in a digital library. Since the historical aerial photographs are gray-scaled and low-resolution images, image retrieval is achieved on the basis of texture feature extraction. Feature extraction methods for geographical image retrieval are Gabor spectral filtering, Laws' energy filtering, and Wavelet transformation, which are all the most widely used in image classification and segmentation. Adaptive image classification supports effective content based image retrieval through composite classifier models dealing with multi-modal feature distribution. The image retrieval methods presented in the paper are evaluated over a test bed of 184 aerial photographs. The experimental results also show the performance of different feature extraction methods for each image retrieval method.

1 Introduction

A digital archive of aerial photography is very useful to environmental scientists as well as business and governmental agencies for the purpose of environmental evaluation, land development planning, land use analysis, and so on. As an example, a collection of historical aerial image photographs can be used for chronologically tracking urban and rural development when it has been digitalized and archived for automatic access into a digital library. The content-based image retrieval in digital libraries helps to relieve the tedious work of manually finding the geographical region of interest. Content-based image retrieval requires the integration of image processing and information retrieval technologies. This is the retrieval of images on the basis of features automatically derived from the images themselves. Texture, color and shape are used the most widely in most researches to describe features in the image. However, the retrieval of the historical aerial image photographs is based only on texture features because they are gray-scaled and low-resolution images. Therefore, more robust feature extraction methods are required to allow effective retrieval results. The feature extraction is described in the next section.

In low resolution aerial images, we cannot apprehend the appearance of a certain objects in detail. Therefore, we need to use regions with a collection of tiny and complicated structures--such as man-made features including buildings, roads, parking lots, airports and bridges--in order to deal with them as texture motifs for image classification/segmentation. We can also regard the shapeless regions of natural resources such as forests, rivers and oceans as texture motifs.

This work presents a texture-based geographical image retrieval system with adaptive and intelligent image classification through on-line model modification. It provides geographical image retrieval over a test bed of 184 aerial photographs ranging from 350 to 650 Kbytes in size.

2 Texture Feature Extraction for Aerial Images Retrieval

Directionality, coarseness, and regularity of patterns appearing on an aerial image are represented by texture. To represent geographical features for aerial image retrieval, there are three popular texture feature extraction methods such as Gabor spectral filtering [1], Laws' energy filtering [2], and Wavelet Transformation [3], all of which have been widely used for various classification and image segmentation tasks.

Gabor filters are useful for dealing with the texture characterized by local frequency and orientation information. Gabor filters are obtained through a systematic mathematical approach. A Gabor function consists of a sinusoidal plane of particular frequency and orientation modulated by a two-dimensional Gaussian envelope. A two-dimensional Gabor filter is given by:

$$G(x, y) = \exp[-\frac{1}{2}(\frac{x}{\sigma_x^2} + \frac{y}{\sigma_y^2})]\cos(\frac{2\pi x}{n_0} + \alpha) \qquad (1)$$

By orienting the sinusoid at an angle α and changing the frequency n_0, many Gabor filtering sets can be obtained. An example of a set of eight Gabor filters is decided with different parameter values (n_0 = 2.82 and 5.66 pixels/cycle and orientations α = 0°, 45°, 90°, and 135°).

Table 1. Laws' Filter Weights and Specifications

Specification	Weight of filter
L5 (Level)	(1,4,6,4,1)
E5 (Edge)	(-1,-2,0,2,1)
S5 (Spot)	(-1,0,2,0,-1)
R5 (Ripple)	(1,-4,6,-4,1)
W5 (Wave)	(-1,2,0,-2,1)

Laws' convolution kernels based on five dimensional vectors are used as an energy filter bank. It consists of 25 filters (Table 1), which can be derived from their weights. Convolving and transposing each other produces various square masks of 25 filters. Each filter is 5x5 matrices and is designed as 5x5 windows. All Laws' masks are directional and illuminant tilt sensitive except L5L5.

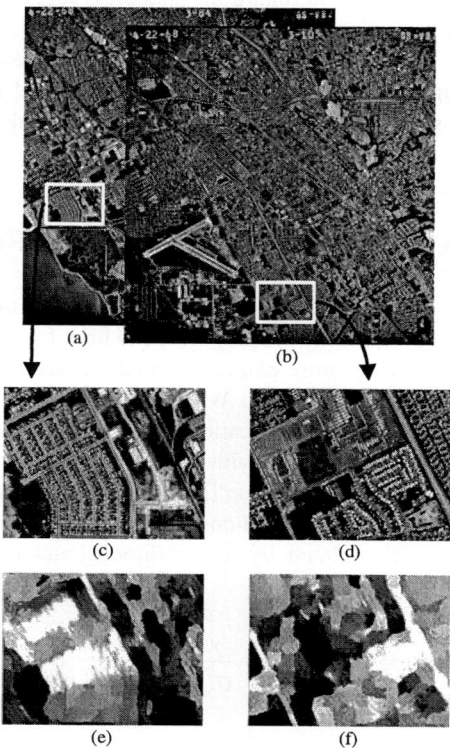

Fig. 1. a) A large aerial image including a query image. b) A large aerial image including a retrieved image. c) A query image. d) A retrieved image. e) Texture features of the query image in (c). f) Texture features of the retrieved image in (d)

A texture feature extraction algorithm based on the wavelet transform provides a non redundant signal representation with accurate reconstruction capability and forms a precise and uniform framework for signal analysis at different scales [4]. The pyramidal wavelet transform is used because of its non data redundancy and less complexity. Basically, in the pyramidal wavelet transform, the original image is decomposed into four sub-images, which are one approximation (LL) and three details (LH, HL, HH) frequency components at each level. The HH, LH, HL and LL subimages represents diagonal details (higher frequencies in both directions, corners), vertical higher frequencies (horizontal edges), horizontal higher frequencies (vertical edges) and lowest frequencies, respectively [5]. The decomposition procedures are performed repeatedly on an approximation component at each level, and hence 3n+1 numbers of sub-images are produced for 'n' level decompositions. Thus, many wavelet transform sub-images can be achieved from different levels, and the variance of each sub-image is used as a texture feature [6]. However, the most significant information appears in middle frequency regions for texture images [7], LH and HL sub-images are selected from each decomposition level to compute the channel variances of a feature image. Since there is no criterion to determine the decomposition level that yields the best discriminations, it is necessary to define the desired (optimal) level. In practice, deeper level decompositions could not contain significant information and will give unreliable data.

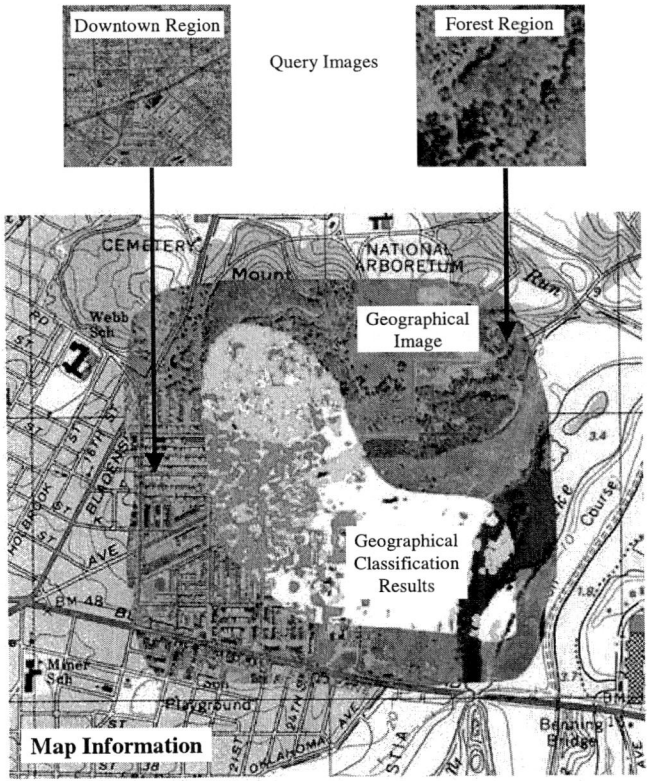

Fig.2. An example of feature classification by RBF models

3 Image Retrieval Using Adaptive Image Classification

This section describes how we adopted a Radial Basis Function based neural network classifier for image retrieval. Radial Basis Function classifiers have been used to model image feature distributions for a variety of research objectives such as image classification and segmentation. In previous researches, we can refer to some methods for modeling image feature data for image retrieval. One method [8] is to build a hybrid neural network for clustering texture patterns in the feature space. In its training phase, feature distributions are partitioned into several clusters through the Kohonen feature map. And then the captured clusters become associated with class labels using a winner-takes-all representation, and class boundaries are finally decided using a learning vector quantization scheme. Another method [9, 10] is to model texture feature data with the Gaussian mixture model, which consists of several Gaussian distribution components corresponding to texture clusters.

A modified Radial Basis Function classier (RBF) [11], with Gaussian distribution as a basis, was chosen for texture data modeling and classification. This is a well-known classifier widely used in pattern recognition and suited for engineering applications. Its well-defined mathematical model allows for further modifications and on-line manipulation with its structure and parameters. It can be easily implemented as a neural network [12]. The RBF classifier models a complex multi-modal data distribution through its decomposition into multiple independent Gaussians. The model can be dynamically adjusted by changing mode parameters over time. Data classification provides a class membership along with a confidence measure of that membership. Two types of model modification [13] are introduced for this work; 1) Self node modification that does not change/shift the node center and adjusts function spread through the feature space, 2) Node Generation that creates a new node due to the increase in the multi-modality of data distribution.

A RBF function F_r consists of a set of basis functions that form localized decision regions. Overlapping local regions formed by simple basis functions can create a complex distribution. For Gaussian distribution, as a basis function, each region is represented by its center and width corresponding to a mean vector and a covariance matrix (μ, Σ). For a multi-modal distribution of a class r, a RBF can be formed through the following linear combination of these basis functions;

$$F_r(X) \; w_0 + \sum_i w_i f_{ri}(X) \qquad (2)$$

where: w_i is the trainable weight vector (for $i = 0, \ldots, N_r$); r is the class membership number; N_r is the number of nodes (basis functions) in class r; and

$$f(X) = \exp[-1/2(X-\mu)^T \Sigma^{-1}(X-\mu)] \qquad (3)$$

Each group of nodes corresponds to a different class. The combination of nodes is weighted. Each node is a Gaussian function with a trainable mean vector and a co-variance matrix. Classification decision yields a class r of the highest $F_r(X)$ value for a sample vector X.

The image retrieval algorithm using adaptive image classification is summarized as follows:

1. Choose the best (primary) filter from a filter bank, which represents a salient feature (Fig. 1(e)) within the query image (Fig. 1(c)). We can obtain a segmented and homogeneous region with the salient feature represented by the filter if the salient feature partially dominates the query image.
2. Find similar images (Fig. 1(d)) to the query image with a threshold for similarity measurement if a dominant region (Fig. 1(f)) in each image is detected when the image is convolved by the primary filter of the query image. When the threshold is low, we can retrieve many candidate images. A collection of these candidate images is an intermediary retrieval result obtained by the primary filter.
3. Select some filters from the bank to complement the primary filter according to a feature reference table in order to analyze the query image in detail. These filters are called a secondary filter set, with which it is possible to represent a variety of features with regard to the segmented homogeneous region.
4. Collect the feature sample vectors from the segmented region according to the results obtained by the convolution with the secondary filter set.
5. Model feature sample vectors in the RBF classifier.
6. Match the candidate images in the intermediary result with the RBF classifier models. Fig. 2 shows an example of feature classification by RBF models. A collection of the matched images is the result obtained by the simple RBF classification method.
7. Modify the RBF classifier to retrieve more images through model modification. Model modification is achieved through the combination of the current models and the feature distributions of the images matched in step 6.
8. Match the candidate images in the intermediary result with the RBF classifier models once again. A collection of the matched images is the result obtained by composite RBF models.

4 Experiments

Experimental data are provided by the UC Berkeley Library Web [14]. They are 184 aerial photographs of the San Francisco Bay area, California, flown in April, 1968 by the U.S. Geological Survey. The scale of the originals is 1:30,000. Each photograph image has the size of approximately 1300 X 1500 pixels with 256 grey-level (the size and resolution of each image are little different from each other). It is cut into about 195 (13 X 15) overlapped sub-images (texture tiles) of size 200 X 200. A test bed for image retrieval has about 35,880 (184 X 195) texture tiles. For evaluation purposes, 30 types of visually similar patterns are provided by human observers. From 10 to 50 texture tiles are also selected for each pattern according to human visual experiences and indexed for retrieval performance evaluation, during which the rest of the images not selected are also used together with the indexed images.

We evaluate the performance of our image retrieval method with different feature extraction methods: 1) Gabor filter bank, 2) Law's energy filter bank, and 3) Wavelet transform filter bank. The Gabor and Law's banks consist of 48 Gabor filters (12 orientations and 4 scales in the frequency domain) and 25 filters, respectively. The Wavelet bank has 24 wavelet filters generated by using three Daubechies wavelets (db1, db2, db3) and five biorthogonal wavelets (bior1.3, bior2.4, bior3.7, bior4.4, bior5.5) at one, two and three scale decomposition.

Table 2 summarizes the performance of the aerial image retrieval methods according to several experimental results.

Table 2. The performance of the aerial image retrieval methods

	Gabor		Law		Wavelet	
	Recall	Precision	Recall	Precision	Recall	Precision
Primary Filter	75%	23.5%	71.4%	20%	69.2%	21%
Simple RBF Model	68%	55.5%	63%	52%	61.6%	53.7%
Composite RBF Model	81.5%	54.5%	78.3%	51.6%	76.2%	51.3%

5 Conclusion

This paper proposed a texture-based geographical image retrieval system with adaptive and intelligent image classification through on-line model modification. Through extensive performance comparisons under several experiments with different feature extraction methods and different retrieval methods, we show that the adaptive image classification improved the average recall-precision rates on aerial images over the simple image retrieval approach. We also show that the Gabor bank outperforms the other banks (Law's and Wavelet banks).

Acknowledgement. This work was supported by a Korea Research Foundation Grant (KRF-2003-003-D00407).

References

1. L. Chen, G. Lu and D. Zhang, Effects of Different Gabor Filter Parameters on Image Retrieval by Texture, Proceedings of the 10th International Multimedia Modeling Conference, pp. 273-278, 2004.
2. A. Gasteratos, P. Zafeiridis, I. Andreadis, An Intelligent System for Aerial Image Retrieval and Classification, LNCS, Vol. 3025, pp. 63-71, 2004.
3. B. Zhang, C. I. Tomai and A. Zhang, An Adaptive Texture Image Retrieval System Using Wavelets, Proceeding of the ICARCV International Conference, Vol. 3, pp. 1210-1215, 2002.
4. M. Unser, Texture classification and segmentation using wavelet frames, IEEE Transactions on Image Processing, Vol. 4, Issue. 11, pp. 1549-1560, 1995.

5. S. Mallat, Multifrequency channel decompositions of images and wavelet models, IEEE Transactions on Acoustics, Speech and Signal Processing, Vol. 37, Issue. 12, pp. 2091-2110, 1989.
6. C. Chen, Filtering methods for texture discrimination, Pattern Recognition Letters, Vol. 20, pp. 783-790, 1999.
7. T. Chang and C. Kuo, A wavelet transform approach to texture analysis, Proceedings of IEEE International Conference on Acoustics, Speech, and Signal Processing, Vol. 4, pp. 661-664, 1992.
8. B. Zhu, M. Ransey and H. Chen, Creating a Large-Scale Content-Based Airphoto Image Digital Library, IEEE Transactions on Image Processing, Vol. 9, Issue. 1, pp. 163-167, 2000.
9. S. Bhagavathy, S. Newsam and B. S. Manjunath, Modeling Object Classes in Aerial Image Using Texture Motifs, Proceedings of Pattern Recognition 16th International Conference, Vol. 2, pp. 981-984, 2002.
10. C. Carson, M. Thomas, S. Belongie, J. M. Jellerstein, and J. Malik, Blobworld: a System for Region-based Image Indexing and Retrieval, Proceedings of the third International Conference on Visual Information Systems, pp. 509-516, 1999.
11. S. Theodoridis, and K. Koutroumbas, Pattern Recognition, Academic Press, 1999.
12. S. Haykin, Neural Networks, Prentice Hall, 2nd edition, 1999.
13. S. W. Baik and P. Pachowicz, On-Line Model Modification Methodology for Adaptive Texture Recognition, IEEE Transactions on Systems, Man, and Cybernetics, Vol. 32, Issue. 7, 2002.
14. http://sunsite.berkeley.edu/AerialPhotos/vbzj.html#index

An Investigation into Applying Support Vector Machines to Pixel Classification in Image Processing

Douglas Clarke, David Albrecht, and Peter Tischer

Monash University,
School of Computer Science and Software Engineering
{dougc, dwa, pet}@csse.monash.edu.au

Abstract. Support Vector Machines (SVMs) have been used successfully for many classification tasks. In this paper, we investigate applying SVMs to classification in the context of image processing. We chose to look at classifying whether pixels have been corrupted by impulsive noise, as this is one of the simpler classification tasks in image processing. We found that the straightforward application of SVMs to this problem led to a number of difficulties, such as long training times, performance that was sensitive to the balance of classes in the training data, and poor classification performance overall. We suggest remedies for some of these problems, including the use of image filters to suppress variation in the training data. This led us to develop a two-stage classification process which used SVMs in the second stage. This two-stage process was able to achieve substantially better results than those resulting from the straightforward application of SVMs.

1 Introduction

In this paper we investigate the application of Support Vector Machines (SVMs) to the image processing domain, in particular the application of SVMs to the classification of features within images. We consider a common problem of image processing, the removal of impulsive noise corruption from images, and develop Support Vector Machine classifiers to detect pixels in an image that are corrupted by impulsive noise.

Impulsive noise is a form of corruption in which the values of a random number of pixels in an image are lost and are replaced by values which are both random and independent of the pixels that are replaced. Impulsive noise corruption can be modelled by salt-and-pepper noise, in which corrupt pixels take on a value at the minimum or maximum pixel intensity (corresponding to a value of either 0 or 255 for 8-bit images) or by a more general model in which corrupt pixels take on a random value distributed uniformly over the range of possible pixel values. This paper deals with noise coming from the second model.

It is desirable to remove impulsive noise corruption from images, both to improve the visual appearance of the image, and to remove corrupt pixel values from further image processing. Many noise filters have been proposed to remove noise corruption from images by replacing pixels corrupted by impulsive noise with an estimate of the pixels' original values in an attempt to reconstruct the original noise-free image. We decompose the problem of removing impulsive noise into two tasks: identifying the noisy pixels in an image, and determining a suitable value with which to replace each noisy pixel.

In this paper, we concentrate on the detection of pixels corrupted by impulsive noise. We treat the detection of noise as a classification problem, and develop Support Vector Machines for categorising the pixels of an image into two groups: pixels corrupted by noise and pixels that represent image structure. A Support Vector Machine classifier is trained on a set of pixels labelled as either "noise" or "uncorrupt" and, following training, its performance is evaluated on a set of unlabelled pixels.

Pixels corrupted by impulsive noise are random-valued and carry no information about the value of the original pixel, and so pixels identified as noise by the SVM can be reconstructed only through interpolation using their non-corrupt neighbours. For some tasks, such as statistical analysis of an image, it is sufficient to identify the corrupt pixels of an image so that they can be omitted from further processing, since pixel replacement through interpolation adds no additional information for analysis.

This paper begins with a brief introduction to Support Vector Machine classifiers. The proposed noise detector is presented in terms of the problems that had to be overcome in the development of an SVM-based approach. In section 2.1 we describe the generation of the training dataset. Next in section 2.2 we improve the distinction between noisy and uncorrupt pixels. In section 2.3 we suppress variation within the class of uncorrupt pixels to improve the accuracy of pixel classification. Finally, in section 2.4 we present a composite approach based on median filtering and a Support Vector Machine, in which a median filter identifies impulsive noise in an image and an SVM corrects misclassifications to prevent image structure from being incorrectly classified as noise.

1.1 Support Vector Machine Classifiers

Support Vector Machines are a machine learning tool for performing such tasks as supervised classification, regression and novelty detection. They have been applied to a wide range of real-world problems including text categorisation, human face detection in images, hand-written character recognition, image retrieval, and the detection of microcalcifications in mammograms [6, 2, 10, 5].

SVM classifiers learn a particular classification function from a set of labelled training examples. The training set consists of n training examples, with each example described by a d-dimensional vector, $\boldsymbol{x} \in \mathbf{R}^d$, labelled as belonging to one of two categories, $y \in \{-1, 1\}$ referred to as the "positive class" and the "negative class". Following training, the result is an SVM that is able to classify previously unseen and unlabelled instances, $\boldsymbol{x}$, into a category based on examples learnt from the training set.

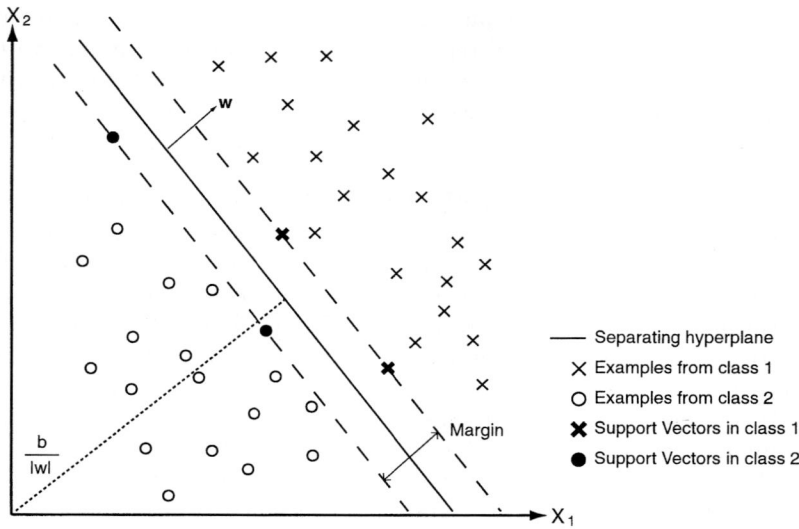

Fig. 1. SVM classification of two classes in a two-dimensional input space

Geometrically, the Support Vector Machine classifier aims to construct a hyperplane that divides $\mathbf{R}^d$ in two, with all training examples in the positive class on one side of the hyperplane, and all examples in the negative class on the other side (see Figure 1). Although there may exist infinitely many hyperplanes that correctly separate the training data, the best SVM classifier is obtained by finding the hyperplane with the maximum "margin". The margin is defined as the distance between the closest training examples in the positive and negative classes to the separating hyperplane [1]. The training examples that determine the margin are known as "support vectors". A trained Support Vector Machine classifies unlabelled points according to the side of the hyperplane on which they fall.

In a typical training set, there will be some examples that unavoidably fall on the wrong side of the hyperplane's decision boundary. In this situation, the separating hyperplane is found by simultaneously maximising the margin between the two classes while minimising the penalty associated with the misclassifications in the training set. The optimum hyperplane, defined by $(\boldsymbol{w} \cdot \boldsymbol{x}) + b = 0$, is found by solving the following quadratic programming problem:

$$\min_{w,b,\xi} \quad \tfrac{1}{2}||\boldsymbol{w}||^2 + C \sum_{i=1}^n \xi_i \tag{1}$$
$$\text{s.t.} \quad y_i(\boldsymbol{x}_i \cdot \boldsymbol{w} + b) \geq 1 - \xi_i$$
$$\xi_i \geq 0 \quad i = 1,\ldots,n$$

where $\xi_i, i = 1, \ldots, n$ are slack variables introduced to allow for examples that fall on the wrong side of the hyperplane, and C is a positive parameter that controls the trade-off between maximising the margin and minimising the training error. This is equivalent to solving the following Lagrangian dual problem, where $\alpha_i, i = 1, \ldots, n$ are the Lagrange multipliers:

$$\max_{\alpha} \quad \sum_{i=1}^{n} \alpha_i - \frac{1}{2} \sum_{i=1}^{n} \sum_{j=1}^{n} \alpha_i \alpha_j y_i y_j \boldsymbol{x}_i \cdot \boldsymbol{x}_j \quad (2)$$
$$\text{s.t.} \quad \sum_{i=1}^{n} \alpha_i y_i = 0$$
$$0 \leq \alpha_i \leq C \quad i = 1, \ldots, n$$

We evaluated two Support Vector Machine algorithms for training, an implementation of the Sequential Minimal Optimisation algorithm [9] and the SVM^{light} package [8]. We obtained similar classification results with either algorithm. The results presented in this paper were obtained using SVM^{light} with a linear kernel and with the Support Vector Machine parameter C determined by SVM^{light}.

2 SVM Detection of Impulsive Noise in Images

Support Vector Machine classifiers learn a particular classification function from a set of labelled training examples. We created training and testing datasets by adding between 1%–20% impulsive noise corruption to an existing image, with the assumption that the original image was initially free of noise and the only noise contained in the image was the impulsive noise that was added.

We examined the effects that a number of parameters had on the performance of the SVM noise classifier. For each set of variables to be evaluated, an array of ten noise-corrupted versions of the same underlying image was generated, in which each image contained an equal level of impulsive noise. The first two images in each set were used to train two Support Vector Machine classifiers independently, while the remaining eight images in the set were used to evaluate the performance of the two trained SVM classifiers. The relative performance of SVMs with different parameter settings was evaluated by calculating the "generalisation performance" of the SVM. The generalisation performance for each SVM consisted of the percentage of noisy pixels and valid pixels in the testing data that were misclassified by the SVM. The misclassification rate was an average of the misclassifications in the eight test images for the two SVM classifiers that were trained.

The examples in the training and test sets were described in a nine-dimensional input space that consisted of the values of each pixel and its eight surrounding neighbouring pixels. This input space was selected because it retained the relationship of each pixel to its neighbours, which we hoped would allow a Support Vector Machine to identify patterns that represented structure such as lines, edges, and corners, and enable these patterns to be distinguished from impulsive noise.

2.1 Training Set Selection

The performance of a Support Vector Machine classifier is dependent on its training and so it is important that the training dataset consists of examples that are representative of the points from the positive and negative classes. We faced two problems in the selection of our training data: reducing the size of the training set and balancing the proportion of training examples from the noise and uncorrupt classes.

The images used in training and testing had dimensions of 512×512 pixels. We found that it was infeasible to create the training set by including every pixel from an image of these dimensions due to the time required to train an SVM on a dataset of this size (over $250,000$ examples). An initial attempt to reduce the size of training dataset was to downsample the training image from 512×512 pixels to a smaller 64×64 pixels. Impulsive noise was then added to the resized image and the training data was generated by taking every pixel in this image to form a training set of roughly 4000 examples. However, this generated a training set with an uneven proportion of examples from the two classes—the proportion of training examples labelled as noise matched the proportion of impulsive noise that was added to the original image. A Support Vector Machine trained on such a biased dataset was found to get caught in a local optimum in which it classified every example into the class that dominated the training set; if the training image contained only 2% impulsive noise, the resulting SVM classified every test example as an uncorrupt pixel.

The problems of training set imbalance and training set size were both overcome by creating the training data by randomly selecting 2000 uncorrupt and 2000 noisy pixels from a full-sized image of dimensions 512×512 pixels. This led to a small training dataset containing 4000 examples with an equal number of examples coming from both classes. In addition, taking a subset of pixels from the full-sized image had the advantage that the spatial properties of pixels in the training image were not affected by resizing the image.

2.2 Improving Class Separation

The generalisation performance of a Support Vector Machine classifier is highly dependent on the positive and negative classes being linearly separable in the input space. If the training set contains two classes that are clearly separable the resulting model will contain few Support Vectors and we conjecture will generalise well to the test set.

Our datasets contained considerable overlap between the "noise" and "uncorrupt" classes. Since we were dealing with noise that takes on a random intensity, there is a probability that a pixel could be corrupted by noise with a value that is close to, or identical to, the original pixel value. This leads to training data that is inseparable, since the same example may be labelled as both a valid pixel and as noise in the dataset. Furthermore, it is somewhat subjective as to whether a pixel that differs only marginally from its neighbours represents noise or is a small feature within the image.

To overcome this problem, examples in the training and test data were labelled as noise only if the original pixel's value had been changed by more than a certain threshold. For example, if a pixel of value x was replaced by noise of value x', the example would be labelled in the dataset as follows (given threshold T):

$$\text{label}(x) = \begin{cases} \text{uncorrupt}, & |x - x'| < T \\ \text{noise}, & |x - x'| \geq T \end{cases} \quad (3)$$

For the remainder of this paper a noise threshold of 25 is used. Although this value excludes one-fifth of the possible values for impulsive noise in an 8-bit greyscale image, it was selected because we believe that impulsive noise with a value that differs from the original pixel value by 25 or less would be visually imperceptible in the image. The use of this threshold produced an SVM with good generalisation performance.

2.3 Reducing the Variation Within the Classes

The detection of impulsive noise in image data is complicated by the large amount of background variation within images, which requires a large training set to define. However, if both training and test images were filtered to remove background structure, while retaining the possible noise in the image, then the task of the Support Vector Machine would be greatly simplified and, we believe, the SVM would generalise better to images outside the training set.

We evaluated the use of a filter to remove the background structure of an image. Training and test images were filtered by either a highpass FIR filter or the Immerkær background-removal filter [7]. The highpass filter was selected for its ability to emphasise the impulsive noise in an image—which appears as high-frequency data in the frequency-domain—making it stand out against the background of the image. The Immerkær filter was proposed as part of a method for estimating the level of additive noise in an image in which the predictable image structure is first removed from the image, leaving only noise (and fine image detail) remaining. Image structure is removed by filtering the source image, X, with the following convolution kernel, resulting in the image Y:

$$Y = \begin{pmatrix} 1 & -2 & 1 \\ -2 & 4 & -2 \\ 1 & -2 & 1 \end{pmatrix} \otimes X \quad (4)$$

The convolution kernel is based on two Laplacian filters, and has the effect of removing all constant, linear, and quadratic variation in the intensity of pixels within the local window.

The effect of applying the highpass filter and Immerkær filter on an initial noise-corrupted image is shown in Figure 2. Figure 4 shows the generalisation performance of a Support Vector Machine trained and tested on images with no filtering, with a highpass filter, and with an Immerkær filter. The median difference is described in the next section.

Fig. 2. Application of pre-processing filters on "Lena" containing 2% noise

2.4 Multistage Classification Using SVMs

Motivated by the significant improvement that the Immerkær background-removal filter had on the generalisation performance of a Support Vector Machine, we had the idea of processing images with the median filter. The median filter is a popular non-linear filter used for removing impulsive noise from images, and is used at the core of many noise removal algorithms. The median filter is capable of effectively suppressing impulsive noise, however, it does so at the expense of the non-corrupt pixels in the image [3,4]. In particular, the median filter is unable to distinguish fine lines from impulsive noise, and so lines in the image are removed or distorted. We recognised that subtracting the median filtered image from its non-filtered counterpart would result in an image containing only the noise in the original image as well as any distortions introduced by the median filter where it misclassified image structure as noise. A Support Vector Machine classifier could then be trained to separate noisy pixels from features removed by the median filter, without the complication of background image variation.

The median filter replaces every pixel with the median value of a surrounding window of the image. For a $(2N+1) \times (2N+1)$ window centered around pixel $x_{i,j}$, the median filter performs the following operation:

$$y_{i,j} = \text{median}(x_{i-N,j-N}, \ldots, x_{i,j}, \ldots, x_{i+N,j+N}) \qquad (5)$$

The "median difference filter" that we developed is described below for source image X,

$$Y = |X - \text{Median}(X)| \qquad (6)$$

We used a median difference filter with a window size of 3×3 pixels in our research.

Figure 3 shows the result of applying the straight median filter to an initial noise-corrupted image, and the corresponding median difference image. Figure 4 presents the generalisation performance of a Support Vector Machine that is applied to the median difference image (corrupted with 2% impulsive noise) and shows that the median difference SVM classifier clearly outperforms other SVM approaches.

Fig. 3. Demonstration of median difference filter on "Lena". For illustrative purposes the image contains 10% noise

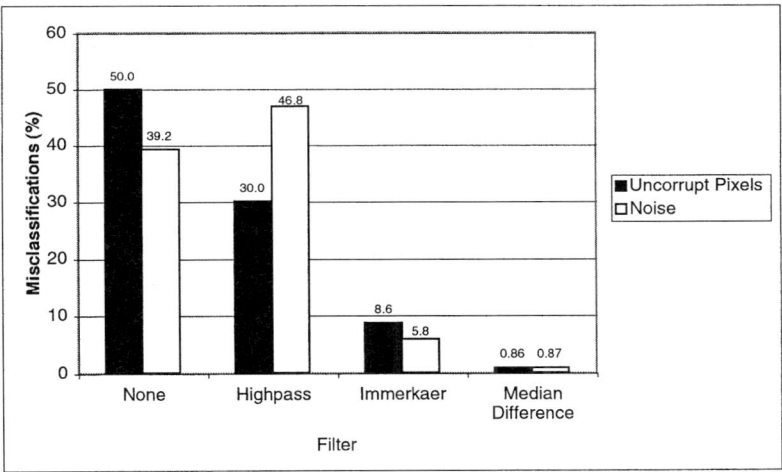

Fig. 4. Plot of generalised error rate for classification of uncorrupt and noisy pixels in test images containing 2% impulsive noise

Fig. 5. The set of test images used for evaluation of proposed SVM technique

3 Comparative Results

In this section we compare the performance of our proposed Support Vector Machine-based impulsive noise detection algorithm against a noise detector based upon the median filter for images corrupted by various levels of impulsive noise. The median filter classifier considers a pixel to be noise if the difference between its value and the median value of its neighbours is greater than a given threshold, T:

$$\text{class}(x_{i,j}) = \begin{cases} \text{noise}, & |x_{i,j} - \text{median}(i,j)| > T \\ \text{uncorrupt}, & |x_{i,j} - \text{median}(i,j)| \leq T \end{cases} \tag{7}$$

Many noise filtering algorithms, including those that treat the detection and removal of noise as a single problem, make use of the median filter—or median filter classifier—to perform implicit noise detection.

Our experiments were performed on 8-bit greyscale images of dimensions 512×512 pixels, which were corrupted with 1%, 2%, 5%, 10%, and 20% random-valued impulsive noise. The Support Vector Machine classifier was trained and tested on images that had been preprocessed with the median difference filter described in Section 2.4. The results in this paper were obtained using the image "Lena", but the trend observed with this image was also observed with other images.

Table 1 presents the 95% confidence interval for the percentage of misclassified pixels in the "noise" and "uncorrupt" classes, using both the proposed SVM classifier and the median filter classifier. These results show that the proposed SVM-based impulsive noise detector is able to perform well even when the level of impulsive noise corruption is high. A summary of the statistical significance of the proposed SVM classifier's better noise detection is given in Table 2. With the exception of the classification of image structure in images corrupted by 1% noise, all tests were statistically significant at below the 5×10^{-5} level of significance. We conjecture that even images with no noise corruption contain pixels that differ significantly from their neighbours, and these pixels are incorrectly classified as noise by the SVM, leading to the slightly higher misclassification rate for image structure in images containing 1%.

The orginal training dataset consisted of 4000 pixels from a 512×512 pixel image. For an image corrupted with 2% impulsive noise, the training set contains only 0.78% of the uncorrupt pixels from the image. Thus the results in Tables 1 and 2 show that the proposed SVM classifier is generalising well from a relatively small training set.

To verify that the Support Vector Machine was indeed learning to identify the characteristics of noise, and not simply learning to identify corruption in the training image, a Support Vector Machine that was trained on the image "Lena" was used to identify noise in the images "Boat" and "Mandrill" (see figure 5). Two Support Vector Machine classifiers were each trained on two separate noise-corrupted versions of the image "Lena" containing 2% impulsive noise. The two trained SVMs were then evaluated on noise classification of eight noise-corrupted versions of the images "Lena", "Boat" and "Mandrill". The median difference

Table 1. Comparison of median filter noise detector versus proposed SVM noise classifier

	Median Filter Classifier		Proposed SVM Classifier	
Noise Level	Misclassified Noise	Misclassified Structure	Misclassified Noise	Misclassified Structure
1%	3.65–4.37%	0.735–0.763%	0.692–0.995%	0.770–0.778%
2%	3.78–4.15%	0.996–1.05%	0.637–0.863%	0.914–0.928%
5%	4.75–5.20%	2.08–2.15%	0.829–0.975%	1.17–1.19%
10%	5.87–6.17%	4.79–4.92%	1.05–1.17%	1.46–1.50%
20%	7.81–8.04%	12.3–12.4%	1.65–1.76%	2.23–2.30%

Table 2. Tests for statistical significance of performance improvement of proposed SVM noise detector

Noise Level	P-Value (Noise)	P-Value (Structure)
1%	2.78×10^{-7}	9.98×10^{-1}
2%	3.99×10^{-10}	4.83×10^{-5}
5%	1.34×10^{-10}	4.85×10^{-11}
10%	5.97×10^{-13}	5.89×10^{-13}
20%	3.15×10^{-14}	3.42×10^{-16}

image was used for all training and test images. Table 3 shows the 95% confidence interval for the percentage of pixels misclassified by the proposed SVM. For comparison, we also include results for an SVM that has been trained and tested on the same underlying image. For example, an SVM that was trained on the image "Boat" containing 2% impulsive noise was tested on eight other versions of "Boat" containing 2% noise.

Table 3. Generalisation of proposed SVM to noise detection outside training image

Image	Trained on "Lena"		Trained on different noise-corrupted version of same image	
	Misclassified Noise	Misclassified Structure	Misclassified Noise	Misclassified Structure
Lena	0.637–0.863%	0.914–0.928%	0.637–0.863%	0.914–0.928%
Boat	1.41–1.62%	2.13–2.16%	1.63–1.86%	1.77–1.81%
Mandrill	5.95–6.48%	14.9–15.7%	11.4–12.1%	6.59–6.93%

We note that performance on "Lena" was better than performance on the other two images. The classifiers trained on "Lena" and "Boat" were more accurate in classifying noise than in classifying structure. However, the reverse was true for "Mandrill". "Mandrill is an image with a large amount of texture and detail. We conjecture that the high level of variation in the image structure in

"Mandrill" causes the classifiers trained on this image to be biased towards capturing structural details correctly. This may explain why the classifier's trained on "Lena" were more accurate in classifying noise on "Mandrill" than the classifiers trained on "Mandrill" itself. Also we conjecture that it may be necessary to include more attributes or to use an SVM with a non-linear kernel to improve the learning of the underlying image structure.

4 Conclusions

In this paper, we have approached the removal of impulsive noise from an image as a classification problem, and have proposed an impulsive noise detection algorithm based on Support Vector Machine classifiers. The performance of the Support Vector Machine classifier was improved by applying domain knowledge in order to generate a balanced training set, to reduce the overlap between the positive and negative classes, and to suppress the variation of examples within each class.

The use of domain knowledge led to a two stage process in which a traditional noise filtering algorithm, the median filter, was used as a first stage to identify impulsive noise in an image, and a Support Vector Machine was then used to correct misclassifications by the median filter. This composite noise classifier performed significantly better than either the median filter or a Support Vector Machine classifier individually. Further work could investigate the replacement of the median filter as a first-stage noise detector with a filter that is appropriate to the level of noise and type of noise in an image.

The results that we have obtained with multi-stage noise detection indicate that Support Vector Machines may be worthwhile as the second stage in a two-stage classification process. Such an approach could be applied to areas outside noise detection, where a Support Vector Machine is used to improve upon an existing technique which, as we have shown with the median filter, is simply used as a black box first-stage classifier. Further work could also investigate the use of other machine learning classifiers to implement the second-stage of the process.

References

1. Burges, C.: A tutorial on Support Vector Machines for pattern recognition. Data Mining and Knowledge Discovery **2** (1998) 121–167
2. Cristianini, N., Shawe-Taylor, J.: An Introduction to Support Vector Machines and other kernel-based learning methods. Cambridge University Press, Cambridge (2000)
3. Davies, E.R.: Edge location shifts produced by median filters: theoretical bounds and experimental results. Signal Process. **16** (1989) 83–96
4. Davies, E.R.: A remanent noise problem with the median filter. In: Proc. 11th IAPR International Conference on Image, Speech and Signal Analysis. Volume 3. (1992) 505–508

5. El-Naqa, I., Yang, Y., Wernick, M., Galatsanos, N., Nishikawa, R.: A Support Vector Machine approach for detection of microcalcifications. IEEE Transactions on Medical Imaging **21** (2002) 1552–1563
6. Hearst, M., Dumais, S., Osuna, E., Platt, J., Schölkopf, B.: Support Vector Machines. IEEE Intelligent Systems **13** (1998) 18–28
7. Immerkær, J.: Fast noise variance estimation. Computer vision and image understanding **64** (1996) 300–302
8. Joachims, T.: Making large-scale SVM learning practical. In Schölkopf, B., Burges, C., Smola, A., eds.: Advances in Kernel Methods - Support Vector Learning, MIT Press (1999) 169–184
9. Platt, J.: Chapter 12. In Schölkopf, B., Burges, C., Smola, A., eds.: Advances in Kernel Methods - Support Vector Learning, MIT Press (1999) 185–208
10. Tong, S., Chang, E.: Support Vector Machine active learning for image retrieval. In: Proceedings of the ninth ACM international conference on Multimedia, ACM Press (2001) 107–118

Applying Image Pre-processing Techniques for Appearance-Based Human Posture Recognition: An Experimental Analysis

M. Masudur Rahman and Seiji Ishikawa

Department of Control Engineering, Kyushu Institute of Technology,
Sensuicho 1-1, Tobata, Kitakyushu 804-8550, Japan
rahman@ss10.cntl.kyutech.ac.jp

Abstract. This paper investigates that loose clothing such as wearing dresses and human body shapes create individual eigenspaces and, as a result, conventional appearance-based method cannot be effective for recognizing human body postures. We introduce *a dress effect* due to loose clothing and *a figure effect* due to various human body shapes in this particular study. This study particularly proposes an image pre-processing by '*Laplacian of Gaussian (LoG)*' filter over input images and a '*mean posture matrix*' for creating an eigenspace in order to overcome the preceding effects. We have tested the proposed approach on various dress environments and body shapes, and robustness of the method has been demonstrated.

1 Introduction

Due to inexpensive mathematical computations, an appearance-based eigenspace (abbr. as ES hereafter) technique has many applications, e.g., human computer interaction, visually mediated interaction and automated visual surveillance. In the past years, we have seen an extensive use of the ES method on capturing the appearances of objects and human faces under various conditions [1-6, 13]. It should be mentioned that the appearance-based ES method was firstly proposed by Murase and Nayar [7] for recognizing 3D object's poses from 2D images. However, PCA algorithm was successfully implemented for human face recognition by Sirovich and Kirby [1]. Besides, several other models have been proposed for the underlying objectives, e.g., separating styles and contents using bilinear models [8], human face detection using one-example views [9], Bayesian rules [10], body pose detection using specialized mapping [11], and spatio-temporal correlation [12].

However, we concentrate on an unexplored area of research, i.e., human body posture recognition using an ES technique which has many expected practical applications such as security. In case of employing ES technique for human body posture recognition, we have found that loose clothing such as wearing clothes and various body shapes have some undesirable effects on shaping the pattern of eigenspaces and we need to overcome these problems for successful representation and recognition of human postures. We introduce notions of *a dress effect* due to loose clothing and *a figure effect* due to various human body shapes in this particular study. We employ image pre-processing by Laplacian of Gaussian (LoG) filter for reducing the dress effect, and a mean posture matrix from some selected posture sets for avoiding the figure effect. This mean posture matrix is used for generating the basic ES. The basic ES is responsible for further recognizing unfamiliar but similar postures. We have succesfully overcome the preceding effects by the proposed methods for human body postures recognition and tentative experimental proofs have been demonstrated in this particular paper.

2   Proposed Approach

2.1   Image Pre-processing

In order to employ an eigenspace in human body posture recognition, posture representation should have generality, i.e., it should solely depend on the posture change and not on the person or dress change. If one employs the original eigenspace technique [7], however, respective eigenspace is inevitably generated each time the person changes his/her dress. This is because it employs gray images for the generation of an eigenspace. We employ blurred edge images of given images to obtain a solely apperance-dependent eigenspace.

A blurred edge image $E(x,y)$ of the original image $I(x,y)$ is defined by

$$E(x, y) = D^2 (G * I(x, y)) \tag{1}$$

G is the gaussian distribution for reducing the texture effect and the resultant image is differentiated by a Laplacian operator D^2. In the proposed technique, the blurred edge images provided by Eq.(1) are employed for generating an eigenspace.

2.2   Computing a Mean Posture Matrix and Proposed Eigenspace

Let us take a blurred edge image $E(x,y)$ and take P successive sampled images x_p ($p=1,2,\ldots,P$). The sampled image x_p having $M_0 \times N_0$ pixel size is converted into a column vector of the form

$$x_p = \left(x_{1p}, x_{2p}, \ldots, x_{N,p} \right)^\mathrm{T}. \tag{2}$$

by arranging pixels in a raster scan manner. Here $N \equiv M_0 \times N_0$. Superscript 'T' denotes transpose of a vector or a matrix.

If person h involves to make respective posture sets, a matrix X^h containing P columns and N rows can be denoted by

$$X^h = \left(x_1^h, x_2^h, \ldots, x_P^h \right). \tag{3}$$

Here $h = 1, 2, \ldots, H$. Taking a particular posture set X^h, an ES can be produced and respective postures are represented in the produced eigenspace. For H humans, the posture curves (graphical representation of ES) corresponding to respective persons should ideally coincide with each other in the ES, which is not the case in practice. Therefore a mean expression of the postures is taken into account.

A mean posture matrix $\overline{X}$ is defined in the following way to obtain a basic ES;

$$\overline{X} = \frac{1}{H}\sum_{h=1}^{H} X^h = (\overline{x}_1, \overline{x}_2, ..., \overline{x}_P), \quad (4)$$

where

$$\overline{x}_p = \frac{1}{H}\sum_{h=1}^{H} x_p^h, \quad (5)$$

which is called a mean image. A mean posture set $\overline{X}$ is a set of average images.

We define a covariance matrix C as follows;

$$C = \overline{X}\overline{X}^T \quad (6)$$

and determine eigenvalues λ_i with its corresponding eigenvectors e_i of the covariance matrix C using an eigen equation $Ce = \lambda e$. The N dimensional space defined by all the eigenvectors of matrix C is compressed via PCA algorithm by choosing only k (k is an integer satisfying $k \ll N$) eigenvectors e_i ($i=1,2,...,k$) corresponding to the largest k eigenvalues to make an ES.

Once we determine the selected eigenvectors employing the mean posture matrix, the successive procedures, i.e., creating eigenspace and posture recognition technique can be found in the literature [7]. The developed ES having edge images and mean posture matrix is defined here as the proposed or basic ES.

3 Experimental Results

3.1 Effect of the Blurred Edge Images

In the performed experiment, a setup is conducted using a camera and 30 different human models ($H=30$) with their presently worn clothes including their different body shapes. A person is asked to stand in front of a fixed video camera and to make a slow turn. The video motion is sampled approximately every 10 degrees yielding 36 (=P) images of different postures. The original sampled image is reduced to a 32×32 pixels image for the sake of memory efficiency. Considerations of occlusion and background issues are out of scope in this particular study. Fig. 1a shows 12 human models out of 30 used in the experiment and 16 (out of 36) body postures of a particular person are also shown in Fig. 1b. These images are submitted to the proposed image processing as described earlier. The result of edge images is also shown in Fig. 1c.

We have generated 30 individual posture curves (single person) as shown in Fig. 2. These posture curves are obtained from individual models and placed in a same axis dimension in order to compare the effect of proposed image processing graphically. It should be noted that these posture curves (Fig. 2b) have generated using LoG images and this is just separate eigenspaces from the respective models. Therefore, we have avoided the averaging the posture sets for this issue, i.e., covariance matrix $C = X^h X^{hT}$. This mean posture matrix is applied for recognizing unknown postures.

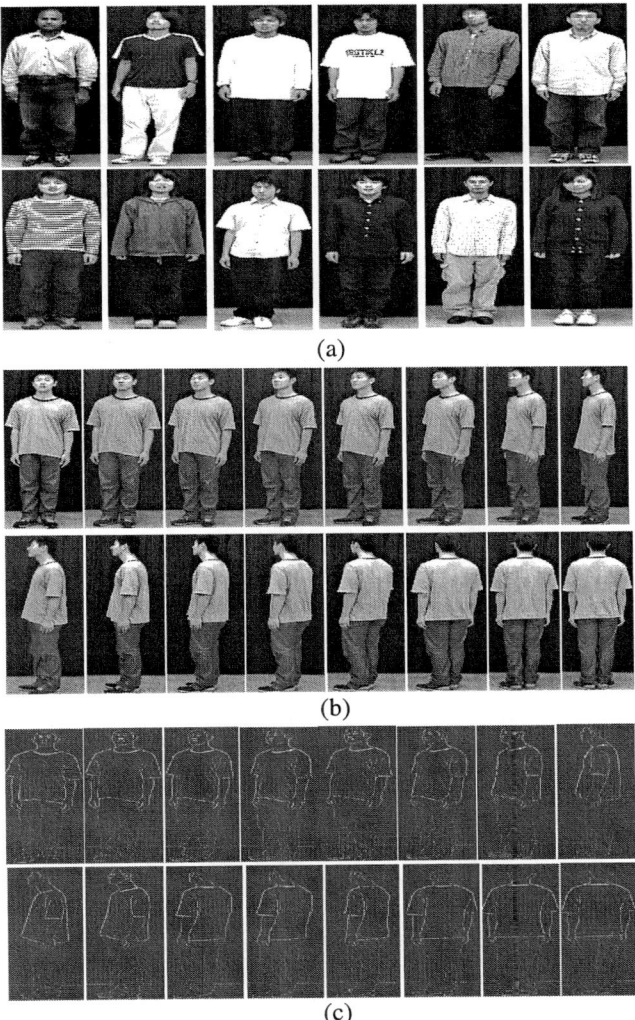

Fig. 1. Human models, postures and processed images: (a) 12 human models out of 30 used in the experiments, (b) 16 postures out of 36 of a model, and (c) blurred edge or LoG images

This performance is just for highlighting the effect of proposed image processing, i.e., LoG images. The posture curves obtained from the conventional method [7] are illustrated in Fig.2a, whereas those derived from the proposed method are depicted in Fig.2b. It is obvious that the dress effect has made the posture curves completely different with each other by the conventional method, though the models' postures are similar. On the other hand, the dress effect has been successfully overcome in the proposed approach as shown in Fig.2b. It is noted that we differentiate between the conventional and proposed method by their input images in creating eigenspace.

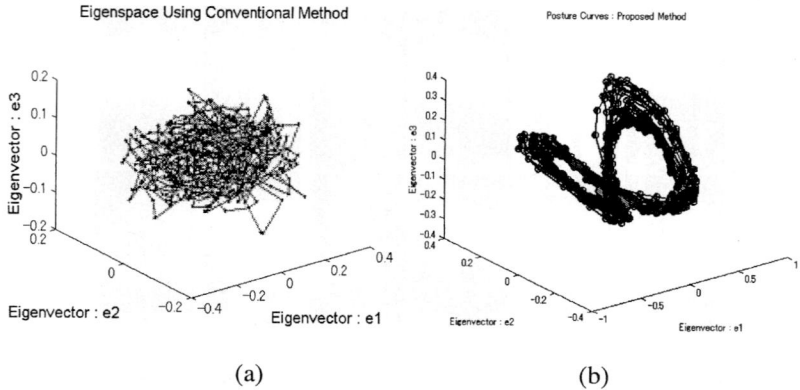

Fig. 2. Individual posture curves obtained from (a) the conventional method and (b) the proposed method

3.2 Recognizing Human Postures Employing the Proposed Eigenspace

We divide all data sets randomly (taking equal number) into three sets, i.e., LS, TS_A and TS_B where LS denotes learning samples and TS denotes testing samples. We employ a leave-and-out or k-fold cross validation method for choosing the learning samples for making the proposed ES so that all data sets can be used either for training or testing. Therefore, when we use LS for generating an ES, TS_A and TS_B data sets remain for testing. Similarly, if we choose TS_A as learning samples, LS and TS_B are used for testing purposes, and *vice versa*. Table 1 shows the distribution of data set for generating the proposed ES and the samples for testing. The average recognition results of each test are also shown in this table. Employing a learning sample such as LS, we calculate a mean data set by Eq.(5) and generate the proposed eigenspace from it. Fig. 3 shows a proposed ES of the data set LS. This proposed ES is used for recognizing image data contained in TS_A and TS_B. Moreover, the leave-and-out method can also arrange the data sets such a way that each time 29 data sets could be used for learning and single data set could be employed for testing. In this case, we have obtained an average of 88.6%. However, if we use more data set, the CPU time will be a bit higher. The recognition rate is calculated dividing the ratio of successful hits and the total postures projected. It is mentioned that we have projected unknown but similar postures onto the basic eigenspace and decided the successful hits based on the minimum description length.

We have obtained an average recognition rate of 71.66% using only the edge images, mean posture matrix are not taken into consideration here, where only one set was used for learning and 29 sets were for testing. This result only highlights the progress of our proposed method. It is noted that the proposed method works only with

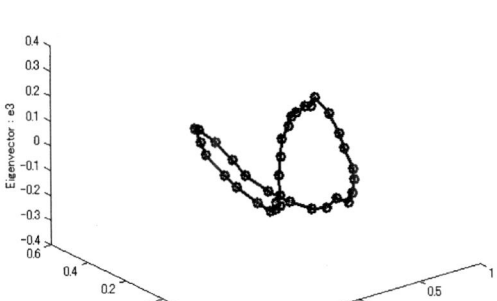

Fig. 3. A proposed eigenspace created from S_A data set

the combined application of LoG image processing and mean posture matrix for creating eigenspace. Classification results between two conventional and the proposed methods are also shown in Table 2. According to the papers of Murase and Nayar [7] and Murase and Sakai [12], we have used the original gray images and silhouette images, respectively for their input images. In these cases, a best-search method has applied for selecting an appropriate learning sample while other data sets are used for testing (i.e., total of 29 data sets) purposes. According to the conventional methods, we need to search a based model for the learning samples and the others will be remaining for testing. Therefore, we have used only one sample for learning and rest of the samples have used for testing. On the other hand, the proposed method calculates a mean posture matrix and we have taken 10 image set for obtaining this mean. Therefore, the rest of 20 samples have used for testing. Obtained higher recognition rates have proved the robustness of the proposed method. In case of time efficiency, we need only 1.5 Sec. (CPU time) using 1 G Htz PC and Matlab implementation software.

Table 1. Data distribution for the proposed ES and recognition

Test	S1-10	S11-20	S21-30	Recognition Rates (avg.)	Average (all data)
(i)	LS	TS_A	TS_B	86.2%	85.6%
(ii)	TS_A	LS	TS_A	83.4%	
(iii)	TS_B	TS_B	LS	87.2%	

Table 2. Classification results between conventional and proposed methods

Methods	Recognition Rates	Test Sets	Eigen Dimension	Mean Square Error
Murase 95[7]	40.05%	29	8	0.0345
Murase 96[12]	71.29%	29	8	0.0345
Proposed ES	85.6%	20	4	0.0345

4 Discussion and Conclusions

This paper has proposed an updated eigenspace technique for human body posture recognition, which allows some image pre-processing techniques. The proposed eigenspace technique has also considered a mean posture matrix for developing the ES. It has successfully reduced the effects of human posture-change due to loose clothing and various body shapes and this result was experimentally shown. We have also compared the proposed method with conventional methods and the obtained results have indicated that the proposed ES method is better than the conventional ones in terms of recognition rates for human body posture recognition. Since our method has employed the image contour and their internal edges, it has more demand in the field of gesture recognition. We have also reduced the processing time by compressing image size and requiring less eigen dimension.

The classification of dresses and human body shapes normally has a large variety. We have employed 30 person's body postures with their presently worn dresses. Since they are mostly from the same society (however there are two models from different nationalities), the body shapes were not so different. Employment of more different types of clothes such as lady's dresses and textured clothes and various body shapes such as Japanese traditional Osumo people are expected to the future study.

Some possible extensions of the proposed method can also be proposed in this section. In particular, the applications of image processing techniques for reducing dress texture effect, generalization (mean) of postures, eigenspace selection may develop some new algorithms in this area for flexible objects recognition where individual eigenspace generating may not be essential. This proposed approach can be of interest to the researchers of various fields and the scope of this study can be extended for recognizing human behavior, activities, motions, gestures, etc.

Bibliography

1. Sirovich, L. and Kirby M.: "Low dimensional procedure for the characterization of human faces", J. Optical Society of America, Vol. 4, No. 3, pp. 519-524(1987).
2. Turk, M.A. and Pentland, A.P.: "Face recognition using eigenfaces, Proc. of the Computer Vision and Pattern recognition", pp. 586-591(1991).
3. Leonardis, A., Bischof, H.: "Robust recognition using eigenimages", *Computer Vision and Image Understanding*, 78, pp.99-118(2000).

4. Ohba, K., Ikeuchi, K.: "Detectability, uniqueness, and reliability of eigen windows for stable verification of partially occluded objects", *IEEE Tran. on Pattern Analysis and Machine Intelligence*, PAMI-9, pp. 1043-1047 (1997).
5. Borotschnig, H., et. al.: "Appearance-based active object recognition", *Image and Vision Computing*, Vol. 18(9), pp. 715-727(2000).
6. Black, M. J., Jepson, A. D.: "Eigen tracking: robust matching and tracking of articulated objects using view-based representation", *Int. Journal of Computer Vision*, Vol. 26(1), pp. 63-84(1998).
7. Murase, H., Nayar, S. K.: "Visual learning and recognition of 3-D objects from appearance", *Int. J. Computer Vision*, 14, 5, 39-50(1995).
8. Tenenbaum, B., Freeman, W. T.: "Separating style and content with bilinear models", *Neural Computation*, 12 (6), pp. 1247-1283(2000).
9. Beymer, D., Poggio, T.: "Face Recognition from one example view", *Proc. of Int. Conf. on Computer Vision*, pp.500-507, 1995.
10. Moghaddam, B., et al.: "Bayesian face recognition", *Pattern Recognition*, Vol.33 pp.1771-1782 (2000).
11. Romer R. and Stan S., "Specialized mapping and the estimation of human body pose from a single image", *IEEE Workshop on Human Motion* (2002).
12. Murase, R. Sakai: "Moving object recognition in eigenspace representation: Gait Analysis and lip reading", *Pattern Recognition Letters*, Vol. 17, pp. 155-162, (1996).
13. Yilmaz, A., Gokmen, M.: "Eigenhill vs. eigenface and eigenedge", *Pattern Recognition*, 34, pp.181-184 (2001).

A Stochastic Approach to Tracking Objects Across Multiple Cameras

Anthony R. Dick and Michael J. Brooks

School of Computer Science, University of Adelaide, Adelaide, SA 5005, Australia
CRC for Sensor, Signal and Information Processing, Technology Park,
Mawson Lakes, SA 5095
{ard, mjb}@cs.adelaide.edu.au

Abstract. This paper is about tracking people in real-time as they move through the non-overlapping fields of view of multiple video cameras. The paper builds upon existing methods for tracking moving objects in a single camera. The key extension is the use of a stochastic transition matrix to describe people's observed patterns of motion both within and between fields of view. The parameters of the model for a particular environment are learnt simply by observing a person moving about in that environment. No knowledge of the environment or the configuration of the cameras is required.

1 Introduction

Tracking moving objects as they are observed by a video camera is a much researched problem in computer vision. Although it is far from solved, there is a variety of existing systems that work quite reliably under certain well documented conditions. A thorough review is beyond the scope of this paper, but some examples are Boujou[1], which tracks point features, Condensation [8] and its variants, which track image contours, and mean-shift methods [2] which track colours. Other tracking systems are specialised to tracking people [1] or certain objects whose shape is known in advance [5].

Many applications, however, demand tracking over a wider area than can be covered by a single camera. For instance, a building may be monitored by a network of surveillance cameras, and ideally a person would be tracked consistently as they move between them [3]. One solution is implement blanket coverage of the building, so that every part of it is visible to at least one camera. If the cameras are calibrated, and the structure of the environment is known, then people will pass from one camera's field of view (FOV) to another at known locations, which act as trigger points for handing over tracking from one camera to the next. This however is impractical for an environment of any size or complexity, due to the number of cameras required and physical constraints on their placement.

---

[1] www.2d3.com

Tracking algorithms will therefore have to deal with "blind spots" where a person is not visible to any camera if they are to operate on a network of cameras monitoring a complex environment. Most tracking algorithms in the computer vision literature are not well suited to this task, because typically they rely on the assumption of smooth motion, using previously observed velocity to predict the future location of their target. An example of this is the Kalman filter [14], and various types of particle filter [8, 4], which are more robust than the Kalman filter to sudden changes but are based on the same underlying assumption. When tracking an object between non-overlapping fields of view, its motion is almost guaranteed not to be smooth. For instance, a person may disappear from the right side of one FOV and then reappear after some time at the top of another FOV, depending on how the cameras are positioned.

This problem has become increasingly apparent in recent years, and has been the subject of some recent research in computer vision. Kettnaker [10] presents a Bayesian approach to tracking objects through FOVs that do not overlap. However this system requires a set of allowable paths, and a set of transition probabilities and their expected duration, to be supplied a priori. This effectively requires that the environment is known in advance, along with the ways in which people move about in it, and the positions of the cameras. In many surveillance applications, this information is difficult or impossible to obtain.

A traffic monitoring system using cameras situated about 2 miles apart along a highway is described in [7, 11]. Cars are identified as they enter each camera's field of view based on both their appearance and positional information from views through which they have previously passed. The surveillance of traffic is well suited to cameras with non-overlapping FOVs, because traffic generally follows well defined paths which extend over long distances.

Recently, work has been carried out on tracking people or objects with more general motion between non-overlapping camera FOVs. This has been approached as a problem of learning the probability of transitions between fields of view from corresponding tracks (e.g. see [9]). However, the correspondence between tracks in different images must be supplied a priori, as training data. Ellis et al. [6] do not require correspondences, instead observing motion over a long period of time and recording each appearance and disappearance. All possible pairings between appearance and disappearance are accumulated in a histogram, and those which occur most consistently are considered the true transitions.

In this paper we describe a system for tracking objects across the FOVs of cameras that do not overlap. The system does not require any knowledge of the cameras' placement or calibration, nor does it need to know anything about the environment it is monitoring. It works by learning a Markov model describing the paths taken by a marker as it is carried around in the environment.

The structure of this paper is as follows. In Section 2, we review a single camera tracking technique which we use as part of our multiple camera tracker. In Section 3, we introduce the Markov model we use to model the motion of objects within and between cameras, and describe how this model is trained for a particular camera setup and environment. Following this the Markov model is combined with the single view tracker to form our multiple view tracking algorithm, described in Section 4. Some illustrative results of the tracker are then presented in Section 5.

2   Tracking Objects with Background Subtraction

Our method for tracking people across multiple cameras is built on an existing technique for tracking within a single camera's field of view. In particular, we implemented the multimodal background subtraction algorithm of Stauffer and Grimson [13].

Background subtraction is a method for object detection that maintains a model of the colour of the background at each pixel; in [13], the model is a mixture of Gaussians. In each frame of video, the likelihood of the current colour of each pixel is computed according to its background model. Based on this likelihood, each pixel is classified as foreground or background. Foreground pixels are those which are not well explained by the background model, and are therefore likely to be interesting objects to track. Clusters of foreground pixels are grouped into objects which can then be tracked as a whole. Stauffer et al. use a Kalman filter to track these objects across frames.

The problem with a Kalman filter is that motion observed in previous frames is used to predict the motion in the current frame. This assumption holds for an object moving smoothly in a single camera's field of view, in an uncluttered environment. However as objects move between camera FOVs, there will inevitably be a discontinuity in their observed motion. Even within a single FOV, if the target object moves behind an obstacle which hides it from view and then reappears at another point in the image, its observed motion is no longer continuous.

We therefore need a tracking algorithm that can cope with discontinuities in order to extend this method to track objects across multiple FOVs. Our algorithm is based on a Markov model, which is introduced in the next section.

3   The Markov Model

We model the movement of each object as a Markov process. A Markov process (or model) is one which at time t can be in any one of N states $S = \{s_1...s_N\}$. The way it progresses between these states is governed by:

- an N dimensional initial state probability vector π, and
- a stochastic $N \times N$ *transition matrix* A, whose (i,j)th element defines the probability of moving from state s_i to s_j.

To cast our tracking system as a Markov model, each camera's field of view is divided evenly into $G \times G$ pixel squares, each of which is associated with a state. The square in which the object currently appears is the current state of the model.

In this context, each element A_{ij} of the transition matrix defines the probability that the object moves from the image region associated with state S_i at frame t to that associated with state S_j at frame $t+1$ (A is stationary). Each coefficient π_i denotes the probability that an object appears for the first time in the region associated with S_i.

This is a very general model of motion, allowing an object to move instantly from any part of any camera FOV to any other. Of course in practice objects do not behave this way. The transition matrix and the initialisation vector need to be assigned values that reflect the way people or objects actually move in the environment under observation.

3.1 Training the Markov Model

We learn appropriate values for A and π from a series of observations. The observations are generated by a person carrying an easily identifiable marker as they move around in the environment. The marker (we used a bright red soccer ball, see Figure 1) is used to ensure the person is tracked reliably, even when there is more than one person moving about in the environment. This was found to be more practical than the alternative, which was to clear the environment of other people and track a single person as they move about.

The marker is tracked simply by finding the image patch whose redness relative to its usual background colour is the highest. If no image patch appears significantly redder than usual, it is assumed that the marker is not currently visible. In practice, this turned out to be very reliable in our rather beige office environment. The training program was left to run in the background for hours on end, without picking up false tracks.

Fig. 1. Training the Markov model. Each 80 by 80 pixel square is assigned a state. Each transition of the red ball between states (the image regions bordered by grid lines, shown here in green) is recorded

To learn values for A and π, we use a simple occurrence counting method. For each frame, as the marker moves between states S_i and S_j in the camera views, the value of A_{ij} is incremented. Similarly, each time a new track is initialised in state S_i, the corresponding value π_i is incremented. Training does not have to be carried out continuously. It was common during experimentation to train the model for a few minutes and then save the current values of A and π, to be loaded up and further refined later on. To prevent A from being dominated by entries in its leading diagonal, which correspond to the marker remaining in the same state, A_{ii} is not incremented if the marker is detected in the same state

S_i in consecutive frames. A_{ii} is incremented, however, if the object appears in state S_i, then disappears for one or more frames, and then reappears in state S_i. After training, A is normalised so that each row sums to 1. π is also normalised so that its entries sum to 1.

This method is analogous to the well known Baum-Welch algorithm [12] for Hidden Markov Models (HMMs), when the states are not hidden (i.e. one can derive the current state of the model from the current observation). The removal of the level of inference that "hides" the states from the observations means that considerably less training data is required for our Markov model than would be needed for the equivalent HMM.

4 Object Tracking

We now apply the Markov model described in the previous section to the results of the object detection method described in Section 2. Recall that having located foreground pixels and connected them to form objects, we have some number of objects detected in the field of view of each camera. These objects are now matched with corresponding objects detected in the previous frame of video.

In practice, it was useful to use Kalman filters as a first pass tracking mechanism. The Kalman filter and the Markov model are complementary, in the sense that the Kalman filter, having a continuous state vector, is better suited to resolving short tracks between frames, whereas the Markov model, having discrete states of $G \times G$ pixels, is better at tracking fast motion or motion that the Kalman filter cannot predict. Thus the Kalman filter will usually pick up objects that have moved slowly and smoothly within the field of view of a single camera, while the remaining objects are then matched using the Markov model, as follows.

First, the current state S_C of each unmatched object is computed by working out the location of its centre. We then consider all objects that disappeared between 2 and K frames ago as candidate matches. The object that disappeared in the location whose state S_D maximises the transition probability A_{DC} is matched with the currently visible object. If the maximum value of A_{DC} is less than the probability that a new track has begun in this location, π_C, the object remains unmatched and is labelled as being previously unseen.

The set of matches that maximise each individual probability may not be the set of matches that maximises the combined probability of all matches. Whenever the probabilities of multiple appearances are maximised by the same disappearance, the matching process is repeated assigning that disappearance to each appearance in turn. The assignment which maximises the combined probability is retained.

5 Results and Observations

We consider a modest network of 3 cameras, all attached to the same desktop PC. The approximate layout of the cameras is shown in Figure 2. Each camera delivers a 320×240 video stream at about 15 frames per second.

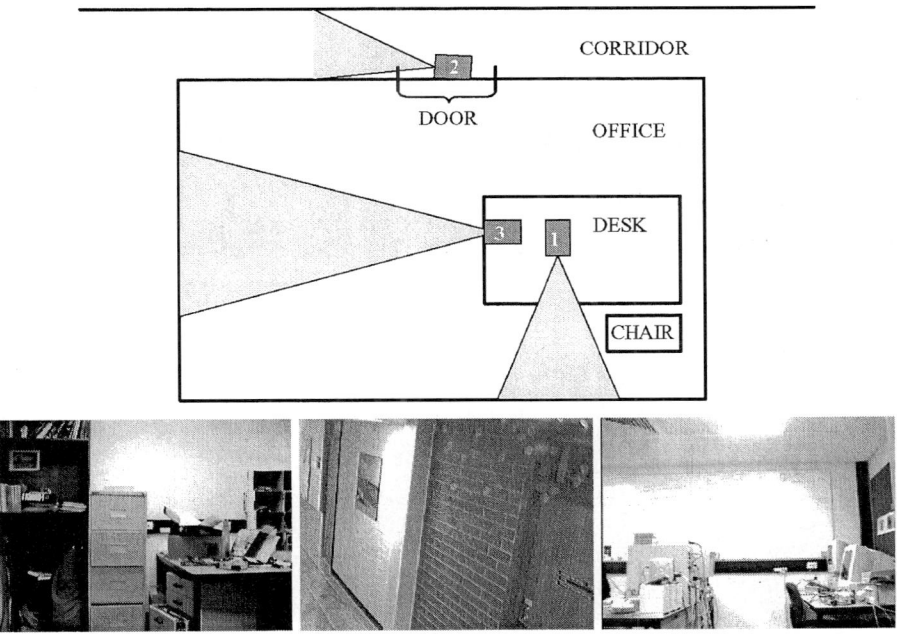

Fig. 2. Top: Camera network layout. Cameras 1 and 3 are on my desk, pointing at right angles to each other. Camera 2 is positioned above the door looking down the corridor outside my office. Bottom: View from cameras 1, 2 and 3

The Markov model was trained sporadically over a period of weeks using the method described in Section 3.1, by the authors and other volunteers carrying the ball around in the office and the corridor outside. The same model parameters were used for all experiments described in this paper. Each state in our model is associated with an 80 × 80 square of pixels, meaning that there is a total of 12 states per camera and 36 states overall. Fortunately, motion in our environment is quite constrained, so although the transition matrix contains 36 × 36 entries, far fewer than that need to be learnt.

Our first set of experiments involves tracking a single person ("Person A") as he moves through this environment, within and between the cameras' fields of view. The sequence of movements is as follows: Person A gets out of his desk chair, then moves right to left through the field of view of camera 1 (Fig 3(a)) to the far side of the office, in the field of view of camera 3 (Fig 3(b)). Not satisfied with this, he then leaves the office and walks down the corridor to an adjacent office. This takes him through the field of view of camera 2, from bottom to top (Fig 3(c),(f),(g)). He then re-enters the office and returns to his chair. This path takes him through the fields of view of all cameras and several blind spots between them.

While this is taking place other people are walking along the corridor outside the office (Fig 3(d),(e)). The main challenges in this experiment are to correctly

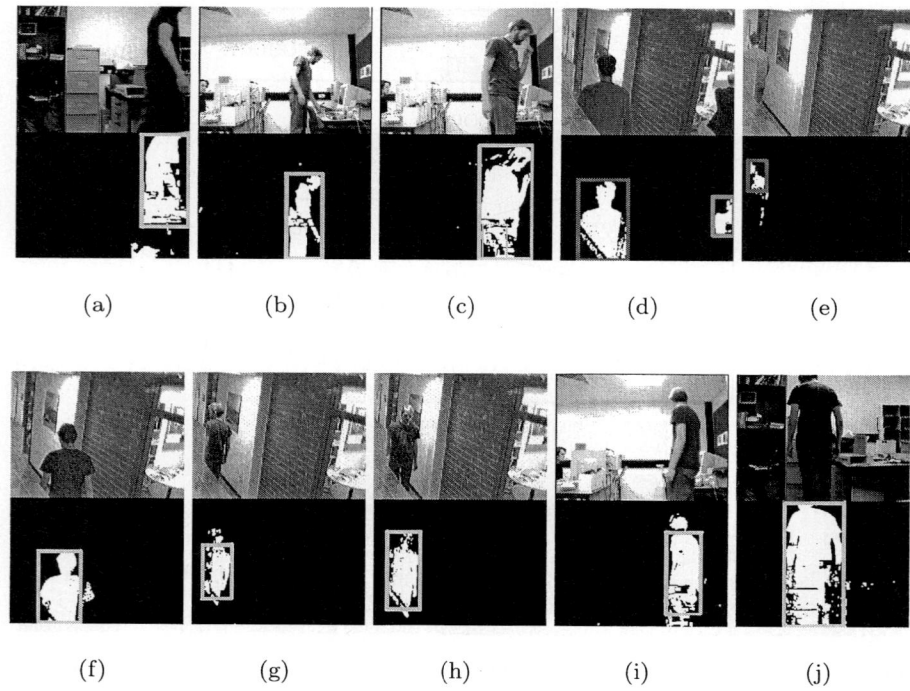

Fig. 3. Snapshots (in order of time) from tracking experiment 1. Each snapshot consists of the video frame (top) and the tracking result (bottom). The subject is successfully tracked through all camera views despite the presence of distractions. Passers-by in the corridor ((d) and (e)), are identified as different people (marked with different colour bounding box), while the subject is identified consistently across all views (same colour) despite disappearing and reappearing several times

link each reappearance of Person A with his disappearance from the previous view, and to track each passerby in the corridor while recognising that each one is the appearance of a new, previously unseen person.

Snapshots of the experiment are shown in Figure 3, in order of time. In each snapshot, the image captured by the relevant camera is shown above the results of the object detection and tracking algorithm. The white pixels in these results are those classified as foreground. Rectangles are drawn around those groups of foreground pixels that are detected as objects and matched to objects in a previous frame. Each object is identified by the colour of its surrounding rectangle. From these results it can be seen that Person A (yellow rectangle) is successfully tracked between views as he moves about in his environment. An example is shown of passers-by who are tracked in the corridor, while Person A is still in his office. The track is successfully maintained for both person A and this passerby.

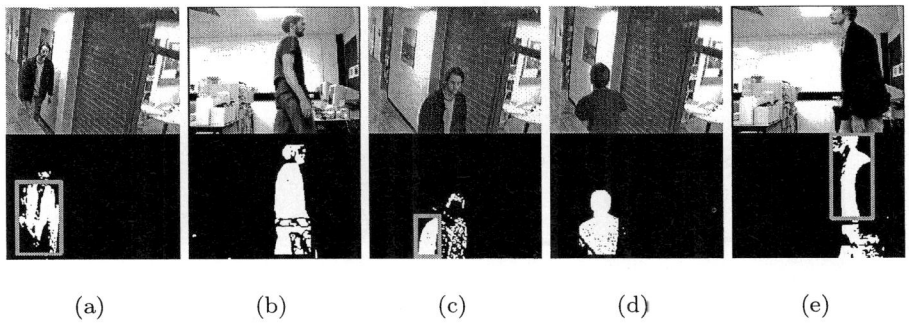

Fig. 4. Snapshots from tracking experiment 2, involving 2 people crossing in the office doorway, out of view of the cameras. The tracks are correctly maintained

A second experiment involves 2 people moving in opposite directions through the camera FOVs. Person A moves from his desk, out of the office and into the corridor. Meanwhile person B moves from an adjacent office, down the corridor and into the office of person A. Persons A and B cross over at the doorway to the office, which is not visible to any camera. The tracker therefore relies on the Markov model to make the correct decision when person A appears in camera 3 and person B appears in camera 2 (the corridor camera), after they cross over. In both cases the tracks are maintained correctly, as shown in Figure 4.

Experiment 3 involves a similar situation, with 2 people moving about in the environment simultaneously. This time, person A leaves his office (Fig 5(a)) and heads down the corridor (Fig 5(c)), exiting at the top of the FOV of the corridor camera. Person B follows A (Fig 5(b),(d)), into the corridor then exits to the bottom of the corridor camera (Fig 5(e)). Persons A and B then reappear and return to their desks (Fig 5(f),(g),(h)).

This sequence shows the ability of the Markov model to decide which disappearance best explains each appearance, based on the location of each. Having been trained, the model knows that it is unlikely to observe a person disappear from the top of the corridor camera and reappear at the bottom, and vice versa.

Experiment 4 shows how the tracker can be misled. Person A is tracked correctly to the door of his office (Fig 6(a),(d)), while at the same time person B exits the office across the corridor (Fig 6(b),(c)). Person B is correctly identified as a new appearance, and then exits to the bottom of the FOV of the corridor camera. Person A then enters the corridor camera from the bottom, and is mistakenly identified as a reappearance of person B (Fig 6(e)). This reflects the Markov model's belief that an appearance at the bottom of corridor camera is more likely to be someone walking along the corridor than exiting the office. This belief is quite reasonable—more people are likely to observed walking along the corridor than exiting person A's office—but wrong in this case.

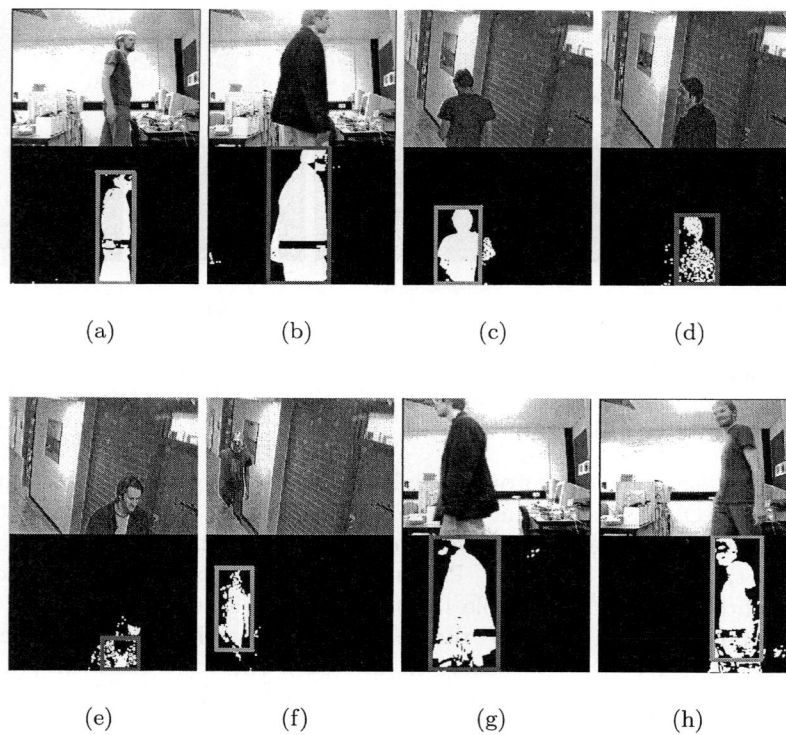

Fig. 5. Person B follows person A out of the office, then turns around. Person A then returns after person B. Both people are correctly identified, despite the fact that person B disappears and reappears. Again, frames are shown in order of time

5.1 Observations

Given the failure case in Experiment 4, it seems like it might be useful to use the appearance of each object to help identify it. However, it was found that due to the difference in lighting, camera characteristics, and their points of view, the appearance of an object could change significantly between cameras. This means that appearance can not be used in a straightforward way to disambiguate appearances and disappearances in camera FOVs. Recognising this, Javed et al. [9] learn the way appearance changes between cameras rather than using similarity of appearance to match objects between views. We intend to investigate similar approaches.

This system operates in real time, at around 5-10 frames per second. The bottleneck is the bandwidth required to capture 3 streams of video on a PC, which could be overcome using specialised capture hardware or by processing the streams on different machines. Computationally the most expensive procedure is the multimodal background subtraction update; in fact once learnt, the Markov model takes very little compute time to apply.

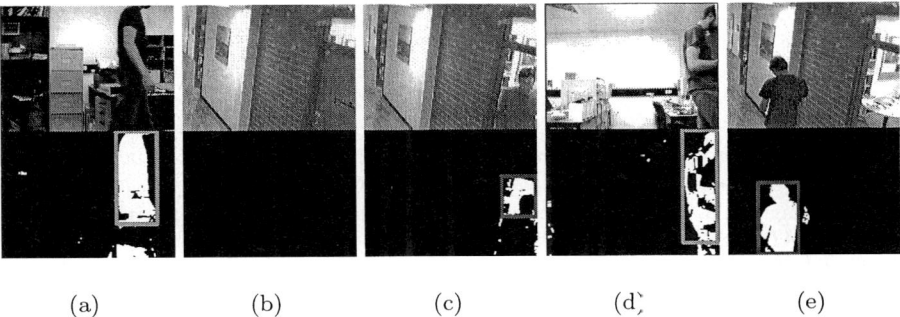

(a) (b) (c) (d) (e)

Fig. 6. A case in which the tracker fails. Person A in the blue shirt is tracked correctly to the door of his office. During this time person B leaves his office, and exits to the bottom of the FOV of camera 2. As person A enters the FOV of camera 1 from below, he is assigned the identity of person B

6 Conclusion and Future Work

In this paper we have introduced a real-time algorithm that uses a Markov model to track objects as they move between the separated FOVs of multiple cameras. We have described the way in which the parameters of the Markov model are learnt and the way it is applied to an existing single camera tracking algorithm.The feasibility of the algorithm has been demonstrated using several scenarios in our office camera network.

There are a number of extensions that could be made to this work. We could extend the Markov model to a Hidden Markov model that combines its motion model probabilistically with the output of the tracker, which would also be expressed probabilistically. It would also be useful to maximise the probability of the observed tracks over the previous N frames rather just the previous 1 frame. The Viterbi algorithm [12] is a well known method for doing this for HMMs. One drawback of Markov models, hidden or not, is that transitions between states occur instantaneously. We plan to incorporate information about transition times by storing a histogram for each transition of the durations observed for that transition during the training phase. This can then be combined with the overall transition probability to disambiguate track discontinuities based on timing.

References

1. J.K. Aggarwal and Q. Cai. Human motion analysis: A review. *Computer Vision and Image Understanding*, 73(3):428–440, March 1999.
2. D. Comaniciu and V. Ramesh. Mean shift and optimal prediction for efficient object tracking. In *ICIP00*, pages Vol III: 70–73, 2000.
3. A.R. Dick and M. J. Brooks. Issues in automated video surveillance. In *Proc. 7th International Conference on Digital Image Computing: Techniques and Applications (DICTA'03)*, pages I:195–204, Sydney, 2003.

4. A. Doucet, N. de Freitas, N. Gordon, and eds. *Sequential Monte Carlo Methods in Practice*. Springer-Verlag, 2001.
5. T. Drummond and R. Cipolla. Application of lie algebras to visual servoing. *International Journal of Computer Vision*, 37(1):21–41, 2000.
6. T. J. Ellis, D. Makris, and J.K. Black. Learning a multi-camera topology. In *Joint IEEE Workshop on Visual Surveillance and Performance Evaluation of Tracking and Surveillance (VS-PETS)*, pages 165–171, 2003.
7. T. Huang and S. Russell. Object identification in a Bayesian context. In *Proceedings of IJCAI*, pages 1276–1283, 1997.
8. M. Isard and A. Blake. Condensation–conditional density propagation for visual tracking. *International Journal of Computer Vision*, 29(1):5–28, 1998.
9. O. Javed, Z. Rasheed, K. Shafique, and M. Shah. Tracking across multiple cameras with disjoint views. In *Proc. IEEE International Conference on Computer Vision*, pages 952–957, 2003.
10. V. Kettnaker and R. Zabih. Bayesian multi-camera surveillance. In *Proc. IEEE Computer Vision and Pattern Recognition*, pages 253–259, 1999.
11. Hanna Pasula, Stuart J. Russell, Michael Ostland, and Yaacov Ritov. Tracking many objects with many sensors. In *Proceedings of IJCAI*, pages 1160–1171, 1999.
12. L. R. Rabiner. A tutorial on hidden markov models and selected apllications in speech recognition. In A. Waibel and K.-F. Lee, editors, *Readings in Speech Recognition*, pages 267–296. Kaufmann, San Mateo, CA, 1990.
13. C. Stauffer and W. E. L. Grimson. Learning patterns of activity using real-time tracking. *IEEE Transactions on Pattern Analysis and Machine Intelligence*, 22(8):747–757, 2000.
14. G. Welch and G. Bishop. An introduction to the Kalman filter. Technical Report 95-041, University of North Carolina at Chapel Hill, 1995.

Caption Detection and Removal in a TV Scene

JongBae Kim* and KyoungKwan Ahn**

*Research Center for Machine Parts and Material Processing,
University of Ulsan, Ulsan, S.Korea
**Department of Mechanical and Automotive Engineering,
University of Ulsan, S.Korea
kkahn@ulsan.ac.kr

Abstract. In this paper, we propose a caption detection and removal technique for reuse of TV scenes using the Multilayer Perceptrons (MLPs) and Genetic algorithms (GAs). The technique first detects the captions in a TV scene using the MLP-based caption detector, and then removes the detected captions using the GA-based region remover. In our technique, the caption removal problem is modeled as an optimization problem, which in our case, is solved by a cost function with isophote constraint that is minimized using a GA. The technique creates an optimal connection of all pairs of isophote disconnected by caption regions. To connect the disconnected isophote, we estimate the value of the smoothness, given by the best chromosome of the GA, and project this value in the isophote direction. Experimental results show a great possibility for automatic removal of captions in TV advertisement scenes.

1 Introduction

These days, we often see indirect advertisement captions in TV scenes. However, indirect advertisement captions are not permitted in public places. Moreover, broadcasters have demonstrated interest in reusing of archive materials for TV programs or on-line distribution to other companies and the general public. Therefore, advertisement captions or text logos are usually erased by hand after taking a picture or are taped over by sticky bands before taking a picture. Since the early days of broadcasting and photography, this work has been done by professional artists. However, these procedures require a lot of time and effort for high performance. If there were an automatic method that could remove a caption in a TV scene without loss of naturalness, it could be efficiently used where automatic removal of a caption is required. Such fields include digital video broadcasting, virtual studios, and translation services. Therefore, one motivation for this investigation comes from the need for a caption removal. For detecting captions in a frame, we used the MLP-based caption detector [1]. Neural network techniques have been applied to solve complex problems in the filed of image processing. Among the numerous neural networks, the MLP network is a particularly efficient model for classification problems [2]. Therefore, MLP networks are employed to train a set of texture discrimination tasks that minimize classification error for the given texture classes, caption region and non-caption region. Additionally, the detected caption regions are removed using a GA-based region remover.

Generally, approaches to image restoration involve optimization of some cost function with constraints [3]. For example, most commonly used cost functions are constrained least-squares (CLS), which directly incorporate prior information about an image through the inclusion of an additional term in the original least-squares cost function. The CLS can be formulated by simultaneously minimizing the data error and a measure of the roughness of the solution as follows:

$$\min_{\hat{f}} \underbrace{\int_{\Omega}(g-\hat{f})^2 d\Omega}_{term\,1} + \alpha \underbrace{\int_{\Omega}(|\nabla \hat{f}|)^2 d\Omega}_{term\,2} \quad (x,y) \in \Omega \qquad (1)$$

The first term in Eq. (1) is the same ℓ_2 residual norm appearing in the least-squares approach and ensures fidelity to the data. The second term is a constraint that captures prior knowledge about the expected behavior of f through an additional ℓ_2 penalty term involving just the image. The regularization parameter α controls the tradeoff between the two terms. This method is based on the addition of a quadratic penalty term to the standard least-squares data fidelity criterion. Usually, the second term in Eq. (1) is chosen as a derivative or gradient operator, which are the 2-D gradient or Laplacian operator, respectively. However, this method is well-known to smooth an image isotropically without preserving discontinuities in intensity. In addition, it is impossible to restore an original image using the linear technique [4]. Thus, we consider the optimization problem of removing a region, which has been disconnected by captions. To prevent the destruction of discontinuities while allowing for isotropically smoothing its uniform areas, we can solve the cost function minimization based on GAs with an isophote (curves of constant intensity) [5].

In the proposed technique, caption removal is computed by the propagation of the best chromosome only in the direction orthogonal to the contour that leads to the isophote. In addition, our technique combines anisotropic diffusion with the GA to restore smooth isophote [6]. Our method optimally connects all pairs of isophote disconnected by captions. The proposed technique views a caption removal problem as an optimization problem, which can be solved by a GA. The GA is capable of searching for global optimum in functions. The principal advantages of GAs are domain independence, non-linearity, and robustness [6]. Our technique very well maintains the surrounding information such as edge or texture. Experimental results demonstrate great possibility of automatic removal of a caption in TV scenes.

2 Overview of the Proposed Method

Given an input of a TV scene taken from a television broadcasting. Output is a removed caption scene. The proposed technique consists of a caption detector and caption remover, as illustrated in Fig 1. The method receives a frame that includes captions in the TV scenes, and then produces a frame that includes the removed captions. We assume that the captions in a frame are noise. Thus, they are automatically removed according to the information of the surrounding area. In the caption detector, the location of a caption in a frame is indicated using the MLP-based caption detector [1]. This step creates a bounding block at each caption region that covers it completely (the bounding box can be larger then the actual caption size). In the caption remover, the removal process performs each caption region detected by the previous step. Before the removal process is performed, an anisotropic diffusion process is first applied to each caption region in order to smoothly (without losing sharpness) create the isophote and reduce the noise. Then, the diffused each caption region is removed by the GA-based caption remover with an isophote constraint [6].

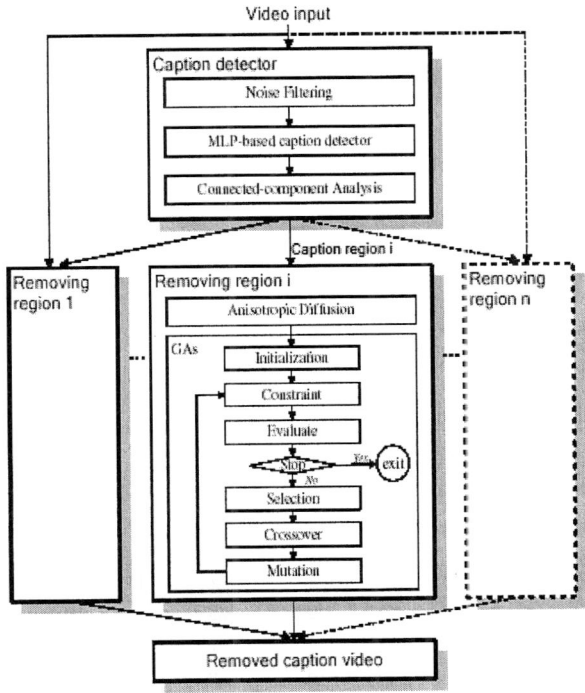

Fig. 1. Flowchart of the proposed method

3 Caption Detection Using MLPs

Caption detection is performed on individual scenes. In this section, we will explain the steps involved in caption detection. The first step is to take an input frame from a TV scene. Before any further processing is performed, the frame's edges are enhanced using a 3×3 mask. Further, a salt and pepper noise removal is performed to remove any noise that was not removed in the previous step. For this purpose we used a mean filter. The second step applies the MLP-based caption detector to the filtered image. Next, a connected component analysis is performed on caption pixels detected in the previous step. Each caption is assumed to give rise to a connected component or a part thereof. All the caption pixels that are present at a certain distance (eight-pixel neighborhood) are merged into a single connected component structure using the heuristics in Ref. [7]. This connected component structure contains the location of the pixels that are connected together. Fig. 2 shows the structure of the MLP for caption detection.

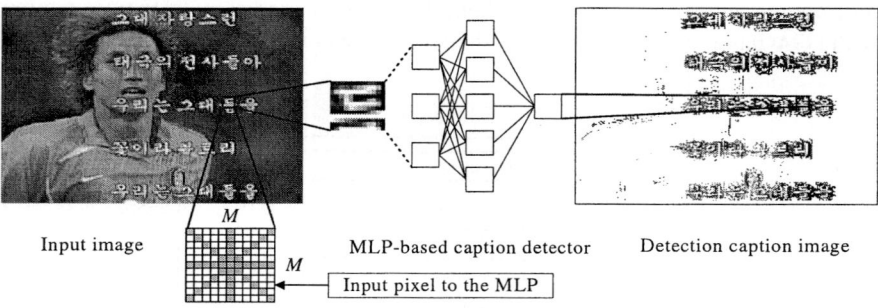

Fig. 2. Structure of the MLP for caption detection

MLPs receive an $M \times M$ pixel region of the image as the input and genetrate a binary image as output. The value of the output node is compared with a threshold value and the class of each pixel is determined. For the input node of network, we used the intensity value of region. Fig. 3 shows an example of the cross-section of an image including the caption regions. As shown in Fig. 3, the intensity of the caption regions is more specific then the intensity of the non-caption regions.

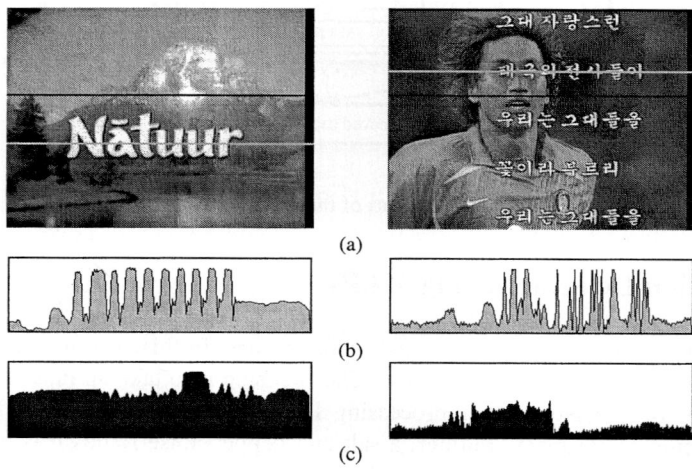

Fig. 3. Intensity variation of caption regions. (a) Input frame, (b) Intensity profile of the caption region, (c) Intensity profile of the non-caption region

After the caption region is detected, we employ a connected component anlaysis to remove the loosely connected pixels of the detected binary caption image and a morphological operator to fill-in the detected binary caption image. Next, to segment each text in the caption region, the caption region vertically and horizontally segments each character using the gradient profile analysis [8]. Fig. 4 shows the text segmentation process for the detected caption regions.

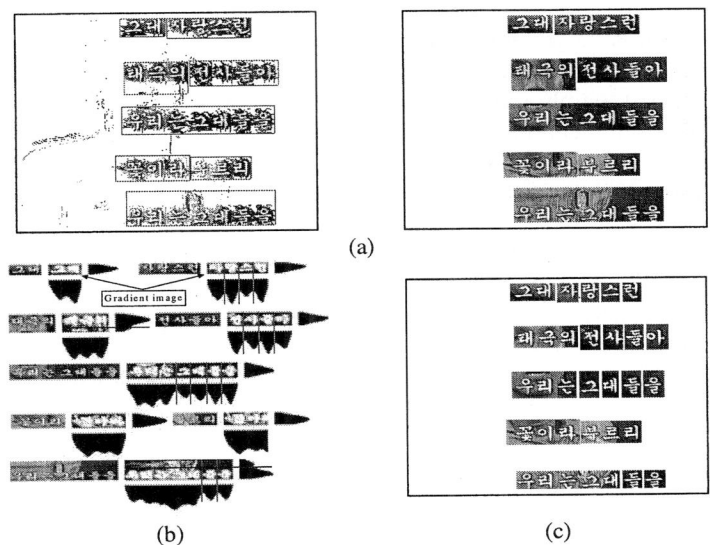

Fig. 4. Example of text segmentation in the detected caption regions. (a) the results of caption detection, (b) x and y-axis projection profiles of caption region, (c) the results of text segmentation

4 Caption Removal Using GAs

During caption removal, each caption region detected by the caption detector is removed using a GA whose inputs are a frame and each caption region. The parameter search procedures of GAs are based upon the mechanism of natural genetics, which are probabilistic in nature and exhibit global search capabilities. GAs work with a population of chromosomes, each representing a possible solution to a given problem at hand. Each chromosome is assigned a fitness value according to how good its solution to the problem is. Highly fit chromosomes are given greater opportunities to mate with other chromosomes in the population. On the other hand, the least fit individuals in the population are less likely to be selected as mates and so disappear from future generations. During each generation, the chromosomes start with random solutions that are then updated and reorganized through GA operators, such as selection, crossover and mutation [6]. After iteratively performing these operations, the chromosomes eventually converge on an optimal solution. For caption removal, the propagation of the best chromosomes is computed only in the direction orthogonal to the contour that leads to the isophote. This method creates an optimal connection of all pairs of disconnected isophote.

4.1 Initial Population and Cost Function

A chromosome that represents a solution to the problem is allocated at a pixel. We used a color vector as a chromosome to represent real values of the image. A chromosome consists of RGB feature vectors that are used to assign a fitness value to the chromosome. Fitness is defined as the minimized cost function between the estimated feature vector and the observed feature vector at the location of the chromosome in the image. The initial chromosome is randomly selected according to the pixel value of the region diffused by anisotropic diffusion. If the pixel value diffused by the diffusion process is X, the initial chromosome at the removed pixel is randomly assigned a value between $X-20$ and $X+20$. Generally, a pixel value in an image is similar to the pixel values of neighboring pixels. The cost function for each chromosome is evaluated by comparing the removed caption image with the original image. In order to find an optimal solution, we use a priori knowledge such as the constraint form of the isophote curvature evolution to reduce the artifacts of restoration. Here, the optimal solution minimizes the isophote curvature of the removed caption pixel, preserves the color values, and is similar to the isophote curvatures of neighboring pixels. The cost function is defined as follows:

$$E = \underbrace{\int_\Omega (\overline{V}_N - \hat{f})^2 d\Omega}_{term 1} + \underbrace{\alpha \int_\Omega |\nabla \hat{f}|(1+|\hat{\kappa}|) d\Omega}_{term 2} + \underbrace{\beta \int_\Omega (\overline{\kappa}_N - |\hat{\kappa}|)^2 d\Omega}_{term 3}, \quad (2)$$

where the term2 and 3 are the constraints, and $\overline{V}_N$ and $\overline{\kappa}_N$ are the average pixel value and the average isophote curvature of neighboring pixels at the restored caption pixel, respectively. $\hat{f}$ and $\hat{\kappa}$ are the estimated pixel and the estimated isophote curvature at the caption pixel to be removed. In Eq. (2), α and β are constants and N is the set of neighboring pixels of the removed caption pixel.

5 Experimental Results

All experiments were performed on a Pentium IV-1.7GHz and implemented using a MS Visual C++. The structure of the MLP-based caption detector uses two hidden layers with 40 nodes per hidden layer, an input layer with 41 nodes of an intensity value at the 11×11 region (as shown Fig. 2), and a threshold value for the output of the discrimination set at 0.5. The parameters for the GA were obtained through several test runs. The probabilities of crossover and mutation were fixed at 0.1 and 0.05, respectively. The population (assuming as initial population the one obtained by an anisotropic diffusion step) and generation size were taken as 512 (a random selection at the diffused R, G and B color channels, 8×8×8=512) and 50, respectively. As mentioned in the section 4, the control parameters of the cost function, α and β, were chosen as 0.15 and 0.3. All examples used frames from advertisement scenes that included captions over TV broadcasting. The size of each frame is 320×240 and a frame rate is 10 frames/s. Fig. 5 shows the results of caption detection and removal from the various test frames.

Fig. 5. Example of caption detection and removal. Test frames (first), detected caption regions (second), and segmented caption region (third), and removed caption frame (last).

Table 1 shows the caption detection rates in test video sequences. Each video sequence (2000 frames, 10 frame/s) is captured from the TV scenes with the various size captions. For experiment, the caption region was manually detected, and compared with the results of caption detection using the MLP-based caption detector and connected component (CC)-based caption detector [9]. The criterion for a correct detection of the caption was the same as in [1, 7]. It shows that MLP-based caption detector performs better than the CC-based caption detector, but that the MLP-based method requires more processing time. Fig. 6 shows the removal results of an image with a caption using our method. The first image in Fig. 6 shows various colors and irregular textures. The first six images of Fig. 6 – clockwise from top left – are an advertisement caption image, an image occluded by a mask, and after 5, 10, 30, and 50 generations of our method.

Table 1. Result of caption detection

Test video	Method	Detection rate (%)	Missed captions	False detections
1	MLP	97.6	8	24
	CC	91.0	15	40
2	MLP	94.5	9	19
	CC	85.7	23	31
3	MLP	95.2	6	19
	CC	81.3	27	37

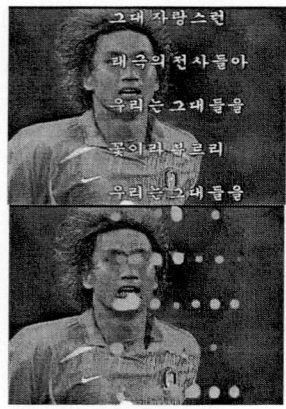 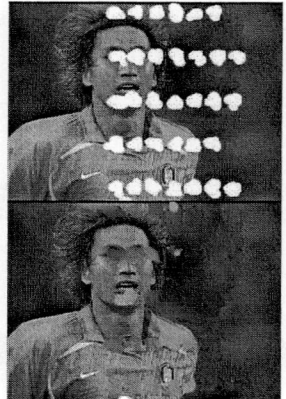 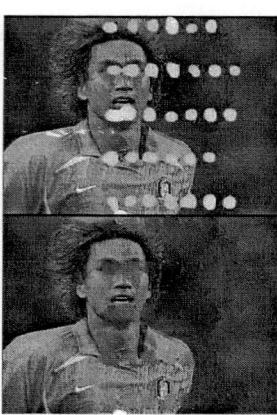

Fig. 6. Results of the caption removal

6 Conclusions

In this paper, we propose a caption detection and removal technique in a TV scene. The caption removal problem is modeled as an optimization problem that can be solved by a cost function with an isophote constraint that is minimized using a GA. In the proposed technique, we estimate the value of smoothness, given by the best chromosomes of the GA, and project this value in the isophotes direction. This method restores the inside of the region using the geometric features of the image from the surrounding area and can be used to make a natural scene. Experimental results demonstrate that the proposed method has sufficiently good performance.

Acknowledgment

This work was supported by the Korea Science and Engineering Foundation (KOSEF) through the research center for machine parts and material processing at University of Ulsan.

References

1. Jung, K.: Neural network-based text location in color images, Pattern Recognition Letter 22 (2001) 1503-1515
2. Huang, Y. L. and Chang, R. F.: Error concealment using adaptive multilayer perceptrons (MLPs) for block-based image coding, Neural comput & Applic 9 (2000) 83-92
3. Geman, D. and Reynolds, G.: Constrained restoration and the recovery of discontinuities, IEEE trans. on PAMI. 14(3) (1992) 367-383
4. Kornoribst, P., Deriche, R.: Image sequence analysis via partial differential equations, Journal of Math. Imaging and Vision 11 (1999) 5-26

5. Sara, R.: Isophotes: the key to tractable local shading analysis, Proceedings of the International Conf. Computer Analysis of Images and Patterns (1995) 416-423
6. Kim, J. B., and Kim, H. J.: Region removal and restoration using a genetic algorithm with isophote constraint, Pattern Recognition Letter 24(9) (2003) 1313-1326
7. Kim, K. I., Jung, K., Park, S. H. and Kim, H. J.: Support vector machines-based text detection in digital video, Pattern Recognition 34(2) (2001) 527-529
8. Kim, J. B., et al.,: Wavelet-based vehicle tracking for automatic traffic surveillance, Proceeding of the IEEE Tencon International Conference 1 (2001) 313-316
9. Zhong, Y., Karu, K., Jain, A. K.: Locating text in complex color images, Pattern Recognition 28(10) (1995) 1523-1535

Enhanced Importance Sampling: Unscented Auxiliary Particle Filtering for Visual Tracking

Chunhua Shen, Anton van den Hengel, Anthony Dick, and Michael J. Brooks

School of Computer Science, The University of Adelaide,
Adelaide, SA 5005, Australia
Cooperative Research Centre for Sensor Signal and Information Processing,
Mawson Lakes, SA 5095, Australia
{chhshen, anton, ard, mjb}@cs.adelaide.edu.au

Abstract. The particle filter has attracted considerable attention in visual tracking due to its relaxation of the linear and Gaussian restrictions in the state space model. It is thus more flexible than the Kalman filter. However, the conventional particle filter uses system transition as the proposal distribution, leading to poor sampling efficiency and poor performance in visual tracking. It is not a trivial task to design satisfactory proposal distributions for the particle filter. In this paper, we introduce an improved particle filtering framework into visual tracking, which combines the unscented Kalman filter and the auxiliary particle filter. The efficient unscented auxiliary particle filter (UAPF) uses the unscented transformation to predict one-step ahead likelihood and produces more reasonable proposal distributions, thus reducing the number of particles required and substantially improving the tracking performance. Experiments on real video sequences demonstrate that the UAPF is computationally efficient and outperforms the conventional particle filter and the auxiliary particle filter.

1 Introduction

The particle filter (PF), also known as sequential Monte Carlo or CONDENSATION [1], has been extensively studied for the sequential time series inference due to its relaxation of the linearity and Gaussianity constraints of the Kalman filter (KF). This method represents the posterior distribution of the states with a group of discrete samples/particles. During the filtering process, these particles are updated to maintain the posterior with the importance sampling technique. In theory the PF algorithm can deal with any nonlinearities or distributions.

In the context of computer vision, its applications includes visual tracking [2, 3, 4, 5, 6], robot localisation [7], structure from motion [8] *etc.* Despite its successful application in those cases, it usually requires a considerable amount of discrete particles to effectively approximate the continuous probabilistic distributions; this results in low efficiency and even prohibitive computational burden for high dimensional state space problems. One solution is to design "optimal" proposal sampling distributions for the importance sampling process, generating less particles in the low posterior probability areas, which contribute little to the state estimation.

The conventional PF [2] for visual tracking adopts the dynamic transition prior (the probabilistic model of the states' evolution) as its proposal distribution. When the dynamic motion model can not capture the subject's motion accurately, the motion predicted by the prior deviates from the true trajectory. This occurs frequently when tracking with a conventional particle filter. In such cases, the likelihood distribution is situated in the prior's tail and sampling from such a prior fails to generate sufficient particles in the high posterior areas [9]. Several approaches have been advanced to relocate the particles to the dominant modes in the likelihood or posterior distribution space with a stochastic or deterministic optimisation method [3, 4, 5, 10, 11].

Alternatively, a learned dynamic model instead of a simple predefined autoregressive model yields better sampling [12, 13]. Nevertheless, such approaches are usually only available for specific motions such as cyclic human walking.

Another way is to design a better proposal. As an *ad hoc* approach, in [14] an auxiliary colour tracker is used to generate proposal distributions for the main tracker. The limitation of this method is that the auxiliary tracker might fail and produce false proposal distributions. A more general approach is "optimal filtering" [15]. It has been shown that the "optimal" importance function should take the most recent observations into consideration [15].

An elegant solution to this problem is the auxiliary particle filter (APF) [9] which generates particles from an importance distribution depending on the most recent observations and then sample from the estimated posterior using this importance distribution. APF has been shown to outperform traditional CONDENSATION algorithm in many applications [7, 9]. In [6] Nait-Charif *et al* have compared APF and CONDENSATION in the context of tracking a person in an overhead view, and better performances are observed when using the APF algorithm. But the improvement is very limited. The reason is that the APF algorithm cannot approximate accurately the one-step ahead likelihood which plays an important role in the algorithm. In this paper, we use an unscented transformation (UT) to alleviate this problem (more discussion is presented in Section 2).

The KF can be used to incorporate the current observation into the PF and consequently to improve the distribution proposal. The unscented particle filter (UPF) is a combination of the unscented Kalman filter (UKF) and the generic PF [16] which has proven to be a better solution for particle filtering based visual tracking [17, 18].

In the context of signal processing, Andrieu *et al* combines UT, UKF and APF for a *jump* Markov system and they obtain promising performances in the application of time-varying autoregressions [19]. Our work is motivated mostly by their strategy.

In this paper we introduce the enhanced importance sampling strategy — the UAPF technique, which uses the UKF to approximate the one-step ahead likelihood for the APF. At the same time, the UKF generates the proposal distributions as the UPF does. This step can utilise the results obtained by the previous UT approximation step, hence little extra computation is involved. This approach then yields efficient sampling and substantial improvement over the conventional PF and the APF algorithm. We apply the UAPF to the visual tracking problem. Experiments on real video sequences demonstrate that the UAPF is computationally efficient and outperforms both the conventional PF and APF.

The structure of the paper is as follows. After the introduction in Section 1, we discuss the optimal sampling technique and present the UAPF algorithm in detail in Section 2. In Section 3 we discuss the application to visual tracking. Experiments on real video sequences are also presented in Section 3, followed by concluding remarks in Section 4.

2   The Unscented Auxiliary Particle Filter

To make this paper self-contained, we first briefly review the technique of Monte Carlo Bayesian filtering, which is described in more detail in [1]. We then summarise the proposed auxiliary particle filter algorithm. Essentially it is an implementation of the APF depending on the UKF. This sampling strategy leads to an enhanced efficient importance sampling distribution and an accurate approximation over the conventional APF. Appealingly, this combination does not introduce much extra computation, which is a critically important factor in real-time visual tracking.

2.1   Bayesian Filtering and the Particle Filter

Visual tracking is usually formulated as Bayesian filtering. Given the Markovian dynamic model $p(\mathbf{x}_t|\mathbf{x}_{t-1})$:

$$\mathbf{x}_t = \mathbf{g}(\mathbf{x}_{t-1}, \mathbf{u}_t) \tag{1}$$

and the observation model $p(\mathbf{z}_t|\mathbf{x}_t)$:

$$\mathbf{z}_t = \mathbf{h}(\mathbf{x}_t, \mathbf{v}_t) \tag{2}$$

at time t, the task is to infer the latent state vectors $\mathbf{x}_t$ based on the observation sequences $\mathbf{z}_{1:t}$. In Eqs. (1) (2), $\mathbf{g}(\cdot,\cdot)$ and $\mathbf{h}(\cdot,\cdot)$ are the system dynamics model and observation model, respectively. Usually they are highly nonlinear. The process and measurement noises at time t are given by $\mathbf{u}_t$ and $\mathbf{v}_t$.

The inference is achieved by

$$p(\mathbf{x}_t|\mathbf{z}_{1:t}) \propto p(\mathbf{z}_t|\mathbf{x}_t)p(\mathbf{x}_t|\mathbf{z}_{1:t-1}) \tag{3}$$

where the prior is the previous posterior propagated across the temporal axis,

$$p(\mathbf{x}_t|\mathbf{z}_{1:t-1}) = \int p(\mathbf{x}_t|\mathbf{x}_{t-1})p(\mathbf{x}_{t-1}|\mathbf{z}_{1:t-1})d\mathbf{x}_{t-1}. \tag{4}$$

When the dynamic and observation models are nonlinear and/or non-Gaussian, the above posterior cannot be analytically computed and one has to resort to numerical approximations such as particle filters. In the visual tracking problem, the dynamic model can be approximated by a linear model while the observation model is usually highly nonlinear.

The essential idea of the particle filter is that the posterior is approximated by a series of discrete particles, each of which includes a state vector $\mathbf{x}_t$ and an associated weight w_t: $\{\mathbf{x}_t^{(n)}, w_t^{(n)}\}_{n=1}^N$, where $\sum_{n=1}^N w_t^{(n)} = 1$ holds. The posterior is formulated as $p(\mathbf{x}_t|\mathbf{z}_{1:t}) = \sum_{n=1}^N w_t^{(n)} \delta(\mathbf{x}_t - \mathbf{x}_t^{(n)})$, where $\delta(\cdot)$ is the Dirac function. Then the integral in Eq. (4) is tractable with this numerical approximation.

Suppose we can sample the particles from an importance density $q(\cdot)$, i.e. $\mathbf{x}_t^{(n)} \sim q(\mathbf{x}_t|\mathbf{x}_{t-1}^{(n)}, \mathbf{z}_{1:t}), (n = 1, \ldots, N)$, then each particle's weight is set to

$$w_t^{(n)} \propto \frac{p(\mathbf{z}_t|\mathbf{x}_t^{(n)}) p(\mathbf{x}_t^{(n)}|\mathbf{x}_{t-1}^{(n)})}{q(\mathbf{x}_t|\mathbf{x}_{t-1}^{(n)}, \mathbf{z}_{1:t})}. \tag{5}$$

Before or after the importance sampling step, a selective re-sampling step is adopted to ensure the efficiency of the particles' evolution [1].

To summarise, we present the complete algorithm for a conventional PF in Fig. 1.

- *Initialisation*:
  Set $t = 1$. Sample N particles $\{\mathbf{x}_{t-1}^{(n)}, w_{t-1}^{(n)}\}_{n=1}^N$ from the prior $p(x_0)$.
- *Re-sampling*:
  Re-sample to obtain N replacement particles $\{\mathbf{x}_{t-1}^{(n)}, \frac{1}{N}\}_{n=1}^N$, according to the weights $w_{t-1}^{(n)}$.
- *Importance sampling*:
  For $n = 1, \ldots, N$, sample N particles $\mathbf{x}_t^{(n)}$ from the importance proposal $q(\mathbf{x}_t|\mathbf{x}_{t-1}^{(n)}, \mathbf{z}_{1:t})$, and evaluate the weights according to Eq. (5). Then normalise the weights.
- Set $t = t + 1$, go to the *Re-sampling* step to process the next frame.

Fig. 1. The particle filtering algorithm

The proposal distribution $q(\cdot)$ is critically important for a successful particle filter because it concerns putting the sampling particles in the useful areas where the posterior is significant. It is known that sampling using the dynamic transition model as the proposal distribution is usually inefficient when the likelihood is situated in the prior's tail or it is highly peaked. In visual tracking the dynamical models cannot accurately predict the true motion trajectory due to unexpected motion. In such cases the conventional PF which samples from the dynamic model is quite likely to put most of the particles in the wrong areas of the state space.

2.2 The Auxiliary Particle Filter

The APF is an improved sampling strategy which performs approximately "optimal" sampling and utilises the most recent observations [9]. It is a one-step look-ahead procedure, in which a particle is propagated to the next time frame in order to help the sampling from the posterior. However, the predictive likelihood is only available by an approximation, i.e., the predictive likelihood $p(\mathbf{z}_t|\mathbf{x}_{t-1}^{(n)})$ is approximated by $\widetilde{p}(\mathbf{z}_t|\mathbf{x}_{t-1}^{(n)})$.

In order to put the particles in useful areas of the state space, the APF re-samples the particles $\{\mathbf{x}_{t-1}^{(n)}, \frac{1}{N}\}_{n=1}^{N}$ according to the values $\pi_t^{(n)} = w_{t-1}^{(n)} \cdot \widetilde{p}(\mathbf{z}_t|\mathbf{x}_{t-1}^{(n)})$. Similar to the standard importance sampling, we sample from a proposal distribution $\mathbf{x}_t^{(n)} \sim q(\mathbf{x}_t|\mathbf{x}_{t-1}^{(n)}, \mathbf{z}_{1:t})$, then the weight associated to each particle should be set to

$$w_t^{(n)} \propto \frac{p(\mathbf{z}_t|\mathbf{x}_t^{(n)})p(\mathbf{x}_t^{(n)}|\mathbf{x}_{t-1}^{(n)})}{q(\mathbf{x}_t|\mathbf{x}_{t-1}^{(n)}, \mathbf{z}_{1:t})\widetilde{p}(\mathbf{z}_t|\mathbf{x}_{t-1}^{(n)})}. \tag{6}$$

In [9] Pitt et al use the values likely to be generated by the dynamic model $p(\mathbf{x}_t|\mathbf{x}_{t-1}^{(n)})$ as the approximation. Although the APF outperforms the conventional PF in many applications [7,9], as pointed out in [19], this approximation of the predictive likelihood could be very poor and lead to performance even poorer than the standard importance sampling if the dynamic model $p(\mathbf{x}_t|\mathbf{x}_{t-1})$ is quite scattered and the likelihood $p(\mathbf{z}_t|\mathbf{x}_t)$ varies significantly over the prior $p(\mathbf{x}_t|\mathbf{x}_{t-1})$. In [6] the authors observe that the APF achieves a little improvement over the stand particle filters in the context of visual tracking.

2.3 The Unscented Transformation and the Unscented Kalman Filter

In this subsection we briefly introduce the UT and UKF. The UKF is the best Kalman filter for nonlinear estimation applications. By including the noise component in the state space, the UKF can be implemented naturally using the UT, which is the basis of UKF and UPF.

Using the UT, the mean and covariance of the Taylor expansion of a nonlinear transformation can be guaranteed to be accurate up to second order. Instead of linearizing using Jacobian matrices, the UT/UKF uses a deterministic sampling strategy to capture the mean and covariance with a small set of carefully selected points named "sigma points" [20]. Therefore, in accuracy, the UT/UKF is better than the extended Kalman filter which approximates the nonlinear transformation with a first-order linearisation. The UKF is also more computationally efficient due to its avoiding the calculation of Jacobian matrices. Note that, unlike the PF, both the EKF and UKF assume unimodal distributions.

Consider the nonlinear tracking problem modelled by the state-space equations (1) and (2), we select $2L+1$ scaled sigma points $\{\widehat{\mathbf{x}}_{t-1}^{(l)}, \widehat{w}_{\mathrm{m},t-1}^{(l)}, \widehat{w}_{\mathrm{P},t-1}^{(l)}\}_{l=0}^{2L}$ at time frame $t-1$, where $\widehat{w}_{\mathrm{m},t-1}^{(l)}$ and $\widehat{w}_{\mathrm{P},t-1}^{(l)}$ are the weights associated with each sigma point[1]. Then the sigma points are propagated through the nonlinear dynamic system eq. (1) ($l = 0, \ldots, 2L$),

$$\widehat{\mathbf{x}}_{t|t-1}^{(l)} = \mathbf{g}(\widehat{\mathbf{x}}_{t-1}^{(l)}, \mathbf{0}). \tag{7}$$

Compute the scaled mean and covariance of $\widehat{\mathbf{x}}_{t|t-1}^{(l)}$

$$\widetilde{\mathbf{x}}_{t|t-1} = \sum_{l=0}^{L} \widehat{w}_{m,t-1}^{(l)} \widehat{\mathbf{x}}_{t|t-1}^{(l)}, \tag{8}$$

$$\widetilde{\mathbf{P}}_{t|t-1} = \sum_{l=0}^{L} \widehat{w}_{P,t-1}^{(l)} (\widehat{\mathbf{x}}_{t|t-1}^{(l)} - \widetilde{\mathbf{x}}_{t|t-1})^{\mathrm{T}} (\widehat{\mathbf{x}}_{t|t-1}^{(l)} - \widetilde{\mathbf{x}}_{t|t-1}). \tag{9}$$

Note that we approximate $\mathbf{x}_{t|t-1}$ and $\mathbf{P}_{t|t-1}$ with the sample mean and covariance of the sigma points set. With the measurement model Eq. (2), we can similarly approximate $\widetilde{\mathbf{z}}_{t|t-1}$ and the covariance by calculating the sample mean and covariance of $\widehat{\mathbf{z}}_{t|t-1}^{(l)} = \mathbf{h}(\widehat{\mathbf{x}}_{t|t-1}^{(l)}, \mathbf{0})$, $l = 0, \ldots, 2L$. In order to implement the UKF, the cross-covariance needs to be calculated in the same way. Finally through *time update* and *measurement update* we can estimate $\mathbf{x}_{t|t}$ and $\mathbf{P}_{t|t}$ with the Kalman filter [20]. With Eq. (8) and the likelihood model the predicted likelihood $\widetilde{p}(\mathbf{z}_t|\mathbf{x}_{t-1}^{(n)})$ can be easily calculated. Moreover, this method also has the advantage of being able to compute the proposal $q(\mathbf{x}_t^{(n)}|\mathbf{x}_{t-1}^{(n)}, \mathbf{z}_{1:t})$ [16, 17].

2.4 The Unscented Auxiliary Particle Filter

Based on the APF and UKF techniques presented above, we use the UT and UKF to compute both the predicted likelihood $\widetilde{p}(\mathbf{z}_t|\mathbf{x}_{t-1}^{(n)})$ and the importance proposal $q(\mathbf{x}_t^{(n)}|\mathbf{x}_{t-1}^{(n)}, \mathbf{z}_{1:t})$. The second step is performed exactly the same as the UPF does. See [16] for more details. This combination yields an enhanced importance sampling strategy—the unscented auxiliary particle filter. For clarity we summarise the unscented auxiliary particle filter algorithm in Fig. 2. Note that a Markov transition kernel with the posterior distribution, such as Metroplis or Gibbs kernel, can be applied to each particle to rejuvenate the trajectory of the particles. This additional step can be used to deal with complex high-dimensional models [16, 22].

3 Visual Tracking with the Unscented Auxiliary Particle Filter

In this section, we describe a visual contour tracking system based on the UAPF technique.

---

[1] Refer to [21] for how to select the sigma points and calculate the weights.

- *Initialisation*:
  Set $t = 1$. Sample N particles $\{\mathbf{x}_{t-1}^{(n)}, w_{t-1}^{(n)}\}_{n=1}^{N}$ from the prior.
- *Auxiliary re-sampling*:
  Re-sample to obtain N replacement particles $\{\mathbf{x}_{t-1}^{(n)}, \frac{1}{N}\}_{n=1}^{N}$, according to the auxiliary weights $\pi_t^{(n)} = w_{t-1}^{(n)} \cdot \widetilde{p}(\mathbf{z}_t|\mathbf{x}_{t-1}^{(n)})$, with normalisation $\sum_{i=1}^{N} \pi_t^{(n)} = 1$. The predicted likelihood is obtained by unscented transformation.
- *Unscented importance sampling*:
  1. Update particles $\mathbf{x}_t^{(n)}$. Estimate the mean and covariance of the state vector, $\widetilde{\mathbf{x}}_t^{(n)}$ and $\widetilde{\mathbf{P}}_{t|t-1}^{(n)}$, with the unscented Kalman filter.
  2. Sample N particles $\{\mathbf{x}_t^{(n)}, w_t^{(n)}\}_{n=1}^{N}$ from the proposal distribution
  $$q(\mathbf{x}_t^{(n)}|\mathbf{x}_{t-1}^{(n)}, \mathbf{z}_{1:t}) = \mathcal{N}(\mathbf{x}_t; \widetilde{\mathbf{x}}_t^{(n)}, \widetilde{\mathbf{P}}_{t|t-1}^{(n)}),$$
  where $\mathcal{N}(\cdot; \cdot, \cdot)$ is the Gaussian distribution.
  3. Compute the particle weights as
  $$w_t^{(n)} = \frac{p(\mathbf{z}_t|\mathbf{x}_t^{(n)}) p(\mathbf{x}_t^{(n)}|\mathbf{x}_{t-1}^{(n)})}{\widetilde{p}(\mathbf{z}_t|\mathbf{x}_{t-1}^{(n)}) q(\mathbf{x}_t^{(n)}|\mathbf{x}_{t-1}^{(n)}, \mathbf{z}_{1:t})}.$$
- Set $t = t + 1$, go to the *Auxiliary re-sampling* step to process the next frame.

Fig. 2. The unscented auxiliary particle filtering algorithm

3.1 The State Space and Dynamics Model

The visual contours we track are elliptic-shaped. Instead of using B-spline representations to model relatively complex shapes [18, 23], we model the shape representations with an ellipse which can be modelled by 5 parameters $\mathbf{x} = \{(O_x, O_y), (R_x, R_y), \theta\}$, which are the centre, axis lengths and orientation angle, respectively, as depicted in Fig. 3.

As most of the motions are full of uncertainties, it is quite difficult to model these motions with an auto-regression (AR) model (or more complex, a mixture of AR models), except for some cyclic motions such as human walking [24]. Even worse, in many scenarios, the camera itself is moving randomly, so we have to consider a combination of the camera's complex movement (pan/tilt/zoom) and the tracked object's motion, it is more unrealistic to learn the dynamic model. Thus it could be problematic to use a predefined first- or second-order AR model to capture the motion of a long video sequence. Consequently to use a motion prior as the sampling proposal could fail to generate particles in the area where the likelihood is significant. However, it is not this paper's intention to explore an elegant motion model. Rather, we assume a constant velocity model for the ellipse centre's motion while a Gaussian random walk for the scale change and the orientation angle's motion, because compared with the global motion of the object, these changes are relatively slower and more difficult to capture.

3.2 The Observation Model and Likelihood Model

The ellipse is centred at (O_x, O_y) and K measurement lines $\varphi^{(k)}$, $(k=1,\ldots,K)$ are constructed passing through the intersection point $(C_x^{(k)}, C_y^{(k)})$, $(k=1,\ldots,K)$ and the ellipse centre (See Fig. 3). Given the current state $\mathbf{x}$, the ellipse in the image coordinate is determined. The measurement line $\varphi^{(k)}$ is also determined. By jointly solving the ellipse equation and the measurement line equation, the intersection point $(C_x^{(k)}, C_y^{(k)})$ can be easily obtained. The observation Eq. (2) is written as,

$$\mathbf{z}_t = \mathbf{h}(\mathbf{x}_t, \mathbf{v}_t) = (C_x^{(k)}, C_y^{(k)}) + \mathbf{v}_t, \quad (k=1,\ldots,K), \tag{10}$$

as stated in Eq. (2), $\mathbf{v}_t$ is the measurement noise. In this paper we assume it is a Gaussian distribution.

Calculating the likelihood is based on this ellipse. As in [18, 23] a Canny edge detector is applied along each measurement line $\varphi^{(k)}$ which has a fixed length L_M. Due to the cluttered background, multiple hypothesis points $\mathbf{z}^{(k)} = \{z_1^{(k)}, \ldots, z_{n_l}^{(k)}\}$[2], may be detected. Among them, at most one point is the true observation belonging to the tracked shape. Under the assumption that (1) the true edge point is normally distributed with zero mean and variance σ^2, (2) the clutter is a Poisson process with density λ, and (3) the density of the clutter features is uniform on the measurement line, the likelihood of the observation at measurement line k is [2, 18],

$$p(\mathbf{z}_t^{(k)}|\mathbf{x}_t) \propto 1 + \frac{1}{\sqrt{2\pi}\sigma h_p \lambda} \sum_{i=1}^{n_l} \exp\left[-\frac{|z_i^{(k)}|^2}{2\sigma^2}\right], \tag{11}$$

where h_p is the prior probability that no true contour edge is detected and $|z_i^{(k)}|$ is the distance of the detected feature point i from the contour. n_l is the number of detected feature points.

Assuming that the feature outputs on a distinct normal line are statistically independent, the overall likelihood for K lines which are roughly even around the ellipse is

$$p(\mathbf{z}_t|\mathbf{x}_t) = \prod_{k=1}^{K} p(\mathbf{z}_t^{(k)}|\mathbf{x}_t). \tag{12}$$

Note that the innovation calculation in [17], which is needed by the measurement update, involves estimation of the mixing weight associated with each detected point; we avoid this estimation by assuming the clutter is uniformly distributed along the measurement line and the detected edges have the same intensities.

---

[2] In the 2D image coordinate, $z_i^{(k)}$ is $(C_x^{(k)}, C_y^{(k)})$. For clarity we omit the time index t.

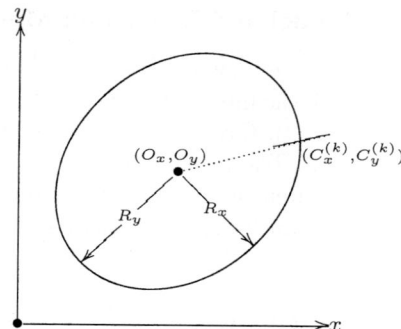

Fig. 3. The state space and the observation model

3.3 Evaluation

We evaluate the UAPF tracking system on two video sequences[3]. The resolution of both of the image sequences is 128 × 96 and they are sampled at 10 frames per second, both in typical office environments.

In these experiments, all the parameters concerned with the particle filter and the measurement process are the same: $N = 500$ particles, the length of measurement line $L_M = 8$ pixels, $\sigma = 4$ pixels and $K = 25$ measurement rays. We start the particle filter by hand. That means the initial states of the particles are manually tuned and the parameters about the dynamical AR model are obtained by analysing the first several frames.

As pointed out in [6], similar results are observed in our experiments that the auxiliary particle filter could merely trivially improve the tracking performances over the conventional PF, when tracking poorly modelled motion. So in this section we only present the comparison between the results obtained by conventional PF and those by the UAPF.

Fig. 4 shows the tracking results on the face tracking with a cluttered background. We see that at frame 18 the conventional PF is easily distracted by the cluttered background when the the head moves in a direction different from what the dynamical model predicts. For the UAPF technique, the current observation is taken into account, so it can get a relatively accurate predicted likelihood which is utilised to generate better proposal distribution. Consequently the particles are placed effectively in those useful areas with significant posterior. Then the UAPF can track the image sequence successfully.

Fig 5 shows the results on a challenging image sequence. The human face is moving back and forth quite quickly. The tracker is easily confused by the clutters when the prior fails to predict the object's motion. The conventional PF tracker fails and never recovers from frame 7 on. However, with the better proposal

---

[3] The test image sequences (courtesy of Dr. Birchfield) are available at the URL address: http://robotics.stanford.edu/~birch/headtracker/seq/

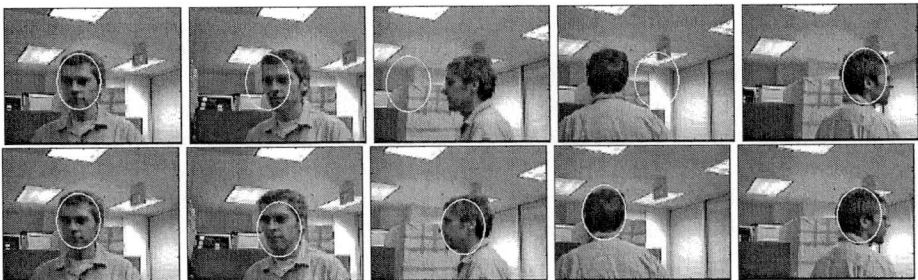

Fig. 4. Tracking results with the conventional PF (top) and the UAPF (bottom). From left to right, the frame numbers are 3, 18, 31, 40 and 50. From frame 18 on, the motion of the tracked object moves towards the inverse direction of the pre-assumed motion direction which makes the conventional PF lose the target. In contrast, the UAPF can track the whole image sequence successfully

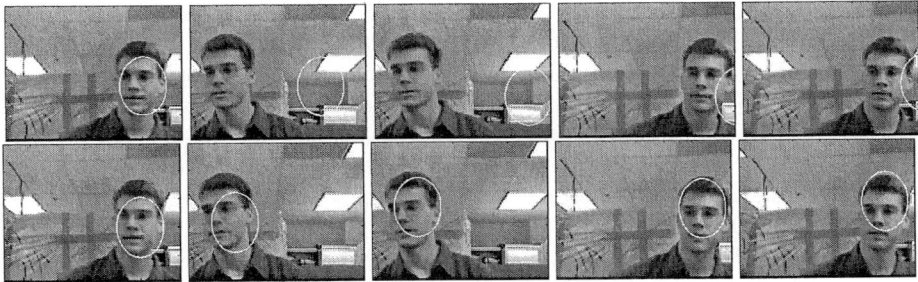

Fig. 5. Tracking results with the conventional PF (top) and the UAPF (bottom). From left to right, the frame numbers are 4, 7, 15, 30. At frame 7, the conventional PF tracker is trapped in a false region when the subject's face changes its motion direction suddenly. The conventional PF tracker fails for most the remaining frames and never be recovered

distributions, the UAPF tracker can track the whole sequence successfully. Please see the tracking video for details[4].

4 Discussion and Conclusion

We have introduced an enhanced importance sampling technique, termed UAPF, for particle filtering in the framework of visual tracking. The UAPF uses the unscented transformation to efficiently predict one-step ahead likelihood and produces more reasonable proposal distributions. We further apply this strategy

---

[4] The tracking results described in this paper can be accessed at the URL address: http://www.cs.adelaide.edu.au/~vision/demo/

to a variety of visual tracking sequences. Experiments on these real-world video sequences show that the UAPF is computationally efficient and outperforms the conventional particle filter and the auxiliary particle filter.

As pointed out in Section 2.4 this method can integrate Markov chain Monte Carlo (MCMC) steps to explore the posterior space, yielding an improved hybrid Monte Carlo filtering [5]. We plan to apply this combination to a high-dimensional problem such as articulated human tracking in which the conventional particle filter is usually deficient [4, 5, 25].

References

1. Doucet, A., de Freitas, N., Gordon, N., eds.: Sequential Monte Carlo Methods in Practice, New York, Springer-Verlag (2001)
2. Isard, M., Blake, A.: CONDENSATION – Conditional density propagation for visual tracking. International Journal of Computer Vision **29** (1998) 5–28
3. Cham, T.J., Rehg, J.M.: A multiple hypothesis approach to figure tracking. In: IEEE Conference on Computer Vision and Pattern Recognition. Volume 2., Fort Collins, Colorado (1999) 239–245
4. Deutscher, J., Blake, A., Reid, I.: Articulated body motion capture by annealed particle filtering. In: IEEE Conference on Computer Vision and Pattern Recognition. (2000)
5. Choo, K., Fleet, D.: People tracking using hybrid Monte Carlo filtering. In: IEEE International Conference on Computer Vision. Volume 2., Vancouver, Canada (2001) 321–328
6. Nait-Charif, H., McKenna, S.J.: Tracking poorly modelled motion using particle filters with iterated likelihood weighting. In: Asian Conference on Computer Vision, Jeju Island, Korea (2004)
7. Vlassis, N., Terwijn, B., Krose, B.: Auxiliary particle filter robot localization from high-dimensional sensor observations. In: IEEE International Conference on Robotics and Automation. Volume 1. (2002) 7–12
8. Qian, G., Chellappa, R.: Structure from motion using sequential Monte Carlo methods. International Journal of Computer Vision **59** (2004) 5–31
9. Pitt, M.K., Shephard, N.: Filtering via simulation: Auxiliary particle filter. Journal of the American Statistical Association **94** (1999) 590–599
10. Chang, C., Ansari, R.: Kernel particle filter: Iterative sampling for efficient visual tracking. In: IEEE International Conference on Image Processing, Barcelona, Spain (2003)
11. Shan, C., Wei, Y., Tan, T., Ojardias, F.: Real time hand tracking by combining particle filtering and mean shift. In: 6th International Conference on Automatic Face and Gesture Recognition, Seoul, Korea (2004)
12. Blake, A., North, B., Isard, M.: Learning multi-class dynamics. In: Advances in Neural Information Processing Systems, The MIT Press (1999) 389–395
13. Pavlovic, V., Rehg, J., MacCormick, J.: Learning switching linear models of human motion. In: Advances in Neural Information Processing Systems, The MIT Press (2000) 981–987

[14] Isard, M., Blake, A.: ICONDENSATION: Unifying low-level and high-level tracking in a stochastic framework. In: 5th European Conference Computer Vision. Volume 1. (1998) 893–908
[15] Doucet, A., Godsill, S., Andrieu, C.: On sequential sampling Monte Carlo sampling methods for Bayesian filtering. Statistics and Computing **10** (2000) 197–208
[16] van der Merwe, R., Doucet, A., de Freitas, N., Wan, E.: The unscented particle filter. Technical Report CUED/F-INFENG/TR 380, Cambridge University Department of Engineering, UK (2000) available at http://cslu.cse.ogi.edu/nsel/research/ukf.html.
[17] Rui, Y., Chen, Y.: Better proposal distributions: Object tracking using unscented particle filter. In: IEEE Conference on Computer Vision and Pattern Recognition. Volume 2., Kauai, Hawaii (2001) 786–793
[18] Li, P., Zhang, T., Pece, A.E.C.: Visual contour tracking based on particle filters. Image and Vision Computing **21** (2003) 111–123
[19] Andrieu, C., Davy, M., Doucet, A.: Efficient particle filtering for jump Markov systems. application to time-varying autoregressions. IEEE Transactions on Signal Processing **51** (2003) 1762–1770
[20] Wan, E.A., van der Merwe, R.: The unscented Kalman filter. In Haykin, S., ed.: Kalman Filtering and Neural Networks. Wiley Publishing (2001)
[21] Julier, S.J., Uhlmann, J.K.: The scaled unscented transformation. In: IEEE American Control Conference, Anchorage AK, USA, IEEE (2002) 4555–4559
[22] Andrieu, C., de Freitas, N., Doucet, A., Jordan, M.I.: An introduction to MCMC for machine learning. Machine Learning **50** (2003) 5–43
[23] Blake, A., Isard, M.: Active Contours. Spinger, Berlin (1998)
[24] Agarwal, A., Triggs, B.: Tracking articulated motion using a mixture of autoregressive models. In: 8th European Conference on Computer Vision. Volume 3., Prague, Czech Republic (2004)
[25] Deutscher, J., Davison, A.J., Reid, I.: Automatic partitioning of high dimensional search spaces associated with articulated body motion capture. In: IEEE Conference on Computer Vision and Pattern Recognition. (2001)

Face Recognition Using Wavelet Transform and Non-negative Matrix Factorization

Neo Han Foon, Andrew Teoh Beng Jin, and David Ngo Chek Ling

Faculty of Information Science and Technology (FIST), Multimedia University,
Jalan Ayer Keroh Lama, Bukit Beruang,
75450 Melaka, Malaysia
{hfneo, bjteoh, david.ngo}@mmu.edu.my

Abstract. This paper demonstrates a novel subspace projection technique via Non-Negative Matrix Factorization (NMF) to represent human facial image in low frequency subband, which is able to realize through the wavelet transform. Wavelet transform (WT), is used to reduce the noise and produce a representation in the low frequency domain, and hence making the facial images insensitive to facial expression and small occlusion. After wavelet decomposition, NMF is performed to produce region or part-based representations of the images. Non-negativity is a useful constraint to generate expressiveness in the reconstruction of faces. The simulation results on Essex and ORL database show that the hybrid of NMF and the best wavelet filter will yield better verification rate and shorter training time. The optimum results of 98.5% and 95.5% are obtained from Essex and ORL Database, respectively. These results are compared with our baseline method, Principal Component Analysis (PCA).

1 Introduction

Faces play an important role in the primary focus of attention in social intercourse, and to identify and verify an identity. Human has the ability to recognize thousand of faces learned throughout their lifetime. Therefore, face recognition is one of the most remarkable abilities of human vision. With its extensive and robust application in security systems, identification of criminals, assistance with speech recognition systems, surveillances and user identifications, it has become a significant research area to the physicists and scientists worldwide.

Unlike human beings who have the excellent capability to recognize different faces, machines are still lacking of this aptitude due to its variation in illuminations, complex backgrounds, visual angles, facial expressions and therefore, face recognition has become a complex and challenge task.

In the early study, [1, 2] found that information in low spatial frequency bands have a dominant role in face recognition. Thereafter, [3] shows that low-frequency components contribute to the global description, while the high-frequency components contribute to the finer details required in the identification task. Nastar et al. [4] have observed the relationship between variation in facial appearance and their deformation spectrum. They found that facial expressions and small occlusions affect the high-frequency spectrum whereas changes in pose or scale of a face affect their low frequency spectrum. Only a change in face will affect all frequency components. Bow [5] demonstrates that the quality of the reconstructed image is very good if the image is restored with the lower half-frequency spectrum. The aforesaid show that the low-frequency components are already sufficient for recognition. Therefore, wavelet transform is proposed for facial images decomposition.

The dimensionality of real world objects is inevitably much higher than can be pictured using the three dimensions we can see. Hence, dimensionality reduction is very important to project the facial images from the high-dimensional space onto a lower-dimensional space. [6] have proposed Principal Component Analysis (PCA) to describe face patterns with a lower-dimensional space than the image space. One of the characteristic of PCA is such that a high dimensional vector can be represented by a small number of orthogonal basis vectors, namely principal components. In this paper, PCA is used as a baseline for comparison.

Next stage will be followed by projected the facial images onto the subspace via NMF. NMF was proposed by Lee and Seung in 1997 [7]. NMF performed similar to PCA but it is based on finding a representation of a local space only using additive constraints. NMF is used in various applications including information retrieval [8], summarizing video [9], music transcription [10] and language model adaptation [11]. NMF imposes the non-negativity constraints in learning basis images. The pixel values of resulting images, as well as coefficients for reconstructions, are all non-negative. This technique preserves much of the structure of the original data and guarantees that both the resulting low-dimensional basis and its accompanying weights are non-negative. For this reason, NMF is considered as a procedure for learning a part-based representation.

In this paper, we investigate the performance when WT and NMF are integrated to take the advantages of these two methods in order to achieve an excellent verification rate in identifying the faces. These results are compared with PCA technique which is our baseline. With the adoption of WT, the training time in NMF can also be reduced significantly.

This paper is organized as follows. Section 2 define wavelet transform based features and their basic properties. In section 3, we describe PCA and NMF properties. Integrated framework of WT and NMF is illustrated in section 4. The experimental results are presented in section 5 and lastly, conclusion is discussed in section 6.

2 Wavelet Transform

Wavelet analysis is a common tool for analyzing localized variation of power within a time series. By decomposing a time series into time-frequency space, dominant modes of variability and how these modes vary in time are able to be determined. The wavelet transform are used for numerous studies in geophysics, including analysis of wave aberration, tropical convection and the dispersion of ocean waves.

The wavelet transform can be used to analyze time series that contain non-stationary power at many different frequencies. Assume that one has a time series, x_n, with equal time spacing and $n=0...N-1$. Also assume that one has a wavelet function, that depends on a non-dimensional "time" parameter. To be "admissible" as a wavelet, this function must have zero mean and be localized in both time and frequency space [12].

The wavelet function is used generically to refer to either orthogonal or non-orthogonal wavelets. In this paper, only the orthogonal wavelet function is used, namely Haar, Daubechies 5 and 10, Symlet 5 and 10, and Spline bior1.1 and 5.5. The basic idea is to represent any arbitrary function $f(x)$ as a superposition of a set of such wavelets or basis functions. The scaling and shifting variables are discretized so that wavelet coefficients can be described by two integers, m and n. Thus, the discrete wavelet transform is given in Equation 1,

$$(W_\psi f(x))(m,n) = \frac{1}{\sqrt{a_o^m}} \sum_k x[k]\psi[a_o^{-m}n-k] \tag{1}$$

where $x[k]$ is a digital signal with sample index k, and $\psi(n)$ is the mother wavelet.

Two-dimensional wavelet transform leads to a decomposition of approximation coefficients at level $j-1$ in four components, the approximations at level j, L_j and the details in three orientations (horizontal, vertical and diagonal), $D_{jvertical}$, $D_{jhorizontal}$ and $D_{jdiagonal}$.

Discrete wavelet transform is used to decompose the facial images into a multiresolution representation in order to keep the least coefficients possible without losing useful image information. Fig. 1(a) depicts the decomposition process by applying a two-dimensional haar wavelet transform of a face image in level 1 and Fig. 1(b) depicts three levels wavelet decomposition by applying haar wavelet transform on the low-frequency band sequentially.

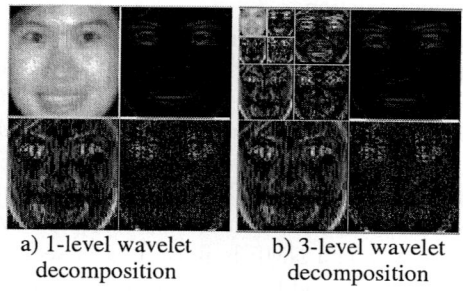

a) 1-level wavelet decomposition   b) 3-level wavelet decomposition

Fig. 1. Face image in wavelet subbands (a) 1-level wavelet decomposition (b) 3-level wavelet decomposition

3 PCA and NMF

3.1 Principle Component Analysis (PCA)

PCA is a linear subspace projection technique used to project data from high-dimensionality subspace onto a lower-dimensionality subspace. Let X_j be N-element one-dimensional image and suppose that we have n such images ($j=1,...,n$). A one-dimensional image column X from the two-dimensional image is formed by scanning all the elements of the two-dimensional image row by row and writing them to the column vector. Then the mean vector, centered data vector and covariance matrix are calculated as in Equation 2, 3 and 4.

$$m = \frac{1}{n}\sum_{j=1}^{n} X_j, \qquad (2)$$

$$d_j = X_j - m, \qquad (3)$$

$$C = \frac{1}{n}\sum_{j=1}^{n} d_j d_j^T \qquad (4)$$

Here $X = (x_1,...,x_N)^T$, $m=(m_1,...m_N)^T$, $d=(d_1,...d_N)^T$. When calculating the covariance matrix, eigenvectors are sorted by decreasing eigenvalues only taking the most representative ones which correspond to the directions of maximum variance. Once the subspace is fully described by a projection matrix, the classification of a new feature vector is accomplished by projecting and finding the nearest training one using Euclidean distance metric.

3.2 Non-negative Matrix Factorization (NMF)

NMF is a method to obtain a representation of data using non-negativity constraints. These constraints lead to a part-based representation in the image subface because they allow only additive, not subtractive, combinations of original data. This is believed to be compatible with the intuition notion of combining parts to form a whole in an accumulative means, and this is how NMF learns a part-based representation [6]. It is also consistent with the physiological fact that the firing rate is non-negative.

Given an initial database expressed by a $n \times m$ matrix X, where each column is an n-dimensional non-negative vector of the original database (m vectors), it is possible to find two new matrices (W and H) in order to approximate the original matrix :

$$X \approx \tilde{X} \equiv WH, \text{ where } W \in \Re^{n \times r}, H \in \Re^{r \times m} \qquad (5)$$

We can rewrite the factorization in terms of the columns of X and H as:

$$x_j \approx \tilde{x}_j = Wh_j, \text{ where } x_j \in \Re^m, h_j \in \Re^r \text{ for } j = 1,...,n \qquad (6)$$

The dimensions of the factorized matrices W and H are $n \times r$ and $r \times m$, respectively. Assuming consistent precision, a reduction of storage is obtained whenever r, the number of basis vectors, satisfies $(n+m)r < nm$. Each column of matrix W contains basis vectors while each column of H contains the weights needed to approximate the corresponding column in V using the basis from W.

In order to estimate the factorization matrices, an objective function has to be defined. We have used the square of Euclidean distance between each column of X and its approximation of $X=WH$ subject to this objective function:

$$\Theta_{NMF}(W,H) = \sum_{j=1}^{n} \|x_j - Wh_j\|^2 = \|X - WH\|^2 \tag{7}$$

This objective function can be related to the likelihood of generating the images in X from the basis W and encoding H. An iterative approach to reach a local minimum of this objective function is given by the following rules [13] :

$$W_{ia} \leftarrow W_{ia} \sum_{\mu} \frac{V_{i\mu}}{(WH)_{i\mu}} H_{a\mu}, \tag{8}$$

$$W_{ia} \leftarrow \frac{W_{ia}}{\sum_{j} W_{ja}}, \tag{9}$$

$$H_{a\mu} \leftarrow H_{a\mu} \sum_{i} W_{ia} \frac{V_{i\mu}}{(WH)_{i\mu}} \tag{10}$$

Initialization is performed using positive random initial conditions for matrices W and H. Convergence of the process is also ensured. Fig. 2 demonstrates the NMF basis figures extracted from our database. These basis provide a sparse and part-based representation of face images.

In face recognition, NMF is performed where $W = (W^T W)^{-1} W^T$. In the feature extraction, each training facial images x_i is projected into the linear space as a feature vector $h_i = Wx_i$. This is then used as a training feature point. A testing face image x_t to be classified is represented as $h_t = Wx_t$. Next we classified them using nearest neighborhood classification scheme, Euclidean distance metric. The Euclidean distance between the testing image and each training image, $d(h_t, h_i)$ is calculated. The testing image is classified to the class to which the closest training image belongs.

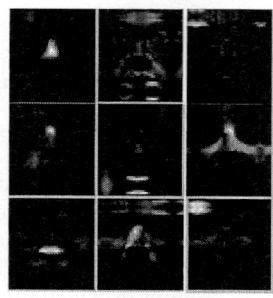

Fig. 2. NMF bases

4 Integrated Framework of Wavelet and Non-negative Matrix Factorization

The integrated framework of wavelet and non-negative matrix factorization (wNMF) produce sparse and part-based images. In addition to that, WT reduce the resolution of the image and decrease the computation load of the feature generation. In this paper, two level of wavelet decomposition is performed on face images. The face image with the low-frequency subband representation, L_l is then subjected to NMF transform as described in Section 3. The block diagram of wNMF feature representation is illustrated in Fig. 3.

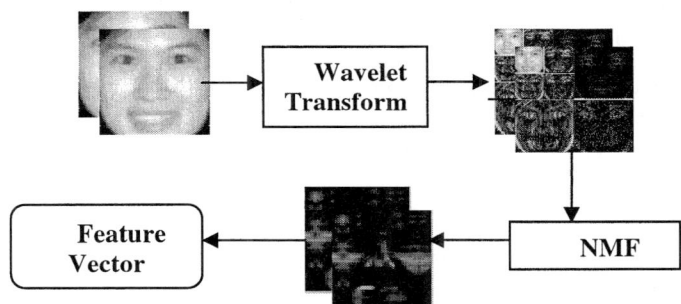

Fig. 3. Block diagram of generating the wNMF features

5 Experimental Results

The experiments were conducted by using *Faces-93* Essex University Face Database (Essex) [14] and Olivetti Research Laboratory (ORL) Database [15]. There are various aspects in the *Faces-93* Essex database which made it appropriate to this experiment. Data capture conditions are subject to photograph at fixed distance from camera, and individuals are asked to speak to produce images of the same individuals with different facial expressions. This database consists of 100 subjects with 10 images for each subject. The set of the 10 images for each subject is randomly partitioned into a training subset of 3 images and a test set of another 5 images. The image size is of 61 x 73 pixels, 256 – level grayscale. The face scale in the images is uniform and there are minor variations in turn, tilt and slant. On the other hand, ORL database contains 40 subjects with 10 images for each subject. The set of the 10 images for each subject is also randomly partitioned into a training subset of 3 images and a test set of another 5 images. The image size is of 92 x 112 pixels, 256 – level grayscale. There are major variations in turn, tilt and slant which we make use of the complexity of this database for our experiments.

For performance evaluation, the error measures of a verification system are False Accept Rate (FAR) and False Reject Rate (FRR) as defined in Equation 11 and 12.

$$FAR = \frac{\text{Number of accepted imposter claims (FA)}}{\text{Total number of imposter accesses}} \times 100\% \quad (11)$$

$$FRR = \frac{\text{Number of rejected genuine claims (FR)}}{\text{Total number of genuine accesses}} \times 100\% \quad (12)$$

A unique measure, Total Success Rate (TSR) is obtained as Equation 13.

$$TSR = \left(1 - \frac{FA + FR}{\text{Total number of accesses}}\right) \times 100\% \quad (13)$$

Another measure, Equal Error Rate (EER) is the datum on the Receiver Operating Characteristics curve where FAR is equal to the FRR.

Firstly, PCA is used to determine the initial face recognition rate. Two different databases were used to test the performance rate. Principal component (pc) is fixed to 100. The result shown that TSR=95.88% with FAR=4.11% and FRR=5% is obtained for Essex database. On the other hand, ORL database achieved TSR=92.31% with FAR=7.69% and FRR=7.5%. This baseline will be used as comparison for further experiments.

Next, an experiment was carried out to verify the performance rate of Non-Negative Factorization (NMF) as shown in Table 1. According to Table 1, different r, the number of basis vectors, were chosen to verify the best performance. $r=10$ to $r=60$ were used for verification rate calculation. The optimum verification rate for Essex Database is EER=1.90% with FAR=1.8%, FRR=2% when $r=40$ whilst ORL database attains EER=7.25% with FAR=7%, FRR=7.5% when $r=20$. There is a significant difference in the verification rate of these two databases as ORL database contains more variations to Essex Database, therefore yield poorer verification rate. Nevertheless both are achieving relatively satisfying results.

Table 1. Comparison of Essex and ORL database with NMF method

Database	r	FAR(%)	FRR(%)	EER(%)
Essex	10	2.50	2.00	2.25
	20	2.20	2.00	2.10
	30	3.00	3.00	3.00
	40	1.80	2.00	1.90
	50	4.90	5.00	4.95
	60	4.80	5.00	4.90
ORL	10	12.00	12.20	12.10
	20	7.00	7.50	7.25
	30	7.40	7.50	7.45
	40	8.00	7.50	7.75
	50	8.00	8.00	8.00
	60	8.00	8.00	8.00

Another experiment was carried out by using a similar set of r to determine the optimum verification rate when NMF is integrated with multiple wavelet filters with decomposition level 2. The optimum result is recorded in Table 2. Integration of haar filter and NMF achieved the best performance when $r=20$ whereas integration of Spline bior5.5 filter and NMF is best when $r=40$ for Essex and ORL database respectively. It can be observed that the optimum r is not big. This indicates that moderately large r of NMF is sufficient to discriminate the different face. Table 3 shows the comparison of PCA, NMF and wNMF for Essex and ORL databases respectively.

Table 2. Comparison of Essex and ORL database with integration of various types of wavelet filters and NMF

Database (Db)	Filter	FAR(%)	FRR(%)	EER(%)
Essex	Haar	1.56	2.00	1.58
	Db5	4.30	4.00	4.15
	Db10	5.00	5.00	5.00
	Sym5	4.60	5.00	4.80
	Sym10	7.70	8.00	7.85
	Bior1.1	5.00	5.00	5.00
	Bior5.5	4.00	4.00	4.00
ORL	Haar	5.90	5.00	5.45
	Db5	5.00	5.00	5.00
	Db10	5.00	5.00	5.00
	Sym5	5.10	5.00	5.05
	Sym10	5.00	5.00	5.00
	Bior1.1	5.00	5.00	5.00
	Bior5.5	4.50	5.00	4.75

Table 3. Comparison of PCA, NMF and wNMF for Essex and ORL database

Db	Method	pc/r	FAR(%)	FRR(%)	TSR(%)
Essex	PCA	100	4.11	5.00	95.90
	NMF	40	1.80	2.00	98.20
	wNMF	20	1.56	2.00	98.50
ORL	PCA	100	7.69	7.50	92.30
	NMF	20	7.00	7.50	93.00
	wNMF	20	4.50	5.00	95.50

Table 4. Training elapse time for Essex and ORL database

Database	WT	Elapse Time (sec)
Essex	Without	534.266
	With	240.094
ORL	Without	398.578
	With	151.547

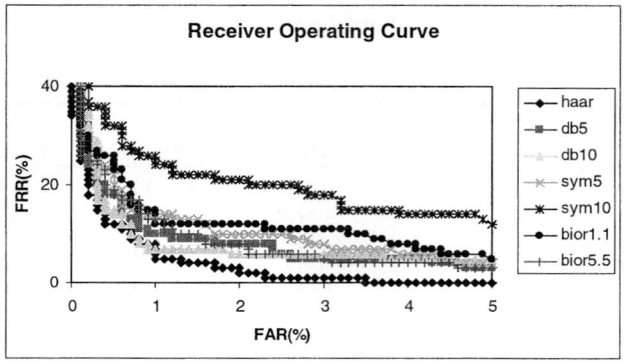

Fig. 4. Integration of various wavelet filters and NMF for Essex database

Table 4 indicates time computation which is implemented on a Pentium 4 2.66 GHz with 256Mb RAM processor. A longer duration is consumed to train the database due to the reason that 1000 iterations are used to update W and H. The difference between these two databases with the hybrid of NMF and WT is 88.547 seconds.

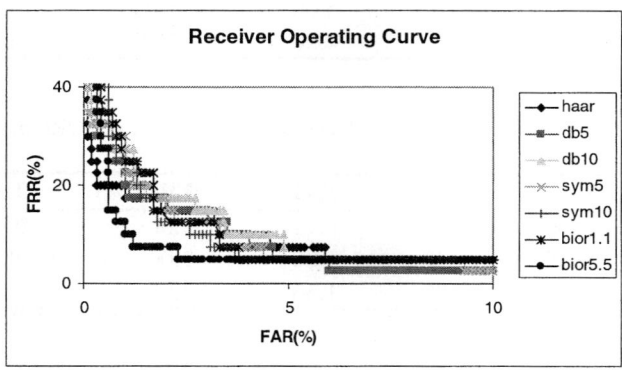

Fig. 5. Integration of various filters and NMF for ORL database

Figure 4 and 5 illustrate the Receiver Operating Characteristics (ROC) curve for the integration of multiple wavelets and NMF for Essex and ORL Database respectively. A ROC curve plots the FRR against FAR at various thresholds. The closer the plot lies to the axis, the better the performance. Thus Figure 4 and 5 reveals that haar filter and spline bior5.5 filter perform the best when the best chosen wavelet is integrated with NMF for both databases.

6 Conclusion

An efficient method for face recognition using Wavelet Transform and Non-Negative Matrix Factorization is presented in this paper. Two databases namely, Essex Database and ORL Database were used throughout the experiments to compare the verification rate. Wavelet analysis produces lower dimension multiresolution representation that alleviates heavy computational load, and also generates noise and minor distortion insusceptible to face wavelet – based template. After wavelet decomposition NMF is performed on the facial images. The results obtained are compared with the PCA technique. The results shown that wavelet and NMF can outperform PCA for better verification rate.

References

1. A.P. Ginsburg, Visual information processing based on spatial filters constrained by biological data, AMRL Technical Report, 1978, pp. 78-129
2. L.D. Harmon, The recognition of faces, Sci. Am. 229 (1973)
3. J. Sergent, Microgenesis of face perception, in: H.D. Ellis, M.A. Jeeves, F. Newcombe, A. Young (Eds.), Aspects of Face Processing, Nijhoff, Dordrecht, 1986
4. C. Nastar, N. Ayache, Frequency-based non-rigid motion analysis, IEEE Trans. Pattern Anal. Mach. Intell. 18 (11) (1996) pp. 1067-1079
5. S. T. Bow, Pattern Recognition and Image Preprocessing, Marcel Dekker, Inc., 1992, pp. 203-274
6. D.D.Lee, H.S.Seung, "Learning the Parts of Obejcts by Non-Negative Matrix Factorization", Nature, vol. 401, pp. 788-791, 1999
7. M.Turk, A.Pentland, Engenfaces for recognition, J. Cognitive Neurosci. 3(1) 71-86, 1991
8. Baowen Xu, Jianjiang Lu, Gangshi Huang, "A Constrained Non-negative Matrix Factorization in Information Retrieval", Proc. of The 2003 IEEE International Conference on Information Reuse and Integration (IRI'2003), October 27-29, 2003, Las Vegas, USA
9. M. Cooper, and J. Foote, "Summarizing Video Using Non-negative Similarity Matrix Factorization", Proc. IEEE Workshop on Multimedia Signal Processing, 2002
10. P.Smaragdis, J.C.Brown, "Non-Negative Matrix Factorization for Polyphonic Music Transcription", IEEE Workshop on Applications of Signal Processing to Audio and Acoustics, 2003
11. M. Novak, R. Mammone, "Use of Non-negative Matrix Factorization for Language Model Adaptation in a Lecture Transcription Task", ICASSP, Salt Lake City, UT, USA, 2001
12. A. Laine. J. Fan, "Texture Classification by Wavelet Packet Signatures", IEEE Trans. Pattern Anal. Machine Intell., Vol. 15, pp. 1186-1191, 1993
13. D.D.Lee, H.S.Seung, "Algorithms for Non-Negative Matrix Factorization", Proceedings of Neural Information Processing Systems, vol. 13, pp. 556-562, 2001

14. Vision Group of Essex University Face Database http://cswww.essex.ac.uk/mv/allfaces/index.html
15. Olivetti Research Laboratory (ORL) Database http://www.uk.research.att.com/facedatabase.html

Modelling-Alignment for Non-random Sequences

David R. Powell[1,2,*], Lloyd Allison[1], and Trevor I. Dix[1,2]

[1] School of Computer Science and Software Engineering,
Monash University, Australia 3800
[2] Victorian Bioinformatics Consortium
{powell, lloyd, trevor}@csse.monash.edu.au

Abstract. Populations of biased, non-random sequences may cause standard alignment algorithms to yield false-positive matches and false-negative misses. A standard significance test based on the *shuffling* of sequences is a partial solution, applicable to populations that can be described by *simple* models. Masking-out low information content intervals throws information away. We describe a new and general method, *modelling-alignment*: Population models are incorporated into the alignment process, which can (and should) lead to changes in the rank-order of matches between a query sequence and a collection of sequences, compared to results from standard algorithms. The new method is general and places very few conditions on the nature of the models that can be used with it. We apply modelling-alignment to local alignment, global alignment, optimal alignment, and the relatedness problem.

Results: As expected, modelling-alignment and the standard prss program from the FASTA package have similar accuracy on sequence populations that can be described by simple models, e.g. 0-order Markov models. However, modelling-alignment has higher accuracy on populations that are *mixed* or that are described by higher-order models: It gives fewer false positives and false negatives as shown by ROC curves and other results from tests on real and artificial data.

An implementation of the software is available via the Web[1].

1 Introduction

Sequence alignment is an important method for discovering patterns and relationships between sequences. The alignment of biological sequences can give clues to common ancestry or to common biological function. Alignment algorithms are used to answer two quite different kinds of questions, (i) Are two (or more) sequences *related* or not? (ii) *How* are two (or more) sequences related, *given* that they are related? There is a "fundamental difference between the searching [for related sequences] and [optimal] alignment operations." – [14]. It is also well known that populations of biased, non-random, low information content sequences may cause algorithms to return false-positive matches and false-negative misses for the first kind of problem and may also cause poor alignments, for the second kind of problem. There are partial solutions, with disadvantages: Masking-out low information content intervals [8] can reduce false-positives but it throws

---
* Partially funded by Australian Research Council Grant A49800558.
[1] http://www.csse.monash.edu.au/~powell/m-align.tar.gz

away some information and raises the question of how low is low? The significance of a possible match is often assessed by comparing its score (or cost) with those obtained when "one member of the protein [say] pair [is] randomized" (shuffled, permuted) – [21]. We call this general kind of significance testing *shuffling*; note that an alignment is calculated under the assumption of random sequences and *then* the shuffling test is applied, possibly to a bad alignment if the sequences are non-random.

We describe a new method, *modelling-alignment* (M-alignment) which incorporates explicit models of sequence populations. It is based on the premise that two sequences are related if one tells something *new* and *useful* about the other, i.e. something not otherwise known. It has a natural null-theory and hypothesis test. Instead of a low information interval being masked-out, it is given a low, but non-zero, weight thus not discarding information.

A high information interval, i.e. a *feature*, is given a high weight; there is a big scoring advantage if it is matched in another sequence. In general this can, and should, change the rank-order of alignments between two sequences and the rank-order of matches between multiple sequences. There is no hard (and arbitrary) threshold for what is a *background* low information interval or for what is a high information feature; there is a continuous spectrum of information content from low to high.

M-alignment is general and places few restrictions on the kind of population model that can be used with it. If the "correct" model is not known in advance there are some sensible candidates to try and a good model can be detected on the basis of information content. Algorithm time-complexity remains $O(n^2)$ for reasonable models. This paper extends work on the 1-state mutation model [2] by applying M-alignment to the relatedness and optimal alignment problems, for both global [21] and local [27] alignment, under the 3-state, affine gap-costs model [13] of mutation.

M-alignment results are compared to those of the prss program – from the FASTA package [22] – which is based on rdf2 [23] with a shuffling significance test. Receiver operating characteristics (ROC) curves show that, as expected, both methods give similar results on simple data, i.e. uniform and 0-order Markov model populations. M-alignment is more accurate, i.e. gives fewer false positives and fewer false negatives, on mixed populations, on populations of mixed sequences, and on populations described by higher-order models.

At this point it is convenient to clarify some of the terminology we use in this paper. We use the term *rank-order* to mean order obtained when items are ranked according to some score. When a group or population of sequences is well explained by a particular model, we say that model is a *population model* for those sequences. An alignment can be seen as a hypothesis of how two (or more) sequences are related. Using information-theoretic techniques we can quantify how likely a hypothesis is, and thus discuss the *probability of an alignment*.

2 Systems and Methods

2.1 Models

There is considerable interest in the compression of biological sequences [15, 19, 24, 3], not so much to save disc space but as a criterion for comparing models of populations of sequences. The terms *biased*, *non-random*, *low information content* and *compressible* are equivalent for our purposes: If DNA bases, say, are generated uniformly at random, an optimal code assigns each one a two-bit code. This follows from Shannon's mathematical theory of communication [26]. If the DNA comes from a biased 0-order model say, shorter codes can be allocated *on average*. For example, if the respective probabilities of an A, T, G or C are [1/2, 1/4, 1/8, 1/8] this leads to optimal codes of [1, 2, 3, 3]-bits respectively, that is 1 3/4-bits on average. For higher-order models, code-words depend on the *context* of previous characters, on the 'k' previous characters for a Markov model of order k. Probabilistic finite-state automata (PFSAs), also known as hidden Markov models, have been used as models [12] of populations of sequences. Each of these models, and many others, can deliver a probabilistic prediction for the next character in a sequence given a context. From Shannon, the length of a code-word for the next character, its *message length*, is the -log of this probability and is a measure of the information content of the character in the context. M-alignment uses this quantity.

2.2 Relatedness and Alignment

The generic dynamic programming algorithm (DPA) for sequence comparison can be used to find various kinds of global alignments depending on how it is instantiated: E.g. Given *scores* of one for a match and zero for mismatch, insert and delete, the DPA finds the longest common subsequence (LCS). Given *costs* of zero for a match and one for mismatch, insert and delete, it finds an optimal alignment under the Levenshtein [18] metric also known as the simple edit-distance [25]. *Affine* gap-costs, for runs of inserts or deletes, are more plausible biologically and Gotoh [13] gave such an alignment algorithm; the key is to have three *states* for each cell in the DPA's matrix, for costs (or scores) *conditional* on diagonal, vertical and horizontal moves.

All of the above DPA variations find a global optimal alignment for some given criterion, or at least under the assumption that, two sequences are related. Shuffling tries to solve the relatedness problem by comparing the score (or cost) of an optimal alignment with the scores (costs) of alignments of the randomized sequences. If the former is not significantly better than the latter the sequences are deemed to be unrelated. The idea is that randomized sequences are *like* their originals in general statistical terms but are otherwise unrelated. Shuffling preserves 0-order statistics of sequences. It can be arranged to preserve 1st-order statistics [11] and even codon usage [5] but it is hard to imagine how to carry it out while preserving the statistics of an arbitrary model particularly if that is a mixture or is high-order.

A different approach to the relatedness problem considers a probabilistic *mutation model*. The costs (scores) of the DPA are replaced by the -log probabilities of match, mismatch, insert and delete. In fact costs and scores can be *normalized* [1] to show the underlying probabilities. An alignment may be seen as just a hypothesis about how sequences are related, and alignment algorithms as encoding the sequences and an alignment in an efficient manner. The alignment that leads to the shortest encoding is the best inference in a statistical sense [28]. The DPA can be used to find a *most probable* alignment, but it can also be modified to calculate the *joint* probability of two sequences:

> An alignment is just a hypothesis. The set of all alignments is exclusive and exhaustive, given that two sequences are related. Rather than selecting the largest probability, their probabilities can therefore be *added*.

This was originally done for a 1-state mutation model [6]. Later, it was extended [4] to 3-state (affine gap-costs) and 5-state (piece-wise linear gap-costs) mutation models, and included the cost (complexity) of models so that simple and complex models can be compared fairly. Such considerations also give a natural *null-theory* that the sequences are not related, i.e. that one tells nothing new or useful about the other. Two sequences are unrelated if their joint probability is less than or equal to the product of their individual probabilities, given by the null-theory.

The next section describes how these methods are extended to local alignment and how the information content of compressible sequences is taken into account in M-alignment.

3   Algorithm

The M-alignment algorithms (i) make use of probabilistic alignment methods for global and local alignment, and (ii) incorporate sequence population models to calculate the information content of characters in context. This is done in combination with the 3-state, affine gap-cost mutation model.

Firstly, probabilistic methods are used to estimate the probability of relatedness of sequences S1 and S2 under *local alignment*, i.e. that there is some configuration S1=A+L+B and S2=C+L'+D where intervals L and L' are related (globally) and intervals A, B, C, and D, which are possibly empty, are not related. A, B, C and D are compressed with the population model. L and L' are compressed with both the population and mutation models, in a way to be described. For the relatedness problem we *sum* over all such configurations, that is over all A, L, B, C, L' and D and all alignments of L with L', still in $O(n^2)$-time. For the optimal local alignment problem we choose the best such configuration.

Secondly, the DPA operates cell by cell on a two-dimensional array. For affine gap-costs, each cell contains three values for the -log probability of S1[1..i] and S2[1..j] conditional on the last operation being an insert, delete or match/mismatch. Each increment involves the -log probabilities of a mutation and of a character from one or both strings as appropriate. The key idea of M-alignment is to obtain the latter from a population model.

Then contribution of an insertion or deletion is calculated as the product or the mutation probability (more on this later), and probability of the character being inserted or deleted. This *character probability* is calculated by using the *population model*. A mismatch is calculated in a similar fashion, except using two probabilities, one for each character. The calculation of a match is slightly different since we have two different probabilities for the same character. For convenience, the probability of a match is multiplied by the *average* of the two character probabilities.

There is the problem of what mutation probabilities to use. This could be addressed by using fixed probabilities as is effectively done with scores in the Smith-Waterman algorithm. Alternatively, and as we do here, the mutation probabilities can be estimated by the algorithm. We do this by starting the probabilities at sensible values, then running the algorithm a number of times re-estimating the mutation probabilities each time. This is simple expectation maximisation which is guaranteed to converge in this case, possibly to a local maximum. The initial mutation probabilities used are calculated by transforming Smith-Waterman costs into probabilities [1]. Note that a side-effect of this is that an explicit probability is given to terminal gaps rather than the somewhat arbitrary zero used in the Smith-Waterman algorithm.

This explanation of the M-alignment algorithm is for the particular case of DNA sequences where the mutations are insertion, deletion, mismatch or match. Instead of simply considering matches and mismatches, it is sometimes useful to use a 4x4 grid of scores to assign a score for aligning each DNA base against each other DNA base. This is very similar to the use substitution matrices when aligning proteins (BLOSUM, PAM, etc.). The modification of M-alignment for this is given in Section 6.

4 Implementation

A version of the DPA was implemented to carry out M-alignment for a 3-state, affine gap-costs mutation model, local alignment. It accepts a population model as a parameter. It is able to return either the -log probability of two sequences being related (by summing alignment probabilities) or an optimal local alignment. The results from testing this program on both real and artificial data are given in the next section.

5 Tests

On the face of it M-alignment appears to address a similar problem as Hidden Markov Model alignment algorithms such as HMMER [10]. Indeed, HMMER and M-alignment have a number of similarities, both use probabilistic modelling, both sum over all possible alignments. *However*, they are for different problems and are therefore difficult to compare fairly. HMMER builds a profile HMM, ideally from a multiple sequence alignment. It is then possible to use this HMM to align against a sequence or search a database. This differs from M-alignment because M-alignment aligns two actual sequences in the presence of a model of the population. However, since M-alignment may use almost any type of model, it would be possible for it to use a HMM profile model, although it is not clear whether this would be useful.

5.1 Generation of Related Sequences

It is easy to generate a typical sequence given a population model. The difficulty is to generate *related pairs* that are typical of the population; uniform random mutations would cause descendants to drift towards the statistics of a uniform model. The solution is to propose a mutation at random and to either accept it or reject it.

We have a sequence, A, and a population model M. The entropy of A under this model shall be written $M(A)$. The length of sequence A will be written $|A|$. The sequence that results from making x mutations to A shall be referred to as A_x. We earlier described the motivation as wanting the mutated sequence to "fit" the population model. To make this precise, what is desired is that as x tends to infinity, the entropy of the mutated sequence, $M(A_x)$, will tend to the entropy of the population model, M, itself.

The method used to mutate sequences was inspired by the Metropolis algorithm [20]. Consider every possible sequence as having a node, S_i, in a graph. An arc between two nodes, S_i and S_j, implies that a single mutation relates the two corresponding sequences. As we make mutations to a sequence, we move between nodes in the graph. In the extreme case where many mutations are made, we want to visit each node with a frequency equal to probability p, where p is probability of that node's sequence under the population model. A sufficient condition for this is to have the probability of taking the arc from S_i to S_j equal to the probability of taking the arc from S_j to S_i.

We will assume a point mutation model for simplicity. That is, we consider making mutations of the form delete a character, insert a character or change a character. For an alphabet of 4 characters, sequence A has $3 \times |A|$ possible change mutations, $|A|$ possible delete mutations and $4 \times (|A| + 1)$ possible insert mutations. If we assume a uniform, or relatively flat, prior on the length of sequences, then we have the requirement when mutating a sequence that on average the number of deletions should be the same as the number of insertions. There is a degree of freedom in choosing the ratio of changes to insertions and deletions. We shall use a probability parameter P_{change} for this. We define two other probabilities in terms of this.

$$P_{insert} = \frac{(1 - P_{change})(4 \times (|A| + 1))}{(5 \times |A| + 4)}$$

$$P_{delete} = \frac{(1 - P_{change})}{(5 + 4/|A|)}$$

When we mutate sequence A, a random choice is made whether to consider an insertion, a deletion or a change mutation using the three above probabilities (note they sum to unity). If a deletion is to be considered, then the position of the deletion is chosen uniform randomly over the length of the sequence. If a change, then the position and character are chosen randomly. If an insertion, then the position and the character to be inserted are randomly selected. The sequence that would result from this mutation is A'. Let q be the probability given to sequence A by the population model, and q' the probability given to sequence A'. If q' is greater than q then the mutation is accepted and A' becomes A_1. Otherwise, the mutation is accepted with probability q'/q. This process is repeated until the desired number of mutations has been made.

Since this method does not preclude a mutation "undoing" previous mutations, the resulting mutated sequence, A_x, may be more similar to A than otherwise expected. This tends to be more likely if M is a very low entropy model.

In the following tests we wish to examine the performance of M-alignment with local alignment. So, we generate related pairs of sequences, L and L', using the above method. Then, unrelated prefixes A and C and suffixes B and D are generated from the population model.

5.2 Results with Artificial Data

Artificial data was used to compare the new M-alignment algorithm with the common Smith-Waterman algorithm using shuffling as a significance test. The benefit of using artificial data is that the conditions can be controlled precisely to clearly illustrate the advantages and disadvantages of techniques. We also know what the answer is.

The implementation used for the Smith-Waterman algorithm was the `prss` program that is part of the FASTA 3.3 package. In all tests, the `prss` program was used with the standard parameters: +5 for a match, -4 for a mismatch, -16 and -4 for the first and subsequent characters in a sequence respectively. The default of 200 uniform shuffles was used to determine the significance of each alignment.

The artificial data was generated using a number of different population models. In all cases, 10 parent sequences were generated from the population model(s). From each parent, 25 child sequences were generated having a mutated subsequence in common with parent. The amount of mutation was varied so some children were similar to their parent and some were very dissimilar. The method of mutation was described in Section 5.1.

The child sequences were considered as the library to be searched, and each parent was used in turn as the query sequence. Thus for each query there were 25 related sequences of differing relatedness and 225 unrelated sequences. This ratio of related to unrelated sequence in the library is high compared to real sequence databases but will suffice for testing purposes. Each parent sequence was compared against every child sequence making 2500 pair-wise comparisons. Of these 2500 comparisons, 250 are between related sequences, and 2250 between unrelated sequences.

To present the results of the tests Receiver Operating Characteristics (ROC) [14, 7] plots are used. Each algorithm tested produces a number measuring the relatedness of the two sequences being compared. This may be the raw Smith-Waterman score, or the p-value found by the `prss` program, or the log odds ratio produce by M-alignment. For each test, the 2500 pair-wise comparisons are ranked in order of significance by this measure. For each possible cut-off value the number of true positives and the number of false positives are counted. Plotted on the y-axis is the ratio of false positives to the total number of unrelated pair-wise comparisons. And on the x-axis the ratio of true positives to the total number of related comparisons. The better an algorithm is at separating related from unrelated sequences the closer its curve will be to the bottom right corner of the ROC plots. Since we are mostly interested in the behaviour for a smallish number of false positives the y-axis is plotted with a log scale. Recall that M-alignment may take as a parameter the model for the sequences. Except where noted otherwise, the M-alignment algorithm is told to fit a 1st order Markov Model to the sequences.

In tests with a simple unbiased model, (i.e. each character occurs with probability 1/4) the raw Smith-Waterman score, the `prss` program and M-alignment perform similarly. For a population model that produces sequences with a simple composition bias, tests showed that the `prss` program and M-alignment perform in a similar manner, while raw Smith-Waterman score is inferior.

Figure 1 shows the results of a test that combines unbiased and biased sequences. Instead of all 10 parent sequences coming from the same population model, 5 come from an unbiased model, and 5 from a 0th order Markov Model (simple composition bias). The shuffling of the `prss` program does account for sequences with a biased composition, but as seen in this test it does not perform as well as M-alignment when

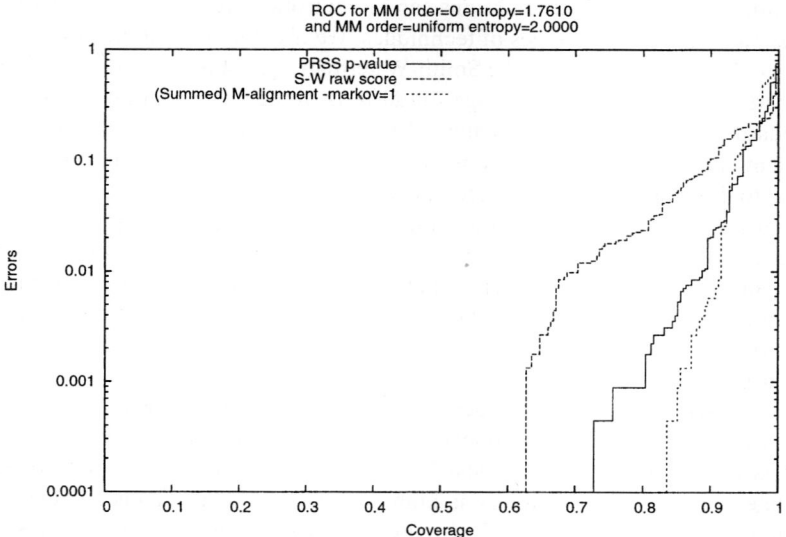

Fig. 1. ROC for a uniform sequence model and biased composition sequences

there are different models in the population. Similar behaviour has been seen when using other combinations of models.

The final test illustrates the benefits if one is able to better model the population. The population model in this test is a little more complicated. This model consists of two sub-models. One is a simple uniform model, and the other a very biased 1st order Markov Model that produces sequences of characters that are TATA-rich. Sequences are generated by choosing one of these two sub-models at random, then using that sub-model to produce a random number of characters. This is repeated a number of times to produce a sequence of sufficient length. This model is, in a sense, a blend between a uniform model, with an entropy of 2 bits per character, and a 1st order model, with an entropy of 1.1 bits per character. Figure 2 shows the results of the different algorithms on sequences of this type. Our algorithm is performing significantly better than the `prss` program. The best performer in this figure is the M-alignment algorithm using the "blendModel". This blendModel was designed with some knowledge of the population model. Specifically, the blendModel knows that the data is produced by a combination of a uniform model and also the exact 1st order model used. It does not know the probability with which these sub-models are chosen, nor the length of the sequences produced by the sub-models. As can be seen in the figure, having this extra knowledge about the population model allows for better separation of related and unrelated sequences. The M-alignment algorithm is superior to the Smith-Waterman algorithms because an arbitrary left-to-right sequence model can be used. Thus, more complex population models may be used with M-alignment to allow better differentiation between related and unrelated sequences.

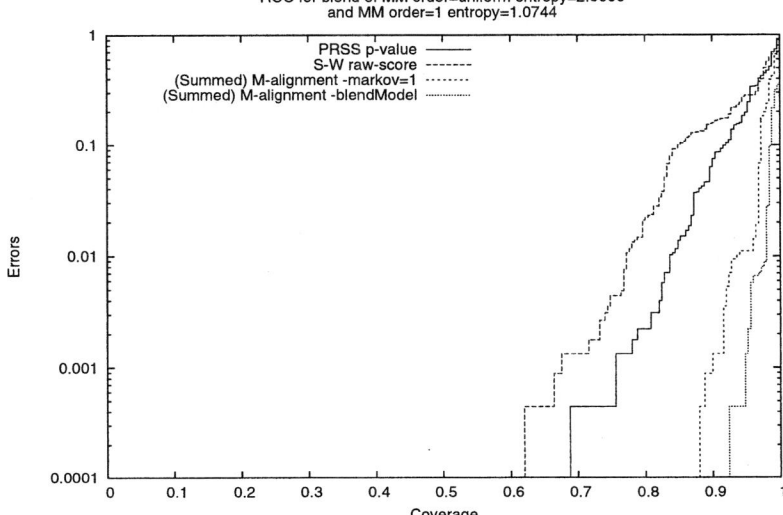

Fig. 2. ROC for a blended model

It may be argued that this test is unfair to the prss program since it would be common practice to mask out low-complexity regions before doing the comparison with the prss program. However, these low-complexity regions do give *some* information about whether the sequences are related, just not as much information as high-complexity regions.

It is clear from the ROC plots that M-alignment is superior to the prss program when sequences are of low complexity, even when it is simply a mixture of uniform and biased composition sequences. However, the prss program performs well on these types of sequence if the population is confined to one type. This may be explained because the prss program does not have a natural cut-off p-value, and indeed the best cut-off depends on the type of the population. M-alignment has a natural cut-off at a log-odds ratio of zero. At zero, both the null model and the alignment model are equally good explanations of the data. In practice, a slightly larger cut-off value would be used; a cut-off of 3 bits indicates the alignment model is 8 times better than the null model, a cut-off of 10 bits gives a confidence of about 99.9% provided population model assumptions are appropriate.

5.3 Results with Real Data

In this section we show that M-alignment also performs well on real genomic DNA sequences. We chose a relatively low information sequence from *Plasmodium falciparum* chromosome 2. The sequence is from the end of the intron and start of the second exon of PFB0010w and of 157 characters in length. This sequence was chosen because PFB0010w is known to be related to a number of genes and pseudo-genes and because it has considerable repetition. Thus this is the type of sequence we expect traditional algorithms to have difficulty with.

This sequence was used in a nucleotide-nucleotide BLAST search against the nr database which was run using the NCBI BLAST server. The default options were used with the exception that filtering was turned off. This search resulted in 60765 "matching" sequences — no matches were found when filtering was on. Each of these 60765 sequences were retrieved with an extra 50 characters at each end so the alignment programs could have some extra context information. The vast majority of these sequences are in fact unrelated to the query sequence. Most of these false positives are due to matching TATA regions. Using M-alignment with a sequence model that correctly apportions weight to such regions should give good results. The model we used, was a fifth-order Markov Model trained on all 60765 matching sequences. A fifth-order model was chosen because it achieved the best compression across the whole population taking into account the complexity of the model. While such a model is not ideal, we assume that most of the sequences are unrelated but do represent a certain population, and that a fifth-order model can capture much of the information about this population. If a sequence is to be said to be related to the query sequence then it must have more in common than simply coming from that population.

The prss and M-alignment programs were then used to do a pair-wise comparison between the query sequence and each of the 60765 matching sequences. Thus, a ranking of all the matching sequences was produced by both programs. M-alignment gives roughly 1300 sequences a significant score, while prss claims more than 10000 significant matches. It is difficult to assess objectively which ordering is better. Our subjective comparison of the two rankings suggests that the M-alignment ranking is superior.

A fragment was taken from pseudo-gene PFB0045c [17], which is known to be distantly related to the gene the query sequence was taken from, PFB0010w. This fragment comes from the region of PFB0045c that corresponds to the intron of PFB0010w. The fragment was not found by the BLAST search. If this fragment is ranked amongst the other sequences it would, ideally, rank fairly high since the vast majority of the 60765 sequences are unrelated to the query sequence. The prss program ranks this fragment at 25499 of 60765, while the M-alignment program ranks it at 241.

6 Proteins

Our use of the M-alignment algorithm has concentrated on DNA sequences thus far, and our implementation is solely for DNA sequences. Here we will briefly describe how it would be possible to extend M-alignment to protein sequences.

When aligning proteins it is not sufficient to simply have a mismatch score (or cost) unlike for DNA. Protein alignment commonly uses a scoring matrix such as PAM [9] or BLOSUM [16] which gives a score for aligning any pair of amino acids. The BLOSUM matrices use the BLOCKS database to calculate the joint probability of two amino-acids occurring together, this is then normalised to account for the bias in appearance of each amino-acid. These are not directly useful to M-alignment. For M-alignment it is necessary to have a *conditional probability* for each pair of amino-acids. So, if we have an alignment that aligns glycine with leucine we need $p(glycine|leucine)$

and $p(leucine|glycine)$, note that these probabilities may be different. It should be straightforward to derive these probabilities from the BLOCKS database. The bias in the appearance of amino acids is then taken into account by the population model.

There are two possible ways to encode each pair of amino acids. We define $Pr(x, y)$ as follows to be the average of these.

$$Pr(x, y|a[1..i-1], b[1..j-1]) = \frac{1}{2}[\, p(y|x)Pr(x|a[1..i-1]) \\ + p(x|y)Pr(y|b[1..j-1])]$$

It is not clear what type of population model would work well for proteins. We have concentrated on DNA sequences thus far because DNA sequences typically have a larger variation in information content than protein sequences.

7 Conclusion

M-alignment in global- and local-, sum-of-all-alignment form performs well at predicting relatedness for various kinds of population. On uniform random populations, accuracy is equivalent to the standard Smith-Waterman program with shuffling; it is hard to see how a significance test based on shuffling could cope well with arbitrary models of populations. M-alignment performs better, as shown by ROC curves, for compressible (non-random) populations if the true population model, or a reasonable model, is known. It can perform badly if a bad model is used, as is to be expected, but it can detect the better of two or more population models on the basis of compression.

M-alignment can be used practically to determine relatedness in small or moderate collections of sequences. It could also be used on a client-computer to post-process, and re-rank, putative matches returned from a large collection of sequences by a fast search algorithm running on a server. This use could reduce false-positives but could not bring back any false negatives. The superior performance of M-alignment was illustrated for this task by using a sequence from *Plasmodium falciparum* chromosome 2.

References

1. L. Allison. Normalization of affine gap costs used in optimal sequence alignment. *Journal of Theoretical Biology*, 161:263–269, 1993.
2. L. Allison, D. R. Powell, and T. I. Dix. Compression and approximate matching. *The Computer Journal*, 42(1):1–10, 1999.
3. L. Allison, D. R. Powell, and T. I. Dix. Modelling is more versatile than shuffling. Technical report, Monash University, School of Computer Science and Software Engineering., 2000.
4. L. Allison, C. S. Wallace, and C. N. Yee. Finite-state models in the alignment of macromolecules. *Journal of Molecular Evolution*, 35:77–89, 1992.
5. S. F. Altschul and B. W. Erickson. Significance of nucleotide sequence alignments: A method for random sequence permutation that preserves dinucleotide and codon usage. *Mol. Biol. Evol.*, 2(6):526–538, 1985.
6. M. J. Bishop and E. A. Thompson. Maximum likelihood alignment of DNA sequences. *J. Mol. Biol.*, 190:159–165, 1986.

7. S. E. Brenner, C. Chothia, and T. J. P. Hubbard. Assessing sequence comparison methods with reliable structurally identifed distant evolutionary relationships. *Proc. Natl. Acad. Sci.*, 95:6073–6078, May 1998.
8. J.-M. Claverie and D. J. States. Information enhancement methods for large scale sequence analysis. *Comp. Chem*, 17(2):191–201, 1993.
9. M. O. Dayhoff, R. M. Schwartz, and B. C. Orcutt. A model of evolutionary change in proteins. *Atlas of Protein Sequence and Structure*, 5:345–352, 1978.
10. S. R. Eddy. Profile hidden Markov models. *Bioinformatics*, 14:755–763, 1998.
11. W. M. Fitch. Random sequences. *Journal of Molecular Biology*, 163:171–176, 1983.
12. M. P. Georgeff and C. S. Wallace. A general selection criterion for inductive inference. In *European Conf. on Artificial Intelligence*, pages 473–482, 1984.
13. O. Gotoh. An improved algorithm for matching biological sequences. *Journal of Molecular Biology*, 162:705–708, 1982.
14. M. Gribskov and N. L. Robinson. Use of receiver operating characteristic (ROC) analysis to evaluate sequence matching. *Computers and Chemistry*, 20(1):25–33, 1996.
15. S. Grumbach and F. Tahi. A new challenge for compression algorithms: genetic sequences. *Inf. Proc. and Management*, 30(6):875–886, 1994.
16. S. Henikoff and J. G. Henikoff. Amino acid substitution matrices from protein blocks. *Proc. Natl. Academy Science*, 89(10):915–919, 1992.
17. R. Huestis and K. Fischer. Prediction of many new exons and introns in *Plasmodium falciparum* chromosome 2. *Molecular and Biochemical Parasitology*, 118:187–199, 2001.
18. V. I. Levenshtein. Binary codes capable of correcting deletions, insertions and reversals. *Soviet Physics Doklady.*, 10(8):707–710, 1966.
19. D. M. Loewenstern and P. N. Yianilos. Significantly lower entropy estimates for natural DNA sequences. Technical Report 96-51, DIMACS, December 1996.
20. N. Metropolis, A. W. Rosenbluth, M. N. Rosenbluth, A. H. Teller, and E. Teller. Equation of state calculations by fast computing machines. *The Journal of Chemical Physics*, 21(6):1087–1092, june 1953.
21. S. B. Needleman and C. D. Wunsch. A general method applicable to the search for similarities in the amino acid sequence of two proteins. *Journal of Molecular Biology*, 48:443–453, 1970.
22. W. R. Pearson. Effective protein sequence comparison. *Meth. Enzymol.*, 266:227–258, 1996.
23. W. R. Pearson and D. J. Lipman. Improved tools for biological comparison. *Proc. Natl. Acad. Sci. USA*, 85:2444–2448, April 1988.
24. E. Rivals, O. Delgrange, J.-P. Delahaye, M. Dauchet, M.-O. Delorme, A. Hénaut, and E. Ollivier. Detection of significant patterns by compression algorithms: the case of approximate tandem repeats in DNA sequences. *CABIOS*, 13(2):131–136, 1997.
25. P. H. Sellers. On the theory and computation of evolutionary distances. *SIAM J. Appl. Math.*, 26(4):787–793, 1974.
26. C. E. Shannon and W. Weaver. *The Mathematical Theory of Communication.* U. of Illinois Press, 1949.
27. T. F. Smith and M. S. Waterman. Identification of common molecular subsequences. *Journal of Molecular Biology*, 147:195–197, 1981.
28. C. S. Wallace and P. R. Freeman. Estimation and inference by compact coding. *Journal of the Royal Statistical Society series B.*, 49(3):240–265, 1987.

Moments and Wavelets for Classification of Human Gestures Represented by Spatio-Temporal Templates

Arun Sharma and Dinesh K. Kumar

School of ECE, RMIT University, PO Box 2476V Melbourne, Australia 3001
s9900960@student.rmit.edu.au
dinesh@rmit.edu.au

Abstract. This paper reports a novel technique to classify short duration articulated object motion in video data. The motion is represented by a spatio-temporal template (STT), a view based approach, which collapses temporal component into a static grey scale image in a way that no explicit sequence matching or temporal analysis is needed, and characterizes the motion from a very high dimensional space to a low dimensional space. These templates are modified to be invariant to translation and scale. Two dimensional, 3 level dyadic wavelet transform applied on these templates results in one low pass subimage and nine highpass directional subimages. Histograms of STTs and of the wavelet coefficients at different scales are compared to establish significance of available information for classification. To further reduce the feature space, histograms of STTs are represented by orthogonal Legendre moments, and the wavelet subbands are modelled by generalized Gaussian density (GGD) parameters - shape factor and standard deviation. The preliminary experiments show that directional information in wavelet subbands improves the histogram-based technique, and that use of moments combined with GGD parameters improves the performance efficiency in addition to significantly reducing complexity of comparing directly the histograms.

1 Introduction

The analysis of video data has become a vital area of research within the computer vision and image understanding community in the last decade. The reason for an in-creased attention towards video data analysis is attributed to not only the falling cost of computational power and the availability of sufficient resources to process large amounts of image data (image sequences) but also to its broad implications for modern day requirements in security, monitoring and surveillance for law enforcement, military applications and use of motion analysis to a wide range of applications across Medi-cine, Sports, Biomechanics and Neuroscience and Motor Control.

Although this technique can be applied to any short duration complex motion of an articulated body, this paper examines it on one of the most studied components in video data - the human motion because it is the driving force in systems related to surveillance, control and analysis. One of the drawbacks of sensing motion by video is the complexity of data processing as compared to other sensors where devices (e.g. gloves, reflectors, electrodes) [1–5] are placed on subjects and in the surroundings to transmit or receive generated signals respectively. This "naturalness and non-intrusive" advantage of video data based on vision sensing approach can be better utilized if the operational complexity of processing the data can be reduced.

This paper proposes to improve the efficiency of our previously reported gesture recognition techniques [6–8], which determined the efficacy of the use of directional information available in wavelet multiresolution decomposition of the spatio-temporal templates (STT) representing action. This is the first step towards developing applica-tions where movement data may be interpreted by machines in normal living and work-ing environments to identify the actions or the subject. This will take the capability of machines into the 'understanding people' domain.

This research has incorporated the techniques proposed by Bobick and Davis [9], Black and Yakoob [10] , Sharma, Dinesh et al [6–8] and Mandal [11]. It is based on the use of view-based representation of actions using STT formed by collapsing tem-poral component and difference of frames (DOF) data, of the video covering the pe-riod of distinct motion, into a static grey scale image. The intensity value at each pixel in this representation is a function of the motion properties at the corresponding spatial location in an image sequence. The temporal history of the movement in the STT is inserted such that the recently moving pixels are brighter [7, 9, 12].

This paper reports a novel research that reduces the complexity of processing video data for classification by condensing the feature space. The authors previously re-ported that wavelet high pass subimages carry important directional information [7], and that the global detail activity available in high pass decompositions significantly improve the classification accuracy [6]. But the complexity of comparing high pass wavelet histograms is very high. This paper reports the efficacy of reducing this com-plexity by modeling highpass wavelet coefficients by generalized Gaussian density (GGD) parameters and by transforming STT histograms into orthogonal Legendre moment's space.

2 Theory: An Overview and Explanation of the Approach

Based on research reported in literature, that actions can be recognized by motion itself [13, 14], that for recognition of actions one only needs the description of the appearance of motion [6–10, 13–15] and that motion can be recognized directly with-out any reference to underlying static images; it can be stated that actions and mes-sages / information can be recognized by description of the appearance of motion without reference to underlying static images, and without a full geometric reconstruc-tion of the moving part [10]. It can also be argued that the static images produced using spatio-temporal template based on the Difference of Frames (DOF) can represent features of temporally localized motion [16].

The hypothesis that similar images have similar color distribution can be extended to grey scale image [17, 18]. Although, histogram based techniques have lower com-plexity as compared to other classical pattern recognition techniques [19–21], authors have reported that performance of the histogram alone is not adequate for motion template classification because it fails to capture the spatial information. However, combining the histogram features with spatial image information provided by the wavelet multiresolution decomposition compensates this drawback [6–8].

The wavelet multiresolution representations are very effective in analyzing informa-tion content of the images by providing a measure of directional activity at each de-composition level in space-frequency domain [22]. At different resolutions, the details of an image generally characterize different physical structures and is useful for pattern recognition algorithms [23].

This paper reports our efforts to improve the efficiency of classification reported in previous papers [6–8] by reducing the dimensionality of feature space by just two GGD parameters (shape factor and standard deviation) to represent wavelet high-pass coefficients and by using limited number of orthogonal Legendre moments to represent STT histograms.

2.1 Modeling of Subband Coefficients

It has been proven that histograms (or pdfs) of highpass wavelet coefficients can be modelled using a generalized Gaussian density (GGD) function, which can be ex-pressed as [23, 24]:

$$p(x) = a \, exp \, \{-|bx|^\gamma\} \quad (1)$$

where γ is the shape parameter of the pdf. The positive constants a and b are given by

$$a = \frac{b\gamma}{2\Gamma(1/\gamma)} \qquad b = \frac{1}{\sigma}\sqrt{\frac{\Gamma(3/\gamma)}{\Gamma(1/\gamma)}} \quad (2)$$

where σ is the *standard deviation* and $\Gamma(.)$ is the standard *gamma* function i.e.

$$\Gamma(z) = \int_0^\infty e^{-t} t^{z-1} dt, \quad z > 0 \quad (3)$$

Figure. 1 show a typical example of a histogram of wavelet subband coefficients to-gether with a fitted GGD using the method reported in [25]. The mean values of the highpass wavelet subimages are very close to zeros. Therefore two parameters, σ (the standard deviation of coefficients) and γ (the shape parameter) can describe the pdf of a highpass subimage.

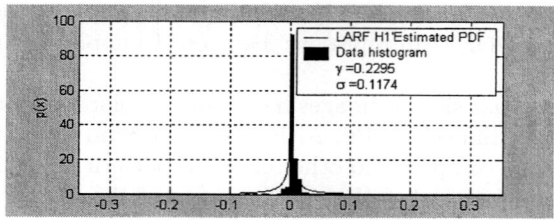

Fig. 1. GGD fit for first level horizontal wavelet coefficients of action Lateral Arm Raise Full

2.2 Moments

By definition regular moments (M_k) are projections of $f(x)$ onto monomials (x^k) and the central moments (μ_k) are projections onto $(x-\bar{x})^k$.

$$M_k = \int_{-\infty}^{+\infty} x^k f(x) dx, \quad \mu_k = \int_{-\infty}^{+\infty} (x-\bar{x})^k f(x) dx \quad for \quad k \geq 0, k \in Z \quad (4)$$

These polynomials are not orthogonal to each other and hence the regular and central moments may have substantial redundancy between them. Therefore, the histograms (*pdf*) of pixel intensities are represented by Legendre moments, which are orthogonal.

Legendre Moments. The Legendre moments of order $K1+K2++Kn$, where n is the space dimension under consideration, are defined [26] by

$$\lambda_{K_1...K_n} = \frac{(2K_1+1)...(2K_n+1)}{2^n} \int_{-\infty}^{+\infty}...\int_{-\infty}^{+\infty} P_{K1}(x_1)...P_{Kn}(x_n) f(x_{1...n})$$
$$\times dx_1...dx_n \text{ where } K_1...K_n = 0,1,...,\infty \quad (5)$$

The Legendre polynomials $P_k(x)$ are a complete orthogonal basis set on the interval [-1,1]. The k_{th} order Legendre polynomial is

$$P_k(x) = \frac{1}{k!2^k} \frac{d^k}{dx^k}(x^2-1)^k = \sum_{j=0}^{k} a_{kj} x^j \quad (6)$$

where a_{kj} the coefficients of x^j are given by Eq. 7 [27].

$$a_{kj} = \sum_{j=0, k \text{ odd} j, k \text{ even}}^{k} \frac{(k+j)!}{2^k ((k-j)/2)!((k+j)/2)!j!} \quad (7)$$

By orthogonality principle, a function can be written as an infinite series expansion in terms of the Legendre polynomial over the square $[-1 \leq x_1, ..., ..., x_n \leq 1]$:

$$f(x_1, ..., ..., x_n) = \sum_{k_1=0}^{\infty}...\sum_{k_n=0}^{\infty} \lambda_{k-1...kn} P_{k_1}(x_1)...P_{k_n}(x_n) \quad (8)$$

where the Legendre moments are computed over the same square. Using Eq. 4, the kth Legendre moment of a function $f(x)$ is defined as:

$$\lambda_k = \frac{(2K+1)}{2} \int_{-\infty}^{+\infty} P_k(x)f(x)dx, \quad for \quad k \geq 0, k \in Z \tag{9}$$

Using Eq. 4 and Eq. 6, λ_k can be written as:

$$\lambda_k = \frac{(2K+1)}{2} \sum_{j=0}^{k} a_{kj} m_j \tag{10}$$

So, the Legendre moments depend on the geometric moments of the same order or lower and can be calculated using Eq. 10.

The STT grey levels range from 0 to 255. Since the Legendre polynomials are orthogonal between [-1,1], the dynamic range of the histogram *(pdf)* is mapped onto this interval.

The *pdf* $f(x)$ can be written as an infinite expansion series in terms of the Legendre polynomial:

$$f(x) = \sum_{k=0}^{\infty} \lambda_k P_k(x) \tag{11}$$

The $f(x)$ can be approximated by the first (N+1) moments as:

$$f'(x) = \sum_{k=0}^{N} \lambda_k P_k(x) \tag{12}$$

The distance between two histograms f and g is given by

$$E = \int_{-1}^{+1} [f'(x) - g'(x)]^2 dx \tag{13}$$

using Eq. 12, it can be written as:

$$= \sum_{k=0}^{N} \frac{2(\lambda_{kf} - \lambda_{kg})^2}{2k+1} = \sum_{k=0}^{N} W_k(\lambda_{kf} - \lambda_{kg})^2, \quad Weight \; W_k = \frac{2}{2k+1} \tag{14}$$

2.3 Discrete Wavelet Transform in Image Processing

The wavelet transform of any image can be successfully implemented by a pair of appropriately designed quadrature mirror filters (QMF's) [22, 23, 28]. Wavelet based image decomposition can be viewed as a form of sub-band decomposition [29]. Each QMF pair consists of a low pass filter (H) and a high pass filter (G), which splits the signal's bandwidth in half. Each filter bank is sampled at half a rate of the previous frequency. By repeating this procedure, it is possible to obtain wavelet transform of any order. The down sampling procedure keeps the scaling parameter constant (n=1/2) throughout successive wavelet transforms. In the case of an image the filtering is implemented in a separable way by filtering the rows and columns.

Figure. 2 shows the 2-D DWT of image at 'level 1' of decomposition. According to the procedure, the image can be transformed into four sub images, namely:

- **LL** sub-image : Both horizontal and vertical directions have low frequencies.
- **LH** sub-image: The horizontal direction has low frequencies and the vertical one has high frequencies.
- **HL** sub-image:The horizontal direction has high frequencies and the vertical one has low frequencies.
- **HH** sub-image: Both horizontal and vertical directions have high frequencies.

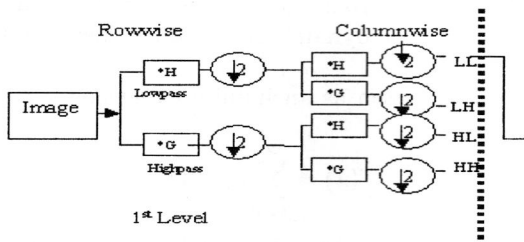

Fig. 2. 1st level Decomposition.,∗ denotes convolution and 2 denotes subsampling

Subsequent levels of decomposition follow the same procedure by decomposing the 'LL' subimage of the previous level (Figure 3).

A three stage dyadic decomposition will create one lowpass subimage (L3) and nine (three each in horizontal (H1, H2, H3), vertical (V1, V2, V3) diagonal (D1, D2, D3) direction) highpass directional subimages, as depicted in Fig. 2. The lowpass subi-mage, a thumbnail version is the low-resolution description of the original image. The highpass subimages provide the fluctuations in the horizontal, vertical diagonal directions.

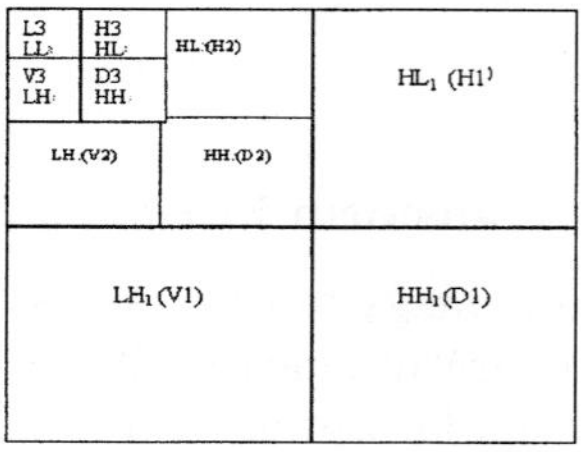

Fig. 3. 3 - Level Multiresolution Decomposition of an image

Fig. 4. Video Frames and Spatio-Temporal Template for Action: Sitting on a Chair

3 Feature Extraction

The spatio-temporal template (STT) of object motion in video data is given by [6, 7]:

$$H_n(x,y) = \max \bigcup_{n=1}^{N-1} B(x,y,n) \times n \qquad (15)$$

where

$$B(x,y,n) = \begin{cases} 1 & \text{if } D(x,y,n) > \Gamma \\ 0 & \text{Otherwise} \end{cases} \qquad (16)$$

and

$$D(x,y,n) = |I(x,y,n) - I(x,y,n-)| \qquad (17)$$

N is total number of frames that capture the motion, Γ is selected threshold, $I(x,y,n)$ is the intensity of each pixel at location x, y at frame/time n and $D(x,y,n)$ is the difference of consecutive frames representing regions of motion. The pixel intensity Hn is a function of motion history at that point and the result is a scalar-value image where more recently moving pixels are brighter [9].

The STT has to be described in terms of suitable features for classification. The grey levels are the temporal descriptors and thus the analysis should be 'global internal' (region based) instead of shape boundary description and its features [29–31].

For an appearance based, view sensitive approach, it is desirable to have action identification technique invariant to the imaging situation [9]. Although, grey level distribution is invariant to image rotation and changes slowly with translation [32], the scale and translation invariance can also be achieved by normalizing the template by using regular moments .(Appendix I: Normalization with respect to translation and scale) [7, 33].

The computation of feature vectors involves representing these templates in terms of histograms (Fig. 6) and wavelet multiresolution coefficients using three-stage dyadic decomposition with db1 wavelet. The highpass wavelet coefficients are modelled by GGD parameters (equations 1 and 2) using the method proposed in [25].

The feature vector computed from the template is compared and matched with a class of feature vectors stored a priori (reference), to establish the correspondence between the given template (of an unknown action) and a predefined action. The classification is done based on minimum distance between two actions represented by template histograms f and g using

$$d_{L_P}(f,g) = \sum_{nk} |f(n_k) - g(n_k)|^p \qquad (18)$$

Measure of similarity between two actions using Legendre moments and GGD parameters is established by L_2 metric:

$$d(f,g) = \sum_{n=0}^{N} W_k(\lambda_{kf} - \lambda_{kg})^2 + \sum_{n=1}^{B}(\sigma_{kf} - \sigma_{kg})^2 + \sum_{k=1}^{B}(\gamma_{kf} - \gamma_{kg})^2 \qquad (19)$$

where, λ s are the Legendre moments, σ and γ are the standard deviation and shape parameters of wavelet subimages respectively. The parameters N and B are number of moments representing histograms f and g, and wavelet subbands respectively

4 Experimentation

Video data was collected for five predefined gestures performed ten times each by seven subjects (Figures 4 - 5). The movement was recorded in 2-D vision-space at 2 meters normal to subject and the window size was an area of 6 sq meters. For each of the experiments, the following constrains were maintained during motion capture:

1. *Related to Movements*: SCMO (Stationary Camera Moving Object), Presence of Single Subject in Scene, Constant Window Size and View Angle, Same pixels are not revisited by motion.
2. *Related to Environment and Subject*: No restriction on colour and tightness of clothes, Subjects of different height, weight, age and both genders, Static back-ground and uniform illumination during the timing window of action

5 Measure of Performance and Methodology for Classification

The efficiency of performance (η) is defined as the ratio of successful matches in the first 20 matches. (e.g. 16 out of 20 gives an accuracy of 80%). Feature vectors were generated for a set of 20 from each of the five gestures (Fig. 4, Fig. 5. The distance measure between test gesture and the stored 100 gestures is computed for similarity.

Efficiency of performance is computed for original templates (DOH), Low pass subimages (LL) and nine highpass subimages (HH) using L1 metric (Eq. 18) cases A,B and C respectively) [7]. Improvement in efficiency is computed by combing directional wavelet histograms (WH) and GGD parameters (WP) respectively with DOH (Cases D and E respectively). Finally, measure of similarity between two actions using Legendre moments and GGD parameters is established by Eq.19.

Fig. 5. Examples of remaining four actions and their spatio-temporal templates (STT)

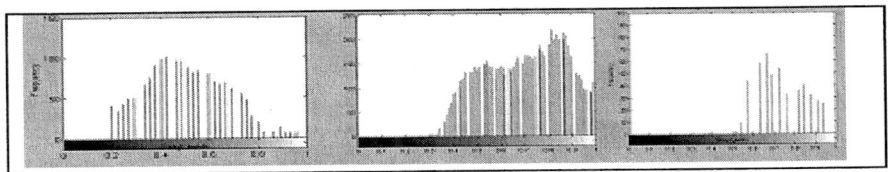

Fig. 6. Examples of STT histograms for Sit, lateral arm raise full and drink

6 Results and Discussions

Table 1 shows the performance efficiency (η) based on various techniques, outlined in section 6, with wavelet decomposition using L1 metric for cases (A-D). L1 metric for DOH and equation 19 for WP are used to compute efficiency for case E.

Table 1. Significance of available information in wavelet lowpass and highpass subimages and improvement in efficiency using wavelet subbands for 3rd level decomposition (B=3)

Case No.	Classification Technique	Efficiency (η)%
A	DOH	87
B	LL	63
C	HH	57
D	DOH+WH	91.5
E	DOH+WP	93

The comparison of template histograms provides an efficiency of 87%. The comparison of 3rd lowpass subimage (L3) of template provides an efficiency of only 63% because of noisy behavior of the lowpass wavelet subimage. It is important to note that comparison of only nine highpass subimages also provide an efficiency of 57%. This shows that although it is possible to discriminate by using the directional information at various scales, the efficiency of accuracy is not significant. Efficiency improves by 4.5% with template histogram and wavelet histograms for 3 levels of decomposition. Replacing subband histograms with wavelet band parameters improves the efficiency by 6%.

In addition to improved performance, the feature space of directional wavelet histograms is significantly reduced using wavelet parameters. Instead of comparing individual bin values, each histogram is compared by just two parameters - shape factor $'\gamma'$ and standard deviation $'\sigma'$.

Table 2 explains the performance efficiency (η) based on moments and wavelet parameters using Eq.19. Moments and wavelet parameters combined provide an

Table 2. Performance of Legendre moments alone and in combination with wavelet subband parametrs - shapefactor and standard deviation

B and N	Performance Efficiency %	
	Moments Alone	Moments + Wavelet parameters($\sigma\&\gamma$)
B=3, N=1	82.5	87.5
B=3, N=15	85	90.5
B=3, N=20	85.5	91

efficiency improvement of 5.5% over moments alone. It is also observed that the efficiency does not improve beyond $N = 15$. For $N = 15$ and $B = 3$, only 21 parameters (15 moments and 6 wavelet parameters) need to be compared. This considerably reduces the dimensionality of feature space but at a marginal decrease in performance.

7 Conclusions

The results demonstrate that the statistical properties of the template and wavelet coefficients can be used to classify short duration movements in video data.. The proposed use of wavelets show that highpass subimages carry important directional information but does not provide significant classification results by itself. The modeling of wavelet coefficients by GGD parameters greatly reduce the feature space with appreciable improvement in efficiency of performance The significant reduction in complexity (15 moments versus all bins) of comparing histograms using Legendre moments is accompanied by a marginal decrease in performance efficiency. The authors are currently attempting to use cascade of features to overcome this drawback.

References

1. Fels, S.S. and G.E. Hinton, *Glove-talk: a neural network interface between a dataglove and a speech synthesiser.* IEEE Transactions on Neural Networks, Jan 1993. 4: p. 2–8.
2. Quam, D.L., *Gesture recognition with a Data-Glove*, in Proceedings of the IEEE Aero-space and Electronics Conference. Jan 1993. p. 755-760.

3. Sturman, D.J. and D. Zeltzer, *A survey of glove-based input.* IEEE Computer Graphics and Applications, Jan1994. 14(1): p. 30-39.
4. Davis, J.W., *Representing and Recognizing Human Motion: From Motion templates to Movement Categories.* International Conference on Intelligent Robots and Systems, Maui, Hawaii, October 29 2001
5. Baudel, T. and M. Beaudouin-Lafon, *Charade:Remote control of objects using free hand gestures.* Communications of the ACM, July 1993. 36(7): p. 28-35.
6. Sharma, A., et al., *Wavelet Directional Histograms of the Spatio-Temporal Templates of Human Gestures.* International Journal of Wavelets, Multiresolution and Information Proc-essing (IJWMIP), 2004. 2(3): p. 1-16.
7. Sharma, A., et al. *Wavelet Directional Histograms for Classification of Human Gestures Represented by Spatio-Temporal Templates.* in IEEE Computer Society:10th International Multi-Media Modelling Conference (MMM 2004). Brisbane, Australia 57-63. January 2004
8. Sharma, A., et al. *Classification of Human Actions using Temporal Templates, Histograms And Orthogonal Moments.* in 7th World Multiconference on Systemics, Cybernetics and In-formatics (SCI 2003). Orlando, USA. July 27-30, 2003
9. Bobick, A.F. and J.W. Davis, *The Recognition of Human Movement using Temporal Tem-plates.* IEEE Transactions on Pattern Analysis and Machine Intelligence(PAMI), March 2001. 23(3): p. 257-267.
10. Black, M.J. and Y. Yakoob. *Tracking and Recognizing Rigid and Non-Rigid Facial Motion Using Local Parametric Models of Image Motion.* in International Conference of Computer Vision. 374-381. 1995
11. Mandal, M.K., S. Panchanathan, and T. Aboulnasr, *Illumination Invariant Image Indexing Using Moments and Wavelets.* Journal of Electronic Imaging, April1998. 7(2): p. 282-293.
12. Masoud, O. and N. Papanikolopoulos. *Human Activity Recognition.* in IEEE Conference on Advanced Video and Signal Based Surveillance. Miami, Florida 157-162. 21-22 July 2003
13. Johnsson, G., Visual Perception of Biological Motion and a Model for Its Analysis. Percep-tion And Psychophysics, 1973. 14(2): p. 201-211
14. Johnsson, G., Visual Motion Perception. Scientific American, June 1975: p. 76-88.
15. Cedras, C. and M. Shah, *Motion Based Recognition.* Image and Vision Computing, March 1995. 13: p. 129 -155
16. Essa, I. and A. Pentland. *Facial Expression Recognition Using a Dynamic Model of Motion Energy.* in International Conference on Computer Vision. Cambridge, MA. June 1995
17. Swain, M.J. and D.H. Ballard, *Color Indexing.* International Journal of Computer Vision, 1991. 7(1): p. 11-32.
18. Stricker, M. and M. Orengo. *Similarity of Color Images.* in Proc. of SPIE:Storage and Re-trieval for Images and Video Databases III. San Jose, CA Vol. 2420381-392. Feb. 1995
19. Belkasim, S., M. Shridhar, and M. Ahmadi, *Pattern Recognition with Moment Invariants: A Comparative Study and New Results.* Pattern recognition, 1991. 24(12): p. 1117-1138
20. Hu, M.-K., *Visual Pattern Recognition by Moment Invariants.* IEEE Transaction on Infor-mation Theory, 1962. 8(2): p. 179-187.
21. Johnsson, G., *Visual Motion Perception.* Scientific American, June 1975: p. 76-88.
22. Mallat, S., *Wavelets for Vision.* Proceedings of the IEEE, April 1996. 84(4): p. 604-614.

23. Mallat, S.G., *A Theory for Multiresolution Signal Decomposition:The Wavelet Representation*. IEEE - Pattern Analysis and Machine Intelligence, July 1989. 11(7): p. 674-693.
24. Birney, K.A. and T.R. Fischer, *On the Modelling of DCT and Subband Image Data for Compression*. IEEE Transaction on Image Processing, Feb 1995. 4(2).
25. Sharifi, K. and G. A.L, *Estimation of Shape parameter for Generalized Gaussian Distribution in Subband decompositions of Video*. IEEE - Transaction on Circuits and Systems for Video Technology, Feb 1995. 5(1).
26. Qjidaa, H. and L. Radouane, *Robust Line Fitting in a Noisy Image by the Method of Moments*. IEEE Trans. on PAMI, November 1999. 21, No 11: p. 1216-1223.
27. Kreyszig, E., *Advanced Engineering Mathematics*. 8 ed. 1999, John Wiley Sons
28. Sarlashkar, A.N.B. and M.J. Malkani. *Feature Extraction Using Wavelet Transform for Neural Network Based Image Classification*. in Proceeding of the Thirtieth Southeastern Symposium in System Theory. Morgantown, WV, USA. 1998.
29. Weiss, L., *Geometric Invariants and Object Recognition*. International Journal of Computer Vision, 1993. 10: p. 207-231.
30. Shavit, E. and A. Jepson, *Motion Understanding Using Phase Portraits*. IJCAI:workshop: Looking at people, 1995.
31. Polana, R. and R. Nelson. *Low Level Recognition of Human Motion*. in IEEE Workshop on Motion of Non-Rigid and Articulated Motion. Austin, Texas 77-82. 1994.
32. Mandal, M.K., T. Aboulnasr, and S. Panchanathan, *Image Indexing Using Moments and Wavelets*. IEEE Transaction on Consumer Electronics, Aug1996. 42(3): p. 557-565.
33. Mukundan, R. and R.K. R, *Moment Functions In Image Analysis, Theory and Application*. 1998, Singapore: World Scientific Publishing Co. Pte. Ltd. 85-87.

Appendix 1

Normalizing the Templates with Respect to Scale and Translation.

$I'(x,y) = I\left(\frac{x}{a} + \overline{x}, \frac{y}{a} + \overline{y}\right)$ $where$ $\left(\overline{x} = \frac{m_{10}}{m_{00}}, \overline{y} = \frac{m_{01}}{m_{00}}\right)(\overline{x}, \overline{y})$ is the centroid of $I(x,y)$ the original template and $a = \sqrt{\frac{\beta}{m_{00}}}$ with β a predetermined value and m_{00} is the $Zero^{th}$ order moment. Note that for a binary image m_{00} is the total number of shape pixels in the image.

Personal Authenticator on the Basis of Two-Factors: Palmprint Features and Tokenized Random Data

Ying-Han Pang, Andrew Teoh Beng Jin, and David Ngo Chek Ling

Faculty of Information Science and Technology, Multimedia University,
Jalan Ayer Keroh Lama, 75450 Melaka, Malaysia
{yhpang, bjteoh, david.ngo}@mmu.edu.my

Abstract. This paper presents a novel two-factor authenticator which hashes tokenized random data and moment based palmprint features to produce a set of private binary string, coined as Discrete-Hashing code. This novel technique requires two factors (random number + authorized biometrics) credentials in order to access the authentication system. Absence of either factor will just handicap the progress of authentication. Besides that, Discrete-Hashing also possesses high discriminatory power, with highly correlated bit strings for intra-class data. Experimental results show that this two-factor authenticator surpasses the classic biometric authenticator in terms of verification rate. Our proposed approach provides a clear separation between genuine and imposter population distributions. This implies that Discrete-Hashing technique allows achievement of zero False Accept Rate (FAR) without jeopardizing the False Reject Rate (FRR) performance, which is hardly possible to conventional biometric systems.

1 Introduction

In the past, secret passwords, ID cards and tokens were the popular approaches for personal recognition. However, with the acceleration of technology recently, these traditional approaches gradually hardly gain reliance from the public since they can easily be duplicated and shared. The cost of management of forgotten passwords, lost, stolen or forged ID cards and tokens, coupled with the decreasing cost and higher reliability of biometric based authentication system, has boosted an extensive implementation of biometric based personal recognition system in our daily activities. Unfortunately, even biometrics also suffers from some inherent biometrics-specific threats [1] and biometric recognition devices have been fooled. A Japanese mathematician and amateur scientist, Tsutomu Matsumoto, reported that he had been able to fool fingerprint recognition devices by molding a "gummy" replica of a human finger [2]. This event arouses a suspicion from the public towards the reliability of the biometric based recognition systems.

Besides that, conventional biometric systems are impossible to gain zero Equal Error Rate (EER), which is zero in False Accept Rate (FAR) and False Reject Rate (FRR). In the conventional biometric systems, the classes are difficult to completely separate in the measurement space. This factor triggers the interdependency problem between FAR and FRR where specification of relatively low FAR, i.e. acceptance of imposters, will output relatively high FRR, i.e. rejection of genuine.

In this paper, a novel two-factor authenticator, which is able to overcome the limitations of the classic biometric recognition system, is proposed. In this proposed system, pseudo random number is inner product with moment based palmprint features to generate a string of random data for each palmprint class (user). Discretization of these strings of random real values into strings of binary bits [0, 1] is implemented based on a predefined threshold value. This set of binary codes is coined as Discrete-Hashing code.

Discrete-Hashing code, abbreviated hereinafter as D-Hashing code, possesses high data capture offset tolerance, with highly correlated bit strings for intra-class data. This means that Discrete-Hashing is able to minimize the intra-class distance but maximize the inter-class distance. Experimental results demonstrate that this proposed approach provides an extremely clear separation between the genuine and imposter populations. This clear separation reveals the additional credit of Discrete-Hashing, which is zero EER achievement. This implies that our proposed method is able to drive off the interdependency problem faced by conventional biometric recognition system and allow acquisition of zero FAR without jeopardizing the FRR performance. Fig. 1 illustrates the overview of our proposed system.

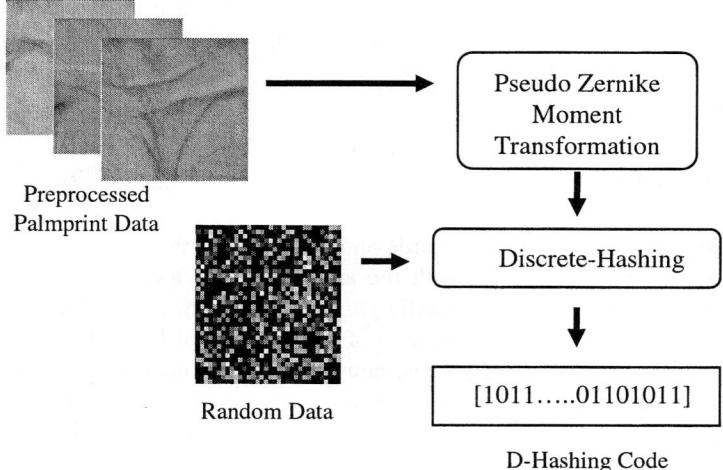

Fig. 1. Block diagram of our proposed system

2 Palmprint Image Preprocessing

Palmprint images captured in the image acquisition stage may have variable sizes and orientations. Moreover, there captured images not only do contain region of interest, denoted hereinafter as ROI, but also contain region of not interest, the trivial objects. Therefore, image preprocessing is a necessary and crucial step in biometric system. A perfect preprocessing always results a more robust and accurate feature extraction, which leads to a tremendous authentication.

During preprocessing, the placement and orientation of ROI is fixed in order to achieve rotational and translational invariants. After the correction of placement orientation, the ROI is extracted. Next, the ROI is converted to a fixed size so that all of the palmprints conform to a same size. Then, intensity normalization algorithm is applied on the extracted ROI to overcome with the low contrast and non-uniform illumination problems. Finally, the preprocessed ROI is input into feature extraction module, see Fig. 2. The details of preprocessing can be referred in [3].

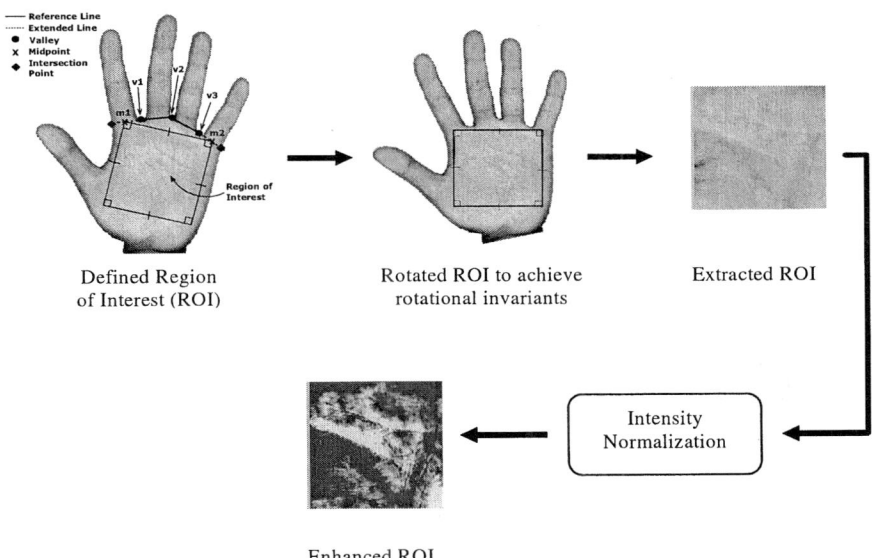

Fig. 2. Palmprint image preprocessing

3 Feature Extractor-Pseudo Zernike Moments

The kernel of pseudo Zernike moments is the set of orthogonal pseudo Zernike polynomials that defined over the polar coordinates inside a unit circle. The two-dimensional pseudo Zernike moments of order p with repetition q of an image intensity function $f(r,\theta)$ are defined as [4][5],

$$PZ_{pq} = \frac{p+1}{\pi} \int_0^{2\pi} \int_0^1 V_{pq}(r,\theta) f(r,\theta) r dr d\theta \quad (1)$$

where Zernike polynomials $V_{pq}(r,\theta)$ are defined as,

$$V_{pq}(r,\theta) = R_{pq}(r)e^{-jq\theta}; \quad \hat{j} = \sqrt{-1} \qquad (2)$$

and

$$r = \sqrt{x^2 + y^2}, \quad \theta = \tan^{-1}\left(\frac{y}{x}\right), \quad -1 < x, y < 1$$

The real-valued radial polynomials are defined as,

$$R_{pq}(r) = \sum_{s=0}^{p-|q|}(-1)^s \frac{(2p+1-s)!}{s!(p+|q|+1-s)!(p-|q|-s)!} r^{p-s}, \quad 0 \le |q| \le p, \, p \ge 0 \qquad (3)$$

and

Since it is easier to work with real functions, PZ_{pq} is often split into its real and imaginary parts, PZ_{pq}^c, PZ_{pq}^s as given below [5]:

$$PZ_{pq}^c = \frac{2(p+1)}{\pi} \int_0^{2\pi}\int_0^1 R_{pq}(r)\cos(q\theta)f(r,\theta)rdrd\theta \qquad (4)$$

$$PZ_{pq}^s = \frac{2(p+1)}{\pi} \int_0^{2\pi}\int_0^1 R_{pq}(r)\sin(q\theta)f(r,\theta)rdrd\theta \qquad (5)$$

where $p \ge 0$, $q > 0$.

4 Discrete-Hashing

The function of Discrete-Hashing is to enhance the offset tolerance of our system. The generated D-Hashing code possesses high intra-class correlation, but relatively low inter-class correlation. In this stage, feature vector, PZ_{pq}, transformed from image function, $f(x,y)$, via pseudo Zernike moment feature extraction approach, is transfigured into a m-length bit string of binary code, $\{0,1\}^m$, by iterated inner product feature vector with a set of pseudo random data. This random data is distributed according to uniform distribution U [-1 1]. Collaboration between pseudo random data and moment based feature vector turns out a robust discriminative power mechanism that results a diminution of intra-class offset.

The progression of Discrete-Hashing is described as below,

1. compute $x(PZ_{pq}, \Re) = $ <feature vector, random data set>, where $<,>$ denotes the inner product process.

2. determine $b(x) = \begin{cases} 0 & ; x < \tau \\ 1 & ; x \ge \tau \end{cases}$, where $|$ is a threshold for assigning a single bit, which will be used to form D-Hashing code.

This procedure is repeated for other sets of random data to attain multiple binary bits for making up a bit string, D-Hashing code, acted as verification key in our proposed authentication system. Here is worth to note that the random data is an orthonormal set $\wp = \{\Re_k ; k = 1,2,3,......,m\}$ which alleviates inter-bit correlations. In other words, each bit $b(x)$ is unassociated to other bits and this trait maximizes the inter-class distance. The D-Hashing code formulation is illustrated in Fig. 3.

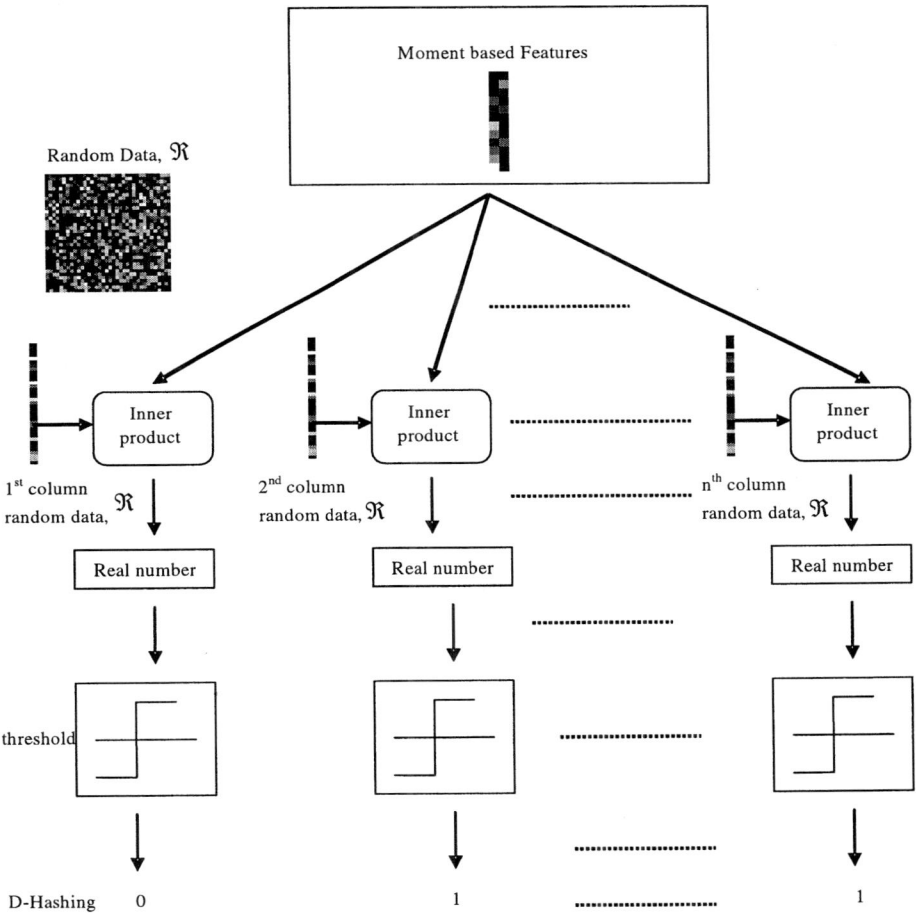

Fig. 3. D-Hashing code formulation

5 Experimental Results and Discussions

Experiments were conducted by using a set of database which possessing 100 different palmprint classes, with six samples for each class. This makes up a total of 600 experimental palmprint samples. For each palmprint pattern, the first, third and fifth sample were used for testing and the rest for enrollment. The region of interest is cropped and converted to 16-bit grayscale. A few palmprint samples are shown in Fig. 4.

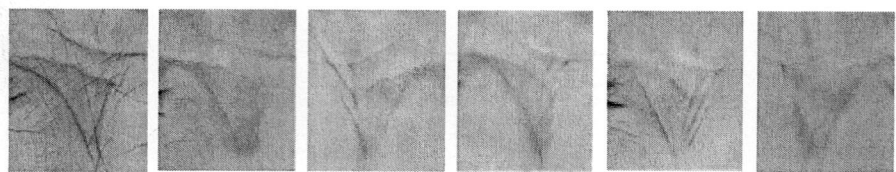

Fig. 4. A few palmprint samples that used in the experiments

The experimental schemes are as follows:

PZM : denoting solely PZM-based scheme.
PZM+D-m: denoting two-factor scheme where m is the bit length.

The experimental data are acquired for m=30, 50 and 70. A simple similarity apparatus, Euclidean distance metric, is adopted in classification phase.

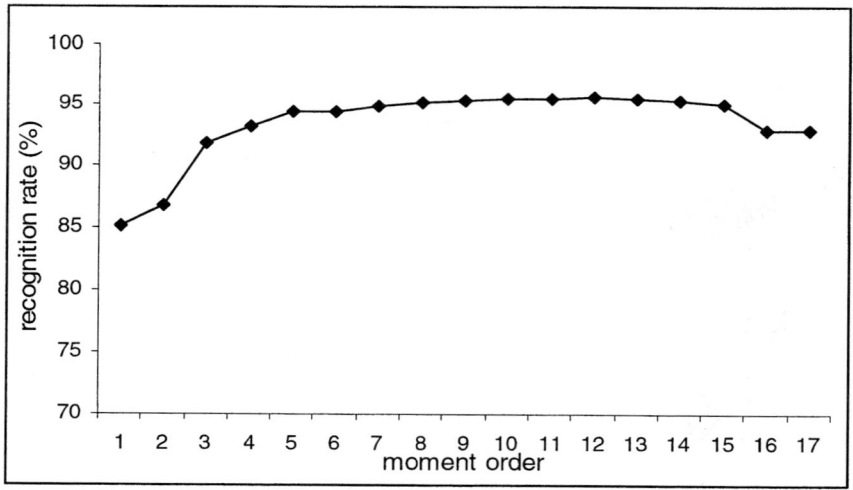

Fig. 5. Plot of recognition rate versus moment order

At the initial stage, pertinent and optimal moment order in representing the palmprint identity is determined. An experiment was conducted using different settings of feature vectors based on the order (h) of pseudo Zernike moments for determining the moments that optimally describe palmprint features. The result of recognition rate is shown in Fig. 5. Moments of order 12, which obtain the highest recognition rate, possesses the best feature vectors that optimally describe the palmprints. Therefore, moments of order 12 are selected for the continuous experiments in this study. Furthermore, the figure also reveals that the higher order of moments, the higher recognition rate of the system. This is because higher order moments capture finer and details about the image [6]. However, this is only true to a certain point as the recognition rate will become stabilize or even worse if the feature length is extended further.

Table 1 shows the comparison between *PZM* and *PZM+D-m* schemes based on the Equal Error Rate (EER) condition where FAR•FRR. It can be observed that *PZM+D-m* schemes perform much better than *PZM* scheme. From the result, *PZM+D-70* scheme yields 0% of FRR when FAR is reduced to zero. This is a significant enhancement to the contemporary biometric systems as the interdependency problem between FAR and FRR is eliminated. Besides, we can see that longer bit length, *m*, produces more impressive result.

Table 1. *PZM* and *PZM+D-m* schemes comparison based in ERR

Schemes	FAR (%)	FRR (%)	TSR (%)
PZM	4.422	4.427	95.578
PZM+D-30	0.535	1.00	99.460
PZM+D-50	0.030	0	99.970
PZM+D-70	0	0	100.00

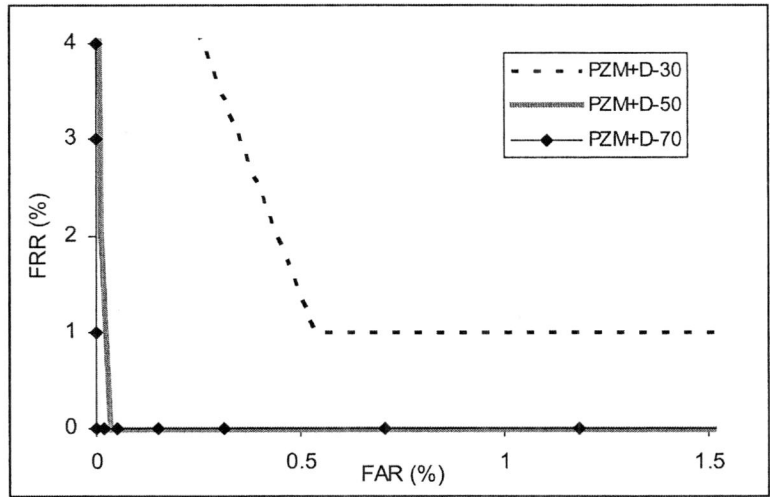

Fig. 6. Receiver Operating Characteristic (ROC) plot for *PZM+D-m* schemes

Fig. 6 depicts dramatic decrement of EER for *PZM+D-m* schemes and its consistent Receiver Operating Characteristic (ROC) plot along the x- and y-axis. The lower and further left on the graph for each curve then the better the performance.

Thus Fig. 6 shows the robustness of *PZM+D*-70 scheme in personal verification. The figure also illustrates the phenomenon of longer bit length, m, produces better result. Introduction of Discrete-Hashing in authentication system is efficient to overcome the trade-off between system FAR and FRR.

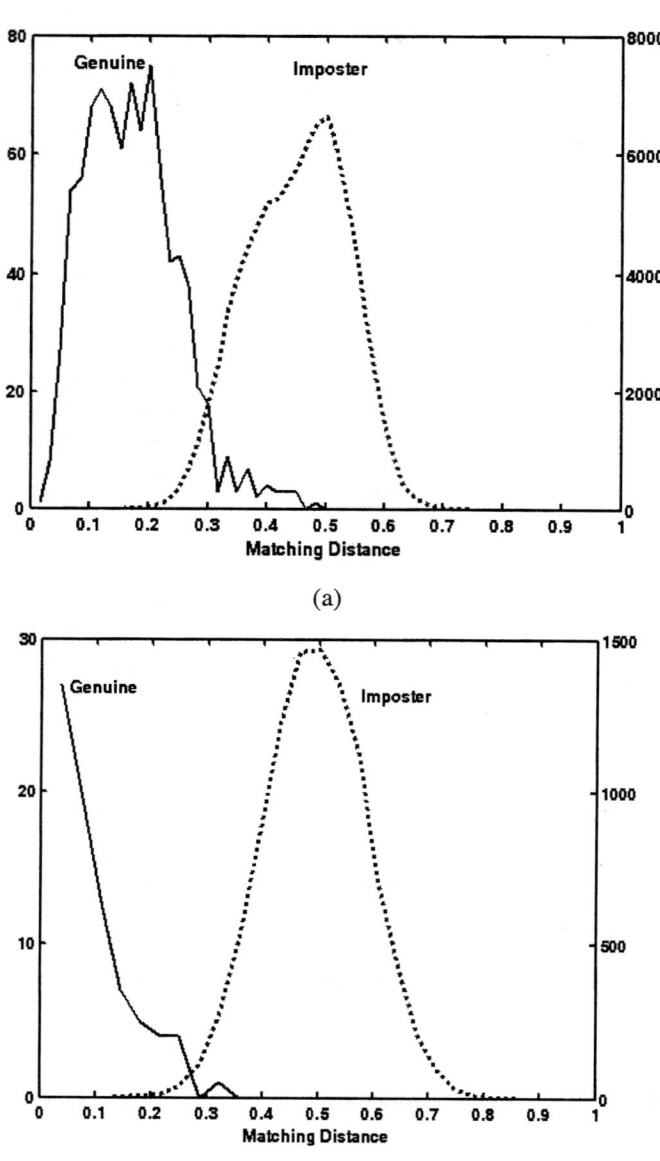

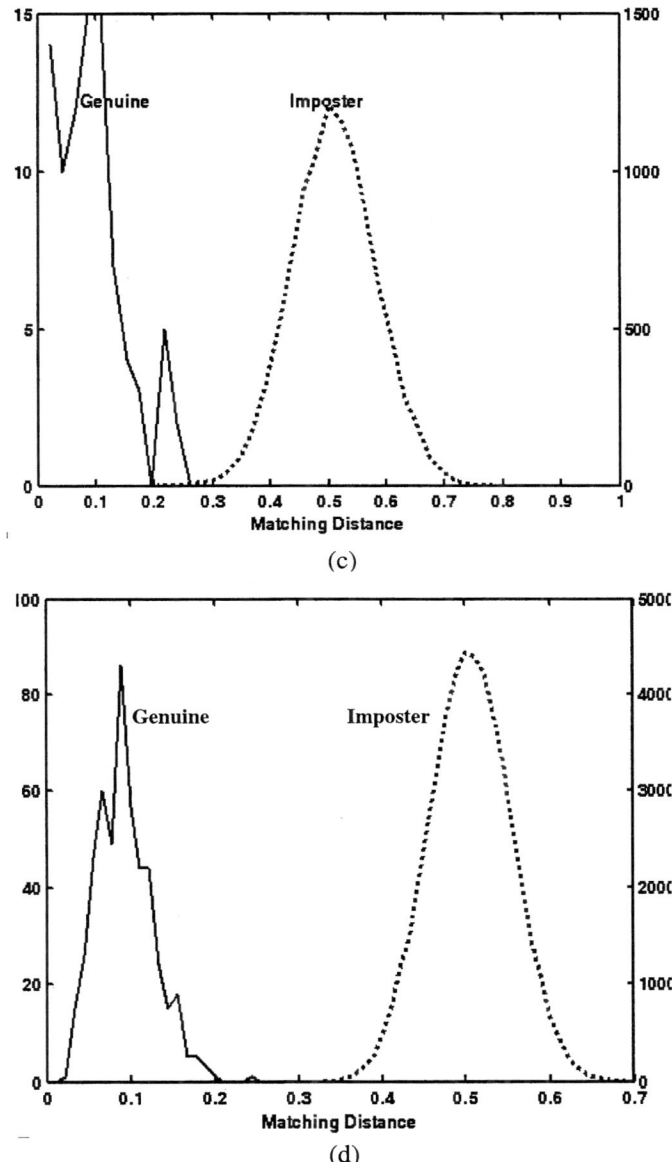

Fig. 7. Genuine and imposter population distribution for (a) PZM scheme, (b) *PZM+D-30* scheme, (c) *PZM+D-50*, and (d) *PZM+D-70*

Fig. 7 illustrates the genuine and imposter population distribution for *PZM* and *PZM+D-m* schemes, respectively. The results show that there is a large overlapping in between the genuine and imposter population distributions for *PZM* scheme, but a small overlapping for $PZM+D$-30 and $PZM+D$-50 schemes and a clear separation for $PZM+D$-70 scheme. This indicates that $PZM+D$-m scheme with suitable bit length, m, outweighs PZM scheme by minimizing the intra-class distance and maximizing the inter-class distance, see Fig. 7. The steeper drop-offs in $PZM+D$-m profiles are apparent compared to the PZM profile. These sharp drop-offs allow achievement of zero FAR without downgrading the FRR performance.

6 Concluding Remarks

Novel framework of two-factor palmprint authentication system is presented in this paper. This two-factor system couples tokenized pseudo random pattern and pseudo Zernike moment based features to generate a set of unique private compact binary code, Discrete-Hashing code. In this paper, pseudo Zernike moments are chosen as feature extractor due to their superior feature representation capability and prominent orthogonality property. Combination between moment based features and random data outcomes a clear separation of the genuine and the imposter frequency distribution, zero EER level where specification of zero FAR does not imperil the performance of FRR, diminution of intra-class offset and expansion of inter-class differential distance. The proposed two-factor palmprint authenticator is able to accomplish an excellent performance with 100% of Total Success Rate (TSR) with zero False Accept rate (FAR) and False Reject rate (FRR).

References

1. Bolle, R. M., Connel, J. H. and Ratha, N. K.: Biometric Perils and Patches. The Journal of the Pattern Recognition Society, Vol. 35, (2002) 2727-2738
2. Tsutomu Matsumoto.: Importance of Open Discussion on Adversarial Analyses for Mobile Security Technology. ITU-T Workshop on Security, Seoul (May 2002)
3. Connie, T., Michael, G.K.O., Andrew, T.B.J. and David, N.C.L: An Automated Biometric Palmprint Verification System. The 3rd International Symp. on Communications & Info. Tech. (ISCIT2003), Thailand, Vol. 2, (2002) 714-719
4. Teh, C.H. and Chin, R.T.: On Image Analysis by the Methods of Moments. IEEE Trans. Pattern Analysis Machine Intell, Vol. 10, (July 1988) 496-512
5. Mukundan, R. and Ramakrishnan, K.R.: Moment Functions in Image Analysis – Theory and Applications. World Scientific Publishing (1998)
6. Pang, Y.H., Andrew, T.B.J and David, N.C.L.: Palmprint Authentication with Zernike moment Invariants. Proceeding of the 3rd International Sym. On Signal Processing and Information technology, MP3-3_ISSPIT2003, Darmstadt, Germany, (December 2003)

Practical Gaze Point Computing Method by 3D Position Estimation of Facial and Eye Features

Kang Ryoung Park

Division of Media Technology, SangMyung University,
7 Hongji-Dong, JongRo-Gu, Seoul,
Republic of Korea

Abstract. This paper addresses the accurate gaze detection method by tracking facial and eye movement at the same time. For that, we implemented our gaze detection system with a wide and a narrow view stereo camera. In order to make it easier to detect the facial and eye feature positions, the dual IR-LED illuminators are also used for our system. The performance of detecting facial features could be enhanced by Support Vector Machine and the eye gaze position on a monitor is computed by a multi-layered perceptron. Experimental results show that the RMS error of gaze detection is about 2.4 degrees (1.68 degrees on X axis and 1.71 degrees on Y axis at the Z distance of 50 cm).

Keywords: Gaze Detection, Facial and Eye Movement.

1 Introduction

Human gaze can provide important information in communication, such as giving cues of people's interest and attention, facilitating turn-taking during conversations, giving reference cues by looking at an object or person, and indicating interpersonal cues such as friendliness or defensiveness [24]. Gaze detection technology is important in many applications. It is applicable to the interface of man-machine interaction, such as the view control in three-dimensional simulation programs. Furthermore, it can help the handicapped to use computers and is also useful for those whose hands are busy doing other things[19]. In addition, it can be used for man-machine interface for wearable computer environment and the manipulation of mouse or keyboard is difficult in such a case. The previous gaze detection researches can be classified into 4 categories. First one is that focused on 2D/3D head motion estimation[2][11]. Second one is that for the facial gaze detection[3-9][12][13][15] and the third one is the eye gaze detection[10][14]. And last one is that considering both head and eye movement has been researched. Ohmura and Ballard et al.[5][6]'s methods and Rikert et al.[9]'s method has the constraints that the user's Z distance should be measured manually and take much time to compute the gaze position. Gee et al.[7] and

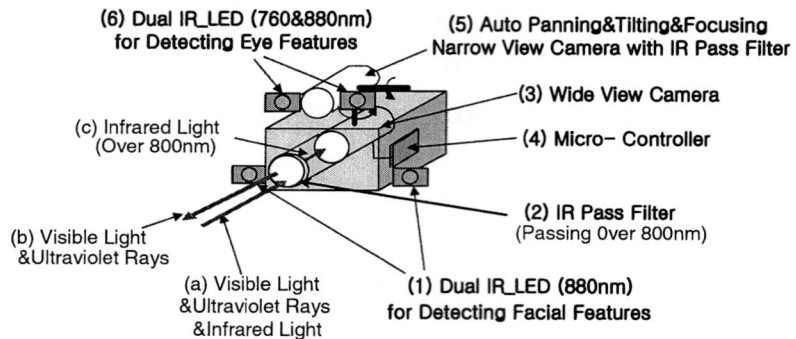

Fig. 1. The gaze detecting system

Heinzmann et al.[8]'s methods only compute gaze direction vector and do not obtain the gaze position on a monitor. In the methods of [12][13], a pair of glasses having marking points is required to detect facial features. The researches of [3][4][16] show the facial gaze detection methods and have the disadvantage that the gaze errors are increased in case that the eye movements happen. To overcome such problems, the research of [17] shows the facial and eye gaze detection, but uses only one wide view camera. In such case, the eye image resolution is too low and the fine movements of user's eye cannot be exactly detected. Wang et al.[1]'s method provides the advanced approaches that combines head pose and eye gaze estimation by a wide view camera and a panning/tilting narrow camera. However, in order to compute the gaze position, their method supposes that they know the 3D distance between two eyes, that between both lip corners and the 3D diameter of eye ball. Also, they suppose there is no individual variation for the 3D distances and diameter. However, our preliminary experiments show that there are much individual variations for the 3D distances/3D diameter and such cases can increase much gaze errors. To overcome above problems, we propose the new method for detecting gaze position.

2 Overall Procedures of Gaze Detecting Algorithm

In this paper, the gaze detection is performed according to following procedures. At first, the facial features are detected in wide view image as shown in section 3. Then, the Z distance between a user and monitor is calculated by our stereo wide/narrow view camera and the facial gaze position is calculated as shown in section 4. After that, the magnified eye image is obtained by panning/tilting/zooming/focusing narrow view camera and the eye feature location is performed as shown in section 5 and 6. Then, the eye gaze position is calculated by multi-layered perceptron and the final gaze position is calculated by the vector summation of facial and eye gaze position as shown in section 7.

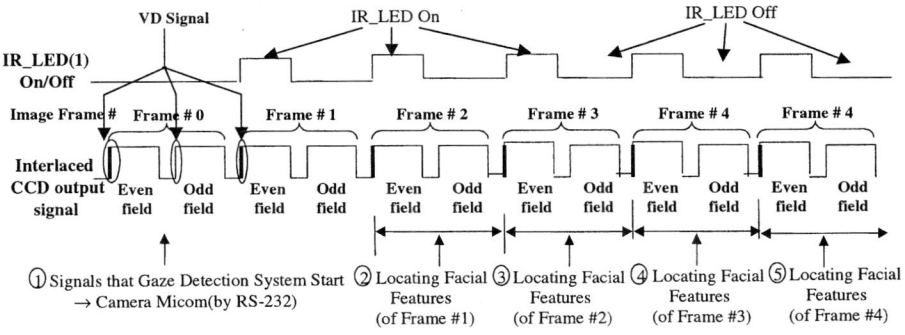

Fig. 2. The on/off controlling of IR-LED illuminator for detecting eye features

3 Localization of Facial Features in Wide View Image

In order to detect gaze position on a monitor, we first locate facial features in wide view images. To detect facial features robustly, we implement a gaze detection system as shown in Fig. 1. The IR-LED(1) is used to make the specular reflections on eyes. Due to the IR pass filter(2) in front of camera lens, the brightness of input image is only affected by the IR-LED(1) excluding external illumination. The reason of using IR-LED(1) of 880nm is that it does not make dazzling to user's eye. When a user starts our gaze detection system, the microcontroller(4) turns on the illuminator(1) synchronized with the even field of CCD signal and turns it off synchronized with the next odd field of CCD signal, successively as shown in Fig. 2[17]. From that, we can get a difference image between the even and the odd image and the specular reflection points on both eyes can be easily detected because their image gray levels are higher than other regions[17]. In addition, we use the Red-Eye effect and the method of changing Frame Grabber decoder value in order to detect more accurate eye position[17]. In general, the NTSC signal from camera has high resolution ($0 \sim 2^{10} - 1$), but the range of A/D conversion by conventional decoder of the Frame Grabber is low resolution ($0 \sim 2^8 - 1$). So, the NTSC signal in high saturated range such as the corneal specular reflection on eye and the some reflection region on facial skin can be represented as same image gray level ($2^8 - 1$), which makes it difficult to discriminate the corneal specular reflection. However, the NTSC signal level of corneal specular reflection is higher than that of other reflection due to the reflectance rate. So, if we make the decoder brightness value lower, there is no high saturated range and the corneal specular reflection and the other reflection can be discriminated easily as shown in Fig. 3. Around the detected corneal specular reflection points, we determine the eye candidate region of 30*30 pixels and locate the accurate eye (iris) center by the circular edge detection method. After that, we detect the eye corner by using eye corner shape template and SVM (Support Vector Machine)[17]. We got 2000 successive image frames for

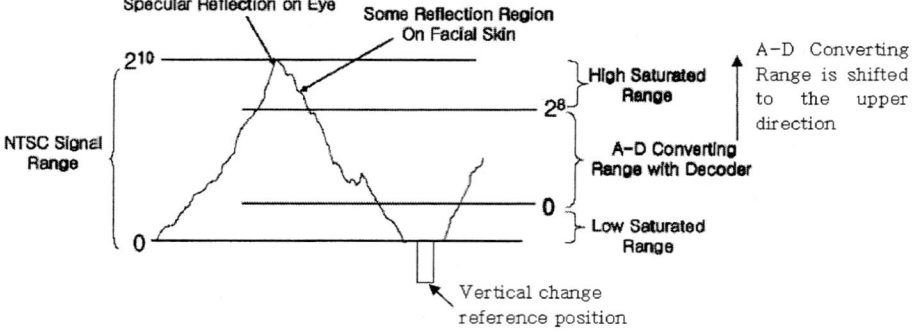

Fig. 3. The NTSC signal range vs. AD conversion range

SVM training and additional 1000 images were used for testing. The parameters used for SVM were selected by our empirical experiments. Experimental results showed the classification error for training data is 0.11% and that for testing data is 0.2%. The classification time of SVM was 8 ms in Pentium-III 866MHz. After locating eye centers and eye corners, the positions of nostrils can be detected by anthropometric constraints in a face and SVM. In order to reduce the effect by the facial expression change, we do not use the lip corners. Experimental results showed that RMS error between the detected feature positions and the actual positions were 1 pixel (of both eye centers), 2 pixels (of both eye corners) and 4 pixels (of both nostrils) in 640×480 pixels image. From those, we use 5 feature points (left/right eye corners of left eye, left/right eye corners of right eye, nostril center) in order to detect facial gaze position.

4 Computing Facial Gaze Position

Based on the detected 2D eye corner center positions, we can pan/tilt the narrow view camera in order to capture the eye image. For that, the Z distance (between the wide view camera and the 3D eye corner positions) should be required in order to determine the accurate angle of panning/tilting supposing that the geometric relationship between the wide and narrow view camera is known. However, the accurate Z distance is difficult to be obtained with single wide view camera and we use the following method in order to determine the angle of panning/tilting. At first, we determine the initial viewing angle of narrow view camera as 4.3 degree(from -2.15 to +2.15 degree, vertically) by empirically and we can obtain the magnified eye image of narrow view camera (the diameter of iris is below 135 pixels at the Z distance of 50 cm). Then, we can detect more accurate 2D eye corner positions by the method as mentioned in section 3. Then, we compute the 3D eye corner positions using the narrow and wide view stereo camera as following. Supposing that P point, which is the left eye corner of right eye, is observed in both wide and narrow view camera as shown in Fig. 4, then we can obtain Eq. (1) [18].

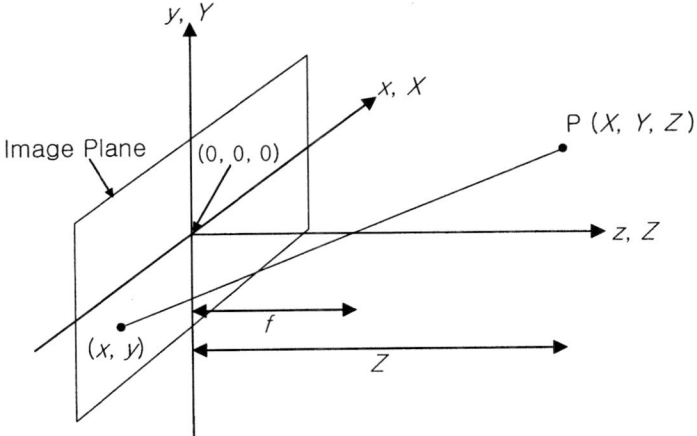

Fig. 4. The perspective projection

$$X_1 = \frac{x_1 * (f_1 - Z_1)}{f_1}, Y_1 = \frac{y_1 * (f_1 - Z_1)}{f_1}$$
$$X_2 = \frac{x_2 * (f_2 - Z_2)}{f_2}, Y_2 = \frac{y_2 * (f_2 - Z_2)}{f_2} \quad (1)$$

where (x_1, y_1) is the observed 2D position in the narrow view camera, (x_2, y_2) is the observed 2D position in the wide view camera and f_1, f_2 are the focal lengths of the narrow view and the wide view camera, respectively. In addition, (X_1, Y_1, Z_1) is the 3D position of P point in the narrow view camera coordinate and (X_2, Y_2, Z_2) is the 3D position of P point in the wide view camera coordinate. Considering the coordinate conversion between the narrow and wide view camera, we can obtain the Z distance (Z_2)[18]. With the calculated the Z distance (Z_2) and Eq. (1), we can obtain the 3D positions(X_2, Y_2, Z_2) of feature point(P) in the wide view camera coordinate. Then, we perform the additional coordinate conversion between the wide view camera coordinate and monitor coordinate. Same rules are applied to the other 4 features points and we can obtain the 3D positions of 5 features (left/right eye corners of left eye, left/right eye corners of right eye, nostril center) in monitor coordinate. For that, additional panning/tilting of the narrow view camera may be required in order to include the other feature points in the narrow view image and it takes little time as below 5 ms. The experimental results show that the RMS error of between the computed 3D positions of 5 features and the actual ones (measured by 3D position tracking sensor) is about 0.781 cm (0.41cm in X axis, 0.45cm in Y axis, 0.49cm in Z axis) for 50 person data. Then, we can determine one facial plane from the computed 3D positions of the 5 features and the normal vector (whose origin exists in the middle of the forehead) of the plane shows a

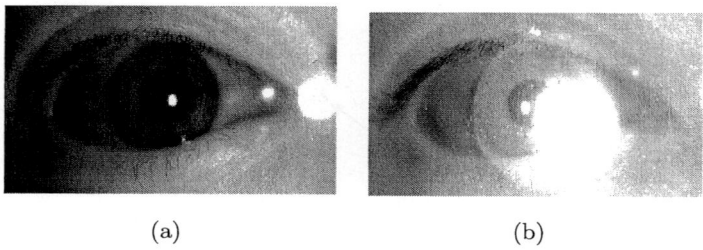

Fig. 5. The eye image having specular reflection on glasses (a)Eye image with left illuminator (b)Eye image with right illuminator

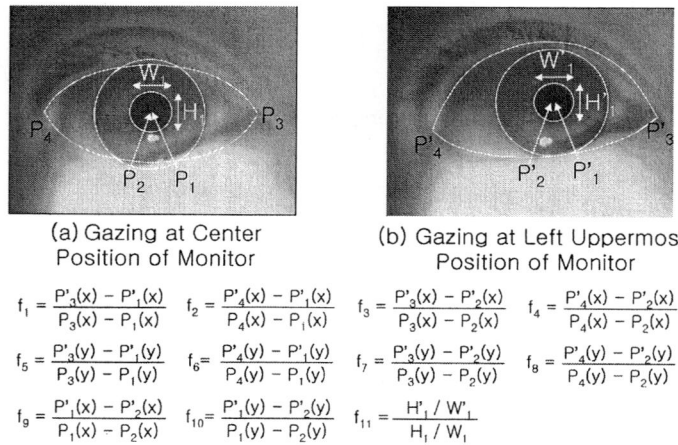

$f_1 = \dfrac{P'_3(x) - P'_1(x)}{P_3(x) - P_1(x)}$ $f_2 = \dfrac{P'_4(x) - P'_1(x)}{P_4(x) - P_1(x)}$ $f_3 = \dfrac{P'_3(x) - P'_2(x)}{P_3(x) - P_2(x)}$ $f_4 = \dfrac{P'_4(x) - P'_2(x)}{P_4(x) - P_2(x)}$

$f_5 = \dfrac{P'_3(y) - P'_1(y)}{P_3(y) - P_1(y)}$ $f_6 = \dfrac{P'_4(y) - P'_1(y)}{P_4(y) - P_1(y)}$ $f_7 = \dfrac{P'_3(y) - P'_2(y)}{P_3(y) - P_2(y)}$ $f_8 = \dfrac{P'_4(y) - P'_2(y)}{P_4(y) - P_2(y)}$

$f_9 = \dfrac{P'_1(x) - P'_2(x)}{P_1(x) - P_2(x)}$ $f_{10} = \dfrac{P'_1(y) - P'_2(y)}{P_1(y) - P_2(y)}$ $f_{11} = \dfrac{H'_1 / W'_1}{H_1 / W_1}$

Fig. 6. The features for eye gaze detection from right eye

gaze vector by head (facial) movements. The gaze position on a monitor is the intersection position between a monitor and the gaze vector.

5   Auto Zooming and Focusing of Narrow View Camera

As mentioned in section 4, we get the eye image in narrow view camera, but the eye image size inevitably becomes small (the diameter of iris is below 135 pixels at the Z distance of 50 cm). In order to compute more accurate eye gaze position, we should get more magnified eye image. So, we implement the zoom lens into our narrow view camera and perform auto zooming operation in narrow view camera. In addition, conventional narrow view camera has small DOF (Depth of Field) and there is the limitation of increasing the DOF with the fixed focal camera. So, we also implement the focus lens into our narrow view camera and perform auto focusing operation in narrow view camera in order to capture clear

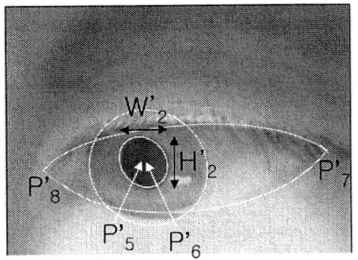
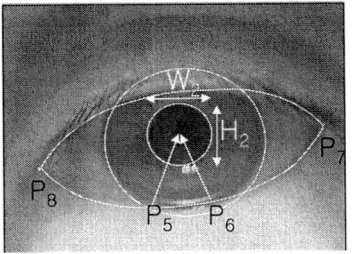

(a) Gazing at Right Lowermost Position of Monitor

(b) Gazing at Center Position of Monitor

$$f_{12} = \frac{P'_7(x) - P'_5(x)}{P_7(x) - P_5(x)} \quad f_{13} = \frac{P'_8(x) - P'_5(x)}{P_8(x) - P_5(x)} \quad f_{14} = \frac{P'_7(x) - P'_6(x)}{P_7(x) - P_6(x)} \quad f_{15} = \frac{P'_8(x) - P'_6(x)}{P_8(x) - P_6(x)}$$

$$f_{16} = \frac{P'_7(y) - P'_5(y)}{P_7(y) - P_5(y)} \quad f_{17} = \frac{P'_8(y) - P'_5(y)}{P_8(y) - P_5(y)} \quad f_{18} = \frac{P'_7(y) - P'_6(y)}{P_7(y) - P_6(y)} \quad f_{19} = \frac{P'_8(y) - P'_6(y)}{P_8(y) - P_6(y)}$$

$$f_{20} = \frac{P'_7(x) - P'_6(x)}{P_7(x) - P_6(x)} \quad f_{21} = \frac{P'_7(y) - P'_6(y)}{P_7(y) - P_6(y)} \quad f_{22} = \frac{H'_2 / W'_2}{H_2 / W_2}$$

Fig. 7. The features for eye gaze detection from left eye

eye image. For auto zooming and focusing, the Z distance between the eye and the narrow view camera is required and we can obtain the accurate Z distance (Z_1) by Eq. (1) and section 4. In the case that the surface of glasses can make the specular reflection which covers the whole eye image, the eye region is not detected and we cannot compute the eye gaze position. So, we turn on the both sided illuminator (Fig. 1(6)) alternately and overcome such problem as shown in Fig. 5.

6 Localization of Eye Features in Narrow View Image

After we get the zoomed/focused eye image (the diameter of iris is more than 230 pixels), we perform the localization of eye features again as shown in Fig. 6 and 7. We detect $P_1 \sim P'_4$ in right eye image as shown in Fig. 6 and also detect $P_5 \sim P'_8$ in left eye image as shown in Fig. 7 for computing eye gaze detection. Here, the P_1 and P'_1 show the pupil center and the P_2 and P'_2 does the iris center. J. Wang et al.[1] uses the method that detects the iris outer boundary by elliptical fitting. However, the upper and lower regions of iris outer boundary tend to be covered by eyelid and inaccurate iris elliptical fitting happens due to the lack of iris boundary pixels. In addition, their method computes eye gaze position by checking the shape change of iris when a user gazes at monitor positions. However, our experimental results show that the shape change amount of iris is very small and it is difficult to detect the accurate eye gaze position with that. So, we use the positional information of both pupil and iris. Also, we use the information of shape change of pupil, which does not tend to be covered by

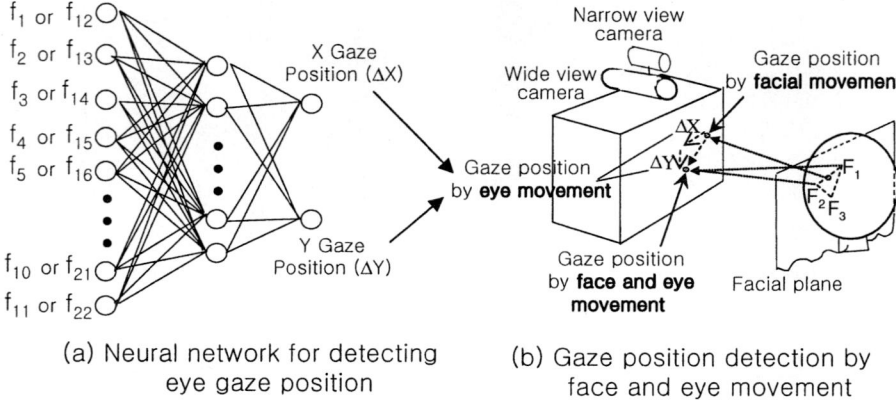

Fig. 8. The neural network for eye gaze detection and gaze position detection by face and eye movement

eyelid. As shown in Fig. 6(b) and 7(a), the shapes of iris and pupil are almost ellipse, when the user gazes at a side position of monitor and we use the canny edge operator to extract edge components and a 2D edge-based elliptical Hough transform. In order to detect the eye corner position, we detect the eyelid as shown in Fig. 6 and 7 using the region-based eyelid template deformation and masking method. Here, we use 2 deformable templates (parabolic shape) for upper and lower eyelid detection, respectively. Experimental results show that RMS errors between the detected eye feature positions and the actual ones are 2 pixels (of iris center), 1 pixel (of pupil center), 4 pixels (of left eye corner) and 4 pixels (of right eye corner). Based on the detected eye features, we select the 22 feature values ($f_1 \sim f_{11}$ are used in case that right eye image can be captured by narrow view camera as shown in Fig. 6 and $f_{12} \sim f_{22}$ are used in case that left eye image can be captured as shown in Fig. 7).

7 Detecting the Gaze Position on a Monitor

In section 4, we explain the gaze detection method only considering head movement. However, when a user gazes at a monitor position, both the head and eyes tend to be moved simultaneously. So, we compute the additional eye gaze position by the detected 22 feature values (as mentioned in section 6) and a neural network (multi-layered perceptron) as shown in Fig. 8(a). The numbers of input nodes, hidden nodes and output nodes are 11, 8 and 2, respectively. They are selected by our empirical experiments. For output function of neural network, we use a limited logarithm function, which shows better performance than that in case of using other functions, like a linear, sigmoid etc. That is because the narrow view camera is above the wide view camera and the 2D eye movement resolution is decreased in case of gazing at the lower positions of the monitor.

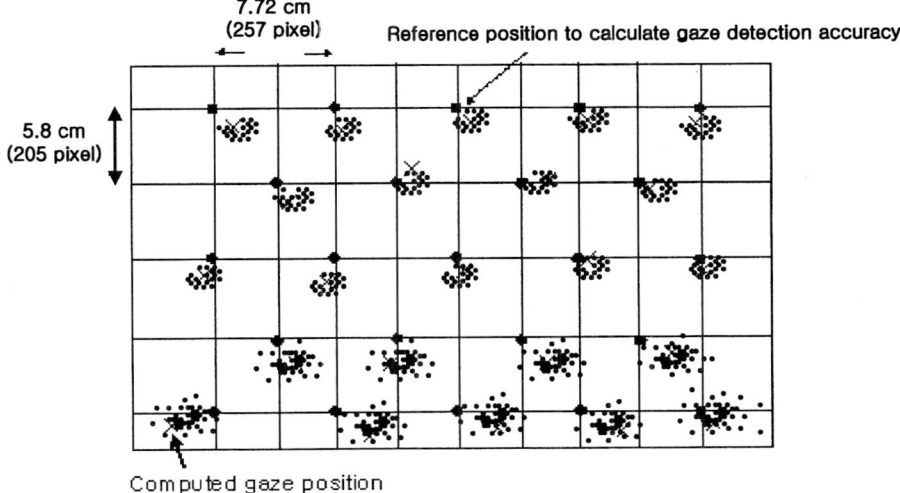

Fig. 9. An example of gaze detection errors on a 19" monitor

The continuous output values of neural network represent eye gaze position on a monitor. After detecting eye gaze position, we can determine a final gaze position based on the vector summation of facial and eye gaze position as shown in Fig. 8(b).

8 Performance Evaluations

The gaze detection error of our method is compared to that of our previous methods[3][4][15][17]. The researches[3][4] compute facial gaze position not considering the eye movements. The research[15] calculates the gaze position by mapping the 2D facial feature position into the monitor gaze position by linear interpolation or neural network without 3D computation and considering eye movements. The method[17] computes the gaze positions considering both head and eye movements, but uses only one wide view camera. The test data are acquired when 95 users gaze at 23 gaze positions on a 19" monitor as shown in Fig. 9. Here, the gaze error is the RMS error between the actual gaze positions and the computed ones. At the 1st experiment, the gaze errors are calculated in two cases as shown in Table 1. The case I shows the gaze error about test data including only head movements and the case II does the gaze error about test data including head and eye movements.

Shown in Table 1, the gaze error of the proposed method is the smallest in any case. Fig. 9 shows an example of the gaze detection errors on a 19" monitor. The reference positions are marked as "black big circle" and the computed gaze positions are shown as "X" and "black small circle". From the Fig. 9, we can

Table 1. Gaze error about test data (cm)

Method	Linear interpol.[19]	Single neural net[19]	Combined neural nets[19]	[3] method	[4] method	[21] method	Proposed method
case I	5.1	4.23	4.48	5.35	5.21	3.40	1.21
case II	11.8	11.32	8.87	7.45	6.29	4.8	2.11

know the gaze errors and the error variations are more increased in lower region of the monitor. That is because two cameras are positioned on the monitor and fine movement of head and eye cannot be seen in case of gazing at the lower positions of the monitor, consequently. At the 2nd experiment, the points of radius 5 pixels are spaced vertically and horizontally at 1.5" intervals on a 19" monitor with monitor resolution of 1280×1024 pixels as such Rikert's research[9]. The RMS error between the real and calculated gaze position is 2.09 cm and it is superior to Rikert's method (almost 5.08 cm). Our gaze error is correspondent to the angular error of 1.68 degrees on X axis and 1.71 degrees on Y axis at the Z distance of 50 cm. In addition, we tested the gaze errors according to user's Z distance. The RMS errors are 2.07cm at 50cm, 2.07cm at 60cm, 2.11cm at 70cm and the performance of our method is not affected by the user's Z position change. Last experiment for processing time shows that our gaze detection process takes about 100ms in Pentium-III 866MHz and it is much smaller than Rikert's method (1 minute in alphastation 333MHz). The research[1] shows the angular error of below 1 degree, but their method supposes that they know the 3D distance between two eyes and that between both lip corners and there is no individual variation for the 3D distances. In addition, they suppose that they know the 3D diameter of eye ball and there is no individual variation for that. However, our preliminary experiments show that there are much individual variations for the 3D distances/3D diameter (from 95 users' test) and such cases can increase much gaze errors (the angular error of more than 5 degree).

9 Conclusions

This paper describes a new gaze detecting method. Experimental results show that the RMS error of gaze detection is about 2.4 degrees (1.68 degrees on X axis and 1.71 degrees on Y axis at the Z distance of 50 cm). In future works, we plan to develop the method to increase the auto zooming/focusing speed to decrease total processing time of gaze detection. In addition, we will test the gaze detection performance with more data in various environment.

References

1. J. Wang and E. Sung, 2002. Study on Eye Gaze Estimation, IEEE Trans. on SMC, Vol.32, No.3, pp.332-350
2. A. Azarbayejani., 1993, Visually Controlled Graphics. IEEE Trans. PAMI, Vol.15, No.6, pp.602-605

3. K. R. Park et al., Apr 2000, Gaze Point Detection by Computing the 3D Positions and 3D Motions of Face, IEICE Trans. Inf.&Syst.,Vol.E.83-D, No.4, pp.884-894
4. K. R. Park, Oct 1999, Gaze Detection by Estimating the Depth and 3D Motions of Facial Features in Monocular Images, IEICE Trans. Fund., Vol.E.82-A, No.10, pp.2274-2284
5. K. OHMURA et al., 1989. Pointing Operation Using Detection of Face Direction from a Single View. IEICE Trans. Inf.&Syst., Vol.J72-D-II, No.9, pp.1441-1447
6. P. Ballard et al., 1995. Controlling a Computer via Facial Aspect. IEEE Trans. on SMC, Vol.25, No.4, pp.669-677
7. A. Gee et al., 1996. Fast visual tracking by temporal consensus, Image and Vision Computing. Vol.14, pp.105-114
8. J. Heinzmann et al., 1998. 3D Facial Pose and Gaze Point Estimation using a Robust Real-Time Tracking Paradigm. Proceedings of ICAFGR, pp.142-147
9. T. Rikert, 1998. Gaze Estimation using Morphable Models. ICAFGR, pp.436-441
10. A.Ali-A-L et al., 1997, Man-machine Interface through Eyeball Direction of Gaze. Proc. of the Southeastern Symposium on System Theory, pp.478-82
11. J. Heinzmann et al., 1997. Robust Real-time Face Tracking and Gesture Recognition. Proc. of the IJCAI, Vol.2, pp.1525-1530
12. Matsumoto-Y, et al., 2000, An Algorithm for Real-time Stereo Vision Implementation of Head Pose and Gaze Direction Measurement. the ICAFGR. pp.499-504
13. Newman-R et al., 2000, Real-time Stereo Tracking for Head Pose and Gaze Estimation. Proceedings the 4th ICAFGR 2000. pp.122-8
14. Betke-M et al., 1999, Gaze Detection via Self-organizing Gray-scale Units. the Proc. of IWRATFG. pp.70-76
15. K. R. Park et al., 2000. Intelligent Process Control via Gaze Detection Technology. EAAI, Vol.13, No.5, pp.577-587
16. K. R. Park et al., 2002. Gaze Position Detection by Computing the 3 Dimensional Facial Positions and Motions. Pattern Recognition, Vol.35, No.11, pp.2559-2569
17. K. R. Park, 2002, Facial and Eye Gaze detection. LNCS, Vol.2525, pp.368-376
18. R. C. Gonzalez et al., 1995, Digital Image Processing, Addison-Wesley
19. Steven C. Chapra et al., 1989, Numerical Methods for Engineers, McGraw-Hill
20. S. Whittaker and B.O'Connail, 1997, The role of vision in face-to-face and mediated communication. In K.E.Finn, A.J.Sellen, and S.B. Wilbur (Eds.), Video-mediated Communication, Lawrence Erlbaum Associates, Mahwah, NJ

A Classification of Ontology Modification

Kevin Lee[1,2] and Thomas Meyer[1]

[1,*] National ICT Australia Sydney Node,
University of New South Wales,
Sydney NSW 2052, Australia
[2] School of Computer Science and Engineering,
University of New South Wales,
Sydney NSW 2052, Australia
{kevin.lee, thomas.meyer}@nicta.com.au

Abstract. Recent research in ontologies and descriptions logics has focused on compromising between expressiveness and reasoning ability, with many other issues being neglected. One major issue that has been neglected is how one should go about in modifying ontologies as inconsistency arises. The central concern of this problem is therefore to determine the most rational way of modifying ontologies, such that no extra knowledge would be retained in or retracted from the knowledge base. The purpose of this paper is to outline the complexities in this and to present some insights into the problem of ontology modification. Description logic (DL) is used in this paper as the underlying logic for the representation of ontology, and ontology modification is performed based on this logic.

Keywords: Ontologies, Description Logics, Belief Revision.

1 Introduction

Description logics are increasingly being seen as an appropriate representation language for defining ontologies [2]. Being fragments of first-order logics, they have a clear and well-understood semantics. Yet, reasoning in these logics can be done much more efficiently than in full first-order logic.

Thus far, research on ontologies and description logics has focused on finding logics with the appropriate level of expressivity for the task at hand, and the development of efficient reasoning in these logics. But many other questions still remain unsolved. For example, when building and integrating ontologies, DL reasoners can be used to derive consequences (like subsumption and instance relationships) and to test for consistency (of one ontology or the integration of different ones). In many cases, these inference services help the users to find errors in the ontology that is being tested (inconsistencies

---

* National ICT Australia is funded by the Australia Government's Department of Communications, Information and Technology and the Arts and the Australian Research Council through Backing Australia's Ability and the ICT Centre of Excellence program. It is supported by its members the Australian National University, University of NSW, ACT Government, NSW Government and affiliate partner University of Sydney.

or unwanted consequences). Although such errors are detected automatically, the ontology engineer must manually change the ontology to correct these errors. It would be preferable if this hard and time-consuming task can (at least partially) be automated by applying known AI techniques from the area of belief revision and the related areas of belief merging and negotiation in particular, to extract information from an inconsistent knowledge base.

Belief revision techniques [6] have been applied in DLs (in Nebel's Ph.D. thesis [19]), but not to the expressive DLs which may be needed for ontologies. The efficient application of these techniques is not just a question of plugging DL algorithms into a belief revision system. Rather, it will involve the development of new algorithms exploiting the structure of the DLs under consideration. The hope is that such algorithms will be well-behaved in practice for the same reasons that the existing algorithms for DLs are well-behaved.

In section 2 we provide a brief introduction to description logics, and in section 3, we describe the problem of inconsistency in description logics and suggest ways for resolving these inconsistencies. In section 4, we present a perference ordering as a guideline for performing ontology modification. This is followed by a discussion on the different kinds of modification relevant to ontologies in section 5.

2 Description Logics

Description Logics are representation languages, specially designed for expressing concepts in a hierarchical structure. They offer inferential capabilities, such as subsumption, instance checking and consistency checking. A knowledge base based on description logic is composed of two separate components, the TBox and the ABox. The ABox contains concept assertions and role assertions. Concept assertions deal with individuals, allocating individuals to concepts. Role assertions, on the other hand, are binary relationships that link up pairs of individuals. The TBox contains terminologies or vocabularies, which can be expressed in terms of concepts or roles. The TBox conveys information by equating each concept to other concepts through the use of connectives, which are defined by the description languages, with the syntax rule governing the formation of complex concepts. Concepts in the TBox can be considered as the representation of a set of individuals in the ABox, and if expressed in terms of roles, it represents a binary relationship between two sets of individuals in the ABox.

For demonstration purposes, we will limit ourselves to just one type of description lanaguage, namely, the $\mathcal{ALU}$, which belongs to the family of attributive languages (or $\mathcal{AL}$-languages), as described in [1]. The attributive language is based on a set of atomic concepts and roles, which are assumed to be pre-defined and will be used as building blocks for more complicated concepts. Construction of concept in $\mathcal{ALU}$ is guided by the following syntax rule:

There are other constructors defined in DLs that can be used to obtain more expressive languages. Other constuctors that are available include full existential quantification and number restrictions.

$$
\begin{array}{rll}
C, D \longrightarrow & A & |\ \text{(atomic concept)}\\
& \neg A & |\ \text{(negation of atomic concept)}\\
& \top & |\ \text{(universal)}\\
& \bot & |\ \text{(bottom concept)}\\
& C \sqcap D & |\ \text{(intersection of concepts)}\\
& C \sqcup D & |\ \text{(union of concepts)}\\
& \forall R.C & |\ \text{(value restriction)}\\
& \exists R.\top & \ \ \text{(limited existential quantification)}
\end{array}
$$

Fig. 1. Syntax Rule for $\mathcal{ALU}$

3 Consistency in Description Logic

In this section, we present the notion of inconsistency in DL as an indication for triggering the ontology modification process, and provide an example on a simple knowledge base in DL.

We define $K = Cn(K_T \cup K_A)$ to be the knowledge base, with K_T and K_A denoting the two components of K, namely the knowledge in the TBox and ABox respectively. An example of such a knowledge base is shown below:

$$K_T = \{Bird \sqsubseteq Animal \sqcap Fly\}$$

$$K_A = \{Bird(Tweety)\}$$

Example 1

Here, we define $Tweety$ as a $Bird$ in K_A, and we define $Bird$ to subsume $Animal$ and Fly in K_T. Also, we assume that that both $Animal$ and Fly are primitve concepts, that is, concepts that cannot be defined any further (refer to later section on basic primitives for more details).

K_T elements can take either of the two forms, namely inclusions and equilities, as denoted by the symbol $\sqsubseteq$ and $\equiv$ respectively, and can be applied to both concepts and roles. K_T can be considered as rules that are imposed onto K_A, and through this we can deduce new knowledge (assertions) not contained in either K_T or K_A. We call this knowledge K_{TA}, and define it as $K - (K_T \cup K_A)$.

$$K_{TA} \supseteq \{Animal(Tweety), Fly(Tweety)\}$$

Note that all tautologies and sentences such as $(Animal \sqcup Unknown)(Tweety)$ are omitted from K_{TA}, as they have little relation to the content of this paper. The above knowledge base is consistent, since $K \not\models \bot$. Note that, if either $K_T \models \bot$ or $K_A \models \bot$, then $K \models \bot$.

Next, consider α as a single sentence. Also, consider the following:

$$\alpha = \{\neg Fly(Tweety)\}$$

If we attempt to incorporate this new piece of knowledge α into our original knowledge base K, we would have an inconsistent knowledge base, since $K_{TA} \cup \{\alpha\} \models \bot$, and therefore $K \cup \{\alpha\} \models \bot$. The main objective of ontology modification is to provide the most rational way of resolving these conflicts, without retracting or retaining any more of the original knowledge in K than is necessary. While it is obvious that ontology modifications are necessary to maintain a consistent knowledge base, it is not clear which part of the knowledge in K should be retained or retracted.

There are two opposing views to this problem. In the machine learning perspective, in particular clustering [9, 10], one can view datums as assertions, while clusters can be viewed as terminologies. In this sense, the formation of clusters is solely dependent on their nearby datums, that is, clusters are a generalised form of datums. If we map this idea to description logics, then the TBox will just be the generalisation of the ABox, which means ABox assertions should prioritise over TBox terminologies, if one is to choose in between the two. Intuitively, since assertions are observations, one would be tempted to believe in them, as human beings (agents) tend to believe in what they see with their own eyes (sensors), and would prefer to give up their belief on things that they do not see, that is, the terminologies. However, from another point of view, where TBox is treated as intensional knowledge and ABox is treated as extensional knowledge, one would arrive at a totally different conclusion. By definition, intensional knowledge of a concept is the set of attributes that are common to all those and only those individuals that are being referred to, whereas extensional knowledge is the set of individuals denoted by the concept. From this definition, one can basically conclude that extensional knowledge is determined by intensional knowledge. Thus, intensional knowledge of TBox is more deeply embedded, and therefore more resistent to change compared to extensional knowledge of the ABox. An example that is consistent with this definition is that of scientific discovery [17], in which theories that are being developed are unlikely to be changed easily, even though there are clear experimental observations that are in conflict with the developed theories.

Basic Primitives. In what follows we will be assuming that agents share a set of primitive concepts in terms of which all other concepts are defined. Without this assumption it seems impossible to perform any kind of ontology modification. Even with this assumption, there are still many difficulties to be resolved. The question of *how* to decide what are the primitive concepts is a very difficult one, as illustrated by a puzzle pointed out by the philosopher David Miller [18], and also in Goodman's paradox [7, 8].

Resolving Inconsistencies. In general, one should always pay special attention to the composition of K in determining how ontology modification should be performed. In this case, consistency between different components of K and α becomes a crucial factor in ontology modification. In this section, we examine the techniques for resolving the inconsistencies as they arise. We introduce the notation K' to represent K after modification. Similarly, we denote K'_T, K'_A and K'_{TA}, as the modifed version of K_T, K_A and K_{TA} respectively,

1. $K \cup \{\alpha\} \not\models \bot$.
   The new piece of knowledge α does not result in any inconsistencies, therefore we can simply incorporate α into K.

2. $K \cup \{\alpha\} \models \bot, K_T \cup \{\alpha\} \not\models \bot$ and $K_A \cup \{\alpha\} \models \bot$.

In this case, we have an inconsistency in $K_A \cup \{\alpha\}$ and we would have to modify K_A to rectify the problem, as modifying K_T or K_{TA} would have no effect on the situation at all. Modification of K_A should resemble the idea of AGM belief change and therefore capture the notion of minimal change.

Another issue we should consider is the effect of modifying K_A. Depending on the interactions between K_T and K_A, the effect on K_{TA} would be varied accordingly. The simplest situation we can have is when there is no interaction between K_T and K_A, that is, none of the assertions in K_A (at least not the ones that would be modified due to α) uses any definition in K_T to make new assertions in K_{TA}, and therefore changes in K_A would not be reflected upon that part of K_{TA} relating to K_T. On the other hand, if interaction exists between K_T and K_A, and if assertions are either added or removed from K_A, then such changes would be reflected upon K_{TA}. This could potentially introduce other inconsistencies in K_{TA} and therefore one should always take K_{TA} into consideration when modifying K_A.

If assertions are being removed from K_A, and as a result assertions that can be derived from K_T need to be removed from K_{TA}, then one can choose to retain these assertions by transferring them to K'_A. One incentive for applying this technique would be to ensure minimal change in K such that $K \cup \{\alpha\}$ is consistent. However, doing so in most cases would not ensure minimal change in K_A. Also, the nature of the transferred knowledge would be changed, as they would no longer be the inferred knowledge of K_T and K_A, but rather it becomes independent of K_T.

Now, consider Example 1 again and this time let $\alpha = \{\neg Bird(Tweety)\}$. Since we have an inconsistency in $K_A \cup \{\alpha\}$, as both $Bird(Tweety)$ and its negated form $\neg Bird(Tweety)$ are in $K_A \cup \alpha$, one would have no choice but to remove $Bird(Tweety)$ from K_A. While removing $Bird(Tweety)$ from K_A would make $K_A \cup \{\alpha\}$ consistent, some knowledge such as $Animal(Tweety)$ and $Fly(Tweety)$ in K_{TA}, would be lost. To retain such knowledge while ensuring consistency, one could simply transfer some of the assertions in K_{TA} to K'_A, that is, transferring either $Animal(Tweety)$ or $Fly(Tweety)$ to K'_A. It should be clear from this example that modifying either K_T or K_{TA} would have no effect on the situation.

3. $K \cup \{\alpha\} \models \bot, K_T \cup \{\alpha\} \models \bot$ and $K_A \cup \{\alpha\} \not\models \bot$.

The situation of having an inconsistency in K_T is similar to that in K_A, in which the only way to resolve the inconsistency would be to make changes to the inconsistent component, which is K_T in this case. Modification of K_T could be done by either strengthening or weakening definitions in K_T. For example, consider Example 1 again, but this time let $\alpha = \{Bird \sqsubseteq \neg Fly\}$. There are two possible solutions to resolve the inconsistency. One is to strengthen the definitions in K_T, that is, by dropping the condition Fly in the original definition, and have $Bird \sqsubseteq Animal \sqcap \neg Fly$ instead. By performing this operation, we are not only admitting that we were incorrect, but also accepting the new condition $\neg Fly$. The alternative solution is by weakening definitions in K_T. In this case, we can weaken $Bird \sqsubseteq Animal \sqcap Fly$ to just $Bird \sqsubseteq Animal$, and avoid having to make judgement on the condition Fly. It should be clear that both the strengthening and weakening techniques can have an effect on K_{TA}. For instance, by changing K_T to $Bird \sqsubseteq Animal$, $Fly(Tweety)$

would no longer be available. However, one could adopt a similar technique as in the case of inconsistent K_A, that is, preserving certain part of the knowledge in K_{TA} by transferring them to K'_A.

4. $K \cup \{\alpha\} \models \bot, K_T \cup \{\alpha\} \not\models \bot$ and $K_A \cup \{\alpha\} \not\models \bot$.
This inconsistency is due to $K_{TA} \cup \{\alpha\} \models \bot$. This problem can be rectified by modifying either K_T or K_A. K_{TA} would shrink eventually, if there is enough knowledge retracted from K_T or K_A. An obvious solution for Example 1 would be to either remove $Bird \sqsubseteq Animal \sqcap Fly$ from the TBox or $Bird(Tweety)$ from the ABox or both. Alternatively, we can weaken the definition in K_T. This is done by identifying a feature from $Tweety$, that can be used to distinguish $Tweety$ from any other birds (or feature from other birds, that is distinct from $Tweety$). In this case, we can weaken the definition $Bird \sqsubseteq Animal \sqcap Fly$ to $Bird \sqsubseteq Animal \sqcap (Fly \sqcup Penguin)$. Here, we could have two situations. If $Penguin(Tweety)$ is in K or α, and that $Tweety$ is the only $Bird$ that is also a $Penguin$, then what we have done is simply making an exception to $Tweety$ and admitting that $Penguin$ can also be a $Bird$. On the other hand, if $Penguin(Tweety)$ is not in either K or α, then we are really just allocating $Tweety$ to a meaningless concept called $Penguin$. Such concept could be substituted by any other concept name, say $unknown(Tweety)$. In fact, we can simply create a concept, substitute $Penguin$ by this concept and have $Tweety$ allocated to it, for instance $unknown(Tweety)$, where the concept $unknown$ can be replaced by any concept name that has never appeared before or will ever be appeared. If such a concept does appear, then we would have a clash in meaning with two concepts having the same label (concept name). This is suggesting that this technique, although effective in resolving inconsistency, should be avoided whenever possible.

5. $K \cup \{\alpha\} \models \bot, K_T \cup \{\alpha\} \models \bot$ and $K_A \cup \{\alpha\} \models \bot$.
When we have a situation where inconsistency exists in both K_T and K_A. Each of the single treatments alone described in 1, 2 and 3 will not be sufficient, instead it is necessary to seek a combination of these treatments. One strategy in resolving inconsistencies in K is by applying both 1 and 2, until both $K_T \cup \{\alpha\} \not\models \bot$ and $K_A \cup \{\alpha\} \not\models \bot$. Now, if $K \cup \{\alpha\}$ still remains inconsistent, then it would be necessary to also apply 3 to resolve inconsistencies in K_{TA}.

4 Preference Ordering for Description Logics

The idea of having a preference ordering for each component in K is based on previous work on epistemic entrenchment [6, 5] in belief revision. Obviously, some terminologies or assertions are more important, and thus should be prioritised over the others. As illustrated in Fig.2, the preference ordering is represented as a cube, with each dimension representing an ordering for each of K_A, K_T and K_{TA}. Each component in K has its own ordering, with the position labelled '0' being the origin, which is also highest priority or priority level 0. The number of priority levels for each of the components is specified at the time the cube is constructed, and one would be required to specify at least the number of priority levels for K_A and K_T. One might also wish to limit the number of priority levels in K_{TA}. The priority levels are positive discrete values, and increase with

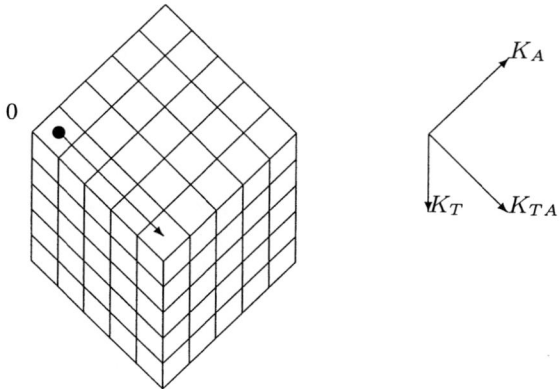

Fig. 2. Preference Ordering for K_T, K_A and K_{TA}

distance from the origin. The higher the priority level value, the lower the priority. Each level contains a set of wffs, and for K_A and K_T, it will be constructed according to one's preferences and can vary in different contexts. One of the interesting features in DL is the idea of dividing K into K_T and K_A. Such a structure allows inferences to be made to generate a natural ordering for K_{TA}.

Here, we propose a method of constructing a preference ordering for K_{TA} based on K_A and K_T. Let K_{Ti} be the set of terminologies for K_T at priority level i and K_{Aj} be the set of assertions for K_A at priority level j. Also, let $|i|$ and $|j|$ be the number of priority levels for K_T and K_A respectively. We define K_T and K_A as follows:

$$K_T = \bigcup_{n=0}^{|i|} K_{Tn}$$

$$K_A = \bigcup_{n=0}^{|j|} K_{An}$$

Next, we define a function called $Inst$ that deduces all the direct logical consequences of a set. We construct K_{TA} as follows:

$$\Gamma_n = \begin{cases} K_{Aj} & \text{if } n = 0; \\ Inst(K_{Ti} \cup \Gamma_{n-1}) & \text{if } n > 0. \end{cases}$$

$$\lim_{n \to \infty} \Gamma_n = Cn(K_T \cup K_A) = K$$

$$K_{TAn} = \Delta\Gamma_{n,n+1} = \Gamma_{n+1} - \Gamma_n$$

The idea is very simple. We first apply the definitions in K_T to K_A to infer a new set of assertions, which will become the set of assertions with the highest priority in K_{TA}. Next, we apply the definitions to the new assertions (those in the highest priority of K_{TA}) we have just generated and infer more assertions, which will be considered as the second highest priority. We repeat the process until either no more assertions can be inferred, or when we run out of priority levels, in which case the level with the lowest priority will store all the remaining assertions.

There are several advantages in this scheme of perference ordering. Firstly, our preference ordering captures the effect of performing inferences, and the more inferences needed to arrive at a particular assertion, the less accurate this knowledge is likely to be, thus we penalise this by giving it a lower priority. Secondly, the fact that each priority level is dependent on the levels above (higher priority) means that if we were to remove one assertion from a particular level, all the levels below it would also be affected. This suggests that, whenever we are performing DL modification, we should always choose to modify assertions in lower priorities first, as it would be less likely to affect other assertions. In this sense, it is consistent with the idea of minimal change. For example, suppose we have the following in K:

$$K_T = \{Bird \sqsubseteq Animal \sqcap Fly, Animal \sqsubseteq \neg Human \sqcap \neg Intelligent\}$$

$$K_A = \{Bird(Tweety)\}$$

We infer the following as the highest priority of K_{TA}:

$$K_{TA0} = \{Animal(Tweety), Fly(Tweety)\}$$

Next, we infer the following based on all previous inferences in K_{TA}:

$$K_{TA1} = \{\neg Human(Tweety), \neg Intelligent(Tweety)\}$$

Now, let $\alpha = Intelligent(Tweety)$, which means we have an inconsistency. While one could change the definiton $Bird \sqsubseteq Animal \sqcap Fly$ to, for instance, $Bird \sqsubseteq Fly$, our preference ordering suggests that we should maintain as many assertions of higher priorities as possible, and be more willing to give up assertions of lower priorities. In this case, since the inconsistency originates from the fact that we have $\neg Intelligent(Tweety)$ in priority level 1, one should attempt to resolve at this particular level, that is, by removing $\neg Intelligent(Tweety)$ from K_{TA}. One way to acheive this is by altering the definition $Animal \sqsubseteq \neg Human \sqcap \neg Intelligent$ to $Animal \sqsubseteq \neg Human$.

5 Discussion

This section will be devoted to a discussion on the more general forms of ontology modification.

5.1 Ontology Alignment

Ontology Alignment is one of the major challenges in ontology modification. The setting is as follows: Two or more agents have different ontologies relating to the same domain. Their purpose is to be able to communicate. What is needed is a method of translation from one ontology to the other. There has been some recent work [11–13, 20, 21] in making use of Channel Theory to perform ontology alignment, in which a method for automatically determining such the ontology translation procedures is defined, under the assumption that all agents share a set of basic primitives on which all other terms are based. In description logics this would amount to the alignment of concepts defined in the TBox. Therefore, if we are to perform ontology modification here, one would probably give higher priorities to the TBox than the ABox.

5.2 Ontology Merging

It is possible to idenitify different types of ontology merging. Merging TBoxes amounts to making sure that different agents use the same terms in identical ways. The goal here is quite unlike that of classical belief merging [14–16]. In belief merging, information from different sources are pooled together, and the requirement is to find a consistent set of beliefs representing the merged information. In the case of merging TBoxes, it seems that either one of the two things could happen. If agents find that they use the same terms in ways that differ only slightly, it would be required of all agents involved to amend their definitions slightly. This is indeed reminiscent of classical belief merging. The other possibility is for them to realise that, although they are using the same term(s), they are really describing sufficiently different concepts. In such a case it would be necessary for both agents to invent new terms to describe the concept of the other one. Perhaps a combination of alignment and merging would be appropriate.

Observe that TBox merging ought not to affect the Aboxes, although it might affect the conclusions that can be drawn, from assertions in the Aboxes, of course. Suppose that a concept in the TBoxes of agents 1 and 2 has been modified slightly; that is, merging has taken place. For example, suppose agent 1's concept of fish in its TBox is of an animal with fins that lives in water, and that its Abox contains the information that Willy is an animal, has fins, lives underwater, and suckles its young. It will then be able to conclude that Willy is a fish. But if, after merging, agent 1's concept of a fish is changed to an animal with fins, living in water, not suckling its young, Willy would no longer be classified as a fish.

A formalisation of TBox merging looks quite different from that of classical merging. For example, one of the basic properties of belief merging is that if all the pieces of information to be merged put together yield a consistent set of sentences, this is what the merged outcome should be. But consider a situation in which agent 1 defines a dog as an animal with four leg that barks, and agent 2 defines a dog as a *large* animal with four legs, that barks. Although these two definitions are consistent, it is unintuitive to take the merged outcome to be these two definitions put together (yielding a definition of a dog as a large animal with four legs that barks). Agent 1 might well reason that agent 2's definition is based on the fact that it has not yet encountered large dogs.

The other type of merging would be Abox merging. This is merging in the classical style, although one would have to make the assumption that TBoxes have already been aligned and merged before ABox merging takes place.

5.3 Ontology Revision

One view of Abox revision is that it is essentially classical revision, but with the provison that everything in the TBox is fixed. Formally, this can be described as classical AGM revision [6], for example, with sentences in the TBox treated similar to logically valid sentences. However, there exists another view of ABox revision. Suppose that Agent 1's definition of a bird is of an animal with feathers. Furthermore, suppose that Agents 1's TBox contains the fact that all birds fly. Now suppose further that I have observed that Agent 1 has observed that Tweety is an animal with feathers, and Agent 1 has been told that Tweety is a bird. Now Agent 1 observed that Tweety cannot fly. This thus creates an inconsistency with information in TBox. One solution to this, of course, is to remove the information that Tweety is a bird. But a more natural solution would seem to be to modify the definition of bird in some way. At the moment it is still unclear as to when to perform the first kind of ABox revision, and when it would be more appropriate to perform the second kind.

6 Future Work

So far, we have provided some insights as to how ontology modification can be performed. However, we have neglected one crucial aspect in ontology modification that relates closely to ontology merging, namely the interpretation of knowledge. Let K be the knowledge base of an agent, say Agent0, and consider α as a piece of new knowledge reaching Agent0. Also, let Fly be a primitve concept. We mentioned earlier that, if $\neg Fly(Tweety)$ is in K and its negated form $Fly(Tweety)$ is α, then $K \cup \{\alpha\}$ will be inconsistent. However, this is not necessarily true, as it depends on whether the concept Fly is actually interpreted the same way in both K and α. If the two interpretations do not equate, then what we really have is in fact $\neg Fly0(Tweety)$ in K and $Fly1(Tweety)$ in α, which means there might not be an inconsistency at all. Future work should therefore be focused on addressing this problem.

7 Conclusion

In this paper, we identified various types of inconsistencies in a typical description language, namely the $\mathcal{ALU}$, and proposed techniques for resolving these inconsistencies. In particular, we looked at the interactions between the different components of the knowledge base, and how they contribute to the ontology modification process. Furthermore, we introduced the idea of a preference ordering based on the nature of inferencing in description logic that can be used as a guide for ontology modification. Such an ordering allows one to distinguish the more prioritised knowledge from the less prioritised ones, and therefore by using this ordering one could decide which part of the knowledge to give up or to retain.

One assumption we have made in this paper is that primitive concepts are being pre-defined as the building blocks for all concepts. This assumption is consistent with the theory by Barwise and Seligman [3, 4], namely Channel Theory, where information flows are based on regularities between agents. The way these regularities are being established, is therefore another interesting area of research in ontology but it is beyond the scope of this paper.

References

1. F. Baader, D. McGuinness, D. Nardi, P. Patel-Schneider. *The description logic handbook: Theory, implementation, and applications.*
2. F. Baader, I. Horrocks, and U. Sattler. *Description Logics for the Semantic Web.* KI V Kunstliche Intelligenz, 4, 2002.
3. J. Barwise and J. Seligman. *The Rights and Wrongs of Natural Regularity.* In Philosophical Perspectives, ed. J. Tomerlin. 331-365. California: Ridgeview, 1994.
4. J. Barwise and J. Seligman. *Information Flow: The Logic of Distributed Systems.* Cambridge University Press, 1997.
5. P. Gardenfors and D. Makinson. *Revisions of knowledge systems using epistemic entrenchment.* In M.y. Vardi, editor, Proceedings of the Second Conference on Theoretical Aspects of Reasoning About Knowledge, pages 83-95. Morgan Kaufmann, Los Altos, California, 1988.
6. P. Gardenfors. *Knowledge in Flux: Modeling the Dynamics of Epistemic States.* The MIT Press, Cambridge, Massachusetts, 1988.
7. N. Goodman. *A Query On Confirmation.* Journal of Philosophy, vol 43, pages 383-385, 1946.
8. N. Goodman. *The New Riddle of Induction.* Journal of Philosophy, vol 63, pages 281-331, 1966.
9. J. Hartigan. *Clustering Algorithms.* John Wiley & Sons, New York, NY, 1975.
10. J. Hartigan. *Distribution Problems in Clustering.* in Classification and Clustering, ed. J. Van Ryzin, Academic Press, New York, NY, 1977.
11. Y. Kalfoglou, M. Schorlemmer. *IF-Map: An Ontology-Mapping Method based on Information-Flow Theory.* Journal of Data Semantics I, LNCS 2800, Springer 2003.
12. R. Kent. *The IFF Approach to Semantic Integration.* Presentation at the Boeing Mini-Workshop on Semantic Integration, 7 November 2002.
13. R. Kent. *Semantic Integration in the IFF.* ISWC'03 Semantic Integration Workshop. Sanibel Island, Florida, USA, 2003.
14. S. Konieczny, R. Pino-Perez. *On the logic of merging.* Proceedings of the 6th International Conference on Principles of Knowledge Representation and Reasoning, KR'98, Trento, Italie, p. 488-498, 1998.
15. S. Konieczny, R. Pino-Perez. *Merging with integrity constraints.* Proceedings of the 5th European Conference on Symbolic and Quantitative Approaches to Reasoning with Uncertainty, ECSQARU'99, London, UK, 1999, Lecture Notes in Artificial Intelligence, vol. 1638, p. 233-244, 1999.
16. S. Konieczny, R. Pino-Perez. *Merging information under constraints: a qualitative framework.* Journal of Logic and Computation, 2000.
17. T. Kuhn. *The Structure of Scientific Revolutions.* University of Chicago Press, 1962.
18. D. Miller. *Popper's Qualitative Theory of Verisimilitude',* British Journal for Philosophy of Science 25, pp. 166-77.
19. B. Nebel. *Reasoning and Revision in Hybrid Representation Systems,* volume 422 of Lecture Notes in Artificial Intelligence. Springer-Verlag, 1990.
20. M. Schorlemmer, Y. Kalfoglou. *Using Information-Flow Theory to Enable Semantic Interoperability.* In Artificial Intelligence Research and Development, volume 100 of Frontiers of Artificial Intelligence and Applications. IOS Press, 2003.
21. M. Schorlemmer, Y. Kalfoglou. *On Semantic Interoperability and the Flow of Information.* ISWC'03 Semantic Integration Workshop. Sanibel Island, Florida, USA, 2003.

Concept Type Hierarchy as Ontology:
An Example Historical Knowledge Base

Dan Corbett[1] and Wendy Mayer[2]

[1] Science Applications International Corporation, McLean, Virginia, USA
[2] Centre for Early Christian Studies, Australian Catholic University,
Brisbane, Queensland, Australia

Abstract. In this paper we explore the issue of using some aspects of the Conceptual Graph Theory formalism to define functions on ontologies. We exploit the formal definitions of type hierarchy and projection to define operations on an ontology, and then illustrate these ideas by demonstrating a knowledge base of historical interactions that was implemented on an ontology defined in this way.

1 Introduction

With the large amount of information (and knowledge) available through the Internet, users are starting to look for effective ways to filter through the information, to find only the information relevant to their work. Instead of using the web to provide documents and raw data, users will instead use a knowledge server to filter and combine the retrieved knowledge to the user's specific purposes. It has been widely acknowledged that the semantics of order-sorted type hierarchies are fundamental both to the retrieval of knowledge from large real-world-size knowledge bases and to the next generation of web technology [Arara and Benslimane 2002; Corbett 2002; Mineau 2002].

An ontology, in the Knowledge Engineering and Artificial Intelligence sense, is a framework for the domain knowledge of an intelligent system. An ontology structures the knowledge, and acts as a container for the knowledge. We exploit the CG formalism by using a concept type hierarchy to act as the framework for the knowledge base. An unpopulated ontology (which is simply a framework for the knowledge) is represented by the type hierarchy without specific individuals, while the populated ontology (the framework, as well as the knowledge of the domain) is represented by a hierarchy and the specific conceptual graphs which instantiate individuals, constraints, situations or concepts.

The Chrysostom web knowledge-base project provides an interesting case for furthering this research. The Chrysostom project is an attempt to model the social world of the late Roman Empire. The underlying ontology captures the knowledge found in a very large body of documents associated with the cities of Antioch in ancient Syria and Constantinople (modern Istanbul) in the fourth and fifth centuries. The initial idea behind the Chrysostom Knowledge Base (CKB) was to capture all of the speeches of the fourth-century orator and bishop John Chrysostom in one, easily accessible location. The point of capturing the knowledge found in the speeches is that they contain a wealth of information about everyday life. Capturing this information in a knowledge base is a significant first step in creating a model of fourth-century society, and also helps to make that information more accessible.

2 Background

Until now, scholars have dipped into these orations selectively, getting bits and pieces of unrelated information. Our research shows that a user can get a distorted picture when not looking across the entire corpus [Allen and Mayer 1993]. Hence, the need for an ontology was twofold: to try to enforce responsible use of the data on scholars, and to provide a uniform framework for the knowledge contained in the speeches.

The Chrysostom knowledge base which runs on top of this ontology makes it possible to search and get every single instance of a piece of knowledge. But because the search is not directly expressed as keywords (due to the nature of the rhetoric, use of broad categories, allusions, etc) the user needs more than the standard keyword search mechanism.

The intent of the project which implements this knowledge base is to extract all information about how society functioned in fourth-century Near-Eastern Helenic cultures. The breadth and variety of the coverage of topics common to the everyday lives of the people of these regions makes this knowledge an extremely valuable resource for researchers of social history.

The original design called for phrases and passages from Chrysostom's speeches to be placed into categories which would then be keyword searchable in an online database. The designers of the CKB soon discovered problems with this design. For example, a historian may want to look for competing uses of public spaces. In a keyword search, this would involve a combination of searches including marketplace, street system, religious building, civic building, plaza, parade, ceremony, and so on. Even then, many concepts would be lost to the user. It is necessary to give the user the ability to find the combination of these *concepts*, not merely a conjunction of the keywords.

Similarly, ideas and concepts may not be directly represented literally in the database. The user may want to find all mention of beggars and begging, for example, but must also search topics related to poverty and homelessness. Concepts may not be directly searchable. For example, the keywords of "psychology", "superstitious behavior" and "value systems" are all unsearchable in the text-based database, but all of these concepts appear in the form of other words or phrases.

The intent was to make all of the speeches (more than 1,000 of them exist in text form) available to any web user. The texts already exist in an accessible form, thanks to the Thesaurus Lingua Graeca Project (TLG), which has been working for more than two decades to put Greek speeches into an electronic form. This combination of concepts and raw text would make a highly useful database of fourth-century life in these cultures. Since the database is so large, including many concepts, many types and categories, and many text passages, our problem was to discover how to best handle the size and complexity of this knowledge base.

In this paper, we will show portions of the CKB, to demonstrate the size and complexity of the ontology. We will then show how lattice operations on the ontology have already improved the performance and accessibility of the knowledge base. We conclude with discussion on how our techniques will further improve this knowledge base, and how the techniques developed for this project will benefit knowledge representation, knowledge retrieval and the semantic web.

3 Projection as an Ontology Operator

We base our formal definition of ontology on the CG Theory definition of canon, as defined in [Mugnier and Chein 1996; Corbett 2003] and others. A canon in the sense discussed here is the set of all CGs which are well-formed, and meaningful in their domain. Canonical formation rules specify how ontologies can be legally built and guarantee that the resulting graphs satisfy "sensibility constraints," called the Canonical Basis. The canonical basis is a set of rules in the domain which specifies how the relations can be legally used, for example that the concept *eats* must have a theme which is *food*.

A type hierarchy can then be established for both the concepts and the relations within a canon. A type hierarchy is based on the intuition that some types subsume other types, for example, every instance of *cat* would also have all the properties of *mammal*. This hierarchy is expressed by a subsumption or generalization order on types. We formalize these ideas below.

Definition 1. Ontology. An ontology is a tuple $(T, I, \forall, ::, B)$ where T is the set of types. We will further assume that T contains two disjunctive subsets C and R containing types for concepts and relations. Relations are functions with arguments, where each $arg_i : R \ \forall \ C$ is a partial function where $arg_i(r)$ indicates the i-th argument of the relation r.

I is the set of individuals, sometimes called referents.

$\forall \ \forall \ T \ \forall \ T$ is the subtype relation. It is assumed to be a lattice (so there are types top ($\top$) and bottom ($\forall$) and lattice operations join (common specialization) and meet (common generalization)).

$:: \ \forall \ I \ \forall \ T$ is the conformity relation. The conformity relation relates type labels to individual markers. This is essentially the relation which ensures that the typing of the concepts makes sense in the domain.

B (also called $\forall$ by some authors) is the Canonical Basis, a function which associates each relation type with the concept types that may be used with that relation. This helps to guarantee well-formed graphs.

An ontology is then a collection of types and individuals, which forms a framework for the knowledge in a domain. The collection is arranged into a hierarchy based on the subtype relation $\forall$. The canon provides the basis for subsumption in the ontology and guarantees consistency among the relations and in the typing of individuals. Note that this hierarchy is not necessarily a taxonomy, in that a type may have multiple supertypes. Further note that there is no point on the hierarchy where we must make a distinction between a type and an instance. Every concept on the hierarchy is treated as a type. A type may have subtypes and supertypes, but there is no need to distinguish these from instances of the types.

This is distinct from the object-oriented objective of objects inheriting all the properties of a class of objects. The essential difference is in, for example, treating a kitchen as you would any generic room. The *type* room can be placed, occupy space, and have specific values for color and number of doors. A *class* of rooms will have attributes, but cannot be said to occupy a space or have specific dimensions, or have a specific count or placement of doors. The generic room can have constraints placed on its attributes, and finally can be specialized into a kitchen. Fundamentally, a generic room can take the place of a specialized room, unlike a class of objects.

The ontology (as a concept type hierarchy) acts as the framework, with conceptual graphs that conform to the hierarchy used to instantiate concepts in the domain. The ontology is populated by creating conceptual graphs which represent actions, ideas, situations or states in the domain. Recall, though, that a conceptual graph need not be a complete description, and will always be treated in the same manner as any other type.

The closest approach to demonstrating an equivalence between FOL and Conceptual Graphs is due to [Amati and Ounis 2000]. They use a restrictive form of CGs, in which each concept type is allowed only one individual to represent it. Once the existential operator has been applied to a generic referent, all concepts of that type must use that one individual. Clearly, this makes it much easier to interpret Conceptual Graphs into FOL. Given that restriction, Amati and Ounis show that graph derivation through projection is sound and complete. They discuss a method for graph deduction on these restricted graphs.

The real significance of the work by Amati and Ounis, and indeed of our own work, is the proof that deduction systems over Conceptual Graphs are not only possible, but also effective ways of handling knowledge comparison and deduction.

4 Projection of Ontology Types

The definitions of consistency and type subsumption in this paper are based on formal concepts of projection and lower bounds from Conceptual Graph Theory [Sowa 1992]. Projection is the operation used to determine subsumption relations, and to find similarities between parts of the knowledge base. A more general type G is said to subsume a more specific type H if G has a projection into H. For example, the type *mammal* would have a projection into the type *cat*.

The set T of types is arranged into a type hierarchy, ordered according to the specificity of each type. Separate type hierarchies are established for the concepts and the relations within a canon, expressed by a generalization order on the types. A type t is said to be more specific than a type s if t specializes some of the concepts from s. Projection is the function which determines the specialization/generalization relation between two concepts.

The following definitions of projection are modified from the standard definition used in recent Conceptual Graph literature [Willems 1995; Mugnier and Chein 1996; Leclère 1997; Corbett 2001]. Rather than defining projection from one graph into another, these definitions represent projection of types, and therefore define the subsumption operator on type hierarchies.

Definition 2. Concept Projection. Given two concept types, $s \forall C$ and $t \forall C'$, s is said to have a projection into t if and only if there is a morphism $h_C: C \forall C'$, such that:

$\forall s \forall C$ and $\forall t \forall C'$, $h_C(s) = t$ only if $type(s) \geq type'(t)$, and $referent(s) = *$ or $referent(s) = referent'(t)$

C is the set of concepts, $type : C \forall T$ indicates the type of a concept, and $referent : C \forall I$ indicates the referent marker of a concept.

Definition 3. Relation Projection. Given two relation types, s and t, s is said to have a projection into t if and only if there is a morphism $h_R: R \forall R'$, such that:

$\forall r \forall R$ and $\forall r' \forall R'$, $h_R(r) = r'$ only if $type(r) \geq type'(r')$
R is the set of relations, and $type : R \forall T$ indicates the type of a relation.

The definition of type subsumption is based on notions of graph projection. Projection and subsumption are defined for individual graphs to help determine their ordering in accordance with the type hierarchy, and to allow unification, deduction and combination of graphs. The topic of graph projection and subsumption is covered in detail in [Corbett 2001] and [Corbett 2003].

This definition of projection then gives us a formal definition for subtype and supertype and for subsumption on the partial order of the types in the hierarchy. The operations of join, meet and unify are now simply applications of the projection operator. Finding types which are compatible (i.e. that can be unified) is now a matter of finding a common subtype (or join) between the two types. If the only common subtype is $\forall$ then there can be no comparison.

In terms of the Chrysostom Knowledge Base, the meet and join operations are used to refine a user's search query. As shown in the following section, a user can start with a general concept and use projection to find more specific concepts, or join can be used to find common specializations between two concepts. Similarly, the meet operator can be used to common generalizations.

5 The Chrysostom Knowledge Base

Given the stated goal of creating a knowledge base of fourth century society, the obvious direction to take was first to define an ontology of the domain, including terminology, relations and concept types. The historical researchers on our team then "filled in" the ontology with the passages from Chrysostom's orations (translated into English) by attaching short passages to the concepts that represent them. Thus, the ontology is populated by the text-based data to create the Chrysostom Knowledge Base. The work of completing the knowledge base continues, as more than a thousand of Chrysostom's works exist, but the knowledge base is implemented and functioning.

The ontology represents the interactions among the concepts in the domain. That is, not just interactions between people, or business transactions, but interactions between, for example, travel and shipping, sea and ship, tools and agriculture, etc. Figure 1 shows a portion of the Chrysostom ontology, including the top of the hierarchy and some of the highest-level types. When complete, the CKB will contain about 65,000 individual text entries spread among more than 1,500 types. At its deepest paths, there are nine layers of subsumption between the top and bottom elements.

It can be seen in Fig. 1 that the highest level types express very broad categories of the things that Chrysostom discusses in his orations. It is possible for any type to have a specialization in common with any other type (a join). For example, the concept "travel" has a join with the concept of "the sea", which is "shipping". The concepts of "plants," "tools," and "occupation" are joined at the concept of "farmer" and "farming."

6 Search Examples

Search on Concrete Concepts

The user interface is implemented as a web-based interface, and there are several ways in which a user can interact with the knowledge base. In our first example, the user is looking for any mention of lodgings for travelers. This user decides to start by entering "hospitality" as a search query. The CKB will respond by showing the subsumed types under hospitality (which is a high-level type). The subsumed types include *festival, meal, visitor* and *provision of lodging*, as shown in Fig. 1. The user interface showing these results is shown in Fig. 2. Our user follows the hierarchy to *provision of lodging* to find two categories, which are two different types of hostels. However, the user can see from the texts mentioned that these words refer to hostels set up for the poor, or for political refugees. The CKB screen shows that *hostel* is a join between *provision of lodging* and *accommodation*, and so the user decides to explore *accommodation* as a promising category. *Accommodation* subsumes two types, *hostel* and *inn*, and it is this latter category that contains the texts that the user is looking for.

Another example is illustrated by the partial CKB hierarchy shown in Fig. 3. (Note that in order to save space, we leave out most of the lattice, such as the explicit top and bottom and other concepts related to the concepts shown here.) Here, our user is interested in finding out about shipping in the ancient world. She searches on the term "shipping" and finds, not surprisingly, that the concept of *shipping* is a join formed between the concepts of *Travel* and *The Sea*. Further, the user finds that there are several categories under shipping that may be of interest, including *personal travel, ship/boat, shipwreck, shipping personnel* and *shipping of goods*. The user navigates through *shipping of goods*, and finds that *trading* also subsumes *shipping of goods*. She then finds text passages of interest under the categories of *import* and *export*.

Concept Type Hierarchy as Ontology: An Example Historical Knowledge Base   265

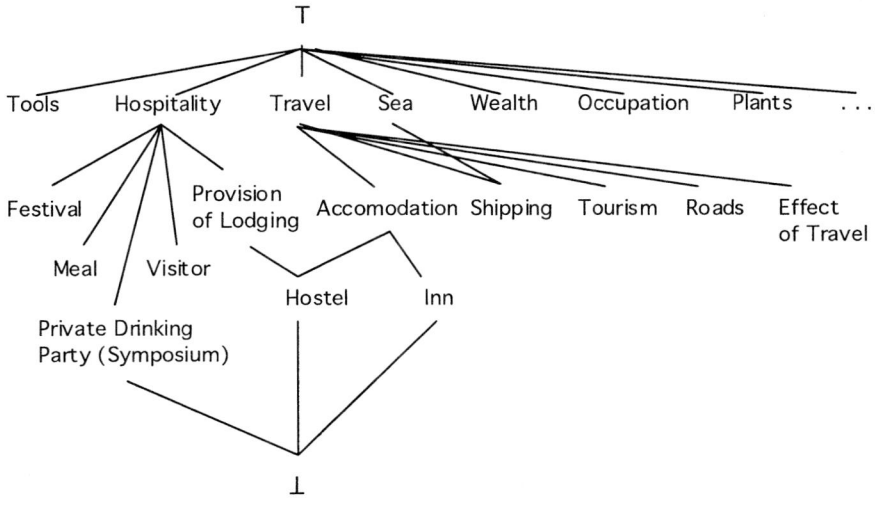

Fig. 1. A portion of the Chrysostom ontology

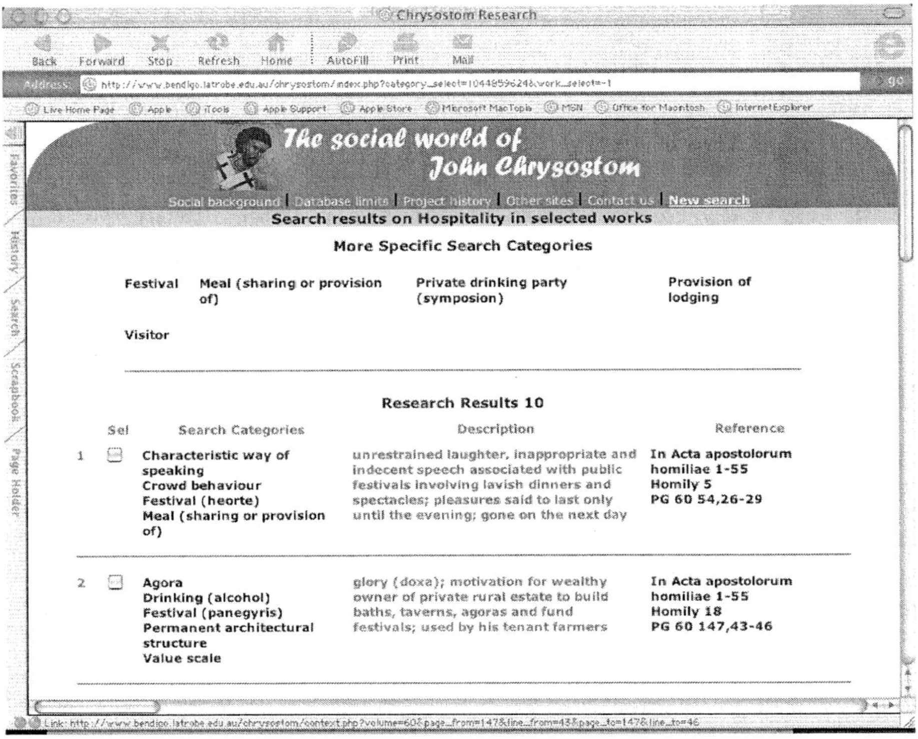

Fig. 2. The user interface to the Chrysostom Knowledge Base

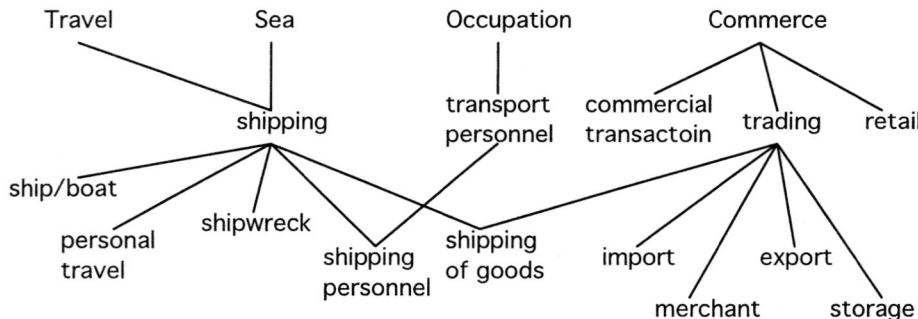

Fig. 3. A portion of the Chrysostom ontology showing shipping and commerce

At any given point in a search, not only is the text that is associated with that concept available, but also the user can click on any of the categories of that text. For example, under *shipwreck*, the user can click on *disaster, captain, crew* or *doctor*. Here, the user did not ask for the join of *disaster* and *personnel* to get *captain*, but the concept of *captain* existed there already, as a join of other concepts. This linking of implied joins (that the user was not searching for) allows greater search and expression of the query.

As a further example, a user is interested in reading about the work methods or environment of the fourth-century bronzesmith. The user may enter the query as "bronzesmith," "metalwork," or even "mallet." As shown in Fig. 4, these queries will yield results which discuss the work practices of metalworkers.

Fig. 4 also includes brief summaries of some of the result passages discovered here, showing that in one case the passage is a reference to how both the bronzesmith and the goldsmith work, and also the need for a source of light. The second passage refers to the bronzesmith's work methods. Not included in the diagram are passages which refer to training in metalwork (said to be combination of theory and practice) decorative metalwork and the use of the concept of metalwork as an example of truly hard work. The user can go to a short text passage where the reference comes from, and the reference numbers in the right column of Fig. 2 are indexes into the TLG where the complete text can be found.

Search on Abstract Concepts
Besides the extensive use in Chrysostom's speeches of analogy and metaphor, users will want to be able to search on abstract concepts. As mentioned earlier, the user can now search for psychology, values, superstitious behavior and other abstract notions. For example, the query "value" will yield many passages associated with values and value scales. From this point, though, the user can follow links to other values expressed in the speeches, such as *honor, debt, behavior, activity of rich people*, and so on. Similarly for the query "superstition," which links to *psychology* and *habitual behavior*.

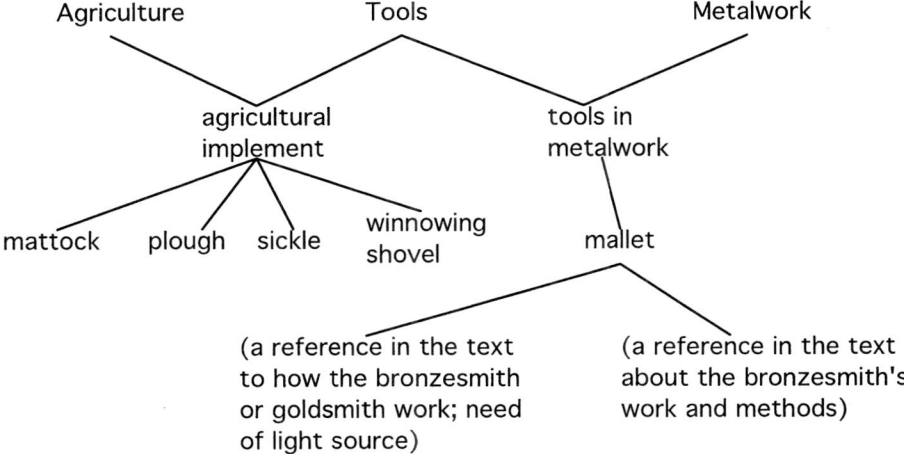

Fig. 4. Another portion of the Chrysostom ontology showing tools

Whether the user starts with a keyword entry or follows links from another concept, all of these concepts have portions of speeches associated with them that give some insight into the lives of people who lived in this time and place. Once the user has found the appropriate concept type, she only has to link to the Greek text to read a short section from the speech. Note that the entire text is not available online, but can be obtained through the TLG.

Note also, that there are text passages associated with nearly all of the types in the ontology. So, the user will not only find short text passages associated with mallet or sickle, but also with *agricultural implement, commercial transaction,* or *transport personnel*. When the original text passage contains these concepts as a general idea, the text is linked to the general concept, rather than something more specific. So, the text data is not only associated with the leaf nodes of the hierarchy, but with nodes at all levels.

7 Future Directions

We have demonstrated the use of type hierarchies and subsumption in this paper, but we haven't yet explored how to use these techniques or unification to retrieve concepts which are hidden in the text because those concepts haven't been made explicit in the type hierarchy. The problem is that it's not always possible to find a join in a straightforward manner. For example, *heatstroke* is a concept that is subsumed by both *summer* and *medical treatment*. However, the join between these two concepts is not explicit in our ontology, and so heatstroke is not searchable in that manner. The user must follow links from either *medicine* or *season* down to the reference on heatstroke.

Our work has now brought us to the point where it will be necessary to create new join terms on the fly. The *heatstroke* example illustrates the direction of the project. In the event of finding a term which may need to be referred to again, there needs to be a mechanism which will create this new concept and place it on the hierarchy. In this case, there will be issues of the subsumption ordering, and how the information is retrieved and indexed.

Exactly how case retrieval and the subsumption ordering, introduced by the unification tool, interact is to be determined. However, the emphasis will be on constructing indices based on the classification of conceptual graph terms into hierarchies complementing the structure of the explored knowledge space. This means that it will be essential to have the knowledge organized into a hierarchical structure which in itself contains much of the semantics for understanding the knowledge, as we have done with the Chrysostom Knowledge Base.

When generating new states the expressiveness of the representation acts to restrict the possibilities requiring consideration. Constraints in the partially elaborated problem statement (ie query) and in the specificity of the corresponding partial solution filter the matching passages. Together with the operation of ordered types in unification, these constraints help to eliminate results which are inappropriate to the state under consideration. Given a computationally efficient implementation of the type system, which is the subject of our future work, a unification tool over conceptual graphs will help to efficiently match appropriate solutions to the partial fragment (or query, keyword, semantic fragment, partial graph) under consideration. In this sense, a unification tool will not only make it easier to create domain rules, but also aid in the retrieval of the solution to the query by making it faster and easier to find appropriate types.

The lattice methods that we employ are domain and representation independent and are based on an abstract data type for partially ordered sets. For a given object domain, a partial order over objects serves as an index to that domain. For example, building designs can be ordered in terms of spatial symmetries, software specification can be ordered by generalization of behavior and social history can be ordered by social role or value systems. The effect is that case retrieval efficiency can be dramatically enhanced.

The knowledge-base which is the subject of our work is unique in that there is no single definition for subsumption, or a "more specific" concept. In fact, it is this feature of a natural database which forces us to enhance the theory behind the semantics of subsumption and type hierarchy, as opposed to the ordering which naturally accompanies databases of artifacts, such as architecture or software constructs.

The point in using a unification tool for conceptual graphs is that conceptual structure term unification is more computationally efficient than standard constraint processing. In our future tool, when a user constrains a query to the database, constraints in the query can be unified with the knowledge-base to produce a result which is very specific to the query. Fewer constraints are solved because constraints are already stored in the hierarchy of the lattice as classifications. This is similar to existing approaches to constraint solving (for example, Baader and Siekmann [Baader and Siekmann 1994]) with the exception that conceptual graphs have the additional semantic power of being a typed and order-sorted structure. Constraints are used, then, to help select appropriate indices and to refine the search result generated by the user's queries.

However, we are still left with several open questions which we hope to address in this project. These questions include the semantic and theoretical support and the implementation techniques of the lattice operators, the efficiency considerations of the indexes and the construction of the lattices. However, these issues are intimately related to the indexing mechanism that we propose to explore. In general, we need to find a conceptual graph solution that helps this historical knowledge-base run in an efficient way when the solutions are many and varied. These issues are directly related to engineering an indexing tool.

Our goal is to automatically create an index into the knowledge base as the query is being formed. The new index item will precisely target the knowledge the user wants to locate, ignoring knowledge that is semantically unrelated, and therefore irrelevant. We achieve this by expanding theory first developed for lattice theory and conceptual graphs to create partially-ordered subsumption hierarchies to index the knowledge.

An example of the use of this sort of indexing of the knowledge can be illustrated by considering a query regarding the travel time between two cities in that time. Ultimately, we want to give the capability to the user to make hypothetical queries that are not explicit in the texts, but can be answered by putting together facts found in the knowledge base. For example, a user may want to query the knowledge base as to whether it would be possible to travel from Constantinople to Antioch in less than ten days. Chrysostom is never explicit on this point, but certain facts about travel do appear in his orations. He discusses military movements, travel by land and by sea, and messengers sent between various cities. Given the time and patience, a researcher in social history could find the answer to the query by reading many speeches, and piecing together the scraps of information they contain.

Our Chrysostom Knowledge Base of the future would allow this sort of query, by matching on the concepts of travel contained in these texts, by performing constraint processing automatically, and by a little use of the knowledge indexing. The new and improved CKB would tell the user that it was possible to travel between those two cities in less than ten days, if the traveler moved by ship.

8 Conclusions

We have demonstrated that the formal definitions of concept and relation type, and of type hierarchies can be used to successfully define an ontology. Using these techniques, we have designed and implemented the Chrysostom Knowledge Base, which contains knowledge of the social history of fourth-century Helenic cultures. The significance of the knowledge is that it contains facts and information about the everyday lives of the people who lived at the time. As such, it is a very valuable resource for researchers studying those cultures. The further significance of this knowledge base is that it is a working implementation of an ontology constructed using concept type hierarchies. The resulting knowledge structure is an ontology of fourth-century social history.

Ultimately, we would like to see the knowledge base instantiated by representing all text passages as conceptual graphs, so that search and indexing is made easier, but we have anecdotal evidence from users that the knowledge base has made research easier because of the lattice structure of the hierarchy.

9 An Invitation

The authors welcome feedback on the Chrysostom Knowledge Base, and invite readers to explore the knowledge base, and its underlying ontology. The CKB can be accessed at: http://www.cecs.acu.e-du.au/chrysostom/

References

Allen, P. and W. Mayer (1993). "Computer and Homily: Accessing the Everyday Life of Early Christians". *Vigiliae Christianae* **47**: 260-280, 1993.

Amati, G. and I. Ounis (2000). "Conceptual Graphs and First Order Logic". *The Computer Journal* **43**(1): 1-12, January, 2000.

Arara, A.A. and D. Benslimane (2002). "Ontology Concept Extraction from Terminologies". In *Proc. Eleventh International Conference on Intelligent Systems*, Boston, Mass, USA, ISCA, July, 2002.

Baader, F. and J. Siekmann (1994). "Unification Theory". *Handbook of Logic in Artificial Intelligence and Logic Programming*. D.M. Gabbay et al, Eds. Oxford, Clarendon Press. **2**: 41-126.

Corbett, D.R. (2001). "Conceptual Graphs with Constrained Reasoning". *Revue d'Intelligence Artificielle* **15**(1): 87-116.

Corbett, D.R. (2002). "Reasoning with Ontologies by Using Knowledge Conjunction in Conceptual Graphs". In *Proc. International Conference on Ontologies, Databases and Applications of Semantics*, Irvine, California, USA, Springer, October, 2002.

Corbett, D.R. (2003). *Reasoning and Unification over Conceptual Graphs*. New York, Kluwer Academic Publishers.

Leclère, M. (1997). "Reasoning with Type Definitions". In *Proc. Fifth International Conference on Conceptual Structures*, Seattle, Washington, USA, Springer-Verlag, August, 1997.

Mineau, G. (2002). "A First Step Toward the Knowledge Web: Interoperability Issues Among Conceptual Graph Based Software Agents, Part I". In *Proc. International Conference on Conceptual Structures*, Borovets, Bulgaria, Springer-Verlag, July, 2002.

Mugnier, M.-L. and M. Chein (1996). "Représenter des Connaissances et Raisonner avec des Graphes". *Revue d'Intelligence Artificielle* **10**(6): 7-56.Sowa, J.F. (1992). "Conceptual Graphs Summary". *Conceptual Structures: Current Research and Practice*. Chichester, UK, Ellis Horwood.

Willems, M. (1995). "Projection and Unification for Conceptual Graphs". In *Proc. Third International Conference on Conceptual Structures*, Santa Cruz, California, USA, Springer-Verlag, August, 1995.

A Dynamic Allocation Method of Basis Functions in Reinforcement Learning

Shingo Iida[1], Kiyotake Kuwayama[1], Masayoshi Kanoh[2],
Shohei Kato[1], and Hidenori Itoh[1]

[1] Dept. of Intelligence and Computer Science, Nagoya Institute of Technology,
Gokiso-cho, Showa-ku, Nagoya 466-8555, Japan
{iida, kuwayama, shohey, itoh}@ics.nitech.ac.jp
[2] Dept. of System Engineering of Human Body, Chukyo University,
101 Tokodachi, Kaizu-cho, Toyota 470-0393, Japan
mkanoh@life.chukyo-u.ac.jp

Abstract. In this paper, we propose a dynamic allocation method of basis functions, an Allocation/Elimination Gaussian Softmax Basis Function Network (AE-GSBFN), that is used in reinforcement learning. AE-GSBFN is a kind of actor-critic method that uses basis functions. This method can treat continuous high-dimensional state spaces, because basis functions required only for learning are dynamically allocated, and if an allocated basis function is identified as redundant, the function is eliminated. This method overcomes the curse of dimensionality and avoids a fall into local minima through the allocation and elimination processes. To confirm the effectiveness of our method, we used a maze task to compare our method with an existing method, which has only an allocation process. Moreover, as learning of continuous high-dimensional state spaces, our method was applied to motion control of a humanoid robot. We demonstrate that the AE-GSBFN is capable of providing better performance than the existing method.

1 Introduction

Many problems with reinforcement learning involve very large state spaces, especially when the state space is multi-dimensional. The curse of dimensionality arises because state spaces grow too large to store all individual state values in a single table. To lessen the curse of dimensionality, function approximators are commonly used, because they require far fewer resources than a table look-up method, and generalize over other parts of the state space. Function approximators commonly use fixed basis functions, such as CMACs [1] and Radial Basis Functions [2]. However, these methods easily break down when they treat continuous high-dimensional state spaces. To avoid this problem, methods of incremental allocation of basis functions, and adaptive state space formation have been proposed [3–6].

In this paper, we propose a dynamic allocation method of basis functions, Allocation/Elimination Gaussian Softmax Basis Function Network (AE-GSBFN),

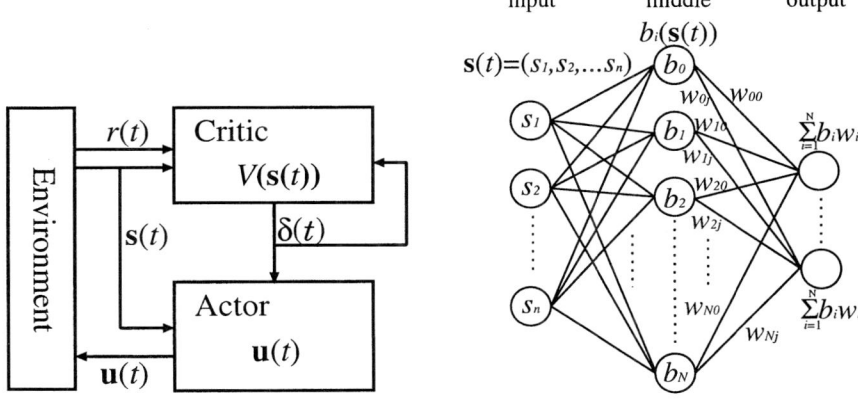

Fig. 1. Actor-critic architecture   **Fig. 2.** Basis function network

in reinforcement learning for treating continuous high-dimensional state spaces. AE-GSBFN is a kind of actor-critic method that uses basis functions, and has allocation and elimination processes. In this method, if a basis function is required for learning, it is allocated dynamically. On the other hand, if an allocated basis function becomes redundant, the function is eliminated. This method can treat continuous high-dimensional state spaces, because the allocation and elimination processes decrease the number of basis functions required for evaluation of the state space. In order to confirm whether this method can avoid a fall into local minima and overcome the curse of dimensionality, we do two experiments: solving a maze and controlling a humanoid robot.

2   Actor-Critic Method

In this section, we describe an actor-critic method using basis functions. We apply this type of method to our method.

Actor-critic methods are TD methods that have a separate memory structure to explicitly represent the policy independent of the value function [2]. Actor-critic methods are constructed by an actor and a critic, as suggested by Figure 1. The policy structure is known as the actor, because it is used to select actions, and the estimated value function is known as the critic, because it criticizes the actions made by the actor.

The actor and the critic each have a basis function network for learning of continuous state spaces. Basis function networks have a three-layer structure as shown in Figure 2, and basis functions are placed in middle-layer units. Repeating the following procedure, in an actor-critic method using basis function networks, the critic correctly estimates the value function $V(s)$, and then the actor obtains actions which maximize $V(s)$.

1. When state $s(t)$ is observed in the environment, the actor calculates the j-th value $u_j(t)$ of the action $\boldsymbol{u}(t)$ as follows [7]:

$$u_j(t) = u_j^{\max} g\left(\sum_i^N \omega_{ij} b_i(s(t)) + n_j(t)\right), \tag{1}$$

where $u_j^{\max}$ is a maximal control value, N is the number of basis functions, $b_i(s(t))$ is a basis function, ω_{ij} is a weight, $n_j(t)$ is a noise function, and $g()$ is a logistic sigmoid activation function whose outputs lie in the range $(-1, 1)$. The Output value of actions is saturated into $u_j^{\max}$ by $g()$.

2. The critic receives the reward $r(t)$, and then observes the resulting next state $s(t + \Delta t)$. The critic provides the TD-error $\delta(t)$ as follows:

$$\delta(t) = r(t) + \gamma V(s(t + \Delta t)) - V(s(t)), \tag{2}$$

where γ is a discount factor, and $V(s)$ is an estimated value function. $V(s(t))$ is calculated as follows:

$$V(s(t)) = \sum_i^N v_i b_i(s(t)), \tag{3}$$

where v_i is a weight.

3. The actor updates weight ω_{ij} using TD-error:

$$\omega_{ij} \leftarrow \omega_{ij} + \beta \delta(t) n_j(t) b_i(s(t)), \tag{4}$$

where β is a learning rate.

4. The critic updates weight v_i:

$$v_i \leftarrow v_i + \alpha \delta(t) e_i, \tag{5}$$

where α is a learning rate and e_i is eligibility trace. e_i is calculated as follows:

$$e_i \leftarrow \gamma \lambda e_i + b_i(s(t)), \tag{6}$$

where λ is a trace-decay parameter.
5. Time is updated.

$$t \leftarrow t + \Delta t. \tag{7}$$

Note that Δt is 1 in general, but we used the description of Δt for interval of the control of humanoid robots.

3 Dynamic Allocation of Basis Functions

In this paper, we propose a dynamic allocation method of basis functions. This method is an extended application of the Adaptive Gaussian Softmax Basis Function Network (A-GSBFN) [8, 3]. A-GSBFN only allocates basis functions, on the other hand, our method allocates and eliminates them. In this section, we first mention A-GSBFN in Section 3.1, and then propose our method, Allocation/Elimination Gaussian Softmax Basis Function Network (AE-GSBFN), in Section 3.2.

3.1 A-GSBFN

Gaussian softmax basis function is used in A-GSBFN, and it is given by the following equation:

$$b_i(\boldsymbol{s}(t)) = \frac{a_i(\boldsymbol{s}(t))}{\sum_{k=1}^{N} a_k(\boldsymbol{s}(t))}, \tag{8}$$

where $a_i(\boldsymbol{s}(t))$ is a radial basis function, and N is the number of radial basis functions. Radial basis function $a_i(\boldsymbol{s}(t))$ in the i-th unit is calculated by the following equation:

$$a_i(\boldsymbol{s}(t)) = \exp(-\frac{1}{2}\|M(\boldsymbol{s}(t) - \boldsymbol{c}_i)\|^2), \tag{9}$$

where $\boldsymbol{c}_i$ is the center of i-th basis function, and M is a matrix that determines the shape of the basis function.

In A-GSBFN, a new unit is allocated if the error is larger than a threshold $\delta_{\max}$ and the activation of all existing units is smaller than a threshold $a_{\min}$:

$$|h(t)| > \delta_{\max} \quad \text{and} \quad \max_i a_i(\boldsymbol{s}(t)) < a_{\min}, \tag{10}$$

where $h(t)$ is defined as $h(t) = \delta(t) n_j(t)$ at the actor, and $h(t) = \delta(t)$ at the critic. The new unit is initialized with $\boldsymbol{c}_i = \boldsymbol{s}$, $\omega_i = 0$.

3.2 Allocation/Elimination GSBFN

In order to perform allocation and elimination of basis functions, we introduce three criteria into A-GSBFN: trace ε_i of activation of radial basis functions [9], additional control time η, and existing time τ_i of radial basis functions. The criteria ε_i and τ_i are prepared for all basis functions, and η is prepared for both networks of the actor and the critic. A learning agent can gather further information on its own states by using these criteria.

We now define the condition of allocation of basis functions.

Definition 1 Allocation.
A new unit is allocated at $\boldsymbol{c} = \boldsymbol{s}(t)$ if the following condition is satisfied at the actor or critic networks:

$$|h(t)| > \delta_{\max} \text{ and } \max_i a_i(\boldsymbol{s}(t)) < a_{\min}$$
$$\text{and } \eta > T_{\text{add}}, \qquad (11)$$

where T_{add} is a threshold. □

Let us consider to use condition (10) for allocation. This condition is only considered for allocation, but it does not consider process after function elimination. Therefore, when a basis function is eliminated, another basis function is immediately allocated at near state of the eliminated function. To prevent immediate allocation, we introduced additional control time η into the condition of allocation. The value of η monitors the length of time that has elapsed since a basis function was eliminated. Note that η is initialized at 0, when a basis function is eliminated.

We then define the condition of elimination using ε_i and τ_i.

Definition 2 Elimination.
The basis function $b_i(\boldsymbol{s}(t))$ is eliminated if the following condition is satisfied in the actor or critic networks.

$$\varepsilon_i > \varepsilon_{\max} \text{ and } \tau_i > T_{\text{erase}}, \qquad (12)$$

where $\varepsilon_{\max}$ and T_{erase} are thresholds. □

The trace ε_i of the activation of radial basis functions is updated in each step in the following manner:

$$\varepsilon_i \leftarrow \kappa \varepsilon_i + a_i(\boldsymbol{s}(t)), \qquad (13)$$

where κ is a discount rate. Using ε_i, the learning agent can sense states which are recently taken by itself. The value of ε_i takes a high value if the agent stays in almost the same state. This situation is considered when the learning fell into a local minimum. Using the value of ε_i, we consider to how avoid the local minimum. Moreover, using τ_i, we consider to how inhibit a basis function from immediate elimination after it is allocated. We therefore defined the condition of elimination using ε_i and τ_i.

4 Experiments

In order to confirm the effectiveness of AE-GSBFN, we did two experiments: solving a maze and controlling a humanoid robot. We first compared AE-GSBFN with A-GSBFN in the maze experiment. We checked performance of the avoidance of local minima in the experiment. We then did the experiment on controlling a humanoid robot to confirm whether AE-GSBFN can treat high-dimensional state space.

4.1 Solving the Maze

Consider the continuous two-dimensional maze shown in Figure 3. This environment has start state $\boldsymbol{S}$ and goal state $\boldsymbol{G}$. In this environment, the learning agent can

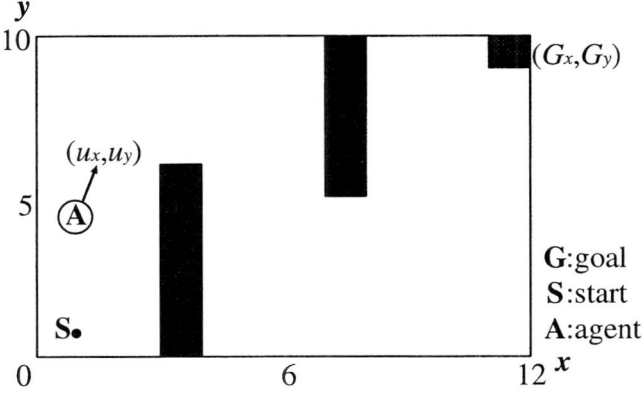

Fig. 3. Maze task

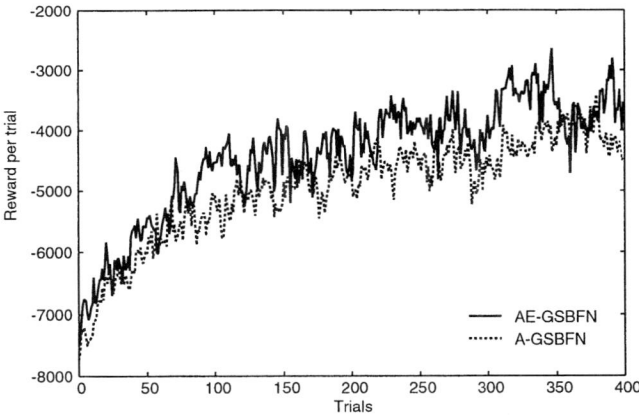

Fig. 4. Rewards per trial

sense G, and takes action $\boldsymbol{u}(t) = (u_x, u_y)$ to reach it. Rewards $r(t)$ are determined by goal state $\boldsymbol{G} = (G_x, G_y)$ and the current state $\boldsymbol{s}(t) = (s_x, s_y)$, as follows:

$$r(t) = -\sqrt{(G_x - s_x)^2 + (G_y - s_y)^2}. \tag{14}$$

One trial terminates when the agent reached $\boldsymbol{G}$ or exceeded 600 steps. We used $u_j^{\max} = 0.5$, $\gamma = 0.9$, $\beta = 0.1$, $\alpha = 0.02$, $\lambda = 0.6$ and $\Delta t = 1$ [step] for parameters in Section 2, $M = \text{diag}(4.0, 4.0)$, $\delta_{\max} = 0.5$ and $a_{\min} = 0.4$ in Section 3.1, and $T_{\text{add}} = 100$ [step], $\kappa = 0.9$, $\varepsilon_{\max} = 5.0$ and $T_{\text{erase}} = 100$ [step] in Section 3.2.

Figure 4 shows the reward per trial with AE-GSBFN and A-GSBFN, and it is desirable that the value is large. The solid line in the figure represents the trial

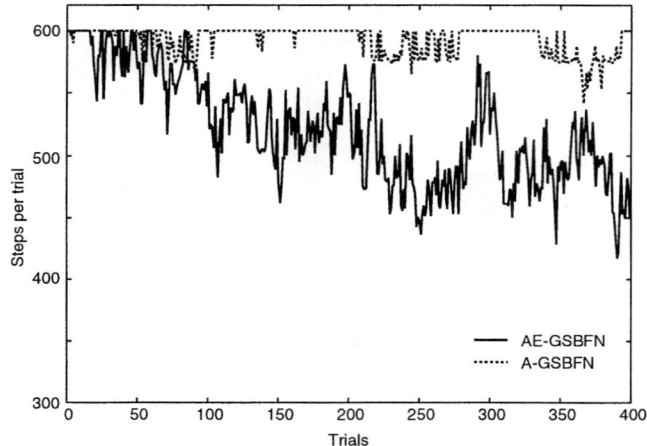

Fig. 5. Average learning curves for AE-GSBFN and A-GSBFN

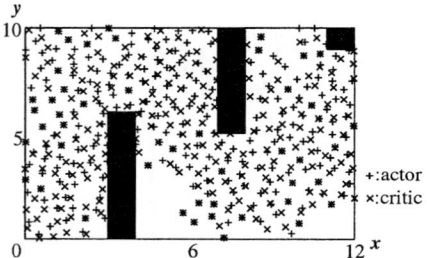

Fig. 6. Allocation of basis functions with AE-GSBFN (actor:243, critic:247). This is a result of successful experiment

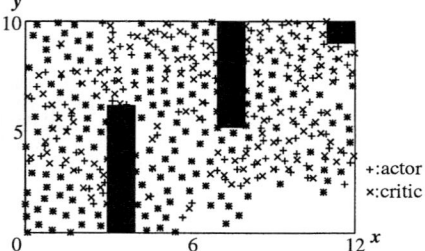

Fig. 7. Allocation of basis functions with A-GSBFN (actor:270, critic:278). This is a result of successful experiment

run with AE-GSBFN and the dotted line is the trial run with A-GSBFN. The results shown in the figure are averaged over 20 repetitions of the experiment. This results indicate that AE-GSBFN obtains more rewards than A-GSBFN. We looked at performances of both method in detail, using the number of steps required to travel from S to G. The curves in Figure 5 represent the number of steps taken by the agent in each trial. Results of the figure are also averaged over 20 repetitions of the experiment. This results indicate that AE-GSBFN traveled from S to G faster than A-GSBFN.

Figures 6 and 7 plot basis functions allocations in successful experiments. In successful experiments, the allocation of basis functions with AE-GSBFN differs little from A-GSBFN. Statistics however indicated that AE-GSBFN achieved G 18 times for 20 repetitions, but A-GSBFN achieved only 9 times. It can be

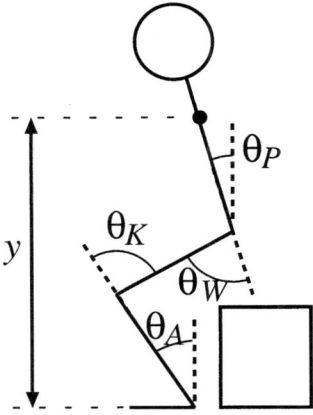
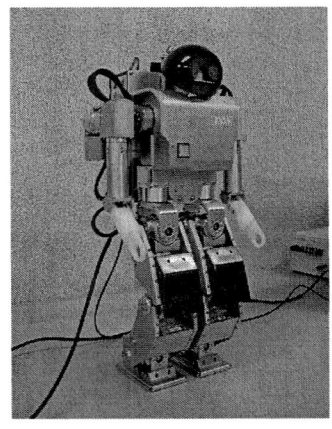

Fig. 8. Learning motion

Fig. 9. HOAP1: Humanoid for Open Architecture Platform

seen that AE-GSBFN performs better than A-GSBFN, and we consider that AE-GSBFN avoided a fall into local minima through the above experiments.

4.2 Controlling Humanoid Robot

In this section, as learning of continuous high-dimensional state spaces, AE-GSBFN is applied to a humanoid robot learning to stand up from a chair (Figure 8). The learning was simulated using the virtual body of the humanoid robot HOAP1 made by Fujitsu Automation Ltd. Figure 9 shows HOAP1. The robot is 48 centimeters tall, weighs 6 kilograms, has 20 DOFs, and has 4 pressure sensors each on the soles of its feet. Both of sensors of angular rate and acceleration are mounted in its breast. To simulate learning, we used the Open Dynamics Engine [10].

The robot can observe the following vector $s(t)$ as its own state:

$$s(t) = (\theta_W, \dot{\theta}_W, \theta_K, \dot{\theta}_K, \theta_A, \dot{\theta}_A, \theta_P, \dot{\theta}_P), \qquad (15)$$

where θ_W, θ_K and θ_A are waist, knee, and ankle angles respectively, and θ_P is the pitch of its body (see Figure 8). Action $u_j(t)$ of the robot is determined as follows:

$$u_j(t) = (\dot{\theta}_W, \dot{\theta}_K, \dot{\theta}_A), \qquad (16)$$

One trial terminates when the robot fell down or time passed over $t_{\text{total}} = 10$ [s]. Rewards $r(t)$ are determined by height y [cm] of the robot's breast:

$$r(t) = \begin{cases} -20 \times \left| \dfrac{l_{\text{stand}} - y}{l_{\text{stand}} - l_{\text{down}}} \right| & \text{(during trial)} \\ -20 \times |t_{\text{total}} - t| & \text{(on failure)} \end{cases}, \qquad (17)$$

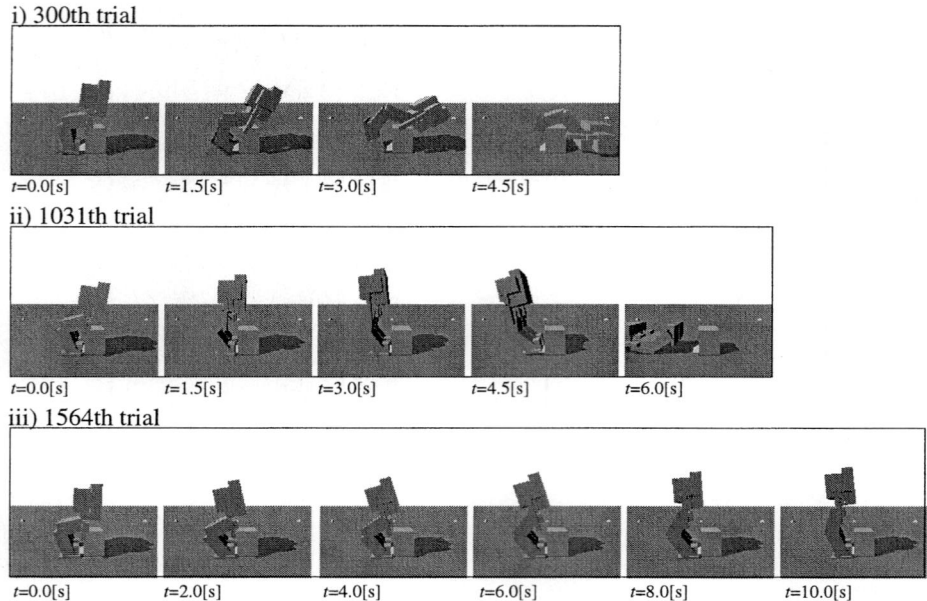

Fig. 10. Learning results

where $l_{\text{stand}} = 35$ [cm] is the position of the robot's breast in an upright posture, $l_{\text{down}} = 20$ [cm] is its center in a falling-down posture. We used $u_j^{\max} = \frac{1}{36}\pi$ [rad], $\gamma = 0.9$, $\beta = 0.1$, $\alpha = 0.02$, $\lambda = 0.6$ and $\Delta t = 0.01$ [s] for parameters in Section 2, $M = \text{diag}(1.0, 0.57, 1.0, 0.57, 1.0, 0.57, 1.0, 0.57)$, $\delta_{\max} = 0.5$ and $a_{\min} = 0.4$ in Section 3.1, and $T_{\text{add}} = 1$ [s], $\kappa = 0.9$, $\varepsilon_{\max} = 5.0$ and $T_{\text{erase}} = 3$ [s] in Section 3.2.

Figure 10 shows learning results. First, the robot learned to fall down backward, as shown by i). Second, the robot intended to stand up from a chair, but fell forward as shown by ii), because it could not yet fully control its balance. Finally, the robot stood up while maintaining its balance, as shown by iii). The number of basis functions in the 2922th trial were 72 in both actor and critic networks. Figure 11 shows experimental result with the humanoid robot HOAP1. The result shows that HOAP1 stand up from a chair as its simulation.

We then compared the number of basis functions in AE-GSBFN with the number of basis functions in A-GSBFN. Figure 12 shows the number of basis functions of the actor, averaged over 20 repetitions. In these experiments, learning with both AE-GSBFN and A-GSBFN succeeded in the motion learning, but the figure indicates that the number of basis functions required by AE-GSBFN is fewer than A-GSBFN. That is, high dimensional learning may be done using AE-GSBFN. Finally, we plot height of the robot's breast in successful experiments in Figures 13 and 14. In the figures, circles denote successful stand-up. The

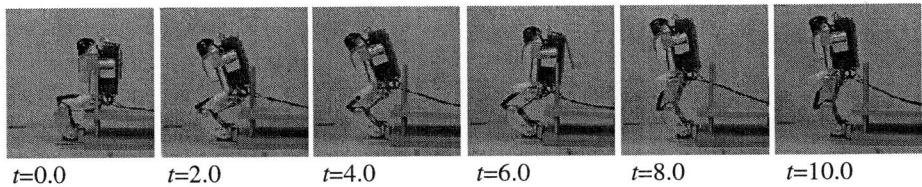

$t=0.0$ $t=2.0$ $t=4.0$ $t=6.0$ $t=8.0$ $t=10.0$

Fig. 11. Experimental result with HOAP1

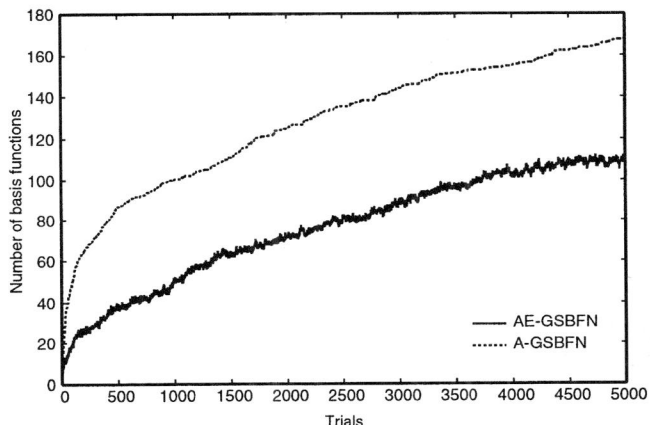

Fig. 12. Number of the basis functions at the actor network (averaged over 20 repetitions).

results show that learning with both AE-GSBFN and A-GSBFN succeeded in the motion learning.

5 Conclusion

In this paper, we proposed a dynamic allocation method of basis functions, AE-GSBFN, in reinforcement learning. Through the allocation and elimination processes, AE-GSBFN overcomes the curse of dimensionality and avoids a fall into local minima. To confirm the effectiveness of AE-GSBFN, it was applied to a maze task and to the motion control of a humanoid robot. We demonstrated that AE-GSBFN is capable of providing better performance than A-GSBFN, and succeeded in enabling the learning of motion control of the robot.

The future work of this study is general comparisons of our method with other dynamic neural networks, for example, Fritzke's Growing Neural Gas [11] and Marsland's Grow When Required Nets [12]. Analysis of the necessity of

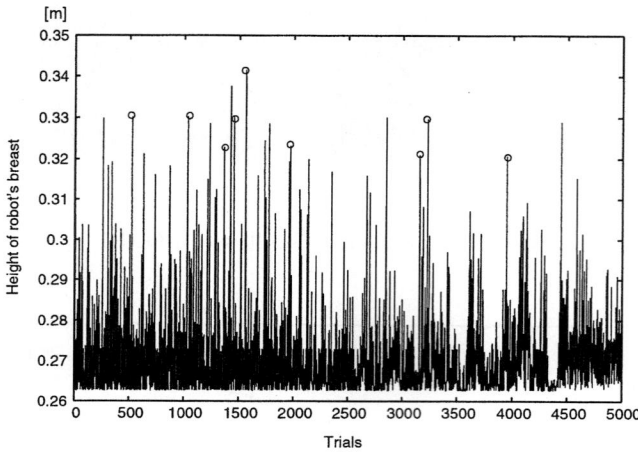

Fig. 13. Height of robot's breast with AE-GSBFN. Circles denote successful stand-up

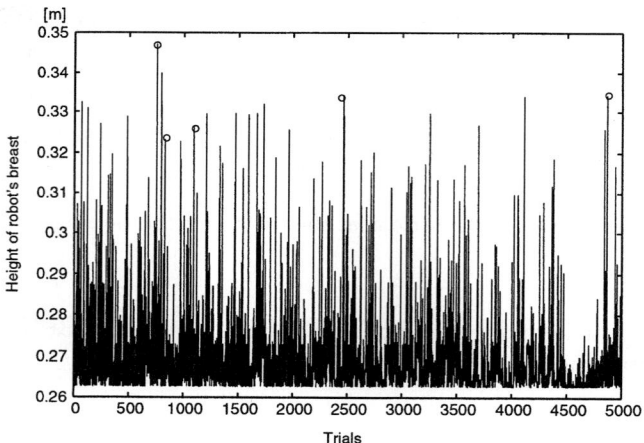

Fig. 14. Height of robot's breast with A-GSBFN. Circles denote successful stand-up

hierarchical reinforcement learning methods proposed by Moromoto and Doya [13] in relation to the chair standing simulation is also important issue for the future work.

References

1. Albus, J.S.: Brains, Behavior, and Robotics. Byte Books (1981)
2. Sutton, R.S., Barto, A.G.: Reinforcement Learning: An Introduction. MIT Press (1998)

3. Morimoto, J., Doya, K.: Reinforcement learning of dynamic motor sequence: Learning to stand up. Proceedings of IEEE/RSJ International Conference on Intelligent Robots and Systems **3** (1998) 1721–1726
4. Samejima, K., Omori, T.: Adaptive state space formation method for reinforcement learning. International Conference on Neural Information Processing (1998) 251–255
5. Takahashi, Y., Asada, M., Hosoda, K.: Reasonable performance in less learning time by real robot based on incremental state space segmentation. IEEE/RSJ International Conference on Intelligent Robots and Systems (1996) 1518–1524
6. Moore, A.W., Atkeson, C.G.: The parti-game algorithm for variable resolution reinforcement learning in multidimensional state space. Machine Learning **21** (1995) 199–234
7. Gullapalli, V.: A stochastic reinforcement learning algorithm for learning real-valued functions. Neural Networks **3** (1990) 671–692
8. Morimoto, J., Doya, K.: Learning dynamic motor sequence in high-dimensional state space by reinforcement learning — learning to stand up —. IEICE **J82-D-II** (1999) 2118–2131 (in Japanese).
9. Kondo, T., Ito, K.: A proposal of an on-line evolutionary reinforcement learning. 13th Autonomous Distributed Symposium (2001) (In Japanese).
10. Smith, R.: (Open Dynamics Engine) http://opende.sourceforge.net/ode.html.
11. Fritzke, B.: Growing self-organizing networks — why? European Symposium on Artificial Neural Networks (1996) 61–72
12. Marsland, S., Shapiro, J., Nehmzow, U.: A self-organizing network that grows when required. Neural Networks **15** (2002) 1041–1058
13. Morimoto, J., Doya, K.: Acquisition of stand-up behavior by a real robot using hierarchical reinforcement learning. International Conference on Machine Learning (2000) 623–630

A Hybrid Classification Approach to Ultrasonic Shaft Signals

Kyungmi Lee and Vladimir Estivill-Castro

School of Computing and Information Technology,
Griffith University, Queensland, Australia
kyungmi.lee@student.griffith.edu.au, v.estivill-castro@cit.gu.edu.au

Abstract. In many applications of machine learning a series of feature extraction approaches and a series of classifiers are explored in order to obtain a system with the highest accuracy possible. In the application we discussed here at least two feature extraction approaches have been explored (Fast Fourier Transform) and Discrete Wavelet Transform, and at least two approaches to build classifiers have also been explored (Artificial Neural Networks and Support Vector Machines). If one combination seems superior in terms of accuracy rate, shall we adopt it as the one to use or is there a combination of the approaches that results in some benefit? We show here how we have combined classifiers considering the misclassification cost to obtain a more informative classification for its application in the field.

Keywords: Industrial applications of AI, Machine learning, Multimodel systems, Pattern analysis in signals, feature extraction, ensemble of classifiers.

1 Introduction

Applications of machine learning evolve through series of feature extraction approaches and a series of classifiers in order to obtain a system with the highest accuracy possible. The industrial application we will discuss here is the classification of ultrasound echoes in an A-scan for long and complex shafts. Although pattern analysis and machine learning techniques have been used with high success in analyzing A-scan data, this is typically in the context of very short signals. There, the task is usually much simpler; in particular, it reduces to detecting the existence of an echo (indicating a fault in the material) or not. But, with long shafts there are many echoes, and in fact there are echoes for where there is no fault (these are known in the field of non-destructive testing as mode-converted echoes). They are the result of reflection and other artifacts of the ultrasound signal navigating and filling the shaft.

To discriminate these echoes from genuine echoes is difficult and some understanding of the physics of the setting suggests at least two approaches to identify features can be used by a classifier. At least two feature extraction approaches have been explored (Fast Fourier Transform(FFT) and Discrete Wavelet Transform(DWT)), and at least two approaches to build classifiers have also been explored (Artificial Neural Networks(ANN) and Support Vector Machines(SVM)). If one combination of feature extraction and classifier seems superior in terms of accuracy rate, shall we adopt it as the one to use or is there a combination of the approaches that results in some benefit? We show here how we have combined classifiers considering the misclassification cost to obtain a more informative classification for its application in the field.

Combining classifiers in machine learning has been mostly considered under the paradigms of 'boosting' [1, 2] and "bagging' [1, 3]. While these alternatives allow to produce a more accurate classifier by combining simpler classifiers, they demand a iterative learning that re-organizes the distribution of cases in the training set. In a sense they are a way to improve a learning paradigm. We believe that in this case there are physical properties that justify the inclusion of the FFT as an informant of the decision process even if the accuracy using DWT is already shown to be superior. Thus, we will not apply boosting or bagging to learning from the DWT(as feature extractor) and SVM(as classifier). While this may improve the accuracy of the classifier, it will potentially ignore important features that the FFT is highlighting.

We have organized this paper as follows. Section 2 provides more details regarding the industrial application. Section 3 describes our analysis based on cost-sensitivity for developing an integrated system. Section 4 describes our empirical evaluation, including the process to extract a training set, followed by conclusions in Section 5.

2   Ultrasonic Flaw Detection for Shafts

Rotating shafts or fixed pins (inside large machinery) are susceptible to failures without apparent warning. Early detection of conditions that lead to in-service failures is necessary and of large economic impact. Failures in shafts are usually preceded by fatigue cracking and this has been detected mainly through non-destructive testing (NDT) techniques using ultrasonic A-scans. A-scan signals taken from shafts are more complicated to interpret. A-scans from other machine parts like plate surfaces or pipe surfaces are shorter and simpler signals, but an A-scan from a shaft is long. Moreover, in a lengthy shaft, an ultrasonic pulse travels many paths echoing off the machined surfaces. Since most shafts are often more complex than a plain solid cylinder (shafts typically have multiple diameter sections or more complex geometry consisting of splines, lubrication and bolt holes), the many reflections from these machined features render it difficult to correctly attribute signals to defects.

Also, the critical faint echoes from a cracked surface may lay somewhere among the multiple secondary echoes. These multiple secondary echoes result from multiple instances of mode conversion between a shear wave and a compression wave as the ultrasonic wave travels the length of the shaft from the

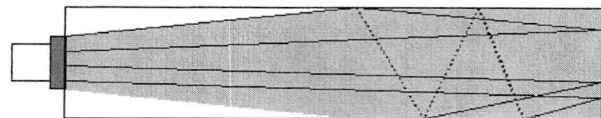

Fig. 1. Ultrasonic pulse generating mode-converted echoes in shaft testing

source. Their position depends on the diameter of the shaft and the various dissipation angles. Figure 1 illustrates the principle behind the generation of mode-converted echoes by showing some illustrative lines of wave propagation of ultrasonic pulse on a lengthy shaft.

These mode-converted echoes may cause misjudgment of the position of features. The problem is then, to discriminate efficiently amongst the large volumes of digital information, the different types of reflectors, and classify them into a) those that correspond to design features of the metal piece (DF), b)those that correspond to flaws, cracks and other defects emerging on the shaft (CR) and c)the multiple reflections and mode-converted echoes (MC) of the two earlier cases a) and b). Among these three causes of echoes, type DF is considered to be easily distinguished compared to other types; namely CR or MC. An issue of further concern in the field is that the signal echoes caused by CR can be confused by fainted echoes caused by MC and vice versa. Consequences of both cases are catastrophic with enormous cost in downtime, consequential damage to associate equipment and potential injury to personnel [4].

To eliminate inconsistent results by even the same human expert, a variety of modern signal processing techniques and artificial intelligence tools have been adopted [5, 6] and these approaches are integrated as automatic ultrasonic signal classification (AUSC) systems. In an AUSC system, ultrasonic flaw signals acquired in a form of digitized data are preprocessed and informative features are extracted using various digital signal processing techniques.

As in most applications of pattern recognition and classification, the main interest for the AUSC research community has been the extraction of effective sets of features from which classification might be performed more efficiently and accurately. While it is hard to determine which set of features is best, it is important to at least identify those that make the process reliable and effective in the field. It is also important to relate some of the features to some of the understanding of the phenomena (in terms of its physics). However, the physics are complex, and the relationship between ultrasonic signal characteristics and flaw classes is not straightforward. Thus, various digital signal processing techniques have been investigated for the determination of features from the raw signal.

Among various feature extraction schemes which have been previously proposed, The Fast Fourier Transform (FFT) has been a useful scheme for extracting frequency-domain signal features [4, 7]. This seems natural when dealing with ultrasound since the most traditional representation of these types of signals is by mathematical Fourier series that identify physically meaningful features like frequency and phase. More recent studies on the ultrasonic flaw classification employ the Discrete Wavelet Transform (DWT) as a part of their feature extraction scheme as DWT provides effective signal compression as well as time-frequency presentation [8, 9].

In their quest for better sets of features for AUSC, many researchers have compared these two feature extraction schemes (FFT and DWT), classifying short signals taken from plate or pipe surfaces and distinguishing corrosive from intact ones. Most comparisons between FFT and DWT showed a superiority of DWT to FFT, for example discriminating the type of flaw (or its non-existence) [10–12]. However, in long shafts there is reasons to believe that phase information is relevant as the creation of a mode-conversion has implications for the phase information.

The first study analyzing feature extraction in more complex ultrasonic signals from shafts [13] also established experimentally that DWT was a potentially stronger feature extraction scheme for feeding Artificial Neural Networks (ANNs). It showed that the DWT scheme enhanced training data, because it could be selected with higher flexibility, and then it could be used for training these networks for in-field ultrasonic shaft signal classification.

The demonstrated superiority of DWT was initially tested only on ANNs as the classifier. However, considering the many difficulties inherent in the ANN learning paradigm (such as generalization control, overfitting and parameter tuning) we remained more conservative about DWT's predominance. We recently made a new comparative experiment involving Support Vector Machines (SVM) instead of ANN models [14]. The experimental results showed once again a superior performance of DWT as the feature extraction scheme in the classification of echoes from ultrasonic signals in long shafts. This confirmed the DWT as indeed superior because it provided better classification with another classifier, namely, the SVM, for which statistical properties indicate robustness in its construction, especially when a limited number of training examples are available.

3 Cost-Sensitive Integrated Classification System

Our goal is to develop a new integrated SVM classifier (ISVM), that is a combined classification system employing efficiently benefits from each of two SVM classifiers using two different feature extraction schemes FFT and DWT. To achieve this, firstly two independent SVM classifiers are constructed, namely FSVM and DSVM. FSVM is a SVM classifier trained with the training data whose features are extracted by the FFT scheme while DSVM is trained using data transformed by the DWT. With these two sub-classifiers, ISVM then sets a new classification rule by which one among FSVM and DSVM is chosen and applied to the classification of new data. That is, the new rule sets which sub-classifier's decision has to be observed for one input to ISVM, mainly based on the comparison of posterior probabilities on each case. The overall structure of ISVM is shown in Figure 2.

The first step for constructing a new combined decision rule is to calculate the posterior probability of every possible hypothesis on each decision made by FSVM or DSVM. The posterior probability is calculated using Bayes theorem

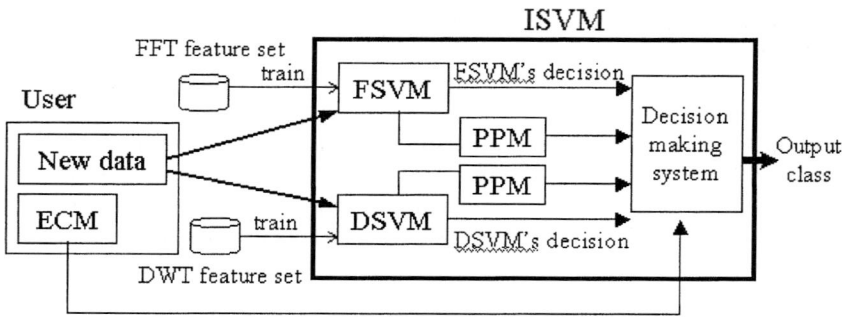

Fig. 2. The overal structure of ISVM

and summarized on a posterior probability table (PPT). In fact, the calculation process using Bayes theorem can be compactly replaced by the representation of the confusion matrix table (CMT) as a PPT as shown in Figure 3.

Generally, CMT shows how well each classifier can recognize each class (sensitivity). For example in Figure 3, we can see how well FSVM performs when classifying MC samples by simply calculating the sensitivity of MC samples in FSVM (this is N_{FMM}/N_{MC}). Also, the performance of FSVM in classifying CR data is N_{FCC}/N_{CR}, which is the sensitivity of CR samples in FSVM.

On the other hand, the posterior probability on PPT reflects the confidence that each class holds after we have made one decision by a classifier. For example,

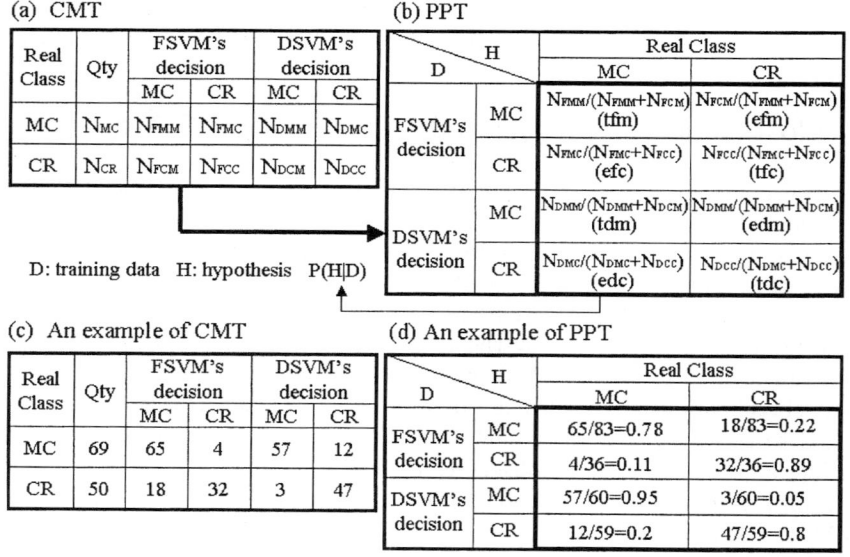

Fig. 3. The relation between CMT(a) and PPT(b) and examples of CMT(c) and PPT(d)

the value *tfm* in the PPT table shown on Figure 3(b) reflects how much we can be confident that the real clsss of an input data would be MC when FSVM classifies an input data as MC. Correspondingly, the value *efm* is the probability that the decision in FSVM, which is MC, would be wrong. Therefore, the value *tfm* is also considered as the degree of trust about the FSVM's decision on MC while value *efm* is the error rate on that decision.

The CMT (Figure 3(a)) summarizes test results through two already constructed classifiers, FSVM and DSVM. Based on the CMT, the trust-rates and error-rates are calculated on each decision. The completed PPT becomes the basis on the further decision which will be made on ISVM. The process for the classification of a new instance in ISVM is divided into two steps as follows.

1. The input data is classified by each sub-classifiers (FSVM and DSVM) respectively, then the results are recorded as F and D.
2. Two posterior probabilities P(CR|F,D) and P(MC|F,D) are compared and CR is assigned to the new instance if P(CR|F,D) is higher than P(MC|F,D) and MC is assigned in the opposite case. Here, values on PPT of each sub-classifiers is used to calculate the posterior probabilities for the combined cases(P(CR|F,D) or P(MC|F,D)).

This decision rule partly employs the theory of naive Bayes classifier and is more or less straightforward if the cost is assigned evenly to different types of misclassification. For example, the final decision made by ISVM is always to follow DSVM's result when the example PPT shown in Figure 3(d) is used. In this case, ISVM is of less interest because the integrated system never will not use the potential of FSVM. In a cost-sensitive environment where one needs to assign different costs to different types of classification error, however, the decision making rule in ISVM becomes more complex.

In conventional or simple classification systems, the costs for making errors in classification is usually same regardless of the type of misclassification. It is, however, impractical to ignore the difference in costs for the different types of errors. In such cost-sensitive environment, the classification system seeks to minimize the total misclassification cost, while the conventional classification seeks to minimize the total number of errors regardless of cost.

In the field of shaft inspection data where we need to predict whether a signal echo is caused by CR(crack) or MC(mode-conversion), two different costs can be assigned. One is the cost of having a crack undetected (assigning the input to class MC when it actually belongs in class CR), and the other is the cost of having a false alarm (assigning the input to class CR when it actually belongs in class MC). Each of both costs are denoted as $c(MC,CR)$ and $c(CR,MC)$ respectively as shown in the error cost matrix (ECM) in Figure 4(a). Here we assume the cost is zero when a case is classified accurately and we exclude the cost of assigning a case to the *unknown* class. This ECM becomes a basic component for constructing the decision making rule in ISVM, consequently which becomes a cost-sensitive classification system.

(a) Error-cost matrix (ECM)

Real Class	Classifier's decision	
	MC	CR
MC	c(MC,MC)=0	c(CR,MC)=b
CR	c(MC,CR)=a	c(CR,CR)=0

(b) Expected risk for each decision

Classifier's Decision		Expected Risk (ER)
FSVM	MC	c(MC,CR)P(CR|FSVM-MC) = a*efm
	CR	c(CR,MC)P(MC|FSVM-CR) = b*efc
DSVM	MC	c(MC,CR)P(CR|FSVM-MC) = a*edm
	CR	c(CR,MC)P(MC|FSVM-CR) = b*edc

Fig. 4. Error costs for each type of misclassification (a) and the calculation formulas of expected risk for each cases (b)

To minimize the expected value of the classification (named expected risk) in a typical error-sensitive classification system, the optimal decision rule is to assign an input pattern **x** to the class k such that:

$$k = \arg\min_{i=1,\ldots,m} \sum_{j=1}^{m} c(i,j) P(j|\mathbf{x}) \qquad (1)$$

where $c(i,j)$ denotes the cost of deciding for class i when the true class is j, m is the number of classes, and $P(j|\mathbf{x})$ denotes the j-th class posterior probability for pattern **x**.

When we apply this rule to the classification of shaft inspection data, the Equation(1) is transformed to:

$$k = \arg\min_{i \in \{CR, MC\}} (c(i, CR) P(CR|x) + c(i, MC) P(MC|x)) \qquad (2)$$

Therefore, the expected risk for every misclassification case in each sub-classifiers FSVM and DSVM is summarized in Figure 4(b) and these values are supplied to the decision making rule in ISVM. As shown in Figure 2, ISVM is an integrated system which consists of two sub-classifiers FSVM and DSVM and a different decision rule is applied depending on types of combination of two sub-decision results from FSVM and DSVM. For one specific shaft inspection data as an input to ISVM, we have four cases in the combination of two decisions by FSVM and DSVM and they are presented in Figure 5. The expected risk (ER) for each of four combinations are also formulated using values calculated through ECM (Figure 4(a)) and PPT (Figure 3(b)). The calculated ER for each hypothesis are compared and the hypothesis with smaller ER is chosen as the final decision in ISVM.

We can present the decision rule in a different way equivalently, which makes the decision rule more explanatory.

- If the decisions of FSVM and DSVM are same and r is smaller than r_1, assign MC.

Sub-classifier's decision		ER for ISVM's decision		Final decision rule (assume $r = \frac{C(MC,CR)}{C(CR,MC)} = a/b$)
FSVM	DSVM	MC	CR	
MC	MC	$a(efm)(edm)$	$b(tfm)(tdm)$	MC if $r \leq r_4$ CR if $r > r_4$ where $r_4 = (tfm * tdm)/(efm * edm)$
CR	CR	$a(tfc)(tdm)$	$b(efc)(edc)$	MC if $r \leq r_1$ CR if $r > r_1$ where $r_1 = (efcm * edc)/(tfc * tdc)$
MC	CR	$a(efm)(tdc)$	$b(tfm)(edc)$	MC if $r \leq r_2$ CR if $r > r_2$ where $r_2 = (tfm * edc)/(efm * tdc)$
CR	MC	$a(tfc)(edm)$	$b(efc)(tdm)$	MC if $r \leq r_3$ CR if $r > r_3$ where $r_3 = (efc * tdm)/(tfc * edm)$

Fig. 5. ER for each hypothesis on ISVM's decision and derived rules for final decision

- If the decisions of FSVM and DSVM are same and r is larger than r_4, assign CR.
- If the decisions of FSVM and DSVM are same and r is between r_1 and r_4, follow their decision.
- If the decisions from FSVM and DSVM are different and r is between r_2 and r_3, follow the opinion of DSVM.
- If the decisions of FSVM and DSVM are different and r is smaller than r_2, assign MC.
- If the decision of FSVM and DSVM are different and r is larger than r_3, assign CR.

4 Empirical Evaluation

The experimental setting consists of four main processes.

1. A set of shaft inspection data, which will be used for training and validation set, is preprocessed and mapped to feature domains using two feature extraction schemes (FFT and DWT).
2. We train two SVM models (temp_FSVM and temp_DSVM) with FFT training data and DWT training data respectively. Test results are obtained through 10-folds cross validation. Based on this test result, a PPT is constructed for each model.
3. Two SVM models (FSVM and DSVM) are trained with the whole set of FFT training data and the whole set of DWT training data respectively. These two trained SVM models become sub-classifiers in ISVM.
4. Separate validation sets for each domains are classified with FSVM and DSVM and those classification results are compared with a result classified by the new developed decision rule of ISVM.

Figure 6 summarizes the steps of our experiment. A more detailed description follows.

A-scan signals were acquired from eight various shafts, ranging between 100mm to 1300mm long by using a probe set to 2 MHz frequency. Signal segments of interest then are selected from the whole ultrasonic A-scan signals. In

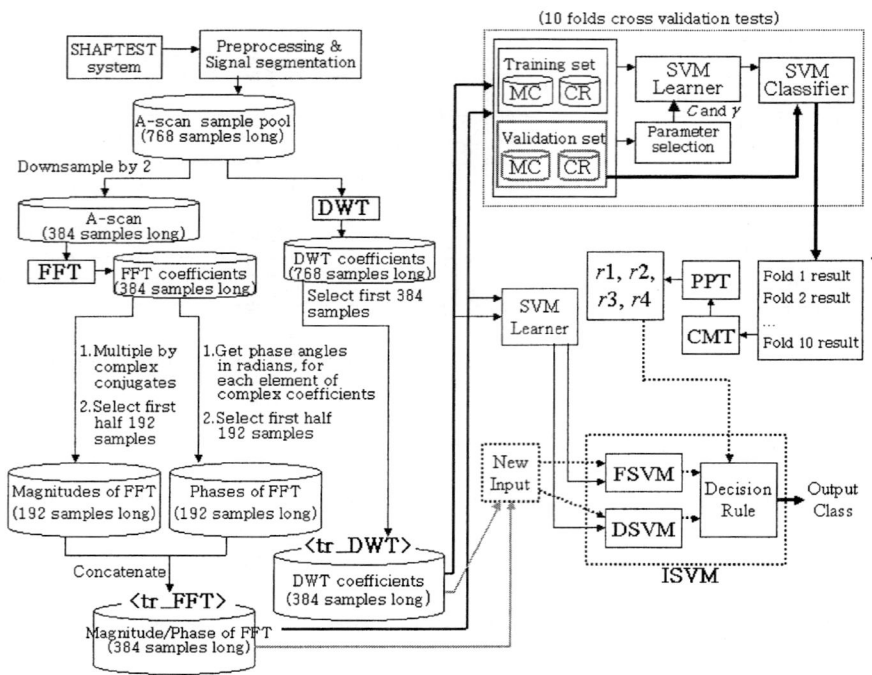

Fig. 6. Flow chart of overall procedure of our experiment

order to apply a consistent way of signal segmentation which is necessary for suppressing time-variance problems with DWT, we used a Systematical echo capturing method with Zero-padding (SZ) [13, 15].

Through this process, we produced a set of time-domain signal vectors of 768 samples long and also recorded whether the signal originated from a crack (CR) or not and whether it was a primary or mode-converted echo (MC). We used $ShafTest^{TM1}$ as a tool to capture these A-scans and build up an initial database of required echoes. For our experiment, 50 CR signals and 69 MC signals were chosen randomly from the sample pool and they were stored as a training set. The remained samples were stored separately so that validation sets can be chosen from the remained sample pool later.

Once an initial database had been built, the time-domain data is mapped to different feature domains: frequency domain using FFT and time-frequency domain using DWT. Through this process, we generate two different sets of feature training data, namely tr_FFT and tr_DWT which would later become the input to the SVM classifiers. In particular, The 768 values of long time-domain vectors delivered by the gate-selection preprocessing, are downsampled into 384 values and then transformed by FFT. For the FFT we concatenated sequences

---

[1] It is a trade mark of CCI Pope.

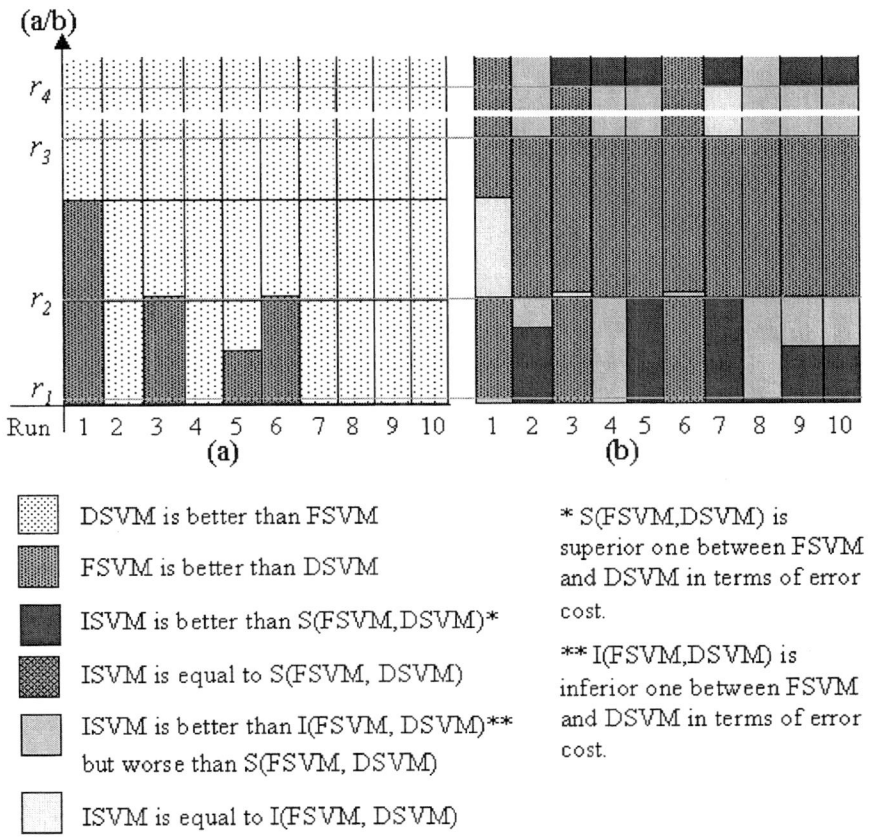

Fig. 7. Experimental results: (a)FSVM *vs* DSVM (b)[FSVM or DSVM]*vs* ISVM

of magnitude components and phase components into a 384 dimensional pattern vector for SVM classification.

On the other hand, the 768 values of long time-domain signal patterns are also converted by DWT. The idea of DWT starts from decomposing discrete time signals into their coarse and detail information by passing them through a high-pass and a low-pass filter respectively. This decomposition is repeated several times only for low-pass filtered signals, and the outputs from high-pass filtering in each decomposition level, presented as DWT coefficients, are concatenated starting with the coarsest coefficients. While, we compressed the 768 values representing the DWT coefficients into 384 samples by discarding the last 384 coefficients which are supposed not containing much information but mainly noise, and these 384 long vector of DWT coefficients are stored as the DWT feature sets. For our experiment, we applied Daubechies wavelets [16] for filtering.

In our new integrated SVM classification system for shaft test, we need to compare the posterior probability each hypothesis holds given that a specific training data has been observed when an error cost matrix is given by a user. Posterior probabilities for each case is summarized in PPM and the steps of constructing PPM is as follows. Firstly, tr_FFT and tr_DWT are divided up into 10 sets. In turn, 9 of these are used to train the SVM classifier, and the remaining set is classified by the constructed SVM classifier. We employed RBF kernel for constructing SVM classifiers as the RBF kernel approach provides nonlinear mapping, requires comparatively small numbers of hyperparameters and has less numerical difficulties. This is repeated with all 10 possible combinations and all the classification results of ten validation sets are concatenated and stored. The statistics of the stored result data is presented on CMT for both FFT data and DWT data and, PPMs are completed in the way explained previously. CMT and PPM for our experiments are same as shown in Figure3(c) and (d) respectively.

On the other hand, two other SVM models are trained by tr_FFT and tr_DWT and they are named as FSVM and DSVM respectively. These two models become sub-classifiers of ISVM and their individual classification performances are compared with ISVM's. As explained previously, the decision making rule set on ISVM requires five parameters: r, r_1, r_2, r_3 and r_4. All values except r are calculated using values in PPMs shown in Figure3(b) and they are 0.037, 0.925, 2.714, 68.16 respectively. With these four values, we can get five possible ranges where r is assumed to be: 1)$r<0.037$, 2)$0.037<r<0.925$, 3)$0.925<r<2.714$ and 4)$2.714<r<68.16$

In order to examine the performance of ISVM compared to FSVM or DSVM, we chose 23 samples randomly from the sample pool which is a remained sample pool after the training set were chosen out previously. These samples are classified by ISVM for each five assumption on r and error cost in each set is calculated. The error cost is also counted on the result classified by single FSVM or DSVM, and they are compared with error cost of ISVM result. These test and comparison process is repeated 10 different times and the results are presented in Figure7. We see that in most scenarios, we obtain more informative and reliable classification by integrating classifiers.

5 Conclusion

When we are to combine the results of classifiers, the machine learning literature offers schemes like boosting and bagging; however, these are mostly effective ways to enhance the predictive value of rough classifications and to re-assign weights to instances in the training set to re-focus the learning on hard instances. But, in the application at hard, there are reasons to believe that the feature extraction methods are obtaining fundamental properties of the signal (like frequency or phase information). We do not want to totally dismiss the outcomes of a classifier based on Fast Fourier Transform despite the classifiers based on Discrete Wavelet Transform have been shown superior. We have presented the first approach in this direction and shown its applicability for this application.

References

1. Bauer, E., Kohavi, R.: An Empirical Comparison of Voting Classification Algorithms: Bagging, Boosting, and Variants. Machine Learning **36** (1999) 105–139
2. Schapire, R.: The boosting approach to machine learning: An overview. In: Proceedings of the MSRI Workshop on Nonlinear Estimation and Classification. (2002)
3. Breiman, L.: Bagging Predictors. Machine Learning **24** (1996) 123–140
4. Cotterill, G., Perceval, J.: A New Approach to Ultrasonic Testing of Shafts. In: Proceedings of the 10th Asia-Pacific Conference on Non-Destructive Testing (APC-NDT). (2001)
5. Katragadda, G., Nair, S., Singh, G.P.: Neuro-Fuzzy Systems in Ultrasonic Weld Evaluation. Review of Progress in Quantitative Nondestructive Evaluation **16** (1997) 765–772
6. Song, S.J., Kim, H.J., Lee, H.: A systematic approach to ultrasonic pattern recognition for real-time intelligent flaw classification in weldments. Review of Progress in Quantitative Nondestructive Evaluation **18** (1999) 865–872
7. Margrave, F.W., Rigas, K., Bradley, D.A., Barrocliffe, P.: The use of neural networks in ultrasonic flaw detection. Measurement **25** (1999) 143–154
8. Obaidat, M.S., Suhail, M.A., Sadoun, B.: An intelligent simulation methdology to characterize defects in materials. Information Sciences **137** (2001) 33–41
9. Simone, G., Morabito, F.C., Polikar, R., Ramuhalli, P., Udpa, L., Udpa, S.: Feature extraction techniques for ultrasonic signal classification. In: Proceedings of the 10th Int. Symposium on Applied Electromagnetics and Mechanics (ISEM 2001). (2001)
10. Polikar, R., Udpa, L., Udpa, S.S., Taylor, T.: Frequency Invariant Classification of Ultrasonic Weld Inspection Signals. IEEE Transactions on Ultrasonics, Ferroelectrics, and Frequency Control **45** (1998) 614–625
11. Redouane, D., Mohamed, K., Amar, B.: Flaw Detection in Ultrasonics Using Wavelets Transform and Split Spectrum. In: Proceedings of the 15th World Conference on Non-Destructive Testing. (2000)
12. Spanner, J., Udpa, L., Polikar, R., Ramuhalli, P.: Neural networks for ultrasonic detection of intergranular stress corrosion cracking. The e-Journal of Nondestructive Testing And Ultrasonics **5** (2000)
13. Lee, K., Estivill-Castro, V.: Classification of Ultrasonic Shaft Inspection Data Using Discrete Wavelet Transform. In: Proceedings of the IASTED international conferences on Artificial Intelligence and appliction, ACTA Press (2003) 673–678
14. Lee, K., Estivill-Castro, V.: Support Vector Machine Classification of Ultrasonic shaft Inspection Data Using Discrete Wavelet Transform. (In: Proceedings of the 2004 International Conference on Machine Learning; Models, Technologies and Applications) 848–854
15. Lee, K., Estivill-Castro, V.: Feature Extraction Techniques for Ultrasonic Shaft Signal Classification. In: Proceedings of the International Conference on Hybrid Intelligent Systems, IOS Press (2003) 479–488
16. Daubechies, I.: Orthogonal bases of compactly supported wavelets. Commun. Pure Appl. Math. **41** (1988) 909–996

A Landmarker Selection Algorithm Based on Correlation and Efficiency Criteria

Daren Ler, Irena Koprinska, and Sanjay Chawla

School of Information Technologies, Madsen Building F09,
University of Sydney NSW 2006, Australia
{ler, irena, chawla}@it.usyd.edu.au

Abstract. Landmarking is a recent and promising meta-learning strategy, which defines meta-features that are themselves efficient learning algorithms. However, the choice of landmarkers is often made in an ad hoc manner. In this paper, we propose a new perspective and set of criteria for landmarkers. Based on the new criteria, we propose a landmarker generation algorithm, which generates a set of landmarkers that are each subsets of the algorithms being landmarked. Our experiments show that the landmarkers formed, when used with linear regression are able to estimate the accuracy of a set of candidate algorithms well, while only utilising a small fraction of the computational cost required to evaluate those candidate algorithms via ten-fold cross-validation.

1 Introduction

With the growing plethora of machine learning algorithms, and both theoretical [18] and empirical [12] results indicating that no single algorithm is generically superior, the issue of selecting an appropriate learning algorithm for a given dataset becomes increasingly important. Traditionally, the common practice is to evaluate all applicable (candidate) algorithms based on some form of *hold-out testing* (e.g. *cross-validation* and *bootstrapping*), and thereby determine which to use (e.g. [14]). However, such evaluation is typically computationally unviable due to the volume of available algorithms. To overcome this, various methods utilising past experience, or meta-knowledge [8], have been proposed. Typically referred to as *meta-learning* [8, 15], such solutions utilise experience on previous datasets (i.e. meta knowledge) to learn hypotheses that characterise the *domains of expertise* of the candidate algorithms. Given the set of all possible datasets, these domains of expertise correspond to subsets in which certain algorithms are deemed to be superior to others.

As in standard machine learning, the success of meta-learning is greatly dependent upon the quality of the features chosen. Various strategies for defining these *meta-features* have been proposed [4, 10, 5, 12, 1, 9]. However, to date there is no consensus on how good meta-features should be chosen. *Landmarking* [13, 6, 7] is an alternative and promising approach that characterises datasets by directly measuring the performance of simple and fast learning algorithms, called landmarkers. The main idea is that the performance of a learning algorithm on a dataset uncovers information about the nature of the dataset [2]. However, the selection of landmarkers is typically done in an ad hoc fashion, with the landmarkers generated focused on characterising the domains of expertise of an arbitrary set of algorithms.

In this paper, we reinterpret the role of landmarkers, defining each as a function over a *set* of learning algorithms that characterises the domain of expertise of *one* specific learning algorithm. Essentially, given a set of candidate algorithms, we wish to generate a set of landmarkers (i.e. for each candidate algorithm, we seek to find one corresponding landmarker), such that each landmarker: (1) is more *efficient* than its counterpart candidate algorithm[1], and (2) corresponds to a domain of expertise that is similar or *correlated* to that of its associated candidate algorithm (i.e. the domains of expertise of the landmarker and associated algorithm roughly overlap in the space of all possible datasets – henceforth labelled the expertise space). Via these new landmarker criteria, we propose a new approach for landmarker generation, where the main idea is to use some subset of the candidate algorithms to landmark each of those candidate algorithms.

The paper is organised as follows. In Section 2, we redefine the role of landmarkers and introduce the new criteria for landmarker selection. The subsequent section introduces a new method for landmarker generation based on the new criteria. Section 4 then describes and discusses the experiments, and corresponding results. The last section concludes the paper and suggests some paths for future work.

2 Establishing Good Meta-attributes: Landmarker Criteria

As is the case with any standard machine learning problem, the performance and success of meta-learning is greatly dependent upon the available inputs and the corresponding features used to describe of the problem. Thus, appropriate meta-features, or in our case, appropriate landmarkers, must be found.

2.1 Redefining Landmarkers

In the literature [13, 6, 7], a landmarker is typically associated with a single algorithm with low computational complexity. Landmarkers have thus far been employed much in the same manner as the prototypical meta-features; they simply serve as meta-features whose purpose is to help define an algorithm-generic expertise space, in which the domain of expertise of *any* candidate algorithm may be defined. This former definition of landmarkers is exemplified in Figure 1 (annotated from [2]). This figure denotes the space of all datasets S, where each rectangle denoted by a l^{old}_i represents the domain of expertise of a landmarker (under the old definition – i.e. each l^{old}_i

---

[1] It may seem that by estimating one candidate algorithm via a set of learning algorithms, we are actually increasing computational complexity. However, as we will see from our proposed landmarker generation algorithm in Section 3, we may limit the set of algorithms from which we construct our landmarkers, such that this set has less computational complexity than the set of candidate algorithms.

corresponds to the domain of expertise of single algorithm), and each dotted ellipse a_i represents the domain of expertise of a candidate algorithm. The general idea is that by noting which landmarker domains of expertise the dataset falls under, it would be possible to induce which candidate algorithm domains of expertise to which it belongs. For example, when a dataset falls within the domains of expertise of l^{old}_3 and l^{old}_4, we may infer that the dataset in question probably belongs to the domain of expertise of a_2. And correspondingly, when another dataset falls within the domains of expertise of l^{old}_2 or similarly, if it does not fall within the domains of expertise of the other l^{old}_i, then it is likely to belong to the domain of expertise of a_1.

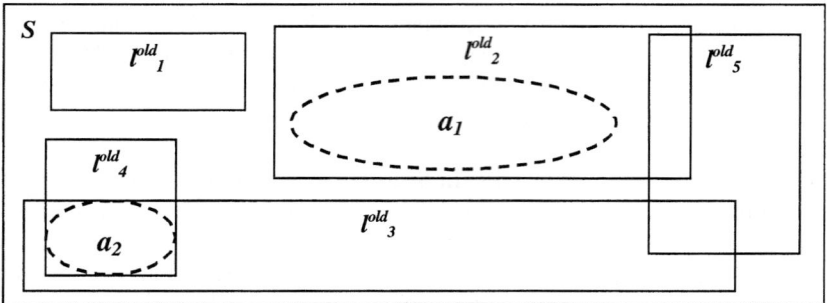

Fig. 1. An example depicting the use of landmarkers under the old definition

We introduce a new perception of landmarkers that defines *each landmarker* to be:

1. A function over *set* of learning algorithms.
2. Specific to *one* candidate algorithm; i.e. the role of the specified landmarker is to characterise only one single algorithm's domain of expertise.

For example, a landmarker for a boosted C4.5 decision tree algorithm could correspond to the accuracies of several learning algorithms such as a decision stump, a naïve Bayes learner, etc. A counterpart of Figure 1, using our new perception of a landmarker is depicted in Figure 4 of Section 2.2 (after further explanation of the criteria used to generate such landmarkers).

This new perception additionally suggests that predicting the domain of expertise of each candidate algorithm should be treated as an isolated learning problem.

The characteristics associated with this new perception of landmarkers (i.e. points 1 and 2 above), are important for two reasons. Firstly, recent empirical results have shown that different candidate algorithms require different characteristics to better predict their domains of expertise (i.e. each meta-feature can have varying significance depending on the candidate algorithm involved) [13, 10, 9]. And secondly, recent work has also shown empirically that estimating the individual predictive accuracy of each candidate algorithm is better than attempting to learn an aggregated concept (e.g. best performing algorithm in the set) over the set of algorithms [11].

Intuitively, while one can consider an overall concept regarding the generic expertise space, this requires that the dataset characteristics be relevant in defining the domain of expertise of _any_ algorithm. This meta-feature space would most likely be very complex, and thus difficult to define. Additionally, with this universal meta-feature paradigm, there is also a much higher probability of learning chance concepts.

2.2 New Landmarking Criteria

In previous landmarking work, two landmarker criteria have been defined: efficiency and bias diversity [13]. The rationale behind the efficiency criteria is obvious – we wish to incur less computational cost than directly evaluating the set of candidate algorithms. Conversely, the rationale behind bias diversity is more vague; the general idea behind bias diversity is to ensure that different landmarkers measure different dataset properties, at least implicitly [13]. This may be interpreted as a criterion that requires the domains of expertise of the landmarkers to be non-correlated.

While these criteria aid to restrict the search space of algorithms (i.e. potential landmarkers), their utility in terms of pinpointing or directing the search for viable landmarkers is questionable. Essentially, the efficiency and bias diversity criteria do not emphasise the selection of landmarkers that would map the domains of expertise of a specific set of candidate algorithms; they do not place any requirement on the relationship between the selected landmarkers and the set of candidate algorithms.

Consequently, it could be interpreted that these criteria seek to find a set of landmarkers that is able to characterise the space of all datasets well enough so that the domain of expertise of _any_ algorithm (i.e. a generic domain of expertise) may be defined. However, these criteria do not ensure the generation of a set of landmarkers that characterises the right dataset features such that there is sufficient generality required to locate the domains of expertise of the given set of candidate algorithms. For example, although the landmarkers depicted in Figure 2 have uncorrelated domains of expertise, they cannot distinguish between the domains of expertise of the five algorithms. This is because the landmarkers do not relate to the algorithms they are meant to characterise. Thus, what landmarker criteria should we then use?

In meta-learning, we are primarily interested in the performance measurements[2] of the algorithms available to us. Thus, to meta-learn, we must map the landmarker measurements to the performance measurement of the candidate algorithm whose domain of expertise we are attempting to learn. This implies that the landmarker for a candidate algorithm should output measurements that are indicative of the performance measurements on that candidate algorithm. More specifically, in order to pick a landmarker for some algorithm, we should ensure that the measurements output by the landmarker are associated or _correlated_ to the performance the candidate algorithm; this would be one way to ensure that the landmarker is related to the target. This may also be explained in terms of the expertise space.

---

[2] Essentially, all the meta-target types are functions of the performance measurements over the candidate algorithms.

Two algorithms whose domains of expertise are overlapping will be closer to each other in a space of all domains of expertise. Conceptually, the distance between two algorithms a and l can be regarded as $\|a - l\|$. Also, we may express $\|a - l\|^2$ as $\|a\|^2 + \|l\|^2 - 2\,a.l$. Thus, if a is close to l, this implies that $\|a - l\|^2$ is small, and thus that $a.l$ is relatively large. This pertains to the correlativity criterion we use to check if a landmarker (e.g. l) is representative of some candidate algorithm (e.g. a). However, in order to operationalise $a.l$, we must move into the space of datasets, as depicted in Figure 3. Thus, we measure correlativity based on r [16] as:

$$r = a.l = \cos\angle(a,l) = \frac{a.l}{\|a\|\,\|l\|} = (\textstyle\sum a_i l_i)/\sqrt{(\sum a_i^2)(\sum l_i^2)} \qquad (1)$$

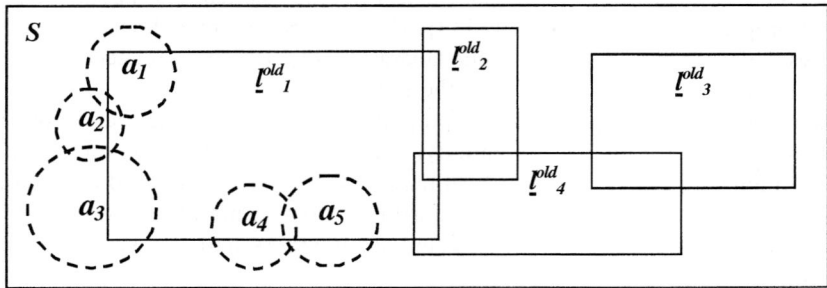

Fig. 2. A scenario in which the bias diversity criteria would fail to map the domains of expertise of the given set of candidate algorithms

It should also not be forgotten that while attempting to derive landmarkers whose measurements are correlated to the cross-validation measurements, the computational cost of running the landmarkers should not exceed the computational cost of performing cross-validation – otherwise there would be no benefit over using cross-validation! Thus, we define the following criteria for landmarkers:

- **Correlativity** – each landmarker should as closely as possible resemble their complex algorithm counterpart; fluctuations in the landmarker performance measurements (e.g. accuracy) should correlate to fluctuations in the same performance measurements of its counterpart algorithm.
- **Efficiency** – the computational cost of running the set of landmarkers should be less (and preferably significantly less) than the computational cost of running all algorithms.

Figure 4 illustrates our new perception of landmarkers in relation to the new criteria. Here, each l_i corresponds to the domain of expertise of the new form of landmarker proposed by us (i.e. a close approximation of the domain of expertise of the candidate algorithm being landmarked). Essentially, by ensuring that a landmarker (i.e. a function over the domains of expertise of several algorithms) correlates to the domain of the candidate algorithm in question, we are able to ensure (or at least quantify) the relevance of the meta-features provided by the landmarkers.

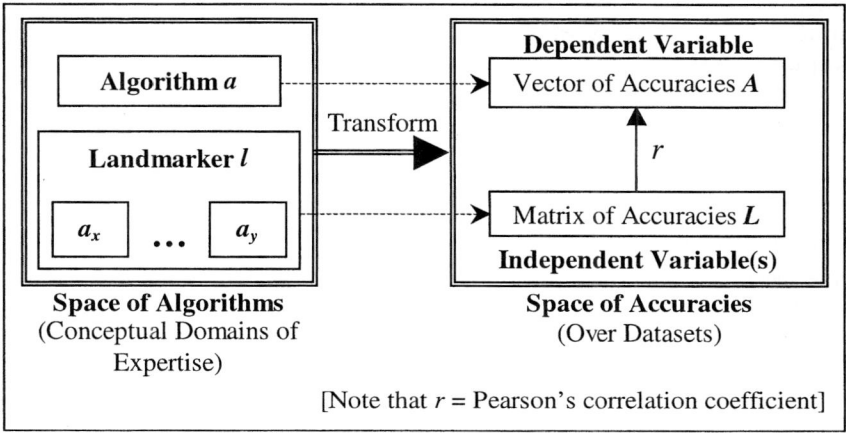

Fig. 3. An example depicting of how *a.l* may be operationalised

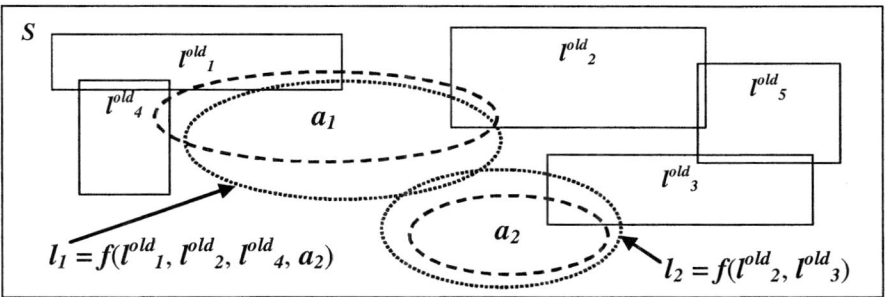

Fig. 4. A scenario illustrating the domains of expertise corresponding to the new version of landmarkers under the new criteria

3 The Proposed Landmarker Generation Approach

A description of the proposed landmarker generation algorithm is given in Figure 5. The general idea of the proposed landmarker generation algorithm is to use a subset of the available algorithms as a landmarker for each of these algorithms. More specifically, given a set of candidate algorithms $A = \{a_1, ..., a_n\}$, we seek to select a set of landmarkers $L' = \{l'_1, ..., l'_n\}$, where each l'_i is the landmarker selected for the algorithm a_i, $l'_i \subset A$, and the union of all $l'_i \in L'$ (written as un-ion(L')) is a (proper) subset of A. For example, given $A = \{a_1, a_2, a_3, a_4\}$, a possible set of selected landmarkers is $L' = \{l'_1, l'_2, l'_3, l'_4\}$, where $l'_1 = \{a_1\}$, $l'_2 = \{a_2\}$, $l'_3 = \{a_1, a_2\}$, $l'_4 = \{a_2\}$.

Input: $A = \{a_1, ..., a_n\}$, a set of candidate algorithms.
Output: $L' = \{l_1', ..., l_n'\}$, a corresponding set of landmarkers where each l_i' is the chosen landmarker for a_i.

Let:
- the powerset of A excluding ϕ and A itself be $L = \{union(L_1), ..., union(L_m)\}$, where $m = 2^n - 2$,
- the powerset of $union(L_i)$ excluding ϕ be $L_i = \{l_1, ..., l_p\}$, with $p = 2^{|union(Li)|} - 1$,
- the mean computational cost of each l_i be denoted $eff(l_i)$, where this mean is over the training datasets, and
- the computational cost of ten-fold cross-validation on the training datasets with A be denoted $eff(A)$.

Landmarker generation algorithm:
[1] For each $union(L_i)$:
[2]   For each $a_j \in A$:
[3]   If $a_j \notin L_i$ then:
[4]   For each $l_k \in L_i$:
[5]   Find $\psi(a_j, l_k) = r^2 + ((eff(A) - eff(l_k))/eff(A))$,
                where r^2 is value of the linear regression function whose
                dependent $= a_j$ and independent(s) $= \{a_x \mid a_x \in l_k\}$
[6]   Let $num\_landmarkers(L_i) = num\_landmarkers(L_i) + 1$
[7]   Find $best\_landmarker(a_j, L_i) = l_y \mid \arg\max_{\forall l_z \in L_i} \psi(a_j, l_z) = \psi(a_j, l_y)$
[8]   Find $mean\_r2(L_i) =$
        $1 / num\_landmarkers(L_i) \sum_{\forall a_j \in A} \psi(a_j, l_x) \mid l_x = best\_landmarker(a_j, L_i)$
[9] Let $L' = \{l_i' \mid l_i' = best\_landmarker(a_i, L_j), L_j = \arg\max_{\forall union(L_k) \in L} mean\_r2(L_k)\}$

Fig. 5. Pseudo code for the proposed landmarker generation algorithm

To choose between the various potential landmarkers, we select the landmarker with the highest combined correlation and efficiency gain. More specifically, for each potential landmarker l_i, we find $r^2(l_i) + ((eff(A) - eff(l_k))/eff(A))$. $r^2(l_i)$ is the mean coefficient of determination obtained over each $a_j - l_i$ pairing (i.e. given the independent(s) l_i, several linear regression functions can be formed, each with l_i paired with a dependent $a_j \in A$). $eff(l_i)$ and $eff(A)$ are the mean computational cost of running l_i and A (i.e. the time taken for training and testing) observed over the training datasets respectively. Note that the values used in the linear regression functions are the accuracy values observed when applying the relevant a_j to a training set of datasets.

This landmarker generation algorithm assumes:

- Several of the algorithms will have similar domains of expertise, and thus, not all have to be used.
- If a candidate algorithm has a very dissimilar domain of expertise (as compared to the other algorithms), that domain of expertise can be correlated to the conjunction of several others.

4 Experiments, Results and Analysis

For our experiments we utilise 10 classification learning algorithms from WEKA [17] (i.e. naïve Bayes, k-nearest neighbour (with k = 1 and 7), support vector machine, decision stump, J4.8 (a WEKA implementation of C4.5), random forest, decision table, Ripper, and ZeroR) and 34 classification datasets randomly chosen from the UCI repository [3]. To evaluate the accuracy of each candidate algorithm on each dataset, stratified ten-fold cross-validation was employed. The effectiveness of the proposed landmarker generation algorithm is evaluated using the leave-one-out cross-validation approach. This corresponds to n-fold cross-validation, where n is the number of instances, which in our case is 34, each pertaining to one UCI dataset.

For each fold we use 33 of the datasets to generate landmarkers as described in Section 3. The resultant set of landmarkers indicates which algorithms must be evaluated and which will be estimated (i.e. the algorithms in $union(L')$, and the remaining $A \setminus union(L')$ respectively). On the dataset left out, we first run the algorithms that must me evaluated and then use their accuracy results to estimate the performance of the other algorithms using the regression functions computed during landmarker generation.

The version of the algorithm described in Section 3 will attempt to find a set of landmarkers L' such that $|union(L')| < |A|$. We have modified the algorithm so that the maximum number of candidate algorithms used by a chosen set of landmarkers (i.e. $|union(L')|$, the landmarker set size of L') may be defined by the user. In our experiments we generate and test all 9 possible landmarker sets sizes ($9 \geq |union(L')| \geq 1$, given that the number of available algorithms is 10).

This leaves us with 9 sets of accuracy *estimates* for each of the candidate algorithms over each of the UCI datasets. Three evaluations are performed over the accuracy estimates:

- Efficiency gained (*EG*): for each held-out dataset and landmarker set size, we compute the percentage of computation saved by employing the landmarker. This saving is the portion of the computational time incurred by conducting ten-fold cross-validation over all the candidate algorithms that is saved by instead running only the algorithms associated with the landmarker in question. For each landmarker set size, we report the mean *EG* recorded over all datasets.
- Rank order correlation (r_s): for each held-out dataset and landmarker set size, we utilise the Spearman's rank order correlation coefficient r_s, to determine the correlation between: (i) the rank order of the accuracies estimated via the landmarkers and regression, and (ii) the rank order of the accuracies evaluated

via ten-fold cross-validation. For each landmarker set size, we report the mean r_s recorded over all datasets.
- Algorithm-pair ordering (AP): for each dataset and landmarker set size, we compare the order of each pair of algorithms (e.g. if $acc(a_1) > acc(a2)$) based on the estimated (via the landmarkers and regression) and evaluated accuracies (via ten-fold cross-validation). For each landmarker set size, we report the mean (across all datasets) of the percentage of pairings in which the order is predicted correctly. Note that there are $^{10}C_2 = 45$ algorithms pairings with 10 algorithms. However, one notices that when all 10 algorithms are employed by the set of landmarkers, no landmarkers are required, and we are simply performing ten-fold cross-validation. Accordingly, for a landmarker set size of x, those x algorithms are evaluated, not estimated. Thus, $^xC_2$ algorithm pairs will correspond to the ordering that is found via ten-fold cross-validation. We denote this as assured AP, which is the accuracy associated with pairings that are guaranteed to be correct.

Table 1. The mean efficiency gained (EG), r_s, algorithm-pair ordering (AP), and r^2 values, and the assured AP value observed from our experiments

No. Algorithms, |union(L')|	Mean EG	Mean r_s	Mean AP	Assured AP	Mean r^2
1	92.9	0.54	71.3	0.0	0.64
2	85.4	0.59	74.1	2.2	0.81
3	84.6	0.68	77.7	6.7	0.89
4	83.1	0.73	80.6	13.3	0.92
5	82.6	0.77	82.4	22.2	0.94
6	67.0	0.83	86.1	33.3	0.94
7	69.4	0.88	89.6	46.7	0.95
8	23.8	0.92	92.7	62.2	0.96
9	8.5	0.97	96.3	80.0	0.97
10*	0.0	1.00	100.0	100.0	NA

* This corresponds to 10-fold cross-validation, which we are comparing against.

Table 1 presents the results from our experiments. It shows the mean EG, the ranking order correlation (mean r_s), the mean accuracy over algorithm-pair orderings (mean AP), the percentage of algorithm-pair orderings guaranteed to be correct (assured AP), and the mean r^2. Each i-th row of the table presents the results of the landmarker set(s) of set size i from each fold. The results show that the landmarkers generated, when used with the linear regression models, are very encouraging. Even when only utilising a single candidate algorithm (i.e. \|union(L')\| = 1), the chosen set of landmarkers is still able to produce a reasonable result (i.e. mean r_s = 0.54, mean AP = 71.3). The efficiency gained is also substantial (i.e. mean EG = 92.9, this means the landmarker only incurred 7.1% of the computational cost that is observed with ten-fold cross-validation on all ten candidate algorithms!). As expected, when we allow the generation algorithm to utilise larger sets of candidate algorithms as landmarkers (i.e. as we allow larger $|union(L')|$), the r^2, r_s, and AP all increase, and the efficiency gained decreases, with all the values approaching the ten-fold cross-validation result.

It should be noted that the computational costs of the algorithms used vary quite drastically. In fact, from Table 1, the large dip in the mean EG of the landmarkers utilised when going from 8 to 9 algorithms is primarily caused by the use of the SVM algorithm, which is significantly more computationally expensive as compared to the other candidate algorithms. However, as our results indicate, the landmarker generation algorithm selects algorithms with higher correlation and lower computational costs, before attempting to utilise the ones with similar levels of correlation, but higher computational costs.

5 Conclusions

In this paper, we have provided a new definition of landmarkers, specifying each to be: (i) a function over a set of learning algorithms, (ii) that is focused on characterising the domain of expertise of one candidate algorithm. Correspondingly, we have identified new criteria for the generation of landmarkers, in that each should be: (i) efficient, and (ii) correlated as compared with its associated algorithm. Based on these criteria, we have proposed a simple landmarker generation algorithm that considers subset combinations of the set of candidate algorithms as landmarkers. The experimental results show that even when the number of algorithms employed by the set of landmarkers is small (and thereby, the gain in efficiency is large – up to a 92.9% saving over the cost of running the entire set of candidate algorithms), the lowest rank order correlation is 0.54, which is a very promising result. Furthermore, as the number of algorithms used by the set of landmarkers increases, the accuracy of the performance estimations approaches that of ten-fold cross-validation, even though the gain in efficiency mostly sustained. These results also suggest that the heuristic employed for the landmarker selection (see Section 3) is a viable one. As future work, we would like to: (i) explore a wider variety of potential landmarkers, (ii) explore the use of different heuristics, (iii) conduct more extensive experimentation, and (iv) ground this approach in a theoretical framework.

References

1. Bensusan, H.: God doesn't always shave with Occam's Razor: learning when and how to prune. Proc. ECML (1998) 119-124
2. Bensusan, H., Giraud-Carrier, C.: Casa Batló is in Passeig de Gràcia or landmarking the expertise space. Proc. ECML, Wkshop. on Meta-learning: Building automatic advice strategies for model selection and method combination (2000) 29-46
3. Blake, C., Merz, C.: UCI repository of machine learning databases. University of California, Irvine, Dept. of Information and Computer Sciences (1998)
4. Brazdil, P., Gama, J., Henery, R.: Characterizing the applicability of classification algorithms using meta level learning. Proc. ECML (1994) 84-102

5. Brazdil, P., Soares, C., Costa, J.: Ranking learning algorithms: Using IBL and meta-learning on accuracy and time results. Machine Learning vol. 50(3) (2003) 251-277
6. Fürnkranz, J., Petrak, J.: An evaluation of landmarking variants. Proc. ECML, Wkshop. on integrating aspects of data mining, decision support and meta-learning (2001) 57-68
7. Fürnkranz, J., Petrak, J., Brazdil, P., Soares, C.: On the use of fast subsampling estimates for algorithm recommendation. Technical Report, Austrian Research Institute for Artificial Intelligence (2002)
8. Giraud-Carrier, C., Vilalta, R., Brazdil, P.: Introduction to the special issue on meta-learning. Machine Learning vol. 54(3) (2004) 187-193
9. Kalousis, A., Hilario, M.: Feature selection for meta-learning. Proc. PAKDD (2001) 222-233
10. Kalousis, A., Hilario, M.: Model selection via meta-learning: a comparative study. Int. J. Artificial Intelligence Tools vol. 10(4) (2001) 525-554
11. Köpf, C., Taylor, C., Keller, J.: Meta-analysis: from data characterisation for meta-learning to meta-regression. Proc. PKDD, Wkshop. on Data Mining, Decision Support, Meta-learning and ILP (2000)
12. Michie, D., Spiegelhalter, D., Taylor, C.: Machine learning, neural and statistical classification. Ellis Horwood (1994)
13. Pfahringer, B., Bensusan, H., Giraud-Carrier, C.: Meta-learning by landmarking various learning algorithms. Proc. ICML (2000) 743-750
14. Schaffer, C.: Technical note: selecting a classification method by cross-validation. Machine Learning vol. 13(1) (1993) 135-143
15. Vilalta, R., Drissi, Y.: A perspective view and survey of meta-learning. J. Artificial Intelligence Review vol. 18(2) (2002) 77-95
16. Wickens, T.: The geometry of multivariate statistics. LEA Publishers (1995)
17. Witten, I., Frank, E.: Data mining: practical machine learning tools with Java implementations. Morgan Kaufmann (2000)
18. Wolpert, D.: The supervised learning no-free-lunch theorems. Proc. Soft Computing in Industry - Recent Applications (2001) 25-42

A Learning-Based Algorithm Selection Meta-Reasoner for the Real-Time MPE Problem

Haipeng Guo[1] and William H. Hsu[2]

[1] Department of Computer Science,
Hong Kong University of Science and Technology
hpguo@cs.ust.hk
[2] Department of Computing and Information Sciences,
Kansas State University
bhsu@cis.ksu.edu

Abstract. The algorithm selection problem aims to select the best algorithm for an input problem instance according to some characteristics of the instance. This paper presents a learning-based inductive approach to build a predictive algorithm selection system from empirical algorithm performance data of the Most Probable Explanation(MPE) problem. The learned model can serve as an algorithm selection meta-reasoner for the real-time MPE problem. Experimental results show that the learned algorithm selection models can help integrate multiple MPE algorithms to gain a better overall performance of reasoning.

1 Introduction

Uncertain reasoning under bounded resources is crucial for real-time AI applications. Examples of these include online diagnosis, crisis monitoring, real-time decision support systems, etc. In these tasks the correctness of a computation depends not only on its accuracy but also on its timeliness. Some mission-critical applications require a hard computation deadline to be strictly enforced where the utility drops to zero instantly if the answer to the query is not returned and a control is not produced. Other soft real-time domains only admit a soft deadline where the utility degrades gradually after the deadline is passed.

Researchers have broadly developed two types of methods to address real-time inference in Bayesian Networks(BNs). The first is to use anytime algorithms (Zilberstein [19]), or flexible computation (Horvitz et al. [7]). These are iterative refinement algorithms that can be interrupted at "any" time and still produce results of some guaranteed quality. Most stochastic simulation and partial evaluation inference algorithms belong to this category. The second method is to combine multiple different inference algorithms where each of these may be more or less appropriate for different characteristics of the problems. The architecture unifying various algorithms often contains a key meta-reasoning component which partitions resources between meta-reasoning and reasoning in order to minimize the overall runtime of problem solving and gain a better overall performance. Work in this category include intelligent reformulation (Breese and Horvitz [2]), algorithm portfolio (Gomes and Selman [5]), cooperative inference (Santos et al. [17]), etc.

This paper is concerned with a specific type of meta-reasoning, namely *algorithm selection*, for the real-time MPE problem with a soft deadline. We use a learning-based approach to induce an MPE algorithm selection model from the training data. The learning needs to be done only once and it takes only a few minutes. Then the learned model is available to anyone as an MPE algorithm selection meta-reasoner. For an input MPE instance, the meta-reasoner(decision trees) can select the best algorithm in only a few seconds and achieve the best overall performance of reasoning. In the following sections we shall first introduce the MPE problem and the algorithm selection problem. Then we shall describe the proposed approach and present the main experimental results. Finally we shall draw the conclusions and discuss future directions.

2 Algorithm Selection for the MPE Problem

2.1 Bayesian Networks and the MPE Problem

A Bayesian network (Pearl [13]) is a pair $(\mathbf{G}, \mathbf{P})$ where $\mathbf{G}$ is a directed acyclic graph whose nodes represent random variables, and $\mathbf{P}$ is a set of Conditional Probability Tables(CPTs) — one for each node in $\mathbf{G}$. An evidence $\mathbf{E}$ is a set of instantiated nodes. An explanation is a complete assignment of all node values consistent with $\mathbf{E}$. The probability of each explanation can be computed in linear time using the chain rule:

$$P(X_1,\ldots,X_n) = \prod_{i=1}^{n} P(X_i|\pi(X_i)), \qquad (1)$$

where $\pi(X_i)$ denotes the parents of node X_i.

MPE is an explanation such that no other explanation has higher probability. It provides the most likely state of the world given the observed evidence. MPE has a number of applications in diagnosis, prediction, and explanation. It has been shown that both exact and approximate MPE are NP-hard (Shimony [15]; Abdelbar and Hedetniemi [1]). Exact MPE algorithms all share a worst-case complexity exponential in the maximal clique size of the underlying undirected graph. So approximate algorithms are necessary for large and complex networks. There are two basic classes of approximate MPE algorithms: stochastic sampling and search-based algorithms. Most of them are anytime algorithms. However, each algorithm may work well on some but poorly on other MPE instances. Under real-time constraints, it would be very helpful if we could know in advance which algorithm is the best for what instances.

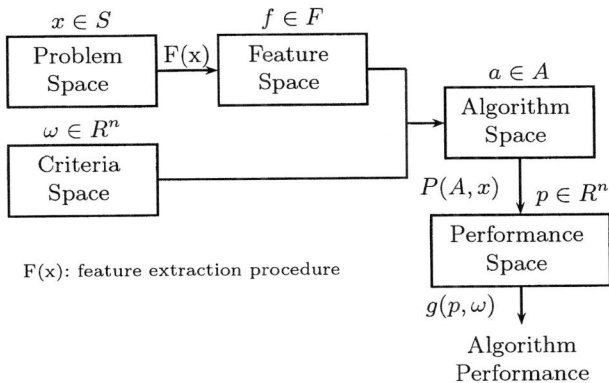

Fig. 1. The abstract model of algorithm selection

2.2 The Algorithm Selection Problem

The algorithm selection problem is to select one among a candidate set of algorithms that solves the input instance the best in some sense. It was first formulated in (Rice [14]). An abstract model of the algorithm selection problem is shown in Fig. 1, where the input instance x in the problem space S is represented as a feature vector f in the feature space. The task is to build a selection mapping between S and the algorithm space A that provides a good (measured by w) algorithm to solve x subject to the constrains that the performance of the algorithm is optimized.

From the point of view of computability theory, the general problem of algorithm selection asks to design a program, or a Turing machine, that takes as inputs the descriptions of two candidate algorithms, and outputs the best one according to some performance criteria such as problem-solving time and solution quality. By applying Rice's theorem it can be shown that the general algorithm selection problem is undecidable (Guo [6]). It implies that, in general, there can be no hope of finding a pure analytical means of automatic algorithm selection only from the descriptions of these algorithms. This general result should not be surprising because the HALTING PROBLEM basically states that in general you can not even tell whether a Turing machine (algorithm) can halt or not given arbitrary input.

3 A Machine Learning-Based Approach for Algorithm Selection

In this paper we turn to a more feasible direction: applying inductive, rather than analytical approach. Our proposed inductive approach relies significantly on experimental methods and machine learning techniques. We are partly motivated by the observation that some easy-to-compute problem features can be used as good indicators of some algorithm's performance on the specific class

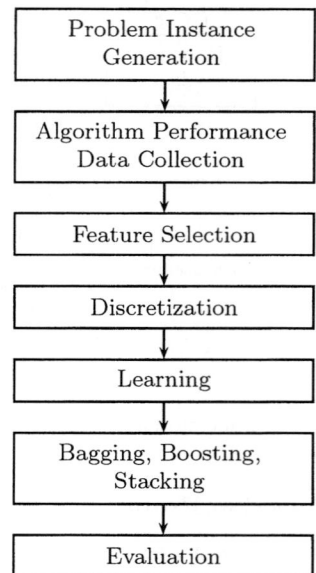

Fig. 2. The machine learning-based approach for algorithm selection

of instances. This knowledge can help select the best algorithm to gain more efficient overall computation. In NP-hard problem-solving, researchers have long noticed that algorithms exploiting special problem instance features can perform on the particular class of instances better than the worst-case scenario. In light of this, two of the main directions of this work are to study different instance features in terms of their goodness as a predictive measure for some algorithm's performance and to investigate the relationships between instance characteristics and algorithms' performance.

Another motivation comes from the inspiration of automating and mimicking human expert's algorithm selection process. In many real world situations, algorithm selection is done by hand by some experts who have a good theoretical understanding to the algorithms and are also very familiar with their runtime behaviors. The automation of the expert's algorithm selection process thus has two aspects: analytical and experimental. We have already known that the first aspect is hard to be automated and compiled into a program. In contrast, automating the experimental aspect is more feasible because of the advancements that have been made in experimental algorithmic (Johnson [11]), machine learning (Witten and Frank [18]), and uncertain reasoning techniques (Horvitz et al. [8]).

The difficulty of automatic algorithm selection is largely due to the uncertainty in the input problem space, the lack of understanding to the working mechanism of the algorithm space, and the uncertain factors of implementations and runtime environments. From the viewpoint of expert systems and machine learning, the algorithm selection system acts as an "intelligent meta-reasoner"

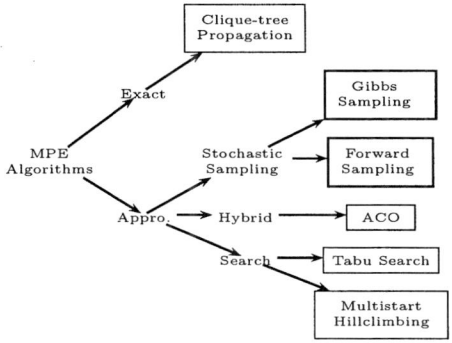

Fig. 3. Candidate MPE algorithms

that is able to learn the uncertain knowledge of algorithm selection from its past experiences and use the learned knowledge (models) to reason on algorithm selection for the input instance in order to make the right decision. This can be formulated as the following machine learning problem:

The algorithm selection learning problem
Task T: selecting the best algorithm, $Best\_Algm(f)$, for instance f.
Measure P: percent of correct selections.
Training data E: algorithm performance data collected from experiments.

Since the target function, $Best\_Algm(f)$, has discrete values, this is indeed a classification problem. An overview of the procedure is shown in Fig. 2. The first two steps, including instance generation and algorithm performance data collection, prepare the training data. The next two steps preprocess the data, including discretization and feature selection. Then in the learning step, machine learning algorithms are applied to induce the predictive algorithm selection model. Also, some meta-learning methods — such as bagging, boosting, and stacking (Witten and Frank [18]) — can be used here to improve the learned predictive models. Finally, the best learned model is evaluated on test data.

4 The Algorithm Space And The Feature Space

4.1 The Algorithm Space

Our candidate MPE algorithms include one exact algorithm: Clique-Tree Propagation(CTP) (Lauritzen and Spiegelhalter [12]); two sampling algorithms: Gibbs Sampling (Pearl [13]) and Forward Sampling (also called Likelihood Weighting) (Fung and Chang [3]) ; two local search-based algorithms: Multistart Hillclimbing and Tabu Search (Glover and Laguna [4]); and one hybrid algorithm combining both sampling and search: Ant Colony Optimization(ACO). These algorithms are chosen because currently they are among the most commonly used MPE algorithms. A classification of these representative algorithms is shown in Fig. 3.

Because of the lack of space, we refer interested readers to (Guo [6]) for detailed descriptions.

4.2 The Instance Feature Space

An MPE instance consists of three components: the network structure, the CPTs, and the evidence.

Network characteristics include network *topological type* and *connectedness*. We distinguish three topological types: polytrees, two-level networks(Noisy-OR), and multiply connected networks. Network connectedness $conn$ is simply calculated as $conn = \frac{n\_arcs}{n\_nodes}$. These two characteristics have a direct influence on the exact inference algorithm's performance. In contrast, sampling algorithms' performance is rarely affected by them.

CPT characteristics include *CPT size* and *CPT skewness*. Since we only consider binary nodes, the maximum number of parents of a node, $max\_parents$, can be used to bound the CPT size. The skewness of the CPTs is computed as follows (Jitnah and Nicholson [10]): for a vector (a column of the CPT table), $v = (v_1, v_2, \ldots, v_m)$, of conditional probabilities,

$$skew(v) = \frac{\sum_{i=1}^{m} |\frac{1}{m} - v_i|}{1 - \frac{1}{m} + \sum_{i=2}^{m} \frac{1}{m}}. \qquad (2)$$

where the denominator scales the skewness from 0 to 1. The skewness of a CPT is the average of the skewness of all columns, whereas the skewness of the network is the average of the skewness of all CPTs. We will see that CPT skewness has a significant influence on the relative performance of sampling and search-based algorithms.

Evidence characteristics includes the *proportion* and the *distribution type* of evidence nodes. Evidence proportion is simply the number of evidence nodes, n_evid, divided by n_nodes: $\frac{n\_evid}{n\_nodes}$. Usually, more evidence nodes implies more unlikely evidence. Hence, the MPE will also be quite unlikely and the probability that it is hit with any sampling scheme is not very high. The distribution of evidence nodes also affects the hardness of MPE instances. If most evidence nodes are "cause" nodes, the problem is called *predictive reasoning*. If most evidence nodes are "effect" nodes, it is called *diagnostic reasoning*. It has been proven that predictive reasoning is easier than diagnostic reasoning (Shimony and Domshlak [16]). In our experiments, we will consider three types of evidence distributions: strictly predictive, strictly diagnostic, and randomly distributed. An inference problem is called "strictly predictive" if the evidence nodes have no non-evidence parents; it is called "strictly diagnostic" if the evidence nodes have no non-evidence children.

We are aware that there might exist some other features that could work as well or even better. These particular features are chosen mainly because domain knowledge, previous literature(Jitnah and Nicholson [10]; Ide and Cozman [9]; Shimony and Domshlak [16]), and our initial experimental experience all

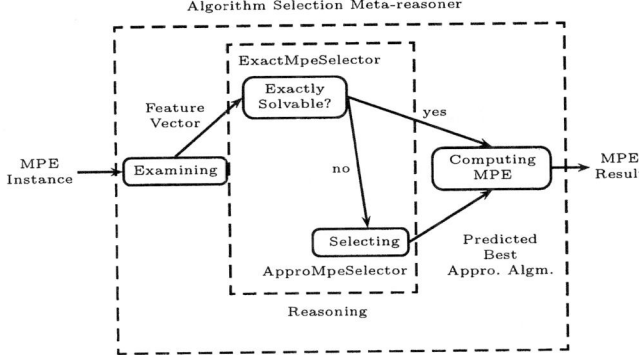

Fig. 4. The algorithm selection meta-reasoner

suggest that they are good indicators of MPE instance hardness and algorithm performance. The other reason is that they are all easy to compute.

5 Experiments and Results

Our first goal is to identify the class of MPE instances for which the exact inference algorithm is applicable. When the exact algorithm is not applicable (most probably due to an out-of-memory error in practice), we need to look at various approximate algorithms. Thus our second goal is to learn the predictive model that can determine which approximate algorithm is the best. Therefore, the algorithm selection meta-reasoner to be learned will consist of two classifiers as shown in Fig. 4: the *ExactMpeSelector* for exact algorithm selection, and the *ApproMpeSelector* for approximate algorithm selection.

5.1 Data Preparation

In the data preparation phase, we first generate MPE instances with different characteristics uniformly at random. The random generation of MPE instances with controlled parameter values is based on a Markov chain method (Ide and Cozman [9]). It is reasonable and necessary to consider only a subset of all possible MPE instances , i.e. the set of "Real World Problems" (RWP). In order to simulate RWP BNs, we first extract the ranges of all characteristic parameter values from a collection of 13 real world samples, call it D_{RWBN}, and then generate networks and MPE instances based on the extracted distributions. The ranges of their characteristic values are as follows: $30 \leq n\_nodes \leq 1,000$; $conn \in [1.0, 2.0]$; $maxParents < 10$; $0.25 < skewness 0.87$. These characteristics information are used to guide the generation of our training datasets.

The first training dataset for learning *ExactMpeSelector*, D_{MPE1}, is generated as follows: we first randomly generate networks with connectedness varying from 1.0 to 2.0(with a step of 0.2) and maximum number of parents varying from 3 to 10. The number of nodes used are $\{30, 50, 80, 100, 120, 150, 200\}$. We then

Table 1. Experiment 1: learning *ExactMpeSelector*

	C45	NaiveB.	BN	Bagg.	Boost.	Stack.
c.a. (%)	94.80	82.79	90.06	94.75	94.81	94.56
s.d. (%)	0.27	0.36	0.24	0.25	0.23	0.45

run exact algorithm CTP on these randomly generated networks and record the performance. To perform inference, CTP first compiles the network into a clique tree. We record the maximum clique size and label the network as "yes" instance if the compilation is successful. Otherwise, if it throws out an out-of-memory error or takes longer than 5 minutes, we label the instance as "no". D_{MPE1} has four numeric attributes: *n_node*, *topology*, *connectedness*, and *maxParents*. The target class, *ifUseExactAlgorithm*, takes boolean values representing whether exact algorithm is applicable or not. We also include these 13 real world networks into D_{MPE1}. The final D_{MPE1} contains a total of 1,893 instances.

The second training dataset for learning *ApproMpeSelector*, D_{MPE2}, only contains two-level and multiply networks. We generate a set of networks with different characteristic values and then run all 5 approximate algorithms on them with different evidence settings. We give each algorithm a fixed number of samples or search points and label the instance using the best algorithm that returns the best MPE value. The total number of samples was 300, 1000, or 3,000. D_{MPE2} has 8 attributes: *n_node*, *topology*, *connectedness*, *maxParents*, *skewness*, *evidPercent*, *evidDistri*, and *n_samples*. The target class is the best algorithm for this instance. D_{MPE2} contains 5,184 instances generated from 192 networks.

5.2 Model Induction

We now apply various machine learning algorithms to induce the predictive algorithm selection models. We consider three different kinds of models: decision tree learning (C4.5), naive Bayes classifier, and Bayesian network learning (K2). We also consider three meta-learning methods to combine multiple models: bagging, boosting and stacking, which all use C4.5 as their base learner. So, total, we have six different learning schemes. Before learning, we also conduct data preprocessing such as discretization and/or feature selection if necessary.

In experiment 1, we run all 6 learning schemes on D_{MPE1}. Table 1 shows the classification accuracies of each learned model. We use the best model out of these 6, i.e. the one that has both high classification accuracy and efficient reasoning mechanism. We can see that boosting(94.81%), C4.5(94.80%), and bagging(94.75%) all have a high classification accuracy. We also notice that NaiveBayes has the worst performance of only 82.79%, which verifies that the features in D_{MPE1} are not independent of each other. Since C4.5 is much simpler and more efficient on reasoning, we use the decision tree learned by C4.5 as the best model for exact MPE algorithm selection: *ExactMpeSelector*.

In experiment 2, we look at feature selection for approximate MPE algorithm selection using D_{MPE2}. Each data case has 9 attributes. The first 8 are MPE

Table 2. Experiment 3: learning *ApproMpeSelector*

	C4.5	NaiveB.	BN	Bagg.	Boost.	Stack.
c.a (%)	77.75	72.77	76.08	75.44	77.16	77.36
s.d. (%)	0.23	0.03	0.01	0.27	0.26	0.32

instance features and the last one is the target class labelling the best approximate MPE algorithm. We apply a GA-wrapped C4.5 feature selection classifier to search for the best feature subset. The wrapper uses C4.5 as the evaluation classifier and a simple genetic algorithm to search the attribute space. The GA's population size and number of generations are 20. The crossover probability is 0.6 and the mutation probability 0.033. The feature subset selected is {*n_node, skewness, evidPercent, evidDistri, n_samples*}. Note that all network structure features are filtered out. The result agrees with our domain knowledge that network structure does not affect approximate algorithms' performance very much. From now on, we will use this selected subset rather than D_{MPE2} itself.

In experiment 3, we apply all 6 machine learning algorithms on the selected feature subset of D_{MPE2} to induce *ApproMpeSelector*. The experimental results(Table 2) show that C4.5 has the highest classification accuracy(77.75%). Because of this and the fact that C4.5 has a much faster reasoning mechanism, we choose it as the best model for *ApproMpeSelector*.

In experiment 4, we study the influences of each individual feature on the relative performance of different algorithms. We partition the training dataset used in experiment 3 by each feature's values and record the number of times of each algorithm being the best at each feature value level. The results are summarized as follows: (1)*Number of Nodes*. *n_nodes* affects the relative performance of two search algorithms, but forward sampling and ACO are almost not affected. When *n_nodes* increases from 50 to 100 multi-start hillclimbing becomes the best algorithm more frequently and the chances for tabu search being the best drops significantly. This can be explained by the constant size of the tabu list used. When network becomes larger while the tabu list remain the same size, the tabu list's influence becomes weaker. This makes it lose its best algorithm position to multi-start hillclimbing. (2)*Number of Samples*. Again, the relative performances of two search algorithms are affected, but forward sampling and ACO's are not. When the given number of samples increases from 300 to 1,000 to 3,000, tabu search becomes the best algorithm more often and multi-start hillclimbing loses its top rank. It seems that Tabu search can utilize available number of search points better than multi-start hillclimbing. (3) *CPT skewness*. Skewness has the most significant influence on the relative performance of these algorithms as shown in Table 3. When the skewness is low, the search space is flat and search algorithms perform much better than sampling algorithms. Multi-start hillclimbing wins the best algorithm two times more than tabu search. When the skewness is around 0.5, ACO outperforms all other algorithms almost all the time. When the skewness increases to 0.9, forward sampling and ACO are the winners and perform equally well. We also notice that forward sampling works better only for highly skewed networks and ACO works for both highly-skewed networks

Table 3. Partitioning D_{MPE2} by CPT Skewness

skewness	Number of Times of Being Best Algorithm				
	gibbs.	forward.	multiHC	tabu	aco
0.1	0	0	1059	512	157
0.5	0	4	9	174	1677
0.9	0	858	9	28	942

and medium-skewed networks. (4)*Evidence Proportion*. The result shows that changing evidence percentage does not affect two search algorithms' relative performance, but it affects forward sampling and ACO. ACO is out-performed by forward sampling as the percentage of evidence nodes increases from 10% to 30%. We should also note that evidence percentage's influence is much weaker than that of skewness. (5)*Evidence Distribution*. The relative performance of multi-start hillclimbing is not affected. Tabu search is only slightly affected. It shows that diagnostic inference is relatively hard for forward sampling but is easy for ACO. In contrast, random distributed evidence is relatively hard for ACO but is easy for forward sampling.

5.3 Model Evaluation

Finally, we evaluate the learned algorithm selection meta-reasoner to verify that it does achieve a better overall performance of reasoning. For a given MPE instance, the meta-reasoner first examines the instance and extracts the feature vector. Then *ExactMpeSelector* is called to determine whether it is exactly solvable. If the classification result is "yes", the system then executes the exact inference algorithm. If it is "no", *ApproMpeSelector* will be used to select the best approximate algorithm. The selected algorithm is then executed and the final MPE value returned. This procedure is shown in Fig. 4.

We first test *ExactMpeSelector* on $D_{MpeTest}$, which contains 405 instances generated in the same way as previous experiments. *ExactMpeSelector* identifies 243 "yes" instances correctly. Then we apply *ApproMpeSelector* on the rest 162 "no" instances. The result shows that there are 123 correctly classified instances and 39 incorrectly classified instances. The classification accuracy is 75.93%.

To show that the algorithm selection system outperforms any single algorithm, we partition these 162 "no" instances into three groups according to their skewness. There are 27 unskewed, 54 medium-skewed, and 81 highly-skewed instances. For each group, we compare the total approximate MPE values returned by each individual algorithm with the total values returned by the algorithm selection system. On medium-skewed and highly-skewed instances, the algorithm selection system returns the largest total MPE values of 6.0×10^{-6} and 0.16. On unskewed instances, the system returns the second largest MPE value of 2.1×10^{-26}. But the largest total, computed by multi-start hill climbing, is only 2.2×10^{-26}. The algorithm selection system's result is almost as good as that. Adding them all together, the algorithm selection system returns the largest total MPE value on all 162 instances.

We also test the system on real BNs. First, all 13 real world networks are correctly classified by ExactMpeSelector. There are 11 "yes" networks. On these networks, all predicted best approximate algorithms also agree with actual best algorithms. The two "no" networks are *link* and *munin1*. *ApproMpeSelector* selects ACO as the best approximate algorithm for both. The actual running of all algorithms on *link* returns all 0, given 5,000 samples. This is due to its huge state space(724 nodes, 5.77×10^{277} states) and low skewness(13,715 out of 20,502 numbers are 0). *munin1* has 189 nodes and 3.23×10^{123} states. Given 5,000 samples, ACO returns the best MPE of 5.93×10^{-8}. Forward sampling finds the second best MPE of 6.61×10^{-9}. All other algorithms just return 0.

In summary, the test results on both artificial and real Bayesian networks verify that the learned algorithm selection meta-reasoner can make reasonable decisions on selecting exact and best approximate MPE algorithms for the input MPE instance and provides a better overall performance.

6 Conclusions and Discussions

We have reported a machine learning-based approach to build an algorithm selection meta-reasoner for the real-time MPE problem. The system consists of two predictive models (classifiers). For an input MPE instance, the first one decides if exact algorithm is applicable. And the second one determines which approximate algorithm is the best. Different MPE instance characteristics have different properties and affect different algorithms' performance. Our experimental results show that CPT skewness is the most important feature for approximate MPE algorithm selection. It reveals that in general search-based algorithms work better on unskewed networks and sampling algorithms work better on skewed networks. Other features, such as *n_nodes*, *n_samples*, *evidPercent* and *evidDistri*, all affect these algorithms' relative performance to some degree, although not as strong as *skewness* does. The learned algorithm selection system uses some polynomial time computable instance characteristics to select the best algorithm for the NP-hard MPE problem and gains the best overall performance in terms of the returned solution quality given the same computational resources. The time of computing features and selecting the best algorithm are negligible comparing to the actual problem solving time. The most important and difficult task in this scheme is to identify the set of candidate features. The main limitation of this method is that the size of training data grows exponentially in the number of features used. The fact that training data are generated from a specific set of real world instances may also limit the learned system's applicable range. In the future this scheme could be applied to algorithm selection of other NP-hard problems and help to build more efficient real-time computation systems.

Acknowledgements

Thanks anonymous reviewers for their valuable comments. This work was partially supported by the HK Research Grants Council under grant HKUST6088/01E.

References

Abdelbar, A. M., Hedetniemi, S. M.: Approximating MAPs for belief networks in NP-hard and other theorems. Artificial Intelligence. **102** (1998) 21–38

Breese, J. S., Horvitz, E.: Ideal reformulation of belief networks. In UAI90. (1990) 129–144

Fung, R., Chang, K. C.: Weighting and integrating evidence for stochastic simulation in Bayesian networks. In UAI89. (1989) 209–219

Glover, F., Laguna, M.: Tabu search. Kluwer Academic Publishers, Boston. (1997)

Gomes, C. P., Selman, B.: Algorithm portfolio design: theory vs. practice. In UAI97. (1997) 190–197

Guo, H.: Algorithm selection for sorting and probabilistic inference: a machine learning-based approach. PhD thesis, Kansas State University. (2003)

Horvitz, E.: Computation and action under bounded resources. PhD thesis, Stanford University. (1990)

Horvitz, E., Ruan, Y., Kautz, H., Selman, B., Chickering, D. M.: A Bayesian approach to tackling hard computational problems. In UAI01. (2001) 235–244

Ide, J. S., Cozman F. G.: Random generation of Bayesian networks. In Brazlian Symposium on Artificial Intelligence, Pernambuco Brazil. (2002)

Jitnah, N., Nicholson, A. E.,: Belief network algorithms: A study of performance based on domain characterization. In Learning and Reasoning with Complex Representations. **1359** Springer-Verlag (1998) 169–188

Johnson, D.: A theoretician's guide to the experimental analysis of algorithms. In M. H. Goldwasser and D. S. Johnson and C. C. McGeoch, editors, Data Structures, Near Neighbor Searches, and Methodology: Fifth and Sixth DIMACS Implementation Challenges. (2002) 215–250

Lauritzen, S. L., Spiegelhalter, D. J.: Local computations with probabilities on graphical structures and their application to expert systems (with discussion). J. Royal Statist. Soc. Series B **50** (1988) 157-224

Pearl, J.: Probabilistic Reasoning in Intelligent Systems: Networks of Plausible Inference. San Mateo, CA, Morgan-Kaufmann. (1988)

Rice, J. R.: The algorithm selection problem. In M. V. Zelkowitz, editors, Advances in computers. **15** (1976) 65–118

Shimony, S. E.: Finding MAPs for belief networks is NP-hard. Artificial Intelligence. **68** (1994) 399–410

Shimony, S. E., Domshlak, C.: Complexity of probabilistic reasoning in directed-path singly connected Bayes networks. Artificial Intelligence. **151** (2003) 213–225

Santos, E., Shimony, S. E., Williams, E.: On a distributed anytime architecture for probabilistic reasoning. Technique Report AFIT/EN/TR94-06. Department of Electrical and Computer Engineering, Air Force Institute of Technology. (1995)

Witten, I. H., Frank, E. Data Mining: Practical Machine Learning Tools and Techniques with Java Implementations. Morgan Kaufmann. (1999)

Zilberstein, S.: Operational rationality through compilation of anytime algorithms. PhD Thesis. University of California at Berkeley. (1993)

A Novel Clustering Algorithm Based on Immune Network with Limited Resource*

Li Jie, Gao Xinbo, and Jiao Licheng

School of Electronic Engineering, Xidian Univ.,
Xi'an 710071, P. R. China

Abstract. In the field of cluster analysis, objective function based clustering algorithm is one of widely applied methods so far. However, this type of algorithms need the priori knowledge about the cluster number and the type of clustering prototypes, and can only process data sets with the same type of prototypes. Moreover, these algorithms are very sensitive to the initialization and easy to get trap into local optima. To this end, this paper presents a novel clustering method with fuzzy network structure based on limited resource to realize the automation of cluster analysis without priori information. Since the new algorithm introduce fuzzy artificial recognition ball, operation efficiency is greatly improved. By analyzing the neurons of network with minimal spanning tree, one can easily get the cluster number and related classification information. The test results with various data sets illustrate that the novel algorithm achieves much more effective performance on cluster analyzing the large data set with mixed numeric values and categorical values.

1 Introduction

Cluster analysis is one of multivariable statistical analysis methods, which is also an important branch of unsupervised classification in statistical pattern recognition [1]. In traditional cluster analysis methods, the objective function based clustering algorithm converts the clustering problem into an optimization problem. Due to having profound functional foundation, this type of based clustering algorithms become the main research topic of cluster analysis, in which c-means algorithm is one of representative algorithms [2]. However, c-means algorithm cannot detect clusters in nonlinear subspaces, since it assumes the clustering prototypes as points in feature space, called clustering centers. To this end, the clustering prototypes are generalized from points to lines, planes, shells and conics, and some c-means type algorithms are proposed with various prototypes, such as c-lines and c-planes ect. algorithms [3, 4]. Therefore, these c-means type algorithms can perform clustering analysis on data sets with different prototypes.

Although the above c-means type algorithms extend the application range of objective function based clustering algorithm, it costs at the increasing of requirements of clustering priori information. For example, the cluster number c,

---

* This project was supported by NFSC (N0.60202004).

and the type of clustering prototypes should be specified in advance, or the algorithm will be misled and results in a wrong partition of data set [2]. Meanwhile, this type of algorithms require that all the prototypes should be with the same form, of course with different parameters. Such requirement limits their practical application of this type of clustering algorithms. In many fields, the handled data set to be analyzed often contains unknown number of subsets with different prototypes. The number of clusters is difficult to automatically determine, especially in high-dimensional feature space.

In recent, a fuzzy clustering algorithm with multi-type prototypes is proposed [5], which integrates the available prototype-based clustering algorithms together. It is evident that the objective function of prototype-based clustering algorithm possesses many local optima, so it is easy to get trap into local optima from improper initialization and results in dissatisfied partition [6, 7]. For this purpose, with the emergence of genetic algorithm (GA), some GA-based clustering algorithms were proposed, which can converge into the global optima with a high probability. However, GA-based methods converge very slowly and easily occur premature phenomenon [8].

For automatic determining the cluster number c, some researchers present self-organized feature mapping (SOFM) to realize the clustering [9]. Although the SOFM can resolve the problem of determining the cluster number, it does not work for analyzing the data set with multi-type prototypes.

Cluster analysis is well known as an unsupervised learning method. However, the above algorithms need priori information, which of course affects their unsupervised performance. With the rising of artificial immune system, an artificial immune network (AIN) is presented to realize the real unsupervised cluster analysis [10]. This new method can obtain good performance for the data set with distinct boundaries among the subsets. For the data set with indistinct boundaries among subsets, it is difficult for this method to achieve the effective network structures. Meanwhile, for the exponential increase of the network scale vs. the data amount and of the cputime vs. the iteration number, the AIN is unsuitable for cluster analysis with large data set. For this purpose, an immune system with limited resource is proposed [11], which solves the problems of time-consuming and network scale explosion, but is not real unsupervised classification.

As an effective tool of data mining, cluster analysis often needs to process large high-dimensional data set, moreover, such data set may be consisting of numeric and categorical attributes. The traditional way to treat categorical attributes as numeric does not always produce meaningful results, because many categorical domains are not ordered. Most existing clustering algorithms either can handle both data types but are not efficient in the case of processing large data sets or can handle large data sets efficiently but are limited to numeric attributes. Few algorithms can do both well, such as k-prototypes and etc [12], however, such method also asks the priori information.

To overcome the drawbacks of the existing algorithms, a novel clustering algorithm with Immune network structure based on limited resource is proposed. It can perform cluster analysis with multi-type prototypes; moreover, it can automatically determine the proper cluster number and cluster structures. Meanwhile, a concept of the fuzzy artificial recognition ball (ARB) is introduce, by which the antigens are identified for data set. Since the fuzzy ARB can adaptive adjust the effect rang according to the excited degree, which overcomes the influence of fuzzy boundary points on the network structure. In addition, by defining a new distance measurement function for samples with different attributes, the proposed algorithm can also analyze the data set with mixed attributes.

2 Clustering Algorithm Based on Evolutionary Immune Networks

The immune network theory, as originally proposed by Jerne in 1974 [13]. Based on the theory of immune network of Jerne, Leandro proposed an evolutionary artificial immune network (EAIN) in 2000 [10]. The main idea of EAIN is as follows. Let $X = \{x_1, x_2, \cdots, x_n\}$ denote a set of n objects, where each object $x_i = [x_{i1}, x_{i2}, \cdots, x_{im}]^T$ is described by m attributes, to characterize a molecular configuration as a point $s \in S^m$. Hence, a point in a m-dimensional space, called shape-spaces, determines the interactions within Ab-Ab and Ag-Ab. The possible interactions within the system will be represented in the form of a connectivity graph. The network model can be formally defined as follows.

Definition 1: The evolutionary artificial immune network is an *edge-weighted graph*, not necessarily fully connected, composed of a set of nodes, called *cells*, and sets of node pairs called *edges* with a number assigned called *weight*, or *connection strength*, specified to each connected edge.

The clusters in the network will serve as *internal images* (*mirrors*) for mapping existing clusters in the data set into existing clusters in the network of cells. As an illustration, suppose there is a data set composed of three regions with high density of data, according to Figure 1(a). A hypothetical network architecture, generated by the learning algorithm to be presented, is shown in Figure 1(b). The numbers within the cells indicate their labels, the numbers next to the connections represent their strengths, and dashed lines suggest connections to be pruned, in order to detect clusters and define the final network structure. Notice the presence of three distinct clusters of cells, each of which with a different number of cells, connections and strengths. These clusters map those of the original data set. Notice also, that the number of cells in the network is much smaller than the number of samples in the data set, characterizing architecture suitable for data compression.

Such clustering method can automatically determine the cluster number and the priori information of clustering prototypes. Unfortunately, when there exists noise in data set, or the boundaries among clusters are indistinct, if noise samples or samples on the cluster boundaries are selected as antigen, the immune system will be activated greatly and make cell proliferation and antibody secretion.

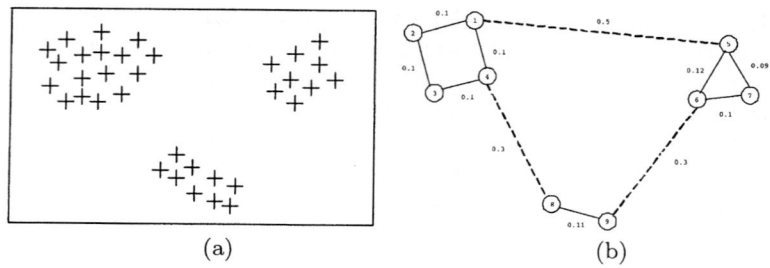

Fig. 1. (a) Available data set with three clusters (b) Network Structure

One thus cannot achieve the clear network structures and cannot obtain the correct classification for the processed data set. Moreover, in this method, the neuron number in the network exponentially increases with iterative number, and the cputime also exponentially increases with the data amount. So, it is unsuitable for the real time processing of large data. In addition, this method can not process data set with categorical attributes either, however, data in data mining often contains both numeric and categorical values. In addition, an obvious drawback of the clustering method based on network structure is to pre-set many parameters in advance.

3 A Novel Clustering Algorithm with Immune Network Structure Based on Limited Resource

In the first place, in order to process such large data sets with mixed numeric and categorical values, we define a new distance measure to realize the aim to combining different attribute features. Let $X = \{x_1, x_2, \cdots, x_n\}$ denote a set of n objects and $x_i = [x_{i1}, x_{i2}, \cdots, x_{im}]^T$ be an object represented by m attribute values. Let c be a positive integer.

3.1 The Definition of Distance Measure

Distance Measure for Numeric Data Clustering. The widely used distance measure is the Euclidean distance [14]. For the data set with real attributes, i.e., $X \subset R^m$, the distance measure between the samples of x_j and p_i can be written:

$$d^2(x_j, p_i) = (x_j - p_i)^T(x_j - p_i) \quad (1)$$

In the novel clustering algorithm, let $P_i = [p_{i1}, p_{i2}, \cdots, p_{ii_n}]$ $i = 1, 2, \cdots, c$, i_n is the number of cell which is contained in the network structure P_i, $p_{ig} = [p_{ig,1}, p_{ig,2}, \cdots, p_{ig,m}]^T$, $g = 1, 2, \cdots, i_n$ is the g-th neuron of the i-th network. The dissimilarity measurement between x_j and the i-th cluster is modified as:

$$d^2(x_j, P_i) = min\{(x_j - p_{ig})^T(x_j - p_{ig}), g = 1, 2, \cdots, i_n\} \quad (2)$$

Distance Measure for Mixed Data Clustering. When X has mixed attributes with numeric and categorical values, assuming that each object is denoted by $x_i = [x_{i1}^r, \cdots, x_{it}^r, x_{i,t+1}^c, \cdots, x_{im}^c]^T$, the dissimilarity between mixed-type objects x_j and network cell p_{ig} can be measured by the Eq.(3).

$$d^2(x_j, p_{ig}) = \sum_{l=1}^{t} |x_{jl}^r - p_{ig,l}^r|^2 + \lambda \cdot \sum_{l=l+1}^{m} \delta(x_{il}^c, p_{ig,l}^c) \qquad (3)$$

where the first term is the squared Euclidean distance measure on the numeric attributes and the second term is the simple matching dissimilarity measure on the categorical attributes. $\delta(\cdot)$ is defined as

$$\delta(a,b) = \begin{cases} 0 & a = b \\ 1 & a \neq b \end{cases} \qquad (4)$$

The weight λ is used to avoid favoring either type of attribute. The influence of λ in the clustering process will be discussed in other paper.

Using Eq.(3) for mixed-type objects, we can obtain dissimilarity measure between x_j and P_i by modifying Eq.(2) for mixed data clustering.

$$d^2(x_j, P_i) = min \sum_{l=1}^{t} |x_{jl}^r - p_{ig,l}^r|^2 + \lambda \cdot \sum_{l=l+1}^{m} \delta(x_{il}^c, p_{ig,l}^c) \qquad (5)$$

In this way, by modifying the distance function, the categorical attributes can be treated as well as numeric attributes. With the new distance function, the available clustering algorithm can process the data set with mixed attributes.

3.2 Recognition Ball

In 1958, Burnet presented that there are corresponding cell systems to various antigen in human body. In the case of an antigen entering into human body, it will select a corresponding cell system and perform reaction. Then this cell system will be activated to proliferate and generate specificity antibody. However, the number of B cells to be generated is finite, which is impossible to unlimited increase exponentially with the increase of the number of antigens. Perelson's theory suggests that there exists a finite number of antibodies which may be said to be representative of an infinite number of antigens [15]. So, Timmis proposed an immune system based on limited resource in 2001 [11], in which a recognition ball is used to represent a kind of similar B cells, moreover, the limitation for resource leads to the competition among B cells, then the B cells with high excited level will be survived.

Fig. 2 shows a diagrammatic representation of the notion of recognition ball: there is a certain volume V in the immune system that contains many paratopes (represented by the dark circles), and epitopes (represented by X). For each antibody (and thus paratope), there is a small surrounding region in shape space called a *recognition ball*, denoted by V_e. Within this recognition ball an antibody

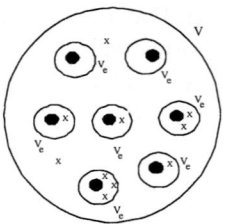

Fig. 2. Recognition ball illustration

can recognize all epitopes, i.e. epitopes will share an affinity with the antibody paratope.

3.3 A Novel Clustering Algorithm with Immune Network Structure Based on Limited Resource

In the resource-limited immune system proposed by Timmis, all the effect radii of the recognition balls are similar, δ. Actually, one hopes that the higher the excitation degree, the larger the effect radius of the recognition, that is to say, it can recognize more antigens. For this purpose, this paper introduces the fuzzy recognition ball to guarantee the effect radius of the recognition ball various vs. the excitation degree.

Let $X = \{x_1, x_2, \cdots, x_n\}$ denote a set of n objects and assuming that each object is denoted by $x_i = [x_{i1}^r, \cdots, x_{it}^r, x_{i,t+1}^c, \cdots, x_{im}^c]^T$, in which the first t components are numeric features, and the last $m-t$ components are categorical features. $ABR_i = [p_{i1}^r, \cdots, p_{it}^r, p_{i,t+1}^c, \cdots, p_{im}^c]^T$ indicates the i-th recognition ball. The detailed clustering algorithm with fuzzy network structure based on limited resource network works is given as follows:

Step 1: Initial recognition balls, determine parameters $MaxR$;

Step 2: Determine the distance d_{ij} between antigen x_j and ARB_i to all the network cells according Eq.(3), then initialize the partition matrix with Eq.(6):

$$w_{ij} = exp(-\frac{d_{ij}^2}{2\sigma_i^2}) \qquad (6)$$

Step 3: Calculate ARB_i's stimulation level s_i according Eq.(7):

$$s_i = \frac{\sum_{j=1}^n w_{ij}}{\sigma_i^2} \qquad (7)$$

Step 4: According $r_i = k \cdot s_i^2$, allocate r_i B cell to fuzzy ARB_i. Compute the total number of B cells $R = \sum r_i$, k is a constant;

Step 5: If $R > MaxR$, remove weakest ARBs, until $R \leq MaxR$;

Step 6: According to the obtained recognition balls to update the partition matrix W with Eq.(8), where $\alpha \in [1\infty)$ is weighting factor;

$$w_{ij} = \left[\sum_k \left(\frac{d_{ij}}{d_{kj}} \right)^{\frac{2}{\alpha-1}} \right]^{-1} \tag{8}$$

Step 7: By using the partition matrix W, update the recognition balls and their effect radii σ_i with Eq.(9) and Eq.(10), in which i_n is the number of objects recognized by i-th ARB, c_i^{max} denotes the categorical label in the l-th attribute with the largest sum of membership degrees over i_n objects;

$$ARB_i = \begin{cases} p_{il}^r = \frac{\sum_{j=1}^{i_n} w_{ij}^\alpha x_{ij}^r}{\sum_{j=1}^{i_n} w_{ij}^\alpha} & l = 1, 2, \cdots, t \\ p_{il}^c = c_l^{max} & l = t+1, \cdots, m \end{cases}, \forall i \tag{9}$$

$$\sigma_i^2 = \frac{\sum_{j=1}^{i_n} w_{ij}^\alpha d_{ij}^2}{\sum_{j=1}^{i_n} w_{ij}^\alpha} \tag{10}$$

Step 8: Perform the clonal and mutation operations on the updated recognition balls. If the stop condition is satisfied, then go to step 9, otherwise return to step 3;

Step 9: Taking the average distance among the antigens within each recognition ball as the threshold of network affinity, then eliminate the recognition balls with affinity less than the threshold to compress the network and to simplify the network structure. Finally, the recognition ball are served as network neurons to perform the corresponding cluster analysis.

After obtaining the final neurons of networks, we have to solve the following two problems. (1) How many clusters contained in data set on earth? (2) How to partition the obtained neurons into categories? Here, we apply the minimal spanning tree (MST) technique to analyze the relationship among neurons. MST is often used to detect and describe the network structure of clusters [16].

Definition 2: A tree is a spanning tree of a graph if it is a sub-graph containing all the vertices of the graph. A *minimal spanning tree* of a graph is a spanning tree with minimum weight. The weight of a tree is defined as the sum of the weights of its constituent edges.

After obtaining the MST of the networks, by detecting the number of valleys in bar plot of the MST, one can determine the cluster number of the given data set. In addition, we detect each distance D_{ij} between any neuron pair (i,j), if D_{ij} is large enough, the neuron pair (i,j) will be disconnected. Finally, the neurons connected in the MST form a category. The number of connected part in the MST corresponds to the cluster number. Thus, if sample x_j belongs to the i-th cluster, we have

$$d^2(x_j, P_i) = min\{d^2(x_j, P_l), \quad l = 1, 2, \cdots, c\} \tag{11}$$

4 Experimental Results and Discussion

To test the effectiveness of the proposed novel clustering algorithm with fuzzy network structure based on limited resource, we present some preliminary experimental results. The novel algorithm is compared with the algorithm based on standard evolutionary immune network and the k-prototype algorithm. The experimental results with various prototype data sets demonstrate the good performance of the novel algorithm.

4.1 Performance Test with Data Set of Homogeneous Prototypes

In order to simplify illustration, we use data records having only three attributes, two numeric values and one categorical value. These records were generated as follows. We first created a set of 2D points, which contains 600 points and has two normal distributions with different variances as shown in Figure 3 (a). We then expanded these points to 3D by adding a categorical value to each point (see Figures 3 (b)). For this data set we deliberately assigned to the majority points in each part an identical categorical value and to the rest other categorical values. For instance the majority of points in the right low part in Figure 3 (b) are assigned categorical value B and the rest in this part are assigned A. All assignments were randomly done.

We apply the proposed novel algorithm to analyze the data set shown in Figure 3 (b). The termination condition is evolutionary generation equal to 10. Figure 3(c) shows the classification result of the novel algorithm, in which circles represent the effect range of the recognition balls (Only two recognition balls are obtained, so the number of classes is $c = 2$). Figure 3(d) presents the classification result of the k-prototype algorithm. It is obvious that the optimal classification is not achieved for the different variances of the two group of data.

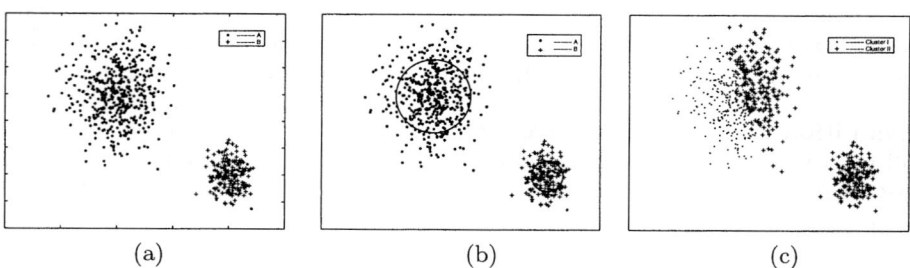

(a)   (b)   (c)

Fig. 3. The test results with data set of homogeneous prototypes.(a) Test data (b) The clustering result of our algorithm (c) Classification result of the k-prototype algorithm

4.2 Performance Test with Data Set of Inhomogeneous Prototypes

In practical applications, one often encounters data set with various prototypes. In this experiment, we design two types of data set with different prototypes as test bed. The first one is a data set with distinct boundaries among clusters. Another is with ambiguous boundaries among clusters.

Data Set with Distinct Boundaries. For the sake of visualization of experimental result, we construct a data set with two numeric attributes and one categorical attribute. First, we generate an erose-shaped data subset, a ring-shaped subset and a spheral subset respectively, and then synthesize these three clusters into a big data set in 2D plane with total 1500 samples as shown in Figure 4 (a). On this data set, the method introduced in section 4.1 is employed to generate a categorical attribute for each sample, as shown in Figure 4 (b). The analysis results of data set shown in Figure 4(b) with the proposed algorithm are presented in Figure 4 (c)-(f). In this experiment, the termination condition is evolutionary generation equal to 10. From Figure 4 (d), it can be obtained that the valley number of the bar plot is just equal to the cluster number. The final classified result is shown in Figure 4 (f), in which all the samples are classified correctly. It is obvious that the proposed clustering algorithm can effectively analyze data set with mixed attributes and erose-shaped prototypes.

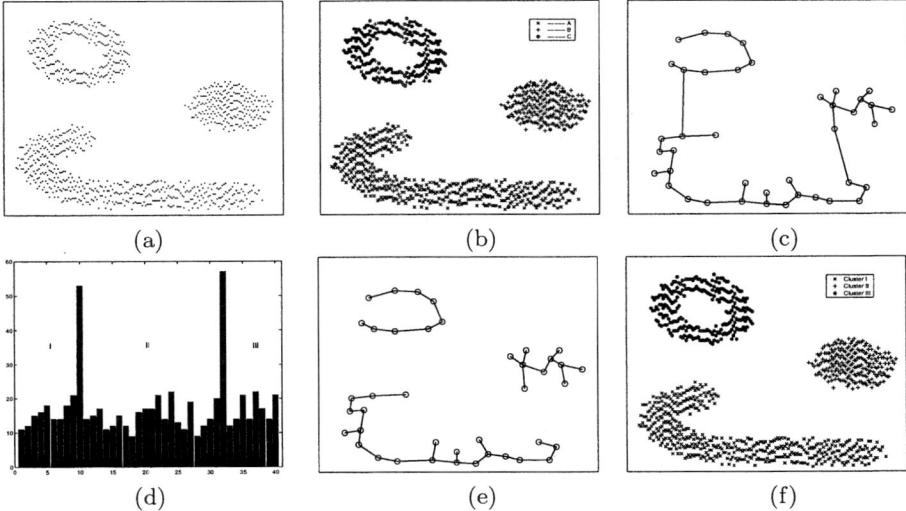

Fig. 4. The test result (I) with data set with different prototypes (a) Three sets of points in 2D with various prototypes (b) Adding the categorical attribute to each point (c) Minimal spanning tree (d) Bar graph generated from the MST (e) Resultant network architecture($N = 39$) (f)The clustering result of our algorithm

Data Set with Indistinct Boundaries. For the data set with multi-type prototypes, if the clusters are well separated, i.e., each cluster has distinct boundary, the traditional fuzzy c-means algorithm can also achieve good classification result. However, in most cases the data set encountered are with indistinct boundaries among clusters. In this case, the available algorithms will not be able to obtain satisfied result.

Based on the same reason as above experiments, we construct a test data set with three attributes as shown in Figure 5 (a). Figure 5 (b)-(d) show the produced MST of network structures, synthetic network structures and its bar plot respectively by the clustering algorithm based on limited recourse. From Figure 5(d), it can be found that the obtained synthetic network structure is well agree with the structure of the original data set, and the proposed algorithm can explore the interior structure of data set very well.

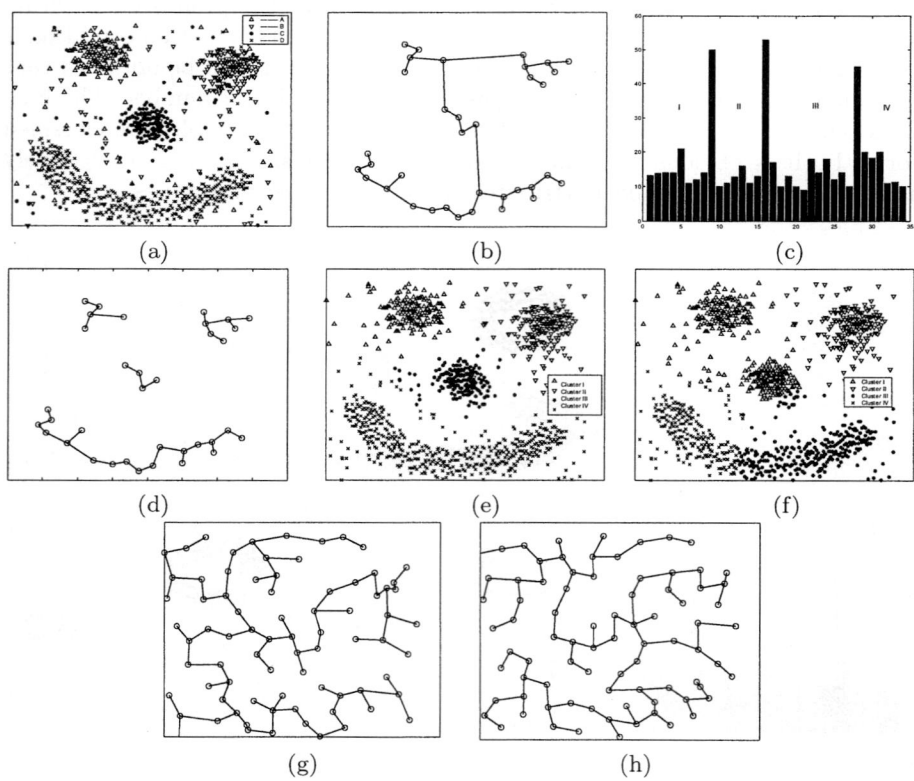

Fig. 5. The test result (II) with data set with different prototypes (a) A synthetic test data set (b) Minimal Spanning Tree (c) Bar graph generated from the MST (d) Resultant network architecture($N = 39$) (e) Classification result of the novel algorithm($\lambda = 2$) (f)Classification result of the k-prototype algorithm (g) MST obtained by EAIN with $\sigma_s = 10$ (h) MST obtained by EAIN with $\sigma_s = 20$

Figure 5 (e) shows the clustering result of the proposed novel algorithm. Although the given data set contains different prototypes with indistinct boundaries, a better classification is still achieved. Since the fuzzy recognition ball is adopted in the novel algorithm, in the case of the samples on the indistinct boundaries, the corresponding recognition ball gets a lower excitation level. For the limited resource, these recognition balls will be eliminated gradually during the competition, which guarantees the final network neurons can represent the typical samples of all classes. Figure 5 (f) is the result of the traditional k-prototype algorithm. Due to the data set contains different prototypes and ambiguous boundaries among clusters; the k-prototype algorithm analyzes the data set with the same prototypes and result in many samples misclassified. Figure 5 (g) and (h) show the MSTs of network neurons generated by the standard EAIN with different values of σ_s. Since the standard EAIN only emphasize the effect of clonal selection, if the samples on the boundaries are selected as antigens, due to the higher Ab-Ag affinity, the corresponding network neurons will be activated and make the proliferation of antibodies with specificity. Moreover, the corresponding network neurons will not be able to remove by either clone compression or network compression. Therefore, the obtained networks cannot clearly reflect the structure of data set. Also the related cluster numbers and classification information will not able to obtained. It thus is impossible to analyze and classify the data set correctly.

4.3 The Expansibility Test of the Novel Algorithm with Large Data Set

To test the expansibility of the novel algorithm with large data set, we plot the curve of CPU time vs. the amount of data set as shown in Figure 6(a), in which the AIS is the standard immune system in section 2, and RLAIS is the proposed algorithm. It can be found that the CPU time of the AIS increase exponentially with the increase of data amount, while the CPU time of the novel algorithm has only a linear increase. In addition, for the same data amount, the new algorithm is faster that the AIS, which make it suitable for the cluster analysis of large data set.

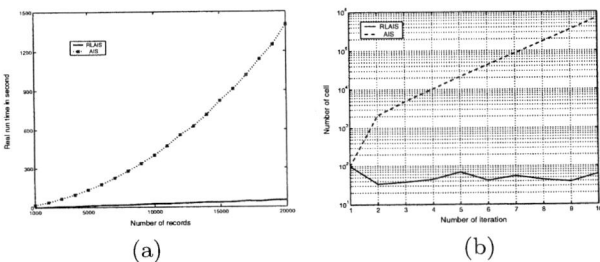

Fig. 6. The test result of the expansibility with large data set(a) The plot of CPU time vs. number of recorders (b) The plot of the neuron number vs. number of iteration

Figure 6 (b) shows the curve of the neuron number vs. the iteration number. With the same number of initialization neurons, the network scale of the AIS increases exponentially, while the network scale of the new algorithm keeps a stable level. It also implies that the proposed algorithm is suitable for cluster analysis of large data set.

5 Conclusion

This paper presents a novel clustering algorithm with fuzzy network structure based on limited resource. By introducing the concept of the fuzzy recognition ball to make the network insensitive to the samples on the fuzzy boundaries, it can obtain the typical samples for all the classes which lead to better classification result. The experimental results illustrate that the novel algorithm can effectively explore the cluster structures of data set. Moreover, it does not depend on the prototype initialization and the priori information of cluster number, which makes it as a real unsupervised learning. Meanwhile, it is noted that the new algorithm only need pre-set the parameter of the maximal resource number, which is very convenient for the actual applications.

References

1. He Qing, Advance of the theory and application of fuzzy clustering analysis, Fuzzy System and Fuzzy Mathematics, **12(2)** (1998) 89–94. (In Chinese)
2. Gao Xinbo: Studies of optimization and applications of fuzzy clustering algorithm, Doctoral Dissertation, Xidian University, Xi'an, China, (1999).
3. Bezdek J.C: Patten Recognition with Fuzzy Objective Function Algorithms. Plenum Press, New York, (1981).
4. Dave R.N. and Bhaswan K: Adaptive fuzzy c-shells clustering and detection of ellipses. IEEE Trans. NN, **3(5)** (1992) 643–662.
5. Gao Xinbo, Xue Zhong, Li Jie: An initialization method for fuzzy clustering with multi-type prototypes, Journal of Chinese Electronics, **27(12)** (1999) 72–75.
6. Hathaway R.J. and Bezdek J.C.: Switching regression models and fuzzy clustering. IEEE Trans. FS, bfseries 3(1) (1993) 195–204.
7. Gath I., Geva A. B.: Unsupervised optimal fuzzy clustering. IEEE Trans. SMC, **11(7)** (1989) 773–781.
8. Li Jie: A GA-based clustering algorithm for large data set with mixed attributes, Proceedings of the Fifth Intenational Conference on Computational Intelligence and Multimedia Applications, (2003) 102–107.
9. William H.H, Loretta S.A, etc.: Self-Organizing Systems for Knowledge Discovery in Large Databases, http://www.kddresearch.org/Publications/ Conference/HAPTW1.pdf
10. Leandro N.C., Fernando J.Z.: An Evolutionary Immune Network for Data Clustering, Proceedings of the IEEE Computer Society Press, SBRN'00, **1**(2000) 84–89.
11. J.Timmis, M.Neal: A resource limited artificial system for data analysis, Knowledge-Based System, **14**(2001) 121–130.
12. Zhexue Huang and K.Ng.Michael: A fuzzy k-modes algorithm for clustering categorical data. IEEE Trans. on FS, August, **7** 1999:446–452.
13. Jerne N.K.: Towards a Network Theory of the Immune System, Ann. Immunol. (Inst. Pasteur) **125C** (1974) 373–389.

14. B. Everitt.: Cluster Analysis. Heinemann Educational Books Ltd., (1974).
15. Wu Minyu, Liu Gongzhi: Medical Immunology, Press of Chinese University of Science and Technology, (1999). (In Chinese)
16. Zahn C.T: Graph-Theoretical Methods for Detecting and Describing Gestalt Clusters, IEEE Trans.on Computers, **C(20)** (1971) 68–86.

A Novel Modeling and Recognition Method for Underwater Sound Based on HMT in Wavelet Domain

Zhou Yue, Kong Wei, and Xu Qing

Institute of Image Processing & Pattern Recognition, SJTU, 200030, China
zhouyue@sjtu.edu.cn

Abstract. To modeling and classify underwater sound, hidden Markov tree (HMT) model in wavelet domain is adopted. Taking advantage of the models, the simulation time sequence of ocean noise can be produced. An improved classification approach based on HMT model and fuzzy maximum and minimum neural net work (FMMNN) is brought forward, which integrates the wavelet coefficients HMT models with FMMNN. The performance of this approach is evaluated experimentally in classifying four types of ocean noises. With an accuracy of more than 86%, this HMT-based approach is found to outperform previously proposed classifiers. Experiments prove that the new method is effective.

Keywords: Hidden Markov Tree Model, Underwater Sound Modeling, Recognition.

1 Introduction

1.1 Underwater Noise

The underwater sound concerned in this paper includes the various ship-radiated noises (called SRN for short) and ocean noise (called OCN for short). They are non-Gaussian signal. Ship-radiated noise can be divided into the three major classes based on generation mechanism, machinery noise, hydrodynamic noise and propeller noise. The spectrum of ship-radiated noise is of two types. One types is broadband noise having a continuous spectra mainly caused by propeller cavitations noise and some machinery noises. Another basic type of noise is tonal noise having discontinuous spectra. This kind of noise, mainly caused by the rotation machinery, consists of tones or sinusoidal components having a spectrum containing line components occurring at discrete frequencies [1]. The ocean noise is mainly composed of biological noise, distant ship traffic noise and noise which is brought by the wind [1].

1.2 Modeling Method Based HMT

There are two types of method to model the SRN. One is the mechanism model, based on not only the mechanism of each acoustic source on the ship, but also the pattern of sound propagation in the sea. Another is based on statistical signal processing. The latter is applied widely because the former is not robust and difficult to test.

Along with the development of the modern signal processing technology, many new theories are brought up, such as wavelet theory etc. Since the wavelet domain provides a natural setting for many applications involving real-word signals [2], the wavelet transform is regarded as an exciting new tool for statistical, signal and image processing. Therefore, the subject of analyzing the SRN in wavelet domain is an active research field.

Although the wavelet transform has the property of the de-correlation, the dependence of wavelet coefficients between two adjacent scales still cannot be ignored. Thus, the hidden Markov tree (HMT) model in wavelet domain is treated as a more effective model, which can match both the statistical dependencies and non-Gaussian property of underwater sound. The model makes use of the intrinsic properties of the wavelet transform between two adjacent scales. It is applied to modeling and classifying underwater sound in this paper.

1.3 Work in This Paper

The paper is organized as follows. In section two, correlative theory of the HMT model is concisely introduced. In section three, the HMT model of the underwater sound is studied. In section four, reconstruction of SRN with the HMT model. In section five, a novel recognition method based on HMT model and FMMNN is proposed, and result is gained. Section six discusses the recognition results and gives the conclusions.

2 Hidden Markov Tree Model in Wavelet Domain

The Haar wavelet and Mallat multi-resolution algorithm are used to represent a signal in terms of shifted and dilated versions of a prototype band pass wavelet function $\psi(t)$, and shifted versions of a low pass scaling function $\phi(t)$. Given a J_0-scale wavelet transform, a signal $z(t)$ can be expressed as follows [3]

$$z(t) = \sum_K u_K \phi_{J_0,K}(t) + \sum_{J=-\infty}^{J_0} \sum_K w_{J,K} \psi_{J,K}(t) \qquad (1)$$

where $w_{J,K} \equiv \int z(t)\psi^*_{J,K}(t)dt$ are wavelet coefficients, and $u_K \equiv \int z(t)\phi^*_{J_0,K}(t)dt$ are scaling coefficients. Binary trees are constructed by the wavelet coefficients, whose roots are on the coarsest scale and branches tend to propagate through the scales (See Fig. 1). The description of the tree can be seen in ref. 3.

Due to Non-Gaussianity of the wavelet transform, a Gaussian mixture model is employed to model the wavelet coefficients distribution density. In a HMT model (see Fig. 1.), w_i is denoted to be the wavelet coefficient. The w_i is associated with a hidden state S_i (if S has two states, $S_i \in H(\text{high}), L(\text{low})$), whose probability mass function (pmf) can be expressed as, $P(S_i = m) = p_i(m)$ (m=H,L)[6]. Conditioning on its state $S_i = m$ (m=H, L), w_i follows a Gaussian distribution with zero mean and variance σ_m. If we let

$$g(x, \mu, \sigma^2) := \frac{1}{\sqrt{2\pi}\sigma} \exp\left\{-\frac{(x-\mu)^2}{2\sigma^2}\right\} \quad (2)$$

denote the Gaussian pdf, then we can write

$$f(w_i | S_i = H) := g(w_i, 0, \sigma_{H,i}^2) \quad (3)$$
$$f(w_i | S_i = L) := g(w_i, 0, \sigma_{L,i}^2)$$

with $\sigma_L^2 > \sigma_H^2$. The marginal pdf $f(w_i)$ is the convex combination of the condition densities

$$f(w_i) = p_i^H g(w_i, 0, \sigma_{H,i}^2) + p_i^L g(w_i, 0, \sigma_{L,i}^2) \quad (4)$$

with $p_i^H = 1 - p_i^L$. p_i^H and p_i^L can be interpreted as the probability that w_i is small or large (in the statistical sense) respectively.

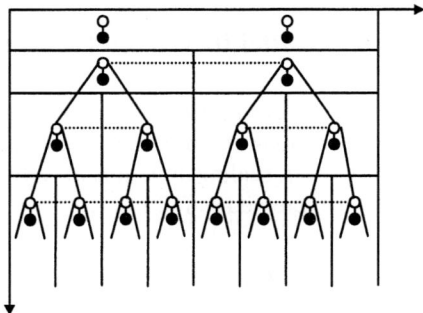

Fig. 1. The framework of the wavelet coefficients tree model. Each node is composed of white dot and black dot. The black dot symbolizes wavelet coefficients, and white dot is the corresponding hidden state S_i. Links represent dependencies between states

The persistence property of wavelet coefficient across scale is modeled by linking the hidden states vertically across scales in a Markov tree. The resulting dependency graph has a binary tree topology that resembles the binary tree topology of the wavelet coefficients. Each sub-band is represented with its own binary; this assumes that the sub-bands are statistically independent.

Each state to state link has a corresponding transition matrix that quantifies statistically the degree of persistence of large/small coefficients:

$$A_i := \begin{bmatrix} p_i^{H \to H} & p_i^{H \to L} \\ p_i^{L \to H} & p_i^{L \to L} \end{bmatrix} \quad (5)$$

with $p_i^{H \to L} = 1 - p_i^{H \to H}$ and $p_i^{L \to H} = 1 - p_i^{L \to L}$.

Denoting the parameters needed to specify a HMT model by the vector $\Theta(p_{s_i}, \varepsilon_{i,\rho(i)}^{mr}, \sigma, \mu)$. Members of Θ are the mixture variances for each state $\sigma_{H,i}$ and $\sigma_{L,i}$, the transition probabilities $\varepsilon_{i,\rho(i)}^{mr}$ and a mass function for the hidden state of the node p_{s_i}. These parameters can be fit to a given set of training data using the Expectation-Maximization (EM) algorithm [3]. The training yields an approximate maximum likelihood estimate of the model parameters given the training data, yielding a good approximation of the joint density function of the wavelet coefficients.

According to the large amount experiments, the parameters of the HMT model are initialized. The mean of the coefficients $\mu_{i,m}$ is 0; the probability of the root state $S_i = m$ (m=H, L) is 0.5; each element in transition probability matrix $\varepsilon_{i,\rho(i)}^{mr}$ is 0.5.

3 HMT Model of Underwater Noise

3.1 Selection of Frequency Band for Analysis

Choosing an appropriate frequency band for analysis is of great importance. Different analysis range of frequency will be selected for different studied objects so that different numbers of the scales are chosen in the wavelet domain. The sample frequency is 1000Hz; maximum scale is 5(or 4) in this paper.

3.2 Pre-processing of Raw Data and Initialization of HMT Model

Since zeros-excursion of the sample is a great disadvantage for performance of the model and classifier, subtracting the mean value from each signal is used to alleviate zero-excursion in the pre-processing.

Considering maximum likelihood estimate is so sensitive to the sample points regarded as outliers, which are larger than three times standard variance (3σ) of sample, that inappropriate normalization method will hurt the accuracy of the resulting model and its classification performance, absolute value of maximum and 3σ are chosen to normalize the samples.

On the other hand, the parameters of the HMT model are initialized according to the large amount of experiments. The mean of the coefficients $\mu_{i,m}$ is 0; the probability of the root state $S_i = m$ (m=H, L) is 0.5; each element in the transition probability matrix $\varepsilon_{i,\rho(i)}^{mr}$ is 0.5.

3.3 Modeling Ship Radiated Noise and Ocean Noise

In the trial, ten Gaussian signals (GDN) are generated. A 5-scale (J=5) discrete wavelet transform and the 2-state ($m = H, L$) HMT model are chosen. The HMT models are trained on each of the ten separately and their corresponding parameters are averaged to be compared with OCN conveniently. Then, ten segments of the ocean noise (OCN1) are sampled by the hydrophone in the calm and quiet midnight sea (3:00-4:00 am); other ten segments of ocean noise (OCN2) are also collected in the day time (7:00-8:00 am), in which there exist many other noise sources, such as distant ship traffic etc. At last, ten segments of SRN are sampled when ships closed with observation spot. Taking advantage of the same parameters (5-scale and 2-state HMT model), the models are constructed on each segment. Because the different samples of the same type have coherence, the average model parameters for each type are required to be compared with each other for the individuality.

The results show that the model parameters of OCN1 match those of the GDN well. In addition, the model parameters of the OCN2 are similar to those of the SRN, since they are contaminated by the noise of the distant ship traffic and other environment noise. The model presents some characters of the ship.

There exits a great difference between model parameters for two types of OCN on the scale 4 and 5. It indicates that ship traffic in distant place is still a dominant source of noise at frequencies around 100Hz. There is a "plateau" or a flattening in observed ambient-noise spectra in this frequency region that coincides remarkable closely with the spectra of SRN. These evidences also indicate that distant ship traffic is a principal source of noise in the range of 50 to 500Hz, though such traffic may occur at a distant of 1000 miles or more from the measurement hydrophone, if hydrophone is sensitive enough. Comparison of the model parameters between OCN and GDN is shown in figure 2. Model parameters of SRN are shown in figure 3.

In figure 2 and 3, there are eight sub-figures respectively; which are arranged like a 2×4 matrix. Thus, we use the index of matrix to represent them. [1, 1] [1, 2]denotes the probability of the root state 1 and state 2. [2, 1] and [2, 2] denote wavelet coefficients variance of state1 and 2 respectively. [1, 3], [4, 1], [2, 3] and [2, 4] denote the transition probability of state1 to 1, 1 to 2, 2 to 1 and 2 to 2. It should be demonstrated that in every sub-figure, the x axis denotes the index of the wavelet coefficients, 16-31 is on the first scale, 8-15 is on the second scale, 4-7 is on the third scale, 2-3 is on the forth scale and the fifth scale.

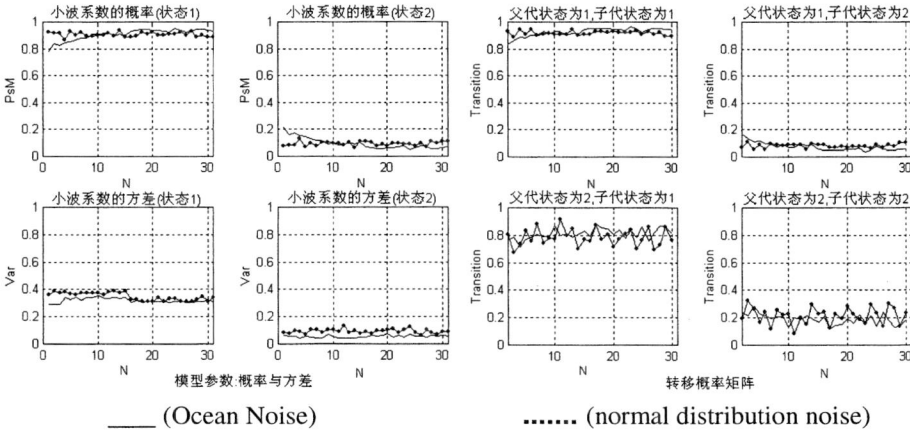

_____ (Ocean Noise) ······· (normal distribution noise)

Fig. 2. Model parameters of the noise background of the sea and normal distribution noise

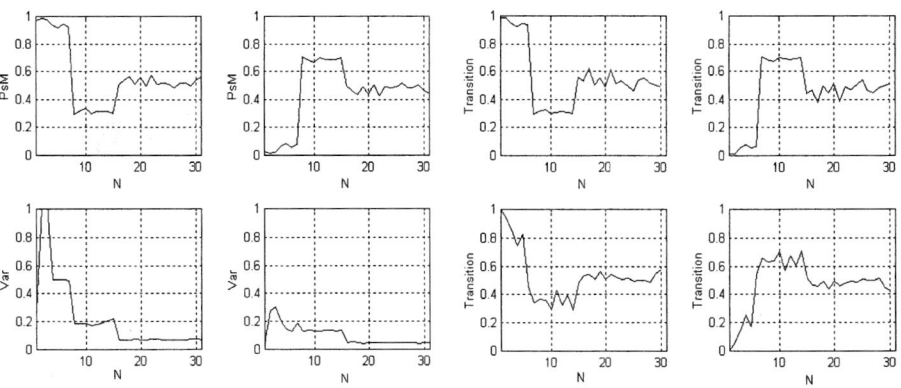

Fig. 3. Model parameters of the ship-radiated noise far from the observe spot

4 Reconstruction of SRN with the HMT Model

The HMT model provides a new way to reconstruct the non-Gaussian signal such as SRN. The HMT models of wavelet coefficients, which are from real-world data, are used in this process.

The goal of our algorithm is to reconstruct a non Gaussian signal using its HMT model. Assumes that the HMT used here models a $J=$ scale wavelet coefficients tree by

$$\Theta(p_{s_i}(m)\varepsilon_{i,\rho(i)}^{mr},\sigma_{i,m}^2,j|i=1,\cdots,2^J-1;m,r=H,L,1\le j\le J).$$

Here W_i represents the wavelet coefficients in the tree. Then the reconstruction algorithm goes as follows:

- importing a HMT model $\Theta(p_{s_i}(m)\varepsilon_{i,\rho(i)}^{mr},\sigma_{i,m}^2,j)$.
- Generate a random number X according to a uniform distribution on $[0,1]$.
- Load the HMT model parameters of the wavelet coefficients
- Set the node index i
- In a tree

If $i=1$ then

    If $X<p_{s_1}(1)$, then W_i is generated by a normal distribution $N(0,\sigma_{i1}^2)$;

    Else W_i is generated by a normal distribution $N(0,\sigma_{i2}^2)$;

Else ($i\ne 1$ or $i\le 2^J-1$)

    If father of the node i is in state $m=H$,

        If $X<\varepsilon_{i,\rho(i)}^{11}$ then W_i is generated by a normal distribution $N(0,\sigma_{i1}^2)$;

        Else W_i is generated by a normal distribution $N(0,\sigma_{i2}^2)$;

    Else (father of the node i is in state $m=L$,)

        If $X<\varepsilon_{i,\rho(i)}^{12}$ then W_i is generated by a normal distribution $N(0,\sigma_{i1}^2)$;

        Else W_i is generated by a normal distribution $N(0,\sigma_{i1}^2)$;

End.
End of restructure of one tree.

- According to restructure of tree shown in Fig.1, all wavelet coefficients are arranged.
- Applied the reverse wavelet transform, a time sequence is gained.
- According to the length requirement of the simulation data we need, the number of tree can be computed, and the repeating computation above will be done.

5 Modeling Recognition System of Underwater Noise Based on the HMT Model

In this paper, another research task is to classify different underwater sound based on HMT model. The class of underwater noises then can be used to identify the type of the ship causing them. Here four types of underwater sounds will be investigated. Type I is ocean noise; type II is the noises caused by oil tanker and container ship; type III is caused by passenger ship; type IV is war ship. These ships have many different characters for function, which have influences on their radiated noises. By HMT model, we can describe these characters from certain aspect respectively.

5.1 Classification of Four Types of Underwater Noise with the HMT Model

Because there are obvious differences between HMT parameters of SRN and OCN described in t section three, emphases studied in this section is how to classify SRN. Have been introduced in the first section, SRN is caused by three factors, including the tonnage, the speed, and the number of the propeller's blades of the ship. They should be reflected on the statistic relationship between wavelet coefficients on different scales. Because HMT model can depict statistic relationship better, it can also characterize the sort attribute of SRN. In the classification process based on HMT model, we divide all samples into two sets. One set is for training, another is for testing. The selection of the training samples is so important that it can directly influent the classification performance of the HMT model. In our case, the training set should be constructed by the representative samples, which are caused by different speed (high and low speed), different tonnage (more than 10,000 ton or less than 10,000 ton), and different ships having same sort attribute.

Supposing that training samples of each class is x_i^k ($k \in K = \{I, II, III, IV\}$; $i = 1, \cdots, n$), the parameters θ_i^k of the HMT model can be trained on each sample. Thus the model set M_i^k ($i = 1, 2, \cdots, n$, $k \in K = \{I, II, III, IV\}$) is gained when training process finish. In the testing process, a new sample O_l (wavelet coefficients is W_l), which is unknown about its sort attribute, can be classified using the maximum likelihood (ML) rule, which is to choose the class which makes the observed data most likely, i.e.

$$m_l = \arg\max_{1 \leq i \leq n}[V_i], \quad V_i = \max_{1 \leq i \leq n, k \in K}[f(W_l|\theta_i^k)] \tag{6}$$

In the classification experiments, samples with a known type are randomly split into training and testing set. The training set contained 55 samples: 10 OCN samples, 15 samples for each of three classes of SRN. The testing set contained 120 sample recordings: 30 samples for each class. The adjustable parameters are chosen as follows: the number of scales in wavelet domain is 5, the number of state of each node is 2(high and low), and the length of sample is 1024 (sample rate is 1000Hz).

The first result is that the method of normalization is very important to classification. Two different normalization methods are applied to the raw data. One takes the maximum as the normalization factor, and another takes three times of standard variance of samples as the normalization factor. For four types of underwater sound, the classification accuracy (80.8%) of the latter method is 3% higher than that of the former one (78.3%).

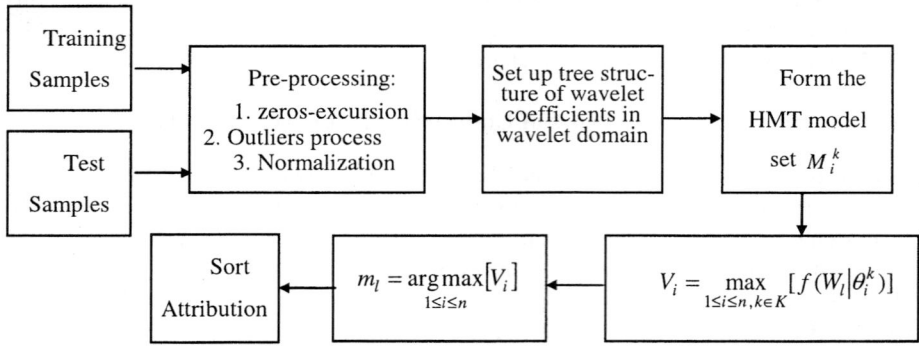

Fig. 4. the framework of the classification based on wavelet domain HMT

Table 1. Classification result of four underwater noises (Based on HMT models)

Class	Number of selected models	Number of samples	Classification based on spectrum and ANN*		Classifier based on HMT model Number of	
			correct tests	Recognition rates	correct tests	Recognition rates
I	5	30	21	70.0%	24	80.0%
II	10	30	22	73.3%	25	83.3%
III	10	30	19	63.3%	21	70.0%
IV	10	30	24	80.0%	27	90.0%
Total	35	120	86	71.7%	97	80.8%

* In the paper, the improved Back-Progagation Neural Network is adopted. The sort attribute of the underwater sound is described by some spectrum characters).

5.2 Improved Classification Method Based on the HMT Model

By analyzing the samples which is classified by mistake, we find some flaws of classification method mentioned in section 5.1. The main flaw is that recognition method (formula 6) lacks fault tolerance. The sort attribute of samples should not be only decided by the model which made the sample have maximum posterior likelihood. We should take into account the behavior of the whole model set. So an improved classification method is proposed as follows.

We still denote x_i^k ($k \in K = \{I, II, III, IV\}$; $i = 1, 2, \cdots n$) to be training samples, and then the HMT model $m_i^k \{\theta_i^k\}$ can be trained respectively. Thus the model set $M = m_i^k$ ($i = 1, 2, \cdots, n$, $k \in K = \{I, II, III, IV\}$) can be gained. For each training sample, we can use a vector to describe its sort attribute. All factors of the vector are the posterior likelihood of x_i^k conditioning on the models M.

$$\begin{aligned} u_l = u_l^i = f(W_l|M) = f(W_l|\theta_i^k) \\ U = \{u_l, l = 1, 2, \cdots, n\} \end{aligned} \quad (7)$$

u_l is regarded as the sort attribute vector of each sample. Using the FMMNN [4-5], we can train a classifier Θ, which uses the vector U as the input and the sort attribute as the output.

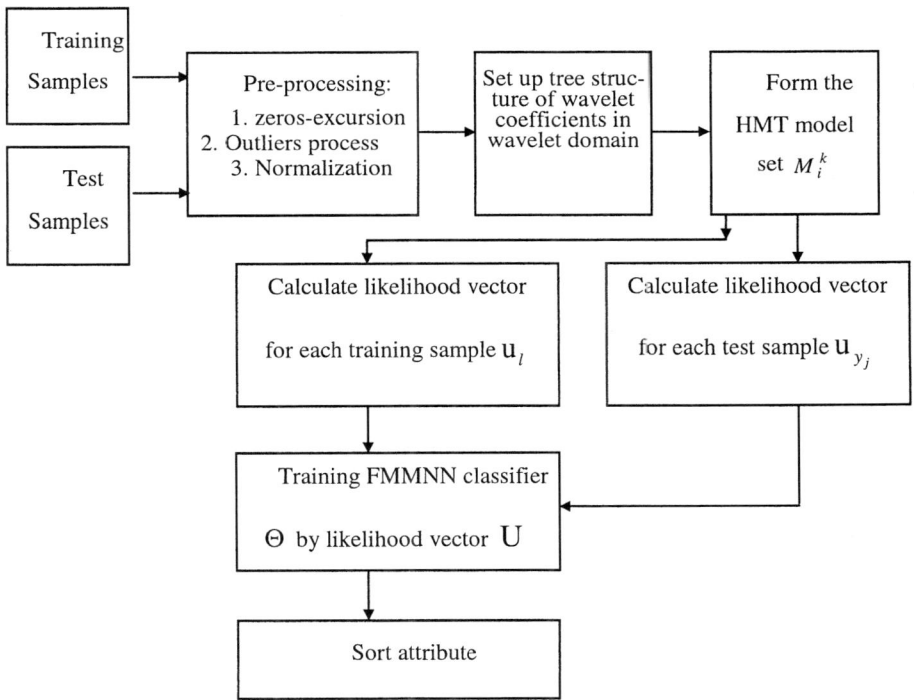

Fig. 5. Sketch of Improved Classification Method Based the HMT Model

Table 2. classification result of four underwater noises (Based on HMT models)

Class	Number of selected models	Number of samples	Improved Classification method based on HMT model	
			Number of correct tests	Recognition rates
I	5	30	25	83.3%
II	10	30	27	90.0%
III	10	30	24	80.0%
IV	10	30	28	93.3%
Total	35	120	97	86.7%

In the testing process, a sort attribute vector u_{y_j} will be gained for one new sample y_j ($j=1,2,\cdots,m$), and then Θ decided the sort attribute of y_j ($j=1,2,\cdots,m$). The sketch of this method is described in figure 5. The classification result of improved method is shown in table 2.

6 Summaries and Concluding

The concept of hidden Markov tree model (HMT) in wavelet domain has been investigated. The HMT-based approach to underwater sound modeling has been studied. The HMT model provides us a good way to analyze and reconstruct the SRN and OCN.

The main factors, such as distance, tonnage, and sailing speed, can influence the parameters of HMT model. Parameters of the same types of ship are coherent at large, and different types of the ships have different parameters. These form the bases of the classification of underwater sound. The HMT-based approach to recognition has been evaluated experimentally for the classification of four types of underwater sound.

The HMT-based classifiers that have been presented in this paper outperform the simple spectrum classifiers, spectrum-based neural network classifiers previously proposed. However, the HMT-based classifiers also have several drawbacks when we study ulteriorly. An improved method based on HMT model is proposed. With an accuracy of more than 86%, this HMT-based approach is found to outperform previously proposed classifiers based on HMT model. Experiments prove that the new method is effective.

No matter whether HMT-based or improved HMT-based method common drawback, which is choosing the HMT model artificially still has. The further work is to find a way to automatically select the HMT model for each class instead of manual work.

References

1. Robert J. Urick: Priciples of Underwater Sound. 3rd edn. McGraw Hill Book Company (1983)
2. D. Donoho and I. Johnstone: Adapting to unknown Smoothness via Wavelet Shrinkage, J. Amer. Stat. Assoc. 90 (1995)1200-1224
3. Matthew S. Crouse et al.: Wavelet-Based Statistical Signal Processing Using Hidden Markov Models, IEEE Trans. Signal Processing, 46(1998) 886-902
4. Simpson P K: Fuzzy Min-Max networks-part 1: classification. IEEE Trans., on Neural Networks, 3(1992) 776-786
5. Simpson P K: Fuzzy Min-Max networks-part 2: clustering. IEEE Trans., on Fuzzy Systems, 1(1993) 32-45

BayesTH-MCRDR Algorithm for Automatic Classification of Web Document

Woo-Chul Cho and Debbie Richards

Department of Computing,
Macquarie University, Sydney, NSW 2109, Australia
{wccho, richards}@ics.mq.edu.au

Abstract. Nowadays, automated Web document classification is considered as an important method to manage and process an enormous amount of Web documents in digital forms that are extensive and constantly increasing. Recently, document classification has been addressed with various classified techniques such as naïve Bayesian, TFIDF (Term Frequency Inverse Document Frequency), FCA (Formal Concept Analysis) and MCRDR (Multiple Classification Ripple Down Rules). We suggest the BayesTH-MCRDR algorithm for useful new Web document classification in this paper. We offer a composite algorithm that combines a naïve Bayesian algorithm using Threshold and the MCRDR algorithm. The prominent feature of the BayesTH-MCRDR algorithm is optimisation of the initial relationship between keywords before final assignment to a category in order to get higher document classification accuracy. We also present the system we have developed in order to demonstrate and compare a number of classification techniques.

1 Introduction

The soaring pace of development enables much information and data to be obtained through the Internet and many documents to be accessed through it by many organizations. Currently, this information exists on the Internet via the Web using the HTML format. To determine the classification of Web documents techniques from document classification are used. Many information societies make use of Web documents and need to classify and search effectively lots of information and data. So algorithms of document classification have been investigated in many scientific fields. A number of key algorithms to classify documents have been developed including: naïve Bayesian algorithm [1], TFIDF (Term Frequency Inverse Document Frequency) algorithm [2], FCA (Formal Concept Analysis) [3], MCRDR (Multiple Classification Ripple Down Rules) [4] and so on. Among these techniques, Bayesian document classification is the method achieving the most promising results for document classification in every language area [5]. However, the naïve Bayes classifier fails to identify salient document features because it extracts every word in the document as a feature. Further, it calculates a presumed value for every word and carries out classification on the basis of it. The naïve Bayes classifier produces many noisy term (stopwords) and ambiguous results, thus affecting classification. This misclassification lowers the precision. So in order to increase precision TFIDF is suggested which uses the Bayesian classification method. This produces less misclassification than the naïve Bayes classifier, but does not reflect the semantic relationships between words and fails to resolve word ambiguity. Therefore it cannot resolve misclassification of documents. In order to solve this problem, we have developed Web Document Classification system which combines both the Bayesian Dynamic Threshold algorithm and the MCRDR algorithm, to produce what we refer to as the BayesTH-MCRDR algorithm. This system applies both the Bayesian algorithm using Dynamic Threshold in order to increase precision and the MCRDR algorithm in order to optimise and construct a knowledge base of related words.

In short, our system first extracts word features from Web documents by using Information Gain [6]. Next, the terms are stemmed using Porter stemming algorithm [7]. Then the documents are classified temporarily by the Bayesian Algorithm, optimized by the MCRDR algorithm and then finally classified. In order to evaluate this system, we compare our approach to Web document classification with the naïve Bayesian, TFIDF, Bayesian-Threshold algorithms and FCA. In addition, we compared document classification by using the stemming algorithm with the document classification by not using it to determine the value of this additional step.

2 Techniques for Web Document Classification

In this section we briefly introduce the key concepts underlying the BayesTH-MCRDR algorithm: Naïve Bayesian, Naïve Bayesian using Threshold, TFIDF and MCRDR. The final subsection describes how we have combined the two techniques.

2.1 Naïve Bayesian

Naïve Bayesian classification [1] uses probability based on Bayes Theorem. This system inputs a vector model of words ($w_1, w_2, \ldots w_n$) for the given document (d), and classifies the highest probability (p) as the class (c) among documents that can observe the given document. That is, as shown in formula (1) the system classifies it as a highest conditional probability class. If we are concerned with only the highest probability class, we can omit Probability (P), because it is a constant and normalizing term. Also, this approach applies the naïve Bayesian assumption of conditional independence on each 'w_t' which is a feature belonging to the same document (see Formula (2)) [1]. So, the naïve Bayesian Classification method decides the highest probability class according to formula (3).

$$\arg\max_{c \in C} P(c \mid d) = \arg\max_{c \in C} P(c \mid w_1, w_2, \ldots, w_n \mid c) \quad (1)$$

$$= \arg\max_{c \in C} P(w_1, w_2, \ldots, w_n \mid c) p(c)$$

$$P(w_1, w_2, \ldots, w_n \mid c) = \prod_{t=1,n} p(w_t \mid c) \quad (2)$$

$$\arg\max_{c \in C} P(c) \prod_{t=1,n} p(w_t \mid c) \qquad (3)$$

2.2 Naïve Bayesian with Threshold

In the definition in section 2.1, the Threshold value of the Naïve Bayesian algorithm is fixed. It results in lower precision when the Naïve Bayesian algorithm classifies documents with low conditional probability. The Naïve Bayesian Threshold algorithm is able to increase the precision of document classification by dynamically calculating the value of the threshold as given in formula (4).

$$
\begin{aligned}
&\text{Category (Class) Set } C = \{c_0, c_1, c_2, c_{3,\ldots}, c_n\}, \quad C_0 = \text{unknown class} \\
&\text{Document Set } D = \{d_0, d_1, d_2, d_{3,\ldots}, d_i\} \\
&\Re(d_i) = \{P(d_i \mid c_1), P(d_i \mid c_2), P(d_i \mid c_3), \ldots, P(d_i \mid c_n)\} \\
&P_{\max}(d_i) = \max\{P(d_i \mid C_t)\}, \quad t = 1,\ldots, n
\end{aligned} \qquad (4)
$$

$$C_{best}(d_i) = \begin{cases} \{c_j \mid P(d_i \mid c_j) = P_{\max}(d_i), \text{ if } P_{\max}(d_i) \geq T\} \\ \qquad\qquad\qquad \text{where } T = 1 - \dfrac{P_{\max}(d_i)}{\sum_{t=1}^{n} P(d_i \mid c_t)} \\ c_0, \qquad\qquad\qquad\qquad otherwise \end{cases}$$

2.3 TFIDF (Term Frequency Inverse Document Frequency)

TFIDF [2], traditionally used in information retrieval, expresses a weight vector based on word frequency of the given document 'd'. In this case, each word weight (W) is calculated by multiplying the Term Frequency (TF) in a given document 'd' and its reciprocal number, Inverse Document Frequency (IDF), of all documents having the word feature. This means that the higher the IDF, the higher the feature (see Formula (5)). That is, if there is a word which has a higher frequency in a certain document, and a lower frequency in other documents, then the word can express the document very well. For document classification we require a prototype vector expressing each class. The prototype vector (c) of each class is calculated as the average of the weight vector of its training document. Only if each class is expressed in a prototype vector, the similarity is calculated by applying the cosine rule between the weight vector of a given document 'd' and each class prototype vector as shown in formula (6).

$$W_i = TF_i \bullet IDF_i \qquad (5)$$

$$\arg\max_{c \in C} \cos(c,d) = \arg\max_{c \in C} \frac{c}{\|c\|} \bullet \frac{d}{\|d\|} \qquad (6)$$

2.4 MCRDR (Multiple Classification Ripple Down Rule)

Kang [4] developed Multiple Classification Ripple Down Rules (MCRDR). MCRDR overcomes a major limitation in Ripple Down Rules (RDR), which only permitted single classification of a set of data. That is MCRDR allows multiple independent classifications. An MCRDR knowledge base is represented by an N-ary tree [4]. The tree consists of a set of production rules in the form "If Condition Then Conclusion".

2.4.1 Creation of Rule

We consider a new *case (present case) A* and two *cornerstone cases B* and *cornerstone cases C*. The cornerstone case is the case that prompted the rule being modified (that is, the rule that currently fires on the present case but which is deemed to be incorrect) to be originally added. The present case will become the cornerstone case for the new (exception) rule. To generate conditions for the new rule, the system has to look up the cornerstone cases in the parent rule. When a case is misclassified, the rule giving the wrong conclusion must be modified. The system will add an exception rule at this location and use the cornerstone cases in the parent rule to determine what is different between the previously seen cases and the present case. These differences will form the rule condition and may include positive and negative conditions (see Formula (7)).

Positive Condition :

$$\text{Present Case (A)} - (\text{Cornerstone Case (B)} \cup \text{Cornerstone Case (C)}) \quad (7)$$

Negative Condition :

$$(\text{Cornerstone Case (B)} \cap \text{Cornerstone Case (C)}) - \text{Present Case (A)}$$

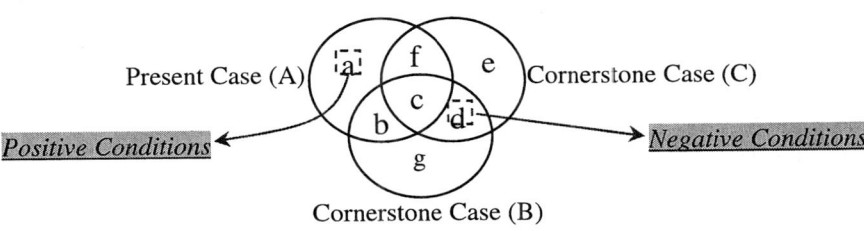

Fig. 1. Difference list {a, not d} are found to distinguish the Present Case (A) from two Cornerstone Cases (B) and (C) [4]

Figure 1 shows a difference list {a, NOT d} between the present case and two cornerstone cases. After the system adds a new rule with the selected conditions by the expert or system, the new rule should be evaluated with the remaining cornerstone cases in the parent rule [4]. If any remaining cornerstone cases are satisfied with the newly added rule, then the cases become cornerstone cases of the new rule [4].

2.4.2 Inference

The inference process of MCRDR is to allow for multiple independent conclusions with the validation and verification of multiple paths [14]. This can be achieved by validating the children of all rules which evaluate to true. An example of the MCRDR inference process is illustrated in Figure 2.

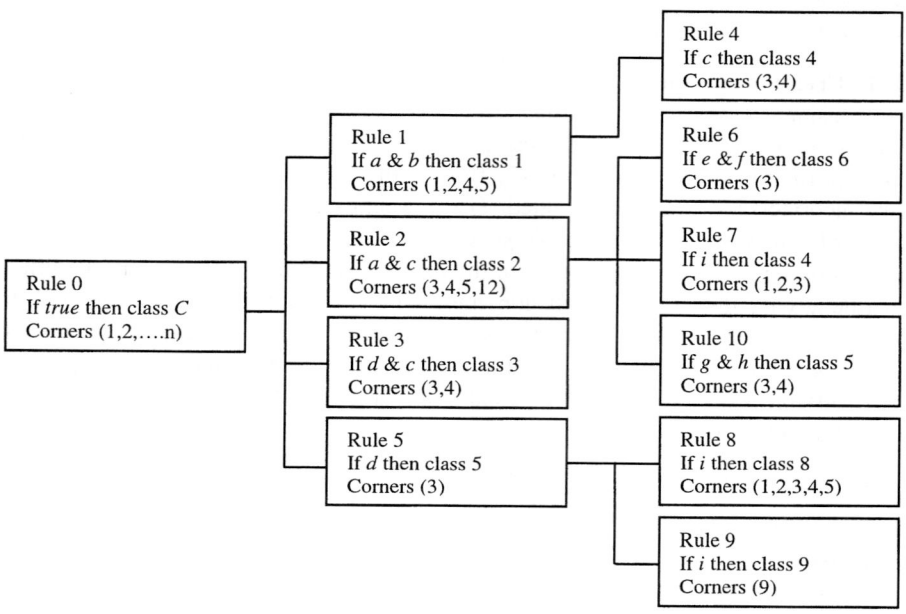

Fig. 2. Knowledge Base and Inference in MCRDR, Attributes: {a, c, d, e, f, h, k} [14]

In this example, a case has attributes {a, c, d, e, f, h, k} and three classifications (conclusion 3, 5 and 6) are produced by the inference. Rule 1 does not fire. Rule 2 is validated as true as both "a" and "c" are found in our case. Now we should consider the children (rules 6, 7, and 10) of rule 2. From comparison of the conditions in children rules with our case attributes, only rule 6 is evaluated as true. Hence, rule 6 would fire to get a *conclusion 6* which is our case classification. This process is applied to the complete MCRDR rule structure in Figure 2. As a result, rule 3 and 5 can also fire, so that *conclusion 3* and *conclusion 5* are also our case classifications.

2.5 FCA (Formal Concept Analysis)

Wille [3] developed Formal Concept Analysis (FCA). FCA is based on the understanding of a concept as an entity of thought, which consists of an extension and intension. Lattice theory is used for representing concepts [8][9]. FCA provides a substitute graphical representation of tabular data that is somewhat instinctive to navigate and use [10]. The fundamental conceptual structure of FCA is the formal context (K). A formal context comprises a set of objects and their attributes. A formal context constitutes a triple (G, M, I). 'G' is the set of objects, 'M' is the set of attributes and 'I' is a binary relation defined between 'G' and 'M'. Their relation is represented as $I \subseteq G \times M$. Hence, we can define a formal context (K) as: K = (G, M, I). If an object g has an attribute m then $g \in G$ is related I to m which is indicated by the relationship $(g, m) \in I$ or gIm. The notion of a formal concept (G, M, I) is represented as a pair (A, B). 'A' is the set of objects ($A \subseteq G$) and 'B' is set of attributes ($B \subseteq M$). Its two operators are:

2.6 BayesTH-MCRDR

The BayesTH-MCRDR algorithm combines the merits of both the Naïve Bayesian using Threshold (BayesTH) and MCRDR algorithms. A new document can be extracted from feature keywords which are obtained through the Information Gain method (see Section 3.1.3). And then, the document is classified by the BayesTH algorithm into a temporary knowledge base (Table 1). At this moment a document is classified, that is assigned a class. The MCRDR algorithm creates new rules based on the feature keywords in the document. In the BayesTH algorithm, the feature keywords are independent of one another. The MCRDR rules represent the semantic relationships between feature keywords and each rule builds each conclusion (classification) through inference of the MCRDR algorithm (Table 2).

Table 1. Table of Temporary Knowledge Base by BayesTH algorithm

Category	Class	Document No	Keyword
Database	Multimedia	1	A, B
	Data Format	2	X, Y, Z

Table 2. Table of Knowledge Base by MCRDR algorithm

Step	Document	Algorithm	Rules (Keywords)	Class
1	1	Bayesian Threshold	A, B	Multimedia
2	1	MCRDR	A&C	Multimedia
3	1	BayesTH-MCRDR	A, B, A&C, A&B, A&B&C	Multimedia

3 Web Document Classification System

We now introduce the system and accompanying process that have been developed. Section 3.1 describes the preprocessing performed on the documents. Section 3.2 describes the implemented system.

3.1 Data Pre-processing

Data preparation is a key step in the data mining process. For us this step involved deletion of stopwords, feature extraction and modeling and document classification. We describe how these were achieved next.

3.1.1 Deletion of Stopwords

The meaning of 'Stopwords' refers to common words like 'a', 'the', 'an', to', which have high frequency but no value as an index word. These words show high frequencies in all documents. If we can remove these words at the start of indexation, we can obtain higher speeds of calculation and fewer words needing to be indexed. The common method to remove these 'Stopwords' is to make a 'Stopwords' dictionary at the beginning of indexation and to get rid of those words. This system follows that technique.

3.1.2 Stemming

Stemming means the process that searches morphological variations for each keyword and transforms various keywords with the same meaning into a keyword. For example, the words "computers", "computing", "compute", "computed", "computable", "computation" in documents or query are transformed into on indexation word "compute". English has the "Stem" which has a certain kinds of meaning and the "Suffix" which stands for variations of morphology. The reason for stemming is to store stems instead of words, and it enables to reduce the size of the index file and to improve the speed of search. Moreover, it prevents the same key words from being represented differently, so it enables us to calculate the keywords precisely and results in improving the quality of the search. Porter [7] developed the Porter Stemming algorithm and it the most popular technique at the moment. The Porter's stemmer does not remove prefixes. It does however handle suffixes and perform string replacement. The Porter's stemmer has various rules for stemming. Each rule is defined by four sub-items which are: Rule Number, Suffix, Replacement String and Stem State. The Rule Number is a unique number allocated to a certain rule. When several rules are satisfied, the rule with the smallest number of conditions will be applied first. The following two conditions should be satisfied in order for a rule to be applied to a given word. Firstly, given words should include the suffix. In these cases, the suffixes in words may be transformed into the Replacement String specified in the rule. If there is NULL suffix, the word is connected with Replacement String, and if there is a NULL Replacement String, suffixes in words are removed.

3.1.3 Feature Extraction

The process of feature extraction is that of determining which keywords will be useful for expressing each document for classification learning. Document modelling is the process of expressing the existence or non-existence, frequency and weight of each document feature based on a fixed feature word [11].

The most basic method to choose word features which describe a document is to use a complete vocabulary set which is based on all words in the document sets. But this requires extensive computation due to a greater number of word features than the number of given documents, and the inclusion of a number of word features which do not assist classification but instead reduce classification power. Some words offer semantics which can assist classification. Selecting these words as word features from the complete word set for the set of documents will reduce effort. In this way we consider Feature Extraction to be Feature Selection or Dimension Deduction. There are various ways to achieve feature selection, but our system uses the well-known Information Gain approach [6] that selects words that have a large entropy difference as word features based on information theory.

$$V = \{w_1, w_2, w_3, w_4, w_5, \ldots, w_n\} \tag{8}$$

$$InforGain(w_k) = P(w_k) \sum_i P(c_i \mid w_k) \log \frac{P(c_i \mid w_k)}{P(c_i)}$$
$$+ P(\overline{w_k}) \sum_i P(c_i \mid w_k) \log \frac{P(c_i \mid \overline{w_k})}{P(c_i)} \tag{9}$$

When the complete set of vocabulary (V) consists of rules (formula (8)) and n words, formula (9) shows the calculation of the information gain for each word w_k. Those words which have the largest information gain are included in the optimized set of word features (K) as in formula (10).

$$K = \{w_1, w_2, w_3, w_4, w_5, \ldots, w_L\}, K \subset V \tag{10}$$

3.1.4 Learning and Classification

In order to do supervised learning and evaluate the accuracy of Web document classification based on BayesTH-MCRDR we must provide classified documents as input. Our system uses the naïve Bayesian learning method as it is a representative algorithm for supervised learning. The Naïve Bayesian classification learning method classifies each Web document with the highest probability class. Where the conditional probability of a given document is low or there is a conflict the system asks the user to choose the most appropriate classification. In situations where either the difference between the two or more highest conditional probabilities is small or the highest conditional probability is low (for example, the highest conditional probability is 0.2 ~ 0.3 and less) we ask the user to intervene. Since precision and trust are closely related, we don't want the system to give an incorrect classification, resulting in the users loss of faith in the system. Hence, when the system can not clearly assign a class, the system assigns the document to 'Others' for the user to deal with (see Formula (4)). In our system the user is able to set the probability threshold 'T' (see Figure 3), above which the system will assign its own conclusion.

3.2 Implementation

The screen dump in Figure 3 displays the key elements of our system which have been developed to evaluate the performance of the implemented algorithms. The screen consists of three parts; the top panel is for choosing which classification rule to apply to the set of Web documents, the second panel allows selection of the class (Communication and Networking, Data Formats, Programming and Development, Information Technology and Multimedia) of the data and whether training (learning) or testing (experiment) data is to be used. The third section on the screen (large lower panel) is used to display the contents of the data for the purposes of evaluating and confirming that the data has been classified into the correct class.

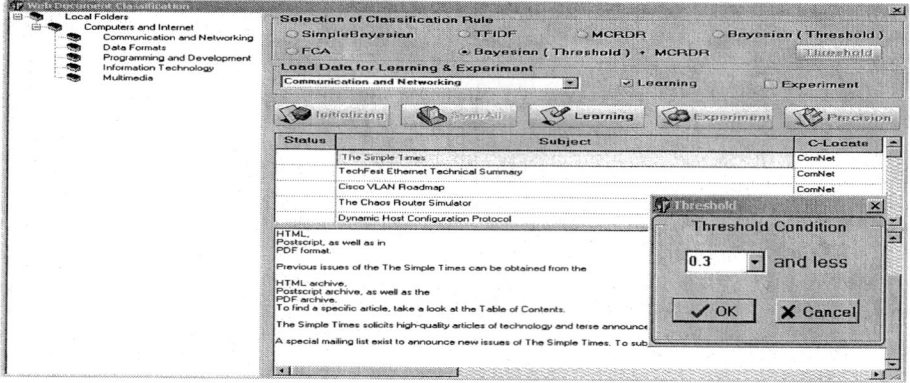

Fig. 3. Web Document Classification System and Control of Threshold value

4 Experiment

4.1 Aims

A key goal of any classification system is to avoid misclassification. Therefore to validate the precision of the BayesTH-MCRDR algorithm for Web document classification, we carried out some experiments. And through the experiments, we compared the classification precision across six different learning methods, and compared the document classification by using stemming algorithm with the document classification by not using it, to discover the differences.

4.2 Data Collection and Set Up

For the experiments we used Web documents provided by the Web directory service at the Yahoo site[1]. We selected one category: Computer and Internet, in order to evaluate the capability of our system. The 'Computer and Internet' category has five sub-categories which are 'Communication and Networking', 'Data Formats', 'Programming and Development', 'Information Technology' and 'Multimedia' (see Fig. 4).

---

[1] http://au.dir.yahoo.com/computers_and_internet/

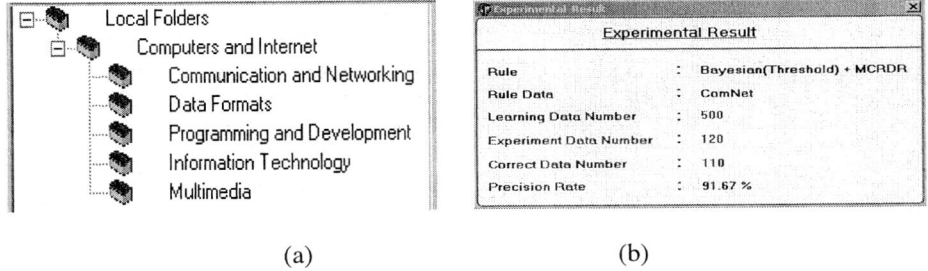

(a)　　　　　　　　　　　　　(b)

Fig. 4. Classified Category (a) for Experiment and Result (b) in the System

We conducted five experiments for each of the five classes. We gave input learning data sets of 100, 200, 300, 400, 500 into each class (increasing 100 per class when experiment each). The total number of learning data is 500 per class. For evaluating precision we used test sets of 120 experimental data at each experiment. The total number of Learning data and Experiment data was 2,500 and 600 each.

4.3 Results

Figure 4(b) shows the evaluation of the precision of each algorithm the user is provided with the precision check function as shown.

	100	200	300	400	500
SB	69.2	70.5	74.8	77.7	80.0
TFIDF	68.5	71.2	74.7	75.3	79.8
B-TH	70.8	71.7	73.3	77.8	81.5
MCRDR	72.3	77.8	79.3	83.2	85.3
FCA	73.8	78.3	78.0	82.3	85.5
BTH-M	76.3	78.4	80.7	85.3	87.5

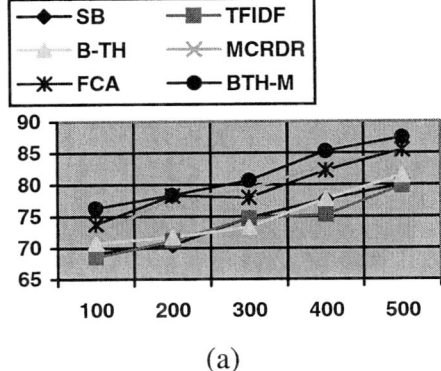

(a)

	100	200	300	400	500
SB	71.8	73.3	76.2	79.8	82.5
TFIDF	70.2	72.5	74.5	77.7	81.2
B-TH	72.3	74.2	77.8	80.7	83.7
MCRDR	74.7	81.7	82.3	85.5	87.8
FCA	76.7	80.8	82.5	84.2	87.0
BTH-M	78.0	82.3	84.2	87.0	89.8

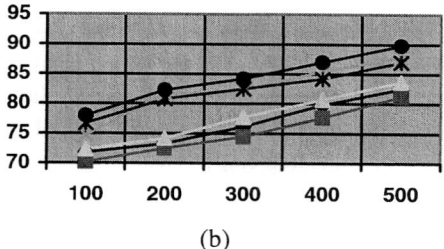

(b)

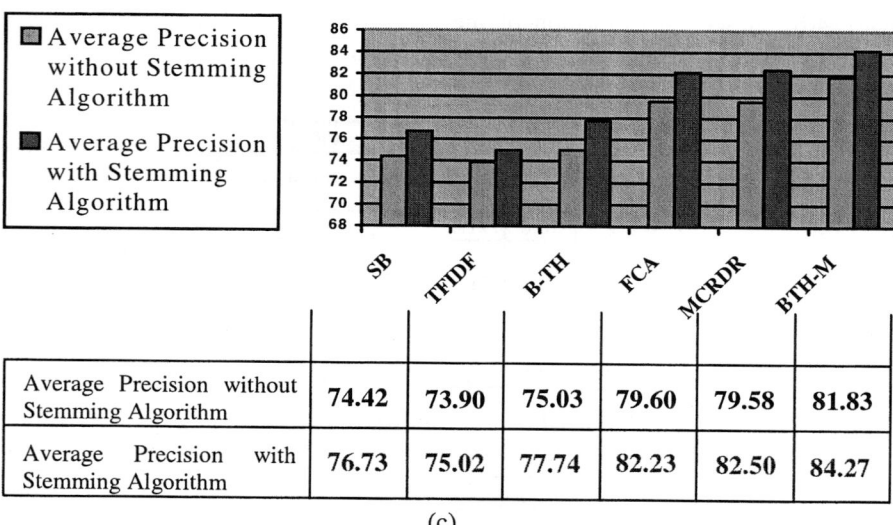

	SB	TFIDF	B-TH	FCA	MCRDR	BTH-M
Average Precision without Stemming Algorithm	74.42	73.90	75.03	79.60	79.58	81.83
Average Precision with Stemming Algorithm	76.73	75.02	77.74	82.23	82.50	84.27

(c)

Fig. 5. *SB: Simple Bayesian; B-TH: Bayesian Threshold; BTH-M: Bayesian Threshold and MCRDR (BayesTH-MCRDR),* (a): Results of average precision for each algorithm per experiment without stemming algorithm. (b): Results of average precision for each algorithm per experiment with stemming algorithm. (c): Compare both results of average precision for each algorithm per experiment without stemming algorithm and results of average precision for each algorithm per experiment with stemming algorithm.

The experimental results show overall precision 74% - 85% for all algorithms even though there are some differences according to the method of classification learning. Specifically, the more documents used in training the higher the classification accuracy, as we expected. Also there are clear differences in classification accuracy (precision) among classification learning methods. Instance that experiment without stemming algorithm, BayesTH-MCRDR shows the highest precision 81.83% in the system. However, TFIDF shows the lowest precision 73.90%. The system, MCRDR and FCA shows similar precision 79.58% and 79.60 respectively. And simple naïve Bayesian and naïve Bayesian algorithm using Threshold show 74.42% and 75.03%, respectively. On the other hand, in the case of the experiment using stemming algorithm, there is an increase in precision of approx. 2.8% in the system. The system, BayesTH-MCRDR shows the highest precision 84.27% and TFIDF shows the lowest precision 75.02%. The simple naïve Bayesian, Bayesian using Threshold, MCRDR and FCA show 76.73%, 77.74%, 82.50% and 82.23% respectively in the system.

5 Conclusions and Further Work

As presented in the paper, we have achieved higher precision by using the BayesTH-MCRDR algorithm than existing classification methods like simple Bayesian classification method, TFIDF classification method, simple Bayesian using Threshold classification method and FCA classification method. The specific feature of this algorithm which enables it to achieve higher precision is the construction of a related word knowledge base from the learning documents before applying the learnt knowledge to the classification of the test set of documents. Also, we found that classification using the Stemming algorithm achieves higher precision than without using the Stemming algorithm. Other research has shown in general that the Bayesian algorithm using a 'Threshold' has better results than the simple Bayesian algorithm. We have achieved even better results using the BayesTH-MCRDR algorithm which has 3% higher precision than the Bayesian Threshold algorithm.

References

1. Mitchell, T.: Machine Learning, McGraw-Hill, International Edition, (1995)
2. Joachims, T.: A probabilistic analysis of the Rocchio algorithm with TFIDF for text categorization, *Proceedings of the 14th International Conference on Machine Learning (ICML-97)*, (1997) 143-151
3. Wille R.: Restructuring lattice theory: an approach based on hierarchies of concepts, *Ordered sets*, 1982, pp.445-470
4. Kang, B.H., Validating Knowledge Acquisition: Multiple Classification Ripple Down Rules, PhD dissertation, School of Computer Science and Engineering at the University of New South Wales, (1995)
5. McCallum, A. and Nigram, K.: A Comparison of Event Models for Naïve Bayes Text Classification, *AAAI-98 Workshop on Learning for Tex Categorization*, (1998)

6. Yang, Y. and Pedersen, J.O.: A Comparative Study on Feature Selection in Text Categorization, *Proceedings of the 14th International Conference on Machine Learning*, (1997) 412-420
7. http://snowball.tartarus.org/porter/stemmer.html
8. Birkhoff, G.: *Lattice Theory 3rd edition*, American Mathematical Society, Incremental Clustering for Dynamic Information Processing, ACM Transactions on Information Processing Systems, 11, 1993, pp. 143-164
9. Ganter, B. and Wille.: R, *General lattice theory 2nd edition*. Birkhauser Verlag, Basel, (1998) 591-605.
10. Ganter, B. and Wille, R.:Formal Concept Analysis – mathematical Foundations Berlin, *Springer Verlag*,(1999).
11. Lewis, D.D.: Feature Selection and Feature Extraction for Text Categorization, *Proceedings of Speech and Natural Language Workshop*, (1992) 212-217

Classification Rule Mining with an Improved Ant Colony Algorithm

Ziqiang Wang and Boqin Feng

Computer Science Department, Xi'an Jiaotong University,
Xi'an 710049, P.R.C (China)
wzqagent@xinhuanet.com

Abstract. This paper presents an improvement ant colony optimization algorithm for mining classification rule called ACO-Miner. The goal of ACO-Miner is to effectively provide intelligible classification rules which have higher predictive accuracy and simpler rule list based on Ant-Miner. Experiments on data sets from UCI data set repository were made to compare the performance of ACO-Miner with Ant-Miner. The results show that ACO-Miner performs better than Ant-Miner with respect to predictive accuracy and rule list mined simplicity.

1 Introduction

Data mining is a progress to extract implicit, nontrivial, previously unknown and potentially useful information (such as knowledge rules, constraints, regularities) from data in database. Mining information and knowledge from large database has been recognized by many researchers as a key research topic in database system and machine learning, and by many industrial companies as an important area with an opportunity of major revenues. There are several data mining tasks, including classification, regression, clustering, dependence modeling, etc. [1]. Each of these tasks can be regarded as a kind of problem to be solved by a data mining algorithm. In this paper, we mainly emphasize the classification task of data mining. Classification rule mining is one of the important problems in the emerging fields of data mining which is aimed at finding a small set of rules from training data set with predetermined targets [1]. There are different classification algorithms used to extract relevant relationship in the data as decision trees which operate performing a successive partitioning of cases until all subsets belong to a single class [2]. This operating way is impracticable except for trivial data sets. There are have been many other approaches for data classification, such as statistical and roughest approaches [1, 3] and neural networks [4]. Although these classification techniques are algorithmically strong, they require significant expertise to work effectively and do not provide intelligible rules.

The classification problem becomes very hard when the number of possible different combinations of parameters is so high that many researches have devoted their attentions to nature-based approaches to find a "good-enough" solution to the classification problem. Especially, there have been numerous attempts to apply genetic algorithms(GAs) [5, 6] in data mining to accomplish classification tasks and achieved better results [7]. In addition, Ant Colony Optimization(ACO) technique [8], which has emerged recently as a new meta-heuristic derived from nature, and has attracted many researchers interests and has been successfully applied to several NP-hard combinatorial optimization problems, but the use of the algorithm for mining classification rule, in the context of data mining, is a research area where few people explored.

To the best of our knowledge, Parpinelli, Lopes and Freitas [9] are the first to propose Ant Colony Optimization(ACO) [8] algorithm for discovering classification rules, with the system Ant-Miner. Their methods use an entropy-based heuristic function. In [10], Liu presented a modified version of Ant-Miner(i.e., Ant-Miner2), where the core heuristic value was based on a simple density estimation heuristic. In addition, Liu [11] further introduced another ant-based algorithm, which uses a different pheromone updating strategy and state transition. In this paper, the objective is to investigate the capability of ACO algorithms to discover classification rule with higher predictive accuracy and much smaller rule list. The remainder of the paper is organized as follows. In the next section, the preliminary knowledge is briefly introduced. In section 3, the Ant-Miner algorithm is analyzed. In section 4, a novel improved algorithm called ACO-Miner is introduced. Section 5 reports computation results when comparing with Ant-Miner across six data sets. Finally, the paper ends with conclusions and directions for future research.

2 Preliminary Knowledge

In general, the problem on mining classification rules can be stated as follows. We are given a large database D, in which each tuple consists of a set of n attributes (features),$\{A_1, A_2, \cdots, A_n\}$. For example, attributes could be name, gender, age, salary range, zip code, etc. Our purpose is to assign each case(object, record, or instance)to one class, out of a set of predefined classes, based on the values of some attributes(called predictor attributes) for the case. In the classification task, the discovered knowledge is usually represented in the form of IF-THEN prediction rules which have the advantage of being a high-level and symbolic knowledge representation contributing towards the comprehensibility of the discovered knowledge. In this paper, knowledge is presented as multiple IF-THEN rules in a classification rules list. Such rules state that the presence of one or more items (antecedents)implies or predicts the presence of other items(consequents). A typical rule has the following form: IF term1 AND term2 AND $\cdots$ THEN class. Where, each term of the rule antecedent is a triple <attribute, operator, value>, such as <age=70>. The rule consequent(THEN part) specifies the class predicted for cases whose predictor attributes satisfy all the terms specified in the rule antecedent. This kind of classification rule representation has the advantage of being intuitively comprehensible for the user.

The ACO algorithm [8] has recently emerged as a new meta-heuristic for hard combination problems. This meta-heuristic belongs to the class of problem-solving strategies derived from nature(other categories including genetic algorithms, immune algorithms, neutral networks, simulated annealing). ACO algorithm has been inspired by colonies of real ants, which deposit a chemical substance called pheromone on the ground. This substance influences the choice they make: the larger amount of pheromone is on a particular path, the larger probability is that an ant selects the path. Artificial ants in ACO algorithm behave in similar way. The ACO algorithm is basically a multi-agent system where low level interactions between single agents (i.e., artificial ants) result in a complex behavior of the whole ant colony. ACO algorithm has been successfully applied to several NP-hard combinatorial optimization problems and achieved better results [12].

3 Overview of Ant-Miner

A high-level description of Ant-Miner [9] is shown in Algorithm 1, the goal of Ant-Miner is to mining classification rules from database. In the following we discuss the key techniques of Ant-Ming, including pheromone initialization, state transition rule, heuristic function, rule pruning and pheromone updating rule.

Algorithm 1: A high-level description of Ant-Miner[9]
TrainingSet={all training cases};
DiscoveredRuleList=[ ];
WHILE(TrainingSet>Max_uncovered_cases);
t=1;
j=1;
Initialize all trails with the same amount of pheromone;
REPEAT
Ant_t starts with an empty rule and incrementally constructs a classification rule R_t by adding one term at a time to the current rule;
Prune rule R_t;
Update the pheromone of all trails by increasing pheromone in the trail followed by Ant_t(proportional to the quality of R_t)and decreasing pheromone in the other trails(simulating pheromone evaporation);
IF(R_t is equal to R_{t-1})
THEN j=j+1;
ELSE j=1;
ENDIF
t=t+1;
UNTIL(t≥No_of_ants)OR (j≥No_rules_converg)
Choose the best rule R_{best} among all rules R_t constructed by all the ants;
Add rule R_{best} to DiscoveredRuleList;
TrainingSet=TrainingSet−{set of cases correctly covered by R_{best}};
END WHILE.

3.1 Pheromone Initialization

The initial amount of pheromone deposited at each path is inversely proportional to the number of values of all attributes, and is defined by the following equation:

$$\tau_{ij}(t=0) = \frac{1}{\sum_{i=1}^{a} b_i} \qquad (1)$$

where a is the total number of attributes, and b_i is the number of possible values that can be taken on by attribute A_i.

3.2 State Transition Rule

Let $term_{ij}$ be a rule condition of form $A_i = V_{ij}$, where A_i is the i-th attribute and V_{ij} is the j-th value of domain of A_i. The probability that $term_{ij}$ is chosen to be added to the current partial rule is given by the following equation:

$$P_{ij}(t) = \frac{\tau_{ij}(t) \cdot \eta_{ij}}{\sum_{i=1}^{a} x_i \cdot \sum_{j=1}^{b_i} (\tau_{ij}(t) \cdot \eta_{ij})} \qquad (2)$$

where $\tau_{ij}(t)$ is the amount of pheromone associated with $term_{ij}$ at iteration t, corresponding to the amount of pheromone currently available in the position i, j of the path being followed by the current ant. η_{ij} is the value of a problem-dependent heuristic function for $term_{ij}$. a is the total number of attributes. x_i is set to 1 if the attribute A_i was not yet used by the current ant, or to 0 otherwise. b_i is the number of values in the domain of the i-th attribute.

3.3 Heuristic Function

For each $term_{ij}$ that can be added to the current rule, Ant-Miner computes the value η_{ij} of a heuristic function that is an estimate of the quality of this term, with respect to its ability to improve the predictive accuracy of the rule. This heuristic function is based on information theory and normalized. The proposed information-theoretic heuristic function is defined as follows:

$$\eta_{ij} = \frac{\log_2 k - H(W|A_i = V_{ij})}{\sum_{i=1}^{a} x_i \cdot \sum_{j=1}^{b_i} (\log_2 k - H(W|A_i = V_{ij}))} \qquad (3)$$

where a, x_i and b_i have the same meaning as above illustration. k is the number of classes. W is the class attribute (i.e., the attribute whose domain consists of the classes to be predicted).

3.4 Rule Pruning

The main goal of rule pruning is to remove irrelevant terms that might have been unduly included in the rule. The basic idea of rule pruning is to iteratively remove one-term at a time from the rule while this process improves the quality of the rule, and the quality of the resulting rule is computed by the following equation:

$$Q = \frac{TP}{TP+FN} \cdot \frac{TN}{FP+TN} \qquad (4)$$

where TP(True Positive) is the number of cases covered by the rule that have the class predicted by the rule. FP(False Positive) is the number of cases covered by the rule that have a class different from the class predicted by the rule. FN(False Negatives) is the number of cases that are not covered by the rule but have the class predicted by the rule. TN(True Negatives) is the number of cases that are not covered by the rule and that do not have the class predicted by the rule.

3.5 Pheromone Updating Rule

Whenever an ant constructs its rule and the rule is pruned, the amount of pheromone in all segments of all paths must be updated. Pheromone updating for a $term_{ij}$ is performed according to the following equation:

$$\tau_{ij}(t+1) = \tau_{ij}(t) + \tau_{ij}(t) \cdot Q, \forall i,j \in R \qquad (5)$$

where R is the set of terms occurring in the rule constructed by the ant at iteration t. Meanwhile, the effect of pheromone evaporation for unused terms is achieved by dividing the value of each τ_{ij} by the summation of all τ_{ij}.

4 Our Proposed Mining Algorithm: ACO-Miner

Although Ant-Miner is a flexible and robust classification mining method, the system has the following drawbacks:1)State transition rule computation is very complex, and lacks of balancing between exploration and exploitation. 2) If rule quality measure Q is very small, evolutionary process will become stagnant. 3)The $H(W|A_i = V_{ij})$ of $term_{ij}$ is always the same when computing heuristic function η_{ij}, regardless of the contents of the rule in which the term occurs. Which is impossible in real application. In order to overcome above drawbacks, we propose an improved classification rule mining algorithm, called ACO-Miner. In the following, we discuss the improved state transition rule, pheromone updating rule and heuristic function.

4.1 Simple State Transition Rule

State transition rule computation of Ant-Miner is very complex. In fact, state transition rule is determined by heuristic function η_{ij} and pheromone τ_{ij}, if we use addition instead of multiplication, and use relative weight to adjust their roles, then we may provide a simple way to compute state transition rule. In addition, in order to provide a direct way to balance between exploration of new terms and exploitation of a priori and accumulated knowledge about the classification, we introduce a parameter $q_0 \in [0,1]$ and a random number q which is uniformly in $[0,1]$. Then, our proposed state transition rule is defined as follows:

IF $q \leq q_0$
THEN choose $term_{ij}$
ELSE Choose $term_{ij}$ according to the following probability

$$P_{ij}(t) = \frac{\beta \cdot \tau_{ij} + (1-\beta) \cdot \eta_{ij}}{\sum_{i=1}^{a} \sum_{j=1}^{b_i} (x_i \cdot (\beta \cdot \tau_{ij} + (1-\beta) \cdot \eta_{ij}))} \quad (6)$$

END IF.

where a, x_i, b_i, τ_{ij} and η_{ij} have the same meaning as above illustration. β is parameter that controls the relative importance of trail versus visibility. Therefore the transition probability is a trade-off between visibility(which says that close terms should be chosen with high probability, thus implementing a greed constructive heuristic) and trail intensity at time t (that says that if there has been a lot of traffic on $term_{ij}$ then it is highly desirable, thus implementing the autocatalytic process).

4.2 Self-Adaptive Pheromone Updating Rule

When an ant constructs its rule and the rule is pruned, the amount of pheromone in all segments of all paths must be updated according to pheromone updating rule in Ant-Miner system. But, if rule quality measure Q is very small (near to zero), evolutionary process will become stagnant. In order to overcome the above drawbacks, we introduce the following self-adaptive pheromone updating rule:

$$\tau_{ij}(t+1) = (1-\rho(t)) \cdot \tau_{ij}(t) + (1-\rho(t)+Q) \cdot \tau_{ij}(t) \quad (7)$$

where Q is the quality measure of constructed rule. $\rho(t)$ is a self-adaptive pheromone evaporation rate, its definition is as follows:

$$\rho(t) = \min\{\rho_{max}, \lambda \cdot \rho(t-1)\} \quad (8)$$

where ρ_{max} is the maximum of $\rho(t)$ which is used to control pheromone evaporation rate, initially, $\rho(t=0) = 0$. λ is a parameter whose value is in $(0.8, 1)$. In the paper, we set $\lambda = 0.85$. Our proposed pheromone updating rule concurrently realizes pheromone accumulation and evaporation, thus avoid stagnation.

4.3 Our Proposed Heuristic Function

Heuristic function computation of Ant-Miner is based on information entropy and normalization, but authors of Ant-Miner consider the $H(W|A_i = V_{ij})$ of $term_{ij}$ is always the same when computing heuristic function η_{ij}, regardless of the contents of the rule in which the term occurs. Consequently, the ants likely converge to a single constructed rule too quickly. This leads premature and a failure to produce alternative potential rules. In order to overcome above drawbacks, we introduce a simple and efficient heuristic function based on idea of Ref. [14]. Our proposed heuristic function is defined as follows:

$$\eta_{ij} = \frac{k - SIG(W, A_i = V_{ij})}{\sum_{i=1}^{a}\sum_{j=1}^{b_i} x_i \cdot (k - SIG(W, A_i = V_{ij}))} \quad (9)$$

where a, x_i, b_i have the same meaning as above illustration. k is the number of classes. $SIG(W, A_i = V_{ij})$ denotes the relevance of attribute-value $A_i = V_{ij}$ to the target classification W, the relevant function is defined as follows:

$$SIG(W, A_i = V_{ij}) = P(A_i = V_{ij}) \cdot P(W|A_i = V_{ij}) - P(W) \quad (10)$$

where W is the class attribute(i.e., the attribute whose domain consists of the classes to be predicted). $P(A_i = V_{ij})$ is the probability of having observed $A_i = V_{ij}$. $P(W|A_i = V_{ij})$ is the probability of observing class W condition on having observed $A_i = V_{ij}$. $P(W)$ is the probability of observing class W.

Note that if $P(W|A_i = V_{ij}) = P(W)$, that is to say $A_i = V_{ij}$ is not relevant to the class W, then the degree of relevance $A_i = V_{ij}$ to W is equal to 0; if $P(W|A_i = V_{ij}) \neq P(W)$, i.e., $A_i = V_{ij}$ is relevant to the class W. The range of this function is$(-1, 1)$. If the value stays positive, then the higher the value, the more relevant the term $A_i = V_{ij}$ with respect to the target class W; if the value is negative, the lower the value, the more relevant the term $\neg(A_i = V_{ij})$ with respect to W. Therefore, using this heuristic function is very convenient and efficient in practice.

5 Experimental Results and Comparison

5.1 Data Set Used and Parameter Setup in ACO-Miner

To evaluate performance of our proposed ACO-Miner algorithm, we have conducted experiment with it on a number of datasets taken from the UCI repository [15]. In Table 1, the selected data sets are summarized in terms of the number of cases, the number of attribute(including categorical and continuous attributes), and the number of the classes of the data set. These data sets have been widely used in other comparative studies. Because ACO-Miner mines rules referring only to categorical attributes, we have discretized continuous attributes by the C4.5-Disc discretization method [16] in a preprocessing step. All the results of the comparison were obtained on a Pentium 4 PC(CPU 2.2GHZ, RAM 256MB).

In the following experiments, ACO-Miner has the following user-defined parameters:

1) Number of ants, i.e., No_of_ ants. Since each ant is associated with a single rule, the larger No_of_ ants, the more candidate rules are needed to evaluate per iteration. In order to have a quicker turn-around time for experiments, we set No_of_ ants=200.

Table 1. Dataset Used in The Experiment

Data Set	#Cases	#Categ.Attrib.	#Contin.Attrib.	#Classes
Ljubljana Breast Cancer	282	9	-	2
Wisconsin Breast Cancer	683	-	9	2
Tic-Tac-Toe	958	9	-	2
Dermatology	366	33	1	6
Hepatitis	155	13	6	2
Cleveland Heart Disease	303	8	5	5

2) Minimum number of cases per rule, i.e., Min_cases_per_rule. In order to enforce at least a certain degree of generality in the discovered rules, each rule must cover at least amount of cases. Then, we set Min_cases_per_rule=8.

3) Maximum number of uncovered cases in the training set, i.e., Max_uncovered _cases. It defines the threshold that the number of training cases that are not covered by any discovered rules. We set Max_uncovered_cases=15.

4) Number of rules used to test convergence of the ants, i.e., No_rules_converge. Since the termination condition of current iteration of WHILE loop is that ants have converged to a single rule(path), we set No_rules_converge=8.

5) In order to control the relative importance of pheromone and heuristic function in state transition rule, we set parameter $\beta=0.4$.

6) In order to provide a direct way to balance between exploration of new terms and exploitation of a priori and accumulated knowledge about the classification, we set parameter $q_0=0.5$.

7) In order to realize self-adaptive pheromone evaporation rate $\rho(t)$, The parameters are needed to set as follows: $\rho_{max} = 0.5$, $\rho(t=0) = 0$, $\lambda = 0.85$.

5.2 Comparison Results

We have evaluated the performance of ACO-Miner by comparing it with Ant-Miner. The first experiment was carried out to compare predictive accuracy of discovered rule lists by well-known ten-fold cross-validation procedure [17]. Each data set is divided into ten partitions, each method is run ten times, using a different partition as test set and the other nine partitions as the training set each time. The predictive accuracies of the ten runs are averaged as the predictive accuracy of the discovered rule list. Table 2 shows the results comparing the predictive accuracies of ACO-Miner and Ant-Miner, where the " ± " symbol denotes the standard deviation of the corresponding predictive accuracy. It can be seen that predictive accuracies of ACO-Miner is higher than those of Ant-Miner.

In addition, We compared the simplicity of the discovered rule list by the number of discovered rules and the average number of literals(conditions) per rule. The results comparing the simplicity of the rule lists discovered by ACO-Miner and Ant-Miner are shown in Table 3 and Table 4. As shown in those tables, taking into number of rules discovered and number of literals per rule,

Table 2. Predictive Accuracy Comparison Between ACO-Miner and Ant-Miner

Data Set	ACO-Miner(%)	Ant-Miner(%)
Ljubljana Breast Cancer	77.14±0.53	75.28±2.24
Wisconsin Breast Cancer	97.15±0.89	96.04±0.93
Tic-Tac-Toe	98.43±0.36	73.04±2.53
Dermatology	96.57±0.74	94.29±1.20
Hepatitis	94.63±0.58	90.00±3.11
Cleveland Heart Disease	78.28±0.45	57.48±1.78

Table 3. Number of Rules Discovered Comparison by ACO-Miner and Ant-Miner

Data Set	ACO-Miner	Ant-Miner
Ljubljana Breast Cancer	6.25±0.23	7.10±0.31
Wisconsin Breast Cancer	4.63±0.12	6.20±0.25
Tic-Tac-Toe	6.47±0.43	8.50±0.62
Dermatology	6.87±0.56	7.30±0.47
Hepatitis	3.07±0.24	3.40±0.16
Cleveland Heart Disease	7.29±0.39	9.50±0.71

Table 4. Number of Literals Per Rule Between ACO-Miner and Ant-Miner

Data Set	ACO-Miner	Ant-Miner
Ljubljana Breast Cancer	1.13	1.28
Wisconsin Breast Cancer	1.58	1.97
Tic-Tac-Toe	1.06	1.18
Dermatology	2.85	3.16
Hepatitis	1.98	2.41
Cleveland Heart Disease	1.45	1.71

Table 5. Running Time Comparison Between ACO-Miner and Ant-Miner

Data Set	ACO-Miner(s)	Ant-Miner(s)
Ljubljana Breast Cancer	46.63	55.28
Wisconsin Breast Cancer	52.39	58.74
Tic-Tac-Toe	57.53	61.18
Dermatology	37.68	49.56
Hepatitis	41.84	56.57
Cleveland Heart Disease	34.75	48.73

ACO-Miner mined rule lists much simpler(smaller) than the rule lists mined by Ant-Miner.

At last, we also compared the running time of ACO-Miner with Ant-Miner. The experimental results are reported Table 5, as expected, we can see that

ACO-Miner's running time is fewer than Ant-Miner's in all data sets. The main reason was that we used addition instead of multiplication in computing state transition rule of ACO-Miner, this reduced ACO-Miner's running time.

In summary, although ACO-Miner need to set more parameter than Ant-Miner, taking into account both the predictive accuracy and rule list simplicity criteria, our proposed ACO-Miner is rather competitive.

6 Conclusions and Future Works

In this paper, we present an ACO-Miner algorithm for data mining, a new method for mining classification rule based on an improvement of Ant-Miner. We have compared the performance of ACO-Miner and Ant-Miner in public domain data sets. Experimental results show that ACO-Miner has a higher predictive accuracy and much smaller rule list than Ant-Miner. Because the application of ACO algorithm in data mining, especially in classification rule mining, is still in infant periods, in future works, our further research directions are as follows. First, we plan to make further experiments to understand system parameters influence on the performance of ACO-Miner, so that, we can set appropriate parameter combinations in term of different classification problems. Second, we will further improve predictive accuracy and rule list simplicity according to investigate other kinds of heuristic function and pheromone updating rule.

References

1. Fayyad, U.M., Piatetsky-Shapiro, G., and Smyth, P.: From data mining to knowledge discovery: an overview. In Advances in Knowledge Discovery & Data Mining, MIT Press(1996)1–34
2. Quinlan, J.R.: Induction of Decision Trees. Machine Learning, 1(1986)81–106
3. Ziarko, W.: Rough Sets, Fuzzy Set and Knowledge Discovery. Springer-Verlag, Berlin(1994)
4. Lu, H., Setiono, R., and Liu, H.: NeuroRule:a connectionist approach to data mining. Proc. of the 21st International Conference on Very large Data Bases, Zurich, Switzerland, Morgan Kaufmann Press(1995) 478–489
5. Fogel, B.: Evolutionary Computation: Toward a New Philosophy of Machine Intelligence. IEEE Press, New York(1994)
6. Goldberg, D.E.: Genetic Algorithms in Search, Optimization, and Machine Learning. Addison-Wesley(1989)
7. Falco, I.D., Iazzetta, A., Tarantino, E., and Cioppa, A.D.: An evolutionary system for automatic explicit rule extraction. Evolutionary Computation 1(2000)450–457
8. Dorigo, M., Maniezzo, V.: The ant system: optimization by a colony of cooperating agents. IEEE Tansactions on System, Man, and Cybernetics 26(1996)1–13
9. Parpinelli, R.S., Lopes, H.S., and Freitas, A.A.: Data mining with an ant colony optimization algorithm. IEEE Transactions on Evolutionary Computing 6(2002)321–332
10. Liu, B., Abbass, H.A., Mckay, B.: Density_based heuristic for rule discovery with ant-miner. The 6th Australia-Japan Joint Workshop on Intelligent and Evolutionary System, Canberra, Australia (2002) 180–184

11. Liu, B., Abbass, H.A., Mckay, B.: Classification rule discovery with ant colony optimization. In Proceeding of the IEEE/WIC International Conference on Intelligent Agent Technology, Beijing, China (2003) 83–88
12. Dorigo, M., Cao, G.D.: Ant algorithms for discrete optimization.Artificial Life 5(1999)137–172
13. Bonabeau, E., Dorigo, M., and Theraulaz, G.:Swarm Intelligence:From Natural to Artificial Systems. Oxford University Press(1999)
14. An, A.: Learning classification rules from data. Computer and Mathematics with Applications 45(2003)737–748
15. Hettich, S., Bay, S.D.: The UCI KDD Archive. URL:http://kdd.ics.uci.edu, 1999
16. Kohavi, R., Sahami, M.: Error-based and entropy-based discretization of continuous features. In Proceeding of Second International Conference Knowledge Discovery and Data Mining, Menlo Park, CA (1996)114–119
17. Weiss, S.M., KulIkowski, C.A.: Computer Systems that Learn. Morgan Kaufmann Press, San Mateo, CA(1991)

Clustering Large Datasets Using Cobweb and K-Means in Tandem

Mi Li, Geoffrey Holmes, and Bernhard Pfahringer

Department of Computer Science,
University of Waikato,
Hamilton, New Zealand
{ml87, geoff, bernhard}@cs.waikato.ac.nz

Abstract. This paper presents a single scan algorithm for clustering large datasets based on a two phase process which combines two well known clustering methods. The Cobweb algorithm is modified to produce a balanced tree with subclusters at the leaves, and then K-means is applied to the resulting subclusters. The resulting method, Scalable Cobweb, is then compared to a single pass K-means algorithm and standard K-means. The evaluation looks at error as measured by the sum of squared error and vulnerability to the order in which data points are processed.

1 Introduction

The clustering task is to partition a dataset D (a set of n points with d dimensions) into meaningful groups (clusters) so that, under a certain definition of similarity, objects within a cluster are similar to one another (high intra-cluster similarity), but differ from objects in other clusters (low inter-cluster similarity). The subject has been explored extensively under various disciplines in the past three decades. A large number of clustering algorithms have been devised in statistics, data mining, pattern recognition, and other fields. However, trials on effective and efficient clustering methods for large databases have only been carried out in recent years due to the emergence of the field of data mining.

Due to the large freedom of choice in the interpretation of the definition, particularly the notion of similarity, many clustering algorithms have been reported in the literature. Moreover, new algorithms are still being devised by data mining practitioners to meet the requirements of different practical applications addressing different aspects of clustering. A form of clustering taxonomy can be derived by dividing the methods into the following five categories: partitioning methods, hierarchical methods, density-based methods, grid-based methods, and model-based methods [8]. Traditional clustering methods and some newly developed algorithms for spatial databases have been discussed in the literature. Some recent, comprehensive reviews can be found in [9, 8, 10]. Many of these methods, however, do not scale to large datasets because they assume that all the data can fit in memory so that multiple scans are feasible.

Given such a wealth of material it seems prudent to try to scale existing methods to a setting where a single scan is the only possible option. Work in this area has focused on scaling of traditional methods, particularly K-means [2–4]. The work presented in this paper builds directly on these contributions by adding a method to their ranks that produces high quality clusters (as measured by sum of squared error) while remaining relatively stable when the order of the data is not randomly presented to the algorithm, for example, when the cluster classes are presented together. This claim is verified in experiments that directly compare with these existing methods.

This paper is organised as follows: first we describe our scaling method of combining Cobweb and K-means. We then compare this algorithm with standard K-means and a single pass scalable algorithm. We report related work, particularly, BIRCH which uses a similar ethos. Finally, we discuss the possible extension of the algorithm to streaming data.

2 Scalable Cobweb

Cobweb [5] is a truly incremental clustering algorithm, which maximizes category utility to build a probabilistic hierarchical tree. The algorithm reads one instance per iteration from a dataset and incorporates it into the tree by descending the tree along an appropriate path to a node where the category utility is maximal after absorbing the instance and updating statistical information (for computation of the probabilities) in each node along the way. To find the proper place to hold the instance, Cobweb tries one, or several, or all of the following four possible operations at each node on the path: (1) place the instance in an existing cluster; (2) create a new cluster by itself; (3) merge the best two clusters with respect to the values of category utility; (4) split a cluster into several clusters by lifting its children one level in the tree to replace itself. The operation resulting in the largest value of category utility is the final choice on that node. This procedure is recursively invoked until a leaf node is reached or a new leaf is created.

Category utility [7] is a measure of increase in predictability of attribute values given a clustering, given an attribute-value pair $a_i = v_{ij}$, where a_i is the ith attribute and v_{ij} is its jth value. For a cluster C_l, the intra-cluster similarity can be described by the conditional probabilities $\Pr[a_i = v_{ij}|C_l]$. A higher value of this probability means that a larger proportion of the members of the cluster C_l shares the specific value v_{ij} of the attribute a_i, so the attribute a_i can be predicted to have the value v_{ij} in the cluster C_l with higher probability. The conditional probability reaches its optimal value 1 when all instances in the cluster C_l have the same value v_{ij} of attribute a_i. Similarly, the inter-cluster similarity can be represented by the following quantities: $\Pr[C_l|a_i = v_{ij}]$. The higher this probability is, the fewer instances there are in clusters other than cluster C_l, which would share the same value v_{ij} of the attribute a_i. An overall measure can be obtained by combining these two probabilities together with the apriori probabilities for each attribute value, summing over all possible combinations:

$$\sum_{l=1}^{|C|} \sum_{i=1}^{|A|} \sum_{j=1}^{|V_i|} \{\Pr[a_i = v_{ij}] \cdot \Pr[C_l|a_i = v_{ij}] \cdot \Pr[a_i = v_{ij}|C_l]\}$$

$|C|$ is the number of clusters in a dataset, and $|A|$ indicates the number of attributes of each instance, and $|V_i|$ represents the number of values of attribute A_i. $\Pr[a_i = v_{ij}]$ is the probability of the attribute a_i having the value v_{ij} in the entire dataset. Using Bayes' rule, and assuming attribute independence, the above formula can be rewritten into:

$$\sum_{l=1}^{|C|} \Pr[C_l] \sum_{i=1}^{|A|} \sum_{j=1}^{|V_i|} \Pr[a_i = v_{ij}|C_l]^2$$

Because category utility is defined as the improvement in the predictability of attribute values given a partitioning over predictability without such a partitioning, category utility is formulated as:

$$CU(C_1, C_2, ..., C_k) = \frac{\sum_{l=1}^{|C|} \Pr[C_l] \sum_{i=1}^{|A|} \sum_{j=1}^{|V_i|} (\Pr[a_i = v_{ij}|C_l]^2 - \Pr[a_i = v_{ij}]^2)}{|C|}$$

The value of category utility will be high when the clustering is good. Maximizing category utility achieves high predictability of a cluster for given variable values and vice versa. Cobweb favours placing an instance into a node that contains instances similar to the incoming one to form a cluster as pure as possible. The original Cobweb algorithm using the above formula only supports nominal attributes. An algorithm called CLASSIT [6] extends the formula to numerical attributes by taking the normal distribution assumption [13]. Applying the probability density function of a normal distribution for every attribute, the above formula can be rewritten as:

$$CU(C_1, C_2, ..., C_k) = \frac{1}{|C|} \sum_{l=1}^{|C|} \Pr[C_l] \frac{1}{2\sqrt{\pi}} \sum_{i=1}^{|A|} (\frac{1}{\sigma_{il}} - \frac{1}{\sigma_i})$$

In this formula σ_i is the standard deviation of the attribute a_i. Clearly, attributes with zero standard deviation will lead to an infinite value in CU, so a parameter named acuity is introduced to impose a minimum variance on each attribute.

The Cobweb algorithm is defined as follows:

1. Initialize the tree by reading in a data point to form the root node.
2. Read in the next data point, and start from the root node.
3. If the node is a leaf, go to step 4. Otherwise, the current node is an internal node. Of the following four operations, choose the one maximizing category utility (locally) and repeat:
   (a) Insert the data point into each of the children of the current node, and choose the one with highest category utility observed.

(b) Create a new leaf for the point and add the leaf to the children of the current node.
(c) Merge the two children found in step (a) that have the highest and the second highest values of category utility by turning the two children of the current node into two children of the merged node, and add the merged node as a child of the current node, then insert the data point into the merged node.
(d) Split the child found in step (a) with the best category utility by raising the level of its children up one level, so that the children of this node become the direct children of the parent of this node. This node is eliminated. Then the data point is inserted as in step (a).
4. When a leaf node is reached, create a new leaf node to hold the data point, then both the old leaf node and the new leaf node are added to a new node as its two children, finally, the new node with two children replaces the original place of the old leaf node to become an internal node of the tree.
5. Check the stopping condition, if it is satisfied, terminate; else, go to the step 2 to begin a new iteration.

The tree constructed in terms of the above steps contains one leaf for every instance. Consequently, the algorithm will output a massive hierarchy for large datasets. To control the growth of the tree, another parameter named 'cutoff' is introduced. If a new node does not produce enough increase in category utility, that node is cut off.

The basic algorithm is deficient in a number of ways. The assumption that the probability distributions on different attributes are independent of each other is sometimes too strong, because correlations may exist between attributes. The quality of clustering is also dependent on the order of the incoming data points. Usually, the algorithm is dealing well with low-dimensional datasets only. Furthermore, Cobweb trees are quite often highly unbalanced making the algorithm inefficient, even impractical, for clustering anything other than small datasets.

This imbalance problem can be addressed with two straightforward measures. One is to limit the number of children each node can have. This is necessary because too many children in each internal node will lead to wasting time on sorting out the best node to place a new data point. We noticed that the standard Cobweb algorithm tends to generate a large number of children for an internal node. It should be noted that Cobweb does not make any restriction on the number of children each node can have (on the width of the tree). After we ran the standard Cobweb on a synthetic dataset, we found that although the height of the generated tree was only five levels, the number of children for some internal nodes was extremely high (up to thirty). On average, each internal node had about eleven children. Lack of restriction on the width of the tree is probably the main reason for degrading performance.

The second measure to keep the tree balanced is to impose an explicit constraint on the height of the tree. There is already a parameter named Cutoff that is set to control the growth of the tree but the value of this parameter is difficult to decide. A small Cutoff value will produce a tree with many leaf nodes containing a single data point because no leaf will actually be cut off. On the contrary, a large Cutoff value will result in a tree with leaf nodes with too many data points in each of them. In a tree like this, the nodes representing many different clusters are merged together. Consequently, it is hard to differentiate the clusters hidden in a dataset. Very little useful information about the clusters can be obtained from such a coarse tree. This will certainly decrease the quality of the final clustering solution. To guarantee efficiency and effectiveness, it is better to limit the height of the tree explicitly.

The purpose of the two constraints on both width and height of the tree is to come to a compromise between a very fine tree with each data point in a separate leaf and a very coarse tree where many data points, possibly coming from different clusters, are punt into single clusters mistakenly and the fine differences among these data points are lost. Our experiments showed that the two constraints do improve the efficiency of the construction of the clustering tree. Still, when a large dataset is clustered, a large number of data points will accumulate in each leaf node because there are fewer leaf nodes in the tree than the number of leaf nodes in a standard Cobweb tree. It is very likely that these data points will consist of points coming from several clusters. Such situations occur so frequently that ignoring them will certainly decrease the quality of clustering.

To address this problem, we add some internal structure to leaf nodes of the tree. Each leaf node keeps a local list of subclusters, allowing for keeping more detailed summary information about all the instances assigned to this leaf node. All local lists coming from all leaves of the tree are further linked together to form a global list that is maintained in main memory. After the construction of the tree, any traditional clustering approach that is capable of handling weighted data points can be utilized to produce the final clustering solution based on this global list of subclusters.

So in order to scale up standard Cobweb to handle larger datasets we have introduced these three scalability extensions:

1. A limit on the number of children each internal node can have.
2. A constraint on the height of the tree.
3. A leaf node has internal structure (a list of subclusters).

The actual clustering procedure is divided into two steps. The first step builds a balanced Cobweb tree with a local list of subclusters stored in each leaf node using the same tree construction approach as standard Cobweb, but with user-defined limits imposed on both the width and height of the tree. The second step employs a traditional clustering method on the global list of all the subclusters of all the leaves to produce the final clustering solution. Any traditional clustering approach that supports weighted data points such as K-means, or CLARANS [11] is suitable, because this step only accesses in-memory data, the sufficient statistics collected in each leaf. the individual data points can be discarded after they are processed, as both the tree building operation and the final clustering can be achieved with the use of sufficient statistics of data points.

Theoretically, if the first (hierarchical) clustering step would output a clustering hierarchy of acceptable quality, then the second step would be redundant. Practically, in our experiments we found that the quality was always improved substantially by including this second (global) clustering step.

Since Scalable Cobweb is based on standard Cobweb it inherits two appealing features. The first feature is incremental clustering that enables our algorithm to conduct only a single scan of the entire dataset. The second feature is the splitting and merging operations that reshape the tree dynamically. This reshaping seems to enable Scalable Cobweb to cope well with arbitrary orderings of training examples.

In the following, we will describe the algorithm and its three scalability extensions in greater depth.

2.1 The Tree-Building Step

In the process of tree building there are two possibilities that the width of a tree is increased, either when a new leaf node is added as a child to an internal node or when the splitting of an internal node has occurred. The merging of two nodes will not lead to the increase in the number of children at a node. When the number of children of a node exceeds the specified upper limit (the maximum number of children of a node allowed), the merging operation of its child nodes is triggered.

The merging can be achieved by either merging the closest pair of nodes according to a certain similarity criterion, or merging the two nodes so that their parent node has the greatest value of category utility after the merging (the greatest CU gain). When merging two child nodes, three different situations can be encountered: either both nodes are leaves, or one node is a leaf, while the other node is an internal node, or both nodes are internal nodes.

When the two nodes are leaves, for example, nodeA and nodeB, firstly, update the statistical information of nodeA using that of nodeB. Then merge the local list of nodeB into that of nodeA. Lastly remove nodeB from the children vector of their parent node. For the second situation, the leaf node nodeA is merged into the non-leaf node nodeB. We need to travel down the internal node nodeB to find the best leaf node nodeC in the successors of nodeB to hold the subclusters in nodeA. There are two criteria to decide which branch we should traverse. One method is to choose the node that is nearest to the nodeA among its siblings. The other method is to choose the node whose parent node has the greatest value of category utility after adding nodeA into the node among its other siblings. If the category utility is used to select the two nodes to merge, then the traverse operation should also be guided by the category utility. We call this approach the category utility guided approach. If we apply other (dis)similarity measures, such as a distance measure, to choose the closest pair of nodes to merge, then the same (dis)similarity measure should be utilized to guide the traverse operation. This approach we call the similarity guided approach. The statistical information of the nodes on the path is updated using that of nodeA. When the two nodes, nodeA and nodeB, are non-leaf nodes, to merge nodeB into nodeA, firstly update the sufficient statistics of nodeA by that of nodeB, then the children of nodeB are added into the children vector of nodeA, and nodeB can be removed. Because the number of children of nodeA is increased, this procedure is recursively called to ensure that the number of children of nodeA satisfies the specified upper limit.

Experiments showed that there is no significant difference in the quality of the final clustering between the two approaches—the similarity guided approach or the category utility guided approach.

In order to efficiently construct the internal subclusters in each leaf, we introduce a proximity threshold to measure the similarity of two data points. When a data point reaches a leaf node (guided by the category utility measure), we traverse the local list of this leaf to see if there is a subcluster that can hold this point. If a subcluster is proven to be similar to this incoming point, that is, the similarity between the subcluster and the point satisfies the proximity threshold, then the point is merged into the subcluster and the statistical information of this subcluster is updated. If no such subcluster can be found in the local list, which means that the new point is quite different from all the subclusters in the local list (and therefore cannot be represented properly by the center of any of the existing subclusters), then a new subcluster is added for this point.

2.2 The Final Clustering Step

Running the first step of the Scalable Cobweb algorithm, a balanced Cobweb tree with subclusters in its leaf nodes is constructed. Typically, each leaf node contains several subclusters, with each subcluster summarizing a group of similar data points. Only sufficient statistics of these groups of data points are kept in subclusters, while the information about individual points is discarded. This hierarchical structure may suffer from two different deficiencies. First, some subclusters in different leaf nodes may contain data points belonging to the same true cluster in the data set. Second, subclusters in any one leaf node may actually belong to different true clusters. Therefore it is necessary to redistribute these subclusters, thus hopefully bringing together the subclusters belonging to the same true cluster. This is the purpose of the second step, which can be considered as a refinement step for producing better quality in the final clustering solution. This step also helps to alleviate the order dependency introduced in the first tree-building step.

In our implementation, the standard K-means algorithm is adopted to regroup the subclusters. It is well known that K-means is a fast algorithm that can deal with high dimensional (up to 100 dimensions) data sets properly. As mentioned in [4], the standard K-means is also quite scalable. Its running time is almost linear in the size of the dataset because the iterations needed for convergence are almost independent of the size of the dataset. Moreover, it possesses two other attractive features: (1) it can take advantage of sufficient statistics to speed up its convergence, and (2) it has the capability of handling instances (data points) with different weights. Therefore, K-means is an attractive choice to use in the second clustering step based on the subclusters generated in the first step. Of course, other algorithms that can deal with weighted instances can also be used in the second step.

In our K-means implementation, the initialization step is different to the standard way of initializing cluster centres. Rather than randomly selecting a subset of the data points, a global mean-based initialization as proposed in [12] is implemented, where the cluster centers are initialized as small perturbations to the global mean of the dataset.

After this second step of clustering, the final output of the algorithm is a flat fixed-size list of clusters, instead of Cobweb's hierarchical clustering tree.

2.3 Outlier Handling

Both standard Cobweb and K-means do not explicitly provide approaches to deal with outliers, but such outliers are to be expected in real-world data, and such outliers can have a strong influence on methods that try to minimize squared error. We have therefore added a simple outlier handling method to Scalable Cobweb, which seems to work quite well in practice. Basically, before the second step of the algorithm commences, any subcluster deemed too small is removed from the list of all subclusters. One may argue that some points that are not actually outliers will be removed as well, and that consequently this procedure may degrade the quality of the final clustering. In fact, rejecting such tiny subclusters should only result in small changes to the final cluster structure and thus should not have any major impact on the final clustering quality. Our experiments support that expectation.

2.4 Memory Management

When large datasets are clustered, the size of the tree may become so large that it cannot fit in the available memory. The following four methods can be utilized to reduce the size of the tree:

1. increase the value of the proximity threshold. This will lead to merging of some subclusters in the leaf nodes to form bigger subclusters;
2. discard small subclusters that only contain very few data points. Usually, the data points in such subclusters are noise, ignoring them will not have much impact on the clustering quality;
3. decrease the upper limit of the number of children that each node can have;
4. decrease the limit on the height of the tree.

The last two methods will result in a reduction of the number of nodes in the tree. All four techniques are able to control the size of the tree, and make room for more data points.

3 Experimental Design

The characteristics of the four datasets used in our experiments are depicted in Table 1. There are two synthetic datasets (Elliptic and Gaussian) and two

Table 1. Dataset characteristics

Dataset	#dims	#examples	#clusters
Gaussian	10	100000	5
Elliptic	2	23000	3
Letter	16	20000	26
Waveform	40	5000	3

real-world datasets (Letter and Waveform) from the UCI repository [1]. The Elliptic dataset contains clusters of elliptic shapes in a 2-dimensional space. The Gaussian dataset contains data points generated by a fixed number of Gaussian distributions, each of which is provided with a random weight. For each distribution the mean and variance are sampled from a uniform distribution on [-5,5] and [0.7, 1.5] respectively.

The two synthetic datasets provide a best-case scenario. The clusters in these synthetic datasets are well separated. All datasets are labeled, in other words, the class label that each data point belongs to is known in advance, so that the correct number of clusters is known in advance and so that ordered experiments could be performed by putting data points with the same class labels together. Experiments were also performed where the datasets were randomized before feeding into an algorithm.

Scalable Cobweb (SC) is measured against standard K-means (StdK) and a single scan method proposed by [4] called Simple Scalable K-means (SSK).[1] SSK is a simplification of the Scalable K-means [2] which attempts to avoid the overhead added by the complicated compression techniques involved in Scalable K-means by simply discarding all points in the buffer after being summarized as sufficient statistics.

Simple Scalable K-means takes the following steps:

1. Initialize the k cluster means.
2. Allocate a discard set for each cluster.
3. Absorb a sample from the dataset.
4. Apply extended K-means to the sample and the discard sets.
5. Update the sufficient statistics with corresponding data points.
6. Purge all singleton data points from the memory.
7. Check the stopping criterion, if satisfied, terminate, else go to step 3.

The extended K-means treats every discard set as a set of weighted data points. This algorithm is several times faster than standard K-means on large datasets [4]. Although a only simple compression mechanism is utilized, the clustering quality is quite often competitive with that of standard K-means.

---

[1] Cobweb is not included in this comparison for runtime and memory reasons.

4 Results

The results of running the three methods on the four datasets are contained in Table 2. These results are rather stable exhibiting only standard deviations of less then one percent. The only exception in terms of variance is the SSK algorithm, which shows more variance in general, and especially so for the Gaussian dataset. The numbers reported in Table 2 are averages over ten runs each. K-means on its own, and also when used internally, has always been run ten times as well using different random initial cluster centres, as K-means is known to be sensitive to the initial choice of cluster centres.

In the case of randomly presented data SC and K-means produce identical results on three of the four datasets. K-means shows a slight improvement on the Letter dataset. SSK is worse than SC on the synthetic data, dramatically so on the Elliptic dataset. On the real datasets SK is better on Letter and marginally better on Waveform.

When the data is ordered the performance on the Letter dataset changes, SC is now better than SSK. It is important to consider the random and ordered rows of SC and SSK. It is clear that SC is stable when the conditions for clustering are in the worst case (ordered). SSK is much less stable particularly on the Gaussian data. No row for ordered K-means has been included in Table 2, as the order of presentation of the data points is not an issue for an algorithm that has random access to all data points and can perform multiple passes over all the data.

In another experiment we investigated the influence the size of the tree has on the quality of clustering. Tree size is controlled by both the maximum height of the tree as well as by the maximum number of children each internal node in the tree is allowed to have. In Table 3 we list results for a few different combinations of parameter values for the Letter dataset, as this is the one dataset where we could expect improvement, as the default setting of Scalable Cobweb does not perform as well as standard K-means. It is obvious that some slight gains can be achieved by larger trees, especially for trees with large enough branching factors.

Table 2. SSE (sum of squared error) for randomized and ordered data

Order	Algorithm	Gaussian	Elliptic	Letter	Waveform
random	SC	1062109	194782	661787	227928
random	SSK	1350113	3227560	628110	227598
random	KMeans	1062109	194782	617100	227767
ordered	SC	1062109	194782	676420	228417
ordered	SSK	5142169	3230641	703831	228222

Table 3. SSE for the Letter dataset and different tree sizes

maxHeight	3	3	3	4	5	10	10
maxChildren	3	6	10	4	5	2	3
SSE	661787	657525	649750	654948	640941	666905	672263

Smaller branching factors do not seem to work as well, even for rather deep trees. This may be seen as a sign of overfitting.

Generally, even though larger trees might improve the clustering quality somewhat, a balance between this improvement and the runtime necessary to achieve it will have to be found. In experiments not reported here for lack of space, we found that the runtime of Scalable Cobweb seems to be dominated by the first phase, the tree-building stage, and that this runtime correlates well with the size of the tree. The second phase (the K-means step) can almost be neglected, as it is very fast dealing only with summary statistics held in main memory. Even multiple runs of K-means for avoiding bad initializations do not change that.

5 Related Work

Scalable Cobweb was inspired by BIRCH [14](Balanced Iterative Reducing and Clustering using Hierarchies). BIRCH uses a memory-resident compact representation (clustering feature tree, or CF-tree, with sufficient statistics in its nodes) to facilitate the clustering process of large datasets. BIRCH like Scalable Cobweb comprises a pre-cluster phase and a cluster phase. The pre-clustering phase builds an initial in-memory CF-tree. In the second phase an appropriate clustering algorithm is used to cluster all entries in leaf nodes of the CF-tree. Here each leaf node is treated as a single point with weight corresponding to the number of data points summarized by this leaf. Experiments have shown that BIRCH scales linearly with the number of data points and produces good clustering with a single scan. The quality can be further improved by a few additional scans. However it is sensitive to the order of the data records.

The most significant difference between BIRCH and Scalable Cobweb is the use of different measures to arrange the tree in the pre-cluster phase. BIRCH uses the sums of cluster feature values to dictate tree growth and management. Since BIRCH was inspired by balanced tree-structured indexes like B-trees the tree management is linked to disk page sizes. In effect, the tree growth is determined by a restricted form of sum of squares error. Scalable Cobweb makes use of category utility and tree height and width restrictions to dictate the form of the pre-cluster tree.

6 Conclusions

An improved Cobweb algorithm has been described that uses three scalability extensions to make standard Cobweb scale up to large datasets. Experiments confirm that the clusters produced by Scalable Cobweb in a single scan of the data are of comparable quality to those produced by standard K-means which employs a multiple scan regime. When compared to a rival scalable algorithm SC is better on synthetic data and generally better when the order of the data is pre-determined, where it exhibits stable behaviour.

Data streams present yet another challenge for clustering algorithms. The data source will be as large as described here, or possibly infinite, but the main challenge is in producing algorithms capable of instantaneous clustering so that instances are clustered at the rate they are traveling down the stream. In such circumstances it would be necessary with the current implementation to periodically perform the tandem cluster phases offline. Producing a Scalable Cobweb algorithm for a streaming environment will be a topic for future work.

References

1. C. Blake, E. Keogh, and C. J. Merz. *UCI Repository of Machine Learning Data Bases*. University of California, Department of Information and Computer Science, Irvine, CA, 1998. [http://www.ics.uci.edu/~mlearn/MLRepository.html]
2. P. S. Bradley, U. M. Fayyad, and C. A. Reina. *Scaling clustering algorithms to large databases*. Microsoft Research, Technical Report, MSR-TR-98-37, June 1998.
3. P. S. Bradley, U. M. Fayyad, and C. A. Reina. *Scaling EM(Expectation-Maximization) clustering to large databases*. Microsoft Research, Technical Report, MSR-TR-98-35, Nov. 1998, Revised Oct. 1999.
4. F. Farnstrom, J. Lewis, and C. Elkan. *Scalability for clustering algorithms revisited*. SIGKDD Explorations Newsletter, Vol.2, Issue 1, pp.1-7, Jul. 2000.
5. D. Fisher. *Knowledge acquisition via incremental conceptual clustering*. Machine Learning, Vol.2, Issue 2, pp.139-172, 1987.
6. J. H. Gennari, P. Langley, and D. Fisher. *Models of incremental concept formation*. Artificial Intelligence, 40:11-61, 1990.
7. M. A. Gluck and J. E. Corter. *Information, uncertainty, and the utility of categories*. In Proceedings of the 7th Annual Conference of the Cognitive Science Society, Irvine, CA, 1985.
8. J. Han, M. Kamber, and A. K. H. Tung. *Spatial clustering methods in data mining: A survey*. In Miller, H. and Han, J. (eds.) Geographic Data Mining and Knowledge Discovery, Taylor and Francis, 2001.
9. A. K. Jain, M. N. Murty, and P. J. Flynn. *Data clustering: A review*.
10. E. Kolatch. *Clustering algorithms for spatial databases: A survey*. Dept. of Computer Science, Univ. of Maryland, College Park, Mar. 2001. ACM Computing Surveys, 31(3):264-323, Sep. 1999.
11. R. Ng and J. Han. *Efficient and effective clustering method for spatial data mining*. Proceedings of the 20th Very Large Databases Conference(VLDB'94), Santiago, Chile, pp.144-155, 1994.
12. C. Ordonez. *Clustering binary data streams with k-means*. 8th ACM SIGMOD Workshop on Research Issues in Data Mining and Knowledge Discovery, San Diego, California, June 2003.
13. I. H. Witten and E. Frank. *Data mining: Practical machine learning tools and techniques with java implementations*. Morgan Kaufmann Publishers, San Francisco, California, 2000.
14. T. Zhang, R. Ramakrishnan, and M. Livny. *BIRCH: An efficient data clustering method for very large databases*. In SIGMOD'96, pp. 103-114, 1996.

Cost-Sensitive Decision Trees with Multiple Cost Scales

Zhenxing Qin, Shichao Zhang, and Chengqi Zhang

Faculty of Information Technology, University of Technology, Sydney,
PO Box 123, Broadway, Sydney, NSW 2007, Australia
{zqin, zhangsc, chengqi}@it.uts.edu.au

Abstract. How to minimize misclassification errors has been the main focus of Inductive learning techniques, such as CART and C4.5. However, misclassification error is not the only error in classification problem. Recently, researchers have begun to consider both test and misclassification costs. Previous works assume the test cost and the misclassification cost must be defined on the same cost scale. However, sometimes we may meet difficulty to define the multiple costs on the same cost scale. In this paper, we address the problem by building a cost-sensitive decision tree by involving two kinds of cost scales, that minimizes the one kind of cost and control the other in a given specific budget. Our work will be useful for many diagnostic tasks involving target cost minimization and resource consumption for obtaining missing information.

1 Introduction

Inductive learning techniques have met great success in building models that assign testing cases to classes (Mitchell 1997, Quinlan 1993). How to minimize misclassification errors has been the main focus of Inductive learning techniques, such as CART (Breiman, Friedman, Olshen and Stone 1984) and C4.5 (Quinlan 1993). However, misclassification error is not the only error in classification problem. Numbers of different types of classification errors are listed in (Turney 2000), and the costs of different types of errors are often very different.

More recently, researchers have begun to consider both test and misclassification costs: (Turney 1995, Greiner, Grove and Roth 2002). The objective is to minimize the expected total cost of tests and misclassifications.

Ling, Yang, Wang and Zhang (2004) proposed a new method for building and testing decision trees that minimizes the sum of the misclassification cost and the test cost. It assumes a static cost structure where the cost is not a function of time or cases. It also assumes the test cost and the misclassification cost have been defined on the same cost scale, such as the dollar cost incurred in a medical diagnosis.

But in practice application, Cost may be measured in very different units. Sometimes we may meet difficulty to define the multiple costs on the same cost scale. It is not only a technology issue, but also a social issue. In medical diagnosis, how much money you should assign for a misclassification cost? Sometimes, a misclassification may hurt a patient's life. And from a point of view from social issue, life is invaluable. So we need to involve both of the two cost scales.

On the other hand, a static cost structure may not enough to handle multiple cost scales. In real world, when involving at least two performance metrics, it is not realistic to expect to minimize both of them always. At that time, a trade-off is needed.

For example, a diagnosis cost may include two kinds of costs in monetary units (test fee - dollars) and temporal units (test time - seconds). For each individual user, it may pay more attention to a specific cost scale. A millionaire prefers a minimal diagnosis mistake (it means minimal misclassification cost), and he would like to pay much more money for more detail tests. But someone else can accept a tolerant misclassification cost by controlling the diagnosis fee in a specific budget (such as the insurance cover limit).

In this paper, we address the problems above by building a cost-sensitive decision tree by involving two kinds of cost scales, which minimizes the one kind of cost and control the other in a given specific budget.

The rest of the paper is organized as follows. In Section 2, we first review the related works. In section 3, we simply introduce the tree-building algorithm based on single cost scale, and discuss the new issues and properties as involving resource control on decision tree. After that, we consider several testing strategies and analyze their relative merits in section 4. Finally, we present our experimental results in section 5 and conclude the work with a discussion of future work in Section 6.

2 Previous Works

More recently, researchers have begun to consider both test and misclassification costs: (Turney 1995, Greiner, Grove and Roth 2002). The objective is to minimize the expected total cost of tests and misclassifications. In Turney's survey article (Turney 2000), a whole variety of costs in machine learning are analyzed, the first two types of costs are the misclassification costs that are the costs incurred by misclassification errors and test costs these are the costs incurred for obtaining attribute values.

In (Zubek, Dietterich, 2002), the cost-sensitive learning problem is cast as a Markov Decision Process (MDP), and an optimal solution is given as a search in a state space for optimal policies. For a given new case, depending on the values obtained so far, the optimal policy can suggest a best action to perform in order to both minimize the misclassification and the test costs.

Similar in the interest in constructing an optimal learner, Greiner, Grove and Roth (2002) studied the theoretical aspects of active learning with test costs using a PAC learning framework. Turney (1995) presented a system called ICET, which uses a genetic algorithm to build a decision tree to minimize the cost of tests and misclassification.

Ling, Yang, Wang and Zhang (2004) proposed a new method for building and testing decision trees that minimizes the sum of the misclassification cost and the test cost. We simply introduce It assumes a static cost structure where the cost is not a function of time or cases. It also assumes the test cost and the misclassification cost have been defined on the same cost scale, such as the dollar cost incurred in a medical diagnosis. We will simply introduce the tree building based on single cost scale as following:

To minimize the total target cost, at each leaf, the algorithm labels the leaf as either positive or negative (in a binary decision case) by minimizing the target misclassification cost. Let us look at a concrete example in (Ling, Yang, Wang and Zhang 2004). Assume that during the tree building process, there is a set of P and N positive and negative examples respectively to be further classified by possibly building a sub-tree. If we assume that $P \times FN > N \times FP$, then if no sub-tree is built, the set would be labeled as positive, and thus, the total target misclassification cost is

$$T = N \times FP$$

Suppose that an attribute A with a test cost C1 is considered for a potential splitting attribute. Assume that A has two values, and there are $P1$ and $N1$ positive and negative examples with the first value, $P2$ and $N2$ positive and negative examples with the second value, and $P0$ and $N0$ positive and negative examples with A's value unknown. Then the total test cost would be

$$(P1+N1+P2+N2) \times C1$$

(i.e., cases with unknown attribute values do not incur test costs). Assume that the first branch will be labeled as positive (as $P1 \times FN1 > N1 \times FP1$), and the second branch will be labeled as negative, then the total misclassification cost of the two branches would be

$$N1 \times FP1 + P2 \times FN1$$

As we have discussed earlier in this section, examples with the unknown value of A stay with the attribute A, and we have assumed that the original set of examples is labeled as positive. Thus, the misclassification cost of the unknowns is $N0 \times FP$. The total cost of choosing A as a splitting attribute would be:

$$T_A = (P1+N1+P2+N2) \times C1 + N1 \times FP1 + P2 \times FN1 + N0 \times FP1$$

If $T_A < T$, where $T = N \times FP1$, then splitting on A would reduce the total cost of the original set, and we will choose such an attribute with the minimal total cost as a splitting attribute. We will then apply this process recursively on examples falling into branches of this attribute. If $T_A \geq T$ for all remaining attributes, then no further sub-tree will be built, and the set would become a leaf, with a positive label. Table 1 is a concrete example Ecoli dataset and figure 1 is the corresponding decision tree.

Table 1. Test and misclassification costs set for Ecoli dataset

A1	A2	A3	A4	A5	A6	FP/FN
50	50	50	50	50	20	800/800

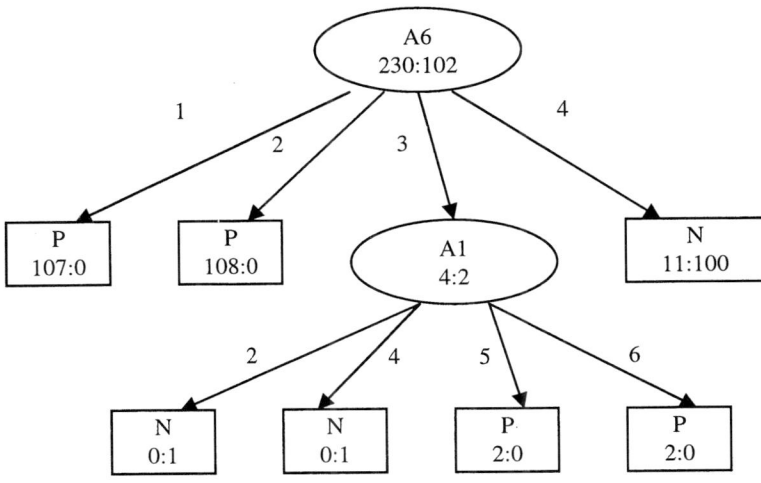

Fig. 1. A decision tree built from the Ecoli dataset (costs are set as in Table 2)

3 Building Decision Tree with Minimal Costs Under Resource Constrains

The goal of our decision-tree learning algorithm is to minimize the sum of target cost on misclassification and test, at the same time, resource cost must less than the resource budget.

We assume test and the misclassification cost contain two kinds of cost – target and resource. Both of the target and resource have been defined on two different cost scales relatively, such as dollar cost and time cost incurred in a medical diagnosis. We assume there is a maximum limit on resource, called resource budget.

Table 2 shows a sample of two cost scales on "Ecoli" dataset. From table 2, we can see that, there are two kinds of costs, cost1 is the target cost, and cost2 is the resource consumption. For example, FP1 = 800 is the target misclassification cost and FP2 = 150 is the resource misclassification cost of false positive.

Table 2. Test and misclassification costs set for "Ecoli" dataset

	FP	FN	A1	A2	A3	A4	A5	A6
Target	800	800	50	60	60	50	50	30
Resource	150	100	10	20	10	10	10	10

3.1 Tree Building Based on Target-First Strategy

There are at least two strategies can be used to involving resource cost in the cost-sensitive decision tree building. The first one is called target-first strategy. It comes from the point of view social issue: target cost is invaluable. It exactly ignore the resource issue and attempts to minimize the total target cost on misclassification and test cost, so we will follow the same building procedure like (Ling, Yang, Wang and Zhang 2004). Exactly the tree-building algorithm is a special case of our target-first strategy when we set all the resource consumption as zero.

As the tree totally ignore resource cost in tree building phase. It means we may pay 100 resource cost to decrease 110 target cost rather than paying 50 resource cost to decrease 100 target. It considers the resource at testing phase. Given a test example, we explore the tree and perform all need test. Once resource budget is exhausted, we stop performing any test and give a result.

3.2 Tree Building Based on Performance-First Strategy

This strategy is exactly the idea of trade-off between target and resource. It uses the target gain ratio to choose potential splitting attributes. Follow the example above, the total target cost of choosing A as a splitting attribute is:

$$T_A = (P1+N1+P2+N2) \times C1 + N1 \times FP1 + P2 \times FN1 + N0 \times FP1$$

We also can calculate the resource consumption of A is

$$C_A = (P1+N1+P2+N2) \times C2 + N1 \times FP2 + P2 \times FN2 + N0 \times FP2$$

If $T_A < T$, where $T = N \times FP1$, then the target cost gain is $T - T_A$, the gain ratio of choosing A as a splitting attribute is

$$R_A = (T - T_A)/C_A$$

Since performance-first strategy involves resource cost during decision tree building, so it is expected to explore deeper along the tree with limited resource. At the same time, we may not have enough resource to perform a test during exploring the tree in testing phase. It means we may stop at an internal node and give a result at once. So the potential result of this internal node should be reserved.

Definition 1: For a internal decision tree node, *potential label* is its class label if the node is labeled as a leaf, and relative target and resource misclassification cost is called *potential leaf cost*.

In testing phase, it uses the similar exploring method as in target-first strategy. Since it involves resource cost during tree building, so test with highest target/resource performance will be perform fist. It is to explore deeper along the tree with limited resource. An example of target-resource cost decision tree is shown as in Figure 2. It is extended from the single scale tree in figure 1.

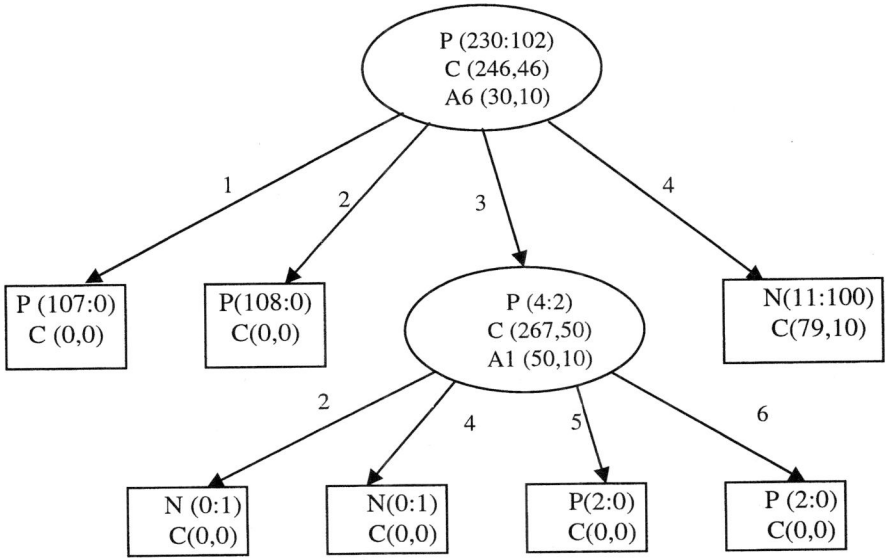

Fig. 2. A decision tree built from the Ecoli dataset (costs are set as in Table 2)

From the Figure 2, we can see that, in each leaf node, we record the class label P or N to represent positive and negative, and the training example data distribution, such as (107,0) at the left child of root node means there is 107 positive and 0 negative examples, finally C(0,0) means 0 target minimal cost and 0 resource cost. In each internal node, we also record the *potential label* with training example distribution and relative cost consumption, such as P (230:102) in root node, and the splitting attribute with test costs, such as A6 (30,10) in root node.

3.3 Resource Control Issues

At the same time of to minimizing the total target cost, we must control the resource consumption less then the specific budget, noted by B. Once resource is exhausted, we will stop exploring further sub-tree and output a leaf according to the target cost. The first issue is how to deal with the cases just going though the threshold B? Firstly, we introduce two concepts first: *confirmed node* and *proposed node*.

Definition 2: Given a test example S and a resource budget B, exploring the decision tree from root node, when we reach an internal node N with the total resource consumption $R(N) \leq B$, attribute value in node N is known but no more resource performing test for the value, then node N is called *proposed node*, and the parent of *N is called confirmed node.*

We stop exploring the decision tree once resource budget can not support further explore, and give users a result based on *confirmed node* and *proposed node*. The former tells users current best decision with resource B, the later tells users the resource needed for further test.

The second issue, how we get minimal target cost with limited resource budget? It exactly comes from single scale tree. Originally, decision tree was built to minimize the misclassification cost based on the statistics information of splitting attributes. Exploring further branches means smaller subset and better class prediction. But further exploring means more tests, also mean more test cost, so minimizing the sum of target cost is also a trade-off problem. We expect our performance-first strategy can provide a best overall performance since the test with best performance was chosen in each branch of decision tree.

4 Performing Tests on Testing Examples with Resource Control

In this section, we discuss some new issues in testing strategies as involving the resource controlling on the cost-minimal decision tree. Our aim is to predict the class of the testing examples with many missing values with the minimal total target cost, and control resource cost in a specific budget. We also use the same test case in (Ling, Yang, Wang and Zhang 2004) to illustrate our test strategies.

Table 3. An example testing case with several unknown values. The true values are in parenthesis and can be obtained by performing the tests (with costs list in Table 2)

A1	A2	A3	A4	A5	A6	Class
?(6)	2	?(1)	2	2	?(3)	P

Cost-minimal decision tree in (Ling, Yang, Wang and Zhang 2004) shows an amazing performance in dealing with testing examples with many missing values. And in order to predict the class of the testing examples with the minimal total cost for this case, four testing strategies were studied. We will briefly introduce them as following, noted as M1 to M4. When meet an unknown value in test example:

The strategy M1, called Optimal Sequential Test (OST), performs extra tests on the unknown values. It uses the tree built with the minimal cost to decide what tests must be performed in sequence.

The strategy M2 stops right there, and uses the ratio of positive and negative examples in that (internal) node to predict the testing example (recall that these ratios are calculated based on training cases which also have unknown values at this node).

The third strategy M3 uses the C4.5's strategy in dealing with missing values by choosing a value according the probabilities of the attribute's all values. Instead of stopping at the node whose attributes value is unknown in the testing case, this strategy will "split" the testing case into fractions according to the training examples, and go down all branches simultaneously.

The fourth and final strategy M4 ignores the attributes with unknown values and uses rest attributes to build a new tree for the test sample.

We can see that M1 performs extra tests for unknown values. So M1 strategy is only for the case with enough resource. Once resource is exhausted, we can choose one of other three strategies to give a result. Strategies M2 & M3 avoid performing tests and predict the testing example with statistics information in nodes. M4 ignores the attributes with unknown values and building a new tree, but it still need to consider the resource consumption as in the original tree. All those three strategies have not any test costs but they may meet the problem of no enough resource as reaching leaf node.

For instance, we test the example of table 3 in decision tree in Figure 2. Assuming we got resource budget B= 10, so we can perform the test in root node, got A6 = 3. Then the example goes down to the 3rd branch of root node, additional resource cost 10 is needed but no enough resource to perform a test for the attribute A1. What should we do now? First, the node is marked as proposed node (proposed to be labeled as Negative with shortage of resource 10). Then we go back to its parent node (root node here) and output it as confirmed node with class label P. We will conduct experiments to compare the three tree building strategies in next section.

5 Experiments

We conducted experiments on five real-world datasets (Ling, Yang, Wang and Zhang 2004, Blake and Merz 1998) and compared the target-first and performance-first tree building strategies against C4.5. These datasets are chosen because they have at least some discrete attributes, binary class, and a good number of examples. The numerical attributes in datasets are discretized first using minimal entropy method (Fayyad and Irani 1993) as our algorithm can currently only deal with discrete attributes. The datasets are listed in Table 4.

Table 4. Datasets used in the experiments

	No. of attributes	No. of examples	Class distribution (P/N)
Ecoli	6	332	230/102
Breast	9	683	444/239
Heart	8	161	98/163
Thyroid	24	2000	1762/238
Austrilia	15	653	296/357

First, we compare the target cost and resource consumption of target-first and performance-first tree building strategies against C4.5 with OST (we assume our resource budget can only support 50 percent of all tests) on all five dataset. The results of target cost and resource consumption are shown as in figure 3 and 4 relatively.

From Figure 3, we can see that performance-first tree strategy outperform the other two in target cost. It means performance-first strategy got a better overall performance with limit resource budget. And in Figure 4, we can see that performance-first strategy also consumes less resource than other two strategies. It means performance-first strategy got a better overall performance, which can get a lower target cost with less resource consumption.

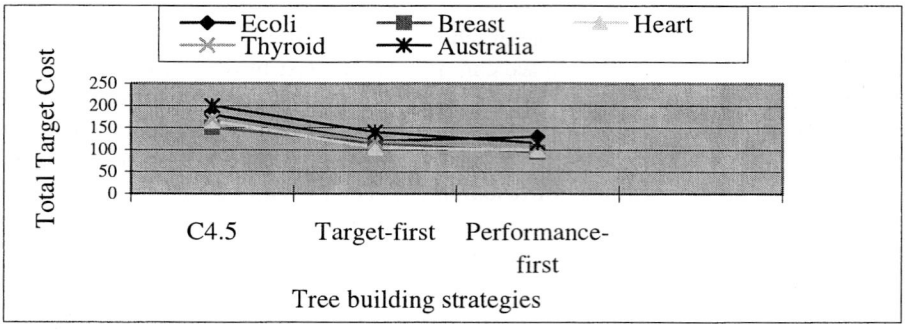

Fig. 3. Comparing of total target cost of three tree building strategies on different datasets

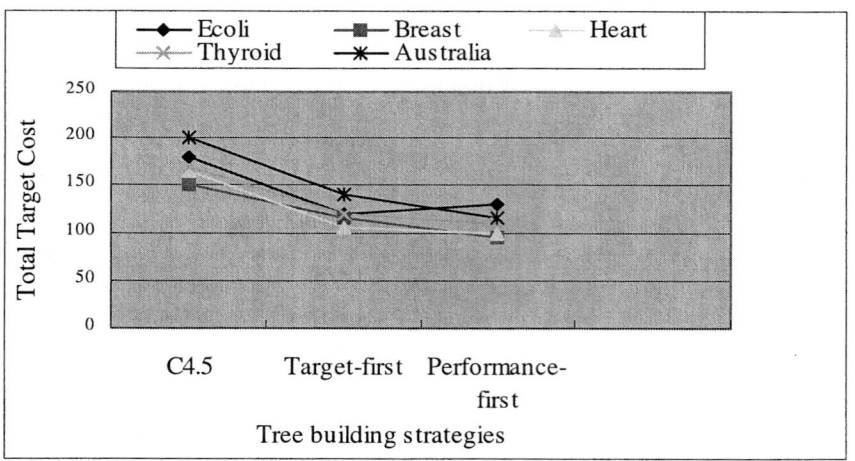

Fig. 4. Comparing of total resource of three tree building strategies on different datasets

To compare the influence of resource budget on three strategies, we conducted an experiment on all the datasets with varying budget B to support a part of all needed tests from 20 to 100 percent. For the more completely usage of resource, we use OST testing strategy first, once the cost is exhaust we use M2 testing strategy to give a result. The result is shown in figure 5. From figure 5, we can see that all target cost will go down as the test examples can explore further branches, then lower total cost are obtained. The performance-first strategy also outperforms the other two in target cost with same resource consumption.

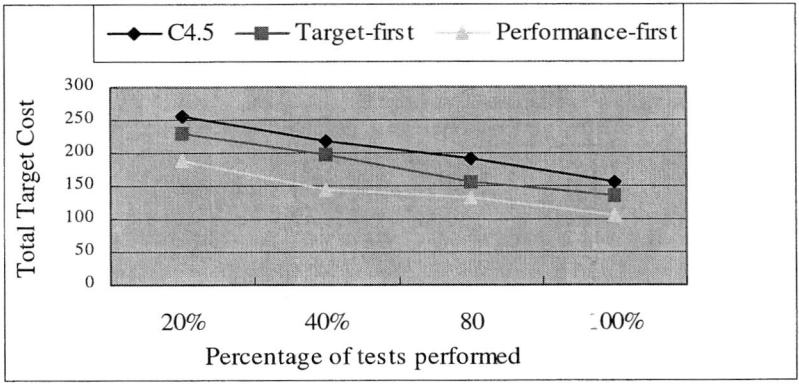

Fig. 5. Comparing of total target cost of three tree building strategies on percentage of tests performed under resource Budget

6 Conclusions and Future Work

In this paper, we presented a simple and novel method to overcome difficulty to define the multiple costs on the same cost scale in building decision trees that minimize the sum of the misclassification cost and the test cost. Our method involves two kinds of cost scales, and minimizes the one kind of cost as control the other one in a given budget. We proposed a new performance-based splitting criterion for attribute selection, and discussed several intelligent testing strategies in single cost scales as involving resource control. Our experiments show that our new decision-tree-building algorithm with performance-based splitting criterion dramatically outperforms the target-first tree building which simply add a resource control on single scales tree. In addition, compared to other related works, our algorithm has a lower cost consumption on most of testing strategies, and is thus more robust and practical.

In the future, we plan to consider how to minimize the total target cost with partial cost-resource exchanging. In some situations, such as medical diagnosis, this scenario is more practical since lot of hospitals provide VIP services. We also want to extend our Optimal Sequential Test to Optimal Batch Test, Also pruning can be introduced in our tree-building algorithm to avoid over-fitting of the data.

References

[1] Charles Ling, Qiang Yang, Jianning Wang and Shichao Zhang (2004), Decision Trees with Minimal Costs. In: *Proceedings of 21st International Conference on Machine Learning*, Banff, Alberta, Canada, July 4-8, 2004.
[2] Turney, P. D. (2000), Types of cost in inductive concept learning, *Workshop on Cost-Sensitive Learning at the Seventeenth International Conference on Machine Learning*, Stanford University, California.
[3] Blake, C. L., and Merz, C. J. (1998), *UCI Repository of machine learning databases* (See [http://www.ics.uci.edu/~mlearn/MLRepository.html]). Irvine, CA: University of California, Department of Information and Computer Science.
[4] Turney, P. D. (1995), Cost-sensitive classication: Empirical evaluation of a hybrid genetic decision tree induction algorithm. *Journal of Articial Intelligence Research*, 2: 369-409, 1995.
[5] Mitchell, T.M. (1997), *Machine Learning*. McGraw Hills
[6] Zubek, V. B., Dietterich, T. G. (2002), Pruning Improves Heuristic Search for Cost-Sensitive Learning. In *Proceedings of the Nineteenth International Conference on Machine Learning*. pp. 27-34, Sydney, Australia.
[7] Greiner, R., Grove, A. J., and Roth D. (2002), Learning cost-sensitive active classiers. Articial Intelligence, 139(2): 137-174, 2002.
[8] Quinlan, J. R. (1993), *C4.5: Programs for Machine Learning*. Morgan Kaufmann, San Mateo, California, 1993.
[9] Breiman, L., Friedman, J. H., Olshen, R. A., and Stone, C. J. (1984), *Classification and Regression Trees*. Wadsworth, Monterey, California, 1984.

Effective Sampling for Mining Association Rules

Yanrong Li and Raj P. Gopalan

Department of Computing, Curtin University of Technology,
Kent street, Bentley, Western Australia 6102
{liyl, raj}@computing.edu.au

Abstract. As discovering association rules in a very large database is time consuming, researchers have developed many algorithms to improve the efficiency. Sampling can significantly reduce the cost of mining, since the mining algorithms need to deal with only a small dataset compared to the original database. Especially, if data comes as a stream flowing at a faster rate than can be processed, sampling seems to be the only choice. How to sample the data and how big the sample size should be for a given error bound and confidence level are key issues for particular data mining tasks. In this paper, we derive the sufficient sample size based on central limit theorem for sampling large datasets with replacement. This approach requires smaller sample size than that based on the Chernoff bounds and is effective for association rules mining. The effectiveness of the method has been evaluated on both dense and sparse datasets.

1 Introduction

Algorithms and techniques for mining association rules in a static large database has been actively studied for more than 10 years since the concept of association rules was first introduced in 1993 by Agrawal et al [1]. However, mining a very large database for association rules is usually time consuming. Sampling is one of the approaches to improve the efficiency of mining. Random sampling of large databases for association rules was first proposed in [2] and more studies followed in [3-7].

Theoretical analyses of sampling large databases for association rules based on binomial distribution and Chernoff bounds were presented in [2, 3]. Sampling was performed with replacement and the sample size was a function of the desired error bound and confidence level. The frequent itemsets found in the sample were verified with the rest of the database. Therefore, the results were not approximations based on the samples. Using only samples to discover the association rules in databases was experimentally evaluated in [4] for sparse databases. Since sample size was empirically chosen as a certain percentage of the original database which is independent of the error bound and confidence level, it is difficult to quantify the quality of the results for a given sample size. A two-phase sampling based algorithm for association rules was presented in [5]. A large initial sample was collected in Phase I to estimate the support of each distinct item in the database and these supports were used in phase II to select representative transactions in the initial sample to form a small final sample that more accurately reflected the itemset supports in the entire database. However, the question remains as to how to determine the initial sample size to ensure its subset, i.e. the small final sample, can effectively discover frequent itemsets. In contrast to [5], a progressive sampling method proposed in [7] starts with a small sample size and progressively increases the sample size until the similarity metric is above a user-specified threshold. Zhang et al [6] sampled large databases without replacement and determined the sample size based on central limit theorem. However the detailed theoretical analysis of errors and the evaluations of effectiveness were not performed.

While the main purpose of sampling a static large disk resident database is to reduce the amount of data to be mined, sampling seems to be the only choice for processing a data stream where data flows faster than it can be processed [8]. Motivated by sampling data streams for mining association rules, we investigate effective sampling methods that not only require small sample sizes but also provide approximation guarantees.

In this paper, we sample the datasets by replacement and derive the sufficient sample size using binomial distribution and central limit theorem (CLT) via different approaches from that of [6]. We theoretically analyze the accuracy of our sampling approach and evaluate its effectiveness on both dense and sparse datasets. We also look at the ways to reduce the number of false frequent itemsets and the number of missed frequent itemsets.

The rest of this paper is organized as follows: Section 2 provides the definitions of association rules. The theoretical analysis of random sampling for association rules is presented in section 3 and the experimental evaluation shown in Section 4. Section 5 discusses the methods to reduce errors and Section 6 contains the conclusion.

2 Association Rules

We give the basic terms needed for describing association rules using the formalism of [1].

Let $I = \{I_1, I_2, ..., I_m\}$ be a set of m distinct items. A transaction T is a non-empty subset of I identified by a *TID* ($T \subseteq I$). A database D is a set of N transactions. A set of items is called an itemset, and an itemset with k items is called a k-itemset. The support p of an itemset X in D, is the proportion of the database that contains X, and $p = y/N$, where y is the number of occurrences of X in D. An itemset is called a *frequent itemset* if its support $p \geq p_t$, where p_t is the *support threshold* specified by users. Otherwise, the itemset is *not frequent*. An association rule is an expression of the form $X \Rightarrow Y$, where non-empty itemsets $X \subseteq I$, $Y \subseteq I$ and $X \cap Y = \phi$. The confidence of the rule is the proportion of transactions that contain both X and Y to those that contain X, i.e., the conditional probability that transactions contain the itemset Y given that they contain the itemset X. An association rule with the *confidence* $\geq$ *confidence threshold* specified by the user is considered as a valid association rule.

Mining association rules can be broken into two steps. All frequent itemsets, also called the *complete frequent itemsets* (CFI) is discovered in the first step and the rules based on the CFI are found in the second step. In this paper, we will look at the problem of sampling for mining CFI.

Many algorithms for mining association rules have been proposed in the literature. We use Apriori [9] for sparse datasets and CTMINE [10] for dense datasets to get the frequent itemsets. Our study is focused on the effectiveness of sampling, and as such independent of the mining algorithms.

3 Sampling Large Databases for Association Rules

In the context of sampling large databases for association rules, a transaction database D of size N is the population that we want to study, and a sample is a subset of D that consists of n transactions selected from the population D. Next, we describe the sampling method we use, derive the sufficient sample size for the sampling method and analyze the accuracy of itemsets' supports computed from a random sample.

3.1 Random Sampling Database with Replacement

There are two kinds of random sampling methods, random sampling with replacement and random sampling without replacement [11]. Random sampling without replacement obtains a sample of size n by selecting n units from the population and at each step every unit in the population not already selected has an equal chance of being selected. Sampling with replacement obtains n units independently and at each step every unit in the population has an equal chance of inclusion in the sample.

We sample D with replacement so that the process of selecting n transactions out of N transactions has all the properties of a Bernoulli process:

- There are n trials;
- There are only two complementary outcomes for each trial, an itemset appears or does not appear in a transaction.
- The probability p of an itemset appearing remains the same from trial to trial. Let q denote the probability that an itemset does not appear in a trial, then $q = 1-p$.
- Each trial is independent. The probability of a transaction being selected in a trial is independent of which transaction has been selected in the previous trials.

The number of times X that an itemset appears in n Bernoulli trials (i.e. the number of times X an itemset appears in a sample), is a binomial random variable and the probability distribution of this discrete random variable follows the binomial distribution[12].

If we denote outcomes of the ith trial as $X_i = ($ $i = 1, 2, \ldots, n)$, where $X_i = 1$ if an itemset appears, and $X_i = 0$ if an itemset does not appear, then the number of appearances of an itemset in the sample is

$$X = \sum_{i=1}^{n} X_i$$

Therefore, $P_s = X/n$, the support of an itemset in the sample, is the sample mean. P_s is an unbiased estimator of p[12].

3.2 Determining the Sufficient Sample Size

According to the central limit theorem (CLT), when the sample size is large, P_s is approximately normally distributed with mean $\mu = p$ and variance $\sigma^2 = pq/n$ [12]. The normal distribution of P_s can be transformed to standard normal distribution of standard random variable

$$Z = (P_s - \mu)/\sigma = (P_s - p)/\sqrt{pq/n}. \tag{1}$$

Therefore we can assert that the probability that Z lies in $[-z_{\alpha/2}, z_{\alpha/2}]$ is $1-\alpha$:

$$\Pr(-z_{\alpha/2} < Z < z_{\alpha/2}) = 1 - \alpha, \tag{2}$$

where $z_{\alpha/2}$ is the Z value above which the area under the standard normal curve is $\alpha/2$. $1-\alpha$ is called *confidence coefficient* in [12] and we call it *confidence level* in our paper since it represents the degree of confidence that Z lies in $[-z_{\alpha/2}, z_{\alpha/2}]$. We can derive the following equation from (1) and (2):

$$\Pr(P_s - z_{\alpha/2}\sqrt{pq/n} < p < P_s + z_{\alpha/2}\sqrt{pq/n}) = 1 - \alpha. \tag{3}$$

Because the normal curve is symmetric, (3) can be decomposed into

$$\Pr(p > P_s + z_{\alpha/2}\sqrt{pq/n}) = \alpha/2 \tag{4}$$

and

$$\Pr(p < P_s - z_{\alpha/2}\sqrt{pq/n}) = \alpha/2. \tag{5}$$

Let's denote the differences between the estimated support of an itemset in a sample RD and its support in the original database D as $\Delta p = |P_s - p|$, then (3) can be rewritten as

$$\Pr(\Delta p < z_{\alpha/2}\sqrt{pq/n}) = 1 - \alpha. \tag{6}$$

Given an error bound e and the confidence level $1-\alpha$ we must choose sample size n such that

$$\Delta p < z_{\alpha/2}\sqrt{pq/n} \le e. \tag{7}$$

Thus we have

$$n \ge z_{\alpha/2}^2 pq/e^2. \tag{8}$$

For an itemset with support p, (8) will give the sufficient sample size that can estimate p with $1-\alpha$ confidence that an error will not exceed e. Since pq has the maximum value of $1/4$ when $p = q = 1/2$, if we choose

$$n \ge \frac{z_{\alpha/2}^2}{4e^2}, \tag{9}$$

we will be at least $1-\alpha$ confident that Δp will not exceed e.

For a given error bound and confidence level, the sample size calculated using (9) which is based on central limit theorem, is much smaller than that based on Chernoff bounds [2, 3]. Table 1 provides some comparisons.

3.3 Accuracy of Sampling

Theorem 1. Given an itemset X whose support is p in D, a confidence level $1-\alpha$, and a random sample RD of size

$$n \geq \frac{z_{\alpha/2}^2}{4e^2},$$

the probability that Δp exceed e is at most α.

Proof.

$$\Pr(\Delta p > e) = \Pr(\Delta p > z_{\alpha/2}\sqrt{1/(4n)})$$
$$\leq \Pr(\Delta p > z_{\alpha/2}\sqrt{pq/n})$$
$$\leq 1 - \Pr(\Delta p < z_{\alpha/2}\sqrt{pq/n})$$
$$\leq \alpha \text{ (apply equation (6))}$$

Table 1. Sufficient sample size

E	α	Chernoff Bounds	CLT
0.01	0.01	26492	16513
0.005	0.01	105966	66049
0.01	0.05	18445	9604
0.005	0.05	73778	38416

Table 2. Database summaries

Dataset Name	N	|R|	T
T10I4D100k	100000	870	10
BMSPOS	515597	1657	7.5
Connect4	67557	129	43

4 Effectiveness of Sampling

The sampling algorithm we use is the same as in [6] except that the random number generated is not unique in order to perform sampling with replacement. We experimentally study the effectiveness of our sampling method on both dense and sparse datasets. The datasets used in the experiment, the measurement of errors, and the experimental results are described below.

4.1 Datasets Studied

We performed experiments on both dense and sparse datasets. The datasets used include: (1) a synthetic sparse dataset, T10I4D100K, generated by the synthetic data generator provided by the QUEST project[13] to simulate market basket data; (2) a sparse real dataset BMSPOS, provided by Blue Martini Software, which contains point-of-sale data from an electronics retailer with the item-ids corresponding to product categories; (3) a dense dataset Connect4 which is gathered from game state information and are available from the UCI Machine Learning Repository[14]. These datasets are benchmarked at FIMI (Frequent Itemsets Mining Implementations Repository)[15]. Table 2 summarizes their characteristics, where N is the number of transactions in a dataset, T is the average transaction length and |R| is the number of distinct items in the dataset.

4.2 Measurement of Errors

We will check errors in the estimation of itemset support and the errors in the estimation of CFI.

We evaluate the errors in itemset support estimation as follows. We take s samples of size n from D, and for each item in D, we count the number of times x that $\Delta p > e$ in s samples and calculate the experimental probability of f that $\Delta p > e, f = x/s$.

The complete frequent itemsets present in D and a sample are denoted as FIo and FIs, respectively. If an itemset exists in FIo but not in FIs, then we call this itemset a *false negative*. If an itemset exists in FIs but not FIo, then we call the itemset a *false positive*. The collection of all the false positives is denoted by Fp and the collection of all the false negatives is denoted by Fn. We measure the errors by

$$fp = |Fp|/|FIs|$$

which represents the proportion of the false frequent itemsets in a sample, and

$$fn = |Fn|/|FIo|$$

which represent the proportion of the frequent itemsets that are missing in a sample.

A set of frequent itemsets FI can be partitioned into ml subsets according to the size of each subset.

$$FI = \bigcup_{l=1}^{ml} FI_l,$$

where FI_l is a set of itemsets with size of l and ml is the size of the longest itemset. We will check the errors in CFI estimation and the errors in each partition of CFI as well.

4.3 Experimental Results

First, we check whether the errors in estimation of itemsets' supports are within the given error bound. According to **Theorem 1**, for a given confidence level $1-\alpha = 0.95$ and a random sample RD of size 9604, the probability that Δp exceed $e = 0.01$ is at most 5%. Following the procedures described in Section 4.2, we perform tests on three datasets to see if the claim holds for our sampling approach. We take 100 samples of size 9604 from each of the datasets to obtain the frequency distribution of f for 1-itemsets in them. The results are given in Table 3. There is only one item in Connect4 with 7% probability that $\Delta p > e$. For each item in the BMSPOS, the probability that $\Delta p > e$ is less than 2% while in T10I4D100K it is 0. The results show that our sampling approach can provide the expected approximation guarantees.

Table 3. Frequency distribution of f in each dataset

	$f(\%)$	0	1	2	3	4	5	6	7
	Connect4(129 items)	106	8	9	1	0	4	0	1
Frequency	BMSPOS(1657 items)	1654	2	1					
	T10I4D100K(870items)	870							

Next, we will check the errors in frequent itemsets estimation. Since different samples may result in different error rates, we take the average outcomes of 50 samples to evaluate the errors. We choose error bound $e = 0.01$ and confidence level $1-\alpha = 0.99$ in our experiments to evaluate the effectiveness of our sampling approach. The sufficient sample size is 16513 for these two figures. We also show for comparison, the experimental results for error bound $e = 0.01$ and confidence level $1-\alpha = 0.95$, which result in a sample size of 9604. Support thresholds are chosen in such a manner that at least frequent itemsets of size 4 can be produced. The following analyses of the experimental results are performed on the samples of size 16513 if the sample size is not explicitly stated.

Figure 1 shows the errors (*fp* and *fn*) for different support thresholds in each dataset. In the figure, the number following *fp* or *fn* is the sample size. It can be seen that the errors fluctuate as the support threshold changes. For Connect4, the errors increase as the support threshold increases while for the other datasets the errors decrease as the support threshold increases. The errors for dense datasets are small for every support threshold computed and the changes of the error are relatively small compared with the changes of support threshold. For example, for Connect4, *fp* and *fn* are 2.6% and 3.4%, respectively when support threshold is 80%, and they change to 4.6% and 4.7%, respectively when the support threshold increases to 95%. For the sparse datasets, the errors are relatively large and so are the changes in errors compared with the changes in support threshold. For instance, in BMSPOS, when the support threshold increases from 0.5% to 1%, the *fp* decreases from 9.3% to 5.4% and *fn* decreases from 8.4% to 6.5%. For all the datasets and all the computed support thresholds, at least 85% of *FIo* is discovered by sampling. It confirms that our sampling approach is effective.

We take a closer look at errors in *FIs* by inspecting each partition $FI_l(l = 1, 2, ..., ml)$ and the results are shown in Figure 2. The errors for frequent 1-itemsets are always small for both dense and sparse datasets. It also reveals that within the overall errors in *FIs*, the errors for each partition may vary dramatically and are not predictable.

The causes of errors *fp* and *fn* in frequent itemsets estimation not only depends on the errors in support estimations of itemsets, but also on two other factors:

(1) The propagation error. If an itemset is missed, then its super sets will be missed; if an itemset is mistaken as a frequent itemset, then its super sets may be mistaken as frequent as well. This is because the association rules mining algorithms apply the apriori principle: if an itemset is frequent, then all its subsets must be frequent. For example, for a sample of Connect4, when $p_t = 95\%$, itemset {109, 121} is

missed in the sample, and its super sets {109, 121, 124}, {109, 121, 127} and {109, 121, 124, 127} are missed, too; Itemset {19 72, 88, 124} is mistaken as frequent itemset, its super sets {19 72, 75, 88, 124} and {19 72, 75, 88, 124, 127} are mistaken as frequent itemsets as well.

(2) The proportion of frequent itemsets whose support is close to p_t. The larger the proportion of the itemsets whose support is close to the specified support threshold p_t, the more likely bigger errors will occur. According to the previous analysis, those itemsets with support $p_t - e < p < p_t + e$ are likely to be missed or mistaken as a frequent itemsets. In Connect4, among those items with support greater than 89%, 13% of them have supports within (89%, 91%); and among those items with supports greater than 84%, only 4% of them have supports within (84%, 86%). Consequently, when $e = 1\%$, 2.27% percentage of the frequent 1-itemsets in the sample is false positives for $p_t = 90\%$ while no false positives presented for $p_t = 85\%$. In both cases, none of the frequent 1-itemsets is missed.

The experimental results also show that both *fp* and *fn* for the samples of size 9604 are bigger than that for the samples of size 16513. This is a tradeoff between sample size (hence efficiency) and the confidence level.

5 Reducing Errors

In this section, we explore the possibility of reducing errors in frequent itemset estimations.

Theorem 2. Given a frequent itemset X in D with $p > p_t$, a random sample RD, and a confidence level $1 - \alpha$, the probability that X is a false negative in RD is at most $\alpha/2$ when the support threshold is lowered to

$$p_{tl} = p_t - z_{\alpha/2}\sqrt{1/(4n)} \tag{8}$$

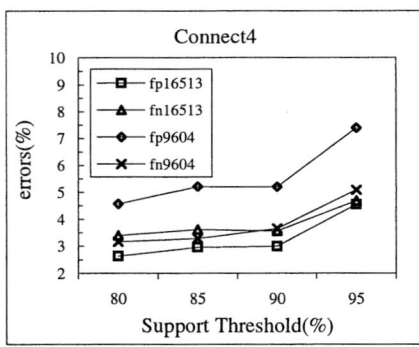
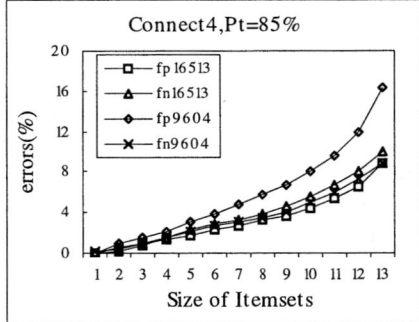

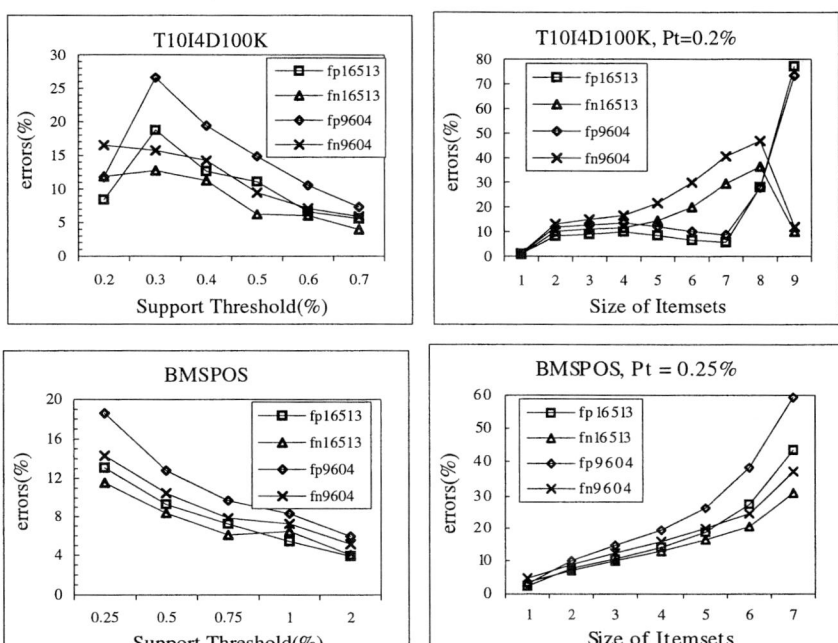

Fig. 1. Errors for different support thresholds   **Fig. 2.** Errors in each partition of *FIs*

Proof. When the support threshold is lowered to p_{tl}, the probability that an itemset X is a false negative in RD equals the probability that the estimated support P_s of X is smaller than p_{tl}.

$$\Pr(P_s < p_{tl}) = \Pr(P_s < p_t - z_{\alpha/2}\sqrt{1/(4n)})$$
$$\leq \Pr(P_s < p - z_{\alpha/2}\sqrt{pq/n})$$
$$\leq \alpha/2 \text{ (apply equation (4))}$$

For $p > p_t \geq 50\%$, $p_t q_t \geq pq$, lowering the support threshold to

$$p_{tl} = p_t - z_{\alpha/2}\sqrt{p_t q_t / n} \tag{9}$$

will give the same confidence level but smaller amount by which the threshold is to be lowered. As a result, less false positives maybe present in the frequent itemsets.

Theorem 3. Given an itemset X with $p < p_t$ in D, a random sample RD, a confidence level $1-\alpha$, the probability that X is a false positive in RD is at most $\alpha/2$ when the support threshold is increased to

$$p_{tu} = p_t + z_{\alpha/2}\sqrt{1/(4n)} \tag{10}$$

Proof. When the support threshold is increased to p_{tu}, the probability that an itemset X in RD is a false positive equals the probability that the estimated support P_s of X is bigger than p_{tu}.

$$\Pr(P_s > p_{tu}) = \Pr(P_s > p_t + z_{\alpha/2}\sqrt{1/(4n)})$$
$$\leq \Pr(P_s > p + z_{\alpha/2}\sqrt{pq/n})$$
$$\leq \alpha/2 \text{ (apply equation (5))}$$

For $p < p_t \leq 50\%$, $p_t q_t \geq pq$, increasing the support threshold to

$$p_{tu} = p_t + z_{\alpha/2}\sqrt{p_t q_t / n} \qquad (11)$$

will give the same confidence level but a smaller amount of increase in threshold. In doing so, less frequent itemsets can be missed as the threshold increases.

If we do not want to miss frequent itemsets present in the original dataset D, then we can lower the support threshold according to equations (8) or (9). On the contrary, if we do not want false frequent itemsets appear in the mined frequent itemsets, we can increase the threshold according to equations (10) or (11). For instance, given $n=16513$, $1-\alpha = 0.99$ and $p_t = 2\%$, p_{tl} and p_{tu} will be 1.72% and 2.28%, respectively, according to equation (9) and (11). We experimented on a sample of BMSPOS for $p_t = 2\%$. When the support threshold is lowered to 1.72%, there is no missed itemsets; when it is increased to 2.28%, only 0.42% are false frequent itemsets. We also notice that when changing the support threshold decreases one type of errors, the other type of errors tends to increase. We will investigate better methods in our future work to reduce both types of errors.

6 Conclusions

Sampling can provide good estimation of complete frequent itemsets where approximate results are acceptable. In this paper, we sampled the large datasets with replacement and derived the sufficient sample size based on binomial distribution and the central limit theorem. For a given confidence level and error bound, our sampling approach requires smaller sample size than that based on the Chernoff bounds but still provides the desired approximation guarantees for supports of itemsets. For applications where the false positives may be very costly, one can increase the support threshold to reduce them. On the other hand, if we want all the frequent itemsets to be discovered, we can lower the support threshold to reduce the number of false negatives. Theorems 2 and 3 can be used to determine the amount by which the support threshold should be varied.

In our future work, we will investigate multi-phase sampling to improve the accuracy and to extend the techniques to mine data streams.

Acknowledgement

The authors wish to thank Dr N. R. Achuthan for valuable discussions with him on the issues of sampling errors.

References

1. Agrawal, R., Imielinski, T. and Swami, A., Mining association rules between sets of items in large databases. in *ACM SIGMOD Conference on Management of Data* (1993).
2. Heikki Mannila, H.T., Inkeri Verkamo, Efficient Algorithms for Discovering Association Rules. in *AAAI Workshop on Knowledge Discovery in Databases* (1994) 181-192.
3. Toivonen, H., Sampling large databases for association rules. in *22th International Conference on Very Large Databases* (1996) 134-145.
4. Zaki, M.J., Parthasarathy, S., Li, W. and Ogihara, M., Evaluation of sampling for data mining of association rules. in *7th International Workshop on Research Issues in Data Engineering High Performance Database Management for Large-Scale Applications* (1997) 42-50.
5. Chen, B., Haas, P. and Scheuermann, P., A New Two Phase Sampling Based Algorithm for Discovering Association Rules. in *SIGKDD '02* (2002).
6. Zhang, C., Zhang, S. and Webb, G.I. Identifying Approximate Itemsets of Interest in Large Databases. *Applied Intelligence, 18* (1). 91-104.
7. S. Parthasarathy, Efficient Progressive Sampling for Association Rules. in *IEEE International Conference on Data Mining* (2002).
8. Babcock, B., Babu, S., Datar, M., Motwani, R. and Widom, J., Models and Issues in Data Stream Systems. in *21st ACM Symposium on Principles of Database Systems* (2002).
9. Borgelt, C., Efficient Implementations of Apriori and Eclat. in *Workshop of Frequent Item Set Mining Implementations* (2003).
10. Gopalan, R.P. and Sucahyo, Y.G., Fast Frequent Itemset Mining using Compressed Data Representation. in *IASTED International Conference on Databases and Applications* (2003).
11. Thomson, S.K. *Sampling*. John Wiley & Sons Inc., (1992).
12. Mendenhall, W. and Sincich, T. *Statistics for Engineering and Sciences*. Dellen Publishing Company, San Francisco (1992).
13. Agrawal, R. and Srikant, R., Fast Algorithms for Mining Association Rules. in *the 20th VLDB Conference* (1994).
14. Blake, C.L. and Merz, C.J., UCI Repository of Machine Learning Databases, Irvine, CA: University of California, Department of Information and Computer Science (1998).
15. Frequent Itemset Mining Dataset Repository, http://fimi.cs.helsinki.fi/data/.

Improving the Centered CUSUMS Statistic for Structural Break Detection in Time Series

Kwok Pan Pang and Kai Ming Ting

Gippsland School of Computing and Information Technology,
Monash University, Victoria 3842, Australia
{ben.pang, kaiming.ting}@infotech.monash.edu.au

Abstract. Structural break is one of the important concerns in non-stationary time series prediction. The cumulative sum of square (CUSUMS) statistic proposed by Brown et al (1975) has been developed as a general method for detecting a structural break. To better utilize this method, this paper analyses the operating conditions of the centered version of CUSUMS using three variables: the percentage of variance change, the post-break data size and the pre-break data size. In traditional approach of the centered CUSUMS, all available data are used for the break detection. Our analysis reveals that one can improve the accuracy of the break detection by either reducing the post-break data size or increasing pre-break data size. Based on our analysis, we propose a modified test statistic. The evidence shows that the modified statistic significantly improves the chance of detecting the structural breaks.

1 Introduction

In forecasting time series, ignoring structural breaks which occur in the time series significantly reduces the accuracy of the forecast (Pesaran and Timmermann, 2003). Since the classical Chow (1960) test was developed, the past decade has seen considerable empirical and theoretical research on structural break detection in time series. Cumulative Sum of Recursive Residual (CUSUM) and Cumulative Sums of Square (CUSUMS) statistics (Brown et al 1975) have been developed as a general method for single structural break detection. Inclan and Tiao (1994) use the CUSUMS for multiple structural break detection. Pesaran and Timmermann (2002) propose Reverse CUSUM for detecting the most recent break. They show that the accuracy of the forecast can be improved if only the data after the most recent break is selected as the training set, instead of using all available data for training in time series which contains structural breaks. Pang and Ting (2003) further extend the idea of Reverse CUSUM and propose a data selection method for time series prediction. All segments that have the same structure as the most recent segment will be grouped together to form an accumulated segment to be used as the new training set. Their result shows that the new data selection can improve time series prediction. The evidence shows that the structural break detection contributes directly to the improved forecasting performance especially when structural change exists. Effective structural break detection can help us collect relevant data and reduce the disturbance or distortion caused by the structural change.

Despite the above research, there is no knowledge about the conditions under which the CUSUMS statistics will perform well. We aim to provide such an analysis in this paper. We focus on the centered version of CUSUMS presented by Brown et al (1975) and analyses under what operating conditions it can perform better in break detection.

This paper first examines the operating conditions of the centered CUSUMS in terms of the percentage of variance change, the pre-break data size and the post-break data size. Then, it investigates the effect of these variables on structural break detection. Based on this analysis, we propose to modify the original centered CUSUM statistic that will significantly improve the accuracy of structural break detection. We evaluate the centered CUSUMS's performance in different situations such as different degrees of structure change and different degrees of noise for single break detections as well as multiple-break detections.

Section 2 briefly describes the background of the centered CUSUMS. We present the result of our analysis: the operating conditions of the centered CUSUMS in section 3, and propose the modified statistic in section 4. The experiments and the results are reported in section 5.

2 Background of CUSUMS

Let $y_1, y_2, \ldots, y_n$ be the time series under consideration. We first convert the series into input and output pairs to be used for ordinary linear regression.
The basic linear regression model we used is having the output y_t with k input variables:

$$y_t = \lambda_1 y_{t-1} + \lambda_2 y_{t-2} + \ldots + \lambda_k y_{t-k} .$$

We use the following notation to denote the observation matrices Y_n and X_n which consists of n observations in the time series.

$$Y_n = \begin{bmatrix} y_1 \\ y_2 \\ \ldots \\ \ldots \\ y_n \end{bmatrix}, \quad X_n = \begin{bmatrix} x_1 \\ x_2 \\ . \\ . \\ x_n \end{bmatrix} = \begin{bmatrix} y_1 & y_2 & . & . & y_{k-1} & y_k \\ y_2 & y_3 & . & . & . & y_{k+1} \\ \ldots & \ldots & . & . & . & \ldots \\ \ldots & \ldots & . & . & . & \ldots \\ y_{n-k+1} & y_{n+k+2} & . & . & . & y_n \end{bmatrix} \text{ and } \beta_n = \begin{bmatrix} \lambda_1 \\ \lambda_2 \\ .. \\ .. \\ \lambda_k \end{bmatrix}$$

Using the observations as the training data, the least square coefficients β_n can be estimated by $\hat{\beta}_n = (X'_n X_n)^{-1} X'_n Y_n$.

The CUSUM and CUSUMS statistics (Brown et al 1975) are defined as follows. The CUSUM statistic is based on the standardized recursive residual w_r:

$$w_r = (y_r - x_r \hat{\beta}_{r-1}) / d_r, \quad r = 2k+1, \ldots, n-1, n \tag{1}$$

where

$$\hat{\beta}_r = (X_r'X_r)^{-1}X_r'Y_r \tag{2}$$
$$d_r = 1 + x_r(X_r'X_r)^{-1}x_r'$$

The CUSUMS is defined in terms of w_r:

$$s_r = \frac{\sum_{i=1}^{r} w_i^2}{\sum_{i=1}^{n} w_i^2}, \quad r = 2k+1,\ldots,n-1,n \tag{3}$$

The centered CUSUMS is defined as:

$$s_{r,n}^* = \frac{\sum_{i=1}^{r} w_i^2}{\sum_{i=1}^{n} w_i^2} - \frac{r}{n}, \quad r = 2k+1,\ldots,n-1,n \tag{4}$$

Note that $s_{r,n}^*$ has zero mean.

The test statistic for structural break detection is:

$$T = \sqrt{\frac{n}{2}} \max_r |s_{r,n}^*|$$

The estimated break location, if T is above a critical value, is defined as:

$$\hat{r} = \arg\max_r |s_{r,n}^*|$$

Under variance homogeneity, Inclan and Tiao (1994) show that $s_{r,n}^*$ behaves like a Brownian Bridge asymptotically. The critical values for structural break detection for different sample sizes are tabulated in Inclan and Tiao (1994).

3 Analysis of Operating Conditions for Centered CUSUMS

In this analysis, we assume two different structures exist in the time series, the break is located at r and their structures can be represented by two different regressions, i.e. $y_t = x_t\beta_a + \xi_t$, $\xi_t \sim N(0,\sigma_a^2)$ for $t = 1,2,\ldots,r$

and

$y_t = x_t\beta_b + \gamma_t$, $\gamma_t \sim N(0,\sigma_b^2)$ for $t = r+1, r+2,\ldots,n$

(I) Let $\tilde{r}$ be the minimum data size required before the structural break for which the centered CUSUMS can detect. Note that the value of $\tilde{r}$ is also representing the break location. Also let n be the size of the data, and α be the significant level required for break detection.

If the break is detected at $r = \tilde{r}$, there must exist a critical value η at the significant level α, where

$$P(\max_r \sqrt{\frac{n}{2}}|s_{r,n}^*| \leq \eta) = 1 - \alpha \tag{5}$$

such that

$$\sqrt{\frac{n}{2}}|s^*_{\tilde{r},n}| = \eta.$$

Let $\sum_{i=1}^{t} w_i^2 = t\sigma_t^2$, and substitute it into (4), then the above equation can be rewritten into

$$\sqrt{\frac{n}{2}}\left(\frac{\tilde{r}}{n}\right)\left|\frac{\sigma_{\tilde{r}}^2}{\sigma_n^2} - 1\right| = \eta$$

Let $\Delta = \left|\frac{(\sigma_{\tilde{r}}^2 - \sigma_n^2)}{\sigma_n^2}\right|$ be the absolute value of the percentage of variance change, the above equation can be further simplified as follows.

$$\tilde{r}\Delta = \eta\sqrt{2n} \tag{6}$$

Or, the minimum data size before the break $\tilde{r}$ can be expressed as:

$$\tilde{r} = \frac{1}{\Delta}\eta\sqrt{2n} \tag{7}$$

(II) With the same approach, let $\dot{n}$ be the minimum data size after the structural break for which the centered CUSUM can detect the structural break. $\dot{n}$ can be expressed as:

$$\dot{n} = (\frac{r^2}{2\eta^2})\Delta^2 \tag{8}$$

When the difference between two structures is very small, σ_n^2 will be close to $\sigma_{\tilde{r}}$ and Δ will be close to zero. On the other hand, when their structure difference is large, σ_n^2 will be much larger than $\sigma_{\tilde{r}}$ and Δ will tend to be a larger value.

The relationship among n, Δ and $\tilde{r}$ for the break detection can be summarized as follows:

Situation I: $\tilde{r}$ versus Δ (when n is fixed)
    (i) if Δ is large, then $\tilde{r}$ can be small
    (ii) if Δ is small, then $\tilde{r}$ must be large

Situation II: $\dot{n}$ versus Δ (when r is fixed)
    (i) if Δ is large, then $\dot{n}$ can be large
    (ii) if Δ is small, then $\dot{n}$ must be small

The above rule for increasing the break detection performance will no longer be valid when Δ tends to zero. It happens when the degree of structure change is too small to show the significance, when the value of n is very close to the break location or when the pre-break data size r is too small. Based on equations (7) and (8), when Δ tends to zero, an invalid estimated $\dot{n}$ or $\tilde{r}$ will be generated, $\tilde{r}$ will tend to be infinitive, and $\dot{n}$ will tend to be zero.

4 Modified Test Statistic

It is interesting to note that large data set can be counter-productive in situation II in terms of using the CUSUMS statistic for break detection. This short-coming has motivated us to modify the statistic, which we will describe in the next section.

In order to determine a more effective data size (n_1) which is smaller than the given data size (n), we propose to modify the original centered CUSUMS statistic as follows:

$$MT_{n_1} = \max_{0 \leq r \leq n_1} \sqrt{\frac{n_i}{2}} \left| \frac{\sum_{i=1}^{r} w_i^2}{\sum_{i=1}^{n_1} w_i^2} - \frac{r}{n_1} \right| \quad , \text{ where } r \leq n_1 \leq n$$

The estimated break location will be obtained by:

$$\hat{r} = \arg\max_{0 \leq r \leq n_1} \sqrt{\frac{n_i}{2}} \left| \frac{\sum_{i=1}^{r} w_i^2}{\sum_{i=1}^{n_1} w_i^2} - \frac{r}{n_1} \right| \quad , \text{ where } r \leq n_1 \leq n$$

In the modified statistic, we will use an adjustable data size n_1 instead of data size n. n_1 is always within the range $r \leq n_1 \leq n$, and it is not fixed. MT_{n_1} will be optimized by selecting an appropriate n_1. As S^*_{r,n_1} behaves like the Brownian Bridge asymptotically, we can use the same critical value for the specified n_1 that are tabulated in Inclan and Tiao (1994).

Note that MT_{n_1} can be computed very efficiently since all the values required are the intermediate values computed by the original statistic.

5 Experiments

We divide the experiments into two sections, the first section of our experiments is designed to verify the analysis conducted in section 3, and it evaluates the centered CUSUMS for the break detection using various pre-break data size (r) and post-break data size $(n-r)$ when a single break exists. The second section is designed to evaluate the performance of the proposed modified statistic for break detection described in section 4. In the experiments, we use the significant level α at 0.01 for the statistical test. The performance will be measured in terms of accuracy, which is the percentage of correct classification.

Every predicted break location falls into one of the following categories:

(i) Correct Classification: If the estimated break location is within boundary (i.e. actual break location ± 10), we classify it to be correct classification.

(ii) Incorrect Classification: If the estimated break location is outside the boundary (i.e. actual break location ± 10), we classify it to be incorrect classification.

In addition, the mean of the absolute deviation (MAD) is used as the second performance measure. We will take the maximum deviation as the measure if no structural break is predicted.

$$\text{Mean of Absolute Deviation (MAD)} = \frac{\sum |P - \hat{P}|}{m}$$

Where P is the actual structural break location, $\hat{P}$ is the estimated structural break location and m is the number the stimulated time series data in that experiment.

For each experiment, we simulated the series 3000 times with different seeds, and we report the performance over 3000 runs. In the experiments, we specify the number of input variables to be 3.

5.1 Validating the Analysis Result for Centered CUSUMS

This experiment aims to validate the relationship among the structural break detection performance, the degree of structural change, pre-break data size and post-break data size. It evaluates the performance of the centered CUSUMS at different pre-break data size (r) and post-break data size ($n-r$) on the single break series in two different situations: (a) with trend changes and (b) with variance changes.

(a) When the Trend Changes

Two single break time series are designed for testing the break detection. The simulation of the data is based on the structures described in table 1. Each series is composed of two segments. Same level of noise that comes with distribution N(0, σ_ε^2) are added into each segment of the same series. Different noise levels (i.e. σ_ε = 0.2, 0.5, 1, 1.2 and 1.5) are used in the experiments.
Two sets of experiments are conducted:

  (i) with a fixed pre-break data size (i.e $r = 100$), we record their structural break detection performance using varied post-break data size (i.e. $n-r$ = 5, 10, 15, 20, 30, 40, 70 and 100).
  (ii) with a fixed post-break data size (i.e. $n-r = 100$), we record their structural break detection performance using varied pre-break data size (i.e. r = 5, 10, 15, 20, 30, 40, 70 and 100).

Table 1. Trend Changes. Description of two single-break series: each series is composed of two segments. The whole sequence of series is $\{y_t, t = 1,2,\ldots,200\}$, and the initial values are specified as: $y_1 = y_2 = y_3 = 50$. The distribution of ε_t is $\varepsilon_t \sim N(0, \sigma_\varepsilon^2)$, σ_ε are specified to be 0.2, 0.5, 1, 1.2 and 1.5

Category of structural change	Segment 1 $\{y_t, t=1,2,\ldots,100\}$	Segment 2 $\{y_t, t=101,102,\ldots,200\}$
Large Structural change	$y_t = 0.6 y_{t-1} + 0.3 y_{t-2} + 0.1 y_{t-3} + \varepsilon_t$	$y_t = 1.1 y_{t-1} + 0.1 y_{t-2} - 0.19 y_{t-3} + \varepsilon_t$
Small Structural change	$y_t = 0.6 y_{t-1} + 0.3 y_{t-2} + 0.1 y_{t-3} + \varepsilon_t$	$y_t = 0.6 y_{t-1} + 0.3 y_{t-2} + 0.105 y_{t-3} + \varepsilon_t$

(b) When the Variance Changes

Two single-break time series with different variance are described in table 2. The test procedure for situation (b) is similar to the test in situation (a).
Two sets of experiments are conducted:

(i) with a fixed pre-break data size (i.e $r = 50$), we record their structural break detection performance using varied post-break data size (i.e. $n-r = 50, 100, 150, 200, 250, 300, 350$ and 400).

(ii) with a fixed post-break data size (i.e. $n-r = 400$), we record their structural break detection performance using varied pre-break data size (i.e. $r = 30, 40, 50, 60, 70, 80, 90$ and 100).

Table 2. Variance changes. Description of two segments: they are formed by two segments with different structures. The whole sequence of series is $\{y_t, t = 1,2,...,500\}$

Category of Structural Change	Segment 1 $\{y_t, t = 1,2,...,100\}$	Segment 2 $\{y_t, t = 101,102,....,500\}$
Large Structural change	$y_t = \varepsilon_{1t}$, $\varepsilon_{1t} \sim N(0,3.24)$	$y_t = \varepsilon_{2t}$, $\varepsilon_{2t} \sim N(0,1)$
Small Structural change	$y_t = \varepsilon_{1t}$, $\varepsilon_{1t} \sim N(0,2.25)$	$y_t = \varepsilon_{2t}$, $\varepsilon_{2t} \sim N(0,1)$

Experiment Results

The results are summarized as follows:

- **Post-break Data Size and the Performance of Centered CUSUMS:**
  With a fixed pre-break data size, reducing the post-break data size enhances the break detection performance, no matter there is a change of a variance or a trend. In the experiment, we examine their break detection performance in terms of the accuracy and MAD. Some sample results are shown in figures 1a-b and 2a-b. The performance at $(n-r)=70$ is always better than those at $(n-r)=100$ when a trend changes in the structure; and the performance at $(n-r)=350$ is always better than those at 400 when there is a variance change in the structure. The relationship between the post-break data size and the break detection performance is clearly shown as the concave curve in figures 1a and 2a. The break detection performance starts to improve when the post-break data size is reduced from the original data size. However, the performance will degrade when the post-break data size is too small.

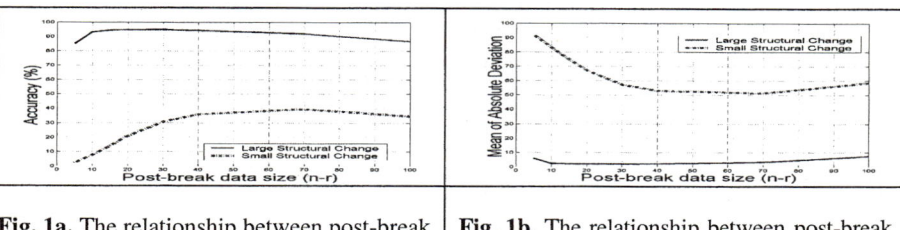

Fig. 1a. The relationship between post-break data size and the accuracy at the noise level $\sigma_\varepsilon = 0.2$ (when a trend changes)

Fig. 1b. The relationship between post-break data size and the mean of absolute deviation at the noise level $\sigma_\varepsilon = 0.2$ (when a trend changes)

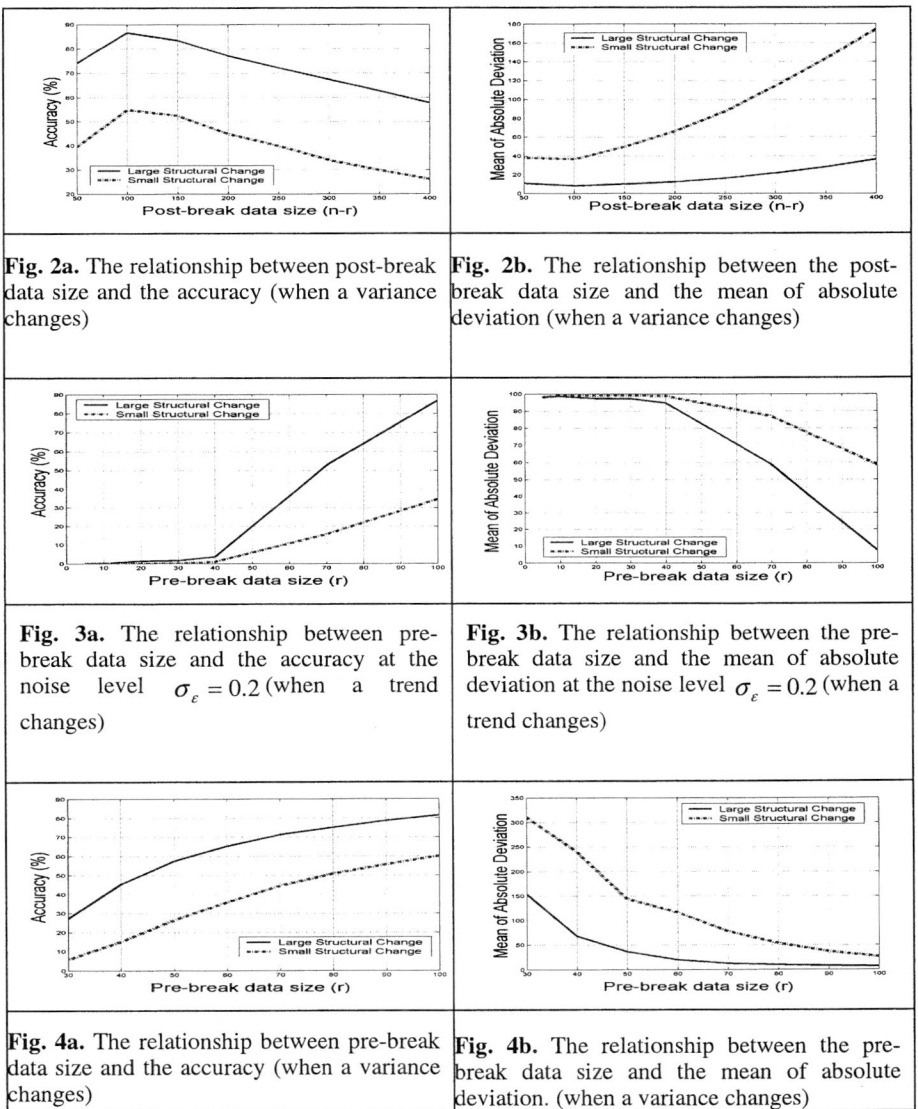

Fig. 2a. The relationship between post-break data size and the accuracy (when a variance changes)

Fig. 2b. The relationship between the post-break data size and the mean of absolute deviation (when a variance changes)

Fig. 3a. The relationship between pre-break data size and the accuracy at the noise level $\sigma_\varepsilon = 0.2$ (when a trend changes)

Fig. 3b. The relationship between the pre-break data size and the mean of absolute deviation at the noise level $\sigma_\varepsilon = 0.2$ (when a trend changes)

Fig. 4a. The relationship between pre-break data size and the accuracy (when a variance changes)

Fig. 4b. The relationship between the pre-break data size and the mean of absolute deviation. (when a variance changes)

- **Pre-break Data Size and the Performance of Centered CUSUMS:**
  With a fixed post-break data size, increasing the pre-break data size improves the break detection performance. Some sample results are shown in both measures in the figures 3a-b and 4a-b.

  Note that not all available results are presented because of lack of space. Similar behavior is observed in all experiments with other noise levels.

5.2 Evaluating the Effectiveness of the Modified Statistic

The following experiment is designed to evaluate the performance of the modified statistic and compare it with the traditional centered CUSUMS statistic:

5.2.1 Time Series with a Single Break

The experiment is designed to evaluate the performance of the modified statistic for the time series in which a single break exists. In the experiment, the series with the large structural change will be used to evaluate the modified statistic in two situations (i.e. trend changes and variance changes) as in section 5.1 (a) and (b).

Experiment Result

The performance of the modified statistic for break detection outperforms the original statistics in both measures in all situations as shown in figures 5 and 6. The modified statistic obviously improves the break detection through the effective post-break data size selection. It significantly increases the accuracy and reduces the mean of the absolute deviation.

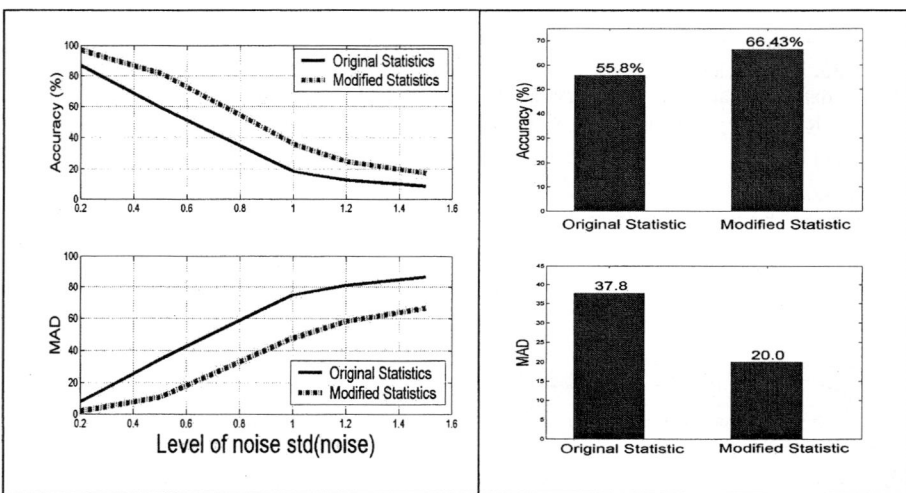

Fig. 5. The performance (in terms of the accuracy and MAD) of the modified statistic and original statistic at different noise level (when a trend changes)

Fig. 6. Performance (in terms of the accuracy and MAD) of modified statistic comparing with the original statistic (when a variance changes)

5.2.2 Time Series with Multiple Breaks

This part of the experiments is to evaluate the performance of the modified statistic for the time series with multiple breaks. The time series is composed of several segments {Seg_1, Seg_2,....,Seg_m}. In the experiments, the modified statistic is evaluated in the following situations.

(a) Trend Changes

Two series with three and seven segments are used here. The characteristics of the series are described in table 3 and 4.

Table 3. Description of the 3-segment series: the sequence of the series is $\{Seg_1, Seg_2, Seg_3\}$. The initial values of the time series are specified as: $y_1 = y_2 = y_3 = 50$. The length of each segment is specified to be 100. The distribution of ε_t is $\varepsilon_t \sim N(0, \sigma_\varepsilon^2)$, $\sigma_\varepsilon = 0.2, 0.5, 1, 1.2$ and 1.5 as in table 1

Seg_1	Seg_2	Seg_3
$y_t = 1.1y_{t-1} + 0.1y_{t-2} - 0.195y_{t-3} + \varepsilon_t$	$y_t = 1.1y_{t-1} + 0.1y_{t-2} - 0.205y_{t-3} + \varepsilon_t$	$y_t = 0.6y_{t-1} + 0.3y_{t-2} + 0.1y_{t-3} + \varepsilon_t$

Table 4. Description of the 7-segment series: the sequence of the series is $\{Seg_1, Seg_2, Seg_3, Seg_4, Seg_5, Seg_6, Seg_7\}$. The length of each segment is specified to be 100, and the initial values of the time series are specified as: $y_1 = y_2 = y_3 = 50$. The distribution of ε_t is $\varepsilon_t \sim N(0, \sigma_\varepsilon^2)$, $\sigma_\varepsilon = 0.2, 0.5, 1, 1.2$ and 1.5 as in table 1

Seg_1, Seg_3, Seg_5	Seg_2, Seg_4, Seg_6	Seg_7
$y_t = 1.1y_{t-1} + 0.1y_{t-2} - 0.195y_{t-3} + \varepsilon_t$	$y_t = 1.1y_{t-1} + 0.1y_{t-2} - 0.205y_{t-3} + \varepsilon_t$	$y_t = 0.6y_{t-1} + 0.3y_{t-2} + 0.1y_{t-3} + \varepsilon_t$

(b) Variance Changes

The characteristics of 3-segment and 7-segment series are described in tables 5 and 6.

Table 5. Description of the 3-segment series: the sequence of the series is $\{Seg_1, Seg_2, Seg_3\}$, the length of each segment is 100

Seg_1, Seg_3	Seg_2
$y_t = \varepsilon_1$, $\varepsilon_1 \sim N(0, 3.24)$	$y_t = \varepsilon_2$, $\varepsilon_2 \sim N(0,1)$

Table 6. Description of the 7-segment series: the sequence of the series is $\{Seg_1, Seg_2, Seg_3, Seg_4, Seg_5, Seg_6,$ and $Seg7\}$, the length of each segment is 100

$Seg_1, Seg_3, Seg_5, Seg_7$	Seg_2, Seg_4, Seg_6
$y_t = \varepsilon_1$, $\varepsilon_1 \sim N(0, 3.24)$	$y_t = \varepsilon_2$, $\varepsilon_2 \sim N(0,1)$

Experiment Result

The modified statistic outperforms the original statistics in both series as shown in figures 7 and 8. It is interesting to note that the performance of the modified statistic remains at the same level, whereas the performance of the original statistic gets worse from 3-segment series to 7-segment series.

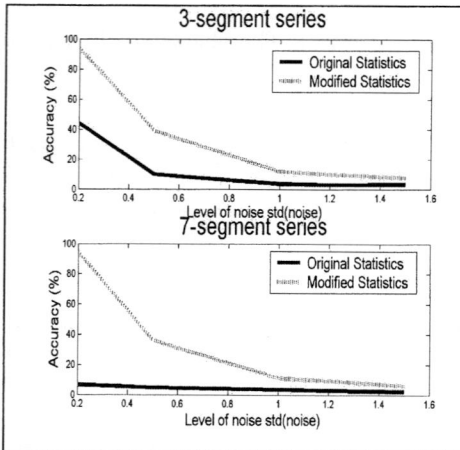
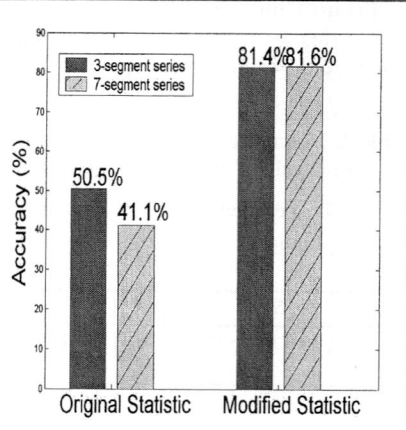

Fig. 7. A comparison of the performance of the modified statistic with the original statistic using the data with 3-segment and 7-segment series when trend changes	**Fig. 8.** A comparison of the performance of the modified statistic with the original statistic using 3-segment and 7-segment series when variance changes

6 Conclusions

This paper makes the following contributions in the structural break detection:

- It provides a better understanding of the operating conditions of the centered CUSUMS for structural break detection. The analysis shows that either the increase of pre-break data size (r) or the reduction of post-break data size ($n-r$) will improve the accuracy of break detection. The second condition implies that it is counter productive to have a data set with a large post-break data size for structural break detection using centered CUSUMS. Though unintuitive at the first glance, the performance of structural break detection highly relate to the post-break data size. An appropriate selection of the post-break data size can significantly improve the performance of break detection.
- The modified centered CUSUMS searches an appropriate post-break data size for break detection. This has led us to an improved version of centered CUSUMS.
- The modified centered CUSUMS is an intensive-computing algorithm. Suppose the data size is n, then $3n^2-3n$ extra arithmetic operations are required for computing the modified centered CUSUMS comparing with the computation of the original centered CUSUMS. In addition, the original centered CUSUMS requires to store n values of the centered CUSUMS statistic in a series consists of n observations, then the modified centered CUSUMS requires to store up to $(n^2+n)/2$ values. Our experiment shows that it takes 0.328 seconds to get the modified centered CUSUMS while original centered CUSUMS needs only 0.109 seconds when the data size is 1000. When we increase the data size up to 5000, the modified centered CUSUMS takes 39.531 seconds while original CUSUMS

takes only 0.922 seconds. Our results show that the increased computation time and space has paid off with an improved performance in break detection.

References

1. Brown, R.L., Durbin, J., and Evans, J.M. (1975) "Techniques for Testing the constancy of Regression Relationship over Time", Journal of Royal Statistical Society, Series B, 37, 149-192.
2. Chow, G. (1960), Tests of equality between sets of coefficients in two linear regressions. Econometrica, Vol. 28, No. 3, 591-605
3. Inclan, C. and Tiao, G. C.. (1994) "Use of Cumulative Sums of Squares for Retrospective Detection of Changes of Variance", Journal of the American Statistical Association, September 1994. Vol. 89, no. 427, 913-923.
4. Pang, K. P. and Ting, K. M. (2003) " Improving Time series prediction by data selection" International Conference on Computational Intelligence for Modeling, Control & Automation, February 2003, 803-813
5. Pesaran, H. and Timmermann, A. (2002) "Market timing and Return Prediction under Model instability", Journal of Empirical Finance, December 2002. Vol. 9, 495-510
6. Pesaran, H. and Timmermann, A., (2003) "How Costly is it to Ignore Breaks when Forecasting the Direction of a Time Series?," Cambridge Working Papers in Economics 0306, Department of Applied Economics, University of Cambridge.

Investigating ID3-Induced Rules from Low-Dimensional Data Cleaned by Complete Case Analysis

Jeanette Auer and Richard Hall

Department of Computer Science and Computer Engineering, La Trobe University,
Bundoora, Victoria, Australia 3085
{auerja, rhall}@cs.latrobe.edu.au

Abstract. While knowledge discovery in databases techniques require statistically complete data, real world data is incomplete, so it must be preprocessed using completeness approximation methods. The success of these methods is impacted by whether redundancy in large amounts of data overcomes incompleteness mechanisms. We investigate this impact by comparing rule sets induced from complete data with rule sets induced from incomplete data that is preprocessed using complete case analysis. To control the incomplete data construction, we apply the well-defined incompleteness mechanisms missing-at-random and missing-completely-at-random to complete data. Initial results indicate that a medium level of pattern redundancy fails to fully overcome incompleteness mechanisms, and that characterizing an appropriate redundancy threshold is non-trivial.

1 Introduction

The knowledge discovery in databases (KDD) process aims to extract new, interesting, correct, and ultimately understandable patterns in large data [1]. Data cleaning is a critical early phase in this process [1-3], and the choice of cleaning method should depend on the incompleteness mechanisms, especially where these methods introduce statistical biases. However, the relationship between cleaning processes and these mechanisms has yet to be characterized [4, 5]. In this paper we investigate the relationships between complete case analysis and some of the incompleteness mechanisms on ID3-induced rules [6] for low-dimensional data with one attribute exhibiting incompleteness.

Incompleteness at the attribute recording level is introduced by at least six factors: designed incompleteness; survey questions overlooked; attribute inapplicability to the current pattern; attribute loss during data merging; equipment failure; deliberate or systematic destruction of data; outright refusal to provide data; and an inability to provide data at pattern collection [4, 7, 8]. Automated knowledge extraction methods require data to be complete across a defined level of features in order measure information gains, rule coverage, or associations [9]. To approximate completeness incomplete records are filled, removed, or otherwise partitioned away from the data that is to be processed by automated knowledge extraction techniques [9, 10].

However, the cleaning processes may introduce biases that attenuate the knowledge quality, meaning the ability of the extracted knowledge to represent the world from which the data was collected. Data can also be incomplete at the level of 'pattern collection' [5, 7], but this level is outside the scope of this paper.

We consider the incompleteness *mechanisms missing at random* (MAR) and *missing completely at random* (MCAR) [4] (see [4, 5, 11-13] for discussions). While these mechanisms are widely cited in statistics literature [13], they appear to have been ignored in the context of KDD, but have been considered in the field of medical informatics [5, 8, 14]. Data is MAR if the probability of observing an attribute value is independent the attribute value itself, after controlling for the values of all other attributes. For example, consider monotone data represented as a rectangular $(n \times K)$ matrix with specific values for each recorded pattern i as $Y=y_{ij}$. Let n be the number of patterns, ($K=2$) be the number of attributes, i be the record number, j be the attribute number, the values of Y_{i1} for observations i, $i=1\ldots n$ be fully recorded, and the values of Y_{i2} for observations i, $i=1\ldots n$ be partially recorded. Such data is MAR if the probability that Y_{i2} is missing depends only on Y_{i2} [4, 11, 12]. Mathematically:

$$\Pr(Y_{ij} = NULL | Y_{i1}, Y_{i2}) = \Pr(Y_{ij} = NULL | Y_{i1}) \qquad (1)$$

In order to test data for the presence of MAR, prior knowledge of the distribution of the values for Y_j is required. However, this distribution is unavailable because the actual values for Y_j that is missing in real world data are unknown. Thus, models induced from MAR data may have an indeterminable number of rules missing.

On the other hand, data is MCAR where the probability of an observation of an attribute value is independent of the attribute value itself or of any other attribute's value [5, 11, 12] (considered by some to be a special case of MAR [5]). For MCAR, R is the probability of incompleteness, and $Y_{complete}$ is the sum of all observed data and missing data. Models derived from MCAR data should represent a UOD at appropriately defined confidence levels [4]. Mathematically:

$$\Pr(R | Y_{complete}) = \Pr(R) \qquad (2)$$

The data cleaning method known as complete-case analysis (CCA), deletes all patterns with missing attribute values [4, 12]. It is trivial to implement, comparatively computationally inexpensive, and it generates patterns complete across a required dimensionality [4, 5]. However, CCA can lead to potential information loss and non-random exclusion of patterns. Potential information loss results when high levels (over 30%) of deletions cause a resulting degradation in induced knowledge quality [4]. Non-random exclusion of patterns occurs when deletions introduce biases into the data, affecting the subsequent induced knowledge quality [5, 12, 15]. Other methods exist to clean data (see [16, 17]) but they are outside the scope of this paper.

Any knowledge extracted from data is descriptive of the 'Universe of Discourse (UOD) for which the data was collected, for example a database of clinical trials of survival analysis [18]. UODs are often described in terms relative to the *domain* rather than in terms relative to the *data* (metadata), as KDD practitioners often focus on domain specifics (patterns) as opposed to similarities across domains (models) [19]. For our investigation to be generalizable across domains, we represent a UOD in terms of three metadata: attribute set size, number of possible values that characterize each attribute, and number of output space values.

This paper is organized into four sections: methodology; results; discussion and conclusions. In the methodology, we discuss how we create master data, attenuated data, and the way that ID3 rules induced from both data are compared. In the results section we graphically compare rule sets extracted from well over half a million trees. The number of data sets from which these trees are induced is the cartesian product of following: eight attributes values over three attributes; six possible output domains; ten copies of each set of data; sixty patterns; two MAR parameter sets plus a MCAR data set of the above form; with three different methods of mapping output classes to patterns.

2 Methodology

To investigate the effectiveness of redundancy in data, both master data and attenuated data is generated. *Master* data is generated that is complete with regards to UODs with the aforementioned metadata. By complete we mean that master data excludes noise and irrelevant attributes. The rule sets extracted from decision trees induced from master data (master trees) are used as a benchmark for rule sets extracted from trees induced from incomplete data. As master rule sets described each UOD, the attenuated rules sets are guaranteed subsets of the master rule set.

Incomplete data is constructed by attenuating the complete data using a single incompleteness mechanism. Attenuated data is processed using CCA prior to decision tree induction. If the incompleteness mechanism has no impact on the induction algorithm, then attenuated data trees will be equivalent to master trees. Equivalency is measured coarsely by comparing the number of attenuated rules induced with respect to the induced master rules (see Figure 1). Maximum rule loss is reported in this set of experiments to determine the baseline for a generalized worse case scenario.

We used low dimensionality metadata parameters: number of predictive attributes {2...5}; domain size of each predictive attribute {2...11}; number of output classes {2...8}; and the pattern draw available to the master set {1...60}. We chose low dimensionality parameters for ease of control and analysis, and to determine if a lower boundary existed above which redundancy always overcomes the incompleteness mechanism. While this low dimensionality is lower than the normal dimensionality associated with KDD processes [20], it is necessary to begin at a lower limit, then grow the dimensionalities, in to precisely characterize either a lower boundary or discrete regions where redundancy effectiveness holds.

Data is generated by taking the cartesian products of the attribute values domain across a specified number of attributes in order to create a balanced, fully characterized set of unique patterns that could be mapped into varying target spaces. The target space mappings are generated by adding an output class to each pattern in one of the following three ways: cycling through the output class space and assigning each subsequent target value to the next pattern in the predictive matrix; shifting the output class space one value and cycling through the space; or by randomly assigning the output targets to each predictive pattern. Incomplete data is created by applying various incompleteness mechanisms to the patterns. For each UOD parameter set, ten separate data were created to minimize possible experimental artifact generation as a result of an aberrant pseudo-random number generation routine. Using cartesian-generated master data ensured that every predictive pattern required all attributes, allowing apriori determination of the master rule domain size, thus the number of rules which were practically generated could be verified against the theoretically-predicted numbers of rules.

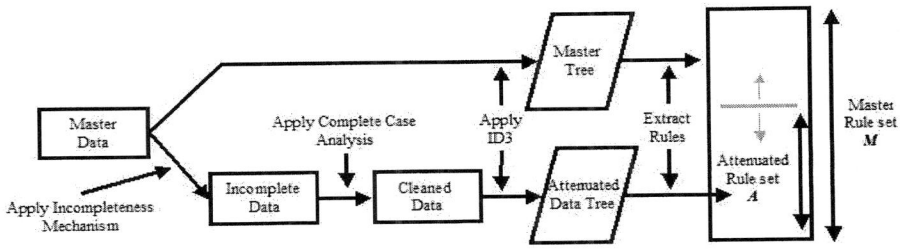

Rules Missing % = A/M * 100

Fig. 1. Experimental design

MAR Data is generated by testing whether a random number is less than the probability threshold for the value of attribute$_2$. If it is lower, then the value of attribute$_2$ is set to NULL, otherwise it remains unchanged [8]. Two sets of MAR data were generated using different probability thresholds. Set$_1$ is made missing at {(0, 10%), (1, 70%), (2, 40%), (3, 40%), ... , (N, 40%)} whilst Set$_2$ is made missing at {(0, 10%), (1, 40%), (2, 40%), ... , ([N-1], 40%), (N, 70%)}; both sets effectively displaying a overall incompleteness of 40%. We investigate this level of incompleteness as it is reported as being typical at the upper end of the range with which KDD practitioners are willing to work [21-23]. We assume that if redundancy can overcome the incompleteness mechanism at 40% it will overcome lower levels of incompleteness. MCAR data is generated by applying a single probability threshold for the value of 40% to each record.

To highlight the difference between MCAR and MAR, a complete worked example (five possible attribute values with two predictive attributes (25 possibilities) with three possible target classes with sequential mapping of target classes to predictive patterns) is shown in Table 1. MAR data with 40% incompleteness requires that the overall probability that an observation is missing be 40% while the actual probability is determined by the value of the attribute itself. Thus, -the probability that the value for attribute Y_{1j} is missing if the actual value was equal to '1' is 10%: if the actual value for attribute Y_{1j} was equal to '2' then the probability that the value was missing is 70%. The overall incompleteness set is shown in Equation 3.

All patterns labeled '✘' would be deleted by CCA. Considering pattern 8 in Table 1 in conjunction with (3), pattern 8's attribute$_1$ value would be set to NULL as 0.5<0.7 (Y_{1j}=2). However, considering pattern 8 with respect to MCAR=40% in Table 1, the value of attribute$_1$ would remain unchanged as 0.5>0.4.

$$P(Y_{1j})_{incomplete} = \begin{cases} 10\%, & if \quad Y_{1j} = 1 \\ 70\%, & if \quad Y_{1j} = 2 \\ 40\%, & if \quad Y_{1j} = 3...5. \end{cases} \qquad (3)$$

Table 1. Example Data Set Showing Complete Data (for two predictive attributes) and those patterns that would be incomplete under the mechanisms MCAR and MAR set one

Pattern J	Random Number	Attribute One Y_{1i}	Attribute Two Y_{2i}	Target Class	Keep pattern under CCA	
					MCAR	MAR
1	0.911694913	1	1	1	✓	✓
2	0.600970673	1	2	2	✓	✓
3	0.96706351	1	3	3	✓	✓
4	0.742055184	1	4	1	✓	✓
5	0.935292748	1	5	2	✓	✓
6	0.72140608	2	1	3	✓	✓
7	0.1404428	2	2	1	✗	✗
8	**0.500062807**	**2**	**3**	**2**	**✓**	**✗**
9	0.33547504	2	4	3	✗	✗
10	0.673162015	2	5	1	✓	✗
11	0.34430932	3	1	2	✗	✗
12	0.139610002	3	2	3	✗	✗
13	0.321159226	3	3	1	✗	✗
14	0.316084394	3	4	2	✗	✗
15	0.476162269	3	5	3	✓	✓
16	0.584894661	4	1	1	✓	✓
17	0.461788968	4	2	2	✓	✓
18	0.440778722	4	3	3	✓	✓
19	0.099157872	4	4	1	✗	✗
20	0.040786828	4	5	2	✗	✗
21	0.778760263	5	1	3	✓	✓
22	0.41587442	5	2	1	✓	✓
23	0.514001777	5	3	2	✓	✓
24	0.222780601	5	4	3	✗	✗
25	0.440115423	5	5	1	✓	✓

ID3 [6] was selected for three reasons: it grows complete un-pruned trees; it is the progenitor of most top down inductive decision tree algorithms; and it can easily be modified to label leaves for which no rules are induced. The first reason means that any rule loss can be categorically identified as being caused only by the application of CCA to the respective incompleteness mechanism. The second reason is that we believe it is likely that ID3 descendents would share both its virtues and vices, thus it means that further investigations of its descendants can be related to the current investigation. Finally, it allows us to trivially identify which master rules our UOD were absent in the attenuated rule sets.

3 Results

All master trees were fully balanced (as expected) and the size of rule sets matched their predicted size (based on the UOD dimensionality). No unresolved rules were observed in any rule sets induced from incomplete data, which means that no contradictions were introduced via attenuation and cleaning. As expected, all attenuated rule sets were subsets of master set.

Initially, we expected that at a certain level of redundancy that rule loss level would approach and remain at the zero level. Unexpectedly, as the number of pattern copies (prior to applications of incompleteness mechanism) increases beyond the initial zero rule loss point we began to observe regions of increasing levels of rule loss, which appears to have some relationship to the underlying master rule size of the UOD. Figure 2 shows the results for applying the incompleteness mechanisms MCAR and MAR to a 3 predictive attribute UOD. Rule loss rates were similar for all mechanisms though the specific rules lost differed from set to set (data not shown). Initial results for 4 and 5 predictive attribute UOD's are consistent with results obtained for the 3 predictive attribute UOD's.

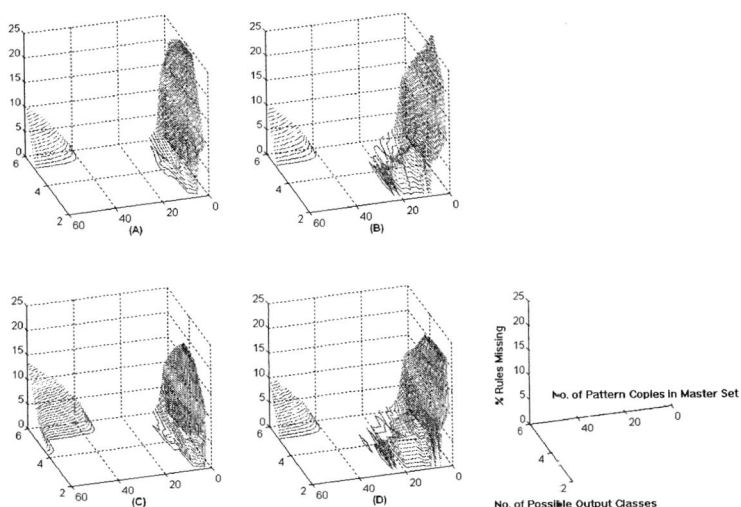

Fig. 2. Rule loss at 40% incompleteness for three predictive attribute UOD's: (A) MCAR, (B) MAR set one, (C) MAR set two, and (D) MAR set one with random output space mappings

To determine if the output space size had an effect on the experimental results, we varied the method of allocation of target to predictive patterns. If target assignment is sequential overall then rule loss rates remained high. However, rule loss dropped to zero for attribute sizes that were multiples of the target domain size (figure 3 & 4). Figures 3A, 3B 3C, 4A, 4B and 4C are generated from sets with sequential output class assignment, figures 3D, 3E 3F, 4F, 4E and 4F are generated from sets with random output class assignment. Randomly allocating output classes to the patterns negated this effect.

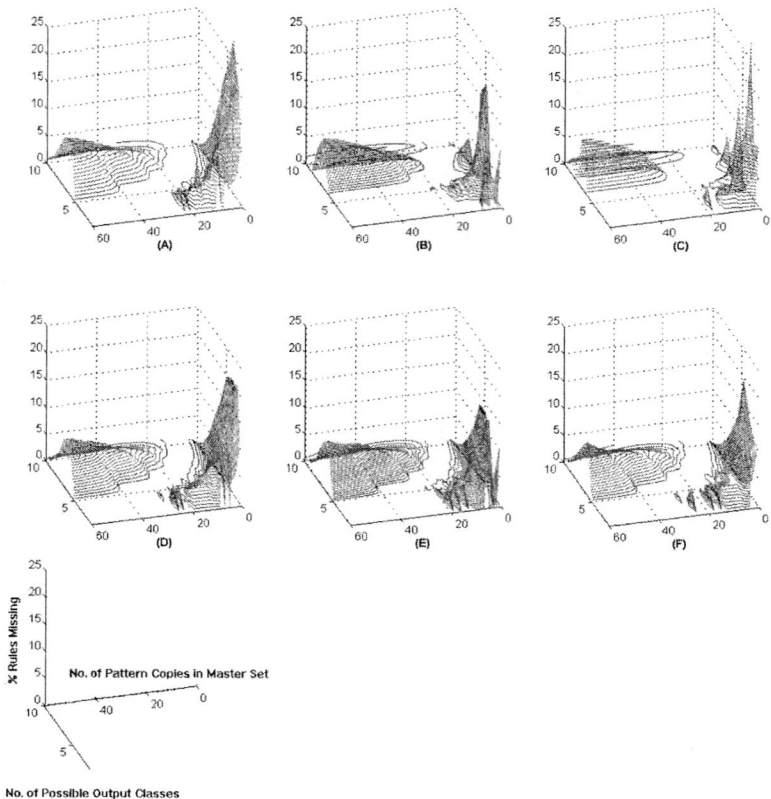

Fig. 3. Domain effect: (A) no limitation on the output space size and sequential output class assignment. (B) limited to output space size equals 3 and sequential output class assignment. (C) limited to output space size equals 4 and sequential target class assignment. (E) no limitation on the output space size and random output class assignment. (F) limited to output space size equals 3 and random output class assignment. (G) limited to output space size equals 4 and random output class assignment

The effect of limiting the number of output classes is clearer when the incompleteness graphs are rotated (see figure 4). Troughs exist at multiples of the output dimension size and likely result from the fact that with the output size domain equals the attribute value size domain size. Random mapping of output target to pattern removed the effect.

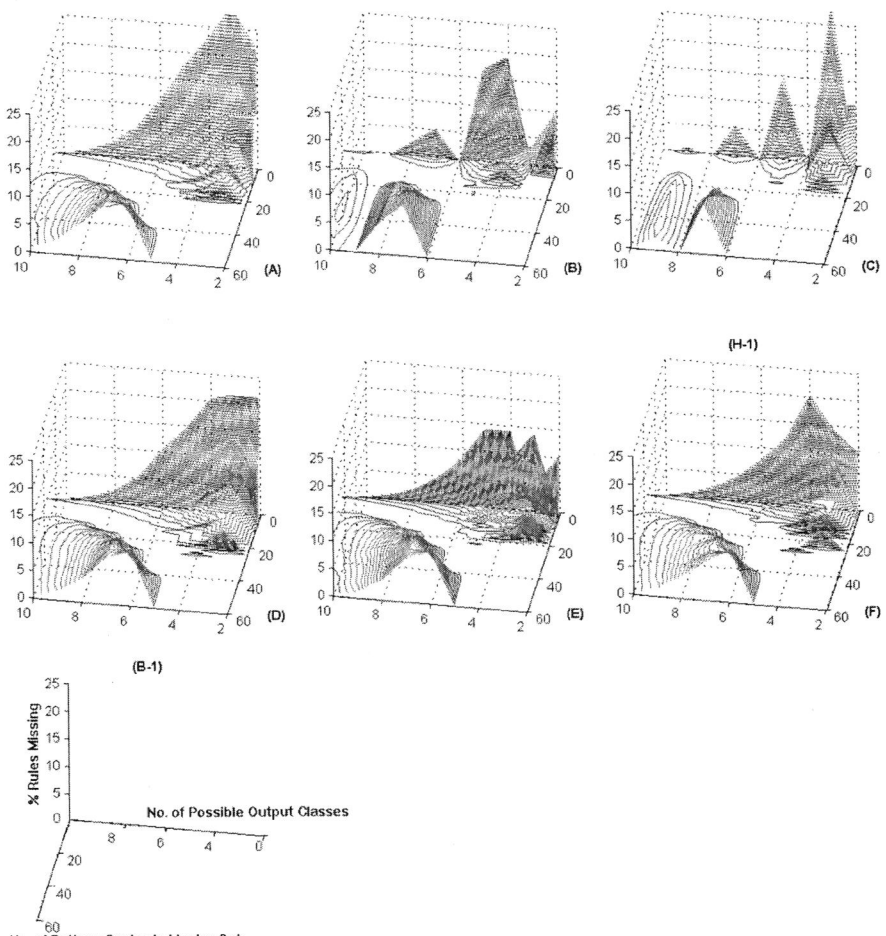

Fig. 4. Domain effect with images rotated 90°: (A) no limitation on the output space size and sequential output class assignment. (B) limited to output space size equals 3 and sequential output class assignment. (C) limited to output space size equals 4 and sequential target class assignment. (E) no limitation on the output space size and random output class assignment. (F) limited to output space size equals 3 and random output class assignment. (G) limited to output space size equals 4 and random output class assignment

The initial high levels of rules missing are to be expected under normal statistical sampling theory. What is not clear is the mechanism leading to increasing rule loss. Repeating the experiment using sequential mapping but with the initial target value shifted up the domain list, returned similar results (data not shown).

4 Discussion

Our results were consistent with statistical sampling theory which indicates that rule loss at low copy number is highly probable [19]. Unexpectedly, we found that under certain conditions, even redundancy levels of 60 pattern copies failed to overcome the incompleteness mechanism. We suspect that the underlying UOD complexity may contributes to this failure, but further investigation is required.

The incompleteness used in this set of experiments (40%) is at the higher end of those reported in the literature [8, 17, 21-23]. Our experiments show that at this level of incompleteness in data (with independent attributes), preprocessed using CCA, ID3 fails to induce up to 10% of the actual knowledge of the domain when compared to complete data. Since our master data are balanced, all rules are equally likely, thus the observed effects are likely to underestimate the loss of rules which would be induced from unbalanced data. If one or more of the attribute values exhibit high incompleteness with regard to the rest of the values, it is likely that higher rule loss rates will be detected. Such data sets are the norm for real-world data.

5 Conclusion

In this paper we investigated whether ID3-induced rules from complete data are different to those induced from incomplete data. Our experiments showed that knowledge induced from incomplete data preprocessed using CCA can contain much fewer rules than knowledge induced from complete data. Unfortunately this result suggests that KDD models being induced from massive amounts of incomplete data, preprocessed using CCA, may be suboptimal.

Our results show that significant portions of the total 'true' rule set can be lost when CCA is used, even for data with large copy numbers. For example, a UOD of four attributes over six possible values (1296 possible patterns) data of approximately 64000 patterns (MAR at 40%) failed to induce all patterns. Therefore, if UOD complexity is a key factor in determining the minimum amount of data needed for induction, then simply having millions of patterns in data is inadequate for extracting high quality knowledge complex domains.

Future work will involve determining if there is exists a mathematical function that describes, in terms of UOD characteristics and incompleteness mechanism, the minimal amount of data is required for optimal knowledge induction. Currently we analyzing whether there is a regular curve over one UOD characteristic set that will lead to a sustained region where rule loss is zero. This function would also provide a confidence metric for knowledge extracted from incomplete data in terms of a UOD.

The methods used by a KDD professional to approximate complete data impacts the quality of the information that can be induced from this data using automatic knowledge acquisition techniques. It appears that in the same way that the KDD process has been modeled, there remains substantial work to model the data cleaning process as a separate entity. While cleaning methods are supposed to maintain the quality of knowledge that can be induced from data, in practice it is difficult to determine which methods to use as none of these methods express knowledge quality in terms of a confidence level. We intend to establish such a level for ID3 and CCA.

Acknowledgement

We would like to thank the Department of Computer Science and Computer Engineering at La Trobe University for its continued support. We would also like to thank Dr. RL Dawe for his valuable input.

References

1. Fayyad, U.M., G. Piatetsky-Shapiro, and P. Smyth, *From data mining to knowledge discovery in databases.* AI Magazine, 1996. **17**(3): p. 37-54.
2. Zhong, N., et al. *KDD process planning.* in *Proceedings of the Third International Conference on Knowledge Discovery and Data Mining.* 1997. Newport Beach, CA, USA: AAAI Press.
3. Pyle, D., *Data Preparation for Data Mining.* 1999, San Francisco, CA: Morgan Kaufmann.
4. Allison, P.D., *Missing Data.* Quantitative Applications in the Social Sciences., ed. M.S. Lewis-Beck. 2001, Iowa City, IA: SAGE Publications.
5. Schafer, J.L. and J.W. Graham, *Missing Data: Our View of the State of the Art.* Psychological Methods, 2002. **7**(2): p. 147-177.
6. Quinlan, J.R., *Induction of Decision Trees.* Machine Learning, 1986. **1**: p. 81-106.
7. Crawford, S.L., J.B. McKinlay, and S.L. Tennstedt, *A comparison of analytic methods for non-random missingness of outcome data.* Journal of Clinical Epidemiology., 1995. **48**: p. 209-219.
8. Demissie, S., et al., *Bias due to missing exposure data using complete-case analysis in the proportional hazards regression model.* Statistics in Medicine., 2003. **22**: p. 545-557.
9. Kusiak, A., *Feature transformation methods in data mining.* IEEE Transactions on Electronics Packaging Manufacturing, 2001. **24**(3): p. 214-221.
10. Ragel, A. and B. Cremilleux, *MVC-a preprocessing method to deal with missing values.* Knowledge-Based Systems, 1999. **12**(5-6): p. 285-291.
11. Rubin, D.B., *Inference and Missing Data.* Biometrika, 1976. **63**(3): p. 581-592.
12. Little, R.J.A. and D.B. Rubin, *Statistical Analysis with Missing Data.* 1987, New York: John Wiley & Sons.
13. Heitjan, D.F. and S. Basu, *Distinguishing Missing at Random and Missing Completely at Random.* American Statistician, 1996. **50**(3): p. 207-213.
14. Allen, A.S. and R.H. Lyles, *Missing data in the 2×2 table: patterns and likelihood-based analysis for cross-sectional studies with supplemental sampling.* Statistics in Medicine., 2003. **22**(4): p. 517-534.
15. Norris, C.M., et al., *Dealing with missing data in observational health care outcome analyses.* Journal of Clinical Epidemiology., 2000. **53**(4): p. 377-383.
16. Walczak, B. and D.L. Massart, *Dealing with missing data. II.* Chemometrics & Intelligent Laboratory Systems, 2001. **58**(1): p. 29-42.
17. Walczak, B. and D.L. Massart, *Dealing with missing data. I.* Chemometrics & Intelligent Laboratory Systems, 2001. **58**(1): p. 15-27.
18. Tsiatis, A.A., M. Davidian, and B. McNeney, *Multiple imputation methods for testing treatment differences in survival distributions with missing cause of failure.* Biometrika, 2002. **89**(1): p. 238-244.
19. Glymour, C., et al., *Statistical inference and data mining.* Communications of the ACM, 1996. **39**(11): p. 35-41.

20. Dey, S. and S.A. Roberts. *On high dimensional data spaces.* in *Third International Conference on Data Mining. Data Mining III. WIT Press. 2002, pp.239-50. Southampton, UK.* 2002.
21. Curran, D., et al., *Identifying the types of missingness in quality of life data from clinical trials. [Review] [29 refs].* Statistics in Medicine., 1998. **17**(5-7): p. 739-56.
22. Allison, P.D., *Multiple imputation for missing data - A cautionary tale.* Sociological Methods & Research., 2000. **28**(3): p. 301-309.
23. Ibrahim, J.G., M.H. Chen, and S.R. Lipsitz, *Missing responses in generalised linear mixed models when the missing data mechanism is nonignorable.* Biometrika, 2001. **88**(2): p. 551-564.

Investigating Learning Parameters in a Standard 2-D SOM Model to Select Good Maps and Avoid Poor Ones

Hiong Sen Tan and Susan E. George

University of South Australia,
Mawson Lakes SA 5095, Australia
tan@cs.unisa.edu.au, susan.george@unisa.edu.au

Abstract. In the self organising map (SOM), applying different learning parameters to the same input will lead to different maps. The question of how to select the best map is important. A map is good if it is relatively accurate in representing the input and ordered. A measure or measures are needed to quantify the accuracy and the 'order' of maps. This paper investigates the learning parameters in standard 2-dimensional SOMs to find the learning parameters that lead to optimal arrangements. An example of choosing a map in a real world application is also provided.

1 Introduction

The Self Organising Map (SOM) [1, 2] is an unsupervised artificial neural network that is able to perform data clustering. Unlike statistical methods or other ways of grouping data the SOM provides a topological ordering where the relationships between data items are made apparent. In fact, relationships within data of high-dimensionality in the input space are reduced to relationships on lower-dimensional output space (typically 1, 2 or 3-dimensions). Maps of more than 3-dimensions are discouraged since visualising the result is complicated beyond 3-dimensions.

The disadvantage of the SOM is that, like other neural network techniques, explaining why a trained network produces a particular result is not simple. In the case of the SOM it is even less straightforward to quantify the network since the data it clusters has no a priori classification to measure classification performance. The map produced is totally dependent on the data and the learning parameters. From the literature, [2], we know several rules of thumb for SOM training, but it is still necessary to evaluate the result maps with respect to some criteria for a good quality map.

The aim of this paper is to investigate what parameter arrangements can lead to a 'good' map in the standard 2-dimensional SOM. Suitable parameter arrangements will reduce the chance of getting poor maps that are twisted or unordered. We use the standard SOM model, in contrast to the variants and extensions of the SOM, such as Growing Cell Structures [3], Growing SOM [4], Tree-Structured SOM [5], and SAM-SOM [6]. Other extensions of the SOM that automatically select parameters have been proposed, Auto SOM [7] and the Parameter-less SOM [8]. However, there is no proof that training the SOM with learning parameter values adjusted automatically during training gives better result than training the SOM with the learning parameter values defined beforehand, and adjusted with respect to the number of training cycles. The detail of the standard 2-dimensional SOM algorithm can be found in [2], and more applied presentations in [9] and [10].

2 The Quality of the Map

This section discusses ways of measuring the quality of SOM maps, first considering a common visualisation method of SOM training that can give an impression of how the map is 'unfolding'. This method of illustrating the SOM learning process is discussed in [2], [10], and [11]. Using a 2-dimensional map with 2-dimensional data means that the connection of neighbouring nodes can be drawn to show the order on the output. The weights of each node are plotted on the x and y coordinates and the neighbouring nodes on the map are connected with lines, e.g. node (0,0) is connected with node (0,1) and (1,0) as shown in Fig. 1. For simplicity, the lines connect only horizontal and vertical (east, west, north and south) neighbours of the node, and do not connect diagonal (north east, south east, north west and south west) neighbours.

Fig. 3 shows four results of training a 5 by 5 SOM with the input from 81 points of a square shown in Fig. 2. It is easy to see that the result maps in Fig. 3(c) and (d) mirror the square input data better than those in Fig. 3(a) and (b). In fact, the maps in Fig. 3(c) and (d) are examples of good maps, i.e. ordered, while the maps in Fig. 3(a) and (b) are examples of poor maps, i.e. unordered and twisted respectively. But, in the comparison of two good maps in Fig. 3(c) and (d), our eyes will not help much. It is even impossible to tell whether one map is better than another without a measure when the data has high dimensionality (more than 3 dimensions) since we cannot represent the weights values with graph coordinates, as in Fig 1. An additional measure or measures are needed, but first, the criteria upon what the measures are based should be determined.

There are at least two criteria that can be used to measure the quality of the map: the accuracy and the order of the map. The accuracy is how well the inputs are represented in the output space. It can be measured by the quantisation error (E_q) [2] as in Equation (1).

$$E_q = \frac{1}{n} \sum_{i=1}^{n} \|x_i - m_c(x_i)\| \qquad (1)$$

where n is the number of inputs and $m_c(x_i)$ is the output that have the closest distance from the input x_i.

The order of the map is whether the map preserves topological order in the input space. The idea is the neighbouring vectors in the input space should be mapped to the neighbouring vectors in the output space. Several measures are proposed to determine whether a map is ordered, such as topographic product [12], topographic function [13], topographic error [14] and Kaski and Lagus' [15]. Since until now there is no single topology preservation measure that is claimed to be better than the others except that the topographic product cannot distinguish the correct folding due to the folded nonlinear input data from the incorrect folding [13], we choose the simple one, i.e. topographic error.

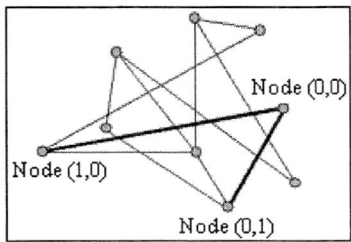

Fig. 1. Neighbouring nodes on the map are connected with lines. The thick line shows node(0,0) is connected to its neighbours, node(0,1) and node(1,0)

Topographic error was proposed by Kiviluoto [14] to measure the continuity of mapping. The neural units which have the best match and second best match weight vectors, w_i and w_j respectively, for input data x on the map have to be adjacent to indicate the continuity of the mapping. The consequence is that some points between x and w_j in the input are mapped to w_i, and the rest to w_j. Otherwise, a local topographic error is indicated. Then, the global topographic error (E_t) of the map can be calculated using the following formula:

$$E_t = \frac{1}{n} \sum_{i=1}^{n} u(x_i) \qquad (2)$$

where $u(x_i) = 1$ if best and second best units are non adjacent and 0 otherwise.

Obviously we want to use the map that most accurately represents the input and also preserves the topology order in the input space. However, in the real world the selection of the measures to justify the quality of the map and the map to be used is related to the application because often there is a trade-off between the accuracy and the order of the map. For example, in our research of clustering documents where the order is slightly more important than accuracy to represent the 'similar' documents close to each other on the map, we use the topographic error as the main measure because the topographic error guarantees that nodes with 'similar' values will be adjacent on the map. We use the quantisation error as the second measure to decide one map is better than another in case both maps have the same topographic error values.

Now, the criteria of a good map have been set and the measures have been chosen, the visual inspection of good maps and not good maps, in Fig. 3, can be justified by the measures, as shown in Table 1. The maps in Fig. 3(c) and (d) are good maps because they have no topographic error while the maps in Fig. 3(a) and (b) are not good maps because their topographic error values are different significantly than those of maps in Fig. 3(c) and (d).

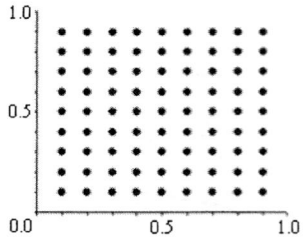

Fig. 2. Input from 81 points in a square

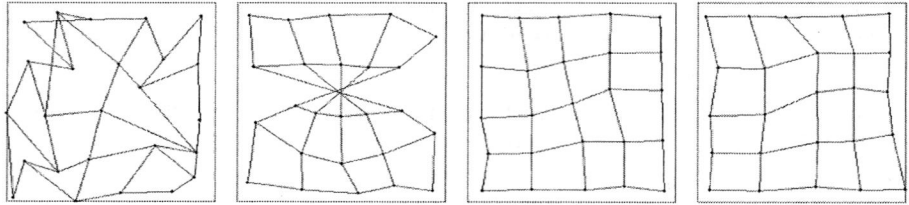

Fig. 3. The examples of result maps. (a) An un-ordered map. (b) A twisted map. (c) and (d) Good maps

The better map of the good maps in Fig. 3(c) and (d) can also be determined. Both of the maps have no topographic error, the map in Fig. 3(c) has quantisation error = 0.00104 while the map in Fig. 3(d) has quantisation error = 0.00095. Thus, the map in Fig. 3(d) is better than the map in Fig. 3(c) as the former is more accurate than the latter. What we need is to actually make sure that the map that is chosen is a good one. We can get several good maps from training the SOM with different parameter arrangements. The suitable parameter arrangements will reduce the chance of getting poor maps that are twisted or unordered. The measures in this case can be used as a yardstick for choosing suitable learning parameters [2], as we do in Section 3.

After we know the suitable parameter arrangements, it is still necessary to train the SOM with several sets of suitable parameter settings, judge the quality with the measures, and choose the best among them based on the measures. We still need to train the SOM with several sets of training parameters even though we know the suitable ones to avoid choosing a poor map instead of good one. The good and poor maps are normally easy to distinguish from the significant difference on their quantisation and topographic error. We should also know that a variety of maps will be produced, even if they have the same quantisation and/or topographic error values. Varfis and Versino [16] showed eight permutations of maps, as seen in Fig. 4. We may choose one of these variations as long as they are good maps.

Table 1. Masurement results of maps in Fig. 3

Map	E_t	E_q
Fig. 3(a)	0.08642	0.00094
Fig. 3(b)	0.06173	0.00172
Fig. 3(c)	0.00000	0.00104
Fig. 3(d)	0.00000	0.00095

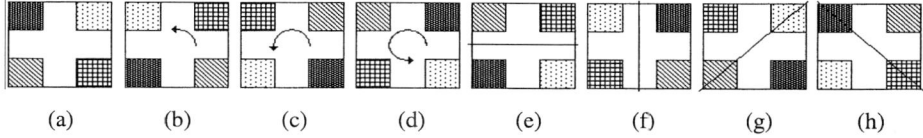

(a) (b) (c) (d) (e) (f) (g) (h)

Fig. 4. The possible permutation of a map. The permutations are with respect to (a). (b) 90° rotation. (c) 180° rotation. (d) 270° rotation. (e) Horizontal flip. (f) Vertical flip. (g) Diagonal flip. (h) Opposite diagonal flip

3 Experiments on the SOM Learning Parameter Arrangement

There are several parameters involved in training the SOM: the number of training cycles, the neighbourhood function, the initial weights, the learning rate, the sequence of inputs and the map size. This section tries to answer what kind of parameter arrangements will lead to a good map.

The SOM either has to be trained until it converges or for a fixed number of training cycles. No proof of the convergence of the SOM, except for 1-dimensional case, has been presented [2]. Fortunately, it is not always necessary to prove the convergence of the map. As long as the SOM is trained with enough training cycles, it can lead to good map production. The lack of training itself can cause the map to not accurately represent the output and hence not to be ordered. Kohonen [2] suggested the number of training cycles should be at least 500 times the number of the map nodes to produce a good map. The research undertaken follows this rule of thumb, for example a 5 by 5 SOM is trained for 12500 training cycles.

The standard SOM model as a clustering technique has drawback similar to K-means algorithm, that is we have to pre-determined the number of formed classes. In the SOM, even though we do not explicitly specify the number of classes we actually limit it with the map size. The bigger map sizes tends to give better results than the smaller ones, but the smaller ones are preferred in some applications for some reasons such as easier visualisation and smaller memory and storage requirement.

3.1 Neighbourhood Value

The neighbourhood should shrink over time. As this research uses the topological rectangle neighbourhood [2], shown in Fig. 5., the question is what the value of the neighbourhood when the training is started and the value when the training is complete. The neighbourhood of the winning node usually ends up with 0, in other words no neighbouring node is updated at the last training cycles.

Fig. 6(a) and (b) show how the maps look when they end up with neighbourhood radius equal to 0 and neighbourhood radius equal to 1, respectively. Both maps are trained for 12500 training cycles with the same map size 5 by 5, same initial weights between 0.1 and 0.9, same sequence of inputs from pre-generated random number, same fixed value 0.1 of learning rate, and started with the same value 2 of neighbourhood radius.

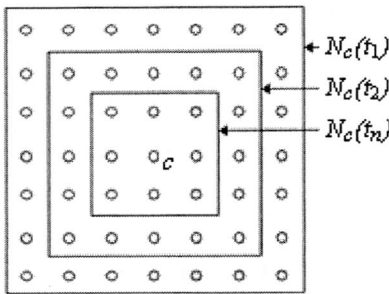

Fig. 5. The topological rectangle neighbourhood where c is the winning node and $N_c(t_i)$ is a group of nodes considered as the neighbours of c including c at discrete time t_i (shown within a square). The size of neighbourhood decreases in time

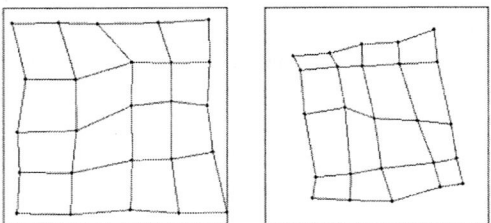

Fig. 6. Result maps with different end values of neighbourhood. (a) Map ends up with neighbourhood radius = 0. (b) Map ends up with neighbourhood radius = 1

From visual inspection, it is clear that the result map in Fig. 6(a) is better than that of Fig. 6(b) because the latter has not spread out maximally. However, both maps have no topographic error, therefore the quantisation error is checked. By looking at the significants different quantisation error of the latter compared to the former, it can be concluded that the latter one is not a good map. Thus, the training should end up with no winning node's neighbour weights being updated.

The SOMs are trained again with the same parameters as the previous ones, except the neighbourhood radius ends up with 0 and starts with various values from the maximum value 4, i.e. the map diameter - 1, to value 1. The results are given in Table 2.

A not good result occurs when the neighbourhood radius starts with 1. This bad result is reasonable because with a neighbourhood that is too small the map will not be ordered and in this particular experiment setting the map is twisted. Three other results show that the neighbourhood can start with values from about half of the map diameter to the maximum value, i.e. map diameter - 1. But there is a significant difference in the learning process as shown in Fig. 7 for the SOM training starting with neighbourhood radius equal to 4 and Fig. 8 for the SOM training starting with neighbourhood radius equal to 2.

When the training is started with maximum neighbourhood radius value that means the weights of all nodes are updated because all nodes are the neighbours of the winning node. As a result, all weights have the same values as shown in Fig. 7(b). Then, this causes the learning process to be slower than in the case where the neighbourhood radius starts with 2. It can be seen that the map in Fig. 7(c) is less spread out than that of Fig. 8(c) after the same period of training cycles, i.e. 5000 training cycles.

From the results shown in Table 2 we conclude the neighbourhood can be started with a value about equal to half of the map diameter.

3.2 Initial Weight

The initial weights are small random values between 0 and 1 as the input data of neural networks are usually scaled to values 0 to 1. Table 3 gives the results for training the SOMs with varying initial weights, all other parameters being equal. The training parameters are: 12500 training cycles, map size 5 by 5, fixed learning rate 0.1, same sequence of inputs from pre-generated random number, and neighbourhood radius starts with 2 and ends with 0.

Table 2. Measurement results for various start values of neighbourhood radius

Neighbourhood radius start value	E_t	E_q
4	0.00000	0.00095
3	0.00000	0.00145
2	0.00000	0.00095
1	0.09877	0.00174

There are only two possible results from these particular parameter setting and different ranges of initial weights, a good map or a twisted map. From the results in Table 3 we can conclude that the initial weights have an impact on the quality of the map, but the ranges of the initial weights do not.

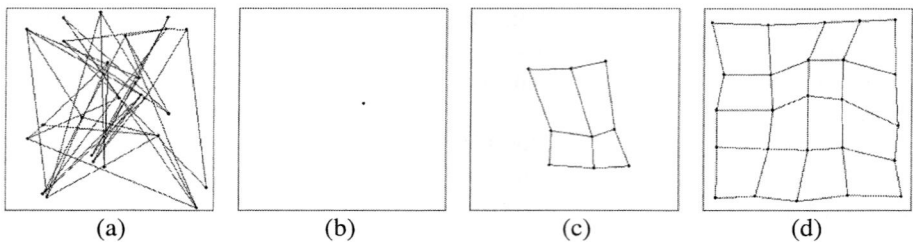

Fig. 7. The learning process of SOM when neighbourhood radius value starts with map diameter - 1. (a) Initial map with random weight values between 0.1 and 0.9. (b) Map after 100 training cycles. (c) Map after 5000 training cycles. (d) Final map after 12500 training cycles

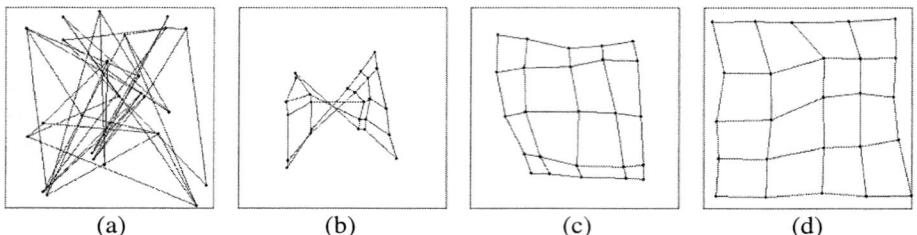

Fig. 8. The learning process of SOM when neighbourhood radius value starts with half of the map diameter. (a) Initial map with random weight values between 0.1 and 0.9. (b) Map after 100 training cycles. (c) Map after 5000 training cycles. (d) Final map after 12500 training cycles

3.3 Input Sequence

The input sequence also contributes to the quality of the map, as shown by the results of training the SOMs, as given in Table 4. The SOMs are trained with the same parameters except the sequence of input is random. The training parameters are: 12500 training cycles, map size 5 by 5, fixed learning rate 0.1, same initial weight values between 0.1 and 0.9, and neighbourhood radius starts with 2 and ends with 0. It is also possible to enter the input sequentially and repeat the sequence. The last row of the table is the result from entering sequentially input no.1 to 81 and repeating them 155 times, so that total training cycles close to 12500, i.e. 12555.

3.4 Learning Rate

The learning rate is between 0 and 1. The learning rate usually starts with a bigger value (close to unity) and ends with the smaller value, usually near to zero for fine adjustment in the last training cycles. It is also possible to use a fixed small value for the learning rate. Table 5 shows the results of training the SOMs with equal parameter values except for the learning rate. The training parameters are 12500 training cycles, map size 5 by 5, same initial weights between 0.1 and 0.9, same sequence of inputs from pre-generated random number, and neighbourhood radius starts with 2 and ends with 0.

Table 3. Measurement results for various values of initial weights

Results are good maps			Results are twisted map		
Initial weights	E_t	E_q	Initial weights	E_t	E_q
0.4 - 0.6	0.00000	0.00095	0.4 - 0.6	0.18519	0.00105
0.3 - 0.7	0.00000	0.00095	0.3 - 0.7	0.18519	0.00105
0.2 - 0.8	0.00000	0.00095	0.2 - 0.8	0.18519	0.00105
0.1 - 0.9	0.00000	0.00095	0.1 - 0.9	0.18519	0.00105
0.0 - 1.0	0.00000	0.00095	0.0 - 1.0	0.18519	0.00105

Table 4. Measurement results for different sequence of inputs

Experiment No.	E_t	E_q	Remark
1.	0.00000	0.00095	
2.	0.13580	0.00060	twisted map
3.	0.13580	0.00079	twisted map
4.	0.00000	0.00068	
5.	0.01235	0.00089	
6.	0.00000	0.00080	

Table 5. Measurement results for various values of learning rate

Fixed learning rate				Decreasing learning rate			
Learning rate		E_t	E_q	Learning rate		E_t	E_q
Start	End			Start	End		
0.05	0.05	0.17284	0.00091	0.1	0.0	0.06173	0.00093
0.1	0.1	0.00000	0.00095	0.2	0.0	0.01235	0.00087
0.2	0.2	0.00000	0.00089	0.3	0.0	0.00000	0.00087
0.3	0.3	0.00000	0.00087	0.4	0.0	0.00000	0.00087
0.4	0.4	0.19753	0.00101	0.5	0.0	0.00000	0.00087
0.5	0.5	0.39506	0.00123	0.6	0.0	0.00000	0.00047
				0.7	0.0	0.00000	0.00088
				0.8	0.0	0.00000	0.00047
				0.9	0.0	0.07407	0.00107
				1.0	0.0	0.00000	0.00088

As it can be seen in the first (left) part of the Table 5, the learning rate can be a small fixed value. But, too small a value can lead to a twisted map and too big a fixed value will lead to an unordered map.

The second (right) part of Table 5 uses a variable learning rate that decreases in time. The following formula is used:

$$\eta_{(t)} = \eta_{(0)} * 1 - ((t - 1) / T) \tag{3}$$

where η(0) is the initial value of learning rate, t is the current training cycle and T is total number of training cycles.

Good maps tend to be produced when the learning rate starts with 0.3 to unity, with exceptions when the learning rate starts with 0.9. The value 0.3 is not the smallest value that can be used to produce a good map and it does not mean the learning rate cannot start with value 0.9 because other parameters such as the initial weight and the sequence of inputs also contribute towards a good map or a poor map.

What can be learned here is that a good map can be produced with a relatively small fixed value of learning rate or with a learning rate that decreases in time. We suggest using the decreasing leaning rate, since from our experiments we found it improves the accuracy. The following simple example from 1-dimensional data supports our finding.

Assume that we have two inputs: 0 and 1, and we would like to project them to 1 by 1 map. We except that the result will be a node with weight value 0.5 regardless the initial weight value. Table 6 gives the results when learning rate 0.1 and number of training cycles 500 are used with different input sequences.

The final weights of presenting random input sequences to the SOM (column 2 of Table 6) are various while ones of presenting fixed input sequences and repeating the sequences for a number of times (column 3 and 4 of Table 6) are uniform. The sequence of the inputs also has an impact on the final weight, as we see in column 3 and 4 of Table 6. The final weight favours the value of the last input presented to the SOM. In column 3 of Table 6 the final weights swing upward to 1 from 0.5 because the sequence of the inputs, which is repeated for a number of times, is 0 then 1, while in column 4 the final weights swing downward to 0 from 0.5 because the sequence of the inputs is 1 then 0.

Table 6 (column 5-7) also shows the result when a decreasing learning rate, start with 0.3 and end with 0.0, is used instead of a fixed small learning rate, i.e. 0.1 in the previous example. By using the decreasing learning rate, the accuracy is improved that is the final weight values are closer to 0.5.

From the result in Table 6, should it be also concluded that using a fixed input sequence and repeating the sequence for a number of times will give better, more accurate, result than using random input sequence? No, it should not. As we mentioned before that if we use fixed input sequence and repeating the sequence for a number of times, the result will swing toward the last inputs. In the trivial example above, the swing is not very strong since the inputs are only two numbers and balanced. In the experiments using more than 5,000 inputs in Section 4, we see that using a random input sequence can produce better result than a fixed input sequence and repeating the sequence for a number of times, as seen in Table 7.

4 Experiments on Clustering More Than 5000 Documents

Up to this point we have identified parameter arrangements of the SOM that can lead to production of good maps. They are: training cycles at least 500 times the number of the map nodes, any initial weight values, neighbourhood radius starts from about half of the map diameter and ends with 0, and decreasing learning rate towards 0. But, we cannot make the parameter values to be chosen automatically because we still do not know the following: what is best start value of the learning rate? and should we use a fixed input sequence or a random input sequence? For this reason, we train the SOM for several times with different parameter arrangements that we have known can lead to production of good maps and choose the best among the results based on their topographic errors and quantisation errors.

Table 7 shows the results of clustering more than 5,000 documents represented by 255 keywords (255 dimensions in input data) on the 2-dimensional SOM size 16 by 16. The neighbourhood radius starts with 8, half of the map diameter and ends with 0. The learning rate value starts with 0.2, 0.3 and 0.4. The input sequences are fixed and random. From the results in Table 7, we choose to use the result of training run #4 since we consider the order is more important than the accuracy of the map in our application. The map is used for browsing to explore the organisation of the documents and to retrieve the desired documents.

Table 6. Results of varying input sequences

Initial weight	With fixed learning rate, i.e. 0.1			With decreasing learning rate, start with 0.3 and end with 0.0		
	Final weight when input sequence is			Final weight when input sequence is		
	Random	0 then 1	1 then 0	Random	0 then 1	1 then 0
0.24608	0.59095	0.52632	0.47368	0.52412	0.50008	0.49992
0.53563	0.41359	0.52632	0.47368	0.47309	0.50008	0.49992
0.79391	0.64353	0.52632	0.47368	0.52413	0.50008	0.49992

Table 7. Meaasurement results of clustering more than 5000 documents

Training run no.	Learning rate start value	E_t	E_q
Fixed sequence of inputs			
1.	0.2	0.20314	0.00024
2.	0.3	0.30078	0.00024
3.	0.4	0.32644	0.00024
Random Sequence of Inputs			
4.	0.2	0.17088	0.00025
5.	0.3	0.18603	0.00022
6.	0.4	0.25303	0.00022

5 Conclusion

In this paper, the quality of the maps produced by the SOM is measured in respect to their accuracy and order. Accuracy describes how accurate the inputs are represented on the output while the order describes how well the relationship among the input data is preserved on the output. The quantisation error is used to measure the accuracy of the map and topographic error is used to measure the order of the map. These two measures, the topographic error and the quantisation error, are then used to find suitable parameters to train the SOM and to choose the best map among available maps from several numbers of training simulations.

We found the following arrangements are suitable to train the SOM to produce good maps. The neighbourhood can start with a value near to half the map diameter and end with 0. Using a decreasing learning rate can produce better results than using a fixed one. The learning rate can start with a value near to unity and end with a value near to 0. The range of initial weights has no impact on the quality of the map but the values of the initial weights do. And, as the input sequence also contributes to the quality of the map, the simulation of training the SOM for a number of times with the parameter arrangement as discussed above is necessary. The simulation serves not only to find the best map among available maps but also to avoid selecting poor maps. The good maps can be differentiated from the poor ones by looking at the significant difference in their topographic error and quantisation error values.

References

1. Kohonen, T., *Self-organized formation of topologically correct feature maps.* Biological Cybernetics, 1982. **43**: p. 59-69.
2. Kohonen, T., *Self-organizing map.* Second Edition ed. Springer Series in Information Sciences, ed. T.S. Huang, T. Kohonen, and M.R. Schroeder. 1995, Berlin Heidelberg: Springer-Verlag.
3. Fritzke, B., *Growing cell structures - a self-organizing network for unsupervised and supervised learning.* Neural Networks, 1994. **7**(9): p. 1441-1460.
4. Alahakoon, D., S.K. Halgamuge, and B. Srinivasan, *Dynamic self-organizing maps with controlled growth for knowledge discovery.* IEEE Transactions on Neural Networks, 2000. **11**(3): p. 601-614.
5. Koikkalainen, P. and K. Oja. *Self-organizing hierarchical feature maps.* in *Proceedings of International Joint Conference on Neural Networks.* 1990. San Diego, CA.
6. Cuadros-Vargas, E. and R.A.F. Romero. *A SAM-SOM family: incorporating spatial access methods into constructive self-organizing maps.* in *Proceedings of International Joint Conference on Neural Networks.* 2002. Honolulu, HI.
7. Haese, K. and G.J. Goodhill, *Auto-SOM: recursive parameter estimation for guidance of self-organizing feature maps.* Neural Computation, 2001. **13**: p. 595-619.
8. Berglund, E. and J. Sitte. *The parameter-less SOM algorithm.* in *Proceedings of the 8th Australian and New Zealand Intelligent Information System Conference (ANZIIS 2003).* 2003. Sydney, Australia: Queensland University of Technology.
9. Lippmann, R.P., *An introduction to computing with neural nets.* IEEE Acoustics, Speech, and Signal Processing Society Magazine, 1987. **4**(2): p. 4-22.
10. Freeman, J.A. and D.M. Skapura, *Neural networks: algorithms, applications and programming techniques.* 1991, Reading, Massachussets: Addison-Wesley.
11. Callan, R., *The essence of neural networks.* Essence of Computing. 1999, London: Prentice Hall Europe.

12. Bauer, H.-U. and K.R. Pawelzik, *Quantifying the neighbourhood preservation of self-organizing feature maps.* IEEE Transactions on Neural Networks, 1992. **3**(4): p. 570-579.
13. Villmann, T., R. Der, and T.M. Martinetz. *A new quantitative measure of topology preservation in Kohonen's feature maps.* in *Proceedings of IEEE International Conference on Neural Networks.* 1994: IEEE.
14. Kiviluoto, K. *Topology preservation in self-organizing maps.* in *The Proceedings of IEEE International Conference on Neural Networks.* 1996. Washington, DC: IEEE.
15. Kaski, S. and K. Lagus. *Comparing self-organizing maps.* in *Proceedings of International Conference on Artificial Neural Networks.* 1996. Bochum, Germany: Springer-Verlag.
16. Varfis, A. and C. Versino, *Selecting reliable Kohonen maps for data analysis.* Artificial Neural Networks, 1992. **2**: p. 1583-1586.

Key Element Summarisation: Extracting Information from Company Announcements

Robert Dale[1,3], Rafael Calvo[2,3], and Marc Tilbrook[1]

[1] Centre for Language Technology, Macquarie University, Sydney
www.clt.mq.edu.au
[2] Web Engineering Group, University of Sydney, Sydney
www.weg.ee.usyd.edu.au
[3] Capital Markets Co-operative Research Centre, Sydney
www.cmcrc.com.au

Abstract. In this paper, we describe KES, a system that integrates text categorisation and information extraction in order to extract key elements of information from particular types of documents, with these informational elements being presented in such a way as to provide a concise summary of the input document. We describe the overall architecture of the system and its components, with a particular focus on the problems involved in handling the names of companies and individuals in this domain.

1 Introduction

Information Extraction (IE [1–3]) is concerned with the process of identifying a pre-specified set of key data elements from a free-text data source, and is widely recognised as one of the more successful spin-off technologies to come from the field of natural language processing. During the 1990s, the DARPA-funded Message Understanding Conferences resulted in a number of systems that could extract from texts, with reasonable results, specific information about complex events such as terrorist incidents or corporate takeovers. These information extraction tasks are manageable because, in each case, some other process has determined that the document being analysed falls within the target domain, and the key information to be extracted is typically only a very small subset of the total content of the document. A major component task in information extraction is **named entity recognition** [4], whereby entities such as people, organizations and geographic locations are identified and tracked in texts; other processing can then take the results of the named entity recognition process to build higher order data structures, effectively determining who did what to who, when and where.

In this paper, we describe KES, an experiment in information extraction where we first use text categorisation to determine the type of document being processed; given the document's type, we can make hypotheses about the kinds of informational elements that can be extracted from that document. After extracting these key elements, we can then produce concise summaries of the input documents, thus saving the user the need to read the source documents in order to determine the central information they contain.

The KES project operates in the domain of financial information. In particular, we have been working with a data set from the Australian Stock Exchange (ASX). This data set consists of a large set of company announcements: these are documents provided by companies to the ASX, who subsequently make them available to users via the web. Many of these documents are required for regulatory purposes, and these regulations impose some requirements on the content of documents. The ASX categorises the documents into a large number of different types, including categories like 'change in shareholding', 'notice of intended takeover', 'statement of director's interests', and so on. Our goal is to take this data set (and similar data sets) and to add value to the documents by making use of language technologies.

In Section 2, we describe the characteristics of our particular problem scenario. Section 3 lays out our approach to solving this problem, and Section 4 elaborates on our approach to the handling of potentially unknown names of organisations and individuals. We conclude by summarising the results produced by our system so far, and pointing to further work in the area.

2 Background

2.1 The Problem

The corpus we are working with is the Signal G document set, a collection of corporate announcements made available by the Australian Stock Exchange (ASX) via their web site. These documents are provided to the ASX by companies in order to adhere to regulatory requirements; in various circumstances, companies are required to provide appropriate documents detailing, for example, changes in shareholding, or intentions to make takeover bids, and the ASX then makes this information available via their web site.[1]

The number of documents involved here is vast: over 100000 documents are submitted to the ASX each year and made available via the web site. This makes it difficult for a user to easily obtain and track information of interest: although the ASX web site permits searching by the stock exchange codes of the companies involved, this still provides only a very limited means of filtering the data.

In order to ease this difficulty, we set out to build a system which could extract key elements of information from this document collection: by deriving this set of structured data from the relatively unstructured data, we would be in a position to facilitate both the indexing and browsing of the documents by allowing a more structured search of their contents and a number of other services. For example, when a company is in the process of taking over another company, it is required to issue frequent updates that report on the relevant changes in

---

[1] See www.asx.com.au. As of mid-2004, the ASX put in place constraints on the use of data gathered from their web site; the experiments reported here pre-date the imposition of those constraints.

shareholding; by extracting this information from the source documents, we can track such events across multiple documents. We can also identify and track individuals across documents, so we can easily provide information about the involvement of particular individuals across a range of companies. With the additional structure added to the documents using IE, we can, for example, provide a messaging service that sends alerts (i.e., emails or SMS messages) based on specific triggers, or even generate speech summaries of important events which can be sent automatically.

2.2 The Corpus

Our corpus consists of a set of 136,630 documents from the year 2000. The ASX categorises the documents it receives into a large set of categories: there are 19 basic report types, subdivided into 176 subtypes. The 19 basic report types are shown in Table 1, with a breakdown showing how many documents from our sample fall into each category.

For our experiment, we focussed on the sub-types of report type 002, as shown in Table 2.

We focussed on this category of reports for three reasons:
– First, the category represents a significant proportion (18.5%) of the documents in our corpus.
– Second, our categorisation technology, as discussed below in Section 3.1, worked very well on these categories.

Table 1. The 19 basic report types in the Signal G Data

	Category	Number
01	Takeover Announcement	4616
02	Security Holder Details	25372
03	Periodic Reports	24323
04	Quarterly Activities Report	6617
05	Quarterly Cash Flow Report	383
06	Issued Capital	21785
07	Asset Acquisition Disposal	3832
08	Notice of Meeting	7381
09	Stock Exchange Announcement	2900
10	Dividend Announcement	1037
11	Progress Report	9169
12	Company Administration	7183
13	Notice of Call (Contributing Shares)	11
14	Other	10481
15	Chairman's Address	1657
16	Letter to Sharareholders	1999
17	ASX Query	1377
18	Warrants	5682
19	Commitments Test Entity Quarterly Reports	825
	Total	136630

Table 2. The subtypes of report type 002

Type	Security Holder Details	# Docs
02/001	Becoming a substantial holder	3763
02/002	Change in substantial holding	8249
02/003	Ceasing to be a substantial holder	1717
02/004	Beneficial ownership - Part 6C.2	5
02/005	Takeover update - Section 689 Notice	2314
02/006	Security holder details - Other	546
02/007	Section 205G Notice - Directors Interests	8778
Total		25372

```
Document date: Fri 20 Jun 2003 Published: Fri 20 Jun 2003 14:37:46
Document No: 298709  Document part: A
Market Flag: N
Classification: Change in substantial holding
SYDNEY AQUARIUM LIMITED                      2003-06-20    ASX-SIGNAL-G

HOMEX - Sydney

++++++++++++++++++++++++++
Commonwealth Bank of Australia decreased its relevant interest in
Sydney Aquarium Limited on 17/06/2003, from 3,970,481 ordinary shares
(18.49%) to 3,763,203 ordinary shares (17.29%).
```

Fig. 1. A simple document of type 02/002

– Third, the documents in this category are relatively predictable in terms of their content, and often quite short.

Figure 1 shows an example of the text contained in a document of type 02/002. This is a very simple example, as are most in this category; by way of contrast, Figure 2 shows a more complex document that reports a change in shareholdings.

In the current ASX web site, accessing this information requires considerable effort on the part of the user. First, they must search the document set by entering the ASX code of the company they are interested in; this results in a list of documents individuated by their titles, with hyperlinks to the PDF and text versions of these documents. It then takes two more clicks to access the text that makes up the document, as shown in Figures 1 and 2; and then, of course, the user has to read through the document to find the information of interest.

2.3 Our Goals

Our goals, then, were to develop techniques for finding the key elements of information in the documents in our corpus. The identification of key elements is essentially an information extraction problem. The idea is that, for certain kinds

```
Document date: Fri 27 Jun 2003  Published: Fri 27 Jun 2003 08:55:58
Document No: 205676   Document part: A
Market Flag: N
Classification: Security holder details - Other , Asset Acquisition
TOLL HOLDINGS LIMITED                            2003-06-27 ASX-SIGNAL-G

HOMEX - Melbourne

++++++++++++++++++++++++++
This is to advise that Toll Group (NZ) Limited has today announced to
the New Zealand Stock Exchange that its holding in Tranz Rail
Holdings Limited has increased by an additional 20,800,000 common
shares at NZ Dollars $0.94 per share. This represents a further
consideration of NZ Dollars $19,552,000. These additional shares now
increase Toll Group (NZ) Limited's holding in Tranz Rail Holdings
Limited to a total of 42,034,153 common shares, representing a 19.99%
shareholding in Tranz Rail.

B McInerney
COMPANY SECRETARY
```

Fig. 2. A more complex document of type 02/002

of documents, we can determine ahead of time specific items of information that those documents contain. In the case of a change of shareholding, for examples, the key elements of information would be the name of the shareholding company, the number of shares it now holds, the company the shares are held in, and the date of the change.

Information that has been extracted from a document can be used in a variety of ways; for example, it can be used to populate a database, and the database might then be searched or analysed in various ways. The focus we have taken so far in KES is that we can add value to documents by producing short summaries of what those documents contain, and we generate those summaries using the key elements we have extracted. By finding the key information and then presenting it in a summarised form, we make it much easier for a user to find information.

3   Our Approach

Our system consists of three processes:

Text Categorisation: We use a text categoriser, trained on human-annotated documents from the Signal G corpus, to determine the report type of each document.

Information Extraction: Given the document's type, we then apply a collection of information extraction routines that are adapted to the specific document types; these locate the key elements of information that are relevant for that document type.

Information Rendering: Once extracted, this information can then be re-presented to users in a variety of forms.

Each of these processes is described in more detail below.

3.1 Text Categorisation

Our text categoriser is described elsewhere [5, 6], and so we will restrict ourselves here to some comments relevant to the present discussion.

The categoriser is trained on the human-categorised data set, and the results for a test set of 7620 documents are shown in Table 3.

Table 3. Categoriser performance on Report Type 02

Category	# Docs	Precision	Recall	F_1
02/001	1109	0.975	0.951	0.963
02/002	2457	0.96	0.957	0.958
02/003	517	0.959	0.972	0.966
02/004	0	0	1	0
02/005	702	0.971	0.984	0.978
02/006	184	0.260	0.586	0.361
02/007	2651	0.986	0.952	0.968

As can be seen from the table, the categoriser works well on all the subtypes of category 02 except for 02/004 (*Beneficial ownership*), for which there were no documents in our set, and 02/006 (*Security holder details–Other*), which is effectively a 'miscellaneous' category. It should also be noted that these results are produced by comparing the categoriser's assignment of report types to that of the human annotators; some preliminary analysis, however, has determined that the human annotators make mistakes, and so it is possible that our categoriser is performing better than these numbers suggest.

3.2 Information Extraction

Information extraction is now a well-developed body of techniques that has been applied in a wide range of contexts. In each case, the general strategy is to construct a template that specifies the elements of information that need to be extracted from documents of a given type, and then to build shallow-processing natural language tools that extract these elements of information. These tools often use simple finite state parsing mechanisms: at the lowest level, the named entities—references to people, places and organisations—will be identified, along with dates, currency amounts and other numerical expressions; then, higher-level finite state machines may identify sentential or clausal structures within which these lower level elements participate. In many cases, the events of interest require the aggregation of information across multiple sentences.

Our information extraction techniques follow this pattern. The templates for two report subtypes are shown in Figures 3 and 4.

Field	Contents
AcquiringParty	a Company or Individual named entity
AcquiredParty	a Company named entity
DateOfTransaction	the date of transaction
NumberOfShares	the number of shares owned as a result of the transaction
PercentageOfShares	the percentage of shares owned as a result in the transaction
ShareType	one of {ordinary, voting, ... }

Fig. 3. Extraction template for 02/001, *Becoming a Substantial Shareholder*

Field	Contents
Director	the name of the director
Company	the Company in which the director has an interest
PreviousNotificationDate	the date of previous notification of interest
InterestChangeDate	the date of change of interest
CurrentNotificationDate	the date of current notification
Holding	a structure consisting of **HoldingCompany**, **NumberOfShares**, and **ShareType**

Fig. 4. Extraction template for 02/007, *Section 205G Notice—Director's Interests*

Documents of report type 02/001 are quite predictable, and in many cases the required data is found by pattern of the following type:[2]

```
$Party became $shareholdertype in $Company on $Date with
$interest of $sharespec
```

Here, $Party and $Company are complex patterns used to identify persons and companies; $shareholdertype, $interest and $sharespec are patterns that match the variety of ways in which information about the nature of the shareholding can be expressed; this is typically distributed over a number of nominal elements separated by prepositions, so we use this fact in anchoring the pattern matching. Table 4 shows the results for a sample document.

A number of report types exhibit similar simplicity; others, however, are more complex, with the information we need to find much more dispersed around the document. In the case of report subtype 02/007, for example, the information is often presented in the form of a table; however, since this table is rendered in plain ASCII text, we need to parse the table to identify the required information. A number of researchers have worked on this particular problem: see, for example, [7,8]. Our techniques for doing this are still being refined, as demonstrated by the significantly poorer extraction performance on this category: Figure 5 shows results for a random test sample of 20 documents

---

[2] This is a simplified representation of a rule in our system.

Table 4. Extraction results for a document of type 02/001

Element	Contents
DocumentCategory	02001
AcquiringPartyASX	TCN
AcquiringParty	TCNZ Australia Investments Pty Ltd
AcquiredPartyASX	AAP
AcquiredParty	AAPT Limited
DateOfTransaction	4/07/1999
NumberOfShares	243,756,813
ShareType	ordinary shares
PercentageOfShares	79.90%

Category	# slots	Found	R	True +ves	P	False +ves	f-score
02001	119	119	1.000	118	0.992	1	0.996
02002	189	188	0.995	188	1.000	1	0.997
02003	60	57	0.950	56	0.982	1	0.966
02005	117	101	0.863	100	0.990	1	0.922
02007	129	69	0.535	68	0.986	1	0.693
Total	614	534	0.870	530	0.993		0.927

Fig. 5. Success rates in extracting key elements

of each of the five 02 subtypes, demonstrating that we do significantly worse on this category.[3] In general, however, the accuracy is high, largely because of the predictability of the documents. The major problems we face are in handling variety and complexity in proper names, a point we return to below in Section 4.

3.3 Information Rendering

Once we have extracted the information, we need to present it to the user in a maximally useful way. We are experimenting with a number of ideas here, including voice synthesis of short sentences that contain the key elements; on the web, we have implemented a mechanism that pops up a box showing the key data fields whenever the mouse is scrolled over the title of the document, thus avoiding the need for several mouse clicks to see what the document contains. The same information could be presented in tabular form to allow sorting or comparison by specific fields and values.

---

[3] The '# slots' column indicates the total number of extractable slot fills available in the sample selected; 'Found' indicates the number of slots extracted; 'R' and 'P' provide the recall and precision figures respectively. The f-score shown is calculated as 2PR/(P+R).

4 Issues in Handling Named Entities

In our domain, we have so far focussed on documents whose structure is relatively well-behaved, so that we achieve high accuracy in extracting the key elements. However, making sense of some of these key elements proves to be a little harder; in particular, the variety of forms of proper names that we find introduces some difficulties into the task. This is particularly the case since we want to resolve, where possible, company names to stock exchange codes, so simply identifying that we have a named entity is not enough; we need to be able to work out what that named entity is.

In this section, we describe some of the problems we face in handling proper names, and outline the solutions we have developed so far.

4.1 Variations in Proper Names

Variations in proper names fall into two broad categories: legitimate variations and misspellings.

Legitimate Variations. Legitimate variations cover cases where multiple names are used for the same entity. In the case of companies, for example, both *Broken Hill Proprietary Limited* and *BHP Ltd* refer to the same organisation. In KES, we attempt to resolve company names to their ASX codes, and so determining that these two terms refer to the same entity is important. Currently, we achieve this by using a small number of heuristics in conjunction with a large manually constructed table of known company names that maps these to their stock codes. One heuristic, for example, looks for substring matches on the 'content-bearing' elements of names, ignoring corporate designators like *Limited* on the basis that these are frequently omitted. There are other heuristics that might be used: in the example just cited, we might employ a mechanism that, on finding an all-caps string like *BHP* in the text, looks for names whose element begin with the letters that make up the abbreviation; however, some initial experiments suggest that this is not very robust.

Legitimate variations are also common in person names: so, for example, *A Smith*, *Mr Smith*, *Alexander Smith* and *Alex Smith* might all refer to the same person. Clearly, the confidence with which identity of reference can be claimed for any two of these strings varies, with the third and fourth being closest, and any assumed co-reference with the second being the riskiest. The problem here, however, is much worse than with company names, since it is not uncommon to find different people sharing exactly the same name.

Misspellings. Misspelled names are rife in our corpus, in large part because of the way in which the document set is constructed: documents are received from companies by fax, and these faxes are scanned, OCRed and then manually edited.[4] Quite apart from spelling errors that might be present in the source

---

[4] As of mid-2003, the ASX has required companies to provide documents as PDF files rather than faxes, but a proportion of these are still produced by scanning.

document, clearly each stage of this process has the chance of adding additional errors. The list below provides a sample set of misspellings of *Perpetual Trustees Australia Limited* found in our corpus:

> Perpectual Trustees Australia Limited
> Perpetual Trustee Australia Limited
> Perpetual Trustee Company Limited
> Perpetual Trustees Astralia Limited
> Perpetual Trustees Australian Limited
> Perpetual Trustes Australia Limited

Our heuristics currently accommodate a range of common misspellings, although clearly there are other methods that might be explored. Integration of a variation of Knuth's Soundex algorithm would address one type of error, where misspellings arise at source; a different approach would be required to handle errors which are clearly introduced by the OCR process.

4.2 Conjunctions of Names

The analysis of conjunctions is a long-standing problem in parsing. The problem is, quite simply, working out what the conjuncts are, given that in many cases some information is assumed to be shared between both conjuncts. This problem surfaces in our corpus in the form of examples like the following:[5]

1. Advent Investors Pty Limited; Enterprise Holdings Pty Limited; Leadenhall Australia Limited; Koneke Pty Limited; Noble Investments Pty Limited; Advent Accounting Pty Limited; Chi Investments Pty Limited
2. James Brenner Skinner, Janice Ivy Skinner, Topspeed Pty Limited, and GN, AW, CM, SM, and SB Skinner

In case (1), we have a long, semi-colon separated list of company names. This case is quite well behaved, with the punctuation effectively removing any problems in parsing. However, it is very common for more ambiguous conjunctions, such as the comma and *and*, to be used in separating elements, as in example (2): here, we need to determine that the first *and* separates complete names, whereas the second *and* separates sets of initials, each of which must be paired-up with the surname *Skinner*. Similar problems occur with proper names like *Centaur and Mining Exploration Limited*, *Investors Trust and Custodial Services*, and *Graham Whelan and G Whelan Pty Limited*: if these strings, or substrings contained within them, appear in our table of company names, we will recognise them appropriately; but there are many company names (for example, of overseas companies) which are not present in our database, and in such cases there is no reliable way of determining whether we have one entity or two.

Currently, we have a prototype parser based around a Prolog Definite Clause Grammar which returns all possible parses of conjunctions, applying heuristics

---

[5] Each of these examples fills a single **AcquiringParty** slot in our extraction process, and so has to be decomposed into its constitiuent elements.

that govern the forms of person names and company names; the results are then filtered these against the known names in the company database. In many cases, however, this still produces more than one possible parse, and so further heuristics are required in order to choose the best parse.

5 Conclusions and Further Work

We have described the components of a system which takes corporate announcements, categorises these into a number of report types, and then uses information extraction techniques to identify specific predefined elements of information in each of these report types. The information so extracted can then be provided to the user in a way that facilitates efficient searching or browsing of the document set, or exported from the database in a variety of other formats.

Our initial prototype performs well for the subset of document types that we have focussed upon, but there are a number of clear directions that we need to pursue next:

1. Although our categoriser performs well, it could still be improved. We are exploring how feedback from the information extraction mechanisms might help the categoriser. For example, if we are unable to identify the information elements for the report type that is ascribed by the categoriser, we can try to extract the elements required for the other report types, and if this is successful, provide this information back to the categoriser. The precise details of how the categoriser can use this information to revise its subsequent categorisation activity remain to be worked out.
2. Our information extraction techniques need to be extended to other report types, and the performance on some of the existing report types needs improvement. The ways forward here are reasonably clear, with a need for more sophisticated mechanisms that can take account of widely dispersed information within a document. Our currently high values for extractions in the simpler document types are obtained largely because the documents' predictability means we can use quite tightly constrained patterns; as we relax these patterns, the scope for error in what we extract increases, and multiple possible values will be found for slots. We then need to develop techniques for choosing amongst alternative solutions.
3. Our handling of the problems posed by variations in proper names and conjunctions of proper names is still relatively limited.

For the last two of these extensions, we are exploring how the system can learn from its previous experience. Some of the techniques required here are quite simple: for example, if reliable data for most slot fills in a template means that an unknown string must correspond to a variant of a particular company name, then this hypothesis about the unknown name can be added to the database so that it is available for the processing of subsequent documents. We are in the process of exploring how best to integrate this kind of information into the system's data sources.

References

1. Cowie, J., Lehnert, W.: Information extraction. Communications of the ACM **39** (1996) 80–91
2. Appelt, D., Hobbs, J., Bear, J., Israel, D., Kameyana, M., Tyson, M.: Fastus: a finite-state processor for information extraction from real-world text. In: Proceedings of the International Joint Conference on Artificial Intelligence (IJCAI'93). (1993)
3. Jackson, P., Moulinier, I.: Natural Language Processing for Online Applications: Text Retrieval, Extraction and Categorization. John Benjamins, Amsterdam (2002)
4. Mikheev, A., Grover, C., Moens, M.: XML tools and architecture for named entity recognition. Markup Languages **1** (1999) 89–113
5. Calvo, R.A.: Classifying financial news with neural networks. In: 6th Australasian Document Symposium. (2001)
6. Calvo, R.A., Williams, K.: Automatic categorization of announcements on the Australian Stock Exchange. (2002)
7. Pinto, D., McCallum, A., Wei, X., Croft, W.B.: Table extraction using conditional random fields. In: Proceedings of SIGIR'03, Toronto, Canada., ACM (2003) 235–242
8. Hurst, M.: The Interpretation of Tables in Texts. PhD thesis, University of Edinburgh, School of Cognitive Science, Informatics (2000)

Knowledge Discovery Using Concept-Class Taxonomies

Venkateswarlu Kolluri[1], Foster Provost[2], Bruce Buchanan[3], and Douglas Metzler[3]

[1]Chitika, Inc., MA 01545
vkolluri@chitika.com
[2]New York University, NY 13576
fprovost@stern.nyu.edu
[3]University of Pittsburgh, PA 15260
buchanan@cs.pitt.edu, metzler@sis.pitt.edu

Abstract. This paper describes the use of taxonomic hierarchies of concept-classes (dependent class values) for knowledge discovery. The approach allows evidence to accumulate for rules at different levels of generality and avoids the need for domain experts to predetermine which levels of concepts should be learned. In particular, higher-level rules can be learned automatically when the data doesn't support more specific learning, and higher level rules can be used to predict a particular case when the data is not detailed enough for a more specific rule. The process introduces difficulties concerning how to heuristically select rules during the learning process, since accuracy alone is not adequate. This paper explains the algorithm for using concept-class taxonomies, as well as techniques for incorporating granularity (together with accuracy) in the heuristic selection process. Empirical results on three data sets are summarized to highlight the tradeoff between predictive accuracy and predictive granularity.

1 Introduction

The importance of guiding the discovery process with domain knowledge has long been recognized [12], but most existing data mining systems do not exploit explicitly represented background knowledge. Recently, taxonomic background knowledge of attributes and attribute value has received attention ([1], [2], [8]). However, while it has been recognized ([9], [11], [12]) that there is often sufficient domain knowledge to generate hierarchies over the (dependent variable) concept-class values as well, in most classification learning research the concept-class variable is assumed to comprise a simple set of discrete values determined by a domain expert. Concept-class, attribute and attribute-value taxonomies are structurally similar, but are distinguished by the role that they play in a particular learning situation as dependent or independent variables.

The practice of leaving to domain experts or data analysts the task of selecting the appropriate levels of analysis [e.g., 8, 17] in situations involving large sets of concept-class values that are inherently hierarchically structured is problematic. Human choosing of appropriate levels of concepts to learn is an inherently labor intensive task that is compounded by the fact that there is not, in general, one ideal generalization level for a given problem. The most useful level is a function not only of the desired conceptual outputs, but also of the data available to drive the learning process. The effects of data availability and the utility of concept class taxonomies are most evident when the data set is small and the concept class value set is relatively large. For instance, in the "bridges" domain, [16], if each type of bridge has only a few examples in a given data set it might be difficult to find sufficient evidence for all specific types of bridges, while there might be evidence for more general types (Figure 1). Thus hierarchical classification learning is a two-fold process. In addition to the search for a set of patterns that best describe a given concept, hierarchical classification involves a search over the concept-class taxonomy to find the concepts that represent the best tradeoffs concerning usefulness and degree of support in the given data set. The approach described here provides for the simultaneous search for rules to predict concepts at all levels of a taxonomic hierarchy, while allowing the user to bias the system to varying degrees of specificity vs. accuracy.

In this paper we describe HRL (Hierarchical Rule Learner), an extension to an existing rule-learning system, RL [14] that demonstrates the feasibility of learning within concept-class taxonomies. We describe why existing methods for evaluating classification models are not sufficient to evaluate hierarchical classification models, introduce the concept of *prediction granularity* of a model that needs to be considered along with predictive accuracy, and show how *granularity* can be incorporated in the learning process. Empirical results on three data sets are summarized to highlight the tradeoffs between predictive accuracy and predictive granularity.

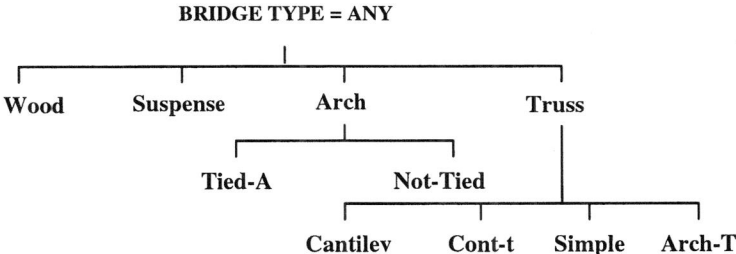

Fig. 1. Bridge concept class taxonomy

2 Hierarchical Rule Learning Using Concept Class Taxonomies

The Hierarchical Rule Learning (HRL) algorithm discovers appropriate concepts within taxonomically structured (dependent) concept-class taxonomies. HRL is an extension of the BFMP learning technique [3], which in turn is a marker-passing based extension of the RL induction system, a descendent of the MetaDENDRAL system [6]. RL is a generate-and-test rule-learning algorithm that performs heuristic search in a space of simple IF-THEN rules containing conjunctions of features (attribute-value pairs).

Figure 2(a) contains a simple database. The location and occupation fields (attributes) contain independent attribute values. The car field is the dependent concept to be learned. In this case the concept values are binary (US made vs. imported). The task consists of learning a set of rules to reliably predict the dependent concept values, e.g., the set of people who own imported cars (i.e., Sam and Mary). Typical top-down inductive learners such as MetaDENDRAL-style learners [6], or decision-tree learners such as C4.5 [15] and CART [5], start with a null rule (which covers everything) and generate additional conjuncts to specialize it, such as *Location = Pittsburgh, Occupation = Research* etc. Each conjunct is matched against the data, and statistics are gathered. The statistics are fed to an evaluation function that decides which conjuncts should be further specialized on the next iteration.

Name	Location	Occupation	Car
Sam	Pittsburgh	Research	Imported
John	Harrisburg	Business	US made
Bob	San Francisco	Research	US made
Tim	Pittsburgh	Business	US made
Mary	Pittsburgh	Research	Imported

Car
Toyota
Dodge
Dodge
Ford
Honda

Fig. 2(a). Cars database **Fig. 2(b).** Cars database class values

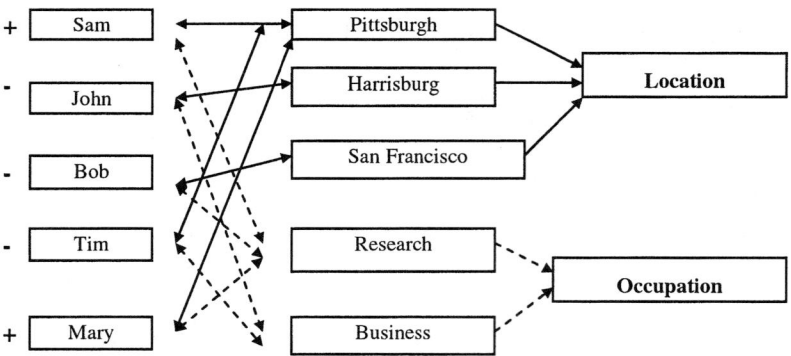

Fig. 2(c). Network representation of the Cars database

BFMP, [3] replaces the matching portion of RL and related algorithms by breadth-first marker propagation, and the collection and counting of markers. In Figure 2(c), attribute values are represented by pointers into the space of values (with a different type of pointer for each type of attribute). BFMP places a class marker on each data item (e.g. Sam) and propagates these markers along attribute links to the value nodes. BFMP then checks the coverage of predicates by counting how many positive and negative markers accumulate on the corresponding value nodes, thereby replacing the matching step in the rule learners. In binary cases such as this, positive markers represent support for the utility of adding that node to specialize the rule under consideration and negative markers represent negative evidence. E.g., the rule

(Location = Pittsburgh ➔ US made) receives two positive markers and one negative. Aronis and Provost [3] showed that rule learning using such marker propagation techniques increases performance over standard pattern matching approaches and is especially effective when dealing with datasets containing large attribute-value sets (with and without attribute-value taxonomies).

HRL extends BFMP to learn appropriate concepts within taxonomically structured (dependent) concept-class value sets. Figure 2(b) shows an alternate dependent concept class (car) for the data set in Figure 2(a) containing individual values, which can be hierarchically ordered as in Figure 4. In such a non-binary learning task, individual markers, (e.g., T, D, F, and H respectively in this case) replace the binary +/- markers, and the negative evidence for a given class at a particular node must be computed as the sum of the markers belonging to the compliment set of class markers.

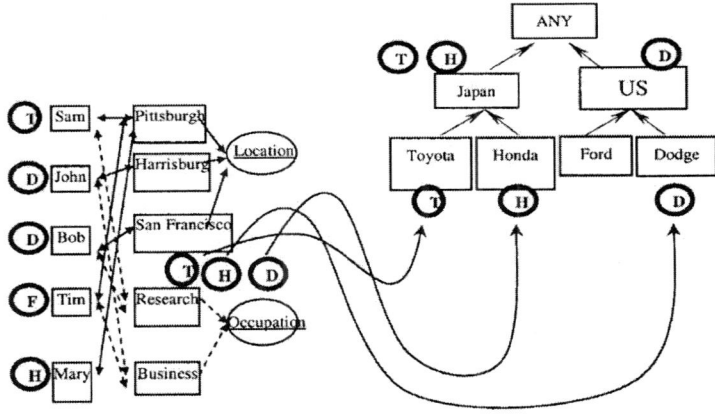

Fig. 3. Extended Car data set network with concept class taxonomy

The left side of Figure 3 shows a network like that shown in Figure 2(c). The individual markers (T, D, F and H) are shown instead of the binary (+/-) markers of Figure 2(c), and the accumulation of those markers are shown for the occupation=research node. These markers are then passed to the class taxonomy shown on the right hand side of Figure 3., and passed up that hierarchy. Although the evidence so far is weak for any rule predicting a particular manufacturer based on occupation=research, it would appear that evidence is gathering for a rule that predicts country=Japan based on occupation=research. The concept class node "Japan" now represents the rule: (Occupation = Research) ➔ (Car = Japan), and it has a "positive" coverage of 2. To calculate the negative coverage for this rule the concept class markers are propagated to the top-level root node "ANY". The difference between the total of all markers gathered at "ANY" and those gathered at the class node "Japan" represents the "negative" coverage of the rule (Occupation = Research) ➔ (Car = Japan). Hence the final coverage statistics for this rule are as follows: *Total* Coverage = 3; Confidence = 2/3= 0.66 Positive coverage = 2, Negative coverage = 1.

HRL can produce multi-level rule sets (models) with rules predicting concept class categories at various levels in the taxonomies. Such hierarchical classification models can make high-level, coarse-grained predictions when insufficient information is available to make precise low-level predictions. The individual rules themselves are useful since they capture structural relationships between the independent features and the dependent concept values at various levels in the concept class taxonomy. Unlike top down learning methods (e.g., [8]), HRL is inherently bottom up, discovering all rules for which there is sufficient support.

3 Working with (Dependent) Concept Class Taxonomies

Heuristics that guide the selection of *"interesting"* rules over hierarchical concept class value sets are fundamentally different from the heuristics needed to select rules with hierarchical attribute value sets. In general, more general attribute values (e.g., location = Pennsylvania rather than location = Pittsburgh) are preferred in the case of attribute value hierarchies, (assuming they are predicting the same concept and have similar statistical evidence), since the coverage of the more general rule will be greater. However, in the case of concept class hierarchies (i.e., a hierarchy used as a set of predicted or dependent variables), more specific values (e.g., Pittsburgh rather than Pennsylvania) will be preferred since the rules will be more informative[1].

The search heuristic of classification learning systems usually attempts to optimize to cover as many positive examples of a class while producing as few false positives as possible [7]. If a classifier needs to select nodes from a class hierarchy however, simple classification accuracy alone is not sufficient as can be seen by noting that the top level rule, (null ➔ ANY, where ANY is the top-level concept in the taxonomy), has 100% coverage and accuracy, but no informative value. On the other hand, fine-grained predictions at the lowest level in a taxonomy are informative but may not be easy to learn if there is insufficient data at that level. In general, more specific rules are more informative but less accurate. Hence the search for "interesting" rules essentially involves a tradeoff between maximizing accuracy and vs. seeking rules of maximum *granularity* (taxonomic specificity).

3.1 Granularity Metrics

In order to capture the intuitive preference for fine-grained (low-level) rules, a measure is needed of taxonomic depth or specificity (which we refer to as *granularity*). A granularity metric should be 1) proportional to the depth of the rule's concept class in the concept class taxonomy, and 2) independent of the given rule's coverage and accuracy (i.e. data-dependant coverage statistics).

---

[1] Other factors may mitigate against these general rules however. Turney [18] pointed out that attribute values may have costs associated with them and a rule that predicts a more general concept may be preferred over a more specific one if the costs of obtaining the predictive attribute values are lower. Model complexity might also influence a user to prefer general rules, since a bias towards lower levels specific rules might generate too many rules.

Simple Granularity Metric: A *simple* approach would be to define the granularity score as the ratio of i, the number of links between the node and the root, and d, the maximum depth of the path along which the node exists. This provides an intuitive scoring scheme that satisfies the two conditions, but leads to inconsistencies in the general case of trees of varying depth.

$$\text{SimpleGranularity} = i/d$$

Absolute Granularity Metric: The *"absolute"* granularity of a node n is defined as:

$$\text{AbsoluteGranularity}(n) = \frac{N - S(n)}{N}$$

where N is the total number of non-root nodes in the taxonomy and $S(n)$ is the number of nodes subsumed under the node n. This assigns a value of 0 to the root node and a value of 1 for all leaf nodes. This is generally intuitive, however if different parts of a taxonomy vary in how well developed they are, one might not want to consider all leaves as equivalently specific. Moreover, this metric is susceptible to changes in the taxonomy, and such changes, if they occur dynamically during a learning process, will invalidate the previously determined information based on the now-changed granularity score.

Relative Granularity Metric:

$$\text{RelativeGranularity}(n) = (1 - \frac{1}{d+1})$$

This measure is sensitive only to d, the depth of n from the root. The root is still 0 while other nodes approach 1 as depth increases. This measure is also susceptible to changes in the taxonomy but only to changes above a node, since it does not involve the number of nodes subsumed under a particular node. On the assumption that taxonomies are more likely to grow dynamically from the leaves or lower conceptual nodes, this measure will less frequently be affected mid-process than would be the absolute granularity metric.

3.2 Rule Quality Measure

Symbolic rule learning systems typically use accuracy (also known as confidence) of individual rules as a selection criterion to pick "interesting" rules. But as explained above, accuracy by itself is not sufficient when dealing with taxonomically structured concept class values. In that case one must utilize a measure of rule granularity (R_g) as well as a measure of rule accuracy (R_{Acc}). Although one could simply sum these, a *weighted linear* combination is more desirable, since it allows users to select an appropriate weighting scheme that suits their preferences:

$$LQ(R,w) = w(R_{Acc}) + (1-w)(R_g)$$

This allows users to explore the models (rule sets) produced by the system under varying emphases on predictive granularity vs. predictive accuracy.

3.3 Model Evaluation

Just as classification accuracy alone is insufficient to guide the rule selection process during learning within taxonomic classes, it is also insufficient for evaluation of the performance of a generated model (rule set). A lower-level, more specific rule is more informative at a given level of accuracy than is a more general rule. Instead of giving equal weight to all correct predictions, a weighted value proportional to the depth of the predicted class node along the path between the root node and the actual class value node can be used to formulate a quality score for evaluating the classification performance:

$$HierarchicalWeighted\ Accuracy = 100 \ x \Sigma c(i/d)/N$$

where for each prediction: c = correctness, i = the level of the predicted class in the class taxonomy, and d = the total depth of the tree path on which the predicted class is, and N = total number of predictions made by the classifier. For example consider a test set in the cars database, (Figure 4) with 10 instances, all of which having the same concept class value, Ford.

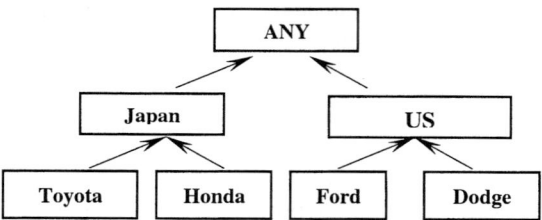

Fig. 4. Cars database taxonomy

If the model predicted all 10 cases as FORD, then its quality value would be: 100 x (10 x 1) / 10 = 100%. If all 10 were predicted to be TOYOTA the quality value would be 0. But if 5 of the 10 predictions were US and 5 were Ford, then the accuracy of the model is: (100 x ((5 x 0.5) + (5 x 1))) / 10 = 75%. In this example, each prediction of type Ford received a value of 1 and each prediction of type US received a value of 0.5, since the node US is halfway between the node FORD and the root node in the concept class taxonomy. Such differential weighting schemes proportional to the depth of the class node capture the notion that there is some information loss when a "correct" higher-level coarse-grained prediction is made. However this approach fails to distinguish between misclassification errors among sibling class nodes vs. error between more distant nodes or the differential costs of different misclassifications, a subject for future work.

4 Empirical Study

We conducted an empirical study to demonstrate the tradeoffs between predictive accuracy and predictive granularity. Three real world data sets, the Soybean data set, the Pittsburgh Bridges data set, and the Imports data set obtained from the UCI-Irvine

ML data repository [4], were used. The data sets were chosen based on the following criteria: large number of concept-classes, and available taxonomic grouping over the set of concept-classes.

In the Soybean domain data set there are 683 instances. The task is to diagnose soybean diseases. There are 19 classes and 35 discrete features describing leaf properties and various abnormalities. The set of 19 classes have been grouped into a two-level concept-class taxonomy as shown in Figure 5.

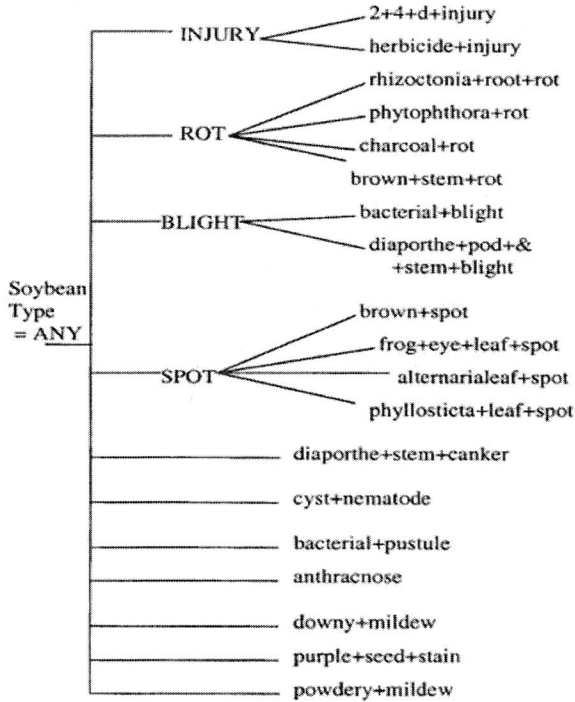

Fig. 5. Soybean concept-class taxonomy

In the Pittsburgh Bridges data set [16], each bridge is described using seven specification properties (e.g., the *river* and *location* of the bridge), and five design properties (e.g., the *material* used). There are 108 instances in this data set. In this study the learning task was to predict the *type* of bridge, given the seven specification properties. There are eight types of bridges: *wood, suspense, tied-a, not-tied, cantilev, cont-t, simple* and *arch*. The Bridges data set's eight concept-class values can be grouped into a two level taxonomy as shown in Figure 1.

The Imports data set [4] consists of 15 continuous, 1 integer and 10 nominal-valued attributes. For this study, the following attributes were used to predict the "make" of the car: *symboling, fuel-type, aspiration, num-of-doors, body-style, drive-wheels, engine-location, engine-type, num-of-cylinders,* and *fuel-system*. The data set contains 114 unique instances. The 22 possible concept-class values (i.e., the make of the car) were grouped into a two-level hierarchy (Figure 6).

To highlight the tradeoffs between predictive accuracy and predictive granularity of the resulting hierarchical classification models, a series of experiments were conducted using the *weighted linear quality metric* (Section 3.2) to guide the HRL system. The weight w, ranging from 0 to 1, can be used to vary emphasis on either the rule confidence, R_{Acc}, or the rule granularity R_g. (Higher w-scores bias the system toward higher predictive accuracy; lower w-scores bias the system towards higher predictive granularity.)

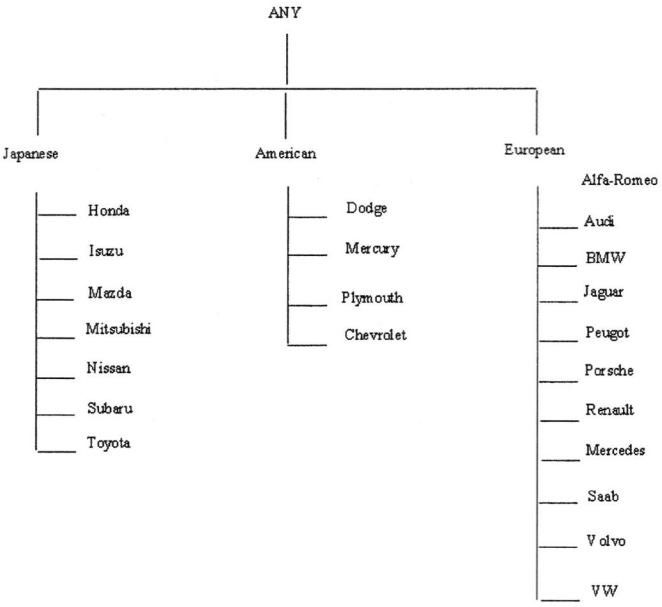

Fig. 6. Imports data set taxonomy

To explore the utility of the various proposed granularity metrics, sets of experiments were conducted using each of the three granularity metrics (Section 3.1). The results obtained with the three granularity metrics at different settings of w in the three domains are summarized in Table 1. The table shows the predictive accuracy and the predictive granularity of the models (rule sets) generated (Section 3.3). The model granularity is the sum of the granularity of all rules in the model. For comparison, the simple-granularity metric was used to compute the predictive granularity of all final models. The results for soybean data using the simple granularity metric are plotted (Figure 7) to highlight the tradeoffs between granularity and accuracy scores.

Results obtained from the HRL experiment with w-score = 1 can be considered as experiments using the "flattened" concept-class value set, using all concept classes in the concept-class taxonomy, but ignoring the structural relationships. As expected, the experiment with w-score of 1 resulted in models with highest accuracy but lowest granularity values, because the learning system was biased to ignore the semantic information implicit in the structural relationships among class nodes in the concept-class taxonomy. But when the w-score was decreased, forcing the learning system to consider the prediction granularity along with the prediction accuracy, a significant increase in the predictive granularity was observed (for all three sets of experiments using different granularity metrics) with a corresponding loss in accuracy.

Table 1. Accuracy-Granularity scores for experiments using Int-HRL in Soybean, Bridges and Imports Domains, respectively

w-score	SimpleGranularity		AbsoluteGranularity		RelativeGranularity	
	Accuracy	Granularity	Accuracy	Granularity	Accuracy	Granularity
1	82.64	58.78	82.70	58.04	84.03	59.44
0.9	83.45	78.54	82.11	76.65	83.02	77.37
0.8	83.88	80.37	80.36	79.66	82.52	79.83
0.7	80.90	85.41	80.17	80.50	82.03	82.27
0.6	79.62	90.71	79.92	86.44	76.26	80.22
0.5	74.08	98.84	79.43	86.05	75.05	80.74
0.4	69.60	100.00	76.69	86.48	72.42	83.87
0.3	52.74	100.00	76.36	88.17	45.19	100.00
0.2	49.15	100.00	50.94	100.00	39.35	100.00
0.1	45.97	100.00	48.47	100.00	36.97	100.00

w-score	SimpleGranularity		AbsoluteGranularity		RelativeGranularity	
	Accuracy	Granularity	Accuracy	Granularity	Accuracy	Granularity
1	72.02	57.05	69.96	57.47	66.80	59.36
0.9	57.58	80.73	59.04	78.48	59.68	83.35
0.8	60.52	85.82	57.55	86.09	58.33	80.24
0.7	54.36	90.54	57.55	88.03	57.23	84.16
0.6	55.85	95.30	58.44	91.34	53.77	86.62
0.5	49.48	100.00	56.64	95.21	52.25	92.88
0.4	51.37	100.00	52.75	99.16	50.89	94.68
0.3	44.27	100.00	41.91	100.00	39.86	100.00
0.2	41.36	100.00	40.35	100.00	39.27	100.00
0.1	36.43	100.00	42.64	100.00	29.44	100.00

w-score	SimpleGranularity		AbsoluteGranularity		RelativeGranularity	
	Accuracy	Granularity	Accuracy	Granularity	Accuracy	Granularity
1	63.96	52.84	66.54	50.00	63.36	50.00
0.9	62.63	69.43	58.94	64.92	60.73	66.25
0.8	57.40	64.18	53.92	65.81	59.60	62.58
0.7	51.35	70.04	61.88	66.29	52.66	68.98
0.6	45.13	86.76	53.41	69.94	54.04	66.55
0.5	31.22	94.58	51.09	79.18	41.34	71.23
0.4	30.18	100.00	38.27	86.46	37.53	84.57
0.3	25.95	100.00	28.87	98.68	21.85	100.00
0.2	26.32	100.00	21.81	100.00	26.07	100.00
0.1	30.39	100.00	28.01	100.00	20.11	100.00

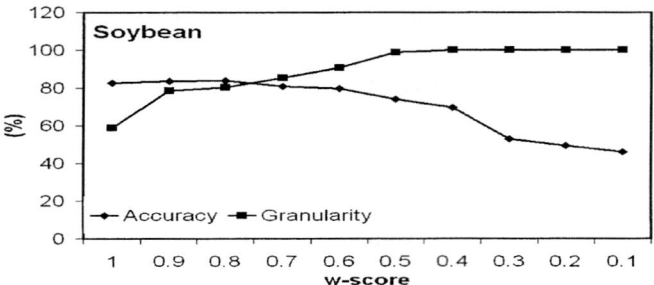

Fig. 7. Accuracy vs. Granularity scores for models generated using the Int-HRL system. Each data point is the average of 10 tests in a 10-fold cross validation experiment

5 Discussion

HRL demonstrates the ability to learn in a space of taxonomically structured (dependent) classes. It produces hierarchical classification models that can be used to classify new instances at differing levels of generality depending on the information available. The use of concept class hierarchies (as opposed to attribute and attribute-value hierarchies) introduces new research issues concerning the heuristics used to estimate the quality of rules. A tradeoff exists between rule accuracy and granularity (specificity) and measurement of the latter is somewhat ambiguous. We introduced three possible metrics for concept-class granularity, each with advantages and disadvantages but it is not yet clear if one is consistently superior to the others. Preliminary results highlight the tradeoffs between predictive granularity and predictive accuracy and indicate similar behavior for the three granularity metrics in each of the domains.

References

1. Almuallim, H., Akiba, Y., and Kaneda, S. (1995). On handling tree-structure attributes in decision tree learning. In *Proc. of the 12th Intl. Conf. on Machine Learning*, Morgan Kaufmann
2. Aronis, J. M., Provost, F. J. and Buchanan, B. G. (1996). Exploiting background knowledge in automated discovery. In *Proc. of the 2nd Intl. Conf. on Knowledge Discovery and Data Mining*, pp: 355--358, Menlo Park, CA, AAAI Press.
3. Aronis, J. M. and Provost, F. J. (1997). Efficient data mining with or without hierarchical background knowledge. *In Proc. of the 3rd Intl. Conf. on Knowledge Discovery and Data Mining*, New Port Beach, CA.
4. Blake, C.L. & Merz, C.J. (1998). UCI Repository of machine learning databases [http://www.ics.uci.edu/~mlearn/MLRepository.html]. Irvine, CA: University of California, Department of Information and Computer Science.
5. Breiman, L., Friedman, J. H., Olsen, R. A., and P. J. Stone (1984). *Classification and regression trees*. Wadsworth International Corp., CA.

6. Buchanan, B. G. and Mitchell, T. M. (1978). *Model-directed learning of production rules*. In D Waterman and F Hayes-Roth, editors, Pattern Directed Inference Systems. Academic Press., New York, NY.
7. Fürnkranz. J. (1999) Separate-and-Conquer Rule Learning. *Artificial Intelligence Review* 13(1) pp:3-54, 1999.
8. Kaufmann, K. A. and Michalski, R. S. (1996). A Method for Reasoning with Structured and Continuous Attributes in the INLEN-2 Multistrategy Knowledge Discovery System. In *Proc. of the 2nd Intl. Conf. on Knowledge Discovery and Data Mining*, pp: 232-238
9. Koller, D. and Sahami, M. 1997 Hierarchically Classifying Documents Using Very Few Words. In Proc. of the 14th Intl. Conf. on Machine Learning, pp. 170-178, San Francisco, CA: Morgan Kaufmann.
10. Krenzelok, E., Jacobsen T., and Aronis J. M. (1995) Jimsonweed (datura-stramonium) poisoning and abuse: an analysis of 1,458 cases. In *Proc. of North American Congress of Clinical Toxicology*, Rochester NY.
11. McCallum, A., Rosenfeld, R., Mitchell, T. and Nigam, K. (1998) Improving Text Classification by Shrinkage in Hierarchy of Classes. In *Proc. Of the 15th Intl. Conf. in Machine Learning*.
12. Michalski, R. S. (1980). Inductive Rule-Guided Generalization and Conceptual Simplification of Symbolic Descriptions: Unifying Principles and Methodology. Workshop on Current Developments in Machine Learning. Carnegie Mellon University, Pittsburgh, PA.
13. Pazzani, M., Merz, C., Murphy, P., Ali, K., Hume, T. and Brunk, C. (1994). Reducing Misclassification Costs. In *Proc of the 11th Intl. Conf. of Machine Learning*, New Brunswick. Morgan Kaufmann
14. Provost, F. J. and Buchanan, B.G. (1995). Inductive Policy: The Pragmatics of Bias Selection. *Machine Learning (20)*.
15. Quinlan, J. R. (1993). *C4.5: Programs for Machine Learning*. Morgan Kaufmann, San Mateo, CA.
16. Reich, R. & Fenves. R. (1989). Incremental Learning for Capturing Design Expertise. Technical Report: EDRC 12-34-89, Engineering Design Research Center, Carnegie Mellon University, Pittsburgh, PA.
17. Taylor, M. G., Stoffel K., and Hendler J. A. (1997) Ontology-based Induction of High Level Classification Rules. In *Proc. of the SIGMOD*
18. Turney, P. D., (1995). Cost-sensitive classification: Empirical Evaluation of a Hybrid Genetic Decision Tree Induction Algorithm, *Journal of Artificial Intelligence Research*, 2, March, 369-409.

Learning the Grammar of Distant Change in the World-Wide Web

Dirk Kukulenz

University of Luebeck, Institute of Information Systems,
Ratzeburger Allee 160, 23538 Luebeck, Germany
kukulenz@ifis.uni-luebeck.de

Abstract. One problem many Web users encounter is to keep track of changes of distant Web sources. *Push services*, informing clients about data changes, are frequently not provided by Web servers. Therefore it is necessary to apply intelligent *pull strategies*, optimizing reload requests by observation of data sources. In this article an adaptive pull strategy is presented that optimizes reload requests with respect to the 'age' of data and lost data. The method is applicable if the remote change pattern may approximately be described by a piecewise deterministic behavior which is frequently the case if data sources are updated automatically. Emphasis is laid on an autonomous estimation where only a minimal number of parameters has to be provided manually.

1 Introduction

Access to the World-Wide Web is currently mainly achieved by keyword-based search, e.g. through Web search engines, or by browsing, which denotes the process of accessing Web objects by the use of hyperlinks. Both strategies assume the Web to be a static information source that doesn't change during a search. However frequently the dynamics of the Web is the focus of the actual search. If a user wants e.g. to keep track of news, stock prices or satellite images, 'static' search strategies like browsing or query search are not suitable.
Basically there exist two strategies to acquire this knowledge, denoted as the *push* and the *pull* strategy [13]. The push strategy implies that a data source itself informs the client about the times of changes. An investigation concerning the push model is presented in [16]. However a push service is difficult to realize in a heterogenous information system as the World-Wide Web. In the pull model it is necessary for a client to predict remote changes in order to initiate reload operations. In order to predict changes it is first necessary to acquire information about a data source, i.e. to detect changes. Basically two strategies are available for this purpose. One is to reload the data source periodically and to compare previous and current data objects. A second strategy in order to detect data changes is provided by the HTTP protocol [7]. Different strategies were developed to acquire optimal cache behavior based on http-headers [9], [19]. Since according to [3] 'last-modified'-headers are only available in 65% of Web pages in

this article we apply the first method in order to register page changes. The main problem discussed in this article is to estimate and to predict change behavior based on an observed history of changes acquired with the above method with a certain precision. The goal is to find an optimal reload policy of remote sources according to quality parameters like amount of lost data and age, that will be introduced in detail in section 2. The reload policy has to minimize costs with respect to network load and the number of Internet connections. This aspect is especially important if a large number of remote data objects is considered.

1.1 Related Research

The problem of realizing continuous queries over data streams seems to be similar to the described problem. However in this field the data stream is usually assumed to be already available [2] while the focus in this article is to make the data stream available, i.e. to optimize the data stream itself. *Web prefetching* is an issue well known from the field of intelligent agents and network optimization [4]. One method applied in this field is the use of Markov processes [8]. In contrast to this article the main concern is usually to predict different data objects from recorded sequences of Web accesses, but not to optimize the times of requests. The consideration of dynamical aspects of the World-Wide Web is a main issue for the development of Web crawlers, Web archives and Web caches. With respect to these applications, diverse statistical methods were presented in order to optimize requests for remote data sources. In [1] an introduction into search engine design and into the problems related to optimal page refresh is given. In [6] aspects of optimal (Web-)robot scheduling are discussed from a theoretical point of view, modeling page change intervals by independent Poisson processes. An empirical analysis of Web page dynamics with respect to statistical properties of intervals between data changes is presented in [3]. One main result is that the distribution of intervals between changes is similar to an exponential distribution. In [20] the problem of minimizing the average level of 'staleness' for web pages and the development of an optimal schedule for crawlers is analyzed based on the assumption of independent and identically distributed time intervals. Assuming a Poisson process for intervals between update times, in [5] an optimized reload frequency estimation is presented.

1.2 Contribution

Many data objects in the Web are updated according to a well defined pattern, e.g. every working day, not at night and not at weekends. For similar update patterns, the assumption of an independent and identical distribution of consecutive time intervals, which is applied in many statistical approaches, is not suitable. In this article we present a reload policy which is optimized for similar 'quasi regular' update patterns. In contrast to a previously presented algorithm for the realization of continuous queries [15], [14] the presented reload policy is adaptive and may register, if the remote change behavior changes and adapt automatically. The estimation depends on specific initial values for the estimation process. One focus in this article is to learn some of these parameters automatically in order to simplify the application of the algorithm for a user. The sequence of time intervals between updates is piecewise approximated by a special kind of a regular grammar we will denote as a *cyclic regular grammar*. Regular grammar inference is a problem well-known from machine learning [10], [12]. Many algorithms were presented to learn regular grammars from positive and negative examples [17], [18]. The cyclic-regular case as defined in section 2 is simpler than the general regular inference problem and may be computed efficiently. We will apply the grammar estimation for the development of a new adaptive reload policy in order to optimize local copies of remote sources.

After a description of the applied model in section 2, in section 3 we propose an algorithm for the grammar estimation and it is shown how this knowledge may be applied to find optimal reload times. The estimation algorithm is illustrated by an example in section 4. In section 5 we present experiments concerning the application of the regular-grammar based reload policy to simulated and real Web data and in section 6 a summary is given and further aspects are discussed.

2 The Model

Let $u_i \in \mathbb{R}^+$ denote the points in time at which the ith update of a Web data object occurs, where $0 \leq u_1 \leq u_2 \leq u_3 \leq u_4 \leq \ldots u_n \leq T \in \mathbb{R}^+, n \in \mathbb{N}$. The interval of time between the $i-1^{th}$ and i^{th} update will be denoted by $t_i := u_i - u_{i-1}, i \in \mathbb{N}$. Let $a_1, a_2, \ldots a_m \in \mathbb{R}^+$ denote the points in time where reload operations are executed, where $0 \leq a_1 \leq a_2 \leq a_3 \ldots \leq a_m \leq T$. For $t \in \mathbb{R}^+$ let $N^u(t)$ denote the largest index of an element in the sequence u that is smaller than t, i.e. $N^u(t) := \max\{n | u_n \leq t\}$. Let $A^u(t) \in \mathbb{R}^+$ denote the size of the time interval since the last update, i.e. $A^u(t) := t - u_{N^u(t)}$. If t is the time of a reload ($t = a_i$ for $i \leq m$), we denote $A^u(t)$ as the *age* of a_i. The age of a local copy denotes how much time since the last remote data update has passed and thus how long an old copy of the data was stored although a new version should have been considered.[1]

Let $Q := \{t_j | j \leq n \in \mathbb{N}\}$ denote the set of time intervals between updates. We assign a symbol $s_i, i \in \mathbb{N}_{\leq n}$ to every element of Q. We call the set of symbols $\Delta := \{s_i | i \leq n\}$ the *alphabet* of the sequence u.

Let S denote a starting symbol, let $r_1, r_2, \ldots r_n$ denote terminals and the symbols $R_1, R_2, \ldots R_n$ non-terminals. In the following we refer to a regular grammar Γ corresponding to the non-deterministic finite automaton in figure 1 as a *cyclic regular grammar*. In figure 1, 'R_0' is a starting state which leads to

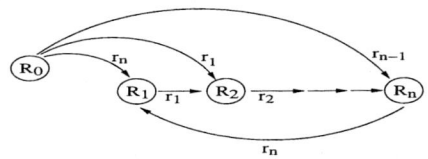

Fig. 1. Nondeterministic automaton corresponding to the grammar $(r_1 r_2 \ldots r_n)^\circ$

---
[1] If a local copy is used as an information source for users, in the respective period of time these users receive the old instead of the new data.

any of n states $R_1, \ldots, R_n$. After this, the list of symbols is accepted in a cyclic way. Every state is an accepting state. To abbreviate this definition we will use the notation: $(r_1 r_2 ... r_n)^\circ := \Gamma$.

The first problem in the following is to describe a sequence of symbols $s_1, s_2 ...$ corresponding to time intervals by a cyclic regular grammar of minimal size. The second problem is to predict further states of the automaton and to find optimal reload times. Finding the optimum means that after each update of the remote data source, the data should be reloaded as soon as possible, i.e. the sum of ages $sumage := \sum_{i=1}^{m} A^u(a_i)$ has to be minimal. The number of reloads should be as small as possible. No change of the data source should be unobserved. The number of lost (unobserved) data objects will be denoted as $\#loss$ in the following.

3 Algorithm for Adaptive Reload Optimization

3.1 Overview, Definitions

The presented algorithm for adaptive reload optimization consists mainly of four components.

A **first component** is responsible for the estimation of time intervals between successive updates. For this purpose the data source is downloaded after constant time periods. One main problem in this context is to find an adequate time period between reload operations in order to capture all remote updates as precisely as possible. In the subsequent section we present a method that is based on the observation of changes in a number of consecutive intervals.

A **second component** of the algorithm determines a sequence of symbols. A number of intervals corresponds to the same symbol. As a motivation for this definition it may be assumed that in many cases in the Web remote update operations are executed by daemon processes after certain time periods. However due to a server and network delay, the time intervals that are actually registered on the client side are slightly different. A symbol represents a cluster which combines these similar intervals, providing a maximal and a minimal length estimation for the interval. A *symbol* is a 3-tuple $s = (i, max, min)$ consisting of a unique identifier i and two length parameters $s.max$ and $s.min$.

A **third component** of the algorithm is responsible for the estimation of a grammar that represents the update behavior of a remote source. A *hypothesis* $H = (\Gamma, s)$ is a 2-tuple consisting of a cyclic-regular grammar Γ and the current state s of the associated finite automaton, according to the enumeration of states in figure 1. In every step of the algorithm after the detection of a symbol, the *default hypothesis* is added to the set of hypotheses. Taking the sequence of symbols registered by the system so far $(r_{i_1}, r_{i_2}, \ldots r_{i_p})$, the *default-hypothesis* is the cyclic regular grammar $(r_{i_1} r_{i_2} \ldots r_{i_p})^\circ$ with the corresponding automaton being in the state '1' according to the enumeration of states in figure 1. This automaton accepts the sequence of input symbols. The last symbol is accepted by a transition from the last state to state '1'. A *prediction* of a hypothesis which is not in the start state (R_0) is the symbol, generated by a transition to the (unique) state following the current state. A *proceed* operation applied to a hypothesis H (*H.proceed*) which is not in the start state '0' converts the current state of H to the subsequent state.

A **fourth component** is finally responsible for the application of the estimation result to an optimal reload policy and for the decision when the estimation becomes false and has to be updated.

3.2 Reload Interval Size and Interval Estimation

Figure 2 shows the basic idea of the interval estimation. The data source is reloaded after constant time periods $a_i - a_{i-1}$ denoted as *sampling interval* (*sampsize*) in the following. By detecting two remote changes (update 2 and 3 in figure 2a) in subsequent reload intervals (interval [3,4] and [7,8]) we acquire a maximal and a minimal estimation for the interval length (min and max in figure 2a).

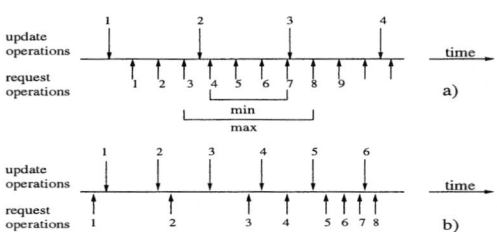

Fig. 2. Determination of a maximal and a minimal estimate for an interval length

An obvious problem with this estimation is that remote changes taking place between two successive reload operations may not be recognized. Therefore it is necessary to find an optimal time interval between successive requests, depending on the remote update behavior. One heuristical approach for this problem is shown in figure 2b. The algorithm is initialized with a reload interval which is known to be too large. After each reload operation the algorithm stores the information whether a change has been detected in the previous interval or not in a queue of size k. This queue contains information about changes being detected by the previous k reload operations. If a new change is detected, the algorithm tests if a previous change is contained in the queue. If this is the case, the reload interval is divided by 2 and the algorithm proceeds. A further question is when to stop with the interval size adjustment, i.e. when the interval size is sufficiently small. One heuristics is to stop the size determination after detection of m successive remote data changes without interval size adjustment.

The reload interval *sampsize* is sufficiently small if the time interval between requests $a_j - a_{j-1}$ is small compared to the time between updates (*sampsize* $\ll \min_i t_i$). It is obvious that the approach above may not lead to optimal results if the variance of update intervals is high. One possible improvement would be to analyses the 'fine' structure after the rough structure (i.e. the large gaps between updates) is known.

```
Symbol-Estimation( newInterval, symbols)
1        for each symbol s in symbols:
2          if newInterval similar to s
             return s
3          define new symbol sn with parameters of newInterval
           add sn to symbols
           return sn
```

Fig. 3. Algorithm component for insertion of new symbols or assignment of new intervals to previously registered symbols by incremental clustering according to a similarity measure

3.3 Symbol Estimation by Incremental Clustering

The previous algorithm generates a sequence of interval estimations some of which are similar. The next step is to cluster similar intervals which are assumed to represent similar remote update intervals. The problem is to find an adequate similarity measure for intervals and to apply it to the interval sequence in order to find the set (and the sequence) of symbols. Figure 3 shows the algorithm component *Symbol-Estimation*, responsible for the learning of new symbols or the assigning of a new interval to a previously registered symbol by incremental clustering of intervals [11]. It depends on the estimation parameters of a new interval (*newInterval*) and the set of previously registered symbols (*symbols*). In step 1 and 2 for each symbol in the set of symbols it is tested if the new parameters of *newInterval* are 'significantly different'. For this purpose the maximal and minimal interval sizes are compared with respect to the sampling size.[2] If this is not true for one symbol, i.e. if the current symbol has already been detected, the respective symbol is returned i.e. the set of symbols isn't changed. If the new interval-parameters are significantly different from all symbols defined so far, a new symbol is inserted into the set *symbols* in step 3. The algorithm is executed for each new detected interval. After the set of symbols has been determined it is easy to assign the previously registered intervals to the symbols by comparison and thereby to compute a sequence of symbols (denoted as *symbolSequence*) from the interval sequence.

3.4 Grammar Estimation

Based on the sequence of symbols detected so far it is now possible to develop hypotheses for the time-based grammar that generated the current symbol sequence. Figure 4 shows the algorithm which takes the sequence of symbols as the input. For every position in the sequence, the whole sequence of symbols ob-

---

[2] Different strategies are conceivable to compare the intervals; the applied method is described in detail in [15].

```
Grammar-Estimation( symbolSequence)
1       set hset = ∅
2       for i=1 to symbolSequence.length()
3           symbol s := symbolSequence.get(i)
4           add the default-hypothesis to hset
5           for each H ∈ hset\{default-hypothesis} do
6               if symbol not equal to prediction of H
7                   delete H from hset
8               else
9                   apply H.proceed
```

Fig. 4. Main algorithm component for the estimation of a cyclic regular grammar

served prior to this position is used to create the *default-hypothesis* (as defined in section 3.1) in step 4 of the algorithm in figure 4. In steps 5 and 6 it is tested for each hypothesis H in the set of hypotheses $hset$ if the prediction of H corresponds to the newly observed symbol. If not, the hypothesis is deleted from the set of hypotheses (step 7). If the prediction is consistent with the observation, the state of the hypothesis is increased in step 9.

3.5 Optimized Adaptive Reload Policy

In this section based on the previous estimation a reload policy is presented for optimal data update that is adaptive and may register if the estimation doesn't represent the remote update pattern (figure 6). It is assumed that the alphabet and the grammar have already been determined. We assume that the current state of the automaton is already known. This state may simply be determined by observing remote changes with a high reload frequency until the symbol sequence observed so far uniquely describes the current state of the automaton (step 1, figure 6) as described in detail in [15]. In steps 2 to 16 a loop is executed that determines at first the unique subsequent symbol according to the automaton H in step 4. According to this symbol an optimal reload time is computed in step 4. The choice of the optimal reload time is depicted in figure 5. The subsequent reload time is chosen such that it is supposed to occur before the next remote update, it corresponds roughly to the estimated minimal interval length between two remote updates (e.g. request 3 has to occur before update 2 in figure 5). Thereby it may be assured that the (symbol-)estimation is not too large in step 8.

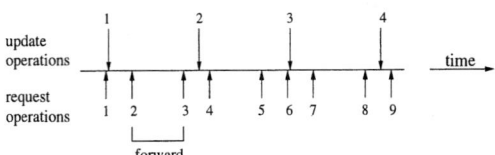

Fig. 5. Determination of an optimal forward interval

The system waits for the respective period of time in step 6, and reloads the remote data. High frequency reload is applied until a change with respect to the current and the previous version of the reloaded data is detected (steps 9 to 14). After the change detection (step 14), the algorithm continues with the prediction of the subsequent symbol in step 4.

One main aspect is how this algorithm may detect an error in the estimation and thereby adapt to changes in the update behavior of the data source. For this purpose the algorithm tests, if a currently predicted symbol corresponds to the currently observed update times. E.g. in the interval between reload 2 and 3 in figure 5 no change of the remote source should occur. This is tested in step 8 of the reload-control algorithm. A second aspect is if the maximal estimated interval length is correct. For this purpose the number of required reloads in the fast forward loop (steps 9 to 14) is counted in step 11. If it is too large (step 12), the interval estimation is obviously false. If the predicted interval doesn't correspond to the observed update-interval the algorithm terminates in step 8 or step 12.

Reload-Control (Input: estimated grammar $\sim H$, sampsize)	
1	find current state of the automaton
2	set $forward := 0$
3	do
4	find next symbol according to automaton H
5	compute optimal reload time t
6	wait until t
7	reload
8	confirm equality between old and new data
9	do
10	$t := t + sampsize$
11	$forward++$
12	if $forward > 3$: stop algorithm
13	wait until t, reload
14	until change detected
15	$forward := 0$
16	until end of observation

Fig. 6. Algorithm to determine optimal reload times based on the grammar estimation in section 3

4 Example

4.1 Grammar Estimation

In order to illustrate the *Grammar-Estimation* algorithm we assume that the system registers a sequence of symbols *ababcab*. After detecting the symbol a, the default hypothesis $H1 := (a)°$ is inserted into the empty set *hset* (table 1) in step 4 of the *Grammar-Estimation* component. This hypothesis is state '1'. In step 2 in table 1 the second detected symbol is b which is different to the

Table 1. Computation steps of the *Grammar-Estimation*-algorithm for the sequence *ababc...*

step	input symbol	reject hypothesis	insert hypothesis	hypotheses/state
1	a		H1:=(a)°	H1/state=1
2	b	H1	H2:=(ab)°	H2/state=1
3	a		H3:=(aba)°	H2/state=2
				H3/state=1
4	b	H3	H4:=(abab)°	H2/state=1
				H4/state=1
5	c	H2,H4	H5:=(ababc)°	H5/state=1
⋮				

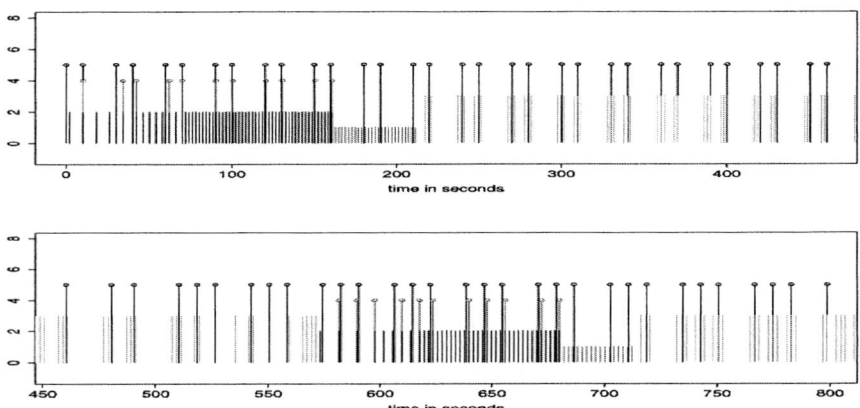

Fig. 7. Visualization of the adaptive reload optimization

prediction of $H1$ ($H1.prectict = a$). Therefore $H1$ is deleted from *hset*. Again, the default hypothesis $H2 := (ab)°$ is added to *hset*. In step 3 the symbol a is detected. In this case the prediction of $H2$ is true. Therefore the state of $H2$ is increased. The default hypothesis $H3 := (aba)°$ is added to hset. This procedure continues until in step 5 the symbol c is detected. In this step $H2$ and $H4$ have to be rejected and the default hypothesis $H5 := (ababc)°$ is added. After consideration of subsequent symbols this hypothesis turns out to be consistent with the sequence *ababcab* and it also turns out to be the smallest one.

4.2 Application Example

Figure 7 shows an application of the complete algorithm. Impulses of length 5 in figure 7 denote times of remote updates. In this example at first the remote update pattern is $(ab)°$ and changes to $(aab)°$ at time ~500 sec (symbol a has a length of 10 seconds; symbol b has a length of 20 seconds). In the first phase of the algorithm (time 1..100 sec) the sampling interval is determined according to section 3.2. Impulses of length 2 denote reload requests. Impulses of length 4 denote detected changes. The detected changes in the interval from 70 to 160 seconds are used for the grammar estimation. Next, the state is determined (impulses of length 1) and the optimized reload is applied (impulses if length 3). At time 570 the algorithm detects an error in the estimation and starts again with the sampling interval estimation.

5 Experiments

In this section we demonstrate the advantages of the adaptive regular reload policy, in the following denoted as the *regular* method, to the policy based on a constant reload frequency, denoted as the *constant* method.[3] Optimization refers to a specific definition of costs, which have to be minimized. For the cost definition we consider the *age* of data *(sumage)* and the number of lost data objects $\sharp loss$ as defined in section 2. The different quality parameters may easily be computed from the sequence of reload operations, which is known and the sequence of remote updates, which is either known or has to be estimated by high-frequency sampling. In the experiments we select the number of downloads of the constant-frequency method such that it is equal to the number of downloads of the regular method. In these experiments the costs created by the estimation process are ignored. These costs only occur once at the beginning of the application. In this respect we consider the costs 'in the limit' and assume that changes in the update behavior that result in a re-estimation are sufficiently rare and therefore don't create significant costs. Figure 8 shows an experiment with generated data which demonstrates the basic properties of the new reload policy. In the experiment a grammar of two symbols $(ab)^\circ$ was considered with a total length of one cycle of 50 seconds (length(a)+length(b)=50 sec). The difference of the two symbol lengths ($|length(a) - length(b)|$) is increased in the experiment (x-axis in figure 8). If e.g. the difference is zero the interval lengths are identical (length(a)=25 and length(b)=25). Figure 8 a) shows that if the interval length difference of the two symbols gets larger, the number of lost data increases when the constant method is applied while it is zero for the regular method. The reason is that the constant method has to consider a reload interval smaller than the smallest update interval in order to capture all updates. Since in this method the reload frequence is constant, this may lead to a large number of (superfluous) reloads; otherwise, if the number of reloads is fix as in the described experiment, the $\sharp loss$ value is likely to increase. Figure 8 b) shows that the age of data (*sumage*) is significantly smaller if the regular method is applied.

---

[3] This method is currently applied by most Web crawlers, Web caches etc. as described in section 1.1.

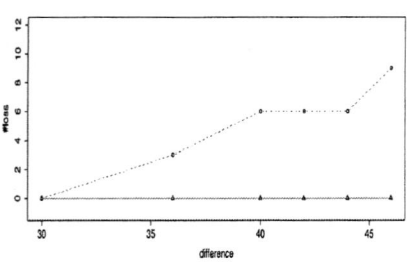 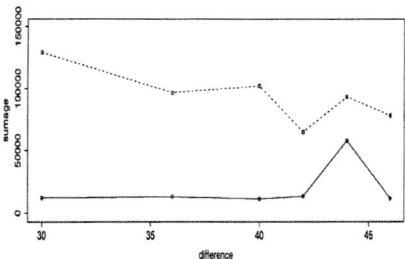

(a) ♯lost for the regular method and the constant method (dashed line)

(b) *sumage* (in seconds) for the regular method and the constant method (dashed line)

Fig. 8. The quality parameters ♯*loss* and *sumage* for a cyclic grammar $(ab)°$ for different interval differences $|length(a) - length(b)|$

Table 2. Comparison of reload policies for different Web pages. Page 1 (http://www.oanda.com) provides financial data. Page 2 (http://www.sec.noaa.gov/rt_plots/xray_5m.html) provides data related to space weather. The reduction of *agesum* applying the regular method ranges from 50% to 90%

	page	loss	sumage (seconds)
constant method	1	0	24143
regular method	1	0	12960
constant method	2	0	50331
regular method	2	0	6233

The previous result may also be shown for real Web pages. In the following experiment a time interval of 5 days is defined. In this time interval the two reload policies are executed and the original update times are determined by fast sampling in order to compute the quality measure. The number of downloads are equal for both systems, which requires that the update behavior has already been determined in an offline step. Table 2 shows the result of a comparison of the different reload policies for different Web pages. Page 1 has the URL http://www.oanda.com. It provides information related to currency exchange. Page 2 (http://www.sec.noaa.gov/rt_plots/xray_5m.html) provides data related to x-radiation from the sun. The results in table 2 show that values for lost data and superfluous data are very similar if as in this example the number of downloads is identical (the length of symbols is similar in this case in contrast to the simulation experiment above). The age of data (*sumage*) may be reduced from 50% up to about 80% for different pages.

6 Conclusion

The article presents an algorithm to estimate the parameters of the update behavior of a distant source that may be approximated piecewise by a specific kind of a regular grammar. The algorithm takes into account that the points in time where data sources in the Web change may usually not be registered exactly. The estimated grammar is used to determine optimal points in time for data reloads with respect to a minimization of the age of data and the amount of lost data. In the experiments it is shown that the age of data may be reduced significantly using the adaptive regular reload policy compared to a constant-frequency based method in the case that changes of the remote update behavior are rare and the respective costs for a re-estimation may be ignored.

The basic idea concerning this research is to develop a personal information system that makes the access to the dynamic properties of the Web for a user as simple as possible. In the article some of the parameters needed for the estimation are determined automatically like the sampling size. However several parameters still have to be provided by a user like the time needed for the sampling size determination, the period of time needed for the grammar estimation, the initial sampling size etc. If the presented results would be used for a personal information system it would still be inconvenient to actually use this tool especially if a large number of data objects has to be considered.

References

1. A.Arasu, J.Cho, H.Garcia-Molina, A.Paepcke, and S.Raghavan. Searching the web. *ACM Trans. Inter. Tech.*, 1(1):2–43, 2001.
2. Shivnath Babu and Jennifer Widom. Continuous queries over data streams. *SIGMOD Rec.*, 30(3):109–120, 2001.
3. Brian E. Brewington and George Cybenko. How dynamic is the Web? *Computer Networks (Amsterdam, Netherlands: 1999)*, 33(1–6):257–276, 2000.
4. Xin Chen and Xiaodong Zhang. Web document prefetching on the internet. In Zhong, Liu, and Yao, editors, *Web Intelligence*, chapter 16. Springer, 2003.
5. Junghoo Cho and Hector Garcia-Molina. Estimating frequency of change. *ACM Trans. Inter. Tech.*, 3(3):256–290, 2003.
6. E. Coffman, Z.Liu, and R.R.Weber. Optimal robot scheduling for web search engines. *Journal of Scheduling*, 1(1):15–29, June 1998.
7. World Wide Web Consortium. W3c httpd. http://www.w3.org/Protocols/.
8. Mukund Deshpande and George Karypis. Selective markov models for predicting web page accesses. *ACM Trans. Inter. Tech.*, 4(2):163–184, 2004.
9. A. Dingle and T.Partl. Web cache coherence. *Computer Networks and ISDN Systems*, 28(7-11):907–920, May 1996.
10. P. Dupont, L. Miclet, and E. Vidal. What is the search space of the regular inference? In R. C. Carrasco and J. Oncina, editors, *Proceedings of the Second International Colloquium on Grammatical Inference (ICGI-94): Grammatical Inference and Applications*, volume 862, pages 25–37, Berlin, 1994. Springer.
11. Brian S. Everitt. *Cluster Analysis*. Hodder Arnold, 2001.

12. E. Gold. Language identification in the limit. *Information and Control*, 10:447–474, 1967.
13. Julie E. Kendall and Kenneth E. Kendall. Information delivery systems: an exploration of web pull and push technologies. *Commun. AIS*, 1(4es):1, 1999.
14. D. Kukulenz. Capturing web dynamics by regular approximation. In *WISE04, International Conference on Web Information Systems Engineering, Brisbane*, 2004.
15. D. Kukulenz. Optimization of continuous queries by regular inference. In *6th International Baltic Conference on Databases and IS*, volume 672 of *Scientific Papers University of Latvia*, pages 62–77, 2004.
16. C. Olston and J.Wildom. Best-effort cache synchronization with source cooperation. In *Proceedings od SIGMOD*, May 2002.
17. J. Oncina and P.Garcia. Inferring regular languages in polynomial update time. *Pattern Recognition and Image Analysis, Perez, Sanfeliu, Vidal (eds.), World Scientific*, pages 49–61, 1992.
18. Rajesh Parekh and Vasant Honavar. Learning dfa from simple examples. *Machine Learning*, 44(1/2):9–35, 2001.
19. D. Wessels. Intelligent caching for world-wide web objects. In *Proceedings of INET-95, Honolulu, Hawaii, USA*, 1995.
20. J. L. Wolf, M. S. Squillante, P. S. Yu, J. Sethuraman, and L. Ozsen. Optimal crawling strategies for web search engines. In *Proceedings of the eleventh international conference on World Wide Web*, pages 136–147. ACM Press, 2002.

Mining Maximal Frequent ItemSets Using Combined FP-Tree

Yuejin Yan[†], Zhoujun Li, Tao Wang, Yuexin Chen, and Huowang Chen

School of Computer Science, National University of Defense Technology,
Changsha 410073, China
[†] Corresponding author: Phn 86-731-4532956
yanyuejin2003@hotmail.com
http://www.nudt.edu.cn

Abstract. Maximal frequent itemsets mining is one of the most fundamental problems in data mining. In this paper, we present CfpMfi, a new depth-first search algorithm based on CFP-tree for mining MFI. Based on the new data structure CFP-tree, which is a combination of FP-tree and MFI-tree, CfpMfi takes a variety pruning techniques and a novel item ordering policy to reduce the search space efficiently. Experimental comparison with previous work reveals that, on dense datasets, CfpMfi prunes the search space efficiently and is better than other MFI Mining algorithms on dense datasets, and uses less main memory than similar algorithm.

1 Introduction

Since the frequent itemsets mining problem (FIM) was first addressed [1], frequent itemsets mining in large database has become an important problem. And the number of frequent itemsets increases exponentially with the increasing of frequent itemsets' length. So the large length of frequent itemset leads to no feasible of FI mining. Furthermore, since frequent itemsets are upward closed, it is sufficient to discover only all maximal frequent itemsets. As a result, researchers now turn to find MFI (maximal frequent itemsets) [4,5,6,7,9,10,13]. A frequent itemset is called maximal if it has no frequent superset. Given a set of MFI, it is easy to analyze some interesting properties of the database, such as the longest pattern, the overlap of the MFI, etc. There are also applications where the MFI is adequate, for example, the combinatorial pattern discovery in biological applications [3].

This paper introduces a new algorithm for mining MFI. We use a novel combined FP-tree in the process of mining, where the right represents sub database containing all relevant frequency information, and the left stores information of discovered MFI that is useful for *superset frequency* pruning. Based on the combined FP-tree, our algorithm takes a novel item ordering policy, and integrates a variety of old and new prune strategies. It also uses a simple but fast superset checking method along with some other optimizations.

The organization of the paper is as follows: Section 2 describes the basic concepts and the pruning techniques for mining MFI. Section 3 gives the MFI mining algorithm, CfpMfi, which does the MFI mining based on the combined FP-tree. In section 4, we compare our algorithm with some previous ones. Finally, in section 5, we draw the conclusions.

2 Preliminaries and Related Works

This section will formally describe the MFI mining problem and the set enumeration tree that represents the search space. Also the related works will be introduced in this section.

2.1 Problem Statement

The problem of mining maximal frequent itemsets is formally stated by definitions 1-4 and lemmas 1-2.

Let $I = \{i_1, i_2, \ldots, i_m\}$ be a set of m distinct items. Let D denote a database of transactions, where each transaction contains a set of items.

Definition 1: (Itemset)
A set $X \subseteq I$ is called an *itemset*. An itemset with k items is called a k-itemset.

Definition 2: (Itemset's Support)
The support of an itemset X, denoted as $\delta(X)$, is defined as the number of transactions in which X occurs as a subset.

Definition 3: (Frequent Itemset)
For a given D, Let ξ be the threshold minimum support value specified by user. If $\delta(X) \geq \xi$, itemset X is called a frequent itemset.

Definition 4: (Maximal Frequent Itemset)
If $\delta(X) \geq \xi$ and for any $Y \supseteq X$, we have $\delta(Y) < \xi$, then X is called a maximal frequent itemset.

According to definitions 3-4, the following lemmas hold.

Lemma 1: A proper subset of any frequent itemset is not a maximal frequent itemset.

Lemma 2: A subset of any frequent itemset is a frequent itemset, a superset of any infrequent itemset is not a frequent itemset.

Given a transactional database D, supposed I is an itemset of it, then any combination of the items in I would be frequent and all these combinations compose the search space, which can be represented by a set enumeration tree [5]. The root of the tree represents the empty itemset, and the nodes at level k contain all of the k-itemsets. The itemset associated with each node, n, will be referred as the node's *head* (n). A complete set enumeration tree of $\{a,b,c,d,e,f\}$ in given order of a,b,c,d,e is shown in figure 1.

The possible extensions of the itemset is denoted as *ctail(n)*, which is a set of items after the last item of *head(n)*. The frequent extensions denoted as *ftail(n)* is a set of items that can be appended to *head(n)* to build the longer frequent itemsets. In depth-first traversal of the tree, *ftail(n)* contains just the frequent extensions of *n*. The itemset associated with each children node of node *n* is set up by appending one of *ftail(n)* to *head (n)*. If a children node of *n* is formed by appending item *i* to *head(n)*, the children node is called a child of *n* at *i*.

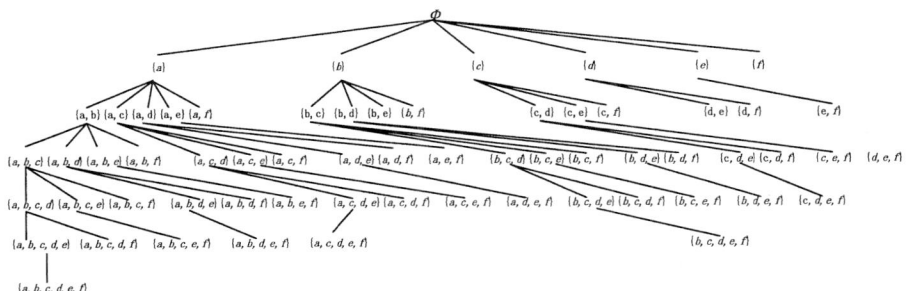

Fig. 1. A Complete Set Enumeration tree of $\{a,b,c,d,e,f\}$

The process of mining is a searching process of the enumeration tree, and it is important to prune the tree efficiently while searching. According to the lemmas 1-2, we introduce theorem 1-3 on pruning.

Theorem 1:(Subset Infrequency Pruning)
If *head(n)* $\cup$ $\{i\}$ is infrequent($i \in$ *ctail(n)*), the node that is the child of *n* at *i* can be pruned from the enumeration tree.

Theorem 2:(Superset Frequency Pruning)
If *head(n)* $\cup$ *ftail(n)* is frequent, all the children nodes of *n* can be pruned from the enumeration tree, and so do all the offspring nodes of *n*.

Superset frequency pruning is also called *looksahead* pruning in MaxMiner. Here we called it *looksahead* pruning with frequent extensions. If *head(n)* $\cup$ *ctail(n)* is frequent, there is a *looksahead* pruning with candidate extensions.

Theorem 3:(*PEP*)
If $\delta(head(n) \cup \{i\}) = \delta(head(n))$, the node that is the child of *n* at *i* can be pruned from the enumeration tree.

Proof: As each transaction contains *head(n)* will also contain item *i*, we can say that any frequent itemset Z containing *head(n)* but not *i*, has the frequent superset $Z \cup \{i\}$, and *i* can be moved from *ftail(n)* to *head(n)*. PEP (Parent Equivalence Pruning) can also be seen as that the children node of *n* at *i* is been composed into *n* and does not need to been searched any more.

2.2 Related Work

Based on the set enumeration tree, we can describe the most recent approaches to MFI mining problem.

The MaxMiner [5] employs a breadth-first traversal policy for the searching. To reduce the search space, it introduced a new pruning technique named as *lookaheads* pruning. To increase the effectiveness of *lookaheads* pruning, MaxMiner dynamically reorders the children nodes, which was used in most of the MFI algorithms after that [4,6,7,9,10].

Mafia [7] is a depth-first algorithm. It uses a vector bitmap representation as in [6], where the count of an itemset is based on the column in the bitmap. All the three pruning methods mentioned in section 2.1 are used in Mafia.

Both MaxMiner and Mafia mine a superset of the MFIs, and require a post-pruning to eliminate non-maximal frequent itemsets. GenMax [9] integrates the pruning with mining to finds the exact MFIs by using two strategies. First, just like that transaction database is projected on current node, the discovered MFI set can also be projected on the node and thus yields fast superset checking; Second, GenMax uses *Diffset* propagation to do fast support computation.

AFOPT [3] uses a data structure called AFOPT tree in which items are ascending frequency ordered to store the transactions in conditional databases with top-town tree traversal strategy. It employs MFI projection generated by pseudo projection technique to test whether a frequent itemset is a subset of one of the discovered MFIs.FPMax* is an extension of the FP-growth method, for MFIs mining only. It uses a FP-tree to store the transaction projection of the original database for each node in the tree. In order to test whether a frequent itemset is the subset of any discovered MFI in *lookaheads* pruning, another tree structure, named MFI-tree, is utilized to keep the track of all discovered MFI, which makes effective superset checking. FPMax* uses an array for each node to store the counts of all 2-itemsets that is a subset of the frequent extensions itemset, this makes the algorithm scan each FP-tree only once for each recursive call emanating from it. The experiment results in FIMI'03 [10] shows that FPMax* has the best performance then for almost all the tested database. FIMfi [13] is also an algorithm base on FP-tree and MFI-tree, and it employs a new item ordering policy and a new method to do superset checking to improve performance.

3 Mining Maximal Frequent Itemsets by CfpMfi

In this section, we discuss algorithm CfpMfi in details.

3.1 Combined FP-Tree

For each node to be searched in the enumeration tree, CfpMfi builds a CFP-tree (combined FP-tree) that is a combination of FP-tree and MFI-tree. The right of the CFP-tree is a FP-tree that stores all relevant frequency information in database and the left of the CFP-tree is a MFI-tree which is used to keep the track of discovered

MFIs for current node. And in the left of the CFP-tree, there is not the field *level* for each node as in MFI-tree of FPMax*. There is also a header for each CFP-tree, and each head entry of CFP-tree has five fields: *item-name, right-node-link, left-node-link, maximal-level* and *maximal-type*. Fields maximal-level and maximal-type are used for subset testing and what they record is defined by definition 5. For an item i in header, we can define the maximal subset of i in CFP-tree as follows.

Definition 5: (i's Maximal Subset in CFP-Tree)
Let S_1 be the itemset represented by the maximal conditional pattern base of i in the left of CFP-tree, for all the conditional pattern bases of i in which the last item's count is more than the threshold ξ in the right of the CFP-tree, and let S_2 be the itemset represented by the maximal base. If $|S_2|>|S_1|$, S_2 is called the right maximal subset of i in CFP-tree, otherwise S_1 is called the left maximal subset of i in CFP-tree.

The field maximal-level at each header entry represents the items' number in S_1 or S_2, and the field maximal-type records the type of the maximal subset of the item in CFP-tree. Figure 2 shows an example of CFP-tree of root when considering extending to the child node $\{e\}$ of root. In the header of the tree, the "T" means the corresponding item that has one left maximal subset, and the "F" means the corresponding item has one right maximal subset.

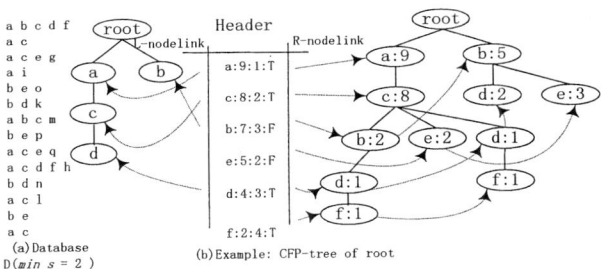

Fig. 2. Example of CFP-tree

According to definition 5, the theorem is given as follows.

Theorem 4:
For a node n, let i be the last item in $head(n)$ and S be its maximal subset in n's CFP-tree, then $head(n) \cup S$ is frequent. Furthermore, if S is the right maximal subset of i in the CFP-tree, $head(n) \cup S$ is a new maximal frequent itemset.

The building process of the CFP-tree of node n in search space is as follows: (1) The header is built after having found all the items that is frequent after combined with $head(n)$. (2) The right part of the CFP-tree associated with the parent node of n is scanned once, the items that do not occur in the header are removed from each conditional pattern base, then the base is inserted into the right of current CFP-tree after being reordered according the order of the header, the extra work needed to be done in the insertion is that the two maximal fields in header entries of the items in the base will be updated after the insertion. (3) Building of the left of CFP-tree is similar to the building of the right in the second step. The first step and the second step are described in procedure 1, and the third step is shown in procedure 2. Figure 3(a) gives the examples of the building of CFP-tree.

Procedure 1: RightBuild
Input : n : current node
i : the item needed to be extended currently
fretail: the frequent extensions itemset for the child of n at i
pepset: a null itemset to store *PEP* items
Output : the new CFP-tree with initialized header and left

(1) Sort the items in *fretail* in the increasing order of support
(2) $pepset = \{i \mid \delta(head(n) \cup \{i\}) = \delta(head(n))$ and i is a frequent extension of $head(n)\}$
(3) Build a head entry for each item in *fretail* but not in *pepset* for the new CFP-tree
(4) For each itemset s according to a conditional pattern base of i in the right of $n.cfptree$
(5)   Delete the items in s but not in *fretail*
(6)   Sort the remaining items in s according to the order of *fretail*
(7)   Insert the sorted itemset into the right of the new CFP-tree
(8) Return the new CFP-tree

Procedure 2: LeftBuild
Input : n : current node
i : the item needed to be extended currently
n': the child of n at i
Output: the CFP-tree with the left initialized

(1) For each itemset s according to a conditional pattern base of i in the left of $n.cfptree$
(2)   Delete the items in s but not in $n'.cfptree.header$
(3)   Sort the remaining items in s according to the order of $n'.cfptree.header$
(4)   Insert the sorted itemsets into the left of $n'.cfptree$
(5) Return $n'.cfptree$

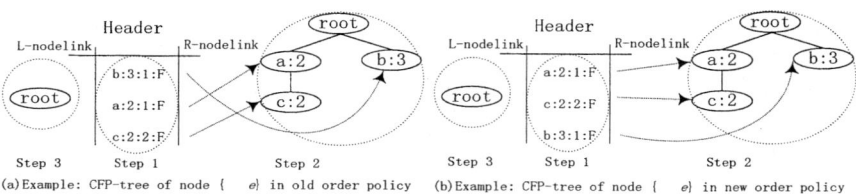

Fig. 3. Examples of constructing CFP-tree

If a new MFI is found, it is used to update the CFP-trees' left of each node within the path from root to current node in search space tree. For example, after considering the node {f}, {f,d,c,a}-{f} is inserted to the left of CFP-trees of root, and after considering the node {d}, {d,b}-{d} is inserted to the left of CFP-trees of root, the left of root's CFP-tree is null when it is initialized, after the two insertion, the CFP-tree is shown as in Figure 2.

3.2 CfpMfi

The pseudo-code of CfpMfi is shown in Figure 6. In each call procedure, each newly found MFI maybe be used in superset checking for ancestor nodes of the current node, so we use a global parameter called *cfpTreeArray* to access the Cfp-trees of ancestor nodes. And when the top call (CfpMfi(*root*,ϕ)) is over, all the MFIs to be mined are stored in the left of *root*'s Cfp-tree in the search space tree.

Lines (4), (9) and (20) are the simple superset checking that will be described in detail in section 3.3. When x is the end item of the header, there is no need to do the checking, for the checking has already been done by the procedure calling current one in line (9) and/or line (20). Lines from (7) to (8) use the optimization array technique introduced in section 3.5. The *PEP* technique is used by call procedure rightbuild in line (18). Lines (5)-(6) and lines (21)-(24) are two *lookaheads* prunings with candidate extensions. The *lookaheads* pruning with frequent extensions is done in lines from (14) to (20). When the condition in lines (11), (15) and (22) is true, all the children nodes of n' are pruned and *ftail*(n') or *ctail*(n') need not to be inserted into the left of *n.CFP-tree* any more. The novel item ordering policy will be introduced in section 3.4 and is used in procedure 1 in line (1). Line (18) builds the header and the right of n'.*CFP-tree*. The *return* statements in line (5), (6), (12), (16) and (23) mean that all the children nodes after n' of n are pruned there. And the *continue* statements in line (13), (17) and (24) tell us that node n' will be pruned, then we can go to consider the next child of n. The left of n'.*CFP-tree* is built by call procedure leftbuild in line (25). After the constructing of the whole n'.*CFP-tree* and the updating of *cfpTreeArray*, CfpMfi will be called recursively with the new node n' and the new *cfpTreeArray*.

Note CfpMfi doesn't employ single path trimming used in FPMax* and AFOPT. If, by having constructed the right of n'.*CFP-tree*, we find out that the right of n'.*CFP-tree* has a single path, the superset checking in line (20) will return *true*, there will be a *lookaheads* pruning instead of a single path trimming.

Procedure: CfpMfi
Input:
    n: a node in search space tree ;
    cfpTreeArray: CFp-trees of all ancestor nodes of n in the path of search space tree from root to n.
(1) For each item x from end to beginning in *header* of *n.CFP-tree*
(2) $h'=h \cup \{x\}$ //h' identifies n'
(3)   if x is not the end item of the header
(4)   if | *ctail*(n') | == *n.CFP-tree.header.x.maximal-level*
(5)   if *n.CFP-tree.header.x.maximal-type* == "T"   return
(6)   else insert $h' \cup$ *ctail*(n') into *cfpTreeArray*   return

(7) if *n.array* is null   count *ftail(n')* using the *n.array*
(8) else   count *ftail(n')* by a scan of the right of *n.CFP_tree*
(9) if | *ftail(n')* | == *n.CFP-tree.header.x.maximal-level*
(10)   if *n.CFP-tree.header.x.maximal-type* == "T"
(11)   if the number of items before *x* in the *n.CFP-tree.header* is | *ftail(n')*|
(12)   return
(13)   else continue
(14)   insert $h' \cup ftail(n')$ into *cfpTreeArray*
(15)   if the number of items before *x* in the *n.CFP-tree.header* is | *ftail(n')*|
(16)   return
(17)   else insert *ftail(n')* into *n.CFP-tree*   continue
(18) *pepset* = ϕ; *n'.CFP-tree* = rightbuild(*n*,*x*, *ftail(n')*,*pepset*)
(19) $h' = h' \cup pepset$
(20) if | *n'.header* | == *n'.CFP-tree.header.lastitem.maximal-level*
(21)   insert $h' \cup ftail(n')$ into *cfpTreeArray*
(22)   if the number of items before *x* in the *n.CFP-tree.header* is | *ftail(n')*|
(23)   return
(24)   else insert *ftail(n')* into *n.CFP-tree*   continue
(25) *n'.CFP-tree* = leftbuild(*n*, *n'*,*x*)
(26) *cfpTreeArray* = *cfpTreeArray* $\cup$ {*n.CFP-tree*}
(27) call CfpMfi(n' , *cfpTreeArray*)

3.3 Implementation of Superset Checking

According to Theorem 2, if *head(n)* $\cup$ *ftail(n)* or *head(n)* $\cup$ *ctail(n)* is frequent, there will be a *lookaheads* pruning, There are two existing methods for determining whether the itemset *head(n)* $\cup$ *ftail(n)* or *head(n)* $\cup$ *ctail(n)* is frequent. The first one is to count the support of *head(n)* $\cup$ *ftail(n)* directly, and this method is normally used in an bread-first algorithms such as in MaxMiner. The second one is to check whether a superset of *head(n)* $\cup$ *ftail(n)* has already been in the discovered MFIs, which is used by the depth-first MFI algorithms commonly [4,7,9,10]. When implementing the superset checking, GenMax uses LMFI to store all the relevant MFIs, and the mapping item by item for *ftail(n)* in the LMFI is needed; In MFI-tree, FPMax* needs only map *ftail(n)* item by item in all conditional pattern bases of *head(n)*. The simple but fast superset checking for *head(n)* $\cup$ *ctail(n)* or *head(n)* $\cup$ *ftail(n)* is firstly introduced in [13]. In CfpMfi, the implementation of superset checking is based on the theorems as follows:

Theorem 5: Let *n'* be the child of *n* at *i*, if the size of *i*'s maximal subset in CFP-tree of *n* is equal to the size of *ftail(n')* or *ctail(n')*, then *head(n')*$\cup$*ftail(n')* or *head(n')* $\cup$ *ctail(n')* is frequent.

Proof: Let *S* be *i*'s maximal subset in CFP-tree of *n*. (1): If *S* is in the left of the CFP-tree, *head(n')* $\cup$ *S* is an subset of some discovered MFIs, then *head(n)* $\cup$ *S* is frequent; According to theorem 4, when *S* is in the right of the CFP-tree, *head(n)* $\cup$ *S* is frequent too. (2): According to the definition of *frq_tail* and *ctail*, we have *ftail(n')* =

{x| x is a item that is bigger than i in header of n' CFP-tree and head(n') ∪ {x} is frquent} and ftail(n') ⊆ ctail(n'), then S ⊆ ftail(n') ⊆ ctail(n'). According to (1) and (2), when the assumption in theorem 5 is right, S = ftail(n') or S = ctail(n') can be hold. Hence, we obtain the theorem.

According to theorem 5, in Cfp-tree, the field *maximal-level* of each *header* entry records the size of the maximal subset, so the superset checking becomes very simple and only needs to check the field with the size of ftail(n') or ctail(n'). Note that superset checking is a frequent operation in the process of mining MFIs. It is because that each new MFI needs to be checked before being added into the discovered MFIs. Then the implementation of superset checking can improve the performance of *lookaheads* pruning efficiently. Furthermore, when the superset checking returns true and the maximal subset is in the right of CFP-tree, it is no need to construct the CFP-trees of n' and n" offspring nodes, there is a *lookaheads* pruning, but the itemset head(n') ∪ ftail(n') or head(n') ∪ ctail(n') is a new MFI, and, as described in procedure 3 in lines (6),(14),(17),(21) and (24), it is used to update the relevant CFP-trees.

3.4 Item Ordering Policy

Item ordering policy appears firstly in [5], and is used by almost all the following MFI algorithms for it can increase the effectiveness of superset frequency pruning. In general, this type of item ordering policy works better in *lookaheads* by scanning the database to count the support of head(n) ∪ ftail(n) in breath-first algorithms, such as in MaxMiner. All the recently proposed depth-first algorithms do the superset checking instead to implement the *lookaheads* pruning, for the counting support of head(n) ∪ ftail(n) costs high in depth-first policy.

FIMfi tries to find a maximal subset of ftail(n), then let the subset in ftail(n) ahead when ordering to gain maximal pruning at a node in question. In CfpMfi, the maximal subset S in definition 5 is the exact subset, and it can be used for this purpose without any extra cost. For example, when considering the node n identified by {e}, we know ftail (n)={a,c,b}, S={a,c}, then the sorted items in ftail(n) is in sequence of a,c,b, the CFP-tree will be constructed as in figure 2(b), the old decreasing order of supports is b,a,c, the CFP-tree will be constructed as in figure 2(a). In the old order policy, the CFP-trees for nodes {e}, {e,a}, and {e,c} will have to be build, but CFpMfi with the new order policy only need to build FP-trees for nodes {e} and {e,b}. Furthermore, for the items in ftail(n)-S, we also sort them in the decreasing order of sup(head(n) ∪ {x}) (x ∈ ftail(n)-S).

4 Experimental Evaluations

In the first Workshop on Frequent Itemset Mining Implementations (FIMI'03) [11], which took place at ICDM'03, there are several algorithms presented recently, which are good for mining MFI, such as FPMax*, AFOPT, Mafia and etc, and FIMfi is a newly presented algorithm in ER 2004 [14], we now present the performance comparisons between CfpMfi and them. All the experiments are conducted on 2.4 GHZ Pentium IV with 1024 MB of DDR memory running Microsoft Windows 2000 Professional. The codes of other three algorithms were downloaded from [12] and all codes of the four algorithms were complied using Microsoft Visual C++ 6.0. Due to the lack of space, only the results for four real dense datasets are shown here. The datasets we used are also selected from all the 11 real datasets of FIMI'03[12], they are chess, Connect, Mushroom and Pumsb_star, and their data characteristics can be found in [11].

4.1 The Pruning Performance of CfpMfi

CfpMfi adopts the new item ordering policy, along with the *PEP* and *lookaheads* pruning with frequent extensions and candidate extensions, to prune the search space tree. Since FPMax* is nearly the best MFI mining algorithm in FIMI'03 and employs FP-tree and MFI-tree structures similar to CFP-tree, we select FPMax* as a benchmark algorithm to test the performance of CfpMfi in pruning. The comparison of the number of CFP-tree' rights built by CfpMfi and FP-trees created by FPMax* is shown in figure 4, in which the number of CFP-tree's rights in CfpMfi is less half of that of FP-trees in FPMax* on all the four dense datasets at all supports. And figure 5 reveals the comparison of the number of CFP-tree' lefts built by CfpMfi and MFI-trees created by FPMax*. And in figure 5, the number of CFP-tree's lefts in CfpMfi is about 30% -70% of that of MFI-trees in FPMax* on all the four dense datasets at all supports. Hence, it is not difficult to conclude from the two figures that by using the new item ordering policy and the pruning techniques, CfpMfi makes the pruning more efficient.

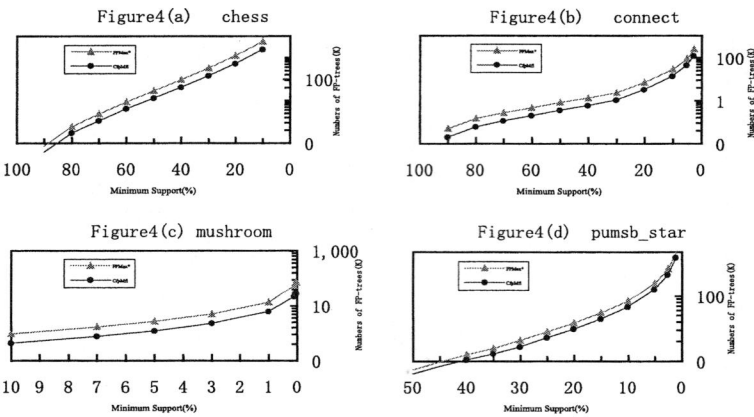

Fig. 4. Comparison of FP-trees' Number

4.2 Performance Comparisons

Figure 6 gives the results of comparison among the five algorithms on the selected dense datasets. For all supports on dense datasets Connect, Mushroom and Pumsb_star, CfpMfi has the best performance. CfpMfi runs around 40% -60% faster than FPMax* on all of the dense datasets. AFOPT is the slowest algorithm on Chess, Mushroom and Pumsb_star and runs 2 to 10 times worse than CfpMfi on all of the

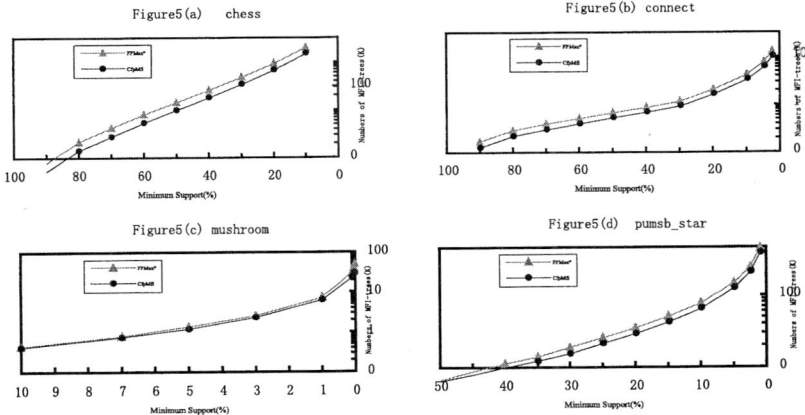

Fig. 5. Comparison of MFI-trees' Number

datasets across all supports. Mafia is the slowest algorithm on Connect, it runs 2 to 5 times slower than CfpMfi on Mushroom and Connect across all supports. On Pumsb_star, Mafia is outperformed by CfpMfi for all the supports though it outperforms FPMax* at lower supports, and on chess CfpMfi outperforms Mafia for the supports no less than 30% but Mafia outperforms FPMax* for the supports no less than 50%. CfpMfi outperforms FIMfi slightly until the lower supports where they cross over. In fact, with the lowest supports 10%, 2.5%, 0.025% and 1% for Chess, Connect, Mushroom and Pumsb_star, CfpMfi is %3, %25, %15 and 30% better than FIMfi respectively.

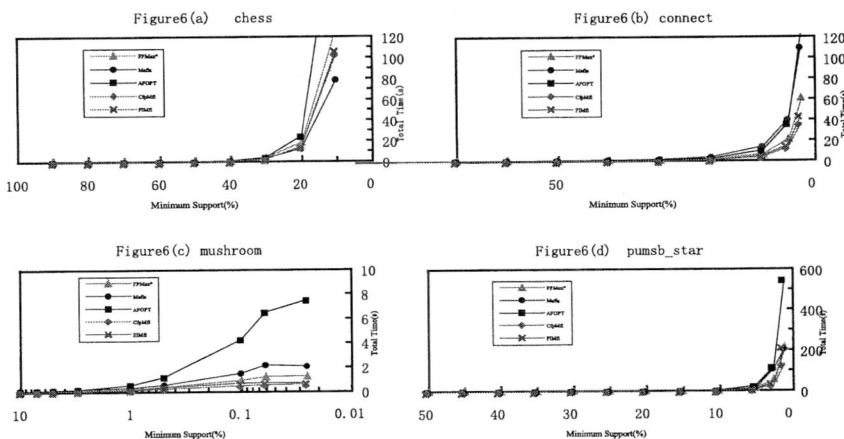

Fig. 6. Performance of Total Time

4.3 Maximal Main Memory Usage Comparisons

Figure 7 gives the results of maximal main memory used by the five algorithms on the selected dense datasets. From the figure, we can see that CfpMfi uses main memory more than FPMax* but less than FIMfi. The figure reveals that by using the compact data structure, CFP-tree, CfpMfi saves more main memory than FIMfi does.

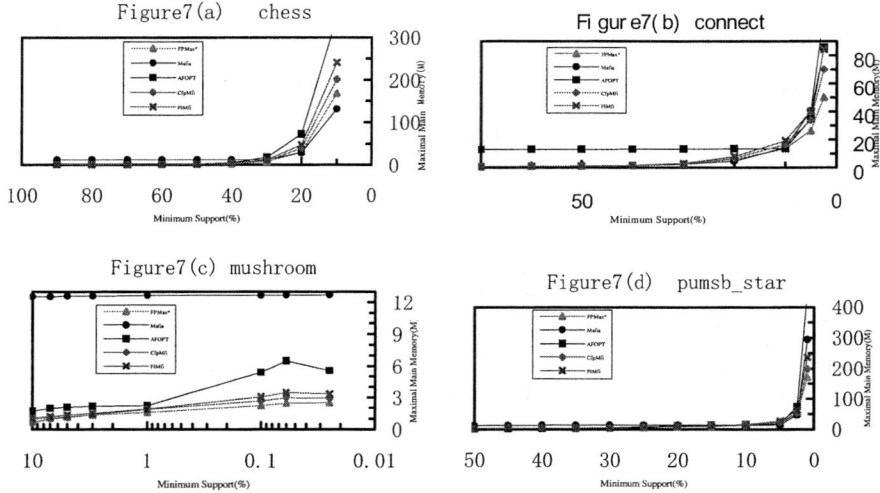

Fig. 7. Performance of Maximal Main Memory Usage

5 Conclusions

We presented CfpMfi, an algorithm for finding maximal frequent itemsets. Our experimental result demonstrates that, on dense datasets, FpMfi is more optimized for mining MFI and outperforms FPMax* by 40% averagely, and for lower supports it is about 10% better than FIMfi. The pruning performance and running time performance comparisons verify the efficiency of the novel ordering policy and the new method for superset checking that presented in [13], and the study of maximal main memory used indicates the compactness of CFP-tree structure. Thus it can be concluded that the new tree data structure, CFP-tree, along with the new ordering policy and some pruning techniques are well integrated into CfiMfi.

Acknowledgements

We would like to thank Guimei Liu for providing the code of AFOPT and Doug Burdick for providing the website of downloading the code of Mafia.

References

[1] R. Agrawal and R. Srikant. Fast algorithms for mining association rules. In Proceedings of the 20th VLDB Conference, Santiago, Chile, 1994.
[2] J. Han, J. Pei, and Y. Yin. Mining Frequent Patterns without Candidate Generation, Proc. 2000 ACM-SIGMOD Int. Conf. on Management of Data (SIGMOD'00), Dallas, TX, May 2000.
[3] L. Rigoutsos and A. Floratos: Combinatorial pattern discovery in biological sequences: The Teiresias algorithm.Bioinformatics 14, 1 (1998), 55-67.
[4] Guimei Liu, Hongjun Lu, Jeffrey Xu Yu, Wei Wang and Xiangye Xiao. AFOPT: An Efficient Implementation of Pattern Growth Approach. In Proceedings of the IEEE ICDM Workshop on Frequent Itemset Mining Implementations, Melbourne, Florida, USA, November 19, 2003.
[5] Roberto Bayardo. Efficiently mining long patterns from databases. In ACM SIGMOD Conference, 1998.
[6] R. Agarwal, C. Aggarwal and V. Prasad. A tree projection algorithm for generation of frequent itemsets. Journal of Parallel and Distributed Computing, 2001.
[7] D. Burdick, M. Calimlim, and J. Gehrke. MAFIA: A Performance Study of Mining Maximal Frequent Itemsets. In Proceedings of the IEEE ICDM Workshop on Frequent Itemset Mining Implementations Melbourne, Florida, USA, November 19, 2003.
[8] M. J. Zaki and C.-J. Hsiao. CHARM: An efficient algorithm for closed association rule mining. TR 99-10, CS Dept., RPI, Oct. 1999.
[9] K. Gouda and M. J. Zaki. Efficiently Mining Maximal Frequent Itemsets. Proc. of the IEEE Int. Conference on Data Mining, San Jose, 2001.
[10] Gösta Grahne and Jianfei Zhu. Efficiently Using Prefix-trees in Mining Frequent Itemsets. In Proceedings of the IEEE ICDM Workshop on Frequent Itemset Mining Implementations, Melbourne, Florida, USA, November 19, 2003.
[11] Bart Goethals and M. J. Zaki. FIMI'03: Workshop on Frequent Itemset Mining Implementations. In Proceedings of the IEEE ICDM Workshop on Frequent Itemset Mining Implementations, Melbourne, Florida, USA, November 19, 2003.
[12] Codes and datasets available at :http://fimi.cs.helsinki.fi/.
[13] Yuejin Yan, Zhoujunli and Huowang Chen. Fast Mining Maximal Frequent ItemSets Based on Fp-tree. In Proceedings of the 23rd International Conference on Conceptual Modeling (ER2004), ShangHai, China, November 8, 2004. (Accepted)
[14] ER 2004: http://www.cs.fudan.edu.cn/er2004/.

Multinomial Naive Bayes for Text Categorization Revisited

Ashraf M. Kibriya, Eibe Frank, Bernhard Pfahringer, and Geoffrey Holmes

Department of Computer Science,
University of Waikato,
Hamilton, New Zealand
{amk14, eibe, bernhard, geoff}@cs.waikato.ac.nz

Abstract. This paper presents empirical results for several versions of the multinomial naive Bayes classifier on four text categorization problems, and a way of improving it using locally weighted learning. More specifically, it compares standard multinomial naive Bayes to the recently proposed transformed weight-normalized complement naive Bayes classifier (TWCNB) [1], and shows that some of the modifications included in TWCNB may not be necessary to achieve optimum performance on some datasets. However, it does show that TFIDF conversion and document length normalization are important. It also shows that support vector machines can, in fact, sometimes very significantly outperform both methods. Finally, it shows how the performance of multinomial naive Bayes can be improved using locally weighted learning. However, the overall conclusion of our paper is that support vector machines are still the method of choice if the aim is to maximize accuracy.

1 Introduction

Automatic text classification or text categorization, a subtopic in machine learning, is becoming increasingly important with the ever-growing amount of textual information stored in electronic form. It is a supervised learning technique, in which every new document is classified by assigning one or more class labels from a fixed set of pre-defined classes. For this purpose a learning algorithm is employed that is trained with correctly labeled training documents. The documents are generally represented using a "bag-of-words" approach, where the order of the words is ignored and the individual words present in the document constitute its features. The features present in all the documents make up the feature space. Since the number of words can be very large, the resulting learning problems are generally characterized by the very high dimensionality of the feature space, with thousands of features. Hence the learning algorithm must be able to cope with such high-dimensional problems, both in terms of classification performance and computational speed.

Naive Bayes is a learning algorithm that is frequently employed to tackle text classification problems. It is computationally very efficient and easy to implement. There are two event models that are commonly used: the multivariate Bernoulli event model and the multinomial event model. The multinomial event model—frequently referred to as multinomial naive Bayes or MNB for short—generally outperforms the multivariate one [2], and has also been found to compare favorably with more specialized event models [3]. However, it is still inferior to the state-of-the-art support vector machine classifiers in terms of classification accuracy when applied to text categorization problems [4–7, 1]. However, recently a new algorithm has been proposed, called "transformed weight-normalized complement naive Bayes" (TWCNB), that is easy to implement, has good running time and is claimed to be nearly as accurate as support vector machines [1]. TWCNB is a modified version of MNB that is derived by applying a series of transformations relating to data and MNB itself.

In this paper we revisit the transformation steps leading from MNB to TWCNB. We show that using TFIDF scores instead of raw word frequencies indeed improves the performance of MNB, and that the same holds for document length normalization. However, our results also show that, depending on the particular text categorization dataset, it may not be necessary to perform the other transformation steps implemented in TWCNB in order to achieve optimum performance. Finally, we show how multinomial naive Bayes can be improved using locally weighted learning.

The paper is structured as follows. In Section 2 we describe our experimental setup. This includes the datasets we have used, how and what kind of features we extracted from them, and the transformations we apply to those features. We also describe the MNB and TWCNB classifiers. In Section 3 we present empirical results comparing standard MNB to TWCNB and support vector machines. Then, in Section 4, we show how MNB can be improved by transforming the input, and compare it again to the other learning algorithms. We also present results for locally weighted learning applied in conjunction with MNB. We summarize our findings in Section 5.

2 Experimental Setup

In this section we describe the datasets we used in our experiments and how we generated features from them. We also discuss the MNB and TWCNB learning algorithms.

2.1 Datasets

For our experiments we have used the 20 newsgroups, industry sector, WebKB, and Reuters-21578 datasets, which are frequently used in the text classification literature. The first three of these are single-label datasets whereas the Reuters-21578 is a multi-label dataset (i.e. with multiple class labels per document).

In the 20 newsgroups data the task is to classify newsgroup messages into one of 20 different categories. The version of the 20 newsgroups data that we have used in our experiments is the one that is referred to as 20news-18828 (available from http://people.csail.mit.edu/people/jrennie/20Newsgroups/). It has all the fields removed from the news messages' header apart from the "from:" and "subject:" fields. All the cross-posted duplicate documents have also been removed, resulting in only 18,828 documents compared with 19,997 in the original 20 newsgroups data.

The industry sector data contains a collection of corporate WWW pages, divided into categories based on the type of company. There are 105 classes and 9,637 documents.

The WebKB data also has a collection of WWW pages and is available from http://www-2.cs.cmu.edu/afs/cs.cmu.edu/project/theo-20/www/data/. The WWW pages are from four computer science departments and split into several categories. Like [2] we used only four of the seven classes in the original data: "student", "faculty", "course", and "project", resulting in 4199 documents.

The Reuters-21578 data is a collection of newswire articles available from http://kdd.ics.uci.edu/. We followed the same approach as [1], using the "ModApte" split into training and test data and removing all classes with no test or training document. This left us with 7770 training and 3019 test documents in 90 classes. Note that a single newswire article may pertain to several categories (i.e. this is a multi-label problem). The standard approach to tackling this problem is to build a binary classifier for each category and that is the method we employed.

2.2 Feature Generation

In the bag-of-words approach each document is represented as a set of words and the number of times each word occurs in the document. In other words, each document has the words as its attributes or features and each attribute can take on an integer value counting the number of times the particular word occurs in the document. The set of words (also called "dictionary") is generated from all the documents present in a dataset. For a particular dataset, we first determine its dictionary by reading all the documents present in it. Then, for each document, we record the number of times each of the words in the dictionary occurs in it including those that did not occur by giving them a value zero. Note that we treated the Reuters-21578 dataset differently than the other datasets in that we determined the dictionary only from the training documents. We formed words by considering only contiguous alphabetic sequences. We also ignored words that were in our list of stopwords for all the datasets apart from WebKB.

For many of the experimental results presented in this paper we converted the word counts of a document using the TFIDF transformation before applying the learning algorithms. The TFIDF transformation takes the original word frequency f and transforms it [1]. Assuming that df is the number of documents containing the word under consideration, and D the total number documents, then the transformed attribute value becomes:

$$TFIDF(word) = log(f+1) \times log(\frac{D}{df}).$$

We also considered normalizing the resulting word vectors to have the same length [1]. We evaluated two options: normalizing to length one and normalizing to the average vector length observed in the dataset. We found that performance can sometimes improve substantially using the latter approach. For conciseness, we shall refer to these conversions as TFIDF and together with normalization as TFIDFN.

2.3 Multinomial Naive Bayes

Let us now discuss how multinomial naive Bayes computes class probabilities for a given document. Let the set of classes be denoted by C. Let N be the size of our vocabulary. Then MNB assigns a test document t_i to the class that has the highest probability $\Pr(c|t_i)$, which, using Bayes' rule, is given by:

$$\Pr(c|t_i) = \frac{\Pr(c)\Pr(t_i|c)}{\Pr(t_i)}, \quad c \in C \tag{1}$$

The class prior $\Pr(c)$ can be estimated by dividing the number of documents belonging to class c by the total number of documents. $\Pr(t_i|c)$ is the probability of obtaining a document like t_i in class c and is calculated as:

$$\Pr(t_i|c) = (\sum_n f_{ni})! \prod_n \frac{\Pr(w_n|c)^{f_{ni}}}{f_{ni}!}, \tag{2}$$

where f_{ni} is the count of word n in our test document t_i and $\Pr(w_n|c)$ the probability of word n given class c. The latter probability is estimated from the training documents as:

$$\widehat{\Pr}(w_n|c) = \frac{1 + F_{nc}}{N + \sum_{x=1}^{N} F_{xc}}, \tag{3}$$

where F_{xc} is the count of word x in all the training documents belonging to class c, and the Laplace estimator is used to prime each word's count with one to avoid the zero-frequency problem [2]. The normalization factor $\Pr(t_i)$ in Equation 1 can be computed using

$$\Pr(t_i) = \sum_{k=1}^{|C|} \Pr(k)\Pr(t_i|k). \tag{4}$$

Note that that the computationally expensive terms $(\sum_n f_{ni})!$ and $\prod_n f_{ni}!$ in Equation 2 can be deleted without any change in the results, because neither depends on the class c, and Equation 2 can be written as:

$$\Pr(t_i|c) = \alpha \prod_n \Pr(w_n|c)^{f_{ni}}, \tag{5}$$

where α is a constant that drops out because of the normalization step.

2.4 Transformed Weight-Normalized Complement Naive Bayes

As mentioned in the introduction, TWCNB [1] has been built upon MNB and is very similar to it. One difference is that the TFIDFN transformation is part of the definition of the algorithm. But the key difference is that TWCNB estimates the parameters of class c by using data from all classes apart from c (i.e. it uses the "complement"). To this end Equation 3 is called "word weight" rather than probability and redefined in the following way:

$$w_{nc} = log(\frac{1 + \sum_{k=1}^{|C|} F_{nk}}{N + \sum_{k=1}^{|C|} \sum_{x=1}^{N} F_{xk}}), \quad k \neq c \wedge k \in C \qquad (6)$$

The word weights are then normalized for each of the classes so that their absolute values sum to one and the classification for test document t_i is based on

$$\text{class}(t_i) = \text{argmax}_c [\log(\Pr(c)) - \sum_n (f_{ni} w_{nc})], \qquad (7)$$

which, because the value of $log(Pr(c))$ is usually negligible in the total, can be simplified to

$$\text{class}(t_i) = \text{argmin}_c [\sum_n (f_{ni} w_{nc})]. \qquad (8)$$

The parallels between MNB and TWCNB can easily be observed if we look at the classification rule for MNB given in [1]:

$$\text{class}(t_i) = \text{argmax}_c [\log(\Pr(c)) + \sum_n f_{ni} \log(\frac{1 + F_{nc}}{N + \sum_{x=1}^{N} F_{xc}})] \qquad (9)$$

This rule is essentially the same as Equation 1 if we drop the denominator, take the log and use Equation 5 instead of Equation 2.

Note that we found TWCNB without normalization of the word weights (which is referred to as "TCNB" in the rest of this paper) to be very similar in performance compared to TWCNB. This will be discussed in more detail in Section 3.

As mentioned earlier, multi-label datasets like Reuters-21578 are usually handled differently than single-label datasets. For multi-label datasets, a classifier's performance is often measured using the precision-recall break-even point, for which we need some kind of document score representative of how likely a document is to belong to a class. Normally, a different classifier is trained for every class: it learns to predict whether a document is in the class (positive class) or not (negative class). This approach is also known as "one-vs-rest". Although this method can be used with MNB, it does not work when used with TWCNB. Unlike MNB, where Equation 2 can be used directly in conjunction with the one-vs-rest method, TWCNB's scores (Equation 7 and Equation 8) cannot be used directly because they are not comparable across different test documents due to the missing normalization step. Hence a different method is used in [1], as described in the appendix of that paper. This method can be called "all-vs-rest". Based on the all-vs-rest approach, TWCNB's score is calculated as follows [8]:

$$docScore(t_i) = \sum_n (f_{ni} w_{nA} - f_{ni} w_{nR}). \qquad (10)$$

In the above, w_{nA} is the word weight with data from all the classes, and w_{nR} is the word weight obtained from the "rest" (i.e. all documents not pertaining to the class that we are computing the score for).

3 Evaluating Standard Multinomial Naive Bayes

In this section we present experimental results comparing MNB with TCNB, TWCNB and linear support vector machines. For learning the support vector machines we used the sequential minimal optimization (SMO) algorithm [9] as implemented in the Weka machine learning workbench [10], using pairwise classification to tackle multi-class problems. Moreover, in the case of the Reuters' data, we fit logistic models to SMO's output based on maximum likelihood [11] because this improved performance significantly. The complexity parameter C was set to 10.

For each of the three single-label datasets mentioned above we present results with a full vocabulary and with a reduced vocabulary of 10,000 words. We pruned the vocabulary by selecting words with the highest information gain. The WebKB and industry sector datasets are collections of web pages, so we also present results obtained by removing HTML tags for these collections. For WebKB we used the top 5,000 words with the highest information gain after removing the tags, and did not remove stopwords. We did so to achieve high accuracy as MNB is reported to have the highest accuracy at 5,000 words [2]. As for TCNB and TWCNB, we also converted the raw word counts for SMO using the TFIDFN conversion, normalizing the document vectors to length one.

To estimate accuracy, we performed 5 runs of hold-out estimation for the 20 newsgroups and industry sector datasets, randomly selecting 80% training and 20% test documents for the 20 newsgroups data, and 50% training and 50% test documents for the industry sector data. For WebKB we performed 10 runs with 70% training and 30% test documents. The results reported are average classification accuracy over all runs. The Reuters-21578 results, however, are reported as precision-recall break-even points. The macro result is the average of the break-even points for all 90 individual Reuters' categories whereas the micro average is the weighted average of the break-even points, with the weight for each class being equal to the number of positive class documents in the test set.

The way we calculated the break-even point for the various classifiers in our experiments is similar to the way it is calculated in the "Bow" toolkit (available from http://www-2.cs.cmu.edu/~mccallum/bow/). First, we obtain the document score for every test document from our classifier and sort these scores in

Table 1. Comparison of MNB with TCNB, TWCNB and SMO

Dataset	MNB	TCNB	TWCNB	SMO with TFIDFN
20news18828-113232words	88.36	91.03	90.91	93.52
20news18828-10000words	86.10	87.98	88.47	92.13
WebKB-NoStoplist-54948words	80.05	79.68	78.46	91.31
WebKB-NoHTMLTagsOrStoplist-5000words	85.98	87.62	85.46	93.24
WebKB-10000words	81.30	85.23	82.12	92.76
IndustrySector-95790words	54.22	92.37	92.36	91.65
IndustrySector-NoHTMLTags-64986words	64.00	88.32	88.28	88.60
IndustrySector-10000words	63.37	87.25	87.33	89.74
Reuters-21578 (Macro)	34.40	69.62	69.46	70.16
Reuters-21578 (Micro)	78.49	86.31	85.78	88.47

descending order. Then, starting from the top of our sorted list, we calculate the precision (i.e. $TP/(TP+FP)$) and recall (i.e. $TP/(TP+FN)$) for each possible threshold in this list (where the threshold determines when something is classified as positive). The break-even point is defined as the point where precision and recall are equal. However, quite often there is no threshold where they are exactly equal. Hence we look for the threshold where the difference between precision and recall is minimum and take their average as the break-even point. If there are several candidates with minimum difference then we use the one which gives the greatest average.

We can see from the results in Table 1 that MNB almost always performs worse than any of the other learning algorithms. This is consistent with previously published results [1]. However, as we shall show in the next section, its performance can be improved considerably by transforming the input.

Our results for the various classifiers are comparable to those that have been published before on these datasets. However, we cannot compare our results for TCNB because it was not evaluated separately from TWCNB in [1]. It is quite evident from Table 1 that the results for TCNB are mostly better than for TWCNB. Hence it appears that word-weight normalization is not necessary to obtain good performance using complement naive Bayes.

4 Improving Multinomial Naive Bayes

In this section we investigate a few ways to increase the accuracy of MNB. Note that these methods have been suggested before in [1] but not evaluated for simple MNB (just for T(W)CNB). As we mentioned earlier, we found that the TFIDF conversion to the data greatly improves the results for MNB. We first present the effect of this conversion on MNB.

The results are shown in Table 2. TFIDF refers to the case where we applied the TFIDF transformation and did not normalize the length of the resulting

Table 2. Effect of the transformed input on MNB

Dataset	MNB	MNB with TFIDF	MNB with TFIDFN$_a$	MNB with TFIDFN
20news18828-113232words	88.36	91.40	92.56	89.69
20news18828-10000words	86.10	89.96	90.93	89.00
WebKB-NoStoplist-54948words	80.05	79.89	80.16	75.14
WebKB-NoHTMLTagsOrStoplist-5000words	85.98	88.05	88.30	84.98
WebKB-10000words	81.30	87.47	87.71	79.86
IndustrySector-95790words	54.22	85.69	88.43	84.09
IndustrySector-NoHTMLTags-64986words	64.00	75.82	81.40	79.69
IndustrySector-10000words	63.37	83.22	85.57	81.77
Reuters-21578 (Macro)	34.40	45.17	42.12	20.08
Reuters-21578 (Micro)	78.49	78.82	76.52	70.94

feature vectors. TFIDFN$_a$ refers to the case where we have normalized the feature vector for each document to the average vector length observed in the data, rather than one. TFIDFN refers to the case where we normalize to length one (i.e. the normalization used in [1]).

The results show that the TFIDF transformation dramatically improves the performance of MNB in almost all cases. TFIDFN$_a$ leads to a further improvement, which is especially significant on the industry sector data (only on the Reuters data there is a small drop compared to TFIDF). TFIDFN, on the other hand, is not very beneficial compared to simple TFIDF. Hence it appears that it is very important to normalize to an appropriate vector length when using normalization in conjunction with MNB. A potential explanation for this is that the Laplace correction used in MNB may start to dominate the probability calculation if the transformed word counts become too small (as they do when the normalized vector length is set to one). A similar effect may be achieved by changing the constant used in the Laplace correction from one to a much smaller value. However, we have not experimented with this option.

Table 3 below shows how the improved MNB with TFIDFN$_a$ compares with TCNB and SMO. Looking at the results we can see that the improved MNB outperforms TCNB in all cases on the 20 newsgroups and WebKB datasets, whereas TCNB outperform MNB on the industry sector and Reuters-21578 datasets. SMO is still superior to all other learning schemes.

The results show that it is not always beneficial to apply T(W)CNB instead of standard MNB. Applying the TFIDF transformation with an appropriate vector length normalization to MNB can lead to better results. Based on our results it is not clear when T(W)CNB produces better results for a given collection of documents. The performance may be related to the skewness of the class distribution because the industry sector data has a skewed class distribution. However, the class distribution of WebKB is also skewed, so there is no clear evidence for this.

Table 3. Comparison of improved MNB with TCNB, and SMO

Dataset	MNB with TFIDFN$_a$	TCNB	SMO with TFIDFN
20news18828-113232words	92.56	91.03	93.52
20news18828-10000words	90.93	87.98	92.13
WebKB-NoStoplist-54948words	80.16	79.68	91.31
WebKB-NoHTMLTagsOrStoplist-5000words	88.30	87.62	93.24
WebKB-10000words	87.71	85.23	92.76
IndustrySector-95790words	88.43	92.37	91.65
IndustrySector-NoHTMLTags-64986words	81.40	88.32	88.60
IndustrySector-10000words	85.57	87.25	89.74
Reuters-21578 (Macro)	42.12	69.62	70.16
Reuters-21578 (Micro)	76.52	86.31	88.47

Note that the good performance of T(W)CNB on the Reuters data can be attributed to the all-vs-rest method discussed in Section 2.4, which is used to obtain the confidence scores for computing the break-even points. In fact, applying the all-vs-rest method to standard MNB results in a classifier that is equivalent to TCNB+all-vs-rest, and produces identical results on the Reuters data. Hence the industry sector data is really the only dataset where T(W)CNB improves on standard MNB.

4.1 Using Locally Weighted Learning

In this section we discuss how MNB can be improved further using locally weighted learning [12]. Our method is essentially the same as what has been applied earlier to the multivariate version of naive Bayes [13], and found to perform very well on other classification problems. The idea is very simple. For each test document we train an MNB classifier only on a subset of the training documents, namely those ones that are in the test document's neighborhood, and weight those documents according to their distance to the test instance. Then, instead of using the feature values of a training instance directly in the MNB formulae (i.e. raw word counts or TFIDF values), we multiply them by the weight of the corresponding training instance. The number of documents in the subset (also called the "neighborhood size") is determined through a user-specified parameter k. Each training document in the subset is assigned a weight which is inversely proportional to its distance from the test document.

In our setting we calculate the Euclidean distance of all the training documents from the test document, and divide all the distances with the distance of the kth nearest neighbor. Then the weight of each training document is computed based on the following linear weighting function:

$$f(d_i) = \begin{cases} 1 - d_i & \text{if } d_i <= 1 \\ 0 & \text{if } d_i > 1 \end{cases} \quad (11)$$

where d_i is the normalized distance of training document i.

This gives a weight zero to all the documents that are further away than the kth nearest one from the test document. Hence those documents are effectively discarded. Once the weights are computed based on this formula, we normalize them so that their sum is equal to the number of training documents in the neighborhood, as in [13]. Note that, unlike [13] we did not normalize the feature values to lie in $[0,1]$ as we found it to degrade performance.

Table 4. Applying LWL to MNB with TFIDFN$_a$

Dataset	MNB	LWL+ MNB with k=50	LWL+ MNB with k=500	LWL+ MNB with k=5000
20news18828-113232words	92.56	93.15	93.65	90.87
20news18828-10000words	90.93	93.29	92.96	89.93
WebKB-NoStoplist-54948words	80.16	77.77	78.10	75.23
WebKB-NoHTMLTagsOrStoplist-5000words	88.30	87.28	88.91	88.63
WebKB-10000words	87.71	83.96	86.37	87.01
IndustrySector-95790words	88.43	89.50	89.53	89.65
IndustrySector-NoHTMLTags-64986words	81.40	85.32	84.03	83.25
IndustrySector-10000words	85.57	86.85	86.29	86.58
Reuters-21578 (Macro)	42.12	56.29	48.18	50.29
Reuters-21578 (Micro)	76.52	84.31	80.30	75.14

Table 4 above gives a comparison of MNB to MNB used in conjunction with locally weighted learning (LWL). We report results for three different subset sizes (50, 500, and 5000). The input data to locally weighted MNB had all the transformations applied to it (i.e. the TFIDF transformation and vector length normalization described above) before the distance calculation was performed to weight the documents. The same transformations were applied in the case of MNB. We can see that in most cases LWL can improve the performance of MNB if the appropriate subset size is chosen, only on the WebKB data there is no improvement. Moreover, optimum (or close-to-optimum) performance is achieved with the smaller subset sizes ($k = 50$ or $k = 500$), and in some cases there appears to be a trend towards better performance as the size becomes smaller (more specifically, on *20news18828-10000words*, *IndustrySector-NoHTMLTags-64986words*, and the Reuters data), indicating that size 50 may not be small enough in those cases. However, we have not experimented with values of k smaller than 50.

Table 5 gives a comparison of SMO with the best results we have been able to achieve with locally weighted MNB. Note that the results for the latter method are optimistically biased because they involve a parameter choice (the neighborhood size) based on the test data. However, even with this optimistic bias for the MNB-based results, SMO performs better in almost all cases, in particular on the WebKB data.

Table 5. Comparison of best results for locally weighted MNB with SMO

Dataset	MNB with TFIDFN$_a$ & LWL	SMO with TFIDFN
20news18828-113232words (k=500)	93.65	93.52
20news18828-10000words (k=50)	93.29	92.13
WebKB-NoStoplist-54948words (k=500)	78.10	91.31
WebKB-NoHTMLTagsOrStoplist-5000words(k=500)	88.91	93.24
WebKB-10000words (k=5000)	87.01	92.76
IndustrySector-95790words (k=5000)	89.65	91.65
IndustrySector-NoHTMLTags-64986words (k=50)	85.32	88.60
IndustrySector-10000words (k=50)	86.85	89.74
Reuters-21578 (Macro) (k=50)	56.29	70.16
Reuters-21578 (Micro) (k=50)	84.31	88.47

5 Conclusions

This paper has presented an empirical comparison of several variants of multinomial naive Bayes on text categorization problems, comparing them to linear support vector machines. The main contribution of this paper is the finding that standard multinomial naive Bayes can be improved substantially by applying a TFIDF transformation to the word features and normalizing the resulting feature vectors to the average vector length observed in the data. If this is done, it can, depending on the dataset, outperform the recently proposed transformed weight-normalized complement naive Bayes algorithm, which also includes the TFIDF transformation and normalization to (unit) vector length, but exhibits two additional modifications—weight normalization and complement-based classification—that appear to represent a departure from standard Bayesian classification. Additionally, we found that the effect of weight-normalization on complement naive Bayes was negligible.

We have also shown how the performance of multinomial naive Bayes can be further improved by applying locally weighted learning. However, even if the best neighborhood size is chosen based on the test data, this improved classifier is still not competitive with linear support vector machines. Hence the overall conclusion is to use support vector machines if their (significantly larger) training time is acceptable, and, if not, to consider standard multinomial naive Bayes with appropriate transformations of the input as an alternative to complement naive Bayes.

References

1. Rennie, J.D.M., Shih, L., Teevan, J., Karger, D.R.: Tackling the poor assumptions of naive Bayes text classifiers. In: Proceedings of the Twentieth International Conference on Machine Learning, AAAI Press (2003) 616–623

2. McCallum, A., Nigam, K.: A comparison of event models for naive Bayes text classification. Technical report, American Association for Artificial Intelligence Workshop on Learning for Text Categorization (1998)
3. Eyheramendy, S., Lewis, D.D., Madigan, D.: On the naive Bayes model for text categorization. In: Ninth International Workshop on Artificial Intelligence and Statistics. (2003) 3–6
4. Joachims, T.: Text categorization with support vector machines: Learning with many relevant features. In: Proceedings of the Tenth European Conference on Machine Learning, Springer-Verlag (1998) 137–142
5. Dumais, S., Platt, J., Heckerman, D., Sahami, M.: Inductive learning algorithms and representations for text categorization. In: Proceedings of the Seventh International Conference on Information and Knowledge Management, ACM Press (1998) 148–155
6. Yang, Y., Liu, X.: A re-examination of text categorization methods. In: Proceedings of the 22nd Annual International ACM SIGIR Conference on Research and Development in Information Retrieval, ACM Press (1999) 42–49
7. Zhang, T., Oles, F.J.: Text categorization based on regularized linear classification methods. Information Retrieval **4** (2001) 5–31
8. Rennie, J.: Personal communication regarding WCNB (2004)
9. Platt, J.: Fast training of support vector machines using sequential minimal optimization. In Schölkopf, B., Burges, C., Smola, A., eds.: Advances in Kernel Methods—Support Vector Learning. MIT Press (1998)
10. Witten, I., Frank, E.: Data Mining: Practical machine learning tools and techniques with Java implementations. Morgan Kaufmann (1999)
11. Platt, J.: Probabilistic outputs for support vector machines and comparisons to regularized likelihood methods. In Smola, A., Bartlett, P., Schölkopf, B., Schuurmans, D., eds.: Advances in Large Margin Classifiers. MIT Press (1999)
12. Atkeson, C.G., Moore, A.W., Schaal, S.: Locally weighted learning. Artificial Intelligence Review **11** (1997) 11–73
13. Frank, E., Hall, M., Pfahringer, B.: Locally weighted naive Bayes. In: Proceedings of the Conference on Uncertainty in Artificial Intelligence, Morgan Kaufmann (2003)

The Effect of Attribute Scaling on the Performance of Support Vector Machines

Catherine Edwards and Bhavani Raskutti

Telstra Research Laboratories, Telstra Corporation,
770 Blackburn Road, Clayton, Victoria, Australia
{Catherine.A.Edwards, Bhavani.Raskutti}@team.telstra.com

Abstract. This paper presents some empirical results showing that simple attribute scaling in the data preprocessing stage can improve the performance of linear binary classifiers. In particular, a class specific scaling method that utilises information about the class distribution of the training sample can significantly improve classification accuracy. This form of scaling can boost the performance of a simple centroid classifier to similar levels of accuracy as the more complex, and computationally expensive, support vector machine and regression classifiers. Further, when SVMs are used, scaled data produces better results, for smaller amounts of training data, and with smaller regularisation constant values, than unscaled data.

1 Introduction

Data preprocessing has been recognised as critically important in data mining to improve both the speed and accuracy of the resultant model [1, 2]. In particular, and as will be shown, simple manipulations of the range of the input data by attribute scaling are computationally inexpensive, and can result in significant performance increases.

This paper presents an empirical investigation of the impact of attribute scaling on the performance of SVM classifiers. We focus on linear binary classifiers (Section 2) and measure the impact of scaling on the accuracy of the classifiers where accuracy is measured in terms of a general classifier goodness measure that is independent of the operating point of the classifier (Section 3). We consider three different scaling techniques that are linear transformations of the attribute space, and change the range and origin of the attribute space (Section 4). Using eight large datasets with differing properties, we study the effect of these scaling methods on classification accuracy when classifier parameters such as training set size are varied (Section 5). Our results show that attribute scaling can vastly improve the accuracy of even simple classifiers, and can thus provide a computationally inexpensive method for achieving high accuracy with a smaller training set size or a less complex classifier (Section 6).

2 Classifiers

Given a labelled m-sample: $\vec{xy}^m := \left((x_1, y_1), ..., (x_m, y_m) \right)$ of patterns $x_i \in X \subset \mathbb{R}^n$ and target values $y_i \in [0, 1]$, our aim is to find a "good" discriminating function $f : X \to \mathbb{R}$

The Effect of Attribute Scaling on the Performance of SVMs 501

that scores the target class instances $y_i = 1$ higher than the background class instances $y_i = 0$. We focus on linear classifiers, namely two linear support vector machines, one ridge regression model and a simple centroid classifier.

2.1 Support Vector Machines (SVML1 and SVML2)

Given the training m-sample as described above, a learning algorithm used by SVMs [3,4,5] outputs a model $f_{\vec{xy}m} : X \rightarrow \mathbb{R}$ defined as the minimiser of the regularised risk functional:

$$f \mapsto ||f||_{\mathcal{H}}^2 + \sum_{i=1}^{m} L([1 - y_i f(x_i)]_+). \tag{1}$$

Here $\mathcal{H}$ denotes a reproducing kernel Hilbert space (RKHS) [5] of real valued functions $f : X \rightarrow \mathbb{R}$ and $||.||_{\mathcal{H}}$ the corresponding norm. $L : \mathbb{R} \rightarrow \mathbb{R}^+$ is a non-negative, convex loss function penalising for the deviation $1 - y_i f(x_i)$ of the estimator $f(x_i)$ from target y_i and $[\xi]_+ := \max(0, \xi)$.

The minimisation of (1) can be solved by quadratic programming [3] with the use of the following expansion known to hold for the minimiser (1):

$$f_{\vec{xy}m}(x) = \sum_{i=1}^{m} \alpha_i y_i k(x_i, x)$$

$$||f_{\vec{xy}m}||_{\mathcal{H}}^2 = \sum_{i,j=1}^{m} \alpha_i \alpha_j y_i y_j k(x_i, x_j)$$

where $k : X \times X \rightarrow \mathbb{R}$ is the kernel corresponding to the RKHS $\mathcal{H}$ [6,7]. The coefficients α_i are unique and they are the Lagrange multipliers of the quadratic minimisation problem corresponding to the constraints $y_i f_{\vec{xy}m}(x_i) > 0$.

The following two types of loss function yield two different SVMs. In both cases, $c > 0$ is a regularisation constant controlling the extent of penalisation:

- **SVML1** or **L1** with "hinge loss" $L(\xi) := c\xi$ is the SVM with linear penalty, and
- **SVML2** or **L2** with the squared hinge loss $L(\xi) := c\xi^2$ is the SVM with quadratic penalty.

2.2 Ridge Regression (RR)

In addition to the SVMs we also use a regularisation network or ridge regression predictor, RR [4,8,6,7]. Formally, this predictor is closely related to SVML2, the only difference being that it minimises a modified risk function (1), with loss $c(1 - y_i f(x_i))^2$ rather than $c[1 - y_i f(x_i)]_+^2$.

2.3 Centroid Classifier (CC)

The centroid classifier [9] is a simple linear classifier with the solution,

$$f_{\vec{xy}m}(x) = \frac{\sum_{i, y_i = +1} k(x_i, x)}{2 \max(1, m_+)} - \frac{\sum_{i, y_i = -1} k(x_i, x)}{2 \max(1, m_-)}$$

where m_+ and m_- denote the numbers of examples with labels $y_i = +1$ and $y_i = -1$, respectively. In terms of the feature space, the centroid classifier implements the projection in the direction of the weighted difference between the centroids of data from each class. Note that the centroid solution approximates the solution obtained by SVMs at very low values of the regularisation constant c [10].

3 Performance Measures

We have used AUC, the area under the receiver operating characteristic (ROC) curve (also known as AROC) as our performance measure. We see this as the natural metric of general goodness of a classifier, capable of meaningful results even if the target class is a tiny fraction of the data [11, 12].

We recall that the ROC curve is a plot of the true positive rate, $P(f(x_i) > \theta|y_i = 1)$, (known as precision), against the false positive rate, $P(f(x_i) > \theta|y_i = -1)$, as a decision threshold θ is varied. The concept of the ROC curve originates in signal detection but it is now used in many other areas, including data mining, psychophysics and medical diagnosis (cf. review [13, 14]). In the last case, AUC is viewed as a measure of the general "goodness" of a test, formalised as a predictive model f in our context, with a clear statistical meaning. According to Bamber's interpretation [15], AUC(f) is equal to the probability of correctly ordering two points, one x_i from the negative and the other x_j from the positive class, by allocating appropriate scores, i.e. $f(x_i) < f(x_j)$. An additional attraction of AUC as a figure of merit is its direct link to the well researched area of order statistics, via U-statistics and Wilcoxon-Whitney-Mann test [15, 16].

There are some ambiguities in the case of AUC estimated from a discrete set in the case of ties, i.e. when multiple instances from different classes receive the same score. Following [15] we implement in this paper the definition

$$AUC(f) = P(f(x_i) < f(x_j)|-y_i = y_j = 1)$$
$$+ 0.5 P(f(x_i) = f(x_j)|-y_i = y_j = 1)$$

expressing AUC in terms of conditional probabilities. Note that the trivial uniform random predictor has an AUC of 0.5, while a perfect predictor has an AUC of 1.

4 Scaling Methods

We define scaling as applying a linear transformation to a set of data that changes its range and origin. Specifically, scaling involves multiplying by a transformation factor a_i, and subtracting a translation factor b_i, both of which are scalars. This is always done relative to each feature, i.e. if the data has m rows of training examples and n columns of features, each column will be scaled individually. This gives an equation in terms of the attribute vector $\hat{x}_i$, the ith column of the matrix, $\forall i, 1 \leq i \leq n$:

$$\hat{z}_i = a_i \hat{x}_i - b_i$$

It is important to note that the scaling factors a_i and b_i for each type of scaling are determined by the training data alone (using only the attribute vector $\hat{x}_i$ in the training set) and that these same factors are subsequently applied to the testing data.

Note that linear scaling of each feature independently preserves the statistical distribution of the data points for that feature, while discarding information about the range and location. Classifiers only need information about the statistical distribution of the positive and negative class data points. Discarding the range and location information has several advantages:

- The score for a particular test instance requires the calculation of a dot product with the test instance vector $\hat{x}$. If one feature has a much larger range than another, the larger feature will dominate (an effect known as feature swamping [17, 2, 18]). This will obscure any classification information contained in the feature with the smaller range. This is a problem if the feature with the larger range is not very predictive. Also, those classifiers that minimise an error function that is sensitive to scale (SVML1, SVML2 and RR) will assign more weight to those features with large ranges at the expense of those features with smaller ranges. Scaling the data reduces this problem.
- Scaling also improves the numerical conditions for those classifiers that converge to a solution (SVML1, SMVL2 and RR) [17, 18]. The algorithms have both a cap on the total number of iterations performed, and a minimum change rate, which limits the optimisation of the machine. Containing the data within a small range increases the likelihood that the solution is reached within those limitations.

This paper compares three types of scaling (Mean0Stdev1, PlusMinus1 and Class-Specific) with unscaled data.

4.1 Mean0Stdev1 Scaling

Mean0Stdev1 scaling transforms the data to have a mean of 0 and a standard deviation of 1. The transformation and translation factors are as follows:

$$a_i = \frac{1}{stdev(\hat{x}_i)} \qquad b_i = \frac{mean(\hat{x}_i)}{stdev(\hat{x}_i)}$$

4.2 PlusMinus1 Scaling

This scale transforms the range of each attribute in the training set to [-1,+1] range. Note that this may not be the range of the scaled test data since the training set may not contain the actual minimum and maximum for every attribute. This is not a significant problem, as there is no requirement that the input data be within this range, however this scale will perform better the closer the sample maximum and minimum are to the population statistics. Thus, as the training set is sampled for on a random basis, as the size of this set increases, so will the performance of this scaling method. The scaling factors a_i and b_i are computed as follows:

$$a_i = \frac{2}{\max(\hat{x}_i) - \min(\hat{x}_i)} \qquad b_i = \frac{\max(\hat{x}_i) + \min(\hat{x}_i)}{\max(\hat{x}_i) - \min(\hat{x}_i)}$$

4.3 Class-Specific Scaling

This scaling method attempts to prejudice the classifier in favour of those features that are likely to be predictive. Intuitively, if for a given feature the positive and negative classes have small variances and significantly different means, that feature is likely to be predictive. If this is the case, we can increase its influence on the classifier as discussed above by increasing the range of its data points. This approach is essentially about making feature swamping work in favour of the classifier.

The transformation factor for each attribute is based on how predictive the model estimates that attribute will be. No translation is performed. Thus,

$$a_i = \frac{mean(\hat{x}_{i+}) - mean(\hat{x}_{i-})}{var(\hat{x}_{i+}) + var(\hat{x}_{i-})} \qquad b_i = 0$$

where $\hat{x}_{i+}$ and $\hat{x}_{i-}$ represent the attribute vector for feature i for the positive and negative class instances respectively. Note that the calculation of the a_i values for all features gives a method for determining which are the most predictive features for that data set. The least predictive features can then be discarded to reduce the amount of computational resources needed for the problem.

5 Experimental Setup

In order to understand the effect of scaling under different training conditions, we considered a number of different classifier settings. First, we explored a range of training set sizes from 50 to 6,400 observations. Next, various values for the regularisation constant were tested - the ends of range (10 and 100,000), and a mid range value (1,000).

The training sets were obtained by randomly selecting a set of 6,400 examples from the main data set of 60,000 to act as the master training set. The remaining observations then became the testing set. Training sets of the appropriate sizes were then randomly extracted from this master training set (choosing the whole set when the training set size is 6,400). The training sets were then scaled using the three methods described above. The testing set was scaled simultaneously, so that the solution produced by the training set was applicable to the testing data. Each training set was then run through the four different classifiers, once with each regularisation constant value. The results were then tested using the appropriately scaled testing set, and the AUC calculated. Note that all sets of observations extracted were stratified - i.e. the proportion of positive and negative class observations was maintained.

5.1 Data Sets

Experiments were performed on eight datasets, from different domains and of different levels of difficulty. The minority class was typically between 10% and 40% of the data. As some of the data sets were smaller than others, a random, stratified selection of 60,000 observations was taken out of each and used as the data set for this experiment.

Telecommunications Churn (Churn10 and Churn31): Data on mobile phone customers of a large telecommunications carrier was used to learn to distinguish between those that churned to a competitor in the following three months and those that didn't. A set of 31 continuous and ordinal variables was used for prediction, including bill and product information. To create a second task, a subset of 10 of these predictors was selected via inspection of initial results, none of which were particularly predictive. This resulted in a difficult to learn task.

Handwritten Digit Recognition (Digit): Data was downloaded from the MNIST handwritten digit database. Each observation consists of a bitmap of 28×28 continuous grayscale values, representing a handwritten digit. This was converted to lower resolution (7×7 pixels) to reduce the dimensionality of the problem. The classification task was to distinguish between the digit '0' and all other digits. To make the problem more challenging, only the top 3 rows of pixels were used, and pixels near the corners which contain little information were discarded, resulting in a 17 dimensional set.

Forest Cover Type (Forest): Data was downloaded from the UCI KDD repository. 30×30 metre cells of forest are classified into one of 7 cover types based on the cell's dominant tree type. The two most populous classes were extracted, and the classification task was to distinguish between these classes. 10 continuous predictors were used.

Housing Mortgage (Housing): Data was downloaded from the U.S. Census Bureau 5% Public Use Microdata Sample (PUMS) containing individual records of the characteristics of a 5% sample of housing units for the state of Florida. Amongst all housing units which had a mortgage, the binary classification task was to distinguish between those for which the mortgage had been paid off and those for which it hadn't. There were 12 continuous or ordinal predictors.

Intrusion Detection (Intrusion): This dataset consists of a random sample of the intrusion detection data used for the 1999 KDD Cup competition. The classification task was to distinguish between normal use and intrusion. The 10 predictors used were a subset of all continuous predictors available with the data, as certain continuous predictors were omitted to make the problem more challenging.

Marital Status (Married): Data was again downloaded from the U.S. Census Bureau PUMS. From this a 1% sample of individual records from the state of California was extracted. The binary classification task was to distinguish between individuals who have been married (whether currently married or not), with individuals who have never been married. The predictors were 11 continuous variables.

Weather Season Prediction (Weather): Data, consisting of 8 continuous or ordinal predictors, was downloaded from the website of the Tropical Atmosphere Ocean project. It contains meteorological measurements from a grid of weather buoys in the Pacific Ocean. Hourly measurements for all buoys over the period from May 1999 to April 2000 were downloaded. The classification task was to distinguish readings made during the northern hemisphere Autumn months from those made in other months.

6 Results

In order to lend statistical significance to our results, performance measurements for each experimental setting were obtained using 10 different randomisations for each setting, computing the mean and standard error of the scores obtained with each set.

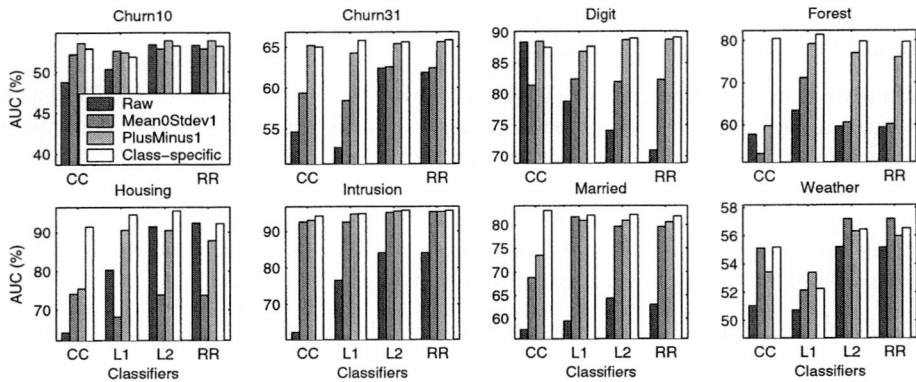

Fig. 1. Impact of scaling on different data sets. Results presented for each of the classifiers: CC (centroid), L1 (SVML1), L2 (SVML2) and RR (ridge regression) and the four scaling methods are averaged over all 10 randomisations, over all training set sizes and where appropriate, over all regularisation constants

Each of the 10 random selections were seeded to ensure that they were consistent across all other experimental settings, i.e. the test and training sets were the same across all settings for a particular randomisation, training set size and data set.

6.1 Classifier and Data Set Interactions

Figure 1 shows the effect of scaling on classifier performance for each data set. The x-axis shows bars grouped into four clusters corresponding to the four classifiers used: CC (centroid), L1 (SVML1), L2 (SVML2) and RR (ridge regression). Each cluster contains four scores, one for each different scaling method: unscaled, Mean0Stdev1, PlusMinus1 and Class-Specific, as shown in the legend. The performance is measured using the mean of the AUC over all randomisations (y-axis). Scores are averaged over all training set sizes, and all regularisation constant values (where appropriate).

Error bars have not been shown in this graph, as the standard error is consistently low. The mean standard error is 0.28% AUC, and the maximum is 1.28% AUC for the forest data set, for SVML1, using the Mean0Stdev1 scaling method. Further, the standard error only exceeds 1% AUC in 3 out of 128 cases.

As seen from Figure 1, there is no single classifier that is the best for all data sets. However, scaled data results in better performance than unscaled data in 30 of the 32 classifier/data set combinations. In particular, the Class-Specific scaling method tends to produce consistent improvements in performance compared to unscaled data, for all classifiers, for six datasets: churn31, forest, housing, intrusion, married and weather. In general, it tends to be the best scaling choice with best or equal best performance in 24 out of the 32 experimental situations shown. PlusMinus1 scaling also tends to

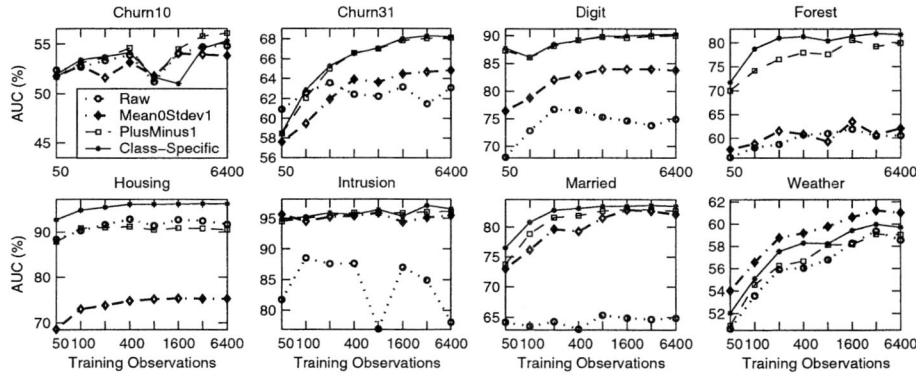

Fig. 2. Impact of scaling and training set sizes on classifier performance for different data sets. Results presented are the mean AUCs, where the means are computed over all randomisations for all classifiers and all regularisation constant values

considerably improve classifier performance and produces the best or equal best score in 10 of the 32 classifier/data set combinations. Overall one of these scales is the best choice in 29 out of 32 situations, and generally there is not a great difference between the performance of these two scaling methods.

The centroid classifier performs better when the Class-Specific scale is used in six data sets, and improves its performance to the point where it is comparable with that of the SVMs and RR. This is noteworthy as the centroid classifier requires no training time, and is thus extremely efficient computationally. Indeed, as a general tendency, the scores for a particular data set are relatively similar over the four classifiers when the data is scaled using the Class-Specific scale. This type of scaling thus seems to reduce the impact of classifier choice significantly.

Mean0Stdev1 scaling varies in effect considerably. It tends to produce improved scores relative to raw data, but not to the same extent as the other two scaling methods. In some cases (e.g. the housing data set) it impairs classifier performance. However for certain data set/classifier combinations (e.g. the weather data set) it actually outperforms the other scaling methods.

Churn10 is the only data set for which scaling has a limited effect. This set performs poorly, with scores only a little better than what a random classification would produce. As described previously, the churn10 data set contains the 10 least predictive attributes from the churn31 data set. Thus it is not surprising that the scores are very low.

6.2 Training Set Size Interactions

Figure 2 shows the effect of training set size increase (x-axis) on AUC (y-axis) for eight different data sets, with the four different types of scaling: unscaled (dotted line), Mean0Stdev1 (dot-dash line), PlusMinus1 (dashed line) and Class-Specific (unbroken

Table 1. Impact of training set size on the standard error of the AUC averaged across all other experimental conditions

Training Set Size	50	100	200	400	800	1600	3200	6400
Standard Error ($\times 10^{-2}$)	5.9	4.2	3.6	2.8	2.7	2.1	1.9	1.5

line). The data shown has been averaged over all randomisations, all classifiers, and all regularisation constant values. Again, the standard error is very low and as such error bars are not shown. However, as shown in Table 1, the mean standard error over all other experimental conditions (as calculated above) drops significantly as the size of the training sample increases.

The trend across all data sets and all scales is for AUC to increase rapidly over the first small increases of training set size (50 to 200 samples), then plateau as the training set size increases further. Scaling seems to have a positive impact on this behaviour, reducing the amount of training data required before the curve flattens out. In particular, the Class-Specific scale tends to decrease the training set size at which the curve plateaus. As such, it is possible to get very good results with small sample sizes.

Raw data is often erratic, depending on the data set (e.g. churn10, churn31, digit, forest and intrusion). However, in seven of the eight data sets, scaling smoothes the curve out significantly. The greatest smoothing effect is seen with the Class-Specific and PlusMinus1 scales. Mean0Stdev1 scaling tends to produce some smoothing effects, but this is often not as pronounced as the other scaling methods (e.g. churn31, forest).

Note that increasing the training set size improves the classifier performance in two key ways. Firstly, more information is available to the classifier, presenting it with a sample that is more representative of the population. Secondly, as the training set size increases, more information becomes available to calculate the scaling statistics. As such, they become progressively closer to the the population statistics. This improves the quality of the scaling method, and thus the classifier performance.

6.3 Effect of Regularisation Constant Values

Figure 3 shows the effect of changing the regularisation constant (c) (x-axis) on AUC (y-axis) for different scaling methods, data sets and classifiers. Each group of twelve graphs corresponds to a data set. The three columns correspond to the different regularisation machines: L1 (SVML1), L2 (SVML2) and RR (ridge regression). The four rows show the four different scaling types: unscaled (Raw), Mean0Stdev1 (M0S1), PlusMinus1 (PM1) and Class-Specific (C-S). Data has been averaged over all training set sizes, and error bars have not been shown as the error is very small.

As we would expect, the trend across all variables is that scores improve as c increases. However, there is significant interaction between the classifier used and the impact of changing c on the performance. For SVML1, scores are often impaired by increasing the regularisation constant, particularly when the data has been preprocessed using the Mean0Stdev1 and PlusMinus1 scaling methods. This is in contrast to SVML2 and RR, which consistently show either improvement or no change as c is increased, across all scaling methods.

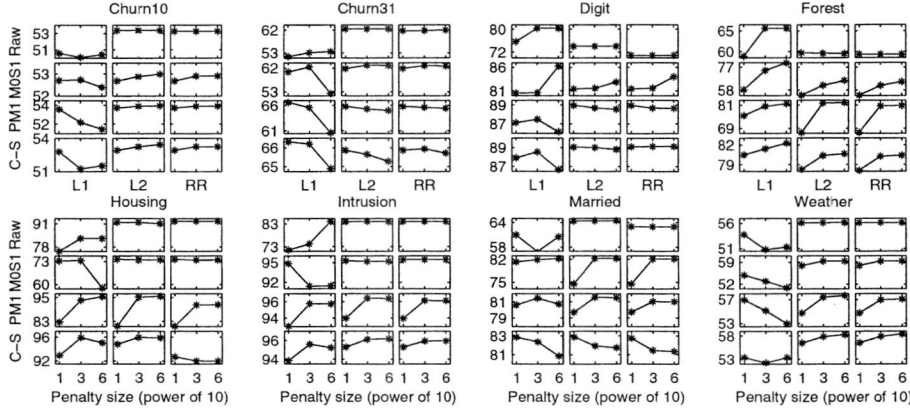

Fig. 3. Effect of regularisation constant (c) for different scaling methods, data sets and classifiers. Results presented are AUCs averaged over all training set sizes and correspond to three machines: L1 (SVML1), L2 (SVML2) and RR (ridge regression) and four scaling methods: unscaled (Raw), Mean0Stdev1 (M0S1), PlusMinus1 (PM1) and Class-Specific (C-S)

There is no clear trend in the interaction between different scaling methods and regularisation constant values. Ideally, the results suggest tuning for the regularisation constant value that gives the best results for a particular data set, classifier and scaling method. However, this requires an investment of time and resources, which is not always possible. We see that there is no evidence that an increase in AUC is likely to result from an increase in c, particularly if the data is scaled. As such, and given that an increase in regularisation constant value correlates to a significant increase in computational resources required, low values of c are recommended in the general case.

7 Discussion and Recommendations

Table 2 shows the overall performance of each form of scaling. The mean AUC and standard error over all experimental conditions is shown in rows 2 and 3 respectively. The last row shows the percentage of times a scaling method provides the best AUC. Notably, all methods of scaling significantly improve the mean score and decrease the mean standard error. Further, scaled data produces the best results in 93.78% of cases. It is clear that simple attribute scaling greatly improves the performance of linear binary classifiers. In particular, the Class-Specific scale tends to be the best choice of scale. It produces the best results in half the experimental conditions, and substantially reduces the effect of experimental vaiable (such a training set size), and thus the standard error.

Table 2. Performance of the three scaling methods, averaged across all experimental conditions

Scaling Method	Unscaled	Mean0Stdev1	PlusMinus1	Class-Specific
Mean AUC %	65.05	69.49	74.30	76.63
Standard Error ($\times 10^{-2}$)	4.1	2.2	1.6	1.4
Best Method (%)	6.22	18.14	25.65	49.99

7.1 Statistical Significance

To test for the statistical significance of these results, paired one-tailed Student's t-tests were used to compare the classification performance of data with and without scaling. All observations were divided into four sets (S_R, S_M, S_P and S_C) based on the form of scaling that the data was preprocessed with (raw, Mean0Stdev1, PlusMinus1 and Class-Specific respectively). The observations in any two of these sets were paired based on the value of the settings of the other experimental variables (data set, classifier, training set size, regularisation constant value and randomisation).

Three null hypotheses were tested for, $H_0^M : \mu_R \geq \mu_M$, $H_0^P : \mu_R \geq \mu_P$ and $H_0^C : \mu_R \geq \mu_C$, where μ_R, μ_M, μ_P and μ_C are the means of S_R, S_M, S_P and S_C respectively. At the significance level $\alpha = 0.001$, all three hypotheses were rejected in favour of the alternative hypotheses, $H_1^M : \mu_R < \mu_M$, $H_1^P : \mu_R < \mu_P$ and $H_1^C : \mu_R < \mu_C$. Thus we can say that, at the 0.1% confidence level, all forms of scaling improve the classification performance.

Further, the extent of the percentage improvement from raw data given by scaling was tested, again using a one tailed Student's t-test with $\alpha = 0.001$. The null hypotheses tested were $H_0^M : 8 \geq \frac{100(\mu_M - \mu_R)}{\mu_R}$, $H_0^P : 15 \geq \frac{100(\mu_P - \mu_R)}{\mu_R}$ and $H_0^C : 18 \geq \frac{100(\mu_C - \mu_R)}{\mu_R}$. Again, these hypotheses were rejected, and thus we can be confident that on average, and at the 0.1% significance level, the three scaling methods, Mean0Stdev1, PlusMinus1 and Class-Specific, improve the classification performance at baseline by 8%, 15% and 18% respectively.

7.2 Recommendations

Based on these results, we can put forward several recommendations, as follows. Scaling should generally be used to improve the performance of linear binary classifiers. Ideally, an initial test run should be performed to determine the optimum scaling method, however if this is not possible, the Class-Specific scaling method should be used.

If only limited resources are available and it is acceptable to achieve classifications that are suboptimal, the centroid classifier with Class-Specific scaling should be used.

If there is only limited training data available (less than 400 samples), the Class-Specific scaling method will typically give the best results.

If the data is scaled, it is generally unnecessary to use large values for the regularisation constant. This will again reduce the computational resources needed for the training task. However, note that if resources permit, small improvements in score can be gained by tuning the value of c to the particular classifier, data set and scaling method.

If the feature space is large, the value of the transformation factor for the Class-Specific scale can be used as a way to choose which features can be discarded. This can further reduce the resources needed for the training.

8 Conclusions and Future Work

We have shown that simple attribute scaling can significantly improve the performance of linear binary classifiers. Furthermore, a particular scaling method, introduced here as the Class-Specific scale, is the best choice of scales to use across all experimental conditions.

Given the extent of the improvements shown here, it would be useful to investigate the effect of attribute scaling on the performance of SVMs with different kernels. Other scaling methods, particularly those that utilise information about the class distribution of each attribute, would also be worth studying further.

Acknowledgements

The permission of the Managing Director, Telstra Research Laboratories (TRL) to publish this paper is gratefully acknowledged. The technical advice and feedback of Herman Ferra, TRL, is gratefully acknowledged.

References

[1] Berry, M., Linoff, G.: Data Mining Techniques: For Marketing, Sales and Customer Support. Wiley, New York (1997)
[2] Pyle, D.: Data Preparation for Data Mining. Morgan Kaufmann Publishers, Inc., California (1999)
[3] Corte, C., Vapnik, V.: Support-vector networks. Machine Learning **20** (1995) 273 – 297
[4] Cristianini, N., Shawe-Taylor, J.: An Introduction to Support Vector Machines and other kernel-based learning methods. Cambridge University Press, Cambridge (2000)
[5] Vapnik, V.: Statistical learning theory. Wiley, New York (1998)
[6] Kimeldorf, G., Whaba, G.: A correspondence between Bayesian estimation of stochastic processes and smoothing by splines. Ann. Math. Statist. **41** (1970) 495–502
[7] Schölkopf, B., Smola, A.J.: Learning with Kernels: Support Vector Machines, Regularization, Optimization and Beyond. MIT Press (2001)
[8] Girosi, F., Jones, M., Poggio, T.: Regularization theory and neural networks architectures. Neural Computation **7** (1995) 219–269
[9] Rocchio, J.J.: Relevance feedback in information retrieval. In Salton, G., ed.: The SMART Retrieval System: Experiments in Automatic Document Processing, Englewood Cliffs, N J, Prentice-Hall Inc. (1971) 313–323
[10] Kowalczyk, A., Raskutti, B.: Exploring Fringe Settings of SVMs for Classification. In: Proceedings of the Seventh European Conference on Principle and Practice of Knowledge Discovery in Databases (PKDD03). (2003)
[11] Bradley, A.: The use of the area under the ROC curve in the evaluation of machine learning algorithms. Pattern Recognition **30(7)** (1997) 1145–1159
[12] Weiss, G., Provost, F.: The effect of class distribution on classifier learning. Technical report, Rutgers University (2001)

[13] Centor, R.: Signal detectability: The use of ROC curves and their analysis. Med. Decis. Making **11** (1991) 102 – 106
[14] Fawcett, T.: ROC Graphs: Notes and practical considerations for data mining researchers. In: HP Labs Tech Report HPL-2003-4. (2003)
[15] Bamber, D.: The area above the ordinal dominance graph and the area below the receiver operating characteristic graph. J. Math. Psych. **12** (1975) 387 – 415
[16] Hand, D., Till, R.: A simple generalisation of the area under the ROC curve for multiple class classification problems. Machine Learning **45** (2001) 171 – 186
[17] Hsu, C., Chang, C., Lin, C.: A practical guide to support vector classification. http://www.csie.ntu.tw/ cjlin/papers/guide/guide.pdf (2003)
[18] Sarle, W.: Neural network FAQ. ftp://ftp.sas.com/pub/neural/FAQ2.html (1997)

Towards Efficient Imputation by Nearest-Neighbors: A Clustering-Based Approach

Eduardo R. Hruschka[1], Estevam R. Hruschka Jr.[2], and Nelson F. F. Ebecken[3]

[1] Universidade Católica de Santos (UniSantos), Brasil
  erh@unisantos.br
[2] Universidade Federal de São Carlos (UFSCAR), Brasil
  estevamr@terra.com.br
[3] COPPE / Universidade Federal do Rio de Janeiro, Brasil
  nelson@ntt.ufrj.br

Abstract. This paper proposes and evaluates a nearest-neighbor method to substitute missing values in ordinal/continuous datasets. In a nutshell, the K-Means clustering algorithm is applied in the complete dataset (without missing values) before the imputation process by nearest-neighbors takes place. Then, the achieved cluster centroids are employed as training instances for the nearest-neighbor method. The proposed method is more efficient than the *traditional* nearest-neighbor method, and simulations performed in three benchmark datasets also indicate that it provides suitable imputations, both in terms of prediction and classification tasks.

1 Introduction

Missing values are a critical problem for data mining methods, which are usually not able to cope with them in an automatic fashion (without data preparation). In general, there are many approaches to deal with the problem of missing values: i) Ignore the instances/attributes containing missing values; ii) Substitute the missing values by a constant; iii) Use the mean or the mode of the instances as a substitution value; and iv) Get the most suitable value to fill the missing ones. The first approach involves removing the instances and/or attributes with missing values. Doing so, the waste of data may be considerable and incomplete datasets can lead to biased statistical analyses. The second approach assumes that all missing values represent the same value, usually leading to considerable distortions. The substitution by the mean/mode value is a common practice and sometimes can even lead to reasonable results. However, it does not take into consideration the between-variable relationships, which are important to the process of missing values substitution. Therefore, the best approach involves filling the missing values with the most suitable ones.

The substitution of missing values, also called *imputation*, should not change important characteristics of the dataset. In this sense, it is necessary to define the important characteristics to be maintained. Data mining methods usually explore relationships between variables and, thus, it is critical to preserve them, as far as possible, when replacing missing values [1]. In other words, the imputation goal is to carefully substitute missing values, trying to avoid the imputation of bias in the dataset. When imputation is performed in a suitable way, higher quality data are produced, and the data mining outcomes can even be improved.

Several imputation methods have been proposed in the literature, and good references can be found in [2]. Some recent works suggest that K-Nearest Neighbors (KNN) methods [3] can be useful for imputation [4,5]. KNN can be defined as a *lazy memory-based* learning process [6] in which the training data is stored in memory and analyzed to find answers to specific queries. As far as the whole training dataset is stored in memory, the computational effort may be high when maintaining a global model to process all queries. To alleviate this problem, a local model can be used to fit the training data only in a region around the location of the query to be answered. This approach originates the usually called *local learning KNN methods*. In addition, indexing methods [3] can also be useful to minimize the computational cost of KNN methods.

In this work, we propose and evaluate an imputation method based on the K-Means clustering algorithm [7,8], which is employed to improve the computational efficiency of imputations based on nearest-neighbors. The paper is organized as follows. The next section describes how the K-Means can be incorporated into the *classical* KNN, originating our proposed imputation method. Besides, Section 2 also describes advantages and disadvantages of such approach, both in terms of efficacy and efficiency. Section 3 reports simulation results in prediction and classification tasks. Finally, Section 4 describes our conclusions and points out some future work.

2   Incorporating K-Means into the Nearest-Neighbor Method

In this section, we first review how to employ the classical KNN for imputation. Then, it is theoretically compared, in terms of efficacy (imputation quality) and efficiency (computational cost), with a clustering-based KNN method. Imputation methods based on KNN assume that missing values of an instance can be substituted by means of the corresponding attribute values of similar complete instances. More specifically, let us consider that each instance is described by a set of N continuous/ordinal attributes. Thus, each instance can be represented by a vector $\mathbf{x}=[x_1,x_2,...,x_N]$. The distance between two vectors (instances) $\mathbf{x}$ and $\mathbf{y}$ will be here called $d(\mathbf{x},\mathbf{y})$. Besides, let us suppose that the *i-th* attribute value ($1 \leq i \leq N$) of vector $\mathbf{u}$ is missing. Imputation methods based on nearest-neighbors compute distances $d(\mathbf{u},\mathbf{y})$, for all $\mathbf{y} \neq \mathbf{u}$, $\mathbf{y}$ representing a complete instance, and use these distances to compute the value to be imputed in u_i. The Euclidean metric is commonly used to compute distances between instances and, considering that the value of the *i-th* attribute is missing, it is given by:

$$d(\mathbf{u},\mathbf{y})_E = \sqrt{(u_1 - y_1)^2 + ... + (u_{i-1} - y_{i-1})^2 + (u_{i+1} - y_{i+1})^2 + ... + (u_N - y_N)^2} \; . \quad (1)$$

In equation (1), the *i-th* attribute is not considered, because it is missing in $\mathbf{u}$. After computing the distances $d(\mathbf{u},\mathbf{y})$ for all $\mathbf{y} \neq \mathbf{u}$, $\mathbf{y}$ representing a complete instance, one or more instances (the more similar ones, which are the neighbors of **u**) are employed to complete u_i. In addition, although equation (1) just considers one missing value (in the *i-th* attribute), one observes that it can be easily generalized for instances with more missing values.

The imputation process by the K-Nearest Neighbor (KNN) method is simple, but it has provided encouraging results [4,5,9]. In clustering problems, this approach is particularly interesting, because in general the clustering process is also based on distances between vectors. In these cases, the inductive bias of the clustering and imputation methods is equal. Besides, KNN methods can be easily adapted to datasets formed by discrete attributes. To do so, one can, for example, substitute the Euclidean distance function by the Simple Matching Approach. However, depending on the dimensionality of the dataset in hand, it can become computationally time consuming. In this sense, it is memory intensive since the entire training set is stored. Besides, classification/estimation is slow since the distance between input (query) instances and those in the training set must be computed. Thus, KNN typically performs better for lower dimensional problems [12].

In this paper, we focus on classification problems, describing a more efficient KNN algorithm for missing values imputation that can be employed in datasets formed by continuous/ordinal attributes. In a nutshell, the K-Means algorithm is first applied in the complete instances **y**, leading to a set of clusters, whose mean vectors (centroids) are, in turn, used as training instances for the *traditional* KNN. From now on, we will call our method KMI (K-Means Imputation), and we propose to apply it separately in the instances of each class (further details in Section 2.4). In summary, the main steps of KMI are:

Algorithm KMI

1 Employ the K-Means Algorithm in the instances without missing values (complete dataset), obtaining K_M cluster centroids (mean vectors);

2 According to the K_M obtained centroids, find the corresponding nearest one for each instance with missing values - equation (1) considering **y** as the centroids and **u** as the instance with missing values;

3 Complete each missing value with the corresponding attribute value of the nearest centroid.

2.1 Brief Review of the K-Means Algorithm

Clustering algorithms that involve the calculation of the mean (centroid) of each cluster are often referred to as K-Means algorithms [7]. These algorithms partition a dataset of N instances into K_M clusters, minimizing the sum of distances among instances and their corresponding cluster centroids. The value of K_M (number of clusters) is usually specified by the user. The distances can be calculated by means of equation (1), but since K-Means is applied in the complete dataset, all attributes are considered. In this work, we employ the K-Means algorithm depicted in Fig.1, where the convergence criterion can be defined either as the maximum number of iterations (t) of steps

2 and 3 or as a function of the difference between centroids of two consecutive iterations.

---
1. Generate a random initial partition of instances into K_M nonempty clusters;
2. Compute the cluster centroids (mean vectors) of the current partition;
3. Assign each instance to the cluster with the nearest centroid;
4. If the convergence criterion has been satisfied, then stop; else, go to step 2.

Fig. 1. Employed K-Means Algorithm

2.2 Efficacy of KNN and KMI

In order to visualize possible advantages and disadvantages of KNN and KMI, let us consider the *pedagogical* dataset (formed by 4 Gaussian distributions, each one composed by 10 instances) depicted in Fig. 2. Both KNN and KMI are designed to fulfill the missing value (represented by ?) of instance $\mathbf{u}=[u_1,u_2,?]$. To do so, these methods take into consideration the available information, i.e., the values of attributes 1 and 2 depicted in Fig. 2, where $\{G1,\ldots,G4\}$ represent four *natural* groups of similar instances. These groups can be *viewed* as four different classes. It is clear that $\mathbf{u}$ is more similar to the instances of G1 (as indicated by the arrow) than to the instances of the other groups. Therefore, it is assumed that one or more instances of this group should be employed to impute u_3.

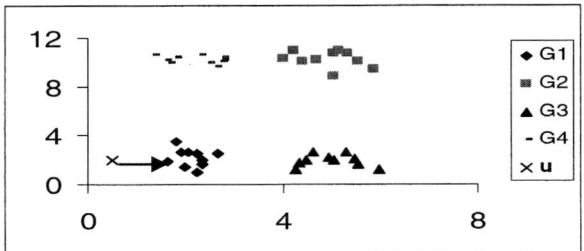

Fig. 2. Hypothetical dataset

Considering KNN, the most similar K_N instances (neighbors) are employed to impute u_3. For instance, the mean vector of K_N instances could be used to impute u_3. Let us call this mean vector as $\mathbf{m}=[m_1,m_2,m_3]$. In this particular case, the third attribute value of the mean vector is imputed in u_3, i.e. $u_3=m_3$. In the hypothetical situation depicted in Fig. 2, a value of K_N more than 10 may cause problems for KNN, because instances very dissimilar of $\mathbf{u}$ (belonging to other groups) would contribute to the imputation of u_3. This problem can be lessened by using the weighted imputation function expressed in Equation (2), where $\mathbf{y}^i$ are the K_N most similar instances in relation to $\mathbf{u}$ and j is the attribute index of the missing value ($j=3$ in our hypothetical case). Doing so, a vector $\mathbf{y}$ contributes to the imputation of u_3 according to its similarity to $\mathbf{u}$. If $d(\mathbf{u},\mathbf{y}^i)=0$, then only instance $\mathbf{y}^i$ is employed to impute the missing value in

u, because in this case **u**=**y**^{i}. Equation (2) also lessens the problem caused by overestimated values of K_N (number of neighbors in the traditional KNN). However, KNN computational cost continues high (this subject is addressed in Section 2.3).

$$u_j = \frac{\sum_{i=1}^{K_N} \frac{1}{d(\mathbf{u}, \mathbf{y}^i)} y_j^i}{\sum_{i=1}^{K_N} \frac{1}{d(\mathbf{u}, \mathbf{y}^i)}} \quad (2)$$

Let us now consider what happens with the application of KMI (K-Means + KNN). In principle, we will consider just the most similar cluster (according to its centroid) for the imputation process. In an ideal situation, the four groups depicted in Fig. 2 would be found by K-Means, and KMI would impute a suitable value in u_3, i.e. the corresponding value of the *mean vector* (centroid) of the most similar group (G1). In this case, if $K_N \leq 10$, KNN would perform a more accurate imputation - by Equation (2) - than KMI. However, for $K_N > 10$, imputation by KMI would be more accurate. Suppose now that $K_M \leq 4$ or that K-Means has not found the *natural* clusters {G1,...,G4}. In both cases, instances from different *natural* groups could be classified in the same cluster. For example, let us suppose that instances of G1 and G3 are *classified* in a single cluster. Under the perspective of imputing u_3, this single cluster would be interesting only if these two groups (G1 and G3) have similar values for y_3. To reduce this problem (without considering computational efficiency issues), one can overestimate (to a certain extent) the value of K_M for two reasons: (i) it favors more compact clusters, formed by few instances, thus providing more accurate imputations; (ii) K-Means may *decrease* K_M, mainly in relation to particular centroid initializations. More specifically, K-means can find less than K_M clusters when, in a set of K_M centroids, at least one is farther from all instances than the others. In some situations, it can be interesting to employ more than one cluster for imputation. For example, let us consider the scenario in which two or more clusters have an equal distance from **u**. In this case, it would be interesting to consider all these clusters for imputation. Another alternative involves the application of equation (2) in the K-Means based imputation.

In theory, the challenge is to find suitable values for K_N and K_M, because, in this case, both methods can provide good results. In practice, however, this is a hard task. Considering KNN, if K_N is set too high, many dissimilar instances in relation to **u** are taken into consideration to impute its missing values. That could deteriorate the quality of the imputed value. On the other hand, if K_N is set too low, the imputation could become badly biased, not appropriately reflecting sampling variability. Similarly, when KMI is concerned, if too high values of K_M are chosen, small clusters are likely to be found, favoring imputations based on small subsets of instances. However, if K_M is set too low, the number of instances in each cluster tends to be high, and very dissimilar instances in relation to **u** may be considered to impute its missing values. In summary, it is really difficult to find the optimal values for K_M and K_N. Under this perspective, it is also important to evaluate the computational costs of KMI and KNN. This subject is addressed in the next section.

2.3 Computational Costs of KNN and KMI

In order to evaluate the computational costs of KNN and KMI, let us call: M as the amount of instances with at least one missing value; C as the amount of instances without missing values (complete dataset); K_N as the number of neighbors for KNN; K_M as the number of clusters for the K-Means Algorithm; and t as the number of iterations for K-Means.

Both methods require the computation of distances between vectors. These distances – given by equation (1) - represent the main computational cost of both KNN and KMI. The required comparisons do not represent significant computational costs when compared with the computation of distances. Thus, the estimated computational cost of KNN is $O(M \cdot C)$, whereas for KMI it is $O(t \cdot K_M \cdot C + M \cdot K_M)$. In practice, M and C are *a priori* known, and the values of both K_M and t are usually defined by the user. With a little notation abuse, the estimated value of K_M that equals the computational costs of KNN and KMI for a fixed t is:

$$K'_M = \frac{M \cdot C}{(t \cdot C + M)} \quad (3)$$

Equation (3) states that if $K_M > K'_M$ then KNN is computationally more efficient than KMI, whereas if $K_M < K'_M$ then KMI is more efficient. Similarly, it would be interesting to estimate K'_N. However, the number of neighbors (K_N) only affects the *comparison phase*, in which the nearest-neighbors are defined. Therefore, it does not significantly influences the computational cost of KNN and, in principle, K'_N could not be estimated. One alternative to circumvent this problem involves comparing the computational costs of KNN and KMI in a situation in which both methods would provide the same efficacy. As previously described (Section 2.2), the efficacy of each method basically depends on the amount of instances employed for imputation. When KMI is concerned, in general it is interesting to consider only the most similar cluster in relation to **u** for imputation. Therefore, in order to provide a fair comparison between KNN and KMI, the value of K_N should be equal to the number of instances of the most similar cluster. However, it is not easy to estimate this number, because it depends on the K-Means result. In this context, a reasonable approach involves assuming that K-Means would provide clusters formed by an equal number of instances, leading to the following relation:

$$K_M = \frac{C}{K_N} \quad (4)$$

In other words, equation (4) relates the number of clusters to the number of neighbors in a way such that both methods take into account approximately the same number of instances to impute the missing values. Now, similarly to the estimation of K'_M - equation (3) - and using equation (4), it is possible to estimate K'_N:

$$K'_N = \frac{t \cdot C + M}{M} \quad (5)$$

Where K'_N equals the computational cost of KNN and KMI, in such a way that both consider approximately an equal number of instances to perform the imputation of missing values. In summary, the computational costs of KNN and KMI depend on the proportion of instances with missing values in relation to the complete dataset, and on K-Means parameters.

2.4 Proposed Method

As described in Sections 2.2 and 2.3, KNN and KMI present advantages and disadvantages concerning both efficacy and efficiency, depending on the characteristics of the dataset in hand and on their parameter values (K_M, t, and K_N). In classification problems, we propose to separate the instances according to their corresponding classes before applying KMI. In this context, let us suppose a classification problem in which there are X classes. Thus, X pairs of {Missing,Complete} datasets {(M_1,C_1), (M_2,C_2),....,(M_X,C_X)} are employed for imputation. In this scenario, the hard task of choosing the value for K_M is attenuated, because K-Means is employed in a *supervised* way, i.e., the information about the class is indirectly inserted in the imputation process. In other words, missing values are imputed only considering corresponding instances of the same class. In this sense, a reasonable approach is to set $K_M=2$, which is the minimum value for this parameter. Doing so, complete instances of each class are summarized by two cluster centroids (mean vectors), and the most similar centroid in relation to each instance with missing values is used for imputation.

Let us see what happens when the computational costs are concerned. To do so, it is not necessary to change the terminology defined in section 2.3. Instead, we assume that the imputation process is being performed in the instances of a single class I, and the concepts described in section 2.3 still remain valid for each pair (M_I,C_I). The only difference is that now we are evaluating KNN and KMI considering the instances of a single class. Anderberg [8] observes that, in general, a number of iterations $t \le 5$ usually will suffice to get suitable solutions by K-Means. Under this perspective, {$t=5, K_M=2$}<<{C,M} and, consequently, KMI becomes of $O(C+M)$, i.e. more efficient than KNN. Obviously, there is a trade-off between efficiency and efficacy (accuracy), and it is necessary to evaluate to what extent it is advantageous to employ more efficient algorithms like KMI. This assessment is highly dependent of the classification problem in hand. Thus, it is useful to perform empirical evaluation in some benchmark datasets. To do so, imputation results are evaluated both in terms of prediction and classification tasks.

3 Simulation Results

3.1 Theoretical Aspects

We are interested in evaluating our imputation method for classification problems in the context of data mining applications. In general, a dataset D is formed by instances with and without missing values. Remember that we call C (complete) the subset of instances of D that do not have missing values, and M (missing) the subset of instances of D with at least one missing value. In this context, imputation methods should carefully *complete* the missing values of M, originating a filled dataset F. In an ideal situation, the imputation method should fill the missing values, originating *filled values*, without inserting bias in the dataset. In a more realistic view, one tries to decrease the amount of inserted bias to acceptable levels, in a way that a dataset D'={C+F}, probably containing more information than D (in the sense that the attributes without missing values in M may contain important information), can be used for data mining (e.g. considering issues such as feature selection, combining multiple models, and so on).

There are two ways of measuring the *bias* inserted by an imputation method: in a prediction task and in a classification task. In a prediction task, one simulates missing values in C. Some known values are removed and then imputed. In this way, it is possible to evaluate how close the imputed values are to the real, known ones. The closer the imputed value to the real one, the better the imputation method is. This alternative is very efficient to compare different imputation methods, because it requires few computations after imputing values, but it does not allow estimating the classifier performance in D'. In other words, although this procedure is valid, the prediction results are not the only important issue to be analyzed. In this sense, the substitution process must also generate values that least distort the original characteristics of D, which are given by the between-variable relationships, defined by each particular classification algorithm. In a more practical view, the known values in M can contain important information, which, in turn, would be lost if their corresponding instances were discarded.

In practical data mining applications, one usually employs different classifiers, choosing the best one according to some criterion of model quality. In this work, we are interested in evaluating the influence of the proposed imputation method in relation to the Average Correct Classification Rate (ACCR) criterion. In fact, the assumption is that the best classifier (BC) - in relation to D and to the available classifiers – provides a suitable model for classifying instances of D. Therefore, it is also important to assess to what extent the imputed values adjust themselves to the BC model(s).

It is a common practice to evaluate classifier performance in a test set. The same concept can be adapted to evaluate the missing values substitution, considering C as the training set and F as the test set. In this context, one can measure the *inserted bias* by the following procedure:

---

1) Evaluate the classifier in a cross-validation process, using dataset C;
2) Evaluate the classifier in dataset F (test set) considering that C is the training set;
3) The estimated inserted bias is the difference between the results achieved in 2) and 1).

Fig. 3. Evaluating the imputation method in a classification context

Looking at Fig. 3, a positive bias is achieved when the Average Correct Classification Rate (ACCR) in F (step 2) is higher than in the cross validation process in C (step 1), i.e. the imputed values are likely to improve the classifier ACCR in D'. By the same token, a negative bias is inserted when the imputed values are likely to worsen the classifier ACCR. Finally, no bias is likely inserted when the accuracies in F and in the cross-validation process are equal (*ideal* situation).

One could argue that a cross-validation process should be performed in both datasets (C and F), comparing the corresponding results. However, it is possible to get different models in C and F. For instance, different decision trees (in terms of selected attributes), but with similar accuracies in a cross-validation process, may be obtained in C and F. In this case, a similar ACCR may not be achieved in D'. In addition, we are interested in evaluating if the imputation process preserves the between-variable relationships, which are defined by each particular classification model. In this sense, the complete dataset is more trustable and, consequently, is its associated model. In other words, verifying how the data in F adjust themselves to the model obtained in C allows estimating the classifier ACCR in D'. Besides, performing cross-validation in both datasets (C and F) is computationally more expensive, because it is necessary to get and evaluate each classifier several times for both C and F.

3.2 Methodology

The KMI was evaluated both in prediction and classification tasks, comparing the obtained results with the traditional KNN for imputation. In order to verify the efficacy of the proposed method (KMI), we compared it to KNN with weighted imputations – equation (2) – and assuming that $K_N=C/K_M$ provides fair comparisons – equation (4). Both methods were evaluated in three scenarios, simulating missing values in proportions of 30%, 50% and 70%, i.e. M=30%C, M=50%C and M=70%C. To do so, we simulated missing values in complete datasets, eliminating some values that are a priori known. In this sense, for each class some instances were randomly chosen, and one of their attribute values was randomly eliminated. Thus, the proportion of instances of each class is maintained in the employed datasets. After inserting missing values, the known values of each attribute were normalized into the range [0,1] to give attributes an equal weight. We performed simulations in 3 datasets that are benchmarks for data mining methods [10] (Iris Plants, Wisconsin Breast Cancer, and Pima Indians Diabetes) and Table 1 summarizes their main characteristics.

Table 1. Summary of Dataset Characteristics

Dataset (# classes)	# instances/class	# attributes	Attribute Type
Iris Plants (3)	{50,50,50}	4	Continuous
Wisconsin Cancer (2)	{444,239}	9	Ordinal
Pima Diabetes (2)	{500,268}	8	Ordinal/Continuous

The simulation results in the prediction task are shown in Table 2, where one observes that KNN has provided slightly better results (smaller average absolute differences between original and imputed values) in most of the performed simulations. As it can be seen in the sequel, these differences have not significantly influenced classification results, which is the most important aspect to be analyzed.

Table 2. Prediction Results: average values for abs(original-imputed)

Method	30% Iris	50% Iris	70% Iris	30% Wisc.	50% Wisc.	70% Wisc.	30% Pima	50% Pima	70% Pima
KNN	0.22	0.19	0.26	1.15	1.12	1.05	12.65	14.85	17.38
KMI	0.21	0.21	0.28	1.22	1.14	1.11	12.73	15.52	17.33

The imputation process must also generate values that least distort the original characteristics of D, which are given by the between-variable relationships, defined by each particular classifier. To evaluate this aspect, we employ the methodology described in Section 3.1, using five classifiers: One Rule, Naïve Bayes, J4.8 Decision Tree, PART and Multilayer Perceptrons. These classifiers are popular in the data mining community, and make part of the WEKA System [11], which was used to perform our simulations, using its default parameters. In a nutshell, One Rule (1R) is a very efficient and simple method that often produces good rules for characterizing the structure in the data. It generates a one-level decision tree, which is expressed in the form of a set of rules that test just one selected attribute. Naive Bayes (NB) uses all attributes and allows them to make contributions to the decision that are equally important, and independent of one another given the class, leading to a simple scheme that works well in practice. J4.8 is the Weka´s implementation of an improved version of the popular C4.5 decision tree learner. PART is a method that provides rules from pruned partial decision trees built using C4.5. It combines the divide-and-conquer strategy of decision trees learning with the separate-and-conquer strategy for rule learning. In essence, to make a single rule, a pruned decision tree is built for the current set of instances. Then, the leaf with the largest coverage is made into a rule and the tree is discarded. Finally, Multilayer Perceptrons are feedforward neural networks (NN) that learn by means of backpropagation algorithms.

In order to estimate the classifier ACCR (Average Correct Classification Rate) in the complete datasets (C), we performed a ten-fold-cross validation (CV) process. Figures 4, 5, and 6 show the simulation results in each dataset, considering the employed classifiers. In these figures, 30%, 50% and 70% represent the proportion of missing values in each simulation, whereas F stand for the datasets filled by either KNN or KMI.

Figures 4, 5, and 6 show that KNN and KMI have provided good and similar classification results in the filled datasets. Since KMI is a more efficient algorithm, our most important results concern about the efficacy of KMI, which is similar to the one provided by KNN. Indeed, KNN has provided better classification results just in 40% of our simulations. Indeed, the most important differences, in terms of classification results in the filled datasets, were equal to 2.22%, 0.63%, and 3.90% in Iris, Wisconsin and Pima respectively. Considering the inserted bias (Fig. 3) both methods (KMI and KNN) have provided equal results in 44.44% of our simulations, whereas KMI has provided better results in 31.11% of our simulations, indicating that KMI provides imputations as suitable as KNN, but in a more efficient way.

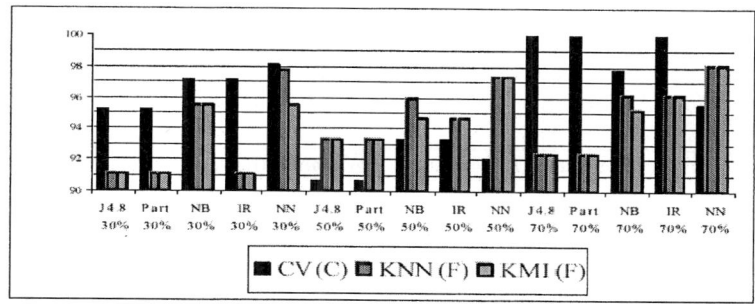

Fig. 4. Average Correct Classification Rate (ACCRs) - Iris Plants

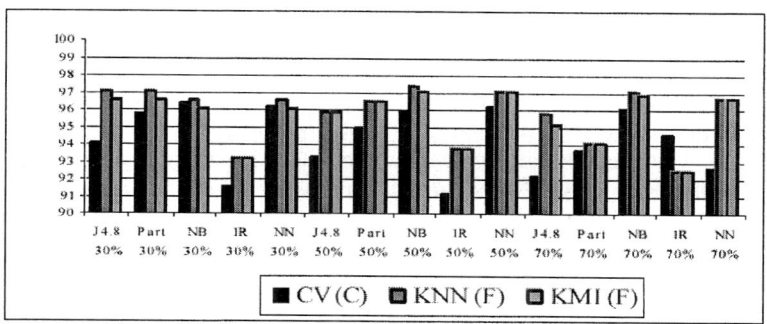

Fig. 5. Average Correct Classification Rate (ACCRs) - Wisconsin Breast Cancer

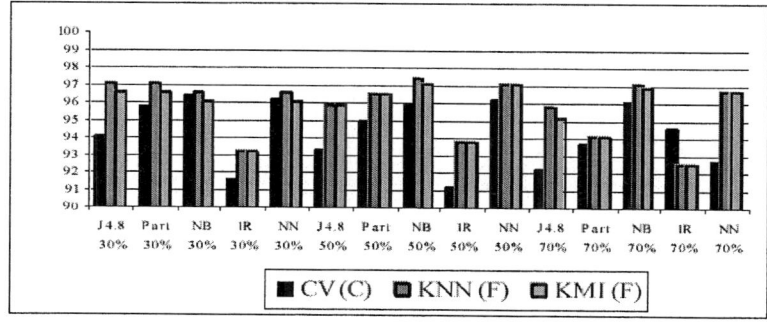

Fig. 6. Average Correct Classification Rates (ACCRs) - Pima Indians Diabetes

Considering the most important estimated inserted biases, Figures 4, 5, and 6 also show that KNN and KMI provided similar performances. Table 3 details the most important inserted biases (positive and negative ones), indicating that KMI has shown worse results just in Pima.

Table 3. Most Important Estimated Inserted Bias in Each Dataset: Bias (bold); imputation method(s) (KNN/KMI/both); classifier; proportion of missing values

Bias (%)	Iris Plants (Fig. 4)	Wisconsin (Fig. 5)	Pima (Fig. 6)
Positive	**5.33**; both; NN; 50%.	**3.97**; both; NN; 70%.	**9.38**; KMI; J4.8; 50%
Negative	**7.62**; both; J4.8/PART; 70%.	**2.16**; both; 1R; 70%.	**7.29**; KMI; 1R; 50%

4 Conclusions

This paper proposed modifications towards improving the efficiency of imputation methods based on nearest-neighbors. In this context, the K-Means algorithm is applied in the complete dataset (without missing values) before the imputation process by nearest-neighbors takes place. Subsequently, the cluster centroids obtained by K-Means are used as *training* instances for the nearest-neighbor method. Particularly, we focused on classification problems, for which we proposed to employ K-Means in a *supervised* way, i.e., missing values are imputed considering just corresponding instances of the same class. Performed simulations in three benchmark datasets indicate that the proposed method provides imputations as suitable as those obtained by means of the traditional K-Nearest Neighbor (KNN) method, both in terms of prediction and classification tasks. Thus, the proposed method is promising.

Our future work will concentrate on performing simulations on real-world datasets, comparing the obtained results with other leading imputation methods. We are also going to evaluate the application of the weighted imputation function in the instances of the clusters found by K-Means. Although it implies in an additional computational cost, the imputations are likely to be even more accurate. In addition, the computational cost can be further minimized by using other reduction techniques such as those proposed in [13]. Finally, we are going to investigate the substitution of K-Means by other efficient algorithms that automatically define the *optimal* number of clusters.

Acknowledgments

Eduardo R. Hruschka acknowledges CNPq (proc. 301.353/03-4) for its financial support. Nelson F.F. Ebecken acknowledges both CNPq and FAPERJ for their financial support.

References

1. Pyle, D., Data Preparation for Data Mining. Academic Press, 1999.
2. Little, R. & Rubin, D. B., Statistical Analysis with Missing Data. Wiley, New York, 1987.
3. Mitchell, T. M. Machine Learning. The McGraw-Hill Companies, Inc, 1997.
4. Hruschka, E. R., Hruschka Junior, E. R., Ebecken, N. F. F. Evaluating a Nearest-Neighbor Method to Substitute Continuous Missing Values. In: The 16th Australian Joint Conference on Artificial Intelligence, Lecture Notes in Artificial Intelligence, v. 2903, pp. 723-734, Springer, 2003.
5. Batista, G. E. A. P. & Monard, M. C., An Analysis of Four Missing Data Treatment Methods for Supervised Learning. Applied Artificial Intelligence. v.17, n.5-6, 519-534, 2003.
6. Atkeson, C. G., Moore, A. W., & Schaal, S., Locally Weighted Learning, Artificial Intelligence Review, 11:11-73, 1997.
7. Everitt, B.S., Landau, S., Leese, M., Cluster Analysis, Arnold Publishers, London, 2001.
8. Anderberg, M. R., Cluster Analysis for Applications, USA, Academic Press, Inc., 1973.
9. Troyanskaya, O. et al., Missing Value Estimation Methods for DNA Microarrays, Bioinformatics, v.17, no. 6, pp. 520-525, 2001.
10. Merz, C.J., Murphy, P.M., UCI Repository of Machine Learning Databases, http://www.ics.uci.edu, Irvine, CA, University of California, Department of Information and Computer Science.
11. Witten, I. H., Frank, E., Data Mining – Practical Machine Learning Tools and Techniques with Java Implementations, Morgan Kaufmann Publishers, USA, 2000.
12. Kennedy, R.L., Lee, Y., Roy, B.V., Reed, C.D., Lippmann,R. P., Solving Data Mining Problems through Pattern Recognition, Prentice Hall PTR, 1997.
13. Wilson, D.R., Martinez, T.R., Reduction Techniques for Instance-Based Learning Algorithms, Machine Learning, 38-3, pp. 257-286, Kluwer Academic Publishers, 2000.

Univariate and Multivariate Linear Regression Methods to Predict Interval-Valued Features

Eufrasio de A. Lima Neto, Francisco A. T. de Carvalho,
and Camilo P. Tenorio

Centro de Informatica - CIn / UFPE, Av. Prof. Luiz Freire,
s/n Cidade Universitaria, CEP: 50740-540 - Recife - PE - Brasil
{ealn, fatc, cpt}@cin.ufpe.br

Abstract. This paper introduces two new approaches to fit a linear regression model on interval-valued data. Each example of the learning set is described by a feature vector where each feature value is an interval. In the first proposed approach, it is fitted two independent linear regression models, respectively, on the mid-point and range of the interval values assumed by the variables on the learning set. In the second approach, is fitted a multivariate linear regression models on these mid-point and range. The prediction of the lower and upper bound of the interval value of the dependent variable is accomplished from its mid-point and range which are estimated from the fitted linear regression models applied to the mid-point and range of each interval values of the independent variables. The evaluation of the proposed prediction methods is based on the average behavior of the *root mean squared error* and the *determination coefficient* in the framework of a Monte Carlo experiment in comparison with the method proposed by Billard and Diday [2].

1 Introduction

Due to the explosive growth in the use of databases new approaches have been proposed to discover regularities and summarize information stored in such large data sets. *Symbolic Data Analysis* (SDA) [1] has been introduced as a new domain related to multivariate analysis, pattern recognition and artificial intelligence in order to extend classical exploratory data analysis and statistical methods to symbolic data. Symbolic data allows multiple (sometimes weighted) values for each variable and new variable types (interval, categorical multi-valued and modal variables) have been introduced. These new variables allow to take into account variability and/or uncertainty present in the data.

This paper concerns the fitting of univariate and multivariate linear regression models to an interval-valued data-set. The classical model of regression for usual data is used to predict the behavior of a dependent variable Y as a function of others independent variables that are responsible for the variability of variable Y. In the case where Y is a vector of multiples response variables, then we have the so called multivariate linear regression model. In both situations, to fit these models on the data, is necessary the estimation of a vector β of parameters from the data vector (or data matrix, in the multivariate case) **Y** and the model matrix **X**, supposed with complete rank p. The estimation using the *method of least square* does not require any probabilistic hypothesis on the variable Y. This method consists in minimize the sum of square of residuals. A detailed study of the univariate and multivariate linear regression models for classical data can be found in Scheffé [7], Draper and Smith [5], Montgomery and Peck [6], among others.

Billard and Diday [2] presented for the first time an approach to fitting a linear regression model to an interval-valued data-set. Their approach consist in fitting a linear regression model on the mid-point of the interval values assumed by the variables on the learning set and applies this model on the lower and upper bounds of the interval values of the independent variables to predict, respectively, the lower and upper bounds of the interval value of the dependent variable. Later, they presented other approaches to fit a linear regression model to the case of histogram-valued data [3], and to take into account taxonomic variables.

This paper introduces two new approaches to fit a linear regression model for interval-valued data which improves the method proposed by Billard and Diday [2]. In the first proposed approach, it is fitted two independent linear regression models, respectively, on the mid-point and range of the interval values assumed by the variables on the learning set. The prediction of the lower and upper bound of the interval value of the dependent variable is accomplished from its mid-point and range which are estimated from the fitted linear regression models applied to the mid-point and range of each interval values of the independent variables. The second approach consist in a multivariate linear regression model of the mid-point and range of the dependent variable over a matrix model X composed by the mid-points and ranges of the independent variables. The prediction of the lower and upper bound of the interval value of the dependent variables are estimated from the fitted multivariate linear regression model applied on the same mid-point and range of each interval values of the independent variables.

In order to show the usefulness of these approaches is predicted, according with the proposed methods and the method presented by Billard and Diday [2] in independent test data sets, the lower and upper bound of the interval values of a variable which is linearly related to a set of independent interval-valued variables. The evaluation of the proposed prediction methods considering different values for the vector of parameters β is based on the estimation of the average behavior of the *root mean squared error* and of the *determination coefficient* in the framework of a Monte Carlo experiment in comparison with the method proposed by Billard and Diday [2].

Section 2 presents the new approaches to fit a linear regression model to interval-valued data. Section 3 describes the framework of the Monte Carlo simulations and presents experiments with artificial interval-valued data sets and with a cardiological interval-valued data set. Finally, the section 4 gives the concluding remarks.

2 Linear Regression Models for Interval-Valued Data

This section explains the method introduced by Billard and Diday [2] to fit a linear regression model on interval-valued data (here named *univariate center method - UCM*) and the methods introduced in this paper (here named *univariate center and range method - UCRM* and *multivariate center and range method - MCRM*).

2.1 Univariate Center Method (UCM)

Let $E = \{e_1, \ldots, e_n\}$ a set of examples which are described by $p+1$ interval-valued variables: Y, and $X_1, \ldots, X_p$. Each example $e_i \in E$ ($i = 1, \ldots, n$) is represented as an interval quantitative feature vector $\mathbf{z}_i = (x_{i1}, \ldots, x_{ip}, y_i)$ where $x_{ij} = [a_{ij}, b_{ij}] \in \Im = \{[a,b] : a, b \in \Re, a \leq b\}$ ($j = 1, \ldots, p$) and $y_i = [y_{Li}, y_{Ui}] \in \Im$ are, respectively, the observed values of X_j and Y.

Let us consider that exist a linear relationship between Y (the dependent variable) and X_j, $j = 1, \ldots, p$ (the p independent predictor variables). Given a new example e, described by $\mathbf{z} = (x_1, \ldots, x_p, y)$ where $x_j = [a_j, b_j]$ ($j = 1, \ldots, p$) and $y = [y_L, y_U]$, the aim is to predict y from x_j ($j = 1, \ldots, p$) through a linear regression model.

Billard and Diday [2] proposed to fit a univariate linear regression model on the mid-point of the interval values assumed by the variables on the learning set and applies this model on the lower and upper bounds of the interval values of the independent variables to predict, respectively, the lower and upper bounds of the interval value of the dependent variable. They compare this approach with the fit of two independent linear regression models, over the lower and upper bounds of the interval-valued variables, and conclude that their approach produce a better performance.

Formally, let us consider again the same set of examples $E = \{e_1, \ldots, e_n\}$ but they are now also described by $p+1$ continuous quantitative variables Y^{md}, and $X_1^{md}, \ldots, X_p^{md}$, which assume as value, respectively, the mid-point of the interval assumed by the interval-valued variables Y, and $X_1, \ldots, X_p$. This means that each example $e_i \in E$ ($i = 1, \ldots, n$) is represented as a continuous quantitative feature vector $\mathbf{w}_i = (x_{i1}^{md}, \ldots, x_{ip}^{md}, y_i^{md})$ where $x_{ij}^{md} = (a_{ij} + b_{ij})/2$ ($j = 1, \ldots, p$) and $y_i^{md} = (y_{Li} + y_{Ui})/2$ are, respectively, the observed values of X_j^{md} and Y^{md}.

The fitted univariate linear regression model is then

$$\mathbf{y}^{md} = \mathbf{X}^{md} \boldsymbol{\beta}^{md} + \boldsymbol{\epsilon}^{md} \qquad (1)$$

where $\mathbf{y}^{md} = (y_1^{md}, \ldots, y_n^{md})^T$, $\mathbf{X}^{md} = ((\mathbf{x}_1^{md})^T, \ldots, (\mathbf{x}_n^{md})^T)^T$, $(\mathbf{x}_i^{md})^T = (1, x_{i1}^{md}, \ldots, x_{ip}^{md})$ ($i = 1, \ldots, n$), $\boldsymbol{\beta}^{md} = (\beta_0^{md}, \ldots, \beta_p^{md})^T$ and $\boldsymbol{\epsilon}^{md} = (\epsilon_1^{md}, \ldots, \epsilon_n^{md})^T$.

If $\mathbf{X}^{md}$ has full rank $p+1 \leq n$, the least squares estimates of $\boldsymbol{\beta}^{md}$ in equation 1 is given by

$$\hat{\boldsymbol{\beta}}^{md} = ((\mathbf{X}^{md})^T \mathbf{X}^{md})^{-1} (\mathbf{X}^{md})^T \mathbf{y}^{md} \qquad (2)$$

Given a new example e, described by $\mathbf{z} = (x_1, \ldots, x_p, y)$ and $\mathbf{z}^{md} = (x_1^{md}, \ldots, x_p^{md}, y^{md})$, where $x_j = [a_j, b_j]$ and $x_j^{md} = (a_j + b_j)/2$ $(j = 1, \ldots, p)$, the value $y = [y_L, y_U]$ of Y will be predicted from the predicted value $\hat{y}^{md}$ of Y^{md} as follow:

$$\hat{y}_L = \hat{y}^{md} = (\mathbf{x}_L)^T \hat{\boldsymbol{\beta}}^{md} \text{ and } \hat{y}_U = \hat{y}^{md} = (\mathbf{x}_U)^T \hat{\boldsymbol{\beta}}^{md} \qquad (3)$$

where $(\mathbf{x}_L)^T = (1, a_1, \ldots, a_p)$, $(\mathbf{x}_U)^T = (1, b_1, \ldots, b_p)$ and $\hat{\boldsymbol{\beta}}^{md} = (\hat{\beta}_0^{md}, \hat{\beta}_1^{md}, \ldots, \hat{\beta}_p^{md})^T$.

In the next section, we introduce a new univariate method which improves the method of Billard and Diday [2].

2.2 The Univariate Center and Range Method (UCRM)

In the method proposed here, is fitted two independent univariate linear regression models, respectively, on the mid-point and range of the interval values assumed by the variables on the learning set. The prediction of the lower and upper bound of the interval value of the dependent variable is accomplished from the mid-point and range which are estimated from the fitted univariate linear regression models applied to the mid-point and range of each interval value of the independent variables.

Let us consider again the same set of examples $E = \{e_1, \ldots, e_n\}$, but they are now also described by $p+1$ continuous quantitative variables Y^r, and $X_1^r, \ldots, X_p^r$ which assume as value, respectively, the range of the interval assumed by the interval-valued variables Y, and $X_1, \ldots, X_p$. This means that each example $e_i \in E$ $(i = 1, \ldots, n)$ is represented as a continuous quantitative feature vector $\mathbf{r}_i = (x_{i1}^r, \ldots, x_{ip}^r, y_i^r)$ where $x_{ij}^r = (b_{ij} - a_{ij})$ $(j = 1, \ldots, p)$ and $y_i^r = (y_{Ui} - y_{Li})$ are, respectively, the observed values of X_j^r and Y^r.

The fitted linear regression model is then

$$\mathbf{y}^r = \mathbf{X}^r \boldsymbol{\beta}^r + \boldsymbol{\epsilon}^r \qquad (4)$$

where $\mathbf{y}^r = (y_1^r, \ldots, y_n^r)^T$, $\mathbf{X}^r = ((\mathbf{x}_1^r)^T, \ldots, (\mathbf{x}_n^r)^T)^T$, $(\mathbf{x}_i^r)^T = (1, x_{i1}^r, \ldots, x_{ip}^r)$ $(i = 1, \ldots, n)$, $\boldsymbol{\beta}^r = (\beta_0^r, \ldots, \beta_p^r)^T$ and $\boldsymbol{\epsilon}^r = (\epsilon_1^r, \ldots, \epsilon_n^r)^T$.

If $\mathbf{X}^r$ has full rank $p+1 \leq n$, the least squares estimates of $\boldsymbol{\beta}^r$ in equation 4 is given by

$$\hat{\boldsymbol{\beta}}^r = ((\mathbf{X}^r)^T \mathbf{X}^r)^{-1} (\mathbf{X}^r)^T \mathbf{y}^r \qquad (5)$$

Given a new example e, described by $\mathbf{z} = (x_1, \ldots, x_p, y)$, $\mathbf{z}^{md} = (x_1^{md}, \ldots, x_p^{md}, y^{md})$ and $\mathbf{z}^r = (x_1^r, \ldots, x_p^r, y^r)$, where $x_j = [a_j, b_j]$, $x_j^{md} = (a_j + b_j)/2$ and $x_j^r = (b_j - a_j)$ $(j = 1, \ldots, p)$, the value $y = [y_L, y_U]$ of Y will be predicted from the predicted values $\hat{y}^{md}$ of Y^{md} and $\hat{y}^r$ of Y^r as follow:

$$\hat{y}_L = \hat{y}^{md} - (1/2)\hat{y}^r \text{ and } \hat{y}_U = \hat{y}^{md} + (1/2)\hat{y}^r \qquad (6)$$

where $\hat{y}^{md} = (\tilde{\mathbf{x}}^{md})^T \hat{\boldsymbol{\beta}}^{md}$, $\hat{y}^r = (\tilde{\mathbf{x}}^r)^T \hat{\boldsymbol{\beta}}^r$, $(\tilde{\mathbf{x}}^{md})^T = (1, x_1^{md}, \ldots, x_p^{md})$, $(\tilde{\mathbf{x}}^r)^T = (1, x_1^r, \ldots, x_p^r)$, $\hat{\boldsymbol{\beta}}^{md} = (\hat{\beta}_0^{md}, \hat{\beta}_1^{md}, \ldots, \hat{\beta}_p^{md})^T$ and $\hat{\boldsymbol{\beta}}^r = (\hat{\beta}_0^r, \hat{\beta}_1^r, \ldots, \hat{\beta}_p^r)^T$.

2.3 The Multivariate Center and Range Method (MCRM)

The second method proposed in this paper consider a multivariate linear regression model of the mid-point and range of the dependent variable over a matrix model X composed by the mid-points and ranges of the independent variables. The prediction of the lower and upper bound of the interval value of the dependent variable is accomplished from the mid-point and range which are estimated from the fitted multivariate linear regression model applied to the mid-point and range of each interval value of the independent variables.

Let us consider again the same set of examples $E = \{e_1, \ldots, e_n\}$, but they are also described by $2(p+1)$ continuous quantitative variables: Y^{md}, Y^r, $X_1^{md}, \ldots$, X_p^{md}, and $X_1^r, \ldots, X_p^r$ which assume as value, respectively, the mid-point and range of the interval-valued variables Y, and $X_1, \ldots, X_p$. This means that each example $e_i \in E$ $(i = 1, \ldots, n)$ is represented as a continuous quantitative feature vector $\mathbf{r}_i = (x_{i1}^{md}, \ldots, x_{ip}^{md}, x_{i1}^r, \ldots, x_{ip}^r, y_i^{md}, y_i^r)$, where $x_{ij}^{md} = (a_{ij} + b_{ij})/2$ and $x_{ij}^r = (b_{ij} - a_{ij})$ $(j = 1, \ldots, p)$ and $y_i^{md} = (y_{Li} + y_{Ui})/2$ and $y_i^r = (y_{Ui} - y_{Li})$ are, respectively, the observed values of X_j^{md}, X_j^r, Y^{md} and Y^r.

The multivariate linear regression model is then denote by

$$\mathbf{Y} = \mathbf{X}\boldsymbol{\beta} + \boldsymbol{\epsilon} \tag{7}$$

where $\mathbf{Y} = ((\mathbf{y}^{md})^T, (\mathbf{y}^r)^T)$, with $\mathbf{y}^{md} = (y_1^{md}, \ldots, y_n^{md})$ and $\mathbf{y}^r = (y_1^r, \ldots, y_n^r)$; $\mathbf{X} = ((\mathbf{x}_1)^T, \ldots, (\mathbf{x}_n)^T)^T$, with $(\mathbf{x}_i)^T = (1, x_{i1}^{md}, \ldots, x_{ip}^{md}, x_{i1}^r, \ldots, x_{ip}^r)$ $(i = 1, \ldots, n)$; $\boldsymbol{\beta} = (\boldsymbol{\beta}^{md}, \boldsymbol{\beta}^r)$, with $\boldsymbol{\beta}^{md} = (\beta_0^{md}, \beta_1^{md}, \ldots, \beta_{2p}^{md})^T$ and $\boldsymbol{\beta}^r = (\beta_0^r, \beta_1^r, \ldots, \beta_{2p}^r)^T$; and $\boldsymbol{\epsilon} = ((\boldsymbol{\epsilon}^{md})^T, (\boldsymbol{\epsilon}^r)^T)$, with $\boldsymbol{\epsilon}^{md} = (\epsilon_1^{md}, \ldots, \epsilon_n^{md})$ and $\boldsymbol{\epsilon}^r = (\epsilon_1^r, \ldots, \epsilon_n^r)$.

If $\mathbf{X}$ has full rank $2p + 1 \leq n$, the least squares estimates of $\boldsymbol{\beta}^k$ $(k = md, r)$ is given by

$$\hat{\boldsymbol{\beta}}^k = ((\mathbf{X})^T \mathbf{X})^{-1} (\mathbf{X})^T \mathbf{y}^k. \tag{8}$$

Given a new example e, described by $\mathbf{z} = (x_1, \ldots, x_p, y)$ and $\mathbf{z}^{md,r} = (x_{i1}^{md}, \ldots, x_{ip}^{md}, x_{i1}^r, \ldots, x_{ip}^r, y^{md}, y^r)$, where $x_j = [a_j, b_j]$, $x_j^{md} = (a_j + b_j)/2$ and $x_j^r = (b_j - a_j)$ $(j = 1, \ldots, p)$, the value $y = [y_L, y_U]$ of Y will be predicted from the predicted values $\hat{y}^{md*}$ of Y^{md} and $\hat{y}^{r*}$ of Y^r as follow:

$$\hat{y}_L = \hat{y}^{md*} - (1/2)\hat{y}^{r*} \text{ and } \hat{y}_U = \hat{y}^{md*} + (1/2)\hat{y}^{r*} \tag{9}$$

where $\hat{y}^{md*} = \tilde{\mathbf{x}}^T \hat{\boldsymbol{\beta}}^{md}$, $\hat{y}^{r*} = (\tilde{\mathbf{x}})^T \hat{\boldsymbol{\beta}}^r$, $(\tilde{\mathbf{x}})^T = (1, x_1^{md}, \ldots, x_p^{md}, x_1^r, \ldots, x_p^r)$, $\hat{\boldsymbol{\beta}}^{md} = (\hat{\beta}_0^{md}, \hat{\beta}_1^{md}, \ldots, \hat{\beta}_{2p}^{md})^T$ and $\hat{\boldsymbol{\beta}}^r = (\hat{\beta}_0^r, \hat{\beta}_1^r, \ldots, \hat{\beta}_{2p}^r)^T$.

3 The Monte Carlo Experiments

In order to show the usefulness of the approaches proposed in this paper, experiments with simulated interval-valued data sets with different degrees of difficulty to fit a linear regression model are considered in this section as well as a cardiological interval-valued data set.

3.1 Simulated Interval-Valued Data Sets

Initially, is considered standard continuous quantitative data sets in $\Re^2$ and $\Re^4$. Each data set (in $\Re^2$ or $\Re^4$) has 375 points partitioned in a learning set (250 points) and a test set (125 points). Each data point belonging to the standard data set is a seed for an interval data (a rectangle in $\Re^2$ or an hypercube in $\Re^4$) and in this way, from these standard data sets, is obtained the interval data sets.

The construction of the standard data set and of the corresponding interval data set is accomplished in the following steps:

s_1) Let us suppose that each random variables X_j^{md} is uniformly distributed in the interval $[a, b]$; at each iteration is randomly selected 375 values of each variable X_j^{md};

s_2) The random variable Y^{md} is supposed to be related to variables X_j^{md} according to $Y^{md} = (\mathbf{X}^{md})^T \boldsymbol{\beta} + \epsilon$, where $(\mathbf{X}^{md})^T = (1, X_1^{md})$ and $\boldsymbol{\beta} = (\beta_0 = U[c,d], \beta_1 = U[c,d])^T$ in $\Re^2$, or $(\mathbf{X}^{md})^T = (1, X_1^{md}, X_2^{md}, X_3^{md})$ and $\boldsymbol{\beta} = (\beta_0 = U[c,d], \beta_1 = U[c,d], \beta_2 = U[c,d], \beta_3 = U[c,d])^T$ in $\Re^4$ and $\epsilon = U[e, f]$; the mid-points of these 375 intervals are calculated according this linear relation;

s_3) Once obtained the mid-points of the intervals, let us consider now the range of each interval. Let us suppose that each random variable Y^r, X_j^r ($j = 1, 2, 3$) is uniformly distributed, respectively, in the intervals $[g, h]$ and $[i, j]$; at each iteration is randomly selected 375 values of each variable Y^r, X_j^r, which are the range of these intervals;

s_4) The interval-valued data set is partitioned in a learning (250 observations) and test (125 observations) data sets.

Table 1 shows nine different configurations for the interval data sets which are used to compare the performance of the **UCM**, **UCRM** and **MCRM** methods in different situations.

Table 1. Data set configurations

C_1	$X_j^{md} \sim U[20, 40]$	$X_j^r \sim U[20, 40]$	$Y^r \sim U[20, 40]$	$\epsilon \sim U[-20, 20]$
C_2	$X_j^{md} \sim U[20, 40]$	$X_j^r \sim U[20, 40]$	$Y^r \sim U[20, 40]$	$\epsilon \sim U[-10, 10]$
C_3	$X_j^{md} \sim U[20, 40]$	$X_j^r \sim U[20, 40]$	$Y^r \sim U[20, 40]$	$\epsilon \sim U[-5, 5]$
C_4	$X_j^{md} \sim U[20, 40]$	$X_j^r \sim U[10, 20]$	$Y^r \sim U[10, 20]$	$\epsilon \sim U[-20, 20]$
C_5	$X_j^{md} \sim U[20, 40]$	$X_j^r \sim U[10, 20]$	$Y^r \sim U[10, 20]$	$\epsilon \sim U[-10, 10]$
C_6	$X_j^{md} \sim U[20, 40]$	$X_j^r \sim U[10, 20]$	$Y^r \sim U[10, 20]$	$\epsilon \sim U[-5, 5]$
C_7	$X_j^{md} \sim U[20, 40]$	$X_j^r \sim U[1, 5]$	$Y^r \sim U[1, 5]$	$\epsilon \sim U[-20, 20]$
C_8	$X_j^{md} \sim U[20, 40]$	$X_j^r \sim U[1, 5]$	$Y^r \sim U[1, 5]$	$\epsilon \sim U[-10, 10]$
C_9	$X_j^{md} \sim U[20, 40]$	$X_j^r \sim U[1, 5]$	$Y^r \sim U[1, 5]$	$\epsilon \sim U[-5, 5]$

These configurations take into account the combination of two factors (range and error on the mid-points) with three degrees of variability (low, medium and high): low variability range ($U[1, 5]$), medium variability range ($U[10, 20]$), high variability range ($U[20,40]$, low variability error ($U[-5,5]$), medium variability error ($U[-10,10]$) and high variability error ($U[-20,20]$).

The configuration C_1, for example, represents observations with a high variability range and with a poor linear relationship between Y and the dependent variables due the high variability error on the mid-points.

In the other hand, the configuration C_9 represent observations with a low variability range and with a rich linear relationship between Y and the dependent variables due the low variability error on the mid-points.

3.2 Experimental Evaluation

The evaluation of the performance of these linear regression models (**UCM**, **UCRM** and **MCRM** approaches) is based on the following measures: the *lower bound root mean-squared error* ($RMSE_L$), the *upper bound root mean-squared error* ($RMSE_U$), the *lower bound determination coefficient* (R_L^2) and the *upper bound determination coefficient* (R_U^2). These measures are obtained from the observed values $y_i = [y_{Li}, y_{Ui}]$ ($i = 1, \ldots, n$) of Y and from their corresponding predicted values $\hat{y}_i = [\hat{y}_{Li}, \hat{y}_{Ui}]$, being denoted by:

$$RMSE_L = \sqrt{\frac{\sum_{i=1}^{n}(y_{Li} - \hat{y}_{Li})^2}{n}} \text{ and } RMSE_U = \sqrt{\frac{\sum_{i=1}^{n}(y_{Ui} - \hat{y}_{Ui})^2}{n}} \quad (10)$$

$$R_L^2 = \left(\frac{Cov(\mathbf{y}_L, \hat{\mathbf{y}}_L)}{S_{\mathbf{y}_L} S_{\hat{\mathbf{y}}_L}}\right)^2 \text{ and } R_U^2 = \left(\frac{Cov(\mathbf{y}_U, \hat{\mathbf{y}}_U)}{S_{\mathbf{y}_U} S_{\hat{\mathbf{y}}_U}}\right)^2 \quad (11)$$

where: $\mathbf{y}_L = (y_{L1}, \ldots, y_{Ln})^T$, $\hat{\mathbf{y}}_L = (\hat{y}_{L1}, \ldots, \hat{y}_{Ln})^T$, $\mathbf{y}_U = (y_{U1}, \ldots, y_{Un})^T$, $\hat{\mathbf{y}}_U = (\hat{y}_{U1}, \ldots, \hat{y}_{Un})^T$, $Cov(\mathbf{y}_\bullet, \hat{\mathbf{y}}_\bullet)$ is the covariance between $\mathbf{y}_L$ and $\hat{\mathbf{y}}_L$ or between $\mathbf{y}_U$ and $\hat{\mathbf{y}}_U$, $S_{\mathbf{y}_\bullet}$ is the standard deviation of $\mathbf{y}_L$ or $\mathbf{y}_U$ and $S_{\hat{\mathbf{y}}_\bullet}$ is the standard deviation of $\hat{\mathbf{y}}_L$ or $\hat{\mathbf{y}}_U$.

These measures are estimated for the **UCM**, **UCRM** and **MCRM** methods in the framework of a Monte Carlo simulation with 100 replications for each independent test interval data set, for each of the nine fixed configurations, as well as for different numbers of independent variables in the model matrix. In each replication, a linear regression model is fitted on the training interval data set for each method (**UCM**, **UCRM** or **MCRM**) and used to predict the interval values of the dependent variable Y on the test interval data set and then, the measures are calculated. For each measure, the average and standard deviation over the 100 Monte Carlo simulation is calculated and then, a statistical t-test is applied to compare the performance of the new approaches proposed in this paper and the performance of the **UCM** method. Additionally, to a more consistence of the results, this procedure is repeated considering 100 different values for the parameter vector $\boldsymbol{\beta}$ selected randomly in the interval $[-10, 10]$.

The comparison between these approaches is achieved by three statistical t-test for independent samples, at a significance level of 1%, applied to each measure considered. For each configuration $C_1, \ldots, C_9$, number of independent variables and methods compared (**UCRM** vs **UCM**, **MCRM** vs **UCM** and **UCRM** vs **MCRM**) is calculated to each measure the ratio of times that the hypothesis H_0 is rejected, considering the 100 different vector of parameters $\boldsymbol{\beta}$.

Concerning the $RMSE_L$ and $RMSE_U$ measures, the null and alternative hypotheses for the three methods are: 1) H_0 : **UCRM** $\geq$ **UCM** versus H_1: **UCRM** < **UCM**; 2) H_0 : **MCRM** $\geq$ **UCM** versus H_1: **MCRM** < **UCM**; 3) H_0 : **MCRM** $\geq$ **UCRM** versus H_1: **MCRM** < **UCRM**.

On the other hand, concerning R_L^2 and R_U^2 measures, the hypotheses are: 1) H_0 : **UCRM** $\leq$ **UCM** versus H_1: **UCRM** > **UCM**; 2) H_0 : **MCRM** $\leq$ **UCM** versus H_1: **MCRM** > **UCM**; 3) H_0 : **MCRM** $\leq$ **UCRM** versus H_1: **MCRM** > **UCRM**.

In the Table 2 we illustrate for the **UCRM** and **UCM** methods, the statistical t-test at a significance level of 1%, for a specific values of the vector of parameters $\boldsymbol{\beta}$ in $\Re^2$ ($\beta_0 = 5, \beta_1 = 1.5$) and $\Re^4$ ($\beta_0 = 5, \beta_1 = 1.5, \beta_2 = -2, \beta_3 = 0.5$).

Table 2. Observed values (and corresponding p-values) of the test statistics following a Students's t distribution with 198 degrees of freedom

Configuration	p	$RMSE_L$		$RMSE_U$		R_L^2 (%)		R_U^2 (%)	
		T	p-value	T	p-value	T	p-value	T	p-value
1	1	-20.26	0.0000	-21.04	0.0000	7.51	0.0000	7.37	0.0000
	3	-33.77	0.0000	-36.12	0.0000	15.66	0.0000	17.46	0.0000
2	1	-41.01	0.0000	-42.18	0.0000	17.10	0.0000	18.51	0.0000
	3	-64.44	0.0000	-64.72	0.0000	31.24	0.0000	36.70	0.0000
3	1	-83.45	0.0000	-87.57	0.0000	39.66	0.0000	36.84	0.0000
	3	-122.14	0.0000	-135.13	0.0000	44.30	0.0000	52.38	0.0000
4	1	-9.81	0.0000	-9.39	0.0000	2.57	0.0055	2.74	0.0034
	3	-20.35	0.0000	-19.59	0.0000	5.30	0.0000	5.47	0.0000
5	1	-25.78	0.0000	-26.02	0.0000	6.56	0.0000	6.09	0.0000
	3	-48.40	0.0000	-52.79	0.0000	16.05	0.0000	14.43	0.0000
6	1	-51.68	0.0000	-54.25	0.0000	20.20	0.0000	17.87	0.0000
	3	-94.70	0.0000	-95.90	0.0000	31.33	0.0000	36.36	0.0000
7	1	-0.83	0.2031	-0.95	0.1717	0.30	0.3805	0.52	0.3010
	3	-2.49	0.0068	-2.63	0.0047	0.86	0.1953	1.05	0.1485
8	1	-3.26	0.0007	-2.63	0.0046	1.51	0.0668	1.21	0.1136
	3	-11.43	0.0000	-10.81	0.0000	3.18	0.0008	3.57	0.0002
9	1	-10.63	0.0000	-9.98	0.0000	5.44	0.0000	4.90	0.0000
	3	-27.55	0.0000	-27.98	0.0000	11.10	0.0000	11.30	0.0000

In the Tables 3 and 4 we show, respectively, the comparison between the **UCRM** vs **UCM** methods and **MCRM** vs **UCM** methods, and present the percentage of rejection of the null hypothesis H_0 for the 100 different configurations of the vector of parameters $\boldsymbol{\beta}$.

From Tables 3 and 4 we can see that the percentage of rejection of the null hypothesis at a significance level of 1%, regardless the number of variables or the performance measure considered, is always higher than 53%. This indicate

Table 3. Comparison between the **UCRM** vs **UCM** methods - Percentage of rejection of the null hypothesis H_0 (T-test for independent samples following a Student's t distribution with 198 degrees of freedom)

Configuration	p	$RMSE_L$	$RMSE_U$	R_L^2 (%)	R_U^2 (%)
1	1	100%	100%	95%	95%
	3	100%	100%	100%	100%
2	1	100%	100%	97%	96%
	3	100%	100%	100%	100%
3	1	100%	100%	98%	98%
	3	100%	100%	100%	100%
4	1	99%	99%	79%	79%
	3	100%	100%	100%	100%
5	1	100%	100%	91%	90%
	3	100%	100%	100%	100%
6	1	100%	100%	97%	96%
	3	100%	100%	100%	100%
7	1	95%	94%	57%	56%
	3	100%	100%	97%	97%
8	1	92%	92%	78%	78%
	3	100%	100%	100%	100%
9	1	99%	99%	88%	87%
	3	100%	100%	100%	100%

Table 4. Comparison between the **MCRM** vs **UCM** methods - Percentage of rejection of the null hypothesis H_0 (T-test for independent samples following a Student's t distribution with 198 degrees of freedom)

Configuration	p	$RMSE_L$	$RMSE_U$	R_L^2 (%)	R_U^2 (%)
1	1	100%	100%	94%	94%
	3	100%	100%	100%	100%
2	1	100%	100%	97%	96%
	3	100%	100%	100%	100%
3	1	100%	100%	97%	98%
	3	100%	100%	100%	100%
4	1	99%	99%	79%	79%
	3	100%	100%	100%	100%
5	1	100%	100%	90%	90%
	3	100%	100%	100%	100%
6	1	100%	100%	97%	96%
	3	100%	100%	100%	100%
7	1	94%	94%	55%	54%
	3	100%	100%	93%	93%
8	1	91%	91%	77%	77%
	3	100%	100%	100%	100%
9	1	98%	97%	86%	87%
	3	100%	100%	100%	100%

that the new approaches (**UCRM** and **MCRM**) in average, considering different vector of parameters β, has a better performance than the **UCM** approach. When the number of independent variables is 3, for the configurations $C_1, C_2, C_3, C_4, C_5, C_6, C_8, C_9$, the null hypothesis H_0 was rejected in 100% of the cases.

Notice that only in the configuration C_7 with $p = 1$ the methods **UCRM** and **MCRM** presented a percentage of rejection of the null hypothesis lower than 78% and 77%, respectively, for the measures R_L^2 and R_U^2. This results was expected because this configuration represents an interval data with a low variability range and with a poor linear relationship due the high variability error on the mid-points.

Additionally, in all configurations, the growing of the number of independent variables produced an increase in the percentage of rejection of the null hypothesis H_0. This means that the performance difference between the **UCRM** and **MCRM** methods and the **UCM** method, increases when the number of independent variables in the model increases.

Now, comparing the configurations $C_1, C_2,$ and C_3, that differ with respect to the error on the mid-points of the intervals, notice that when the variability of the error decreases, the percentage of rejection of the null hypothesis H_0 increases. This shows that, as much linear is the relationship between the variables as higher is the statistical significance of the difference between the new approaches and the current method. We arrive the same conclusion comparing the configurations (C_4, C_5, C_6) and (C_7, C_8, C_9).

On the other hand, comparing the configurations C_1, C_4 and C_7, that differ with respect to the variability on the range of the intervals, notice that when the interval's range decreases, the percentage of rejection of the null hypothesis H_0 decreases too. This result was expected because if the range of the intervals approaches zero, we would have the **UCM** method as an special case of the **UCRM** and **MCRM** methods. We have a similar conclusion comparing the configurations (C_2, C_5, C_8) and (C_3, C_6, C_9).

Finally, concerning the comparison of the performance of the **UCRM** and **MCRM** methods, the results obtained in the experimental process indicated that the null hypothesis was never rejected at a significance level of 1%, regardless the number of variables, the performance measure considered or the configuration. This means that the average performance of **MCRM** is not better than the **UCRM** methods. Moreover, how the **MCRM** method use the double of variables in the model matrix **X**, when compared with the **UCRM** method, we conclude that the **UCRM** method is preferred.

3.3   Cardiological Interval-Valued Data Set

This data set concerns the record of the pulse rate Y, the systolic blood pressure X_1 and diastolic blood pressure X_2 for each of eleven patients (see [2]). Table 5 shows this interval data set. The aim is to predict the interval values y of Y (the dependent variable) from x_j ($j = 1, 2$) through a linear regression model.

Table 5. Cardiological interval data set

u	Pulse rate	Systolic blood pressure	Diastolic blood pressure
1	[44-68]	[90-100]	[50-70]
2	[60-72]	[90-130]	[70-90]
3	[56-90]	[140-180]	[90-100]
4	[70-112]	[110-142]	[80-108]
5	[54-72]	[90-100]	[50-70]
6	[70-100]	[130-160]	[80-110]
7	[63-75]	[60-100]	[140-150]
8	[72-100]	[130-160]	[76-90]
9	[76-98]	[110-190]	[70-110]
10	[86-96]	[138-180]	[90-110]
11	[86-100]	[110-150]	[78-100]

The performance of the **UCRM** and **MCRM** methods in comparison with the **UCM** method is evaluated through the calculation of $RMSE_L$, $RMSE_U$, R_L^2 and R_U^2 measures on this cardiological interval data set. These measures evaluate the performance of the models identifying the best fit on the data set. For the **UCM** method, we have: $RMSE_L = 11.0942$, $RMSE_U = 10.4136$, $R_L^2 = 0.3029$, $R_U^2 = 0.5347$. For the **UCRM** method, we have: $RMSE_L = 9.8096$, $RMSE_U = 8.9414$, $R_L^2 = 0.4154$, $R_U^2 = 0.6334$; and for the **MCRM** method we have: $RMSE_L = 8.5748$, $RMSE_U = 7.4185$, $R_L^2 = 0.5325$, $R_U^2 = 0.7293$.

From these results we conclude the **UCRM** and **MCRM** methods outperforms the **UCM** method also on this cardiological interval data set. In contrast with the results of the simulated test data sets, the **MCRM** method presented a better performance when compared with the **UCRM** method. However, this result was observed in the simulated training data set and show an overfitting of the **MCRM** method over the data. In the real data set this result occurred due the reduced number of observation and the double of parameters used in this method when compared with the **UCRM** method.

4 Concluding Remarks

In this paper, we presented two new methods to fit a linear regression model on interval-valued data. The first method fits two independent linear regression models, respectively, on the mid-point and range of the interval values assumed by the variables on the learning set. The second approach fits a multivariate linear regression models on the mid-point and range of the interval values assumed by the variables on the learning set. This means that in this model the prediction of the mid-point (and the range) of the interval value of the dependent variable is a linear function of the mid-point and range of each interval value assumed by the independent variables. In both approaches, the prediction of the lower and upper bound of the interval value of the dependent variable is accomplished from the mid-point and range which were estimated from the fitted linear regression models applied to the mid-point and range of each interval value of the independent variables. Thus, with these new approaches, is possible to reconstruct the bounds of the interval value of the dependent variable in a more efficiency way.

The Monte Carlo simulations showed that the superiority of the methods introduced in this paper, measured by the percentage of rejection of the null hypothesis concerning the *root mean-squared error* and *determination coefficient* measures, when compared with the **UCM** method, is statistically significant. In particular, the performance difference between **UCRM** (or **MCRM**) and the **UCM** methods, increases when the number of independent variables considered in the model increases or when the linear relationship between the variables is stronger, and decreases when the interval's range decreases. This last result was expected because if the range of the intervals approaches zero, we would have the **UCM** method as an special case of the **UCRM** and **MCRM** methods. The **UCRM** method is preferred when compared with the **MCRM** method because the number of variables in the **UCRM** method is smaller than the **MCRM** method. Finally, the **UCRM** and **MCRM** methods outperforms the **UCM** method also in the cardiological interval data set.

Acknowledgments. The authors would like to thank CNPq and CAPES (Brazilian Agencies) for their financial support.

References

1. Bock, H.H. and Diday, E.: Analysis of Symbolic Data: Exploratory Methods for Extracting Statistical Information from Complex Data. Springer, Berlin Heidelberg (2000)
2. Billard, L., Diday, E.: Regression Analysis for Interval-Valued Data. Data Analysis, Classification and Related Methods: Proceedings of the Seventh Conference of the International Federation of Classification Societies, IFCS-2000, Namur (Belgium), Kiers, H.A.L. et al. Eds, Vol. 1 (2000), Springer, 369–374
3. Billard, L., Diday, E.: Symbolic Regression Analysis. Classification, Clustering and Data Analysis: Proceedings of the Eighenth Conference of the International Federation of Classification Societies, IFCS-2002, Crakow (Poland), Jajuga, K. et al. Eds, Vol. 1 (2002), Springer, 281–288
4. Billard, L., Diday, E.: From the Statistics of Data to the Statistics of Knowledge: Symbolic Data Analysis. Journal of the American Statistical Association, Vol. 98 (2003) 470-487
5. Draper, N.R., Smith, H.: Applied Regression Analysis. John Wiley, New York (1981)
6. Montgomery, D.C., Peck, E.A.: Introduction to Linear Regression Analysis. John Wiley, New York (1982)
7. Scheffé, H.: The Analysis of Variance. John Wiley, New York, (1959)

Using Classification to Evaluate the Output of Confidence-Based Association Rule Mining

Stefan Mutter[1,2], Mark Hall[2], and Eibe Frank[2]

[1] Department of Computer Science, University of Freiburg, Freiburg, Germany
mutter@informatik.uni-freiburg.de
[2] Department of Computer Science, University of Waikato, Hamilton, New Zealand
{mhall, eibe}@cs.waikato.ac.nz

Abstract. Association rule mining is a data mining technique that reveals interesting relationships in a database. Existing approaches employ different parameters to search for interesting rules. This fact and the large number of rules make it difficult to compare the output of confidence-based association rule miners. This paper explores the use of classification performance as a metric for evaluating their output. Previous work on forming classifiers from association rules has focussed on accurate classification, whereas we concentrate on using the properties of the resulting classifiers as a basis for comparing confidence-based association rule learners. Therefore, we present experimental results on 12 UCI datasets showing that the quality of small rule sets generated by Apriori can be improved by using the predictive Apriori algorithm. We also show that CBA, the standard method for classification using association rules, is generally inferior to standard rule learners concerning both running time and size of rule sets.

1 Introduction

Association rule mining is a widely-used approach in data mining. Association rules are capable of revealing all interesting relationships in a potentially large database. However, a major problem in association rule mining is its complexity. Even for moderate-sized databases it is intractable to find all the relationships. This is why a mining approach defines an interestingness measure to guide the search and prune the search space. Therefore, the result of an association rule mining algorithm is not the set of all possible relationships, but the set of all interesting ones. The definition of the term interesting, however, depends on the application. The different interestingness measures and the large number of rules make it difficult to compare the output of different association rule mining algorithms. There is a lack of comparison measures for the quality of association rule mining algorithms and their interestingness measures. In this paper we focus on *confidence-based* association rule mining. Here the term 'confidence-based' refers to those association rule learners that use the confidence (i.e. accuracy) of a rule as the interestingness measure.

Association rule mining algorithms are often compared using time complexity. That is an important issue of the mining process, but the quality of the resulting rule set is ignored. On the other hand there are approaches that investigate the discriminating power of association rules and use them to solve classification problems. This research area is called *classification using association rules*. An important aspect of classification using association rules is that it can provide quality measures for the output of the underlying mining process. The properties of the resulting classifier can be the basis for comparisons between different confidence-based association rule mining algorithms. A certain mining algorithm is preferable when the mined rule set forms a more accurate, compact and stable classifier in an efficient way.

The introduction of these quality measures—particularly the accuracy of the classifier—kills two birds with one stone. First, we are interested in the comparison of the quality of different confidence-based mining algorithms. Therefore, we use classification using association rules. Secondly, classification using association rules can be improved itself by using a mining algorithm that prefers highly accurate rules. In this paper we compare two different rule mining strategies combined with several different approaches to classification using association rules.

The rest of the paper is organised as follows. In Section 2 we explain the mining, pruning, and classification algorithms used for our study. Section 3 describes our experimental methodology, followed by a discussion of results. We present our conclusions in Section 4.

2 Algorithms

The algorithmic approach for classification using association rules can be divided into three fundamental parts: association rule mining, pruning, and classification.

2.1 Association Rule Mining

We used two different methods for rule mining—the Apriori algorithm introduced by Agrawal and Srikant [1] that has become a standard approach and the predictive Apriori algorithm published by Scheffer [11]. The most significant difference between the two relates to how the interestingness of an association rule is measured. Although both are confidence-based, the confidence is estimated differently. Both algorithms start the same way by building frequent item sets. An item set is called frequent when its support is above a predefined minimum support. It is possible to construct frequent item sets in reasonable time because of their support-based downward closure. An item set X of length k is frequent if and only if all subsets of X with length $k - 1$ are frequent. This property allows the search space to be pruned substantially.

Rule discovery using Apriori is straightforward. For every frequent item set f and every non-empty subset s of f, Apriori outputs a rule of the form $s \Rightarrow (f - s)$ if and only if the confidence of that rule is above the user-specified threshold. The confidence is simply the accuracy of the rule. The rules are ranked according to this confidence value. If two or more rules share the same confidence they are ordered using their support and secondly the time of discovery. Hence Apriori's interestingness measure is the confidence of a rule.

The interestingness measure of predictive Apriori suits the requirements of a classification task. It tries to maximise the expected accuracy of an association rule instead of the accuracy on the training data (as measured by the simple confidence measure in

Apriori). The probability of a correct prediction given the database under consideration is called the predictive accuracy. Scheffer [11] defines it in the following way:

Let D be a database whose individual records r are generated by a static process P, let $X \Rightarrow Y$ be an association rule. The predictive accuracy $c(X \Rightarrow Y) = Pr(r \text{ satisfies } Y | r \text{ satisfies } X)$ is the conditional probability of $Y \subseteq r$ given that $X \subseteq r$ when the distribution of r is governed by P [11].

The confidence $\hat{c}(X \Rightarrow Y)$ of an association rule $X \Rightarrow Y$ is the relative frequency of a correct classification in the training database. Hence the confidence value is optimistically biased. However, it can be corrected using the support of the rule under consideration by computing the expected predictive accuracy $E(c(r)|\hat{c}(r), s(X))$ of a rule $r\ X \Rightarrow Y$ given its confidence $\hat{c}$ and the support of the rule body $s(X)$. Scheffer [11] calculates it as

$$E(c(r)|\hat{c}(r), s(X)) = \frac{\int cB[c, s(X)](\hat{c}(r))P(c)dc}{\int B[c, s(X)](\hat{c}(r))P(c)dc}$$

using Bayes formula and exploiting the fact that the likelihood $P(\hat{c}(r)|c(r), s(X))$ can be modeled by the binomial distribution $B[c, s(X)](\hat{c}(r))$. $P(c)$ is the prior distribution. We use discretisation to approximate these integrals. Scheffer suggests dividing the predictive accuracy c into 100 discrete intervals and using the midpoint of each interval for calculation.[1] Because of discretisation the above integrals become sums over all possible (100) values of c. The second problem to cope with is the prior distribution. In order to estimate it, for each discretised predictive accuracy value, the fraction of association rules which have this accuracy is counted. Thus, to derive the real prior distribution we would have to investigate the space of all association rules which is intractable. The solution is to draw many association rules at random under the uniform distribution. Scheffer suggests drawing 1000 random association rules for each possible length.[1] In addition, predictive Apriori has an inherent pruning strategy that prefers more general rules. Therefore it searches for the n best rules according to the following criteria:

1. the predictive accuracy of the rule is among the n best and
2. it is not subsumed by a rule with at least the same predictive accuracy

The parameter n is user specified. These criteria differ slightly from the ones published in the predictive Apriori paper [11] where all n best rules are not subsumed by any other rule in that list. This version of the predictive Apriori algorithm originates from an unpublished manuscript by Scheffer [10]. In our opinion it better suits the requirements of a classification task, because highly accurate rules which are subsumed by less accurate ones remain part of the output.

In contrast to Apriori, predictive Apriori uses an increasing support threshold. Out of each frequent item set rules are generated and added to the best n rules so far if the above conditions apply. If one rule has to be deleted out of the list of the best n because of subsumption, we have to recursively re-run the rule generating procedure because another rule which previously did not make it into the best n could now qualify for inclusion.

---

[1] In personal communication via e-mail.

```
1. Input: rule set sorted according to interestingness measure
2. For all rules r in sorted order DO:
3.      For all training instances d DO:
4.          If r covers d Then
5.              mark d.
6.              If r classifies d correctly Then
7.                  mark r.
8.          If r is marked Then
9.              delete all instances d that are marked.
10.             insert r into an intermediate classifier C
11.             select the majority class label out of the training instances d as default.
12.             For all training instances DO:
13.                 classify using C and count the total number of errors made by C.
14.         Else
15.             delete all marks from each training instance d.
16. Find the rule $r_{min}$ with the lowest number of errors.
17. From $r_{min}$ accept all subsequent rules as long as the error does not increase. The last rule accepted is $r_{stop}$.
18. Delete all rules after $r_{stop}$.
19. The default class associated with $r_{stop}$ is the default class of the classifier.
```

Fig. 1. The CBA pruning algorithm. The scheme is an adapted version of Liu et al. [6]

Note that association rules in their general form cannot be used directly for a classification task. The head Y of an association rule $X \Rightarrow Y$ (with rule body X) has to be restricted to one attribute-value-pair. The attribute of this attribute-value-pair is consequently the class attribute. An association rule of this form is called a *class association rule*. We have adapted both algorithms to mine class association rules. For Apriori, we used the method described by Liu et al. [6]. The training data is divided into n subsets— one for each class. Frequent item sets are then found for each subset separately. For each frequent item set a rule is generated by appending a consequent which is the class label of the subset from which it was mined.

Predictive Apriori constructs rules out of frequent item sets generated from all the data (after the class attribute has been deleted) and considers generating a rule for each value of the class attribute for every frequent item set. As before, a rule is kept if its expected predictive accuracy is among the n best. In addition, the prior distribution has to be estimated for class association rules.

2.2 Pruning

Pruning is an essential step in classification using association rules and a crucial difference between existing approaches. A very simple strategy is to bound the number of rules without any closer inspection of the rules themselves. An advantage of this strategy in a comparative study of association rule mining algorithms is that it does not change the sort order induced by the rule miner.

The second pruning approach used in this paper is the pruning method introduced by Liu et al. [6] in their CBA algorithm. It consists of an obligatory and an optional pruning step. The obligatory pruning step is summarised in Figure 1. Our implementation of CBA cannot reproduce all the results from the CBA paper [6]. However, using the algorithmic step in line 17 of Figure 1 (deleting all rules after r_{stop} and not after r_{min} as described in the CBA paper [6]) we were able to reproduce some of the results. The optional pruning step is based on the pessimistic error-rate-based pruning as introduced by Quinlan [8]. It works the following way: for every mined rule r $X \Rightarrow Y$ where $X = x_1 \wedge \ldots \wedge x_n$ is a conjunction of items x_i, the algorithm checks to see if removing any single item from rule r results in a reduction of the pessimistic error rate. If so, r is pruned. When used, error-based pruning is always performed as a preprocessing step before the obligatory pruning step.

2.3 Classification

For a set of classification rules there are two fundamental approaches to using them for classification: a weighted vote algorithm or a decision list classifier.

The simplest voting scheme is a majority vote where each rule r is equally weighted with weight $w(r) = 1$. In addition we explored a weighting scheme using the inverse function $f(x) = \frac{1}{x}$ for weighting. For each rule r its weight $w(r)$ is calculated using:

$$w(r) = \frac{1}{rank(r)}$$ where $rank(r) \in \{1, \ldots, R\}$ and R is the number of rules.

This weighting scheme emphasises the difference between the top-ranked rules and the bottom-ranked ones, because rules at the bottom of the sorted list only get a little weight and so only have a small influence.

The standard classifier for classification using association rules—the CBA algorithm [6]—is a decision list classifier. Compared to pruning, classification is very simple in CBA. It just searches the pruned and ordered list for the first rule that covers the instance to be classified. The prediction is the class label of that classification rule. If no rule covers the instance, CBA uses the default class calculated during pruning (see Figure 1). If the decision list is empty, the majority class of the training instances will be assigned to each test instance as default. CBA uses a rule limit. It stops the search for association rules after investigating 80000 rules regardless whether they fulfil the requirements of the minimum support and confidence or not. In our experiments we did not use this cutoff—instead we varied the number of rules mined in order to better explore the behaviour of the association rule learners.

3 Experiments

For our experiments we used 12 datasets from the UCI repository [2], shown in Table 1. A rule mining strategy is preferable if it allows a compact and accurate classifier to be formed from the mined set of rules. Therefore we used the following performance measures:

- the percentage of instances correctly classified in the test set,
- the average rank of the first rule that covers and correctly predicts a test instance,
- the number of mined rules generated by a class association rule miner,
- the number of rules after the pruning step,
- the time required for mining, and
- the time required for pruning.

In every experiment the support threshold s_{min} of Apriori was set to 1% of all instances and the confidence threshold $\hat{c}_{min}$ was set to 0.5—the standard thresholds for

Table 1. The UCI datasets used for the experiments and their properties. In the led7 dataset 10% of the instances are noisy

Dataset	Instances	Numeric attributes	Binary attributes	Nominal attributes	Classes	Missing values (%)
balance	625	4	0	0	3	0.0
breast-w	699	0	0	9	2	0.3
ecoli	336	7	0	0	8	0.0
glass	214	9	0	0	6	0.0
heart-h	294	6	3	4	2	20.4
iris	150	4	0	0	3	0.0
labor	57	8	3	5	2	35.7
led7	1000	0	7	0	10	0.0
lenses	24	0	0	4	3	0.0
pima	768	8	0	0	2	0.0
tic-tac-toe	958	0	0	9	2	0.0
wine	178	13	0	0	3	0.0

support and confidence. When indicated, we restricted the number n of mined rules for Apriori and predictive Apriori (the only input parameter for predictive Apriori).

Class association rule mining as well as association rule mining in general is only possible for nominal attributes.[2] Therefore we needed to discretise the numeric attributes in our datasets for these methods. We used Fayyad and Irani's [4] maximum entropy method for discretisation. To process missing values at classification time, they were treated as different from all other attribute values. All experimental results were obtained using one ten-fold stratified cross-validation. We report statistically significant results at the 5% significance level using the corrected resampled t-test proposed by Nadeau and Bengio [7] and applying a Bonferroni adjustment as suggested by Salzberg [9]. In addition we show the standard deviation for each result. All algorithms used in the experiments were implemented within the WEKA machine learning framework [12].[3]

3.1 Compactness of Rule Sets

As Table 2 shows, Apriori mines considerably more rules than predictive Apriori but most of them are pruned in the final set of classification rules. The advantage of predictive Apriori is that it generates fewer rules right from the start.

3.2 Rule Ranking

In this section we investigate whether highly accurate and general rules are preferred by the ranking system of the mining algorithms. To this end we measured the average rank of the first rule that covered an instance and predicted it correctly. For this comparison, both association rule mining algorithms mined the 100 highest ranked rules for every dataset. We calculated a default class which is the majority class in the training instances. If no rule covered a test instance and the default class predicted the instance correctly, the count was set to the number of mined rules incremented by one, otherwise it was set to the number of mined rules incremented by two. The results are summarised in

---

[2] Association rule mining for numeric-valued attributes is still an open area of research.
[3] WEKA is available from http://www.cs.waikato.ac.nz/ml/weka

Table 2. The compactness of the rule sets mined by different association rule mining algorithms. Table (a) compares the number of mined rules when we do not restrict their number. The number of rules left after error-based pruning is shown in (b) and (c) shows the size of the final rule set used by CBA when it receives the rules from Table (b) as input

Dataset	Apriori	Pred. Apriori
balance	72.2 ± 13.07	78.7 ± 10.29•
breast-w	5124.9 ± 65.50	906.8 ±325.34o
ecoli	888.2 ± 152.35	304.4 ± 22.51o
glass	6055.2 ± 454.27	472.1 ±144.56o
heart-h	19886.8 ± 757.08	324.9 ± 18.71o
iris	96.5 ± 14.25	29.8 ± 8.34o
labor	96084.3 ±5569.42	228.9 ± 21.79o
led7	510.6 ± 13.50	1565.9 ± 20.44•
lenses	121.8 ± 3.52	28.8 ± 10.03o
pima	3311.4 ± 311.11	179.5 ± 43.16o
tic-tac-toe	7642.5 ± 42.23	6289.6 ±105.04o
wine	87427.9 ±5066.97	1034.2 ±714.36o

o, • statistically significant improvement or degradation
(a)

Dataset	Apriori	Pred. Apriori
balance	28.9 ± 2.23	50.9 ± 2.85•
breast-w	2975.9 ± 105.44	137.9 ± 46.91o
ecoli	333.2 ± 24.52	221.2 ± 16.45o
glass	1661.6 ± 161.29	307.6 ± 93.20o
heart-h	1242.2 ± 62.28	188.4 ± 10.31o
iris	28.4 ± 3.27	13.5 ± 1.35o
labor	79371.8 ±4747.00	62.0 ± 7.90o
led7	330.5 ± 15.76	1053.3 ± 22.18•
lenses	31.4 ± 2.91	10.6 ± 4.43o
pima	461.0 ± 46.47	87.0 ± 18.05o
tic-tac-toe	1180.8 ± 17.84	1731.9 ± 28.83•
wine	36396.5 ±3710.72	554.3 ±383.79o

o, • statistically significant improvement or degradation
(b)

Dataset	Apriori	Pred. Apriori
balance	14.1 ±0.57	14.1 ± 0.57
breast-w	103.5 ±4.84	37.8 ±11.28o
ecoli	19.8 ±2.35	20.3 ± 1.83
glass	27.3 ±2.45	22.7 ± 2.87o
heart-h	38.8 ±3.39	33.1 ± 2.85o
iris	5.6 ±0.84	5.6 ± 0.70
labor	26.7 ±2.45	8.7 ± 1.83o
led7	60.4 ±3.24	62.0 ± 2.91•
lenses	20.2 ±1.03	2.6 ± 2.76o
pima	39.7 ±6.62	39.0 ± 6.63
tic-tac-toe	155.8 ±5.92	166.6 ± 6.52•
wine	30.7 ±5.06	7.6 ± 5.27o

o, • statistically significant improvement or degradation
(c)

Figure 2. Predictive Apriori outperforms Apriori in two third of the datasets. This fact indicates that predictive Apriori tends to rank high quality rules higher. The problem with using Apriori's confidence-based ordering without a support-based correction is that rules with low support tend to have high confidence. These rules are very specific and prone to noise.

3.3 Accuracy

In the context of a comparison of mining algorithms a weighted classifier with non-uniform weights emphasises the importance of a good rule ranking induced by the mining algorithms. This is because the higher the ranking of a rule is, the more strongly weighted is its prediction. The overall accuracy on a test set is higher for that mining algorithm that has a better sorting of the mined rules according to their accuracy. Figure 3 illustrates the results.

The predictive Apriori algorithm with an inversely weighted classifier outperforms Apriori on every data set except for balance. For both algorithms the number of mined rules was restricted to 100. The inverse weighting function relies on the discriminative

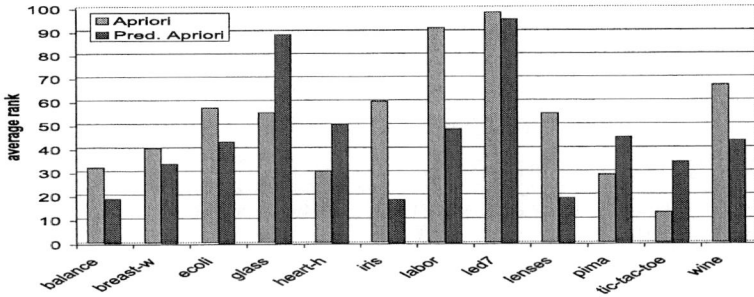

Fig. 2. The differences in the rule ranking between the mining algorithms. Apriori and predictive Apriori both mine the best 100 rules. The figure shows the average rank of the first rule that covers and correctly predicts a test instance. All differences except for breast-w, pima and wine are significant at the 5% level

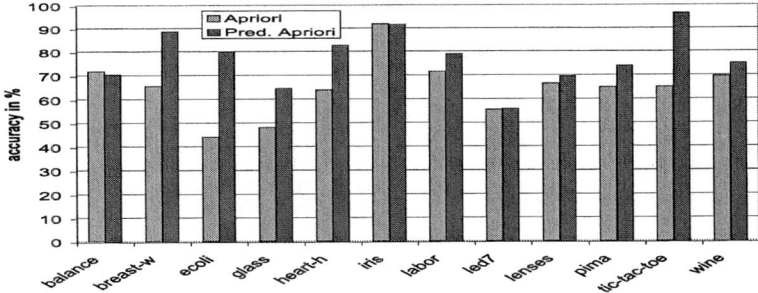

Fig. 3. The accuracies for different association rule mining algorithms using inversely weighted classifiers. The number n of mined rules was restricted to 100. Differences for breast-w, ecoli, heart-h, pima and tic-tac-toe are significant at the 5% level

power of the top ranked rules, because the classifier assigns much higher weights to them. This fact indicates that the predictive Apriori algorithm tends to rank high-quality rules at the top.

The next classification algorithm we used to compare our rule mining strategies is the majority vote algorithm. The main focus in this comparison is different than in the previous case. Here we are not interested in the individual ordering. A majority vote algorithm cannot provide any insights into this, because every rule has the same weight independent of the ranking. Instead, the majority vote algorithm can be used to evaluate how many rules are necessary to build an accurate classifier. The results can be found in Table 3.

They reveal an interesting property. For a small number of mined rules the accuracy using predictive Apriori is higher than that for Apriori. To build a comparable classifier with Apriori's rules the majority vote classifier needs more classification rules. A compact rule set built by predictive Apriori is better than a compact one built with Apriori. Apriori

Table 3. The accuracies of different mining algorithms using a majority vote classifier. The number n of mined rules was varied. The information about statistical significance is calculated separately for each n

Data Set	Pred. Apriori Apriori $n = 10$	Pred. Apriori Apriori $n = 100$	Pred. Apriori Apriori $n = 200$
balance	73.92± 5.20 74.40± 6.63	73.29± 5.41 76.46± 4.81	73.29± 5.41 76.46± 4.81
breast-w	65.47± 0.47 65.47± 0.47	88.65± 8.65 65.47± 0.47•	90.94± 9.24 65.47± 0.47•
ecoli	68.14± 7.72 42.56± 1.21•	76.81± 2.85 43.44± 2.56•	73.23± 5.32 68.12± 5.09
glass	49.09± 3.53 50.04± 9.11	61.06± 8.38 48.59± 5.80•	71.04± 7.88 46.71±11.90•
heart-h	77.52± 5.29 63.95± 1.43•	82.00± 6.34 63.95± 1.43•	84.38± 7.28 63.95± 1.43•
iris	90.67± 9.00 90.00±12.67	91.33± 9.45 92.67± 7.34	91.33± 9.45 92.00± 7.57
labor	80.67±15.46 64.67± 3.22•	86.67±15.32 73.33±15.07•	90.00±14.05 81.00±17.36
led7	27.60± 2.59 23.90± 2.51•	56.20± 4.57 56.10± 3.78	67.40± 5.19 64.40± 4.88•
lenses	70.00±28.11 63.33±32.20	68.33±33.75 68.33±33.75	68.33±33.75 68.33±33.75
pima	65.89± 1.71 65.11± 0.36	73.96± 4.18 65.11± 0.36•	72.93± 5.31 67.18± 4.76•
tic-tac-toe	74.21± 2.48 65.34± 0.43•	92.48± 3.09 65.34± 0.43•	85.38± 3.86 67.22± 1.51•
wine	65.36±21.14 65.23±10.53	77.71±26.79 66.90± 7.90	78.82±27.65 52.97±13.27•

Data Set	Pred. Apriori Apriori $n = 500$	Pred. Apriori Apriori $n = 700$	Pred. Apriori Apriori $n = 1000$
balance	73.29± 5.41 76.46± 4.81	73.29± 5.41 76.46± 4.81	73.29± 5.41 76.46± 4.81
breast-w	92.51± 9.95 65.90± 1.51•	91.65± 9.83 85.11± 3.76	90.36± 9.69 88.55± 4.03
ecoli	77.08± 6.04 74.98± 4.75	77.08± 6.04 79.18± 4.09	77.08± 6.04 79.77± 2.25
glass	63.9o± 7.56 60.24± 7.30	61.15± 4.94 63.10± 6.30	61.15± 4.94 63.48± 7.62
heart-h	82.34± 8.54 71.85±10.34•	82.34± 8.54 79.99± 5.42	82.34± 8.54 83.02± 6.35
iris	91.33± 9.45 92.00± 7.57	91.33± 9.45 92.00± 7.57	91.33± 9.45 92.00± 7.57
labor	80.67±17.34 76.00±20.05	80.67±17.34 77.67±24.09	80.67±17.34 76.00±17.69
led7	69.80± 4.42 72.40± 4.38o	74.60± 5.36 72.40± 4.50•	74.20± 5.07 72.40± 4.50
lenses	68.33±33.75 68.33±33.75	68.33±33.75 68.33±33.75	68.33±33.75 68.33±33.75
pima	74.49± 6.30 72.14± 4.51	74.49± 6.30 72.53± 4.91	74.49± 6.30 70.71± 3.59
tic-tac-toe	76.62± 2.39 97.91± 1.64o	75.79± 2.26 97.39± 1.80o	72.55± 1.49 98.01± 1.67o
wine	77.71±26.92 65.13±11.47	73.79±24.64 66.34±11.89	70.39±22.11 69.64±18.40

o, • statistically significant improvement or degradation

is able to catch up when the number of rules is increased. Using the best 1000 rules, Apriori has one significant win over predictive Apriori and no significant losses.

We also used a CBA decision list instead of majority voting. In this case—when the main focus is on different mining algorithms—we used CBA without error-based pruning. We observed the same behaviour as for the majority vote algorithm. For a small number of rules predictive Apriori outperforms Apriori as shown in Table 4.

3.4 Comparison with Standard Classification Techniques

We compared CBA to three standard techniques—one decision tree learner and two rule learners. The standard decision tree inducer C4.5 [8] was used. Every path in the tree from the root to a leaf node is considered as a rule. We also included JRip, WEKA's implementation of Cohen's RIPPER algorithm [3], and the PART algorithm for constructing decision lists from partial trees [5]. All three algorithms used their default parameters. In this section we compare the compactness and the accuracy of class association rules to that of the standard techniques.

Table 5 shows the results for the compactness, i.e. the number of rules used for classification. Even though using predictive Apriori results in a slightly smaller set of rules, the result of the comparison to the standard techniques is clear. The three algorithms C4.5, JRip and PART generate fewer rules than CBA. However, with respect to accuracy, Table 6 shows that CBA achieves results comparable to the standard rule learners.

Table 4. The accuracies of different mining algorithms using CBA without error-based pruning. The number n of mined rules was varied. The information about statistical significance is calculated separately for each n

Data Set	Pred. Apriori $n = 10$	Apriori	Pred. Apriori $n = 100$	Apriori	Pred. Apriori $n = 200$	Apriori
balance	66.73± 7.77	68.15± 4.74	71.50± 5.97	71.50± 5.97	71.50± 5.97	71.50± 5.97
breast-w	93.97± 3.40	89.40± 3.51●	94.25± 3.55	90.10± 4.32●	93.11± 3.20	94.97± 3.29
ecoli	68.72± 8.98	61.91± 2.63●	80.37± 2.43	62.79± 3.54●	80.07± 2.72	74.99± 5.31●
glass	47.66± 5.24	51.41± 8.60	70.56± 7.94	51.45± 5.79●	71.97± 8.77	49.11±11.21●
heart-h	77.86± 4.47	64.98± 1.19●	81.66± 7.03	68.36± 5.39●	79.94± 7.12	65.67± 3.86●
iris	90.67±10.04	93.33± 5.44	92.67± 6.63	92.67± 6.63	92.67± 6.63	92.67± 6.63
labor	67.00±12.81	70.00 ±11.86	81.00±20.61	74.00 ±19.93	79.00±19.50	72.67±16.54
led7	27.50± 2.59	23.90± 2.51●	62.40± 4.01	61.10± 4.72●	71.40± 5.50	68.70± 5.21●
lenses	68.33±33.75	61.67±28.38	63.33±32.20	66.67±30.43	63.33±32.20	66.67±30.43
pima	65.89± 1.71	65.11± 0.36	73.44± 4.81	65.11± 0.36●	74.09± 4.18	68.23± 5.62●
tic-tac-toe	100.00± 0.00	69.84± 2.49●	100.00± 0.00	74.85± 5.31●	100.00± 0.00	100.00± 0.00
wine	76.05±19.91	78.10±12.45	76.60±20.88	87.03± 7.61	79.38±21.25	86.05±10.21
Data Set	Pred. Apriori $n = 500$	Apriori	Pred. Apriori $n = 1000$	Apriori	Pred. Apriori n not restricted	Apriori
balance	71.50± 5.97	71.50± 5.97	71.50± 5.97	71.50± 5.97	71.50± 5.97	71.50± 5.97
breast-w	93.11± 3.26	95.40± 3.53○	93.97± 3.55	95.55± 2.92○	93.97± 3.55	95.13± 3.03
ecoli	80.07± 2.72	79.47± 7.12	80.07± 2.72	80.65± 3.24	80.07± 2.72	80.65± 3.24
glass	71.97± 8.77	57.08± 7.77●	71.97± 8.77	61.26±10.88●	71.97± 8.77	71.97± 8.77
heart-h	80.29± 6.39	76.60± 9.10	80.29± 6.39	80.97± 7.51	80.29± 6.39	80.63± 7.20
iris	92.67± 6.63	92.67± 6.63	92.67± 6.63	92.67± 6.63	92.67± 6.63	92.67± 6.63
labor	79.00±19.50	68.00± 8.64	79.00±19.50	77.67±19.88	79.00 ±19.50	79.00±19.50
led7	72.00± 5.16	72.30± 5.10	72.00± 5.16	72.30± 5.10	72.00± 5.16	72.30± 5.10
lenses	63.33±32.20	66.67±30.43	63.33±32.20	66.67±30.43	63.33±32.20	66.67±30.43
pima	74.09± 4.18	71.23± 3.83	74.09± 4.18	74.09± 4.81	74.09± 4.18	74.10± 4.48
tic-tac-toe	100.00± 0.00	100.00± 0.00	100.00± 0.00	100.00± 0.00	98.85± 1.44	99.06± 1.25
wine	79.38±21.25	87.12± 9.05	79.38±21.25	91.60± 7.08	79.38±21.25	93.82± 6.71

○, ● statistically significant improvement or degradation

Table 5. The compactness of CBA compared to standard techniques. CBA performed error-based pruning and did not restrict the number of rules output by the association rule miner

Dataset	CBA + Apriori	C4.5	JRip	PART	CBA + pred. Apriori
balance	14.10±0.57	39.60±6.00●	12.20±2.53	37.69±4.17●	14.10± 0.57
breast-w	103.50±4.84	28.00±6.00○	12.60±1.35○	10.10±3.03○	37.80±11.28○
ecoli	19.80±2.35	18.30±1.89	9.00±1.41○	13.60±2.17○	20.30± 1.83
glass	27.30±2.45	22.60±2.76○	8.20±0.92○	14.50±1.27○	22.70± 2.87○
heart-h	38.80±3.39	5.40±2.55○	3.30±0.67○	7.20±1.55○	33.10± 2.85○
iris	5.60±0.84	4.70±0.48○	3.90±0.74○	3.80±1.32○	5.60± 0.70
labor	26.70±2.45	3.60±1.43○	3.60±0.52○	3.40±0.84○	8.70± 1.83○
led7	60.40±3.24	29.10±2.51○	15.20±1.55○	28.60±1.65○	62.00± 2.91●
lenses	20.20±1.03	3.60±0.52○	0.00±0.00○	3.60±0.52○	2.60± 2.76○
pima	39.70±6.62	19.20±6.53○	3.30±0.67○	7.50±1.18○	39.00± 6.63
tic-tac-toe	155.80±5.92	90.60±4.50○	10.60±1.43○	40.20±3.77○	166.60± 6.52●
wine	30.70±5.06	5.40±0.70○	3.90±0.57○	4.60±0.70○	7.60± 5.27○

○, ● statistically significant improvement or degradation

3.5 Time Complexity

Pruning a rule set output by predictive Apriori takes less time than pruning one output by Apriori, because predictive Apriori prunes away many rules during the search using its inherent pruning strategy (see Section 2.1). Nonetheless, predictive Apriori is much slower during mining. Table 7 shows the results. In comparison to standard learners, it

Table 6. The accuracy of CBA compared to standard techniques. CBA performed error-based pruning and did not restrict the number of rules output by the association rule miner

Dataset	CBA + Apriori	C4.5	JRip	PART	CBA + pred. Apriori
balance	71.50± 5.97	76.65± 3.77o	80.80± 3.56o	83.54± 4.93o	71.50± 5.97
breast-w	94.12± 3.55	94.69± 2.46	94.13± 2.73	94.26± 3.79	92.25± 3.92•
ecoli	81.26± 3.08	84.23± 7.51	82.16± 6.63	83.60± 6.36	80.96± 2.78
glass	70.13± 9.19	66.75± 7.94	68.66± 8.74	68.14± 7.21	68.25± 8.02
heart-h	79.98± 8.26	81.07±11.22	78.95± 9.30	81.02± 7.55	79.97± 9.03
iris	94.00± 5.84	96.00± 5.62	94.67± 6.13	94.00± 5.84	94.00± 5.84
labor	81.33±21.44	73.67±22.52	77.00±19.53	78.67±17.58	79.33±18.84
led7	72.30± 5.10	72.40± 4.55	71.90± 5.04	72.80± 4.85	72.20± 5.18
lenses	50.00±26.06	81.67±33.75o	75.00±32.63o	81.67±33.75o	66.67±38.49
pima	74.36± 4.83	73.83± 5.66	75.14± 3.68	75.27± 3.93	72.79± 3.78
tic-tac-toe	79.85± 1.84	85.07± 4.49o	97.81± 1.81o	94.47± 3.15o	78.70± 2.01•
wine	94.44± 5.86	93.86± 5.52	91.57± 9.27	93.27± 5.80	76.11±26.97

o, • statistically significant improvement or degradation

Table 7. The time complexity of the three standard machine learning techniques and CBA during training. CBA performed error-based pruning and did not restrict the number of rules. The times in brackets are the times for CBA's pruning method including error-based pruning

Dataset	CBA + Apriori	C4.5	JRip	PART	CBA + pred. Apriori
balance	0.28(0.23)	0.05o	0.48	0.09o	2.42(0.24)•
breast-w	28.90(27.00)	0.01o	0.31o	0.02o	283.56(1.40)•
ecoli	0.85(0.62)	0.02o	0.10o	0.04o	8.66(0.31)•
glass	5.82(2.93)	0.03o	0.10o	0.05o	46.81(0.34)•
heart-h	29.28(14.04)	0.02o	0.04o	0.04o	297.26(1.02)•
iris	0.03(0.02)	0.00o	0.01o	0.00o	0.78(0.03)•
labor	344.49(198.14)	0.00o	0.00o	0.00o	370.19(0.06)•
led7	5.23(4.21)	0.03o	0.22o	0.05o	50.05(5.37)•
lenses	0.02(0.02)	0.00o	0.00o	0.00o	0.26(0.00)•
pima	6.54(4.90)	0.05o	0.19o	0.06o	50.16(1.59)•
tic-tac-toe	23.89(15.60)	0.02o	0.44o	0.06o	2342.79(17.31)•
wine	170.23(48.30)	0.01o	0.03o	0.01o	2908.09(0.21)•

o, • statistically significant improvement or degradation

also shows that learning classifiers based on class association rules involves considerably more computation. The numbers are seconds of runtime on a 2.60 GHz Pentium(R) 4 with 1 GB of memory.

4 Conclusions

This paper has provided a comparative study of classification using association rules. In particular we have shown how to use this classification approach to evaluate the quality of a set of association rules generated by a confidence-based miner.

More specifically, we applied this methodology to the comparison of Apriori with predictive Apriori. Concerning the quality of the mined rule set, predictive Apriori is able to mine a high quality set of association rules. Its ranking metric—the expected predictive accuracy—makes sure that high-quality rules are ranked closer to the top. The rule ordering induced by the predictive accuracy outperforms Apriori's confidence-based ordering. The results also show that the rule set needed to build an accurate classifier is smaller when predictive Apriori is used. However, our experiments have shown that the time complexity of predictive Apriori is worse.

In addition, we have provided some benchmarks for the standard classifier in this research area—the CBA algorithm. Liu et al. [6] compare their algorithm to C4.5. We extended the comparison by including other state-of-the-art rule learners. In our opinion, CBA (in its standard combination with Apriori as class association rule mining algorithm) has comparable accuracy to standard techniques. However, CBA needs more rules and is slower than the standard techniques. We also found that CBA with predictive Apriori is slightly less accurate than CBA with Apriori. However, this is only true if a large number of association rules is generated. Predictive Apriori can improve classification using association rules when it is used to generate a small set of rules.

References

1. Agrawal R. and Srikant R. Fast Algorithms for Mining Association Rules. In *Proc. of the 20th Int. Conf. on Very Large Data Bases*, pages 475–486. Morgan Kaufmann, 1994.
2. Blake C. and Merz C. UCI Repository of machine learning databases. http://www.ics.uci.edu/~mlearn/MLRepository.html, 1998.
3. Cohen W. Fast Effective Rule Induction. In *Machine Learning: Proc. of the 12th Int. Conf.*, pages 115–123. Morgan Kaufmann, 1998.
4. Fayyad U. and Irani K. Multi-interval discretization of continuous-valued attributes for classification learning. In *Proc. of the 13th Int. Joint Conf. on Artificial Intelligence*, pages 1022–1027. Morgan Kaufmann, 1993.
5. Frank E. and Witten I. Generating Accurate Rule Sets Without Global Optimization. In *Machine Learning: Proc. of the 15th Int. Conf.*, pages 152–160. Morgan Kaufmann, 1998.
6. Liu B., Hsu W. and Ma Y. Integrating Classification and Association Rule Mining. In *Proc. of the 4th Int. Conf. on Knowledge Discovery and Data Mining*, pages 80–86. The AAAI Press, 1998.
7. Nadeau C. and Bengio Y. Inference for the generalization error. *Advances in Neural Information Processing Systems*, 12:307–313, 1999.
8. Quinlan J. *C4.5: Programs for Machine Learning*. Morgan Kaufmann, 1993.
9. Salzberg S. On Comparing Classifiers: Pitfalls to Avoid and a Recommended Approach. *Data Mining and Knowledge Discovery*, 1(3):317–327, 1997.
10. Scheffer T. Finding Association Rules That Trade Support Optimally against Confidence. Unpublished manuscript.
11. Scheffer T. Finding Association Rules That Trade Support Optimally against Confidence. In *Proc. of the 5th European Conf. on Principles and Practice of Knowledge Discovery in Databases*, pages 424–435. Springer-Verlag, 2001.
12. Witten I. and Frank E. *Data Mining: Practical machine learning tools and techniques with Java implementations*. Morgan Kaufmann, 2000.

Analyzing the Effect of Query Class on Document Retrieval Performance

Pawel Kowalczyk, Ingrid Zukerman, and Michael Niemann

School of Computer Science and Software Engineering,
Monash University,
Clayton, Victoria 3800, Australia
{pawel, ingrid, niemann}@csse.monash.edu.au

Abstract. Analysis of queries posed to open-domain question-answering systems indicates that particular types of queries are dominant, e.g., queries about the identity of people, and about the location or time of events. We applied a rule-based mechanism and performed manual classification to classify queries into such commonly occurring types. We then experimented with different adjustments to our basic document retrieval process for each query type. The application of the best retrieval adjustment for each query type yielded improvements in retrieval performance. Finally, we applied a machine learning technique to automatically learn the manually classified query types, and applied the best retrieval adjustments obtained for the manual classification to the automatically learned query classes. The learning algorithm exhibited high accuracy, and the retrieval performance obtained for the learned classes was consistent with the performance obtained for the rule-based and manual classifications.

1 Introduction

The growth in popularity of the Internet highlights the importance of developing systems that generate responses to queries targeted at large unstructured corpora. These queries vary in their informational goal and topic, ranging from requests for descriptions of people or things, to queries about the location or time of events, and questions about specific attributes of people or things. There is also some variation in the success of question-answering systems in answering the different types of queries.

Recently, there has been some work on predicting whether queries can be answered by the documents in a particular corpus [1, 2]. The hope is that by identifying features that affect the "answerability" of queries, the queries can be modified prior to attempting document retrieval, or appropriate steps can be taken during the retrieval process to address problems that arise due to these features.

In this paper, we investigate the use of query type as a predictor of document retrieval performance in the context of a question answering task, and as a basis for the automatic selection of a retrieval policy. The first step in our study consisted of performing two types of query classification: a coarse-grained classification, which was performed by means of a rule-based mechanism, and a finer-grained classification, which was done manually. We considered these two types of classification because finer-grained classes are believed to be more informative than coarser-grained classes when extracting answers to queries from retrieved documents [3]. However, prior to committing to a particular classification grain, we must examine its effect on document retrieval performance (as document retrieval is the step that precedes question answering).

Our analysis of the effect of query type on document retrieval performance shows that performance varies across different types of queries. This led us to experiment with different types of adjustments to our basic document retrieval process, in order to determine the best adjustment for each type of query. The application of specific adjustments to the retrieval of documents for different query types yielded improvements in retrieval performance both for the coarse-grained and the finer-grained query classes.

In the last step of our study, we applied a supervised machine learning technique, namely Support Vector Machines (SVMs) [4], to learn the finer-grained query types from shallow linguistic features of queries, and used the query-type-based retrieval adjustments to retrieve documents for the learned classes.[1] Our results for both the machine learning algorithm and the document retrieval process are encouraging. The learning algorithm exhibited high accuracy, and the resultant retrieval performance was consistent with the performance obtained for the rule-based and manually-derived query categories.

In the next section, we review related research. In Section 3, we describe our document retrieval procedure. Next, we describe our data set, discuss our rule-based classification process and our manual classification process, and present the results of our experiments with the adjustments to the retrieval procedure. In Section 5, we describe the data used to train the SVM for query classification, and evaluate the performance of the SVM and the retrieval performance for the automatically learned classes. In Section 6, we summarize the contribution of this work.

2   Related Research

Our research is at the intersection of query classification systems [5, 6, 3] and performance prediction systems [1, 2].

Query classification systems constitute a relatively recent development in Information Retrieval (IR). Radev et al. [5] and Zhang and Lee [3] studied automatic query classification based on the type of the expected answer. Their work was motivated by the idea that such a classification can help select a suitable answer in a document when performing an open-domain question-answering task. Radev et al. compared a machine learning approach with a heuristic (hand-engineered) approach for query classification, and found that the latter approach outperformed the former. Zhang and Lee experimented with five machine learning methods to learn query classes, and concluded that when only surface text features are used, SVMs outperform the other techniques. Kang and Kim's study of query classification [6] was directed at categorizing queries according to the task at hand (informational, navigational or transactional). They postulated that appropriate query classification supports the application of algorithms dedicated to particular tasks.

---

[1] The automation of the finer-grained classification is necessary in order to incorporate it as a step in an automatic document-retrieval and question-answering process.

Our work resembles that of Zhang and Lee in its use of SVMs. However, they considered two grains of classifications: coarse (6 classes) and fine (50 classes), while we consider an intermediate grain (11 classes). More importantly, like Kang and Kim, we adjust our retrieval policy based on query class. However, Kang and Kim's classes were broad task-oriented classes, while we offer finer distinctions within the informational task.

Performance-prediction systems identify query features that predict retrieval performance. The idea is that queries that appear "unpromising" can be modified prior to attempting retrieval, or retrieval behaviour can be adjusted for such queries. Cronen-Townsend *et al.* [1] developed a *clarity score* that measures the coherence of the language used in documents which "generate" the terms in a query. Thus, queries with a high clarity score yield a cohesive set of documents, while queries with a low clarity score yield documents about different topics. Zukerman *et al.* [2] adopted a machine learning approach to predict retrieval performance from the surface features of queries and word frequency counts in the corpus. They found that queries were "answerable" when they did not contain words whose frequency exceeded a particular threshold (this threshold is substantially lower than the frequency of stop words, which are normally excluded from the retrieval process). This finding led to the automatic removal of such words from queries prior to document retrieval, yielding significant improvements in retrieval performance. The work described in this paper predicts retrieval performance from surface features of queries (by first using these features to classify queries). However, it does not consider corpus-related information. Additionally, unlike the system described in Zukerman *et al.* that modifies the queries, our system dynamically adjusts its retrieval behaviour.[2]

3 Document Retrieval

Our retrieval mechanism combines the classic vector-space model [7] with a paraphrase-based query expansion process [8, 2]. This mechanism is further adjusted by considering different numbers of paraphrases (between 0 and 19) and different retrieval policies. Below we describe our basic retrieval procedure followed by the adjustments.

Procedure *Paraphrase&Retrieve*

1. *Tokenize, tag and lemmatize the query.*
   Tagging is performed using Brill's part-of-speech tagger [9]. Lemmatizing consists of converting words into *lemmas*, which are uninflected versions of words.
2. *Generate replacement lemmas for each content lemma in the query.*
   The replacement lemmas are the intersection of lemmas obtained from two resources: WordNet [10] and a thesaurus that was automatically constructed from the Oxford English Dictionary. The thesaurus also yields similarity scores between each query lemma and its replacement lemmas.

---

[2] We also replicated Zukerman *et al.*'s machine learning experiments. However, since our document retrieval technique combines the vector-space model with boolean retrieval (Section 3), the results obtained when their machine learning approach was used with our system differed from Zukerman *et al.*'s original findings.

3. *Propose paraphrases for the query using different combinations of replacement lemmas, compute the similarity score between each paraphrase and the query, and rank the paraphrases according to their score.*

   The similarity score of each paraphrase is computed from the similarity scores between the original lemmas in the query and the corresponding replacement lemmas in the paraphrase.

4. *Retain the lemmatized query plus the top K paraphrases* (the default value for K is 19).

5. *Retrieve documents for the query and its paraphrases using a paraphrase-adjusted version of the vector-space model.*

   For each lemma in the original query or its paraphrases, documents that contain this lemma are retrieved. Each document is scored using a function that combines the *tf.idf (term frequency inverse document frequency)* score [7] of the query lemmas and paraphrase lemmas that appear in the document, and the similarity score between the paraphrase lemmas that appear in the document and the query lemmas. The tf.idf part of the score takes into account statistical features of the corpus, and the similarity part takes into account semantic features of the query.

6. *Retain the top N documents* (at present $N = 200$).

3.1 Adjustments to the Basic Retrieval Procedure

The adjustments to our retrieval procedure pertain to the number of paraphrases used for query expansion and to the retrieval policy used in combination with the vector space model. The effect of these adjustments on retrieval performance is discussed in Sections 4.1 and 4.2.

Number of Paraphrases. We consider different numbers of paraphrases (between 0 and 19), in addition to the original query.

Retrieval Policies. Our system features three boolean document retrieval policies, which are used to constrain the output of the vector-space model: (1) *1NNP*, (2) *1NG (1 Noun Group)*, and (3) *MultipleNGs*.

- *1NNP* – retrieve documents that contain at least one proper noun (NNP) from the query.[3] If no proper nouns are found, fall back to the vector space model.
- *1NG* – retrieve documents that contain the content words of at least one of the noun groups in the query, where a noun group is a sequence of nouns possibly interleaved by adjectives and function words, e.g., "Secretary of State", "pitcher's mound" or "house".
- *MultipleNGs* – retrieve documents that contain at least g NGs in the query, where $g = \min\{2, \#\text{ of NGs in the query}\}$.

---

[3] NNP is the tag used for singular proper nouns in parsers and part-of-speech taggers. This tag is part of the Penn Treebank tag-set (http://www.scs.leeds.ac.uk/amalgam/tagsets/upenn.html).

4 Query Classification and Retrieval Adjustment

Our dataset consists of 911 unique queries from the TREC11 and TREC12 corpora. These queries were obtained from logs of public repositories such MSNSearch and AskJeeves. Their average length is 8.9 words, with most queries containing between 5 and 12 words. The answers to these queries are retrieved from approximately 1 million documents in the ACQUAINT corpus (this corpus is part of the NIST Text Research Collection, http://trec.nist.gov). These documents are newspaper articles from the New York Times, Associated Press Worldstream (APW), and Xinhua English (People's Republic of China) news services. Thus, the task at hand is an example of the more general problem of finding answers to questions in open-domain documents that were not designed with these questions in mind (in contrast to encyclopedias).

We first extracted six main query features by automatically performing shallow linguistic analysis of the queries. These features are

1. *Type of the Initial Query Words* – corresponds mostly to the first word in the query, but merges some words, such as "what" and "which", into a single category, and considers additional words if the first word is "how".
2. *Main Focus* – the attribute sought in the answer to the query, e.g., "How *far* is it from Earth to Mars?" (similar components have been considered in [11, 12]).
3. *Main Verb* – the main content verb of the query (different from auxiliary verbs such as "be" and "have"), e.g., "What book did Rachel Carson *write* in 1962?". It often corresponds to the head verb of the query, but it may also be a verb embedded in a subordinate clause, e.g., "What is the name of the volcano that *destroyed* the ancient city of Pompeii?".
4. *Rest of the Query* – e.g., "What is the name of the volcano that destroyed *the ancient city of Pompeii*?".
5. *Named Entities* – entities characterized by sequences of proper nouns, possibly interleaved with function words, e.g., "Hong Kong" or "Hunchback of Notre Dame".
6. *Prepositional Phrases* – e.g., "*In the bible*, who is Jacob's mother?".

After the shallow analysis, the queries were automatically classified by a rule-based system into six broad categories which represent the type of the desired answer.

1. **location**, e.g., "In what country did the game of croquet originate?".
2. **name**, e.g., "What was Andrew Jackson's wife's name?".
3. **number**, e.g., "How many chromosomes does a human zygote have?".
4. **person**, e.g., "Who is Tom Cruise married to?".
5. **time**, e.g., "What year was Alaska purchased?".
6. **other**, which is the default category, e.g., "What lays blue eggs?".

The rules for query classification considered two main factors: type of the initial query words (feature #1 above), and main-focus words (feature #2). The first factor was used to identify location, number, person and time queries ("where", "how [much | many | ADJ]", "[who | whom | whose]" and "when" respectively). The main focus words were then used to classify queries whose initial word is "what", "which" or "list". For example, "country", "state" and "river" indicate location (e.g., "What is the *state* with the smallest population?"), and "date" and "year" indicate time (e.g., "What *year* was the light bulb invented?").

Table 1. Breakdown of automatically derived categories for TREC11 and TREC12 queries; performance for 19 paraphrases and 1NNP retrieval policy; best retrieval adjustment and best performance (measured in *answerable queries*)

Query type	# of queries	# of queries with answers	Performance 19/1NNP	Best performance	
			ans queries (%)	#para/policy	ans queries (%)
location	172	167	137 (82.0%)	8/MultNG	149 (89.2%)
name	63	60	45 (75.0%)	1/MultNG	49 (81.7%)
number	169	147	109 (74.1%)	0/MultNG	122 (83.0%)
person	61	55	48 (87.3%)	19/NNP	48 (87.3%)
time	143	138	115 (83.3%)	19/MultNG	124 (89.9%)
other	303	275	191 (69.5%)	12/MultNG	204 (74.2%)
total	911	842	645 (76.6%)		696 (82.7%)

Table 1 shows the breakdown of the six query categories, together with the retrieval performance when using our default retrieval method (19 paraphrases and the 1NNP retrieval policy), and when using the retrieval adjustment that yields the best retrieval performance for each query class. The first column lists the query type, the second column shows the number of queries of this type, and the third column shows the number of queries for which TREC participants found answers in the corpus (obtained from the TREC judgment file).[4] The retrieval performance for our default method appears in the fourth column. The fifth and sixth columns present information pertaining to the best performance (discussed later in this section).

We employ a measure called *number of answerable queries* to assess retrieval performance. This measure, which was introduced in [2], returns the number of queries for which the system has retrieved at least one document that contains the answer to a query. We use this measure because the traditional precision measure is not sufficiently informative in the context of a question-answering task. For instance, consider a situation where 10 correct documents are retrieved for each of 2 queries and 0 correct documents for each of 3 queries, compared to a situation where 2 correct documents are retrieved for each of 5 queries. Average precision would yield a better score for the first situation, failing to address the question of interest for the question-answering task, namely how many queries have a chance of being answered, which is 2 in the first case and 5 in the second case.

As seen from the results in the first four columns of Table 1, there are differences in retrieval performance for the six categories. Also, the other category (which is rather uninformative) dominates, and exhibits the worst retrieval performance. This led to two directions of investigation: (1) examine the effect of number of paraphrases and retrieval policy on retrieval performance, and (2) refine the query classification to increase the specificity of the "other" category in particular.

---

[4] TREC releases a judgment file for all the answers submitted by participants. For each submitted answer (and source document for that answer) the file contains a number which represents a degree of correctness. Thus, at present, when assessing the performance of our retrieval procedure, we are bounded by the answers found by previous TREC participants.

4.1 Effect of Number of Paraphrases and Retrieval Policy on Performance

We ran all the combinations of number of paraphrases and retrieval policies on our six query classes (a total of 60 runs: 20 × 3), and selected the combination of number of paraphrases and retrieval policy that gave the best result for each query type (where several adjustments yielded the same performance, the adjustment with the lowest number of paraphrases was selected). The fifth and sixth columns in Table 1 show the results of this process. The fifth column shows the number of paraphrases and retrieval policy that yield the best performance for a particular query type, and the sixth column shows the number of answerable queries obtained by these adjustments. As can be seen from these results, the retrieval adjustments based on query type yield substantial performance improvements.

4.2 Manual Refinement of Query Classes

We re-examined the automatically derived query classes with a view towards a more precise identification of the type of the desired answer (as stated above, the hope is that this more precise categorization will help to find answers in documents). At the same time, we endeavoured to define categories that had some chance of being automatically identified. This led us to the 11 categories specified below. These classes include five of the six previously defined categories (name was split between person and attribute). The queries in the six original classes were then manually re-tagged with the new classes.

1. **location**, e.g., "In what country did the game of croquet originate?".
2. **number**, e.g., "How many chromosomes does a human zygote have?".
3. **person**, e.g., "Who is Tom Cruise married to?".
4. **time**, e.g., "What year was Alaska purchased?".
5. **attribute** – an attribute of the query's topic, e.g., "What is Australia's *national blossom*?".
6. **howDoYouSay** – the spelling-out of an acronym or the translation of a word, e.g., "What does DNA stand for?".
7. **object** – an object or the composition of an object, e.g., "What did Alfred Nobel invent?".
8. **organization** – an organization or group of people, e.g., "What *company* manufactures Sinemet?".
9. **process** – a process or how an event happened, e.g., "How did Mahatma Gandhi die?". It is worth noting that 80% of the queries in this category are about how somebody died.
10. **term** – a word that defines a concept, e.g., "What is the fear of lightning called?".
11. **other** – queries that did not fit in the other categories, e.g., "What is the chemical formula for sulfur dioxide?".

Table 2 shows the breakdown of the 11 query categories (the original categories are asterisked), together with the retrieval performance obtained for our default retrieval policy (19 paraphrases, 1NNP). As for Table 1, the first column lists the query types, the second column shows the number of queries of each type, and the third column shows the number of queries which were deemed correct according to the TREC judgment file. The retrieval performance for our default method appears in the fourth column. The fifth

Table 2. Breakdown of manually tagged categories for TREC11 and TREC12 queries; performance for 19 paraphrases and 1NNP retrieval policy; best retrieval adjustment and best performance (measured in *answerable queries*)

Query type	# of queries	# of queries with answers	Performance 19/1NNP ans queries (%)	Best performance #para/policy	Best performance ans queries (%)
*location	206	198	163 (82.3%)	6/MultNG	175 (88.4%)
*number	187	163	120 (73.6%)	6/MultNG	135 (82.8%)
*person	118	106	88 (83.0%)	2/NNP	90 (84.9%)
*time	144	139	116 (83.5%)	19/MultNG	125 (89.9%)
attribute	121	112	81 (72.3%)	4/MultNG	85 (75.9%)
howDoYouSay	21	20	10 (50.0%)	4/NNP	12 (60.0%)
object	13	13	8 (61.5%)	0/1NG	11 (84.6%)
organization	26	25	22 (88.0%)	0/1NG	24 (96.0%)
process	35	30	21 (70.0%)	0/MultNG	25 (83.3%)
term	30	27	11 (40.7%)	0/1NG	13 (48.1%)
*other	10	9	5 (55.6%)	0/MultNG	6 (66.7%)
total	911	842	645 (76.6%)		701 (83.3%)

and sixth columns contain the retrieval adjustments yielding the best performance, and the result obtained by these adjustments, respectively. As can be seen from these results, the retrieval adjustments based on the finer-grained, manually-derived query types yield performance improvements that are similar to those obtained for the coarser rule-based query types.

It is worth noting that there is nothing intrinsically important that distinguishes these 11 categories from other options. The main factor is their ability to improve system performance, which spans two aspects of the system: document retrieval and answer extraction. Since the finer categories are more informative than the coarser ones, the hope is that they will assist during the answer extraction stage. Our results show that this will not occur at the expense of retrieval performance.

5 Using Support Vector Machines to Learn Query Classes

The SVM representation of each query has 11 parts, which may be roughly divided into three sections: coarse properties (3 parts), fine-grained properties (6 parts), and WordNet properties (2 parts).

- **Coarse Properties** – these are properties that describe a query in broad terms.
    - headTarget – the target or topic of the question, which is the first sequence of proper nouns in the query, and if no proper nouns are found then it is the first noun group, e.g., for the query "Who is Tom Cruise married to?", the headTarget is "Tom Cruise".
    - headConcept – the attribute we want to find out about the target, e.g., for the query "What is the currency of China?", the headConcept is "currency".

- headAction – the action performed on the target, which is mostly the head verb of the query, e.g., "married" in the above query about Tom Cruise.
- **Fine Properties** – these properties correspond to the six query features extracted from the query by performing shallow linguistic analysis (Section 4): (1) *type of the initial query words*, (2) *main focus*, (3) *main verb*, (4) *rest of the query*, (5) *named entities*, and (6) *prepositional phrases*. They provide additional detail about a query to that provided by the coarse properties (but *main focus* and *main verb* often overlap with headConcept and headAction respectively).
- **WordNet Properties** – these properties contain the WordNet categories for the top four WordNet senses of the *main verb* and *main focus* of the query.[5]
  - verbWNcat – e.g., "marry" has two senses, both of which are *social*, yielding the value *social: 2*.
  - focusWNcat – e.g., "currency" has four senses, two of which are *attribute* (which is different from our `attribute` query type), one *possession*, and one *state*, yielding the values *attribute: 2, possession: 1, state: 1*.

Each of these parts contains a bag-of-lemmas (recall that words are lemmatized), which are modified as follows.
- Proper nouns are replaced by designations which represent how many consecutive proper nouns are in a query, e.g., "Who is Tom Cruise married to?" yields `who be 2NNP marry`.
- Similarly, abbreviations are replaced by their designation.
- Certain combinations of up-to three query-initial words are merged, e.g., "what is the" and "who is".

The SVM was trained as follows. For each query type, we separated the 911 queries into two groups: queries that belong to that type and the rest of the queries. For instance, when training to identify `person` queries, our data consisted of 118 positive samples and 793 negative samples. Each group was then randomly split in half, where one half was used for training and the other half for testing, e.g., for our `person` example, both the training set and the test set consisted of 59 positive samples and 397 negative samples.[6]

Table 3 shows the recall and precision of the SVM for the 11 manually-derived query types, where recall and precision are defined as follows.

$$\text{Recall} = \frac{\text{number of queries in class } i \text{ learned by the SVM}}{\text{number of queries in class } i}$$

$$\text{Precision} = \frac{\text{number of queries in class } i \text{ learned by the SVM}}{\text{number of queries attributed by the SVM to class } i}$$

Also shown is the retrieval performance for the learned classes after the application of query-type-based retrieval adjustments. Both results were obtained from 20 trials.

---

[5] These properties perform word-sense collation, rather than word-sense disambiguation.

[6] We also used another training method where the 911 queries were randomly split into two halves: training and testing. We then used the queries of a particular class in the training set, e.g., `person`, as positive samples (and the rest of the training queries as negative samples). Similarly any queries of that class that were found in the test set were considered positive samples (and the rest of the queries were negative samples). Although both methods yielded consistent results, we prefer the method described in the body of the paper, as it guarantees a consistent number of positive training samples.

Table 3. Recall and precision obtained by SVM for 11 manually derived categories for TREC11 and TREC12 queries; average retrieval performance for SVM-learned queries

Query type	# of queries	# of queries (with ans)	SVM performance (average over 20 runs)		Retrieval performance (avg. 20 runs, best adjustment)
			Recall (STDV)	Precision (STDV)	ans queries (STDV)
*location	206	198	0.93 (0.02)	0.93 (0.04)	87.8% (2.1%)
*number	187	163	0.96 (0.02)	0.99 (0.01)	82.6% (3.0%)
*person	118	106	0.95 (0.03)	0.82 (0.04)	85.0% (2.8%)
*time	144	139	1.00 (0.01)	0.99 (0.01)	88.7% (3.4%)
attribute	121	112	0.84 (0.05)	0.90 (0.04)	74.7% (3.9%)
howDoYouSay	21	20	0.86 (0.13)	0.81 (0.09)	62.3% (12.2%)
object	13	13	0.74 (0.18)	0.90 (0.12)	82.7% (12.2%)
organization	26	25	0.62 (0.13)	0.91 (0.09)	91.9% (6.6%)
process	35	30	0.97 (0.03)	0.99 (0.02)	85.1% (6.8%)
term	30	27	0.99 (0.02)	0.83 (0.04)	46.2% (10.1%)
*other	10	9	0.42 (0.19)	0.77 (0.23)	68.2% (16.4%)
total	911	842	0.92	0.93	82.6%

As seen from the results in Table 3, six of the learned classes had over 93% recall, and seven classes had over 90% precision. The other class had a particularly low recall (42%) and also a rather low precision (77%). However, this is not surprising owing to the amorphous nature of the queries in this class (i.e., they had no particular distinguishing features, so queries belonging to other classes found their way into other, and other queries wandered to other classes). The organization class had a high precision, but a lower recall, as some organization queries were wrongly identified as person queries (this is a known problem in question answering, as it is often hard to distinguish between organizations and people without domain knowledge). The object class exhibited this problem to a lesser extent. Some attribute queries were mis-classified as location queries and others as person queries. This explains the lower recall obtained for attribute, and together with the organization problem mentioned above, also explains the lower precision obtained for person (location is less affected owing to the larger number of location queries).

Overall, although we used only a modified bag-of-words approach, we obtained better results for our fine-grained classification than those obtained by Zhang and Lee [3] for a coarse classification (the best performance they obtained with an SVM for bag-of-words was 85.8%, for n-grams 87.4%, and for a kernel that takes into account syntactic structure 90.0%). This may be attributed to our use of WordNet properties, and our distinction between coarse, fine and WordNet properties. Also, it is worth noting that the features considered significant by the SVM for the different classes are intuitively appealing. For instance, examples of the modified lemmas considered significant for the location class are: "city", "country", "where" and "where be", while examples of the modified lemmas for the time class are: "year", "date", "when" and "when be".

The retrieval performance shown in the last column of Table 3 is consistent with that shown in Table 2. That is, the retrieval performance obtained for the automatically-learned classes was not significantly different from that obtained for the manually-tagged classes.

6 Conclusion

We have studied two aspects of the question-answering process – performance prediction and query classification – and offered a new contribution at the intersection of these aspects: automatic selection of adjustments to the retrieval procedure based on query class. Overall, our results show that retrieval performance can be improved by dynamically adjusting the retrieval process on the basis of automatically learned query classes.

In query classification, we applied SVMs to learn query classes from manually tagged queries. Although our input was largely word based, our results (averaged over 20 runs) were superior to recent results in the literature. This may be attributed to the breakdown of query properties into coarse-grained, fine-grained and WordNet-based.

In performance prediction, we first used coarse-grained query classes learned by a rule-based system as predictors of retrieval performance, and as a basis for the dynamic selection of adjustments to the retrieval procedure. This yielded improvements in retrieval performance. Next, finer-grained, manually-derived classes were used as the basis for the dynamic selection of retrieval adjustments. Retrieval performance was maintained for these finer-grained categories. This is an encouraging result, as fine-grained categories are considered more useful than coarse-grained categories for answer extraction. Finally, the retrieval adjustments were applied to the SVM-learned, fine-grained query categories, yielding a retrieval performance that is consistent with that obtained for the manually-derived categories. This result demonstrates the applicability of our techniques to an automated question-answering process.

Acknowledgments

This research is supported in part by the ARC Centre for Perceptive and Intelligent Machines in Complex Environments. The authors thank Oxford University Press for the use of their electronic data, and Tony for developing the thesaurus.

References

1. Cronen-Townsend, S., Zhou, Y., Croft, W.B.: Predicting query performance. In: SIGIR'02 – Proceedings of the 25th ACM International Conference on Research and Development in Information Retrieval, Tampere, Finland (2002) 299–306
2. Zukerman, I., Raskutti, B., Wen, Y.: Query expansion and query reduction in document retrieval. In: ICTAI2003 – Proceedings of the 15th International Conference on Tools with Artificial Intelligence, Sacramento, California (2003) 552–559
3. Zhang, D., Lee, W.S.: Question classification using Support Vector Machines. In: SIGIR'03 – Proceedings of the 26th ACM International Conference on Research and Development in Information Retrieval, Toronto, Canada (2003) 26–32

4. Vapnik, V.: Statistical Learning Theory. Wiley-Interscience, New York (1998)
5. Radev, D., Fan, W., Qi, H., Wu, H., Grewal, A.: Probabilistic question answering from the Web. In: WWW2002 – Proceedings of the 11th World Wide Web Conference, Honolulu, Hawaii (2002) 408–419
6. Kang, I.H., Kim, G.: Query type classification for Web document retrieval. In: SIGIR'03 – Proceedings of the 26th ACM International Conference on Research and Development in Information Retrieval, Toronto, Canada (2003) 64–71
7. Salton, G., McGill, M.: An Introduction to Modern Information Retrieval. McGraw Hill (1983)
8. Zukerman, I., Raskutti, B.: Lexical query paraphrasing for document retrieval. In: COLING'02 – Proceedings of the International Conference on Computational Linguistics, Taipei, Taiwan (2002) 1177–1183
9. Brill, E.: A simple rule-based part of speech tagger. In: ANLP-92 – Proceedings of the Third Conference on Applied Natural Language Processing, Trento, IT (1992) 152–155
10. Miller, G., Beckwith, R., Fellbaum, C., Gross, D., Miller, K.: Introduction to WordNet: An on-line lexical database. Journal of Lexicography **3** (1990) 235–244
11. Moldovan, D., Harabagiu, S., Pasca, M., Mihalcea, R., Girju, R., Goodrum, R., Rus, V.: The structure and performance of an open-domain question answering system. In: ACL2000 – Proceedings of the 38th Annual Meeting of the Association for Computational Linguistics, Hong Kong (2000) 563–570
12. Zukerman, I., Horvitz, E.: Using machine learning techniques to interpret WH-questions. In: ACL01 Proceedings – the 39th Annual Meeting of the Association for Computational Linguistics, Toulouse, France (2001) 547–554

Combined Word-Spacing Method for Disambiguating Korean Texts

Mi-young Kang, Aesun Yoon, and Hyuk-chul Kwon

Korean Language Processing Lab., School of Electrical & Computer Engineering,
Pusan National University, San 30, Jangjeon-dong,
609-735, Busan, Korea
{kmyoung, asyoon, hckwon}@pusan.ac.kr
http://klpl.re.pusan.ac.kr

Abstract. In this paper, we propose an automatic word-spacing method for a Korean text preprocessing system in resolving the problem of context-dependent word-spacing. The current method combines the stochastic-based method and partial parsing. First, the stochastic method splits an input sentence into a candidate-word sequence using word unigrams and syllable bigrams. Second, the system engages a partial parsing module based on the asymmetric relation between the candidate-words. The partial parsing module manages the governing relationship using words which are incorporated into the knowledge base as having a high-probability of spacing-error words. These elements serve as parsing trigger points based on their linguistic information, and they determine the parsing direction as well as the parsing scope. Combining the stochastic- and linguistic-based methods, the current automatic word-spacing system becomes robust against the problem of context-dependant word-spacing. An average 8.98% amelioration of the total error rate is obtained for inner and external data.

1 Introduction

Compared with Chinese and Japanese which do not use any spaces or other delimiters excepting punctuation marks within a sentence, Western European languages are somewhat easy to break into meaningful semantic units because 'words'[1] are delimited by spaces.[10], [11] Korean words are delimited by spaces like words in Western European languages. A Korean word can be composed of one or several concatenated morphemes of different linguistic features which are equivalent to a phrase in English. This spacing unit is called a 'word', 'eo-jeol', or 'morpheme cluster' in Korean linguistic literature. In this paper, we adopt the term 'word' in order to refer to 'an alphanumeric cluster of morphemes` located between two blanks in Korean. Korean

---

[1] The concept of word is not easy to define. Generally, words are linguistically-considered atomic elements: they are the indivisible building blocks of syntax.

normative grammar prescribes word-spacing rules.[2] The word-spacing error in Korean is the second-most frequent[3] among other errors that we encounter while processing Korean texts. It is due to the ignorance of word-spacing rules or simple omission of a space when typing. Sometimes, writers commit word-spacing errors on purpose. (For example, users commit word-spacing errors on purpose due to word-count limits from opinion pages in a daily newspaper which should be written with less than 100 words). Violation of those word-spacing constraints in Korean induces linguistic errors and ambiguities in the lexical interpretation of parts of speech, because there are many homographs of different parts-of-speech (POS) in Korean which can be disambiguated only by their spacing status. Resolving those ambiguities created by word-spacing errors, therefore, is crucial in Korean-language-processing application domains such as information retrieval, Optical Character Recognition (OCR), Text-to-Speech Synthesis (TTS), Korean text editing, among others. In information retrieval systems, a morphological analysis of query words or phrases fails when there is a word-spacing error. Also, a correct recognition of word boundary cannot be expected if target documents are not processed with regard to word-spacing. Besides, the correct conversion of Korean text to phonemes in developing TTS is impossible when there are word-spacing errors in the text.

Several studies have proposed automatic word-spacing methods for Korean text. Among these previous studies on word-spacing, we can distinguish (a) rule-/knowledge-based approaches and (b) the stochastic approach. Rule-/knowledge-based approaches use morphological analysis and heuristic linguistic knowledge. [6], [9] Nevertheless, a disadvantage is the amount of language that has to be treated without the possibility of expanding this knowledge base and applying it to natural language processing. Contrary to rule/ knowledge-based methods, the stochastic approach has advantages in set-up time and cost savings and the capability of coping with unregistered words. [4], [5], [7], [10], [11] However, the stochastic method shows a strong training-data-dependency and data sparseness. Data sparseness becomes more serious while processing agglutinative languages such as Korean. In such languages, using syllable statistics at the right-hand boundary of a word exacerbates the data sparseness problem. Therefore, word-spacing errors in Korean need to be processed while taking into consideration Korean language particularity.

For the implementation of an efficient word-spacing system for Korean-text preprocessing, this paper proposes an automatic word-spacing method to resolve the

---

[2] The following rules are found in The Revised Korean Spelling System and Korean Standard Language (officially announced by the Ministry of Education and which came into effect in March, 1989.):
- a postposition is attached to a preceding noun;
- a dependent noun appears with a space in a sentence;
- a space is placed in every four-digit number in the Korean numeric system; and others.

In addition, the following word-spacing rules are commonly accepted by Korean normative grammar even though they are not prescribed in RKSSKSL:
- a determiner is used with a space on both sides;`
- an adverb appears in a sentence with a space on both sides; and others.

Furthermore, some word-spacing rules in Korean are facultative.

[3] See Table 3 in the text.

problem of context-dependent word-spacing in Korean. Our current method combines (a) the stochastic-based method which splits an input sentence into a candidate-word sequence using word unigrams and syllable bigrams; (b) the method of dynamic extension of a candidate-word list using the 'longest match strategy' based on the viable-prefix; and (c) the partial parsing module based on the asymmetric relation between candidate words. To achieve this aim, the current paper is composed of five sections. Following this introduction, Section 2 presents our ongoing automatic word-spacing system which uses syllable bi-grams, word stochastic information, and the dynamic extension of a candidate-word list using the 'longest match strategy' based on the viable-prefix and the dynamic selection of candidate words. Section 3 discusses an automatic word-spacing algorithm based on partial parsing with a heuristic linguistic knowledge base and the combined word-spacing system. Section 4 presents the results of our experiments. Finally, in section 5, we give concluding comments and suggestions for future studies.

2 Korean Word-Spacing Based on Word Unigrams and Syllable Bigrams (Ongoing Work)

Our first attempt to construct an automatic word-spacing method for Korean text pre-processing is based on the stochastic information extracted from a large training database which was composed of articles of two different newspaper companies (Corpus A and B) and of three years' worth of news broadcasting scripts (Corpus C). Arabic numerals, Roman-alphabet letters, symbols, among others, were all included in the word count. Seven patterns of Arabic numerals were extracted. First, we extracted five patterns according to one-digit numbers, two-digit numbers, three-digit numbers, four-digit numbers and more than five-digit numbers. Second, every figure located on both sides of one period were grouped in one pattern in order to consider float. Finally, IP addresses, dates (year•month•day), subsection numbering (chapter•section•subsection), times (hour•minute•second) and others used with more than two periods were grouped in one pattern. Each of those patterns was treated as one word with regard to word-spacing.

Table 1. Words and Disyllables in the Training Data (Corpus A, B and C)

Total N° of different word unigrams	1,950,068
Total N° of word unigrams	33,643,884
Total N° of different syllable bigrams	391,732
Total N° of syllable bigrams	90,235,529

Word-Spacing Based on Word Unigrams and Syllable Bigrams. Word-spacing probabilities are estimated, in our current word-spacing system, by using a maximum likelihood estimator with two parameters: word probability $P(W)$, which means in this paper the probability that a sequence could be a possible word estimated by relative word frequencies; odds favoring the inner-spacing probability (P_{innerS}) of a disyllable at the current k^{th} possible word boundary compared to the rate of no-inner-spacing probability. When an input sentence is given, the most probable word sequence is selected among candidate-word sequences applying the following estimator.[4]

The optimal sentence

$$= \arg\max_{S} \prod_{k=1}^{n} P(W_k) \frac{P_{innerS}(LS \ of \ W_k, FS \ of \ W_{k+1})}{1 - P_{innerS}(LS \ of \ W_k, FS \ of \ W_{k+1})} \qquad \text{(Eq. 1)}$$

$$P_{innerS}(LS \ of \ W_k, FS \ of \ W_{k+1})$$
$$= \frac{freq(LS \ of \ W_k \# FS \ of \ W_{k+1})}{freq(LS \ of \ W_k \# FS \ of \ W_{k+1}) + freq(LS \ of \ W_k \phi FS \ of \ W_{k+1})} \qquad \text{(Eq. 2)}$$

If $k = n$, then $P_{inneS}(LS \ of \ W_k, FS \ of \ W_{k+1}) = 0.5$; $W_k = k^{th}$ word; FS = First syllable; LS = Last syllable; #: spacing (word boundary); $\emptyset$: absence of spacing.

Smoothing Method Based on Syllable Bigrams. In order to mitigate data sparseness, we use a stochastic smoothing approach using a 'longest match strategy' based on the syllable bigram statistics. This smoothing method estimates the inner-spacing probability of each disyllable starting from the last syllable of a stochastic candidate word, attaches each syllable while the inner spacing probability of each successive disyllable, $P_{innerS}(x_1, x_2)$, $P_{innerS}(x_2, x_3)$,...and $P_{innerS}(x_{n-1}, x_n)$, is over a threshold, and selects the longest word among the unseen candidate-words. The inner data varies according to the training corpus. It is extracted at the same distribution ratio as a given corpus in the whole training corpora.

Comparison of Stochastic Models. We can compare our stochastic model's performance with other stochastic-based studies on Korean word-spacing. Lee D.G. et al. (2003) treated word-spacing problems such as POS tagging using a hidden Markov model (HMM), and found the most likely sequence of word-spacing tags T = (t1, t2, ..., tn) for a given sentence of syllables S = (s1, s2, ..., sn) with the equation: $\arg\max_{T} p(T|S)$. The best result is given by the model using syllable tri-grams: it shows a 93.06% word-unit precision with POS-tagged corpus by ETRI. And a syllable bigram-based model of Kang, S.S. and Woo C.W (2001) shows a 71.22% word-unit precision according to the experiment by Lee D.G. et al. (2003). Compared with these stochastic models, our method using word unigrams and syllable bigrams shows a better performance, a 93.39% word-unit precision, with the test data equivalent to that used by Lee D.G. et al. (2003) (i.e. ExT 2 in Table 4). Some would consider that our system would use more system memory with a stochastic candidate-words list than that using tri-grams. However, as shown in Table 2, our model using word unigrams and syllable bigrams with smoothing based on syllable bigrams requires a relatively small memory size compared with the model using syllable trigrams.

---

[4] We observed that the computation of logarithms avoids underflow, and that the multiplication of odds favoring the inner spacing probability of a disyllable by the exponent of a power m produces the best performance.

Table 2. Memory Comparison of Stochastic Models

Stochastic Models	Total memory size of the total N° of different words
Syllable Bigram	4.1MB
Syllable Bigram + Word Unigram	4.1MB + 25.1MB = 29.2MB
Syllable Trigram	63.7MB

3 Combined Word-Spacing Method Rule- and Knowledge-Based Word-Spacing Module

Our basic system provides a list of possible words based on word unigram information. The word-unigram-based model is an intuitively natural approach to the word-spacing problem and requires a relatively small memory size compared with the model using syllable trigrams. However, the model naturally induces data sparseness because of the agglutinative morphology of Korean and semantic and syntactic ambiguities which can be removed only by considering the candidate-words' contexts. In this section, we propose a method combining the stochastic model and the rule-/knowledge-based model.

Agglutinative Morphology and Linguistic Ambiguity. In Korean, sequences of suffixes are productively and successively attached to the ends of word stems and determine most of the grammatical relations. In the following examples, various suffixes successively attach to the stem *namgi*.[5, 6]

(1) a. namgi-nim-i # nam-gi-si-eoss-da
    Namgi-H-Nom /to stay-CS-H-Past-E "Mr. Namgi left something"
 b. nam-gi-si-eoss-da-lago # ha-go # us-da
    to stay-{CS|*Nol}-H-Past-E-QS /to deliver (a speech)-Conj /to smile-E "to smile saying that (somebody) left (something)"
 c. nam-gi   to stay-Nol "the staying"

The form *namgi* can be disambiguated only by considering its context. It can be analyzed as a noun considering noun suffixes such as *-nim* <Hon>, *-ga* <Nom>, among others: (1-a) ***namgi****-nim-i*; as a causative verb stem derived from another verb stem *nam-* considering verb endings or verb pre-endings (verb suffixes) attached to it: (1-a) ***nam-gi****-si-eoss-da* and (1-b) ***nam-gi****-si-eoss-da-lago*; and as a derived noun from a verb with nominal suffix *-gi* (1-c). Moreover, we can find some sub-chains of the whole used as spaced words: *#nam-gi-si-eoss-da-lago#*; *#nam-gi-si-eoss-da#*; *#nam-gi#*. This variability of a word boundary produces a higher difficulty in processing the word-spacing of Korean than of English, in which fewer morphemes for inflec-

---

[5] Throughout this paper, we adopt the Revised Romanization of Korean, released on July 4, 2000 by the South Korean Ministry of Culture and Tourism.
[6] Symbols and Abbreviations: |: separation; -: morphological boundary; *: unacceptable form; { }: alternative elements; W: word; Acc: accusative; Auxvb: auxiliary verb; Adv: adverb; CS: causative suffix; Conj: conjunction; D: determiner; E: verbal ending; H: honorific suffix; N: noun; Nom: nominative; Nol: nominal suffix; Past: past tense; Post: postposition; Pfx: Prefix; QS: quotation suffix used in indirect narrative; Sfx: suffix;

tion simultaneously encode several meanings. [1] A large number of conjugated forms of each Korean verb are possible considering all the possible combinations among verbal stems, verbal pre-endings and verbal endings.

Word-Spacing Errors and Linguistic Ambiguities. There is a word-spacing problem due to linguistic ambiguities that the statistical method can hardly overcome and can only be resolved by considering enough of the context of the word being checked.

(2) Ambiguity between a postposition and a noun
 a. banghag{-|*#}nae # don-eul # da # sseo{-|#}beoli-da
  vacation-{all through<Sfx>|*inside<N> /money-Acc /all<Adv> /to spend-Conj{-|#}Auxvb-E "Somebody spent all his money all through the vacation."
 b. haggyo # nae.
  school /inside<N> "the inside of school"
(3) Ambiguity between a prefix and a noun
 a. geum{-|*#}segi # choego{-|#}haengsa
  {this<Pfx>|*gold<N>}-century /the greatest<N> /event<N> "The greatest event of the century"
 b. geum # paljji gold /wristlet "a gold wristlet"
(4) Ambiguity between a determiner and a part of a noun
 a. chongal # su{*-|#}bal-eul # sso-da
  ball /{*care|many<D>}/round-acc /to shot-E "to shot many rounds of shot"
 b. hwanja # subal invalid /care "care for an invalid"

The same morpheme, *nae* in (2), can be interpreted as a postposition 'all through' when it is used without a space on its left side, or as a noun 'inside' when it is used with a space. The same morpheme *geum* in (3) can prefix 'this' without a space on its right side or the noun 'gold' with a space. The forms *subal* and *su#bal* in (4) differ only regarding the inner space. They are analyzed as a noun and a sequence of a determiner 'many rounds of shot' and its determined noun.

Constructing Spacing-Error Checking Rules. In order to mitigate data-sparseness due to the agglutinative morphology of Korean and remove linguistic ambiguities, it is necessary to understand the factors that influence spacing-errors found in real texts. Table 3 shows the summary of frequencies for each error type identified by our recent experiment on an earlier system which was carried out with Corpus A of approximately 19 million words (see Table 1). The result shows that 1,404,777 words were rejected by running a Korean grammar checker.[7]

Table 3. Error Types in Web-Documents

Error Types	N° of Erroneous Words	Frequency (%)
Grammatical Errors	222,516	15.84
Spacing Errors	**334,899**	**23.84**
Spelling Errors	846,940	60.29
Verbal Conjugation Errors	421	0.03
Total	1,404,777	100.00

---

[7] The Korean Grammar Checker is used in Pusan National University [3].

According to the results in Table 3, the word-spacing error in Korean is the second-most frequent among other errors that we encounter while processing Korean texts. Based on statistical results and heuristic evidence obtained while treating various word-spacing error types in the texts, error analysis makes possible the building of an adequate knowledge base. These linguistic conditions can be used to make correction rules based on a morph-syntactical analysis or on collocation and anti-collocation, which are then incorporated into the knowledge base. Each rule is composed of a Word Potentially Involved in Word-spacing Error (WPI) and its one or more targets' information. The WPI triggers partial parsing. While the singularity of the WPI should be respected, the target can be the subject of several rules: an eventual dependent could be a target of a different WPI. Our current system provides about 800 words or patterns as WPIs which trigger partial parsing.

```
Rule (number) =
    {Word Potentially Involved in Word-spacing Error, Parsing Direction;
     Negligible Words' Linguistic Information;
     Compatible or Incompatible Words' Linguistic Conditions;
     Correction (Splitting, Attachment)}
```

Fig. 1. Knowledgebase of Word-spacing Rules

There are approximately 1,541 rules in our system that are related to context-dependant word-spacing error correction. And, 9,407 words or patterns and 15,679 rules are dedicated to compound nouns.

Word-Spacing Error Correction Based on Partial Parsing Method. We engage the partial parsing method based on the rule-/knowledge-based approach in order to resolve context-dependant word-spacing problems. The orientation of the parsing to detect and correct grammatical and semantic errors in our system is constructed with respect to a WPI [8]. The partial parsing module is triggered when this WPI is detected. Partial parsing proceeds from a selected WPI until its target (i.e. a word that forms a collocation or anti-collocation with it), or no other possible targets, are found. The word-spacing module implemented with partial parsing provides three possible checking directions a posteriori: right-hand parsing, left-hand parsing, and conditional parsing.

---

[8] Our partial parsing method deals with knowledge based on dependency grammar. Nevertheless, this is rather far from classical dependency grammar. Whereas dependency grammar describes order and restrictions in the same formula, our system tolerates different descriptions for each case. But in the current word-spacing module, the governor in our system is not conceived in a linguistic sense but as a word potentially involved in word-spacing error (WPI) that the system identifies when checking a sentence and which selection as governor doesn't burden the spacing system since the system always has to have the fewest rules possible in order to avoid lowering the efficiency of the system. We refer reader to [3] for further discussion on the parsing trigger and parsing direction.

Consider first the WPI having a 'right-hand headed relation' with their targets. For example, we can find many spacing errors between the POS of a homograph, *nae* in (2-a). It can be attached only to a noun [+time] as a suffix. Otherwise, it should be spaced from its left-hand noun as another noun. The construction of Korean compound nouns such as *choego{- | #}haengsa* in (3-a) is endocentric, with the possible exception of coordinated structures. It means that they have a head on the right-hand side in a construction. This linguistic aspect is reflected as such in the parsing direction of our system. Our system controls the semantic and lexical scope of each noun belonging to a compound noun in order to check if the collocation relation is established or not. The form *geum* in (3-a) is often mis-split in real texts, producing semantic ambiguity. The form is included as a WPI, in the knowledge base, having a 'left-hand headed relation' with its targets. When it is attached to a noun [+time], there is compatibility between the WPI and the target. Otherwise, the morpheme is interpreted as a noun. Finally, we have a 'conditional WPI'. We call a 'conditional WPI' a syntactic entity that can govern its target regarding the semantic or morpho-syntactic state of the element situated on its other wing. Many Korean writers confuse *subal* with *su#bal*. Thus *subal* in (4-a) triggers parsing as a WPI and selects a verb *sso-da* 'to shoot' as its target. However, the WPI needs to satisfy the co-occurrence condition with the item on its other wing, *chongal* 'ball'. *subal* is not compatible with *chongal*. Thus correction of *su#bal* by splitting proceeds.

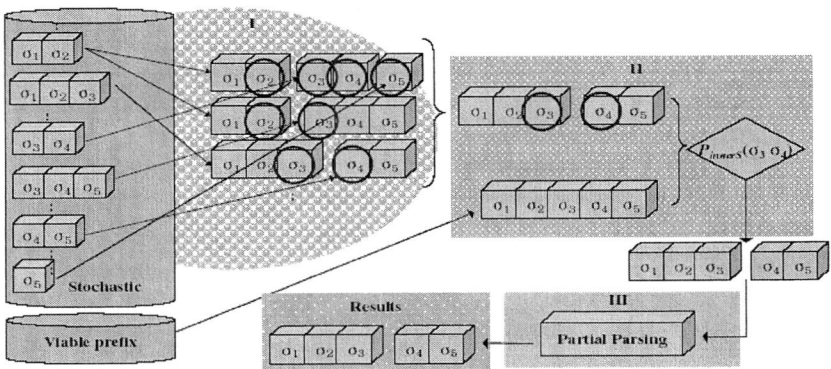

Fig. 2. Combined Word-spacing Module

Combined Word-Spacing Model. The current combined word-spacing model provides: (I) the stochastic-based method which splits an input sentence into a candidate-word sequence using word unigrams and syllable bigrams; (II) the method of dynamic extension of the candidate-word list using the 'longest match strategy' based on the viable-prefix which searches the longest candidate-word which can be analyzed morphologically. The extension does not proceed using the stochastic method based on syllable bigrams in the combined model, in the interests of the efficiency of partial parsing The 'longest match strategy' based on the viable-prefix suggests dynamically possible words and includes them among possible k^{th} candidate words, and the system dynamically selects a candidate-word by estimating the inner-spacing probability of disyllables located at the boundary of stochastic-based words (i.e. σ_3 and σ_4 at the step II in the Figure 2). If this value is under the threshold, the system selects the word from the stochastic word list and, if the value is over the threshold, the system selects the longest-radix word; and (III) the partial parsing method based on the asymmetric relation between candidate words selected by applying methods (I) and (II). The word-spacing module based on statistic and partial parsing is depicted as follows:

4 Experimentation

For the test of our stochastic word-spacing model's performance, two types of test data were provided: (a) the inner test data extracted at the same distribution ratio as a given corpus over the whole training data, Corpus A, B, and C, and (b) three external test data, each extracted from the Sejong Project's processed and balanced corpus (ExT 1), the POS-tagged corpus by ETRI(Electronics and Telecommunications Research Institute) (ExT 2): and from special opinion pages in a daily newspaper on the web of less than 100 words (Ext 3).

Table 4. Test Data Suite

	N° of Sentences	N° of Words	N° of Syllables
Inner	2,000	25,020	103,196
ExT 1	2,000	13,971	40,353
ExT 2	2,000	17,191	52,688
ExT 3	2,000	12,504	40,088

Table 5. Experimental Results (PP: Partial parsing)

		Stochastic Model Without Smoothing	Knowledge-based Dynamic Extension	With Partial Parsing
InT	Pw	98.45%	98.46%	98.52%
	Rw	98.19%	98.00%	97.98%
ExT 1	Pw	90.91%	97.81%	98.07%
	Rw	93.63%	97.77%	97.95%
ExT 2	Pw	90.43%	98.88%	99.02%
	Rw	94.61%	99.01%	99.12%
ExT 3	Pw	86.88%	93.60%	94.09%
	Rw	90.89%	94.73%	95.01%

The system test was preceded by removing spaces from the input test data and selecting according to the following two evaluation measures: (a) correctly spaced words compared to the total number of words created by the system (word-unit precision, Pw); and (b) correctly spaced words compared to the total number of words in the test document (word-unit recall, Rw). The result of stochastic automatic word-spacing with dynamic expansion of the candidate-word list using stochastic smoothing is shown in the following Table.

The system thus becomes robust against ambiguity that would be encountered because of word-spacing errors while processing Korean texts. And a similar performance is provided for inner and balanced standard external data (ExT 1) (98.52% and 98.07% respective word-unit precisions). The performance observed with text from opinion pages in a daily newspaper (ExT 3) is lower than that with other test data. This kind of text is especially intricate because it contains stylistic errors that require complete reconstitution of sentences. In these types of text, due to the constraint of the number of words, users commit spacing errors purposely and produce especially intricate text. Therefore, even though we could obtain only a 94.09% word-unit precision, which is lower than with other test data, it is very encouraging in preprocessing Korean texts.

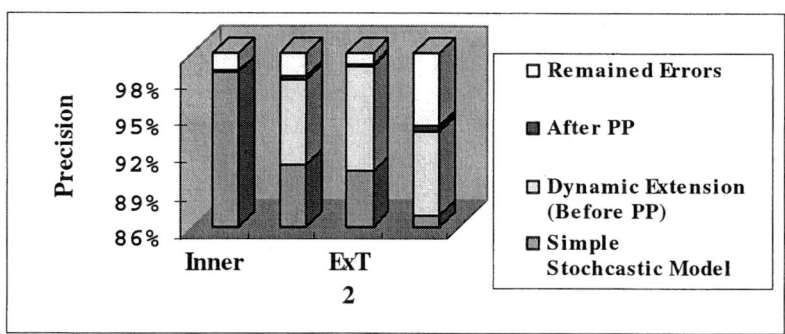

Fig. 3. Amelioration of total error rate

By smoothing with the dynamic extension of the candidate-word list based on the viable prefix, a high amelioration of performance was observed for the inner and the external data. The system thus compensates for the data sparseness problem in the simple stochastic method. Figure 3 shows that, according to different test data, about 2.81% of words are not processed correctly after applying methods (I) and (II). Most of those errors are context-dependant word-spacing problems. Implementing the combined word-spacing method using partial parsing, context-dependant word-spacing problems are resolved and 3.90%, 11.87%, 12.50% and 7.66% amelioration is obtained on the total error rate for Inner, ExT 1, ExT 2 and ExT 3 respectively as depicted in Figure 3.

6 Conclusions and Further Research

In this paper we have implemented an automatic word-spacing system which combines (a) a stochastic-based method based on word unigram and syllable bigram, (b) a normalization of data sparseness in providing a candidate-words list extension using the 'longest match strategy' based on the viable-prefix and (c) the rule-/knowledge-based method using partial parsing. This combined method efficiently (a) normalizes data sparseness due to Korean agglutinative morphology where chains of suffixes are commonly attached to the ends of stems, and therefore there is considerable risk in using the syllable statistics for the right-hand boundary of a word, and (b) resolves semantic and syntactic ambiguities concerning word-spacing which remain after applying only stochastic and dynamic candidate-words list extension. Using partial parsing, semantic and syntactic ambiguities are removed and an average 8.98% amelioration of the total error rate is obtained for inner and external data. Thus our method becomes robust against homographs, the meanings of which can only be disambiguated by spacing.

Our further research will develop a predictive algorithm for unseen words in order to extract linguistic categorical information from a training corpus of different types of texts so that it can be applied to Korean text preprocessing, and to define the optimal combining algorithm between the statistical spacing method and the rule-based spacing method.

Acknowledgements

This work was supported by National Research Laboratory Program (Contract Number: M1-0412-00-0028-04-J00-00-014-00).

References

1. Comrie, B.: Language Universals and Linguistic Typology, Blackwell (1989)
2. Grefenstette, G.: What is a Word, What is a Sentence, Problems of Tokenization Proceedings of the conference on computational lexicography and text research (1994)
3. Kang, M.Y., Yoon, A.S., Kwon, H.C.: Improving Partial Parsing Based on Error Pattern Analysis for Korean Grammar Checker, TALIP Volume 2, Issue 4, ACM (2003) 301-323
4. Kang, M.Y., Choi, S.W., Kwon, H.C.: A Hybrid Approach to Automatic Word-spacing in Korean, LNCS Vol.3029 (2004) 284 - 294
5. Kang, S.S., Woo C.W.: Automatic Segmentation of Words Using Syllable Bigram Statistics. Proceedings of 6th Natural Language Processing Pacific Rim Symposium (2001) 729-732
6. Kang, S.S.: Korean Morphological Analysis and Information Retrieval, Hongleunggwahag Publisher, Seoul (2002)
7. Lee, D.G., Lee, S.Z., Lim, H.S., Rim, H.CH.: Two Statistical Models for Automatic Word Spacing of Korean Sentences, Journal of KISS(B): Software and Applications, Vol. 30. 4, (2003) 358~370

8. Manning, C.D., Schütze, H.: Foundations of Statistical Natural Language Processin The MIT Press, Cambridge London (2001)
9. Sim, CH.M., Kwon, H.CH.: Implementation of a Korean Spelling Checker Based on Collocation of Words, Journal of KISS(B): Software and Applications, Vol. 23. 7 (1996) 776-785
10. Teahan, W. J., McNab R., Wen, Y., Witten, I. H.: A compression-based algorithm for Chinese word segmentation, Computational Linguistics, Vol 26. 3 (2000) 375 – 393
11. Tsutsumi, J., Nitta, T., Ono, K., Jiang, S.D., Nakaishi, M.: Segmenting a Sentence into Morphemes using Statistic Information between Words, Proceedings of Coling'94 (1994) 227-233
12. Korean Standard Pronunciation Dictionary, Edited by Kim, S.T et al., Eomungak (1993)

Extraction of Shallow Language Patterns: An Approximation of Data Oriented Parsing

Samuel W. K. Chan

Dept. of Decision Sciences,
The Chinese University of Hong Kong,
Hong Kong, China
swkchan@cuhk.edu.hk

Abstract. This paper presents a novel approach to extracting shallow language patterns from text. The approach makes use of an attributed string matching technique which is based on two major but complementary factors: *lexical similarities* and *sentence structures*. The technique takes full advantage of a huge number of sentence patterns in a Treebank, while preserving robustness, without being bogged down into a complete linguistic analysis. The ideas described are implemented and an evaluation of 5,000 Chinese sentences is examined in order to justify its statistical significances.

1 Introduction

Identifying language patterns is a fundamental task in natural language processing. Competent speakers of a language hardly ever fail to recognize the language patterns, like verb-object pairs, various phrases structures, semi-idiomatic expressions, and platitudes of that language. Even though these patterns have been found useful in various application areas, including information extraction, textual summarization, and even bilingual alignment, the demands for a highly efficient sentence patterns extraction system are still mounting.

One of the most important sentence patterns is the case frame which can be used to represent the meaning of sentences [10]. In general, a case frame is to be understood as an array of slots, each of which is labelled with a case name, and eventually possibly filled with a case filler, the whole system representing the underlying structure of an input sentence. Certainly, one approach to extracting the case frames is to obtain a full parse of a sentence. However, having a complete parse tree for a sentence is difficult in many cases. An alternative approach is the shallow parsing which tries to circumvent the complexity of full parsing and analyzes a sentence at the level of phrases and the relations between them [1]. As a branch in shallow parsing, data-oriented parsing (DOP) models embody the assumption that humans produce and interpret natural language utterances by invoking representations of their concrete past language experiences, rather than the rules of a consistent and non-redundant competence grammar [3]. DOP models usually maintain large corpora of sentences annotated with syntactic and semantic structures. New input sentences are analyzed by combining partial structures from the corpus. The occurrence frequencies of these structures are employed to estimate which of the resulting analyses are the most suitable patterns for the input sentence.

In this research, a shallow but effective sentence chunking process is designed and developed. This sentence chunking process is to extract all the phrases from the input sentences, without being bogged down into deep semantic parsing and understanding. On the other hand, while several criteria for recognizing sentence patterns, such as case frames, in sentences have been considered in the past, none of the criteria serves as a completely adequate decision procedure. Most of the studies in computational linguistics do not provide any hints on how to map input sentences into case frames automatically, particularly in Chinese [6]. Our second objective is to assign the extracted phrases into their corresponding case roles based on a corpus of utterances annotated with labeled trees or subtrees. One of our primary goals in this research is to design a shallow but robust mechanism which can extract Chinese sentence patterns [14, 15, 4, 5]. Even though the classical syntactic and semantic analysis in Chinese is extremely difficult, if not impossible, to systematize in the current computational linguistics research, this DOP does not require any deep linguistic analysis to be formalized. Consequently, the annotated sentences will give piecemeal the underlying semantic representation, without being mired into the formalism. The organization of the paper is as follows. The related work in DOP and text chunking are first described in Section 2. We have employed a corpus annotated with the labeled trees. The characteristics of the Treebank that supports our approach will also be explained. In this research, each Chinese token will have two attributes, namely Part-of-Speech (*POS*) and Semantic Classes (*SC*). Any input sentence can be viewed as an attributed string. The detailed discussion on how an attributed string matching algorithm can be used in the shallow patterns extraction is shown in Section 3. The system has already been implemented using Java language. In order to demonstrate the capability of our system, an experiment with 5,000 sentences is conducted. It is explained in Section 4 followed by a conclusion.

2 Related Work

A number of systems have been developed to perform shallow parsing. The early approaches in shallow parsing that mainly came out of the Message Understanding Conferences (MUC) have demonstrated their capabilities for extracting noun groups, verb groups, and particles [11]. For example, the FASTUS is a system which is designed for extracting information from free text. One of the applications is to mark text with annotations that indicate items of interest, such as names of people or companies. It also fills up database templates with information that could be then entered into a relational database [2]. Similarly, the SPARKLE (Shallow PARsing for acquisition of Knowledge for Language Engineering) aims to develop shallow parsing technology in four European languages together with corpus-based lexical acquisition techniques, and deploy parsers in multilingual information retrieval and speech dialogue systems (http://www.informatics.susx.ac.uk/research/nlp/sparkle/sparkle.html). Their shallow parsing is carried out by a generalized

LR parser, which uses a unification-based phrasal grammar of POS tags. The resulting parses will serve for acquiring lexical information.

Extracting shallow language patterns involves chunking sentences into segments. Motivated by the psycholinguistic evidence which demonstrates that intonation changes or pauses would affect the language understanding processes in humans [12], Abney proposes the concept of text chunking as a first step in the full parsing [1]. A typical chunk of a text is defined as consisting of a single content word surrounded by a constellation of function words, matching a fixed template. Church also uses a simple model for finding non-recursive NPs in sequence of POS tags [9]. Turning the sentence chunking as a bracketing problem, Church calculates the probability of inserting both the open and close brackets between POS tags. Each chunking alternative is ranked and the best alternative is selected. In a somewhat similar vein, using transformation-based learning with rule-template referring to neighboring words, POS tags and chunk tags, Ramshaw and Marcus identify essentially the initial portions of non-recursive noun phrases up to the head, including determiners [18]. These chunks are extracted from the Treebank parses, by selecting NPs that contain no nested NPs. While the above approaches have been proposed to recognize common subsequences and to produce some forms of chunked representation of an input sentence, the recognized structures do not include any recursively embedded NPs. As the result, the resultant fragments bear little resemblance to the kind of phrase structures that are normally appeared in linguistics.

While the state of the art in computational linguistics is to make use of the knowledge encoded in Treebank to analyze sentence structures, two major issues have to be clarified beforehand. First, what formalism do we assume to annotate the corpus utterances? Second, what kinds of trees do we extract from the corpus, and how do we recombine them? In this paper, we address the first issue by adopting the Sinica Chinese Treebank [7]. In contrast to the English and Chinese Penn Treebank which takes a straightforward syntactic approach [16, 21], the Information-based Case Grammar (ICG) in Sinica Chinese Treebank stipulates that each lexical entry contains both semantic and syntactic features. The grammar indicates the way that lexical tokens in the sentences are related to each other. That is, grammatical constraints are expressed in terms of linear order of thematic roles and their syntactic and semantic restrictions. This tree structure has the advantage of maintaining phrase structure rules as well as the syntactic and semantic dependency relations. The latest version of Sinica Treebank (v.2.1), released in early 2004, contains about 55,000 trees with 300,000 words. The Treebank contains a compact bundle of syntactic and semantic information, with more than 150 different types of POS and 50 semantic roles.

On the other hand, while it may be too computationally demanding to have a full syntactic and semantic analysis of every sentence in every text, Sima'an addresses the second issue and presents a *Tree-gram* model, a typical example of DOP, which integrates bilexical dependencies, and conditions its substitutions based on the structural relations of the trees that are involved [19]. The basic ideas of the Tree-gram model are to (i) take a corpus of utterances annotated with labeled trees; (ii) decompose every corpus tree into a set of subtrees; (iii) perform parsing as the union of the best possible subtrees based on a stochastic tree substitution grammar. In this research, we propose an algorithm in extracting shallow language patterns by matching any input Chinese sentence with the trees in the Treebank using an approximate pattern matching technique. Different from the stochastic tree substitution grammar proposed in the Tree-gram model, our approach, characterized by an optimization technique, looks for a transformation with a minimum cost, or called *edit distance*. While the concept of edit distance is commonly found in the conventional pattern matching techniques [13, 20], we take a step further in applying the technique in data-oriented parsing. The detailed discussion of the algorithm is shown as follows.

3 Shallow Language Patterns Extraction Using Attributed String Matching Algorithm

The algorithm is essentially accomplished by applying a series of edit operations to an input sentence to change it to every tree in the Treebank. Every edit operation has been associated with a cost and the total cost of the transformation can be calculated by summing up the costs of all the operations. This edit distance reflects the dissimilarity between the input sentence and the trees. Instead of analyzing the exact Chinese tokens appearing in the sentence, extended attributes of each token in both input sentence and the trees, with their POS and semantic classes, are used. The closely matched tree, i.e., the one with minimum cost or edit distance, is selected and the corresponding phrase structures and semantic role tags delineated in the tree are unified with the input sentence.

Let two given attributed strings A and B denoted as $A = a_1 a_2 a_3 \ldots a_m$ and $B = b_1 b_2 b_3 \ldots b_n$, where are a_i, b_j the ith and jth attributed symbols of A and B respectively. Each attributed symbol represents a primitive of A or B. Generally speaking, to match an attributed string A with another B means to transform or edit the symbols in A into those in B with a minimum-cost sequence of allowable edit operations. In general, the following three types of edit operations are available for attributed symbol transformation.

(a) *Change*: to replace an attributed symbol a_i with another b_j, denoted as $a_i \rightarrow b_j$.
(b) *Insert*: to insert an attributed symbol b_j into an attributed string, denoted as $\lambda \rightarrow b_j$ where λ denotes a null string.
(c) *Delete*: to delete an attributed symbol a_i from an attributed string, denoted as $a_i \rightarrow \lambda$.

[Definition 1]
An *edit sequence* is a sequence of ordered edit operations, $s_1, s_2, \ldots s_p$ where s_i is any of the following three types of edit operations, *Change, Insert, Delete*.

[Definition 2]
Let R be an arbitrary nonnegative real cost function which defines a cost $R(a_i \rightarrow b_j)$ for each edit operation $a_i \quad b_j$. The cost of an edit sequence $S = s_1, s_2, \ldots s_p$ to be

$$R(S) = \sum_{i=1}^{p} R(s_i) \qquad (1)$$

[Definition 3]
For two strings A ad B with length m and n respectively, $D(i, j)$ denotes the edit distance, which is the minimum number of edit operations, needed to transform the first i characters of A into first j characters of B, where $1 \leq i \leq m$ and $1 \leq j \leq n$. In other words, if A has m letters and B has n letters, then the edit distance of A and B is precisely the value $D(m, n)$.

The following algorithm has been proposed for computing every edit distances $D(i, j)$ [13].

[Algorithm A]

$D(0, 0) := 0$;
for $i := 1$ **to** m **do** $D(i, 0) := D(i-1, 0) + R(a_i \rightarrow \lambda)$;
for $j := 1$ **to** n **do** $D(0, j) := D(0, j-1) + R(\lambda \rightarrow b_j)$;
for $i := 1$ **to** m **do**
    for $j := 1$ **to** n **do**
    begin
        $m1 := D(i, j-1) + R(\lambda \rightarrow b_j)$;
        $m2 := D(i-1, j) + R(a_i \rightarrow \lambda)$;
        $m3 := D(i-1, j-1) + R(a_i \rightarrow b_j)$;
        $D(i, j) := \min(m1, m2, m3)$;
    end

Our attributed string matching in case role annotation is to make use of the algorithm above and modify the cost function $R(.)$ for various edit operations. In our approach, each Chinese token has two attributes, i.e., Part-Of-Speech (POS) and Semantic Class (SC). Let S be an input sentence and the T be a tree in the Sinica Treebank, s_i and t_j be two tokens in S and T with attribute $\langle POS_i, SC_i \rangle$ and $\langle POS_j, SC_j \rangle$ respectively. We define the cost function for a *change* operation $s_i \rightarrow t_j$ to be

$$R(s_i \rightarrow t_j) = u(POS_i, POS_j) + v(SC_i, SC_j) \tag{2}$$

where $u(POS_i, POS_j)$ defines the partial cost due to the difference between the POS of the tokens. The POS tags from the Chinese Knowledge Information Processing Group (CKIP) of Academia Sinica are employed [8]. The tags involve 46 different types of POS which can further refine into more than 150 subtypes. In order to figure out the cost function $u(\cdot,\cdot)$, in our system, all the POS tags are organized into a tree structure using XML with an associated hard-coded cost function. Figure 1 shows a fragment of XML of the nouns (Na) which is divided into in-collective (Nae) and collective (Nal) nouns which are then divided ultimately into in-collective concrete uncountable nouns (Naa), in-collective concrete countable nouns (Nab), in-collective abstract countable nouns (Nac), in-collective abstract uncountable nouns (Nad). The cost function $u(\cdot,\cdot)$ will reflect the difference based on the tag Toll encoded in the XML as shown in Figure 1. For example, the cost for changing a word having POS from Naa to Nab,

u(Naa, Nab) = Toll(Naa→Nal1) + Toll(Nal1→Nab) = 1 + 1 = 2

Similarly,
u(Naa, Naea) = Toll(Naa→Na11)+Toll(Na11→Na1)+Toll(Na1→Na)+
Toll(Na→Nae)+Toll(Nae→Naea)= 7

```
<Na Toll="4" Level="2">
  <Na1 Toll="2" Level="3">
    <Na11 Toll="1" Level="4">
      <Naa Toll="1" Level="5" />
      <Nab Toll="1" Level="5" />
    </Na11>
    <Na12 Toll="1" Level="4">
      <Nac Toll="1" Level="5" />
      <Nad Toll="1" Level="5" />
    </Na12>
  </Na1>
  <Nae Toll="2" Level="3">
    <Naea Toll="1" Level="4" />
    <Naeb Toll="1" Level="4" />
  </Nae>
</Na>
```

Fig. 1. Tree structure of Nouns (Na) based on the CKIP Academia Sinica

The function $u(\cdot,\cdot)$ partially indicates the alignment of the syntactic structure of the input sentence and the sentence appeared in the Treebank. The second term in equation (2) defines the other partial cost due to the semantic differences. In our approach, the lexical tokens in the both sentences are identified using a lexical source similar to the Roget's Thesaurus. The lexical source is a bilingual thesaurus with an *is-a* hierarchy. An *is-a* hierarchy can be viewed as a directed acyclic graph with a single root. Based on the *is-a* hierarchy in the thesaurus, we define conceptual distance d between two notional words by their shortest path lengths [17].

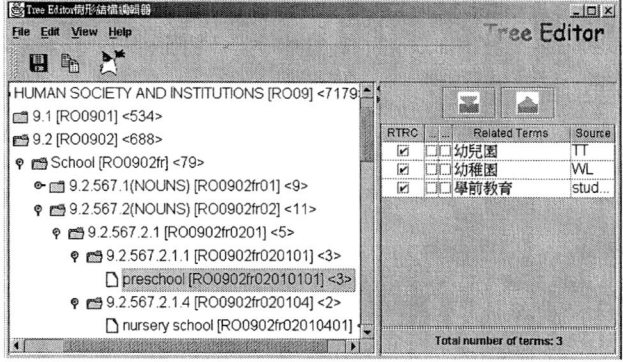

Fig. 2. *is-a* hierarchy in the bilingual thesaurus

Figure 2 shows one of our *is-a* hierarchies in our bilingual thesaurus using our Tree Editor. While the upward links correspond to generalization, the specialization is represented in the downward links. For example, the upward link from 幼稚園 (preschool) to 學校 (school) indicates that 學校 (school) is more general than 幼稚園 (preschool) and the lexical tokens in the same terminal subclass, such as 幼稚園 (preschool), 幼兒園 (nursery school), or 幼兒中心 (day-care centre), are of the same meaning. The hierarchies demonstrated in the thesaurus are based on the idea that linguists classify lexical items in terms of similarities and differences. They are used to structure or rank lexical items from more general to the more special. Given two tokens t_1 and t_2 in an *is-a* hierarchy of the thesaurus, the distance d between the items is defined as follows:

$$d(t_1, t_2) = \text{minimal number of } \textit{is-a} \text{ relationships in the shortest path between } t_1 \text{ and } t_2 \quad (3)$$

The shortest path lengths in *is-a* hierarchies are calculated. Initially, a search fans out through the *is-a* relationships from the original two nodes to all nodes pointed to by the originals, until a point of intersection is found. The paths from the original two nodes are concatenated to form a continuous path, which must be a shortest path between the originals. The number of links in the shortest path is counted. Since $d(t_1, t_2)$ is positive and symmetric, $d(t_1, t_2)$ is a metric which means (i) $d(t_1, t_1) = 0$; (ii) $d(t_1, t_2) = d(t_2, t_1)$; (iii) $d(t_1, t_2) + d(t_2, t_3) \geq d(t_1, t_3)$. At the same time, the semantic similarity measure between the items is defined by:

$$v(t_i, t_j) := \begin{cases} d(t_i, t_j) & \text{if } d(t_i, t_j) \leq d_{max} \\ \textit{MaxInt} & \text{otherwise} \end{cases} \quad (4)$$

where d_{max} is proportional to the number of lexical items in the system and *MaxInt* is a maximum integer of the system. This semantic similarity measure defines the degree of relatedness between tokens. Obviously, strong degree of relatedness exists between the lexical tokens under the same nodes. For the cost of the insert and delete operations, we make use the concept of *collocation* which measures how likely two tokens are to co-occur in a window of text. To better distinguish statistics based ratios, work in this area is often presented in terms of the mutual information, which is defined as

$$MI(t_{j-1}, t_j) = \log_2 \frac{P(t_{j-1}, t_j)}{P(t_{j-1}) \times P(t_j)} \quad (5)$$

where t_{j-1} and t_j are two adjacent tokens. While $P(x, y)$ is the probability of observing x and y together, $P(x)$ and $P(y)$ are the probabilities of observing x and y anywhere in the text, whether individually or in conjunction. Note that tokens that have no association with each other and co-occur together according to chance will have a mutual information number close to zero. This leads to the cost function for insertion and deletion shown in equation (6) and (7) respectively.

$$R(\lambda \rightarrow t_j) = \begin{cases} K \times |z| & \text{if } 0 \geq z > \varepsilon \\ \textit{MaxInt} & \text{otherwise} \end{cases} \quad (6)$$

where $z = \min \{MI(t_{j-1}, t_j), MI(t_j, t_{j+1})\}$

$$R(t_j \to \lambda) = \begin{cases} L \times |MI(t_{j-1}, t_{j+1})| & \text{if } 0 \geq MI(t_{j-1}, t_{j+1}) > \varepsilon \\ MaxInt & \text{otherwise} \end{cases} \quad (7)$$

where K, L, ε are three constants relied on the size of the corpus.

Obviously, the insertion operation will be penalized if the co-occurrence between the newly inserted token and its neighbors is low. Similarly, the deletion operation is most likely to happen if there is a high co-occurrence between the adjacent pairs after the deletion. Using the above cost functions for the three edit operations, the tree in the Treebank with minimum cost is identified to best approximation of the input sentence S and its relevant case roles tags will be adopted. Shallow language patterns, with all the recursively embedded structures, are then extracted based on the case role tags appeared in the Treebank. Experimental results and an illustration of the patterns extracted are shown in the following section.

4 Experimental Results

We have implemented the system using Java JDK1.4.2 under Sun Microsystems. The whole system development is designed under Unified Modeling Language (UML) using Rational Rose. To show the efficiency of the proposed algorithm, a series of experiments are performed.

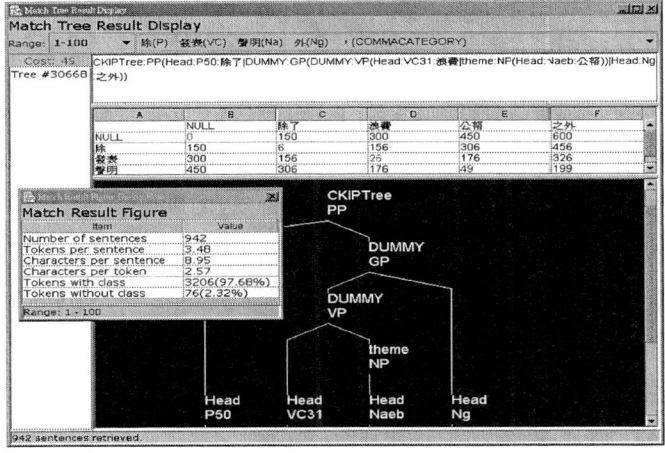

Fig. 3. Graphical User Interface (GUI) in the shallow language patterns extraction

In our experiment, for every input sentence, the best matching tree with minimum edit distance in the Treebank is calculated as shown in Algorithm A. The Information Case Grammar (ICG) of the best matching tree in the Treebank will be adopted. Figure 3 shows the graphical user interface which includes the cost matrix generated and the corresponding ICG structure of the input sentence. We have tested the system with 5,000 input sentences. The detailed results are shown in Table 1. The average sentence length is around 10.5 characters per sentence. In order to let the readers to visualize the relevance of the edit distance with the underlying tree structure, Figures 4 and 5 show two sentences clearly with edit distance equal to 15 and 64 respectively. The sentence

議員商討總統出兵一事 (S1)

(in English, *The senators discuss the issue on sending troops initiated by the president*)

has a small edit distance, equal to 15, with the tree shown in Figure 4.

Table 1. Analysis of 5,000 sentences in the experiment

Edit distance	# of sentences	Average # of tokens	Average edit distance	% of sentences having incomplete semantic classes
0-25	336	5.24	21.06	2.32
0-50	1556	6.15	34.42	9.01
0-75	2841	6.67	46.94	11.08
0-100	5000	6.62	65.94	11.93

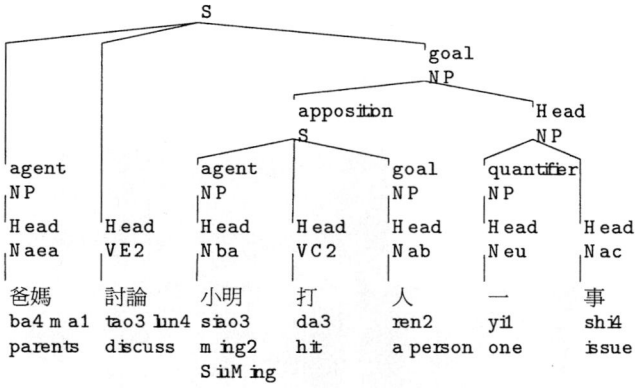

Fig. 4. Tree in the Treebank which closely matches, edit distance equal to 15, with the input sentence shown in (S1)

The sentence is then chunked into phrases, ⟨議員⟩ (*The senators*), ⟨商討⟩ (*discuss*), and ⟨總統出兵一事⟩ (*the issue on sending troops initiated by the president*), which are further tagged with *agent*, *act*, and *goal* respectively by taking the advantage of annotation in the Treebank. Certainly, the phrase 〈總統出兵一事〉 (*the issue on sending troops initiated by the president*) can be further chunked into more details 〈總統出兵〉 (*sending troops initiated by the president*), 〈一事〉 (*the issue*).

Table 2. Language patterns extracted from the input sentence (S1)

@SP[	議員商討總統出兵一事	The senators discuss the issue on sending troops initiated by the president
Agent	〈議員〉	The senators
Act	〈商討〉	discuss
Goal	@AP[〈總統出兵〉]AP, @NP[〈一事〉]NP	@AP [(sending troops initiated by the president)] AP, @NP [(the issue)] NP
]SP		
@AP[	總統出兵	sending troops initiated by the president
Agent	總統	the president
Act	出	sending
Goal	兵	troops
]AP		

This chunking not only provides the basic semantic tag for each constituent, it also reflects the language patterns of the input sentence. The corresponding pattern extracted is shown in Table 2. As shown in Table 2, the language patterns extracted are indicated by the square brackets together with the explicit semantic tags. While the sentence pattern is marked with @SP[...], the embedded phrases are marked by different tags, such @AP[...] for apposition phrase, or @PP[...] for position phrase. Similarly, in Figure5, the upper sentence is coming from the Treebank *T* while the lower one represents the input sentences *S*. Due to the similarity, in terms of the edit distance, of the matched pair, the syntactic structure of the sentence from the Treebank is transplanted to the input sentence. As a result, each token in the input sentence will inherit the associated roles from the target sentence. For example, the Chinese sentence shown in Figure 5,

可惜國家財政萬分困難 (S2)
(in English: *Unfortunately, the national budget is so tight*)

The sentence is chunked into 〈可惜〉 (*unfortunately*), and 〈國家財政萬分困難〉 (*the national budget is so tight*) which is further chunked into 〈國家財政〉 (*national budget*), 〈萬分〉 (*so*), 〈困難〉 (*tight*). At the same time, 〈國家財政萬分困難〉 (*national budget is so tight*), 〈國家財政〉 (*national budget*), and 〈萬分〉 (*so*) are annotated as the *goal, main theme* and *degree* of Sentence S2 respectively.

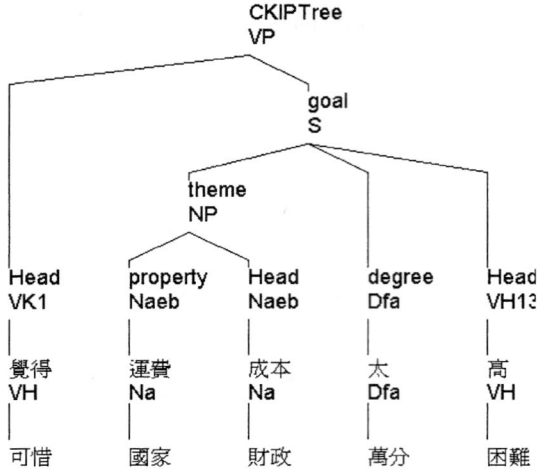

Fig. 5. Sentence with edit distance equal to 64

As with other text analysis, the effectiveness of the system appears to be dictated by recall and precision parameters where recall (R) is a percentage of how many correct case roles can be identified while precision (P) is the percentage of case roles, tackled by the system, which are actually correct. In addition, a common parameter F is used as a single-figure measure of performance as in follows,

$$F = \frac{(\beta^2 + 1) \times P \times R}{\beta^2 \times P + R} \quad (8)$$

We set $\beta =1$ to give no special preference to either recall or precision. The recall, precision and F value are 0.84, 0.92 and 0.878 respectively. It is worthwhile to mention that, as shown in Table 1, more than 500 sentences have incomplete semantic classes which mainly come from proper nouns, unknown words, proverbs or even short phrases. While the boundaries between words and phrases in Chinese are not easy to differentiate, the performance, due to the coverage of semantic classes in our thesaurus, does not deteriorate much in our system. This tolerance ability provides the graceful degradation in our case role annotation. While other systems are brittle and working only in all-or-none basis, the robustness of our system is guaranteed even though more than 10% of tokens having their *SC* tags missing.

5 Conclusion

In this paper, we have illustrated a shallow technique in which language patterns are extracted in forms of chunks of phrases or words. The chunks are further tagged with case roles. Although the technique does not require a full syntactic parse to pursue semantic analysis, the recursively embedded phrases can also be identified without pain. While we have demonstrated that it is much easier to work out the approximate parse of individual actual sentences than to try to determine what all possible manifestations of a certain rule or grammatical constructs are, our linguistic sequence analysis is inspired by the research into bio-molecular sequences, such as DNA and RNA in protein. Bio-molecular scientists believe that *high sequence similarity usually implies significant function or structural similarity*. It is characteristic of biological systems that objects have a certain form that has arisen by evolution from related objects of similar but not identical form. This *sequence-to-structure* mapping is a tractable, though partly heuristic, way to search for functional or structural universality in biological systems. With the support from the results as shown in this paper, we conjecture this *sequence-to-structure* phenomenon appears in our sentences. The sentence sequence encodes and reflects the more complex linguistic structures and mechanisms described by linguists. While our system does not claim to deal with all aspects of language, we suggest an alternative, but plausible, approach to handle the real corpus.

Acknowledgement

The work described in this paper was partially supported by a grant from the Research Grants Council of the Hong Kong Special Administrative Region, China (Project No. CUHK4438/04H).

References

[1] Abney, S. (1991). Parsing by chunks. In Berwick, R., Abney, S. & Tenny, C. (Eds.), *Principle-Based Parsing*. Kluwer Academic.
[2] Appelt, D. E., Hobbs, J. R., Bear,J., Israel, D., Tyson,M. (1993). FASTUS: a finite-state processor for information extraction from real-world text. *Proceedings of the Thirteenth International Joint Conference on Artificial Intelligence*, vol. 2, 1172-1178.
[3] Bod, R., Scha, R., & Sima'an, K. (2003). *Data-Oriented Parsing*. Stanford: California, CSLI.
[4] Chan, S.W.K. (2004). Extraction of Textual Salient Patterns: Synergy between Lexical Cohesion and Contextual Coherence. *IEEE Transactions on Systems, Man and Cybernetics, Part A: Systems and Humans*, 34, 2, 205-218.
[5] Chan, S.W.K., & Franklin, J. (2003). Dynamic context generation for natural language understanding: A multifaceted knowledge approach. *IEEE Transactions on Systems, Man and Cybernetics, Part A: Systems and Humans*, 33, 1, 23-41.
[6] Chao, Y.-R. (1968). *A Grammar of Spoken Chinese*. University of California Press.
[7] Chen, F.-Y., Tsai, P.-F., Chen, K.-J., & Huang, C.-R. (2000). Sinica Treebank. [in Chinese] *Computational Linguistics and Chinese Language Processing*, 4, 2, 87-103.
[8] Chen, K.-J., Huang, C.-R., Chang, L.-P., & Hsu. H.-L. (1996). Sinica Corpus: Design Methodology for Balanced Corpora. *Proceedings of the 11th Pacific Asia Conference on Language, Information, and Computation (PACLIC II)*, Seoul Korea, 167-176.
[9] Church, K. (1988). A stochastic parts program and noun phrase parser for unrestricted text. *Proceedings of Second Conference on Applied Natural Language Processing*, Austin, Texas.

[10] Fillmore, C.J. (1968). The case for case. In E. Bach & R.T. Harms (Eds.), *Universals in Linguistic Theory*, 1-90. Holt, Rinehart & Winston.
[11] Gaizauskas, R., & Wilks, Y. (1998). Information extraction: Beyond document retrieval. *Journal of Documentation*, 54, 1, 70-105.
[12] Gee, J., & Grosjean, F. (1983). Performance structures: A psycholinguistic and linguistic appraisal. *Cognitive Psychology*, 15, 4, 411-458.
[13] Gusfield, D. (1997). *Algorithms on Strings, Trees, and Sequences: Computer Science and Computational Biology*. Cambridge University Press.
[14] Her, O. S. (1990). *Grammatical functions and verb subcategorization in Mandarin Chinese*. The Crane publishing Co.
[15] Li, Y. C. (1971). *An investigation of Case in Chinese Grammar*. Set On Hall University Press.
[16] Marcus, M., Santorini, B. and Marcinkiewicz, M. (1993). Building a large annotated corpus of English: The Penn Treebank. *Computational Linguistics*, 19, 2, 313-330.
[17] Rada, R., Mili, H., Bicknell, E., and Blettner, M. (1989) Development and application of a metric on semantic nets. *IEEE Transactions on Systems, Man, and Cybernetics*, 19, 1, 17-30.
[18] Ramshaw, L. A., & Marcus, M.P. (1995). Text chunking using transformation-based learning. *Proceedings of the Third Workshop on Very Large Corpora*, 82-94.
[19] Sima'an, K. (2000). Tree-gram parsing: lexical dependencies and structural relations. *Proceedings of the 38th Annual Meeting of the Association for Computational Linguistics*, 53-60, Hong Kong.
[20] Tsay, Y.T., & Tsai, W.H. (1989). Model-guided attributed string matching by split-and-merge for shape recognition. *International Journal of Pattern Recognition and Artificial Intelligence*, 3, 2, 159-179.
[21] Xia, F., Palmer, M., Xue, N., Okurowski, M.E., Kovarik, J., Chiou, F.-D., Huang, S., Kroch, T., & Marcus, M. (2000). Developing Guidelines and Ensuring Consistency for Chinese Text Annotation. *Proceedings of the second International Conference on Language Resources and Evaluation (LREC-2000)*, Athens, Greece.

Improving the Presentation of Argument Interpretations Based on User Trials

Ingrid Zukerman, Michael Niemann, and Sarah George

School of Computer Science and Software Engineering,
Monash University,
Clayton, Victoria 3800, Australia
{ingrid, niemann, sarahg}@csse.monash.edu.au

Abstract. The interpretation of complex discourse, such as arguments, is a difficult task that often requires validation, i.e., a system may need to present its interpretation of a user's discourse for confirmation. In this paper, we consider the presentation of discourse interpretations in the context of a probabilistic argumentation system. We first describe our initial approach to the presentation of an interpretation of a user's argument; this interpretation takes the form of a Bayesian subnet. We then report on the results of our preliminary evaluation with users, focusing on their criticisms of our system's output. These criticisms motivate a content enhancement procedure that adds information to explain unexpected outcomes and removes superfluous content from an interpretation. The discourse generated by this procedure was found to be more acceptable than the discourse generated by our original method.

1 Introduction

The interpretation of complex discourse, such as arguments, is a difficult task that often requires validation. That is, if a system is uncertain about its understanding of a user's discourse, it should present its interpretation for confirmation or correction. In this paper, we describe the content enhancement component of a probabilistic argumentation system currently under development. Our system receives arguments from users, interprets these arguments in the context of its domain knowledge, and generates responses. The arguments take the form of Natural Language (NL) sentences linked by means of argument connectives. A sample argument is shown in the top left of Figure 1, and its gloss appears in the top right of the Figure. Given an internal representation of an interpretation or an argument (right-hand side of Figure 1), our content enhancer determines information to be added to or removed from this representation to make its presentation more acceptable to people.

Our system uses Bayesian networks (BNs) [1] as its knowledge representation and reasoning formalism. Our domain of implementation is a murder mystery, for which we have designed several BNs. Each BN can support a variety of scenarios, depending on the instantiation of the evidence nodes. The murder mystery used for this paper is represented by means of a 32-node BN, which is illustrated in Figure 2 (the evidence

Argument
The neighbour saw Mr Green in the garden at 11
IMPLIES
Mr Green had the opportunity to murder MrBody
 [ALittleUnlikely]

Gloss
Even though the neighbour saw Mr Green in the garden at 11, Mr Green possibly did not have the opportunity to murder Mr Body

Original interpretation
The neighbour seeing Mr Green in the garden at 11 implies that he very probably was in the garden at 11, which implies that he probably was not in the garden at the time of death. This implies that he possibly did not have the opportunity to murder Mr Body.

Interpretation (Bayesian subnet)

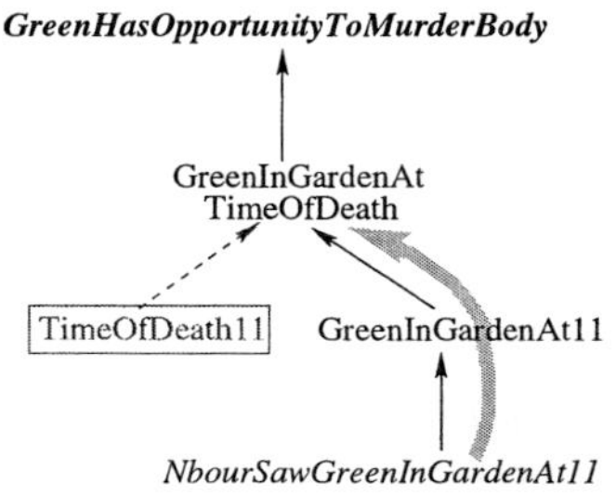

GreenHasOpportunityToMurderBody
↑
GreenInGardenAt
TimeOfDeath

TimeOfDeath11   GreenInGardenAt11
↑
NbourSawGreenInGardenAt11

Enhanced interpretation
Even though the neighbour saw Mr Green in the garden at 11, the time of death not being 11 implies that Mr Green probably was not in the garden at the time of death, which implies that he possibly did not have the opportunity to murder Mr Body.

Fig. 1. Sample argument and interpretation

nodes are boxed, the observed evidence nodes are boldfaced and boxed, and the arrows show the causal relationships between the nodes).

The interaction between a user and the system proceeds as follows. The user first obtains information about a murder (in our examples Mr Body was murdered), and then builds an argument regarding the guilt or innocence of a particular suspect (Mr Green). The argument is typically composed of a sequence of implications leading from observable evidence to the argument goal, where each implication is composed of one or more antecedents and a consequent. Our system's discourse interpretation component matches the user's sentences with the nodes in the BN, and then derives an interpretation by finding a concise reasoning path or graph (a subnet of the domain BN) that connects the nodes in the argument, taking into consideration the information obtained by the user and the inference patterns within the BN. When generating an interpretation, the system attempts to make the structure and beliefs in the Bayesian subnet as similar as possible to what was stated by the user, within the limitations of its world model. This means that sometimes the beliefs in an interpretation do not match exactly the user's stated beliefs.

The black arcs and nodes in the Bayesian subnet at the bottom right of Figure 1 illustrate an interpretation generated for the argument at the top left of the Figure; the italicized nodes in the subnet are those mentioned in the argument (this interpretation may also be traced in the bottom right-hand side of Figure 2). The text corresponding to this interpretation appears in the middle left of Figure 1. Our content enhancer adds the grey, boxed node to the subnet in Figure 1, and skips the node overwritten by the thick grey arrow. The resultant interpretation is then presented to the user both in the same format as the argument and in the textual form shown in the bottom left of Figure 1.

In the next section, we describe our preliminary trial with users, focusing on their criticisms of our system's interpretations. In Section 3, we present the content enhancer we implemented to address these concerns, followed by the results of our evaluation. We then discuss related research, and present concluding remarks.

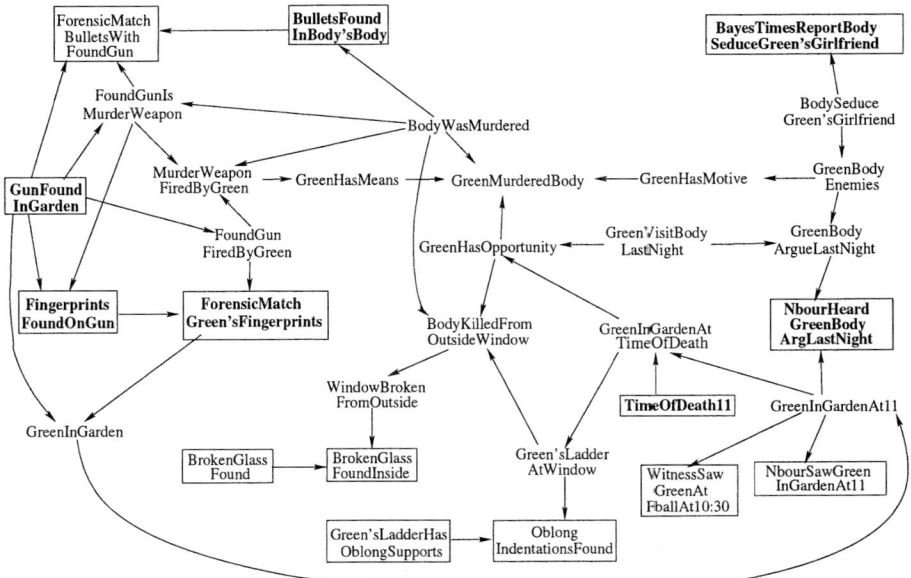

Fig. 2. Sample domain BN

2 Preliminary Trial – Results

Our initial generation technique consisted of simply following the links in the Bayesian subnet corresponding to an interpretation, and presenting the *canonical sentences* that are associated with each node in the subnet. For instance, the canonical sentence for GreenHasOpportunityToMurderBody is "Mr Green *have* the opportunity to murder Mr Body" (the verb "have" is inflected during the realization process). This process yields the text labelled "Original interpretation" in Figure 1.

The belief in a node being true is divided into the following seven belief categories: {VeryLikely, Likely, ALittleLikely, EvenChance, ALittleUnlikely, Unlikely, VeryUnlikely}, which are based on those offered in [2]. When rendered in English, they yield the following terms: {"very probable", "probable", "possible", "maybe"} – the probabilities under 0.5 are rendered in English by negating the verb, e.g., "Mr Green probably *did not* murder Mr Body".[1]

Our preliminary trial was designed to evaluate the performance of our argument interpretation component. We prepared four pencil-and-paper evaluation sets, each comprising of a short argument and between one and three candidate interpretations generated by our system. Each set was shown to between 15 and 23 subjects. Our subjects were asked to assess each interpretation, and to comment on aspects of the interpretations they liked or disliked. Although there was general acceptance of our system's interpre-

---

[1] We conducted trials to test people's understanding of these linguistic representations of the belief categories in comparison to alternative wordings. The above terms yielded the most consistent understanding (with the lowest standard deviation).

tations and its reasoning, our subjects' comments focused on the information included to describe these interpretations. Their concerns were that the interpretations were not presented in a concise yet complete manner that fully represents how the propositions in an interpretation influence each other. The original interpretation in Figure 1 illustrates two of the problems which are typical of those pointed out by our trial subjects: too little information and too much information. The inference from "Mr Green being in the garden at 11" to "Mr Green *not* being in the garden at the time of death" appears to be a non-sequitur, i.e., the information provided is insufficient to make sense of this inference. The inference from "the neighbour seeing Mr Green in the garden at 11" to "Mr Green being in the garden at 11" was viewed as being superfluous, i.e., too much information is being presented.

Below we summarize the main problems identified by our trial users.

- **Too Much Detail** – users became annoyed when obvious inferences (such as the second example above) were stated.
- **Discrepancies Between the Beliefs in an Argument and in Its Interpretation** – users were disconcerted when the system claimed to have interpreted an argument, but the beliefs that were presented differed from the beliefs stated within the argument (recall that our system cannot always match a user's stated beliefs with those obtained in the Bayesian subnet).
- **Increase in Certainty** – users objected to inferences where the consequent had a greater degree of certainty than its antecedents, e.g., "Mr Green *probably* had the means to murder Mr Body. Therefore, Mr Green *very probably* murdered Mr Body".
- **Large Change in Certainty** – users accepted small decrements in certainty, e.g., from "probable" to " possible". However, they objected to inferences where the belief in the consequent was substantially different from the belief in the antecedent (regardless of whether the difference represented an increase or a decrease in the level of certainty), e.g., the inference in Figure 1 from "Mr Green very probably being in the garden at 11" to "Mr Green probably *not* being in the garden at the time of death".

3 Enhancing the Content of a Presentation

Our content enhancement process identifies the above problems computationally, and addresses them by adding information to an interpretation or removing information.

3.1 Too Much Detail

In order to avoid unnecessary detail in the description of an interpretation, we used the following rule to identify potentially superfluous nodes, with the aim of removing them.

Rule 1

If $Node_B$ is between $Node_A$ and $Node_C$ ($Node_A \rightarrow Node_B \rightarrow Node_C$) AND
  $Node_B$ is similar to $Node_A$ AND
    BeliefCategory($Node_B$) = BeliefCategory($Node_A$) THEN
$Node_B$ is superfluous (its omission yields the implication '$Node_A \rightarrow Node_C$')

Table 1. Sample nodes removed from our trial interpretations

(a) The neighbour saw Mr Green in the garden at 11 [VeryLikely] IMPLIES [OMITTED] **Mr Green was in the garden at 11 [VeryLikely]** IMPLIES Mr Green was in the garden at the time of death [VeryLikely]
(b) The neighbour heard Mr Green arguing with Mr Body last night [VeryUnlikely] IMPLIES [OMITTED] **Mr Green and Mr Body had a loud argument last night [VeryUnlikely]** IMPLIES Mr Green visited Mr Body last night [VeryUnlikely]

As stated in Section 2, each node in the BN is associated with a canonical sentence which represents the information in the node. These sentences are used in two ways: (1) to find the best match with the statements in a user's argument in order to map the argument onto the BN, and (2) to assess the similarity between two nodes for the application of Rule 1. For both usages, the similarity between two sentences is estimated by means of a modified version of the cosine similarity measure [3], which calculates the angle between the vectors comprising the words in the sentences. Our version ignores stop words (high frequency words that are generally ignored for retrieval purposes) and proper nouns that are common to most nodes, e.g., "Green" and "Body", and takes into account synonyms and near synonyms, e.g., "glass" and "window". For the node-similarity usage, if the (normalized) similarity score between an antecedent node and a consequent node exceeds a threshold, then the nodes are regarded as similar, thereby satisfying the second antecedent of Rule 1. If the nodes also have the same level of certainty, then the consequent node may be treated as superfluous and removed.

Clearly, Rule 1 may yield several candidates for omission along a reasoning path. However, we want to avoid removing too many nodes in order to safeguard against too much information being lost. This is done by applying a greedy algorithm that inspects each node along a reasoning path, and ranks the nodes according to their similarity score with respect to their antecedent. These nodes are then considered for removal in highest-to-lowest order of similarity score. However, no node can be removed if it was in the original argument or if it is the consequent of an already removed node. For instance, given $A \rightarrow B \rightarrow C \rightarrow D$, if B is similar to A and they have the same belief, then B is omitted, and C can not be removed even if it is similar to A. If only C and D were found to be similar, then C will be omitted, as the consequent D was in the original argument.

Table 1 displays fragments from two of the interpretations shown to our trial subjects, highlighting the information omitted as a result of the application of Rule 1. The application of this rule reduces the verboseness of the output by removing propositions that a reader can easily deduce from their antecedent.

3.2 Discrepancies Between Beliefs

As stated in Section 1, the interpretation generated by the system does not always match the beliefs in a user's argument. For instance, say the user states that fact A being true implies that fact B is Likely to be true. The system will endeavour to find a path from the node corresponding to A to the node corresponding to B that makes B Likely. However, the system's beliefs are restricted by what can be calculated from the *Conditional Probability Tables (CPTs)* of the nodes in the BN.[2] Hence, it is possible that the closest belief our system can obtain for B is ALittleLikely.

If such a discrepancy in belief occurs, then the following information is included in the presentation.

- A preamble such as the following: "I know this is not quite right, but it is the best I could do given what I believe about this situation".
- An explanation at each point of discrepancy, e.g., "I know that your belief is stronger, but this is the closest I can come up with".

At the knowledge representation level, the system could update its inference patterns to match the user's. In the context of BNs, this involves modifying the CPTs for the offending implications. However, this is a complex process, with far-reaching implications with respect to the system's inference patterns. This type of solution is left for future investigation, as the CPTs in our system are regarded as static.

3.3 Increase in Certainty and Large Change in Certainty

Given an implication such as $A \rightarrow B$, users generally accepted inferences that yielded the same or a slightly weaker belief in B than the belief in A (a belief is weaker if it leans towards greater uncertainty about whether a fact is true or false, i.e., even chance). However, as indicated above, they objected to all other belief changes between antecedents and consequents. This situation is identified by means of the following rule.

Rule 2

For $Node_A$ [$BeliefCategory_A$] $\rightarrow$ $Node_B$ [$BeliefCategory_B$]:
// increase in certainty
If $BeliefCategory_A$ is weaker than $BeliefCategory_B$ OR
// large change in certainty
$BeliefCategory_A$ differs from $BeliefCategory_B$ by more than 1 level THEN
a "leap" in belief has occurred

Some of the identified leaps in belief are due to the CPTs of the implications in the reasoning path, and can be justified only by explaining the CPTs (a task that is outside the scope of this paper). However, most of these leaps are due to influences from nodes that are not part of the initial interpretation, and should be included in the presentation of the interpretation to make it acceptable to users. These influencing nodes are siblings of the antecedents of the offending implications. That is, they are nodes

---

[2] The CPT of a node represents the influence of its parent nodes in the BN on the beliefs in this node. The CPTs in our BN were derived from human knowledge of the domain.

Algorithm *SelectInfluences(Implication, BN)*

1. Get Antecedents and Consequent for the Implication
2. For each Sibling of Antecedents that is an influence node
   (a) // Decreasing belief between antecedent and consequent
       If Belief(Antecedent) > Belief(Consequent) THEN
       i. If BeliefCategory(Sibling) = BeliefCategory(Consequent) THEN
          store Sibling as a `StandardInfluence`
       ii. Else if BeliefCategory(Sibling) < BeliefCategory(Consequent) THEN
           store Sibling as an `LargeInfluence`
       iii. Else //BeliefCategory(Sibling) > BeliefCategory(Consequent)
            if BeliefCategory(Antecedent) > BeliefCategory(Sibling) THEN
            store Sibling as a `WeakInfluence`
   (b) // Increasing belief between antecedent and consequent
       If Belief(Antecedent) < Belief(Consequent) THEN
       i. If BeliefCategory(Sibling) = BeliefCategory(Consequent) THEN
          store Sibling as a `StandardInfluence`
       ii. Else if BeliefCategory(Sibling) > BeliefCategory(Consequent) THEN
           store Sibling as an `LargeInfluence`
       iii. Else // BeliefCategory(Sibling) < BeliefCategory(Consequent)
            if BeliefCategory(Antecedent) < BeliefCategory(Sibling) THEN
            store Sibling as a `WeakInfluence`
3. Add the influences in the highest-ranked category to the implication

Fig. 3. Algorithm for selecting influence nodes

connected to the consequent of these implications, e.g., TimeOfDeath11 is a sibling of GreenInGardenAt11 in Figure 1. However, not every sibling is necessarily an influence, and not all siblings that are influences should be included in an interpretation. For instance, a sibling node that represents unobserved evidence is not an influence (the evidence has not been gathered, hence the value of this node is unknown). In contrast, an influencing node must either be an observed evidence node, or it must be influenced by a neighbouring node that is an observed evidence node. Also, we aim to include in an interpretation the minimum number of influences that explain the belief in a consequent. Hence, weak influences will be omitted if stronger influences are present.

After a leap in belief has been identified in an implication, algorithm *SelectInfluences* is activated in order to determine which influence nodes to present (Figure 3).[3] To this effect, our algorithm divides the influencing siblings of the implication's antecedents into three categories based on the strength of the belief in each sibling compared to the strength of the belief in the consequent and the antecedents: large > standard > weak. For example, a sibling with a large influence is one that has a more extreme belief than the consequent. Such a sibling is estimated to have a strong "pull" in its own direction, and hence provides a good explanation for the current (unintuitive) belief in the consequent. Since our system tries to minimize the number of inclusions in an interpretation, it adds to the implication only the nodes in the highest non-empty category.

---

[3] For clarity of exposition, we show only the "positive" version of the *SelectInfluences* algorithm. This version works for siblings that increase the belief in a consequent when they are true, and decrease its belief when they are false. The "mirror image" of this version is applied when a false sibling yields a true belief in the consequent, and a true sibling yields a false belief.

Upon completion of this enhancement step, the nodes added to each implication are incorporated in the presentation of the implication by means of appropriate connectives. For instance, additive expressions, such as "together with", are used when presenting nodes that explain increases in certainty (provided the nodes are on the same side of EvenChance as the antecedent), while adversative expressions, such as "however" and "despite", are used when presenting nodes that explain reductions in certainty or movements across the EvenChance divide.

To illustrate the workings of algorithm *SelectInfluences*, let us consider the argument fragments in Table 2, which appeared in interpretations shown to our trial subjects (the argument goal in these interpretations was either GreenMurderedBody or GreenHasOpportunity). These fragments exhibit changes in certainty which our subjects found confusing, and which were made more understandable by the addition of influence nodes.

The interpretation fragment in Table 2(a) goes from Mr Green *very probably* being in the garden to Mr Green *possibly not* being in the garden at 11. This is a case of a decrease in belief (Step 2a) coupled with a large drop in certainty. Our algorithm examines the siblings of GreenInGarden, which are NbourSawGreenInGardenAt11, WitnessSawGreenAtFootballAt10:30 and NbourHeardGreenBodyArgueLastNight (Figure 2), in order to find the strongest negative influences that explain this decrease in belief (even though GreenInGardenAtTimeOfDeath is a sibling of the antecedent, it is not considered because it is already part of the interpretation as the consequent of GreenInGardenAt11). First our algorithm determines whether a sibling has a negative influence, and if it does, the sibling is assigned an influence category. However, in this example the first two siblings are unobserved evidence nodes, which do not contribute to the information content of the interpretation. Hence, the only candidate for inclusion in the interpretation is NbourHeardGreenBodyArgueLastNight. This node is assigned the large influence category, as

Table 2. Sample nodes added to our trial interpretations

(a) Large change in certainty, decrease in belief – addition of `LargeInfluence`
Mr Green was in the garden [VeryLikely]
BUT
[ADDED] The neighbour heard Mr Green arguing with Mr Body last night [VeryUnlikely]
IMPLIES
Mr Green was in the garden at 11 [ALittleUnlikely]
(b) Large change in certainty, decrease in belief – addition of `LargeInfluence`
Mr Green had the means to murder Mr Body [Likely]
BUT
[ADDED] Mr Green had the opportunity to murder Mr Body [ALittleUnlikely]
IMPLIES
Mr Green murdered Mr Body [EvenChance]
(c) Increase in certainty, increase in belief – addition of `StandardInfluence`
Mr Green visited Mr Body last night [ALittleUnlikely]
BUT
[ADDED] Mr Green was in the garden at the time of death [VeryLikely]
IMPLIES
Mr Green had the opportunity to murder Mr Body [VeryLikely]

its belief category is more extreme than that of the consequent, and it is then added to the interpretation.

The interpretation fragment in Table 2(b) goes from Mr Green *probably* having the means to murder Mr Body to him *maybe* murdering Mr Body. This is also a case of a decrease in belief (Step 2a), and decrease in certainty. Our algorithm examines the siblings of GreenHasMeans, which are BodyWasMurdered, GreenHasMotive and GreenHasOpportunity (Figure 2), in order to find the strongest negative influences. Since BodyWasMurdered has a positive influence, it is dropped from consideration, but the other two siblings have a negative influence: GreenHasOpportunity has a large influence, and GreenHasMotive has a standard influence. As indicated above, if stronger influences are present, weaker influences are not added to an interpretation, as we are trying to minimize the number of inclusions in an interpretation. Hence, only GreenHasOpportunity is added.

Finally, the interpretation fragment in Table 2(c) goes from Mr Green *possibly not* visiting Mr Body last night to Mr Green *very probably* having the opportunity to murder Mr Body. This is a case of an increase in belief (Step 2b) and an increase in certainty. Our algorithm considers the siblings of GreenVisitBodyLastNight, which are BodyKilledFromOutsideWindow, GreenInGardenAtTimeOfDeath and GreenMurderedBody (Figure 2), in order to find the strongest positive influences that explain this increase in belief. GreenInGardenAtTimeOfDeath has the strongest influence (standard), so it is the only node added to the interpretation.

4 Evaluation

Our evaluation of the content enhancer was conducted as follows. We constructed three evaluation sets, each consisting of two presentations of an interpretation. One of the presentations was generated using our original approach, and the other by post-processing this presentation with the content enhancer. Two of the evaluation sets were from the initial trial (Section 2) and one was new.[4] This set was added in order to evaluate all aspects of the content enhancer. For one of the evaluation sets, the content enhancer removed nodes from the interpretation that it felt contained superfluous information (Section 3.1). For the other two sets, the enhancer added influencing nodes to the interpretations (Section 3.3). One of these interpretations included a large decrease in belief and the other included a small increase in belief.

The three evaluation sets were shown to 20 subjects, including 6 of the subjects who participated in the initial trial (the other subjects of this trial were unavailable). The subjects came from several populations, which included staff and students in the School of Computer Science and Software Engineering at Monash University, and friends of the authors. The subjects belonged to several age groups and exhibited different levels of computer literacy. In our experiment, we first gave our subjects a definition and example of an interpretation, and told them that the aim of the experiment was to compare our original method for the presentation of BIAS' argument interpretations with our new method. The subjects were then shown the three evaluation sets. However, they were

---

[4] The interpretation for one of the original evaluation sets was not affected by the content enhancer. Also, due to modifications performed to the interpretation system since the initial trial, the interpretations generated for another evaluation set differed from the original ones.

not told which presentation was generated by the original method and which by the enhanced method, and had no knowledge of the BN used to derive the interpretations. This yielded a total of 60 judgments, where 48.3% favoured the new output, 15% were indifferent, and 36.7% favoured the old output.

For the evaluation set which had nodes removed from the presentation, the results were widely spread, suggesting that people's opinions regarding what is superfluous differ substantially, and may depend on contextual information. 30% of the trial subjects preferred the post-processed presentation, 35% were indifferent, and 35% preferred the original interpretation. 40% of the subjects felt that the original interpretation was verbose, but 25% of the subjects thought that the original interpretation was lacking in information to fully explain its reasoning path and beliefs. Also, our subjects' comments indicated that the information they found lacking from the post-processed interpretation was not necessarily related to the removed node. For the evaluation sets which had nodes added to the interpretations, the results clearly favour the enhanced presentations. 57.5% of the trial subjects preferred the new interpretations, compared to 37.5% who preferred the original ones, and 5% who were indifferent. 45% of the subjects felt that the expanded presentations were too verbose regardless of whether they preferred them or not, while 17.5% thought that the expanded presentations still lacked information. Only 7.5% thought that the original presentations were already too verbose. This indicates that the subjects preferred to know more about the system's reasoning, but still had problems with its presentation. These problems may be partially attributed to the presentation of the nodes as full canonical sentences, which makes the interpretations appear repetitive in style, and hence may have an adverse influence on acceptance.

In general, our subjects' comments point to the difficulty of conducting user trials in a commonsense domain. Our BN contains only limited domain knowledge (included by the authors), which may differ from the beliefs and expectations of our subjects. This explains why our subjects may have considered the presented information insufficient to account for the system's inferences, irrespective of the modifications made by the content enhancer. Some of the subjects also felt that for an interpretation to be acceptable, they had to make assumptions about what other information the system was basing its beliefs on, even though they had no knowledge of the structure of the BN. Future developments in the system will work on establishing these assumptions and including them in the presentations.

In addition, a limitation of our approach is that its similarity measure only approximates the similarity between the content of propositions. As a result, our system may omit propositions that appear similar to stated propositions according to our measure, but are in fact dissimilar in content. In contrast, our system retains propositions that are dissimilar in form to stated propositions, even if they convey a similar meaning. This indicates that a more sophisticated measure of propositional similarity is required to determine whether nodes may be omitted from a presentation.

5 Related Research

The mechanism presented in this paper enhances the content of discourse generated from BNs.

BNs have become pervasive in recent years. However, the explanation of Bayesian reasoning has been considered only by a few researchers [4, 5, 6]. Druzdzel [4] and McConachy et al. [5] studied different aspects of the presentation of BNs. Druzdzel focused on the reduction of the number of variables being considered, verbal expressions of uncertainty, and qualitative explanations, which were generated by tracing the influence of the nodes in a BN. McConachy et al. applied attentional models to the construction of probabilistic arguments, and studied probabilistic argumentation patterns and argumentation strategies. Jitnah et al. [6] extended this work by considering strategies for the presentation of rebuttals to users' arguments. Our work follows the last two contributions. However, it is worth noting that these systems generated arguments, while we present interpretations of arguments. In addition, the presentations generated by these systems hinged on discrepancies between the system's world model and the user's, while our presentations rely on the features of an interpretation itself.

Several NLG systems consider the addition or removal of information to improve planned discourse. The research reported in [7, 8, 9] considers the addition of information to planned discourse to prevent or weaken a user's erroneous inferences from this discourse. In contrast, the mechanism presented in this paper adds information to explain reasoning steps that a user may find difficult to understand. The work described in [5, 9, 10] considers the omission of information that may be inferred by a user from planned discourse. Our omission mechanism is most similar to that described in [5]. However, they used spreading activation and partial Bayesian propagation to determine whether a node may be omitted, while we use a simple word similarity measure and belief comparison.

6 Conclusion

We have offered a mechanism developed on the basis of user trials, which enhances the content of argument interpretations for presentation. This is done through the removal of superfluous information and the inclusion of information that explains unintuitive effects. Our mechanism was developed in the context of BNs. However, it is also applicable to non-Bayesian systems (provided belief is represented). Further, although our current results focus on interpretations, our procedures are also applicable to arguments.

Our evaluation of the content-enhancer shows that the post-processed presentations have a positive effect on users' acceptance of the system's interpretations, in particular in regard to the addition of information. In the near future, we propose to further refine the node-removal component of our algorithm, and to improve the node-addition component to include assumptions made by the system. We also intend to conduct additional user trials with more complex arguments.

Acknowledgments

This research is supported in part by the ARC Centre for Perceptive and Intelligent Machines in Complex Environments.

References

1. Pearl, J.: Probabilistic Reasoning in Intelligent Systems. Morgan Kaufmann Publishers, San Mateo, California (1988)
2. Elsaesser, C.: Explanation of probabilistic inference for decision support systems. In: Proceedings of the AAAI-87 Workshop on Uncertainty in Artificial Intelligence, Seattle, Washington (1987) 394–403
3. Salton, G., McGill, M.: An Introduction to Modern Information Retrieval. McGraw Hill (1983)
4. Druzdzel, M.: Qualitative verbal explanations in Bayesian Belief Networks. Artificial Intelligence and Simulation of Behaviour Quarterly (1996) 43–54
5. McConachy, R., Korb, K.B., Zukerman, I.: Deciding what not to say: An attentional-probabilistic approach to argument presentation. In: Proceedings of the Twentieth Annual Conference of the Cognitive Science Society, Madison, Wisconsin (1998) 669–674
6. Jitnah, N., Zukerman, I., McConachy, R., George, S.: Towards the generation of rebuttals in a Bayesian argumentation system. In: Proceedings of the First International Natural Language Generation Conference, Mitzpe Ramon, Israel (2000) 39–46
7. Joshi, A., Webber, B.L., Weischedel, R.M.: Living up to expectations: Computing expert responses. In: AAAI84 – Proceedings of the Fourth National Conference on Artificial Intelligence, Austin, Texas (1984) 169–175
8. van Beek, P.: A model for generating better explanations. In: Proceedings of the Twenty-Fifth Annual Meeting of the Association for Computational Linguistics, Stanford, California (1987) 215–220
9. Zukerman, I., McConachy, R.: WISHFUL: A discourse planning system that considers a user's inferences. Computational Intelligence **17** (2001) 1–61
10. Horacek, H.: A model for adapting explanations to the user's likely inferences. User Modeling and User-Adapted Interaction **7** (1997) 1–55

Reliable Unseen Model Prediction for Vocabulary-Independent Speech Recognition

Sungtak Kim and Hoirin Kim

School of Engineering,
Information & Communications University,
119, Munjiro, Yuseong-gu, Daejeon, 305-714, Korea
{stkim, hrkim}@icu.ac.kr

Abstract. Speech recognition technique is expected to make a great impact on many user interface areas such as toys, mobile phones, PDAs, and home appliances. Those applications basically require robust speech recognition immune to environment and channel noises, but the dialogue pattern used in the interaction with the devices may be relatively simple, that is, an isolated-word type. The drawback of small-vocabulary isolated-word recognizer which is generally used in the applications is that, if target vocabulary needs to be changed, acoustic models should be re-trained for high performance. However, if a phone model-based speech recognition is used with reliable unseen model prediction, we do not need to re-train acoustic models in getting higher performance. In this paper, we propose a few reliable methods for unseen model prediction in flexible vocabulary speech recognition. The first method gives optimal threshold values for stop criteria in decision tree growing, and the second uses an additional condition in the question selection in order to overcome the over-balancing phenomenon in the conventional method. The last proposes two-stage decision trees which in the first stage get more properly trained models and in the second stage build more reliable unseen models. Various vocabulary-independent situations were examined in order to clearly show the effectiveness of the proposed methods. In the experiments, the average word error rates of the proposed methods were reduced by 32.8%, 41.4%, and 44.1% compared to the conventional method, respectively. From the results, we can conclude that the proposed methods are very effective in the unseen model prediction for vocabulary-independent speech recognition.

1 Introduction

The potential application areas using voice interface are enormous. Voice control of consumer devices such as audio/video equipments in home has both commercial potential and well defined functionality that could benefit in user interface. Automotive applications also form a very important area of interest, where the convenience and safety issues play an important role on the choice of the user interface. In addition, user interface using speech recognition is expected to make a great impact on toys, mobile phones, PDAs, and so on. Those applications basically require robust speech recognition immune to environment and channel noises, but the dialogue pattern used in the interaction with the devices will be relatively simple, that is, an isolated-word type. The most straightforward way to implement small vocabulary isolated-word recognizers, which seem to be widely used in the practical applications, is to use speaker-dependent technology. However, training a specific user's speech before the real use could be too inconvenient. Hence, speaker-independent technology is often used, especially when the vocabulary size increases. Even though we may use speaker-independent technology, we cannot avoid changing the target vocabulary occasionally, for example, adding new words or replacing the recognition vocabulary. In this case, we usually have to re-train acoustic models in order to achieve high performance. But, if a reliable unseen model prediction is possible, we do not need to re-train acoustic models to get higher performance.

In this paper, we propose a few reliable methods based on modified binary decision trees for unseen model prediction. Many recognition systems have used binary decision trees for state tying and unseen model prediction. Binary decision trees with splitting questions attached to each node provide an easy representation to interpret and predict the structures of given data set[1]. For more accurate tree-based state tying and unseen model prediction, several factors such as stop criteria, question sets, and question selection in each node should be considered. Of these factors, our approaches focus on stop criterion and question selection, and then we devise a new hybrid construction scheme for decision tree combining two approaches. For the stop criterion, we tried to determine an optimal threshold value which allows getting a proper tree size for state tying and unseen model prediction. For the question selection, we added a new condition that enables candidate question to use sufficient training data and to guarantee higher log-likelihood on YES nodes. By using two-stage scheme for decision trees, firstly we can get fairly trained models, and then make the models more effective in the aspects of state tying and more efficient in the aspects of unseen model prediction.

In Chapter II, we briefly review the state tying process based on decision tree. In Chapter III, we present the three proposed methods for accurate unseen model prediction and state tying. Then, the baseline system, the experiments and results are given in Chapter IV and Chapter V. Finally, in Chapter VI, we summarize this work and present ideas for future work.

2 Decision Tree-Based State Tying

Although many other split criteria could be used in decision trees, most of decision tree-based state tying algorithms have used two fundamental criteria, which are likelihood and entropy criteria [2],[3],[4]. The similar probability distributions have to be shared or merged since the basic aim of tree-based state tying is to reduce the number of model parameters and to make the shared parameters more robust. Therefore, the triphone states, whose estimated probability distributions are close to each other in a viewpoint of a distance measure, are tied together. In this paper, we use a log-likelihood gain as the distance measure. The log-likelihood gain is obtained by using the following equation [5].

$$G(A,B) = (LL(A) + LL(B)) - LL(AB)$$

$$= \frac{1}{2}\left(n_A \log \frac{\sum_{d=1}^{D}\sigma_{d,AB}^2}{\sum_{d=1}^{D}\sigma_{d,A}^2} + n_B \log \frac{\sum_{d=1}^{D}\sigma_{d,AB}^2}{\sum_{d=1}^{D}\sigma_{d,B}^2}\right) \quad (1)$$

Here AB is the parent node of nodes A and B in the binary decision tree, therefore A and B are the child nodes of the parent node AB. n_X is the number of training vectors assigned to node X, and $\sigma_{d,X}$ is the variance of component d of node X.

The formula for the log-likelihood gain can be easily rewritten in a form which only contains sum and squared sum of the observation vector components together with the observation counts. Therefore the equations for computing means and variances of training vectors in each node can be expressed as

$$\tilde{\mu}_{d,X} = \frac{1}{n_X}\sum_{s \in X} n_s \mu_{d,s} \quad (2)$$

$$n_X = \sum_{s \in X} n_s \quad (3)$$

$$\tilde{\sigma}_{d,X}^2 = \frac{1}{n_X}\left(\sum_{s \in X} n_s \sigma_{d,s}^2 + \sum_{s \in X} n_s \mu_{d,s}^2\right) - (\tilde{\mu}_{d,X})^2 \quad (4)$$

where s is a state index, $\tilde{\mu}_{d,X}$ is the mean of component d of node X, $\mu_{d,s}$ is the mean of component d of state s, and n_s is the number of training vectors in the state s. $\tilde{\sigma}_{d,X}^2$ and $\sigma_{d,s}^2$ are the variances of component d of the node X and the state s, respectively. By means of these equations, the re-training computation for each tree construction can be simplified.

3 The Proposed Methods for Unseen Model Prediction

3.1 Modified Stop Decision (MSD) for Optimal Tree Growing

In tree-based unseen model prediction, the tree size becomes a very important factor deciding the accuracy of the predicted models. As the size of tree is larger, the tree has finer resolution due to many leaf nodes. And, if there are many unseen models to be predicted, it is desirable for the tree to get fine resolution. On the other hand, if there are many seen models in the state pool of root node, the probability of observing unseen models will be low. At that time, the size of trees may be reduced because decision trees do not need to get fine resolution.

There is another stop criterion, using minimum number of training vectors of node [6]. In a viewpoint of unseen model prediction, the criterion is not proper because it does not consider whether the probability of observing unseen models is low or not. To overcome those defects, we propose a method that determines optimal threshold value for stop criteria. The method reflects the probability of observing unseen models on the threshold. Then, the threshold values will make trees to get optimal size for more accurate unseen model prediction. A new function for determining optimal threshold values in the state pool of each tree is defined as

$$\text{Threshold} = \eta \times N_{seen} \times LL_{norm} \quad (5)$$

$$LL_{norm} = \frac{\text{Log-likelihood of state pool}}{\text{Number of feature vectors in state pool}}$$
$$= -\frac{1}{2}\left(D\log 2\pi + \log \sum_{d=1}^{D} \sigma_d^2 + D\right) \quad (6)$$

where η is a weighting factor to control the number of tied sates, N_{seen} is the number of seen models in the state pool, LL_{norm} is the normalized log-likelihood of the training vectors in the state pool, D is the dimension of feature vectors, and σ_d^2 is the variance of component d of feature vectors. In Eq. (5), N_{seen} controls the threshold value for reliable unseen model prediction. That is, as N_{seen} is larger, the threshold value becomes higher. This is motivated from the fact that, if there are many seen models in the state pool, the probability of observing unseen models to be predicted will be smaller and the tree does not need to get fine resolution for unseen model prediction. On the other hand, if N_{seen} is small, the threshold value must be lower, since the probability of observing unseen models will be higher and the tree needs to get high resolution. On the other hand, LL_{norm} is determined by the variance of feature vectors in the state pool, and it controls the threshold value in the aspect of state tying. That is, as the variance in the state pool becomes larger, the threshold value will be lower. If the state pool has a larger variance, the decision trees should have lots of tied states as possible. This is reasonable for robust state tying because, as the variance of state pool is larger, we need a larger tree and the threshold value must be lower. In conclusion, N_{seen} and LL_{norm} mutually compensate for reliable unseen model prediction and state tying.

3.2 Reliable Question Selection (RQS) Focused on the YES Node

In the tree-based state tying with the likelihood-based framework, the common criterion[5],[7],[8] of choosing a question is formulated as

$$Q^* = \arg\max_Q (G(A,B)) \quad (7)$$

where G(A,B) is the log-likelihood gain in node AB. G(A,B) is expressed in Eq. (1). The drawback of using Eq. (7) is that this does not guarantee sufficient training vectors nor higher log-likelihood in the YES node even though the chosen question has the maximum log-likelihood gain. In binary tree-based unseen model prediction, the YES node is more important than the No node because the YES node reflects the context effect of the question itself better than that of the NO node. From the fact, it seems to be desirable that we choose the question providing sufficient training vectors to the YES node and having higher log-likelihood in the node for accurate unseen model prediction.

Thus we propose a new criterion of choosing the question to provide sufficient training vectors and higher log likelihood to the YES node as follows.

$$Q^* = \arg\max_Q (G(A,B)) \quad \text{if } n_A > n_{ave} \quad (8)$$

$$n_{ave} = \frac{1}{N}\left(\sum_{n_s \leq 2\sigma} n_s\right) \quad (9)$$

where n_A is the number of training vectors in the YES node, n_{ave} is the average number of the training vectors for states in the state pool, and N is the total number of states in the state pool. In Eq. (9), n_{ave} is the number of training vectors in states that are included in the confidence interval 95%. Here we assume that the number of the training vectors in states has a Gaussian distribution. So, we do not use too large or too small number of training vectors in states to get n_{ave}.

By using this technique, decision trees can guarantee that YES nodes have a sufficient number of training vectors and higher log-likelihood. In result, we can precisely predict unseen models by using the reliable question selection.

3.3 Two-Stage Decision Tree (TSDT) Combining the RQS and MSD Algorithms

When we use triphone models as acoustic models, it is very difficult to construct a training database so that all the possible triphone models have a similar number of training vectors in each model. If the numbers of training vectors in models are significantly different from one another, the decision tree would not be constructed precisely because the likelihood of models may be very sensitive to how many models are trained as shown in Eq. (1) and Eq. (7). In other words, as models are better trained, the likelihood of models is higher. Thus the decision tree using the likelihood framework will be too much dependent on the given training database. In the result, the accuracy of the unseen model prediction for vocabulary-independent speech recognition will be degraded severely.

To overcome this problem, we propose a method that the state of each model has the same number of training vectors as possible. We design a two-stage decision tree: at first we generate a tree from the RQS method with zero threshold value, and next we construct the final tree from the MDS method. In stage 1, we construct a decision tree with RQS method, and assign the probability distribution of shared state in each leaf node to the probability distribution of original states in the leaf node. So, the original models become evenly trained models. Finally at stage 2 we can construct the decision tree which is less dependent on the training database. The two-stage decision tree algorithm is summarized as follows (see also Figure 1).

TSDT Algorithm

- Step 1: Cluster states of seen models by using the RQS method with the threshold zero.
- Step 2: Assign fairly trained states to original states in each leaf node.
- Step 3: Reconstruct thes decision trees by using the MSD method.

Thus Step 1 and Step 2 construct evenly trained acoustic models. Step 3 makes reliable tied models for unseen model prediction by using models sufficiently trained from previous steps.

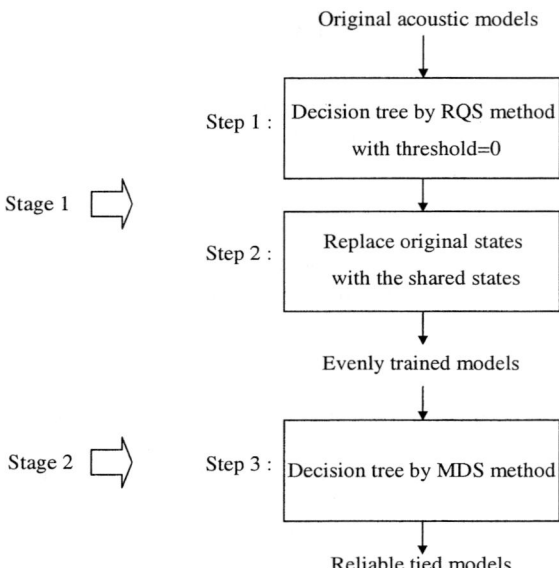

Fig. 1. The process of the TSDT method

4 Baseline System

At first, the input speech is pre-emphasized using the first order FIR filter with a coefficient of 0.97. The samples are blocked into overlapping frames of 20ms and each frame is shifted at a rate of 10ms. Each frame is windowed with the Hamming window. Every frame is characterized by the total 39th order feature vectors. The feature vectors are composed of 13 mel frequency cepstral coefficients (MFCC), their first-order temporal regression coefficients (ΔMFCC), and their second-order temporal regression coefficients ($\Delta\Delta$ MFCC). Hidden Markov model-based triphones are trained with 3 states left-to-right structure for acoustic modeling.

One decision tree is constructed for every states of each center phone, and all triphone models with the same center phone are clustered into the corresponding root node according to the state position. To get tied states, a decision tree is built using a top-down procedure starting from the root node of the tree. Each node is split according to the phonetic question that results in maximum increase in the likelihood on the train data from Eq. (1). Different phone questions have been investigated in [9],[10], but we have used only simple phone questions because the focus in this work is not on those variations. The likelihood gain due to a node split can be calculated efficiently from pre-calculated statistics of the reconstructed states by using Eq. (2), Eq(3), and Eq (4). The process is repeated until the likelihood gain falls below a threshold. In baseline system, we used a same threshold for each decision tree. After this process is done, states reaching the same leaf node of each decision tree are regarded as similar and so tied. Fig. 2(a) shows this procedure. The resulting clusters of tied states are then retrained and multiple-mixture Gaussian distribution HMMs are estimated.

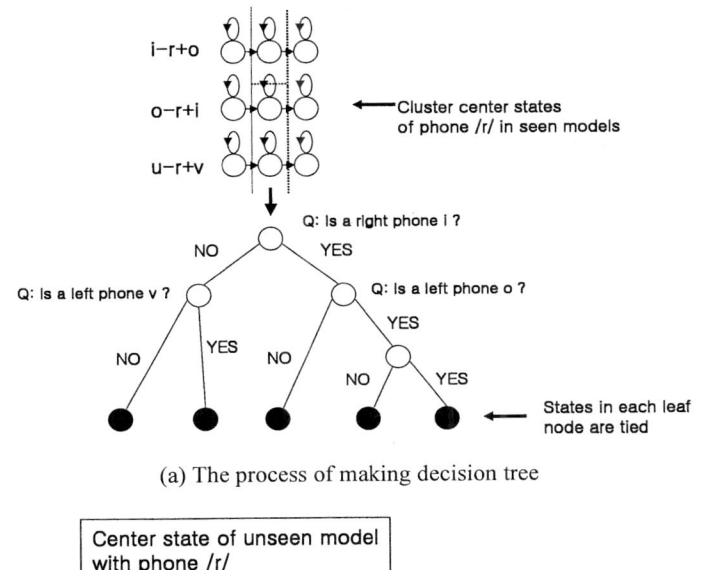

(a) The process of making decision tree

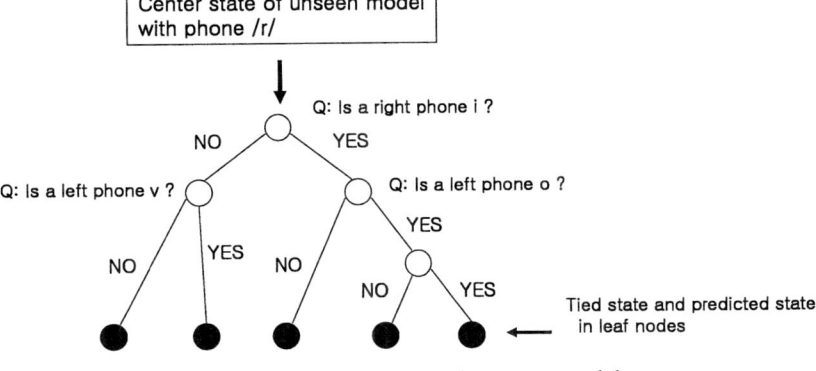

(b) The process of predicting the unseen models

Fig. 2. An example of decision tree structure in case of center states

When unseen models are observed due to new words added to the vocabulary in-recognition process, the unseen models are predicted by answering to the phonetic questions which already determined in training process and traversing the decision tree from the root node to a final leaf node as shown in Fig. 2(b). The most similar leaf node determined by the decision tree is used as the unseen models.

5 Evaluation

5.1 Speech Data

Speech database used in this work is composed of the PBW(Phonetically Balanced Words) 452 DB and the FOW(Frequently Observed Words) 2000 DB. The PBW 452 DB consists of 452 isolated Korean words, each of which is uttered twice by 70 speakers including 38 males and 32 females. The FOW 2000 DB consists of 2,000 isolated Korean words, each of which is spoken once by two speakers including one male and one female. The FOW 2000 DB includes all the 452 words that are vocabulary of the PBW 452 DB, and the other 1,548 words are different from the words of the PBW 452 DB. These speech data are sampled at 16 kHz and quantized in 16 bit resolution. We used the PBW 452 DB for training and the FOW 2000 DB for test.

For various experiments of vocabulary-independent speech recognition, we established four different test situations from FOW 2000 DB as follow.

- Case 1: The test vocabulary is totally different from the training vocabulary.
- Case 2: The test vocabulary is different from the training vocabulary by 75 %.
- Case 3: The test vocabulary is different from the training vocabulary by 50 %.
- Case 4: The test vocabulary is different from the training vocabulary by 25 %.

The number of words in the test vocabulary for each case is shown in Table 1 where the number of distinct words in the training vocabulary is 452.

Table 1. Number of test words in each case

	S	D	Total distinct words
Case 1	0	1,548	1,548
Case 2	452	1,356	1,808
Case 3	452	452	904
Case 4	452	151	603

In Table 1, S represents the number of words which are the same as the training vocabulary, D represents the number of words which are different from the training vocabulary.

5.2 Performance Comparison of the Conventional Algorithm and the Proposed Methods

In this experiment, we compared the performances of the baseline algorithm and the proposed methods. The baseline algorithm gets a number of tied states according to the same log-likelihood gain values as the threshold values of trees, and the proposed methods get the number of tied states according to the control factor η in Eq. (5).

Table 2. Word recognition accuracies(%) of the baseline and the proposed methods in case 1

# of states	Baseline	MDS	RQS+ MDS	TSDT
1,261	90.31	91.21	91.80	92.18
1,338	89.92	91.21	91.60	91.67
1,397	89.86	91.60	92.18	92.18
1,465	90.05	91.80	91.99	92.25
1,531	89.66	91.67	92.44	92.51

Table 3. Word recognition accuracies(%) of the baseline and the proposed methods in case 2

# of states	Baseline	MDS	RQS+ MDS	TSDT
1,261	92.48	93.03	93.25	93.81
1,338	92.20	92.98	93.58	93.58
1,397	92.37	93.20	94.14	93.92
1,465	92.48	93.36	93.86	93.92
1,531	92.15	93.14	94.08	94.19

Table 4. Word recognition accuracies(%) of the baseline and the proposed methods in case 3

# of states	Baseline	MDS	RQS+ MDS	TSDT
1,261	96.79	97.23	97.23	97.68
1,338	97.35	96.79	97.57	97.68
1,397	97.12	97.01	97.46	97.90
1,465	97.35	97.23	97.35	97.79
1,531	96.90	97.68	97.68	98.23

Table 5. Word recognition accuracies(%) of the baseline and the proposed methods in case 4

# of states	Baseline	MDS	RQS+ MDS	TSDT
1,261	98.84	99.50	99.00	99.34
1,338	99.00	99.50	99.17	99.50
1,397	99.00	99.34	99.34	99.50
1,465	99.34	99.34	99.34	99.67
1,531	99.17	99.34	99.34	99.67

The following tables show the word recognition accuracies of the baseline and the proposed methods in each vocabulary-independent situation. After the tree-based clustering procedure that is based on single Gaussian mixture models, the number of mixture components of all pdfs in all experiments was enlarged to 7 Gaussians per

HMM state. That is, all of the following recognition accuracies were obtained on 7 Gaussians per state.

These results show that the proposed methods have higher or comparable recognition performances when they are compared to the baseline system. Especially, the two-stage decision tree (TSDT) method outperforms other methods in whole cases. To show the effects of the proposed methods in vocabulary-independent speech recognition, the average ERR (Error Reduction Rate) of each case is given in Table 6.

Table 6. Average ERR (%) of the proposed methods

	Case 1	Case 2	Case 3	Case 4
MDS	15.3	10.5	3.0	35.9
RQS+ MDS	20.3	18.9	12.3	17.6
TSDT	21.9	20.2	26.0	50.0

6 Conclusion

In this paper, we proposed three effective methods to construct decision trees for reliable unseen model prediction in vocabulary-independent speech recognition. The MDS method determines the optimal threshold values for accurate state tying and unseen model prediction, the RQS+ MDS method chooses a question guaranteeing sufficient training vectors and higher log-likelihood in the YES nodes, and the TSDT method is a type of model compensation that aligns the new probability distributions to the original models in order to make original ones fairly trained. From experimental results, we could know that these methods were more effective on realistic vocabulary-independent speech recognition corresponding to case 4. The TSDT method was effective on all cases of test environments.

References

1. X. Huang, A. Acero, and H. Hon, "*Spoken Language Processing*," Prentice Hall, 2001.
2. J. Duchateau, K. Demuynck, and D. Van Compernolle, "Novel Node Splitting Criterion in Decision Tree Construction for Semi-Continuous HMMs," in *Proc. of Eurospeech '97*, pp.1183-1186, 1997.
3. S. J. Young, J. J. Odell, and P. C. Woodland, "Tree-Based State Tying for High Accuracy Acoustic Modeling," in *Proc. of Human Language Technology Workshop*, Plainsboro, pp. 307-312, 1994.
4. Mei-Yuh Hwang, Xuedong Huang, and Fileno A. Alleva, "Predicting Unseen Triphone with Senones," *IEEE Trans. Speech and Audio Processing*, Vol. 4, No. 6, pp. 412-419, Nov. 1996.
5. K. Beulen and H. Ney, "Automatic question generation for decision tree based state tying," in *Proc. of ICASSP '98*, pp. 805-808, 1998.

6. Wolfgang Reichl and Wu Chou, "Robust Decision Tree State Tying for Continuous Speech Recognition," *IEEE Trans. Speech and Audio Processing*, Vol. 8, No. 5, pp. 555-566, Sept. 2000.
7. Daniel Willett, Christoph Neukirchen, J. Rottland, and Gerhard Gigoll, "Refining Tree-based State Clustering by means of Formal Concept Analysis, Balanced Decision Tree and Automatically Generated Model-Sets," in *Proc. of ICASSP '99*, Vol. 2, pp. 565-568. 1999.
8. T. Kato, S. Kuroiwa, T. Shimizu, and N. Higuchi, "Efficient mixture Gaussian synthesis for decision tree based state tying," in *Proc. of ICASSP '01*, Vol. 1, pp. 493-496, 2001.
9. R. Kuhn, A. Lazarides, Y. Normandin, and J. Brousseau, "Improved decision trees for phnetic modeling," in *Proc. of ICCASSP '95*, pp.552-555.
10. A. Lazarides, Y. Normandin, and R. Kuhn, "Improving decision trees for acoustic modeing," in *Proc. of ICSLP '96*, pp. 1053-1056.

Voice Code Verification Algorithm Using Competing Models for User Entrance Authentication

Heungkyu Lee* and Hanseok Ko**

*Dept. of Visual Information Processing,
**Dept. of Electronics and Computer Engineering,
Korea University, Seoul, Korea
hklee@ispl.korea.ac.kr, hsko@korea.ac.kr

Abstract. In this paper, we propose a voice code verification method for an intelligent surveillance guard robot, wherein a robot prompts for a code (i.e. word or phrase) for verification. In the application scenario, the voice code can be changed every day for security reasoning and the targeting domain is unlimited. Thus, the voice code verification system not only requires the text-prompted and speaker independent verification, but also it should not require an extra trained model as an alternative hypothesis for log-likelihood ratio test because of memory limitation. To resolve these issues, we propose to exploit the subword based anti-models for log-likelihood normalization through reusing an acoustic model and competing with voice code model. The anti-model is automatically produced by using the statistical distance of phonemes against a voice code. In addition, a harmonics-based spectral subtraction algorithm is applied for a noisy robust system on an outdoor environment. The performance evaluation is done by using a common Korean database, PBW452DB, which consists of 63,280 utterances of 452 isolated words recorded in silent environment.

1 Introduction

For surveillance task, a lot of manpower at the sentry is placed on duty to guard the premises against unauthorized personnel for 24 hours. To lessen the time and overload of human guards at post, an intelligent surveillance guard robot is desirable. The surveillance guard robot takes the role of detecting and authorizing a person entering into the perimeter of the secured area as well as passing the status warning. This system includes detection, recognition and tracking by using multiple sensors such as stereo cameras, IR cameras and array microphones. Under such an environment, a robot prompts for a code (i.e. word or phrase) for verification. In the application scenario, the voice code can be changed every day for security reasoning and the targeting domain is unlimited. Thus, the voice code verification system not only requires the text-prompted and speaker independent verification but also it should not require an extra trained model such as a filler or garbage model for an alternative hypothesis model in a log-likelihood ratio test (LRT). This is due to the memory limitation on an embedded DSP (Digital Signal Processing) hardware system that we developed.

This paper is motivated by the task where the system does not need to know the speaker and has only to verify whether the uttered voice code is correct or not on a specific area. Mostly, confidence measure (CM) for this task is used to verify the uttered observation sequences after or during calculating the probability of a word W being recognized by an ASR system. Besides the utterance verification [1][2], a filler model or garbage model can be used for these purposes. However, most algorithms require the extra model trained for a garbage model or anti-model [3]. But a limited memory size of our proposed embedded system prevents the algorithm from using and storing the extra alternative hypothesis model. Thus, the method that does not require the extra trained model and the re-use of the acoustic model is investigated for the voice code utterance verification. Generally, a log-likelihood ratio test is applied to verify the utterance in this field of utterance verification where the verification step requires the alternative model for doing this task. To manage this problem, the anti-models that are re-usable from an acoustic model and can compete with a voice code model should be considered.

Our proposed system uses a two-pass strategy using a SCHMM (Semi-Continuous Hidden Markov Model)-based recognition [4] and verification step as in Figure 1. In the first pass, recognition is performed via a conventional Viterbi beam search algorithm that segments the test utterance into the N-best strings of phoneme hypotheses. In the second pass, voice code verification is performed. It computes a confidence measure that determines whether or not to reject the recognized voice code [5]. This paper is organized as follows. In Section 2, we describe the voice code verification method using sub-word based anti-models. In Section 3, we conduct the representative experiments. Finally, the conclusive remarks are presented and we discuss the results on performance of the proposed methods.

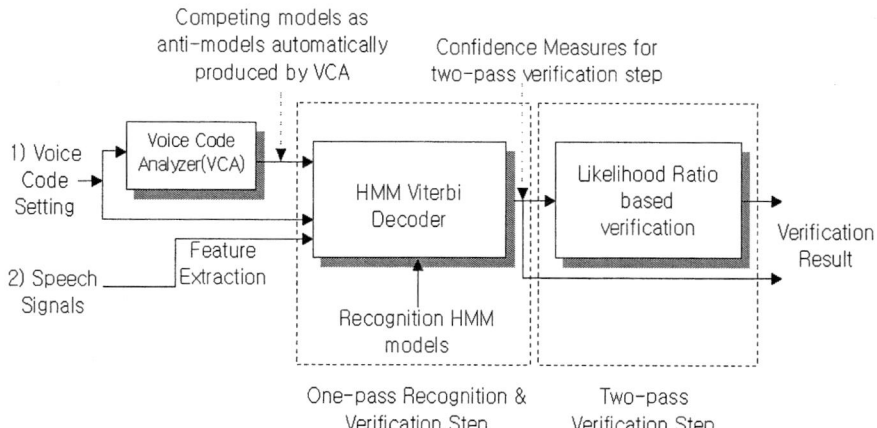

Fig. 1. The block-diagram of the voice code verification

2 Voice Code Verification

2.1 Competing Models as Anti-models

The a posteriori probability used for the likelihood normalization method in text-prompted speaker verification is given by

$$p(S_c, W_c / O) = \frac{p(O/S_c, W_c) p(S_c, W_c)}{\sum_i \sum_j \{p(O/S_i, W_j) p(S_i, W_j)\}} \approx \frac{p(O/S_c, W_c)}{\sum_i \sum_j p(O/S_i, W_j)} \quad (1)$$

where S_i is a speaker and S_c is the claimed speaker. W_i is a text and W_c is the prompted text. $p(S_i, W_j)$ is the simultaneous probability for speaker i and text j. $p(O/S_c, W_c)$ is the probability of the claimed speaker's HMM corresponding to the prompted text. In the voice code verification, S_c and S_i can be ignored because this is a speaker independent verification. Thus, the equation (1) can be simplified as

$$p(W_c / O) \approx \frac{p(O/W_c)}{\sum_j p(O/W_j)} \quad (2)$$

This is the same with the likelihood normalization method for utterance verification in a conventional ASR algorithm. In equation (2), W_c becomes the uttered word sequence, $p(O/W_j)$ is approximated by the summation of the n highest likelihoods by using the parallel phoneme HMM networks for all registered words. As a result, if the speaker information is ignored, the text-prompted verification technique is equal to the conventional ASR algorithms as a pattern classification problem using the maximum a posteriori (MAP) decision rule to find the most likely sequence of words as follows.

$$W_k = \arg \max_j L(O/W_j) \quad (3)$$

where $L(O/W_j)$ is the likelihood of an observation sequence O given word W_j. In a text-prompted verification, this is the time that the number of a given word, j is equal to one. At this time, when someone speaks a false word for a text-prompted verification, we cannot verify the uttered word because we have no normalized models to test a likelihood score. Thus, we need the models to increase the likelihood score more than the one of claimed voice code model when someone speaks the false voice code. But, we do not want the previously trained models (filler or garbage model) for likelihood normalization because the memory of our system is limited. To cope with these problems, we reuse the original acoustic model for the alternative hypothesis model. Alternative hypothesis models as anti-models can be made automatically through the analysis of phoneme information with respect to the prompted text word. In this paper, we propose the construction method of anti-models by using the statistical distance of phonemes against the voice code. This reused anti-model can be used for competing with the prompted voice code as follows.

$$W_k = \arg\max_j L(O/W_0, \overline{W_1}, ..., \overline{W_j}) \quad (4)$$

where W_0 is a prompted voice code, $\overline{W}$ is a competing model to be used for likelihood normalization, and the combination of anti-phonemes. W_k is a concatenation of syllable units that can be written as

$$W_k = S_1^k S_2^k \cdots S_N^k \quad (5)$$

where N is the number of a syllable. In addition, a syllable unit is a concatenation of context independent phoneme units that can be written as

$$S_k = P_1^k P_2^k \cdots P_M^k \quad (6)$$

where M is the number of the phoneme. Finally, this context independent phoneme unit is changed into a context dependent phoneme unit after anti-phoneme units are constructed. Then, the anti-phoneme units become the context dependent model.

As you see in equation (4), in the first pass, Viterbi algorithm is employed to find the most likelihood word W_k. In this step, prompted voice code is first verified as in given;

$$PVC = \begin{cases} true & if \ j=0 \\ false & else \end{cases} \quad (7)$$

If the verification result, PVC is true, the second pass to test a likelihood score is followed. In this sub-section, we describe the automatic construction method of anti-models that opposes to the statistical distance according to the manner and place of articulation, and tongue advancement and aperture. At first, the prompted voice text is automatically changed into a phoneme string, produced using a grapheme to phoneme (G2P) converter through the text analysis. Then, the following rules for construction of anti-models are applied. The voice code can be composed of a concatenation of a syllable, S that is the set of phonemes. A voice code, W_0 is expressed by

$$W_0 = \{S_1, S_2, ..., S_N\} \quad (8)$$

where N is the total number of syllable of a given voice code. At first, when a person says a similar word, this may result in a verification success. This occurs when any person says the word as follows.

$$\overline{W_1^1} = \{\overline{S_1}, S_2, ..., S_N\} \quad (9)$$
$$\overline{W_2^1} = \{S_1, \overline{S_2}, ..., S_N\}..., $$
$$\overline{W_N^1} = \{S_1, S_2, ..., \overline{S_N}\}$$

where N is the number of anti-syllable models for the first method and the variable, $\overline{s}$ is the anti-syllable. This sometimes results in a verification success. Thus, we can use the equation (9) as anti-models to prevent the false acceptance through competing with a voice code model when a person says a similar password. The anti-syllable model can be constructed using a concatenation of an anti-phoneme against each syllable unit as

$$\overline{S_N} = \{\overline{P_1}, \overline{P_2}, ..., \overline{P_M}\} \qquad (10)$$

The criterion to select the anti-phoneme is to use the method to classify phonemes according to the manner and place of articulation, and tongue advancement and aperture as in Table 1, which is matched in order between phoneme and anti-phoneme. Table 2 depicts the matched phoneme set between Korean and English for your understanding. In this paper, we use the 44 phonemes set for Korean voice code verification. The anti-phoneme is chosen the one to one matching between phoneme and anti-phoneme. To make the anti-model of each syllable, the corresponding syllable in the prompted voice code is changed into an anti-syllable using the anti-phoneme according to the Table 1 after the text is changed into the phoneme list using a grapheme to phoneme converter, where it needs a parsing process to find the each syllable that is composed of consonant and vowel. In the Korean language, a syllable can be composed of "C+V", "C+V+C" and "V+C" where V is the vowel and C is the consonant. A Korean syllable can be classified into 9 groups as in Table 3. Using this rule, a given text is classified into the syllable lists [7][8].

Table 1. The anti-model production rules using statistical distance of phonemes

		Phoneme to Anti-phoneme	Standard
Consonant	Phoneme	ㄱ ㅋ ㄲ ㅇ ㄷ ㅌ ㄸ ㅅ ㅆ ㅈ ㅊ ㅉ ㄴ ㄹ ㅂ ㅍ ㅃ ㅁ ㅎ	Manner and place of articulation
	Anti-phoneme	ㅃ ㅂ ㅂ ㅂ ㄲ ㄱ ㄱ ㅃ ㅂ ㄲ ㄱ ㄱ ㄲ ㄱ ㄱ ㄱ ㄱ ㄱ ㅂ	
Vowel	Phoneme	ㅏ ㅑ ㅓ ㅣ ㅢ ㅟ ㅜ ㅠ ㅡ ㅔ ㅐ ㅚ ㅙ ㅖ ㅗ ㅛ ㅕ ㅝ ㅘ ㅞ ㅒ	Tongue advancement and aperture
	Anti-phoneme	ㅟ ㅜ ㅟ ㅏ ㅏ ㅏ ㅣ ㅏ ㅏ ㅟ ㅟ ㅏ ㅏ ㅏ ㅣ ㅏ ㅏ ㅔ ㅣ ㅏ ㅏ	

Table 2. Matching table between Korean and English phoneme

	Consonent						Vowel				
ㄱ	g	ㅋ	kh	ㅊ	ch	ㅏ	a	ㅛ	yo	ㅕ	yv
ㄴ	n	ㅌ	th	ㅈ	j	ㅓ	v	ㅠ	yu	ㅑ	ya
ㄷ	d	ㅍ	ph	ㅉ	jj	ㅗ	o	ㅐ	yae	ㅞ	we
ㄹ	r	ㅎ	h	ㅇ	ng	ㅜ	u	ㅖ	ye	ㅢ	eui
ㅁ	m	ㄲ	gg	ㅆ	ss	ㅡ	eu	ㅘ	wa	ㅝ	Wv
ㅂ	b	ㄸ	dd			ㅣ	i	ㅚ	we	ㅙ	we
ㅅ	s	ㅃ	bb			ㅒ	e	ㅟ	wi	ㅖ	e

Table 3. Korean syllable production rules

Syllable	Word production rules	Group	Group number	Comments
CV	CV/CV	CV/CV (PART1)	1	
	CV/CVC			
	CV/VC	CV/V (PART2)	2	
	CV/V			
CVC	CVC/CV	CVC/C (PART3)	3	
	CVC/CVC			
	CVC/VC	CVC/V (PART4)	1	It follows the rule part 1 according to the Korean utterance rule.
	CVC/V			
VC	VC/CV	VC/C (PART5)	4	
	VC/CVC			
	VC/VC	VC/V (PART6)	5	It follows the rule part 7 according to the Korean utterance rule.
	VC/V			
V	V/CV	V/CV (PART7)	5	
	V/CVC			
	V/VC	V/V (PART8)	6	
	V/V			

The second, when any person utters the similar word that includes all parts of a prompted voice code, it often results in a verification success. It would be the time that any person utters a false text as follows

$$\overline{W_1^2} = \{S_1, S_2, ..., S_N, \overline{S_{N+1}}\},$$
$$\overline{W_2^2} = \{S_1, S_2, ..., S_N, \overline{S_{N+1}}, \overline{S_{N+2}}\}, ..., \quad (11)$$
$$\overline{W_M^2} = \{S_1, S_2, ..., S_N, \overline{S_{N+1}}, \overline{S_{N+2}}, ..., \overline{S_{N+M}}\}$$

where M is the number of anti-syllable models to compete with a given voice code model, and anti syllable, $\overline{S_{N+M}}$ is matched to its syllable, S_N. To prevent this case, we use the equation (11) as anti-models. The anti-syllable model also can be constructed using Table 1 or 2.

The third, when any person says a similar word that is some part of the password text, this also often results in a verification success. This happens when any person says a text as follows.

$$\overline{W_1^3} = \{S_1\},$$
$$\overline{W_2^3} = \{S_1, S_2\}, ..., \quad (12)$$
$$\overline{W_{N-1}^3} = \{S_1, S_2, ..., S_{N-1}\}$$

where $N-1$ is the number of anti-syllable models. To prevent this case, we use the equation (12) as anti-models. In addition, we can use anti-models contrary to the equation (12) as follows.

$$\overline{W_1^4} = \{\overline{S_1}\}$$
$$\overline{W_2^4} = \{\overline{S_1}, \overline{S_2}\}...,$$
$$\overline{W_{N-1}^4} = \{\overline{S_1}, \overline{S_2},..., \overline{S_{N-1}}\}$$
(13)

Finally, the following anti-model is applied.

$$\overline{W_1^5} = \{\overline{S_1}, \overline{S_2},..., \overline{S_N}\}$$
(14)

After these anti-models are constructed through the analysis of a given voice code, all anti-models are used for competing with a voice code model. These models would increase the likelihood score of anti-models while the likelihood score is reduced when someone speaks a false word or phrase.

2.2 Voice Code Verification Using Sub-word Based Anti-models

In the second pass, the voice code verification task is applied. Generally, a sub-word based utterance verification or out- of-vocabulary rejection method is based on a likelihood ratio test. The major difficulty with an LRT in utterance verification is how to model the alternative hypothesis, where the true distribution of the data is unknown and an alternative hypothesis usually represents a very complex and composite event. Given a decoded sub-word in an observed segment, we need a decision rule by which we assign the sub-word to either hypothesis H_0 or H_1. For the binary testing problem, one of the most useful tests for decision is the Neyman-Pearson Lemma. For a given number of observations, which minimizes the error for one class while maintaining the error for the other class constant, is a likelihood ratio test as follows.

$$LRT(X) = \frac{P(X/H_0)}{P(X/H_1)} = \frac{P(O_n/\lambda_n)}{P(O_n/\overline{\lambda_n})} \geq \eta$$
(15)

where H_0 means that the hypothesis is true and H_1 means that the hypothesis is false, λ is the sub-word model, $\overline{\lambda}$ is the anti-subword model, and X is the uttered input observation that the number of a sub-word is N as follows.

$$X = \{O_1, O_2,..., O_N\} = \{O_1^{t_1}, O_{t_1+1}^{t_2},..., O_{t_{N+1}}^{t_N}\}$$
(16)

The sub-word alignment and log-likelihood value are obtained on a log domain through the Viterbi segmentation. For the normalization of likelihood ratio, an average frame log-likelihood ratio (LLR), $R(n)$ is defined as

$$R_n = \frac{1}{l_n}[\log P(O_n/\lambda_n) - \log(O_n/\overline{\lambda_n})]$$
(17)

The dynamic range of a sub-word based likelihood ratio is higher. This can affect the overall performance. One way to limit the dynamic range of the sub-word confidence measure is to use a sigmoid function of the form.

$$R_n = \frac{1}{l_n}\left[\log P(O_n/\lambda_n) - \frac{1}{nBest}\sum_{m=1}^{nBest}\log(O_n/\overline{\lambda_m})\right] \quad (18)$$

In this equation (18), dynamic range of sub-word based log likelihood ratio is high. This can affect to the overall performance. One way to limit the dynamic range of the sub-word confidence measure is to use a sigmoid function of the following form.

$$U_n = \frac{1}{1+\exp(-\alpha \times (R_n - \tau))} \quad (19)$$

where τ and α are location and weighting parameters. The log confidence score has a slope of α when the log likelihood score is less than zero.

2.3 Confidence Measure

For an effective voice code verification, we need to define a function to combine the results of sub-word tests. The confidence measure (CM) for an input utterance O can be represented as

$$CM(O) = f(CM_1, CM_2, ..., CM_N) \quad (20)$$

where $f()$ is the function to combine the verification scores. This is defined as a function of their likelihood ratios. It can be considered as a joint statistic for overall word-level verification. The first confidence measure CM_1 is based on a frame-duration normalization, which is defined as follows:

$$CM_1 = \frac{1}{L}\sum_n^N (l_n * R_n) \quad (21)$$

where N is the total number of sub-words in the utterance, and L is the total number of utterance frames, $L = \sum_{n=1}^{N} l_n$. The second one CM_2 is based on a syllable segment-based normalization. It is a simple average of a log likelihood of all the syllables.

$$CM_2 = \frac{1}{N}\sum_n^N R_n \quad (22)$$

$$CM_3 = \exp\left(\frac{1}{N}\sum_{n=1}^{N}\log R_n\right) \quad (23)$$

$$CM_4 = \frac{1}{N}\sum_{n=1}^{N} U_n \quad (24)$$

$$CM_5 = \exp\left(\frac{1}{N}\sum_{n=1}^{N}\log U_n\right) \quad (25)$$

where equation (22) and (23) are the arithmetic and geometric means of the unweighted sub-word level confidence scores, and equation (24) and (25) are the arithmetic and geometric means of the sigmoid weighted sub-word score.

For every confidence measure, a specific threshold is set up. If its value is below the threshold, the candidate is discarded from the verification task. Thus, it results in a voice code verification failure.

3 Evaluation of Proposed System

3.1 Experimental Condition

For speech input to verify the uttered voice code, the sampling rate is 11KHz 16bit, and speech signals are analyzed within 125ms frame with 10ms lapped into 26th order feature vector that has 13th order MFCCs including log energy and their 1st and 2nd derivatives. A training data set consists of about 120,000 utterances of 6,000 isolated words set recorded in an office environment. In addition, we used a different speech corpus for testing the data set, which is PBW452DB, Korean Common DB. It consists of 63,280 utterances of 452 isolated words recorded in a silent environment.

3.2 Experimental Results

We applied an utterance verification technique using an N-best alternative hypothesis model for likelihood normalization in an LRT. In our previous work [6] on utterance verification, several utterance verification methods are simulated. Our method, the Bayesian fusion technique showed the performance higher than any other methods. However, we applied the 5-best technique that is easy to implement and has a low computing time on a DSP board.

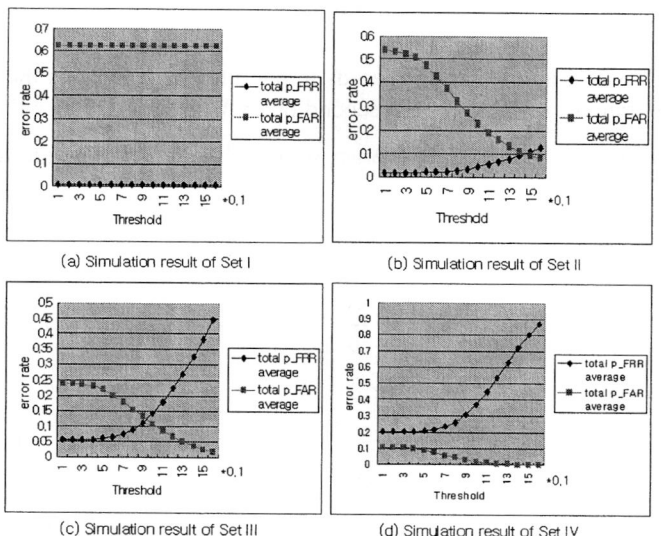

(a) Simulation result of Set I

(b) Simulation result of Set II

(c) Simulation result of Set III

(d) Simulation result of Set IV

Fig. 2. Simulation results of the second approach using statistical distance of phonemes

For a voice code verification simulation, an anti-model making routine for likelihood normalization against a log-likelihood score of voice code is implemented as in Section 2. The simulation is done using the total anti-models as in equations (9), (11), (12), (13) and (14). At first, we evaluated by using four categories of the set. Set I is the anti-model set using equation (14), set II is the anti-model set using equations (11) and (14), set III is the anti-model set using equations (11), (12) and (14) and set IV is the anti-model set using equations (9), (11), (12) and (14). As shown in (a) of Figure 2, set I has a high FAR while FRR is low. In set II, the EER is 0.09. However, it cannot cope with various situations as described in Section II. Thus, we did extra simulations about set II. The (b) of Figure 2 is the time that we use $M=1$ of equation (11). When we use $M=3$ (method II), FRR and FAR are improved as in Figure 3, (a).

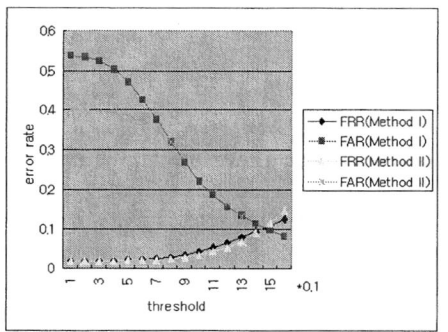
(a) Comparison result of the set II using method I, II

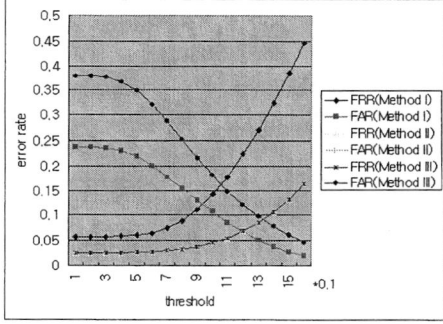
(b) Comparison result of the set III using method I, II, III.

Fig. 3. Comparison results using anti-models set

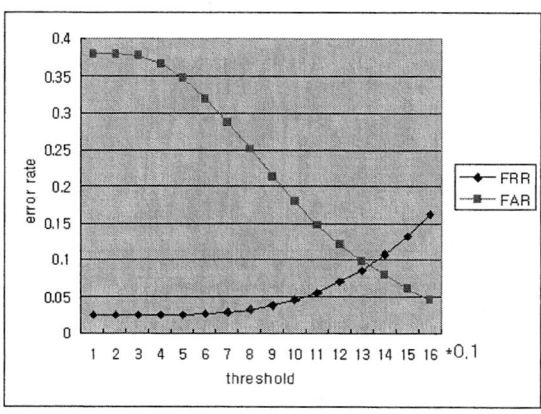

Fig. 4. Final result using all anti-models

Using the result of (a) in Figure 3, we combined the anti-models using equations (12) and (13). In (b) of Figure 3, Method I is the method using equations (11), (12) and (14). Method II is the method using equations (11), (13) and (14). Method III is the method using equations (11), (12), (13) and (14). Method II and III showed the similar result. However, method III is a bit improved and also can cope with the any utterance of people very well. Finally, to method III of set III, we combined anti-models using equation (9) as in Figure 4. The curve shape and result of final method is similar with method III of Figure 3, (b). But the final result is a bit improved than method III of Figure 3, (b). In addition, the EER is 0.08. This result is improved by 16% than the one of utterance verification result in our previous work [6].

This system usually is utilized on an outdoor surveillance region. Thus, this requires a noise robust voice code verification to cope with not only environmental noise, but also other white noises. To resolve this problem, a harmonics-based spectral subtraction algorithm [9] is applied for preprocessing the noise. First, experiment is conducted by the Aurora 2 evaluation procedure under a continuous digits recognition tasks. Test sets are reproduced using TIDigits of which the entire speech data are down-sampled to 8 Khz and various realistic noises are added artificially. The feature vector order is 39 and is composed of 13 order static MFCC (c1-c12+log energy), its derivatives and accelerations. For comparison, a spectral subtraction algorithm and nonlinear algorithm are evaluated as in Table 4. As you can see in Table 4, the HSS showed that the proposed algorithm is more robust than other algorithms. A notable advantage of the proposed scheme is that it does not require an exact SNR estimate in various noise conditions.

Next, HSS is applied to the voice code verification experiment, which is also conducted using PBW452DB. The simulation result is shown in Table 5. In a babble noise environment, EER did not show the rapid decrease of EER. However, in white noise, EER showed a rapid decrease of EER. But, It brought about a 40% relative improvement than when there was no harmonics-based spectral subtraction algorithm.

Table 4. Word accuracies on Aurora2 mis-matched training/testing condition(%)

	Baseline	SS	NSS	HSS
Baseline	60.06	77.89	78.20	80.59
CMN	71.16	78.56	78.73	82.00

Table 5. EER of voice code verification under babble and white noise environments

		EER(Equal error Rate)			
		Clean	5dB	10dB	15dB
Clean DB	FRR	0.076738	-	-	-
	FAR	0.109624	-	-	-
Babble noise	FRR	-	0.088653	0.088069	0.089238
	FAR	-	0.096128	0.095923	0.095385
White noise	FRR	-	0.518268	0.376042	0.221871
	FAR	-	0.362295	0.320828	0.218299

4 Discussions and Conclusions

The key point is to use the competing models that are anti-models using a statistical distance of phonemes. This idea is due to the fact that the alternative model always follows the same state as the target model. Thus, if we can do the modeling of the alternative hypothesis very well, we thought that the voice code verification task could be solved by competing against each other without extra trained models such as filler or garbage models. As you saw the simulation result, we know that the use of a lot of anti-models degraded the detection probability while the use of a few anti-models degraded the false acceptance rate. Thus, the proper number of anti-models that can compete with the voice code model should be used. In addition, outdoor noise is an important issue that should be considered. Under this condition, the speaker verification rate is very low and also the voice code verification rate is the same. Even though we applied a harmonic-based spectral subtraction algorithm, some other algorithms should also be used for compensating the verification rate on an outdoor environment where wind or rain noise exists, and so on.

As a result, our proposed method for a text-prompted and speaker independent verification provided a voice code verification function without an extra trained model such as filler or garbage models for likelihood normalization through the reuse of a general acoustic model. In experiment, the performance evaluation is done by using a common Korean database, PBW452DB, which consists of 63,280 utterances of 452 isolated words recorded in a silent environment. The result is improved by 16% higher than the result of utterance verification result. In addition, simulation result showed that the performance is higher under noisy environment than in any other algorithms when we applied the harmonics-based spectral subtraction algorithm compared to general spectral subtraction and nonlinear spectral subtraction.

Acknowledgements

This work was supported by grant No. 2003-218 from the Korea Institute of Industrial Technology Evaluation & Planning Foundation.

References

[1] Hui Jiang, Chin-Hui Lee, "A new approach to utterance verification based on neighborhood information in model space," Speech and Audio Processing, IEEE Transactions on, Volume: 11, Issue: 5, Sept. 2003.
[2] Tomoko Matsui, Sadaoki Furui, "Likelihood normalization for speaker verification using a phoneme- and speaker-independent model," Speech Communication 17(1995) 109-116.
[3] Bing Xiang, Berger, T. "Efficient text-independent speaker verification with structural Gaussian mixture models and neural network," Speech and Audio Processing, IEEE Transactions on, Volume: 11, Issue: 5, Sept. 2003, pp447-456.
[4] X. Huang, A. Acero and H. Hon, *Spoken Language Processing*, Prentice Hall PTR, 2001

[5] F. Wessel, R. Schluter, K. Macherey, and H. Ney, "Confidence measures for large vocabulary continuous speech recognition," IEEE Trans. Speech Audio Processing, vol. 9, Mar. 2001.
[6] Taeyoon Kim and HANSEOK KO, Uttrance Verification Under Distributed Detection and Fusion Framework," , Eurospeech 2003, pp. 889~892, Sep, 2003.
[7] Hansang Park, B.A., M.A., "Temporal ans spectral Characteristics of Korean Phonation Types," Doctor of philosophy degree thesis, The university of Taxas at Austin, August, 2002.
[8] Willian J. Hardcastle and John laver, "The Handbook of Phonetic Sciences," Blackwell publishers Ltd, 1997.
[9] Jounghoon Beh and Hanseok Ko, "A Novel Spectral Subtraction Scheme For Robust Speech Recognition: Spectral Subtraction using Spectral Harmonics of Speech," ICME 2003, III 633 ~ III 636, Jul, 2003

A Logic Based Approach for Dynamic Access Control

Vino Fernando Crescini and Yan Zhang

School of Computing and Information Technology,
University of Western Sydney,
Penrith South DC, NSW 1797, Australia
{jcrescin,yan}@cit.uws.edu.au

Abstract. The *PolicyUpdater*[1] system is a fully-implemented access control system that provides policy evaluations as well as dynamic policy updates. These functions are achieved by the use of a logic-based language $\mathcal{L}$ to represent the underlying access control policies, constraints and update propositions. The system performs authorisation query evaluations and conditional policy updates by translating the language $\mathcal{L}$ to a normal logic program in a form suitable for evaluation using the *Stable Model* semantics.

1 Introduction

Recent advances in the information security field have produced a number of different approaches to access control, some of which are logic-based, e.g. [5,7]. Bertino, et. al. [1] proposed an approach based on ordered logic with ordered domains. Jajodia, et. al. [6] on the other hand, proposed a general access control framework that features handling of multiple policies. However, these approaches lack the necessary details to address the issues involved in implementing a system based on these approaches.

The *Policy Description Language* or *PDL*, developed by Lobo, et. al. [8], is designed for representing event and action oriented generic policies. *PDL* was later extended by Chomicki, et. al. [3] to include a constraint mechanism called *policy monitors*. Bertino, et. al. [2], again took *PDL* a step further by extending *policy monitors* to support preferred constraints. While these languages possess enough expressive power to be used for most access control applications, systems based on these languages will not have the ability to perform dynamic policy updates.

To overcome these limitations, we propose the PolicyUpdater access control system. This system, with its own access control language, $\mathcal{L}$, allows policies to be represented as logical facts and rules with variable resolution and default propositions, and provides a mechanism to conditionally and dynamically perform a sequence of policy updates, as well as query evaluation.

The rest of this paper is organised as follows. In Section 2, the paper introduces language $\mathcal{L}$ with its formal syntax, semantics and some examples. Section 3 addresses the issues associated with domain consistency and query evaluation. Finally, Section 4 ends the paper with some concluding remarks.

---

[1] Web page at http://www.cit.uws.edu.au/~jcrescin/projects/policyupdater/index.html

2 Language $\mathcal{L}$: Syntax and Semantics

Language $\mathcal{L}$ is a first-order logic language that is used to represent a policy base for an authorisation system. Two key features of the language are: (1) providing a means to conditionally and dynamically update the existing policy base and (2) having a mechanism by which queries may be evaluated from the updated policy base.

2.1 Syntax

Logic programs of language $\mathcal{L}$ are composed of language statements, each terminated by a semicolon ";" character. Comments may appear anywhere in the logic program and, like C, language $\mathcal{L}$ comments are delimited by the "/*" and "*/".

Components of Language $\mathcal{L}$

Identifiers. The most basic unit of language $\mathcal{L}$ is the identifier. Identifiers are used to represent different components of the language, and is defined as an upper or lower case alphabet character, followed by 0 to 127 characters of alphabet, digit or underscore characters. There are 3 types of identifier, each defined by the following syntax:

```
[a-zA-Z]([a-zA-Z0-9_]){0,127}
```

- *Entity Identifiers* represent constant entities that make up a logical atom. They are divided further into 3 types, with each type again divided into the *singular entity* and *group entity* categories: *Subjects* (e.g. alice, lecturers); *Access Rights* (e.g. read, write, own); and *Objects* (e.g. file, database, directory). This type of identifier must start with a lowercase character.
- *Policy Update Identifiers* are used for the sole purpose of naming a policy update. These identifier names are then used as labels to refer to policy update definitions and directives. As labels, identifier of this class occupy a different namespace from entity identifier. For this reason, policy update identifier share the same syntax with entity identifier.
- *Variable Identifiers* are used as entity identifier place-holders. To distinguish them from entity and policy update identifiers, variable identifier are prefixed with an upper-case character.

Atoms. An atom is composed of a relation with 2 to 3 entity or variable identifier that represent a logical relationship between the entities. There are 3 types of atoms:

- *Holds.* An atom of this type states that the subject identifier sub holds the access right identifier acc for the object identifier obj.

    ```
    holds(<sub>, <acc>, <obj>)
    ```

- *Membership.* This type of atom states that the singular identifier elt is a member or element of the group identifier grp. It is important to note that identifier elt and grp must be of the same base type (e.g. subject and subject group).

```
memb(<elt>, <grp>)
```

- *Subset.* The subset atom states that the group identifier $grp1$ and $grp2$ are of the same types and that group $grp1$ is a subset of the group $grp2$.

```
subst(<grp1>, <grp2>)
```

Facts. A fact makes a claim that the relationship represented by an atom or its negation holds in the current context. Facts are negated by the use of the negation operator "!". The following shows the formal syntax of a fact:

```
[!]<holds_atom>|<memb_atom>|<subst_atom>
```

Expressions. An expression is either a fact, or a logical conjunction of facts, separated by the double-ampersand characters "&&".

```
<fact1> [&& <fact2> [&& ...]]
```

Atoms that contain no variables, i.e. composed entirely of entity identifiers, are called *ground atoms*. Similarly, facts and expressions composed of ground atoms are called *ground facts* and *ground expressions*, respectively.

Definition Statements

Entity Identifier Definition. All entity identifiers (subjects, access rights, objects and groups) must first be declared before any other statements to define the entity domain of the policy base. The following entity declaration syntax illustrates how to define one or more entity identifiers of a particular type.

```
ident sub|acc|obj[-grp] <ent_id>[, ...];
```

Initial Fact Definition. The initial facts of the policy base, those that hold before any policy updates are performed, are defined by using the following definition syntax:

```
initially <ground_exp>;
```

Constraint Definition. Constraints are logical rules that hold regardless of any changes that may occur when the policy base is updated. The constraint rules are true in the initial state and remain true even after a policy update is performed.

The constraint syntax below shows that for any state of the policy base, expression $ex1$ holds if expression $ex2$ is true and there is no evidence that $ex3$ is true. The *with absence* clause allows constraints to behave like default propositions, where the absence of proof that an expression holds satisfies the clause condition of the proposition.

It is important to note that the expressions $ex1$, $ex2$ and $ex3$ may be non-ground expressions, which allows identifier occurring in these expressions to be variables.

```
always <ex1> [implied by <ex2> [with absence <ex3>]];
```

Policy Update Definition. Before a policy update can be applied, it must first be defined by using the following syntax:

```
<up_id>([<var_id>[, ...]]) causes <ex1> if <ex2>;
```

up_id is the policy update identifier to be used in referencing this policy update. The optional var_id list are the variable identifier occurring in the expressions $ex1$ and $ex2$ and will eventually be replaced by entity identifier when the update is referenced. The postcondition expression $ex1$ is an expression that will hold in the state after this update is applied. The expression $ex2$ is a precondition expression that must hold in the current state before this update is applied.

Note that a policy update definition will have no effect on the policy base until it is applied by one of the directives described in the following section.

Directive Statements

Policy Update Directives. The policy update sequence list contains a list of references to defined policy updates in the domain. The policy updates in the sequence list are applied to the current state of the policy base one at a time to produce a policy base state upon which queries can be evaluated. The following four directives are the policy sequence manipulation features of language $\mathcal{L}$.

Adding an Update into the Sequence. Defined policy updates are added into the sequence list through the use of the following directive:

```
seq add <up_id>([<ent_id>[, ...]]);
```

where up_id is the identifier of a defined policy update and the ent_id list is a comma-separated list of entity identifier that will replace the variable identifier that occur in the definition of the policy update.

Listing the Updates in the Sequence. The following directive may be used to list the current contents of the policy update sequence list.

```
seq list;
```

This directive is answered with an ordinal list of policy updates in the form:

```
<n> <up_id>([<ent_id>[, ...]])
```

where n is the ordinal index of the policy update within the sequence list starting at 0. up_id is the policy update identifier and the ent_id list is the list of entity identifier used to replace the variable identifier place-holders.

Removing an Update from the Sequence. The syntax below shows the directive to remove a policy update reference from the list. n is the ordinal index of the policy update to be removed. Note that removing a policy update reference from the sequence list may change the ordinal index of other update references.

```
seq del <n>;
```

Computing an Update Sequence. The policy updates in the sequence list is not applied until the *compute* directive is issued. The directive causes the policy update references in the sequence list to be applied one at a time in the same order that they appear in the list. The directive also causes the system to generate the policy base models against which query requests can be evaluated.

```
compute;
```

Query Directive. A ground query expression may be issued against the current state of the policy base. This current state is derived after all the updates in the update sequence have been applied, one at a time, upon the initial state. Query expressions are answered with a *true*, *false* or an *unknown*, depending on whether the queried expression holds, its negation holds, or neither, respectively. Syntax is as follows:

```
query <ground_exp>;
```

Example 1 The following language $\mathcal{L}$ program code listing shows a simple rule-based document access control system scenario.

In this example, the subject $alice$ is initially a member of the subject group $grp2$, which is a subset of group $grp1$. The group $grp1$ also initially holds a *read* access right for the object $file$. The constraint states that if the group $grp1$ has *read* access for $file$, and no other information is present to conclude that $grp3$ do not have *write* access for $file$, then the group $grp1$ is granted *write* access for $file$. For simplicity, we only consider one policy update $delete\_read$ and a few queries that are evaluated after the policy update is performed.

```
ident sub alice;
ident sub-grp grp1, grp2, grp3;
ident acc read, write;
ident obj file;

initially memb(alice, grp2) && subst(grp2, grp1);
initially holds(grp1, read, file);

always holds(grp1, write, file)
  implied by holds(grp1, read, file)
  with absence !holds(grp3, write, file);

delete_read(SG0, OS0) causes !holds(SG0, read, OS0);

seq add delete_read(grp1, file);

compute;

query holds(grp1, write, file);
query holds(alice, read, file);
```

∎

2.2 Semantics

After giving a detailed syntactic definition of language $\mathcal{L}$, we now define its formal semantics.

Domain Description of Language $\mathcal{L}$

Definition 1. *The domain description $\mathcal{D_L}$ of language $\mathcal{L}$ is defined as a finite set of ground initial state facts, constraint rules and policy update definitions.*

In addition to the domain description $\mathcal{D_L}$, language $\mathcal{L}$ also includes an additional set: the sequence list ψ. The sequence list ψ is an ordered set that contains a sequence of references to policy update definitions. Each policy update reference consists of the policy update identifier and a series of zero or more identifier entities to replace the variable place-holders in the policy update definitions.

Language $\mathcal{L}^*$ In language $\mathcal{L}$, the policy base is subject to change, which is triggered by the application of policy updates. Such changes bring forth the concept of policy base states. Conceptually, a state may be thought of as a set of facts and constraints of the policy base at a particular instant. The state transition notation $PB \xrightarrow{u} PB'$ shows that a new state PB' is generated from the current state PB after the policy update u is applied.

This concept of a state means that for every policy update applied to the policy base, a new instance of the policy base or a new set of facts and constraints are generated. To precisely define the underlying semantics of domain description $\mathcal{D_L}$ in language $\mathcal{L}$, we introduce language $\mathcal{L}^*$, which is an extended logic program representation of language $\mathcal{L}$, with state as an explicit sort.

Language $\mathcal{L}^*$ contains only one special state constant S_0 to represent the initial state of a given domain description. All other states are represented as a resulting state obtained by applying the Res function.

The $Res(u, \sigma)$ function takes a policy update reference u, where $u \in \psi$, and the current state σ as input arguments and returns the resulting state after update u has been applied to state σ. Given an initial state S_0 and a sequence list ψ, each state σ_i ($0 \leq i \leq |\psi|$) may be represented as $\sigma_0 = S_0, \sigma_1 = Res(u_0, \sigma_0), \ldots, \sigma_{|\psi|} = Res(u_{|\psi|-1}, \sigma_{|\psi|-1})$. Substituting each state with a recursive call to the Res function, the final state $S_{|\psi|}$ is defined as $S_{|\psi|} = Res(u_{|\psi|-1}, Res(\ldots, Res(u_0, S_0)))$.

Entities. The entity set $\mathcal{E}$ is a union of six disjoint entity sets: single subject $\mathcal{E}_{ss}$, group subject $\mathcal{E}_{sg}$, single access right $\mathcal{E}_{as}$, group access right $\mathcal{E}_{ag}$, single object $\mathcal{E}_{os}$ and group object $\mathcal{E}_{og}$. We also define three additional entity sets: $\mathcal{E}_s$, $\mathcal{E}_a$ and $\mathcal{E}_o$, which are unions of their respective singular and group entity sets. Each entity in set $\mathcal{E}$ corresponds directly to the *entity identifier s* of language $\mathcal{L}$.

Atoms. The main difference between language $\mathcal{L}$ and language $\mathcal{L}^*$ lies in the definition of an atom. Atoms in language $\mathcal{L}^*$ represent a logical relationship of 2 to 3 entities in a particular state. That is, language $\mathcal{L}^*$ atoms have an extra parameter to specify the state in which they hold. In this paper, atoms of language $\mathcal{L}^*$ are written with the hat character ($\hat{holds}$, $\hat{memb}$ and $\hat{subst}$) to differentiate from the atoms of language $\mathcal{L}$. The atom set $\mathcal{A}^\sigma$ is the set of all atoms in state σ.

Facts. In language $\mathcal{L}^*$, a fact states whether an atom or its negation holds in a particular state. A fact f in state σ is formally defined as $f^\sigma = [\neg]\alpha$, $\alpha \in \mathcal{A}^\sigma$.

Translating Language $\mathcal{L}$ to Language $\mathcal{L}^*$. Given a domain description $\mathcal{D_L}$ of language $\mathcal{L}$, we translate $\mathcal{D_L}$ into an extended logic program of language $\mathcal{L}^*$, as denoted by $Trans(\mathcal{D_L})$. The semantics of $\mathcal{D_L}$ is provided by the answer sets of program $Trans(\mathcal{D_L})$. Before we can fully define $Trans(\mathcal{D_L})$, we must first define the following functions:

The $CopyAtom()$ function takes two arguments: an atom of language $\mathcal{L}^*$ at some state and new state. The function returns an equivalent atom of the same type and with the same entities, but in the new state specified.

Another function, $TransAtom()$, takes an atom α of language $\mathcal{L}$ and an arbitrary state σ. It then returns a language $\mathcal{L}^*$ atom of the same type in state σ, with the same given entities. The other function, $TransFact()$, is similar to the $TransAtom()$ function, but instead of translating an atom, it takes a fact from language $\mathcal{L}$ and a state then returns the equivalent fact in language $\mathcal{L}^*$.

Initial Fact Rules. Translating initial fact expressions of language $\mathcal{L}$ to language $\mathcal{L}^*$ rules is a trivial procedure: translate each fact that make up the initial fact expression of language $\mathcal{L}$ with its corresponding equivalent initial state atom of language $\mathcal{L}^*$. For example, the following code shows a language $\mathcal{L}$ *initially* statement:

```
initially holds(bob, read, file) && memb(alice, users);
```

in language $\mathcal{L}^*$, the above statement is translated to:

$\hat{holds}(bob, read, file, S_0) \leftarrow$
$\hat{memb}(alice, users, S_0) \leftarrow$

Constraint Rules. Each constraint rule in language $\mathcal{L}$ is expressed as a series of logical rules in language $\mathcal{L}^*$. Given that all variable occurrences have been grounded to entity identifiers, a constraint in language $\mathcal{L}$, with $m, n, o \geq 0$ may be represented as:

```
always a0 && ... && am
    implied by b0 && ... && bn
    with absence c0 && ... && co;
```

Each fact in the *always* clause of a language $\mathcal{L}$ constraint corresponds to a new rule, where it is the consequent. Each of these new rules will have expression b in the *implied by* clause as the positive premise and the expression c in the *with absence* clause as the negative premise.

$$\hat{a_0} \leftarrow \hat{b_0}, \ldots, \hat{b_n}, not\ \hat{c_0}, \ldots, not\ \hat{c_o}$$
$$\ldots$$
$$\hat{a_m} \leftarrow \hat{b_0}, \ldots, \hat{b_n}, not\ \hat{c_0}, \ldots, not\ \hat{c_o}$$

For example, given a policy update reference in the sequence list ψ (i.e. $|\psi| = 1$) and the following language $\mathcal{L}$ code fragment:

```
always holds(bob, read, f1) && holds(bob, write, f1)
    implied by memb(bob, grp)
    with absence !holds(bob, own, f1);
```

The following shows the language $\mathcal{L}^*$ translation:

$\hat{holds}(bob, read, f1, S_0) \leftarrow \hat{memb}(bob, grp, S_0), not\ \neg\ \hat{holds}(bob, own, f1, S_0)$
$\hat{holds}(bob, write, f1, S_0) \leftarrow \hat{memb}(bob, grp, S_0), not\ \neg\ \hat{holds}(bob, own, f1, S_0)$
$\hat{holds}(bob, read, f1, S_1) \leftarrow \hat{memb}(bob, grp, S_1), not\ \neg\ \hat{holds}(bob, own, f1, S_1)$
$\hat{holds}(bob, write, f1, S_1) \leftarrow \hat{memb}(bob, grp, S_1), not\ \neg\ \hat{holds}(bob, own, f1, S_1)$

Policy Update Rules. With all occurrences of variable place-holders grounded to entity identifiers, a language $\mathcal{L}$ policy update can then be translated to language $\mathcal{L}^*$. In language $\mathcal{L}^*$, policy updates are represented as a set of implications, with each fact in the postcondition expression as the consequent and precondition expression as the premise. However, the translation process must also take into account that the premise of the implication holds in the state before the policy update is applied and that the consequent holds in the state after the application [10]. For example, given an update sequence list $\psi = \{grant\_read, grant\_write\}$ and the following language $\mathcal{L}$ policy update definitions:

```
grant_read()
    causes holds(bob, read, file) if memb(bob, readers);
grant_write()
    causes holds(bob, write, file) if memb(bob, writers);
```

The following shows the language $\mathcal{L}^*$ translation:

$\hat{holds}(bob, read, file, S_1) \leftarrow \hat{memb}(bob, readers, S_0)$
$\hat{holds}(bob, write, file, S_2) \leftarrow \hat{memb}(bob, writers, S_1)$

Inheritance Rules. All properties held by a group are inherited by all the members and subsets of that group. This rule is easy to apply for subject group entities. However, careful attention must be given to access right and object groups. A subject holding an access right for an object group implies that the subject also holds that access right for all objects in the object group. Similarly, a subject holding an access right group for a particular object implies that the subject holds all access rights contained in the access right group for that object.

A conflict is encountered when a particular property is to be inherited by an entity from a group of which it is a member or subset, and the contained entity already holds the negation of that property. This conflict is resolved by giving negative facts higher precedence over its positive counterpart: by allowing member or subset entities to inherit its parent group's properties only if the entities do not already hold the negation of those properties.

The following are the inheritance constraint rules to allow the properties held by a subject group to propagate to all of its members that do not already hold the negation of the properties. For all s_s, s_g, a, o, σ where $s_s \in \mathcal{E}_{ss}, s_g \in \mathcal{E}_{sg}, a \in \mathcal{E}_a, o \in \mathcal{E}_o$ and $S_0 \leq \sigma \leq S_{|\psi|}$:

$$\hat{holds}(s_s, a, o, \sigma) \leftarrow \hat{holds}(s_g, a, o, \sigma), \hat{memb}(s_s, s_g, \sigma), not \neg \hat{holds}(s_s, a, o, \sigma)$$
$$\neg \hat{holds}(s_s, a, o, \sigma) \leftarrow \neg \hat{holds}(s_g, a, o, \sigma), \hat{memb}(s_s, s_g, \sigma)$$

The rules below represent inheritance rules for subject groups to allow subsets to inherit properties held by their supergroup. Note that there is also a set of corresponding rules to represent membership and subset inheritance for access right and object groups. For all $s_{g1}, s_{g2}, a, o, \sigma$ where $s_{g1}, s_{g2} \in \mathcal{E}_{sg}, a \in \mathcal{E}_a, o \in \mathcal{E}_o$ and $S_0 \leq \sigma \leq S_{|\psi|}$:

$$\hat{holds}(s_{g1}, a, o, \sigma) \leftarrow$$
$$\quad \hat{holds}(s_{g2}, a, o, \sigma), \hat{subst}(s_{g1}, s_{g2}, \sigma), not \neg \hat{holds}(s_{g1}, a, o, \sigma)$$
$$\neg \hat{holds}(s_{g1}, a, o, \sigma) \leftarrow \neg \hat{holds}(s_{g2}, a, o, \sigma), \hat{subst}(s_{g1}, s_{g2}, \sigma)$$

Transitivity Rules. Given three group entities G, G' and G''. If G is a subset of G' and G' is a subset of G'', then G must also be a subset of G''. The following rules ensure that the transitive property holds for subject groups. Note that similar rules exist to ensure that the transitive property also holds for access right and object groups. For all $s_{g1}, s_{g2}, s_{g3}, \sigma$ where $s_{g1}, s_{g2}, s_{g3} \in \mathcal{E}_{sg}$ and $S_0 \leq \sigma \leq S_{|\psi|}$:

$$\hat{subst}(s_{g1}, s_{g3}, \sigma) \leftarrow \hat{subst}(s_{g1}, s_{g2}, \sigma), \hat{subst}(s_{g2}, s_{g3}, \sigma)$$

Inertial Rules. Intuitively, all facts in the current state that are not affected by a policy update should be carried over to the next state after the update. In language $\mathcal{L}^*$, this rule must be explicitly stated as a constraint. Formally, the inertial rules are expressed as follows. For all $\hat{\alpha}, u$, there is an $\hat{\alpha}'$ where $\hat{\alpha} \in \mathcal{A}^\sigma$, $u \in \psi$ and $\hat{\alpha}' = CopyAtom(\hat{\alpha}, Res(u, \sigma))$:

$$\hat{\alpha}' \leftarrow \hat{\alpha}, not \neg \hat{\alpha}'$$
$$\neg \hat{\alpha}' \leftarrow \neg \hat{\alpha}, not \hat{\alpha}'$$

Definition 2. *Given a domain description $\mathcal{D_L}$ of language $\mathcal{L}$, its language $\mathcal{L}^*$ translation $Trans(\mathcal{D_L})$ is an extended logic program of language $\mathcal{L}$ consisting of: (1) initial fact rules, (2) constraint rules, (3) policy update rules, (4) inheritance rules, (5) transitivity rules, and (6) inertial rules, as described above.*

By using the above definition, we can now state a theorem that defines the maximum number of rules generated in a translation $Trans(\mathcal{D_L})$ given a domain description $\mathcal{D_L}$. With this theorem, we show that the size of the translated domain $|Trans(\mathcal{D_L})|$ is only polynomially larger than the size of the given domain $|\mathcal{D_L}|$.

Theorem 1 (Translation Size[2]). *Given a domain description $\mathcal{D_L}$; the sets $\mathcal{S}_i$, $\mathcal{S}_c$ and $\mathcal{S}_u$ containing the initially, constraint and policy update statements in $\mathcal{D_L}$, respectively; the set of all entities $\mathcal{E}$ in $\mathcal{D_L}$, including its subsets $\mathcal{E}_s$, $\mathcal{E}_a$, $\mathcal{E}_s$, $\mathcal{E}_{ss}$, $\mathcal{E}_{as}$, $\mathcal{E}_{os}$, $\mathcal{E}_{sg}$, $\mathcal{E}_{ag}$, $\mathcal{E}_{og}$; the set $\mathcal{A}$ containing all the atoms in $\mathcal{D_L}$; the maximum number of facts M_i in any statement in $\mathcal{S}_i$; the maximum number of facts M_c in the always clause of any statement in $\mathcal{S}_c$; the maximum number of facts M_u in the postcondition of any statement in $\mathcal{S}_u$; and finally the sequence list ψ.*

$$|Trans(\mathcal{D_L})| = \\
M_i\,|\mathcal{S}_i| + M_c\,|\mathcal{S}_c|\,|\psi| + M_u\,|\psi| + |\psi|\,(|\mathcal{E}_{sg}|^3 + |\mathcal{E}_{ag}|^3 + |\mathcal{E}_{og}|^3) + 2\,|\mathcal{A}|\,|\psi| + \\
2|\psi|\,(\,|\mathcal{E}_{ss}|\,|\mathcal{E}_{sg}|\,|\mathcal{E}_a|\,|\mathcal{E}_o| + |\mathcal{E}_s|\,|\mathcal{E}_{as}|\,|\mathcal{E}_{ag}|\,|\mathcal{E}_o| + |\mathcal{E}_s|\,|\mathcal{E}_a|\,|\mathcal{E}_{os}|\,|\mathcal{E}_{og}|\,) + \\
2|\psi|\,(\,|\mathcal{E}_{sg}|^2\,|\mathcal{E}_a|\,|\mathcal{E}_o| + |\mathcal{E}_s|\,|\mathcal{E}_{ag}|^2\,|\mathcal{E}_o| + |\mathcal{E}_s|\,|\mathcal{E}_a|\,|\mathcal{E}_{og}|^2\,)$$

3 Domain Consistency Checking and Evaluation

A domain description of language $\mathcal{L}$ must be consistent in order generate a consistent answer set for the evaluation of queries. This section considers two issues: the problem of identifying whether a given domain description is consistent, and how query evaluation is performed given a consistent language domain description. Before these issues can be considered, a few notational constructs must first be introduced. Given a domain description $\mathcal{D_L}$ composed of the following language $\mathcal{L}$ statements:

```
initially a_0 && ... && a_m && !b_0 && ... && !b_n;
always   c_0 && ... && c_o && !d_0 && ... && !d_p
  implied by e_0 && ... && e_q && !f_0 && ... && !f_r
  with absence g_0 && ... && g_s && !h_0 && ... && !h_t;
update()
  causes i_0 && ... && i_u && !j_0 && ... && !j_v
  if k_0 && ... && k_w && !l_0 && ... && !l_x;
```

We define the 6 sets of ground facts:

$\mathcal{F}^+_{int} = \{a_z \mid 0 \leq z \leq m\}$, $\mathcal{F}^+_{con} = \{c_z \mid 0 \leq z \leq o\}$, $\mathcal{F}^+_{upd} = \{i_z \mid 0 \leq z \leq u\}$,
$\mathcal{F}^-_{int} = \{b_z \mid 0 \leq z \leq n\}$, $\mathcal{F}^-_{con} = \{d_z \mid 0 \leq z \leq p\}$, $\mathcal{F}^-_{upd} = \{j_z \mid 0 \leq z \leq v\}$

Additionally, we use the complementary set notation $\overline{\mathcal{F}}$ to denote a set containing the negation of facts in set $\mathcal{F}$, i.e. $\overline{\mathcal{F}} = \{\neg\rho \mid \rho \in \mathcal{F}\}$. Furthermore, we define the following functions. Let γ be an initial, constraint or policy update definition statement of language $\mathcal{L}$:

$$Eff(\gamma) = \begin{cases} \{a_0, \ldots, a_m, \neg b_0, \ldots, \neg b_n\}, & \text{if } \gamma \text{ is an initially statement} \\ \{c_0, \ldots, c_o, \neg d_0, \ldots, \neg d_p\}, & \text{if } \gamma \text{ is a constraint statement} \\ \{i_0, \ldots, i_u, \neg j_0, \ldots, \neg j_v\}, & \text{if } \gamma \text{ is a policy update statement} \end{cases}$$

$$Def(\gamma) = \begin{cases} \emptyset, & \text{if } \gamma \text{ is an initially statement} \\ \{g_0, \ldots, g_s, \neg h_0, \ldots, \neg h_t\}, & \text{if } \gamma \text{ is a constraint statement} \\ \emptyset, & \text{if } \gamma \text{ is a policy update statement} \end{cases}$$

$$Pre(\gamma) = \begin{cases} \emptyset, & \text{if } \gamma \text{ is an initially statement} \\ \{e_0, \ldots, e_q, \neg f_0, \ldots, \neg f_r\}, & \text{if } \gamma \text{ is a constraint statement} \\ \{k_0, \ldots, k_w, \neg l_0, \ldots, \neg l_x\}, & \text{if } \gamma \text{ is a policy update statement} \end{cases}$$

Definition 3. *Given a domain description $\mathcal{D_L}$ of language $\mathcal{L}$, two ground facts ρ and ρ' are mutually exclusive in $\mathcal{D_L}$ if:*

$$\rho \in \{\mathcal{F}^+_{int} \cup \overline{\mathcal{F}^-_{int}} \cup \mathcal{F}^+_{con} \cup \overline{\mathcal{F}^-_{con}} \cup \mathcal{F}^+_{upd} \cup \overline{\mathcal{F}^-_{upd}}\} \text{ implies}$$
$$\rho' \notin \{\mathcal{F}^+_{int} \cup \overline{\mathcal{F}^-_{int}} \cup \mathcal{F}^+_{con} \cup \overline{\mathcal{F}^-_{con}} \cup \mathcal{F}^+_{upd} \cup \overline{\mathcal{F}^-_{upd}}\}$$

Simply stated, a pair of mutually exclusive facts cannot both be true in any given state. The following two definitions refer to language $\mathcal{L}$ statements.

Definition 4. *Given a domain description $\mathcal{D_L}$ of language $\mathcal{L}$, two statements γ and γ' are complementary in $\mathcal{D_L}$ if one of the following conditions holds:*

1. *γ and γ' are both constraint statements and $Eff(\gamma) = \overline{Eff(\gamma')}$.*
2. *γ is a constraint statement, γ' is an update statement and $Eff(\gamma) = \overline{Eff(\gamma')}$.*

Definition 5. *Given a domain description $\mathcal{D_L}$, $\mathcal{D_L}$ is said to be normal if it satisfies all of the following conditions:*

1. $\mathcal{F}^+_{int} \cap \mathcal{F}^-_{int} = \emptyset$
2. *For all constraint statements γ in $\mathcal{D_L}$, $\overline{Eff(\gamma)} \cap Pre(\gamma) = \emptyset$.*
3. *For any two constraint statements γ and γ' in $\mathcal{D_L}$, $Def(\gamma) \cap Eff(\gamma') = \emptyset$.*
4. *For any two complementary statements γ and γ' in $\mathcal{D_L}$, there exists a pair of ground expression $\epsilon \in Pre(\gamma)$ and $\epsilon' \in Pre(\gamma')$ such that ϵ and ϵ' are mutually exclusive.*

With the above definitions, we can now provide a sufficient condition to ensure the consistency of a domain description.

Theorem 2 (Domain Consistency[2]). *A normal domain description of language $\mathcal{L}$ is also consistent.*

Basically, only consistent domain descriptions can be evaluated in terms of user queries. For this reason, Theorem 2 may be used to check whether a domain description is consistent.

Definition 6. *Given a consistent domain description $\mathcal{D}_\mathcal{L}$, ground query expression ϕ and a finite sequence list ψ, we say query ϕ holds in $\mathcal{D}_\mathcal{L}$ after all policy updates the in sequence list ψ have been applied, denoted as $\mathcal{D}_\mathcal{L} \models \{\phi, \psi\}$, if and only if for every fact $\rho \in \phi$, $TransFact(\rho, S_{|\psi|})$ is in every answer set of $Trans(\mathcal{D}_\mathcal{L})$.*

Definition 6 shows that given a finite list of policy updates ψ, a query expression ϕ may be evaluated from a consistent language $\mathcal{L}$ domain $\mathcal{D}_\mathcal{L}$. This is achieved by generating a set of answer sets from the normal logic program translation $Trans(\mathcal{D}_\mathcal{L})$. ϕ is then said to hold in $\mathcal{D}_\mathcal{L}$ after the policy updates in ψ have been applied if and only if every answer set generated contains every fact in the query expression ϕ.

Example 2. Given the language $\mathcal{L}$ program listing in Example 1 and the sequence list $\psi = \{delete\_read(grp1, file)\}$. The following shows the results of each query ϕ:

$\phi_0 = holds(grp1, write, file)$: TRUE
$\phi_1 = holds(alice, read, file)$: FALSE

∎

4 Conclusion

In this paper, we have presented the PolicyUpdater system, a logic-based authorisation system that features query evaluation and dynamic policy updates. This is made possible by the use of a first-order logic language, $\mathcal{L}$, for defining, updating and querying of access control policies. As we have shown, language $\mathcal{L}$ is expressive enough to represent constraints and default rules. The full PolicyUpdater system implementation is presented in [4].

One possible future extension to this work is to integrate temporal logic in language $\mathcal{L}$ to allow temporal constraints to be expressed in access control policies. This extension will be useful in e-commerce applications where authorisations are granted or denied based on time dependent policies.

References

1. Bertino, E., Buccafurri, F., Ferrari, E., Rullo, P., A Logic-based Approach for Enforcing Access Control. *Journal of Computer Security*, Vol. 8, No. 2-3, pp. 109-140, IOS Press, 2000.
2. Bertino, E., Mileo A., Provetti, A., Policy Monitoring with User-Preferences in PDL. In *Proceedings of IJCAI-03 Workshop for Nonmonotonic Reasoning, Action and Change*, pp. 37-44, 2003.

---

[2] The proof of these theorems are presented in the full version of this paper [4].

3. Chomicki, J., Lobo, J., Naqvi S., A Logic Programming Approach to Conflict Resolution in Policy Management. In *Proceedings of KR2000, 7th International Conference on Principles of Knowledge Representation and Reasoning*, pp. 121-132, Kaufmann, 2000.
4. Crescini, V. F., Zhang, Y., *PolicyUpdater - A System for Dynamic Access Control.* 2004 (manuscript).
5. Halpern, J. Y., Weissman, V., Using First-Order Logic to Reason About Policies. In *Proceedings of the 16th IEEE Computer Security Foundations Workshop*, pp.187-201, 2003.
6. Jajodia, S., Samarati, P., Sapino, M. L., Subrahmanian, V. S., Flexible Support for Multiple Access Control Policies. *ACM Transactions on Database Systems*, Vol. 29, No. 2, pp. 214-260, 2001.
7. Li, N., Grosof, B. N., Feigenbaum, J., Delegation Logic: A Logic-based Approach to Distributed Authorization. *ACM Transactions on Information and System Security*, Vol. 6, No. 1, pp. 128-171, 2003.
8. Lobo, J., Bhatia, R., Naqvi, S., A Policy Description Language. In *Proceedings of AAAI 16th National Conference on Artifcia l Intelligence and 11th Conference on Innovative Applications of Artificial Intelligence*, pp. 291-298, AAAI Press, 1999.
9. Simons, P., Efficient Implementation of the Stable Model Semantics for Normal Logic Programs. *Research Reports, Helsinki University of Technology*, No. 35, 1995.
10. Zhang, Y., Logic Program Based Updates. *ACM Transactions on Computational Logic*, 2004 (to appear).

A New Neighborhood Based on Improvement Graph for Robust Graph Coloring Problem

Songshan Guo[+], Ying Kong[+], Andrew Lim[*], and Fan Wang[*,@]

[+]Dept. of Computer Science, Zhongshan (Sun Yat-sen) University,
Guangzhou, China
[*]Dept. of Industrial Engineering and Engineering Management,
Hong Kong University of Science and Technology,
Clear Water Bay, Hong Kong
fanwang@ust.hk

Abstract. In this paper, we propose a new neighborhood structure based on the improvement graph for solving the Robust Graph Coloring Problem, an interesting extension of classical graph coloring. Different from the traditional neighborhood where the color of only one vertex is modified, the new neighborhood involves several vertices. In addition, the questions of how to select the modified vertices and how to modify them are modelled by an improvement graph and solved by a Dynamic Programming method. The experimental results clearly show that our new improvement graph based k-exchange cycle neighborhood improves the accuracy significantly, especially for large scale heuristic search.

1 Introduction

The graph coloring problem is a well-known NP-hard problem, which has numerous applications in the real engineering and business world [18]. The goal of the graph coloring problem is to use the minimal number of colors to color the vertices of a given graph, with the constraint that a pair of adjacent vertices must receive different colors. Since it has been proved that the graph coloring problem is an NP-hard problem [9], a lot of heuristic algorithms have been proposed, such as the greedy coloring algorithm [15], successive augmentation [2], tabu search based algorithm [6], simulated annealing based algorithm [11] [4] and evolutionary based algorithm [5]. Furthermore, the well-known second DIMACS challenge benchmarks have also been set up to compare different problem solving methods [12].

The Robust Graph Coloring Problem (RGCP), is a widely used extension in uncertainty management from the classical graph coloring problem, which was first introduced in [19]. RGCP focuses on building robust coloring for a given graph by a fixed number of colors, taking into consideration the possibility of penalizing those coloring where both vertices of an missing edge having the same

---

[@] Corresponding Author

color. The penalty function depends on the application domain. One case study of RGCP application, namely "airline crew robust assignment" motivated from an airline, is presented in [14].

We have presented a genetic algorithm to solve the RGCP [14]. In that paper, the major contribution is the new effective partition based encoding method and the genetic algorithm. Different with that paper, in this paper, we focus on creating effective neighborhood structures. A new improvement graph based neighborhood structure is presented, comparing with the traditional operator where we just modify the color of a single vertex every time. A local search algorithm is then developed to compare the performances of such two neighborhoods. From the experimental results for various sizes of graph, the new improved graph based neighborhood obtains better accuracy.

This paper is organized as follows: in Section 2, the RGCP is stated formally. In Section 3, the encoding method of search space is discussed. The two neighborhood structures are then presented in Section 4. We develop a local search algorithm in Section 5 and provide the experimental results in Section 6. Finally, Section 8 presents the conclusions.

2 Problem Statement

The RGCP can be defined formally as follows: Given the graph $G = (V, E)$ with $|V| = n$, a positive integer c and a penalty set $P = \{p_{ij}, (i,j) \in \overline{E}\}$, the objective function of RGCP is to find

$$\min R(G) \equiv \sum_{(i,j)\in \overline{E}, C(i)=C(j)} p_{ij} \qquad (1)$$

where C is a coloring mapping, i.e., $C : V \to 1, 2, \cdots, c$ satisfying $C(i) \neq C(j), \forall (i,j) \in E$. Any RGCP instance is characterized by (G, c, P). Depending on various application domains, the penalty set may have different definitions.

Since the NP-hardness of RGCP has been proved in (Yanez 2003), the above binary programming method can only solve very small instances optimally in acceptable computing time.

3 Search Algorithm

3.1 Encoding

A partition approach is applied to the search space encoding, where a set of vertices belonging to a class will be assigned the same color [14]. In other words, a solution can be present as $\{V_1, V_2, \cdots V_c\}$, where $V_i = \{j | C(j) = i, 1 \leq j \leq n\}, 1 \leq i \leq c$. It is definite that partition based encoding can represent any coloring solutions, feasible or unfeasible.

3.2 Neighborhood 1: Single Vertex Coloring Modification

The first method for neighborhood construction is Single Vertex Color Modification. The operator first randomly selects one vertex $v_i (1 \leq i \leq n)$ among all n

vertices in the graph. Then, the new color of v_i is assigned a fixed or random color, e.g. $C_{new}(v_i) = c', c' \neq C(v_i)$ where c' is given by randomization or determination.

3.3 Neighborhood 2: Improvement Graph

We first define the improvement graph transformed from a given graph with a fixed coloring mapping. For a given graph $G = (V, E)$ and a coloring mapping $C, C : V \to 1, 2, ..., c$, we define the improvement graph $G' = (V', E')$ as follows:
1. $V' = V$;
2. $(i, j) \in E'$, iff $C(i) \neq C(j)$;
3. The weight of the directed edge (i, j), $w(i, j)$, is defined as the reduction (positive or negative) of $R(G)$ when we empty the color of vertex i and change the color of vertex j from $C(j)$ to $C(i)$.

Then, we define the "k-exchange cycle" in an improvement graph G': a k-exchange cycle is a simple cycle in G', which consists of exact k successive edges, e.g. $\{(s_i, e_i)|(s_i, e_i) \in E', \forall 1 \leq i \leq k\}$ satisfying that (1) $(s_i, e_i) \neq (s_j, e_j), \forall 1 \leq i, j \leq k, i \neq j$; and (2) $s_1 = e_k, s_i = e_{i-1} \forall 1 < i \leq k$. We call the sum of the weights of all k edges along the cycle the weight of the k-cycle, e.g. $\sum_{\forall (s_i, e_i) \in EC} w(s_i, e_i)$. By a k-exchange cycle in an improvement graph, we have a new neighborhood operator for the coloring mapping of the corresponding graph, where we $C(e_i) = C(s_i)$ for all i from 1 to k. In the mean while, the reduction of $R(G)$ is equal to the weight of the exchange cycle. It is easy to know that the advantage of this new neighborhood is that the color distribution K is kept unchanged. On the other hand, compare with the previous "single vertex coloring modification", this new operator can affect more vertices in the same operation.

Since there are a lot of k-exchange cycles in an improvement graph, we need to find the optimal one with the maximum reduction of $R(G)$. A Dynamic Programming (DP) method is developed to find the optimal k-exchange cycle.

A few denotations are first defined:

p_k: a path, e.g. the consequence of k vertices $v_{i1}, v_{i2}, ..., v_{ik}$ covers the edges $(v_{i1}, v_{i2}), (v_{i2}, v_{i3}) \cdots$ and $(v_{i(l-1)}, v_{ik})$.

$Length(p_k)$: the length of the path p_k, e.g. k

$cycle(p_k)$: the cycle corresponding to the path p_k, e.g. the cycle along $v_{i1}, v_{i2}, ..., v_{ik}, v_{i1}$

$w(cycle(p_k))$: the total reduction of $R(G)$ along the cycle p_k. In other words, it is the sum of the weights of all edges belonging to $cycle(p_k)$, e.g. $w(cycle(p_k)) = \sum_{(v_i, v_j) \in cycle(p_k)} w(v_i, v_j)$

$s(p_k)$: the first vertex of the path p_k, e.g. v_{i1}

$e(p_k)$: the last vertex of the path p_k, e.g. v_{ik}

$p_k + v$: the new path with an added vertex v at the end of the original path p_k.

Based on the definition of the k-exchange cycle, the following DP formula is applied to obtain the best k-exchange cycle, where the p_k represents the path of the best k-exchange cycle, $cycle(p_k)$.

$$p_{k+1} = max^{-1}_{p_k + v}\{w\left(cycle(p_k + v)\right) | \forall v \in \Omega\} \text{ for all } p_k, k \geq 2 \quad (2)$$

where $\Omega = \{v | v \in V(G') \text{ and } (e(p_k), v) \in E(G') \text{ and } C(v_i) \neq C(v_j) \forall v_j \in p_k\}$

We illustrate the DP algorithm for seeking the best k^*-exchange cycle as Algorithm 1. Here, k^*-exchange cycle is marked as the best cycle among all h-exchange cycles where h is from 1 to k. The DP constructs the best exchange cycle in the order of length k. First, all single edges with negative weight are added into the search candidate list - $List$. They are considered as all possible best paths with length $k = 1$. Then, the best paths with length from 2 to k are obtained by iteration based on the DP equation(2). During the DP iteration, the best path with the maximum reduction of $R(G)$ is remarked. Finally, the best k^*-exchange cycle is determined.

Since the "longest path problem" is NP-complete [9], the computational complexity should be exponential if the above DP search covers the whole search space. To balance the solution accuracy with the running time, we create a candidate list management scheme (Algorithm 2) similar to the Beam Search. We set $List$ to be a sorted doubly linked list where the elements represent the candidate paths in decreasing order of w. In each time a new candidate path is found, it will be inserted into $List$ by sort. There is an importation parameter to control the maximum size of the $List$, $MaxListLength$. Once the length of the $List$ exceeds the fixed maximum length, the last element of the $List$ will be removed to keep the length. If the $MaxListLength$ is big enough, the DP can guarantee to produce the optimal solution for the k^*-exchange cycle. On the other hand, a small $MaxListLength$ may lose the optimal solution. However, it can reduce the search space efficiently.

3.4 Local Search

We illustrate the local search algorithm for solving the RGCP in Algorithm 3. The basic idea of the local search is that it starts from an initial solution and repeatedly replaces it with a better solution in its neighborhood until a better solution could not be found in the neighborhood structure.

Algorithm 3 Local search for solving RGCP

1: $coloring \leftarrow$ Call Initial Solution Generation;
2: $Improvement \leftarrow true$; remarks if there is a new better solution found
3: **repeat**
4:    construct the neighborhood structure $N(coloring)$ of $coloring$;
5:    **if** find any solution $coloring'$ from $N(coloring)$ so that $R'(coloring) < R(coloring)$ **then**
6:       $coloring \leftarrow coloring'$;
7:    **else**
8:       $Improvement \leftarrow false$;
9:    **end if**
10: **until** Not $Improvement$
11: **return** $coloring, R$;

Algorithm 1 DP Algorithm for find best k-exchange cycle

1: $List \leftarrow \phi$;
2: $w_{best} \leftarrow 0$;
3: **for all** (v_i, v_j) such that $(v_i, v_j) \in E(G'), w(v_i, v_j) > 0$ **do**
4:     $Add(List, (v_i, v_j))$;
5:     **if** $w(cycle(v_i, v_j)) > w_{best}$ **then**
6:        $w_{best} = w(cycle(v_i, v_j))$
7:     **end if**
8: **end for**
9: **for** $l = 1$ to $k - 1$ **do**
10:     $p \leftarrow Pop(List)$;
11:     **for all** v such that $(e(p), v) \in E(G')$ and $w(p + v) > 0$ and $color[v_j] \neq color[v] \, \forall v_j \in p$ **do**
12:        $p' \leftarrow p + v$;
13:        **if** $(v, s(p)) \in E(G')$ and $w(cycle(p')) > w_{best}$ **then**
14:           $w_{best} \leftarrow w(cycle(p'))$;
15:           $p_{best} \leftarrow p'$;
16:        **end if**
17:        **if** $Length(p) \leq k - 1$ **then**
18:           $Add(List, p')$;
19:        **end if**
20:     **end for**
21: **end for**
22: **return** $cycle(p_{best}), w_{best}$;

Algorithm 2 Algorithm of candidate list management - $Add(List, p)$

1: Insert p into $List$ in the decreasing order of $w(cycle(p))$;
2: **if** $Length(List) > MaxListLength$ **then**
3:     delete $List[Length]$;
4: **end if**

4 Experimental Results

4.1 Test Data And Experimental Environment

We have designed four sizes of test data to evaluate the performance of various meta-heuristics in different sizes of graph: Small Size ($n = 10, 15, 20$), Middle Size ($n = 50, 100$), Large Size ($n = 250, 500$) and Huge Size ($n = 1000$). There are 15 test sets in total, 7 sets for Small Size, 3 sets for Middle Size, 4 sets for Large Size and 1 set for Huge Size. For each test set, we have randomly generated 50 instances where the missing edge penalties are generated with the uniform distribution in the interval [0,1]. The graph density is fixed to be 0.5. For our experiments, we use a Pentium 4 personal computer with a 1GHz CPU and 256MB RAM.

4.2 Comparison of Neighborhood Structures

In Table 1, the performance comparison between single vertex color modification and improvement graph based k-exchange cycle are provided for Small, Middle, Large and Huge Size, in terms of accuracy ($R(G)$) and running time. These computational results are obtained when we give enough time for running the different methods, where the stopping criteria is that the search is finished when there is no improvement on $R(G)$ for five continual iterations.

Table 1. Comparison on neighborhood structure

n	c	single vertex color modification		k-exchange cycle	
		$R(G)$	Runing Time	$R(G)$	Running Time
10	4	3.67	0.00s	2.96	0.00s
10	5	2.36	0.00s	1.54	0.02s
15	5	7.63	0.01s	6.62	0.01s
15	6	5.68	0.01s	3.99	0.01s
20	5	15.92	0.00s	14.22	0.01s
20	8	7.15	0.02s	3.81	0.02s
20	10	3.86	0.01s	1.46	0.06s
50	18	18.62	0.02s	7.28	0.37s
100	35	32.79	0.14s	10.87	1.04s
100	50	8.40	3.00s	1.55	0.45s
250	70	93.98	5.23s	44.27	9.57s
250	90	51.18	6.58s	15.39	7.59s
500	150	113.50	68.02s	52.37	88.37s
500	250	23.67	69.65s	1.27	78.79s
1000	400	61.33	552.34s	18.40	687.19s

For the above results, it is clear that the new improvement graph based neighborhood outperforms the single vertex color modification. Especially for Large Size and Huge Size, the new neighborhood obtains much better accuracy. For instance, for the case $(n, c) = (1000, 400)$, the new neighborhood achieves $R(G) = 18.40$, improving 70% relatively. In addition, the running time of such two neighborhood are in the same level.

Configuration of k-Exchange Cycle. As presented in Section 4, a DP method is applied to find the best k-exchange cycle under several configurations including k setting and the management scheme of the candidate list. In Table 2, the performance of the local search with k-exchange cycle are illustrated where k is set from 3 to 7 with the sort candidate list management (the maximum length is 10). The corresponding running time is shown in Table 3. The note $k - sort/unsort - MaxListLength$ remarks one configuration.

From the results of performance vs. k, running time increases with the increase of k slowly. The performance in accuracy for different k is not diverse. Hence, $k = 4$ with the shortest running time is the best choice.

Table 2. Performance of k-exchange cycle with different k on $R(G)$

n	c	3-sort-100	4-sort-100	5-sort-100	6-sort-100	7-sort-100
10	4	2.96	2.96	2.96	2.96	2.96
10	5	1.55	1.54	1.54	1.54	1.54
15	5	6.62	6.62	6.62	6.62	6.62
15	6	4.01	3.99	3.93	3.96	3.96
20	5	14.22	14.22	14.22	14.22	14.22
20	8	4.04	3.81	3.85	3.85	3.83
20	10	1.56	1.46	1.46	1.46	1.46
50	18	7.85	7.28	7.35	7.14	7.13
100	35	11.99	10.87	10.73	10.56	10.56
100	50	1.68	1.55	1.56	1.53	1.52
250	70	46.97	44.27	43.24	42.12	42.35
250	90	16.17	15.39	14.48	14.29	13.76
500	150	53.86	52.37	49.96	48.30	48.53
500	250	1.11	1.27	1.13	1.01	1.04
1000	400	16.16	18.40	17.44	16.53	15.89

Table 3. Average Running Time Per Instance of k-exchange Cycle with Different k's (in second)

n	c	3-sort-100	4-sort-100	5-sort-100	6-sort-100	7-sort-100
10	4	0.00	0.00	0.00	0.00	0.01
10	5	0.02	0.02	0.02	0.02	0.01
15	5	0.01	0.00	0.00	0.00	0.02
15	6	0.02	0.00	0.00	0.02	0.00
20	5	0.00	0.00	0.00	0.00	0.00
20	8	0.04	0.02	0.02	0.02	0.02
20	10	0.02	0.06	0.05	0.06	0.06
50	18	0.50	0.37	0.53	0.34	0.41
100	35	0.76	1.04	0.90	0.70	1.06
100	50	0.76	0.45	0.51	0.84	0.90
250	70	9.48	9.57	8.07	7.81	7.33
250	90	11.45	7.59	8.47	8.27	7.58
500	150	114.18	88.37	96.11	94.04	78.17
500	250	134.62	78.79	77.01	71.77	61.58
1000	400	2261.62	687.19	725.49	738.55	733.65

To asses the efficiency of the management of candidate list to balance accuracy and running time, in Table 4 and Table 5, accuracy and running time comparison among three management schemes are presented for $k = 4$, including unlimited candidate list (4-unsort), sort candidate list with maximum size of 100 (4-sort-100) and sort candidate list with maximum size of 200 (4-sort-200).

Table 4. Performance of different candidate list management on $R(G)$

n	c	4-unsort	4-sort-100	4-sort-200
10	4	2.96	2.96	2.96
10	5	1.54	1.54	1.69
15	5	6.62	6.62	7.23
15	6	3.99	3.99	4.19
20	5	14.22	14.22	14.22
20	8	3.81	3.81	3.82
20	10	1.46	1.46	1.60
50	18	7.24	7.28	7.32
100	35	10.79	10.87	10.56
100	50	1.51	1.55	1.52
250	70	42.16	44.27	44.33
250	90	14.08	15.39	14.82
500	150	47.71	52.37	49.26
500	250	0.83	1.27	1.08
1000	400	13.44	18.40	15.58

Table 5. Average running time per instance of k-exchange cycle with different candidate list management (in second)

n	c	4-unsort	4-sort-100	4-sort-200
10	4	0.00	0.00	0.03
10	5	0.01	0.02	0.00
15	5	0.00	0.00	0.00
15	6	0.02	0.00	0.02
20	5	0.00	0.00	0.00
20	8	0.02	0.02	0.06
20	10	0.05	0.06	0.26
50	18	0.65	0.37	0.62
100	35	1.36	1.04	1.80
100	50	1.32	0.45	0.33
250	70	13.01	9.57	9.00
250	90	12.51	7.59	11.48
500	150	159.68	88.37	108.61
500	250	148.38	78.79	111.80
1000	400	3010.93	687.19	1452.32

It is clear that the order of running time from the slowest to the fastest is 4-unsort, 4-sort-200 and 4-sort-100. However, the order of accuracy from the best to the worst is also 4-unsort, 4-sort-200 and 4-sort-100. In other words, the larger size of the candidate list (the more running time), the higher accuracy in terms of management scheme of k-exchange cycle.

5 Conclusions

In this paper, we have proposed a new neighborhood structure based on the improvement graph for solving the Robust Graph Coloring Problem, an interesting extension of classical graph coloring. Different from the traditional neighborhood where the color of only one vertex is modified, the new neighborhood involves several vertices. In addition, the questions of how to select the modified vertices and how to modify them are modelled by an improvement graph and solved by a Dynamic Programming method. A local search algorithm has been developed to provide the computational results of performance comparison on various sizes of graph. The experimental results clearly show that our new improvement graph based k-exchange cycle neighborhood obtains much better performance than the traditional neighborhood, especially for large scale heuristic search.

References

1. Barthelemy, J.P. Guenoche, A. 1991. *Trees and Proximity Representations.* John Wiley Sons, New York.
2. Brelaz, D. 1979. New methods to color vertices of a graph. *Communications of ACM* 22 251-256.
3. Chaitin, G.J. 1982. Register allocation and spilling via graph coloring. *SIGPLAN '82 Symposium on Compiler Construction, Boston, Mass. June 1982*, 17 98-105.
4. Chams, M., Hertz, A., Werra, D.de. 1987. Some experiments with simulated annealing for coloring graphs. *European Journal of Operational Research* 32 260-266.
5. Costa, D., Hertz, A., Dubuis, O. 1995. Embedding a sequential procedure within an evolutionary algorithm for coloring problems. *Journal of Heuristics* 1 105-128.
6. Dorne, R., Hao, J.K. 1998. Meta-heuristics: Advances and Trends in Local Search Paradigms for Optimization, *Chapter 6: Tabu search for graph coloring T-colorings and set T-colorings.* Kluwer Academic, 77-92.
7. Galinier, P., Hao, J.K. 1999. Hybrid evolutionary algorithm for graph coloring. *Journal of Combinatorial Optimization.* 3 379-397.
8. Gamst, A. 1986. Some lower bounds for a class of frequency assignment problems *IEEE Transactions of Vehicular Technology.* 35(1) 8-14.
9. Garey M.R., Johnson, D.S. 1979. *Computer and Intractability.* Freeman, San Francisco.
10. Halldorsson, M.M. 1990. A still better performance guarantee for approximate graph coloring. Technical Report 91-35, DIMACS, New Brunswick, NJ.
11. Johnson, D.S., Aragon C.R., McGeoch, L.A., Schevon C. 1991. Optimization by simulated annealing: an experimental evaluation; part ii, graph coloring and number partitioning. *Operations Research*, 39(3) 378-406.
12. Johnson D.S., Trick, M.A. 1996. *Proceedings of the 2nd DIMACS Implementation Challenge, DIMACS Series in Discrete Mathematics and Theoretical Computer Science.* American Mathematical Society. 26.
13. Joslin, D.E., Clements, D.P. 1998. Squeaky wheel optimization. *the National Conference on Artificial Intelligence, AAAI-1998*, Edmonton, Alberta, Canada.
14. Kong, Y., Wang, F., Lim, A. Guo, S.S. 2003. A New Hybrid Genetic Algorithm for the Robust Graph Coloring Problem. *Proceeding of Australian Conference on Artificial Intelligence 2003* 125-136.

15. Korte, B., Vygen, J. 2002. *Combinatorial Optimization*. Springer-Verlag, second edition, 2002.
16. Kubale, M., Jackowski, B. 1985. A generalized implicit enumeration algorithm for graph coloring. *Communications of the ACM*. 28 412-418.
17. Opsut, R.J., Roberts, F.S. 1981. On the fleet maintenance, Mobile radio frequency, task assignment and traffic phasing problems. *The Theory and Applications of Graphs*. John Wiley Sons, New York. 479-492.
18. Pardalos, P.M., Mavridou, T., Xue, J. 1998. The Graph Coloring Problems: A Bibliographic Survey. *Handbook of Combinatorial Optimization*. Kluwer Academic Publishers. 2 331-395.
19. Yanez, J. Ramirez, J. 2003. The robust coloring problem. *European Journal of Operational Research*. 148(3) 546-558.

An Extension of the H-Search Algorithm for Artificial Hex Players

Rune Rasmussen and Frederic Maire

School of SEDC (Information Technology Faculty),
Queensland University of Technology,
P.O. Box 2434, Brisbane QLD 4001, Australia
r.rasmussen@student.qut.edu.au, f.maire@qut.edu.au

Abstract. Hex is a classic board game invented in the middle of the twentieth century by Piet Hein and rediscovered later by John Nash. The best Hex artificial players analyse the board positions by deducing complex virtual connections from elementary connections using the H-Search algorithm. In this paper, we extend the H-search with a new deduction rule. This new deduction rule is capable of discovering virtual connections that the H-search cannot prove. Thanks to this new deduction rule, the horizon of the artificial Hex players should move further away.

1 Introduction

The Danish engineer and poet Piet Hein invented the game of Hex and presented it at the Niels Bohr Institute of Theoretical Physics in 1942. The game of Hex is a strategic two-player game on a rhombic board (see Fig. 1) The aim of the game for the player Black is to connect the North and South sides of the board with an unbroken chain of black stones. Similarly, the aim of player White is to connect the East and West sides with an unbroken chain of white stones. The first player to make such a connection wins the game. Players can never tie in a game of Hex [1]. The standard size for a Hex board is 11x11 but some players prefer to play on larger boards (like 19x19).

In 1948, John F. Nash rediscovered the game of Hex and presented it at Princeton University. Hex is solvable in polynomial space but is NP-hard [2]. On reason why creating an artificial player for Hex is difficult is that the branching factor of the game tree for Hex is large (much larger than Chess). In fact, it has the same branching factor as Go. In 1949, John Nash proved the existence of a winning strategy for the opening player. However, this proof does not provide a winning strategy.

In 1953, Claude Shannon and E. F. Moore of the Bell Telephone Laboratories devised the first artificial Hex player. The Shannon and Moore's Hex player considers a Hex board as an electric resistor network with a potential on the player's sides. A move by the player makes short circuit connections in the network and a move by the opponent makes open circuits in the network. Shannon and Moore used the resistance of the network as an evaluation function to evaluate board positions [3]. In other words, the connecting player tries to minimise and the opponent tries to maximise the resistance of the network.

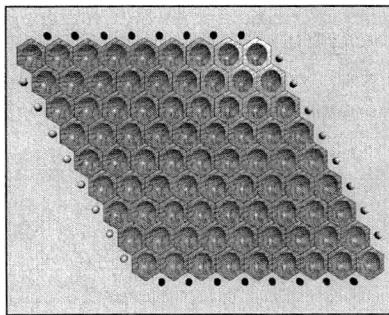

Fig. 1. A 9x9 board. The player Black tries to connect the North and South edges of the board. The player White tries to connect the East and West edges of the board

A more recent evaluation functions for the game of Hex is the Queen-Bee distance [4, 5]. The Queen-Bee distance measures the degree of connection a cell has to an edge of the board by estimating how many moves the connecting player needs to secure the connection. The Queen-Bee distance assumes that the opponent will try to prevent the connection by playing the best available cell for the connecting player. This assumption leads to a recursive definition of the Queen-Bee distance. In particular, if a cell x is empty, the Queen-Bee distance of x is equal to the $1+2^{nd}$ best Queen-Bee distance among all the neighbours y of x. Evaluating the degree of a connection between groups of stones is a key concept in Hex. A *virtual connection* between two groups of stones is an unavoidable connection.

The H-Search algorithm deduces complex virtual connections from elementary connections. Vadim Anshelevich is the pioneer of this approach. His player, 'Hexy', uses the H-Search algorithm and was the winner of the 2000 Computer Olympiads for the game of Hex [6, 7]. The strength of 'Hexy' is its ability to discover virtual connections. Another artificial player that makes use of the H-Search algorithm is 'Six'. 'Six' was the winner of the 2003 Computer Olympiads for the game of Hex [8].

In this paper, we extend the H-Search algorithm with a new deduction rule. This deduction rule can find virtual connections that the H-Search algorithm fails to find. Our deduction rule is a process that mimics the way humans play Hex. Section 2 describes the H-Search algorithm and its deduction rules. Section 3 presents our new deduction rule. Section 4 examines an edge connection template that our new deduction rule can solve, but that is beyond the deductive capability of the standard H-Search.

2 The H-Search Algorithm

The H-Search algorithm deduces virtual connections. However, there are trivial connections that do not require deduction. If two stones of the same colour sit on adjacent cells, then these stones are *virtually connected*. By definition, A *group* is a single empty cell or is a mono-coloured connected component (all the stones are of the same colour) [6, 7]. A group provides a waypoint for making connections. By convention, the four sides of the board constitute four distinct groups where the colour of the side is the colour of its group. A player wins when two side-groups become connected.

The H-Search algorithm solves sub-games. A sub-game is the restriction of the game to a region of the board. In this region, one player, the *connecting player*, tries to connect two distinguished groups while the other player tries to prevent that connection.

Formally, a *sub-game* is a triple (x, C, y) where x and y are disjoint groups and C is a set of cells such that $x \cap C = y \cap C = x \cap y = \emptyset$. If x or y are groups of stones then the stones have the connecting player's colour. The groups x and y are called the *targets* and the set C is called the *carrier*. The H-Search algorithm involves two types of connections. A sub-game is a virtual connection or a *strong sub-game* if the connecting player can win the sub-game even when playing second. In addition, a sub-game is a *weak sub-game* if the connecting player can win when playing first. The H-Search algorithm involves two deduction rules, the AND rule and the OR rule.

Theorem 1: The AND Deduction Rule

Let sub-games (x, A, u) and (u, B, y) be strong sub-games with a common target u and targets $x \cap y = \emptyset$. In addition assume $\{x, u, y\} \cap (A \cup B) = \emptyset$ and $A \cap B = \emptyset$. If u is a group of stones then the sub-game $(x, A \cup B, y)$ is a strong sub-game. If u is an empty cell then the sub-game $(x, A \cup u \cup B, y)$ is a weak sub-game.

Theorem 2: The OR Deduction Rule

Let (x, A_k, y) be of weak sub-games for $1 \leq k \leq m$ with common targets x and y. If $\bigcap_{k=1}^{m} A_k = \emptyset$ then the sub-game (x, A, y) where $A = \bigcup_{k=1}^{m} A_k$ is a strong sub-game.

The H-Search algorithm derives complex connections from elementary connections. The H-Search algorithm applies the AND deduction rule first and applies it to pairs of strong sub-games. In Fig. 2, 'A' and 'B' denote strong sub-games. When the H-Search algorithm deduces a new strong sub-game, it appends it to the strong sub-game list and applies the AND deduction on another pair of strong sub-games. When the H-Search algorithm deduces a weak sub-game, it appends it to the weak sub-game list and applies the OR deduction rule on the subset of weak sub-games with the same targets. In Fig. 2, $\{A_k\}_k$ denotes that set. At the end of one OR deduction the H-Search performs AND deduction. The algorithm terminates when it exhausts the sub-game sets.

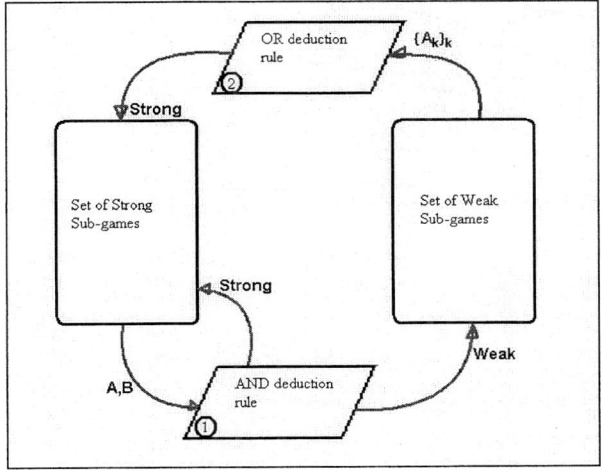

Fig. 2. The H-Search applies the AND rule first. Whenever, H-Search deduces a weak sub-game, it immediately applies the OR deduction

2.1 Sub-game Decomposition

The sub-game sets provide a connection database for the player. The player may use this database to enhance its evaluation function. A player can also use the hierarchical AND-OR decomposition of a connection into more elementary connections to select the sequence of right moves to secure a virtual connection. Sub-game decomposition provides a policy for making connections. A *policy* is a mapping from state (a board position) to action (a move) [9]. A *tactic* is a policy for securing a connection between two targets in a sub-game [10, 11]. For example, suppose that a strong sub-game was derived by applying the AND deduction rule on the strong sub-games (x, A, u) and (u, B, y). If the opponent plays in the carrier A, then the connecting player will query the sub-game (x, A, u) for a reply move that secures the sub-game (x, A, u). Similarly, suppose that a strong sub-game was derived by applying the OR deduction rule on the weak sub-games (x, A_k, y) for $1 \leq k \leq m$. If the opponent plays at $z \in \bigcup_{k=1}^{m} A_k$, then the connecting player will find a sub-game with carrier A_i, such that $z \notin A_i$ and secure the weak sub-game (x, A_i, y). That is the connecting player transforms (x, A_i, y) into a strong sub-game after querying (x, A_i, y).

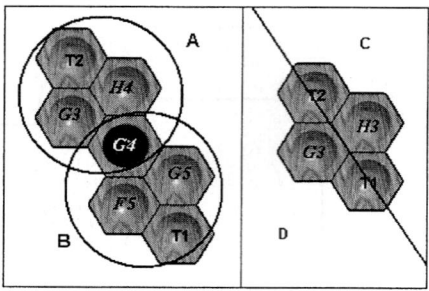

Fig. 3. The AND rule deduced the left sub-game and the OR rule deduces the right sub-game

In Fig. 3, the AND rule is the deducing rule for the left strong sub-game and the OR rule is the deducing rule for the right sub-game. The tactic for the left sub-game is the aggregation of the tactic of strong connection 'A' and the tactic of strong connection 'B'. The tactic for the right strong sub-game is the combination of the tactic of the weak connection 'C' and the tactic of the weak connection 'D'. If the opponent moves on G3, the connecting player moves on H3 (and reciprocally).

3 Extension of the OR Deduction Rule

In Theorem 2, when the intersection of the weak sub-games is empty then the OR deduction rule deduces a strong sub-game. If the OR deduction rule fails, can some other deduction rules prove these failed OR connections? The new deduction rule that follows can prove some connections obtained from failed OR deductions. In Theorem 2, if the intersection of weak sub-games is not empty then the OR deduction fails. Hayward refers to this non-empty intersection as the *must-play* (MP) *region* [12]. In Fig. 4, the cell "MP" is the must-play region. If the opponent moves outside of the must-play region, then the connecting player will be able to transform the weak sub-game into a strong sub-game.

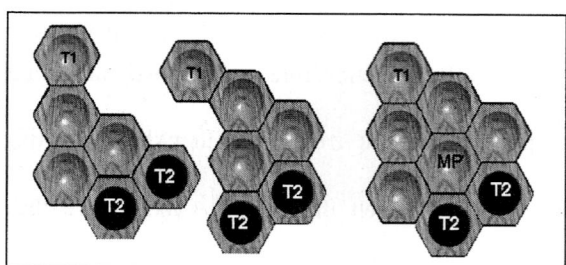

Fig. 4. Two weak sub-games between T1 and T2. The cell MP is the intersection of the carriers of the two weak connections and is the "must-play" region that prevents the connection

The new deduction rule that follows can deduce failed OR deductions. This deduction rule must generate the sub-game tactics explicitly as its search is more complex than the H-search. The new deduction rule deduces a sub-game and a tactic at the same time. Here, a tactic is a decision tree where the opponent's moves are stored on the edges of the tree, and the connecting player's reply-moves are stored at the vertices of the trees. We refer to this decision tree as a *tactical decision tree*.

3.1 The Must-Play (MP) Deduction Rule

The Must-Play (MP) deduction rule is a guided search of the game tree of a failed OR deduction sub-game. We can assume that the opponent picks his moves in the MP region to block the connecting player; otherwise, the connecting player would immediately secure the connection. The connecting player moves to extend on the targets' groups. This deduction rule is a post H-Search rule as it relies on weak and strong connections to deduce new connections.

In Fig. 5 left, T1 and T2 are the targets of a weak sub-game where the set A is the must-play region. The cell x is a cell in the must-play region where the opponent could move and the set $\{a,b,c,d,..\}$ are candidate moves for connecting player. These candidate moves strongly connect with target T1 and at worst weakly connect with target T2. A similar set of moves for the player lie near target T2. For the sake of simplicity, we only consider the set that lie near target T1.

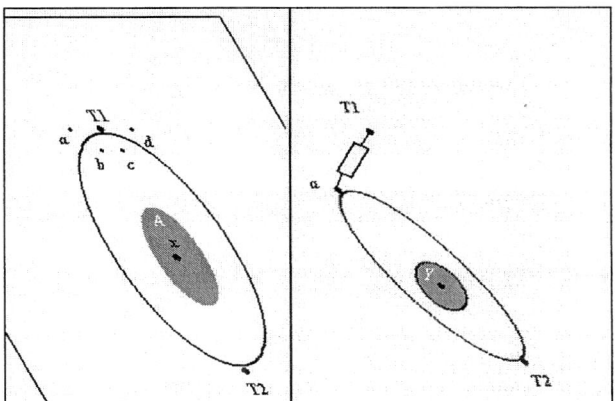

Fig. 5. The MP deduction rule is a guided search of the game tree where the opponent's moves are in must play regions. The connecting player's moves build a strongly connected component on the targets that at worst weakly connect to the other target

If the player extends target T1 with a move on cell 'a' and this move strongly connects with target T2 then the MP deduction rule has found a winning sequence of moves. The rule inserts the sequence into the tactical decision tree. In Fig. 5 right, if the move on cell 'a' weakly connects with target T2, then there is a must-play region Y between extended target T1 and target T2. The MP deduction rule reiterates the search for a move by the opponent in this new must-play region. If the MP deduction rule finds a solution for every possible move by the opponent in the must-play regions then there is a strong sub-game for targets T1 and T2.

The pseudo code in Fig. 10 is a recursive search that captures the duality between the opponent's moves in the must-play regions and the player's reinforcing moves near the targets. The search depth sets the maximum number of null deductions (see pseudo code). Unlike traditional search techniques, the search depth does not necessarily give better results. Setting the search depth too deep adds redundancy to the final sub-game and tactic. The search depth is a parameter that has to be fine-tuned for use in a competitive player.

4 Results

In this section, we show that our new deduction rule can deduce an edge template that the H-Search algorithm cannot deduce. The edge template of interest is the strong connection between a cell on the fifth row and a side (see Fig. 6). This edge template is one of the many template that can be found in the book 'Hex Strategy: Making the Right Connections' by Cameron Browne [10].

Theorem 3: The H-Search Algorithm cannot deduce the edge template of Fig. 6.

Proof: Assume, on an empty board, the fifth row sub-game in Fig. 6 is H-Search deducible. Either the top rule is the AND rule or the top rule is the OR rule. Assume first that the AND rule is the top deducing rule. From Theorem 1, the AND rule deduces a strong sub-game when the common cell is a stone group. However, this is impossible here as the board is empty. Therefore, the AND rule is not the deducing rule.

The OR deduction rule must therefore be the deducing rule. From Theorem 2, the intersection of all weak sub-games with targets T1 and T2 must be empty. However, we will exhibit a move for the opponent that prevents the connecting player from making any weak connection.

The fatal opponent move is on the cell labelled 'A'. By Theorem 2, the player must have a weak sub-game with targets T1 and T2. Since the AND rule is the only rule that can deduce a weak sub-game the player can move on a cell that strongly connects to T1 and T2. Of all of the cells that strongly connect to T1, only those with the labels 'a', 'b', 'c' and 'd' could also strongly connect with target T2.

Assume one of these cells also strongly connects with T2. Let that cell be either 'a' or 'b'. By Theorem 2, the intersection of weak sub-games between either 'a' or 'b' and the target T2 is empty. If the opponent moves on the cell with the label 'B' then either 'a' or 'b' is weakly connected to T2. However, neither 'a' or 'b' is weakly connected to T2 via the cells 'a', '1', '2' or the cells 'b', 'c', 'y'. Therefore, the cells 'a' and 'b' must weakly connect to T2 via the cell 'x'. However, the cells 'B' and 'A' have the opponent's stones such that 'x' is weakly connected to T2. Therefore, 'a' and 'b' neither weakly nor strongly connect with T2 via 'x', however, this contradicts the assumption that the player's move on 'a' or 'b' strongly connects T1 and T2 because Theorem 2 only deals with weak sub-games and there are none.

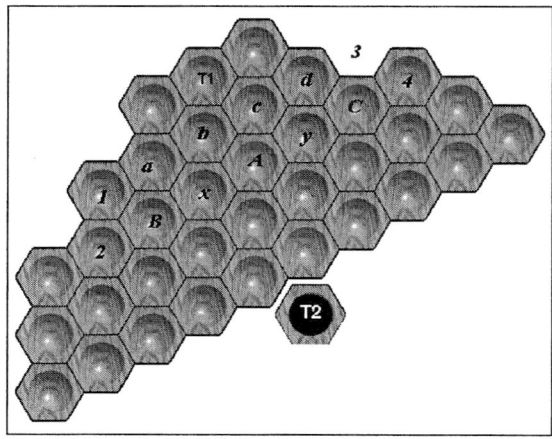

Fig. 6. An edge template; a strong connection is between T1 and T2 (T2 is a side)

Let the cell be either 'c' or 'd' that strongly connect with T2. By Theorem 2, the intersection of weak sub-games between either 'c' or 'd' and the target T2 is empty. If the opponent's move on cell 'C' then either 'c' or 'd' weakly connects to T2. However, neither 'c' or 'd' weakly connects to T2 via the cells 'd', '3', '4' or the cells 'c', 'b', 'x'. Therefore, the cells 'c' and 'd' must weakly connect to T2 via the cell 'y'. However, the cells 'A' and 'C' have the opponent's stones such that 'y' is weakly connected to T2. Therefore, 'c' and 'd' neither weakly nor strongly connect with T2 via 'y', however, this contradicts the assumption that the player's move on 'c' or 'd' strongly connects T1 and T2 because Theorem 2 only deal with weak sub-games and there are none.

Since no move by the player on cells 'a', 'b', 'c' or 'd' strongly connects to T2 given the opponent's first move was on the cell 'A' and these cells are the only possible candidates, the assumption that the OR deduction rule did deduce this fifth-row sub-game is a contradiction. Therefore, the H-Search algorithm cannot deduce a fifth row sub-games on an empty board.

Theorem 4: The MP deduction rule can deduce the edge template of Fig. 6.

One way to prove this theorem would be to display the tactical tree returned by our program. However, a printout of such a tree would exceed the page limit for this paper (The full proof tree is available via e-mail request and an extract can be found in the appendix). Our proof is a computer program that demonstrates the deductive property of the MP deduction rule. This computer program is a test-bed for the MP deduction rule. It provides a view of the proof trees and a window where the user can make moves in a sub-game and the computer returns a response from the sub-game tactic. In Fig. 8, a screen shot of that computer program places emphasis on strong connections with the side of the board. In addition, we present an argument using the MP deduction rule that proves a key solution path for the sub-game in Fig. 6.

Proof: In Fig. 7, if the opponent makes move '1' in the must-play region then the connecting player can make move '2' and strongly extend target T1. The MP deduction rule continues a search path that has the opponent's moves in must-play regions as '1', '3', '5' and '7' and the player's moves as '2', '4', '6' and '8'. The moves '2', '4' and '6' by the player strongly extend the target T1 and move eight strongly extends the target T2. In addition, the cells with the label 'a' form a weak carrier between the T1 and T2 extensions and the cell with the label 'b' forms a separate weak carrier between the T1 and T2 extensions. Since, these two carriers are disjoint, by Theorem 1 T1 and T2 strongly connect.

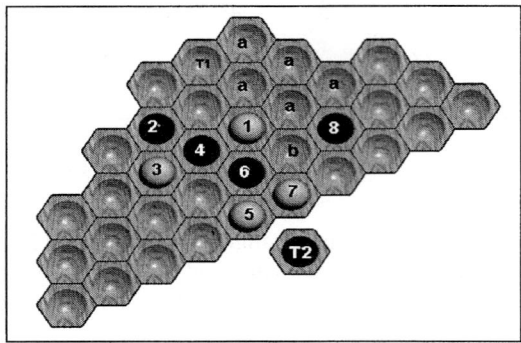

Fig. 7. A solution path discovered by the MP deduction rule

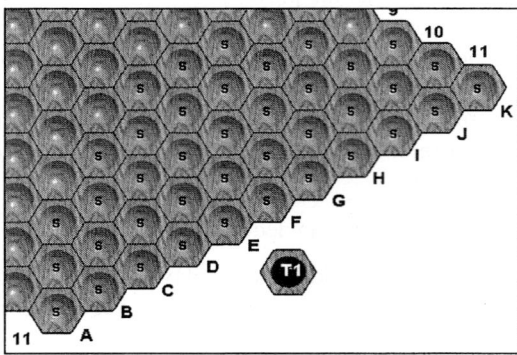

Fig. 8. A test run of the MP deduction rule implementation gives the cells with label 'S' as strong connections with the side target T1. There are three fifth-row strong connections

5 Conclusion

Hex is the game that kick-started the connection game genre in the middle of the twentieth century. Despite its simple rules, Hex is a subtle strategic game that can provide a test-bed for the development of general principles of combining tactics into strategies. In this paper, we describe an extension of the OR deduction rule that allows the automatic discovery of new connection. The MP deduction rule is an efficient search of the game tree of a failed OR deductions. Indeed, to prove that a sub-game is strong, this rule only considers the relevant candidate moves of the opponent. This rule dramatically prunes the game tree of the connection by exploiting the MP region. For example, since the carrier of the edge-template of Fig. 6 has 35 empty cells, its full game tree is of depth 35 with 35-factorial different possible games. The MP deduction rule in this case is equivalent to looking ahead 35 moves in advance. The MP deduction rule is efficient because it also uses heuristics to generate a set of candidate moves for the connecting player. The MP deduction rule could be made complete by testing all possible reply-moves of the connecting player, but at a computational cost that would not be a good trade-off for an artificial player, as testing many failed OR-deductions is more worthwhile in competitive conditions.

References

[1] M. Gardener, "The Game of Hex," in *The Scientific American Book of Mathematical Puzzles and Diversions*. New York: Simon and Schuster, 1959.
[2] S. Even, Tarjan R.E., "A Combinatorial Problem Which is Complete in Polynomial Space," *Journal of the Association for Computing Machinery*, vol. 23, pp. 710-719, 1976.
[3] W. J. Duffin, "Electricity and Magnetism," 4th ed. London: McGraw-Hill, 1990, pp. 46-81.
[4] J. Van Rijswijck, "Are Bees Better Than Fruitflies?," in *Department of Computing Science*. Edmonton: University of Alberta, 2002.
[5] J. Van Rijswijck, "Search and Evaluation in Hex," in *Department of Computing Science*. Edmonton: University of Alberta, 2002.
[6] V. V. Anshelevich, "A Hierarchical Approach to Computer Hex," *Artificial Intelligence*, vol. 134, pp. 101-120, 2002.
[7] V. V. Anshelevich, "An Automatic Theorem Proving Approach to Game Programming," presented at Proceedings of the Seventh National Conference of Artificial Intelligence, Menlo Park, California, 2000.
[8] G. Melis, Hayward, R., "Hex Gold at Graz: Six Defeats Mongoose," *to appear ICGA Journal*, 2003.
[9] S. Russell, Norvig, P., *Artificial Intelligence a Modern Approach*, Second ed. Upper Saddle River: Pearson Education, 2003.
[10] C. Browne, *Hex Strategy:Making the Right Connections*. Natick: A. K. Peters, 2000.
[11] C. Browne, "Connection Games," A. K. Peters, 2004.
[12] R. Hayward, Björnsson, Y., Johanson, M., Kan M., Po, N., Van Rijswijck, J., *Advances in Computer Games: Solving 7x7 HEX: Virtual Connections and Game-State Reduction*, vol. 263. Boston: Kluwer Achedemic Publishers, 2003.

Appendix

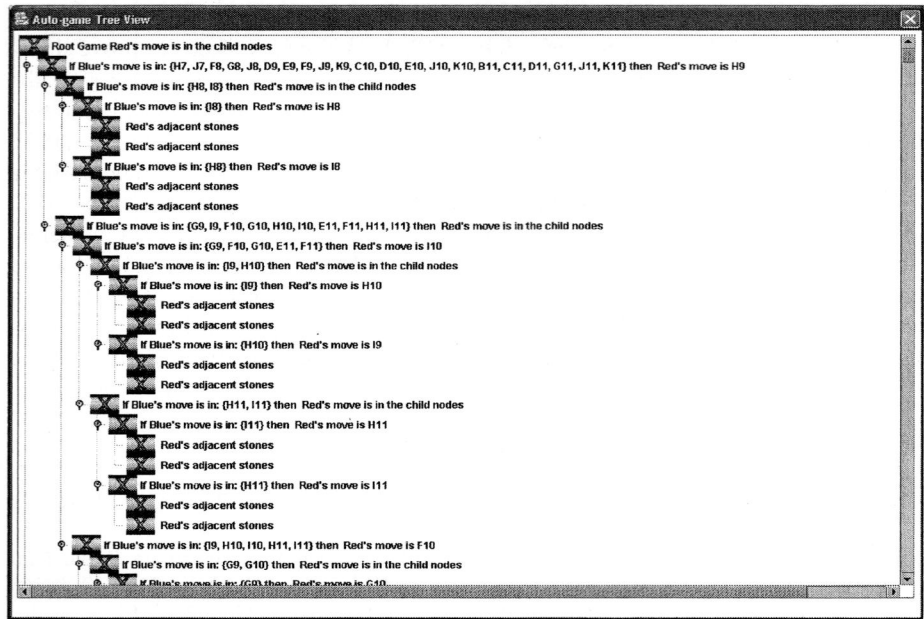

Fig. 9. A screen shot of the part of the tree derived by the MP deduction rule for the edge template of Fig. 6. The target T1 is at position I7 (see Fig. 8 for the coordinates). The depth of the tree is 11 and the number of nodes of 1008. The "Red's adjacent stones" leaves correspond to adjacent cells (elementary strong connections)

```
function MP_Deduction(targetA, targetB, Depth) returns a SubGame, Tactic

Inputs:
  targetA:  The first target
  targetB:  The second target
  Depth:    The deepest level in the search

if not hasWeak(targetA, targetB)) or hasStrong(targetA, targetB) then
  return null

Must_Play := GetMustPlayRegion(targetA, targetB)

Played_Moves := { targetA, targetB }
Result := null
for cell ∈ Must_Play do
  Played_Moves := Played_Moves ∪ {cell}
  Result := Search_On_Player(Stack_A, Stack_B, Played_Moves, Depth, 1)
  Played_Moves := Played_Moves - {cell}
  if Result ≠ null then
    TheSubGame := BuildSubGame(Result, targetA, targetB)
    TheTactic := BuildTactic(Result, targetA, targetB)
    return TheSubGame, TheTactic

end // for
return null
```

```
function Search_On_Player(StackA, StackB, Played, Depth, Level) returns a Tactic

Inputs:
  StackA: The stack of strong connections that extends the first target group
  StackB: The stack of strong connections that extends the second target group
  Played: The set of moves that the search has made
  Depth:  The depth of the search
  Level:  The current level of the search

if Level > Depth then
  return null

if Exists_A_Cell_That_Strongly_Connects(StackA, StackB) then
  return BuildStrongConnectionTactic(StackA, StackB)

for stack ∈ { StackA, StackB} do
  for cell := Strongly_Connected_AND_Deducible_With(stack) do
    StrongTactics := Get_StrongTactics(cell, stack)
    for game ∈ StrongTactics do
      if IsEmpty( {cell ∪ game } ∩ Played_Moves ) then
        Push(stack, game)
        Played_Moves := Played_Moves ∪ {cell}
        Result := Search_On_Opponent(StackA, StackB, Played, Depth, Level + 1)
        Played_Moves := Played_Moves - {cell}
        Pop(stack)
        if Result not null then
          return Result
end // for
return null
```

```
function Search_On_Opponent(StackA, StackB, Played, Depth, Level) returns a Tactic

Inputs:
  StackA: The stack of strong connections that extends the first target group
  StackB: The stack of strong connections that extends the second target group
  Played: The set of moves that search has made
  Depth:  The depth of the search
  Level:  The current level of the search

TheConnectionTactic := Create_ConnectionTactic()
Must_Play := Get_Must_Play_Region_Between_Stacks(StackA, StackB)
Result := null
for cell ∈ Must_Play do
  Played_Moves := Played_Moves ∪ {cell}
  Result := Search_On_Player(Stack_A, Stack_B, Played_Moves, Depth, Level + 1)
  Played_Moves := Played_Moves - {cell}
  if Result = null then
    return null

  Add_Transition_To(TheConnectionTactic, Result)
end // for
```

Fig. 10. Pseudo code for the MP deduction rule

Applying Constraint Satisfaction Techniques to 3D Camera Control

Owen Bourne and Abdul Sattar

Institute for Integrated and Intelligent Systems,
Griffith University,
PMB50 Gold Coast Mail Centre, QLD 9726
[o.bourne, a.sattar]@griffith.edu.au

Abstract. Controlling an autonomous camera in three-dimensional virtual environments is a difficult task which manifests itself in many interactive computer graphics applications, such as computer games. In this paper, we represent this problem as a constraint satisfaction problem which is often over-constrained. A range of complex requirements, such as frame coherence, occlusion and camera holes can be elegantly represented as constraints. We then apply both complete and incomplete search methods to find the optimal camera placement. An interactive computer games application was developed to experimentally evaluate these methods. Our experimental results and a discussion with related studies conclude that our approach is sophisticated both in modelling and solving the difficult task of 3D camera control.

1 Introduction

Controlling an autonomous camera in three-dimensional (3D) virtual environments is a difficult task which manifests itself in many interactive computer graphics applications. Medical imaging [13, 17], computer games [12] and guided exploration [6] are a few examples where autonomous cameras are required to provide suitable views of the scene as the user interacts with the environment. The automated camera system is expected to consistently provide a suitable view of the target object(s) for the user. This includes maintaining visibility of the target and occasionally allowing limited free-roaming before the camera manipulates its view and/or position to maintain the visibility of the target.

Automatically controlling the camera in 3D environments is a non-trivial task. A camera controlling algorithm must be able to calculate suitable position and orientation properties of the camera for each frame of animation (usually at 60 frames-per-second or higher for real-time applications). Essentially it has to deal with a range of complex requirements, such as:

- *Frame coherence*, which defines that camera positions across consecutive frames must be related to each other to avoid jerky movements;
- *Occlusion*, where the line-of-sight between the camera and the target becomes blocked by scene geometry;

- *Camera holes*, where the camera becomes trapped in a position where suitable movements cannot be made;
- *Camera cutting*, where the camera makes large-scale movements with a dramatic change in orientation between consecutive frames; and
- *Unnecessary movements*, where the camera moves before it is necessary.

The camera control system often finds it difficult to satisfy all of these requirements. There is a need to adequately represent these constraints such that suitable solutions could be efficiently determined. Camera control problems are potentially over-constrained, meaning perfect solutions may not be possible. However, the best partial solutions have to be identified, such that the automated camera system can function in an acceptable manner.

A Constraint Satisfaction Problem (CSP) is a triple $\langle V, D, R \rangle$, with a set of variables V, a domain D of values for each variable V, and a set of relations R [8]. A constraint is defined as a relation over a set of variables that restricts the valid instantiations of the variables. The problem is to determine an assignment to the variables such that all of the constraints are satisfied. If there is no consistent assignment, then the problem is termed an over-constrained problem [10].

In this paper, we apply the constraint satisfaction paradigm to effectively represent the 3D camera control problem. We found that the complex requirements could be easily represented as constraints and the whole problem of providing suitable views of the target becomes a constraint satisfaction problem. However, it is an over-constrained problem because there are often conflicting requirements involved in the problem domain. We evaluated both a branch and bound approach as well as a greedy local search method to find the optimal solution to the problem by relaxing some constraints. All constraints were assigned a cost to ensure some constraints were more relaxed than others. To demonstrate the elegance of the constraint satisfaction paradigm in representing the 3D camera control problem, we developed an interactive computer game. The game was designed to test the automated camera system with complex and dynamic virtual environments. We demonstrate through experimentation within this application that local search can be effectively applied to the camera control problem with performance benefits over the commonly used complete methods.

The rest of the paper is organized as follows; Section 2 describes how the 3D camera control problem can be modelled as a CSP. Section 3 details our experimental study that includes the design of the interactive computer game, implementation of the standard branch and bound, and local search methods, and analysis of the results. Section 4 compares our work with related research. Finally we conclude the paper with a few remarks on future research.

2   3D Camera Control as a Constraint Satisfaction Problem

3D camera control involves placing the camera in the best possible position to provide an unobstructed view of the target in virtual environments. An automated camera control system is required in many domains which utilize interactive computer graphics. Each of these domains demands efficient and robust autonomous control of the virtual camera.

The camera control problem is often represented as an optimization problem where the goal is to find the solution with the minimal cost. There are a number of features specific to automated camera control (directly captured as constraints) which must be dealt with in real-time.

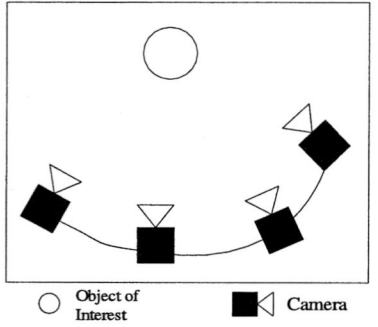

(a) Good Frame Coherence.

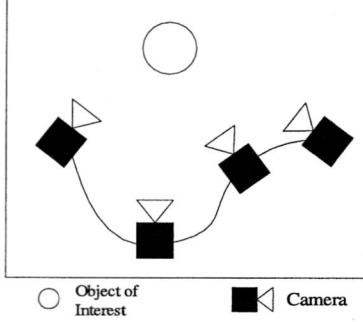

(b) Poor Frame Coherence.

Fig. 1. Frame coherence

Frame coherence requires that camera positions across consecutive frames must be related to each other to avoid jerky movements. Most solvers do not solve the current frame in relation to previous frames, causing the violation of frame coherence. Figure 1 illustrates frame coherence with each camera representing a consecutive frame. Figure 1(a) shows a camera with good frame coherence, as a smooth line can be drawn between the subsequent positions. Figure 1(b) shows a camera with poor frame coherence, as a smooth line cannot be drawn between the subsequent positions;

Occlusion is where the line-of-sight between the camera and the target becomes (or is in danger of becoming) blocked by scene geometry. In Figure 2(a), if the camera moves to the left or right its view of the target will become blocked by one of the occluders;

Camera holes are where the camera becomes trapped in a position where suitable movements cannot be made. This often happens when the camera is moved into a corner or backed against a wall (Figure 2(b)). The camera cannot make movements in any direction, either because it will collide with scene geometry, or because it will move too close to (or past) the target;

Camera cutting is where the camera makes dramatic (physically impossible) movements in position or orientation between consecutive frames, and *Unnecessary movements* are where the camera moves before it is necessary. This is directly related to frame coherence. The camera should remain at rest until it is necessary for it to move.

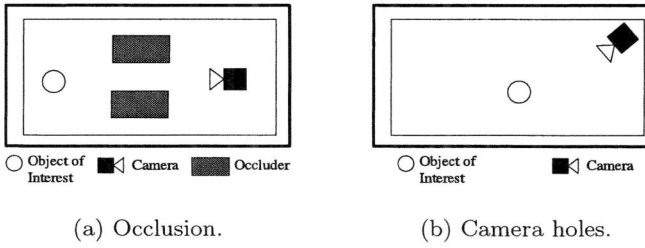

(a) Occlusion.   (b) Camera holes.

Fig. 2. Camera positioning difficulties

2.1 Representing 3D Camera Control as a Constraint Satisfaction Problem

It is natural to represent the camera position (X,Y,Z axes) as the problem variables (V in the formal definition). The domain for each variable consists of all points in one dimension which the camera can occupy (D in the formal definition). The domain can be optimized by restricting the upper and lower bounds to realistic values based on previous movement data (e.g. camera velocity).

The camera control problem in our representation is often over-constrained, meaning we cannot always find a zero cost solution. The cost of a solution is calculated by summing the cost of violating each of the constraints. Each constraint is assigned a cost, and the more the constraint is violated, the more impact it has on the overall cost of the solution.

Consider a simple trailing behaviour (where the camera follows the target around the environment), which can be obtained by implementing two constraints: *distance* and *height*. The *distance* constraint is used to force the camera to maintain a specified distance from the target, while the *height* constraint forces the camera to maintain a specified height in relation to the target.

Frame coherence and unnecessary movements (which are implicitly related) are addressed using a multiple constraint approach. We defined two frame coherence constraints: *distance* and *rotation*. *Distance* constrains the distance the camera can move in a frame based on the distance the camera has moved in previous frames (with a preset level of variance to allow for acceleration/deceleration), resulting in smooth movement between frames. *Rotation* operates similarly, ensuring smooth rotation of the camera based on the angular displacement of the camera from previous frames. Unnecessary movement is eliminated with the frame coherence constraints, causing the camera to remain at rest until such time that the cost of constraint violation increases sufficiently to force a camera movement to reduce the cost of the solution.

Occlusion and camera holes are addressed with a visibility constraint. The visibility constraint coarsely determines visible and non-visible areas in the domain, determined by rays intersecting geometry. Each potential solution is evaluated by calculating the risk of violating the visibility of the target. Non-visible areas behind occluders or close to objects influence the cost of the visibility constraint, causing the camera to prefer lower cost solutions further away from the non-visible areas.

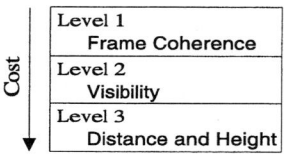

Fig. 3. Cost hierarchy

The assignment of costs in our representation occurs in three layers, where higher layers have bigger cost values (Figure 3). The first layer contains the constraints that are most important, and therefore are assigned the highest cost when violated. Frame coherence is considered to be the most important visual property of our camera system (as failing to have smooth movement can cause motion sickness), so is in the first layer. The second layer contains constraints whose satisfaction is important, but not mandatory. The constraint defining visibility of our target is in this second layer, as smooth movement is presently more important to us than visibility. The third layer contains constraints dictating the general behaviour of the camera, which can be violated more readily to satisfy constraints in higher layers. This layer includes our distance and height constraints.

2.2 Constraint Solving

While there are various complete search heuristics which provide benefits in some problems [8], the nature of the camera control problem largely negates their use. The search tree for camera control is very wide (large domains) and not very deep (usually between 1 and 7 variables, depending on the representation and implementation) as shown in Figure 4. As many of the heuristics in complete search (such as backjumping and conflict-directed backjumping) work best when pruning search trees of considerable depth, these heuristics provide little benefit on our search tree.

Local search provides an efficient method of finding reasonable solutions to large and difficult problems quickly [14]. However, the major drawback of using

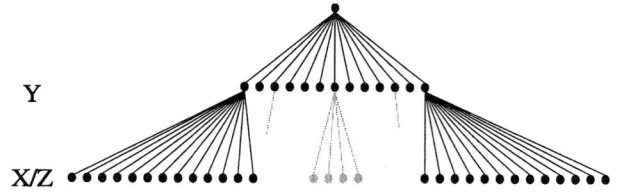

Fig. 4. The search tree for the 3D camera control problem

local search in the camera control problem is that we are attempting to find our best solution (minimum cost), which cannot be guaranteed by local search.

The randomized nature of local search also tends to violate the frame coherence properties of the camera more readily than complete search. In order to increase the likelihood of finding the best solution (or one close to it), we must increase the maximum potential solutions that the algorithm can evaluate. This has the obvious disadvantage of reducing performance, and so a trade-off between speed and accuracy must be achieved.

2.3 Algorithms

Two algorithms are considered in this study: a branch and bound search and a greedy local search.

The Branch and Bound algorithm is essentially a backtracking search that provides a mechanism to search inconsistent portions of the search tree in over-constrained situations [10]. A cost is associated with the violation of each constraint, and the solution with the best cost is the solution that has violated the fewest constraints. The standard form of the algorithm typically sets the cost of all constraint violations to 1, although different costs are assigned to each constraint in our implementation. The search continues into inconsistent portions of the search tree providing that the cost of the partial solution is not higher than the previously identified best cost, or a pre-defined maximum cost.

The Local Search algorithm used in our experiments initially instantiates each variable to a random value from its domain. The cost of this initial solution is then evaluated. If not all constraints are satisfied (solution has a non-zero cost), a variable is selected at random and assigned a new value from its domain. The new cost is then calculated iteratively until either a solution is found, or the maximum number of attempts have been made. More effective heuristics (such as Tabu lists [11]) can be used to extend the basic local search algorithm, providing potentially better and quicker solutions.

3 Experimental Study

We now present an evaluation of our camera control system on an interactive 3D computer game. The computer games domain was chosen as it encapsulates all of the requirements of 3D camera control. Other domains were not pursued as they failed to encapsulate all of these requirements. Computer games also provide an increasingly realistic environment for evaluating artificial intelligence methodologies [15].

3.1 Interactive Computer Game

We have developed a 3D game engine in order to evaluate the real-time performance of our constraint-based camera representation. A 3D game engine was used because it provides stricter requirements than other domains (such as guided exploration). The camera module of a 3D game engine must be able to deal with dynamic environments as well as an unpredictable, user-controlled target. Computationally, the camera module for a 3D game engine must execute quickly, as other processes (such as artificial intelligence and physics) must also be executed per frame while maintaining an efficient and consistent framerate.

The core of our 3D game engine uses a hierarchy of bounding volumes (axially-aligned bounding boxes) to represent the objects in the virtual environment [1]. This representation is used to optimize rendering, collision detection and the evaluation of the visibility constraint (ray intersection). Ray intersections with bounding volumes are much more efficient than ray intersections with the large number of polygons represented by the bounding volumes.

Our 3D game engine supports the generation and playback of animation traces, allowing the animation of the target through the environment to be stored and used for the evaluation of constraint solvers. The ability to play back animation traces removes the necessity for our constraint solvers to be executed visually within our system, and for the solvers to be run in batches with varying parameters for constraint costs.

For the evaluation of the constraint solvers, an animation trace of a targets path through a test virtual environment was generated. Each constraint solver was then executed on the animation trace, generating the camera's orientation and position for each frame. The results were then viewed through the game engine to evaluate the visual properties of the solution.

Fig. 5. Screenshots of the 3D game engine

The screenshots in Figure 5 show two non-consecutive frames for a test run. As evidenced in the screenshots, the camera maintains the same distance and height relations between itself and the target over time. The direction the camera faces the target is loosely constrained, which is why we see both a back and front facing view of our target.

3.2 Results

Both the branch and bound and local search algorithms were run on the same animation trace with the same cost assignments for the constraints. The branch and bound algorithm used a granularity (or resolution) of 0.01 while local search used a granularity of 0.00001 (our target is approximately 30 units wide), giving local search many more possible solutions to choose from. The reason for the difference is that branch and bound is too computationally expensive to run at such high granularities with the current domain sizes.

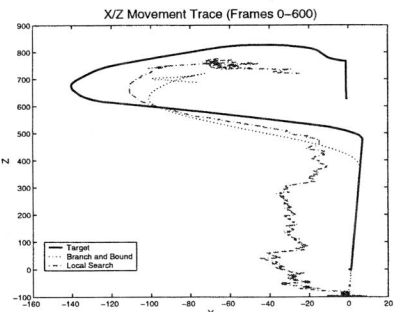

Fig. 6. Movement trace

Figure 6 shows a partial trace of the movement of the target and the camera paths generated by the branch and bound and local search algorithms (using constraint costs: Height = 1.0, Distance = 1.0, Frame Coherence Distance = 1.0, Frame Coherence Rotation = 5.0). As can be seen, local search exhibits less consistent movement than branch and bound. This is in part due to the random nature of the algorithm, and also in part due to the limited number of evaluations made by the local search algorithm (50,000 per frame) in comparison to the branch and bound algorithm (216,360,000 per frame). Allowing more moves to be made by the local search algorithm produces smoother movement while increasing computation time.

Branch and bound search solved the problem in an average of 120 seconds/frame, while local search solved the problem in an average of 0.05 seconds/frame. Both algorithms had small variations in solution time due to small changes in the domain size caused by dynamic domain selection. Branch and bound search does not provide anywhere near real-time performance, whereas local search achieves close to real-time performance without any optimizations or the use of heuristics.

3.3 Analysis

As we expected, local search generates solutions more quickly at higher granularities than branch and bound, due to the limited number of evaluations. However, local search must be run at higher granularities to obtain good visual results, as at lower granularities it provides poor visual results regardless of the number of evaluations allowed. Our tests show that local search is significantly faster than branch and bound, while providing similar visual results. This indicates that complete search strategies are unnecessary in this domain.

It is difficult to compare our results against existing work, due to differences in the environment data, different constraint representations, different hardware and different constraint solving methods. As such, a simple and direct comparison between our approach and existing work could not be performed. Comparisons based solely on computational time indicate that our approach is more efficient than existing approaches in [4, 2, 12].

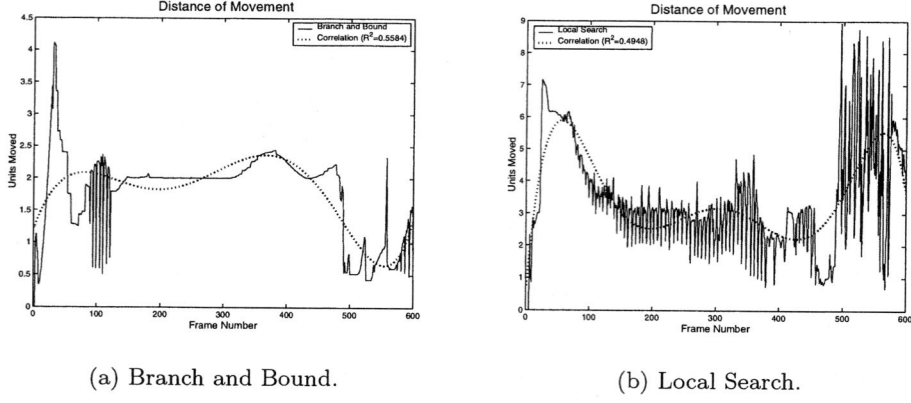

(a) Branch and Bound. (b) Local Search.

Fig. 7. Comparison of visual results

Figures 7(a) and 7(b) show the relative movements made by the camera generated by each respective algorithm. These graphs provide us with a method to numerically evaluate the frame coherence generated by a given constraint solver. Using regression analysis, a 6th order polynomial is fitted to the movement plots of the camera. The correlation co-efficient (R^2) value represents how close to a smooth (and optimally frame coherent) movement the constraint solver generated (values closer to ±1 are good, values close to 0 are poor). Local search generated a correlation co-efficient of 0.4948, in comparison to 0.5584 for branch and bound on our test case. Branch and bound provides slightly smoother visual results, as supported by our regression analysis results.

4 Related Work

Potential fields have been applied to the 3D camera control problem [6, 5]. They work by defining repulsive forces around the virtual environment which interact with the camera, moving it away from obstacles. The camera's movement follows the path of least resistance through the potential fields. This approach satisfies the frame coherence requirements, but is also prone to getting stuck in inter-frame local minima. Tweaking the potential fields is required to obtain desirable results, and the pre-processing generation of the potential fields is time-consuming. In our approach, no pre-processing of the environment is necessary, and the camera module is independent of all sub-systems and can be easily placed in any 3D virtual environment without pre-processing the environment.

Constraint satisfaction algorithms have been applied to virtual camera control in numerous publications [3, 4, 2, 7, 9, 12, 16]. Deficiencies in constraint representation have restricted the applicability of various constraint solvers. The use of complete search (often generate-and-test) is common. The evaluation of visibility as a post-constraint step is a contributor to the difficulty in applying arbitrary constraint solvers. A potential solution must be evaluated for visibility after the constraint solver has nominated the potential solution, often using a costly visibility evaluation function (ray-casting is common). This does not allow for the visibility information to influence the constraint search. In Bares and Lester [3] visibility problems are addressed by separating multiple targets into their own viewports. In our approach, we evaluate visibility as a constraint. This allows visibility to influence and help direct the constraint search, and also removes the necessity for post-constraint visibility evaluation.

Frame coherence was not explicitly addressed in any representation until defined as a problem in 3D camera control by Halper et al. [12]. In Halper et al.'s representation, prediction of target movement is used to find solutions resulting in smooth camera movements. Frame coherence is not considered a constraint, but is the result of predicting where the camera should be in future frames and moving the camera towards that goal. This does not provide any guarantee that frame coherence will be satisfied, as it is entirely dependent on the algorithm used to predict the targets movements. In our approach, frame coherence is represented as 2 constraints that must be satisfied to a certain degree (by exploiting our cost structure), otherwise the solution is deemed as invalid.

The representation by Christie et al. models camera movement as a constrained combination of pre-defined motions [7]. Their approach provides for some frame coherent results, and the camera's motion can be reasonably accurately represented as a few distinct motions. However, pre-defining the camera's motions disallows the dynamic property available with constraints, and does not account well for unexpected movements required by the camera (in response to the targets movements) that are not represented as an existing movement. In our approach, the camera's movements are entirely defined by the constraints relating the camera's position to the target.

More effective domain selection strategies have been attempted by Bares et al. [2]. While restricting the domain size is critical to achieving real-time performance, the approach by Bares et al. still provides a relatively coarse search space. The search space also does not appear to scale effectively in correlation to the movement of the camera (changes in velocity). Our approach uses dynamic domain selection based on the camera's movement from the previous frames. This provides a fine resolution when the camera is moving slowly, and a coarse resolution when moving quickly.

5 Conclusion

We have provided an expressively rich representation of the 3D camera control problem as a constraint satisfaction problem. This representation uses a form of constraint hierarchies to derive preferred behaviour from the camera by specifying some constraints as more important in the cost of the solution than others. These hierarchies provided consistent and desirable behaviour from our camera module with the use of a minimal number of constraints to address the issues associated with 3D camera control. Frame coherent results were achieved through the use of specialized constraints.

Our representation method provided the ability to apply arbitrary constraint satisfaction algorithms (including local search methods) to our test cases, rather than the generate-and-test methods commonly used with existing representations. The comparison of complete and incomplete search methods on the sample animation trace produced results indicating that local search algorithms can be effectively and efficiently applied to 3D camera control. As a consequence, problems posed in our representation can be solved more quickly than in existing approaches through the use of local search techniques.

We have applied and tested our representation on an interactive computer game application. The nature of the 3D camera control problem was examined after experimental trials were run with our test application. The 3D camera control problem is often over-constrained due to limitations in the granularity (or resolution) of our search space. The problem is not always over-constrained.

We have provided a method for numerically evaluating frame coherence. Rather than using qualitative methods (such as "it looks smooth"), we used regression analysis to provide a quantitative value measuring how closely the camera's actual movement corresponds to a preferred smooth movement.

5.1 Future Directions

Additional constraints to provide more controlled behaviour can be investigated. Further investigation into heuristics appropriate for broad search trees is necessary. A more complete investigation comparing the effectiveness and efficiency of complete and local search algorithms on a variety of domains of the 3D camera control problem will be interesting to investigate. The integration of the camera module into an increasingly complex and dynamic virtual environment, along with multiple targets, can be investigated.

References

1. Tomas Akenine-Möller and Eric Haines. *Real-Time Rendering*. A K Peters, 2002.
2. William Bares, Scott McDermott, Christina Boudreaux, and Somying Thainimit. Virtual 3D camera composition from frame constraints. In *Eight ACM International Conference on Multimedia*, pages 177–186, Marina Del Ray, California, USA, October 30 - November 4 2000.

3. William H. Bares and James C. Lester. Intelligent multi-shot visualization interfaces for dynamic 3D worlds. In *1999 International Conference on Intelligent User Interfaces (IUI'99)*, pages 119–126, Los Angeles, California, USA, January 5-8 1999.
4. William H. Bares, Somying Thainimit, and Scott McDermott. A model for constraint-based camera planning. In *AAAI 2000 Spring Symposium Series on Smart Graphics*, pages 84–91, Stanford, California, USA, March 20-22 2000.
5. Steffi Beckhaus. Guided exploration with dynamic potential fields: The Cubical-Path system. *Computer Graphics Forum*, 20(4):201–210, December 2001.
6. Steffi Beckhaus, Felix Ritter, and Thomas Strothotte. CubicalPath - dynamic potential fields for guided exploration in virtual environments. In Brian A. Barsky, Yoshihisa Shinagawa, and Wenping Wang, editors, *Pacific Graphics 2000*, pages 387–395, Hong Kong, October 3-5 2000. IEEE Press.
7. Marc Christie, Eric Languenou, and Laurent Granvilliers. Modeling camera control with constrained hypertubes. In Pascal Van Hentenryck, editor, *Principles and Practice of Constraint Programming (CP2002)*, pages 618–632, Ithaca, New York, USA, September 2002. Springer.
8. Rina Dechter. Backtracking algorithms for constraint satisfaction problems - a survey. January 29 1997.
9. Steven M. Drucker and David Zeltzer. Intelligent camera control in a virtual environment. In *Graphics Interface '94*, pages 190–199, Banff, Alberta, Canada, May 1994.
10. Eugence C. Freuder and Richard J. Wallace. Partial constraint satisfaction. pages 63–110, 1996.
11. Fred Glover. Tabu search - part I. *ORSA Journal on Computing*, 1(3):190–206, 1989.
12. Nicolas Halper, Ralf Helbing, and Thomas Strothotte. A camera engine for computer games: Managing the trade-off between constraint satisfaction and frame coherence. *Computer Graphics Forum*, 20(3), 2001.
13. Lichan Hong, Shigeru Muraki, Arie Kaufman, Dirk Bartz, and Taosong He. Virtual voyage: Interactive navigation in the human colon. In *24th International Conference on Computer Graphics and Interactive Techniques (SIGGRAPH'97)*, pages 27–34. ACM Press, August 6-8 1997.
14. Holger H. Hoos and Thomas Stützle. Local search algorithms for SAT: An empirical evaluation. *Journal of Automated Reasoning*, 24(4):421–481, May 2000.
15. John E. Laird and Michael van Lent. Human-level AI's killer application: Interactive computer games. In *AAAI*, pages 1171–1178, Austin, Texas, USA, July 30 - August 3 2000. AAAI Press.
16. E. Languenou, F. Benhamou, F. Goualard, and M. Christie. The virtual cameraman: an interval constraint based approach. In *Constraint Techniques for Artistic Applications (Post ECAI'98 Workshop)*, Brighton, UK, August 24 1998.
17. Anna Vilanova, Andreas König, and Eduard Gröller. VirEn: A virtual endoscopy system. *Machine Graphics and Vision*, 8(3):469–487, 1999.

Constraints from STRIPS — Preliminary Report

Norman Foo[1], Pavlos Peppas[2], and Yan Zhang[3]

[1] NICTA, and The School of Computer Science and Engineering,
University of New South Wales, Sydney NSW 2052, Australia
[2] Dept of Business Administration, University of Patras, 26110 Patras, Greece
[3] School of Computing and Information Technology, University of Western Sydney,
NSW 2747, Australia

Abstract. We re-visit the problem of converting action specifications into system constraints by re-examining it in the very simple setting of STRIPS. This has the merit of making many thorny issues relatively transparent. The paper is in the form of an extended summary of ongoing work and many of the results are merely outlined. But sufficient details are included to indicate where we will be taking things further, and to encourage others to pursue the same objectives. These objectives are in some sense a kind of reverse-engineering, as the database community is evidently familiar with the idea of starting with constraints and then deriving action specifications from them. However in AI reactive systems, action specifications are often the primary entity, so techniques to unearth the implicit constraints can facilitate better designs.

1 Introduction

Despite (or perhaps because of) its simplicity, STRIPS [Fikes and Nilsson 71] is possibly the most widely used method for specifying actions in dynamic domains. It precedes much more sophisticated languages like the situation calculus [Shanahan 97], but unlike them it needs only an intuitive grasp of logic to use. Moreover it is easily and efficiently programmable in simple Prolog, or procedural languages like Java. For a large number of applications in areas such as planning, device specifications, and network protocols that do not require elaborate (as distinct from large) theories, the simplicity of STRIPS outweighs the known limitations [Lifschitz 86] of its expressiveness that is rectified in, say, the situation calculus. This feature is particularly attractive because it lends itself to rapid prototyping of action specifications for testing and revising. AI domains that are *reactive* are particularly suited for STRIPS-like action specifications because they can be described as domains in which the action plans are very shallow and action ramifications [Shanahan 97] are completely known. In such domains the typical action can be paraphrased as "if the system is in a state in which condition A holds, do action B so that it gets to a state in which C holds". An popular example of a highly reactive domain is the robot soccer competition.

In this paper, we focus on the kinds of simple domains that occur widely in practice and re-visit a topic that we had treated in much greater generality in the past [Foo, et.al. 97] [Zhang and Foo 96], and which has been addressed again very recently [Lin 04]. There are several over-lapping motives for this re-visit, but all stemming from the simplicity attribute of STRIPS. First, its restricted expressiveness for simple domains eanbles us to highlight ontological issues without distraction by technicalities. Ontology here is not about the usual taxonomies of objects, etc., but about choices in the modelling of "real" systems, and involve issues such as the correctness of specifications relative to these choices, the adequacy of the language chosen, and the extraction of implicit systems information from action specifications. These are crucial questions in knowledge representation that are often avoided because they are either considered too hard or incapable of meaningful formal inquiry. We make a small start here. Second, the concepts of system laws, and the soundness and completeness of the specifications are easily grasped in this framework. Finally, there is no need for the relatively heavy logical and model-theoretic machinery that were used in [Zhang and Foo 96] and Lin [Lin 04] but were necessary there because they allowed more expressive languages.

While the aim here is to extract logical theories from STRIPS specifications, we attempt to keep the logical formalism to a minimum. To assist intuition, we use the well-worn blocks world domain as a running example; other examples are adduced to discuss ontology.

2 Review of STRIPS

This is a brief review of STRIPS to establish the vocabulary. It was invented to specify *actions*, and intended to capture in a natural way the notion of discrete-time *state change*. The states are represented as a (usually finite) set of logical *ground atoms*, and an action has the effect of changing this set, by deleting some and adding new ones. Thus the *post-conditions* of actions consists of specifying a *delete-list* and an *add-list* — it is customary to drop the hyphens, so we will do so below. Actions can be parametised by variables that are instantiated or bound to particular constants for any one action instance. Moreover, before an action can be executed, it has to satisfy a *pre-condition* which is often merely a test to see if certain ground atoms are in the state. An elaboration that does not complicate STRIPS semantics include pre-conditions that are clauses; one that does complicate it enormously are post-conditions that are disjunctions of atoms, and hence we eschew that here.

As an example, consider a blocks world where we adopt the convention that upper case letters stand for variables and lower case for constants which name particular blocks. The number of blocks is finite, and there is one non-block constant *table*, signifying the surface of the table. The only predicates[1] are $on(\_,\_)$ and $clear(\_)$, where, as usual, $on(b,c)$ means the b is on block c, $table(b)$ means the block b is on the table, and $clear(b)$ means the block b has nothing on it.

A state of the world is given by a collection of such ground atoms. For instance, let state $S1$ be:

$on(b,c), on(c,e), table(e), clear(b), on(d,f), table(f), clear(d)$.

---

[1] For simplicity we omit the *in-hand(_)* predicate.

We use the standard notation that $S \models \alpha$ to signify that the logical formula α holds (is true) in a state S; for the above, $S1 \models on(b,c)$ and similarly for the other atoms in $S1$. It is conventional to assume unique names (UNA), and also to invoke the closed world assumption (CWA) which is the formal analog of Prolog negation-as-failure. The UNA says that all constants are distinct, and the CWA (in this simple encoding of states) says that the negation of a ground atom that holds in a state if that atom is missing from it. For instance, from the UNA $S1 \models b \neq c$, and from the CWA $S1 \models \neg table(b)$ and $S1 \models \neg on(b,e)$. In the presence of the CWA, all states are effectively *complete*, i.e., for each *literal* α, either $S \models \alpha$ or $S \not\models \alpha$.

Here are the more or less standard blocks world actions, to which we assign names for ease of continuing reference.

$unstack(X)$
$precondition : on(X,Y), clear(X)$
$deletelist : on(X,Y)$
$addlist : table(X), clear(Y)$

$move(X,Z)$
$precondition : on(X,Y), clear(X), clear(Z)$
$deletelist : on(X,Y), clear(Z)$
$addlist : on(X,Z), clear(Y)$

$stack(X,Y)$
$precondition : table(X), clear(X), clear(Y)$
$deletelist : table(X), clear(Y)$
$addlist : on(X,Y)$

In these specifications, multiple predicate occurences in the components signify conjunctions, e.g., the precondition for $unstack(X)$ is that both $on(X,Y)$ and $clear(X)$ must be present, and its addlist says that the atoms $table(X)$ and $clear(Y)$ are to be added as effects. Although the language of logic is used, an *operational* way to interpret the actions is as follows: given a state S (of ground atoms), we can execute an action if there is some *unifier* σ of its component atoms with S, in which case delete (respectively, add) from S those (unified) atoms (respectively, to) S. This is equivalent to executing a Prolog meta-rule of the form

$assert(addlist) \,||\, retract(deletelist) \leftarrow precondition$

after successful unification. The $||$ signifies parallel execution.

For example, in the state $S1$ above, one unifier yields the action $unstack(d)$ with deletelist $on(d,f)$, and addlist $table(d), clear(f)$. The resulting state $S2$ is $on(b,c)$, $on(c,e), table(e), clear(b), table(f), clear(d), table(d), clear(f)$.

All of these ideas are well-known and should be familiar to anyone who has examined planning in a Prolog framework. The novelty begins in the next section where we will explain that this view, combined with reasoning about consistency, reveals an intuitive connection with logical constraints.

3 Possible Constraints

A *system constraint* is a formula that all legal states of a system must satisfy. In the blocks world domain one such constraint is $\neg(on(A, B) \wedge on(A, C))$ which says (with the UNA on variable names) that blocks cannot be on top of two distinct blocks. System constraints are sometimes called the *laws* of the system.

An *action constraint* is a formula that holds in all states that result from the action. Thus any state that arises from the action will satisfy the action constraint. In sub-section 3.1 we will indicate how action constraints of the class of actions of a system are related to system constraints. One way to think about action constraints is that they restrict the kinds of states that can result from an action. Suppose β is a constraint of the action ϕ. Then $\neg \beta$ would describe the states that cannot be the result of action ϕ. It is at least plausible that there is enough information in STRIPS specifications for such constraints to be extracted, and sub-section 3.1 will explain how this can indeed be done.

An *action invariant* is a formula α such that if it satisfies the action precondition, and the action is executed, then the formula also satisfies the resulting state; more formally $S \models \alpha \Rightarrow S' \models \alpha$, where S and S' are the states before and after the action respectively. Therefore, an action invariant is of necessity also an action constraint since it satisfies the resulting state of the action by definition. Section 3 exploits this relationship to suggest candidates for invariants by producing a set of constraints for each action, using the insight in the previous paragraph.

Our (informal) definition of an action invariant should strike a chord with readers familiar with imperatvie program development or proving. Reasoning about segments of programs (loops being the most common) often involve the discovery of invariants that are the core of the operational meaning of the segments. Trivial invariants abound — any tautology will do — so the interesting invariants are those that are "tight" or stringent, and the latter are often arrived at by examining the pre-conditions and post-conditions of the segment. So it is with actions in STRIPS where any tautology is a system constraint, an action constraint and an action invariant.

The initial aim of our paper is to discover the tight constraints and invariants. The final aim is to elevate some of these invariants to the level of system constraints. Although we will discuss the latter in section 4, the idea can be summarized as follows. Suppose there are a finite number of actions $\phi_1, \ldots, \phi_k$ with respective action invariants $\lambda_1, \ldots, \lambda_k$. Then any λ_i is also a system constraint if it is an action invariant for all ϕ_i for $1 \leq i \leq k$. Action constraints will be used as candidates for action invariants, so ultimately it is action constraints that will be the candidates for system constraints.

Figure 1 summarizes the relationships among action constraints, action invariants and system invariants.

The subsections below examine the components in STRIPS specifications and show that they contain implicit information that can be used to extract action constraints as candidates for action invariants, and also suggest ontological alternatives. In these subsections, by constraint we will mean action constraint.

3.1 Reasoning About Addlists and Deletelists

The presumed intention of the addlist and the deletelist as effects of an action is for *correct state update*.

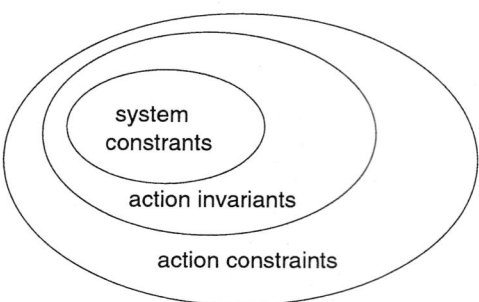

Fig. 1. Relationships between constraints and invariants

This can be seen in, e.g., the $unstack(d)$ instantiated action on state $S1$ above. Suppose, contrary to intention, we use the use its addlist components $table(d), clear(f)$ to add to $S1$ but neglect to remove its deletelist component $on(d, f)$. The resulting "state" $S3$ will have a subset of atoms $table(d), clear(f), on(d, f)$. This is intuitively wrong as now block d is both on the table and on block f; moreover it says that block f is clear, so adding to the confusion. A little reflection will show that for any action, adding atoms of an addlist but not removing atoms of a deletelist is the same as permitting both the atoms of the addlist and deletelist to co-exist in the resulting "state", which is an incorrect update. In fact, incorrect updates can also result from co-existence of *parts* of an addlist and deletelist.

We may reason similarly with the other action specifications. This leads to a postulate that captures these intuitions.

Addlist-Deletelist Consistency Postulate:
If state S is updated to state S' via a STRIPS action with addlist atom set $Add = \{a_1, \ldots, a_n\}$ and deletelist atom set $Del = \{d_1, \ldots, d_m\}$ then $\neg(a'_1 \wedge \ldots \wedge a'_j \wedge d'_1 \wedge \ldots \wedge d'_k)$, where $\{a'_1, \ldots, a'_j\} \subseteq Add$ and $\{d'_1, \ldots, d'_k\} \subseteq Del$, are candidates for action constraints.

We can generalize this by lifting the constants to variables in the obvious manner. For brevity, call the generalized version the *Add-Del postulate*.

Besides this intention there is an implicit assumption that a specification is *parsimonious* — it does not try to delete an atom that is not in the state to be updated, nor does it try to add an atom that is already present. This implies that if an action on state S has atoms $a_1, \ldots, a_n$ in its addlist and atoms $d_1, \ldots, d_m$ in its deletelist, then the atoms $d_1, \ldots, d_m$ are all in S but none of $a_1, \ldots, a_n$ are in it. Conversely, in the updated state S' all of the atoms $a_1, \ldots, a_n$ are in it, but none of $d_1, \ldots, d_m$. Logically, the closed world assumption equates the absence of an atom to its negation. Hence any of the possible constraints proposed by the Add-Del postulate is satisfied by both S and S'. But the action is only possible if S also satisfies its precondition. Thus we have the following:

Proposition 1. *The possible constraints from the Add-Del postulate are action invariants.*

In the examples below, distinct variables should (as is the convention with STRIPS specifications) be interpreted as unifying with distinct constant names, denoting distinct objects.

Applying the above to the $unstack(X)$ action above yields the following formulas.

$\neg(on(X, Y) \wedge table(X) \wedge clear(Y))$
$\neg(on(X, Y) \wedge table(X))$
$\neg(on(X, Y) \wedge clear(Y))$

The first formula is implied by the other two. The interesting question ' suggested by the example is this: which (subset) among the three formulas are the *correct* or truly intended constraints? Of course in a simple and familiar setting such as the blocks world we can quickly make a judgement — the second and third formulas suffice, and are the *essential* correct ones. The first formula is therefore redundant.

The potential for combinatorial explosion is revealed by considering the what the Add-Del postulate suggests for the $move(X, Z)$ action. It gives the following possible candidates for action constraints:

$\neg(on(X, Y) \wedge on(X, Z))$
$\neg(on(X, Y) \wedge clear(Y))$
$\neg(clear(Z) \wedge on(X, Z))$
$\neg(clear(Z) \wedge clear(Y))$
$\neg(on(X, Y) \wedge clear(Z) \wedge on(X, Z))$
$\neg(on(X, Y) \wedge clear(Z) \wedge clear(Y))$
$\neg(on(X, Z) \wedge clear(Y) \wedge on(X, Y))$
$\neg(on(X, Z) \wedge clear(Y) \wedge clear(Z))$
$\neg(on(X, Z) \wedge clear(Y) \wedge clear(Z) \wedge on(X, Y))$

Which subset among these are the essential correct ones, and which are redundant? One way to attempt an answer is to notice that the shorter ones (the first four) imply the longer ones (the last five), so if any of the the shorter ones can be established to be correct, some of the longer ones will be redundant. On the other hand, for any of the longer ones to be essential, it must be the case that the shorter ones that imply it are incorrect. Because of the familiarity of this domain, we can again easily judge which ones are essential. The first formula $\neg(on(X, Y) \wedge on(X, Z))$ is about the *uniqueness of block locations*. The next two *define the meaning* of $clear(X)$ as nothing is on block X; given that these formulas are satisfied in a state S only when a suitable bindings exist, they translate to the equivalent constraint $clear(X) \leftrightarrow \neg \exists Y on(Y, X)$. The fourth formula does not convey any useful information, but (like the rest) is nevertheless an action invariant since $clear(Z)$ is true in S but false in S', and $clear(Y)$ is false in S but true in S'. Due to subsumption, we may ignore the remainder.

It is helpful to pause for a moment to compare this with a mainstream activity in databases (see e.g., [Lawley, Topor and Wallace 93]) for which our approach may be regarded as a converse. The formal rendition of that work in our vocabulary would be this: *Start with constraints; then given the add-list of actions, derive appropriate preconditions and delete-lists.* As is well-known from standard work in programming language semantics, there is a trade-off among these entities but it is the weakest preconditions that are sought (presumably to make the scope of action application as wide as possible). Our approach here is therefore a kind of reverse-engineering. It treats the action specifications as primary entities, hypothesizing that they express an intended, underlying and implicit semantics that are action constraints, action invariants and system constraints. A remark made by one reviewer is helpful: both action and system contraints can be viewed as static, the former being local and the latter being global; on the other hand action invariants are dynamic.

3.2 Ontology

In less familiar domains the kind of judgement that we exercised in the blocks world to select the correct action constraints from the possible ones suggested by the Add-Del postulate may not be so immediate. The next example illustrates this. Consider a domain in which there are two switches and in an electric circuit in which there is also a light. The STRIPS specification of this system uses three propositiions — $sw1$, $sw2$ for saying that the respective switches are turned on, and $lightoff$ for saying that the light is off. Here is an attempted specification of an action for turning on the light.

$TurnOn$
$precondition : lightoff$
$deletlist : lightoff$
$addlist : sw1, sw2$

The Add-Del postulate suggests these as possible action constraints:

$\neg(sw1 \land lightoff)$
$\neg(sw2 \land lightoff)$
$\neg(sw1 \land sw2 \land lightoff)$

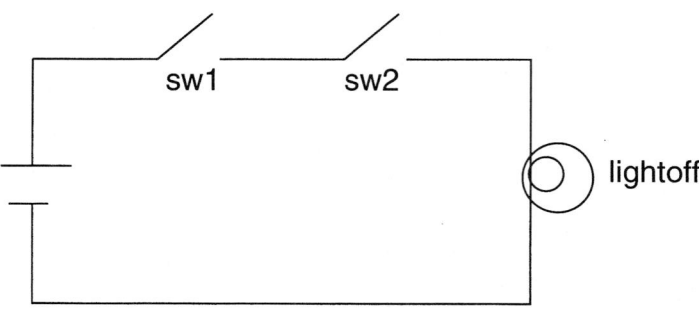

Fig. 2. Switches in series

The first formula is incorrect if there is a state SS such that $SS \models sw1 \land lightoff$. Hence we should look for a system in which this is so. A system in which there is such a state is shown in figure 2. As this system can also invalidate the second formula, this leaves only the longer third formula as the correct constraint. An alternative is a system in which the first and second formulas are indeed constraints, and the third is therefore redundant. A system in which this is the case is shown in figure 3. This example shows how questions about which among the possible formulas suggested by the Add-Del postulate are actual action constraints can trigger off a search for alternative *ontologies*. This search is *extra-logical*, for there is nothing in the implicit logic of STRIPS that can inform the ultimate choice. However, it is interesting that it can nevertheless *suggest* what to look for. For many domains the *modelling* enterprise is tentative and iterative, for we may be guessing at the internal structure of a black box. The use of the preceding method is to decide which experiments to run — or what questions to ask the persons who wrote the action specifications — in a search for possible invalidation of (short) possible constraints so that an ontological judgement can be made.

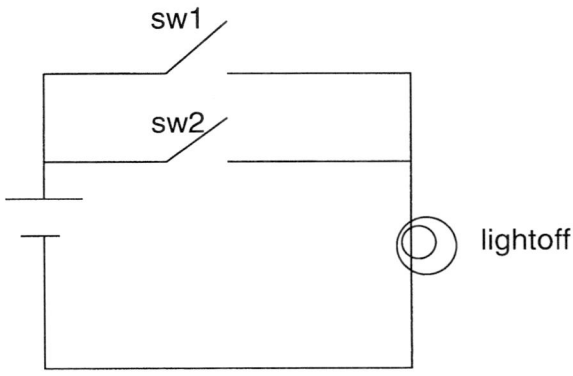

Fig. 3. Switches in parallel

3.3 Reasoning About Preconditions

Analogous to our dissection of the intended meaning of addlists and deletelists, we now examine the pre-condition component of an action specification. For an action $\phi(X)$ consider why its (non-trivial) pre-condition $\pi(X)$ might be written. The intention appears to be that the action a state S satisfying $\pi(c)$ the action $\phi(c)$ can be safely executed by updating S with the addlist and deletelist accordingly. Importantly, if S does not satisfy $\pi(c)$, then $\phi(c)$ must *not* be executed. This suggests that whenever S does not satisfy $\pi(c)$ but (parts of) the addlist and deletelist are nevertheless used to update S, the resulting state is incorrect. This looks rather formidable except that in fact much of its apparent complexity is already accounted for by the Add-Del postulate. Let the set of atoms in the pre-condition be Pre. Then the possible constraints can be expressed as:

$$\neg(\neg(p_1 \wedge \ldots \wedge p_k) \wedge C)$$

where $\{p_1, \ldots, p_k\} \subseteq Pre$ and C is one of the candidate action constraints from the Add-Del postulate.

An example of this is the pre-condition for the $stack(X, Y)$ action. Assume that the component $clear(Y)$ does not hold. By the constraint above this is equivalent to the existence of some Z (distinct from X) such that $on(Z, Y)$ holds. Then one possible constraint is $\neg(\neg clear(Y) \wedge on(X, Y))$ where the $on(X, Y)$ is from the addlist, and this formula is equivalent to $\neg(on(Z, Y) \wedge on(X, Y))$, another familiar constraint.

Since an action invariant is of the form "if $S \models C$, then after action ϕ $S' \models C$", the possible constraints that arise from considering preconditions are trivially action invariants because the precondition C is false in each of them.

4 System Contraints

We now examine how action invariants can be elevated to system constraints. In preparation for this we need some concepts that are analogous to well-known ones in dynamical sytems theory. By the notation $S\phi S'$ we mean that applying action ϕ to state S yields the state S'. This notation extends naturally to a sequence of actions $\phi^1, \ldots, \phi^n$ where $S_0\phi^1 S_1 \ldots \phi^n S_n$ has the obvious meaning, and we say that S_n is *reachable from* S_0 (via that action sequence). The actions ϕ^i will be from a set $\Phi = \{\phi_1, \ldots, \phi_m\}$ of actions, so to describe arbitrary sequences of actions on states using such actions we may say that the previous sequence $S_0, S_1, \ldots, S_n$ is a Φ-*trajectory*. Thus S' is reachable from S if there is a Φ-trajectory that begins with S and ends with S'. $Reach(S, \Phi)$ is the set of states reachable from S via the set Φ of actions; if Σ is a set of states, $Reach(\Sigma, \Phi)$ is the set $\bigcup_{S \in \Sigma} Reach(S, \Phi)$. Thus, $Reach(\_, \Phi)$ may be viewed as a map from sets of states to sets of states, i.e, if Γ is the set of all states, $Reach(\_, \Phi) : \Gamma \to \Gamma$.

Given an action ϕ let $\Sigma(\phi)$ denotes the states that satisfy the action invariants of ϕ, i.e. $\Sigma(\phi) = \{S | S \models \psi \text{ and } \psi \text{ is an invariant of } \phi\}$.

Proposition 2. $\Sigma(\phi)$ *is a fixed point of* $Reach(\_, \{\phi\})$.

Proof: If $S \in \Sigma(\phi)$ then by definition of $\Sigma(\phi)$, if S' is the result of action ϕ on S, $S' \in \Sigma(\phi)$. Hence, by induction, $\Sigma(\phi)$ is closed under any number of applications of ϕ, and therefore $\Sigma(\phi) \subseteq Reach(\Sigma(\phi), \{\phi\})$. On the other hand, if $S \in Reach(\Sigma(\phi), \{\phi\})$, there is a sequence $S_0, S_1, \ldots, S_n = S$ such that $S_0\phi S_1, S_1\phi S_2, \ldots, S_{n-1}\phi S$ and $S_0 \in \Sigma(\phi)$. By closure of $\Sigma(\phi)$ under repeated application of ϕ, $S \in \Sigma(\phi)$, so $Reach(\Sigma(\phi), \{\phi\}) \subseteq \Sigma(\phi)$.

What is the largest collection of such fixed points across all actions? To answer this question, let us consider two actions ϕ_1 and ϕ_2, and the sets $\Sigma(\phi_1)$ and $\Sigma(\phi_2)$. Also, for brevity we write $\phi(S)$ to mean the state S' that results after applying action ϕ to state S. Recall that if the invariants of ϕ are also invariants for all other actions then these invariants are system constraints. So if ϕ_1 and ϕ_2 were the only actions, a guess at the generalization of proposition 2 might be the following: $\Sigma(\phi_1) \cap \Sigma(\phi_2)$ is a fixed point of $Reach(\_, \{\phi_1, \phi_2\})$. There is a slight problem with this. While certainly $S \in \Sigma(\phi_1) \cap \Sigma(\phi_2)$ implies $\phi_1(S) \models \psi_1$ and $\phi_2(S) \models \psi_2$ for invariants ψ_1 of ϕ_1 and ψ_2 of ϕ_2, it may not be the case that $\phi_1(S) \models \psi_2$ or $\phi_2(S) \models \psi_1$. If we want ψ_1 and ψ_2 to be system invariants, what we really need is for each of them to be invariants also for the other action. In effect we need to have $\psi_1 \wedge \psi_2$ be an action invariant for both actions. This motivates the generalization below.

Let $\Sigma(\Phi)$ denote the states that satisfy the action invariants of every ϕ in Φ, i.e. $\Sigma(\Phi) = \{S | S \models \psi, \ \psi \ is \ an \ invariant \ of \ \phi, \ and \ \phi \in \Phi\}$. The following proposition has a proof which is a generalization of that of proposition 2.

Proposition 3. $\Sigma(\Phi)$ *is a fixed point of* $Reach(\_, \Phi)$.

As an example, the action constraints in the blocks world domain above are also system constraints.

We conclude with some observations about anomalous components of states in the blocks world that exemplify similar situations in other domains. A *local anomaly* is a part of a state that violates system constraints. In the STRIPS convention of ground atoms representing state, this is simply a collection of atoms (subset of the state) that do not satisfy a system constraint. We can summarize the observations below by saying that local anomalies can be *quarantined*.

Consider a state that has an atom $on(b, b)$. Ontologically this is nonsense, but nothing in the object-level STRIPS excludes it. It formally fails the pre-condition for all actions (block b is never $clear$!) that either tries to delete or move it, or to stack on it. So, if we begin with a state that has this we are stuck with it forever. But if we start with "normal" states we can never reach one that has such a local anomaly. What some people may find disturbing is this: unless we write a constraint that precludes such atoms, none of the action (and therefore, systems) constraints can exclude states from containing anomalous atoms. However, we may console ourselves with two facts. If we begin with non-anomalous states, then all trajectories will remain non-anomalous. And, if we had such anomalous atoms, in a sense they will be *irrelevant* as they can never participate in any action.

Now consider another kind of local anomaly for which there is provably no first-order constraint that excludes it. This example suffices to highlight the problem: let there be a chain of atoms $on(a_1, a_2), on(a_2, a_3), \ldots, on(a_{k-1}, a_k)$. This is just an elaboration of the pervious one, but to exclude it requires a formula for transitive closure — none exists if the chain length is not known. But the same consoling remarks apply to such chains.

5 Conclusion

We have re-visited an old problem in a new light using a very simple and familiar action specification language. In doing so we are able to explain in highly intuitive terms some results that are potentially useful in practical domains. In a somewhat more technical section we made connections with standard dynamical systems theory and fixed points to explain the connection between single actions and a family of actions.

Acknowledgement

The reviewers provided insightful and critical comments that helped us clarify our exposition. In particular, one reminded us about the converse methodology in databases to our approach, and this placed our report in a clearer perspective. The work of the first author was performed in the Kensington laboratory of the National ICT Australia, which is funded through the Australian Government's *Backing Australia's Ability* initiative, in part by the Australian Research Council.

References

[Fikes and Nilsson 71] Fikes, R. E. and Nilsson, N. J., " STRIPS: A New Approach to the Application of Theorem Proving to Problem Solving", *Artificial Intelligence*, 2, 1971, 189-208.

[Foo, et.al. 97] Foo, N., Nayak, A., Pagnucco, M., Peppas, P., and Zhang, Y., "Action Localness, Genericity and Invariants in STRIPS", Proceedings of the Fifteenth International Joint Conference on Artificial Intelligence, IJCAI'97, pp. 549-554, Nagoya, August 1997, Morgan Kaufmann.

[Lifschitz 86] Lifschitz, V., "On the Semantics of STRIPS", in *Reasoning about Actions and Plans*, ed. M. Georgeff and A. Lansky, Morgan Kaufmann Publishers, 1986, 1-9.

[Lin 04] Lin, F., "Discovering State Invariants", Proceedings of the Ninth International Conference on Principles of Knowledge Representation and Reasoning, KR'04, 536-544, Whistler, 2004.

[Shanahan 97] Shanahan, M., *Solving the Frame Problem: A Mathematical Investigation of the Common Sense Law of Inertia*, MIT Press, 1997.

[Lawley, Topor and Wallace 93] Lawley, M., Topor, R. and Wallace, M., "Using Weakest Preconditions to Simplify Integrity Constraint Checking", Proceedings of the Australian Database Conference, 1993.

[Zhang and Foo 96] Zhang, Y. and Foo, N., "Deriving Invariants and Constraints from Action Theories" , Fundamenta Informaticea, vol. 30, 23-41, 1996.

Embedding Memoization to the Semantic Tree Search for Deciding QBFs

Mohammad GhasemZadeh, Volker Klotz, and Christoph Meinel

FB-IV Informatik, University of Trier,
D-54286 Trier, Germany
{GhasemZadeh, klotz, meinel}@TI.Uni-Trier.DE

Abstract. Quantified Boolean formulas (QBFs) play an important role in artificial intelligence subjects, specially in planning, knowledge representation and reasoning [20]. In this paper we present ZQSAT (sibling of our FZQSAT [15]), which is an algorithm for evaluating quantified Boolean formulas. QBF is a language that extends propositional logic in such a way that many advanced forms of reasoning can be easily formulated and evaluated. ZQSAT is based on ZDD, which is a variant of BDD, and an adopted version of the DPLL algorithm. The program has been implemented in C using the CUDD package. The capability of ZDDs in storing sets of subsets efficiently enabled us to store the clauses of a QBF very compactly and led us to implement the search algorithm in such a way that we could store and reuse the results of all previously solved subformulas with few overheads. This idea along some other techniques, enabled ZQSAT to solve some standard QBF benchmark problems faster than the best existing QSAT solvers.

Keywords: DPLL, Zero-Suppressed Binary Decision Diagram (ZDD), Quantified Boolean Formula (QBF), Satisfiability, QSAT.

1 Introduction

Propositional satisfiability (SAT) is a central problem in computer science with numerous applications. SAT is the first and prototypical problem for the class of NP-complete problems. Many computational problems such as constraint satisfaction problems, many problems in graph theory and forms of planning can be formulated easily as instances of SAT.

Theoretical analysis has showed that some forms of reasoning such as: belief revision, non monotonic reasoning, reasoning about knowledge and STRIPS-like planning have computational complexity higher than the complexity of the SAT problem. These forms can be formulated by quantified Boolean formulas and be solved as instances of the QSAT problem . Quantified Boolean formula satisfiability (QSAT) is a generalization of the SAT problem. QSAT is the prototypical problem for the class of PSPACE-complete problems. With QBFs we can represent many classes of formulas more concisely than conventional Boolean formulas.

ZDDs are variants of BDDs. While BDDs are better suited for representing Boolean functions, ZDDs are better for representing sets of subsets. Considering all the variables appearing in a QBF propositional part as a set, the propositional part of the formula can be viewed as a set of subsets, this is why using ZDDs for representing a formula could potentially be beneficial. This idea is used in a number of related works [8, 10, 2] where the SAT problem is considered. They use ZDDs to store the CNF formula and the original DP algorithm to search its satisfiability. We also found ZDDs very suitable for representing and solving QSAT problems.

We represent the clauses in the same way in a ZDD, but we employ an adopted version of the DPLL [9] algorithm to search the solution. In fact, our adopted version simulates the "Semantic tree method in evaluating QBFs". It benefits from an adopted unit-mono-resolution operation which is very fast thanks to the data structure holding the formula. In addition, it stores all already solved subformulas along their solutions to avoid resolving same subproblems. Sometimes the split operation generates two subproblems which are equal. With ZDDs it is very easy to compare and discover their equality, therefore our algorithm can easily prevent solving both cases when it is not necessary. There are some benchmark problems which are known to be hard for DPLL (semantic tree) algorithms. ZQSAT is also a DPLL based algorithm, but it manages to solve those instances very fast. ZQSAT is still slow in some QBF instances, this is why we can not claim ZQSAT is the best conceivable algorithm, but it is the first work that shows how ZDDs along memoization can be used successfully in QBF evaluation.

2 Preliminaries

2.1 Quantified Boolean Formulas

Quantified Boolean formulas are extensions of propositional formulas (also known as Boolean formula). A Boolean formula like $(x \vee (\neg y \rightarrow z))$ is a formula built up from Boolean variables and Boolean operators like conjunction, disjunction, and negation. In quantified Boolean formulas, quantifiers may also occur in the formula, like in $\exists x(x \wedge \forall y(y \vee \neg z))$. The $\exists$ symbol is called existential quantifier and the $\forall$ symbol is called universal quantifier. A number of normal forms are known for each of the above families. Among them, in our research, the *prenex normal form* and *conjunctive normal form (CNF)* are important. In many problems including SAT and QSAT, normal forms do not affect the generality of the problem, instead they bring the problem in a form that can be solved more easily.

Definition 1. *A Boolean formula is in conjunctive normal form (CNF) if it is a conjunction of disjunctions of literals, that is, $\phi = c_1 \wedge c_2 \wedge \ldots \wedge c_n$, where $c_i = (l_{i1} \vee \ldots \vee l_{im_i})$ and l_{ij} is a negative or positive literal. The disjunctions are referred as clauses.*

Each Boolean formula can be transformed into a logically equivalent Boolean formula which is in conjunctive normal form (CNF). Generally this transformation can not be done efficiently.

Definition 2. *A QBF Φ is in prenex normal form, if it is in the form:*

$$\Phi = Q_1 V_1 Q_2 V_2 \ldots Q_n V_n \phi,$$

where $Q_i \in \{\forall, \exists\}$, V_i ($1 \leq i \leq n$) are disjoint sets of propositional variables and ϕ is a propositional formula over the variables $x_1, \ldots, x_n$. The expression $Q_1 V_1 Q_2 V_2 \ldots Q_n V_n$ is called the prefix and ϕ the matrix of Φ.

2.2 The DPLL Algorithm for the SAT Problem

Most former and recent SAT solvers are in some way extensions of the DPLL [9] algorithm. DPLL tries to find a satisfying assignment for a CNF formula by making an exhaustive search. Each variable is assigned with a truth-value (true or false) which leads to some simplifications of the function. Since the function is in CNF, the assignment can be done efficiently. If an assignment forces the formula to be reduced to false then a backtrack will take place to make another possible assignment. If none of the possible assignments satisfy the function then the function is unsatisfiable. In order to prune the search space we have to consider unit clauses. A unit clause is a clause with exactly one literal. For example in $f = (a \vee \neg b \vee \neg c) \wedge (a \vee \neg c \vee d) \wedge (b) \wedge (a \vee b \vee c)$, the third clause is a unit clause. Unit resolution is the assignment of proper truth values to the literals appearing in unit clauses and removing them from the formula. For instance, in the above example, b receives the value true, which lets f be simplified to: $f_1 = (a \vee \neg c) \wedge (a \vee \neg c \vee d)$. If all literals in a clause simplify without satisfying the clause then DPLL immediately returns "UNSATISFIABLE", but if all the clauses satisfy and be removed then it returns "SATISFIABLE". When no more simplification is possible, DPLL splits the simplified function over one of the remaining variables (which can receive either the value true or false). This step removes one variable, and consequently a number of clauses. Two smaller CNF formulas will be generated of which at least one must be satisfiable to make the original formula satisfiable.

2.3 The Semantic Tree Approach for the QSAT Problem

This method is very similar to the DPLL algorithm. It iteratively splits the problem of deciding a QBF of the form $Qx\,\Phi$ into two subproblems $\Phi[x = 1]$ and $\Phi[x = 0]$ (the unique assignment of each x respectively with true or false), and the following rules:

- $\exists x\,\Phi$ is valid iff $\Phi[x = 1]$ or $\Phi[x = 0]$ is valid.
- $\forall x\,\Phi$ is valid iff $\Phi[x = 1]$ and $\Phi[x = 0]$ is valid.

Figure 1 displays the pseudocode of this algorithm, which we have called QDPLL.

The differences between QDPLL (for QBFs) and the DPLL algorithm (for Boolean satisfiability) can be enumerated as follows:

1. In the Unit-Resolution step (line 1), if any universally quantified variable is found to be a unit clause then the procedure can immediately conclude the UNSAT result and terminate.
2. In the Mono-Reduction step (line 1), if any universally quantified variable is found to be a mono-literal, then it can be removed from all the clauses where it occurs (rather than removing the clauses, as it applies to existentially quantified mono literals). We call a literal *monotone* if its complementary literal does not appear in the matrix of the QBF. The Mono-Reduction step can result in new unit clauses. Therefore the procedure must continue line 1 as long as new simplifications are possible.

```
Boolean QDPLL( Prenex-CNF   F )
{
1   F=Simplify F by repeated Unit-Resolution removal of subsumed
      clauses and possible Mono-Reductions;

2   if (F is primitive ) return Solution;
    // the same as in DPLL, if F include Empty-Clause return
    // UNSAT, but if F is Empty return SATISFIABLE

3   F0,F1=choose x as the splitting variable; Split F;
              // Very little freedom in choosing variables.

4   Solution=DPLL(F0);
5   if (Solution==TRUE   and   Existential_Literal(x) ) return TRUE;
6   if (Solution==FALSE and   Univarsal_Literal(x)   ) return FALSE;

    // for the other two cases
7   return DPLL(F1);
}
```

Fig. 1. The semantic tree approach for QBFs

3. In the splitting step (line 3), there is a little freedom in choosing the splitting variable. In fact, in a block of consecutive variables under the same kind of quantifier we are allowed to consider any order, but before processing all the variables in the leftmost block we are not allowed to assign values to any variable from other blocks. In other words, Iterations of quantified blocks must be considered exactly in the same order as they appear in the QBF prefix. As an example in the QBF $\forall x_1 \forall x_2 \forall x_3 \exists y_1 \exists y_2 \exists y_3 \forall z_1 \forall z_2 \forall z_3 \phi$, all x_i must be assigned before any assignment for any y_j take place, in the similar way, all y_j must be assigned before any assignment for any z_k take place, but we are allowed to consider any order when we are processing the variables of for example x block.

4. After solving one of the branches, even if the result is true (line 7), it could be necessary to solve the other branch as well. Due to universal variables allowed to appear in QBFs, the false result (line 6) for one of the branches can signify the UNSAT result and terminate the procedure without checking the other branch.

From another point of view, this method searches the solution in a tree of variable assignments. Figure 2 [13] displays the semantic tree for:

$$\Phi = \exists y_1 \forall x \exists y_2 \exists y_3 (C_1 \wedge C_2 \wedge C_3 \wedge C_4),$$

where:

$C_1 = (\neg y_1 \vee x \vee \neg y_2), C_2 = (y_2 \vee \neg y_3), C_3 = (y_2 \vee y_3),$ and $C_4 = (y_1 \vee \neg x \vee \neg y_2).$

We can follow the tree and realize that Φ is invalid. A very interesting point can be easily seen in the tree. It is the duplication problem in semantic tree method, namely, the same subproblem can appear two or more times during the search procedure. In a

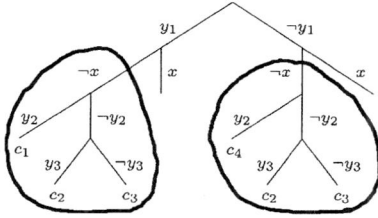   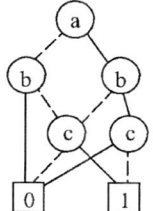 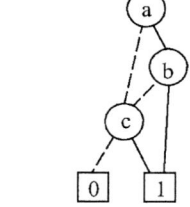

Fig. 2. A semantic tree proof   **Fig. 3.** BDD versus ZDD

big QBF this situation can frequently happen in different levels. The superiority of our algorithm which we will present later, is its possibility to detect and avoid to examine such duplications repeatedly.

2.4 BDDs Versus ZDDs

Here we give a very short background for BDDs and ZDDs. Several years ago, Binary Decision Diagrams (BDDs) [5, 6, 21, 3, 16] and their variants [4] entered the scene of the computer science. Since that time, they have been used successfully in industrial CAD tools. In many applications, specially in problems involving sparse sets of subsets, the size of the BDD grows very fast and causes inefficient processing. This problem can be solved by a variant of BDD, called ZDD (Zero suppressed Binary Decision Diagrams) [17, 1]. These diagrams are similar to BDDs with one of the underlying principles modified. While BDDs are better suited for the representation of functions, ZDDs are better suited for the representation of covers (set of subsets). Considering all the variables appearing in a QBF (propositional part) as a set, the propositional part of the formula can be viewed as a set of subsets, this is why using ZDDs for representing a formula could potentially be beneficial. As an example [18], in Figure 3, the left diagram displays the ZDD representing $S = \{\{a,b\}, \{a,c\}, \{c\}\}$, and the right diagram displays $F = (a \wedge b \wedge \neg c) \vee (a \wedge \neg b \wedge c) \vee (\neg a \wedge \neg b \wedge c)$, which is the characteristic function of S. In a ZDD (or BDD) we represent an internal node by $P(x, \Gamma_0, \Gamma_1)$ where x is the label of the node, and Γ_1, Γ_0 are SubZDDs rooted in it 'Then-child' and 'Else-child' respectively. The size of a ZDD Γ, denoted by $|\Gamma|$, is the number of its internal nodes.

3 Our Algorithm

ZQSAT is the name we used for our QSAT solver. The major points which are specific to our algorithm are:

1. Using ZDDs to represent the QBF matrix (the formula clauses). (We adopted this idea from [8, 10, 2] then established the specific rules suitable for QBF evaluation).
2. Embedding memoization to overcome mentioned duplication problem (to avoid solving the same subproblem repeatedly).

Figure 4 displays the pseudocode for MQDPLL, which stands for our 'DPLL with memoization' procedure. This procedure forms the search strategy used by ZQSAT.

```
Boolean MQDPLL( Prenex-CNF   F  )
  {
1  if ( F is Primitive or AlreadySolved ) return Solution;
2  S=Simplify F by repeated Unit-Resolution, removal of
      subsumed clauses and possible MonoLiteral-Reductions;
3  if ( S is Primitive or AlreadySolved )
      {Add F along with the Solution to SolvedTable;
      return Solution; }

4  F0,F1=choose x as the splitting variable then Split S;
5  Solution=DPLL(F0);  // Why this branch? Read in text !!
6  if (F0==F1) or
      (Solution==TRUE  and  Existential-Literal(x) ) or
      (Solution==FALSE and  Univarsal-Literal(x)    )
      {Add F along with the Solution to SolvedTable;
      return Solution; }
7  Solution=DPLL(F1);
8  Add F along with the Solution to SolvedTable;
   return Solution;
  }
```

Fig. 4. MQDPLL: Our 'DPLL with memoization' procedure

MQDPLL is different from QDPLL in some aspects. Firstly, it benefits from a memoization strategy (dynamic programming tabulation method) to store and reuse the results of already solved subproblems (lines 1, 3, 6, 8 in the above pseudocode). Secondly, the situation where the two subfunctions f_0 and f_1 are equal can be detected and the subproblem would be solved only once (line 6).

In line 4, the algorithm needs to choose a variable for the splitting operation. At this point we must respect the order of iterations of quantification blocks, but when we are working with a quantification block we are allowed to choose any variable order. In our implementation we used the order which appears in the initial QBF formula. In fact we tried to investigate other possibilities, but since we obtained no benefits in our first effort we did not continue to investigate the issue in detail. We believe in this regard we can potentially find useful heuristics in our future research.

In line 5, the algorithm needs to choose the next branch (F0 or F1) to continue the search process. There are a number of possibilities like: always F0 first, always F1 first, random choice, according to the number of nodes in the ZDDs representing F0 and F1, according to the indices appearing in the root nodes of the ZDDs representing F0 and F1, Considering the number of positive/negative appearance of the variables in F0 and F1 clauses and so on. We tried most of these possibilities and realized that in our implementation they behave more or less the same, but we still believe that at this point we can potentially improve the performance of our algorithm.

Storing all already solved subproblems and detecting the equality of two subproblems (functions) is usually very expensive. We managed to overcome these difficulties thanks to ZDDs. This data structure lets us to store the QBF matrix very efficiently and allowed us to store every subfunction created in the splitting step or obtained after the simplification operations, with no or very little overheads (see Figure 5).

3.1 Using ZDDs to Represent a CNF Formula

A ZDD can be used to represent a set of subsets. We use this property to represent the body of the QBF, which is supposed to be a propositional function in CNF. Since each propositional CNF formula ϕ can be represented as a set of sets of literals $[\phi]$ we can represent a CNF formula by means of a ZDD. In ZDDs, each path from the root to the 1-terminal corresponds to one clause of the set. In a path, if we pass through $x_i = 1$ (toward its 'Then-child'), then x_i exists in the clause, but if we pass through $x_i = 0$ (toward its 'Else-child') or we don't pass through x_i, then x_i does not exist in the clause.

To represent the sets of clauses, i.e., a set of sets of literals, we assign two successive ZDD indices to each variable, one index for positive and the next for its complemented form [8]. Figure 5 shows how this idea works for a small CNF formula [10, 2]. In ZDDs (like BDDs), the variable order can considerably affect the shape and size of the resulting graph. As we pointed out earlier, in evaluating QBFs, the variable selection is strongly restricted. In general the order of the prefix must be respected. In representing and evaluating a QBF like $\Phi = \exists x_1 \ldots \forall x_n \phi$ using ZDDs, we consider the extended literal order $x_1 \leq \neg x_1 \leq \ldots \leq x_n \leq \neg x_n$. The following theorem [8] gives a good estimate for the size of the ZDD representing a CNF formula in the mentioned method.

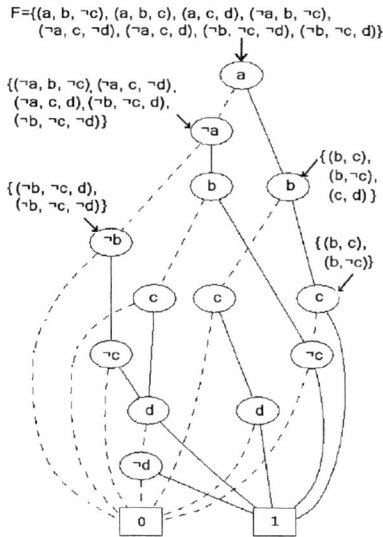

Fig. 5. ZDD encoding of a CNF formula

Theorem 1. *Let f be a formula in conjunctive normal form. The number of nodes of the ZDD Γ_f encoding the set of clauses of f is always at most equal to the total number of literals of f.*

Due to the page limit we removed the proof (please contact the authors for the proof).

3.2 Benefits of Using ZDDs Along Our MQDPLL-Algorithm

In Figure 5, we can also see another interesting characteristic of the ZDDs, that is, their possibility of sharing nodes and subgraphs. In fact each node in a ZDD stands for a unique function. In our search procedure, after the simplification operations and after the splitting step, new functions arise. We noticed that many of these functions are the same, therefore we let ZQSAT to retain all already produced functions along their solutions, to prevent resolving the same functions (memoization). We mentioned earlier, this idea is embedding dynamic programming/memoization to the DPLL Algorithm. In fact, after inserting this possibility, ZQSAT managed to solve the instances known to be hard for DPLL-based methods very fast (see Table 1).

Considering ZDDs as the data structure holding the formula affects the search algorithm and its complexity considerably. Operations like detecting the unit clauses, detecting mono variables, performing the unit/mono resolution and detecting the SAT/UNSAT conditions depend strongly on the data structure holding the formula. Here we give some rules concerning these operations. The rules can be derived from the basic properties known for QBFs, some lemmas presented in [7] and the properties of representing CNF clauses in a ZDD. Performing these operations with other data structures is often much slower. Reminding that Minato [17] has presented efficient algorithms for set operations on ZDDs. His algorithms are mostly based on dynamic programming and efficient caching techniques. We used them (through the CUDD package) in our research work.

In the following rules we suppose we have read the clauses and represented them in a ZDD Γ. The rules are applicable when we are examining the satisfiability of Γ:

Rule 1 **(Finding All Unit Clauses):** A unit clause is a clause with exactly one literal. If the literal is universally quantified, then the clause and subsequently the QBF is unsatisfiable. If the literal is existentially quantified, then the truth value of the literal can be determined uniquely. Let $\Gamma = P(l_1, \Gamma_1, \Gamma_2)$ be a ZDD where l_1 is the topmost literal in the variable order, then the literal l_2 is a unit clause in Γ iff:

- $l_2 = l_1$ and Γ_1 contains the empty set. In other words, the literal appearing in the root of the ZDD is a unit clause if moving to its Then-child followed by moving always toward the Else-child leads us to the 1-terminal.
- $l_2 \in var(\Gamma_2)$ and l_2 is a unit clause in Γ_2. Note: if $l_2 \in var(\Gamma_1)$ then it can not be a unit clause.

Finding all unit clauses can be accomplished in at most $(2 \cdot n - 1)/2$ steps, where n is the number of variables in the set of clauses represented by Γ.

Rule 2 **(Trivial UNSAT):** If x is a unit-clause and it is universally quantified, then the QBF formula is unsatisfiable. This operation needs only one comparison instruction and can be done during the step of finding the unit clauses.

Rule 3 **(Trivial UNSAT):** If x is an existentially quantified unit-clause and its complementary literal is also a unit clause, then the QBF formula is unsatisfiable. This operation can be performed during the identification of unit clauses.

Rule 4 **(Variable Assignment/Splitting Operation):** Let $\Gamma = (x, \Gamma_1, \Gamma_2)$ be our ZDD. Considering x to be `true`, simplifies Γ to $Union(Then(\Gamma_2), Else(\Gamma_2))$. Similarly considering x to be `false`, simplifies Γ to $Union(\Gamma_1, Else(\Gamma_2))$. This operation is quadratic in the size of the ZDD.

Rule 5 **(Propagation of a Unit Clause):** If x is a unit clause and is located in the root node then Γ can be simplified to Γ_2. If Γ_2 has complement of x in its root then the result will be: $Union(Then(\Gamma_2), Else(\Gamma_2))$. On the other hand, if x is a unit clause but not located in the root node then, first we must remove all the clauses including x as a literal from Γ by $\Gamma' = Subset0(\Gamma, x)$. After this we must remove the complementary literal of x, denoted by $\overline{x}$ from Γ' by $\Gamma'' = Union(Subset1(\Gamma', \overline{x}), Subset0(\Gamma', \overline{x}))$.

Rule 6 **(Mono Variables):** A literal l is monotone if its complementary literal does not appear in the QBF. If l is existentially quantified we can replace it by `true`, which simplifies Γ to Γ_2, but if l is universally quantified we must replace it by `false`, which simplifies Γ to $Union(\Gamma_1, \Gamma_2)$.

Rule 7 **(Detecting SAT/UNSAT):** If the ZDD reduces to the 1-terminal then the QBF is SAT. Similarly, if the ZDD reduces to 0-terminal then the QBF is UNSAT. This operation needs only one comparison instruction.

These rules are the basic stones in implementing the operations needed in ZQSAT, specially the unit resolution and mono literal reduction in MQDPLL procedure.

4 Experimental Results

We evaluated our algorithm by different known benchmarks presented in QBFLIB (QBF satisfiability LIBrary) [19]. We run ZQSAT along the best existing QBF-Solvers such as QuBE [12], Decide [20], Semprop [14] and QSolve [11]. The platform was a Linux system on a 3000-Mhz, 2G-RAM desktop computer. We also considered 1G-RAM limit which were never used totally by any of the above programs, and a 900 second timeout which was enough for most solvers to solve many of benchmark problems.

The results we obtained show that ZQSAT is very efficient and in many cases better than state-of-the-art QSAT solvers. It solves many instances which are known hard for DPLL (semantic-tree) method, in a small fraction of a second (see Table 1 and Table 2). Like almost all other QSAT solvers it is inefficient in solving random QBFs. According to the well known counting theorem, the representation and evaluation of random instances could not be done efficiently [16]. In the following we give more detailed information.

Structured Formulas: Most structured Formulas come form real word problems represented as a QBF. We used the benchmarks of Letz [19] and Rintanen [20]. The benchmarks of Letz include instances known to be hard for DPLL (tree-based) QBF solvers. ZQSAT is also a DPLL based algorithm, but it manages to solve those instances very fast. In a real problem there are always some connections between its components, which remain in some form in its corresponding QBF representation. This feature causes similar subproblems to be generated during the search step, also assignment of values to

Table 1. Comparison of the runtimes of different QBF solvers over a number of QBFs. The instances are hard for tree-based QBF solvers (see Letz [19])

| Problem | ZQSAT | QuBE | | Decide | Semprop | QSolve | Z | Nr. Lookup | | No. Mem. |
tree-exa-		BJ	Rel					Total	Succ	Rec.Calls
10-10	< .01	< .01	< .01	< .01	< .01	< .01	1	49	14	1277
10-15	< .01	< .01	< .01	0.06	0.01	< .01	1	79	24	40957
10-20	< .01	< .01	0.01	1.89	0.27	< .01	1	109	34	1310717
10-25	< .01	0.01	0.07	63.95	8.51	< .01	1	139	44	not solved
10-30	< .01	0.11	0.75	(?)	273.28	0.03	1	169	54	not solved
2-10	< .01	< .01	< .01	< .01	< .01	< .01	1	31	6	not solved
2-15	< .01	< .01	< .01	0.01	< .01	< .01	1	51	11	not solved
2-20	< .01	0.01	< .01	0.1	0.01	< .01	1	71	16	not solved
2-25	< .01	0.12	< .01	1.16	0.1	0.04	1	91	21	not solved
2-30	< .01	1.29	< .01	12.9	1.06	0.53	1	111	26	not solved
2-35	< .01	14.42	< .01	144.16	11.98	5.85	1	131	31	not solved
2-40	< .01	158.41	< .01	(?)	130.19	65.73	1	151	36	not solved
2-45	< .01	(?)	< .01	(?)	(?)	729.7	1	171	41	not solved
2-50	< .01	(?)	< .01	(?)	(?)	(?)	1	191	46	not solved
(?): Not solved in 900 seconds										

variables causes sharp simplification on generated subformulas. Therefore, our memoization idea helps very much in these circumstances. Table 1 shows how ZQSAT is faster than other recent QBF solvers in evaluating these benchmark problems.

The four rightmost columns in the table are provided to show the role and effect of our memoization idea. The two columns which stand for the number of lookups (total, successful) give us an estimate of the hit ratio, i.e. 'successful lookups' versus 'all lookups', which in our implementation is the same as the total recursive DPLL calls'. We must be careful analyzing these numbers, because the number of total calls depends strongly (sometimes exponentially) on the number of successful lookups. In order to avoid such a misinterpretation we provided the rightmost column which displays the number of DPLL recursive calls when no memoization is considered. In this condition our implementation only managed to solve three smallest instances of Letz benchmarks (in above mentioned platform and our 900 second time out). The column labeled with 'Z' is in connection with construction of the initial ZDD for the formula. In fact we realized that even in failing benchmarks, ZQSAT managed to make the initial ZDD soon.

Next, we considered the benchmarks of Rintanen, where some problems from AI planning and other structured formulas are included. They include some instances form blocks world problem, Towers of Hanoi, long chains of implications, as well as the bw-large.a and bw-large.b blocks world problems. The experimental results for these benchmarks are presented in Table 2. This table shows that ZQSAT works well on most instances. We are comparable and in many cases better than other solvers. Let us mention that 'Decide' is specially designed to work efficiently for planning instances.

In Table 2 we see that our implementation could not solve any instance of blocksworld. We observed that MQDPLL benefited very few times from the already solved subformulas. In other words, our pruning method was not successful for this problem. In fact this is a matter of pruning strategy, different pruning strategies behave differently facing various sets of QBF benchmarks.

Table 2. Comparison of different QBF solvers on a number of QBFs from the set of benchmarks of Rintanen [20, 19]

Problem tree-exa-	ZQSAT	QuBE BJ	QuBE Rel	Decide	Semprop	QSolve	Z	Nr. Lookup Total	Nr. Lookup Succ	No. Mem. Rec.Calls
B*3i.5.4	(?)	(?)	(?)	1.84	(?)	(?)	1	(?)	(?)	not solved
B*3ii.4.3	(?)	0.81	0.01	0.01	2.25	(?)	1	(?)	(?)	not solved
B*3ii.5.2	(?)	23.25	0.41	0.02	65.76	(?)	1	(?)	(?)	not solved
B*3ii.5.3	(?)	(?)	33.12	0.36	160.93	(?)	1	(?)	(?)	not solved
B*3iii.4	(?)	0.25	0.01	< .01	12	(?)	1	(?)	(?)	not solved
B*3iii.5	(?)	(?)	0.48	0.1	0.53	(?)	1	(?)	(?)	not solved
B*4i.6.4	(?)	(?)	264.76	1.28	(?)	(?)	1	(?)	(?)	not solved
B*4ii.6.3	(?)	(?)	27.64	1.1	(?)	(?)	1	(?)	(?)	not solved
B*4ii.7.2	(?)	(?)	(?)	2.28	(?)	(?)	1	(?)	(?)	not solved
B*4iii.6	(?)	(?)	13.62	0.59	(?)	(?)	1	(?)	(?)	not solved
B*4iii.7	(?)	(?)	(?)	67.28	(?)	(?)	1	(?)	(?)	not solved
C*12v.13	2.66	0.12	1.41	0.19	0.06	1.96	1	72	11	12310
C*13v.14	3.76	0.26	3.44	0.38	0.13	6.52	1	78	12	24600
C*4v.15	5.27	0.55	9.17	0.77	0.27	21.98	1	84	13	49178
C*15v.16	7.08	1.22	24.21	1.62	0.54	62.53	1	90	14	98332
C*16v.17	9.43	3.09	60.68	3.31	1.14	205.72	1	96	15	196638
C*17v.18	12.49	5.86	148.58	6.9	2.43	633.44	1	102	16	393248
C*18v.19	16.2	12.87	352.21	14.4	5.12	(?)	1	108	17	786466
C*19v.20	21.01	31.93	840.26	30.29	10.59	(?)	1	114	18	1572900
C*20v.21	26.69	91.23	(?)	61.93	22.24	(?)	1	120	19	3145766
C*21v.22	33.17	195.12	(?)	129.24	46.61	(?)	1	126	20	not solved
C*22v.23	40.8	494.26	(?)	272.24	98.53	(?)	1	132	21	not solved
C*23v.24	50.24	(?)	(?)	571.12	202.3	(?)	1	138	22	not solved
i*02	< .01	< .01	< .01	< .01	< .01	< .01	1	8	0	8
i*04	< .01	< .01	< .01	< .01	< .01	< .01	1	14	0	14
i*06	< .01	< .01	< .01	0.01	< .01	< .01	1	20	0	20
i*08	< .01	< .01	< .01	0.14	0.02	0.01	1	26	0	26
i*10	< .01	0.01	< .01	1.12	0.14	0.07	1	32	0	32
i*12	< .01	0.04	< .01	8.69	1.04	0.5	1	38	0	38
i*14	< .01	0.18	< .01	65.27	7.74	3.69	1	44	0	44
i*16	< .01	0.74	< .01	482.97	56.88	27.04	1	50	0	50
i*18	< .01	3.12	< .01	(?)	423.41	200.82	1	56	0	56
i*20	< .01	13.06	< .01	(?)	(?)	(?)	1	62	0	62
T*10.1.iv.20	2.65	(?)	(?)	0.58	(?)	(?)	1	43	0	43
T*16.1.iv.32	26.08	(?)	(?)	7.38	(?)	(?)	1	66	0	66
T*2.1.iv.3	< .01	< .01	< .01	< .01	< .01	< .01	1	10	0	10
T*2.1.iv.4	< .01	< .01	< .01	< .01	< .01	< .01	1	10	0	10
T*6.1.iv.11	(?)	2.1	205.75	4.78	2.25	3.66	1	(?)	(?)	not solved
T*6.1.iv.12	0.24	0.79	29.44	0.04	0.4	2.65	1	27	0	27
T*7.1.iv.13	(?)	37.45	(?)	63.87	39.7	134.02	1	(?)	(?)	not solved
T*7.1.iv.14	0.5	12.25	521.59	0.09	5.22	64.17	1	30	0	30
(?): Not solved in 900 seconds										

Random Formulas: For random formulas we used the benchmarks of Massimo Narizzano [19]. ZQSAT is inefficient in big unstructured instances. ZDDs are very good in representing sets of subsets, but they are less useful, if the information is unstructured. ZDDs explore and use the relation between the set of subsets. Therefore if there is no relation between the subsets (clauses) then it could not play its role very well. Fortunately, in real word problems there are always some connections between the problem components. In our effort to investigate why ZQSAT is slow on the given instances, we found that in these cases the already solved subformulas were never or too few times used again, also the mono and unit resolution functions could not reduce the size of the (sub)formula noticeably.

5 Conclusion

In this paper we have presented ZQSAT, an algorithm to evaluate quantified Boolean formulas. The experimental results show how it is comparable and in some cases faster than the best existing QBF solvers. However, we still do not claim ZQSAT is the best conceivable algorithm, but it shows how ZDDs along memoization can be used successfully in QBF evaluation.

References

1. Olaf Achröer and Ingo Wegener. The Theory of Zero-Suppressed BDDs and the Number of Knight's Tours. *Formal Methods in System Design*, 13(3), November 1998.
2. Fadi A. Aloul, Maher N. Mneimneh, and Karem A. Sakallah. ZBDD-Based Backtrack Search SAT Solver. In *International Workshop on Logic and Synthesis (IWLS)*, pages 131–136, New Orleans, Louisiana, 2002.
3. www.bdd-portal.org. http://www.bdd-portal.org/.
4. Jochen Bern, Christoph Meinel, and Anna Slobodová. OBDD-Based Boolean manipulation in CAD beyound current limits. In *Proceedings 32nd ACM/IEEE Design Automation Conference*, pages 408–413, San Francisco, CA, 1995.
5. Randal E. Bryant. Graph-based algorithms for Boolean function manipulation. *IEEE Transactions on Computers*, C-35:677–691, 1986.
6. Randal E. Bryant and Christoph Meinel. *Ordererd Binary Decision Diagrams in Electronic Design Automation*, chapter 11. Kluwer Academic Publishers, 2002.
7. Marco Cadoli, Marco Schaerf, Andrea Giovanardi, and Massimo Giovanardi. An Algorithm to Evaluate Quantified Boolean Formulae and Its Experimental Evaluation. *Journal of Automated Reasoning*, 28(2):101–142, 2002.
8. Philippe Chatalic and Laurent Simon. Multi-Resolution on Compressed Sets of Cluases. In *Proceedings of the 12th IEEE International Conference on Tools with Artificial Intelligence (ICTAI'00)*, 2000.
9. M. Davis, G. Logemann, and D. Loveland. A machine program for theorem proving. *Communication of the ACM*, 5:394–397, 1962.
10. Karem A. Sakallah Fadi A. Aloul, Maher N. Mneimneh. Backtrack Search Using ZBDDs. In *International Workshop on Logic and Synthesis (IWLS)*, page 5. University of Michigan, June 2001.
11. Rainer Feldmann, Burkhard Monien, and Stefan Schamberger. A Distributed Algorithm to Evaluate Quantified Boolean Formulae. In *Proceedings of the 17th National Conference on Artificial Intelligence (AAAI-2000)*, 2000.
12. Enrico Giunchiglia, Massimo Narizzano, and Armando Tacchella. QUBE: A System for Deciding Quantified Boolean Formulas Satisfiability. In *Proceedings of the International Joint Conference on Automated Reasoning*, pages 364–369, 2001.
13. Reinhold Letz. Efficient Decision Procedures for Quantified Boolean Formulas. Vorlesung WS 2002/2003 TU Muenchen: Logikbasierte Entscheidungsverfahren.
14. Reinhold Letz. Lemma and Model Caching in Decision Procedures for Quantified Boolean Formulas. In *Proceedings of TABLEAUX 2002*, pages 160–175. Springer Berlin, 2002.
15. C. Meinel M. GhasemZadeh, V. Klotz. FZQSAT: A QSAT Solver for QBFs in Prenex NNF (A Useful Tool for Circuit Verification) . In *International Workshop on Logic and Synthesis (IWLS)*, pages 135–142. California, USA, June 2004.
16. Christoph Meinel and Thorsten Theobald. *Algorithms and Data Structures in VLSI Design*. Springer, 1998.

17. S. Minato. Zero-suppressed BDDs for set Manipulation in Combinatorial Problems. In *proceedings of the 30th ACM/IEEE Design Automation Conference*, 1993.
18. Alan Mishchenko. An Introduction to Zero-Suppressed Binary Decision Diagrams. http://www.ee.pdx.edu/ alanmi/research/dd/zddtut.pdf, June 2001.
19. QBFLIB - Quantified Boolean Formulas Satisfiability Library. http://www.mrg.dist.unige.it/ qube/qbflib/.
20. Jussi Rintanen. Improvements to the Evaluation of Quantified Boolean Formulae. In *Proceedings of the 16th International Joint Conference on Artificial Intelligence (IJCAI-99)*, pages 1192–1197, 1999.
21. Ingo Wegener. *Branching Programs and Binary Decision Diagrams – Theory and Applications*. SIAM Monographs on Discrete Mathematics and Applications, 2000.

On Possibilistic Case-Based Reasoning for Selecting Partners in Multi-agent Negotiation

Jakub Brzostowski and Ryszard Kowalczyk

School of Information Technology,
Swinburne University of Technology, Hawthorn, Victoria 3122, Australia
{jbrzostowski, rkowalczyk}@it.swin.edu.au

Abstract. The paper proposes an approach for selecting partners in multi-agent negotiation with the use of possibilistic case-based reasoning. It predicts the possibility of successful negotiation with other agents based on their past negotiation behaviour and the derived qualitative expected utility for the current situation. The proposed approach allows the agents to select their most prospective negotiation partners based on a small sample of historical cases of previous negotiations even if they are different from the current situation. Partner selection models for both independent and correlated negotiation agents are detailed and demonstrated with simple scenarios.

1 Introduction

Negotiation is a decentralised decision-making process of finding efficient agreements between two or more partners in the presence of limited common knowledge and conflicting preferences. It is a key mechanism for distributing tasks, sharing resources, composing services and forming coalitions in multi-agent environments (e.g. [1], [2]). In relatively small environments a self-interested agent can typically achieve its best results by negotiating with all agents that offer their services (also resources, capabilities etc) and then choosing an agreement or deriving a compound agreement that best satisfies its negotiation objectives (e.g. maximal payoff). However negotiation can be expensive in terms of the computational time and resources, and it can also be impractical to negotiate with a large number of agents, especially in open dynamic environments. More importantly it is always desirable to negotiate with the agents with whom there is a higher chance of successful negotiation and reaching better agreements. Therefore selection of most prospective partners for negotiation is of critical importance to the practicality and efficiency of multi-agent negotiation.

The problem of partner selection is related to coalition formation that has widely been studied in game theory and multi-agent interactions. However most of the work in that area is concerned with decision mechanisms for forming coalitions, and optimal coalition structures and their pay-off divisions (e.g. [3], [4]), with little devotion to the negotiation partner selection context. A related work by Banerjee and Sen [5] considers the problem of an agent deciding on which partnership of other agents to interact with given a number of the required interactions and a model of the environment in the form of payoff structures of each of these partnerships. The proposed probabilistic decision theory based procedure for making the partner selection requires a considerable history of repeated interactions for deriving probability distributions and makes a strong assumption of the availability of the payoff structure for the partnership. The selection problem of agents for negotiation has been addressed by Fatima et al in [1] where the authors study the influence of the agents information states on the negotiation equilibrium. The results obtained are useful for decision making in situations where an agent has the option of choosing whom to negotiate with on the basis of the amount of information that agents have about their opponents.

In this paper we propose an approach for selecting partners in multi-agent negotiation with the use of possibilistic case-based reasoning. It employs the principles of possibility based decision theory [6] for predicting the possibility of successful negotiation with other agents based on their past negotiation behaviour and the derived qualitative expected utility for the main agent. This method does not assume any specific payoff structure and allows the agent to select its most prospective negotiation partners based on a small sample of historical cases of previous negotiations even if they are different from the current situation. The proposed approach resembles some principles of the possibilistic case-based reasoning used to design bidding strategies in agent auctions presented in [7][8]. However our approach focuses on the partner selection problem that can involve different combinations of agents rather then deciding on a value of the single attribute bid. Moreover our approach considers situations of both independent and correlated negotiation agents and proposes the corresponding possibilistic case-based reasoning models using the discrete form of possibility distribution.

The remainder of the paper is organized as follows. Section 2 briefly presents some preliminaries including the problem outline and the principles of possibility-based decision theory. The possibilistic case-based decision models of the indepependent and correlated case-based reasoning for selecting negotiation partners are detailed in Section 3. Illustrative examples of calculations for the proposed models are presented in Section 4. Finally, Section 5 presents the generalization of the models, and the conclusions and further work are presented in Section 6.

2 Preliminaries

2.1 Problem Definition

There are a number of agents offering services to the main agent that can use them individually or aggregate in a compound service. The main agent needs to select one or more agents as the most prospective negotiation partners with whom the possibility of successful negotiation and reaching the best agreement is the highest. The selection procedure needs to take into account potential dependencies between the prospective partners. We apply possibility based decision theory [6] to model the negotiation behaviour of the agents. Possibility theory is a complementary approach to probability theory. It provides the decision theoretical basis for prediction of the outcomes based on small historical data. If the set of historical data is sufficiently large a statistical approach could be used for calculating the probability of occurrence of particular outcome as an alternative. However if there are very few cases of repeated situations the probability theory can be less appropriate. We apply case-based reasoning assuming a principle that: *"the more similar are the situations, the more possible that the outcomes are similar"*. This principle allows us to apply the information stored in the history of previous cases to the current problem even if a sample of the historical data consists some inconsistencies such as two cases with the same situation but different outcomes.

2.2 Possibility-Based Decision Theory

The main assumption of Possibility-based Decision Theory [6] is that every decision d induces a possibility distribution describing uncertainty about the actual outcome. Let $X = \{x_1, \ldots, x_p\}$ denote a set of outcomes and d is a decision or act. Then the possibility distribution π_d is a function specifying which outcome is more plausible after making a decision d: $\pi_d : X \rightarrow V$, where V is a linear valuation scale with $inf(V) = 0$ and $sup(V) = 1$. The utility function $u(x)$ assigns to each outcome a degree of preference in a set U: $u : X \rightarrow U$. Similarly $inf(U) = 0$ and $sup(U) = 1$. It is often assumed that $U = V$ [6]. Choosing the best decision means to choose possibility distribution by which the value of some functional $\mathcal{U}$ is the highest [9]. If $\mathcal{U}(\pi_d) \leq \mathcal{U}(\pi_{d'})$ then we prefer the decision d' over d ($d \preceq d'$). The functional $\mathcal{U}$ may be defined in the terms of pessimistic and optimistic qualitative utilities:

$$QU^-(\pi|u) = min_{x \in X} max(1 - \pi(x), u(x))$$

$$QU^+(\pi|u) = max_{x \in X} min(\pi(x), u(x))$$

where $QU^-(\pi|u)$ and $QU^+(\pi|u)$ are neccesity and possibility measures respectively or in other words, the Sugeno integrals of the utility function u with respect to the necessity and possibility measures respectively [6].

3 Possibilistic Case-Based Decision Model

To find partners for negotiation we calculate the qualitative expected utility based on the possibility of succesfull negotiation with other agents. To do this we model negotiation behaviour of other agents and specify the utility of main agent. The issues of negotiation are attributes corresponding to the agents providing services. This attributes may be availibilities (or other aggregated characteristics) of services provided by agents which we are negotiating with. Without losing the generality we initially consider the main agent negotiating with two other agents. (the generalised case for multiple agents is presented later) Let (a_1^t, a_2^t) denote the negotiation requirement of the main agent where $a_i^t \in [0, 1]$.

We assume that the agents will not offer more than the requirement. Therefore our decion space is a cartesian product defined by a rectangle $[0, a_1^t] \times [0, a_2^t]$.

We store the historical data in a following way. Every situation i is described by four parameters $s^i = (a_1^i, a_2^i, c_1^i, c_2^i)$ and every outcome is described by two parameters $o^i = (\Delta a_1^i, \Delta a_2^i)$ where

- a_1^i and a_2^i the initial requirements of main agent in the i-th negotiation with the first and second agent
- c_0^i and c_1^i parameters specyfing main agent's utility during the i-th negotiation
- Δa_1^i and Δa_2^i values of the agreement after the i-th negotiation with the first and second agent proportional to the requirement

We define utility function of the main agent as $\nu(x_1, x_2) = p(x_1 \otimes x_2)$ where:

$$p(x) = \begin{cases} 1 & \text{if } x > c_1^t \\ \frac{x - c_0^t}{c_1^t - c_0^t} & \text{if } c_0^t \leq x \leq c_1^t \\ 0 & \text{if } x < c_0^t \end{cases}$$

where x are all possible outcomes of negotiation with other agents obtained as an aggregation: $x = x_1 \otimes x_2$. $\otimes$ is a t-norm and we assure it as the product operator $x = x_1 \cdot x_2$ in our further calculations.

Assume that we have a history of $t - 1$ negotiations for other agents H^{t-1}:

$$H^{t-1} = \{r^i = (s^i, o^i); i \leq t - 1\}$$

An example of the history is presented in Table 1.

Table 1. Example of history with five cases and the current situation

i	a_1^i	a_2^i	c_0^i	c_1^i	Δa_1^i	Δa_2^i
1	0.9	0.8	0.2	0.6	0.5	0.62
2	0.8	0.6	0.35	0.4	0.62	0.66
3	0.85	0.7	0.25	0.4	0.58	0.81
4	0.95	0.97	0.5	0.8	0.73	0.61
5	0.9	0.8	0.2	0.6	0.72	0.5
t	0.9	0.8	0.2	0.6		

We model negotiation behaviour of potential partners in terms of possibility theory by applying the principle "the more similar are the situation desription attributes, the more possible that the outcome attributes are similar". Based on the history we construct the fuction $\mu^t(y)$ as a prediction about possibility of succesfull negotiation:

$$\mu^t(y) = Max_{(s^i, o^i) \in H^{t-1}} S(s^i, s^t) \otimes P(o^i, y) \tag{1}$$

where S and P are similarity relations [10] comparing situations and outcomes, respectively. $\otimes$ is a t-norm which can be defined: $a \otimes b = Min(a,b)$. We assume the final function describing the possibility of succesful negotiation is decreasing because if the agent agrees on some value with some degree of possibility p it should also be able to agree on every lower value with at least such a degree p. Therefore we need to modify the function obtained by formula (1). The modification will be described in the next section. Function before modification will be called the density of possibility distribution and function after modification will be called the possibility distribution.

3.1 Independent Case-Based Reasoning

We consider first the modelling of two agents separately. We calculate the possibility distribution encoding the possibility of the agent to agree on the value of attribute (ag. availability) during the negotiation. We apply the possibilistic principle mentioned in previous section for the first agent to obtain its density function:

$$\mu_1^t(y_1) = Max_{(s^i, o^i) \in H^{t-1}} S((a_1^i, c_0^i, c_1^i), (a_1^t, c_0^t, c_1^t)) \otimes P(\Delta a_1^i, y_1)$$

Similarly for the second agent:

$$\mu_2^t(y_2) = Max_{(s^i, o^i) \in H^{t-1}} S((a_2^i, c_0^i, c_1^i), (a_2^t, c_0^t, c_1^t)) \otimes P(\Delta a_2^i, y_2)$$

Now we give the full description of calculation for the one-dimensional possibility distributions. To obtain the density functions μ_1^t, μ_2^t we divide the interval $[0,1]$ corresponding to the first agent into m subintervals and consider only the discrete points $\eta_k \in \{\eta_1, \eta_2, \ldots, \eta_m\} \subset [0,1]$. In a case of the second agent we divide the interval $[0,1]$ into p intervals and obtain p discrete points $\theta_l \in \{\theta_1, \theta_2, \ldots, \theta_p\} \subset [0,1]$. Of course the values of m and p may be equal. Now we have to calculate a vector $P_1^i = P_1(\Delta a_1^i)$ for the outcome Δa_1^i of every situation i in the history corresponding to the first agent.

$$P_1^i = P_1(\Delta a_1^i) = [P(\Delta a_1^i, \eta_1), P(\Delta a_1^i, \eta_2), \ldots, P(\Delta a_1^i, \eta_m)]$$

This calculations can be done iteratively, i.e. every P_1^i can be calculated as a auxiliary vector after negotiation number i. Analogically we calculate the vector $P_2^i = P_2(\Delta a_2^i)$ corresponding to the second agent:

$$P_2^i = P_2(\Delta a_2^i) = [P(\Delta a_2^i, \theta_1), P(\Delta a_2^i, \theta_2), \ldots, P(\Delta a_2^i, \theta_p)]$$

where P is the similarity relation. Having the sequences of auxiliary vectors: $\{P_1^i\}_{i \leq t-1}$ and $\{P_2^i\}_{i \leq t-1}$ we calculate for our current situation $s^i = (a_1^i, a_2^i, c_0^i, c_1^i)$ the sequences of comparisons with all situations in the history for the first agent:

$$\{S_1^i\}_{i \leq t-1} = \{S((a_1^i, c_0^i, c_1^i), (a_1^t, c_0^t, c_1^t))\}_{i \leq t-1}$$

and for the second one:

$$\{S_2^i\}_{i \leq t-1} = \{S((a_2^i, c_0^i, c_1^i), (a_2^t, c_0^t, c_1^t))\}_{i \leq t-1}.$$

Having the sequence of vectors P_1^i and the sequence of values S_1^i we now make an aggregation $S_1^i \otimes P_1^i$ for every $i \leq t-1$:

$$S_1^i \otimes P_1^i = [S_1^i \otimes P(\Delta a_1^i, \eta_1), S_1^i \otimes P(\Delta a_1^i, \eta_2), \ldots, S_1^i \otimes P(\Delta a_1^i, \eta_m)]$$

The same for the second agent:

$$S_2^i \otimes P_2^i = [S_2^i \otimes P(\Delta a_2^i, \theta_1), S_2^i \otimes P(\Delta a_2^i, \theta_2), \ldots, S_2^i \otimes P(\Delta a_2^i, \theta_p)]$$

The vectors are calculated for every case i in the history H^{t-1}. Having all the vectors we can finaly obtain the functions μ_1^t and μ_2^t by aggregating all the vectors (for sake of notaion simplicity we state only i instead of (s^i, o^i)):

$$\mu_1^t = [\mu_1^t(\eta_1), \mu_1^t(\eta_2), \ldots, \mu_1^t(\eta_m)] =$$
$$[Max_i S_1^i \otimes P(\Delta a_1^i, \eta_1), Max_i S_1^i \otimes P(\Delta a_1^i, \eta_2), \ldots, Max_i S_1^i \otimes P(\Delta a_1^i, \eta_m)]$$

Function μ_2^t corresponding to the second agent:

$$\mu_2^t = [\mu_2^t(\theta_1), \mu_2^t(\theta_2), \ldots, \mu_2^t(\theta_p)] =$$
$$[Max_i S_2^i \otimes P(\Delta a_2^i, \theta_1), Max_i S_2^i \otimes P(\Delta a_2^i, \theta_2), \ldots, Max_i S_2^i \otimes P(\Delta a_2^i, \theta_p)]$$

The functions μ_1^t and μ_2^t are treated as densities of the possibility distributions. They specify how likely are the agents to agree on the values of attributes Δa_1^t and Δa_2^t during the negotiation. In terms of possibility measures it can be defined as follows

$$\prod(\{\Delta a_1^t\}) = \mu_1^t(\Delta a_1^t) \qquad \prod(\{\Delta a_2^t\}) = \mu_2^t(\Delta a_2^t)$$

If it is possible that an agent can agree on the value of attribute Δa_1^t then it is also possible that possibility of a lower value is at least the same. So we need to calculate $\prod(\eta_k \leq \Delta a_1^t) = \prod([\Delta a_1^t, 1])$ (Figure 1). The final possibility distributions are obtained from the possibilistic distribution densities in the following way:

$$\pi_1^t(\Delta a_1^t) = \prod([\Delta a_1^t, 1]) = sup\{\prod(\{\eta_k\}) \mid \eta_k \geq \Delta a_1^t\} = \qquad (2)$$
$$= sup\{\mu_1^t(\eta_k) \mid \eta_k \geq \Delta a_1^t\}$$

$$\pi_2^t(\Delta a_2^t) = \prod([\Delta a_2^t, 1]) = sup\{\prod(\{\theta_l\}) \mid \theta_l \geq \Delta a_2^t\} = \qquad (3)$$
$$= sup\{\mu_2^t(\theta_l) \mid \theta_l \geq \Delta a_2^t\}$$

The joined possibility distribution specyfing how likely are both agents to agree on values $(\Delta a_1^t, \Delta a_2^t)$ during the negotiation can be obtained in the following way:

$$\pi^t(\Delta a_1^t, \Delta a_2^t) = \pi_1^t(\Delta a_1^t) \otimes \pi_2^t(\Delta a_2^t)$$

where $\otimes$ is a t-norm defined as before. To be able to select one or more agents for negotiation we need to find a set of points maximizing the expected qualitative

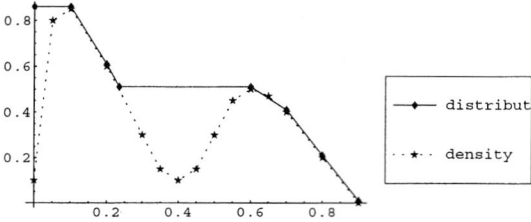

Fig. 1. Example of possibility distribution density and possibility distribution

utility in the decision space. By this points we mean the outcomes which are optimaly good for the main agent and its partners. Such outcomes (or rather a set of outcomes) - $\mathcal{P}^t$ can be obtained by aggregating the main agent's utility function and the qualitative utilities of other agents predicted by our model:

$$\mathcal{P}^t = argMax_{(y_1,y_2) \in [0,1]^2} \pi^t(y_1, y_2) \otimes \nu^t(y_1, y_2) \qquad (4)$$

Considering the point $(b_1^t, b_2^t) \in \mathcal{P}^t$ which is closest to the point $(1,1)$ we can determine whom to negotiate with. We consider this point because it has the highest utility in the set $\mathcal{P}^t$. If the absolute difference of coordinates divided by $Max\{b_1^t, b_2^t\}$ exceeds some level $\epsilon \in [0,1)$:

$$\frac{|b_1^t - b_2^t|}{Max\{b_1^t, b_2^t\}} \geq \epsilon \qquad (5)$$

then we choose only one of agents for negotiation for whom the corresponding coordinate is larger (for instance if $b_1^t \geq b_2^t$ then we choose A_1). If the condition (5) is not satisfied the the possibility of succesful negotiation with both agents is sufficiently undiscriminated and we have to negotiate with both agents: $\{A_1, A_2\}$.

3.2 Correlated Case-Based Reasoning

In some situations there may be some correlation between the two agents with which we are negotiating, e.g. an attribute of one agent may depend on an attribute of the second one. Therefore we consider the case in which the possibility distribution is calculated in a twodimensional form from the beginning. We apply the possibilistic principle in two dimensional cases as follows:

$$\mu^t(y_1, y_2) = Max_{(s^i, o^i) \in H^{t-1}} S((a_1^i, a_2^i, c_0^i, c_1^i), (a_1^t, a_2^t, c_0^t, c_1^t)) \\ \otimes P((\Delta a_1^i, \Delta a_2^i), (y_1, y_2))$$

The outcomes of every historical case are rescaled in the same way as in the previous section. The decision space which is defined by a square $[0,1]^2$ is divided into $m \times p$ rectangles and we consider only discrete points $(\eta_k, \theta_l) \in [0,1]^2$.

For every case r^i in the history we calculate an auxiliary matrix $P^i = P(o^i)$ depending on the outcome $o^i = (\Delta a^i_1, \Delta a^i_2)$ as follows:

$$P^i = P(o^i) = P(\Delta a^i_1, \Delta a^i_2) = [P(\Delta a^i_1, \Delta a^i_2), (\eta_k, \theta_l))]_{k \leq m, l \leq p}$$

As in the previous sections this calculation can be done iteratively. Having the sequence of matrices $\{P^i\}_{i \leq t-1}$ we calculate a sequence of comparisons of our current situation with all situations in the history H^{t-1}:

$$\{S^i\}_{i \leq t-1} = \{S(s^i, s^t)\}_{i \leq t-1} = \{S((a^i_1, a^i_2, c_0, c_1), (a^t_1, a^t_2, c_0, c_1))\}_{i \leq t-1}$$

Having the sequence of matrices P^i and the sequence of values S^i we can make an aggregation $S^i \otimes P^i$ for every $i \leq t-1$:

$$S^i \otimes P^i = [S^i \otimes P((\Delta a^i_1, \Delta a^i_2), (\eta_k, \theta_l))]_{k \leq m, l \leq p}$$

Having all the matrices we can finaly obtain the function μ^t by aggregating the matrices (for sake of notation simplicity we state only i instead of (s^i, o^i)):

$$\mu^t = [Max_i S^i \otimes P((\Delta a^i_1, \Delta a^i_2), (\eta_k, \theta_l))]_{k \leq m, l \leq p}$$

The function μ^t specifies how likely are the agents to agree on the values of attributes $(\Delta a^i_1, \Delta a^i_2)$ during the negotiation and is treated as density of possibility distribution. In terms of possibility measures it can be defined as follows:

$$\prod(\{o^t\}) = \prod(\{\Delta a^i_1, \Delta a^i_2\}) = \mu^t(\Delta a^i_1, \Delta a^i_2)$$

If it is possible for the agents to agree on the values of attributes Δa^t_1 and Δa^t_2 then it is also possible for them to agree on every smaller value on at least the same level of possibility. So we can calculate $\prod([\Delta a^t_1, 1] \times [\Delta a^t_2, 1])$. The final possibility distribution is obtained from the possibilistic distribution density in following way:

$$\pi^t(o^t) = \prod([\Delta a^t_1, 1] \times [\Delta a^t_2, 1]) =$$
$$= sup\{\mu^t(\eta_k, \theta_l) \mid \eta_k \geq \Delta a^t_1, \theta_l \geq \Delta a^t_2\} =$$
$$= sup\{sup\{\mu^t(\eta_k, \theta_l) \mid \eta_k \geq \Delta a^t_1\} \quad \theta_l \geq \Delta a^t_2\}$$

The selection of agents for negotiation is done in the same way as in the previous section.

4 Example of Calculations

4.1 Independent Reasoning Case

To demonstrate the proposed approach we make calculations based on the historical data from Table 1 in Section 3: The results are shown in Figure 2. It can be noted that in the case $s^{t=6} = (0.9, 0.2, 0.6)$ the density of possibility

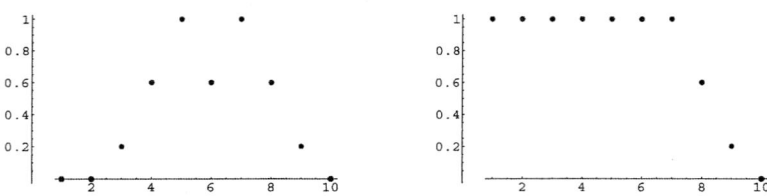

Fig. 2. Density of possibility distribution for the first agent - $\mu_1^t = [0, 0, 0.2, 0.6, 1, 0.6, 1, 0.6, 0.2, 0]$ and its possibility distribution - $\pi_1^t = [1, 1, 1, 1, 1, 1, 1, 0.6, 0.2, 0]$

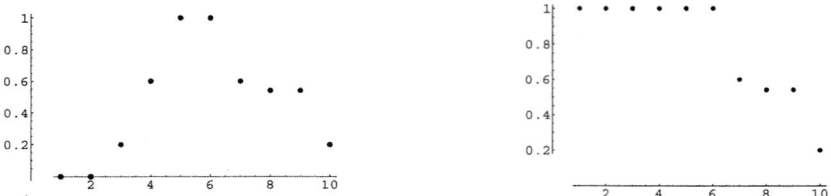

Fig. 3. Density of possibility distribution for the second agent - $\mu_2^t = [0, 0, 0.2, 0.6, 1, 1, 0.6, 0.54, 0.54, 0.2]$ and its possibility distribution - $\pi_2^t = [1, 1, 1, 1, 1, 1, 0.6, 0.54, 0.54, 0.2]$

distribution for the first agent has two equally important maxima. It means that in the history we have two cases which have the same input values as our current case (we observe full similarity between current situation and the situations $s^1 = (0.9, 0.2, 0.6)$ and $s^5 = (0.9, 0.2, 0.6)$). The outputs of s^1 and s^5 are $\Delta a_1^1 = 0.5, \Delta a_1^5 = 0.72$. Therefore the maxima are situated in points 0.5 and 0.72. The third case in the history $s^3 = (0.85, 0.7, 0.25)$ is the third most similar situation to our current one and its outcome is $\Delta a_1^3 = 0.58$. The high value (0.6) in this point corresponds to the similarity of s^3 and s^t. The next step is the calcultion of possbility distribution π_1^t (Figure 2). The calculations for the second agent are analogous and the results are plotted in fugure (3). Having the possbility distributions of two services π_1^t and π_2^t we aggregate them with t-norm and obtain joint possibility distribution π^t (Figure 4):

$$\pi^t(y_1, y_2) = \pi_1^t(y_1) \otimes \pi_2^t(y_2)$$

We aggregate the possibility distribution π^t with the utility function ν^t and obtain the optimal decision set:

$$\mathcal{P}^t = argMax_{(\eta_k, \theta_l) \in [0,1]^2} \pi^t(\eta_k, \theta_l) \otimes \nu^t(\eta_k, \theta_l)$$

From Figure 5 we see that the set of points with expected utility 0.54 is: $\mathcal{P}^6 = \{(0.8, 0.8), (0.7, 0.9), (0.8, 0.9)\}$. From the set we choose the point $(0.8, 0.9)$. The values of coordinates are close: $|0.9 - 0.8| = 0.1$. Therefore criterion (5) is not satisfied and we have to negotiate with both agents $\{A_1, A_2\}$.

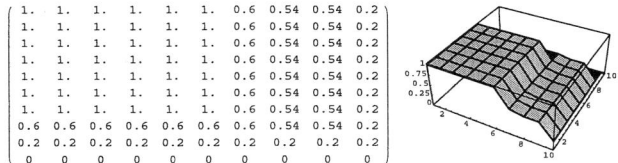

Fig. 4. Possibility distribution - π^t

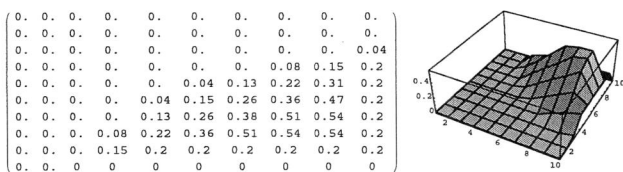

Fig. 5. Function $\pi^t \otimes \nu^6$

4.2 Correlated Reasoning Case

For the case $s^{t=6} = (0.9, 0.8, 0.2, 0.6)$ the distribution density has two strong equally important maxima (Figure 6). As discussed in previous sections this means that in the history we have two cases with input identical to our current one. These are the cases s^1 and s^5. The values of outcomes of these situations are: $(\Delta a_1^1, \Delta a_2^1) = (0.5, 0.62)$ and $(\Delta a_1^5, \Delta a_2^5) = (0.72, 0.5)$. That is why the maxima occur in these points. We observe another weaker maximum (0.77) in point (0.58, 0.81). This point corresponds to third case in the history $s^3 = (0.85, 0.7, 0.25, 0.4)$ with the outcome $(\Delta a_1^3, \Delta a_2^3) = (0.58, 0.81)$. The next step is the calculation of two-dimensional possibility distribution (Figure 7). The determination of optimal decision set and selection of agents for negotiation is done in the same way as in previous section.

5 Multilateral Case

The selection of agents for negotiation can be generalized to the multiagent case. In this situation we have to choose a subset of m agents $\{A_{j_1}, A_{j_2}, \ldots, A_{j_m}\}$ from

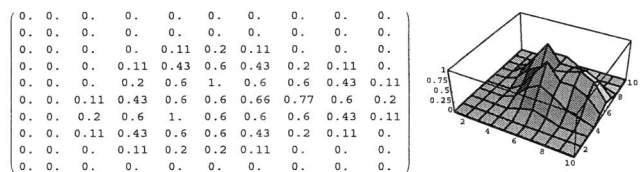

Fig. 6. Density of twodimensional possibility distribution - μ^6

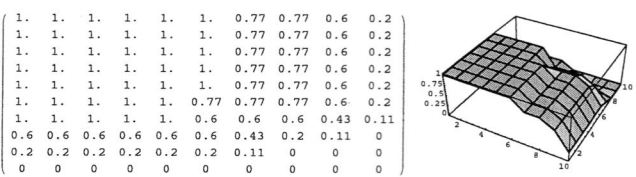

Fig. 7. Two-dimensional possibility distribution - π^6

a set of n candidates $\{A_1, A_2, \ldots, A_n\}$ for negotiation. First of all we need utility function of agent A_0. Analogous as in Section 3 we define it as:

$$\nu(y_1, y_2, \ldots, y_n) = p(y_1 \cdot y_2 \cdot \ldots \cdot y_n)$$

We store the historical data as a sequence of pairs $r^i = (s^i, o^i)$ where the situation is described by $n+2$ numbers: $s^i = (a_1^i, a_2^i, \ldots, a_n^i, c_0^i, c_1^i)$ and outcome is described by n numbers $o^i = (\Delta a_1^i, \Delta a_1^i, \ldots, \Delta a_n^i)$. Analogically as in Section 3.1 we model separately every agent A_i. Based on the possibilistic case-based reasoning we obtain predictions of behaviour for every agent A_i in a form of the possibility distribution π_i^t. Then we calculate a joint possibility distribution specyfing the prediction about all agents:

$$\pi^t(y_1, y_2, \ldots, y_n) = \pi_1^t(y_1) \otimes \pi_2^t(y_2) \otimes \ldots \otimes \pi_n^t(y_n)$$

where $\otimes$ is as usually a t-norm. Having the prediction about partners of agent A_0 and its utility function we can make an aggregation to obtain the optimal decision set $\mathcal{P}^t$:

$$\mathcal{P}^t = argMax_{(y_1, y_2, \ldots, y_n)} \pi^t(y_1, y_2, \ldots, y_n) \otimes \nu^t(y_1, y_2, \ldots, y_n)$$

Next we choose from the set $\mathcal{P}^t$ the point $(b_1^t, b_2^t, \ldots, b_n^t)$ nearest to point $(1, 1, \ldots, 1)$ because it is most beneficial for the main agent and order its coordinates to obtain a sequence $b_{j_1}^t, b_{j_2}^t, \ldots, b_{j_n}^t$ ($b_{j_1}^t \geq b_{j_2}^t \geq \ldots \geq b_{j_n}^t$). From this ordering we derive the order of agents $j_1, j_2, \ldots, j_n$. The earlier the agent is in the sequence the higher possibilistic expected utility meaning that it is more beneficial to negotiate with the agent then with others later in the order. If we want to choose a subset of agents for negotiation from the whole set of agents we have to determine division of the ordering into two parts. The criterion may have a following form: we choose agents $A_{j_1}, A_{j_2}, \ldots, A_{j_s}$ for negotiation if the condition

$$\frac{|\frac{1}{s}\sum_{i=1}^{s} b_{j_i} - \frac{1}{n-s}\sum_{i=s+1}^{n} b_{j_i}|}{Max\{\frac{1}{s}\sum_{i=1}^{s} b_{j_i}, \frac{1}{n-s}\sum_{i=s+1}^{n} b_{j_i}\}} \geq \epsilon \qquad (6)$$

is satisfied, where ϵ is some treshold. Criterion (6) states that if the mean values of two clusters are distant enough we choose the first cluster of agents for negotiation.

6 Conclusions and Future Work

The paper proposed a possibilistic case-based reasoning for selecting negotiation partners. We constructed the prediction about possibility of succesful negotiation in the terms of possibility distribution. This information was applied for calculation of the qualitative expected utility for the current situation. This approach allows the agent to select a subset of the best partners which are most promising for negotiation based on their behaviour in previous negotiations. Two models of selecting partners were considered for the independent and correlated negotiation agents.

In our future work we will consider more parameters that could be taken into acount in situation description and analyse which parameters influence the outcome mostly. We will use the possbilistic case-based reasoning for the decision making during the whole negotiation process. We will also consider multi-attribute partners selection and multi-stage negotiation extending the model proposed in this paper.

References

1. Jennings, N.R., Faratin, P., Lomuscio, A., Parson, S., Sierra, C., Wooldridge, M.: Automated negotiation: Prospects, methods and challenges. International Journal of Group Decision and Negotiation **10** (2001) 199–215
2. Rosenschein, J., Zlotkin, G.: Rules of Encounter: Designing Conventions for Automated Negotiation among Computers. MIT Press (1994)
3. Sandholm, T., Lesser, V.R.: Coalitions among computationally bounded agents. Artificial Intelligence **94** (1997) 99–137
4. Klusch, M., Gerber, A.: Dynamic coalition formation among rational agents. IEEE Intelligent Systems **17** (2002) 42–47
5. Banerjee, B., Sen, S.: Selecting partners. In Sierra, C., Gini, M., Rosenschein, J.S., eds.: Proceedings of the Fourth International Conference on Autonomous Agents, Barcelona, Catalonia, Spain, ACM Press (2000) 261–262
6. Dubois, D., Prade, H.: Possibility theory as a basis for qualitative decision theory. In Mellish, C., ed.: Proceedings of the Fourteenth International Joint Conference on Artificial Intelligence, San Francisco, Morgan Kaufmann (1995) 1924–1930
7. Garcia, P., Gimenez, E., amd J. A. Rodriguez-Aguilar, L.G.: Possibilistic-based design of bidding strategies in electronic auctions. In: Proceedings of the Thirteen European Conference on Artificial Intelligence. (1998) 575–579
8. Gimenez-Funes, E., Godo, L., Rodriguez-Aguilar, J.A., Garcia-Calves, P.: Designing bidding strategies for trading agents in electronic auctions. In: Proceedings of the Third International Conference on Multi-Agent Systems. (1998) 136–143
9. Godo, L., Zapico, A.: On the possibilistic-based decision model: Characterization of preference relations under partial inconsistency. The Int. J. of Artificial Intelligence, Neural networks, and Complex Problem-Solving Technologies **14** (2001) 319–333
10. Dubois, D., Prade, H.: Fuzzy set modelling in case-based reasoning. International Journal of Intelligent Systems **13** (1998) 345–373

Set Bounds and (Split) Set Domain Propagation Using ROBDDs

Peter Hawkins, Vitaly Lagoon, and Peter J. Stuckey

Department of Computer Science and Software Engineering,
The University of Melbourne, Vic. 3010, Australia
{hawkinsp, lagoon, pjs}@cs.mu.oz.au

Abstract. Most propagation-based set constraint solvers approximate the set of possible sets that a variable can take by upper and lower bounds, and perform so-called set bounds propagation. However Lagoon and Stuckey have shown that using reduced ordered binary decision diagrams (ROBDDs) one can create a practical set domain propagator that keeps all information (possibly exponential in size) about the set of possible set values for a set variable. In this paper we first show that we can use the same ROBDD approach to build an efficient bounds propagator. The main advantage of this approach to set bounds propagation is that we need not laboriously determine set bounds propagations rules for each new constraint, they can be computed automatically. In addition we can eliminate intermediate variables, and build stronger set bounds propagators than with the usual approach. We then show how we can combine this with the set domain propagation approach of Lagoon and Stuckey to create a more efficient set domain propagation solver.

1 Introduction

It is often convenient to model a constraint satisfaction problem (CSP) using finite set variables and set relationships between them. A common approach to solving finite domain CSPs is using a combination of a global backtracking search and a local constraint propagation algorithm. The local propagation algorithm attempts to enforce consistency on the values in the domains of the constraint variables by removing values from the domains of variables that cannot form part of a complete solution to the system of constraints. Various levels of consistency can be defined, with varying complexities and levels of performance.

The obvious representation of the true domain of a set variable as a set of sets is too unwieldy to solve many practical problems. For example, a set variable which can take on the value of any subset of $\{1, \ldots, N\}$ has 2^N elements in its domain, which rapidly becomes unmanageable. Instead, most set constraint solvers operate on an approximation to the true domain of a set variable in order to avoid the combinatorial explosion associated with the set of sets representation. One such approximation [4, 7] is to represent the domain of a set variable by upper and lower bounds under the subset partial ordering relation. A *set bounds* propagator attempts to enforce consistency on these upper and lower bounds. Various refinements to the basic set bounds approximation have been proposed, such as the addition of upper and lower bounds on the cardinality of a set variable [1].

However, Lagoon and Stuckey [6] demonstrated that it is possible to use reduced ordered binary decision diagrams (ROBDDs) as a compact representation of both set domains and of set constraints, thus permitting *set domain* propagation. A domain propagator ensures that every value in the domain of a set variable can be extended to a complete assignment of all of the variables in a constraint. The use of the ROBDD representation comes with several additional benefits. The ability to easily conjoin and existentially quantify ROBDDs allows the removal of intermediate variables, thus strengthening propagation, and also makes the construction of propagators for global constraints straightforward.

Given the natural way in which ROBDDs can be used to model set constraint problems, it is therefore worthwhile utilising ROBDDs to construct other types of set solver. In this paper we extend the work of Lagoon and Stuckey [6] by using ROBDDs to build a set bounds solver. A major benefit of the ROBDD-based approach is that it frees us from the need to laboriously construct set bounds propagators for each new constraint by hand. The other advantages of the ROBDD-based representation identified above still apply, and the resulting solver performs very favourably when compared with existing set bounds solvers.

Another possibility that we have investigated is an improved set domain propagator which splits up the domain representation into fixed parts (which represent the bounds of the domain) and non-fixed parts. This helps to limit the size of the ROBDDs involved in constraint propagation and leads to improved performance in many cases.

The contributions of this paper are:

– We show how to represent the set bounds of (finite) set variables using ROBDDs. We then show how to construct efficient set bounds propagators using ROBDDs, which retain all of the modelling benefits of the ROBDD-based set domain propagators.
– We present an improved approach for ROBDD-based set domain propagators which splits the ROBDD representing a variable domain into fixed and non-fixed parts, leading to a substantial performance improvement in many cases.
– We demonstrate experimentally that the new bounds and domain solvers perform better in many cases than existing set solvers.

The remainder of this paper is structured as follows. In Section 2 we define the concepts necessary when discussing propagation-based constraint solvers. Section 3 reviews ROBDDs and their use in the domain propagation approach of Lagoon and Stuckey [6]. Section 4 investigates several new varieties of propagator, which are evaluated experimentally in Section 5. In Section 6 we conclude.

2 Propagation-Based Constraint Solving

In this section we define the concepts and notation necessary when discussing propagation-based constraint solvers. Most of these definitions are identical to those presented by Lagoon and Stuckey [6], although we repeat them here for self-containedness.

Let $\mathcal{L}$ denote the powerset lattice $\langle \mathcal{P}(U), \subseteq \rangle$, where the *universe* U is a finite subset of $\mathbb{Z}$. A subset $K \subseteq \mathcal{L}$ is said to be *convex* if and only if for any $a, b \in K$ and any $c \in \mathcal{L}$ the relation $a \subseteq c \subseteq b$ implies $c \in K$. A collection of sets $C \subseteq \mathcal{L}$ is said to be an *interval* if there are sets $a, b \in \mathcal{L}$ such that $C = \{x \in \mathcal{L} \mid a \subseteq x \subseteq b\}$. We then refer to C by the shorthand $C = [a, b]$. Clearly an interval is convex.

For any finite collection of sets $x = \{a_1, a_2, \ldots, a_n\}$, we define the convex closure operation $conv : \mathcal{L} \to \mathcal{L}$ by $conv(x) = [\cap_{a \in x} a, \cup_{a \in x} a]$.

Let $\mathcal{V}$ denote the set of all set variables. Each set variable has an associated finite collection of possible values from $\mathcal{L}$ (which are themselves sets).

A *domain* D is a complete mapping from the fixed finite set of variables $\mathcal{V}$ to finite collections of finite sets of integers. We often refer to the *domain of a variable* v, in which case we mean the value of $D(v)$. A domain D_1 is said to be *stronger* than a domain D_2, written $D_1 \sqsubseteq D_2$, if $D_1(v) \subseteq D_2(v)$ for all $v \in \mathcal{V}$. A domain D_1 is equal to a domain D_2, written $D_1 = D_2$, if $D_1(v) = D_2(v)$ for all variables $v \in \mathcal{V}$. We extend the concept of convex closure to domains by defining $ran(D)$ to be the domain such that $ran(D)(x) = conv(D(x))$ for all $x \in \mathcal{V}$.

A *valuation* θ is a set of mappings from the set of variables $\mathcal{V}$ to sets of integer values, written $\{x_1 \mapsto d_1, \ldots, x_n \mapsto d_n\}$. A valuation can be extended to apply to constraints involving the variables in the obvious way. Let *vars* be the function that returns the set of variables appearing in an expression, constraint or valuation. In an abuse of notation, we say a valuation is an element of a domain D, written $\theta \in D$, if $\theta(v_i) \in D(v_i)$ for all $v_i \in vars(\theta)$.

Constraints, Propagators and Propagation Solvers. A constraint is a restriction placed on the allowable values for a set of variables. We define the following *primitive set constraints*: (membership) $k \in v$, (non-membership) $k \notin v$, (constant) $u = d$, (equality) $u = v$, (subset) $u \subseteq w$, (union) $u = v \cup w$, (intersection) $u = v \cap w$, (difference) $u = v \setminus w$, (complement) $u = \bar{v}$, (cardinality) $|v| = k$, (lower cardinality bound) $|v| \geq k$, (upper cardinality bound) $|v| \leq k$, where u, v, w are set variables, k is an integer, and d is a ground set value. We can also construct more complicated constraints which are (possibly existentially quantified) conjunctions of primitive set constraints.

We define the *solutions* of a constraint c to be the set of valuations θ that make that constraint true, ie. $solns(c) = \{\theta \mid (vars(\theta) = vars(c)) \wedge (\ \theta(c))\}$.

We associate a *propagator* with every constraint. A propagator f is a monotonically decreasing function from domains to domains, so $D_1 \sqsubseteq D_2$ implies that $f(D_1) \sqsubseteq f(D_2)$, and $f(D) \sqsubseteq D$. A propagator f is *correct* for a constraint c if and only if for all domains D:

$$\{\theta \mid \theta \in D\} \cap solns(c) = \{\theta \mid \theta \in f(D)\} \cap solns(c)$$

This is a weak restriction since, for example, the identity propagator is correct for any constraints.

A *propagation solver* $solv(F, D)$ for a set of propagators F and a domain D repeatedly applies the propagators in F starting from the domain D until a fixpoint is reached. In general $solv(F, D)$ is the weakest domain $D' \sqsubseteq D$ which is a fixpoint (ie. $f(D') = D'$) for all $f \in F$.

Domain and Bounds Consistency. A domain D is *domain consistent* for a constraint c if D is the strongest domain containing all solutions $\theta \in D$ of c. In other words D is domain consistent if there does not exist $D' \sqsubseteq D$ such that $\theta \in D$ and $\theta \in solns(c)$ implies $\theta \in D'$.

A set of propagators F maintain domain consistency for a domain D if $solv(F, D)$ is domain consistent for all constraints c.

We define the *domain propagator* for a constraint c as

$$dom(c)(D)(v) = \begin{cases} \{\theta(v) \mid \theta \in D \land \theta \in solns(c)\} & \text{if } v \in vars(c) \\ D(v) & \text{otherwise} \end{cases}$$

Since domain consistency is frequently difficult to achieve for set constraints, instead the weaker notion of bounds consistency is often used. We say that a domain D is *bounds consistent* for a constraint c if for every variable $v \in vars(c)$ the upper bound of $D(v)$ is the union of the values of v in all solutions of c in D, and the lower bound of $D(v)$ is the intersection of the values of v in all solutions of c in D.

A set of propagators F maintain set bounds consistency for a constraint c if $solv(F, D)$ is bounds consistent for all domains D.

We define the *set bounds propagator* for a constraint c as

$$sb(c)(D)(v) = \begin{cases} conv(dom(c)(ran(D))(v)) & \text{if } v \in vars(c) \\ D(v) & \text{otherwise} \end{cases}$$

3 ROBDDs and Set Domain Propagators

We make use of the following Boolean operations: $\land$ (conjunction), $\lor$ (disjunction), $\neg$ (negation), $\rightarrow$ (implication), $\leftrightarrow$ (bi-implication) and $\exists$ (existential quantification). We denote by $\exists_V F$ the formula $\exists x_1 \cdots \exists x_n F$ where $V = \{x_1, \ldots, x_n\}$, and by $\bar{\exists}_V F$ we mean $\exists_{V'} F$ where $V' = vars(F) \setminus V$.

Binary Decision Trees (BDTs) are a well-known method of representing Boolean functions on Boolean variables using complete binary trees. Every internal node $n(v, f, t)$ in a BDT r is labelled with a Boolean variable v, and has two outgoing arcs — the 'false' arc (to BDT f) and the 'true' arc (to BDT t). Leaf nodes are either 0 (false) or 1 (true). Each node represents a single test of the labelled variable; when traversing the tree the appropriate arc is followed

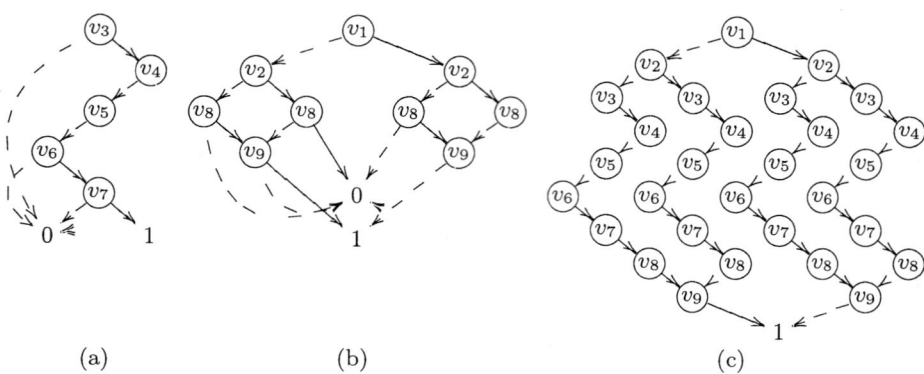

Fig. 1. ROBDDs for (a) $L\overline{U} = v_3 \wedge \neg v_4 \wedge \neg v_5 \wedge v_6 \wedge v_7$ (b) $R = \neg(v_1 \leftrightarrow v_9) \wedge \neg(v_2 \leftrightarrow v_8)$ and (c) $L\overline{U} \wedge R$ (omitting the node 0 and arcs to it). Solid arcs are "then" arcs, dashed arcs are "else" arcs

depending on the value of the variable. Define the size $|r|$ as the number of internal nodes in an ROBDD r, and $VAR(r)$ as the set of variables v appearing in some internal node in r. A Binary Decision Diagram (BDD) is a variant of a Binary Decision Tree that relaxes the tree requirement, instead representing a Boolean function as a directed acyclic graph with a single root node by allowing nodes to have multiple parents. This permits a compact representation of many (but not all) Boolean functions.

Two canonicity properties allow many operations on a BDD to be performed very efficiently [3]. A BDD is said to be *reduced* if it contains no identical nodes (that is, nodes with the same variable label and identical then and else arcs) and has no redundant tests (no node has both then and else arcs leading to the same node). A BDD is said to be *ordered* if there is a total ordering $\prec$ of the variables, such that if there is an arc from a node labelled v_1 to a node labelled v_2 then $v_1 \prec v_2$. A *reduced ordered* BDD (ROBDD) has the nice property that the function representation is canonical up to variable reordering. This permits efficient implementations of many Boolean operations.

We shall be interested in a special form of ROBDDs. A *stick ROBDD* is an ROBDD where for every internal node $n(v, f, t)$ exactly one of f or t is the constant 0 node.

Example 1. Figure 1(a) gives an example of a stick ROBDD representing the formula $v_3 \wedge \neg v_4 \wedge \neg v_5 \wedge v_6 \wedge v_7$. Figure 1(b) gives an example of a more complex ROBDD representing the formula $\neg(v_1 \leftrightarrow v_9) \wedge \neg(v_2 \leftrightarrow v_8)$. One can verify that the valuation $\{v_1 \mapsto 1, v_2 \mapsto 0, v_8 \mapsto 1, v_9 \mapsto 0\}$ makes the formula true by following the path right, left, right, left from the root.

3.1 Modelling Set Domains Using ROBDDs

The key step in building set domain propagation using ROBDDs is to realise that we can represent a finite set domain using an ROBDD.

If x is a set variable and $A \in D(x)$ is a subset of $\{1, \ldots, N\}$, then we can represent A as a valuation θ over the Boolean variables $V(x) = \{x_1, \ldots, x_N\}$, where $\theta_A = \{x_i \mapsto 1 \mid i \in A\} \cup \{x_i \mapsto 0 \mid i \notin A\}$. The domain of x can be represented as a Boolean formula ϕ which has as solutions $\{\theta_A \mid A \in D(x)\}$. We will order the variables $x_1 \prec x_2 \cdots \prec x_N$.

An ROBDD allows us to represent (some) subsets of $\mathcal{P}(\{1, \ldots, N\})$ efficiently. For example the subset $S = \{\{3,6,7,8,9\}, \{2,3,6,7,9\}, \{1,3,6,7,8\}, \{1,2,3,6,7\}\}$, where $N = 9$, is represented by the ROBDD in Figure 1(c). In particular, an interval can be compactly represented as a stick ROBDD of a conjunction of positive and negative literals (corresponding to the lower bound and the complement of the upper bound respectively). For example the subset $conv(S) = [\{3,6,7\}, \{1,2,3,6,7,8,9\}]$ is represented by the stick ROBDD in Figure 1(a).

3.2 Modelling Primitive Set Constraints Using ROBDDs

We will convert each primitive set constraint c to an ROBDD $B(c)$ on the Boolean variable representations $V(x)$ of its set variables x. By ordering the variables in each ROBDD carefully we can build small representations of the formulae. The *pointwise* order of Boolean variables is defined as follows. Given set variables $u \prec v \prec w$ ranging over sets from $\{1, \ldots, N\}$ we order the Boolean variables as $u_1 \prec v_1 \prec w_1 \prec u_2 \prec v_2 \prec w_2 \prec \cdots u_n \prec v_n \prec w_n$.

By ordering the Boolean variables pointwise we can guarantee linear sized representations for $B(c)$ for each primitive constraint c except those for cardinality. The size of the representations of $B(k \in v)$ and $B(k \notin v)$ are $O(1)$, while $B(v = w)$, $B(v = d)$, $B(v \subseteq w)$, $B(u = v \cup w)$, $B(u = v \cap w)$, $B(u = v \setminus w)$, $B(v = \bar{w})$ and $B(v \neq w)$ are all $O(N)$, and $B(|v| = k)$, $B(|v| \leq k)$ and $B(|v| \geq k)$ are all $O(k \times (N - k))$. For more details see [6].

3.3 ROBDD-Based Set Domain Propagation

Lagoon and Stuckey [6] demonstrated how to construct a set domain propagator $dom(c)$ for a constraint c using ROBDDs. If $vars(c) = \{v_1, \ldots, v_n\}$, then we have the following description of a domain propagator:

$$dom(c)(D)(v_i) = \exists_{V(v_i)}(B(c) \land \bigwedge_{j=1}^{n} D(v_j)) \quad (1)$$

Since $B(c)$ and $D(v_j)$ are ROBDDs, we can directly implement this formula using ROBDD operations. In practice it is more efficient to perform the existential quantification as early as possible to limit the size of the intermediate ROBDDs. Many ROBDD packages provide an efficient combined conjunction and existential quantification operation, which we can utilise here. This leads to the following implementation:

$$\phi_i^0 = B(c)$$
$$\phi_i^j = \begin{cases} \exists_{V(v_j)}(D(v_j) \land \phi_i^{j-1}) & 1 \leq i, j \leq n,\ i \neq j \\ \phi_i^{i-1} & i = j \end{cases} \quad (2)$$
$$dom(c)(D)(v_i) = D(v_i) \land \phi_i^n$$

The worst case complexity is still $O(|B(c)| \times \Pi_{j=1}^n |D(v_j)|)$. Note that some of the computation can be shared between propagation of c for different variables since $\phi_i^j = \phi_{i'}^j$ when $j < i$ and $j < i'$.

4 Set Bounds and Split Domain Propagation

4.1 Set Bounds Propagation Using ROBDDs

ROBDDs are a very natural representation for sets and set constraints, so it seems logical to try implementing a set bounds propagator using ROBDD techniques. Since set bounds are an approximation to a set domain, we can construct an ROBDD representing the bounds on a set variable by approximating the ROBDD representing a domain. Only a trivial change is needed to the set domain propagator to turn it into a set bounds propagator.

The bounds on a set domain can be easily identified from the corresponding ROBDD representation of the domain. In an ROBDD-based domain propagator, the bounds on each set variable correspond to the *fixed* variables of the ROBDDs representing the set domains. A BDD variable v is said to be *fixed* if either for every node $n(v, t, e)$ t is the constant 0 node, or for every node $n(v, t, e)$ e is the constant 0 node. Such variables can be identified in a linear time scan over the domain ROBDD. For convenience, if ϕ is an ROBDD, we write $[\![\phi]\!]$ to denote the ROBDD representing the conjunction of the fixed variables of ϕ. Note that if ϕ represents a set of sets S, then $[\![\phi]\!]$ represents $conv(S)$. For example, if ϕ is the ROBDD depicted in Figure 1(c), then $[\![\phi]\!]$ is the ROBDD of Figure 1(a).

We can use this operation to convert our domain propagator into a bounds propagator by discarding all of the non-fixed variables from the ROBDDs representing the variable domains after each propagation step. Assume that $D(v)$ is always a stick ROBDD, which will be the case if we have only been performing set bounds propagation. If c is a constraint, and $vars(c) = \{v_1, \ldots, v_n\}$, we can construct a set bounds propagator $sb(c)$ for c thus:

$$\phi_0 = B(c)$$
$$\phi_j = \exists_{VAR(D(v_j))}(D(v_j) \wedge \phi_{j-1}) \qquad (3)$$
$$sb(c)(D)(v_i) = \overline{\exists}_{V(v_i)}(D(v_i) \wedge [\![\phi_n]\!])$$

Despite the apparent complexity of this propagator, it is significantly faster than a domain propagator for two reasons. Firstly, since the domains $D(v)$ are sticks, the resulting conjunctions ϕ_j are always decreasing (technically nonincreasing) in size, hence the corresponding propagation is much faster. Overall the complexity can be made $O(|B(c)|)$.

As an added bonus, we can use the updated set bounds to simplify the ROBDD representing the propagator. Since fixed variables will never interact further with propagation they can be projected out of $B(c)$, so we can replace $B(c)$ by $\exists_{VAR([\![\phi_n]\!])}\phi_n$. In practice it turns out to be more efficient to replace $B(c)$ by ϕ_n since this has already been calculated.

This set bounds solver retains many of the benefits of the ROBDD-based approach, such as the ability to remove intermediate variables and the ease of construction of global constraints, in some cases permitting a performance improvement over more traditional set bounds solvers.

4.2 Split Domain Propagation

One of the unfortunate characteristics of ROBDDs is that the size of the BDD representing a function can be very sensitive to the variable ordering that is chosen. If the fixed variables of a set domain do not appear at the start of the variable ordering, then the ROBDD for the domain in effect can contain several copies of the stick representing those variables. For example, Figure 1(c) effectively contains several copies of the stick in Figure 1(a). Since many of the ROBDD operations we perform take quadratic time, this larger than necessary representation costs us in performance.

In the context of groundness analysis of logic programs Bagnara [2] demonstrated that better performance can be obtained from an ROBDD-based program analyzer by splitting an ROBDD up into its fixed and non-fixed parts. We can apply the same technique here.

We split the ROBDD representing a domain $D(v)$ into a pair of ROBDDs $(L\overline{U}, R)$. $L\overline{U}$ is a stick ROBDD representing the Lower and Upper set bounds on $D(v)$, and R is a Remainder ROBDD representing the information on the unfixed part of the domain. Logically $D = L\overline{U} \wedge R$. We will write $L\overline{U}(D(v))$ and $R(D(v))$ to denote the $L\overline{U}$ and R parts of $D(v)$ respectively.

The following result provides an upper bound of the size of the split domain representation (proof omitted for space reasons):

Proposition 1. *Let D be an ROBDD, $L\overline{U} = [\![D]\!]$, and $R = \exists_{VAR(L\overline{U})} D$. Then $D \leftrightarrow L\overline{U} \wedge R$ and $|L\overline{U}| + |R| \leq |D|$.*

Note that $|D|$ can be $O(|L\overline{U}| \times |R|)$. For example, considering the ROBDDs in Figure 1 where $L\overline{U}$ is shown in (a), R is in (b) and $D = L\overline{U} \wedge R$ in (c) we have that $|L\overline{U}| = 5$ and $|R| = 9$ but $|D| = 9 + 4 \times 5 = 29$.

We construct the split propagator as follows: First we eliminate any fixed variables (as in bounds propagation) and then apply the domain propagation on the "remainders" R. We return a pair $(L\overline{U}, R)$ of the new fixed variables, and new remainder.

$$\phi_0 = B(c)$$
$$\phi_j = \exists_{VAR(L\overline{U}(D(v_j)))}(L\overline{U}(D(v_j)) \wedge \phi_{j-1})$$
$$\delta_i = \exists_{V(v_i)} (\phi_n \wedge \bigwedge_{j=1}^{n} R(D(v_j))) \quad (4)$$
$$\beta_i = L\overline{U}(D(v_i)) \wedge [\![\delta_i]\!]$$
$$dom(c)(D)(v_i) = (\beta_i, \exists_{VAR(\beta_i)} \delta_i)$$

For efficiency each δ_i should be calculated in an analogous manner to ϕ_i^n of Equation (2).

There are several advantages to the split domain representation. Proposition 1 tells us that the split domain representation is effectively no larger the simple domain representation. In many cases, the split representation can be substantially smaller, thus speeding up propagation. Secondly, we can use techniques from the bounds solver implementation to simplify the ROBDDs representing the constraints as variables are fixed during propagation. Thirdly, it becomes possible to mix the use of set bounds which operate only on the $\overline{LU}$ component of the domain with set domain propagators that need complete domain information.

5 Experimental Results

We have extended the set domain solver of Lagoon and Stuckey [6] to incorporate a set bounds solver and a split set domain solver. The implementation is written in Mercury [9] interfaced with the C language ROBDD library CUDD [8].

A series of experiments were conducted to compare the performance of the various solvers on a 933Mhz Pentium III with 1 Gb of RAM running Debian GNU/Linux 3.0. For the purposes of comparison benchmarks were also implemented using the ic_sets library of ECL^{i}PS^e v5.6 [5]. Since our solvers do not yet incorporate an integer constraint solver, we are limited to set benchmarks that utilise only set variables.

5.1 Steiner Systems

A commonly used benchmark for set constraint solvers is the calculation of small Steiner systems. A Steiner system $S(t, k, N)$ is a set X of cardinality N and a collection C of subsets of X of cardinality k (called 'blocks'), such that any t elements of X are in exactly one block. Steiner systems are an extensively studied branch of combinatorial mathematics. If $t = 2$ and $k = 3$ we have the so-called Steiner Triple Systems, which are often used as benchmarks [4, 6]. Any Steiner system must have exactly $m = \binom{N}{t}/\binom{k}{t}$ blocks (Theorem 19.2 of [10]).

We use the same modelling of the problem as Lagoon and Stuckey [6], extended for the case of more general Steiner Systems. We model each block as a set variable $s_1, \ldots, s_m$, with the constraints:

$$\bigwedge_{i=1}^{m}(|s_i| = k) \quad (5)$$

$$\wedge \bigwedge_{i=1}^{m-1} \bigwedge_{j=i+1}^{m} (\exists u_{ij}.u_{ij} = s_i \cap s_j \wedge |u_{ij}| \leq (t-1)) \wedge (s_i < s_j) \quad (6)$$

A necessary condition for the existence of a Steiner system is that $\binom{N-i}{t-i}/\binom{k-i}{t-i}$ is an integer for all $i \in \{0, 1, \ldots, t-1\}$; we say a set of parameters (t, k, N) is admissible if it satisfies this condition [10]. In order to choose test cases, we ran each solver on every admissible set of (t, k, N) values for $N < 32$. Results are given for every test case that at least one solver was able to solve within a time limit of 10 minutes. The labelling method used in all cases was sequential 'element-not-in-set' in order to enable accurate comparison of propagation performance.

Table 1. Performance results on Steiner Systems. The time and number of fails needed to find a solution or prove unsatisfiability are reported. × denotes abnormal termination on a test-case, either due to global/trail stack overflow in the case of ECL^{i}PS^e, or due to allocating too many BDD variables for the ROBDD solvers. '—' denotes failure to complete a testcase within 10 minutes. In all cases the domain solver and the split solver have the same number of fails

Problem	Separate Constraints							Merged Constraints				
	ECL^{i}PS^e		Bounds		Domain		Split	Bounds		Domain		Split
	Time/s	Fails	Time/s	Fails	Time/s	Fails	Time/s	Time/s	Fails	Time/s	Fails	Time/s
S(2,3,7)	0.6	10	**0.1**	10	**0.1**	0	0.2	**0.1**	8	**0.1**	0	**0.1**
S(3,4,8)	1.0	21	0.2	21	0.9	0	0.9	**0.1**	18	0.2	0	0.2
S(2,3,9)	16.7	1,394	5.9	1,394	2.1	100	3.1	0.3	325	**0.2**	9	**0.2**
S(2,3,13)	—	—	—	—	—	—	—	—	—	253.1	24,723	350.6
S(2,4,13)	4.0	313	1.9	313	3.6	32	3.1	**0.2**	157	0.3	0	0.3
S(2,3,15)	7.7	65	7.9	65	43.3	0	49.7	**0.7**	56	2.8	0	3.5
S(2,4,16)	—	—	—	—	—	—	—	—	—	1.3	15	1.2
S(2,6,16)	—	—	—	—	—	—	—	—	—	162.4	15,205	166.3
S(3,4,16)	162.0	289	×	×	×	×	×	24.5	274	—	—	—
S(2,5,21)	6.9	421	6.7	421	227.6	0	120.3	**0.9**	413	2.9	0	2.9
S(3,6,22)	115.4	1,619	×	×	×	×	×	19.5	1,608	—	—	—
S(2,3,31)	×	×	×	×	×	×	×	62.1	280	—	—	—

To compare the raw performance of the bounds propagators we performed experiments using a model of the problem with primitive constraints and intermediate variables u_{ij} directly as shown in Equations 5 and 6. The same model was used in both ECL^{i}PS^e and ROBDD-based solvers, permitting comparison of propagation performance, irrespective of modelling advantages. The results are shown in "Separate Constraints" section of Table 1. In all cases the ROBDD bounds solver performs better than ECL^{i}PS^e, with the exception of two cases which the ROBDD-based solvers cannot solve due to a need for an excessive number of BDD variables to model the intermediate variables (no propagation occurs in these cases).

Of course, the ROBDD representation permits us to merge primitive constraints and remove intermediate variables, allowing us to model the problem as m unary constraints and $\binom{m}{2}$ binary constraints (containing no intermediate variables u_{ij}) corresponding to Equations 5 and 6 respectively. Results for this improved model are shown in the "Merged Constraints" section of Table 1. Lagoon and Stuckey [6] demonstrated this leads to substantial performance improvements in the case of a domain solver; we find the same effect evident here for all of the ROBDD-based solvers.

With the revised model of the problem the ROBDD bounds solver outstrips the ECL^{i}PS^e solver by a significant margin for all test cases. Conversely the split domain solver appears not to produce any appreciable reduction in the

Table 2. First-solution performance results on the Social Golfers problem. Time and number of failures are given for all solvers, and the ROBDD peak live node count for ROBDD-based solvers. A first-fail "element-in-set" labelling strategy is used in all cases. "—" denotes failure to complete a test case within 10 minutes. The cases 5-4-3, 6-4-3, and 7-5-5 have no solutions

Problem	ECL^{i}PS^e		Bounds			Domain			Split		
w-g-s	time /s	fails	time /s	fails	size ×10³	time /s	fails	size ×10³	time /s	fails	size ×10³
2-5-4	16.2	10,468	**0.2**	30	41	**0.2**	0	44	**0.2**	0	43
2-6-4	107.6	64,308	1.5	2,036	**117**	0.4	0	129	**0.3**	0	124
2-7-4	210.8	114,818	5.1	4,447	**212**	1.0	0	346	**0.9**	0	325
2-8-5	—	—	—	—	—	5.3	0	1,367	4.4	0	**1,342**
3-5-4	30.8	14,092	**0.3**	44	**82**	0.8	0	199	0.6	0	189
3-6-4	200.0	83,815	5.5	2,357	**212**	3.4	0	952	**2.9**	0	919
3-7-4	404.8	146,419	16.7	5,140	**366**	5.5	0	1,504	4.8	0	1,419
4-5-4	39.5	14,369	**0.6**	47	**137**	2.0	0	487	1.6	0	461
4-6-5	—	—	106.2	19,376	**425**	187.9	0	4,159	131.1	0	2,880
4-7-4	560.2	149,767	31.7	5,149	**500**	24.7	0	2,139	**17.6**	0	2,004
4-9-4	95.4	19,065	**6.0**	139	**1,545**	395.7	0	13,137	256.9	0	5,615
5-4-3	—	—	454.8	103,972	**137**	**52.9**	**3,812**	543	63.1	**3,812**	613
5-5-4	—	—	10.6	2,388	**242**	5.8	18	1,333	**4.0**	18	1,128
5-7-4	—	—	54.8	5,494	**616**	67.5	0	3,054	**48.2**	0	2,476
5-8-3	**12.0**	**2,229**	2.1	19	**761**	10.3	0	2,046	10.9	0	2,192
6-4-3	—	—	569.8	90,428	**118**	**32.7**	**1,504**	440	36.9	**1,504**	612
6-5-3	—	—	3.9	495	**159**	**2.7**	34	441	**2.1**	34	414
6-6-3	**8.0**	**1,462**	—	—	—	3.6	7	699	2.9	7	709
7-5-3	—	—	—	—	—	37.8	**528**	1,058	31.2	**528**	1,082
7-5-5	—	—	—	—	—	static fail					

BDD sizes over the original domain solver, and so the extra calculation required to maintain the split domain leads to poorer performance.

5.2 Social Golfers

Another common set benchmark is the "Social Golfers" problem, which consists of arranging $N = g \times s$ golfers into g groups of s players for each of w weeks, such that no two players play together more than once. Again, we use the same model as Lagoon and Stuckey [6], using a $w \times g$ matrix of set variables v_{ij} where $1 \leq i \leq w$ and $1 \leq j \leq g$. It makes use of a global partitioning constraint not available in ECL^{i}PS^e but easy to build using ROBDDs.

Experimental results are shown in Table 2. These demonstrate the split domain solver is almost always faster than the standard domain solver, and requires substantially less space. Note that the BDD size results are subject to the operation of a garbage collector and hence are only a crude estimate of the relative sizes. This is particularly true in the presence of backtracking since Mercury has a garbage collected trail stack.

As we would expect, in most cases the bounds solver performs worse than the domain solvers due to weaker propagation, but can perform substantially better (for example 4-9-4 and 5-8-3) where because of the difference in search it explores a more productive part of the search space first (first-fail labelling acts differently for different propagators). Note the significant improvement of the ROBDD bounds solver over the ECL^{i}PS^e solver because of stronger treatment of the global constraint.

6 Conclusion

We have demonstrated two novel ROBDD-based set solvers, a set bounds solver and an improved set domain solver based on split set domains. We have shown experimentally that in many cases the bounds solver has better performance than existing set bounds solvers, due to the removal of intermediate variables and the straightforward construction of global constraints. We have also demonstrated that the split domain solver can perform substantially better than the original domain solver due to a reduction in the size of the ROBDDs.

Avenues for further investigation include investigating the performance of a hybrid bounds/domain solver using the split domain representation, and investigating other domain approximations in between the bounds and full domain approaches.

References

[1] F. Azevedo. *Constraint Solving over Multi-valued Logics*. PhD thesis, Faculdade de Ciências e Tecnologia, Universidade Nova de Lisboa, 2002.

[2] R. Bagnara. A reactive implementation of Pos using ROBDDs. In *Procs. of PLILP*, volume 1140 of *LNCS*, pages 107–121. Springer, 1996.

[3] R. E. Bryant. Symbolic Boolean manipulation with ordered binary-decision diagrams. *ACM Comput. Surv.*, 24(3):293–318, 1992. ISSN 0360-0300. doi: http://doi.acm.org.mate.lib.unimelb.edu.au/10.1145/136035.136043.

[4] C. Gervet. Interval propagation to reason about sets: Definition and implementation of a practical language. *Constraints*, 1(3):191–246, 1997.

[5] IC-PARC. The ECLiPSe constraint logic programming system. [Online, accessed 31 May 2004], 2003. URL http://www.icparc.ic.ac.uk/eclipse/.

[6] V. Lagoon and P. Stuckey. Set domain propagation using ROBDDs. In M. Wallace, editor, *Procs. of the 8th Int. Conf. on Constraint Programming*, LNCS, page to appear. Springer-Verlag, 2004. Also at http://www.cs.mu.oz.au/~pjs/papers/cp04-setdom.ps.

[7] J.-F. Puget. PECOS: a high level constraint programming language. In *Proceedings of SPICIS'92*, Singapore, 1992.

[8] F. Somenzi. CUDD: Colorado University Decision Diagram package. [Online, accessed 31 May 2004], Feb. 2004. http://vlsi.colorado.edu/~fabio/CUDD/.

[9] Z. Somogyi, F. Henderson, and T. Conway. The execution algorithm of Mercury, an efficient purely declarative logic programming language. *Journal of Logic Programming*, 29(1–3):17–64, 1996.

[10] J. H. van Lint and R. M. Wilson. *A Course in Combinatorics*. Cambridge University Press, 2nd edition, 2001.

User Friendly Decision Support Techniques in a Case-Based Reasoning System

Monica H. Ou[1], Geoff A.W. West[1], Mihai Lazarescu[1], and Chris Clay[2]

[1] Department of Computing,
Curtin University of Technology,
GPO Box U1987, Perth 6845, Western Australia, Australia
{ou, geoff, lazaresc}@cs.curtin.edu.au
[2] Royal Perth Hospital,
Perth, Western Australia, Australia
claycd@iinet.net.au

Abstract. This paper describes methods to enable efficient use and administration of a CBR system for teledermatology in which the users are assumed to be non-computer literate. In particular, a user-friendly interface to enable a general practitioner to decide a diagnosis with the minimum number of questions asked is proposed. Specifically, we propose a technique to improve the usefulness of a decision tree approach in terms of general rather than specific questions. Additionally, we describe a new technique to minimise the number of questions presented to the user in the query process for training the CBR system. Importantly we apply FCA technique to enable the consultant dermatologist to validate new knowledge and supervised the incremental learning of the CBR system.

1 Introduction

Teledermatology is defined as the practice of dermatological services at a distance [1]. However, current systems lack decision support abilities and human interaction [2]. Our aim is to develop a Web-based CBR (Case-Based Reasoning) system that can be used to provide decision support to general practitioners (GPs) for diagnosing patients with dermatological problems. CBR has been successfully applied to medical diagnosis, such as in PROTOS and CASEY [3].

There are many machine learning techniques that have been developed for classification and learning. Most commercial CBR tools support case retrieval using Nearest Neighbor or Inductive Decision Trees due to the simplicity of the algorithms and good classification performance [3]. CBR is a popular approach that has been applied to various domains, most of the research having been focused on the classification aspect of the system. However, relatively little effort has been put on the human computer interaction aspect of CBR. The users of the system (i.e. the GPs and consultant) are mostly non-computer experts although they are experts in the medical domain. The important aspects of this research that need to be addressed are as follows:

1. How to enable non-computer experts to easily and efficiently interact with the system during the diagnosis process.
2. How to improve the comprehensibility of the rules generated by machine learning techniques such as decision trees.
3. Provide a simple but effective mechanism for validating and maintaining the knowledge base. The CBR system needs maintenance on a regular basis as new cases get added to the database. These tasks are to be done by a consultant dermatologist who is a domain expert but may not be a computer expert. The system needs to enable the non-computer expert to easily detect and visualise the inconsistency between the previous and new input cases.

This paper proposes a general methodology to provide easy to use decision support for the GPs, and describes a supervised incremental learning approach via the consultant. The objectives required to be developed to assist the GPs are: To reduce the number of questions presented to the user during the querying process to minimise the consultation time, and to handle the attribute visualisation problem caused by the output of the decision tree classification algorithm. The decision tree partitions the attribute values into a binary format of "yes/no", which makes it hard for the non computer science literate user to understand.

Normally CBR systems are allowed to learn by themselves. The analogy here is the GP would take the current case, compare with those in the CBR, and once satisfied, add the case to the database. In our case, the valid cases are chosen by another user (the consultant) after reviewing each case. The inconsistent or ambiguous cases can then be visualised and handled by the consultant. The FCA technique is used to enable learning of the CBR system by the consultant. FCA is a mathematical theory which formulates the conceptual structure, and displays relations between concepts in the form of concept lattices which comprise attributes and objects [4,5]. A lattice is a directed acyclic graph in which each node can have more than one parent, and the convention is that the superconcept always appears above all of its subconcepts. FCA has been used as a method for knowledge representation and retrieval [6,7], conceptual clustering [5], and as a support technique for CBR [8]. Overall, FCA is used to:

1. Help the consultant supervise the incremental learning of the CBR system.
2. Validate the consistency between current and previous knowledge.
3. Represent the differences between the current and previous cases with the use of context tables and concept lattices. The lattice is recreated as the table changes when each new case is added. Sudden changes in the rules would necessitate new attributes to be added, old cases to be examined and reviewed, or the new unclassified case stored in some repositories by the consultant for later referral.

Initial discussion with various GPs reveals a significant issue with the decision support system. Importantly there is opposition to various autonomous techniques for decision making. The GPs need to supervise the diagnosis process. In addition, the consultant needs to supervise the CBR system.

Overall, the objective is to provide tools to allow GPs and consultants (non-experts in artificial intelligence and computer science) to use and train a CBR system in an efficient way. In addition, it is important to provide the GP user of our system with a flexible and user-friendly GUI interface as well as minimising the amount of time spent on each task. The expected outcome of using the system is that it will be beneficial and effective to both the GPs and the consultants and reduce the travelling costs for patients.

2 Overall System Architecture

The CBR system involves asking questions for appropriate symptoms, and returning the most likely diagnosis for that particular complaint. We define protocols, apply a decision tree classification technique, and define a general methodology for validating and maintaining the knowledge base by the consultant. In developing the system, we require a convenient way of storing all the past cases and allowing the new cases to be added easily to the case-base.

2.1 The Data

The data we use in our experiments consist of patient records for the diagnosis of dermatological problems. The dataset is provided by Dr C. Clay. It contains patient details, symptoms and importantly, the consultant's diagnosis. Each patient is given an identification number, and episode numbers are used for multiple consultations for the same patient. The data has 17 general attributes and consists of cases describing 22 diagnoses [9]. Data collection is a continuous process with new cases added to the case-base after consultant diagnosis.

2.2 Defined Protocols

Knowledge acquisition and validation continue to be problematic in knowledge-based systems due to the modelling nature of these tasks. For these reasons our focus is to design a CBR decision support system that disallows automatic update. All new knowledge is to be validated by the consultant dermatologist. The reason for this is that the CBR system requires human expert supervision in order to ensure that the decision and learning are correct. This is particularly important as some of the new cases might be inconsistent with the previous cases in the knowledge base.

During knowledge elicitation with the consultant, we identified protocols which reflect the way the GP should use the decision support system for diagnosing patients with skin problems. As shown in Figure 1, the GP performs diagnosis if and only if confident. In other words, the GP may use the system to *assist* them with the diagnoses process. Otherwise, the GP ultimately needs to consult a consultant by emailing the patient's case history for evaluation. The consultant may need to go through different stages if unsure about the diagnosis. The stages include requiring the GP to perform trials of therapy (e.g. micro biology, blood tests, imaging etc), use video conferencing with the GP and the patient, face-to-face consultation, consult with peers in Perth, peers in Australia,

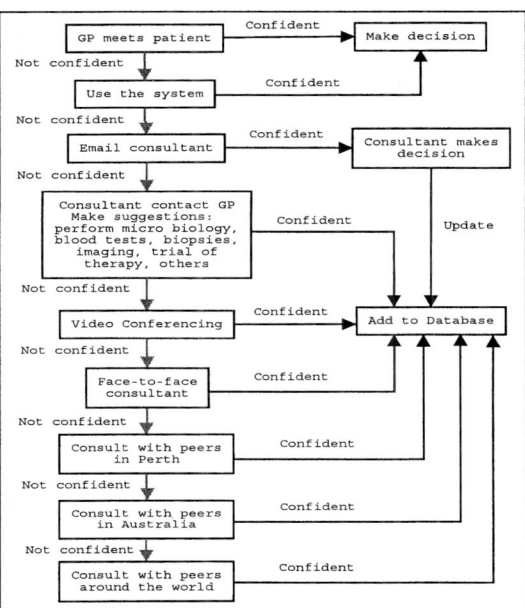

Fig. 1. The process of using the system

and finally consult with peers around the world. However, if the consultant is confident, then the new diagnosed case can get added to the database.

2.3 Classification

An important issue in CBR is generalisation across all the cases. The problem with CBR is how to ask questions in the right format. For example, it is poor to ask questions for which the answer is *"yes"/"no"*. It is much better and more user-friendly for the system to ask a more general question such as *"Where does the lesion occur?"*. Rather than a number of separate *"yes"/"no"* questions, such as *"Does the lesion occur on your leg?"*. However, *"yes"/"no"* and related type answers are what a decision tree asks. This is usually acceptable when the computer is giving the answer, and not a human.

This research involves using J48 [10]. It is the Weka[1] implementation of the C4.5 decision tree algorithm [11] for inducing the rules. In Figure 2, the CBR engine generates classification rules based on the data stored in the database. Most importantly these rules are reformulated into simpler rules represented by 17 general user-friendly questions that could be used to ask the GP. These questions are typically used by GPs in the real world during the GP-Patient diagnosis. The general questions are defined by the consultant dermatologist, and cover the 17 topics concerned with diagnosis.

---

[1] www.cs.waikato.ac.nz/ml/weka [Last accessed: March 2, 2004].

There are two different approaches available to the GP. The GP may enter some general information about the patient provided that there is some knowledge about the possible diagnosis. Based on the given information, the system chooses the next most appropriate question to ask. Alternatively, the GP may provide no information by going straight to the first question that gets generated by the system. For both options, the query process continues until the GP feels confident about the diagnosis, or the system finds the matching symptom of the current case with a past case. Then the system returns the most appropriate diagnosis for the particular complaint. In addition, the system returns a list of close matches that are ranked in terms of similarity between current and past cases. Currently, the similarity measure is defined by the distance between two vectors (i.e. the current case is compared with the past cases in the knowledge base). The reason for calculating and displaying the close matches is to alert the GP of other possible diagnoses that appear to have features which are similar to those of the current case.

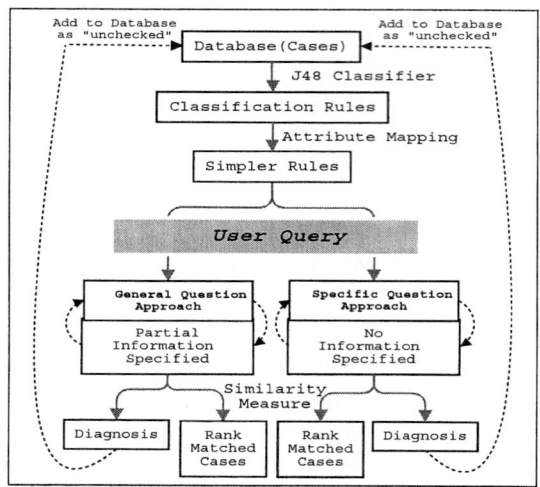

Fig. 2. The CBR classification sequence and GP interrogation process

2.4 Knowledge Validation and Maintenance

The case being diagnosed by the GP is stored in the database and marked as 'unchecked'. This means the diagnosed case needs to be checked by an authorised consultant before deciding whether or not to add it to the knowledge base. In most cases, if the consultant disagrees with the conclusion they are required to specify the correct conclusion and select some features in the case to justify the new conclusion. The correctly classified new case is then stored in the database.

One of the difficult tasks in using expert systems is the requirement for updating and maintaining of the knowledge base. It is important to make sure new knowledge/cases are consistent with past knowledge. We apply FCA to visually check for consistency between new and past cases. If adding a new case will dramatically change the lattice, then the consultant can easily see the changes in the lattice and needs to determine if the new case added is valid. Figure 3 presents the process of knowledge validation and maintenance. J48 is used to automatically partition the continuous attribute values. The attribute-value pair of the rules are automatically extracted and represented as a formal context which show relations between the attributes and the diagnosis. The formal context gets converted to a concept lattice for easy visualisation as a hierarchical structure of the lattices. As each new case gets added, the formal context gets updated and a new lattice is generated. The differences between the two lattices are highlighted to reflect the changes and inconsistency as the result of adding each new case.

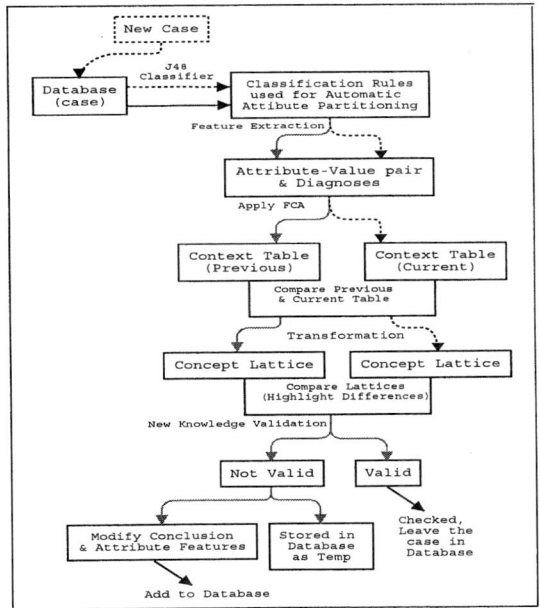

Fig. 3. Knowledge base validation and maintenance

It is important to emphasize that such a system has to be as accurate as possible and certainly not contain rules or data that are contradictory. It is vital that the expert (consultant) be confident the rules and data are valid. This process cannot be done automatically as it requires a human expert to constantly check for consistency in the current knowledge base and maintain the quality of the data as new cases get added.

2.5 Attribute Visualisation and Minimising the Querying Process

Generally, the output (e.g. decision rules) generated by machine learning algorithms are usually hard to understand and be interpreted by human users, especially for non-computing experts. Therefore, our objective is to have a System-GP query process not dissimilar to the GP-Patient query process. This means it is better to ask a more general question rather than a number of separate *"yes"/"no"* questions. The question is how do we derive these general questions from the essentially *"yes"/"no"* questions a decision tree generates.

Flexibility is also the key issue to consider when designing a decision support system. It is also recommended to allow the GP to give answers to general questions before the query begins. Again, this gives the GPs the flexibility and removes dependence on the order in which questions are generated by the tree and allows many rules to be satisfied in advance leading to increased efficiency.

3 Decision Support for General Practitioners

3.1 A Technique for Minimising the Querying Process

This paper describes a new approach for minimising the querying process to shorten the number of steps the user needs to perform. The technique is expected to be particularly useful to GPs in terms of saving the amount of time spent for identifying the possible diagnosis.

Based on decision rules generated from the C4.5 algorithm, the normal querying process starts from the root of the decision tree. That means the root of the tree forms the first question that gets presented to the GP. The root is usually the best attribute for disambiguating the most classes/cases and may not be obvious to the GP as a useful attribute. It is also not good to ask the same first question for each new case as this would not be liked by the GP and would lead to the system not being used. It is preferable to initially acquire partial information from the GP and then present the subsequent questions related to the given information. We provide the system with both the options and concentrate here on the second approach.

Success of the second approach is highly dependent on the amount of information provided by the GP. The more information the GP specifies, the fewer questions there are left to be answered. The second option involves two main stages in the querying process:

1. The system starts off by displaying the general questions directly to the GP.
   (a) The GP chooses the general questions and the corresponding answers based on the condition/symptoms of the patient.
   (b) Submit the information to the CBR engine for back-end processing.
   (c) The system eliminates all the rules that do not correspond to the selected questions.
2. The system displays the first question that corresponds to the information initially given by the GP.
   (a) The system extracts the matched rules from the existing rule collection.
   (b) Based on the pattern in the rules, it presents the first question by calculating the common parent node of the entered attributes. This helps determine which part of the tree the matching should focus on.

(c) Then based on the retrieved answer, it gets the remaining matched rules.
(d) Process "c" repeats until there is only one rule existing in the collection. Then the system displays the diagnosis to the GP.

We provide some explicit examples to illustrate the interaction between the user and the CBR system. The results show that our technique requires fewer steps to get to the solution compared to the standard decision tree. This is because you get decisions based on the same attribute occurring at more than one level in the tree, e.g. a rule concerning the time of onset of a rash. At one level it may be ≤ 6 weeks, further down it is ≤ 3 weeks. A general question asking for when the onset occurred would satisfy both decisions. The proposed technique helps solve the problem of asking redundant questions. Note that the number of questions X is usually less than n, as many nodes in a tree are concerned with the same attribute. The worse case is for $X = n$, where n is the depth of the tree.

The tree shown in Figure 4 is used to demonstrate the attribute matching when the user provides partial information at the initial phase. The demonstration is based on a few scenarios.

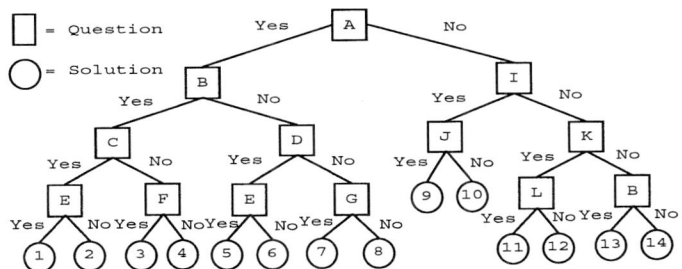

Fig. 4. A sample decision tree

- If the user enters $E = Yes$, $D = Yes$, then the next question the system displays to the user would be $B = Yes$ or No? The system asks for the answer to B for confirmation. If $B = No$, then it returns solution number 5, because E is the last node in the tree and no other pattern matches these two entered attributes. Note, there is no need to ask C, due to the existence of D. Compared with the standard decision tree query approach, ours involves fewer questions.
- If the user enters only one attribute such as $E = Yes$, since $E = Yes$ belongs to different branches of the tree, the system asks B (because B is the common node of the two patterns). If the answer is Yes, then C is the next question to ask; else D is asked.
- If the user enters $B = No$ and $G = No$. Then the next node to ask is A which is the parent of the two entered attributes. If $A = Yes$, then ask D. If $D = No$, then return solution number 7; else if $D = Yes$, ask E and return solution 5 or 6 by answer to E. This can avoid asking the intermediate node.

As can be seen from the example, the querying process is good for minimising the number of questions presented to the GP.

3.2 Attribute Visualisation Technique

We transform the generated attribute-valued pair from the J48 classifier to a more user friendly attribute grouping and naming. This is necessary because it is hard for the users of our system (mainly the GPs and the consultant) to understand the meaning of the attributes in these rules (see Figure 5). The purpose of attribute grouping is to improve the comprehensibility of the query-based information presented to the GP. A step-by-step procedure for performing attribute mapping is as follows:

1. Identify related attributes that may belong to the same general question.
2. Group all the related attributes into a conceptual element.
3. Specify a higher level name (commonsense name) that best describes the conceptual element.
4. Perform the attribute mapping, i.e. map the attributes that are in the decision rules to the specified commonsense names.

The attribute mapping technique also prevents the same type of attribute being asked more than once (which occurs because an attribute may be used on different levels of the tree for partitioning). We present a simple example to illustrate the concept of attribute mapping. The classification rules generated by J48 are in the format shown in Figure 5.

---

1. $(treatments\_antifungalCream\_moderatResult) = Y \Longrightarrow SeborrhoeicDermatitis$
2. $(treatments\_antifungalCream\_moderatResult = N) \rightarrow (sites\_onset\_upperArm = Y) \rightarrow (lesion\_status = 3) \Longrightarrow KeratosisPilaris$
3. $(treatments\_antifungalCream\_moderatResult = N) \rightarrow (sites\_onset\_upperArm = Y) \rightarrow (lesion\_status = 4) \Longrightarrow Urticaria$
4. $(treatments\_antifungalCream\_moderatResult = N) \rightarrow (sites\_onset\_upperArm = N) \rightarrow (cur\_meds\_septrin = Y) \Longrightarrow ErythemaMultiforme$

Fig. 5. Sample classification rules from J48

We perform attribute mapping to produce simpler rules, so that the attributes will belong to different general groups with meaningful names. For example, rule 1 in Figure 5, rather than having to ask the GP *"treatments_antifungalCream-moderateResults = Y"*, it is better to ask *"What treatments do you have?"*, then provide the GP with a list of answers to the question. The rule simply means "If after application of the antifungal cream, the result is moderate, then the diagnosis would be Seborrhoeic Dermatitis". Currently these approaches are being evaluated with the help of various GPs to determined how useful this is.

4 Supervised Incremental Learning by Consultant

It is important to validate the rules extracted from the past cases to determine if they are correct and consistence and reliable enough to accurately classify new cases. This validation process is to prevent new cases that contradict the existing cases from being added into the knowledge base. Note the consultant is the person who, being the expert, adds new cases to the system and as a consequence has to be able to check to see if new rules generated from the modified case database are valid.

We combine FCA and CBR classification for validating new knowledge and need to evaluate the usefulness of this approach. The incorporation of FCA into CBR has enabled a concept lattice to be built automatically from a context table. The table consists of attribute-value pairs that are generated by the decision tree learning algorithm. The decision tree is used to partition the continuous attribute values (e.g. duration of illness) into a binary format. The modelling of the validation process will benefit the consultant in many ways:

1. Provide visual representation of the concept.
2. Graphically visualise the changes in the classification rules as new cases are added to the knowledge base.
3. Detect any inconsistency between previous and the new case.

4.1 Formal Context

Of interest to the consultant is how each new case will affect the knowledge in the case base. The context table is a useful tool for representing the conceptual differences between the previous and current cases.

The formal context (C) is derived from the attribute-value pairs generated by the decision tree. It is defined as follows.

Definition: A formal context $C = (D, A, I)$, where D is a set of diagnoses, A is a set of attributes, and I is a binary relation which indicates diagnosis d has attribute a.

Table 1 shows a simple example of a formal context of our system using only a subset of mixed types attribute for simplicity. The objects on each row represent the diagnosis D, whereas the attributes on each column represent a set of related symptoms A, and the relation I is marked by the "X" symbol. In this case each X shows the important attributes for each of the diagnoses.

As the consultant enters each new case, the context table will be affected which reflects the changes in attributes and diagnoses. The relationship between the attribute and diagnosis (marked"X") will also change accordingly. By comparing the relationships between certain attributes and diagnoses in the new context table with the previous table we can determine if the existing concepts have changed dramatically. The changes are measured by the degree of similarity between the previous and current concepts. The measurement is based on the

Table 1. Formal context using a subset of related attributes

	progressive	fluctuating	static	remitting	intermittent	age>20	age<=20
Atopic eczema		X	X		X		
Plaque psoriasis	X	X	X				
Pustular psoriasis	X		X				
Guttate psoriasis	X		X			X	X
Allergic contact dermatitis		X		X		X	X
Irritant contact dermatitis		X	X			X	X
Pompholyx			X	X			
Lichen planus	X		X				
Discoid eczema	X	X	X	X			X
Varicella (chicken pox)	X						X
Herpes simplex					X		
Molluscum contagiosum	X		X				
Verruca vulgaris	X		X			X	
Pityriasis rosea	X		X			X	
Impetigo	X		X				
Cellulitis	X		X				
Folliculitis	X	X	X				
Furunculosis	X						

matching number of attributes and the relationships which correspond to the diagnosis. A minor difference indicates a small degree of variation.

If the concept changes significantly, then the consultant needs to check to see if the new case is in fact valid. If the case is invalid, the consultant is required to change the conclusion or the attribute features to satisfy the new case or store the case in a repository for later use (refer to Figure 3). With the help of the consultant, the stored instances will be used to train the CBR system.

4.2 Concept Lattices

The formal context shown in Table 1 can be expressed in a form of a concept lattice. Initially, a concept lattice is generated from the current specified formal context table. However, as the consultant adds a new case, the system presents a new lattice based on the new specified context. The previous lattice is stored and compares with the new lattice. The nodes and links in the lattices are highlighted in different colours to illustrate the differences. The two lattices are expected to change very slightly. If however, there is dramatic changes in the new lattice, then obviously there is a serious inconsistency between the current and previous cases. Once again, the consultant is required to change the conclusion or the attribute features to satisfy the new case (refer to Figure 3).

5 Conclusions

This paper presents a general methodology to extract and represent knowledge from the CBR system and the consultant to produce easy to use decision support for GPs. We use a new approach to minimise the querying process of a decision tree compared to the standard decision tree. In addition, we propose a technique to improve the visualisation of the attributes. Of importance to the CBR system is how to validate new knowledge and maintain consistency of the knowledge base. We apply FCA to analyze the knowledge base and highlight the inconsistency after each new case is added. The new methodology not only gives a new way to handle the querying process with the minimum number of questions, but also helps to provide a logical and user-friendly interface for the CBR system. The proposed use of FCA for validating the new concept and supervise the incremental learning of the CBR system have shown through interaction with a consultant.

Acknowledgements

The research reported in this paper has been funded in full by a grant from the AHMAC/SCRIF initiative administered by the NHMRC.

References

1. Wootton, R., Oakley, A., eds.: Teledermatology. Royal Society of Medicine Press Ltd, London, UK (2002)
2. Tait, C.P., Clay, C.D.: Pilot Study of Store and Forward Teledermatology Services in Perth, Western Australia. Australian Journal of Dermatology (1999) Research Report. Royal Perth Hospital, Australia.
3. Watson, I.: Applying Case-Based Reasoning: Techniques for Enterprise Systems. Morgan Kaufmann Publishers, USA (1997)
4. Ganter, B., Wille, R.: Formal Concept Analysis: Mathematical Foundations. Springer, Heidelberg (1999)
5. Ganter, B.: Computing with Conceptual Structures. In: Proc. of the 8th International Conference on Conceptual Structure, Darmstadt, Springer (2000)
6. Cole, R. Eklund, P., Amardeilh, F.: Browsing Semi-structured Texts on the Web using Formal Concept Analysis. Web Intelligence (2003)
7. Richards, D.: Visualizing Knowledge Based Systems. In: Proceedings of the 3rd Workshop on Software Visualization, Sydney, Australia (1999) 1–8
8. Díaz-Agudo, B., Gonzalez-Calero, P.A.: Formal Concept Analysis as a Support Technique for CBR. Knowledge-Based System **7** (2001) 39–59
9. Ou, M.H., West, G.A.W., Lazarescu, M.: Dealing with Decision Costs in CBR in Medical Applications. In: Proceedings of the 16th Australian Joint Conference on Artificial Intelligence AI-03, Perth, Australia (2003) 666–677
10. Witten, I., Frank, E.: Data Mining: Practical Machine Learning Tools and Techniques with Java Implementations. Morgan Kaufmann Publishers, USA (2000)
11. Quinlan, J.R.: C4.5 Programs for Machine Learning. Morgan Kaufmann Publishers, USA (1993)

Longer-Term Memory in Clause Weighting Local Search for SAT

Valnir Ferreira Jr. and John Thornton

Institute for Integrated and Intelligent Systems,
Griffith University,
PMB50 Gold Coast Mail Centre , QLD 9726
{v.ferreira, j.thornton}@griffith.edu.au

Abstract. This paper presents a comparative study between a state-of-the-art clause weighting local search method for satisfiability testing and a variant modified to obtain longer-term memory from a global measure of clause perturbation. We present empirical evidence indicating that by learning which clauses are hardest to satisfy, the modified method can offer significant performance improvements for a well-known range of satisfiable problems. We conclude that our method's ability to learn, and consequently to offer performance improvement, can be attributed to its ability to obtain information from a global measure of hardness, rather than from the contextual perspective exploited in previous works.

1 Introduction

Local search methods have attracted substantial attention in the research community due to their ability to efficiently find solutions to satisfiability testing (SAT) problems that are too large for complete search methods. SAT problems are of significant practical and theoretical interest as many real-world applications like artificial intelligence reasoning, constraint satisfaction, and planning can be formulated in this way. The problem consists of finding an assignment for the Boolean variables in a propositional formula that makes the formula true [2]. Local search methods for SAT work by iteratively modifying the value of one variable in the problem from true to false or vice-versa. These variable flips are typically performed so as to minimise an evaluation function that maps any given variable assignment x to the number of unsatisfied clauses under x. The methods follow this heuristic until a satisfying assignment is found (all clauses are satisfied) or until either a maximum run-time or number of flips is reached.

Clause weighting local search methods (CWLS) modify a basic local search by having individual weights assigned to all clauses in the SAT problem, thus dynamically changing the evaluation function and the search landscape as the search progresses. Since the introduction of weighted local search more than a decade ago [4, 6], several improvements have been proposed, the most relevant ones being the discrete Lagrangian method (DLM) [9], and SAPS [3], which at the time of its publication achieved state-of-the-art performance on a range of benchmark SAT problems. Recently, the pure additive weighting scheme (PAWS) was introduced [7] and shown to give significant performance improvements over SAPS on a range of challenging well-known SAT problems from the SATLIB[1] and DIMACS[2] libraries, as well as on a set of SAT-encoded random binary CSPs from the phase transition region.

In this work, we hypothesise that the performance of clause weighting local search methods such as PAWS can be significantly enhanced by learning which clauses are globally hardest to satisfy, and by using this information to treat these clauses differentially. Our work is principally motivated by (a) the fact that there seems to be some speculation and little empirical results on this topic, and (b) the belief that we can improve the performance of CWLS methods for SAT by identifying and exploiting implicit longer-term clause dependencies.

2 Learning While Weighting

Several works have investigated whether clause weights in CWLS methods should be seen as useful information, and therefore be interpreted as learning how to better search SAT instances. These works propose that by dynamically modifying their weight profile while searching a given instance, CWLS methods are in fact rendering the underlying search space easier. This idea was used for many years as an explanation for the efficiency of these methods in general. The work on WGSAT [1] offered some better insights into this topic by concluding that clause weights can only offer information that is limited and contextual (i.e. related to the last few assignments), and should therefore be interpreted only as a source of short-term memory. As the search moves away from a particular context, such information is no longer relevant in the new context. This is a reason why all successful CWLS methods need efficient ways to adjust clause weights as the search progresses, as it is by doing so that they can maintain the weight profile relevant to the context in which they are searching. To this end, most methods can be divided into those that adjust their weight profiles multiplicatively, and those that do it additively.

Multiplicative methods use floating point clause weights and increase/decrease multipliers that combined give the weight profile a much finer granularity. Additive methods, on the other hand, assign integer values to clause weights and increase/decrease amounts, which results in a coarser clause weight distribution. Given that CWLS methods rely on their weight profiles for search guidance, and given the tightly coupled relationship between these weight profiles and the selection of candidate variables to flip (which ultimately impinges on a method's runtime), we currently believe that the efficiency of additive methods like PAWS can be partially explained by the fact that additive methods make less distinction between candidate costs and thus consider a larger domain of candidate moves [7]. One can see why it would be desirable to derive guidance from information

---

[1] http://www.satlib.org
[2] http://dimacs.rutgers.edu/Challenges/Seventh/PC

that is of a long-term nature, rather than short-term, or contextual. Intuitively, longer-term memory is desirable because it could lead to the development of better flipping heuristics that would take into account global information such as which clauses are hardest to satisfy or which clauses have been unsatisfied the most during the search. To our knowledge, such information is currently not explored by even the most efficient methods.

In an attempt to exploit longer-term memory for remembering and avoiding local minima, DLM was extended [10] with a *special increase* sub-procedure that picks a set C of clauses (the size of C is problem dependent and varies between the number of all false clauses and the number of clauses in the problem) and then computes the ratio between the maximum clause weight in C and the mean weight of all clauses in C. If this ratio is larger than a problem dependent threshold, then the weight of the clause with the maximum clause weight in C is increased by 1. Note that the special increase sub-procedure is called at the end of DLM's clause re-weighting stage, so it can be seen as the adding of an extra penalty to that single most heavily weighted clause. The use of special increases was shown to have flattened the distribution of the number of times clauses had to be re-weighted during the search, with the resulting algorithm showing improved performance over the original DLM for a range of hard satisfiable instances from the DIMACS library. The effect that the special increase has on the weight profile is interesting as, given the resulting better performance, it could point towards a correlation between a less rugged search space and the method's ability to find a solution more efficiently.

The usefulness of clause weights for learning how to better search SAT instances has been brought back into the spotlight recently in [8]. In this work, SAPS was run on a given problem until a solution was found, and the corresponding clause weights at that point were recorded. These weights were then used to generate the so-called weighted instances, i.e., instances where the weight of each clause is initialised to the value the clause had *at the end* of the preceding successful run, rather than to one. The authors then propose that if a method can find a solution to the weighted instance by performing less flips than it would for the corresponding unweighted instance, then the weights carried over from the previous run would be truly making a difference (i.e. making the instance easier). Note that this is the same as restarting the method while maintaining all clause weights unmodified. The authors then go on to say that "if all clause weights represent *knowledge* that the algorithm has accumulated about the search space, then the modified SAPS algorithm is starting with all knowledge *a priori*". Then, a set of relatively easy instances[3] was used to test this hypothesis, and the results demonstrated that there was no significant difference between the two methods, which led to the conclusion that there was no evidence to support the claim that the creation of modified landscapes by

---

[3] Unweighted SAPS was able to solve 9 out of 10 instances in less than 200,000 flips; 8 of which it was able to solve in less than 35,000 flips.

CWLS methods render instances any easier, and so the belief that this can be seen as a form of learning is incorrect and should be dismissed.

The main criticism we level at this approach is that it tries to harness knowledge from clause weights in an innefective way. It uses the weight profile recorded at the time when the method found a solution to initialise the weights of clauses of a new instance where variables are randomly instantiated to values potentially different from the ones assigned to them when the weight profile was recorded. In our view, this type of weight usage is doomed to fail, as there is substantial evidence (for instance [1]) to support the fact that clause weights used in this way are context dependent, i.e., at any point in time during the search they will provide a short-term memory that only goes back a few instantiations (more or less, depending on the weight adjustment mechanism being used by the CWLS method). Alternatively, the heuristic we introduce and explain throughout the remainder of this paper is able to explore longer-term information derived from a global, rather than contextual, measure of clause perturbation that is available as a by-product of the weight update mechanism that is common to CWLS methods.

3 PAWS+US

PAWS is an additive CWLS method for SAT that achieves state-of-the-art performance on a range of hard satisfiable SAT problems. Figure 1 shows the augmented version of PAWS, modified to accommodate what we call the *usual suspects* heuristic (US). The usual suspects are the clauses that emerge from a run as the most heavily weighted, according to a cumulative list that logs the number of times each clause was weighted during the search. We call this modified method *PAWS+US* to distinguish it from the standard PAWS. The methods only differ in respect to the clause weight initialisation (lines 4-8) and weight update (lines 19-26) procedures. In all other respects, PAWS+US is identical to the standard PAWS presented in [7].

The method begins by randomly instantiating all variables in the problem. PAWS initialises all clause weights to 1, whereas PAWS+US initialises the weight of the US clauses to their special weight increment (*inc*), and the weight of other clauses to one. After this initialisation stage, the search begins and while a solution is not found and the search is not terminated (either by reaching a maximum predetermined time or number of flips) the method builds, at every iteration, a list L of candidate flips, where an element of L is a variable that, if flipped, would reduce the objective function the most (lines 10-16). Then, with probability 1-P_{flat}[4] it randomly selects and flips a variable from L, and with probability P_{flat} it takes a flat move, i.e., a variable flip that would leave the value of the

---

[4] P_{flat} is one of two parameters of PAWS that determines the probability for a flat move. We found that P_{flat} can be treated as a constant, and its value was set at 15% for all experiments reported here.

objective function unchanged (lines 17-18). If no potential improvement is found (i.e. any variable flip would result in an increased value for the objective function, and hence the method has reached a local minimum), then a weight update is performed. At this stage PAWS adds one to the weight of every unsatisfied clause, whereas PAWS+US adds a special weight increment value (inc) to the US clauses that are unsatisfied at this point and one to every other false clause (lines 20-22). After the weight update stage is finished, if $MaxInc$[5] consecutive weight increases have taken place, then a weight decrease is performed whereby every weighted clause ($c_j \mid w_j > 1$) has its weight subtracted by one.

```
1.  procedure PAWS+US
2.  begin
3.      generate random starting point
4.      for each clause cᵢ do:
5.          if PAWS then set clause weight wᵢ ← 1
6.          else if PAWS+US then set clause weight wᵢ ← incᵢ
7.          end if
8.      end for
9.      while solution not found and not terminated do
10.         best ← ∞
11.         for each literal xᵢⱼ in each false clause fᵢ do
12.             Δw ←change Σw in false clause caused by flipping xᵢⱼ
13.             if Δw < best then L ← xᵢⱼ and best← Δw
14.             else if Δw = best then L = L ∪ xᵢⱼ
15.             end if
16.         end for
17.         if best < 0 or (best = 0 and probability ≤ P_flat) then
18.             randomly flip xᵢⱼ ∈ L
19.         else
20.             if PAWS then for each false clause fᵢ do: wᵢ ← wᵢ + 1
21.             else if PAWS+US then for each false clause fᵢ do: wᵢ ← wᵢ + incᵢ
22.             end if
23.             if # times clause weights increased % MaxInc = 0 then
24.                 for each clause cⱼ | wⱼ > 1 do: wⱼ ← wⱼ − 1
25.             end if
26.         end if
27.     end while
28. end
```

Fig. 1. The PAWS method with the US extension

4 Empirical Study

The first part of our empirical study involved creating the lists of usual suspects for each of the 25 problems in our test set. In order to determine the US list

---

[5] $MaxInc$ is another parameter of PAWS used to determine the point in the search where a weight decrease will be performed.

for a problem, we ran PAWS 100 times with optimal values for $MaxInc$[6] while keeping a counter of the number of times each clause was weighted during the search (i.e. the clause was false at the time a weight increase was performed). We then obtained the mean number of weight increases for every clause over the 100 runs, and ordered the resulting list in descending order of weight increases. This resulting list is used to determine the US clauses for a run of PAWS+US. The method requires two extra parameters in addition to $MaxInc$, namely the usual suspects list length (LL) and the usual suspects weight increment (Inc). For this study we considered list lengths between 1 and 10 and weight increments between 2 and 5. Initially, we also tried list lengths consisting of the top 5 and top 10% most heavily weighted clauses but due to discouraging results we decided not to consider these list lengths further. For each of the 40 possible (Inc, LL) pairs for a problem, PAWS+US was run 100 times and the statistics for these runs were collected. For example, if PAWS+US(Inc:2,LL:5) is used on a problem p, the top 5 clauses from p's US list will have their weight incremented by 2 (instead of the standard weight increment of 1) every time a weight increase is performed and the clause is unsatisfied. Note here the important distinction between the US heuristic and the heuristic discussed above used with SAPS to investigate the usefulness of clause weights for learning how to better search SAT instances. The US lists provide global information of a longer-term nature that is used to treat the US clauses differentially throughout the search every time a weight increase takes place whereas the approach previously discussed uses contextual information obtained at the end of one search to instantiate the weights of clauses in a subsequent search. There is no differential treatment of these clauses in any way. Therefore, in comparison, we can say that our approach first *learns* which clauses are typically hardest to satisfy and then uses this information to treat these clauses differentially.

Our problem set originates from one of our previous studies [7] and is significantly diverse as it draws problems from four different domains. SATLIB's -med and -hard instances correspond to the median and hardest instances as found by a run of SAPS with optimal parameters on the respective original sets flat100, flat200, uf100 and uf250. From DIMACS we use the two most difficult graph colouring problems (g125.17 and g250.29) and the median and hardest 16-bit parity learning problems (par16-2-c and par16-3-c). For the random 3-SAT problems, we first generated 3 sets of problems (400, 800 and 1600 variable sets) from the 4.3 clause-to-variable ratio hard region. To these sets we added the f400, f800, and f1600 problems from DIMACS and repeated the procedure described above to determine the median and hardest instances, which resulted in the 6 random 3-SAT problems (f400, f800 and f1600 -med and -hard). Finally, a range of random binary CSPs (also from the accepted 4.3 ratio hard region) were generated and transformed into SAT instances using the multi-valued encoding procedure described in [5]. These problems were divided into 3 sets of 5 problems each according to the number of variables (v), the domain size (d)

---

[6] Optimal values for the $MaxInc$ parameter were determined in [7].

Table 1. Results for the SATLIB and DIMACS problems

Problem	Solver	Settings	Success (%)	Time (s) mean median	Flips mean median	Wilcoxon t: time f: flips
SATLIB						
bw_large.a	PAWS	Max:34	100	0.05 / 0.05	3,107 / 2,533	
	PAWS+US	Inc:3,LL:5	100	0.04 / 0.04	2,330 / 1,805	*0.0000t *0.0170f
bw_large.b	PAWS	Max:50	100	0.40 / 0.29	47,001 / 31,620	
	PAWS+US	Inc:4,LL:2	100	0.29 / 0.22	31,448 / 22,474	*0.0212t *0.0314f
bw_large.c	PAWS	Max:5	100	10.23 / 7.53	1,245,757 / 888,581	
	PAWS+US	Inc:5,LL:2	100	6.29 / 5.11	720,611 / 569,357	*0.0003t *0.0001f
bw_large.d	PAWS	Max:4	100	14.85 / 11.64	1,369,449 / 1,054,353	0.2946t 0.4211f
	PAWS+US	Inc:5,LL:3	100	14.75 / 11.05	1,314,033 / 1,050,479	
ais10	PAWS	Max:52	100	0.14 / 0.10	16,253 / 10,220	0.1609t 0.1579f
	PAWS+US	Inc:5,LL:2	100	0.16 / 0.11	18,820 / 12,020	
flat100-med	PAWS	Max:16	100	0.05 / 0.04	10,498 / 6,162	0.1429t 0.1633f
	PAWS+US	Inc:3,LL:1	100	0.05 / 0.04	8,991 / 6,180	
flat100-hard	PAWS	Max:46	100	0.13 / 0.09	38,252 / 26,326	*0.0117t *0.0180f
	PAWS+US	Inc:3,LL:4	100	0.09 / 0.07	27,032 / 18,682	
flat200-med	PAWS	Max:9	100	0.56 / 0.41	177,173 / 125,979	0.1813t 0.1952f
	PAWS+US	Inc:2,LL:2	100	0.50 / 0.38	160,767 / 116,965	
flat200-hard	PAWS	Max:74	100	10.44 / 7.37	3,343,427 / 2,365,859	0.1979t 0.2062f
	PAWS+US	Inc:2,LL:2	100	9.24 / 6.54	2,976,442 / 2,097,565	
uf100-hard	PAWS	Max:15	100	0.03 / 0.03	2,993 / 2,288	*0.0024t 0.3680f
	PAWS+US	Inc:2,LL:8	100	0.02 / 0.03	2,843 / 2,288	
uf250-med	PAWS	Max:15	100	0.05 / 0.04	6,766 / 4,675	0.0632t *0.0220f
	PAWS+US	Inc:2,LL:1	100	0.04 / 0.04	4,721 / 3,686	
uf250-hard	PAWS	Max:18	100	1.26 / 0.80	316,767 / 200,491	0.4567t 0.4040f
	PAWS+US	Inc:5,LL:9	100	1.11 / 0.72	261,294 / 165,989	
DIMACS						
g125.17	PAWS	Max:4	100	11.81 / 7.93	719,942 / 486,419	0.3484t 0.3675f
	PAWS+US	Inc:3,LL:1	100	11.80 / 7.01	724,633 / 424,301	
g.250.29	PAWS	Max:4	100	32.71 / 26.35	382,086 / 285,976	0.3475t 0.2520f
	PAWS+US	Inc:4,LL:2	100	31.93 / 27.59	383,378 / 325,129	
par16-3-c	PAWS	Max:40	97	14.46 / 10.97	3,928,952 / 2,980,095	0.2157t 0.2694f
	PAWS+US	Inc:3,LL:5	100	13.88 / 10.48	3,816,071 / 2,890,594	
par16-2-c	PAWS	Max:36	99	16.15 / 10.63	4,421,398 / 2,903,163	0.0909t 0.0919f
	PAWS+US	Inc:3,LL:1	97	17.66 / 12.04	4,820,909 / 3,280,032	

and the constraint density from the originating CSP (c), which resulted in the 30v10d40c, 30v10d80v and 50v15d80c problem sets from which the hardest of 5 problems was added to our problem set.

Local search run-times for the same problem can vary greatly due to different starting points and subsequent randomised decisions. For this reason, empirical studies have traditionally reported on statistics such as mean, median and standard deviation obtained from many runs on the same problem as a means to

Table 2. Results for the random binary CSP and random 3-SAT problems

Problem	Solver	Settings	Success (%)	Time (s) mean median	Flips mean median	Wilcoxon t: time f: flips
Random 3-SAT						
f400-med	PAWS	Max:9	100	0.19 / 0.14	42,862 / 29,140	
	PAWS+US	Inc:3,LL:4	100	0.12 / 0.08	23,526 / 12,869	*0.0001t *0.0001f
f400-hard	PAWS	Max:11	100	5.84 / 4.73	1,367,508 / 1,108,036	
	PAWS+US	Inc:3,LL:1	100	3.72 / 2.84	861,328 / 654,044	*0.0101t *0.0085f
f800-med	PAWS	Max:9	100	0.55 / 0.39	107,092 / 73,492	*0.0011t *0.0012f
	PAWS+US	Inc:3,LL:1	100	0.92 / 0.61	186,309 / 119,224	
f800-hard	PAWS	Max:10	100	4.07 / 2.50	912,512 / 529,681	
	PAWS+US	Inc:2,LL:1	100	4.11 / 2.14	870,033 / 443,084	0.4679t 0.3833f
f1600-med	PAWS	Max:10	100	1.97 / 1.51	406,891 / 273,914	0.2800t 0.3323f
	PAWS+US	Inc:3,LL:3	100	2.13 / 1.53	418,190 / 291,807	
f1600-hard	PAWS	Max:11	99	31.10 / 22.97	5,144,062 / 3,795,800	
	PAWS+US	Inc:2,LL:10	100	23.73 / 16.69	3,501,171 / 2,501,328	*0.0273t *0.0033f
SAT-encoded random binary CSPs						
30v10d40c	PAWS	Max:7	100	0.23 / 0.16	26,142 / 16,439	*0.0011t *0.0006f
	PAWS+US	Inc:2,LL:2	100	0.47 / 0.29	61,088 / 35,478	
30v10d80c	PAWS	Max:7	100	0.12 / 0.10	10,677 / 8,164	0.2217t 0.2204f
	PAWS+US	Inc:3,LL:1	100	0.14 / 0.10	13,775 / 10,297	
50v15d80c	PAWS	Max:5	100	2.01 / 1.53	136,914 / 105,270	*0.0170t *0.0170f
	PAWS+US	Inc:4,LL:1	100	2.87 / 2.14	197,701 / 147,661	

ascertain one algorithm's superiority over another. As the standard deviation is only informative for normally distributed data, and local search run-time and run-length distributions are usually not normally distributed, we recently proposed that the nonparametric Wilcoxon rank-sum test be used to measure the confidence level of these assertions [7]. The test requires that the number of flips or run-times from two sets of observations A and B be sorted in ascending order, and that observations be ranked from 1 to n. Then, the sum of the ranks for distribution A is calculated and its value can be used to obtain, using the normal approximation to the Wilcoxon distribution, the z value that will give the probability P that the null hypothesis $H_0 : A \geq B$ is true. The Wilcoxon value in tables 1 and 2 give the probability P that the null hypothesis $A \geq B$ is true, where A is the distribution of the number of flips (or run-times) that has the smaller rank-sum value. We record the P value against distribution A, and take $P < 0.05$ to indicate with an asterisk that A is *significantly* less than B.

For all experiments, we set the maximum flip count to 20 million flips and the maximum time limit to infinity. All experiments were performed on a Sun supercomputer with 8 × Sun Fire V880 servers, each with 8 × UltraSPARC-III 900 MHz CPU and 8 GB memory per node. All statistics were derived from 100 runs of the algorithms.

We analyse our results from three different perspectives: the individual problem level, the problem domain level, and the overall level, where we consider a method's performance over the whole problem set. The results for PAWS were obtained using the the best known setting for $MaxInc$, whereas for PAWS+US we used the same $MaxInc$ and picked the optimal of 40 possible (Inc, LL) combinations based on a criteria of greatest completion rate, followed by the smallest mean number of flips. At the problem level, PAWS+US offers significantly better performance both in terms of run-time and number of flips for nine problems (uf100-hard time only, and uf250-med flips only). This means that for these nine problems the use of at least one (the optimal), and sometimes more (Inc, LL) pairs significantly improves PAWS's performance. PAWS, on the other hand, is significantly better for three of the problems.

When the analysis is taken to the problem domain level, PAWS+US is better (but not significantly) than PAWS for the random 3-SAT and SATLIB problems, whereas the reverse is true for the random binary CSPs, as demonstrated by the run-time and run-length distributions in table 2. By inspecting the distributions for the DIMACS problems in table 1, however, we can say with certainty that neither method dominates. Overall, PAWS's run-length distribution is slightly better than PAWS+US's, whereas it is not possible to determine either method's dominance in regards to the run-time distribution, as demonstrated in Figure 2.

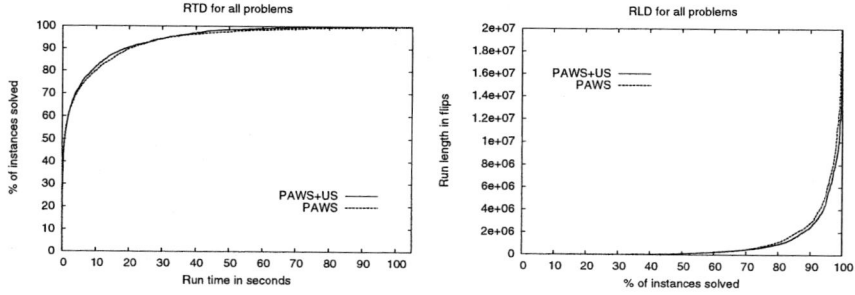

Fig. 2. The performance of PAWS and PAWS+US on the whole problem set, with optimal parameter settings for both methods as shown in tables 1 and 2

For those problems where PAWS+US significantly outperformed PAWS, we observed that the improvement was generally not limited to optimal (Inc, LL) settings only, as was the case of problem bw_large.c for example, as shown in figure 3. This result, together with the others where PAWS+US gave significant improvements, can be interpreted as evidence that the use of the global knowledge afforded by the special treatment dispensed to the US clauses does indeed render the instance easier for the CWLS method, irrespective of the rate of weight increase dictated by the setting of Inc.

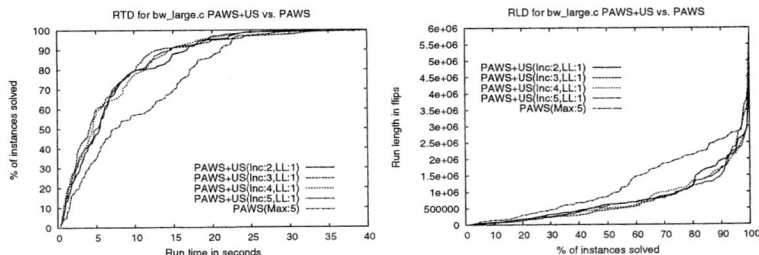

Fig. 3. RTD and RLD comparisons between PAWS($Max : 5$) and PAWS+US($Inc : \{2,...,5\}, LL : 1$) for the bw_large.c problem showing the method's stability w.r.t. the different settings of Inc

We also decided to investigate the existence of an inter-parametric dependency between a (LL, Inc) pair and $MaxInc$. We re-ran our experiments, this time using 4 additional settings for $MaxInc$ (we used optimal $MaxInc \pm 2$), which allowed us to investigate ($4 \times 10 \times 5$) Inc, LL and $MaxInc$ combinations. For all but three problems we observed that modifying the value of $MaxInc$ generally resulted in performance degradation, which indicates that the US heuristic generally works *in combination with* already optimally tuned values of $MaxInc$, and that its introduction does not create the need for re-tuning the host method's parameter. Two problems for which improvements were observed were flat100-med, and flat200-med, as for these we found at least one $(Inc, LL, MaxInc)$ triple that resulted in a reduction in the P value derived from using the Wilcoxon rank-sum test to less than 0.05, indicating that should these settings be used, the method would give a significant improvement over PAWS. However, we concluded that this improvement does not justify the expensive search required to find these triples. The third problem, f1600-hard, was the exception to the rule as most triples with a $MaxInc = 10$ (instead of PAWS's optimal setting of 11) resulted in significant improvements over the already significantly better performance obtained by PAWS+US($Inc : 2, LL : 10$). Furthermore, we found that the setting of $MaxInc = 10$ only works well in combination with the US and not in isolation. Figure 4 is used to illustrate these findings.

As previously mentioned, and according to observations not reported here, we found that generally PAWS+US gives the best performance when combined with the best known setting for $MaxInc$, settings which were found in [7] by testing 72 distinct values between 3 and 75. For this study, finding the optimal (Inc, LL) pair for PAWS+US involved searching on a space of (4×10) possible combinations, and then using this optimal pair in combination with the best setting for $MaxInc$. Therefore, in practice, the cost of tuning PAWS+US is equivalent to searching on the space of the 40 possible combinations. This

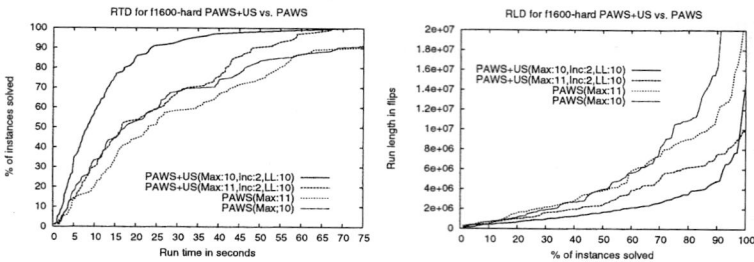

Fig. 4. RTD and RLD comparisons between PAWS($Max : \{10, 11\}$) and PAWS+US($Max : \{10, 11\}, Inc : 2, LL : 10$) for the f1600-hard problem, where a one step change in the weight decrease parameter resulted in yet another significant performance increase by PAWS+US

compares positively against most multiplicative CWLS methods such as SAPS, where the tuning of highly sensitive multipliers typically requires searching on a larger space of possible combinations.[7]

5 Conclusion

Our results challenge the conclusions reached in previous works [8], which stated that no meaningful information could be derived from clause weights in CWLS methods. These works attempted to acquire meaningful information by examining clause weights at the end of a search, despite existing evidence [1] that information acquired in this fashion is of limited applicability due to its contextual nature. Furthermore, these methods did not consider using the acquired information to alter the way clauses are treated.

In contrast, we propose that our results support our hypothesis that CWLS methods can learn from clause weights, and that the significant performance improvement offered by PAWS+US can be attributed to (a) its ability to learn which clauses are globally hardest to satisfy, and (b) its ability to use this information to treat these clauses differentially.

As is the case with most empirical evaluations of local search methods, we found that our heuristic can offer performance improvements at the problem level, but this advantage tends to disappear as we shift the perspective to the overall level and consider all problems in combination. However, given that PAWS+US offered significant improvements over the state-of-the-art performance for approximately 40% of the problems in our test set, we believe that these initial results represent a well-founded motivation for future work. One interesting research path is the development of a better understanding of the

---

[7] The search space of SAPS's α, ρ and P_{smooth} parameters in our investigation of additive vs. multiplicative methods [7] was approximately ($20 \times 20 \times 5$).

factors underlying our method's successes and failures. Another is on extending the US heuristic to incorporate neighbourhood weighting.

References

1. Jeremy Frank. Learning short-term weights for GSAT. In *Proceedings of the 14th National Conference on Artificial Intelligence (AAAI'97)*, pages 384–391, Providence, Rhode Island, July 1997. MIT Press.
2. Ian Gent and Toby Walsh. Towards an understanding of hill-climbing procedures for SAT. In *Proceedings of the 11th National Conference on Artificial Intelligence (AAAI'93)*, pages 28–33, Washington, D.C., July 1993. MIT Press.
3. Frank Hutter, Dave Tompkins, and Holger Hoos. Scaling and probabilistic smoothing: Efficient dynamic local search for SAT. In *Proceedings of CP-02*, volume 2470 of *LNCS*, pages 233–248, Ithaca, New York, September 2002. Springer Verlag.
4. Paul Morris. The breakout method for escaping from local minima. In *Proceedings of the 11th National Conference on Artificial Intelligence (AAAI'93)*, pages 40–45, Washington, D.C., July 1993. MIT Press.
5. Steven Prestwich. Local search on sat-encoded CSPs. In *Proceedings of the 6th International Conference on Theory and Applications of Satisfiability Testing (SAT 2003)*, Portofino, Italy, May 2003. Springer.
6. Bart Selman and Henry Kautz. Domain-independent extensions to GSAT: Solving large structured satisfiability problems. In *Proceedings of the International Joint Conference on Artificial Intelligence (IJCAI'93)*, pages 290–295, Chambery, France, August 1993. Morgan Kaufmann.
7. John Thornton, Duc Nghia Pham, Stuart Bain, and Valnir Ferreira Jr. Additive versus multiplicative clause weighting for SAT. In *Proceedings of the 20th National Conference on Artificial Intelligence (AAAI'04)*, pages 191–196, San Jose, California, July 2004. MIT Press.
8. Dave Tompkins and Holger Hoos. Warped landscapes and random acts of SAT solving. In *Proc. of the Eighth International Symposium on Artificial Intelligence and Mathematics - AMAI, AI&M 1-2004*, Fort Lauderdale, Florida, January 2004.
9. Benjamin Wah and Yi Shang. Discrete lagrangian-based search for solving MAX-SAT problems. In *Proceedings of the 15th International Joint Conference on Artificial Intelligence (IJCAI'97)*, pages 378–383, Nagoya, Japan, August 1997. Morgan Kaufmann.
10. Zhe Wu and Benjamin Wah. Trap escaping strategies in discrete lagrangian methods for solving hard satisfiability and maximum satisfiability problems. In *Proceedings of the 16th National Conference on Artificial Intelligence (AAAI'99)*, pages 673–678, Orlando, Florida, July 1999. MIT Press.

Natural Landmark Based Navigation

E. Lazkano, A. Astigarraga, B. Sierra, J. M. Martínez-Otzeta, and I. Rañó

Dept. of Computer Science and Artificial Intelligence,
University of the Basque Country
ccplaore@si.ehu.es
http://www.sc.ehu.es/ccwrobot

Abstract. The work described in this paper presents a goal oriented navigation system in a behavior-based manner. The main contributions are, in first place the in-depth study of local navigation strategies and, on the other hand, the use of natural landmarks, namely corridors and emergency exit panels. Eliminating the centralized control of modules the system performs the task as a result of the combination of many relatively simple and light weight behaviors that run concurrently.

1 Introduction

The ability to navigate is probably one of the main skills needed by a mobile robot in order to function autonomously in its environment. Without such ability, the robot would not be able to avoid dangerous obstacles, reach energy sources or come back home after an exploration of its environment. Although many animals have shown that they are very good at navigating, autonomous navigation in unknown environments is a complicated task for engineered robots. This is not the case with biological navigation systems, which navigate in robust ways exploiting a collection of specialized behaviors and tricks (Webb, 1995; Collett et al., 2001). Therefore, research efforts have been aimed at incorporating biologically inspired strategies into robot navigation models (Trullier et al., 1997; Mallot and Franz, 2000). Behavior-based (Brooks, 1986; Matarić, 1997) (BB) navigation systems are clearly influenced by biomimetic navigational mechanisms, in which navigation is the process of determining and maintaining a trajectory to a goal location (Mallot and Franz, 2000). The main question is not the classic "Where am I?" (Levitt and Lawton, 1990; Borenstein et al., 1996), but "How do I reach the goal?"; a question that not always requires the knowledge of the starting position. Thus, navigating can be accomplished by the abilities of wandering around and recognizing the desired goal. Biological navigation strategies fall into two groups: (1) **Local navigation or local strategies** that allow the robot to move in its immediate environment, in which only the objects or places that are in the perceptual range of the robot's sensors are useful; (2) **Way finding** involves moving in environments in which relevant cues may be outside the current range of robot perception. These strategies rely on local navigation behaviors to move from one place to another, allowing the robot to find places or goals that could not be reached using local strategies only.

The main project that we are involved in, consists of creating a robust navigational architecture for a mobile robot following an incremental BB design methodology. For such a work, we make use of an holonomic B21 model from RWI named Marisorgin. Despite the low computational power available (2 Pentium running at 120 MHz), she has a wide range of sensing capabilities including a CCD camera mounted on a pan tilt head, sonars, infrareds, bumpers and an electronic compass. The environment the robot moves on is a typical office-like semi-structured environment. The rooms are rectangular in shape and wide halls are connected by narrow corridors. The navigational task is depicted in figure 1. It consists of going from the laboratory to the library hall and coming back again after visiting Otzeta's office, placed in the corridor parallel to the laboratory's one (route-B). The complete path amounts up to 150m. Note that the

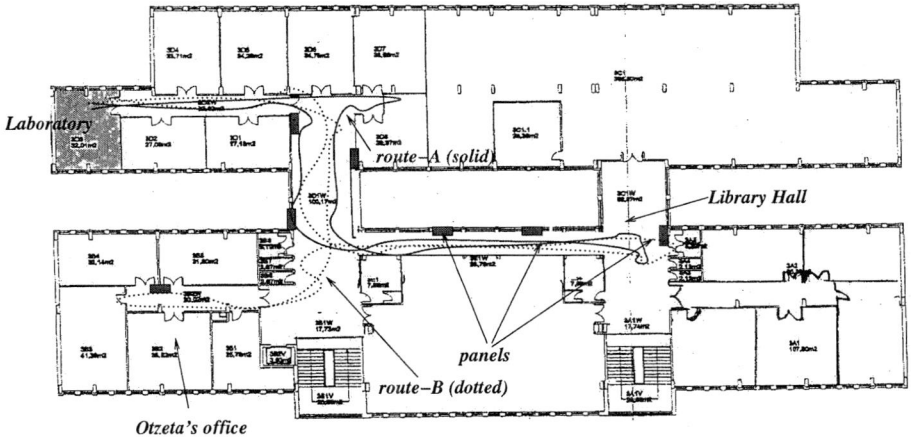

Fig. 1. The robot's niche and the routes A and B

whole navigational task can not be accomplished relying only on local navigational behaviors; it is not enough to give the robot a unique preferred compass orientation to fullfill the task; the orientation to follow must be changed so that different locations can be achieved. Therefore, landmark identification processes act as perceptual triggers to extract natural features from the environment (corridors and emergency exit panels) and make the robot follow the drawn nominal route. Since way finding strategies depend on local navigation routines, we find it is crucial to solve those local navigation mechanisms adequately in order to evolve the system to more complex way finding capabilities. Sections 2 and 3 are fully devoted to describe how those behaviors should be designed, combined and evaluated. After the assessment of appropriate wandering control system, section 4 explains the landmark identification processes added that define the global navigation strategy needed to fulfill the task. The paper ends describing some experimental results and conclusions in section 5.

2 Methodological Issues

Two main questions arise when building behavior-based control architectures. Basic behaviors must be defined and combined to get the overall effective behavior, but (1) what must those basic behaviors be? and (2) how must they be combined in order to get a good performance? The global description of the behaviors must be accompanied by a formal definition of the inputs and outputs, and the function performed by each one. Following (Arkin, 1998), each behavior "i" can be expressed as a triplet (S_i, R_i, β_i) where S_i is the domain of stimuli, R_i is the range of possible responses and β_i represents the mapping function from stimuli to response. Each sensor stimuli belongs to a domain or class and has a strength. Not every behavior produces a response at every time. Some behaviors produce effective responses only when the input activation exceeds a threshold level for activating its corresponding binary flag (f_i).

Motor responses can be separated into two components: *strength* or magnitude of the response; and *orientation* or direction of action for the response. For our needs, motor response can be expressed in terms of translational and rotational velocities: $\forall r_j \in R_i \quad r_j = [w_j^i, v_j^i]$. Not every behavior produces a motor response: behaviors called *Perceptual Triggers* (PT) have the function of activating/deactivating behaviors or identifying goals.

Once the basic set of behaviors is defined and formalized, still the hard question about how the motor responses of the behavior collection must be converted into motor commands remains. More formally, the coordination function $\rho = C(G * B(S)) = C(G * R)$ is the vector encoding the global motor response where $R = B(S)$ is the behavior response to input stimuli S, and G is the behavior activation vector, i.e, the activation flag determined by each behavior.

The taxonomy of action selection mechanisms is classified in two main branches: competitives and cooperatives (Arkin, 1998; Pirjanian, 1999). In **competitive** strategies, active behaviors compete to reach the actuators and only the output of the winner has effect in the robot's behavior. (Brooks, 1986), (Maes, 1989) and (Rosenblatt, 1995) are examples of competitive action selection mechanisms. The alternative are **cooperative** strategies, where the responses of the different behaviors all contribute to the overall response generally by means of a weighted vectorial sum (Arkin, 1989). The final output is not the output of a single behavior but the combination of the outputs of the different active ones.

Last, but not least, to implement a control architecture it is a good policy to develop the tools needed to easily build and debug the different behaviors. The

SORGIN software framework (Astigarraga et al., 2003) is a set of data structures and the library of functions associated to those objects, specifically developed for behavior-based control architecture engineering. From a generic point of view, global behavior can be considered as a network of coupled concurrent active entities -threads- interacting asynchronously among them in some way. SORGIN identifies these active entities with software components and defines their interaction, creating thus a principled method of modularity and behavior libraries. SORGIN has been developed using the "C" programming language and Posix threads, both standard and portable elements.

3 Local Navigation

Nominal paths are those imposed by local navigation strategies but are also dependent on the environment that enforces "comfortable" ways of traversing the different segments or locations. Nominal paths are better suited for landmark identification than just wandering behaviors (Nehmzow, 1995). Having that idea on mind, a nominal path for the robot has been defined that is essentially a subtask of the overall task, but available using only local strategies: go from the lab to the library hall and come back again (see figure 1, route-A). This task can be accomplished just wandering in a preferred compass orientation. We identified four basic skills or behaviors. Every non PT behavior will output a three-dimensional vector of the type (f_i, w_i, v_i) and the PT behaviors will just output the confidence level of the perceived landmark.

- The *corridor-follower* (corr) maintains the robot at a centered position with respect to the left and right side obstacles or walls. It also must control the obstacles in front of the robot and decide the translational velocity according to the free space the robot has in its front: $(f_{corr}, w_{corr}, v_{corr})$.
- The *obstacle-avoider* (oa) behavior avoids any obvious obstacle detected by the robot: (f_{oa}, w_{oa}, v_{oa}).
- The *goal-follower* (gf) behavior takes a goal orientation and attempts to reach that goal based on the difference between the final desired orientation and current orientation: (f_{gf}, w_{gf}, v_{gf}).
- The *stop* (b) behavior stops the robot when it collides with an object: $(f_b, 0, 0)$.

For the work described in this paper, two different coordination mechanisms are tried: a completely competitive one, where the winner is selected according to a preset fixed hierarchy:

$$\rho = \{(v_i, w_i)/\forall index_j < index_i \ \ f_j = 0, j \in \{b, oa, corr, oa\}\}$$

where the *index* function returns the priority of the behavior in the hierarchical organization. And a more cooperative one where the global response is a weighted sum of different motor responses. For the latter, the weights have been experimentally selected and are fixed over time:

$$\rho = \sum_{i \in \{b,oa,corr,gf\}} weight_i * (v_i, w_i); \quad weights = \begin{bmatrix} f_b \\ (1-f_b)f_{oa}(1-0.1f_{corr}) \\ (1-f_b)f_{corr}(0.75-0.65f_{oa}) \\ (1-f_b)(1-f_{oa})(1-0.75f_{corr}) \end{bmatrix}$$

3.1 Experimental Setup and Evaluation

Although all the modules developed were incrementally built and tested, and both action selection mechanisms produce qualitatively the same behavior, are they significatively different? which is better suited for navigation? When a single behavior is to be evaluated, the most straightforward method is to run an experiment several times and give the overall performance. On the other hand, to measure the goodness of the more complex emergent behavior is much more difficult. Robot behavior is encapsulated in its trajectory (Nehmzow and Walker, 2003) and some numerical values can be defined to measure the properties of that trajectory (Pirjanian, 1998). This is precisely the approach adopted for measuring the differences between both controllers. But, as far as we know, there is not a standard quantitative way to measure the performance of the system by means of behavior assessment. That is probably the main lack of the field of Intelligent Robotics and Autonomous Systems.

The following attributes have been identified:

- The goal must be satisfied, i.e the robot must complete the journey. Distance represents how straight ahead the robot has achieved the goal.
- Collisions must be avoided. So, bumpers should not activate and it is desirable that infrareds activate few times. The activation flags of the behaviors can be used as a measure: $\overline{f_{oa}}$ and $\overline{f_b}$.
- The distance to obstacles must be equilibrated at left and right sides so that she traverses the corridors smoothly. The sonar module groups some left and right side sonar values and uses the difference between left and right to center the robot in narrow corridors. That difference could give a hint about this attribute: $\overline{l-r}$.
- Also, the compass heading must be as close as possible to the desired value: $\Theta_d - \Theta$. It must be pointed out that only two desired headings are given to the robot, one for going to the library and one for returning back to the lab.
- Velocity changes should be smooth in face of abrupt changes but smoothness might not affect reactivity. The averaged rotational and translational velocities and their standard deviations should be a reflection of the path smoothness: $\overline{v} \pm \sigma_v$, $\overline{w} \pm \sigma_w$.

It is important to note that, when working with mobile robots in real environments, it is almost impossible to replicate an experiment in identical conditions. Although variations are unavoidable, the experiments must be done in such a way that the effect of the variability is minimized, settling the same initial conditions, position and heading for the different runs.

Table 1. Results obtained during the experimentation

day	t (s)	$\bar{v} \pm \sigma_v$	dist.(m)	$\bar{w} \pm \sigma_w$	$l - r$	$\Theta_d - \Theta$	$\overline{f_b}$	$\overline{f_{ir}}$
co	1003	0.13±0.047	132.40	0.15±8.259	-583.281	2.930±68	0	0.092±0.29
cm	881	0.14±0.043	126.52	-0.19±11.204	-628.122	8.259±64	0	0.034±0.18
co	1014	0.14±0.042	117.62	0.17±8.137	-600.122	2.695±67	0	0.074±0.26
cm	837	0.15±0.035	123.88	0.21±11.208	-641.901	9.679±65	0	0.020±0.14
co	989	0.13±0.042	130.55	0.18±8.342	-512.110	3.315±67	0	0.078±0.27
cm	1114	0.14±0.039	157.07	0.17±11.791	-595.180	28.495±72	0	0.021±0.14
co	873	0.14±0.036	122.22	-0.25±8.020	-505.090	7.127±64	0	0.043±0.20
cm	865	0.15±0.035	125.43	0.20±11.266	-529.245	11.186±64	0	0.014±0.12
co	858	0.14±0.036	121.84	-0.24±8.048	-328.323	8.992±64	0	0.040±0.20
cm	884	0.14±0.046	124.64	-0.23±11.190	-672.886	8.291±63	0	0.031±0.17
co	882	0.14±0.038	122.60	-0.23±8.077	-617.304	7.291±65	0	0.049±0.22
cm	1074	0.11±0.067	122.44	-0.16±10.929	-328.842	3.991±59	0	0.078±0.27
co	897	0.14±0.043	122.89	-0.23±7.340	-258.812	6.573±63	0	0.061±0.24
cm	904	0.14±0.044	125.66	-0.20±11.248	-473.025	8.302±64	0	0.025±0.16
co	964	0.13±0.053	123.39	-0.20±7.727	-405.432	5.851±62	0	0.098±0.30
cm	875	0.14±0.044	125.13	-0.21±11.159	-643.928	7.862±63	0	0.028±0.17
co	882	0.14±0.049	122.60	-0.23±7.906	-569.394	7.910±64	0	0.050±0.22
cm	2207	0.14±0.038	301.48	-0.12±12.483	-205.100	60.83±64	0	0.071±0.26
co	980	0.13±0.043	131.03	0.17±8.226	-497.606	4.198±68	0	0.009±0.01
cm	921	0.13±0.049	124.34	0.22±11.169	-427.896	10.42±62	0	0.031±0.17
$\overline{Co}$	934.2	0.136	124.71	-0.072	-487.75	5.688	0	0.06
$\overline{Cm}$	1056.2	0.138	145.66	-0.030	-514.61	15.731	0	0.04

Table 1 shows the results obtained. Last row shows the averaged values for the whole set of runs. No collision occurs during the 20 runs and thus, the overall behavior shows the safetiness property in both controllers. Concerning the infrared sensors activations, the competitive coordination (cm) maintains the robot further away from obstacles than the cooperative (co) one because the sonar module acts also as an obstacle avoider.

Looking to path smoothness, the deviation of the rotational velocity is higher in the competitive runs, reflecting a more oscillatory behavior. The translational velocity is also a little bit higher in the competitive behavior. But this fact gets blurred when the robot has difficulties in finding the corridor in her way back to the lab. The cooperative schema helps the sonar module to find the corridor because of the compass module contribution to the velocities (figure 2).

As expected, the variation of the difference between the left and right side sonars is big, but the difference maintains the sign over all runs. The negative sign is due to the wall-following behavior that emerges when traveling along wide halls.

Figure 3 shows the ratios of the activation flags for the different behaviors. For the competitive runs, these ratios shows the degree of competition among the

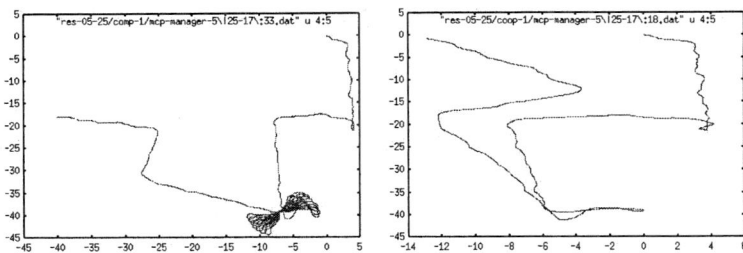

Fig. 2. Robot trajectories for competitive and cooperative runs

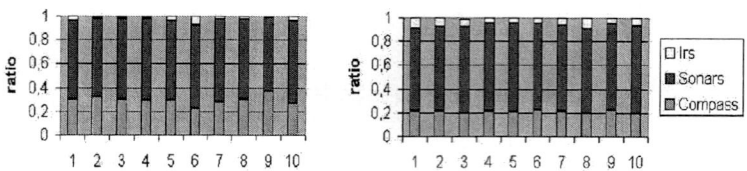

Fig. 3. Ratio of flag activations during the 10 trials

behaviors. The same values are extracted for the cooperative runs, although it must be remarked that for these cases the output of the system is a combination of the different velocities. Taking all those facts into account, we conclude that the overall behavior performance is better in the cooperative controller. More experiments have been done with the environment full of students to see the persistence for attaining the target and the robot is able to achieve the goal even when the natural trajectory of the robot is intentionally perturbed.

4 Natural Landmarks for Perceptual Triggered Response

To perform the global task (figure 1, route-B) the robot needs more knowledge that must be properly combined with the capability of wandering in a preferred compass orientation. More specifically, the robot needs to recognize some environmental properties, namely *landmarks*, that will change the orientation to follow according to the situation and the task. Some authors define landmarks as potentially visible real world objects at known locations (Greiner and Isukapalli, 1994); but landmarks are not necessarily restricted to real world objects and can be considered as such features of the environment detected by the robot sensors (Nehmzow and Owen, 2000), either by visual sensors (Trahanias et al., 1999; Popescu, 2003; Franz et al., 1998; Mata et al., 2002; Rizzi et al., 2001) or by proximity sensors and odometry (Thrun, 1998; Burgard et al., 1998), (Owen and Nehmzow, 1998; Bengtsson and Baerveldt, 2003).

The environment can be provided with specific landmarks so that the robot can easily identify different locations. Instead, we chose to extract environmental characteristics that can be recognized by robot sensors. In the approach presented in this paper we combine emergency exit panels and corridor identification for navigation.

Emergency Exit Panel Recognition: Emergency exit panels are international natural landmarks mandatory in every public building that must follow some shape, color and location standards (European "Council Directive 92/58/EEC of 24 June 1992 on the minimum requirements for the provision of safety and/or health signs at work"[1]). They must be put in every junction or

---

[1] Official Journal L 245, 26/08/1992 P. 0023 - 0042.

intersection where the wrong way to the exit may be taken. This can be very helpful for the robot to identify crossroads. An emergency exit panel must be put from every evacuation origin to a location where the emergency exit or the panel that indicates it is clearly visible. They must be clearly visible even when the lighting is off.

To extract the panel from the background in the image, a simple thresholding is enough to appropriately segment the green areas of the image (see figure 4).

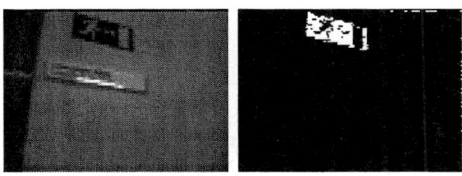

Fig. 4. Original and segmented images

To classify an image as containing or not a panel, instead of using image correlation functions we applied a Multi Layer Perceptron (MLP) neural network trained using as input vector the quadratic weighted sums of 20 × 20 sized image blocks, resulting 28 input neurons. The training image set contained the inputs of 220 images, taken from the nominal trajectory and with constant pan and tilt values. The neural net has a single hidden layer of 3 neurons and the output is a binary vector that classifies the image as containing or not a panel. Applying a leaving-one-out (LOO) validation technique, and after a training period of 1000 epochs for each set, we obtained a validated performance of 97.27%.

Corridor Identification: A posterior analysis of the data collected during the previous phase showed that corridors presented very strong properties that make them identifiable. We consider the same physical corridor as being different depending on the way the robot is following it. Corridors can be followed in the environment from North to South (NS) or from South to North (SN) and this produces two different robot behaviors. The compass allows to disambiguate those situations. Equation (1) shows the single rule applied for corridor identification. The i subindex stands for NS or SN direction and θ, for the current compass reading.

$$corridor\_id_i(t) = \begin{cases} 1 \text{ if } \theta \in [\theta^i_{min}, \cdots, \theta^i_{max}] \text{ and } sonars < TH \\ 0 \text{ else} \end{cases} \quad (1)$$

To make the corridor identification more robust, instead of trusting just on a single sonar and compass reading, we maintain a belief value of being in each corridor using the weighted sum of a fixed size FIFO buffer that contains the results of the corridor identification behavior for the last BSIZE readings[2].

---

[2] For the experimental done $BSIZE = 100$.

4.1 Integration of Landmark Identification Processes in the Control Architecture

The top level task is constructed combining all the above explained behaviors using a finite state automata (FSA) that acts as a sequencer. The landmark detection subsystems continuously process their inputs looking for new landmarks. If a landmark is detected, the robot executes actions that guide herself to the direction of the goal and re-positions according to the location in order to identify a new exit panel. When the robot identifies a new exit panel, a new compass heading is given that makes her go towards a new location. This schema of sequentially changing the compass target heading and the pan and tilt positions after landmark detection encodes the information needed to do the task in a simple and efficient way.

In order to ensure that transitions occur effectively, preserve the system from noise and make it more robust, we applied the previously explained landmark identificators in the following manner:

- *exit_panel_id*: The emergency exit panel recognition based on the MLP gives as output the mean value of the last 10 images. This value gives a measure of the confidence level (cl) of the recognition process. In spite of the defined confidence level, the positive identification relies in a few snapshots. We made the confidence level affect the global translational velocity of the robot according to $v' = (1 - cl).v$ to slow down the robot when a panel is being recognized so that he does not lose its sight.
- *corridor_id:* The corridor identification processes also make use of a confidence level, Bel_i (see equation (2)). But to act as perceptual triggers the output is defined as:

$$\begin{cases} 1 & \text{if } Bel_i > 0.6 \quad \text{in corridor} \\ 0 & \text{if } Bel_i < 0.1 \quad \text{not in corridor} \\ 0.5 & \text{else} \quad \text{uncertainty} \end{cases} \quad (2)$$

Only when they send the value "1" as output the automata will consider being in a corridor. There is an uncertainty range due to transitions and disturbances and it is indicated by a 0.5 output. There is no change in the global state while uncertainty remains.

5 Results, Conclusions and Further work

Figure 5 shows two typical plots of the outputs of the different landmark recognition behaviors together with the changes in the state of the FSA during a complete path. The stairs-like line displays changes in the state number (multiplied by 0.1 for scale purposes). These changes show that the complete state sequence that corresponds to the defined full path, has been met. The robot is capable of catching the visual landmarks needed to force the robot to go into the corridor. Concerning the corridor identification behaviors, the uncertainty range helps to have robust state transitions and the robot is capable of completing the full path without getting lost in spite of corridor width irregularities.

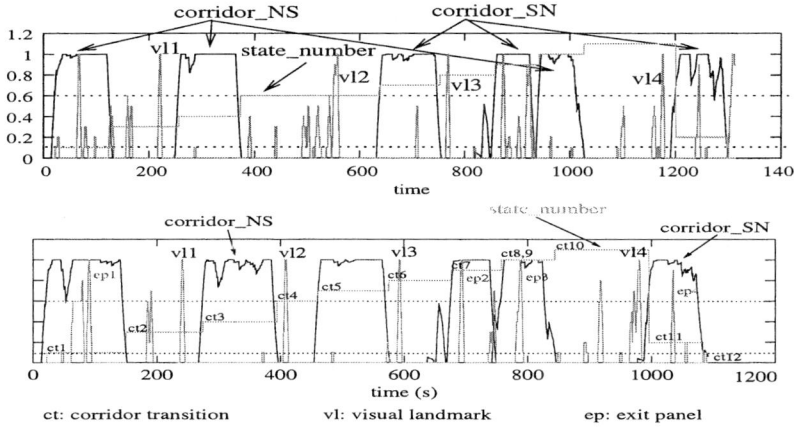

Fig. 5. Landmark identification state of a complete path

The results show that the landmark identification system can be used by the robot to effectively fulfill the task. We think that the presented system could be adapted to many environments and hence, it is not particular to our environment. Of course, every module can be improved. A zoomed camera and adaptive pan and tilt angle selection mechanism could help to adjust the image according to the distance to the wall for actively searching the landmark (Aloimonos, 1993) when the robot traverses the panel area out of the nominal orientation due for example to people playing with the robot. On the other hand, corridor belief is always properly maintained due to the nature of the landmark, and the performance is not affected by the presence of open doors or people walking around.

Up to now, the robot only is able to follow a predefined route defined by a sequence of landmarks. Information about the whole environment should be distributed along the control architecture to somehow provide the system with planning capabilities and route selection mechanisms.

Acknowledgements. This work was supported by the Gipuzkoako Foru Aldundia under grant OF761/2003.

References

Aloimonos, J. (1993). *Active Perception*. Lawrence Erlbaum Assoc Inc.

Arkin, R. (1989). Motor schema-based mobile robot navigation. *International Journal of Robotics Research*, 8(4):92–112.

Arkin, R. C. (1998). *Behavior-Based Robotics*. MIT Press.

Astigarraga, A., Lazkano, E., Rañó, I., Sierra, B., and Zarautz, I. (2003). SORGIN: a software framework for behavior control implementation. In *CSCS14*, volume 1, pages 243–248.

Bengtsson, O. and Baerveldt, A. (2003). Robot localization based on scan-matching – estimating the covariance matrix for the IDC algorithm. *International Journal Robotics and Autonomous Systems*, 1–2(44):131–150.

Borenstein, J., Everett, B., and Feng, L. (1996). *Navigating Mobile Robots: Systems and Techniques*. A. K. Peters.

Brooks, R. A. (1986). A robust layered control system for a mobile robot. *IEEE Journal of robotics and automation*, RA–26:14–23.

Burgard, W., Derr, A., Fox, D., and Cremers, A. B. (1998). Integrating global position estimation and position tracking for mobile robots: the dynamic markov localization approach. In *Proceedings of the IEEE/RSJ International Conference on Intelligent RObot and Systems*.

Collett, T. S., Collett, M., and Wehner, E. (2001). The guidance of desert ants by extended landmarks. *The IEEE Journal of Experimental Biology*, 204:1635–1639.

Franz, M. O., Schölkopf, B., Mallot, H. A., and Bülthoff, H. H. (1998). Where did I take the snapshot? scene-based homing by image matching. *Biological Cybernetics*, 79:191–202.

Greiner, R. and Isukapalli, R. (1994). Learning to select usefule landmarks. In *Proceedings of the Twelfth National Cnference on Artificial Intelligence*, pages 1251–1256. AAAI Press/MIT Press.

Levitt, T. S. and Lawton, D. T. (1990). Qualitative navigation for mobile robots. *Artificial Intelligence*, 44(3):305–360.

Maes, P. (1989). The dynamic of action selection. In *Proceedings of the 1989 International Joint Conference on Artificial Intelligence, Detroit*, pages 991–997.

Mallot, H. A. and Franz, M. A. (2000). Biomimetic robot navigation. *Robotics and Autonomous System*, 30:133–153.

Mata, M., Armingol, J., de la Escalera, A., and Salichs, M. (2002). Learning visual landmarks for mobile robot navigation. In *Proceedings of the 15th world congress of the International Federation of Autonomic Control*.

Matarić, M. (1997). Behavior–based control: examples from navigation, learning and group behavior. *Journal of Experimental and Theoretical Artificial Intelligence*, 9:323–336.

Nehmzow, U. (1995). Animal and robot navigation. *Robotics and Autonomous Systems*, 15(71–81).

Nehmzow, U. and Owen, C. (2000). Experiments with manchester's fourty two in unmodified large environments. *Robotics and Autonomous Systems*, 33:223–242.

Nehmzow, U. and Walker, K. (2003). Is the behavior of a mobile robot chaotic? In *Proceedings of the Artificial Intelligence and Simulated Behavior*.

Owen, C. and Nehmzow, U. (1998). Map interpretation in dynamic environments. In *Proceedings of the 8th International Workshop qon Advanced Motion Control*.

Pirjanian, P. (1998). *Multiple Objective Action Selection and Behavior Fusion using Voting*. PhD thesis, Institute of Electronic Systems, Aalborg University, Denmark.

Pirjanian, P. (1999). Behavior coordination mechanisms – state of the art. Technical Report iris-99-375, Institute of Robotics and Intelligent Systems, USC.

Popescu, N. (2003). Robust self-localization of a robot by intelligent fuzzy system. In *14th Conference on Control Systems and Computer Science*, pages 175–179.

Rizzi, A., Duina, D., Inelli, S., and Cassinis, R. (2001). A novel visual landmark matching for a biologically inspired homing. *Pattern Recognition Letters*, 22:1371–1378.

Rosenblatt, J. K. (1995). DAMN: A distributed architecture for mobile navigation. In *Proc. of the AAAI Spring Symp. on Lessons Learned from Implememted Software Architectures for Physical Agents*, pages 167–178, Stanford, CA.

Thrun, S. (1998). Learning maps for indoor mobile robot navigation. *Artificial Intelligence*, 99(1):21–71.

Trahanias, P. E., Velissaris, S., and Oraphanoudakis, S. C. (1999). Visual recognition of workspace landmarks for topological navigation. *Autonomous Robots*, 7:143–158.

Trullier, O., Wiener, S. I., Berthoz, A., and Meyer, J. A. (1997). Biologically-based artificial navigation systems: Review and prospects. *Progress in Neurobiology*, 51:483–544.

Webb, B. (1995). Using robots to model animals: a cricket test. *Robotics and Autonomous Systems*, 16:117–134.

A Novel Approach for Simplifying Neural Networks by Identifying Decoupling Inputs

Sanggil Kang[1] and Wonil Kim[2]

[1] Department of Computer, College of Information Engineering,
The University of Suwon, Suwon, Gyeonggi-do, Korea
sgkang@suwon.ac.kr
[2] Dept. of Digital Contents, College of Electronics and Information Engineering,
Sejong University, Seoul, Korea
wikim@sejong.ac.kr

Abstract. This paper proposes a novel approach for modeling partially connected feedforward neural networks (PCFNNs) by identifying input type which refers to whether an input is coupled or uncoupled with other inputs. The identification of input type is done by analyzing input sensitivity changes by varying the magnitude of input. In the PCFNNs, each input is linked to the neurons in the hidden layer in a different way according to its input type. Each uncoupled input does not share the neurons with other inputs in order to contribute to output in an independent manner. The simulation results show that PCFNNs outperform fully connected feedforward neural networks with simple network structure.

1 Introduction

Fully connected feedforward neural networks (FCFNNs) have been commonly used for input-output mapping (IOM) problems [1, 2] due to their generalization ability. However, the structure of FCFNNs is complex because each neuron in a lower layer is connected to every neuron in the next higher layer, which causes redundant connections to exist in them. By trimming these useless connections, the structure of the networks can become simpler without deteriorating their performance or sometimes even better [3]. According to [4], the trimmed networks can be called as partially connected feedforward neural networks (PCFNNs).

Various trimming techniques have been proposed, such as optimal brain damage (OBD) [5-7], optimal brain surgeon (OBS) [8], etc. OBD eliminates the weights with low saliency which is obtained by estimating the approximation of the second derivative of the network error with respective to each weight. The less salient, the less important the weight is. In order to improve the way to obtain the approximation, OBS is often used despite of its computational expense. In OBS, networks can be easily overfit because they need to be trained until the error reaches to the minimum, as addressed in [6]. Finnoff et al. [7] avoided this problem by introducing a pruning method called autoprune [9], however, a constant threshold (35% of all weights in the first pruning step and 10% in each following step) for classifying unnecessary connections and necessary connections is not convincing for every case. This disadvantage makes their method less valuable. Prechelt modified the autoprune technique by adjusting the threshold during training in order to adapt the evolution of the weights. However, his technique is suitable for only small networks. In most trimming techniques, it is difficult to provide the obvious threshold with which the connections are usually classified into the 'important' or 'unimportant' to outputs. This problem is caused by the blackbox learning style [10] of neural networks. In this paper, we obtain a priori information of inputs, which helps the networks be amendable to understand their input-output relationship to some extent. Sometimes, the information can solve the dilemma for determining the threshold.

In this paper, the information is defined as input type which refers to whether an input is coupled or uncoupled with other inputs in generating output. In other words, the coupled inputs multiplicatively contribute to output and the uncoupled inputs additively. The definition of the input type is reflected on structuring a network, that is, the uncoupled inputs do not share neurons in the hidden layer with any other inputs, while the coupled inputs share those among them. If all inputs are coupled then an FCFNN is structured because all inputs share all neurons due to description above. If uncoupled inputs exist, a PCFNN can be structured. The main task of our work is to identify the input types. The identification is done by analyzing input sensitivity changes computed by varying the amplitude of inputs.

The remainder of this paper is structured as follows: Section 2 presents the theoretical representation of the sensitivity change according to the input type; Section 3 describes the way to structure PCFNNs from the identified input types; Section 4 presents examples and shows that PCFNNs can replace with FCFNNs without deteriorating their performances; Section 5 summarizes conclusions and potential future direction.

2 Theoretical Input Sensitivity Change

For convenience, the input sensitivity analysis is done for the uncoupled input-output mapping (UIOM) and coupled input-output mapping (CIOM), separately. We refer the UIOM as the nonlinear generalization function whose inputs are all uncoupled, while those of the CIOM are all coupled. For instance, all inputs of the former contribute to output with an additive fashion but the latter with a multiplicative fashion in this paper. Also, only the multi input single output system is taken into consideration for deriving the theoretical equations because those of the multi input multi output system are straightforward.

2.1 Uncoupled Input-Output Mapping

Assume there are a generating function composed of input vector $X = [x_1, x_2, \cdots, x_n]$ and target (or true output) y and an FCFNN trained with the data as following:

$$y = \sum_{i=1}^{n} f_i(x_i) \text{ and } \hat{y} = g(X, W) \tag{1}$$

where $f_i(x_i)$ is a function of input x_i, $\hat{y}$ and g are the network[1] output and the net function of the network, respectively. W is a set of weights. The network output can be expressed in terms of the target and the network error, denoted as e.

$$\hat{y} = y + e \qquad (2)$$

The input sensitivity of the network output with respective to input x_j can be obtained by

$$S_j = \frac{\partial \hat{y}}{\partial x_j} = \frac{\partial y}{\partial x_j} + \frac{\partial e}{\partial x_j} = \frac{\partial y}{\partial x_j}, \quad \forall j \qquad (3)$$

where S_j is the sensitivity of x_j and $\partial e / \partial x_j = 0$ if it is assumed that e is independent of the inputs. In order to analyze the sensitivity changes, input x_i is varied by an amount of Δx_i. The varied input, denoted as $x_{\Delta x_i}$, and the modified input vector, denoted as $X_{\Delta x_i}$, can be expressed as:

$$x_{\Delta x_i} = x_i + \Delta x_i \text{ and } X_{\Delta x_i} = \{x_1, x_2, \cdots, x_{\Delta x_i}, \cdots, x_n\} \qquad (4)$$

At this time, let's train the FCFNN with the original target y and $X_{\Delta x_i}$ instead of X. The additional FCFNN can also be expressed as:

$$\hat{y}_{\Delta x_i} = g_{\Delta x_i}(X_{\Delta x_i}, W_{\Delta x_i}) \qquad (5)$$

where $\hat{y}_{\Delta x_i}$ and $g_{\Delta x_i}$ are the additional network output and its net function, respectively. $W_{\Delta x_i}$ is a set of weights in the retrained network. If Δx_i is relatively very small to x_i enough to apply Taylor Series Expansion (TSE) then $g_{\Delta x_i}(X_{\Delta x_i}, W_{\Delta x_i})$ can be approximated as:

$$g_{\Delta x_i}(X_{\Delta x_i}, W_{\Delta x_i}) \approx g(X, W_{\Delta x_i}) + \Delta x_i \cdot g'_{\Delta x_i}(X, W_{\Delta x_i}) \qquad (6)$$

where $g'_{\Delta x_i}$ is the derivative of $g_{\Delta x_i}$ in terms of x_i. In the TSE, only the first-order derivative is considered in order to have the simple closed forms of the sensitivity changes which will be shown later. Also, for classifying inputs into the uncoupled input and the coupled input, it is not an issue whether considering the second-order derivative or not. For further understanding, readers can refer to Appendix, which explains the higher order derivative does not impact on the classification. From Equation (6), if W obtained in the first training can be used as the initial weights of the additional training and if it can also be assumed that the network is well trained enough that $W_{\Delta x_i}$ can be very close to W, then the $g(X, W_{\Delta x_i})$ can be approximated to $g(X, W)$. Too small value of Δx_i is a necessary condition to satisfy the previous assumptions. Equation (6) can be modified as

---

[1] Network is interchangeable with FCFNN or PCFNN in this paper.

$$g_{\Delta x_i}(X_{\Delta x_i}, W_{\Delta x_i}) \approx g(X,W) + \Delta x_i \cdot g'(X,W) \tag{7}$$

Thus,

$$\hat{y}_{\Delta x_i} = \hat{y} + \Delta x_i \frac{\partial(y+e)}{\partial x_i} = \hat{y} + \Delta x_i \cdot f_i'(x_i) \tag{8}$$

From the additional network, the closed form of the theoretical sensitivity of each input can be obtained by

$$S_{j,\Delta x_i} = \frac{\partial \hat{y}_{\Delta x_i}}{\partial x_j} \approx \begin{cases} \frac{\partial \hat{y}}{\partial x_i} + \Delta x_i \cdot f_i'(x_i) + \Delta x_i \cdot f_i''(x_i), & \text{for } i = j \\ \frac{\partial \hat{y}}{\partial x_i}, & \text{for } i \neq j \end{cases} \tag{9}$$

where ' and " are the notations of the first derivative and the second derivative. Therefore, the sensitivity changes due to Δx_i are obtained by Equation (9) – Equation (3).

$$\Delta \delta_{j,\Delta x_i} = \begin{cases} \Delta x_i \cdot f_i'(x_i) + \Delta x_i \cdot f_i''(x_i), & \text{for } i = j \\ 0, & \text{for } i \neq j \end{cases} \tag{10}$$

2.2 Coupled Input-Output Mapping

In a manner similar to that in Section 2.1, the theoretical representation of the sensitivity changes for the coupled input-output mapping can be obtained by starting from Equation (8). Let's have a generating function expressed as:

$$y = h\left(\prod_{i=1}^{n} f_i(x_i)\right) \tag{11}$$

where h is a nonlinear function. The retrained network output and the sensitivity equations are

$$\hat{y}_{\Delta x_i} = \hat{y} + \Delta x_i \cdot f_i'(x_i) \cdot h'\left(\prod_{j=1}^{n} f_j(x_j)\right) \cdot \prod_{j \neq i}^{n} f_j(x_j) \tag{12}$$

$$\frac{\partial \hat{y}_{\Delta x_i}}{\partial x_j} \approx \begin{cases} \frac{\partial \hat{y}}{\partial x_j} + \frac{\partial \Delta x_i}{\partial x_j} f_j'(x_j) \cdot h'\left(\prod_{m=1}^{n} f_m(x_m)\right) \cdot \prod_{m \neq i}^{n} f_m(x_m) + \Delta x_i \cdot f_j''(x_j) \cdot h'\left(\prod_{m=1}^{n} f_m(x_m)\right) \cdot \prod_{m \neq i}^{n} f_m(x_m) \\ \quad + \Delta x_i \cdot f_m''(x_m) \cdot h''\left(\prod_{m=1}^{n} f_m(x_m)\right) \cdot \left(\prod_{m \neq i}^{n} f_m(x_m)\right)^2, \quad \text{for } i \neq j \\ \frac{\partial \hat{y}}{\partial x_j} + \Delta x_i \cdot f_i'(x_i) \cdot f_j'(x_j) \cdot \left(h''\left(\prod_{m \neq j}^{n} f_m(x_m)\right) \cdot \prod_{m \neq i}^{n} f_m(x_m) + h'\left(\prod_{m=1}^{n} f_m(x_m)\right) \cdot \prod_{m \neq i,j}^{n} f_m(x_m)\right), \\ \quad \text{for } i = j \end{cases} \tag{13}$$

where $\Delta \delta_{j,\Delta x_i}$ is the rest terms of $\partial \hat{y}_{\Delta x_i}/\partial x_j$.

From Equations (10) and (13), we can be inferred that the sensitivity changes of the uncoupled inputs are not correlated with a variation on any other input, while those of the coupled inputs are correlated among them.

2.3 Algorithm of the Identification of Input Type

Based on the above theoretical inference, the derived equations can be applied to only the ideal situation in which there is no corruption in data. In real situation, it is highly possible that data is corrupted, so networks cannot be well trained, which makes us hesitate to directly apply the derived equations to the identification. Nevertheless, our method can be still applicable with the relative comparison of the sensitivity changes. For instance, if the sensitivity change of an input is relatively very small, compared to those of the other inputs, it may not matter that the input is considered as an uncoupled input.

Step 1: Train an FCFNN with $X = [x_1, x_2, \cdots, x_n]$ and y
Step 2: Calculate MSE_0 (mean square error) from the network
Step 3 : Estimate $S_j, \forall j$
Step 4 :
    For $i = 1$ To $i = n$
        For $\sigma \in$ a set of predetermined values
        $\Delta x_i = \sigma \cdot x_i$
        Train the additional network with $X_{\Delta x_i}$ and y until
            $MSE_0 \approx MSE_i$ //mean square error from the additional networks
        Estimate $S_{j,\Delta x_i}$, calculate $\Delta \delta_{j,\Delta x_i}$ for $\forall j$ and save them
    End
    End
Step 5 : Calculate the mean (denoted as $\overline{\Delta \delta}_{j,\Delta x_i}$)of the saved $\Delta \delta_{j,\Delta x_i}$
Step 6 : Make a decision of the type of each input by relative comparison of $\overline{\Delta \delta}_{j,\Delta x_i}$, $\forall j$

Fig. 1. The algorithm of identifying the type of each input

As demonstrated in the previous section, the accuracy of the sensitivity analysis depends on the training performance of the additional network. Thus, a way to vary an input can be critical of whether the additional network can be well trained or not. We choose a fraction of inputs as an input variation express as

$$\Delta x_i = \sigma \cdot x_i \qquad (14)$$

where σ is a fraction value of inputs. As shown in (10) and (13), the value of σ is one of essential factors of deciding the value of $\Delta\overline{\delta}_{j,\Delta x_i}$. Too small value of σ produces a slight fluctuation in the sensitivity changes between the uncoupled inputs and the coupled inputs so it is sometimes vague to classify them into coupled or uncoupled. To avoid the problem, an appropriate value needs to be chosen to produce a salient difference between them to some extent, without seriously deteriorating the training performance. Also, the conditions for training the additional networks, such as the initial values, the training method, etc., should be same as those of the original networks, in order to facilitate the analysis. Also, the additional networks should be trained until their performances are very close to that of the original network. Usually, the mean square error (MSE) is commonly used as the measurement of the performance. For a reliable decision, the process of the estimation of input sensitivity changes is repeated as increasing the value of σ and the mean of the sensitivity changes is analyzed as in Figure 1, where $\Delta\overline{\delta}_{j,\Delta x_i}$ is the mean sensitivity change of input.

3 Modeling Partially Connected Three-Layered Feedforward Neural Networks

From the identified input types, a PCFNN can be modeled if there is at least one uncoupled input. In the PCFNN, each input is linked to the neurons in the hidden layer in the different way according to its input type. The uncoupled inputs do not share the

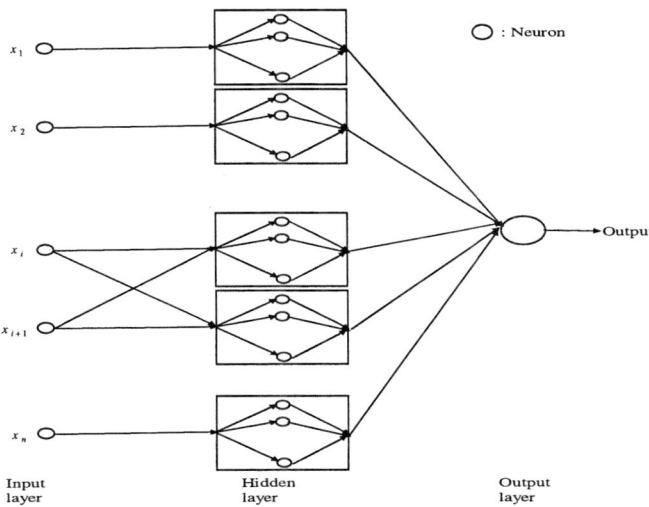

Fig. 2. An example of PCFNNs

neurons with other inputs in order to contribute to output in an uncoupled manner. On the other hand, the coupled inputs share the neurons with one another. For instance, in Figure 2, inputs x_1, x_2, and x_n are uncoupled but x_i and x_{i+1} are coupled each other. However, the hidden layer should be fully connected to the output layer in order all inputs to contribute to output. Otherwise, the uncoupled inputs linked to the neurons, which are insulated to the output layer, do not contribute to output at all. Thus, our method is suitable for modeling three-layered PCFNNs in which only one hidden layer exists and the activation function in the output layer is the linear. However, the three-layered networks resolve many practical mapping problems. Each input is linked to a group of neurons as depicted in rectangular box as shown in Figure 2. Each group can have different number of neurons for optimizing the network performance. The number of combinational trial of the neurons in the groups will be required for obtaining the optimal performance. The exhaustive searching for the optimal number of the neurons is very expensive so equivalent number is usually assigned, as done in the next section.

4 Experiment

This section presents and interprets the experimental results of the identification of the input types in accordance with the algorithm. The experiments were done using three simple generated mapping examples as following:

Case 1: $y = \exp(-x_1^2) + 1/(1-x_2)^7 + 5 \cdot x_3$
Case 2: $y = \exp(-x_1^2) \cdot 1/(1-x_2)^7 \cdot 5 \cdot x_3$
Case 3: $y = \exp(-x_1^2) \cdot 1/(1-x_2)^7 + 5 \cdot x_3$

where the inputs are uniformly distributed with a range of $[0,1]$ and 1,000 patterns for each training and test data. The additional networks are trained until satisfying the

Table 1. Mean sensitivity changes for no corruption in data

Case	Varied input	$\Delta\bar{\delta}_{1,\Delta x_i}$	$\Delta\bar{\delta}_{2,\Delta x_i}$	$\Delta\bar{\delta}_{3,\Delta x_i}$
1	x_1	0.72	0.00	0.00
	x_2	0.00	0.32	0.00
	x_3	0.00	0.00	0.57
2	x_1	0.36	0.42	0.25
	x_2	0.45	0.64	0.58
	x_3	0.56	0.67	0.54
3	x_1	0.44	0.54	0.00
	x_2	0.35	0.65	0.00
	x_3	0.00	0.00	0.44

condition $MSE_0 - \alpha \le MSE_i \le MSE_0 + \alpha$, where $\alpha = 10^{-6}$ obtained from an empirical experience. When estimating the input sensitivities from the trained networks, the normally distributed random noise with zero mean and 10^{-4} variance is added to the inputs. The predetermined fraction values are $\sigma = 0.05, 0.1, 0,15$, and 0.2. Throughout all of the following experiments, the results are written to the nearest one hundredth for the values of input sensitivities.

4.1 For no Corruption in Data

For Case 1, the mean sensitivity changes (MSC) of each input is not affected by varying other inputs so all input are considered as uncoupled. For instance, $\Delta\overline{\delta}_{2,\Delta x_i}$ and $\Delta\overline{\delta}_{3,\Delta x_i}$ of inputs x_2 and x_3 are zeroes when x_1 is varied. It has the same mechanism in MSC of the inputs when x_2 and x_3 are varied, respectively. For Case 2, those of all inputs are affected by varying any one of them so all inputs are considered as coupled as presented in Table 1. Similarly, x_1 and x_2 are considered as coupled and x_3 is uncoupled for Case 3.

Table 2. Mean sensitivity changes for corruption in data

Case	γ	Varied input	$\Delta\overline{\delta}_{1,\Delta x_i}$	$\Delta\overline{\delta}_{2,\Delta x_i}$	$\Delta\overline{\delta}_{3,\Delta x_i}$
1	0.1	x_1	0.56	0.01	0.02
		x_2	0.04	0.36	0.05
		x_3	0.01	0.03	0.44
	0.3	x_1	1.15	2.11	1.23
		x_2	0.99	2.36	1.56
		x_3	2.17	2.22	3.21
2	0.1	x_1	0.78	0.88	0.65
		x_2	0.62	0.72	0.89
		x_3	0.31	0.44	0.98
	0.3	x_1	1.54	0.78	2.01
		x_2	1.96	1.86	1.12
		x_3	0.76	1.12	1.56
3	0.1	x_1	0.34	0.27	0.03
		x_2	0.37	0.51	0.02
		x_3	0.01	0.02	0.56
	0.3	x_1	1.33	1.14	0.43
		x_2	1.15	1.42	0.89
		x_3	0.67	0.44	0.76

4.2 For Corruption in Target

Corrupted target, denoted as $\tilde{y}$, can be obtained by adding random noise to y. The random noise was generated with zero mean and γ^2 variance, where γ is a fraction of the mean of the generated target values. For $\gamma = 0.1$ and 0.3, the same process as Section 4.1 was done, however the relative comparison of MSC is performed.

For $\gamma = 0.1$, of Case 1, $\Delta\overline{\delta}_{1,\Delta x_1} = 0.56$, $\Delta\overline{\delta}_{2,\Delta x_1} = 0.01$, and $\Delta\overline{\delta}_{3,\Delta x_1} = 0.02$ when x_1 is varied, as shown in Table 2. Where, 0.01 and 0.02 are too small in comparison with 0.56 so it may not be a matter that input x_1 is considered as uncoupled with x_2 and x_3. Similarly, x_2 and x_3 can also be considered as uncoupled. However, for $\gamma = 0.3$, the mean sensitivities of all inputs are affected from varying any one of them so they all are considered as coupled. For example, $\Delta\overline{\delta}_{1,\Delta x_1} = 1.15$, $\Delta\overline{\delta}_{2,\Delta x_1} = 2.11$, and $\Delta\overline{\delta}_{3,\Delta x_1} = 1.23$ when x_1 is varied. The MSCs of x_2 and x_3 are so big compared to that of x_1. For Case 2, all inputs are identified as coupled for all the values of γ. For Case 3, the type of each input can be correctly identified when $\gamma = 0.1$. However, all inputs are identified as coupled when $\gamma = 0.3$.

4.3 Comparison of the Performances of FCFNNs and PCFNNs

In this section, the performances of FCFNNs and PCFNNs are compared for Cases 1 and 3 in order to show that the PCFNNs modeled from the identified input types are

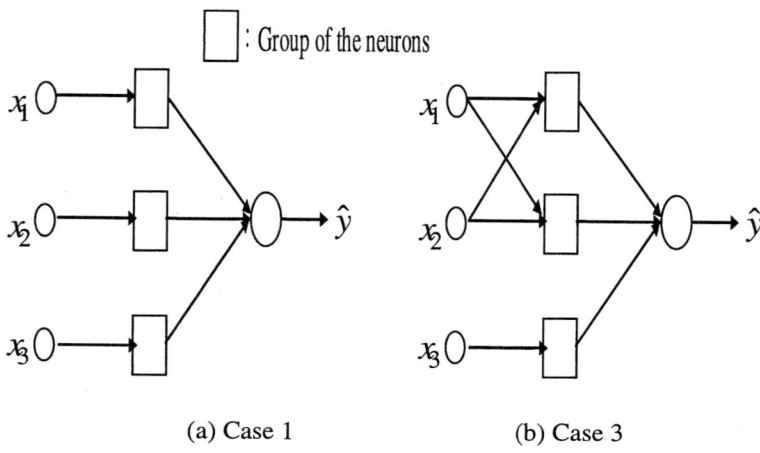

(a) Case 1   (b) Case 3

Fig. 3. PCFNNs for Case 1 and Case 3

simpler than FCFNNs without deteriorating their generalization abilities which is the performances for the test data (people are usually not interested in the performance of the training data). The root mean square error (RMSE) was used as the measurement of their performances. For the fair comparison of FCFNNs and PCFNNs, the same number of neurons is assigned to each network. To avoid the exhaustive search of the optimal number of neurons in each group, the equivalent number of neurons is assigned for the convenience. The number of the training epoch is 500 for each network. For Case 1, each input does not share the groups of neurons as viewed in Figure 3 (a). For Case 3, inputs x_1 and x_2 share the groups of neurons but input x_3 does not as in Figure 3 (b). For Case 1, there exist 27 and 45 connections for modeling FCFNNs when the total number of neurons in the hidden layer is assigned to 9 and 15. By modeling PCFNNs, 18 and 30 connections (67% of the total number of neurons) are saved without deteriorating the network performance or even slightly better as shown in Table 3. Also, the 12 and 20 connections (44%) are saved for Case 3.

Table 3. Results of the performances of PCFNNs and FCFNNs

Case	γ	The number of neurons in the hidden layer	RMSE of the test data		The number of connections by PCFNNs
			PCFNNs	FCFNNs	
1	0	9	0.03	0.04	18(67%)
		15	0.04	0.06	30(67%)
	0.1	9	0.07	0.07	18(67%)
		15	0.06	0.07	30(67%)
3	0	9	0.006	0.006	12(44%)
		15	0.004	0.006	20(44%)
	0.1	9	0.01	0.02	12(44%)
		15	0.01	0.03	20(44%)

5 Conclusion

In this paper a new method for structuring PCFNNs from identified input types was proposed. The identification of the input type was done by the analysis of the input sensitivity changes by varying the magnitude of each input. As shown in the experimental results, our method can work even when the target is corrupted with tolerance. From our empirical experience, when the sensitivity change of an input is less than 10% of that of a varied input, the input can be considered as the uncoupled input. It is also shown that the modeled PCFNNs are simpler than FCFNNs without deteriorating the generalization ability.

On the negative side, it is difficult to verify the method of identifying input type in practical situations because the true physical input types are not usually known. Only the performance comparison of PCFNNs and FCFNNs can give a cue whether the types of inputs are well identified or not. If PCFNNs can replace with FCFNNs, we can conclude the inputs are well identified.

References

1. M. Mangeas, A.S. Weigend, and C. Muller, "Forecasting electricity demand using nonlinear mixture of experts," *World Congress on Neural Networks*, vol. 2, pp. 48-53, 1995
2. D.M. Bates, *Nonlinear Regression Analysis and Its Applications*, Wiley, 1998
3. D. Elizondo, and E. Fiesler, "A survey of partially connected neural networks," *International Journal of Neural Systems*, vol. 8, nos. 5 & 6, pp. 535-558, 1997
4. S. Kang, and C. Isik, "Partially connected neural networks for mapping problems," *Proc. 5th International Conference on Enterprise Information Systems*, Angers, France, pp. 469-473, 2003
5. Y. Le Cun, J.S. Denker, and S.A., Solla, "Optimal brain damage," *Advances in neural information processing systems*, vol. 2, pp. 598-605, 1990
6. L. Prechelt, "Connection pruning with static and adaptive pruning schedules," *Neural computing*, vol. 16, pp. 49-61, 1997
7. W. Finnoff, F. Hergert, and H.G. Zimmermann, "Improving model selection by nonconvergent methods," *Neural Networks*, vol. 6, pp. 771-783, 1993
8. B. Hassibi, D.G. Stork, and C. Wolff, "Optimal brain surgeon: extensions and performance comparisons," *Advances in neural information processing systems*, vol. 6, pp.263-270, 1994.
9. M.C. Mozer, and P. Smolensky, "Using relevance to reduce network size automatically," *Connection Science*, vol. 1, no. 1, pp.3-16, 1989.
10. J. Sjoberg, Q. Zhang, L. Ljung, A. Benveniste, B. Deylon, P.Y. Glorennec, H, Hjalmarsson, and A. Juditsky, "Nonlinear black-box modeling in system identification: a unified overview," *Automatica*, vol. 31, no. 12, pp.1691-1724, 1995.

Appendix

Let's see what the impact of the sensitivity changes if we consider the second derivative part of the Taylor series expansion in (6).

$$g_{\Delta x_i}(X_{\Delta x_i}, W_{\Delta x_i}) \approx g_{\Delta x_i}(X, W_{\Delta x_i}) + \Delta x_i \cdot g'_{\Delta x_i}(X, W_{\Delta x_i}) + \frac{1}{2} \cdot \Delta x_i^2 \cdot g''_{\Delta x_i}(X, W)$$

$$\approx y + e + \Delta x_i \cdot \frac{\partial(y+e)}{\partial x_i} + \frac{1}{2} \cdot \Delta x_i^2 \cdot \frac{\partial^2(y+e)}{\partial^2 x_i}$$

$$= \hat{y} + \Delta x_i \cdot f'_i(x_i) + \frac{1}{2} \cdot \Delta x_i^2 \cdot f''_i(x_i) \tag{A.1}$$

$$\Delta \delta_{j,\Delta x_i} \approx \begin{cases} \Delta x_i \cdot f'_i(x_i) + \Delta x_i \cdot (1 + \Delta x_i) \cdot f''_i(x_i) + \frac{1}{2} \cdot \Delta x_i \cdot f'''_i(x_i), & \text{for } i = j \\ 0, & \text{for } i \neq j \end{cases} \tag{A.2}$$

As shown in (A.2), the varied input has a sensitivity change as the same as when only the first derivative part was considered. With the same way, for the coupled input-output mapping, we can verify that the second derivative term does not give an impact on the classification of input types.

Aggregation of Foraging Swarms

Long Wang[1], Hong Shi[1], Tianguang Chu[1], Weicun Zhang[2], and Lin Zhang[3]

[1] Intelligent Control Laboratory, Center for Systems and Control,
Department of Mechanics and Engineering Science,
Peking University, Beijing 100871, P. R. China
{longwang, hongshi, chutg}@pku.edu.cn
[2] Automation Department, University of Science and Technology Beijing,
Beijing 100083, P. R. China
weicunzhang@263.net
[3] Computer Science Department, Naval Postgraduate School,
Monterey, CA93943, USA
linzhang@yahoo.com

Abstract. In this paper, we consider an anisotropic swarm model with an attraction/repulsion function and study its aggregation properties. It is shown that the swarm members will aggregate and eventually form a cohesive cluster of finite size around the swarm center. We also study the swarm cohesiveness when the motion of each agent is a combination of the inter-individual interactions and the interaction of the agent with external environment. Moreover, we extend our results to more general attraction/repulsion functions. The model in this paper is more general than isotropic swarms and our results provide further insight into the effect of the interaction pattern on individual motion in a swarm system.

1 Introduction

In nature swarming can be found in many organisms ranging from simple bacteria to more advanced mammals. Examples of swarms include flocks of birds, schools of fish, herds of animals, and colonies of bacteria. Such collective behavior has certain advantages such as avoiding predators and increasing the chance of finding food. Recently, there has been a growing interest in biomimicry of forging and swarming for using in engineering applications such as optimization, robotics, military applications and autonomous air vehicle [1]–[10]. Modeling and exploring the collective dynamics has become an important issue and many investigations have been carried out [11]–[16]. However, most available results in the literature are on the isotropic swarms, sound results on the anisotropic swarms are relatively few. The study of anisotropic swarms is very difficult though anisotropic swarming is a ubiquitous phenomenon, including natural phenomena and social phenomena [17]–[22].

Gazi and Passino [2] proposed an isotropic swarm model and studied its aggregation, cohesion and stability properties. Subsequently, Chu, Wang and Chen [4] generalized their model, considering an anisotropic swarm model, and obtained the properties of aggregation, cohesion and completely stability. The concept of coupling matrix in the swarm model reflects the interaction strength between different individuals. The coupling matrix considered in [4] is symmetric, that is, the interaction between two individuals is reciprocal. In this paper, due to the asymmetry of social, economic and psychological phenomena, we will study the behavior of anisotropic swarms when the coupling matrix is completely asymmetric. The results given in this paper extend the corresponding results on isotropic swarms [2, 7] and anisotropic swarms [4, 5, 6] to more general cases and further illustrate the effect of the interaction pattern on individual motion in swarm systems. Moreover, we also study the aggregation properties of the anisotropic swarm under an attractant/repellent profile. Our results have potential applications in coordination and formation control of multiple autonomous mobile robots, and in collective evolution of robot society.

In the next section we specify an individual-based continuous-time anisotropic swarm model in Euclidean space which includes the isotropic model of [2] as a special case, and we also study the agent motion when the external attractant/repellent profile is considered. In Section 3, under some assumption on the coupling matrix, we show that the swarm exhibits aggregation. In Section 4, we extend the results in Section 3 by considering a more general attraction/repulsion function. We summarize our results in Section 5.

2 Anisotropic Swarms

We consider a swarm of N individuals (members) in an n-dimensional Euclidean space. We model the individuals as points and ignore their dimensions. The equation of motion of individual i is given by

$$\dot{x}^i = \sum_{j=1}^{N} w_{ij} f(x^i - x^j), \ i = 1, \cdots, N, \qquad (1)$$

where $x^i \in R^n$ represents the position of individual i; $W = [w_{ij}] \in R^{N \times N}$ with $w_{ij} \geq 0$ for all $i, j = 1, \cdots, N$ is the coupling matrix; $f(\cdot)$ represents the function of attraction and repulsion between the members. In other words, the direction and magnitude of motion of each member is determined as a weighted sum of the attraction and repulsion of all the other members on this member. The attraction/repulsion function that we consider is [2]

$$f(y) = -y\left(a - b\exp\left(-\frac{\|y\|^2}{c}\right)\right), \qquad (2)$$

where a, b, and c are positive constants such that $b > a$ and $\|y\|$ is the Euclidean norm given by $\|y\| = \sqrt{y^T y}$.

In the discussion to follow, we always assume $w_{ii} = 0, i = 1, \cdots, N$ in model (1). Moreover, we assume that there are no isolated clusters in the swarm, that is, $W + W^T$ is irreducible.

Note that the function $f(\cdot)$ constitutes the social potential function that governs the interindividual interactions and is attractive for large distances and repulsive for small distances. By equating $f(y) = 0$, one can find that $f(\cdot)$ switches sign at the set of points defined as $\mathcal{Y} = \{y = 0 \text{ or } \|y\| = \delta = \sqrt{c \ln (b/a)}\}$. The distance δ is the distance at which the attraction and repulsion balance. Such a distance in biological swarms exists indeed [3]. Note that it is natural as well as reasonable to require that any two different swarm members could not occupy the same position at the same time.

Remark 1: The anisotropic swarm model given here includes the isotropic model of [2] as a special case. Obviously, the present model (1) can better reflect the asymmetry of social, economic and psychological phenomena [17]–[22].

In the above model, the agent motion was driven solely by the interaction pattern between the swarm members, i.e., we didn't consider the external environment's effect on agent motion. In what follows, we will consider the external attractant/repellent profile and propose a new model.

Following [14], we consider the attractant/repellent profile $\sigma : R^n \to R$, which can be a profile of nutrients or some attractant/repellent substances (e.g. nutrients or toxic chemicals). We also assume that the areas that are minimum points are "favorable" to the individuals in the swarm. For example, we can assume that $\sigma(y) > 0$ represents a noxious environment, $\sigma(y) = 0$ represents a neutral, and $\sigma(y) < 0$ represents attractant or nutrient rich environment at y. (Note that $\sigma(\cdot)$ can be a combination of several attractant/repellent profiles).

In the new model, the equation of motion for individual i is given by

$$\dot{x}^i = -h_i \nabla_{x^i} \sigma(x^i) + \sum_{j=1}^{N} w_{ij} f(x^i - x^j), \ i = 1, \cdots, N, \qquad (3)$$

where the attraction/repulsion function $f(\cdot)$ is same as given in (2), $h_i \in R^+ = (0, \infty)$, and w_{ij} is defined as before. $-h_i \nabla_{x^i} \sigma(x^i)$ represents the motion of the individuals toward regions with higher nutrient concentration and away from regions with high concentration of toxic substances. We assume that the individuals know the gradient of the profile at their positions.

In the discussion to follow, we will need the concept of weight balance condition defined below:

Weight Balance Condition: Consider the coupling matrix $W = [w_{ij}] \in R^{N \times N}$, for all $i = 1, \cdots, N$, we assume that $\sum_{j=1}^{N} w_{ij} = \sum_{j=1}^{N} w_{ji}$.

The weight balance condition has a graphical interpretation: consider the directed graph associated with the coupling matrix, weight balance means that, for any node in this graph, the weight sum of all incoming edges equals the weight sum of all outgoing edges [8]. The weight balance condition can find physical interpretations in engineering systems such as water flow, electrical current, and traffic systems.

3 Swarm Aggregation

In this section, theoretic results concerning aggregation and cohesiveness of the swarms (1) and (3) will be presented. First, it is of interest to investigate collective behavior of the entire system rather than to ascertain detailed behavior of each individual. Second, due to complex interactions among the multi-agents, it is usually very difficult or even impossible to study the specific behavior of each agent.

Define the center of the swarm members as $\bar{x} = \frac{1}{N}\sum_{i=1}^{N} x^i$, and denote $\beta_{ij} = \exp\left(-\frac{\|x^i - x^j\|^2}{c}\right)$. We first consider the swarm in (1), then the equation of motion of the center is

$$\dot{\bar{x}} = -\frac{a}{N}\left[\sum_{i=1}^{N}\sum_{j=1}^{N} w_{ij}(x^i - x^j)\right] + \frac{b}{N}\sum_{i=1}^{N}\left[\sum_{j=1}^{N} w_{ij}\beta_{ij}(x^i - x^j)\right]$$

$$= -\frac{a}{N}\sum_{i=1}^{N}\left(\sum_{j=1}^{N} w_{ij} - \sum_{j=1}^{N} w_{ji}\right)x^i + \frac{b}{N}\sum_{i=1}^{N}\left[\sum_{j=1}^{N} w_{ij}\beta_{ij}(x^i - x^j)\right].$$

If the coupling matrix W is symmetric, by the symmetry of $f(\cdot)$ with respect to the origin, the center $\bar{x}$ will be stationary for all t, and the swarm described by Eqs. (1) and (2) will not be drifting on average [4]. Note, however, that the swarm members may still have relative motions with respect to the center while the center itself stays stationary. On the other hand, if the coupling matrix W is asymmetric, the center $\bar{x}$ may not be stationary. An interesting issue is whether the members will form a cohesive cluster and which point they will move around. We will deal with this issue in the following theorem.

Theorem 1: Consider the swarm in (1) with an attraction/replusion function $f(\cdot)$ in (2). Under the weight balance condition, all agents will eventually enter into and remain in the bounded region

$$\Omega = \left\{x : \sum_{i=1}^{N} \|x^i - \bar{x}\|^2 \leq \rho^2\right\},$$

where

$$\rho = \frac{2bM\sqrt{2c}\exp(-\frac{1}{2})}{a\lambda_2};$$

and $M = \sum_{i,j=1}^{N} w_{ij}$; λ_2 denotes the second smallest real eigenvalue of the matrix $L + L^T$; $L = [l_{ij}]$ with

$$l_{ij} = \begin{cases} -w_{ij}, & i \neq j, \\ \sum_{k=1, k \neq i}^{N} w_{ik}, & i = j; \end{cases} \quad (4)$$

Ω provides a bound on the maximum ultimate swarm size.

Proof. Let $e^i = x^i - \bar{x}$. By the definition of the center $\bar{x}$ of the swarm and the weight balance condition, we have

$$\dot{\bar{x}} = \frac{b}{N}\sum_{i=1}^{N}\left[\sum_{j=1}^{N}w_{ij}\beta_{ij}(x^i - x^j)\right].$$

Then, we have

$$\dot{e}^i = -a\sum_{j=1}^{N}w_{ij}(x^i - x^j) + b\sum_{j=1}^{N}w_{ij}\beta_{ij}(x^i - x^j) - \frac{b}{N}\sum_{i=1}^{N}\left[\sum_{j=1}^{N}w_{ij}\beta_{ij}(x^i - x^j)\right].$$

To estimate e^i, let $V = \sum_{i=1}^{N}V_i$ be the Lyapunov function for the swarm, where $V_i = \frac{1}{2}e^{iT}e^i$. Evaluating its time derivative along the solution of system (1), we have

$$\dot{V} = -a\sum_{i=1}^{N}\sum_{j=1}^{N}w_{ij}e^{iT}(e^i - e^j) + b\sum_{i=1}^{N}e^{iT}\left\{\sum_{j=1}^{N}w_{ij}\beta_{ij}(x^i - x^j)\right.$$
$$\left. -\frac{1}{N}\sum_{k=1}^{N}\left[\sum_{j=1}^{N}w_{kj}\beta_{kj}(x^k - x^j)\right]\right\}$$
$$\leq -ae^T(L \otimes I)e + b\sum_{i=1}^{N}\sum_{j=1}^{N}w_{ij}\beta_{ij}\|x^i - x^j\|\|e^i\|$$
$$+\frac{b}{N}\sum_{i=1}^{N}\left[\sum_{k=1}^{N}\sum_{j=1}^{N}w_{kj}\beta_{kj}\|x^k - x^j\|\right]\|e^i\|,$$

where $e = (e^{1T}, \cdots, e^{NT})^T$, $L \otimes I$ is the Kronecker product of L and I with L as defined in Eq. (4) and I the identity matrix of order n.

Note that each of the functions $\exp\left(-\frac{\|x^i - x^j\|^2}{c}\right)\|x^i - x^j\|$ is a bounded function whose maximum is achieved at $\|x^i - x^j\| = \sqrt{c/2}$ and is given by $\sqrt{c/2}\exp(-(1/2))$. Substituting this into the above inequality and using the fact that $\|e^i\| \leq \sqrt{2V}$, we obtain

$$\dot{V} \leq -ae^T(L \otimes I)e + 2bM\sqrt{c}\exp\left(-\frac{1}{2}\right)V^{\frac{1}{2}}. \tag{5}$$

To get further estimate of $\dot{V}$, we only need to estimate the term $e^T(L \otimes I)e$. Since

$$e^T(L \otimes I)e = \frac{1}{2}e^T((L + L^T) \otimes I)e,$$

we need to analyze $e^T((L + L^T) \otimes I)e$. First, consider the matrix $L + L^T$ with L defined in Eq. (4), we have $L + L^T = [\tilde{l}_{ij}]$, where

$$\tilde{l}_{ij} = \begin{cases} -w_{ij} - w_{ji}, & i \neq j, \\ 2\sum_{k=1, k\neq i}^{N}w_{ik}, & i = j. \end{cases} \tag{6}$$

Under the weight balance condition, we can easily see that $\lambda = 0$ is an eigenvalue of $L+L^T$ and $u = (l, \cdots, l)^T$ with $l \neq 0$ is the associated eigenvector. Moreover, since $L+L^T$ is symmetric and $W+W^T$ (hence, $L+L^T$) is irreducible, it follows from matrix theory [8] that $\lambda = 0$ is a simple eigenvalue and all the rest eigenvalues of $L + L^T$ are real and positive. Therefore, we can order the eigenvalues of $L + L^T$ as $0 = \lambda_1 < \lambda_2 \leq \lambda_3 \leq \cdots \leq \lambda_n$. Moreover, it is known that the identity matrix I has an eigenvalue $\mu = 1$ of n multiplicity and n linearly independent eigenvectors

$$u^1 = \begin{bmatrix} 1 \\ 0 \\ \vdots \\ 0 \end{bmatrix}, \quad u^2 = \begin{bmatrix} 0 \\ 1 \\ \vdots \\ 0 \end{bmatrix}, \quad \cdots, \quad u^n = \begin{bmatrix} 0 \\ 0 \\ \vdots \\ 1 \end{bmatrix}.$$

By matrix theory [8], the eigenvalues of $(L + L^T) \otimes I$ are $\lambda_i \mu = \lambda_i$ (of n multiplicity for each i). Next, we consider the matrix $(L + L^T) \otimes I$. $\lambda = 0$ is an eigenvalue of n multiplicity and the associated eigenvectors are

$$v^1 = [u^{1T}, \cdots, u^{1T}]^T, \cdots, v^n = [u^{nT}, \cdots, u^{nT}]^T.$$

Therefore, $e^T((L + L^T) \otimes I)e = 0$ implies that e must lie in the eigenspace of $(L + L^T) \otimes I$ spanned by eigenvectors $v^1, \cdots, v^n$ corresponding to the zero eigenvalue, that is, $e^1 = e^2 = \cdots = e^N$. This occurs only when $e^1 = e^2 = \cdots = e^N = 0$. However, this is impossible to happen for the swarm system under consideration, because it implies that the N individuals occupy the same position at the same time. Hence, for any solution x of system (1), e must be in the subspace spanned by eigenvectors of $(L + L^T) \otimes I$ corresponding to the nonzero eigenvalues. Hence, $e^T((L + L^T) \otimes I)e \geq \lambda_2 \|e\|^2 = 2\lambda_2 V$. From (5), we have

$$\dot{V} \leq -a\lambda_2 V + 2bM\sqrt{c}\exp(-\tfrac{1}{2})V^{\frac{1}{2}}$$
$$= -\left[a\lambda_2 V^{1/2} - 2bM\sqrt{c}\exp(-\tfrac{1}{2})\right]V^{\frac{1}{2}}$$
$$< 0$$

whenever

$$V > \left(\frac{2bM\sqrt{c}\exp(-1/2)}{a\lambda_2}\right)^2.$$

Therefore, any solution of system (1) will eventually enter into and remain in Ω.

Remark 2: The discussions above explicitly show the effect of the coupling matrix W on aggregation and cohesion of the swarm.

Remark 3: The weight balance condition is more general than the case when the coupling matrix W is a symmetric matrix [2, 4, 5, 6, 7].

Remark 4: From Theorem 1, we see that, under the weight balance condition, the motion of the swarm center only depends on the repulsion between the swarm members.

Remark 5: Theorem 1 shows that the swarm members will aggregate and form a bounded cluster around the swarm center.

From the above discussions, we know that if we ignore the influence on agent motion from external environment, under the weight balance condition, the motion of the swarm center only depends on the repulsion between the swarm members, and all agents will eventually enter into and remain in a bounded region around the swarm center. In what follows, we will study the aggregation properties of the swarm system when the attractant/repellent profile is taken into account.

The equation of the motion of the swarm center now becomes

$$\dot{\bar{x}} = -\frac{1}{N}\sum_{i=1}^{N} h_i \nabla_{x^i}\sigma(x^i) - \frac{a}{N}\sum_{i=1}^{N}\left(\sum_{j=1}^{N} w_{ij} - \sum_{j=1}^{N} w_{ji}\right)x^i$$
$$+ \frac{b}{N}\sum_{i=1}^{N}\left[\sum_{j=1}^{N} w_{ij}\beta_{ij}(x^i - x^j)\right].$$

Before we discuss cohesiveness of the swarm, we first make an assumption.

Assumption 1: There exists a constant $\bar{\sigma} > 0$ such that

$$\|\nabla_y \sigma(y)\| \le \bar{\sigma}, \quad \text{for all } y.$$

Assumption 1 implies that the gradient of the profile is bounded. This assumption is reasonable since almost all profiles we encounter such as plane and Gaussian profiles are with bounded gradient.

The following theorem shows that the swarm system still exhibits aggregation behavior when the external profile is taken into account.

Theorem 2: Consider the swarm in (3) with an attraction/replusion function $f(\cdot)$ in (2). Under the weight balance condition and Assumption 1, all agents will eventually enter into and remain in the bounded region

$$\overline{\Omega} = \left\{x : \sum_{i=1}^{N} \|x^i - \bar{x}\|^2 \le \rho^2\right\},$$

where

$$\rho = \frac{2bM\sqrt{2c}\exp(-\frac{1}{2}) + \frac{4\bar{\sigma}(N-1)}{N}(\sum_{i=1}^{N} h_i)}{a\lambda_2};$$

and M and λ_2 are defined as in Theorem 1. $\overline{\Omega}$ provides a bound on the maximum ultimate swarm size.

Proof. Let $e^i = x^i - \bar{x}$. By the definition of the center $\bar{x}$ of the swarm and the weight balance condition, we have

$$\dot{\bar{x}} = -\frac{1}{N}\sum_{i=1}^{N} h_i \nabla_{x^i}\sigma(x^i) + \frac{b}{N}\sum_{i=1}^{N}\left[\sum_{j=1}^{N} w_{ij}\beta_{ij}(x^i - x^j)\right].$$

Define the Lyapunov function as $V = \sum_{i=1}^{N} V_i$, where $V_i = \frac{1}{2} e^{iT} e^i$. Evaluating its time derivative along the solution of system (3), we have

$$\dot{V} = -a \sum_{i=1}^{N} \sum_{j=1}^{N} w_{ij} e^{iT} (e^i - e^j) + b \sum_{i=1}^{N} \sum_{j=1}^{N} w_{ij} \beta_{ij} e^{iT} (x^i - x^j)$$
$$- \frac{b}{N} \sum_{i=1}^{N} \left[\sum_{k=1}^{N} \sum_{j=1}^{N} w_{kj} \beta_{kj} e^{iT} (x^k - x^j) \right] \quad (7)$$
$$- \sum_{i=1}^{N} e^{iT} \left[h_i \nabla_{x^i} \sigma(x^i) - \frac{1}{N} \sum_{k=1}^{N} h_k \nabla_{x^k} \sigma(x^k) \right].$$

Furthermore, by assumption, we have

$$\dot{V} \leq -a \sum_{i=1}^{N} \sum_{j=1}^{N} w_{ij} e^{iT} (e^i - e^j) + b \sum_{i=1}^{N} \sum_{j=1}^{N} w_{ij} \beta_{ij} \|x^i - x^j\| \|e^i\|$$
$$+ \frac{b}{N} \sum_{i=1}^{N} \left[\sum_{k=1}^{N} \sum_{j=1}^{N} w_{kj} \beta_{kj} \|x^k - x^j\| \right] \|e^i\|$$
$$+ \sum_{i=1}^{N} \left\| h_i \nabla_{x^i} \sigma(x^i) - \frac{1}{N} \sum_{k=1}^{N} h_k \nabla_{x^k} \sigma(x^k) \right\| \|e^i\|$$
$$\leq -a \sum_{i=1}^{N} \sum_{j=1}^{N} w_{ij} e^{iT} (e^i - e^j)$$
$$+ 2bM\sqrt{c} \exp(-\frac{1}{2}) V^{1/2} + \frac{2\sqrt{2}\bar{\sigma}(N-1)}{N} (\sum_{i=1}^{N} h_i) V^{1/2}.$$

By analogous discussions as in the proof of Theorem 1, we have

$$\dot{V} \leq -a \lambda_2 V + 2bM\sqrt{c} \exp(-\frac{1}{2}) V^{1/2} + \frac{2\sqrt{2}\bar{\sigma}(N-1)}{N} \left(\sum_{i=1}^{N} h_i \right) V^{1/2}$$
$$= -\left[a \lambda_2 V^{1/2} - 2bM\sqrt{c} \exp(-\frac{1}{2}) - \frac{2\sqrt{2}\bar{\sigma}(N-1)}{N} \left(\sum_{i=1}^{N} h_i \right) \right] V^{1/2}$$
$$< 0$$

whenever

$$V > \left(\frac{2bM\sqrt{c} \exp(-1/2) + \frac{2\sqrt{2}\bar{\sigma}(N-1)}{N} \left(\sum_{i=1}^{N} h_i \right)}{a \lambda_2} \right)^2.$$

Therefore, any solution of system (3) will eventually enter into and remain in $\overline{\Omega}$.

Remark 6: Theorem 2 shows that, with bounded attractant/repellent profile, the swarm members will aggregate and form a bounded cluster around the swarm center. The motion of the swarm center depends on the repulsion between the swarm members and the weighted average of the gradient of the profile evaluated at the current positions of the individuals.

Of course, not all profiles are bounded. In the case of unbounded profile, in order to ensure the swarm to be ultimately bounded, the gradient of the profile at x^i should have a "sufficiently large" component along e^i so that the influence of the profile does not affect swarm cohesion. The following theorem addresses this issue.

Theorem 3: Consider the swarm in (3) with an attraction/replusion function $f(\cdot)$ in (2). Assume that there exist constants A_σ^i, $i = 1, \cdots, N$, with $A_\sigma = \min_i A_\sigma^i > -\frac{a\lambda_2}{2}$ such that

$$e^{iT}\left[h_i \nabla_{x^i}\sigma(x^i) - \frac{1}{N}\sum_{k=1}^N h_k \nabla_{x^k}\sigma(x^k)\right] \geq A_\sigma^i \|e^i\|^2$$

for all x^i and x^k. Then, under the weight balance condition, all agents will eventually enter into and remain in the bounded region

$$\overline{\Omega} = \left\{x : \sum_{i=1}^N \|x^i - \overline{x}\|^2 \leq \rho^2\right\},$$

where

$$\rho = \frac{2bM\sqrt{2c}\exp(-\frac{1}{2})}{a\lambda_2 + 2A_\sigma};$$

and M and λ_2 are defined as in Theorem 1. $\overline{\Omega}$ provides a bound on the maximum ultimate swarm size.

Proof. Following the proof of Theorem 2, from (7), we have

$$\dot{V} \leq -a \sum_{i=1}^N \sum_{j=1}^N w_{ij} e^{iT}(e^i - e^j) + b \sum_{i=1}^N \sum_{j=1}^N w_{ij}\beta_{ij}\|x^i - x^j\|\|e^i\|$$
$$+ \frac{b}{N}\sum_{i=1}^N \left[\sum_{k=1}^N \sum_{j=1}^N w_{kj}\beta_{kj}\|x^k - x^j\|\right]\|e^i\| - A_\sigma\|e\|^2$$
$$\leq -a \sum_{i=1}^N \sum_{j=1}^N w_{ij} e^{iT}(e^i - e^j)$$
$$+ 2bM\sqrt{c}\exp(-\tfrac{1}{2})V^{1/2} - 2A_\sigma V.$$

By analogous discussions as in the proof of Theorem 1, we have

$$\dot{V} \leq -(a\lambda_2 + 2A_\sigma)V + 2bM\sqrt{c}\exp(-\tfrac{1}{2})V^{1/2}$$
$$= -\left[(a\lambda_2 + 2A_\sigma)V^{1/2} - 2bM\sqrt{c}\exp(-\tfrac{1}{2})\right]V^{1/2}$$
$$< 0$$

whenever

$$V > \left(\frac{2bM\sqrt{c}\exp(-1/2)}{a\lambda_2 + 2A_\sigma}\right)^2.$$

Therefore, any solution of system (3) will eventually enter into and remain in $\overline{\Omega}$.

4   Further Extensions

In Sections 2 and 3 we considered a specific attraction/repulsion function $f(y)$ as defined in (2). In this section, we will consider a more general attraction/repulsion function $f(y)$. Here $f(y)$ constitutes the social potential function that governs the interindividual interactions and is assumed to have a long range attraction and short range repulsion nature. Following [13], we make the following assumptions:

Assumption 2: The attraction/repulsion function $f(\cdot)$ is of the form

$$f(y) = -y[f_a(\|y\|) - f_r(\|y\|)], y \in R^n, \tag{8}$$

where $f_a : R_+ \to R_+$ represents (the magnitude of) attraction term and has a long range, whereas $f_r : R_+ \to R_+$ represents (the magnitude of) repulsion term and has a short range, and R_+ stands for the set of nonnegative real numbers, $\|y\| = \sqrt{y^T y}$ is the Euclidean norm.

Assumption 3: There are positive constants a, b such that for any $y \in R^n$,

$$f_a(\|y\|) = a, \quad f_r(\|y\|) \le \frac{b}{\|y\|}. \tag{9}$$

That is, we assume a fixed linear attraction function and a bounded repulsion function.

Analogous to Theorems 1–3, in this case, we can also obtain the following three theorems.

Theorem 4: Consider the swarm in (1) with an attraction/replusion function $f(\cdot)$ in (8) and (9). Under the weight balance condition, all agents will eventually enter into and remain in the bounded region

$$\Omega^* = \left\{ x : \sum_{i=1}^{N} \|x^i - \bar{x}\|^2 \le \rho^2 \right\},$$

where $\rho = \frac{4bM}{a\lambda_2}$; and λ_2 and M are defined as in Theorem 1; Ω^* provides a bound on the maximum ultimate swarm size.

Theorem 5: Consider the swarm in (3) with an attraction/replusion function $f(\cdot)$ in (8) and (9). Under the weight balance condition and Assumption 1, all agents will eventually enter into and remain in the bounded region

$$\overline{\Omega}^* = \left\{ x : \sum_{i=1}^{N} \|x^i - \bar{x}\|^2 \le \rho^2 \right\},$$

where
$$\rho = \frac{4bM + \frac{4\bar{\sigma}(N-1)}{N}(\sum_{i=1}^{N} h_i)}{a\lambda_2};$$

and M and λ_2 are defined as in Theorem 1. $\overline{\Omega}^*$ provides a bound on the maximum ultimate swarm size.

Theorem 6: Consider the swarm in (3) with an attraction/replusion function $f(\cdot)$ in (8) and (9). Assume that there exist constants A_σ^i, $i = 1, \cdots, N$, with $A_\sigma = \min_i A_\sigma^i > -\frac{a\lambda_2}{2}$ such that

$$e^{iT}\left[h_i \nabla_{x^i}\sigma(x^i) - \frac{1}{N}\sum_{k=1}^{N} h_k \nabla_{x^k}\sigma(x^k)\right] \geq A_\sigma^i \|e^i\|^2$$

for all x^i and x^k. Then, under the weight balance condition, all agents will eventually enter into and remain in the bounded region

$$\overline{\Omega}^* = \left\{x : \sum_{i=1}^{N} \|x^i - \bar{x}\|^2 \leq \rho^2\right\},$$

where
$$\rho = \frac{4bM}{a\lambda_2 + 2A_\sigma};$$

and M and λ_2 are defined as in Theorem 1. $\overline{\Omega}^*$ provides a bound on the maximum ultimate swarm size.

Following the proof of Theorems 1–3, we can prove Theorems 4–6 analogously.

5 Conclusions

In this paper, we have considered an anisotropic swarm model and analyzed its aggregation. Under the weight balance condition, we show that the swarm members will aggregate and eventually form a cohesive cluster of finite size around the swarm center. The model given here is a generalization of the models in [2, 4, 5, 6, 14], and can better reflect the asymmetry of social, economic and psychological phenomena [17]–[22]. The results obtained in this paper have potential applications in coordination and formation control of multiple autonomous mobile robots, and in collective evolution of robot society.

Acknowledgement

This work was supported by the National Natural Science Foundation of China (No. 10372002 and No. 60274001) and the National Key Basic Research and Development Program (No. 2002CB312200).

References

1. Passino, K.M.: Biomimicry of bacterial foraging for distributed optimization and control. IEEE Control Systems Magazine 22 (2002) 52–67
2. Gazi, V., Passino, K.M.: Stability analysis of swarms. IEEE Trans. Automat. Contr. 48 (2003) 692–697
3. Warburton, K., Lazarus, J.: Tendency-distance models of social cohesion in animal groups. J. Theoretical Biology 150 (1991) 473–488
4. Chu, T., Wang, L., Chen, T.: Self-organized motion in anisotropic swarms. J. Control Theory and Applications 1 (2003) 77–81
5. Chu, T., Wang, L., Mu, S.: Collective behavior analysis of an anisotropic swarm model. Proc. of the 16th International Symposium on Mathematical Theory of Networks and Systems (2004) 1–14
6. Shi, H., Wang, L., Chu, T.: Swarming behavior of multi-agent systems. Proc. of the 23rd Chinese Control Conference (2004) 1027–1031
7. Liu, B., Chu, T., Wang, L., Hao, F.: Self-organization in a group of mobile autonomous agents. Proc. of the 23rd Chinese Control Conference (2004) 45–49
8. Horn, R.A., Johnson, C.R.: Matrix Analysis. New York: Cambridge Univ. Press (1985)
9. Arkin, R.: Behavior-Based Robotics. Cambridge MA: MIT Press (1998)
10. Pachter, M., Chandler, P.: Challenges of autonomous control. IEEE Control Systems Magazine 18 (1998) 92–97
11. Liu, Y., Passino, K.M., Polycarpou, M.M.: Stability analysis of one-dimensional asynchronous swarms. IEEE Trans. Automat. Contr. 48 (2003) 1848–1854
12. Liu, Y., Passino, K.M., Polycarpou, M.M.: Stability analysis of m-dimensional asynchronous swarms with a fixed communication topology. IEEE Trans. Automat. Contr. 48 (2003) 76–95
13. Gazi, V., Passino, K.M.: A class of attraction/repulsion functions for stable swarm aggregations. Proc. IEEE Conf. Decision Contr. 3 (2002) 2842–2847
14. Gazi, V., Passino, K.M.: Stability analysis of social foraging swarms. IEEE Trans. Systems, Man, and Cybernetics, Part B: Cybernetics 34 (2004) 539–557
15. Jadbabaie, A., Lin, J., Morse, A.S.: Coordination of groups of mobile autonomous agents using nearest neighbor rules. IEEE Trans. Automat. Contr. 48 (2003) 988–1001
16. Czirok, A., Vicsek, T.: Collective behavior of interacting self-propelled particles. Physica. A. 281 (2000) 17–29
17. Anderson, P., Arrow, K.J., Pines, D.: The Economy as an Evolving Complex System. New York: Addison-Wesley (1988)
18. Boabeau, E., Dorigo, M., Theraulaz, G.: Swarm Intelligence: From Natural to Artificial Systems. Oxford, UK : Oxford Univ. Press (1999)
19. Axelord, R.M.: The Complexity of Cooperation: Agent-Based Models of Competition and Collaboration. New Jersey: Princeton Univ. Press (1997)
20. Waldrop, M.M.: Complexity: The Emerging Science at the Edge of Order and Chaos. New York: Youchstone Books (1993)
21. Holland, J.H.: Hidden Order: How Adaptation Builds Complexity. New York: Addison-Wesley (1996)
22. Kauffman, S.: At Home in the Universe: The Search for Laws of Self-Organization and Complexity. Oxford, UK : Oxford Univ. Press (1996)

An ACO Algorithm for the Most Probable Explanation Problem

Haipeng Guo[1], Prashanth R. Boddhireddy[2], and William H. Hsu[3]

[1] Department of Computer Science,
Hong Kong University of Science and Technology
hpguo@cs.ust.hk
[2] Department of Plant Pathology
[3] Department of Computing and Information Sciences,
Kansas State University
{reddy, bhsu}@ksu.edu

Abstract. We describe an Ant Colony Optimization (ACO) algorithm, ANT-MPE, for the most probable explanation problem in Bayesian network inference. After tuning its parameters settings, we compare ANT-MPE with four other sampling and local search-based approximate algorithms: Gibbs Sampling, Forward Sampling, Multistart Hillclimbing, and Tabu Search. Experimental results on both artificial and real networks show that in general ANT-MPE outperforms all other algorithms, but on networks with unskewed distributions local search algorithms are slightly better. The result reveals the nature of ACO as a combination of both sampling and local search. It helps us to understand ACO better, and, more important, it also suggests a possible way to improve ACO.

1 Introduction

Bayesian networks (BNs) (Pearl 1988) are the currently dominant method for uncertain reasoning in AI. They encode the joint probability distribution in a compact manner by exploiting conditional independencies. One of the main purposes of building a BN is to conduct probabilistic inference - i.e. to compute answers to users' queries, given exact values of some observed evidence variables. This paper is concerned with a specific type of Bayesian network inference: finding the Most Probable Explanation (MPE). MPE is the problem of computing the instantiation of a Bayesian network that has the highest probability given the observed evidence. It is useful in many applications including diagnosis, prediction, and explanation. However, MPE is NP-hard (Littman 1999).

Ant Colony Optimization (ACO) is a recently developed approach that takes inspiration from the behavior of real ant colonies to solve NP-hard optimization problems. The ACO meta-heuristic was first introduced by Dorigo(1992), and was recently defined by Dorigo, Di Caro and Gambardella(1999). It has been successfully applied to various hard combinatorial optimization problems.

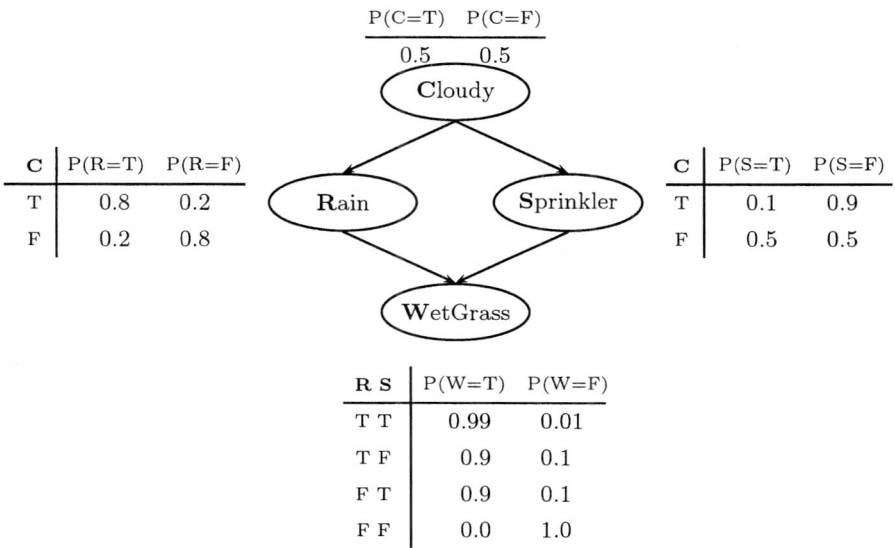

Fig. 1. The Sprinkler Network

In this paper we present the first application of ACO to the MPE problem. In section 2 we briefly introduce MPE and the related work. Then we describe our ANT-MPE algorithm in section 3. In section 4 we present the experimental results, including tuning ANT-MPE's parameters and comparing it with four other sampling and local search-based approximate MPE algorithms. Finally we summarize our findings and conclude with some discussions.

2 The MPE Problem

2.1 Bayesian Networks and The MPE Problem

A Bayesian network (Fig.1) is a Directed Acyclic Graph (DAG) where nodes represent random variables and edges represent conditional dependencies between random variables. Attached to each node is a Conditional Probability Table (CPT) that describes the conditional probability distribution of that node given its parents' states. Distributions in a BN can be discrete or continuous. In this paper we only consider discrete ones. BNs represent joint probability distributions in a compact manner. Let $\{X_1, \ldots, X_n\}$ be the random variables in a network. Every entry in the joint distribution $P(X_1, \ldots, X_n)$ can be calculated using the following chain rule:

$$P(X_1, \ldots, X_n) = \prod_{i=1}^{n} P(X_i | \pi(X_i)), \tag{1}$$

where $\pi(X_i)$ denotes the parent nodes of X_i. Figure 1 shows a simple BN with 4 nodes, the Sprinkler network (Russell and Norvig 2003).

Let (G, P) be a Bayesian network where G is a DAG and P is a set of CPTs, one for each node in G. An evidence E is a set of instantiated nodes. An explanation is a complete assignment of all node values consistent with E. Each explanation's probability can be computed in linear time using (1). For example, in the Sprinkler network (Fig. 1), suppose we have observed that the grass is wet, i.e. the $E = \{W = \mathbf{T}\}$. One possible explanation of this is: $\{ C = \mathbf{T}, R = \mathbf{T}, S = \mathbf{F}, W = \mathbf{T}\}$. Its probability is:

$$P(C = \mathbf{T}, R = \mathbf{T}, S = \mathbf{F}, W = \mathbf{T})$$
$$= P(C = \mathbf{T})P(R = \mathbf{T}|C = \mathbf{T})P(S = \mathbf{F}|C = \mathbf{T})P(W = \mathbf{T}|S = \mathbf{F}, R = \mathbf{T})$$
$$= 0.5 \times 0.8 \times 0.9 \times 0.9 = 0.324.$$

MPE is an explanation with the highest probability. It provides the most likely state of the world given the observed evidence. MPE has a number of applications in diagnosis, abduction and explanation. Both exact and approximate MPE are NP-hard (Littman 1999, Abdelbar and Hedetniemi 1998). Therefore approximate and heuristic algorithms are necessary for large and dense networks.

2.2 Related Work

Clique-tree propagation is the most popular exact inference algorithm(Lauritzen and Spiegelhalter 1988). It is efficient for sparse networks but can be very slow and often runs out-of-memory for dense and complex ones. The same is true for other exact algorithms such as variable elimination and cutset conditioning. In fact, all exact inference algorithms share a worst-case complexity exponential in the induced treewidth (same as the largest clique size) of the underlying undirected graph,

Approximate MPE algorithms trade accuracy for efficiency so that they can at least find a near-optimal explanation in a reasonable amount of time on some large instances where exact algorithms fail. There are two basic categories of approximate algorithms: stochastic sampling and search-based algorithms. Their main advantage is that the running time is fairly independent of the topology of the network and linear in the number of samples or search points.

Stochastic sampling algorithms can be divided into importance sampling algorithms (Fung and Chang 1989) and Markov Chain Monte Carlo (MCMC) methods (Pearl 1988). They differ from each other in whether samples are independent or not. Both can be applied to a large range of network sizes. But with a large network and unlikely evidence, the most probable explanation can also be very unlikely. Thus the probability of it being hit by any sampling schemes will be rather low. This is the main weakness of sampling algorithms.

Search algorithms have been studied extensively in combinatorial optimization. Researchers have applied various search strategies to solve MPE, for example, the best first search (Shimony and Charniack 1999), linear programming

(Santos 1991), stochastic local search (Kask and Dechter 1999), genetic algorithms (Mengshoel 1999), etc. More recently, Park (2002) tried to convert MPE to MAX-SAT, and then use a MAX-SAT solver to solve it indirectly. Other local search algorithms often use some heuristics to guide the search in order to avoid getting stuck into local optimal. The most popular heuristics include Stochastic Hillclimbing, Simulated Annealing (Kirkpatrick et al. 1983), Tabu Search (Glover et al. 1997), etc.

3 Ant Algorithms to Solve MPE

Ant algorithms were inspired by the foraging behavior of real ant colonies, in particular, by how ants can find the shortest paths between food sources and nest. Ants deposit on the ground a chemical substance called pheromone while walking from nest to food sources and vice versa. This forms pheromone trails through which ants can find the way to the food and back to home. Pheromone provides indirect communications among ants so that they can make use of each other's experience. It has been shown experimentally (Dorigo, Di Caro and Gambardella 1999) that this foraging behavior can give rise to the emergence of shortest paths when employed by a colony of ants.

Based on this ant colony foraging behavior, researchers have developed ACO algorithms using artificial ant systems to solve hard discrete optimization problems. In an ant system, artificial ants are created to explore the search space simulating real ants searching their environment. The objective values to be optimized usually correspond to the quality of the food and the length of the path to the food. An adaptive memory corresponds to the pheromone trails. Also, the artificial ants can make use of some local heuristic functions to help make choose among a set of feasible solutions. In addition, a pheromone evaporation mechanism is usually included to allow the ant colony to slowly forget its past history. By doing so it can direct the search towards new directions that have not been explored in the past.

ACO was first used on the Travelling Salesman Problem (Dorigo and Gambardella 1997). From then on it has been applied to the Job-Shop Scheduling Problem (Colorni et al. 1994), to the Graph Coloring Problem (Costa and Hertz 1997), to the Quadratic Assignment Problem (Gambardella et al. 1999), to the Vehicle Routing Problem (Bullnheimer 1999), etc.

In the following of this section we describe how to apply ACO to solve the MPE problem.

3.1 An Ant System for MPE

The Ants. In an MPE ant system, artificial ants build MPE solutions (explanations) by moving on the Bayesian network from one node to another. Ants must visit all nodes in the *topological order* defined by the network, i.e. before a node X_i is visited all its parents, $\pi(X_i)$, must be visited. When an ant visit X_i, it must take a *conditional branch* which is a number in the CPT. For evidence nodes E, ants are only allowed to take the branches that agree with E. The memory of each ant contains the nodes it has visited and the branches selected.

The Pheromone Tables, the Heuristic Function Tables, and the Ant Decision Tables. Each node has 3 tables: *the Pheromone Table (PT), the Heuristic Function Table (HFT)*, and *the Ant Decision Table (ADT)*. All three tables have the same structure as the CPTs. The PTs store pheromone values accumulated on each conditional branch. HFTs represent heuristics used by ants. They are exactly the same as CPTs and are kept unchanged. ADTs are used by ants to make the final decision of choosing which branch to take.

How to Update These Tables and Build the Tour. The ADT, $A_i = [a_{ijk}]$, of node X_i is obtained by the composition of the local pheromone trail values τ_{ijk} with the local heuristic values η_{ijk} as follows:

$$a_{ijk} = \frac{[\tau_{ijk}]^\alpha [\eta_{ijk}]^\beta}{\sum_j [\tau_{ijk}]^\alpha [\eta_{ijk}]^\beta} \qquad (2)$$

where j is the jth row and k the kth column of the corresponding ADT at the ith node. α and β are two parameters that control the relative weight of pheromone trails and heuristic values.

The probability with which an ant chooses to take a certain conditional branch while building its tour is:

$$p_{ij} = \frac{a_{ij\pi_i}}{\sum_j a_{ij\pi_i}} \qquad (3)$$

where π_i is the column index of the ADT and its value is conditioned on the values of parent nodes of ith node. This is equivalent to randomly simulate the ADT.

After ants have built their tour (an explanation), each ant deposits pheromone $\Delta\tau_{ijk}$ on the corresponding pheromone trails (the conditioned branches of each node on the tour). The pheromone value being dropped represents solution quality. Since we want to find the most probable explanation, we use the probability of the selected tour as the pheromone value. Suppose the generated tour is $\{x_1, \ldots, x_n\}$, the pheromone value is as follows:

$$\Delta\tau_{ijk} = \begin{cases} P(x_1, \ldots, x_n) & \text{if } j = x_i, k = \pi(x_i) \\ 0 & \text{otherwise} \end{cases} \qquad (4)$$

where the $P(x_1, \ldots, x_n)$ is computed by the chain rule in (1).

Updating the PTs is done by adding a pheromone value to the corresponding cells of the old PTs. Each ant drops pheromone to one cell of each PT at each

Algorithm 1 ANT-MPE

1: **Input** — an MPE instance (G, P, E);
2: **Output** — an explanation $u = (u_1, \ldots, u_n)$;
3: **Begin** ANT-MPE(G, P, E)
4: **Initialization**: initialize α, β, ρ, $n\_iterations$, n_ants, $best\_trail$, PTs, HFTs, ADTs;
5: **while** $n\_iterations > 0$ **do**
6:    updating ADTs using PTs and HFTs;{Equation 2}
7:    generating n_ants ant trails by random sampling from ADTs according to the topological order;{Equation 3}
8:    computing each trail's probability and updating $best\_trail$;{Equation1}
9:    updating PTs by dropping pheromone, pheromone evaporation;{Equation 4 & 5}
10:    $n\_iterations - -$;
11: **end while**
12: **Return** $best\_trail$;
13: **End** ANT-MPE.

node, i.e., the jth row, kth column of the PT at ith node. After dropping the pheromone, an ant dies. The pheromone evaporation procedure happens right after the ants finish depositing pheromone. The main role of pheromone evaporation is to avoid stagnation when all ants end up selecting the same tour. In summary, PTs are updated by the combination of pheromone accumulation and pheromone evaporation as follows:

$$\tau_{ijk} = (1 - \rho)\tau_{ijk} + \Delta\tau_{ijk} \qquad (5)$$

where $\tau_{ijk} = \sum_{l=1}^{m} \Delta\tau_{ijk}$, m is the number of ants used at each iteration, and $\rho \in (0, 1]$ is the pheromone trail decay coefficient.

3.2 The ANT-MPE Algorithm

Given the above ant system, we design an ACO algorithm, ANT-MPE, for MPE. It is listed in Algorithm 1. In the initialization step, we set pheromone values to a small positive constant on all pheromone tables, set ADTs to 0, and set HFTs to the same as CPTs. After initialization, we generate a batch of ants for several iterations. At each iteration, we first update the ant decision tables from the current pheromone tables and the heuristic function tables. Then ants use the ant decision tables to build tours, evaluate them by CPTs, and save the best trail. Then pheromone is dropped and the pheromone tables are updated. The pheromone evaporation is triggered right after. This procedure stops when the number of iterations runs out. The best solution so far is returned as the approximate MPE.

4 Results

4.1 Test Datasets

The CPT skewness of a network is computed as follows (Jitnah and Nicholson 1998): for a vector (a column of the CPT table), $v = (v_1, v_2, \ldots, v_m)$, of conditional probabilities,

$$skew(v) = \frac{\sum_{i=1}^{m} \left| \frac{1}{m} - v_i \right|}{1 - \frac{1}{m} + \sum_{i=2}^{m} \frac{1}{m}}. \tag{6}$$

where the denominator scales the skewness from 0 to 1. The skewness for one CPT is the average of the skewness of all columns, whereas the skewness of the network is the average of the skewness of all CPTs.

We used both real world and randomly generated networks to test ANT-MPE. CPT skewness was used as the main control parameter when generating random networks because we knew from domain knowledge that it would affect the instance hardness for sampling and local search algorithms. We had collected 11 real world networks. The size and skewness of these real world networks are listed in Table 6. We can see that on average most real world networks are skewed. In fact only one network's skewness(*cpcs54*) is less than 0.5 and the average skewness is about 0.7. In our experiment, we considered three different levels of skewness: {skewed(0.9), medium(0.5), unskewed(0.1)}.

The number of nodes we used for random network generation were 100 and 200. All networks were too dense to be solved exactly. All nodes were binary variables. Another factor was the evidence. In all experiments, 10% nodes were randomly selected as the evidence nodes and their values were also randomly selected. The default number of ants for each experiment was set to 3,000.

4.2 Experiment 1: Tuning α, β, and ρ in ANT-MPE

In experiment 1 we used 100 randomly generated multiply connected networks to tune the parameter values in ANT-MPE. These networks were divided into 5 groups by their skewness and number of nodes: {*skewed*100, *medium*100, *unskewed*100, *medium*200, *unskewed*200}. Each group contained 20 networks.

The weight of pheromone trails, α, and the weight of local heuristic function, β, are two most important parameters for ant algorithms. We first ran ANT-MPE on all 100 networks with 5 different combinations of (α, β) values: {(0, 5), (1, 0), (1, 5), (3, 5), (5, 1)}. The pheromone evaporation rate ρ was set to 0.01 for all runs. We gave each parameter setting 3,000 ants and compared the approximate MPE values returned. When a parameter setting returned the highest value, we counted one "win" for it. When it returned the lowest value, we counted one "loss" for it. Note that they could tie with each other.

The result is listed in Table 1. We can see that: (1) When $\beta = 0$, the local heuristic function was not being used, it never won and lost 97 out of 100

Table 1. Different (α, β) values on skewed, medium, unskewed networks with 100 and 200 nodes

(α,β)	skewed100		medium100		unskewed100		medium 200		unskewed 200		total	
	win	loss	win	loss	win	loss	win	loss	win	loss	win	loss
(0, 5)	17	0	16	0	6	0	14	0	6	0	59	0
(1, 0)	0	20	0	20	0	18	0	20	0	19	0	97
(1, 5)	17	0	15	0	8	0	15	0	10	0	65	0
(3, 5)	17	0	15	0	6	0	16	0	4	0	58	0
(5, 1)	16	0	0	0	0	2	0	0	0	1	16	3

times. When $\beta = 5$, it never lost and the number of wins increased to around 60. This indicates the importance of local heuristic function, i.e. the conditional probability tables. (2) When we set β to its best value 5 and let α be 0, 1 and 3, number of wins peaked at $\alpha = 1$ as 65. This can be explained as follows: when $\alpha = 0$, the communications between ants are not exploited so the search performance will be correspondingly affected; when $\alpha = 3$, the communications are overemphasized and the search can be trapped into local optima too early. (3) Different parameter settings tied with each other more frequently on skewed networks than on unskewed networks. This was because skewed networks' solution spaces were also skewed thus making them easier for ant algorithms comparing to those unskewed ones. Basically most parameter settings were able to find the same best MPE. Also note that on these more difficult unskewed networks, (1, 5) always got the best performance.

So we took (1, 5) as the best (α, β) values. This result also agreed with Dorigo's finding (1997) on the TSP problem. We used it as our default (α, β) values in all other experiments. We also tuned ρ in the same way using 5 different values: $\{0, 0.001, 0.01, 0.05, 0.5\}$. But the results did not show the dominance of any ρ value over others excepted that 0.1 was slightly better than others. So we just used $\rho = 0.1$ in all other experiments. Because of the lack of space, we do not list the detail results here.

4.3 Experiment 2: Algorithm Comparison on Randomly Generated Networks

In experiment 2, we compared ANT-MPE with four other sampling and local search-based approximate MPE algorithms: Forward Sampling, Gibbs Sampling, Multi-Start Hillclimbing, and Tabu Search on two randomly generated test datasets. Again, all networks were exactly intractable. On the first test dataset, we ran all algorithms and counted the number of times each algorithm "won" the competition. So far, the most effective way to fairly compare different heuristic algorithms is to allow all algorithms to consume the same amount of computation resources, with distinctions being based on the quality of solutions obtained (Rardin 2001). In our experiments, we gave each algorithm a given number of samples(or equivalently, ants and search-points) and then compared the quality of solutions returned. The algorithm returned the highest MPE was

Table 2. Experiment 2.1: number of times of each algorithm being the best

	Best Algorithm				
	Gibbs Sampling	Forward Sampling	Multi-start HC	Tabu Search	ANT-MPE
counts	0	366	697	139	1,390
percentage	0%	14.12%	26.89%	5.36%	53.63%

Table 3. Experiment 2.1: grouped by #samples

#samples	Number of Times of Being the Best Algorithm				
	Gibbs Sampling	Forward Sampling	Multi-start HC	Tabu Search	ANT-MPE
300	0	106	283	0	475
1,000	0	124	262	3	475
3,000	0	136	152	136	440

Table 4. Experiment 2.1: grouped by skewness

skewness	Number of Times of Being the Best Algorithm				
	Gibbs Sampling	Forward Sampling	Multi-start HC	Tabu Search	ANT-MPE
0.1	0	0	694	135	35
0.5	0	0	1	1	862
0.9	0	366	2	3	493

labelled as "winner". We also record when the highest MPE was found by each algorithm. If two algorithms returned the same value, the one that used less resources was labelled as "winner". On the second test dataset, we compared the total approximate MPE values returned by each algorithm.

Experiment 2.1: Algorithm Comparison by Number of WINs. The test dataset here contained 2,592 randomly generated MPE instances. Number of nodes was set to 100. The skewness had three levels: skewed(0.9), medium(0.5), or unskewed(0.1). Each level contained 864 instances. Number of samples had three values as well: 300, 1,000, or 3,000. Each group also contained 864 instances. The results are summarized in Table 2, Table 3 and Table 4.

Table 2 basically shows that in general ANT-MPE outperforms all other algorithms. Table 3 shows that number of samples does not significantly affect ANT-MPE. It only slightly influences two search algorithms' relative performance. Table 4 gives the most interesting result. We can see that (1) on skewed networks ANT-MPE generally outperforms all other algorithms, while Forward Sampling still can compete; (2) on medium networks, ANT-MPE dominates; (3) on unskewed networks, search algorithms outperforms ANT-MPE. Fortunately, most real world networks are not unskewed. This is because skewness in fact

Table 5. Experiment 2.2: Total MPE Probabilities Returned by Each Algorithm

skewness	Total MPE Probabilities Returned by Each Algorithm				
	Gibbs Sampling	Forward Sampling	Multi-start HC	Tabu Search	ANT-MPE
0.1	4.7×10^{-29}	1.0×10^{-27}	2.2×10^{-26}	7.9×10^{-27}	1.1×10^{-26}
0.5	1.4×10^{-14}	2.8×10^{-8}	6.2×10^{-9}	1.6×10^{-7}	6.0×10^{-6}
0.9	1.9×10^{-46}	0.14	1.4×10^{-10}	2.5×10^{-14}	0.16

indicates the structure of the probabilistic domain and real world distributions are all structured to some degree. Therefore we can expect that ANT-MPE would work well on most real world networks.

Experiment 2.2: Algorithm Comparison by the Returned MPE Probabilities. In this experiment we ran all algorithms on 162 randomly generated networks. They were divided into three groups: 27 unskewed networks, 54 medium networks, and 81 skewed networks. For each group, we collected the total approximate MPE probabilities returned by each algorithm. The result is shown in Table 5. It shows that in terms of the returned MPE probabilities, ANT-MPE outperforms all other algorithms on both skewed and medium networks. On unskewed networks, Multi-start Hillclimbing(2.2×10^{-26}) is only slightly better than ANT-MPE(1.1×10^{-26}). ANT-MPE is the second best and it is still at the same order of magnitude as Multi-start Hillclimbing. So we can draw the conclusion that in general ANT-MPE outperforms all other algorithms.

4.4 Experiment 3: Algorithm Comparison on Real Networks

In experiment 3 we ran on all algorithms on 11 real world networks. Each run was given 3,000 samples. We compared the exact MPE probability, the MPE probability returned by the best approximate algorithm, and the MPE probability returned by ANT-MPE. We used Hugin to compute the exact MPE. The result is listed in Table 6.

ANT-MPE was the best for 7 of 10 networks where the results were available. Forward Sampling were the best for *alarm* and *insurance* because they returned the MPE earlier. But ANT-MPE was able to find the same MPE later on. Multi-start Hillclimbing outperformed ANT-MPE on *cpcs54*, whose skewness was only 0.25. But ANT-MPE was the second best on *cpcs54* and Multi-start Hillclimbing was only slightly better. We can say that in general ANT-MPE outperformed all other algorithms on the real world test dataset.

5 Concluding Remarks

We have described an ant algorithm, the ANT-MPE, for the MPE problem. To our knowledge, this is the first application of ACO to MPE. The empirical results show that in general ANT-MPE outperforms other sampling and search

Table 6. Test Results on 11 Real World Bayesian Networks

Network	#Nodes	Skewness	Exact MPE	Best Appro. Algorithm	Returned by Best Algo.	Returned by ANT-MPE
alarm	37	.84	0.04565	Forward Sampling	0.04565	0.04565
barley	413	.87	3.67×10^{-37}	N/A	N/A	N/A
cpcs179	179	.76	0.0069	ANT-MPE	0.0069	0.0069
cpcs54	54	.25	1.87×10^{-11}	Multi-start HC	1.28×10^{-11}	5.78×10^{-12}
hailfinder	56	.50	1.44×10^{-12}	ANT-MPE	2.11×10^{-13}	2.11×10^{-13}
insurance	27	.70	0.002185	Forward Sampling	0.002185	0.002185
pigs	441	.55	5.03×10^{-88}	ANT-MPE	1.31×10^{-141}	1.31×10^{-141}
water	32	.75	3.08×10^{-4}	ANT-MPE	3.08×10^{-4}	3.08×10^{-4}
munin2	1003	.89	8.74×10^{-37}	ANT-MPE	1.23×10^{-37}	1.23×10^{-37}
munin3	1041	.55	2.49×10^{-37}	ANT-MPE	7.07×10^{-40}	7.07×10^{-40}
munin1	189	.88	N/A	ANT-MPE	5.93×10^{-8}	5.93×10^{-8}

algorithms on both artificial and real networks. More specifically, on skewed networks ANT-MPE generally outperforms other algorithms, but Forward Sampling are competent; on medium networks ANT-MPE basically dominates; on unskewed networks, local search algorithms outperform ANT-MPE, but they are only slightly better and ANT-MPE is the second best.

This result is interesting because it reveals ant algorithms' nature as a combination of sampling and local search. The sampling part comes from the fact that each individual ant can use CPTs as heuristic functions to explore new trails. The search part is that a colony of ants can exchange information through pheromone trails so as to cooperatively "learn" how to find the best solution. Basically, if we set α to 0, then ACO becomes Forward Sampling, because it only uses CPTs as the heuristic functions when generating ant trails(samples). With the use of pheromone trails($\alpha \neq 0$), ANT-MPE manages to outperform Forward Sampling on both unskewed and medium networks while performing equally well on skewed networks. As the skewness decreases, the solution space becomes more "flat" and the number of local optima increases. It is well-known that as the number of local optima increases, most likely the search space becomes harder to explore. This makes it more difficult for sampling algorithms, while simple search heuristic like random restart will have more chances to explore new areas in the solution space. That is why search algorithms outperform ANT-MPE on unskewed networks. This result implies that as a combination of sampling and local search, ACO's search aspect is weaker than its sampling aspect. This can be verified by the importance of β values as shown in experiment 1. It also suggests a possible way to improve ACO. If we can detect that the solution space is flat, then we can change ants' strategy to favor exploration more than exploitation so as to gain a better overall performance.

Possible future work include conducting similar algorithm comparison experiments on other NP-hard problems to see if the same conclusion regarding to instance hardness and algorithm performance can be drawn there.

Acknowledgements

Thank anonymous reviewers for their valuable comments. This work was partially supported by the HK Research Grants Council under grant HKUST6088/01E.

References

Abdelbar, A. M., Hedetniemi, S. M.: Approximating MAPs for belief networks in NP-hard and other theorems. Artif. Intell. **102** (1998) 21–38

Bullnheimer, B.: Ant Colony Optimization in Vehicle Routing. Doctoral thesis, University of Vienna. (1999)

Colorni, A., Dorigo, M., Maniezzo, V., Trubian, M.: Ant system for Job-Shop Scheduling. Belgian Journal of Operations Research, Statistics and Computer Science. **34(1)** (1994) 39–53

Costa, D., Hertz, A.: Ants can colour graphs. Journal of the Operational Research Society. **48** (1997) 295–305

Dorigo, M.: Optimization, Learning and Natural Algorithms. Ph.D.Thesis, Politecnico di Milano, Italy. (1992)

Dorigo, M., Di Caro, G., Gambardella, L. M.: Ant algorithms for discrete optimization. Artificial Life, **5(2)** (1999) 137-172

Dorigo, M., Gambardella, L. M.: Ant Colonies for the Traveling Salesman Problem BioSystems. **43** (1997) 73-81

Fung, R., Chang, K. C.: Weighting and integrating evidence for stochastic simulation in Bayesian networks. In Uncertainty in Artificial Intelligence 5. (1989) 209–219

Gambardella, L. M., Taillard, E., Dorigo, M.: Ant colonies for the quadratic assignment problem. Journal of the Operational Research Society. **50** (1999) 167–176.

Glover, F., Laguna, M.: Tabu search. Kluwer Academic Publishers, Boston. (1997)

Jitnah, N., Nicholson, A. E.,: Belief network algorithms: A study of performance based on domain characterization. In Learning and Reasoning with Complex Representations. **1359** Springer-Verlag (1998) 169–188

Kask, K., Dechter R.: Stochastic local search for Bayesian networks. In Workshop on AI and Statistics 99. (1999) 113–122

Kirkpatrick, S., Gelatt, C. D., Vecchi, M. P.: Optimization by simulated annealing. Science, Number 4598. **220** (1983) 671–680

Littman, M.: Initial experiments in stochastic search for Bayesian networks. In Procedings of the Sixteenth National Conference on Artificial Intelligence. (1999) 667–672

Lauritzen, S. L., Spiegelhalter, D. J.: Local computations with probabilities on graphical structures and their application to expert systems (with discussion). J. Royal Statist. Soc. Series B **50** (1988) 157-224

Mengshoel, O. J.: Efficient Bayesian Network Inference: Genetic Algorithms, Stochastic Local Search, and Abstraction. Computer Science Department, University of Illinois at Urbana-Champaign. (1999)

Park, J. D.: Using weighted MAX-SAT engines to solve MPE. In Proceedings of the 18th National Conference on Artificial Intelligence (AAAI). (2002) 682–687

Pearl, J.: Probabilistic Reasoning in Intelligent Systems: Networks of Plausible Inference. San Mateo, CA, Morgan-Kaufmann. (1988)

Rardin, R. L., Uzsoy, R.: Experimental evaluation of heuristic optimization algorithms: a tutorial. Journal of Heuristics. **7** (2001) 261–304

Russell, S., Norvig, P.: Artificial Intelligence: A Modern Approach. Prentice Hall, NJ. (2003)

Santos, E.: On the generation of alternative explanations with implications for belief revision. In UAI91. (1991) 339–347

Shimony, S. E., Charniak, E.: A new algorithm for finding MAP assignments to belief network. In UAI 99. (1999) 185–193

Designing a Morphogenetic System for Evolvable Hardware

Justin Lee and Joaquin Sitte

Smart Devices Laboratory,
Faculty of Information Technology,
Queensland University of Technology,
GPO Box 2434, Brisbane, Qld 4001, Australia

Abstract. Traditional approaches to evolvable hardware (EHW), using a direct encoding, have not scaled well with increases in problem complexity. To overcome this there have been moves towards encoding a growth process, which however have not shown a great deal of success to date. In this paper we present the design of a morphogenetic EHW model that has taken the salient features of biological processes and structures to produce an evolutionary and growth model that consistently outperforms a traditional EHW approach using a direct encoding, and scales well to larger, more complex, problems.

1 Introduction

Evolvable hardware (EHW) uses simulated evolution to evolve circuits which are then evaluated for their fitness in producing the desired behaviour as required for solving a particular problem. EHW is generally implemented on reconfigurable hardware, such as field programmable gate arrays (FPGAs), which consist of a lattice of configurable logic blocks (CLBs), typically consisting of some arrangement of basic logic gates, multiplexors, and flip-flops, that can be configured to perform various digital logic functions. The functionality of the CLBs and the connections between CLBs can be configured by downloading a bitstream to the device to produce the desired circuit. FPGAs allow evolving solutions to be tested in situ, which is well suited to embedded applications such as robot controllers and image processing.

While evolvable hardware has proven to be successful in the evolution of small novel circuits, it has been limited in its applicability to complex designs, largely due the use of direct encodings in which the chromosome directly represents the device's configuration. A practical approach to solving this problem for specific application domains has been function-level evolution, involving the use of higher-level primitives such as addition, subtraction, sine, etc. (see [1–3] as examples). Although this scales the ability of EHW to solve more complex problems, it comes at the price of higher gate counts, designer bias and loss of potential novelty in solutions, thus countering some of the original motivations for EHW.

A separation between genotype (the chromosome) and phenotype (the generated circuit), and a way of generating the phenotype from the genotype (a growth process), is the approach taken by nature to evolve complex organisms, and has increasingly been seen as a means of scaling EHW to more complex problems without losing its ability to generate novelty. By encoding a growth process, known as morphogenesis, rather than an explicit configuration, the complexity is moved from the genotype to the genotype-phenotype mapping. Although there have been some successes with using morphogenetic approaches in generating neural networks [4-6] and tessallating patterns [7], there has been little success in EHW, and furthermore, existing approaches have not shown that morphogenesis does aid in scaling evolution to more complex problems.

We have undertaken an in-depth examination of biological development and by extracting the features from this that we judged to be useful and applicable to development within the constraints of EHW, we were able to come up with a complete bio-inspired morphogenetic EHW system for the Xilinx Virtex series of FPGAs, that includes biologically inspired genetic operators, chromosome structure and genetic code, along with cellular processes driven by gene expression and simple inter-cell signalling. Details of the design and design decisions are given in section two. Section three presents the results of using our morphogenetic system and compares this with a traditional direct encoding scheme, and in section four we conclude.

2 Design of a Cell-Based Morphogenetic EHW System

There are several issues that need to be resolved in the design of a developmental system for EHW. What abstractions can be usefully adapted from biology to EHW; what processes and structures should be emulated in a simulated cell; how to map from a cellular model to the FPGA hardware and at what level of abstraction should the hardware be manipulated; and, what genetic model and encoding should be used. These issues are dealt with in the following sections.

2.1 Mapping to FPGA

The level of abstraction for evolution and development to manipulate the FPGA resources can range from directly manipulating the bitstream, or the individual configurable components, to manipulating higher level constructs, as in functional EHW or with a hardware description language such as VHDL. We chose to manipulate the FPGA at the logic-gate level, using the Java JBits API provided by Xilinx for the Virtex [8], so as to avoid too much designer bias and to allow evolution freedom to explore novelty.

There is a spectrum of approaches as to how to map from a cellular model to the underlying hardware of the FPGA. On one extreme it may be a totally simulated cellular model, with no correspondance between the components and processes of development and the underlying hardware, with only the result of development being implemented on the FPGA. To the other extreme where all aspects of development, such as proteins, signal pathways, etc, correspond to actual physical resources on the FPGA. After an in-depth look at both the Virtex architecture (see [9] for details) and biological developmental processes we decided on a model in which the developmental process is closely tied to the FPGA structure. Rather than trying to evolve or design simulated developmental mechanisms and structures, we directly use the underlying FPGA structure for implementing much of the developmental process. For example, rather than designing special signaling proteins and signal receptors, we let the FPGA routing resources act as signals to the connecting CLBs (see [10] for more details). This approach counters some of the difficulties involved in having simulated developmental processes distinct from the underlying medium. Problems such as the computational expense and arbitrariness of various aspects of development, such as rates of diffusion of signal proteins, determining which proteins are signals, what the extent of signal spread is, and matching them to receptors, which themselves need to be designed somewhat arbitrarily or evolved.

Cells too are mapped directly to the underlying FPGA architecture, so that each cell may correspond to either a CLB slice or logic element, according to the user's specification. The decision to map to slice or logic element, rather than CLBs, was made due to the functional independence of these elements in the Virtex: logic elements are functionally independent for most functions, while slices may either utilise two independent 4-input function generators or combine these into a single 5-input function generator.

2.2 Biological Developmental Processes

Biologically speaking, development is the process by which a multicellular organism is formed from an initial single cell. Starting from a single cell, a simple embryo is formed comprised of a few cell types organised in a crude pattern, which is gradually refined to generate a complex organism comprised of many cell types organised in a detailed manner. This model of the development process is known as epigenesis, and is comprised of five major overlapping processes: growth, cell division, differentiation, pattern formation and morphogenesis [11]. Growth brings an increase in the size of the organism through changes in cell size, or cell division, or depositing of materials (such as bone) into the extracellular matrix; cell division increases the number of cells, and may occur in conjuction with, or independently from the growth phase; differentiation is responsible for producing the cells with specialised structures and functionality through changes to cells' patterns of gene expression; pattern formation organises and positions cells to generate an initially rough body plan which is then further refined by morphogenesis, which is responsible for coordinating the dynamic behaviours of cells in the developing embryo to collectively generate tissues and organs of differing shapes and structures.

Although growth and cell division are essential in biological organisms, their applicability to our EHW model is limited by the fixed mapping from cells to hardware that we have chosen. The underlying FPGA hardware has a fixed structure, with FPGA logic cells (CLBs) being fixed in both shape and in their physical relationship to each other (having a regular matrix pattern), with only their connectivity and function being variable. Although pattern formation is not directly applicable for the same reasons, there are some abstractions from pattern formation that are still relevant, such as axis specification and polarisation. In the biological process of pattern formation, one of the first tasks undertaken in the embryo is to determine the principal body axis, and polarisation. This may be determined by the asymmetric distribution of maternal gene products in the egg, or require a physical cue from the environment. For performing morphogenesis in EHW, axis specification and polarisation may also be inportant, and in our case is provided by axis specific simulated cytoplasmic determinant molecules preplaced at run-time. Morphogens are chemical gradients that produce graded responses from cells according to concentration. These are the primary biological mechanism for determining location along an embryonic axis. In our EHW system, simulated morphogens are also used for this purpose, to give information as to a cell's position relative to the input and output cells on the CLB matrix.

The processes which are most useful to our model are differentiation and morphogenesis, through which cells coordinate their behaviour. These two processes are closely entwined, and both have gene expression central to their functioning.

Gene Expression. The whole developmental process is largely driven and controlled by the mechanics of gene expression. This is the process by which proteins signal cellular state to activate genes, which in turn are able to effect changes in cell state by the production of further proteins which may be used as signals or cellular building blocks. This provides a view of the cell as a set of parallel processing elements (genes) controlled by the interactions between their programs encoded in the chromosome and their environment as represented by proteins detectable by the cell.

There are two particular types of protein that have important roles in development, these being transcription factors (TFs) and components of signaling pathways. Transcription factors control gene expression by binding at sites on the regulatory regions of a gene, hence playing a major role in the coordination of developmental processes; whereas signaling pathways are necessary for cells to be able to perceive external signals [11]. The mechanics of signaling pathways are quite complex, and not necessary for EHW. What is necessary is that signals from other cells can be detected and effect the expression of genes within the receiving cell. In our model all proteins are treated as transcription factors, so that choosing which effect gene expression can be decided by evolution (via elements that can bind at binding sites) rather than arbitrarily by the designer, however simulated TF molecules that are only used for controlling gene expression are also provided and correspond to non-coding messenger RNA in higher-level organisms, which are able to encode higher-level architectural plans [12].

Control of gene expression can take place at any of the intermediate stages of transcription, RNA processing, mRNA transport, mRNA degradation, and protein activity. Transcription of DNA, whereby the coding region of a gene is transcribed to an RNA molecule prior to translation into a protein, is the first level of regulation of gene expression and hence the developmental process, and is generally the most important level of control in gene expression [13, 11]. As gene regulation at the transcription level appears to be the most important level of gene regulation, and for reasons of simplicity and limiting computational expense, we chose to regulate gene expression solely at this level in our system. Furthermore, the results achieved by Reil [14] who used a gene expression model with transcriptional regulation, demonstrated that gene regulation using a simple model is able to produce many of the properties exhibited in nature.

Cell Differentiation. Generally speaking, cells all contain the same genetic information, however, their specialised structures and functionality differ according to the proteins present within the cell, and this is determined by which genes are expressed. Differentiation is the process by which different patterns of gene expression are activated and maintained to generate cells of different types. Which genes, and hence proteins, are expressed differs between cells according to what cytoplasmic determinants are inherited at cell division, and what extracellular signals are received. Cytoplasmic determinants are molecules, such as transcription factors, that bind to the regulatory regions of genes and help to determine a cell's developmental fate (i.e. pattern of gene expression that causes the cell to differentiate in a particular manner). Although cell division is not applicable to our developmental model, the use of pre-placed cytoplasmic determinants to differentiate cells, at specially designated IO cells for example, may be useful.

Induction, whereby a signal received from another cell is able to affect the receiving cell's developmental fate, is used to control differentiation and pattern formation in development. An inductive signal may be used to instruct a cell to choose one fate over others, or be required to allow a cell already committed to a particular developmental pathway to continue towards differentiation. Inductive signals may occur over various ranges and may produce a single standard response in the responding cell, or a graded response dependent on signal concentration, in which case it is called a morphogen [11]. Induction and other forms of signaling (both from within and without the cell) can be readily applied to EHW with fixed cell structures, and along with gene expression, are probably the most important mechanisms of developmental biology in their applicability to EHW.

Morphogenesis. Morphogenesis is the process by which complex structures, such as tissues and organs, are generated through the utilisation of cell behaviours. Cells are able to produce many individual and collective behaviours, such as changes of shape and size, cell fusion and cell death, adherence and dispersion, movements relative to each other, differential rates of cell proliferation, and cell-extracellular matrix interactions [11].

Obviously many of these behaviours are not directly applicable to developmental processes in EHW where there is a fixed mapping between cells and the underlying hardware structure. Cell behaviours here are limited to changes in connectivity (routing) and function. Of the biological behaviours listed above, only cell-cell and cell-extracellular matrix interactions are applicable to our EHW system. Cell death, was not used in our system, but would be simple to implement, by disabling connections to and from the dead cell, and could be used to isolate faulty regions of the underlying hardware. The notion of an extracellular matrix, a network of macromolecules secreted by cells into their local environment, also has some relevance to our system, for interactions between cells and the matrix inducing differentiation. The extracellular matrix could be used to correspond to the inter-CLB cell routing resources, specifically the programmable interconnection points (PIPs) used to connect lines from other CLBs to lines that can connect to the local CLB's inputs or outputs. Cell-cell interactions, in contrast, deal only with directly connectable lines between CLBs. In the current version of our EHW system, only directly connectable single-length lines (between neighbouring CLBs) are used, providing cell-cell interactions, but ruling out cell-extracellular matrix interactions.

2.3 Cell Model

Biological cells contain structures such as a cell wall to stop swelling or shrinking and a cell membrane that allows the passing of small molecules, and are filled with a substance known as the cytoplasm. These and other cell structures do not need to be explicitly represented in simulated cells with a fixed size and mapping to the underlying FPGA hardware. This also applies to the metabolic processes required for cell maintenance in biological systems. We have chosen a simple cell model loosely based on prokaryote (bacterial) cells, containing a single chromosome, proteins and a number of RNA polymerase enzymes (currently based on the number of genes in the chromosome). Ribosome, which is required to translate messenger RNA to proteins, does not need explicit representation, as the transcription-level gene regulation model we use only requires the simulation of the RNA polymerase enzyme responsible for transcription. Translation is treated as an indivisible part of the transcription process, which, although not biologically correct, meets the functional requirements of our model.

There are three kinds of proteins detectable within the cell, two of which are present in the cell, these being the simulated transcription factors and the non-simulated FPGA gate-level logic settings, and the other is the receiving end of a signaling pathway that corresponds to a shared FPGA routing resource. All proteins that correspond to underlying FPGA gate-level settings, have one protein per logic resource present in the cell (signaling pathways are present in the originating cell), and these are present for the entire duration of the cell's life. Simulated transcription factors, however, don't need to be unique within the cell, nor does every possible TF need to be present in the cell, and TFs have a lifespan.

2.4 Genetic Model

Chromosome Model. In the design of the encoding of the chromosome and genes, one of the first considerations was allowing a variable number of genes and preconditions for their expression. Requiring a preset number of genes would introduce unnecessary designer bias and constrain evolution's ability to find optimal solutions.

Another important factor that was taken into consideration is the importance of neutral mutations and junk DNA. When a mutation to the genotype makes no change to the resulting phenotype, this is known as a neutral, or silent, mutation. This occurs frequently in nature due to the redundancy of the genetic code (the mapping from the triplet sequences of bases of RNA, known as codons, to amino acids), where a mutation (or "wobble") at the third position in a codon often codes for the same amino acid [15]. Neutral mutations are important as they allow movements in genotype space with no changes in fitness, which gives the population the ability to take mutations that are not immediately beneficial. Thus the population is able to drift along neutral ridges [16], rather than sacrificing its current fitness, which may significantly aid the evolutionary search. Instead of becoming trapped in sub-optimal regions of the landscape a population is able to continue moving through genotype space in search of areas that allow further increases in fitness. Neutral mutations have been shown to significantly aid evolutionary search for evolving telecommunications networks [17] and evolvable hardware [16, 18].

Junk DNA is used to denote sections of the chromosome that have no function, and so can collect mutations, but may later be activated. This may happen, for example, through gene duplication where a mutation on a gene's promoter site deactivates that gene (acting as a gene switch), allowing neutral mutations to take place on the duplicate, which may later be reactivated [19]. See also the work of Burke et al. [20] on the exploitation of variable length genomes for utilising junk DNA, and Harvey and Thompson's work which utilised 'junk' sections of the genome in EHW [16].

To exploit these factors we decided on a variable length chromosome and a base-4 encoding along with a codon-based genetic code. A variable length chromosome allows evolution to decide how many genes are required for the problem at hand, while also providing space for junk DNA. A base-4 chromosome was chosen as it allows us to constrain the mutation operators and gives more redundancy for neutral mutations. A codon-based genetic code was decided on to facilitate neutral mutations on genes' coding region: most single base mutations will result in either no change or a change to a related gene product, especially for mutations in the third base of a codon.

Gene Model. Genes are bounded by initiation and terminator sites. The initiation sites contain zero or more regulator regions and a promoter region. RNA polymerase recognises promoter regions as starting points for gene transcription, which continues until the terminator site is reached. Regulatory elements control where and when the gene is transcribed, and the rate of transcription. With this in mind a gene structure loosely based on that of prokaryotes (in particular the operon model) was decided on, giving a gene structure as shown in Figure 1.

Enhancers and repressors are determined by their location on the gene relative to the promoter. Enhancers are located upstream of promoter, where they act to attract the polymerase enzyme for gene transcription, while repressors

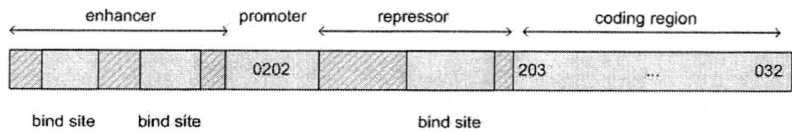

Fig. 1. Gene Structure

are located between the promoter and gene coding region, thus blocking polymerase from transcription. Transcription factors (either simulated or proteins that correspond to the underlying FPGA hardware resources) bind to repressors and enhancers to effect the activation of the associated gene. Within regulatory regions (enhancers and repressors), there are bind sites to which these can bind. These are identified by special signature sequences, allowing a variable number of bind sites per regulator. FPGA resources are able to be bound to several bind sites concurrently, but TFs are only able to bind to a single bind site, and remain attached for their remaining lifespan.

The gene coding region encodes for FPGA gate-level logic and simulated molecules, and allows multiple of these to be encoded per gene. There are, however, no introns and exons, only a sequence of codons which encode gene products. A start codon, analogous to the AUG start codon in nature, is used to indicate where to start transcription, and a stop codon (eg UGA, UAA, UAG) is used to indicate where transcription terminates. Gene products are decoded to an intermediate format (analogous to a chain of amino acids) by mapping each resource type (such as 'LUT') and attribute (eg LUT 'F'), to a specific codon, as given in the genetic code, and then by further decoding that resource's settings (eg a 16 bit LUT configuration) from the following codons according to the resource's own code. This format is then further decoded to produce JBits class constants and settings values for manipulating the FPGA configuration bitstream. Our genetic code was specifically designed for use with EHW systems where the number of resources to be set per CLB is not predetermined, such as when encoding a growth process.

Binding of FPGA resources to bind sites on genes' regulatory regions is done using a related coding scheme, with the only difference being in the first codon of the code, which differs slightly to allow the differentiation between local-to-cell FPGA resources, and connecting resources which may have the originating cell's state queried, as required for implementing signalling pathways.

Genetic Operators. Evolution cannot occur without genetic operators to search the genotype space. The most commonly used operators in evolutionary computation are crossover and mutation. Although these were inspired by biological counterparts, biological crossover in particular has little resemblance to its simulated operator. In nature crossover requires two DNA molecules with a large region of homology (nearly identical sequence), usually hundreds of base pairs long, so that the exchange between two chromosoms is usually conservative [21]. Taking inspiration from this, we have implemented a homologous crossover operator that uses a variant of the longest common substring, implemented using Ukkonen's algorithm for constructing suffix trees in linear time [22], but with a random common substring being chosen and biased towards longer matches. 1-point crossover is then performed at the boundary of the randomly chosen subsequence.

Mutation in our system is also biologically inspired. Mutations of a single base may involve a mutation of an existing base to another character in the DNA alphabet, and may be of two kinds: transversions (A-T or G-C) and transitions (A-G or T-C). Many of these mutations will have no effect on the encoded protein due to the redundancy of the genetic code, and thus aid in evolutionary search. Other mutations may involve the insertion or deletion of bases in a sequence, which may cause a frame shift in the codons downstream, and will have a serious effect on the encoded protein which is generally deleterious [21]. Another type of mutation involves the reversal of a section of the chromosome and is known as inversion. We have provided analogs of each of these kinds of mutation.

3   Experiments

This set of experiments is aimed at testing whether our morphogenetic system can successfully generate complex circuit structures and to compare its performance and scalability against a direct encoding. We ran two sets of experiments, the first involved routing on a 5x5 CLB matrix (containing 100 cells) from an input in the center of the west edge of the matrix to an output at the center of the east edge of the matrix. Evolution must also connect the input and output cells to dedicated routing CLBs on the outside (of the evolvable region) neighbour. For the second set of experiments we increased the size of the CLB matrix to 8x8 (containing 256 cells), and the number of inputs and outputs to 4 each. Inputs are placed in the center of the West edge of the CLB matrix, 2 input locations per CLB, while outputs are spread evenly across the East edge of the CLB matrix, requiring evolution to learn not just how to connect horizontally across the matrix, but also how to spread vertically from the middle outwards.

To route from inputs to outputs would generally be trivial, and so we have severely constrained the routing lines available. Each cell is mapped to a logic element, giving 4 cells to a single CLB. Each cell is then limited to a slimmed down subset of resources, with only one input used per LUT, giving 4 possible LUT functions (output 0 or 1, pass or invert signal). Each cell is able to drive the input of a LUT in 3 or 4 of the neighbouring CLBs. The set of lines available to each cell were chosen such that it is not possible to directly route horizontally from the West to East edges of a CLB matrix, and it is also necessary for lines to be routed through each of the 4 distinct cell (logic element) types. Fitness, in both experiments, was based on how much progress was made in routing a signal, possibly inverted, from the inputs to the outputs, noting that we don't care what the relationship between the different inputs and outputs are, only that all inputs are connected and one or more of these drives the outputs. See [10] for more details on the FPGA resources allocated to each cell type and the algorithm used for calculating fitness.

For each set of experiments twenty evolutionary runs were done with a population size of 100 and using a steady state genetic algorithm with tournament selection without replacement. The crossover rate was set at 80%, mutation at 2%, inversion at 5%, and for the variable length chromosomes used with the morphogenetic approach, a base insert/delete rate of 0.1% was used with 50-50 chance of insertion or deletion. Each evolutionary run was continued until a solution with 100% fitness was found or until a sufficient number of generations had passed without an improvement in the maximum fitness attained (1000 generations for the first set of experiments, and 1500 with a minimum of 5000 generations for the second). For the morphogenesis approach, growth is done for a minimum of 30 steps, with fitness evaluated at each step, and growth continued if the maximum phenotype fitness for this genotype increased in the last 15 (minimum growth steps/2) growth steps, or if phenotype fitness is increasing. The genotype's fitness is given by the maximum phenotype fitness achieved during growth. Note that TFs and morphogens were not used in these experiments.

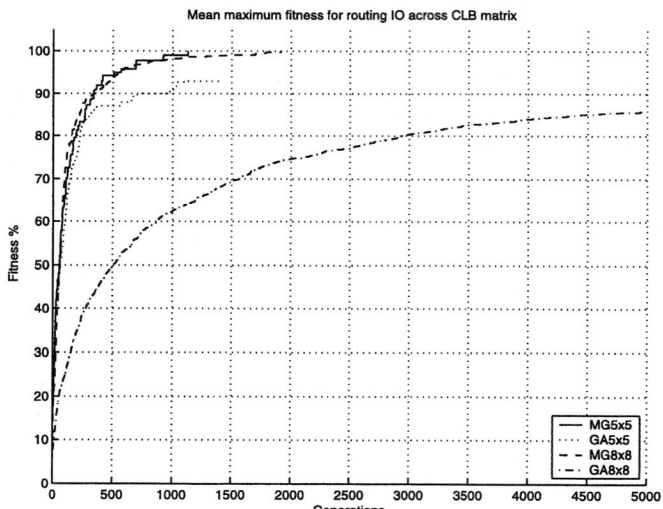

Fig. 2. Mean maximum fitness for routing IO across CLB matrix

In the first set of experiments the direct encoding approach was able to find a 100% solution in 13 out of the 20 runs, with the average number of generations required for successful runs being 531.0769 with a standard deviation (SD) of 340.5768. The morphogenetic approach was able to find a 100% solution every time, and took an average of 458.5 generations (SD=283.9556), 36.95 growth steps, and had on average 9.9 genes and a chromosome length of 5690.35 bases. In the second set of experiments the morphogenetic approach was again able to find a 100% solution on each run, taking an average of 1001.7 generations

(SD=510.5647), 49.95 growth steps, and had 5.65 genes and chromosome length of 3461.4 bases. The direct encoding approach, however, was unable to find any 100% solution, with maximum fitness values reaching a mean of 86.6406% (SD=3.0930%), and taking on average 4647.1 generations (SD=1756.9). The highest fitness achieved by the direct encoding approach was 93.75% which occurred at generation 9954. This run was continued up to 35,000 generations and reached a maximum of 96.875% at generation 16,302. Figure 2 show the mean maximum fitness over all runs for both approaches on the two experiments (up to generation 5000).

From Figure 2 it is evident that the morphogenetic approach (denoted by MG) not only outperforms the direct encoding approach (denoted by GA), but also scales very well, with the more complex problem (MG8x8) keeping pace with the simpler problem (MG5x5) up until the last few fitness percentage points where there is a lag of around 800 generations until it catches up. This is in complete contrast to the direct encoding approach, where it took 5000 generations to reach the same point that took 500 generations on the simpler problem.

4 Conclusion

In this paper, we have introduced our morphogenetic system for evolvable hardware and shown how we chose its key characteristics based on an in-depth investigation of biological developmental and genetic processes. By closely coupling the gate-level state of the underlying hardware with a simple, yet flexible, gene expression model to drive development we have avoided introducing too many assumptions and overheads, while allowing a great deal of redundancy for neutral pathways through evolutionary space, and have come up with a system that not only outperforms a standard direct encoding approach to EHW, but scales well to increases in problem complexity.

References

1. Higuchi, T., Murakawa, M., Iwata, M., Kajitani, I., Liu, W., Salami, M.: Evolvable hardware at function level. In: IEEE International Conference on Evolutionary Computation. (1997) 187–192
2. Clark, G.R.: A novel function-level EHW architecture within modern FPGAs. In: Proceedings of the 1999 Congress on Evolutionary Computation (CEC99). Volume 2. (1999) 830–833
3. Kalganova, T.: An extrinsic function-level evolvable hardware approach. In: Proceedings of the Third European Conference on Genetic Programming (EUROGP2000), Lecture Notes in Computer Science. Volume 1802., Edinburg, UK, Springer-Verlag (2000) 60–75
4. Jakobi, N.: Harnessing morphogenesis. Technical Report CSRP 423, School of Cognitive and Computer Science, University of Sussex, Sussex (1995)
5. Eggenberger, P.: Cell interactions as a control tool of developmental processes for evolutionary robotics. In: Proceedings of SAB '96. (1996) 440–448

6. Roggen, D., Floreano, D., Mattiussi, C.: A morphogenetic evolutionary system: Phylogenesis of the poetic circuit. In Tyrrell, A.M., Haddow, P.C., Torresen, J., eds.: Proceedings of the 5th International Conference on Evolvable Systems: From Biology to Hardware ICES 2003. Volume 2606 of Lecture Notes in Computer Science., Trondheim, Norway, Springer (2003) 153–164
7. Bentley, P., Kumar, S.: Three ways to grow designs: A comparison of evolved embryogenies for a design problem. In: Proceedings of the Genetic and Evolutionary Conference (GECCO '99). (1999) 35–43
8. Guccione, S., Levi, D., Sundararajan, P.: Jbits: Java based interface for reconfigurable computing. In: Second Annual Military and Aerospace Applications of Programmable Devices and Technologies Conference (MAPLD), Laurel, MD (1999)
9. Xilinx Inc.: Virtex 2.5 V Field Programmable Gate Arrays: Product Specification, DS003 (V2.5). http://direct.xilinx.com/bvdocs/publications/ds003.pdf (2001)
10. Lee, J., Sitte, J.: A gate-level model for morphogenetic evolvable hardware. In: Proceedings of the 2004 IEEE International Conference on Field-Programmable Technology (FPT'04), Brisbane, Australia (2004)
11. Twyman, R.: Instant Notes in Developmental Biology. BIOS Scientific Publishers limited, Oxford (2001)
12. Mattick, J.S.: Non-coding RNAs: the architects of eukaryotic complexity. EMBO reports **2** (2001) 986–991
13. Reil, T.: Models of gene regulation - a review. In Maley, C., Boudreau, E., eds.: Artificial Life 7 Workshop Proceedings, MIT Press (2000) 107–113
14. Reil, T.: Dynamics of gene expression in an artificail genome - implications for biological and artificial ontogeny. In Floreano, D., Mondada, F., Nicoud, J., eds.: Proceedings of the 5th European Conference on Artificial Life, Springer Verlag (1999) 457–466
15. Crick, F.: Codon-anticodon pairing; the wobble hypothesis. Journal of Molecular Biology **19** (1966) 548–555
16. Harvey, I., Thompson, A.: Through the labyrinth evolution finds a way: A silicon ridge. In Higuchi, T., ed.: Proceedings of the First International Conference on Evolvable Systems: From Biology to Hardware, Springer-Verlag (1996) 406–422
17. Shipman, R., Shakleton, M., Harvey, I.: The use of neutral genotype-phenotype mappings for improved evolutionary search. BT Technology Journal **18** (2000) 103–111
18. Thompson, A.: Notes on design through artificial evolution. In Parmee, I.C., ed.: Adaptive Computing in Design and Manufacture V, London, Springer-Verlag (2002) 17–26
19. Ohno, S.: Evolution by Gene Duplication. Springer Verlag, Berlin (1970)
20. Burke, D.S., Jong, D., A., K., Grefenstette, J.J., Ramsey, C.L., Wu, A.S.: Putting more genetics into genetic algorithms. Evolutionary Computation **6** (1998) 387–410
21. Winter, P., Hickey, G., Fletcher, H.: Instant Notes in Genetics. 2nd edn. BIOS Scientific Publishers limited, Oxford (2002)
22. Ukkonen, E.: On-line construction of suffix trees. Algorithmica **14** (1995) 249–260

Evaluation of Evolutionary Algorithms for Multi-objective Train Schedule Optimization

C.S. Chang and Chung Min Kwan

National University of Singapore Department of Electrical and Computer Engineering,
10 Kent Ridge Road, Singapore 119260
{eleccs, g0301034}@nus.edu.sg
http://www.nus.edu.sg

Abstract. Evolutionary computation techniques have been used widely to solve various optimization and learning problems. This paper describes the application of evolutionary computation techniques to a real world complex train schedule multiobjective problem. Three established algorithms (Genetic Algorithm GA, Particle Swarm Optimization PSO, and Differential Evolution DE) were proposed to solve the scheduling problem. Comparative studies were done on various performance indices. Simulation results are presented which demonstrates that DE is the best approach for this scheduling problem.

1 Introduction

The problem of minimizing operating costs and maximizing passenger comfort of a medium sized mass rapid transit (MRT) system is multiobjective and conflicting. It is affected by factors such as the dispatch frequency of trains; dwell time at passenger stations, waiting time for passengers as well as how smooth a train travels. Recently, evolutionary algorithms were found to be useful for solving multiobjective problems (Zitzler and Thiele 1999) as it has some advantages over traditional Operational Research (OR) techniques. For example, considerations for convexity, concavity, and/or continuity of functions are not necessary in evolutionary computation, whereas, they form a real concern in traditional OR techniques. In multiobjective optimization problems, there is no single optimal solution, but rather a set of alternative solutions. These solutions are optimal in the wider sense that no other solutions in the search space are superior to (dominate) them when all objectives are simultaneously considered. They are known as pareto-optimal solutions. Pareto-optimality is expected to provide flexibility for the human decision maker.

In this paper, three pareto-based approaches for solving the multiobjective train scheduling problem were investigated. The paper is organized as follows: The formulation of the problem is detailed in section 2 followed by the proposed algorithms in section 3. Experiments are then presented in section 4 and conclusions are drawn in section 5.

2 Formulation of Problem

2.1 Motivation

Modern MRT systems are concerned with providing a good quality of service to commuters without compromising safety. An important assessment on the quality of service is the comfort level of the passengers. Besides the quality of service, decision makers of MRT system are also concerned with minimizing the operating costs of running the system. However, under normal conditions operating costs could be minimized only with passenger comfort level compromised. There is hence a need to find the optimal set of solutions for these conflicting objectives.

In our work a spreadsheet database was created for the study of various train parameters and their effect on operating costs. The database enables key parameters to be adjusted, and supports a framework for generating a predetermined train schedule. The set of train schedules can subsequently be fed into an algorithm known as Automated Train Regulator (ATR) [1] for dynamic simulation of the schedule, fine tuning, and the study of possible conflicts encountered during implementation. The piece of work seeks to automate the process of optimizing the predetermined timetable by employing evolutionary algorithms; where the schedule is previously tuned manually. The process is extended to incorporate a simple passenger discomfort function to demonstrate the feasibility of the algorithms in the multiobjective case. The whole task is simplified by making some assumptions. a.) Only key variables affecting the operating costs and passenger comfort level are considered. b.) Certain fixed costs like the salary of the train drivers, transport allowances, the number of working hours per day etc are fixed in advance. c.) Passenger flows during different periods of a working or festive day are also known in advance.

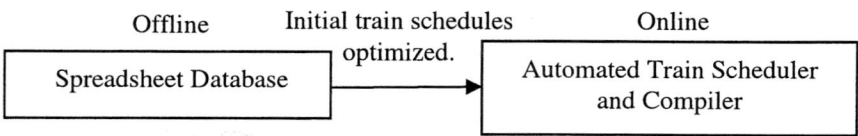

Fig. 1. Spreadsheet and Scheduler Relationship

2.2 Key Variables and Constraints

The following equations define the basic relationship of the variables affecting the multi-objective optimization problem. Essentially the operating cost increases with the increase of the number of trains T in the system.

$$\text{No. of trains } T = \text{Cycle Time} / \text{Headway} . \tag{1}$$

$$\text{Cycle Time} = \text{Run Time} + \text{Layover Time} + \text{Dwell Time} . \tag{2}$$

The passenger comfort level is defined to be affected by the headway in a simple model:

$$\text{Passenger Comfort Level} = \alpha \, (\text{headway})^2. \tag{3}$$

Where the headway, run time, layover time and dwell time in the above equations are identified as key variables to be optimized. An explanation for the key variables is provided below.

Headway. This is defined as the distance (time gap) between two successive trains traveling in the same direction on the same track.

Dwell Time. This is part of the cycle time taken by a train to stop at a particular station. This key variable is affected by passenger flow and the times taken by passengers to board/ alight each train.

Run Time and Coast Level. The run time of a train is defined as the time taken for its journey to travel between stations. Coast level describes the train movement profile and the amount of energy usage. As illustrated in a train velocity-time profile between adjacent stations (Fig. 2), the train is accelerated after departure from the first station. When it reaches its desired velocity, the train can either (**a**) remain powering (Coast Level 0) to cover a given distance within the shortest time but requiring the highest energy consumption; (**b**) turn the motive power on and off at certain desired velocities (Coast Level 1), or (**c**) turn off the motive power completely (Coast Level 2) for the longest run time but consuming the lowest energy.

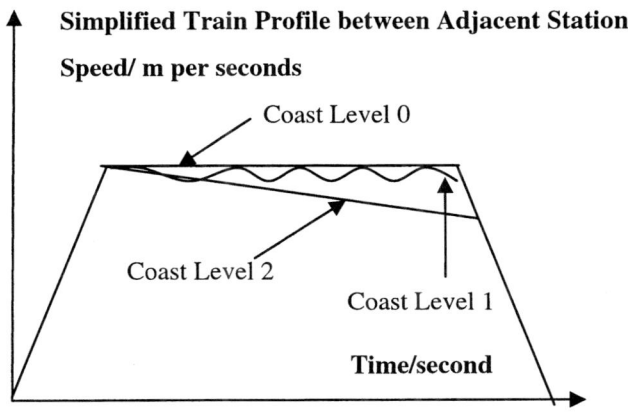

Fig. 2. Train Profile and Coast Level

Layover Time. This is the time taken for a train to reverse its direction at a terminal station, which includes the time taken for changing the train driver and completing other procedures required at the terminal station.

Hard Constraints (Safety). These are associated with the safe running of trains, passenger safety and proper train functioning. (Cannot be violated)

- Minimum headway – this must be observed at all times to ensure a safe distance between a train from the train immediately ahead/behind
- Minimum routine inspection time at terminal stations – minimum time involved at terminal stations for routine inspections of trains to ensure a safe journey
- Minimum dwell time – ensures that trains stay long enough at each station.
- Speed limits – limits the train speed at track locations of high curvature or entry/exit points of underground/ over-ground sections
- Maximum allowable passenger loading –limits the maximum number of passengers allowed in a train

Soft Constraints (Quality of Service). These are associated with the quality of service and passenger comfort, which include:

- Policy Headway – This is the maximum allowable headway set at peak hours to ensure that passengers would be able to receive a minimum quality of service.

2.3 Objective Function

The objective function of our train scheduling problem is to minimize the operation cost and passenger discomfort level, subjected to the various constraints in section 2.2. The problem statement is stated as follows:

Minimize $f(x) = f_1(x), f_2(x)$ where $f_1(x)$ = Operating costs, $f_2(x)$ = Passenger Discomfort level (Subjected to Safety and Quality of service constraints). (4)

where the passenger discomfort level is the inverse of passenger comfort level as defined in equation (3), and both objectives are conflicting.

3 Optimization Methods

The multi-objective train scheduling problem as defined in previous section is a complex problem which could not be solved by conventional OR techniques. The use of the spreadsheet database allows evolutionary algorithms to be employed elegantly; avoiding the complexities of the mathematical equations governing the objective functions as these are handled by the spreadsheet itself. Three techniques are adopted to solve the multi-objective train scheduling problem, GA, PSO and DE. PSO strictly belongs to a special class known as swarm optimization that is inspired by the choreography of a bird flock; it is included in our analysis to provide interesting alternative for comparison with the conventional evolutionary algorithms.

Pareto-based approach (Goldberg) [2] is preferred and adopted in this work because it is able to provide a whole range of non-dominated solutions, providing flexibility for the decision maker to select and adopt the best solution as he/she deemed fit. Non-pareto methods like the weighted sum (Horn 1997) [3] is difficult to implement in this work because there is no common metric between the different criteria, leading to difficulties in setting a suitable weight.

3.1 Multi-objective Evolutionary Computation Algorithm

Many well known pareto-based algorithms are available to be adopted in solving the train-scheduling problem. [4,11,13]. For comparison purposes, care must be taken to ensure that the algorithms are as generic as possible and could be used for all three algorithms without providing unfair advantage. The generic multiobjective algorithm adopted in our work is listed as follows (modified from SPEA, [4])

```
1. Generate an initial population P and create the
empty external nondominated set P'(Pareto front set).

2. Copy the nondominated members of P into P'.

3. Remove solutions within P' which are covered by any
other member of P'.

4. If the number of externally stored nondominated so-
lutions exceeds a given maximum N', prune P' by means of
clustering. (N' = Pruned Pareto front set)

5. Calculate the fitness of each individual in P as
well as in P'. (Fitness evaluation)

6. Apply (GA, PSO or DE) to the problem.

7. If the maximum number is reached, then stop, else go
to step 2.
```

3.2 Methodology and Design of Proposed Solutions

In the comparative study between the three algorithms proposed, the main challenge is to ensure that algorithms could be compared in a meaningful and fair way. Two design steps were adopted to achieve it. The first step involves studying the three algorithms and identifying the parameters to be kept constant to ensure a fair comparison. Subsequently, the second stage involves preliminary studies to tune the set of control parameters for each proposed algorithm.

3.2.1 Techniques and Identification of Control Parameters

Most common evolutionary computation techniques follow roughly the same process [5]: 1.)Encoding of solutions to the problem as a chromosome; 2.) A function to evaluate the fitness, or survival strength of individuals; 3.) Initialization of the initial population; selection operators; and reproduction operators. For the three algorithms proposed, the components are listed as follows:

Table 1. Main components for the various algorithms

	GA	PSO	DE
Encoding	Real	Real	Real
Selection	Roulette Wheel	See equation 5 and 6 [8,9]	See equation 7 and 8 [10,11]
Reproduction	Mutation, Crossover [6,7]		
Population size	30	30	30

The various equations as listed in the tables are as follows:

$$\underline{v}_i = w * \underline{v}_i + c1 * rand1 * (\underline{pbest}_i - \underline{present}_i) + c2 * rand2 * (gbest - \underline{present}_i). \quad (5)$$

$$\underline{present}_i = \underline{present}_i + \lambda * \underline{v}_i. \quad (6)$$

Equations (5) and (6) are modifying equations for the PSO algorithm. The adjustments of the individual candidate solutions are analogous to the use of a crossover operator in conventional evolutionary computation method. $\underline{v}_i$ represents the velocity vector of the ith particular candidate solution of the population; $\underline{pbest}_i$ is the ith candidate solution's best experience attained thus far; $\underline{present}_i$ is the current position along the search space of the ith candidate; rand1 and rand2 are random terms in the range from 0 to 1; gbest represents the best candidate solution in the particular generation and c1, c2, w and are weight terms. The detailed workings could be found in [8,9].

$$\underline{v}_i = \underline{x}_{i,G} + \lambda.(\underline{x}_{best,G} - \underline{x}_{r1,G}) + F.(\underline{x}_{r2,G} - \underline{x}_{r3,G}). \quad (7)$$

$$\underline{u}_j = \underline{v}_j \text{ for } j = \langle n \rangle_D, \langle n+1 \rangle_D, \ldots \ldots \langle n+L-1 \rangle_D \quad (8)$$

$$\underline{u}_j = \underline{x}_j \quad \text{otherwise}$$

In the DE process, equations (7) and (8) detail the population modification process. Equation (7) is analogous to the mutation process while equation (8) is analogous to the crossover process in conventional evolutionary algorithms. The term $\underline{v}_i$ in equation (7) represents the ith trial vector; $\underline{x}_{i,G}$ is the ith candidate solution of the current generation G; $\underline{x}_{best,G}$ is the best candidate solution of the current generation; $\underline{x}_{r2,G}$ and $\underline{x}_{r3,G}$ are randomly selected candidate solutions within the population size; λ and F are weight terms and finally the term $\underline{u}_j$ represents the jth element that has gone through the process of crossover based on a crossover probability of CR. The detailed workings could be found in [10,11].

In our comparative studies, it is considered a common practice that they must have the same representation, operators, and parameters to ensure a fair comparison. In this part of work the population size (30), coding type (Real) and the method of initializing the population size (random) are identified as components to be kept constant. The other control parameters relating to the three algorithms (Mutation, Crossover for GA; C1, C2, w, λ for PSO; λ, F, crossover for DE) are allowed to be tuned.

The next part presents the preliminary studies done to tune the various control parameters.

3.2.2 Tuning and Customization of Algorithms

The control parameters for each algorithm were determined through extensive experimentation. The tuned control parameters are summarized as follows:

Table 2. Tuned Control Parameters for GA, PSO, DE

Parameter for EA	GA	PSO	DE
Population size	30	30	30
Coding Type	Real number	Real number	Real number
Selection and Reproduction mechanisms	0.8 (One-point crossover)	2 (C1 & C2)	0.5 to 0 (linear decrease,λ)
	Roulette Wheel (**Selection**)	4.0 to 2.0 (linear decrease, **w**)	4.0 to 0 (linear decrease, **F**)
	Mutation rate Decreases linearly (starts with 0.02, decreases to 0)	0.8 (λ)	0.3 (**crossover**)

Many available techniques for controlling and selecting the parameters for a general multi-objective evolutionary algorithm are discussed [5]. In our work however, simple forms of dynamic tuning were used in all three algorithms and it is deemed sufficient for our application based on the satisfactory results obtained for the single unconstrained optimization case. The rationale of incorporating such a variation was due to its simplicity and fast implementation. It allows for a large exploration of the search space at the initial stage (global exploration) and a faster convergence after sufficient iterations (local fine tuning). Simplicity in implementation will facilitate customization of the algorithms in future for formulating a more comprehensive way to control the parameters, which will lead to generalizability and customization. Further work may lead to adaptive control and other forms of more complex control for parameter tuning.

4 Simulation Results and Analysis

The East-West line of a typical medium sized MRT system was used for testing the feasibility of the developed algorithms. The test system consists of 26 passenger stations studied at morning peak. All simulations were carried out on the same

Pentium 4 PC (2.4 GHz). 30 independent runs were performed per algorithm to restrict the influence of random effects. Initial population was the same for each run for the different algorithm. The termination condition for each simulation is 500 iterations. Analysis is performed in two stages—the first stage consists of testing the three algorithms on the single objective of operating costs aimed at verifying the feasibility of the algorithms. Subsequently the second stage solves the complete multi-objective train scheduling problem. The computer program for the optimization process is written in Microsoft Visual C#, under the .NET framework.

4.1 Stage 1—Operating Cost as SINGLE Objective

To gain insight and confidence in the three proposed algorithms, simulations were performed for operating costs as a single objective (Passenger comfort level omitted) with the optimal known in advance as the optimization processes were run under no constraints. This stage is necessary to ensure the workability of the proposed algorithms before embarking on the full multiobjective optimization. The range of variables and their expected optimized values are listed as follows:

Table 3. Variables for optimization *(UP and DOWN directions)*

Variables	Allowable Range	Expected Optimal
Headway	60s to 180s	180s
Total Dwell time	540s to 1080s	540s
Layover time	120s to 240s	120s
Coast level	0 to 2	2

The results for each algorithm converged to their expected optimized values as shown in Table 6 and Fig. 3. Referring to the results, it was noted clearly that GA falls behind PSO and DE in performance. In terms of the amount of time taken to run the optimization process GA clocked a time of 14 minutes, which is about 16% slower than PSO and 27% slower than DE. Moreover, GA was not able to produce as good a result as either PSO or DE. It is concluded at this stage that GA is inferior to both PSO and DE.

There is a close contention between PSO and DE. While DE takes a faster time (11minutes) to complete the simulation, with PSO (12 minutes) lagging by 9%, PSO converges at a faster rate compared to DE (shown in Fig. 7.) At this stage therefore, it is not clear which is the best algorithm for our application. However, the feasibility of all the algorithms have been demonstrated through this stage; as all are shown to be capable for the single objective train operation costs optimization.

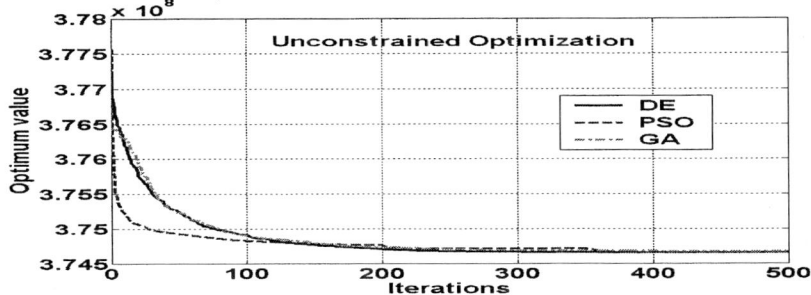

Fig. 3. Results for Unconstrained Optimization (*Averaged over 30 runs*)

Table 4. Results and Comparison (*Average Values over 30 runs*)

Type of comparison	GA	PSO	DE
Average Time taken	14mins	12mins	11mins
Convergence	>500 iterations	About 280 iterations	About 320 iterations
Final Headway West Bound	179	179	179
Final Headway East Bound	179	179	179
Final Dwell time West Bound	540	540	540
Final Dwell time East Bound	542	540	540
Final Layover time West Bound	120	120	120
Final Layover time East Bound	122	120	120
Final Coast level	2	2	2
Lowest Cost Achieved (Testing Values)	374040350	374035708	374035708

4.2 Stage 2 – Multi-objective Optimization

Having gained the initial confidence on the feasibility of the algorithms, the challenge in this stage is to determine the optimal set of solutions for the multiobjective problem defined in equation (4). Based on the passenger comfort level defined in equation (3), the parameter α is set to be 0.01. The termination condition for the multiobjective case has been set to 800 iterations to avoid premature termination. Population size (N) and the maximum number of externally stored nondominated solutions (N′) was set to 30. Control parameters of the three algorithms were kept as determined earlier.

A random search algorithm (Rand) was added to serve as an additional point of reference [4, 12]. This probabilistic algorithm was performed with the GA algorithm without any selection, mutation and crossover.

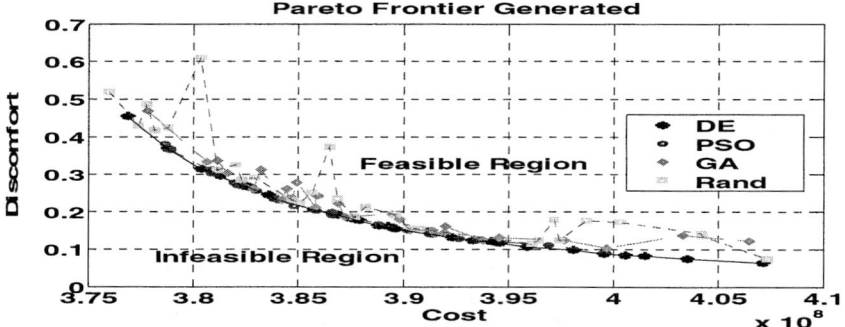

Fig. 4. Best Pareto-Front Generated for the Multi-Objective problem (*30 runs, N and N′ are both set to 30*)

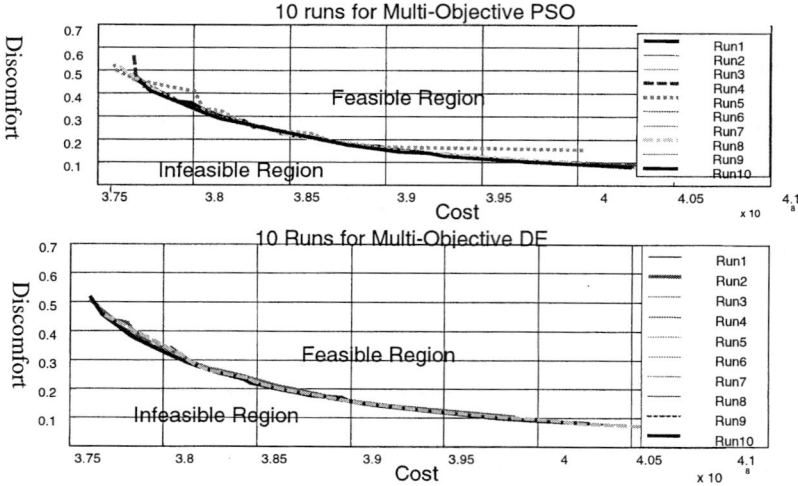

Fig. 5. 10 Independent runs for PSO and DE (*GA and Rand omitted as they are shown to be inferior to PSO and DE*)

To provide a fair comparison in the multiobjective scenario, certain concepts in the MOPSO method [13] was adopted and the global best term in the PSO update equations (the term gbest) was replaced by a repository storage used to store the positions of the particles that represent nondominated vectors. In terms of DE, an alternative form of equation (7) was used (Storn and Price, Scheme DE 1) which does not take into account $\underline{x}_{best,G}$. $\underline{x}_{i,G}$ has also been replaced by the term $\underline{x}_{r1,G}$, a randomly selected candidate within the population size. The results for the simulations are as follows:

The results were obtained by running 30 independent runs and plotting the best non-dominated front extracted for each algorithm over the 30 runs. In an additional plot (Fig. 5) the figures showing 10 independent runs for two algorithms provide an additional insight into the problem. It was noted that the multi-objective DE and multi-objective PSO were able to maintain consistent results showing minimal deviation (Except one for PSO).

Table 5. Results of Multiobjective Optimization Based on number of points (A) is dominated by (B) (*30 runs, best results taken*)

(A)	No. of solution points dominated by (B)				
	Rand	GA	PSO	DE	Mean
Rand	--	11	27	28	22
GA	3	--	20	20	14.3
PSO	0	0	--	0	0
DE	0	0	0	--	0

A useful quantitative measure adopted from [4, 12 coverage] was used to aid in the evaluation process. It displays the number of solution points generated by an algorithm (A) that is dominated by another algorithm (B). (See Table 5) The higher the mean demonstrates that the more that particular type of algorithm is dominated by others. From the results it is seen that Rand is most dominated by other algorithms (as expected) while GA is the second worse. DE and PSO are not dominated by each other (with a mean of 0) However, it was noted that DE was able to provide a better spread of solutions compared to PSO. Based on the qualitative process of spread as well as the consistency of results demonstrated in Fig. 5, DE was shown to perform better in this piece of work.

5 Discussion

From the results presented certain points are drawn. Firstly, evolutionary algorithms are shown to work well with the single objective of operation costs in section 4.1, where the three algorithms presented were able to effectively reach the unconstrained optimized values. The successful results demonstrated in section 4.1 allowed section 4.2 to be carried out meaningfully (else there would be no basis of multiobjective optimization if the single case failed). While not clearly observable in the single objective case, DE has been shown superior based on the two performance criteria presented in section 4.2. We would therefore draw the conclusion that DE overall outperforms the other two algorithms. While experimentally this is shown, the authors have not been able to define mathematically why DE is superior to others in this type of problems. Future work seeks to expand the complexity of the problem (by bringing in more objectives, dropping certain assumptions) as well as bring in other forms of evolutionary algorithms for more extensive testing.

6 Conclusion

This study compared three evolutionary algorithms on a multiobjective train scheduling problem. By breaking up the analysis into two stages, we seek to first verify the feasibility of the algorithms in the single objective of operating costs and subsequently extending the work to the multiobjective case of operating costs and passenger comfort. The capabilities of all the three algorithms have been demonstrated in both the stages, with DE showing remarkable performance. Future work would seek to include the use of evolutionary algorithms in more complex mass rapid transit planning operations.

References

1. C.S. Chang, Chua C.S., H.B. Quek, X.Y. Xu, S.L., Ho, "Development of train movement simulator for analysis and optimization of railway signaling systems", *Proceeding of IEE conference on development of Mass Transit Systems, 1998, pp. 243-248.*
2. D.E. Goldberg, *Genetic Algorithms in Search, Optimization, and Machine Learning.* Reading, MA: Addison-Wesley, 1989.
3. J. Horn, "F1.9 Multicriteria decision making," in *Handbook of Evolutionary Computation,* T. Back, D.B. Fogel, and Z. MIchalewicz, Eds. Bristol, U.K.: Inst. Phys. Pub., 1997
4. E. Zitzler, L. Thiele, "Multiobjective Evolutionary Algorithms: A Comparative Case Study and the Strength Pareto Approach", *IEEE Trans. on Evolutionary Computation,* vol. 3, No. 4, Nov 1999
5. Engelbrecht, A.P., "Computational Intelligence: An Introduction," Hoboken, N.J.: J. Wiley & Sons, c2002.
6. C.S. Chang, W.Q. Jiang, S. Elangovan, "Applications of Genetic Algorithms to determine worst-case switching overvoltage of MRT systems", *IEEE Proc- electrPowerApp,* vol. 146, No.1, Jan 1999.
7. J.X. Xu, C.S.Chang, X.Y. Wang, "Constrained multiobjective global optimization of longitudinal interconnected power system by Genetic Algorithm", IEE Proc Gener.Transm..Distrib.,Vol. 143. No.5, Spetember 1996, pp. 435-446
8. J. Kennedy, and R.C. Eberhart. "Swarm Intelligence", Morgan Kaufmann Publishers, 2001
9. (Particle Swarm Optimization Tutorial), X. Hu, Available: http://web.ics.purdue.edu/~hux/ tutorials.shtml
10. R. Storn, K. Price, "Differential Evolution—A simple and efficient adaptive scheme for global optimization over continuous space", Technical Report TR-95-012, ICSI

11. C.S. Chang, D.Y. Xu, and H.B. Quek, "Pareto-optimal set based multiobjective tuning of fuzzy automatic train operation for mass transit system", IEE Proc-Electr. Power Appl., Vol. 146, No. 5, pp. September 1999, pp 577-587
12. E. Zitzler and L. Thiele, "Multiobjective optimization using evolutionary algorithms – A comparative case study," in *5th Int. Conf. Parallel Problem Solving from Nature (PPSNV)*, A.E. Eiben, T. Back, M. Schoenauer, and H.-P. Schwefel, Eds. Berlin, Germany: Springer-Verlag, 1998, pp. 292-301.
13. C.A. Coello Coello, G. Toscano, M.S. Lechuga, "Handling Multiple Objectives with Particle Swarm Optimization," *IEEE Trans. on Evolutionary Computation,* vol. 8, No. 3, June 2004

Fuzzy Modeling Incorporated with Fuzzy D-S Theory and Fuzzy Naive Bayes

Jiacheng Zheng[1] and Yongchuan Tang[2]

[1] College of Economics, Zhejiang University,
Hangzhou, Zhejiang Province, 310027, P. R. China
hzcc@mail.hz.zj.cn
[2] College of Computer Science, Zhejiang University,
Hangzhou, Zhejiang Province, 310027, P. R. China
yongchuan@263.net

Abstract. In fuzzy model, the consequent of fuzzy rule is often determined with degrees of belief or credibility because of vague information originating from evidence not strong enough and "lack of specificity". In this paper, we present a fuzzy model incorporated with fuzzy Dempster-Shafer Theory. The consequent of fuzzy rule is not fuzzy propositions, but fuzzy Dempster-Shafer granules. The salient aspect of the work is that a very simplified analytic output of fuzzy model which is a special case of Sugeno-type fuzzy model is achieved when all fuzzy sets in fuzzy partition of the output space have the same power (the area under the membership function), and the determination of basic probability assignments associated with fuzzy Dempster-Shafer belief structure using fuzzy Naive Bayes. The construction method of fuzzy Naive Bayes and an learning strategy generating fuzzy rules from training data are proposed in this paper. A well-known example about time series prediction is tested, the prediction results show that our fuzzy modeling is very efficient and has strong expressive power to represent the complex system with uncertain situation.

1 Introduction

Fuzzy system modeling has been proven an important and efficient technique to model the complex nonlinear relationship. Fuzzy rules are the key of the fuzzy system modeling. Each fuzzy rule is an if-then rule, "if" part is the antecedent of the rule and "then" part is the consequent of the rule. Both antecedent and consequent can considered as fuzzy propositions representing fuzzy sets of the input space and output space. A certainty factor is often associated with each fuzzy rule, which represents how certain the antecedent implies the consequent.

Yager and Filev [1] discussed the methodology of including the probabilistic information in the output of the fuzzy system based on fuzzy Dempster-shafer theory, and investigated two kinds of uncertainty. In their discussions, for the certainty degree of each rule, the consequent was formed as a Dempster-Shafer belief structure which just has two focal elements; for the additive noise to systems output, the consequent was formed as a Dempster-Shafer belief structure in which each focal element has the same membership function. In the same frame, Binaghi and Madella [2] discussed fuzzy

Dempster-Shafer reasoning for rule-base classifiers, where the consequent of the fuzzy rule is represented as a Dempster-Shafer belief structure in which each focal element is a crisp set representing the class label. Tang and Sun [9] presented a fuzzy classifier where each fuzzy rule represented a probability distribution of class labels, which is a special belief structure.

In this work, we extend aforementioned works for fuzzy system modeling based on fuzzy Dempster-Shafer theory. The consequent of fuzzy rule is also a fuzzy Dempster-Shafer belief structure in which focal elements set includes all fuzzy sets in fuzzy partition of the output space. The salient aspects of this work are that a simplified analytic fuzzy model is achieved and the determination of basic probability assignments associated with focal elements is complemented by fuzzy Naive Bayes. The basic probability number of focal element is explained as the conditional probability of this focal element given the antecedent of the fuzzy rule, and is determined by fuzzy Naive Bayes method. A learning strategy of generating fuzzy rules from training data is proposed, and the construction method of fuzzy Naive Bayes from training data is also presented.

In what follows, we review some basic ideas of Dempster-Shafer theory which are required for our procedure. We next discuss the fundamentals of fuzzy system modeling based on Mamdani reasoning paradigm. Then fuzzy Naive Bayes is introduced for computing the basic probabilities of the focal elements in fuzzy Dempster-Shafer belief structure. The fuzzy system modeling incorporated with fuzzy Dempster-Shafer theory is presented in fourth part. In fifth part, a simplified analytic expression output structure is achieved when all fuzzy sets in fuzzy partition of output space have the same power(the area under the membership function). The learning strategy of generating fuzzy rules from training data and basic probabilities assignments using fuzzy Naive Bayes are discussed in sixth part. the seven part shows the experimental results when this simplified fuzzy system modeling is applied to a well known time series prediction problem. The final part is our conclusions.

2   Dempster-Shafer Theory of Evidence

We introduce some basic concepts and mechanisms of the Dempster-Shafer theory of evidence [3] [4] [5] [8] which required for our procedure. The Dempster-Shafer theory is a formal framework for plausible reasoning providing methods to represent and combine weights of evidence. Let Θ be a finite set of mutually exclusive and exhaustive events or hypotheses about problem domain, called the frame of discernment.

A Dempster-Shafer belief structure, information granule m, is a collection of non-null subsets of Θ, $A_i, i = 1, \ldots, n$, called focal elements, and a set of associated weights $m(A_i)$, called basic probability assignment (PBA). This PBA must be such that:

$$m(A_i) \in [0,1], \qquad m(A_i) \neq 0, \qquad \sum_i m(A_i) = 1 \qquad (1)$$

When our knowledge is of the form of a Dempster-Shafer theory belief, because of the imprecision in the information, when attempting to try to find the probabilities associated with arbitrary subsets of Θ we can't find exact probabilities but lower and upper probabilities.

Firstly one measure, Bel, is introduced to capture the relevant information. Let B be a subset of Θ, we define

$$\text{Bel}(B) = \sum_{A_i \subseteq B} m(A_i), \tag{2}$$

Then we define Pl

$$\text{Pl}(B) = 1 - \text{Bel}(\overline{B}). \tag{3}$$

One advantage of Dempster-Shafer theory is its capability to express degrees of ignorance, that is the belief in an event and the belief in its opposite do not necessarily add up to one like in probability theory. A situation of total ignorance is characterized by $m(\Theta) = 1$.

Assume that m_1 and m_2 are two independent belief structures on a frame of discernment Θ, with focal elements $A_i, i = 1, \ldots, n_1$, and $B_j, j = 1, \ldots, n_2$. Then the conjunction of m_1 and m_2 is another belief structure $m = m_1 \oplus m_2$ whose focal elements are all the subsets F_k of Θ, where $F_k = A_i \cap B_j$ and $F_k \neq \emptyset$.

The basic probability numbers associated with each F_k are defined as

$$m(F_k) = \frac{1}{1-T}(m_1(A_i) * m_2(B_j)) \tag{4}$$

where

$$T = \sum_{\substack{i,j \\ A_i \cap B_j = \emptyset}} m_1(A_i) * m_2(B_j).$$

Now the concept of the fuzzy Dempster-Shafer belief structure can be introduced. A fuzzy Dempster-Shafer belief structure is a Dempster-Shafer belief structure with fuzzy sets as focal elements [6]. When we combine two fuzzy Dempster-Shafer belief structures using a set operation ∇, we simply uses its fuzzy version.

3 Fuzzy System Modeling

There are two types fuzzy models or fuzzy inference systems: Mamdani-type and Sugeno-type[10][11]. These two types of fuzzy models vary somewhat in the way outputs are determined. In this investigation we use Mamdani-type fuzzy model.

Assume we have a complex, nonlinear multiple input single output relationship. The technique of Mamdani-type fuzzy model allows us to represent the model of this system by partitioning the input space and output space. Thus if $X_1, X_2, \ldots, X_n$ are the input variables and Y is the output variable we can represent the non-linear function by a collection M "rules" of the form

$$R(r) : \text{If } (X_1 \text{ is } A_r^1) \text{ and } (X_2 \text{ is } A_r^2) \text{ and } \ldots (X_n \text{ is } A_r^n) \text{ then } Y \text{ is } B_r$$
$$\text{with certainty factor } \alpha_r; \tag{5}$$

Where if U_i is the universe of discourse of X_i then A_j^i is a fuzzy subset of U_i and with V the universe of discourse of Y then B_i is a fuzzy subset of V. And $r = 1, 2, \ldots, M$, M is the total number of rules, α_r ($0 < \alpha_r \leq 1$) is the importance factor or certainty factor of the rth rule.

Assume the input to the Mamdani-type fuzzy inference system consists of the value $X_i = x_i$ for $i = 1, 2, \ldots, n$. The procedure for reasoning consists of the following steps [1]:

1. Calculate the firing level of each rule τ_r

$$\tau_r = \bigwedge_i [A_r^i(x_i)] \text{ or } \prod_i [A_r^i(x_i)] \qquad (6)$$

2. Associate the importance or certainty factor α_r with τ_r

$$\pi_r = \tau_r \times \alpha_r \qquad (7)$$

3. Calculate the output of each rule as a fuzzy subset F_r of Y where

$$F_r(y) = \bigwedge [\pi_r, B_r(y)] \qquad (8)$$

4. Aggregate the individual rule outputs to get a fuzzy subset F of Y where

$$F(y) = \bigvee_r [F_r(y)] \qquad (9)$$

5. Defuzzify the aggregate output fuzzy subset

$$\bar{y} = \frac{\sum_i y_i F(y_i)}{\sum_i F(y_i)} \qquad (10)$$

The learning process of fuzzy system often proceed to adjust the fuzzy sets in the rule base firstly, then go ahead tuning the importance factors or certainty factors, or learn all parameters simultaneously [12][13][14][15][16].

4 Fuzzy Naive Bayes

4.1 Naive Bayes

The simplest Bayesian Belief Network is so-called Naive Bayes. It just has two levels nodes and it has the simple structure (V, A, P) proposed in Fig. 1. The Naive Bayes has been successfully used to the classification problem and achieved the remarkable effect. This Naive Bayes learns from observed data the conditional probability of each variable X_i given the value of the variable Y. Then the computation of the probability $P(Y|X_1, \ldots, X_n)$ can be done by applying Bayes rule. This computation is feasible by making the strong assumption that the variables X_i are conditionally independent given the value of the variable Y.

$$P(Y|X_1, \ldots, X_n) = \frac{P(X_1, \ldots, X_n|Y)P(Y)}{P(X_1, \ldots, X_n)} = \frac{\prod_i P(X_i|Y)P(Y)}{P(X_1, \ldots, X_n)}. \qquad (11)$$

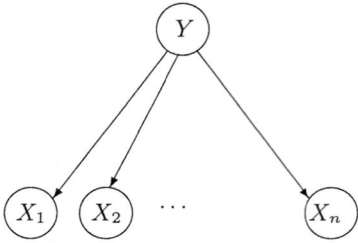

Fig. 1. Naive Bayes

4.2 Fuzzy Naive Bayes

The fuzzy Naive Bayes is a simple and direct generalization of the Naive Bayes [7]. Both have the same graphical structure (see Fig. 1), the only difference between them is that the variables in the fuzzy Naive Bayes are linguistic variables which can take the fuzzy subsets as their values.

In the fuzzy Naive Bayes, each variable takes the linguistic values in which each linguistic value associates with a membership function. Let $\{A_j^i : j = 1, 2, \ldots, k_i\}$ is the fuzzy partition of the domain of the variable X_i, and $\{B_i : i = 1, 2, \ldots, p\}$ is the fuzzy partition of the domain of the variable Y. Assume the elements in the observed data set D have the form $\overline{X} = [X; y]$, and X is a n dimensional vector $[x_1, x_2, \cdots, x_n]$. So one way to compute the prior probabilities assigned to the node Y is proposed as follows:

$$P(Y = B_k) = \frac{\sum_{\overline{X} \in D} B_k(y)}{\sum_{k=1}^{p} \sum_{\overline{X} \in D} B_k(y)}. \tag{12}$$

And the conditional probabilities of other nodes can be estimated from the observed data as follows:

$$P(X_i = A_j^i | Y = B_k) = \frac{\sum_{\overline{X} \in D} A_j^i(x_i) B_k(y)}{\sum_{j=1}^{k_i} \sum_{\overline{X} \in D} A_j^i(x_i) B_k(y)}. \tag{13}$$

Where x_i is the i-th component of the vector $\overline{X} \in D$.

5 Fuzzy System Modeling with Dempster-Shafer Belief Structure

In Mamdani-type model described in section 3, the consequent of each rule consists of a fuzzy subsets B_r and a certainty factor α_r (see formula (5)). The use of fuzzy subset implies a kind of uncertainty associated with the output of a rule. This kind of uncertainty is called possibilistic uncertainty and is the reflection of a lack of precision in describing the output. The certainty factor of each rule represents how certain the relationship between the antecedent and the consequent of this rule is, and it reflects another kind of uncertainty related to the lack of specificity in the rules. Uncertain evidence can induce only a belief that is more or less strong, thus admitting degrees of belief. Proceeding in this way, a natural extension of the fuzzy systems model is to consider the consequent to be the fuzzy Dempster-Shafer belief structure. Thus we shall now consider the output of each rule to be of the form

$$Y \text{ is } m_r \tag{14}$$

where m_r is a belief structure with focal elements $B_{r,j}$, where $B_{r,j} \in \{B_1,\ldots,B_p\}$ ($j = 1,\ldots,p$), $\{B_1,\ldots,B_p\}$ is a fuzzy partition of the output space V and $m_r(B_{r,j})$ is basic probability number of focal element $B_{r,j}$. Thus, the fuzzy rule of fuzzy model in section 3 has the following form

$$R(r): \text{ If } (X_1 \text{ is } A_r^1) \text{ and } (X_2 \text{ is } A_r^2) \text{ and } \ldots (X_n \text{ is } A_r^n) \text{ then } Y \text{ is } m_r \tag{15}$$

The value $m_r(B_{r,j})$ represents the degree of credibility or probability that the output of the rth rule lies in the set $B_{r,j}$. So rather than being certain as to what is the output set of a rule we have some randomness in the rule. According to this new form of the fuzzy rule, the fuzzy reasoning involves the integration of the propagation of evidence within the fuzzy rules.

Assume the input to this fuzzy inference system consists of the value $X_i = x_i$ for $i = 1, 2, \ldots, n$. The new procedure for reasoning in fuzzy model with belief structure consists of the following steps

1. Calculate the firing level of each rule τ_r

$$\tau_r = \bigwedge_i \left[A_r^i(x_i)\right] \text{ or } \prod_i \left[A_r^i(x_i)\right] \tag{16}$$

2. Determine the outputs of individual rules from their firing levels and consequent

$$\hat{m}_r = \varphi(\tau_r, m_r) \tag{17}$$

where φ is the implication operator and $\hat{m}_r$ is a fuzzy belief structure on V. The focal elements of $\hat{m}_r$ are $F_{r,j}$, fuzzy subsets of V, defined as

$$\mu_{F_{r,j}}(y) = \tau_r \wedge \mu_{B_{r,j}}(y) \text{ or } \mu_{F_{r,j}}(y) = \tau_r * \mu_{B_{r,j}}(y) \tag{18}$$

where $B_{r,j}$ is a focal element of the fuzzy belief structure m_r. The basic probability number associated with $F_{r,j}$ are given by

$$\hat{m}_r(F_{r,j}) = m_r(B_{r,j}) \tag{19}$$

3. Aggregate rule outputs, applying the non-null producing operation $\triangledown$, to combine fuzzy belief structures

$$m = \bigoplus_{r=1}^{M} \hat{m}_r \tag{20}$$

for each collection $\mathcal{F}_k = \{F_{1,j_1^k}, F_{2,j_2^k}, \ldots, F_{M,j_M^k}\}$ where F_{r,j_r^k} is a focal element of $\hat{m}_r$, we have a focal element E_k of m

$$E_k = \triangledown_{r=1}^{M} F_{r,j_r^k} \tag{21}$$

when the operation $\triangledown$ is *average* operation, the focal element E_k is defined as

$$\mu_{E_k}(y) = \frac{1}{M} \sum_{r=1}^{M} \mu_{F_{r,j_r^k}}(y) \qquad (22)$$

and its basic probability number is

$$m(E_k) = \prod_{r=1}^{M} \hat{m}_r(F_{r,j_r^k}) \qquad (23)$$

Hence, the output of the fuzzy model is a fuzzy Dempster-Shafer belief structure m with focal elements $E_k, k = 1, \ldots, p^M$.

4. Defuzzify the fuzzy belief structure m to obtain the singleton output

$$\bar{y} = \sum_{k=1}^{p^M} \bar{y}_k m(E_k) \qquad (24)$$

where $\bar{y}_k$ is the defuzzified value of the focal element E_k

$$\bar{y}_k = \frac{\sum y \mu_{E_k}(y)}{\sum \mu_{E_k}(y)} \qquad (25)$$

Thus y is essentially the expected defuzzified value of the focal elements of m.

6 A Simplified Analytic Fuzzy Model

We have noticed that the number (p^M) of focal elements of fuzzy belief structure m discussed in last section exponentially increases as the number of fuzzy rules increases. This deficiency may make the fuzzy model presented be useless. But by introducing some constraints on the model we can obtain an analytic and tractable representation of the reasoning process. The constrains focus on three aspects: the *production* operation is taken as the implication operation, the *average* operation is taken as the aggregation operation, and the power of each fuzzy subsets in fuzzy partition of the output space are the same.

We still consider the fuzzy model involving M fuzzy rules of the following form

$$R(r) : Antecedent_r \text{ Then } Y \text{ is } m_r \qquad (26)$$

where m_r is a fuzzy belief structure with focal elements $B_{r,j}(j = 1, \ldots, p)$ having associated basic probability numbers $m_r(B_{r,j}) = \alpha_{r,j}$, $\sum_{j=1}^{p} \alpha_{r,j} = 1$. Here $B_{r,j} \in \{B_1, B_2, \ldots, B_p\}$ and $\{B_1, B_2, \ldots, B_p\}$ is fuzzy partition of the output space.

Under these constrains, we may rewrite the reasoning process of the fuzzy model as the following steps:

1. Calculate the firing level of the rules $\tau_1, \tau_2, \ldots, \tau_M$.
2. Calculate the output of the rules $\hat{m}_1, \hat{m}_2, \ldots, \hat{m}_M$ where each $\hat{m}_r$ has focal elements defined as follows:

$$\mu_{F_{r,j}}(y) = \tau_r \mu_{B_{r,j}}(y), \; j = 1, \ldots, p; \; \hat{m}_r(F_{r,j}) = \alpha_{r,j}. \tag{27}$$

3. Determine the output of the system, which is a fuzzy belief structure m with focal elements $E_k (k = 1, \ldots, p^M)$ and basic probability numbers $m(E_k)$ defined using formulas (22) and (23).
4. Calculate the defuzzified values $\bar{y}_k$ of the focal elements E_k by applying Eq. (25)

$$\begin{aligned}
\bar{y}_k &= \frac{\sum_y y \mu_{E_k}(y)}{\sum_y \mu_{E_k}(y)} = \frac{\sum_y y \sum_{r=1}^M \mu_{F_{r,j_r^k}}(y)}{\sum_y \sum_{r=1}^M \mu_{F_{r,j_r^k}}(y)} \\
&= \frac{\sum_y y \sum_{r=1}^M \tau_r \mu_{B_{r,j_r^k}}(y)}{\sum_y \sum_{r=1}^M \tau_r \mu_{B_{r,j_r^k}}(y)} = \frac{\sum_{r=1}^M \tau_r \sum_y y \mu_{B_{r,j_r^k}}(y)}{\sum_{r=1}^M \tau_r \sum_y \mu_{B_{r,j_r^k}}(y)}
\end{aligned} \tag{28}$$

we have the constraint that the power of each fuzzy subsets B_j in fuzzy partition $\{B_1, B_2, \ldots, B_p\}$ are equal. The power of fuzzy subset B_j is defined as $S_j = \sum_y \mu_{B_j}(y)$. Hence we assume S_j be S for $j = 1, \ldots, p$. It follows that

$$\bar{y}_k = \frac{\sum_{r=1}^M \tau_r \bar{\bar{y}}_{j_r^k}}{\sum_{r=1}^M \tau_r} \tag{29}$$

where $\bar{\bar{y}}_{j_r^k}$ is the defuzzified value of fuzzy subset B_{r,j_r^k} which belongs to fuzzy partition $\{B_1, B_2, \ldots, B_p\}$.

5. Defuzzify fuzzy belief structure m to obtain the singleton output of the system

$$\bar{y} = \sum_{k=1}^{p^M} \bar{y}_k m(E_k) = \frac{\sum_{k=1}^{p^M} \sum_{r=1}^M \tau_r \bar{\bar{y}}_{j_r^k} \prod_{t=1}^M \alpha_{t,j_t^k}}{\sum_{r=1}^M \tau_r} = \frac{\sum_{r=1}^M \tau_r \sum_{k=1}^{p^M} \bar{\bar{y}}_{j_r^k} \prod_{t=1}^M \alpha_{t,j_t^k}}{\sum_{r=1}^M \tau_r} \tag{30}$$

Reorganizing the terms in formula (30) and Considering that $\sum_{j=1}^p \alpha_{r,j} = 1$ we obtain

$$\bar{y} = \frac{\sum_{r=1}^M \tau_r \sum_{j=1}^p \bar{\bar{y}}_j \alpha_{r,j}}{\sum_{r=1}^M \tau_r} = \frac{\sum_{r=1}^M \tau_r \gamma_r}{\sum_{r=1}^M \tau_r} \tag{31}$$

where $\bar{\bar{y}}_j$ is the defuzzified value of the fuzzy subset B_j. We observe that the quantity $\gamma_r = \sum_{j=1}^p \bar{\bar{y}}_j \alpha_{r,j}$ is independent of the current input value to the fuzzy model: it depends only on the rth rule. So it is possible to calculate the γ_r before reasoning process. We can rewrite the rules in the simplified following form of

$$R(r) : Antecedent_r \; Then \; Y \; is \; H_r \tag{32}$$

where $H_r = \{1/\gamma_r\}$ is a singleton fuzzy set defined by the value γ_r. And the defuzzified output of the simplified fuzzy model will be

$$\bar{y} = \frac{\sum_{r=1}^{M} \tau_r \gamma_r}{\sum_{r=1}^{M} \tau_r} \qquad (33)$$

7 A Learning Strategy of Fuzzy Belief Structures

We firstly discuss the antecedent construction steps. Each example, from the training data set, is translated into the antecedent of one rule in which each input variable is represented by means of one fuzzy proposition. For example, assume $[x_1^r, x_2^r, \ldots, x_n^r, y_r]$ be an input vector, then the antecedent candidate will be

$$Antecedent_r = \text{If } X_1 \text{ is } A_{r(1)}^i \text{ and } \ldots, \text{ and if } X_n \text{ is } A_{r(n)}^n \qquad (34)$$

where $\mu_{A_{r(i)}^i}(x_i^r) = \max_{1 \le j \le k_i} \mu_{A_j^i}(x_i^r)$, k_i is the number of fuzzy regions in the universe of discourse of variable X_i.

Then only one of those initial antecedent candidates being the same is kept, and others are removed. Hence the antecedent construction is completed, suppose there are M antecedents which will be used to generate the rules.

For each antecedent $Antecedent_r$ just constructed, one rule may be generated as the form of

$$R(r): Antecedent_r \text{ then } Y \text{ is } m_r \qquad (35)$$

where the focal elements of m_r are $B_i, i = 1, \ldots, p$, and basic probability numbers are $\alpha_{r,i}, i = 1, \ldots, p$. The determination of basic probability number $\alpha_{r,i}$ is resolved by interpreting $\alpha_{r,i}$ as the conditional probability of fuzzy proposition "Y is B_i" given the antecedent $Antecedent_r$. It means

$$\alpha_{r,i} = P(B_i|Antecedent_r) = P(B_i|A_{r(1)}^1, \ldots, A_{r(n)}^n) \qquad (36)$$

The formula (36) can be computed out from a fuzzy Naive Bayes constructed from the same training data. In the third section, the details of constructing a fuzzy Naive Bayes from a training data set is investigated. This fuzzy Naive Bayes has two levels nodes, see Fig. 1. The only one node in the first level represents the output variable Y, and the nodes in the second level represent the input variables $X_i, i = 1, \ldots, n$. The conditional probabilities associated with each node is estimated by formulas (12) and (13) from training data. So the formula (36) is computed out using Bayes rule by formula (11).

8 Experiment

We test the fuzzy model based on fuzzy belief structure by predicting a time series that is generated by the following Mackey-Glass (MG) time-delay differential equation.

$$\dot{x}(t) = \frac{0.2x(t-\tau)}{1+x^{10}(t-\tau)} - 0.1x(t) \tag{37}$$

This time series is chaotic, and so there is no clearly defined period. The series will not converge or diverge, and the trajectory is highly sensitive to initial conditions. This is a benchmark problem in the neural network and fuzzy modeling research communities [7] [15].

To obtain the time series value at integer points, we applied the fourth-order Runge-Kutta method to find the numerical solution to the above MG equation. Here we assume $x(0) = 1.2, \tau = 17$, and $x(t) = 0$ for $t < 0$. For each t, the input training data for the fuzzy model is a four dimensional vector of the form, $X(t) = [x(t-18), x(t-12), x(t-6), x(t)]$. The output training data corresponds to the trajectory prediction, $y(t) = x(t+6)$. For each t, ranging in values from 118 to 1117, there will be 1000 input/output data values. We use the first 500 data values for the fuzzy model training (these become the training data set), while the others are used as checking data for testing the identified fuzzy model.

In our experiment, we use the gaussian-type membership function which has the form of

$$\exp\frac{(x-c)^2}{-2\sigma^2} \tag{38}$$

Let each universe of discourse of variables be a closed interval $[l, u]$, in our experiment, l, u be the minimal value and maximal value of each dimension of all training data respectively. And if the universe $[l, u]$ is partitioned into N fuzzy regions $A_i (i = 1, \ldots, N)$ which have the gaussian-type membership function defined in formula (38), then in our experiment, A_i is defined as

$$\mu_{A_i}(x) = \exp\frac{(x-c_i)^2}{-2\sigma_i^2}, \forall x \in [l, u]. \tag{39}$$

Where $c_i = l + \frac{(i-1)(u-l)}{N-1}$, $\sigma_i = \frac{u-l}{2(N-1)\sqrt{\ln 4}}$, such that $\mu_{A_i}(c_i) = 1$ and $\mu_{A_i}(\frac{c_i+c_{i+1}}{2}) = \mu_{A_{i+1}}(\frac{c_i+c_{i+1}}{2}) = 0.5$.

We have done a series of tests, when the number of fuzzy subregions of each universe of discourse of variables varies from 3 to 18, Fig. 2 illustrates the mean square errors (MSE) for training data and test data respectively. The test results show that the performance increases as the number of fuzzy subregions partitioning each universe increase. When the number of fuzzy subregions of each universe of discourse of variables is 16, Fig. 3 and Fig. 4 illustrate the prediction results of the fuzzy model based on fuzzy belief structure. Their MSE are 0.8279 and 0.7985 respectively.

9 Conclusions

In this work we present a fuzzy model which has more knowledge representing power. This fuzzy model is an extension of Mamdani-type fuzzy model, and can includes the

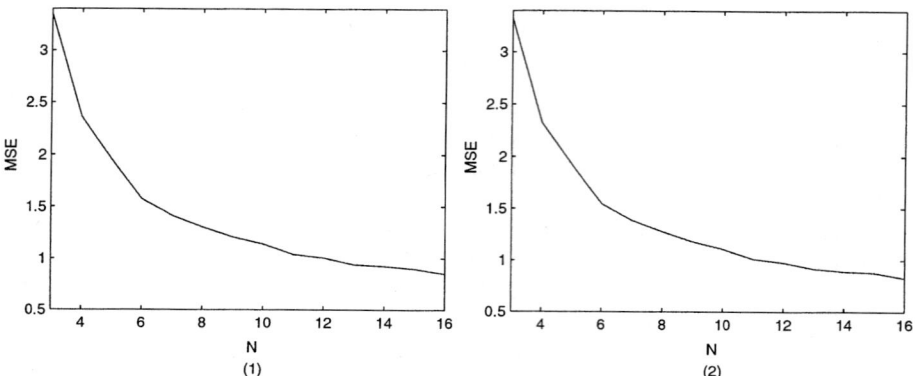

Fig. 2. (1) the mean square errors for training data; (2) the mean square errors for test data

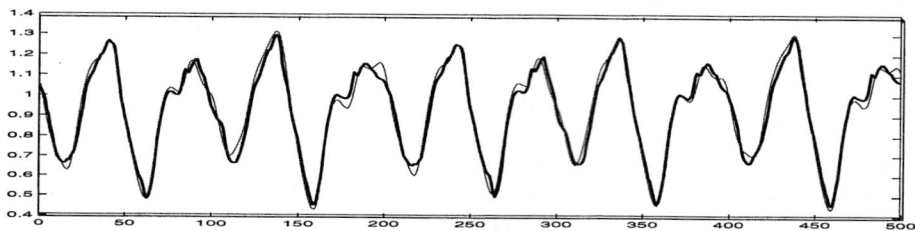

Fig. 3. The thin line is the expected output of the training data; the thick line is the prediction output of the fuzzy model

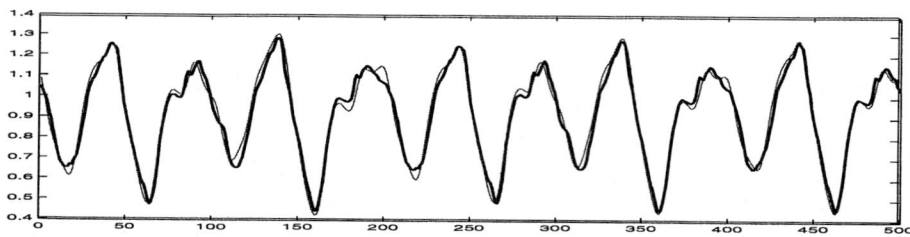

Fig. 4. The thin line is the expected output of the test data; the thick line is the prediction output of the fuzzy model

randomness in the model. In this fuzzy model, the consequent of each rule is a fuzzy Dempster-Shafer belief structure which takes the fuzzy partition of the output space as the collection of focal elements.

The salient aspect of this work is that we achieve a simplified and analytic fuzzy model when each focal element, fuzzy subset in fuzzy partition of the output space, has the same power. In this simplified analytic fuzzy model, the computation complexity has decreased, and the fuzzy model is reduced to Sugeno-type fuzzy model. The basic probability number of each focal element is interpreted as the conditional probability of focal element given the antecedent of the rule, so we use the fuzzy Naive Bayes to compute these conditional probabilities.

Acknowledgements

This work has been partially supported by China Postdoctoral Science Foundation (No. 2003034514), Hubei Province Young Elitist Project (No. 2002AC001), the National Basic Research Program of China (Grant No. 2002CB312106), Science & Technology Plan of Zhejiang Province (Grant No. 2004C33086).

References

1. Yager, R.R., Filev, D.P.: Including probabilistic uncertainty in fuzzy logic controller modeling using dempster-shafer theory. IEEE transactions on systems, man and cybernetics **25** (1995) 1221–1230
2. Binaghi, E., Madella, P.: Fuzzy dempster-shafer reasoning for rule-based classifiers. International Journal of Intelligenct Systems **14** (1999) 559–583
3. Dempster, A.P.: A generalization of bayesian inference. J. Royal Stat. Soc. (1968) 205–247
4. Shafer, G.: A Mathematical Theory of Evidence. Princeton University Press, Princeton, NJ (1976)
5. Dempster, A.P.: Upper and lower probabilities induced by a multi-valued mapping. Ann. Mathematical Statistics **38** (1967) 325–339
6. Yen, J.: Generalizing the dempster-shafer theory to fuzzy sets. IEEE transactions on systems, man and cybernetics **20** (1990) 559–570
7. Tang, Y., Xu, Y.: Application of fuzzy Naive Bayes and a real-valued genetic algorithm in identification of fuzzy model. Information Sciences (2004) In Press.
8. Tang, Y., Sun S., Liu, Y.: Conditional Evidence Theory and its Application in Knowledge Discovery, Lecture Notes in Computer Science 3007 (2004), 500–505.
9. Tang Y., Sun S., A mixture model of classical fuzzy classifiers, Lecture Notes in Computer Science 3129 (2004), 616–621.
10. LEE, C.C.: Fuzzy logic in control systems: fuzzy logic controller-part 1. IEEE transactions on systems, man, and cybernetics **20** (1990) 404–419
11. LEE, C.C.: Fuzzy logic in control systems: fuzzy logic controller-part 2. IEEE transactions on systems, man, and cybernetics **20** (1990) 419–435
12. Blanco, A., Delgado, M., Requena, I.: A learning procedure to identify weighted rules by neural networks. Fuzzy Sets and Systems **69** (1995) 29–36
13. Cheong, F., Lai, R.: Constraining the optimization of a fuzzy logic controller using an enhanced genetic algorithm. IEEE transactions on systems, man, and cybernetics-part B: Cybernetics **30** (2000) 31–46
14. Kasabov, N., Kim, J., Kozma, R.: A fuzzy neural network for knowledge acquisition in complex time series. Control and Cybernetics **27** (1998) 593–611
15. Russo, M.: Genetic fuzzy learning. IEEE transactions on evolutionary computation **4** (2000) 259–273
16. Yager, R.R., Filev, D.P.: Unified structure and parameter identification of fuzzy models. IEEE transactions on systems, man and cybernetics **23** (1993) 1198–1205
17. Kleiter, G.D.: Propagating imprecise probabilities in bayesian networks. Artificial Intelligence **88** (1996) 143–161

Genetic Algorithm Based K-Means Fast Learning Artificial Neural Network

Yin Xiang and Alex Tay Leng Phuan

Nanyang Technological University
aslptay@ntu.edu.sg

Abstract. The K-means Fast Learning Artificial Neural Network (KFLANN) is a small neural network bearing two types of parameters, the tolerance, δ and the vigilance, μ. In previous papers, it was shown that the KFLANN was capable of fast and accurate assimilation of data [12]. However, it was still an unsolved issue to determine the suitable values for δ and μ in [12]. This paper continues to follows-up by introducing Genetic Algorithms as a possible solution for searching through the parameter space to effectively and efficiently extract suitable values to δ and μ. It is also able to determine significant factors that help achieve accurate clustering. Experimental results are presented to illustrate the hybrid GA-KFLANN ability using available test data.

1 Introduction

K-Means Fast Learning Artificial Neural Network (KFLANN) has the ability to cluster effectively, with consistent centroids, regardless of variations in the data presentation sequence [6], [7], [12]. However, its search time on parameters δ and μ for clustering increases exponentially compared to the linear increase in the input dimension. A Genetic Algorithm (GA) was used to efficiently orchestrate the search for suitable δ and μ values, thus removing the need for guesswork. The hybrid model, GA-KFLANN, shows that the technique indeed has merit in fast completion as well as accurate clustering. Although the δ and μ values obtained provided sub-optimal clustering results, these results were still within acceptable clustering tolerance. This paper also provides an introduction to the K-means Fast Learning Artificial Neural Network (KFLANN) and a description of how the Genetic Algorithm was weaved into the algorithm to support the effective search for the required parameters.

1.1 The KFLANN Algorithm

The basic architecture of the KFLANN is shown in Fig. 1 [3], [4], [5]. It has 2 layers, the input and output layer, and a set of weight vectors connecting the 2 layers. The KFLANN is a fully connected network.

The number of output nodes can increase according to the classification requirements, determined indirectly by the δ and μ parameters. As each new cluster is formed, a new output node is created and the weight vectors of the new output node are assimilated with the exemplar values. The algorithm of the KFLANN follows.

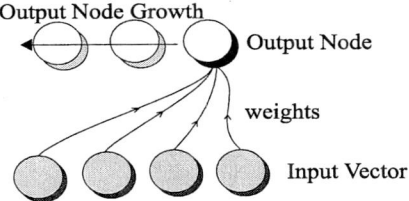

Fig. 1. The Architecture of KFLANN

1.1.1 Algorithm of KFLANN

Notation μ: vigilance value
δ_i: tolerance value of the ith attribute
n: the number of input attributes
I_i: the ith input node
W_{ji}: weight connecting the ith input node and the jth output neuron
$D[a] = 1$ if $a > 0$. Otherwise $D[a] = 0$.

1. Initialize network with μ between 0 and 1. Determine and set δ_i for $i = 1, 2, 3, \ldots,$ n. The values of μ and δ affect the behaviors of the classification and learning process.

2. Present the next pattern to the input nodes. If there are no output clusters present, GOTO 6.

3. Determine the set of clusters that are possible matches using equation (1). If there are no output clusters GOTO 6.

$$\frac{\sum_{i=1}^{n} D\left[\delta_i^2 - (W_{ji} - I_i)^2\right]}{n} \geq \mu \tag{1}$$

4. Using criteria in equation (2) determine the winning cluster from the match set from Step 3. Normalize W_{ji} and I_i. The following distance is calculated between the normalized versions.

$$winner = \arg\min_{j} \left[\sum_{i=0}^{n} (W_{ji} - I_i)^2\right] \tag{2}$$

5. When the Winner is found. Add vector to the winning cluster. If there are no more patterns, GOTO 7. Else GOTO 2.

6. No match found. Create a new output cluster and perform direct mapping from input vector into weight vector of new output cluster. If there are no more patterns, GOTO 7. Else GOTO 2.

7. Re-compute cluster center using K-means algorithm. Find the nearest vector to the cluster center in each cluster using equation (2). Place the nearest vector in each cluster to the top of the training data and GOTO 2.

After each cycle of clustering with all exemplars, the cluster centers are updated using K-means algorithm. This is *Step 7* of the KFLANN algorithm. A comparison between each cluster center and patterns in respective cluster is then conducted to determine the nearest point to each cluster center. The algorithm then assigns this point as the new centroid.

1.1.2 Parameter Search for δ and μ

The KFLANN algorithm is able to cluster effectively only if the correct δ and μ values are used [7]. As illustrated in Fig. 2, the δ values indirectly determine the clustering behaviour of the algorithm. A larger δ provides lesser clusters (a), while a smaller δ provides more clusters (b). Since the characteristic spread of data is sometimes unknown, the δ values are still very much a guessing game. The results of a brute-force combinatorial exhaustive search [12] are used to compare with the results obtained from the GA search presented in this paper. This original brute-force algorithm tries all possible combinations of tolerance and vigilance values. For example, if there are n attributes in an exemplar and each tolerance has m steps on its value range, m^n modifications have to be made on tolerance values totally. The high price of the exhaustive search provides the motivation for better alternatives.

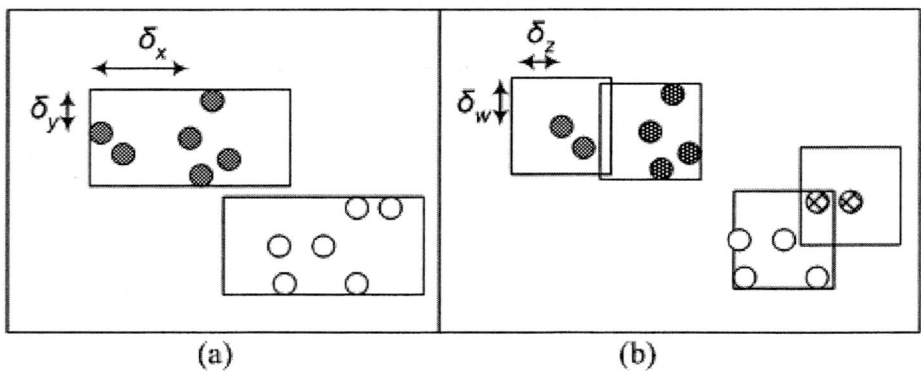

Fig. 2. Different clusters are formed for the same data set when δ is varied

1.2 The Genetic Algorithm

Genetic Algorithms are guided, yet random search algorithms for complex optimization problems and are based on principles from natural evolutionary theory. GAs are computationally simple yet powerful and do not require the search space to be continuous, differentiable, unimodal or of a functional form.

The GA process is illustrated in Fig. 3. To obtain solutions, the problem space is initially encoded into a relevant format, suitable for evolutionary computation. The parameters of the search space are encoded in the form known as *chromosomes* and each indivisible parameter in a chromosome is called a *gene*. A collection of such strings is called a *population*. Initially, a random population is created, which represents different points in the search space. An *objective* and *fitness* function is associated with each string that represents the degree of *goodness* of the chromosome. Based on the principle of survival of the fittest, a few of the strings are reproduced and each is assigned a number of copies that go into the mating pool. Biologically inspired operators like *crossover* and *mutation* are applied on these strings to yield a new generation of chromosomes. The process of reproduction, crossover and mutation continues for a fixed number of generations or till a termination condition is satisfied. [10]

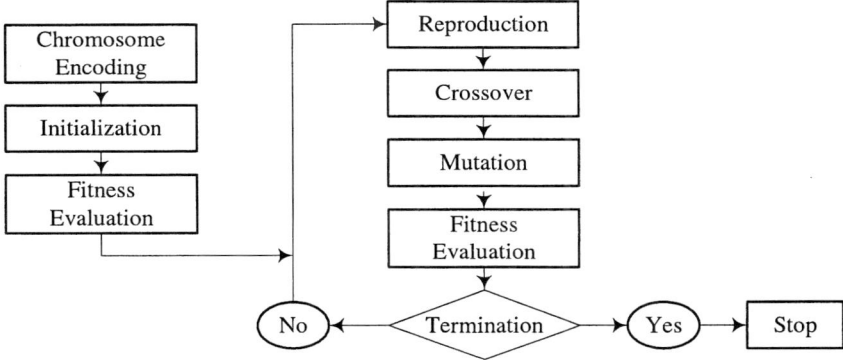

Fig. 3. The GA process

GA is useful when a sub-optimal solution is sufficient. The self-evolving nature and likeliness to reach a near-optimal condition regardless of dimensionality, is the strong motivation for introducing GA into KFLANN.

1.2.1 Chromosome Encoding

The chromosomal encoding for the GA-KFLANN consists of two parts: the control genes (ConG) and the coefficient genes (CoeG). The ConG are a string of binary numbers, which are used to turn on or off the corresponding features to achieve the goal of feature selection. Whereas, the CoeG are a sequence of real numbers representing tolerance and vigilance values to control the behaviour of KFLANN. The ConG may not be used when all features are fully utilized in a clustering problem. For the purpose of discussion, the Iris flower dataset is now used as an example to illustrate the encoding required for GA computations. The δ and μ are first converted into chromosomal equivalents as shown in Fig. 4. CoeG shown in shaded pattern represent those turned off by their corresponding ConG.

1.2.2 Population Initialization

In the 1st generation of the GA, ConG (if used) are randomly assigned to the value '1' or '0', while CoeG are randomly initialized to values between the upper bound and the lower bound of tolerance or vigilance of features from the input data. Since tolerance value (δ) is the maximum distance of how far a pattern in a cluster can be

Population								
Control Genes				Coefficient Genes				
				Tolerance δ				Vigilance μ
				Sepal length	Sepal width	Petal length	Petal width	
1	1	1	1	0	0.88	0.56	0.40	//////	0.75
2	0	0	1	1	//////	//////	0.17	0.47	0.5
⋮									
n	1	1	1	1	0.73	0.65	0.34	0.12	1.0

Fig. 4. Sample Chromosome Encoding for the Iris Dataset

from the cluster center in each attribute [12] as shown in Fig. 2, the upper bound of tolerance for each attribute can be set to half of the maximum distance among data points in that attribute, while the lower bound can be assigned to the minimum distance. For example, assume there are 5 data points: (0, 0), (1, 1), (3, 4), (5, 0), and (2, 6). The upper bound for the 1st dimension is (5-0)/2 = 2.5, while the lower bound is 1, which is the minimum distance among data points. Therefore, tolerance δ_1 shall be initialized in the range [1, 2.5]. Similarly tolerance δ_2 can be found in the range [1, 3].

1.2.3 Fitness Evaluation

Fitness evaluation of the clustering results is the key issue for GA. A good fitness evaluation can make GA produce proper tolerance and vigilance values and lead KFLANN to the optimal clustering, while a poor one can cause GA to converge towards a wrong direction and lead to inaccurate clustering.

Within-group variance $\sigma_{W_i}^2$ for each cluster i and between-group variance σ_B^2 can be easily computed from the output of KFLANN for each clustering result. And the two types of variance satisfy the following equation:

$$\sigma_T^2 = \sigma_W^2 + \sigma_B^2 \qquad \sigma_W^2 = \sum_{i=1}^{k} \sigma_{W_i}^2 \qquad (3)$$

where σ_T^2 is the total variance. Since σ_T^2 is fixed for a data set, a natural criterion for grouping is to minimize σ_W^2, or, equivalently, maximize σ_B^2 [1]. Moreover, the clustering with the maximum between-group variance and minimum within-group variance means highly dense clusters and good data compression. Thus, a possible evaluation criterion can be formed as maximizing the term: σ_B^2 / σ_W^2.

It works reasonably well for data sets without overlapping patterns, but not so well as expected with overlapping clusters. An additional term used in fitness evaluation is a Boolean variable, convergence, representing whether a clustering converges. The whole term is expressed as follows:

$$fitness = (convergence + 1) \times \sigma_B^2 / \sigma_W^2 \qquad (4)$$

This is to ensure that converged clustering has much higher fitness value and force the GA to produce tolerance and vigilance that can make KFLANN converge and form consistent centroids.

1.2.4 Reproduction

Solution strings from the current generation are copied into a mating pool according to the corresponding fitness values. Strings with higher fitness values will likely be represented in higher numbers in the mating pool, which means δ and μ generating higher clustering accuracy will more likely survive and pass their values to the next generation. This is because that there is a higher chance for δ and μ with higher clustering accuracy to hit the respective correct settings. Stochastic Universal Sampling (SUS) is the most popular reproduction strategy and utilized in this paper.

1.2.5 Crossover

Crossover is a probabilistic process that exchanges information between two parent chromosomes in the mating pool for generating two child chromosomes, so that proper settings of parameters can be grouped together into a single child chromosome. For example, one parent has the best setting of sepal length, while another has proper petal width value. A better clustering result will be achieved if the 2 good settings can be grouped together into just one offspring.

Two types of crossover operators are implemented in this paper since the ConG and CoeG make use of different encoding schemes. Uniform crossover is applied to the ConG while convex crossover is applied to the CoeG. In uniform crossover a template of the same length as ConG is randomly generated to decide which parent to contribute for each bit position. For example, 2 parents are shown in Table 1, one is underlined and the other is italic. Bits from parent 1 are passed to offspring 1 if the corresponding bits in the template are of value '1'; otherwise those bits are passed to offspring 2. This rule works in reverse way for parent 2. Therefore, the 1st four and last two bits of parent 1 are passed to offspring 1, while the rest goes to offspring 2. Similarly, parent 2 contributes different parts to offspring 1 and 2 respectively according to the template.

Table 1. An Example of Uniform Crossover

	Parent	Template	Offspring
1	1001011	1111001	1001*101*
2	*0101101*		*0101*011

If x and y are the CoeG of two parents, then convex crossover is of the following form:

$$x' = \lambda x + (1-\lambda)y \tag{5}$$

$$y' = (1-\lambda)x + \lambda y \tag{6}$$

where x' and y' are the corresponding CoeG of two children. λ is set to 0.7 in this paper.

1.2.6 Mutation

Mutation operation randomly picks up a gene in the generated offspring strings and changes its value properly in order to allow the GA to escape from a local optimal to search for a global optimal. Two types of mutation operators are used in this paper like the described crossover above. Normal mutation is applied to the ConG while dynamic mutation is applied to the CoeG.

For a given string, if the gene x is selected for mutation, then the offspring x' = 1 – x if x is a control gene. If x is a coefficient gene, then x' is selected with equal probability from the two choices:

$$x' = x + r(u-x)(1-\frac{t}{T})^b \qquad x' = x - r(x-l)(1-\frac{t}{T})^b \tag{7}$$

$x \in [l, u]$
r: a random number chosen uniformly from [0, 1]
t: current generation number
T: the maximum number of generations
b: degree of nonuniformity.

1.2.7 Population Replacement

It is possible that offsprings become weaker than the parents as some good genes in the parents may be lost. Therefore, elitism strategy is used by copying the best or best few parents into the next generation to replace the worst children.

1.3 Hybrid Model of GA-KFLANN

The architecture of the GA-KFLANN is illustrated in Fig. 5. The original KFLANN takes tolerance and vigilance values produced by the GA to cluster the input data set with selected features by GA. After the KFLANN converges or a predefined number of cycles have been reached, the fitness values of the clustering results are evaluated and fed back to GA to generate the next population of better parameters. This process continues until a preset number of generations of GA have been reached or no much improvement on the fitness value can be observed.

2 Experiments and Results

2.1 Iris Data Set

Fisher's paper [8] is a classic in the field and is referenced frequently to this day. The data set contains 150 random samples of flowers from the Iris species: Setosa, Versicolor, and Virginica. From each species there are 50 observations with 4 attributes each in centimeters.

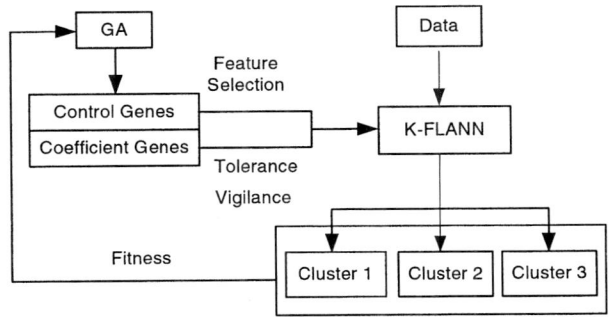

Fig. 5. The Architecture of GA-KFLANN

2.1.1 Results Without Control Genes (ConG)

Test results of data mining are exercised without ConG on the Iris data, which means that feature selection is turned off, and the best 4 outcomes of a run are shown in Table 2.

Table 2. The Best 4 Results of a Run of Iris Data Clustering without ConG

# Of Clusters	Fitness	Accuracy
4	3.95417	85.3%
3	3.85691	88.0%
3	3.52583	86.7%
2	3.32374	66.7%

There is a nonlinear relation between fitness and accuracy because Versicolor and Virginica are not linearly separable from each other. This makes the fitness evaluation as mentioned previously function poorly since maximizing the between group variance B does not work properly. Therefore, clustering with higher fitness may not have higher accuracy. Row No. 2 has the clustering with the highest accuracy and desired number of clusters.

Table 3 shows the comparison between the GA-KFLANN and the exhaustive search on Iris data set. The highest accuracy considered here includes not only accuracy itself in Table 2 but also the number of clusters.

The exhaustive search yielded better accuracy but required more processing time on Iris clustering. Another consideration is that the exhaustive search actually did feature selection as well but the GA-KFLANN did not. Therefore, the exhaustive search is expected to have higher accuracy but the GA-KFLANN has greater potential in both completion time and accuracy.

Table 3. Comparison between GA-KFLANN and Exhaustive Search on Iris Data Clustering

	Accuracy	Completion Time
GA-KFLANN	88.0%	< 1 minute
Exhaustive Search	96%	5 minutes

2.1.2 Results With Control Genes (ConG)

Table 4 shows the best 4 results in a run of Iris data clustering with ConG and the table is sorted according to the fitness of clustering. The attributes with a tick "√" indicate the presence of the attribute to achieve the accuracy. The number of clusters is recorded in the first column.

Table 4. The Best 4 Results of a Run of Iris Data Clustering with ConG

# Of Clusters	Fitness	Accuracy	Sepal Length	Sepal Width	Petal Length	Petal Width
6	20.7	72.7%	√			
4	13.5	86.7%			√	
3	12.5	89.3%				√
3	10.8	96%			√	√

It is clear that the last two rows have higher accuracy and the desired number of cluster. Petal width provides most information in clustering comparing to other features of Iris. Therefore, petal width is a main factor in determination of the Iris classification and the GA-KFLANN was able to perform well in both feature selection and clustering on the Iris data.

Table 5 shows the comparison among the GA-KFLANN, the exhaustive search and K-Nearest Neighbour (K-NN) on Iris data set. All 3 methods achieved high accuracy, but the GA-KFLANN showed superior potential on effective and efficient search because it took much less time for completion.

Table 5. Comparison of Different Clustering Algorithms on Iris Data

	Accuracy	Completion Time	Reference
GA-KFLANN	96%	< 1 minute	
Exhaustive Search	96%	5 minutes	[12]
K-NN	95.1%		[9]

2.2 Wine Data

This data was obtained from a chemical analysis of wines grown within the region of Italy, but were derived from three different cultivators. The analysis determined the quantities of 13 constituents found in each of the three types of wines. There were 178 instances of wine samples in the data set.

2.2.1 Results Without Control Genes (ConG)

The results in Table 6, of wine clustering without using ConG took only 2 minutes to generate. The highest accuracy with the correct number of clusters was however only 70.2%. In comparison, the exhaustive search on wine data set achieved 95.51% [12]. The exhaustive search however yielded this high accuracy at the expense of speed, which took 2 weeks to solve 5 attributes.

Table 6. The Best 5 Results of a Run of Wine Data Clustering without ConG

# Of Clusters	Fitness	Accuracy
3	6.21352	64.6%
3	5.86033	70.2%
3	4.42048	65.2%
4	3.54305	66.9%
3	2.34613	68.0%

2.2.2 Results with Control Genes (ConG)

Table 7 shows the results of wine clustering with ConG enabled to select features.

Table 7. The Best 4 Results of a Run of Wine Data Clustering with ConG

Attributes													Fitness	Accuracy
1	2	3	4	5	6	7	8	9	10	11	12	13		
√	√			√	√			√	√				1.21	60.11%
√	√	√			√		√	√				√	0.765	58.42%
	√		√	√	√		√						0.716	39.89%
√		√			√			√	√				0.669	90.44%

Alcohol (Item 1), Alcalinity of ash (Item 4), Flavanoids (Item 7), Colour intensity (Item 10), Hue (Item 11)

The highest accuracy achieved currently was 90.44% and this was achieved in 2 minutes. In comparison, the highest accuracy achieved in the exhaustive search was 95.51% in 2 weeks. Results of a K-NN in [9] achieved 96.7% accuracy. The features discovered to be significant using exhaustive search were Flavanoids (Item 7), Colour intensity (Item 10) and Proline (Item 13).

It is clear that the exhaustive search can achieve higher accuracy in clustering and locate the most significant factors, while the GA-KFLANN has relatively lower accuracy and more factors selected due to its random evolutionary nature. However, the exhaustive search also takes unacceptable long time to complete. Therefore, the GA-KFLANN shows greater potential in clustering as well as feature selection.

2.3 Wisconsin Breast Cancer Data

This breast cancer databases was obtained from the University of Wisconsin Hospitals, Madison from Dr. William H. Wolberg [11]. There were 699 patterns from 2 classes and 9 attributes. Table 8 shows the results of breast cancer clustering sorted according to fitness value.

Four results out of five have higher than 90% accuracy and the highest one achieved is 95.6%. The last row of Table shows the number of appearance for each attributes and it is clear that attribute 3, 4, 5 and 9 appear more frequently than others.

Table 8. The Best 5 Results of a Run of Wisconsin Breast Cancer Data Clustering

Attributes									Fitness	Accuracy
1	2	3	4	5	6	7	8	9		
	√			√	√		√	√	20.3	90.7%
√		√	√			√			16.8	89.4%
	√	√	√	√				√	7.34	91.5%
	√	√	√	√	√		√	√	7.34	91.5%
		√	√	√		√		√	2.81	95.6%
1	3	4	4	4	2	2	2	4		

Therefore, some evidence from the clustering results supports that the 4 attributes likely to be the significant in representing the dataset were, Uniformity of Cell Shape (Item 3), Marginal Adhesion (Item 4), Single Epithelial Cell Size (Item 5), Mitoses (Item 9).

The GA-KFLANN seemed to perform well in this data set. As there were too many attributes, it was not viable to conduct an exhaustive search. However, a comparison was made with K-NN, which achieved 96.6% accuracy on this data set [2]. Both performed pretty good clustering.

3 Conclusions

Although the data used were from well-known sources which have been investigated by many, the emphasis of the experiments was on the technique which was used to boost searching, extract the features from the data and get accurate clustering. From the 3 data sets, the analysis resulted in the determination of significant factors. This information was extracted without the need to have an understanding of the data. Further investigations are underway to determine if there is a proper fitness evaluation method to guide the search of GA for optimal clustering parameters.

References

[1] B. Everitt, *Cluster Analysis*, 2nd ed., New York, Halsted Press, 1980.
[2] B. Ster and A. Dobnikar, Neural Networks in Medical Diagnosis: Comparison with Other Methods,, In A. Bulsari et al., editor, Proceedings of the International Conference EANN '96, pp 427-430, 1996.
[3] D. J. Evans and L. P. Tay, *Fast Learning Artificial Neural Networks for Continuous Input Applications*, Kybernetes, Vol. 24, No. 3, 1995.
[4] L. P. Tay and D. J. Evans, "Fast Learning Artificial Neural Network (FLANN II) Using Nearest Neighbour Recall", *Neural Parallel and Scientific Computations*, Vol. 2, No. 1, 1994.
[5] L. P. Tay and S. Prakash, K-Means Fast Learning Artificial Neural Network, an Alternative Network for Classification, ICONIP, 2002.
[6] L. P. Wong and L. P. Tay, Centroid Stability with K-Mean Fast Learning Artificial Neural Networks, IJCNN, Vol.2, pp 1517 – 1522, 2003.
[7] L. P. Wong, J. Xu and L. P. Tay, Liquid Drop Photonic signal using Fast Learning Artificial Neural Network, ICICS, Vol.2, pp. 1018- 1022, 2003.
[8] R. A. Fisher, "The Use of Multiple Measurements in Taxonomic Problems", *Annual Eugenics*, 7, Part II, 179-188, 1936.
[9] S. D. Bay, Combining Nearest Neighbor Classifiers through Multiple Feature Subsets, Proc. 17th Intl. Conf. on Machine Learning, pp. 37-45, Madison, WI, 1998.
[10] U. Maulik and S. Bandyopadhyay, "Genetic Algorithm-Based Clustering Technique", *Pattern Recognition*, Vol. 33, No. 9, pp. 1455-1465, 2000.
[11] W. H. Wolberg and O. L. Mangasarian, "Multisurface Method of Pattern Separation or Medical Diagnosis Applied to Breast Cytology", *Proceedings of the National Academy of Sciences*, U.S.A., Vol. 87, pp 9193-9196, 1990.
[12] X. Yin and L. P. Tay, Feature Extraction Using The K-Means Fast Learning Artificial Neural Network, ICICS, Vol.2, pp. 1004- 1008, 2003.

Immune Clonal Selection Network

Haifeng Du[1,2], Xiaoyi Jin[3,4], Jian Zhuang[2], Licheng Jiao[1], and Sun'an Wang[2]

[1] Institute of Intelligent Information Processing, Xidian University,
710071, Xi'an, China
{Haifengdu72, lchjiao1}@163.com
[2] Industry Training Center, Xi'an Jiaotong University,
710049, Xi'an, China
{Haifengdu72, jian_zhj}@163.com
[3] Institute for Population and Development Studies, Xi'an Jiaotong University,
710049, Xi'an, China
Xiaoyijin@163.com
[4] School of economy and finance, Xi'an Jiaotong University,
710071, Xi'an, China
Xiaoyijin@163.com

Abstract. Based on the Antibody Clonal Selection Theory of immunology, the general steps of ICSA (Immune Clonal Selection Algorithm) are presented in this paper. The network framework of ICSA is put forward, and the dynamic characters of ICSA are analyzed based on the Lyapunov theory. Then, this paper gives a novel Artificial Immune System Algorithm, Pseudo- Grads Hybrid Immune Clonal Selection Network (GHICSN). The simulation results of some functions optimization indicate that GHICSN improves the performance of ICSA to some extent.

1 Introduction

Artificial Immune System (AIS) algorithms are inspired by the information processing model of the vertebrate's immune system[1]. Clonal selection theory is very important for the immunology, and attracts much attention from the artificial intelligence researchers, who had explored successively a few clonal algorithms based on imitating clonal mechanism from various viewpoint[2], [3]. However, applications of the antibody clonal mechanisms in AIS are still rare.

Some discussion about the similarities and differences between Artificial Neural Networks (ANN) and Artificial Immune Systems can be found in reference [4], and the relations between EAs and ANN are explored in reference [5]. As we know, ANN is one of the full-blown artificial intelligence technology correspondingly, and has self-contained research system and theory framework. In this paper, we mainly analyze the network framework of immune clonal selection algorithm and discuss its convergence based on the Lyapunov theory, which implicates not only a new way to study immune clonal selection algorithm but also a novel reference for analyzing other artificial immune system algorithms. We proceed as follows: Section 2 provides a description of the ICSA. Section 3 introduces the network framework of ICSA. Pseudo- Grads Hybrid Immune Clonal Selection Network (GHICSN) is described in Sections 4. Finally, Section 5 states some conclusions.

2   Immune Clonal Selection Algorithm

There are mainly two kinds of theories about the mechanism of biology generating special antibody that aims at such kind of antigen, one is the model theory based on the adaptability, and the other is clonal selection theory based on selection. The highlight of the argument is whether the ability of antibody proliferation is determined by evolution or gained by antigen stimulation [6]. In fact, antibody proliferation can be divided into two stages. Before antigen stimulation, all of the cells generated by variety antibody of the organism can be considered as a junior repertoire, and its information is determined by billions of years' evolution and heredity. After stimulation, the cells with relevant antibody (receptors) will be selected and cause clonal proliferation. After stimulated by antigens again and again, hypermutation takes place in the V-area. The cells with high affinity antibody proliferate selectively, and cause antibody style transformation until the antibody is mature. During this process of clonal selection, some biologic characters such as learning, memory and antibody diversity can be used by artificial immune system.

Some researchers such as De Castro have stimulated the clonal selection mechanism in different ways, then proposed different Clonal Selection Algorithms one after another[4], [5]. Just like evolutionary algorithms, the artificial immune system algorithms work on an encoding of the parameter set rather than the parameter set itself.

Without loss of generality, we consider the following global optimization problem P:

$$\text{maximize} \quad f(x) \quad \text{subject to} \quad d \leq x \leq u \tag{1}$$

where, $x = \{x_1, x_2, \cdots, x_m\} \in \Re^m$ is a variable vector, $d = \{d_1, d_2, \cdots, d_m\}$ and $u = \{u_1, u_2, \cdots, u_m\}$ define the feasible solution space, namely, $x_i \in [d_i, u_i]$ $i = 1, 2, \cdots, m$, $f(x)$ is the objective function. In AIS, it can be described as $\max\{f(\hbar^{-1}(a))\}$, Where $a = \{a_1, a_2, \cdots, a_l\}$ is the antibody coding of the variable x, described by $a = \hbar(x)$, and x is called the decoding of antibody a, described as $x = \hbar^{-1}(a)$. The set I is called the antibody space, f is the positive real function in the set I, and f is called the antibody-antigen affinity function. According to biological terms, in the antibody a, a_i is considered as the evolutionary gene called allele, whose probable values are correlated with the coding method. Let ℓ be the number of the possible values of a_i. For binary coding and decimal coding, there are $\ell = 2$ and $\ell = 10$ accordingly. Generally, antibody bit string is divided into m parts, and the length of each part is l_i, where $l = \sum_{i=1}^{m} l_i$, and each part is denoted as $x_i \in [d_i, u_i]$ $i = 1, 2, \cdots, m$. Especially, for binary coding, we use the decoding method as follow:

$$x_i = d_i + \frac{u_i - d_i}{2^{l_i} - 1}\left(\sum_{j=1}^{l_i} a_j 2^{j-1}\right) \tag{2}$$

and the antibody space is:

$$I^n = \{A : A = (a_1, a_2 \cdots a_n),\ a_k \in I,\ 1 \le k \le n\} \tag{3}$$

where the positive integer n is the size of antibody population. The antibody population $A = \{a_1, a_2 \cdots a_n\}$, which is an n-dimension group of antibody a, is a point in the antibody group space I^n.

Clearly, the definition given above doesn't follow the definition of biology strictly since it doesn't distinguish antibody from B cell. For convenience, the immune clonal selection algorithms (ICSA), discussed in this paper, has its antibody population evolved as following:

$$A(k) \xrightarrow{T_c^C} Y(k) \xrightarrow{T_g^C} Z(k) \widetilde{\cup} A(k) \xrightarrow{T_s^C} A(k+1) \tag{4}$$

For $X = \{x_1, x_2, \cdots, x_n\}$ and $Y = \{y_1, y_2, \cdots, y_n\}$, $\widetilde{\cup}$ operation is defined as follow:

$$X \widetilde{\cup} Y \equiv \bigcup_{i=1}^{n} \{x_i \cup y_i\} \tag{5}$$

Inspired by the Antibody Clonal Selection Theory of Immunology, the major elements of Clonal Operator are described as follows, and the antibody population at time k is represented by the time-dependent variable $A(k)$.

Clonal Operating T_c^C: Define the following:

$$Y(k) = T_c^C(A(k)) = [T_c^C(a_1(k)),\ T_c^C(a_2(k)),\ \cdots,\ T_c^C(a_n(k))]^T \tag{6}$$

Where $y_i(k) = T_c^C(a_i(k)) = I_i \times a_i(k)$ $i = 1, 2 \cdots n$, I_i is q_i-dimension row vector with all its elements being 1. $T_c^C(a_i(k))$ is called q_i clone of antibody a_i

$$q_i(k) = g(n_c, f(a_i(k)), \Theta_i) \tag{7}$$

Θ_i indicates the affinity of antibody i and other antibodies, and the paper simply defines it as follow:

$$\Theta_i = \min\{D_{ij}\} = \min\{\exp(\|a_i - a_j\|)\} \quad i \ne j; i, j = 1, 2, \cdots, n \tag{8}$$

$\|\bullet\|$ is an arbitrary norm, for binary coding, we use Hamming distance, but for decimal coding we generally use Euclidean distance. Θ_i is generally normalized, namely $0 \le \|\bullet\| \le 1$, clearly, the bigger the antibody affinity is, namely the more the similarities, the stronger the antibody-antibody restraint is, and the smaller Θ_i is. Especially when antibody affinity is 0, Θ_i is 1. Furthermore, $D = (d_{ij})_{n \times n}$ $i, j = 1, 2, \cdots, n$ is an antibody-antibody affinity matrix. D is a symmetric matrix, which denotes the diversity of population.

Generally, q_i is estimated as follow:

$$q_i(k) = \text{Int}\left(n_c * \frac{f(a_i(k))}{\sum_{j=1}^{n} f(a_j(k))} * \Theta_i \right) \quad i = 1, 2 \cdots n \tag{9}$$

Where $n_c > n$ is a given value related to the clone scale, Int(•) is supremum function, Int(x) rounds the elements of x to the least integer bigger than x. So, for the single antibody, the clone scale is adjusted self-adaptively by the antibody-antigen affinity and antibody-antibody affinity. Moreover, when it is constrained less by antibody, and stimulated more by antigen, the clone scale is also bigger, or else, it becomes smaller.

Immune Genic Operating T_g^C : Crossing and Mutation are the main operators in Immune Genic Operating. According to the information exchanging characters of the Monoclonal and the Polyclonal in biology, Monoclonal Operator is defined as only adopting the mutation in the step of immune genic operating, but the Polyclonal Operator adopting both Crossing and Mutation. It need to be pointed out here that clonal selection operator in this paper is just used for reference of the mechanism of the immunology, rather than for following the concepts of the immunology completely. Even for the Monoclonal Selection Operator, it doesn't mean a singular antibody but just reserves more information from parent compared to the Polyclonal Selection Operator. According to immunology, affinity maturation and antibody diversity depend on hypermutation of antibody, but not crossover and recombination that the affinity is mature and the generating of antibody diversity. Thus, it is different from genetic algorithms where Crossover is main operator but Mutation is background operator, that in clonal selection algorithms, Mutation is emphasized. In this paper, without special explanation, the immune genic operating only involves mutation operator, and Monoclonal Selection Algorithms is called ICSA.

According to the mutation probability p_m^i, the cloned antibody populations are mutated, $Z(k) = T_g^C(Y(k))$.

Clonal Selection Operating T_s^C : $\forall i = 1, 2, \cdots n$, $z_i(k)$ can be given as:

$$z_i(k) = \max\{z_i(k)\} = \{z_{ij}(k) \mid \max f(z_{ij}) \quad j = 1, 2, \cdots q_i\} \tag{10}$$

then, for $T_s^C(z_i(k) \cup a_i(k) \to a_i(k+1))$

$$a_i(k+1) = \begin{cases} z_i(k) & f(a_i(k)) \leq f(z_i(k)) \\ z_i(k) & f(a_i(k)) > f(z_i(k)) \end{cases} \tag{11}$$

After the clonal operating, the new antibody population is
$A(k+1) = \{a_1(k+1), a_2(k+1), \cdots, a_n(k+1)\}$, which are equivalent with memory cells and plasma cells after biology clonal selection, and special differences between them haven't been made in the operator.

In practical application, either no improvement over continuous iterations or limited iterations, or both are adopted as terminated conditions. Here, the termination condition is defined as follow:

$$\left| f^* - f^{best} \right| < \varepsilon \tag{12}$$

Where f^* is the optimal solution of objective function f, f^{best} is the best objective function value of temporary generation. When $0 < \left| f^* \right| < 1$, f^{best} is:

$$\left| f^* - f^{best} \right| < \varepsilon \left| f^* \right| \tag{13}$$

3 The Network Framework of ICSA

The network framework of ICSA can be described as Fig 1. The network is very similar to multilayer feed-forward neural networks. In this section, using for reference of the research method of the neural network, we will analyze the immune clonal selection algorithm, especially the stability.

Consider maximizing the function P: $\max\{f(e^{-1}(a)): a \in I\}$, so the effect of the last layer of the network is to select the optimum from the antibodies, and the network model as follows:

$$A(k+1) = \bigcup_{i=1}^{n} f^{-1}\left\{ \max\left[f(a_i(k)) \cup \left(\bigcup_{j=1}^{q_i(k)} f(\hbar_{ij}(a_i(k))) \right) \right] \right\} \tag{14}$$

$$Y(k+1) = g\left\{ \bigcup_{i=1}^{n} f^{-1}\left\{ \max\left[f(a_i(k)) \cup \left(\bigcup_{j=1}^{q_i(k)} f(\hbar_{ij}(a_i(k))) \right) \right] \right\} \right\} \tag{15}$$

where $z_{ij} = \hbar_{ij}(a_i(k)) = \hbar(a_i(k)) = a_i(k) + \Delta a_{ij}(k)$ $i = 1, 2, \cdots n$ $j = 1, 2, \cdots q_i$

$q_i(k)$ is determined by Eq. (9). The network is dynamic as the result of $q_i(k)$ is indefinite. For the convenience of analyzing, we choose $q_i(k) = q_i = \max_k \{q_i(k)\}$.

A two-layer feed-forward artificial neural network with span connections can be expressed as follow [7]:

$$y(k) = f\left[\sum_{h_1}^{H_1} a_{h_1} f\left[\sum_{i=0}^{N} a_{ih_1} x_i(k) \right] + \sum_{j=0}^{N} a_j x_j(k) \right] \tag{16}$$

where x, a, y represent the inputs, the weight values and the outputs separately.

Comparing the Eq. (15) and (16), we could see that their basic frameworks are the same except for the substitution of the Boolean calculation such as "and" for the arithmetic calculation of the typical neural network. Therefore, the clonal selection algorithm is also called immune clonal selection network in this paper. But the immune clonal algorithm and the neural network are two different algorithms after all, at least they have some differences. The weight value of this network is invariably 1, but that of the ordinary neural network is variable. In fact, only two parameters of this network need to be adjusted. They are $q_i(k)$ and $\Delta a_{ij}(k)$ where $q_i(k)$ controls the framework of the network and $\Delta a_{ij}(k)$ influences the efficiency and the performance of the algorithm, so $\Delta a_{ij}(k)$ is a key to adjust algorithm. They are also different in learning algorithm. Immune clonal algorithm accomplishes the random search that is directed by probability by adopting genic operation (mainly with crossover and mutation). But the neural network is mainly by the iterative learning.

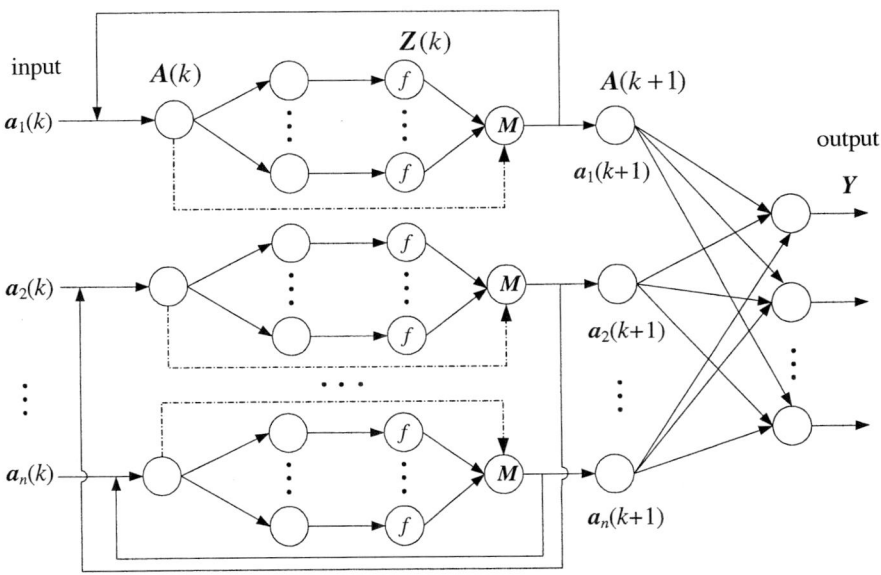

Fig. 1. The network framework of ICSA

However, note that the framework of the immune clonal algorithm is similar to the artificial neural network. So we can analyze the immune clonal selection algorithm in virtue of the research method of the neural network. We mainly discuss the stability of the immune clonal selection algorithm in the text.

Define the error function as $e = y^d - y^*$, where y^d is optimum value of the problem and y^* is optimum value of the outputs. Generally, $y^* = f\left(\hbar^{-1}(a^*)\right)$ $a^* \in A \in B^*$. Because we want the maximum value of the question P, we have $e \geq 0$.

We define the Lyapunov function as follow:

$$V(k) = \frac{e^2(k)}{2} = \frac{(y^d - y^*(k))^2}{2} \tag{17}$$

$$\Delta V(k) = V(k+1) - V(k) = \frac{1}{2}\left(e^2(k+1) - e^2(k)\right) \tag{18}$$

$$\Delta V(k) = (e(k+1) - e(k))\left(e(k) + \frac{1}{2}(e(k+1) - e(k))\right)$$
$$= \Delta e(k)\left(e(k) + \frac{1}{2}\Delta e(k)\right) \tag{19}$$

where $\Delta e(k) = e(k+1) - e(k)$. Obviously, the necessary condition of $\Delta V(k) < 0$ is $\Delta e(k) \times e(k) < 0$, considering that $e \geq 0$. Therefore, the algorithm is convergent only when the tracks formed by the immune clonal selection algorithm fall into the fourth quadrant in the plane.

Furthermore, due to the Taylor series,

$$y^*(k+1) - y^*(k) = -\Delta e(k) = \left[\frac{\partial y^*(k)}{\partial a^*}\right]^T \times [a^*(k+1) - a^*(k)] + o[a^*(k+1) - a^*(k)] \tag{20}$$

We have the mark that $a^*(k+1) - a^*(k) = \Delta a^*(k)$. The sign of $\Delta e(k)$ can't be influenced by the high order infinitesimal in the Eq. (21) when the $\Delta a^*(k)$ is small enough. This can be stated as follow:

$$\operatorname{sgn}(\Delta e(k)) = \operatorname{sgn}\left(-\left[\frac{\partial y^*(k)}{\partial a^*}\right]^T \times [a^*(k+1) - a^*(k)]\right) \tag{21}$$

So:

$$\Delta V(k) \approx -\left[\frac{\partial y^*(k)}{\partial a^*}\right]^T \Delta a^*(k)e(k) + \left(\left[\frac{\partial y^*(k)}{\partial a^*}\right]^T \Delta a^*(k)\right)^2 \tag{22}$$

If we only consider the sign, the equal mark in (22) is satisfied.

If $\Delta a^*(k) = \eta \nabla f = \eta \frac{\partial y^*(k)}{\partial a}$, we have that

$$\Delta V(k) \approx -\left\|\frac{\partial y^*(k)}{\partial a^*}\right\|^2 \left(\eta e(k) - \eta^2 \left\|\frac{\partial y^*(k)}{\partial a^*}\right\|^2\right) \tag{23}$$

If $\Delta V(k) < 0$ is satisfied, we get

$$\eta e(k) - \eta^2 \left\| \frac{\partial y^*(k)}{\partial a^*} \right\|^2 > 0 \qquad (24)$$

Therefore

$$0 < \eta < \min_k \left(\frac{e(k)}{\left\| \frac{\partial y^*(k)}{\partial a^*} \right\|^2} \right) \qquad (25)$$

So we can have the theory as follow:

Theorem 1: The algorithm is convergent and the dynamic course decided by the algorithm is gradually reaching the stability when the individual in the antibodies changes by the rule that $\Delta a_{ij}(k)$, which comes from the equation $h_{ij}(a_i(k)) = h(a_i(k)) = a_i(k) + \Delta a_{ij}(k)$ $i = 1,2,\cdots n$ $j = 1,2,\cdots c_i$, alters along the Grads of the affinity function and the step length is decided by the Eq. (25).

As analyzed above, the algorithm must be convergent provided that the antibodies evolve along the Grads of the affinity function and by some certain step length in the macro view no matter what operations (such as cross, aberrance and so on) the immune gene have in the micro view. The convergent speed of the algorithm evolving course and the characteristic of the converging course are decided by η, which is consistent with the iterative principle in the neural network.

4 Pseudo-Grads Hybrid Immune Clonal Selection Network

Theorem 1 gives the sufficient condition of the convergence, but the mechanism of Clonal Selection Theory determines that ICSA pays more attention to the genic operation. It is obvious that stochastic operation (Immune Genic Operation) can not make sure that the evolution works along the grads of affinity function. On the other hand, because of the complexity of the question to be optimized, the grads of affinity function can not be acquired easily; in addition, the learning methods of artificial neural network based on grads are easily convergent to local optimum and emphasize grads too much. All these may lose the universal characteristics of feeble methods. So, in practice, it is difficult to carry out the algorithm strictly according to Theorem 1. In this section, we will define Pseudo-Grads and proposed a novel Artificial Immune System Algorithm, Pseudo-Grads Hybrid Immune Clonal Selection Network.

Compared with evolutionary algorithms, immune clonal selection algorithms gives more attention to local search combined with global search, and because of clonal mechanism, it is possible to use multi-strategy in changing an antibody. Based on the discussions, this paper gives a novel Artificial Immune System Algorithm, Pseudo-Grads Hybrid Immune Clonal Selection Network (GHICSN). Define

$$g_i(k) = \begin{cases} a_i(k) - a_i(k-1) & f(a_i(k)) > f(a_i(k)) \\ 0 & f(a_i(k)) \le f(a_i(k)) \end{cases} \quad i = 1, 2, \cdots n; \quad k = 1, 2, \cdots \quad (26)$$

as pseudo-grads.

Accordingly, the genic operating of Immune clonal selection algorithm can be described as:

$$\Delta a_i(k) = \begin{cases} \eta_r \times g_i(k) & rnd < p_g \text{ and } g_i(k) \ne 0 \\ gene - operator & rnd \ge p_g \text{ or } g_i(k) = 0 \end{cases} \quad (27)$$

Namely, if parents come well, the corresponding children adopt pseudo-grads to improve the individuals (with certain probability pg), which is a local certain search. Otherwise, adopt immune genic operating. Where η_r is a real vector.

In order to validate our approach, the GHICSN is executed to solve the following test function and compared with ICSA and standard Evolution Programming algorithm (EP) [8].

$$\min f_1(x, y) = x^2 + y^2 - 0.3 \times \cos(3\pi x) + 0.3 \times \cos(4\pi y) + 0.3 \quad x, y \in [-1,1] \quad (28)$$

f_1 is the third Bohachevsky test function, whose global optimal value is -0.1848 at [0,-0.23] and [0,0.23].

$$\min f_2(x, y) = \left\{ \sum_{i=1}^{5} i \cos[(i+1)x + i] \right\} \times \left\{ \sum_{i=1}^{5} i \cos[(i+1)y + i] \right\} \quad x, y \in [-10,10] \quad (29)$$

f_2 is the Shubert testing function, there are 760 local minimum values and 18 of them are global minimum solutions, the optimal value is -186.73.

$$\min f_3(x, y) = (x^2 + y - 11)^2 + (x + y^2 - 7)^2 \quad x, y \in [-6,6] \quad (30)$$

f_3 is the Himmelbaut test function, there are a lot of local minimum values, and 4 of them are global minimum solutions. The optimal value is 0 at [3, 2], [3.5844, -1.8482], [-2.8051, 3.1313] and [-3.7793, -3.2832].

$$\min f_4(x, y) = (x^2 + y^2)^{0.25} \left(\sin^2 50(x^2 + y^2)^{0.1} + 1.0 \right) \quad x, y \in [-5.12, 5.12] \quad (31)$$

f_4 is the Schaffer1test function, its global optimal value is 0 at [0,0].

In order to show justness, we set the parameters as shown in table 1. For function f_4, ICSA and GHICSN adopt the (μ, λ) selection strategy [8], where λ is 0.5μ.

All algorithms adopt Gaussion mutations, namely

$$x_i' = x_i + 0.1 \times N_i(0,1) \times \sqrt{|f(X)|} \quad (32)$$

For GHICSN, η_r is:

$$\eta_r = 0.01 \times \sqrt{|f(X)|} \quad (33)$$

Table 1. The given algorithm parameters

Function	ε	EP		ICSA			GHICSN			
		Pop size	mutation probability	Pop size	q_i	mutation probability	Pop size	q_i	Mutation probability	p_g
f_1	10^{-3}	40	0.1	10	4	0.5	10	4	0.5	0.7
f_2	10^{-1}	40	0.1	10	4	0.5	10	4	0.5	0.7
f_3	10^{-3}	40	0.1	10	4	0.5	10	4	0.5	0.6
f_4	10^{-2}	40	0.1	40	5	0.5	40	5	0.5	0.7

Table 2 shows 20-time independent experiment results. It denotes that ICSA and GHICSN have better ability when compared with EP. It also shows that GHICSN has better stability and higher convergent speed compared with ICSA. In addition, for functions f_1, f_2 and f_4, EP sometimes can not break away from the local optimal value, but ICSA and GHICSN avoid it effectively. For the function f_1, f_2 and f_4, here only circumstances when the algorithm can break away from the local optimal value are considered.

Table 2. Simulation Results

function	The generation that it can find the optimal solutionh										
	EP				ICSA				GHICSN			
	max	min	Mean	std	max	min	mean	std	max	min	mean	std
f_1	1080	200	593.7	235.6	4360	280	832	883.5	1720	200	646	339.0
f_2	4880	1000	2346	1012.1	5360	480	2722	1530.5	5040	440	2506	1365.7
f_3	1400	280	936	294.9	650	350	518	90.7	600	250	425	86.6
f_4	38640	640	7804	10449	10400	800	3080	2287.2	8600	1200	2920	1830

Farther, the relatively changing of the objective function denotes the algorithm's diversity essentially. For functions f_1 and f_2, the change of objective function in each experiment is shown in Fig 2 and Fig 3. It can be seen that ICSA and GHICSN keep the population diversities better when compared with EP. And for multi-optimal objective functions, ICSA and GHICSN can find the different optimal points while EP only finds one optimal point.

Obviously, GHICSA's ability is effected by η_r and p_g. The choice of η_r is interrelated with idiographic problem, so we mainly discuss the effect of p_g.

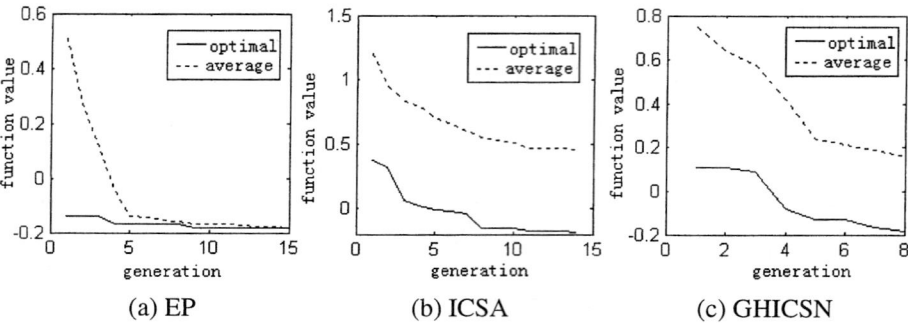

Fig. 2. The changing of the function value for f_1

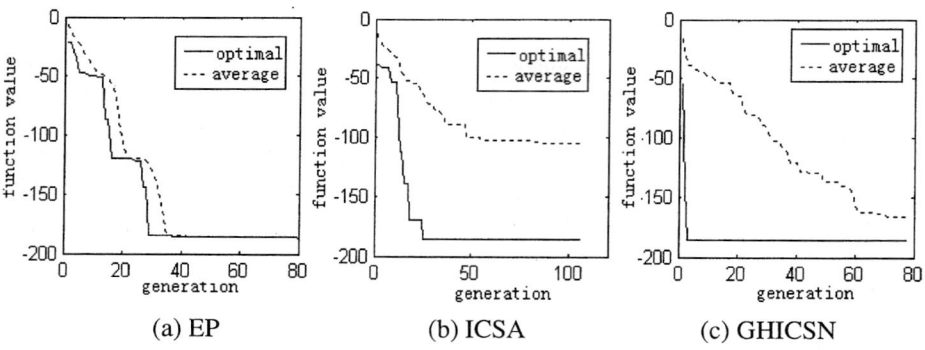

Fig. 3. The changing of the function value for f_2

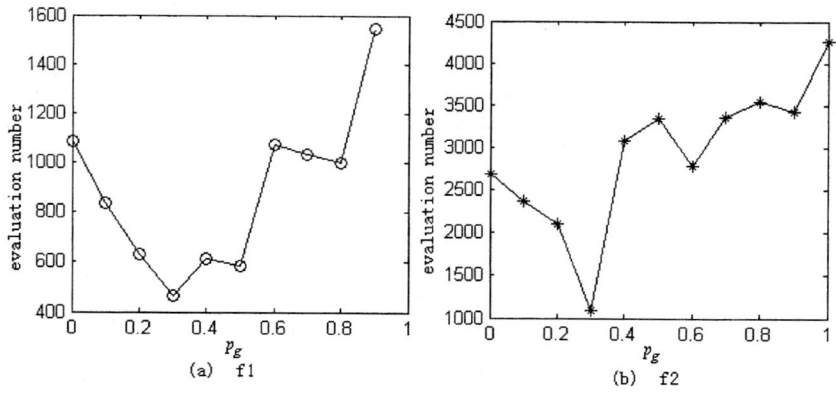

Fig. 4. The impact of p_g in GHICSA

Fig 4 shows 10-time independent experiment results when p_g changed from 0 to 1. y-axis denotes the evaluation function number of GHICSN for function f_1 and f_2. It shows that when $p_g \approx 0.3$ GHICSN has the best ability. The conclusion also applies to s others functions. But if using Grads search only, it is easily convergent to local optimal value. So in GHICSN, the operator based on Pseudo- Grads is only an assistant.

5 Conclusion and Prospect

In this paper, the network framework of immune clonal selection algorithm is put forward, and the dynamic characters of ICSA based on the Lyapunov theory are analyzed, especially the stability. Then we defined Pseudo-Grads and proposed a novel Artificial Immune System Algorithm, Pseudo-Grads Hybrid Immune Clonal Selection Network. Theoretical analysis and simulations show that the ability of ICSA was improved to certain extent after using Pseudo-Grads search. In a word, the main purpose of this paper is providing a new way to study immune clonal selection algorithm and exploring a new hybrid intelligent system.

Further simulations indicate that the amelioration based on Pseudo-Grads is not always effective for all functions. On one hand, just as forenamed, the operator based on Pseudo-Grads is only an assistant in GHICSN, if p_g is not fit (easily too large, we propose $p_g \leq 0.3$), it is easily convergent to local optimal value. On the other hand, Pseudo-Grads is different from the standard Grads, it only emphasizes on the changing direction of variants and does not mention the objective function, which reduces the Pseudo-Grads search's ability of local search. Modifying the Pseudo-Grads adaptively according to idiographic problem to improve the ability of GHICSN is our further research.

References

1. Dasgupta, D., Forrest, S.: Artificial Immune Systems in Industrial Applications. In: John, A. M., Marcello, M.V. (eds.): Proceedings of the Second International Conference on Intelligent Processing and Manufacturing of Materials, Vol. 1. IEEE, Hawaii (1999) 257–267
2. De Castro, L.N., Von Zuben, F.J.: The Clonal Selection Algorithm with Engineering Applications. In: Whitley, D., Goldberg, D.E., Cantú-Paz, E., Spector, L., Parmee, I.C., Beyer, H. (eds.): Proceedings of the Genetic and Evolutionary Computation Conference. Morgan Kaufmann, Las Vegas (2000) 36–37
3. Kim,J., Bentley, P.J.: Towards an Artificial Immune System for Network Intrusion Detection: an Investigation of Clonal Selection with a Negative Selection Operator. In: IEEE Neural Networks Council (ed.): Proceedings of the 2001 Congress on Evolutionary Computation, Vol. 2. IEEE, Seoul Korea (2001) 1244 –1252
4. Dasgupta, D.: Artificial neural networks and artificial immune systems: similarities and differences. In: Tien, J.M.(ed.):1997 IEEE International Conference on Computational Cybernetics and Simulation, IEEE, Orlando(1997) 873–878
5. Hu X.C.: Comparison of Genetic Algorithm and Neural Network Technology. http://www.ics.hawaii.edu/~sugihara/research/.

6. Lu, D.Y., Ma, B.L.: Modern Immunology. Shanghai technology education publishing company, Shanghai (1998)
7. Hagan, M.T., Demuth, H.B. Beale, M.H.: Neural Network Design. 1st edn. China Machine Press, Beijing (2002)
8. Michalewicz, Z.: Genetic Algorithms + Data Structures = Evolution Programs. 3rd edn. Springer-Verlag, Berlin Heidelberg New York (1996)

Performance Improvement of RBF Network Using ART2 Algorithm and Fuzzy Logic System

Kwang Baek Kim[1] and Cheol Ki Kim[2]

[1] Dept. of Computer Engineering, Silla University, Busan, Korea
[2] Div. of Computer Engineering, Miryang National University, Busan, Korea
gbkim@silla.ac.kr

Abstract. This paper proposes an enhanced RBF network that enhances learning algorithms between input layer and middle layer and between middle layer and output layer individually for improving the efficiency of learning. The proposed network applies ART2 network as the learning structure between input layer and middle layer. And the auto-tuning method of learning rate and momentum is proposed and applied to learning between middle layer and output layer, which arbitrates learning rate and momentum dynamically by using the fuzzy control system for the arbitration of the connected weight between middle layer and output layer. The experiment for the classification of number patterns extracted from the citizen registration card shows that compared with conventional networks such as delta-bar-delta algorithm and the ART2-based RBF network, the proposed method achieves the improvement of performance in terms of learning speed and convergence.

1 Introduction

Many studies on improving the learning time and the generalization ability of the learning algorithm of neural network have been performed. As a result, RBF (Radial Basis Function), which has been used for multivariate analysis and interpolation of statistics, was used for organizing the neural network model by Brommhead and Low for the first time. Then RBF network was proposed by Watanabe et al. [1]. RBF network has the characteristics of short learning time, generalization and simplification etc., applying to the classification of learning data and the nonlinear system modeling.

The RBF network is a feed-forward neural network that consists of three layers, input layer, middle layer and output layer. In the RBF network, because the operations required between layers are different, learning algorithms between layers can be mutually different. Therefore, the optimum organization between layers can be separately constructed [2]. Approaches to the composition of layers in the RBF network are classified to three types: The first type is the 'fixed centers selected at random' which selects nodes of the middle layer randomly from the learning data set. The second is the 'self-organized selection of centers' which decides the middle layer according to the form of self-organization and applies the supervised learning to the output layer. The last one is the 'supervised selection of centers' which uses the supervised learning for the middle layer and the output layer. The middle layer of the RBF network executes the clustering operation, classifying input data set to homogeneous clusters. The measurement of homogeneity in clusters is the distance between vectors in clusters. And the classification of input data to a cluster means that the distances between input data and each vector in the cluster are shorter than or equal to the fixed radius. But, the use of a fixed radius in clustering causes wrong classifications. Therefore the selection of the organization for middle layer determines the overall efficiency of the RBF network [3]. Therefore, this paper proposes and evaluates the enhanced RBF network that uses ART2 to organize the middle layer efficiently and applies the auto-turning method of adjusting learning rate and momentum using the fuzzy control system for the arbitration of the connected weight between middle layer and output layer.

2 Related Studies

2.1 Delta-Bar-Delta Algorithm

Delta-bar-delta algorithm [4], which improved the quality of backpropagation algorithm, enhances learning quality by arbitrating learning rates dynamically for individual connected weights by means of making delta and delta-bar.

The formula of making delta is as follows: In this expression, i, j and k indicate the input layer, the middle layer and the output layer, respectively.

$$\Delta_{ji} = \frac{\partial E}{\partial w_{ji}} = -\delta_j x_i \tag{1}$$

$$\Delta_{kj} = \frac{\partial E}{\partial w_{kj}} = -\delta_k z_j \tag{2}$$

The formula of making delta-bar is as follows:

$$\overline{\Delta}_{ji}(t) = (1-\beta) \cdot \overline{\Delta}_{ji}(t) + \beta \cdot \overline{\Delta}_{ji}(t-1) \tag{3}$$

$$\overline{\Delta}_{kj}(t) = (1-\beta) \cdot \overline{\Delta}_{kj}(t) + \beta \cdot \overline{\Delta}_{kj}(t-1) \tag{4}$$

The value of parameter β in formula (4) is the fixed constant between 0 and 1.0. The variation of learning rate in terms of the change direction of delta and delta-bar is as follows: If the connected weight changes to the same direction in the successive learning process, the learning rate will increase. At this point delta and delta-bar has the same sign. On the other hand, if the signs of delta and delta-bar are different, the learning rate will decrease as much as the ratio of 1-γ of the present value. The formula of the learning rate for each layer is as follows:

$$\begin{aligned}\alpha_{ji}(t+1) &= \alpha_{ji}(t) + k & \text{if } \overline{\Delta}_{ji}(t-1) \cdot \Delta_{ji}(t) &> 0 \\ &= (1-\gamma) \cdot \alpha_{ji}(t) & \text{if } \overline{\Delta}_{ji}(t-1) \cdot \Delta_{ji}(t) &< 0 \\ &= \alpha_{ji}(t) & \text{if } \overline{\Delta}_{ji}(t-1) \cdot \Delta_{ji}(t) &= 0\end{aligned} \tag{5}$$

$$\alpha_{kj}(t+1) = \alpha_{kj}(t) + k \quad \text{if } \overline{\Delta_{kj}}(t-1) \cdot \Delta_{kj}(t) > 0$$
$$= (1-\gamma) \cdot \alpha_{kj}(t) \quad \text{if } \overline{\Delta_{kj}}(t-1) \cdot \Delta_{kj}(t) < 0 \quad (6)$$
$$= \alpha_{kj}(t) \quad \text{if } \overline{\Delta_{kj}}(t-1) \cdot \Delta_{kj}(t) = 0$$

2.2 ART2-Based RBF Network

The learning of ART2-based RBF network is divided to two stages. In the first stage, competitive learning is applied as the learning structure between input layer and middle layer. And the supervised learning is accomplished between middle layer and output layer [5][6]. Output vector of the middle layer in the ART2-based RBF network is calculated by formula (7), and as shown in formula (8), the node having the minimum output vector becomes the winner node.

$$O_j = \frac{1}{N} \sum_{i=1}^{N} \left(x_i - w_{ji}(t) \right) \quad (7)$$

$$O_j^* = Min\{O_j\} \quad (8)$$

where $w_{ij}(t)$ is the connected weight value between input layer and middle layer.

In the ART2-based RBF network, the node having the minimum difference between input vector and output vector of the hidden layer is selected as the winner node of the middle layer, and the similarity test for the winner node selected is the same as formula (9).

$$O_j^* < \rho \quad (9)$$

where ρ is the vigilance parameter in the formula.

The input pattern is classified to the same pattern if the output vector is smaller than the vigilance parameter, and otherwise, to the different pattern. The connected weight is adjusted to reflect the homogeneous characteristics of input pattern on the weight when it is classified to the same pattern. The adjustment of the connected weight in ART2 algorithm is as follows:

$$w_{j^*i}(t+1) = \frac{w_{j^*i}(t) \cdot u_n + x_i}{u_n + 1} \quad (10)$$

where u_n indicates the number of updated patterns in the selected cluster.

The output vector of the middle layer is normalized by formula (11) and applied to the output layer as the input vector.

$$z_i = 1 - \frac{O_j}{N} \quad (11)$$

The output vector of the output layer is calculated by formula (12).

$$O_k = f\left(\sum_{j=1}^{M} w_{kj} \cdot z_j \right) \quad (12)$$

$$f(x) = \frac{1}{1+e^{-x}} \tag{13}$$

The error value is calculated by comparing the output vector with the target vector. The connected weight is adjusted like formula (15) using the error value.

$$\delta_k = (T_k - O_k) \cdot O_k \cdot (1 - O_k) \tag{14}$$

$$w_{kj}(t+1) = w_{kj}(t) + \alpha \cdot \delta_k \cdot z_j \tag{15}$$

3 Enhanced RBF Network

The enhanced RBF network applies ART2 to the learning structure between the input layer and the middle layer, and proposes the auto-turning method of arbitrating learning rate for the adjustment of the connected weight between the middle layer and the output layer. When the absolute value of the difference between the output vector and the target vector for each pattern is below 0.1, it is classified to the accuracy, and otherwise to the inaccuracy. Learning rate and momentum are arbitrated dynamically by applying the numbers of the accuracy and the inaccuracy to the input of the fuzzy control system. Fig. 1 shows the membership function to which the accuracy belongs, whereas Fig. 2 shows the membership function to which the inaccuracy belongs.

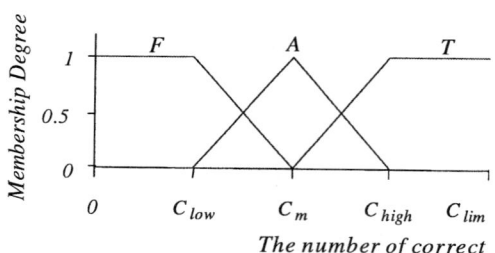

Fig. 1. The membership function to which the accuracy belongs

The values of C_{low} and C_{high} are calculated by formula (16) and (17).

$$C_{low} = \log_2(N_i + N_p) \tag{16}$$
$$\begin{pmatrix} N_i : \text{the number of input nodes} \\ N_p : \text{the number of patterns} \end{pmatrix}$$

$$C_{high} = C_{\lim} - C_{low} \tag{17}$$

In Fig. 1 and 2, F, A and T are the linguistic variables indicating false, average and true, respectively. When the rule of controlling fuzzy to arbitrate the learning rate is expressed with the form of *if ~ then*, it is as follows:

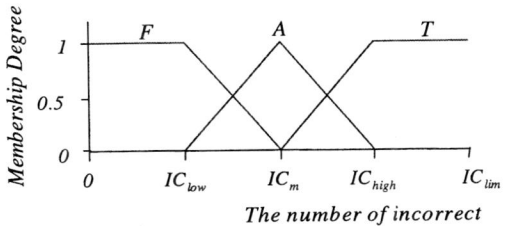

Fig. 2. The membership function to which the inaccuracy belongs

- R_1 : If correct is F, incorrect F Then α is B
- R_2 : If correct is F, incorrect A Then α is B
- R_3 : If correct is F, incorrect T Then α is B
- R_4 : If correct is A, incorrect F Then α is M
- R_5 : If correct is A, incorrect A Then α is M
- R_6 : If correct is A, incorrect T Then α is M
- R_7 : If correct is T, incorrect F Then α is S
- R_8 : If correct is T, incorrect A Then α is S
- R_9 : If correct is T, incorrect T Then α is S

Fig. 3 shows the output membership function calculating the learning rate, which is going to be applied to learning.

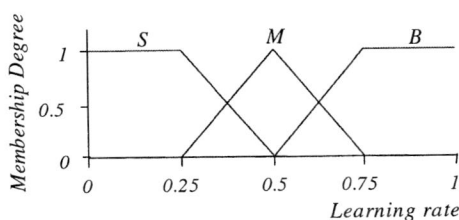

Fig. 3. The membership function of learning rate

In Fig. 3, S, M and B are the linguistic variables indicating small, medium and big, respectively. When accuracy and inaccuracy are decided as the input value of the fuzzy control system, membership degrees of accuracy and inaccuracy for each membership function are calculated. After the calculation of membership degree for each member function, the rule of fuzzy control is applied and the inference is accomplished by means of Max-Min inference procedure. Defuzzification of the gain output was achieved through the center-of-gravity computation [7]. Formula (18) shows the center of gravity, which is used for the defuzzification.

$$\alpha = -\frac{\sum \mu(y) \cdot y}{\sum y} \tag{18}$$

Momentum is calculated by formula (19).

$$\mu = \zeta - \alpha \tag{19}$$

where ζ is the parameter between 1.0 and 1.5, which is given empirically.

4 Experiments and Performance Evaluation

We implemented the enhanced RBF network proposed with C++ Builder 6.0 and executed the experiment for performance evaluation on IBM compatible PC in which Intel Pentium-IV CPU and 256MB RAM were mounted.

We analyzed the number of epoch and the convergence by applying 136's number patterns having 10×10 in size, which are extracted from the citizen registration cards, to the conventional delta-bar-delta method, the ART2-based RBF network and the learning algorithm proposed in this paper. Fig. 4 shows the patterns which were used for training. Table 1 shows target vectors.

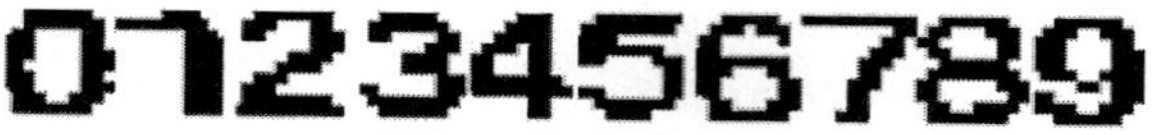

Fig. 4. Example of training patterns

Table 1. Target vectors which were used for training

	0	1	2	3	4	5	6	7	8	9
	0	0	0	0	0	0	0	0	1	1
Target value	0	0	0	0	1	1	1	1	0	0
	0	0	1	1	0	0	1	1	0	0
	0	1	0	1	0	1	0	1	0	1

Table 2 shows parameters of each algorithm which were used for the experiment and Table 3 shows the result of training.

In Table 2, α indicates the learning rate, ρ the vigilance parameter of ART2, ζ the parameter for calculation of momentum, and β, κ, γ parameters fixed by delta-bar-delta algorithm. The experiment have been executed 10 times under the criterion of classifying input pattern to the accuracy when the absolute value of the difference between the output vector of input pattern and the target vector is below $\varepsilon(\varepsilon \leq 0.1)$ in 10000's epoch executions. The fact that the proposed method is more enhanced than conventional methods in terms of learning speed and convergence is verified in Table 3. Moreover, the proposed method did not react sensitively to the number of learning and the convergence, whereas conventional methods did. Consequently, the proposed method had good convergence ability, and took less learning time than the Delta-bar-Delta method and ART2-based RBF network.

Table 2. Parameters which were used for training

Learning method / Parameter	α	ρ	ζ	β	κ	γ
Delta-bar-Delta	0.5			0.7	0.005	0.2
ART2-based RBF network	0.5	0.1				
Proposed method		0.1	1.0			

Table 3. Comparison of the convergence among each algorithm

Learning method / Result of Learning	# of experiment	# of success	# of average epoch
Delta-bar-delta	10	2	2793
ART2-based RBF network	10	10	2710
Proposed method	10	10	1464

Fig. 5 shows the graph for the change rate of TSS (Total Sum of Square) of error according to the number of epoch. As shown in Fig. 5, the proposed method has faster speed of primary convergence and smaller TSS of error than conventional methods.

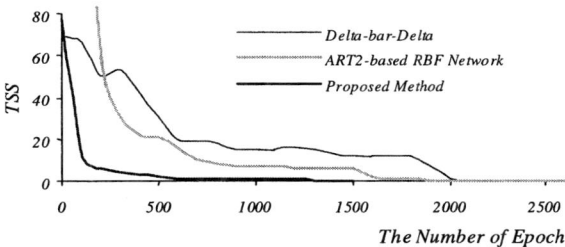

Fig. 5. Graph of total sum of square

Through experimental results, we found that the proposed method spent less time for training compared with the conventional training method, and had good convergence ability.

5 Conclusions

The learning of the ART2-based RBF network is divided to two stages. At the first stage the competitive learning is performed between input layer and middle layer, and at the second stage the supervised learning is performed between middle layer and output layer. An enhanced RBF network is proposed in this paper, which uses ART2 algorithm between input layer and middle layer to enhance the efficiency of learning of conventional ART2-based RBF network and applies the auto-tuning method of arbitrating learning rate and momentum automatically by means of the fuzzy control system to arbitrate the weight value efficiently between middle layer and output layer. In the proposed auto-tuning method of learning rate and momentum, when the absolute value of the difference between the output vector and the target vector for input pattern is below ε, input pattern is classified to the accuracy, and otherwise to the inaccuracy. Then, applying the numbers of the accuracy and the inaccuracy to the fuzzy control system, the learning rate is arbitrated dynamically. The momentum is arbitrated dynamically by using the adjusted learning rate, so that the efficiency of learning is enhanced.

The experiments of applying the proposed method to the classification of number patterns extracted from the citizen registration card shows 2 results related to performance: First, the proposed method did not react sensitively to the number of learning and the convergence, whereas conventional methods did, and second, the total sum of square has decreased remarkably than conventional methods. Therefore, the efficiency of learning in the proposed method is enhanced than conventional neural networks.

The study on the method generating the optimized middle layer by enhancing the efficiency of ART2 algorithm will be the subject of study in the future.

References

1. Watanabe M., Kuwata K., and Katayma R.: Adaptive Tree Structured Self Generating Radial Basis Function and its Application to Nonlinear Identification Problem. Proceedings of IIZUKA. (1994) 167-170
2. Lo J.: Multi-layer Perceptrons and Radial Basis Functions are Universal Robust Approximators. Proceedings of IJCNN. (**2**) (1998) 1311-1314
3. Panchapakesan C., Ralph D., and Palaniswami M.: Effects of Moving the Centers in an RBF Network. Proceedings of IJCNN. (**2**) (1998) 1256-1260
4. Jacobs R. A.: Increased rates of convergence through learning rate adaptation. IEEE Transactions on Neural Networks. **1(4)** (1988) 295-308
5. Pandya A. S., and Macy R. B.: Neural Networks for Pattern Recognition using C++. IEEE Press and CRC Press. (1995)
6. Kim K. B., Jang S. W., and Kim C. K.: Recognition of Car License Plate by Using Dynamical Thresholding Method and Enhanced Neural Networks. Lecture Notes in Computer Science. LNCS 2756. (2003) 309-319
7. Jamshidi M., Vadiee N., and Ross T. J.: Fuzzy Logic and Control. Prentice-Hall. (1993)

Solving Rotated Multi-objective Optimization Problems Using Differential Evolution

Antony W. Iorio and Xiaodong Li

School of Computer Science and Information Technology,
Royal Melbourne Institute of Technology University,
Melbourne, Vic. 3001, Australia
{iantony, xiaodong}@cs.rmit.edu.au
http://goanna.cs.rmit.edu.au/~xiaodong/ecml/

Abstract. This paper demonstrates that the self-adaptive technique of Differential Evolution (DE) can be simply used for solving a multi-objective optimization problem where parameters are interdependent. The real-coded crossover and mutation rates within the NSGA-II have been replaced with a simple Differential Evolution scheme, and results are reported on a rotated problem which has presented difficulties using existing Multi-objective Genetic Algorithms. The Differential Evolution variant of the NSGA-II has demonstrated rotational invariance and superior performance over the NSGA-II on this problem.

1 Introduction

Traditional genetic algorithms that use low mutation rates and fixed step sizes have significant trouble with problems with interdependent relationships between decision variables, but are perfectly suited to many of the test functions currently used in the evaluation of genetic algorithms [1]. These test functions are typically linearly separable and can be decomposed into simpler independent problems. Unfortunately, many real-world problems are not linearly separable, although linear approximations may sometimes be possible between decision variables.

Interdependencies between variables can be introduced into a real-coded functional problem by rotating the coordinate system of the test function. A rotated problem is not amenable to the directionless step-sizes and low mutation rates that Genetic Algorithms typically use. Although the NSGA-II is a very robust multi-objective optimization algorithm it suffers from the same limitations as traditional Genetic Algorithms on these problems.

Previous work has reported on the poor performance of a number of MOEAs, including the NSGA-II, on a rotated problem [2]. Rotated problems typically require correlated self-adapting mutation step sizes in order to make timely progress in optimization. In contrast, Differential Evolution has previously demonstrated rotationally invariant behaviour in the single objective domain [3]. This provides motivation to further demonstrate the worth of DE as a technique for addressing rotated multi-objective optimization problems. Our survey of the literature found that no work has explicitly demonstrated rotationally invariant behaviour in multi-objective problems, therefore we propose a simple alteration to the NSGA-II to make it rotationally invariant. The mutation and crossover operators within the NSGA-II have been replaced with a Differential Evolution algorithm for generating candidate solutions. Differential Evolution has all the desired properties necessary to handle complex problems with interdependencies between input parameters, without the implementation complexity and computation cost of some self-adaptive Evolutionary Strategies [3].

A number of experiments have been conducted on a uni-modal rotated problem from the literature [2]. We have found that integrating Differential Evolution within the NSGA-II achieves rotational invariance on this problem.

The following section provides a brief introduction to the important concepts of Multi-objective Optimization, Differential Evolution, and Rotated Problems. Section 3 discusses the proposed model the Non-dominated Sorting Differential Evolution (NSDE) which integrates Differential Evolution with the NSGA-II. Section 4 outlines the performance metrics used in this study. Section 5 describes the experiments that were conducted, followed by the parameter settings and discussion of results in Section 6 and 7. The outcomes of this work and some possible future directions are outlined in Section 8.

2 Background

2.1 Multi-objective Optimization

Multi-objective optimization deals with optimization problems which are formulated with some or possibly all of the objective functions in conflict with each other. Such problems can be formulated as a vector of objective functions $\mathbf{f}(\mathbf{x}) = (f_1(\mathbf{x}), f_2(\mathbf{x}), ..., f_n(\mathbf{x}))$ subject to a vector of input parameters $\mathbf{x} = (x_1, x_2, ..., x_m)$, where n is the number of objectives, and m is the number of parameters. A solution $\mathbf{x}$ dominates a solution $\mathbf{y}$ if objective function $f_i(\mathbf{x})$ is no worse than objective function $f_i(\mathbf{y})$ for all n objectives and there exists some objective j such that $f_j(\mathbf{x})$ is better than $f_j(\mathbf{y})$. The non-dominated solutions in a population are those solutions which are not dominated by any other individual in the population. Multiobjective evolutionary optimization is typically concerned with finding a diverse range of solutions close to the Pareto-optimal front, which is the globally non-dominated region of the objective space.

A number of evolutionary multiobjective algorithms have been developed since the late 80s, and the NSGA-II [2] is typically regarded as one of the best.

The criteria for evaluating the performance of a multiobjective evolutionary algorithm are different from those for assessing the performance of single objective algorithms. Generally, a multi-objective optimization produces a set of solutions. Therefore, we need to assess the final solution set in terms of uniform coverage of the Pareto-optimal front, closeness to the front, and spread across the front. In section 4 we will outline in more detail the performance metrics used in this study.

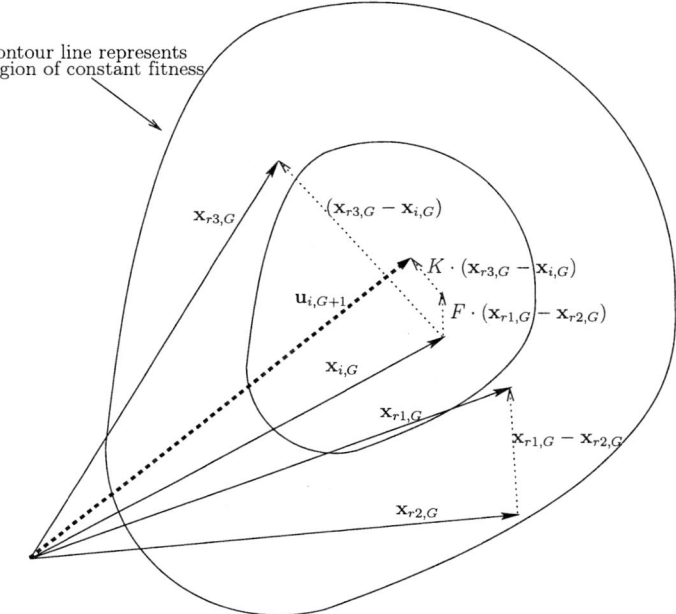

Fig. 1. The above figure shows the vector addition and subtraction necessary to generate a new candidate solution in *DE/current-to-rand/1*

2.2 Differential Evolution

Differential Evolution is a population-based direct-search algorithm for global optimization [4]. It has demonstrated its robustness and power in a variety of applications, such as neural network learning [5], IIR-filter design [6], and the optimization of aerodynamic shapes [7]. It has a number of important characteristics which make it attractive as a global optimization technique, and the reader is referred to [3] for an excellent introduction to DE which covers this in more detail. The primary property of Differential Evolution that will be the topic of study in this paper is rotational invariance.

Differential Evolution differs from other EAs in the mutation and recombination phase. Unlike stochastic techniques such as Genetic Algorithms and Evolutionary Strategies, where perturbation occurs in accordance with a random quantity, Differential Evolution uses weighted differences between solution vectors to perturb the population.

$$randomly\ select\ r_1, r_2, r_3 \in \{1, 2, ..., n\};\ r_1 \neq r_2 \neq r_3 \neq i \quad (1)$$
$$\mathbf{u}_{i,G+1} = \mathbf{x}_{i,G} + K \cdot (\mathbf{x}_{r3,G} - \mathbf{x}_{i,G}) + F \cdot (\mathbf{x}_{r1,G} - \mathbf{x}_{r2,G})$$

The Differential Evolution variant used in this work is known as *DE/current-to-rand/1* (Equation 1), and is rotationally invariant [3]. The population of a

Differential Evolutionary Algorithm is typically randomly initialised within the initial parameter bounds. At each generation G, the population undergoes perturbation. Three unique individuals, or solution vectors denoted by $\mathbf{x}$, are randomly selected from the population. The coefficient K is responsible for the level of combination that occurs between $\mathbf{x}_{r3,G}$ and the current individual $\mathbf{x}_{i,G}$. The coefficient F is responsible for scaling the step size resulting from the vector subtraction $\mathbf{x}_{r1,G} - \mathbf{x}_{r2,G}$. Figure 1 details the relationship between the vectors responsible for the generation of a new candidate solution. Typically in the single-objective case, if the new individual $\mathbf{u}_{i,G+1}$, evaluates better than the currently selected individual $\mathbf{x}_{i,G}$, then the current individual is replaced with the new one. The algorithm iterates over i from 1 to n, where n is the size of the population.

2.3 Multi-objective Differential Evolution

Differential Evolution has also been applied to multi-objective problems. One of the first examples of this was to tune a fuzzy controller for the automatic operation of a train, although the cost function transformed the objectives of punctuality, comfort, and energy usage into the degenerate case of a single objective [8]. The Pareto Differential Evolutionary Algorithm (PDE) uses non-dominated solutions for reproduction, and places offspring back into the population if they dominate the current parent [9, 10]. This PDE was also extended into a variant with self-adaptive crossover and mutation [11]. Multi-objective DE has also been applied to minimize the error and the number of hidden units in neural network training. The resulting Pareto-front is the tradeoff between these two objectives [12]. The non-dominated sorting, ranking, and elitism techniques utilised in the NSGA-II have also been incorporated into a Differential Evolution method [13]. Another approach involving Pareto-based evaluation has also been applied to an Enterprise Planning problem with the two objectives of cycle time and cost [14], and also compared with the Strength-Pareto Evolutionary Algorithm [15].

2.4 Rotated Problems

A function can be rotated through one or more planes in the parameter space, where the number of planes is determined by the dimensionality of the problem. A problem with D dimensions in the parameter space has $D(D-1)/2$ possible planes of rotation. A problem rotated through all possible parameter space planes means that every variable has interdependencies with every other.

In order to generate a rotated problem, each solution vector $\mathbf{x}$ is multiplied by a rotation matrix $\mathbf{M}$, and the result is assigned to $\mathbf{y}$ (Equation 2). The new vector is then evaluated on each of the objective functions.

Figure 2 demonstrates the effect of rotation on the multi-objective problem in Equation 2 with two input parameters. The shapes of the functions stay the same, but their orientations change.

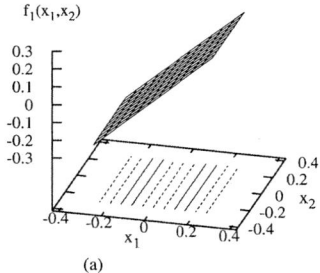
(a)

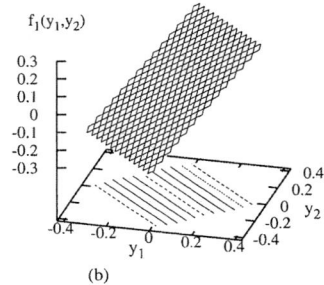
(b)

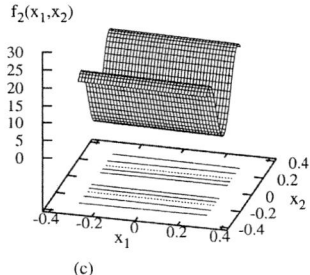
(c)

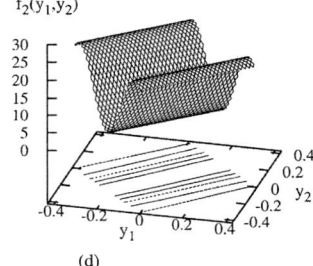
(d)

Fig. 2. The above figure shows the effect of a 45-degree rotation on the x_1x_2 plane on function f_1 and f_2. Before rotation, the functions are aligned with the coordinate system ((a) and (c)), and after rotation they are not ((b) and (d))

$$\text{minimize} \quad f_1(\mathbf{y}) = y_1 \text{ and } f_2(\mathbf{y}) = g(\mathbf{y})exp(-y_1/g(\mathbf{y}))$$
$$\text{where} \quad g(\mathbf{y}) = 1 + 10(D-1) + \sum_{i=2}^{D} \left[y_i^2 - 10\cos(4\pi y_i)\right] \quad (2)$$
$$\text{and} \quad \mathbf{y} = \mathbf{Mx}, \; -0.3 \leq x_i \leq 0.3, \; for \; i = 1, 2, ..., D.$$

It is apparent from the contour plots in Figure 2 that before rotation the functions are aligned with the coordinate system. In which case, it is possible to make progress in the search by perturbing the parameters x_1 and x_2 independently. With rotated problems, significant progress in the search can only proceed by making simultaneous progress across all parameters within a solution vector. Consider Figure 3, where the elliptical contour represents a region of constant fitness. The point $\mathbf{v}$ can be perturbed along both the x_1 and x_2 axes, and any location along the dashed line will be an improvement over any point along the contour, assuming that the global optimum is centered on the coordinate axis. After rotation, progress from perturbing the same rotated point $\mathbf{v}'$ will be lower. This is because the interval of potential improvement for each of the decision variables is reduced, meaning that the search will progress more slowly when the parameters are only perturbed independently of each other. Another aspect

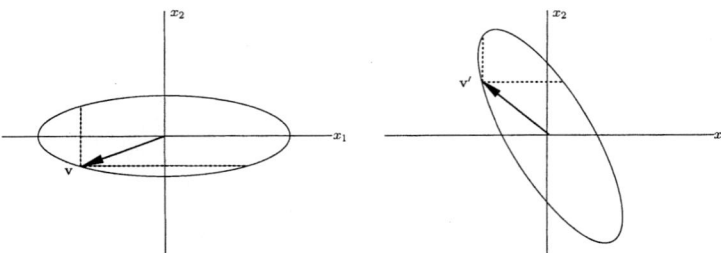

Fig. 3. The above figure demonstrates how rotation can reduce the interval of possible improvement. When the function is aligned with the coordinate axes, the improvement interval (dashed line) is larger than when the function is rotated away from the coordinate axes. The ellipse represents the region of constant fitness. Vector **v** and **v'** represent the same point in the search space before and after rotation respectively

of rotated problems is that points can easily be trapped along a valley line in the search space and can only make progress with simultaneous improvements over all input parameters (Figure 4). The point **v** can easily be perturbed in the x_1 axis to find the global minimum in the center of the coordinate system. The same point **v'** after rotation is still on the valley, but now it can not progress to a point of improved fitness by only moving along the direction of the coordinate axes (dashed line) because any such perturbation will be to a point of lower fitness in the search space. Typically the valley can be found easily, but the search often becomes trapped at this location. Only a simulatenous improvement in all parameters will result in the discovery of fitter solutions. On these types of problems, the small mutation rates frequently used in Genetic Algorithms are known to be even less efficient than a random search [1]. Self-adaptation has been relatively successful at solving this sort of problem using Evolutionary Strategies, but it requires the learning of appropriate correlated mutation step sizes and

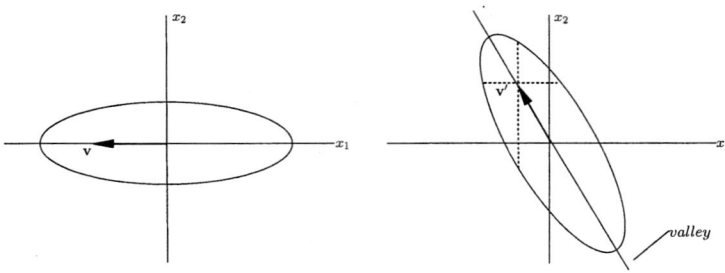

Fig. 4. The above figure demonstrates how rotation can trap points along the valley. If the point **v'** moves anywhere along the dashed lines it will be towards a point in the parameter space of lower fitness. Vector **v** and **v'** represent the same point in the search space before and after rotation respectively

it can be rather computationally expensive when D becomes large [3]. Differential Evolution is an attractive solution to this problem because of its ability to adapt to the fitness landscape through the correlation of mutation step sizes by sampling multiple times the difference between randomly selected solution vectors.

3 NSDE: A Simple Modification to the NSGA-II

The NSGA-II algorithm uses elitism and a diversity preserving mechanism. N offspring are created from a parent population of size N. The combined population of size $2N$ is sorted into separate non-domination levels. Individuals are selected from this combined population to be inserted into the new population, based on their non-domination level. If there are more individuals in the last front than there are slots remaining in the new population of size N, a diversity preserving mechanism is used. Individuals from this last front are placed in the new population based on their contribution to diversity in the population. The algorithm then iterates until some termination condition is met. The NSGA-II uses a real-coded crossover and mutation operator but in the multi-objective implementation of *DE/current-to-rand/1*, NSDE (Non-dominated Sorting Differential Evolution), these mutation and recombination operators were not used, and were replaced with Differential Evolution. In the single objective implementation of the Differential Evolution, if the new candidate $u_{i,G+1}$ evaluates better than the current individual $x_{i,G}$, the current individual is replaced with the new individual. In the multi-objective implementation this is not possible because we do not know which individual is better until all candidates are sorted together and assigned to a non-domination level. Therefore, $u_{i,G+1}$ is first added to the new candidate offspring population. New candidates are generated using *DE/current-to-rand/1* until the candidate offspring population is filled up to size N. The new individuals are then evaluated on the objective functions, and then subjected to the combined non-dominated sorting described above. For further details regarding the implementation of the NSGA-II, the reader is referred to [2].

4 Performance Metrics

A number of performance metrics have been proposed for the purposes of comparing multiobjective optimization algorithms [16]. An analysis of different performance assessment techniques is provided in [17].

We use the following performance metrics introduced by Zitzler [18]. These metrics are frequently employed in the literature and we use them here to facilitate the comparison of the results with others. Secondly, they do not attempt to combine coverage, convergence or spread measures into a scalar, but provide these measures as distinct results. This assists any evaluation of the algorithms in relation to these measures. The * designates we have used the objective space variant of these metrics only. Because metrics alone are probably insufficient to assess the performance of a multiobjective optimization algorithm [16], we have also provided plots of the non-dominated solutions (Figure 5).

$$\mathcal{M}_1^*(Y') := \frac{1}{|Y'|} \sum_{p' \in Y'} \min\{||\mathbf{p}' - \bar{\mathbf{p}}||^*; \bar{\mathbf{p}} \in \bar{\mathbf{Y}}\} \qquad (3)$$

$$\mathcal{M}_2^*(Y') := \frac{1}{|Y' - 1|} \sum_{p' \in Y'} |\{\mathbf{q}' \in \mathbf{Y}'; ||\mathbf{p}' - \mathbf{q}'||^* > \sigma^*\}| \qquad (4)$$

$$\mathcal{M}_3^*(Y') := \sqrt{\sum_{i=1}^n \max\{||\mathbf{p}_i' - \mathbf{q}_i'||^*; \mathbf{p}', \mathbf{q}' \in \mathbf{Y}'\}} \qquad (5)$$

Y' is the set of objective vectors corresponding to the non-dominated solutions found, and $\bar{Y}$ is a set of uniform Pareto-optimal objective vectors. $\mathcal{M}_1^*(Y')$ provides a measure of convergence to the Pareto-optimal front by giving the average distance from Y' to $\bar{Y}$. The smaller the value of $\mathcal{M}_1^*(Y')$ the better, as the distance between Y' to $\bar{Y}$ should be minimised. This metric is useful when the true Pareto-front is known, although other metrics for measuring convergence to the front are appropriate when this is not the case [16].

$\mathcal{M}_2^*(Y')$ describes how well the solutions in Y' cover the front. $\mathcal{M}_2^*(Y')$ should produce a value between $[0, |Y'|]$ as it estimates the number of niches in Y' based on the niche neighbourhood size of σ^*. A niche neighbourhood size, $\sigma^* > 0$, is used in Equation 4 to calculate the distribution of the non-dominated solutions. Objective vectors outside the niche range are counted for each objective vector p' in Y'. The higher the value for $\mathcal{M}_2^*(Y')$ the better the coverage is across the front, according to σ^*.

$\mathcal{M}_3^*(Y')$ measures the spread of Y', which provides an indication of how well the search has spread to the extremes of the Pareto-optimal front. Large values of $\mathcal{M}_3^*(Y')$ are desired.

None of these metrics can be considered individually. For example, a good convergence of the population towards the Pareto-front may also have a poor coverage across the front, or vice versa.

5 Experiments

Experiments were conducted on the rotated problem described in section 2.4. The dimensionality of the parameter space was 10, resulting in 45 possible planes of rotation. Rotations were performed on each plane, introducing non-linear dependencies between all parameters. In order to demonstrate the rotational invariance of the NSDE on the problem, we performed experiments with 0 degrees of rotation (no parameter interactions) up to 45 degrees of rotation, at 5 degree intervals. Each experiment was run 30 times, for a total of 800 generations (80,000 evaluations) for each run. For comparative purposes the same experiments were performed with the NSGA-II as well. Results are presented in Figure 5, and Table 1.

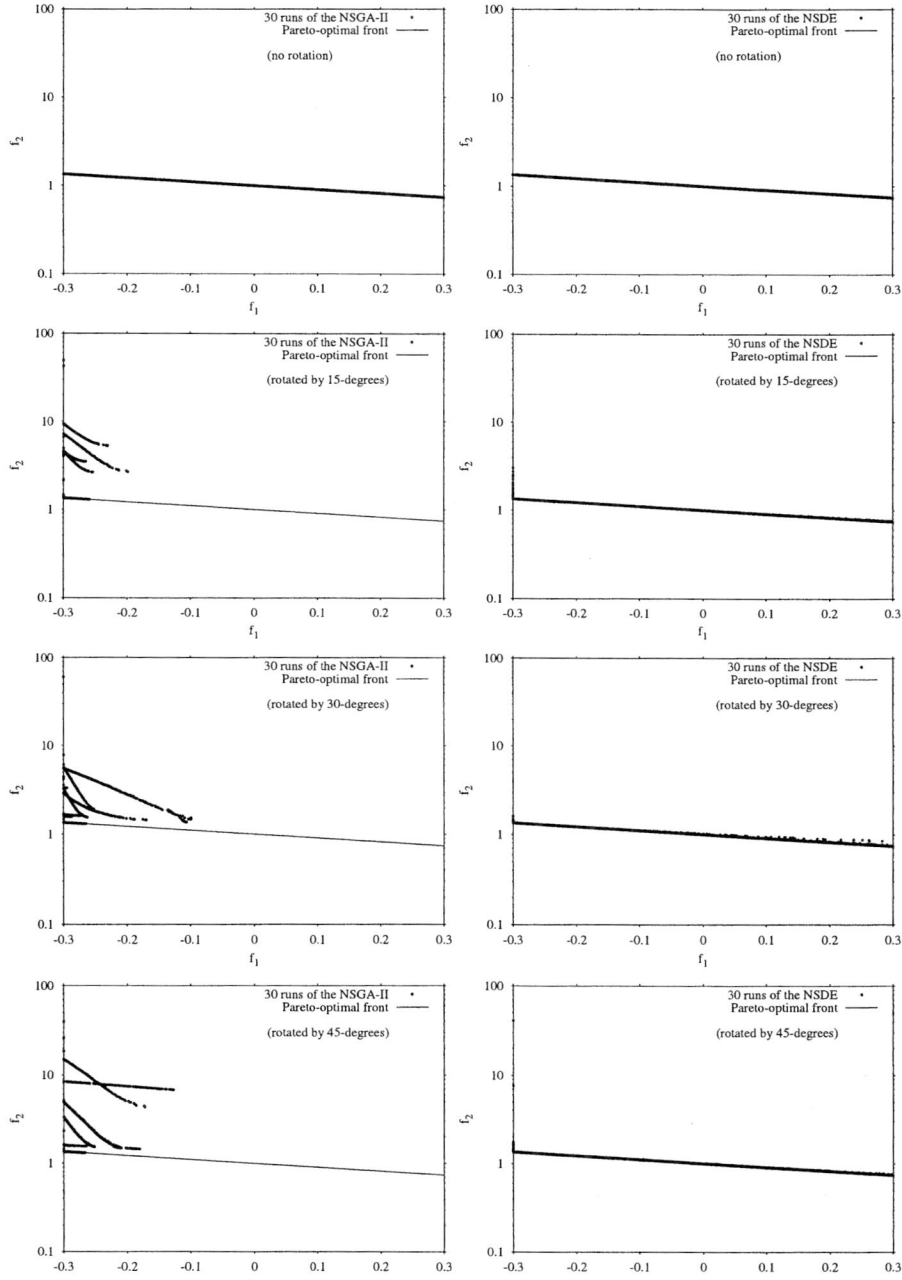

Fig. 5. Each of the left and right plots respectively show 30 runs of the NSGA-II and the NSDE algorithm on the rotated problem, with successively increasing degrees of rotation on all planes

Table 1. $\mathcal{M}_1^*$, $\mathcal{M}_2^*$, $\mathcal{M}_3^*$, and the number of evaluations (averaged over 30 runs). R_d represents the rotated problem where d is the degree of rotation on each plane

Metric	Algorithm	R_0	R_5	R_{10}	R_{15}	R_{20}
$\mathcal{M}_1^*$	NSGA-II	6.26E-04 ±7.55E-05	2.42E-02 ±9.31E-02	1.49E+00 ±3.07E+00	1.14E+00 ±1.62E+00	3.49E-01 ±6.85E-01
	NSDE	2.22E-03 ±1.97E-04	3.76E-03 ±5.22E-03	5.60E-03 ±1.18E-02	2.95E-01 ±7.51E-01	1.10E-01 ±4.16E-01
$\mathcal{M}_2^*$	NSGA-II	9.86E+01 ±7.00E-02	8.56E+01 ±2.46E+00	6.87E+01 ±2.42E+01	5.35E+01 ±2.35E+01	6.41E+01 ±1.98E+01
	NSDE	9.85E+01 ±5.49E-02	9.85E+01 ±1.28E-01	9.85E+01 ±2.14E-01	9.86E+01 ±2.22E-01	9.85E+01 ±4.68E-01
$\mathcal{M}_3^*$	NSGA-II	1.10E+00 ±5.48E-06	5.44E-01 ±3.33E-01	6.47E-01 ±7.94E-01	5.37E-01 ±6.27E-01	8.66E-01 ±1.52E+00
	NSDE	1.10E+00 ±7.48E-04	1.10E+00 ±1.79E-02	1.11E+00 ±3.68E-02	1.12E+00 ±8.01E-02	1.17E+00 ±3.56E-01

Metric	Algorithm	R_{25}	R_{30}	R_{35}	R_{40}	R_{45}
$\mathcal{M}_1^*$	NSGA-II	3.71E-01 ±5.47E-01	5.18E-01 ±7.91E-01	8.97E-01 ±2.08E+00	8.17E-01 ±1.79E+00	1.01E+00 ±1.87E+00
	NSDE	2.36E-03 ±4.41E-19	1.38E+00 ±1.07E+00	3.86E-03 ±5.06E-03	2.29E-02 ±6.26E-02	5.82E-01 ±9.78E-01
$\mathcal{M}_2^*$	NSGA-II	6.94E+01 ±2.66E+01	5.22E+01 ±3.61E+01	5.24E+01 ±3.42E+01	4.60E+01 ±3.39E+01	5.11E+01 ±3.75E+01
	NSDE	9.86E+01 ±5.22E-01	9.85E+01 ±1.19E-01	9.85E+01 ±3.13E-01	9.83E+01 ±1.36E+00	9.86E+01 ±2.00E-01
$\mathcal{M}_3^*$	NSGA-II	9.34E-01 ±1.22E+00	8.39E-01 ±1.47E+00	5.61E-01 ±9.51E-01	7.95E-01 ±1.75E+00	1.43E+00 ±2.32E+00
	NSDE	1.32E+00 ±5.81E-01	1.10E+00 ±3.14E-02	1.09E+00 ±5.03E-02	1.11E+00 ±1.50E-01	1.28E+00 ±9.62E-01

6 Parameter Settings

A population size of 100 was used for both the NSDE and the NSGA-II. A crossover rate of 0.9 and mutation rate of 0.1 were used with the NSGA-II. η_c and η_m are parameters within the NSGA-II which control the distribution of the crossover and mutation probabilities and were assigned values of 10 and 50 respectively. The choice of the NSGA-II parameters is the same as the parameter values previously used on this rotated problem in other work [2]. For the NSDE, F was set to 0.8 and K was set to 0.4. Suggestions from the literature helped guide our choice of parameter values for the NSDE [3]. The niche neighbourhood size σ^* described in section 4, for the metric $\mathcal{M}_2^*(Y')$, was set to 0.01.

7 Results and Discussion

From Table 1 it is apparent that the NSDE maintains a significantly better convergence ($\mathcal{M}_1^*$), coverage ($\mathcal{M}_2^*$), and spread ($\mathcal{M}_3^*$) than the NSGA-II. Figure 5 contains plots of 30 runs of the final non-dominated set after 80,000 evaluations. These figures further demonstrate that the NSDE consistently converged closely to the Pareto-optimal front, independently of the degree of rotation.

The only difference between the NSDE and the NSGA-II is in the method of generating new individuals. NSDE uses the step sizes of Differential Evolution which are adaptively adjusted to the fitness landscape. In contrast, the NSGA-II uses real-coded crossover and mutation operators. It is obvious that the cause of the poor performance by the NSGA-II on the rotated problem is because the perturbation of variables through mutation and crossover is not correlated. We have demonstrated that Differential Evolution can provide rotationally invariant behaviour on a multi-objective optimization problem, and we expect this should be true for other rotated problems as well. It is significant that such striking results were obtained from such a simple variation of the NSGA-II.

8 Conclusion

Outside of Evolutionary Strategies, Differential Evolution is currently one of a few techniques for solving multi-objective optimization problems with interdependencies between variables. The striking results on the single test problem we have investigated in this preliminary study suggest that further work is worthwhile. Currently we are investigating a number of even harder rotated problems, incorporating some of the features of existing test functions, such as multi-modality, non-uniformity, and discontinuities.

References

1. Salomon, R.: Re-evaluating Genetic Algorithm Performance Under Coordinate Rotation of Benchmark Functions: A Survey of Some Theoretical and Practical Aspects of Genetic Algorithms. In: Bio Systems, Vol. 39, No. 3. (1996) 263–278
2. Deb, K., Pratap, A., Agarwal, S., Meyarivan, T.: A Fast and Elitist Multiobjective Genetic Algorithm: NSGA-II, In: IEEE Trans. Evol. Comput., Vol. 6, No. 2. (2002) 182–197
3. Price, K V.: An Introduction to Differential Evolution. In: Corne, D., Dorigo, M., and Glover, F. (eds.): New Ideas in Optimization. McGraw-Hill, London (UK) (1999) 79–108
4. Price, K. V.: Differential evolution: a fast and simple numerical optimizer. In: Smith, M., Lee, M., Keller, J., Yen., J. (eds.): Biennial Conference of the North American Fuzzy Information Processing Society, NAFIPS. IEEE Press, New York (1996) 524–527
5. Ilonen, J., Kamarainen, J.-K., Lampinen, J.: Differential Evolution Training Algorithm for Feed-Forward Neural Networks. In: Neural Processing Letters Vol. 7, No. 1 (2003) 93-105
6. Storn, R.: Differential evolution design of an IIR-filter. In: Proceedings of IEEE International Conference on Evolutionary Computation ICEC'96. IEEE Press, New York (1996) 268-273

7. Rogalsky, T., Derksen, R.W. and Kocabiyik, S.: Differential Evolution in Aerodynamic Optimization. In: Proceedings of the 46th Annual Conference of the Canadian Aeronautics and Space Institute. (1999) 29–36
8. Chang, C. S. and Xu, D. Y.: Differential Evolution of Fuzzy Automatic Train Operation for Mass Rapid Transit System. In: IEEE Proceedings of Electric Power Applications Vol. 147, No. 3 (2000) 206-212
9. Abbass, H. A., Sarker, R. and Newton, C.: PDE: A Pareto-frontier Differential Evolution Approach for Multi-objective Optimization Problems. In: Proceedings of the 2001 Congress on Evolutionary Computation (CEC'2001) Vol. 2 (2001) 971-978
10. Abbass, H. A. and Sarker, R.: The Pareto Differential Evolution Algorithm. In: International Journal on Artificial Intelligence Tools Vol. 11, No. 4 (2002) 531-552
11. Abbass, H. A.: The Self-Adaptive Pareto Differential Evolution Algorithm. In: Proceedings of the 2002 Congress on Evolutionary Computation (CEC'2002) Vol. 1, IEEE Press, (2002) 831-836
12. Abbass, H. A.: A Memetic Pareto Evolutionary Approach to Artificial Neural Networks. In: Proceedings of the Australian Joint Conference on Artificial Intelligence, Adelaide, Australia, Lecture Notes in Artificial Intelligence Vol. 2256, Springer-Verlag, (2001) 1-12
13. Madavan, N. K.: Multiobjective Optimization Using a Pareto Differential Evolution Approach. In: Proceedings of the 2002 Congress on Evolutionary Computation (CEC'2002) Vol. 2, IEEE Press, (2002) 1145-1150
14. Xue, F.: Multi-Objective Differential Evolution and its Application to Enterprise Planning. In: Proceedings of the 2003 IEEE International Conference on Robotics and Automation (ICRA'03) Vol. 3, IEEE Press, (2003) 3535-3541
15. Xue, F., Sanderson, A. C. and Graves, R. J.: Pareto-based Multi-objective Differential Evolution. In: Proceedings of the 2003 Congress on Evolutionary Computation (CEC'2003) Vol. 2, IEEE Press, (2003) 862-869
16. Okabe, T., Jin, Y. and Sendhoff B.: A Critical Survey of Performance Indicies for Multi-Objective Optimisation. In: Proceedings of the 2003 Congress on Evolutionary Computation (CEC'2003) Vol. 2, IEEE Press, (2003) 878-885
17. Zitzler, E., Thiele, L., Laumanns, M., Fonseca, C. M., Fonseca, V. G.: Performance Assessment of Multiobjective Optimizers: An Analysis and Review. In: IEEE Trans. Evol. Comput., Vol. 2, No. 2. (2003) 117–132
18. Zitzler, E., Deb, K. and Thiele, L.: Comparison of multiobjective evolutionary algorithms: Empirical results. *Evolutionary Computation*, 8(2):173-195, April (2000).

Sub-structural Niching in Non-stationary Environments

†Kumara Sastry, ‡Hussein A. Abbass, and †David Goldberg

†Illinois Genetic Algorithms Laboratory, University of Illinois, 117, Transportation Building, 104, S. Mathews Av. Urbana, IL 61801
{kumara, deg}@illigal.ge.uiuc.edu
‡Artificial Life and Adaptive Robotics Laboratory (ALAR), School of Information Technology and Electrical Engineering, University of New South Wales, Australian Defence Force Academy, Canberra, ACT 2600, Australia
h.abbass@adfa.edu.au

Abstract. Niching enables a *genetic algorithm* (GA) to maintain diversity in a population. It is particularly useful when the problem has multiple optima where the aim is to find all or as many as possible of these optima. When the fitness landscape of a problem changes overtime, the problem is called non–stationary, dynamic or time–variant problem. In these problems, niching can maintain useful solutions to respond quickly, reliably and accurately to a change in the environment. In this paper, we present a niching method that works on the problem substructures rather than the whole solution, therefore it has less space complexity than previously known niching mechanisms. We show that the method is responding accurately when environmental changes occur.

1 Introduction

The systematic design of genetic operators and parameters is a challenging task in the literature. Goldberg [14] used Holland's [21] notion of building blocks to propose a design–decomposition theory for designing effective *genetic algorithms* (GAs). This theory is based on the correct identification of substructures in a problem to ensure scalability and efficient problem solving. The theory establishes the principles for effective supply, exchange and manipulation of sub–structures to ensure that a GA will solve problems quickly, reliably, and accurately. These types of GAs are called *competent* GAs to emphasize their robust behavior for many problems.

A wide range of literature exists for competent GAs. This literature encompasses three broad categories based on the mechanism used to unfold the substructures in a problem. The first category is Perturbation techniques which work by effective permutation of the genes in such a way that those belonging to the same substructure are closer to each other. Methods fall in this category include the messy GAs [16], fast messy GAs [15], gene expression messy GAs [22], linkage identification by nonlinearity check GA, linkage identification by monotonicity detection GA [27], dependency structure matrix driven GA [34], and linkage identification by limited probing [20].

The second category is linkage adaptation techniques, where promoters are used to enable genes to move across the chromosome; therefore facilitating the emergence of genes' linkages as in [7]. The third category is probabilistic model building techniques, where a probabilistic model is used to approximate the dependency between genes. Models in this category include population-based incremental learning [3], the bivariate marginal distribution algorithm [29], the extended compact GA (ecGA) [19], iterated distribution estimation algorithm [5], and the Bayesian optimization algorithm (BOA) [28].

When the fitness landscape of a problem changes overtime, the problem is called non–stationary, dynamic or time–variant problem. To date, there have been three main evolutionary approaches to solve optimization problems in changing environments. These approaches are: (1) diversity control either by increasing diversity when a change occurs as in the hyper–mutation method [8], the variable local search technique [33] and others [4, 23]; or maintaining high diversity as in redundancy [17, 9, 10], random immigrants [18], aging [12], and the thermodynamical GAs [26]; (2) memory-based approaches by using either implicit [17] or explicit [25] memory; and (3) speciation and multi–populations as in the self-organizing-scouts method [6].

Niching is a diversity mechanism that is capable of maintaining multiple optima simultaneously. The early study of Goldberg, Deb and Horn [13] demonstrated the use of niching for massive multimodality and deception. Mahfoud [24] conducted a detailed study of niching in stationary (static) environments. Despite that many of the studies found niching particularly useful for maintaining all the global optima of a problem, when the number of global optima grows, the number of niches can grow exponentially.

In this paper, we propose a niching mechanism that is based on the automatic identification and maintaining sub–structures in non–stationary problems. We incorporate bounded changes to both the problem structure and the fitness landscape. It should be noted that if the environment changes either unboundedly or randomly, on average no method will outperform restarting the solver from scratch every time a change occurs. We use a dynamic version of the *extended compact genetic algorithm* (ecGA) [19], called the *dynamic compact genetic algorithm* (dcGA) [1]. We show that the proposed method can respond quickly, reliably, and accurately to changes in the environment. The structure of the paper is as follows: in the next section, we will present dcGA and niching, then a feasibility study to test niching is undertaken followed by experiments and discussions.

2   Dynamic Compact Genetic Algorithm (dcGA)

Harik [19] proposed a conjecture that linkage learning is equivalent to a good model that learns the structure underlying a set of genotypes. He focused on probabilistic models to learn linkage and proposed the ecGA method using the *minimum description length* (MDL) principle [30] to compress good genotypes into partitions of the shortest possible representations. The MDL measure is a tradeoff between the information contents of a population, called compressed population complexity (CPC), and the size of the model, called model complexity (MC).

The CPC measure is based on Shannon's entropy [31], $E(\chi_I)$, of the population where each partition of variables χ_I is a random variable with probability p_i. The measure is given by

$$E(\chi_I) = -C\sum_i^\sigma p_i \log p_i \qquad (1)$$

where C is a constant related to the base chosen to express the logarithm and σ is the number of all possible bit sequences for the variables belonging to partition χ_I; that is, if the cardinality of χ_I is ν_I, $\sigma = 2^{\nu_I}$. This measures the amount of disorder associated within a population under a decomposition scheme. The MDL measure is the sum of CPC and MC as follows

$$\text{MDL} = N\sum_I \left(-C\sum_i^\sigma p_i \log p_i\right) + \log(N)2^{\nu_I} \qquad (2)$$

With the first term measures CPC while the second term measures MC.

In this paper, we assume that we have a mechanism to detect the change in the environment. Detecting a change in the environment can be done in several ways including: (1) re–evaluating a number of previous solutions; and (2) monitoring statistical measures such as the average fitness of the population [6]. The focus of this paper is not, however, on how to detect a change in the environment; therefore, we assume that we can simply detect it. The *dynamic compact genetic algorithm* (dcGA) works as follows:

1. Initialize the population at random with n individuals;
2. If a change in the environment is being detected, do:
   (a) Re–initialize the population at random with n individuals;
   (b) Evaluate all individuals in the population;
   (c) Use tournament selection with replacement to select n individuals;
   (d) Use the last found partition to shuffle the building blocks (building block–wise crossover) to generate a new population of n individuals;
3. Evaluate all individuals in the population;
4. Use tournament selection with replacement to select n individuals;
5. Use the MDL measure to recursively partition the variables until the measure increases;
6. Use the partition to shuffle the building blocks (building block–wise crossover) to generate a new population of n individuals;
7. If the termination condition is not satisfied, go to 2; otherwise stop.

Once a change is detected, a new population is generated at random then the last learnt model is used to bias the re–start mechanism using selection and crossover. The method then continues with the new population. In ecGA, the model is re-built from scratch in every generation. This has the advantage of recovering from possible problems that may exist from the use of a hill–climber in learning the model.

In the original ecGA and dcGA, the probabilities are estimated using the frequencies of the bits after selection. The motivation is that, after selection, the population contains only those solutions which are good enough to survive the selection process. Therefore, approximating the model on the selected individuals inherently utilizes fitness information. However, if explicit fitness information is used, problems may arise from the magnitude of these fitness values or the scaling method.

Traditional niching algorithms work on the level of the individual. For example, re-scaling the fitness of individuals based on some similarity measures. These types of niching require the niche radius, which defines the threshold beyond which individuals are dissimilar. The results of a niching method are normally sensitive to the niche radius. A smaller niche radius would increase the number of niches in the problem and is more suitable when multiple optima are located closer to each other, while a larger niche radius would reduce the number of niches but will miss out some optima if the optima are close to each other. Overall, finding a reasonable value for the niche radius is a challenging task.

When looking at ecGA, for example, the variables in the model are decomposed into subsets with each subset represents variables that are tight together. In a problem with m building blocks and n global optima within each building block, the number of global optima for the problem is n^m. This is an exponentially large number and it will require an exponentially large number of niches. However, since the problem is decomposable, one can maintain the niches within each building block separately. Therefore, we will need only $n \times m$ niches. Obviously, we do not know in advance if the problem is decomposable or not; that is the power of ecGA and similar models. If the problem is decomposable, it will find the decomposition, we can identify the niches on the level of the sub–structures, and we save unnecessary niches. If the problem is not decomposable, the model will return a single partition, the niches will be identified on the overall solution, and we are back to the normal case. ecGA learns the decomposition in an adaptive manner, therefore, the niches will also be learnt adaptively.

We propose two types of niches in dcGA for dynamic environments. We will call them Schem1 and Schem2 respectively. For each sub-structure (partition), the average fitness of each schema s is calculated for partition χ_I as follows:

$$\text{Fit}(s \in \chi_I) = \frac{\sum_i^p \grave{f}_{is}}{\sigma} \quad (3)$$

$$\grave{f}_{is} = \begin{cases} \grave{f}it_i & if \ i \mapsto s \\ 0 & otherwise \end{cases} \quad (4)$$

where, fit_i is the fitness value of individual i, $\grave{f}_{is}$ is the fitness value of individual i if the schema s is part of i and 0 otherwise. The schema fitness is calculated in Schem1 using the previous equation. In Schem2, the schema fitness is set to zero if its original value is less than the average population fitness. In theory, it is good to maintain all schemas in the population. In practice, however, maintaining all schemas will disturb the convergence of the probabilistic model. In addition, due to selection, some below average schemas will disappear overtime. Therefore, the choice will largely depend on the problem in hand. The dcGA algorithm is modified into Schem1 and Schem2 by calculating the probabilities for sampling each schema based on the schema fitness rather than the frequencies alone. This re–scaling maintains schemas when their frequencies is small but their average fitness is high.

3 Feasibility of the Method

Before we proceed with the experiments in the non–stationary environment, we need to check the performance of the method on a stationary function. The function we use here is trap–4. Trap functions were introduced by Ackley [2] and subsequently analyzed in details by others [11, 14, 32]. A trap function is defined as follows

$$trap_k = \begin{cases} high & \text{if } u = k \\ low - u * \frac{low}{k-1} & otherwise \end{cases} \quad (5)$$

where, low and $high$ are scalars, u is the number of 1's in the string, and k is the order of the trap function.

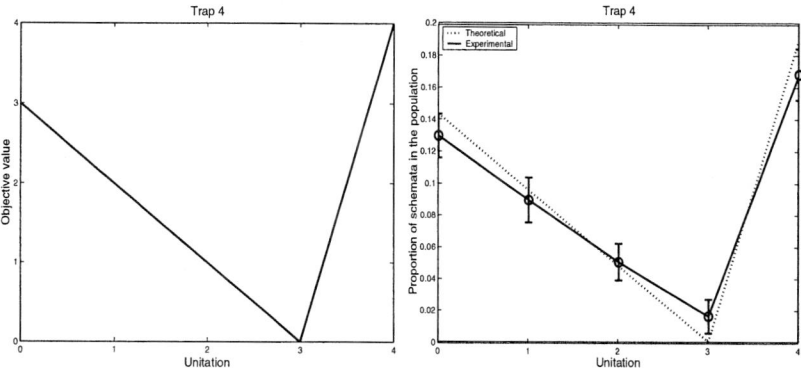

Fig. 1. On left, trap–4. On right, theoretical and experimental fitness sample

Figure 1–left depicts the trap–4 function we use in this experiment. The first key question in these experiments is whether or not during the first generation of niching, the niching method correctly samples the actual fitness function. We define a unitation as a function which counts the number of 1's in a chromosome. Given an order k trap, the theoretical proportion of a schema s with a unitation of i is calculated as follows:

$$p(s = i) = \frac{C(k, i) \times f(s = i)}{\sum_{j=0}^{k} C(k, j) \times f(s = j)} \quad (6)$$

Figure 1–right depicts the theoretical and experimental proportion of the schemas, where it is clear that the building blocks exist in proportion to their schema fitness.

Once we ensure that the building block exists in proportion to their fitness, the second question to answer is whether the niching method we propose is sufficient to maintain the relative proportion of the different schemas correctly. Figure 2 confirms this behavior, where one can see that the niching method was able to maintain the relative proportion of the different schemas.

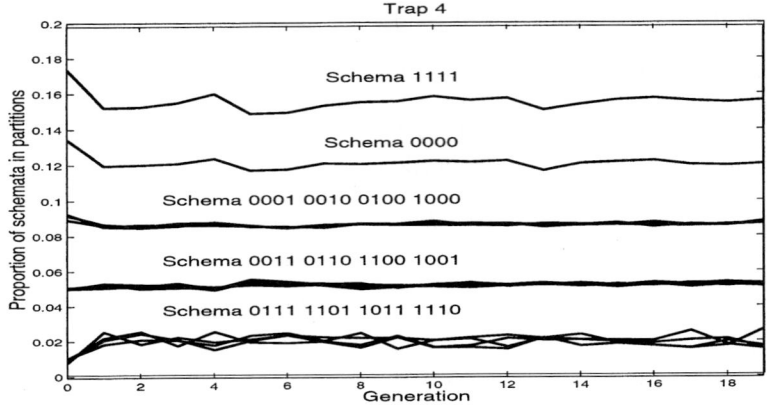

Fig. 2. The modified trap function 4 in a changing environment

We can conclude from the previous experiment that the niching method is successful in maintaining the schemas. These results do not require any additional experiments in a changing environment where the environment switches between the already maintained schemas. For example, if the environment is switching between schema 0000 and schema 1111 as the global optima, the previous results is sufficient to guarantee the best performance in a changing environment. One of the main reason for that is the environment is only manipulating the good schemas. However, what will happen if the bad schemas become the good ones and the environment is reversing the definition of a good and bad schemas. We already know that the maintenance of all schemas will slow down the convergence and because of selection pressures, below average schemas will eventually disappear. Therefore, we construct our experimental setup in a changing environment problem with two challenging problems for niching. The first problem alters the definition of above and below average schemas, while the second problem manipulates the boundaries of the building blocks (switching between two values of k).

4 Experiments

We repeated each experiment 30 times with different seeds. All results are presented for the average performance over the 30 runs. The population size is chosen large enough to provide enough samples for the probabilistic model to learn the structure and is fixed to 5000 in all experiments. Termination occurs when the algorithm reaches the maximum number of generations of 100. We assume that the environment changes between generations and the changes in the environment are assumed to be cyclic, where we tested two cycles of length 5 and 10 generations respectively. The crossover probability is 1, and the tournament size is 16 in all experiments based on Harik's default values.

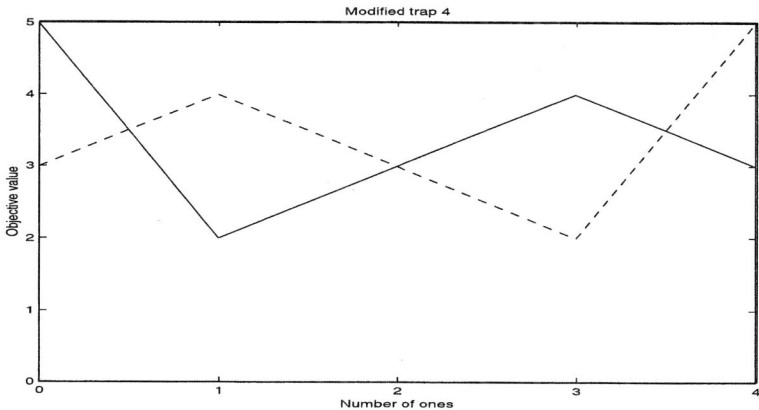

Fig. 3. The modified trap function 4 in a changing environment

4.1 Experiment 1

In the initial set of experiments, we modified the trap function of order 4 to break the symmetry in the attractors. In this section, we choose $low = k$, $high = k+1$. Symmetry can be utilized by a solver to easily track optima. The new function is visualized in Figure 3. At time 0 and in even cycles, the optimal solution is when all variables are set to 0's and the second attractor is when the sum of 1's is equal to 3. When the environment changes during the odd cycles, the new solution is optimal when all variables are set to 1's and the new deceptive attractor is when the sum of 1's is 1 or alternatively the number of 0's is 3.

Figure 4 depicts the behavior of the three methods using the modified trap–4 function. By looking at the results for dcGA, the response rate (*i.e.* the time between a change and reaching the new optimal solution) is almost at the edge of 5 for 20 building blocks. This means that the algorithm requires on average 5 generations to get close to the new optimal. By looking at the cycle of length 10, it becomes clearer that the algorithm takes a bit more than 5 generations (between 6-7 generations) to converge.

When looking at Schem1, we can see that the algorithm takes longer in the first phase to get to the optimal solution. On the average, it takes 30 generations to do so. We will call this period the "warming up" phase of the model. The niching method delays the convergence during this stage. However, once the warming up stage is completed, the response rate is spontaneous; once the change occurs, a drop occurs then the method recovers instantly and gets back to the original optima. By comparing Schem1 and Schem2, we find the two methods are very similar except for the warming–up stage, where Schem2, which uses the above average schemas only, has a shorter time to warm-up than Schem1.

4.2 Experiment 2

In this experiment, we subjected the environment under a severe change from linkage point of view. Here, the linkage boundary changes as well as the attractors. As being

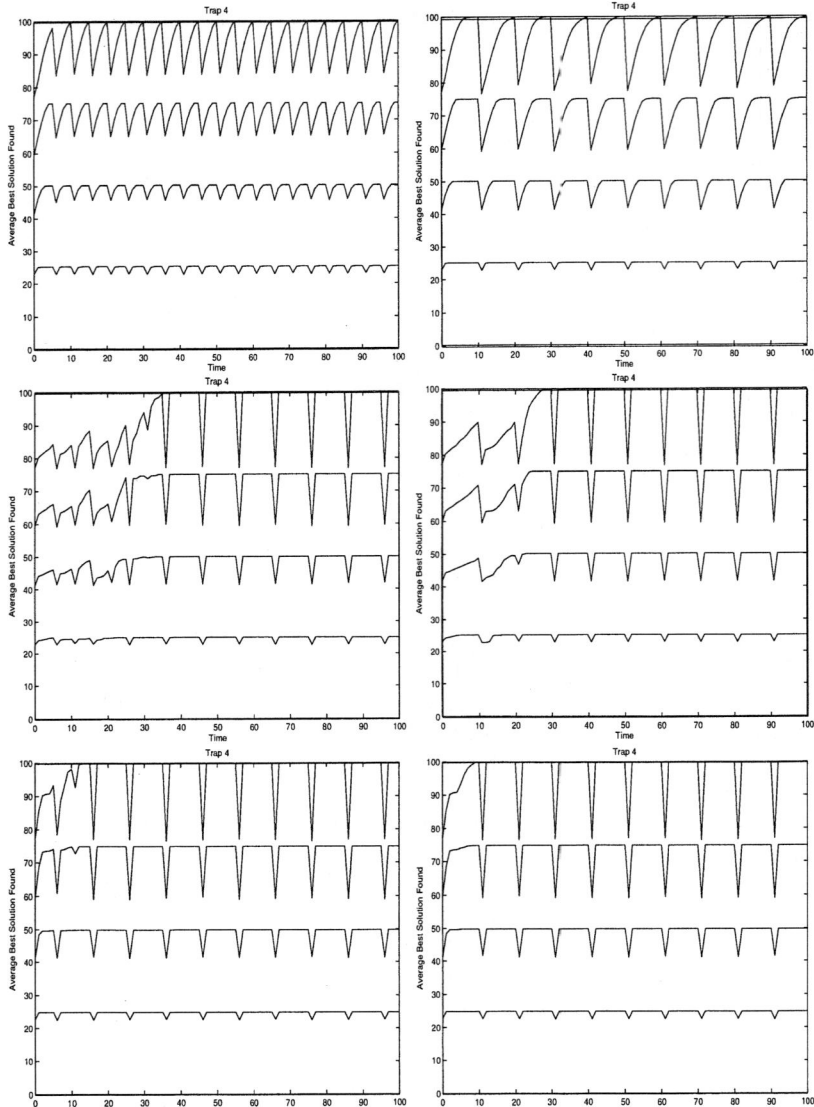

Fig. 4. Modified Trap 4 (left) Cycle 5 (Right) Cycle 10, (top) dcGA, (middle) Schem1, (Bottom) Schem2. In each graph, the four curves correspond to 5, 10, 15, and 20 building blocks ordered from bottom up

depicted in Figure 5, the environment is switching between trap–3 with all optima at 1's and trap–4 with all optima at 0's. Moreover, in trap–3, a deceptive attractor exists when the number of 1's is 1 while in trap–4, a deceptive attractor exists when the number of 1's is 3. This setup is tricky in the sense that, if a hill climber gets trapped at the

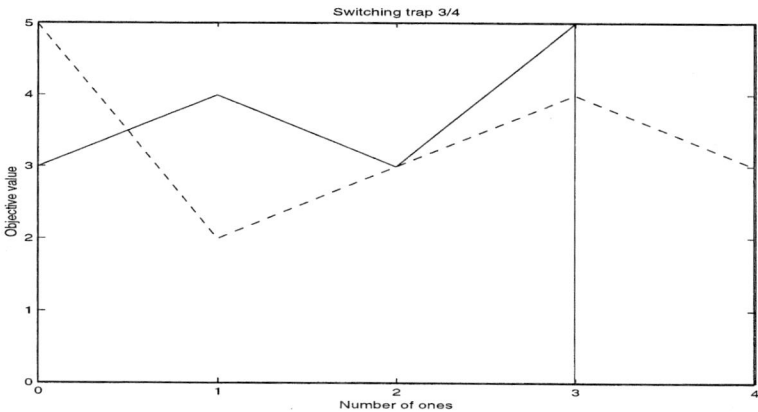

Fig. 5. The switching trap function with k=3,4 in a changing environment

deceptive attractor for trap–4, the behavior will be good for trap–3. However, this hill–climber won't escape this attractor when the environment switches back to trap-4 since the solution will be surrounded with solutions of lower qualities. This setup tests also whether any of the methods is behaving similar to a hill–climber.

Figure 6 shows the performance of dcGA, Schem1, and Schem2. We varied the string length between 12 and 84 in a step of 12 so that the string length is dividable by 3 and 4 (the order of the trap). For example, if the string length is 84 bits, the optimal solution for trap 4 is $5 \times \frac{84}{4} = 105$ and for trap 3 is $5 \times \frac{84}{3} = 120$. Therefore, the objective value will alternate between these two values at the optimal between cycles. The results in Figure 6 are very similar to the previous experiment. The dcGA method responds effectively to environmental changes but Schem1 and Schem2 respond faster. Also, the warming up period for Schem1 is longer than Schem2.

5 Conclusion

In this paper, we presented a niching method based on an automatic problem decomposition approach using competent GAs. We have demonstrated the innovative idea that niching is possible on the sub–structural level despite that the learning of these sub–structures is adaptive and may be noise. We tested changes where the functions maintain their linkage boundaries but switches between optima, as well as drastic changes where the functions change their optima simultaneously with a change in their linkage boundaries. In all cases, niching on the sub–structural level is a robust mechanism for changing environments.

Acknowledgment

This work was sponsored by the Air Force Office of Scientific Research, Air Force Materiel Command, USAF, under grant F49620-00-0163 and F49620-03-1-0129, by the

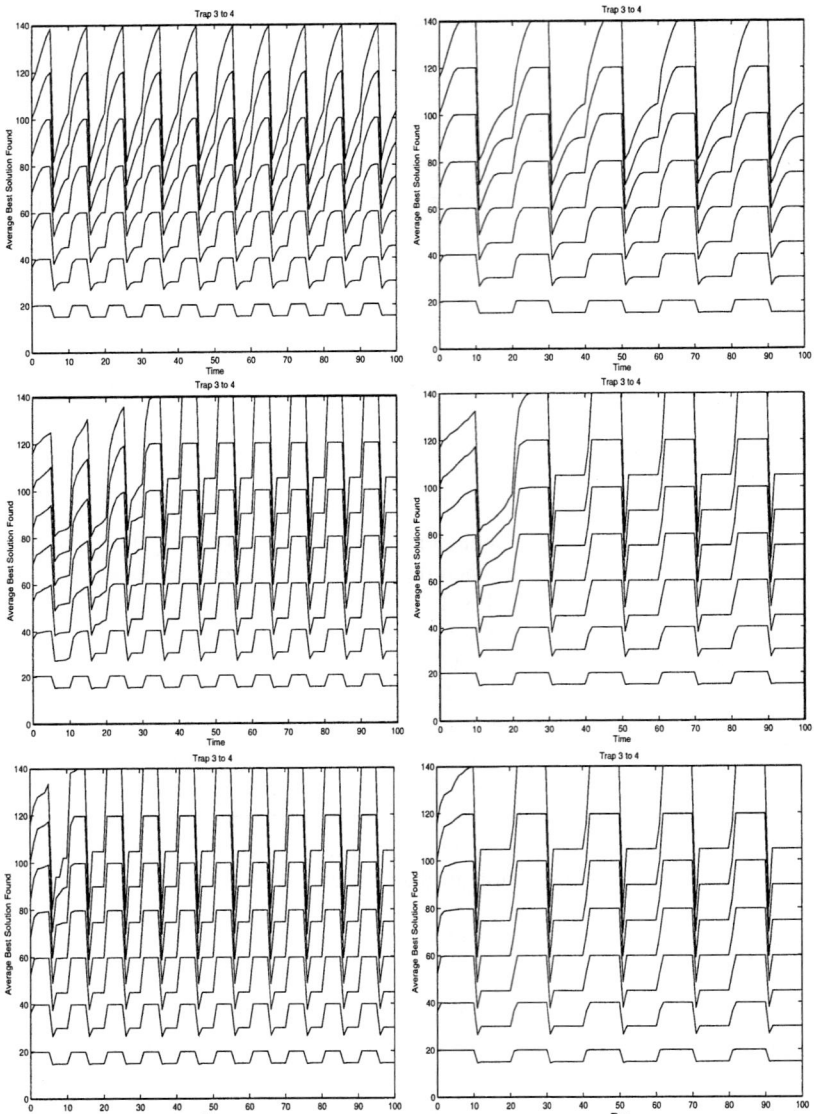

Fig. 6. Switching Trap 3–4 (left) Cycle 5 (Right) Cycle 10, (top) dcGA, (middle) Schem1, (Bottom) Schem2. In each graph, the seven curves correspond to strings of length 12, 24, 36, 48, 60, 72, and 84 bits ordered from bottom up

Technology Research, Education, and Commercialization Center (TRECC), at UIUC by NCSA and funded by the Office of Naval Research (grant N00014-01-1-0175), the National Science Foundation under ITR grant DMR-99-76550 (at Materials

Computation Center), ITR grant DMR-0121695 (at CPSD), the Dept. of Energy under grant DEFG02-91ER45439 (at Fredrick Seitz MRL), the University of New South Wales SSP Scheme, and the Australian Research Council (ARC) Centre on Complex Systems grant number CEO0348249.

References

1. H.A. Abbass, K. Sastry, and D. Goldberg. Oiling the wheels of change: The role of adaptive automatic problem decomposition in non–stationary environments. Technical Report Illigal TR-2004029, University of Illinois, Urbana–Champaign, 2004.
2. D.H. Ackley. *A connectionist machine for genetic hill climbing.* Kluwer Academic publishers, 1987.
3. S. Baluja. Population–based incremental learning: A method for integrating genetic search based function optimization and competitive learning. Technical Report CMU-CS-94-163, Carnegie Mellon University, 1994.
4. C. Bierwirth and D.C. Mattfeld. Production scheduling and rescheduling with genetic algorithms. *Evolutionary Computation*, 7(1):1–18, 1999.
5. P. Bosman and D. Thierens. Linkage information processing in distribution estimation algorithms. *Proceedings of the Genetic and Evolutionary Computation Conference*, pages 60–67, 1999.
6. J. Branke. *Evolutionary Optimization in Dynamic Environments.* Kluwer Academic Publishers, Boston, 2001.
7. Y.-p. Chen. *Extending the Scalability of Linkage Learning Genetic Algorithms: Theory and Practice.* PhD thesis, University of Illinois at Urbana-Champaign, Urbana, IL, 2004. (Also IlliGAL Report No. 2004018).
8. H.G. Cobb. An investigation into the use of hypermutation as an adaptive operator in genetic algorithms having continuous, time-dependent nonstationary environments. Technical Report AIC-90-001, Naval Research Laboratory, 1990.
9. P. Collard, C. Escazut, and E. Gaspar. An evolutionnary approach for time dependant optimization. *International Journal on Artificial Intelligence Tools*, 6(4):665–695, 1997.
10. D. Dasgupta. Incorporating redundancy and gene activation mechanisms in genetic search. In L. Chambers, editor, *Practical Handbook of Genetic Algorithms*, pages 303–316. CRC Press, 1995.
11. K. Deb and D.E. Goldberg. Analyzing deception in trap functions. *Foundations of Genetic Algorithms*, pages 93–108. Morgan Kaufmann, 1993.
12. A. Ghosh, S. Tstutsui, and H. Tanaka. Function optimisation in nonstationary environment using steady state genetic algorithms with aging of individuals. *IEEE International Conference on Evolutionary Computation*, pages 666–671. IEEE Publishing, 1998.
13. D. E. Goldberg, K. Deb, and J. Horn. Massive multimodality, deception, and genetic algorithms. *Proceedings of parallel problem solving from nature II*, pages 37–46. Elsevier Science Publishers, 1992.
14. D.E. Goldberg. *The design of innovation: lessons from and for competent genetic algorithms.* Kluwer Academic Publishers, Massachusetts, USA, 2002.

15. D.E. Goldberg, K. Deb, H. Kargupta, and G. Harik. Rapid, accurate optimization of difficult problems using fast messy genetic algorithms. *Proceedings of the Fifth International Conference on Genetic Algorithms, San Mateo, California*, pages 56–530. Morgan Kauffman Publishers, 1993.
16. D.E. Goldberg, B. Korb, and K. Deb. Messy genetic algorithms: motivation, analysis, and first results. *Complex Systems*, 3(5):493–530, 1989.
17. D.E. Goldberg and R.E. Smith. Nonstationary function optimisation using genetic algorithms with dominance and diploidy. *Second International Conference on Genetic Algorithms*, pages 59–68. Lawrence Erlbaum Associates, 1987.
18. J.J. Grefenstette. Genetic algorithms for changing environments. *Proceedings of Parallel Problem Solving from Nature*, pages 137–144. Elsevier Science Publisher, 1992.
19. G. Harik. *Linkage Learning via Probabilistic Modeling in the ECGA*. PhD thesis, University of Illinois at Urbana–Champaign, 1999.
20. R. B. Heckendorn and A. H. Wright. Efficient linkage discovery by limited probing. *Proceedings of the Genetic and Evolutionary Computation Conference*, pages 1003–1014, 2003.
21. J. H. Holland. *Adaptation in Natural and Artificial Systems*. University of Michigan Press, Ann Arbor, MI, 1975.
22. H. Kargupta. The gene expression messy genetic algorithm. In *Proceedings of the IEEE International Conference on Evolutionary Computation*, pages 814–819, Piscataway, NJ, 1996. IEEE Service Centre.
23. S.C. Lin, E.D. Goodman, and W.F. Punch. A genetic algorithm approach to dynamic job shop scheduling problems. In *Seventh International Conference on Genetic Algorithms*, pages 139–148. Morgan Kaufmann, 1997.
24. S.W. Mahfoud. *Bayesian*. PhD thesis, University of Illinois at Urbana-Champaign, Urbana, IL, 1995. (Also IlliGAL Report No. 95001).
25. N. Mori, S. Imanishia, H. Kita, and Y. Nishikawa. Adaptation to changing environments by means of the memory based thermodynamical genetic algorithms. *Proceedings of the Seventh International Conference on Genetic Algorithms*, pages 299–306. Morgan Kaufmann, 1997.
26. N. Mori, H. Kita, and Y. Nishikawa. Adaptation to changing environments by means of the thermodynamical genetic algorithms. *Proceedings of Parallel Problem Solving from Nature*, volume 1411 of *Lecture Notes in Computer Science*, pages 513–522, Berlin, 1996. Elsevier Science Publisher.
27. M. Munetomo and D. Goldberg. Linkage identification by non-monotonicity detection for overlapping functions. *Evolutionary Computation*, 7(4):377–398, 1999.
28. M. Pelikan, D. E. Goldberg, and E. Cantú-Paz. Linkage learning, estimation distribution, and Bayesian networks. *Evolutionary Computation*, 8(3):314–341, 2000. (Also IlliGAL Report No. 98013).
29. M. Pelikan and H. Mühlenbein. The bivariate marginal distribution algorithm. In R. Roy, T. Furuhashi, and P. K. Chawdhry, editors, *Advances in Soft Computing - Engineering Design and Manufacturing*, pages 521–535, London, 1999. Springer-Verlag.
30. J. J. Rissanen. Modelling by shortest data description. *Automatica*, 14:465–471, 1978.
31. Claude E. Shannon. A mathematical theory of communication. *The Bell System Technical Journal*, 27(3):379–423, 1948.
32. D. Thierens and D.E. Goldberg. Mixing in genetic algorithms. *Proceedings of the Fifth International Conference on Genetic Algorithms (ICGA-93)*, pages 38–45, San Mateo, CA, 1993. Morgan Kaufmann.

33. F. Vavak, K. Jukes, and T.C. Fogarty. Learning the local search range for genetic optimisation in nonstationary environments. In *IEEE International Conference on Evolutionary Computation*, pages 355–360. IEEE Publishing, 1997.
34. T.-L. Yu, D. E. Goldberg, A. Yassine, and Y.-P. Chen. A genetic algorithm design inspired by organizational theory: Pilot study of a dependency structure matrix driven genetic algorithm. *Artificial Neural Networks in Engineering*, pages 327–332, 2003. (Also IlliGAL Report No. 2003007).

Suitability of Two Associative Memory Neural Networks to Character Recognition

Orla McEnery, Alex Cronin, Tahar Kechadi, and Franz Geiselbrechtinger

Department of Computer Science,
University College Dublin, Belfield, Dublin 4, Ireland
alex.cronin@ucd.ie

Abstract. The aim of the current study is to assess the suitability of two Associative Memory (AM) models to character recognition problems. The two AM models under scrutiny are a One-Shot AM (OSAM) and an Exponential Correlation AM (ECAM). We compare these AMs on the resultant features of their architectures, including recurrence, learning and the generation of domains of attraction. We illustrate the impact of each of these features on the performance of each AM by varying the training set size, introducing noisy data and by globally transforming symbols. Our results show that each system is suited to different character recognition problems.

1 Introduction

Neural networks have interesting features such as learning and generalization abilities, adaptivity, the capability of modelling nonlinear relationships, and massive parallelism [1–4] them very good candidates to model very complex systems where traditional optimization methods are not applicable. Many methods of learning and network architectures have been developed in an attempt to satisfy the needs of such systems [5–7].

Associative memory (AM) models are a class of nonlinear artificial neural networks that have been developed to model applications in the field of pattern recognition. They originate from the linear associative memory proposed by Kohonen and Steinbuch [8, 9]. Research performed in the area of feedback associative memories by Hopfield [10, 11] resulted in AM models becoming a very attractive area of study [12]. AM models constitute a neural-network paradigm and possess very interesting features such as efficiency (in computational terms), distributed data storage and parallel flow of information that make them robust in tolerating errors of individual neurons. However, they can have problems in the areas of memory capacity and application dependency [13, 14].

In this study, we focus on comparing and contrasting two AM models, a One-Shot Associative Memory (OSAM) [13] and an Exponential Correlation Associative Memory (ECAM) [14]. Both AM models are supervised neural networks, and therefore have prototype patterns ("solutions") stored in memory.

Both models were previously reported as yielding excellent test results [13, 14]. The OSAM builds on the work of done with the ECAM and claims many advantages. The OSAM is one-shot neural network and thus less complex than the ECAM as there is no requirement for convergence or stabilization of the network. Whereas the ECAM may not stabilize quickly enough to facilitate real time applications. The OSAM's [13] successes are illustrated using a data set that serves to highlight only the advantages and none of the disadvantages of the OSAM over the ECAM. This data set comprised of only 16 prototype patterns which were distorted to a maximum of 6.5%. In our work, we wish to complete the picture, illustrating both the strengths and weaknesses of each with respect to distinct sub-domains of the character recognition problem.

We identify the features on which the two AM models differ, and study the behavior of both, with respect to these aspects, in Section 2. Given these architectural similarities and dissimilarities, we investigate the suitability of each aspect of each AM model in solving a character recognition problem. Our chosen application area is complex due to the fact that symbol formation varies between users, and that individual users symbol formation is not consistent.

These AM models have previously been used in pattern classification domains. However, we have undertaken a more in-depth comparison of the application of these models to the domain of character recognition. These AM models including their algorithms are well presented in [13, 14]. Our experimental results clearly show the boundaries and limitations of these two networks, and identify the features of each that make them appropriate for different sub-domains of character recognition.

2 OSAM and ECAM Models

Both the OSAM and the ECAM are supervised networks and store prototype patterns to which the input patterns can be associated. The storage capacity of both these AMs achieves the theoretical maximum of 2^n prototype patterns where n is the number of elements in each prototype [15]. They both have the same number of layers and the same number of neurons. Each input layer is composed of n neurons each of which accepts a component of an n-bit input pattern. Each hidden layer is made up of m neurons. It is here that the network calculates the similarity of an input pattern to a prototype pattern. Each output layer consists of n neurons which output the prototype pattern which is the most similar to an input pattern. Both the input patterns and prototype patterns are coded as n-bit bipolar patterns. Each prototype has a symbol identity. We call the set of all prototype patterns in each AM that have the same symbol identity, a *prototype identity set*.

The OSAM is a feed-forward network while the ECAM is recurrent. Each network also has a different method of determining the similarity of an input pattern to a prototype pattern. We compare and contrast the OSAM and the ECAM based on the key aspects of AM models, which are recurrence, learning (internal representation of prototypes, calculation of weights and similarity measure) and domain of attraction of prototypes.

2.1 Recurrence

The ECAM is a recurrent AM. Output continues to be reapplied as input until certain termination conditions are fulfilled. These conditions are either the output pattern matches the previous input pattern and therefore no further stabilization can take place, or the user defines a maximum number of recursions, implicitly defining an amount of time they are willing to wait for a solution, and the final output is then returned.

The OSAM is not a recurrent AM. It is purely a one-shot feed-forward memory. However, it achieves stabilization by dynamically updating the learning rate in its training phase. This will be discussed in more detail in Section 2.2.

2.2 Learning

Both the OSAM and the ECAM employ a learning rate which governs stabilization of the networks although the structure and nature of each is very different. Both are determined in the training phase and utilized in the testing phase. The training phase of the OSAM is as follows. In the hidden layer, the prototypes are compared using Hamming distance [16] (bit difference) to determine how much they differ from each other. A weights matrix is calculated from the prototype patterns and a set of α-values. These α-values are the learning rates for each prototype, and are initially generated using global and local similarities, which work together to establish which components of a prototype pattern are significant in distinguishing it from all other prototypes. The more similar a component is, both locally and globally, the less significant it is considered to be. This is due to the fact that the comparison of inputs and prototypes is based on the differences between them. These α-values are further refined by using the optimization algorithm defined by Wu and Batalama [13] until a stable state has been reached. The more significant components of a prototype pattern are assigned an α-value closer to one and the less significant components are assigned an α-value closer to zero.

In the training phase of the ECAM the prototype patterns are stored in memory and the learning rate, γ, is chosen. γ is a rational number greater than 0 and is the same for all components of all prototype patterns. We concur that a maximum recognition rate can be achieved if γ is set to 1.0 [14].

In the testing phase of the OSAM, inputs are applied to the network, and compared against the prototypes in the hidden layer. The initial output of the hidden layer represents the prototypes that are potential "winners". There are three possible situations: if no prototype is associated with the input, then the input will not be recognized; if there is one potential winner, the input will be associated with that prototype; and if there is more than one potential winner, the one with the minimum Hamming distance from the input pattern will be the ultimate winner. The final output in all cases is a reference to which prototype, if any, the input is associated with. The output layer then maps the output of the hidden layer to the appropriate prototype pattern. The final output of the network is an exact replica of the prototype that the input has been associated with.

The testing phase of the ECAM involves the application of input patterns to the AM. In the hidden layer the ECAM uses a correlation equation to determine the negated normalized Hamming distance of an input pattern to each prototype pattern in memory; this set of values is the ECAM's first measure of similarity. These values are then distributed over a greater range by the use of a scaling factor, $(1+\gamma)$, in the weighting function, to result in a new set of similarity values. In the output layer, these final values are averaged to determine this iteration's output. This output is then re-applied to the network until stabilization occurs (see Section 2.1 for termination conditions).

2.3 Domain of Attraction of a Prototype Pattern

AM models work by associating an input pattern with a prototype pattern stored in memory. The domain of attraction of a prototype defines the area of the input space (the set of all possible inputs to the network) that is associated with a prototype pattern. Both the OSAM and ECAM have domains of attraction that are disjoint. However, they are produced and act in different ways, resulting in static domains of attraction in the OSAM and dynamic domains of attraction in the ECAM.

In the OSAM, the domains of attraction are calculated purely on the basis of the difference between prototypes. This difference is determined by the minimum Hamming distance between each prototype pattern and all other prototype patterns. This minimum Hamming distance is used to calculate the radius of that prototype's domain of attraction, r (Figure 1(a)). Therefore, the domain of attraction is completely defined by its radius. An input will be associated with a particular prototype if the Hamming distance between the input and that prototype is less than the radius for that prototype (Figure 1(b)), or vice versa (Figure 1(c)). As the domains of attraction are determined purely on the basis of the prototypes, they are defined in the learning phase and remain static during the testing phase.

In the ECAM, the domain of attraction into which an input falls cannot be calculated prior to the application of that input pattern to the network. The calculation of the domains of attraction of the ECAM has been shown to be NP hard, and may only be discovered by the application of all possible input patterns to the network [17]. At the end of the training phase, prior to the application of an input to the ECAM, the domain of attraction of the prototype contains one element, the prototype itself (Figure 1(d)). When an input is applied to the network, we do not know which prototype pattern's domain of attraction it is in. It is only when the network stabilizes to the steady output of a prototype pattern, that we can conclude that the input is in the domain of attraction of that particular prototype. We now know that one input is in the domain of attraction of the prototype (Figure 1(e)), but in order to establish its domain of attraction we will need to find the set of all inputs such that each input is associated with the prototype pattern (Figure 1(f)). As such, the domains of attraction are incrementally defined during the testing phase, and therefore, are dynamic in nature. This is one of the key advantages of the ECAM.

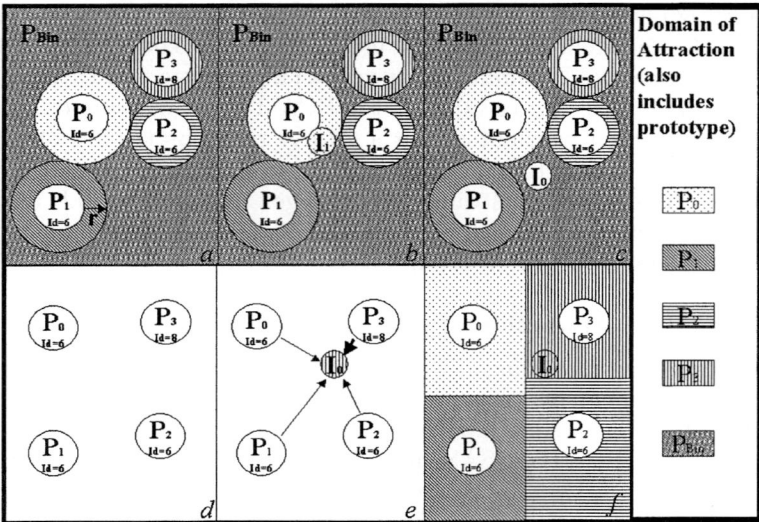

Fig. 1. Illustration of the formation and consequence of the domains of attraction for the OSAM (a,b,c) and the ECAM (d,e,f)

In the OSAM, the complete calculation of the domains of attraction are necessary prior to applying input; this is not the case in the ECAM. Because the set of domains of attraction must cover the entire input space of the ECAM, there is potential for confusion in areas of the input space distant from prototype patterns, resulting in mis-recognition. The fact that the ECAM uses the averaged weighted distance of all prototype patterns from an input pattern to determine its output means that if, for example, there are four prototype patterns equally close to an input and three of them share the same identity then it is likely that one of the prototypes from this prototype identity set will be returned.

2.4 Bin Prototype

In the OSAM, the domains of attraction for prototypes collectively cover only a subsection of the input space. The complement of this subsection represents the domain of attraction of the bin prototype (Figure 1(a)). If an input does not map into the domain of attraction of any prototype pattern, it is said to map into the domain of attraction of the bin prototype. In contrast, the domains of attraction of the ECAM cover the entire input space. (Figure 1(f)).

3 Experimental Analysis

Each prototype and input of these AMs consists of an n-bit bipolar vector of $\pm 1s$. We have generated these in the following fashion. Our software logs a set of $\{x, y\}$ coordinates between a pen-down and pen-up event when each symbol is

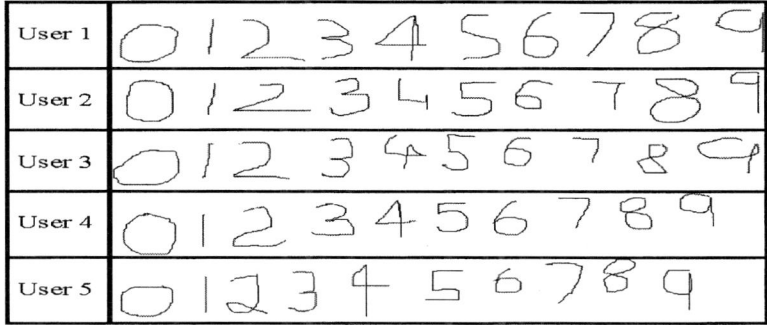

Fig. 2. Sample of the handwritten symbols, 0 to 9, from each of five distinct users

drawn. In order to ensure a continuous set of $\{x, y\}$ coordinates, an interpolation algorithm is employed to supplement those coordinates generated by the mouse. A 20 × 20 matrix is generated to represent the $\{x, y\}$ coordinates of the plotted symbol, with a default component value of -1 and a value of $+1$ representing a plotted point. This is then mapped to a vector. The symbol has now been encoded as a 400-bit bipolar pattern of ±1s suitable to be used as input to our networks. The range of symbols used to test both AMs were the digits 0 to 9.

Experiments were run to determine the recognition rate of each of the AMs, to determine the influence of varying the size of the training set, the effect of noisy input data, and the effect of global transformation of input data.

3.1 Influence of Varying Training Set Size

Each of five users generated 20 unique symbols to represent each of the digits 0 to 9, 1000 symbols in all (Figure 2). Users were free to write the symbols as they saw fit, with the sole constraint that each symbol had to be represented by one pen-stroke, as this is a current restriction of our software. This set was broken into two further base sets; a prototype base set of 750 patterns and an input set of 250 patterns. 15 prototype sets were created in total from the prototype base set; three sets of 50, 100, 150, 200 and 250 prototypes (containing 1,2,3,4 and 5 symbols respectively, generated by each user for each of the digits 0 to 9). The results represent overall recognition and mis-recognition at each of the different *prototype densities* (the number of prototypes stored in the memory of an AM), as well as the percentage of each symbol recognised or mis-recognised.

In the OSAM, recognition was low, ranging from 5.9% to 7.7% averaged over all symbols. Writing varies enormously both between and within users, and as such, the differences between these inputs and the stored prototypes were larger than the domains of attraction would allow for recognition. Increasing the number of prototypes for each symbol did not appear to influence the recognition rates. This is in contrast to the ECAM, whose average recognition increased from 51% to 70%. The increase in average recognition rates corresponded to the

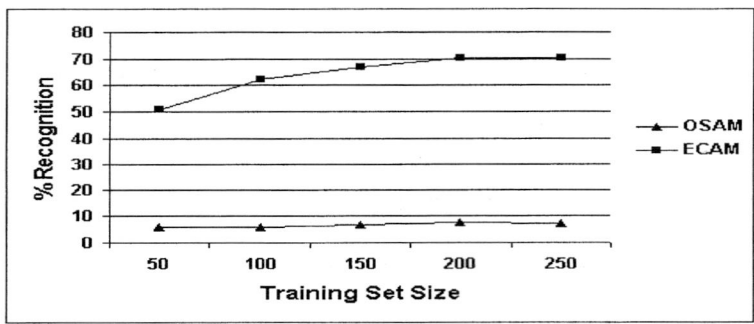

Fig. 3. Average recognition rates for the OSAM and ECAM with increasing training set size

increase in the number of prototypes for each symbol, with recognition being higher with more prototypes for each symbol (Figure 3).

In the ECAM, there can be recognition, mis-recognition and non-recognition. The recognition rates have been presented above. Non-recognition occurs when no pattern identity is returned by the AM, and will happen when the network has not reached a stable state, in which case, further iterations of the network will resolve this, or when the learning rate has not been set to an optimal value. Mis-recognition occurs when the wrong prototype identity is returned by the AM, and in the case of the ECAM, the mis-recognition rates are equal to 100% minus the recognition rate, as the learning rate was optimal. Mis-recognition does not occur in the way one might imagine. Although certain symbols may appear similar to one another when examined by the naked eye e.g. 7 and 1, these symbol sets are not confused in the same way by the ECAM; the confusion is a function of the ECAM's similarity metric and will be examined in future work.

Although the overall recognition by the OSAM was low, none of the inputs were mis-recognized. This can be explained by the fact that the similarity metric used in this AM is very strict, and that any input that is not similar enough to a prototype will be associated with the bin prototype.

With regard to individual symbol recognition in the OSAM, all symbols excluding 1 were recognized at rates of at most 10%. The recognition of inputs representing the symbol 1 ranged from 49.3% to 64%. In the ECAM, individual symbol recognition was much higher than in the OSAM. Again, the symbol 1 was recognized at a much higher rate than the other symbols, with recognition ranging between 92 and 100%.

The domains of attraction of the 1's prototype identity set occupies a well defined area of the input space. They are adjacent and there are few if any domains of attraction of other prototype identity sets in this area of the input space. This is due to the fact that the prototypes for 1 are very similar to one another and very dissimilar to prototype patterns for other symbols. Therefore if an input falls within this area of the input space it will be assigned the identity 1. The input patterns for 1s vary little, and overlap strongly with the well defined

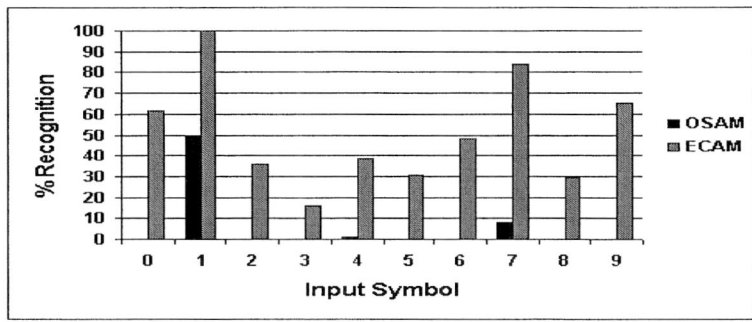

Fig. 4. Symbol recognition rates for the OSAM and ECAM with a prototype density of 50

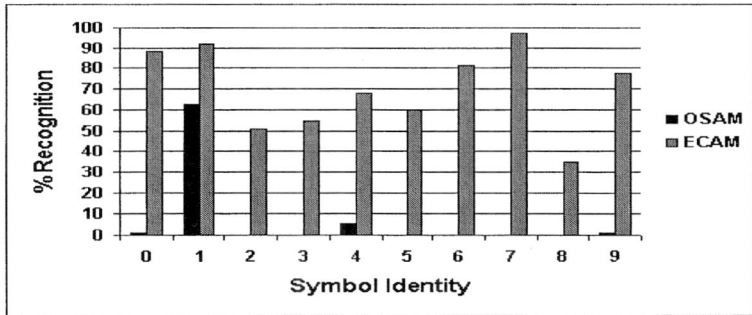

Fig. 5. Symbol recognition rates for the OSAM and ECAM with a prototype density of 250

area of the domains of attraction of the prototypes of the prototype identity set 1.

In the OSAM, the variation of prototype density had no impact on recognition rates at a symbol by symbol level. However, with the ECAM, the higher the prototype density, the greater the recognition. This is illustrated in Figure 4 and Figure 5. Figure 4 shows the individual symbol recognition with a prototype density of 50, and Figure 5 shows it with a prototype density of 250. It is clear from these figures that the change in prototype density has no major impact on the recognition of the individual symbols in the OSAM. However, when we compare these two figures with reference to the ECAM, we can see that the levels of symbol recognition at the prototype density of 250 were, in general, higher than the level of recognition with a prototype density of 50.

The fact that recognition did not differ significantly with an increase in prototype density in the OSAM suggests that although there are more of prototypes stored in memory, they cover a similar amount of the input space. The individual domains of attraction are bigger with smaller number of prototypes for each symbol, but the number of domains of attraction is higher with a larger number of prototypes. Therefore, there is an offset between the size and the number of the domains of attraction.

3.2 Influence of Noisy Data

To simulate noisy input data, which is one of the commonest problems associated with typed-text recognition, we distorted a set of 50 prototypes, 5 prototypes per symbol, in the following three ways: by flipping between zero and 200 individual bits; by flipping between zero and 40 sets of five bits; and by flipping between zero and 20 sets of ten bits. Maximum distortion was 50%.

The OSAM was 100% accurate in recognizing inputs up to the point where the distance between an input and a prototype exceeded the radius of the domain of attraction for that prototype. This is explained by the fact that the domains of attraction are disjoint and are defined purely by their radius. If an input does not fall within the domain of attraction, it is associated with the bin prototype, and as such, is not recognized (Figure 1(a)).

For example, if the radius of a prototype was 28, then the OSAM was successful in recognizing up to 28 single bit inversions, up to 5 sets of five-bit inversions (25 bits), and up to 2 sets of 10-bit inversions (20 bits). If an input did not fall within the domain of attraction, then they were not associated with any of the prototypes stored in the neural network. The minimum, maximum and average radii for one of the prototype sets tested consisting of 50 prototypes, and the radius of another prototype set consisting of 10 prototypes, are shown in Table 1. This shows that as the number of prototypes increases, the radii decrease.

Table 1. Minimum, Maximum and Average Radii for each symbol of a prototype set of 50, and the radius for each symbol of a prototype set of 10, in the OSAM

	Symbol	0	1	2	3	4	5	6	7	8	9
50 prototypes	Min Radius	26	6	19	28	20	21	26	25	26	28
	Max Radius	37	10	30	36	35	33	34	28	35	31
	Avg Radius	30.6	8.2	25.2	32.2	31.4	27.6	29.8	25.8	31.0	29.2
10 prototypes	Radius	33	29	31	40	44	31	31	29	40	30

In the ECAM, high accuracy tending towards 100% was found for flipping up to 100 bits, irrelevant of whether or not the bits were flipped in sets of 1, 5 or 10. Flipping greater numbers of bits resulted in lower accuracy. Although the ECAM has a greater tolerance to noise than the OSAM, we have no measure of confidence as to the accuracy of recognition, due to its ability to mis-recognise.

3.3 Influence of Entire Symbol Shift

The original $\{x, y\}$ coordinates which represented the prototypes were shifted by w coordinates to the right to generate new input coordinates, such that the

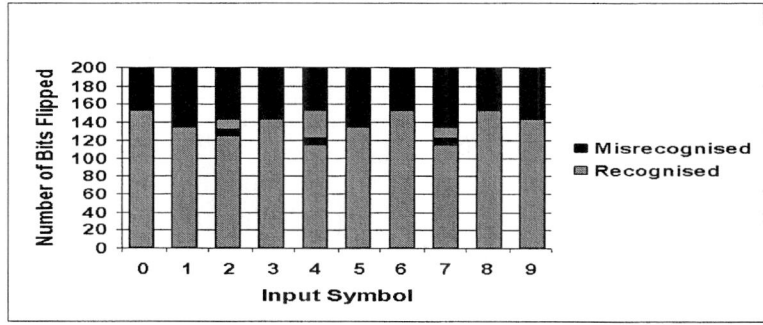

Fig. 6. Recognition and mis-recognition of noisy input by the ECAM

new x coordinate equalled $(x + w)$. The prototype vector was generated as in Section 3, paragraph 1. We preformed 4 tests in which w took on the integer values 0,1,2, and 3.

In the case of the OSAM, when the prototype images were shifted zero bits, recognition was 100%. When they were shifted one, two or three bits to the right, recognition was 0% in all cases. This was due to the fact that the measure of similarity between inputs and prototypes is based on the bit-by-bit comparison between them. When the entire image is shifted, although the symbol shape is the same as it was before the shift, the bit difference between the images is greatly increased, thus similarity is decreased. This shows that the OSAM is dependant on the exact position of the pattern. This is due to the similarity value being defined by the radius of the domain of attraction. When the patterns were shifted, the differences between them and their corresponding prototypes became larger than the radius of the domain of attraction of that prototype.

The ECAM performed very differently to the OSAM in this area. This is shown in Figure 7. When the prototype images were shifted zero, one, two and three bit to the right, the average recognition rates were 100%, 84%, 62% and 42%, respectively, and mis-recognition rates were 0%, 16%, 37% and 57%, respectively. Therefore, when the images were shifted to the right, the recognition rate steadily fell as a result of the way the ECAM's similarity metric is defined [14].

4 Conclusion

We compared two AM models (OSAM and ECAM) on a functional and architectural level and highlighted the features which make the OSAM more suited to typed text recognition and the ECAM more suited to handwriting recognition.

The OSAM did not benefit from varying the training set size, with recognition rates remaining relatively static. Whereas the ECAM benefited greatly with recognition rates rising from 51% to 71%. This is because of the dynamic nature of the ECAM's domains of attraction, which ensures association of all inputs with a prototype.

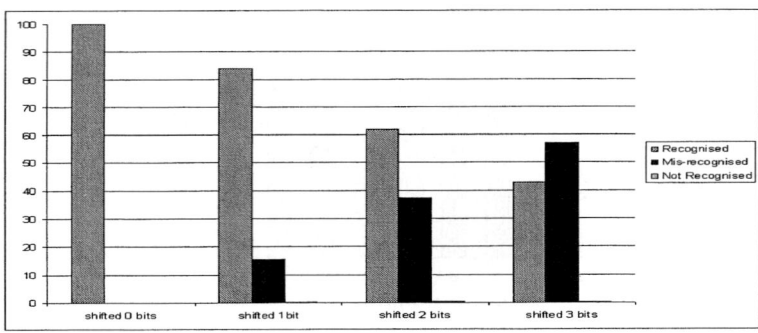

Fig. 7. Impact of shifting images on recognition, mis-recognition and non-recognition rates in the ECAM

When such random distortion as would be expected in scanned typed-text was introduced to the inputs, the OSAM was 100% accurate in recognizing inputs within the domain of attraction, defined by its radius. The ECAM recognition tended towards 100% accuracy, as far as 25% distortion, and thereafter, the recognition rate declined steadily. Because the ECAM can mis-recognize prototypes, we have restricted confidence in its result.

When we globally transformed prototypes and used them as inputs, the OSAM failed to recognize them, as all inputs lay outside the domains of attraction, whereas the ECAM succeeded in recognizing the inputs proportionate to the degree of transformation, indicating more graceful degradation.

Based upon the above, we conclude that both the OSAM and ECAM are appropriate for different areas of the character recognition problem domain. The reliability of the OSAM ensures its successful application in the area of small distortions in the input set, i.e. the recognition of typed text, and the flexibility of the ECAM facilitates its application to the area of handwriting recognition.

In the future, we hope to refine each system's performance in their niche areas, and extend the range of symbols that both systems can recognize, to include the full range of alpha-numeric and mathematical symbols. We aim to validate our findings with other commonly available data sets. We hope to test the OSAM further with typed text, to support our conclusions from the current study.

References

1. Zurada, J.: Introduction to Artificial Neural Systems. West Publishing Company, St. Paul, MN (1992)
2. Skapura, D.: Building Neural Networks. Addition-Wesley Publishing Company (1995)
3. Serbedzija, N.: Simulating artificial neural networks on parallel architectures. Computer **29** (1996) 56–70

4. Tan, C., Quah, T., Teh, H.: An artificial neural network that models human decision making. Computer **29** (1996) 45–54
5. Setiono, R., Liu, H.: Symbolic representation of neural networks. Computer **29** (1996) 71–77
6. Shang, Y., Wah, B.: Global optimisation for neural network training. Computer **29** (1996) 45–54
7. Jain, A., Mao, J., Mohiuddin, K.: Artificial neural networks: A tutorial. Computer **29** (1996) 31–44
8. Kohonen, T.: Correlation matrix memories. IEEE Trans. Comput. **21** (1972) 353–359
9. Kohonen, T.: Associative Memory: A System-Theoretical Approach. Springer-Verlag, New-York (1977)
10. Hopfield, J.: Neural networks and physical systems with emergent collective computational abilities. In: Nat. Acad. Sci.,. Volume 79. (1982) 2554–2558
11. Hopfield, J.: Neurons with graded response have collective computational properties like those of two-state neurons. In: Nat. Acad. Sci.,. Volume 81. (1984) 3088–3092
12. Wu, Y., Pados, D.: A feedforward bidirectional associative memory. IEEE Trans. Neural Networks **11** (2000) 859–866
13. Wu, Y., Batalama, N.: An efficient learning algorithm for associative memories. IEEE Trans. on Neural Networks **11** (2000) 1058–1066
14. Chieuh, T., Goodman, R.: Recurrent correlation associative memories. IEEE Trans. on Neural Networks **2** (1991) 275–284
15. Chou, P.A.: The capacity of the kanerva associative memory. IEEE Trans. on Information Theory **35** (1989) 281–298
16. Hamming, R.W.: Error detecting and error correcting codes. The Bell System Technical Journal **26** (1950) 147–160
17. DasGupta, B., Siegelmann, H.T., Sontag, E.D.: On the complexity of training neural networks with continuous activation functions. IEEE Transactions on Neural Networks **6** (1995) 1490–1504

Using Loops in Genetic Programming for a Two Class Binary Image Classification Problem

Xiang Li and Vic Ciesielski

School of Computer Science and Information Technology,
RMIT University, GPO Box 2476V, Melbourne, Victoria 3001
{xiali, vc}@cs.rmit.edu.au

Abstract. Loops are rarely used in genetic programming (GP), because they lead to massive computation due to the increase in the size of the search space. We have investigated the use of loops with restricted semantics for a problem in which there are natural repetitive elements, that of distinguishing two classes of images. Using our formulation, programs with loops were successfully evolved and performed much better than programs without loops. Our results suggest that loops can successfully used in genetic programming in situations where domain knowledge is available to provide some restrictions on loop semantics.

1 Introduction

Loops are powerful constructs in programming and they provide a mechanism for repeated execution of a sequence of instructions. However, there is very little use of looping constructs in programs evolved by genetic programming. There are four reasons for this. Firstly, loops are hard to evolve. It is necessary to evolve the start and end points and the body. In some cases, an index variable is needed and the start, end points and body need to be consistent. Secondly, it takes longer to evaluate programs with loops. Some mechanisms must be implemented to handle infinite loops. Thirdly, there is a large class of useful problems which can be solved without loops. Fourthly, it is often possible to put the looping behaviour into the environment or into a terminal. For example, in the usual solution to the Santa Fe ant problem [1], the evolved program is repetitively invoked by the environment until some maximum number of steps has been exceeded or the solution has been found. The evolved program contains no loops.

1.1 Goals

The aim of this paper is to establish whether loops can be used in genetic programming for a problem with natural repeating elements and whether there are advantages for doing this. We have chosen to work with an artificially constructed binary image classification problem.

In particular, we will investigate :

1. How can for-loops be incorporated into evolved programs for image classification?
2. Will the classifiers with loops need more/fewer generations to evolve?
3. Are the classifiers with loops better than the classifiers without loops, that is, more accurate, smaller, more understandable?
4. What are the differences between decision strategies in the evolved loop and non-loop programs?

Our expectations are that for-loops can be applied to the classification problem and that programs with for-loops will be smaller in size and easier to analyse and thus more understandable.

2 Related Work

There are few reports in the literature on the use of loops in genetic programming. However, there is a definite increasing trend on applying GP for image analysis.

Koza [2–p135] described how to implement loops with automatically defined functions. Kinnear [3] used an iterative operator with an index value to evolve a sorting algorithm. Langdon [4] utilized a 'forwhile' construct to evolve a list data structure. Maxwell [5] developed a method to deal with infinite loops by calculating partial fitness of the program after restricting execution time.

Zhang and Ciesielski [6] have used GP for the object detection. In [6], they describe the process, terminals and a fitness function for classifying sets of objects ranging from relatively easy to very difficult. They found that GP was better than a neural network for the same problems. Roberts and Howard [7] used GP to learn a strategy for detecting faces in a cluttered scene. Ross et al. [8] successfully evolved mineral identification function for hyperspectral images by GP. However, none of these works has utilized loops for solving the object classification problem.

In [9], we have explored the use of for-loops with restricted semantics on a modified Santa Fe ant problem [10]. This work showed that by controlling the complexity of the loop structures, it is possible to evolve smaller and more understandable solutions. Our success with loops on the modified ant problem has encouraged us to look into problems involving a two dimensional grid. To classify objects according to shape is one such problem.

3 Syntax and Semantics of the FOR-LOOPS

For simplicity we assume that images are stored in a one dimensional array and that the pixels will be referenced by image[i]. The syntax is:

(FOR-LOOP START END METHOD)

METHOD is a function selected from {plus, minus}. START and END are randomly generated integers and restricted to a range within the possible pixel locations. If END is greater than START, the for-loop will transverse through the image from the START position to the END position and do the calculation indicated by the METHOD. For example, if METHOD is plus, the for-loop will add up the pixel values in image[START] to image[END] and return the sum. If START is greater than END, the for-loop will calculate the result in the reverse order. The for-loop will return the pixel value of the position if START and END are the same. In this implementation of looping, infinite loops are not possible and no special actions are necessary in fitness calculation.

Strongly typed genetic programming (STGP) [11] is used in the experiments. The way STGP works allows multiple data types and enforces closure by only generating parse trees which satisfy the type constraints. Crossover and mutation operations will only swap or mutate functions and terminals of the same type. In this implementation a for-loop function returns a type of double. START and END are of type position and METHOD returns a method type (see Table 2).

4 The Binary Image Classification Problem

Our image classification problem involves distinguishing two objects of interest, circles and squares.

The objects are the same size and, in the first classification task, are centered in a 16x16 grid. The pictures were generated by first constructing full squares and circles and then randomly removing groups of pixels or individual pixels to make the classification task non trivial. Examples of these images are shown in Figure 1.

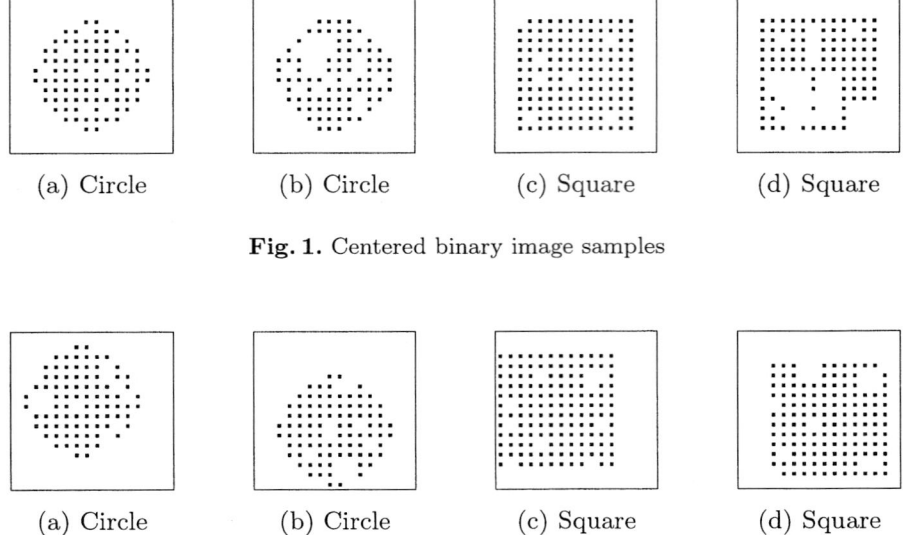

(a) Circle   (b) Circle   (c) Square   (d) Square

Fig. 1. Centered binary image samples

(a) Circle   (b) Circle   (c) Square   (d) Square

Fig. 2. Shifted binary image samples

Table 1. Definition of Terminals and Functions, The Normal Approach

NODES	DESCRIPTION
RandDouble::Terminal	Generates a double value between 0-100.00
RandPos::Terminal	Generates a random position between 0-255, denoted by symbol 'image'. It returns the pixel value in the corresponding square.
d+::Function	Takes two double values, adds them together and returns the result.
d-::Function	Takes two double values, subtracts the second from the first and returns the result.

Table 2. Definition of Extra Terminals and Functions, The Loop Approach

NODES	DESCRIPTION
RandPosition::Terminal	Generates a random position between 0-255, denoted by symbol 'PosImg'.
MinusMethod::Terminal	An indicator of the minus operation
PlusMethod::Terminal	An indicator of the plus operation
ForLoop::Function	Takes 3 arguments. The first two are position indicators, the third argument is a function indicator. The loop will transverse the positions and perform the calculation indicated by Function.

The second classification task involves shifted images. The centered objects have been randomly moved in the horizontal or vertical direction. This increases the difficulty of the task. Examples of the shifted images are shown in Figure 2.

The task of the experiments is to let GP to evolve a classifier by learning from training images and then use it on the test images to determine whether they are squares or circles. A successful classifier should correctly classify the training images and the testing images. In our formulation, classifiers indicate a square when they return a value greater than or equal to 0; classifiers indicate a circle when the return value is less than 0.

Small classifiers evolved with a small computation cost are desirable. For each problem, we will evolve classifiers without loops (normal) and with loops (loops) and compare accuracy, size and computation cost, convergence behaviour.

The terminals and functions used by normal approach can be seen in Table 1.

In the loop approach, GP will have all the functions and terminals of the normal approach shown in Table 1, as well as the extra terminals and functions in Table 2. The extra terminal RandPosition is different from terminal RandPos. RandPos returns a pixel value {0, 1}, while RandPostion returns the position value {0 to 255}. PlusMethod and MinusMethod are the arithmetic function indicators used in the ForLoop function.

PARAMETER NAME	VALUES
Population Size	100
Generation Number	2000
Mutation/Crossover/Elitism Rate	28 % / 70 % / 2 %
Tree Depth	min : 1 max : 7
Initialisation Method	Ramped half-and-half, where grow and full method each deliver half of initial population
Selection Method	Proportional fitness
Termination Criteria	100 % accuracy on training set or 2000 generations reached

Fig. 3. Parameters Settings, the Image Classification Problem

It is the fitness measure which directs the genetic search, reorganising and moving the population towards a solution. The fitness of the image classification problem is not computed directly from the value returned by the classifier, but determined by the consequences of the execution. We use the classification error rate as the fitness, see Equation 1.

$$fitness = \frac{Number\ of\ Errors}{Total} \qquad (1)$$

4.1 Experiments

In this study, experiments with the normal method used the functions and terminals shown in Table 1. Experiments with the loop approach used extra nodes as shown in Table 2. The values of other GP variables are illustrated in Table 4.1. There are 32 (16 squares/16 circles) pictures in the training set and 18 (9 squares/9 circles) in the test set.

4.2 Experimental Results

Figures 4, 5, 7, 8, 9 show data gathered during the experiments. In the figures, *centered-normal* indicates the experiments were done on centered images using the normal terminals functions listed in Table 1. *Centered-loops* indicates the experiments used the extra loop functions and terminals on centered images (see Table 2). *Shifted* indicates the experiments were on shifted images.

Figures 4 and 5 show the overall convergence behaviour of the population. Figure 4 shows the cumulative probability of success for getting a perfect classifier. A perfect classifier means that the evolved program that classifies all the training and test images correctly. If a classifier passes the training set, but fails to identify all the testing images, it is considered a failure. The graph shows that for the centered images the loop method is much more likely to generate a successful classifier. At 600 generations, 82 of the 1000 loop runs had succeeded while only 52 of the normal runs without loop were successful. The difference is even more pronounced on the more difficult shifted image problem. After 2,000 generations, 36 of the 100 loop runs had succeeded while only 2 of runs without loops were successful. Figure 5 shows the mean average training fitness which is consistent with success rates shown in Figure 4.

Figure 6 shows the mean average fitness with one standard deviation on centered images. Programs with loops demonstrate a signification wider variance than those without.

Figure 7 shows the mean best program fitness. The best program refers to the best evolved classifier in the training process. This may not be a successful classifier. There is not much difference in the mean best program fitness for the centered images between both approaches, even though Figure 4 shows that there are more successes by the loop method. This is because classifiers using loops have a larger variation in fitness difference, see Figure 6. The bad runs dominate the good runs. For shifted images, there is a significant difference. Classifiers evolved without loops do not perform well. This trend is further shown by the fitness of the best runs on the testing set as shown in Figure 8.

Figure 8 follows the same pattern as Figure 7. The loop method performs much better for shifted images and programs with loops have a wider variation in fitness. For the centered problem in figure 8, none of the approaches actually get perfect solutions in all runs, but, because of the scale of the Y axis, it appears that zero fitness is reached. For centered problems, figures 7 and 8 show that the loops approach tends to get better solutions quicker in training, but suffers from overfitting and does not perform as well as the normal approach in testing.

Figure 9 shows the average size of the programs. Initially, we expected that programs with loops would be much smaller in size, but the results revealed that this was not the case. There are no wide differences for classifiers on the centered images or on the shifted images. The reason for this is that GP quickly found smaller sized solutions to correctly identify all the objects in the training set by the normal method and evolution stopped. However, most of these are premature solutions and do not perform well on the test set. Figure 9 also shows that, for the centered images, both approaches resulted perfect classification of the training data after about 800 generations and training stopped. Shifted image classification is a harder problem and, in our experiments, neither of the approaches resulted in correct classification of the training set. The programs took longer to evolve. We observed that as fitness improved (see Figure 7), there was a decrease in size for the loop method and a slight bloating [12] in the normal method.

4.3 Analysis of the Solutions

In this section, we analyse the solutions found by both methods on the two types of sample images and compare the decision strategies.

Figure 10 lists one of the smallest classifiers evolved by the normal method and figure 16 shows the points examined to distinguish the objects. The solution is small and elegant. It uses only two positions and took 4,797 evaluations to find. However, this solution has found an idiosyncrasy in the data and is clearly not general.

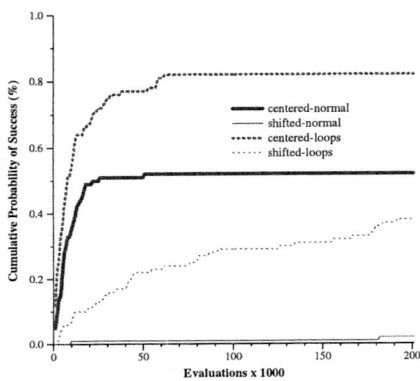

Fig. 4. Cumulative probability of success, average of 100 runs

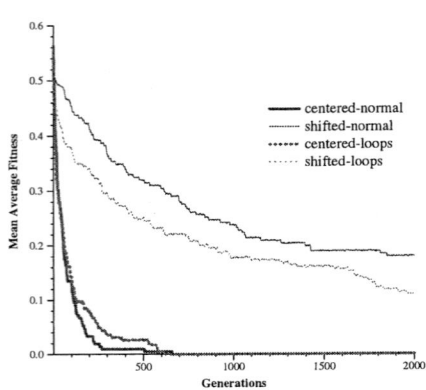

Fig. 5. Mean average training program fitness, average of 100 runs

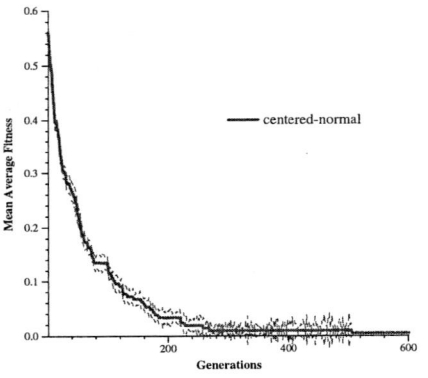

Fig. 6. Mean average fitness, with one standard deviation, centered images

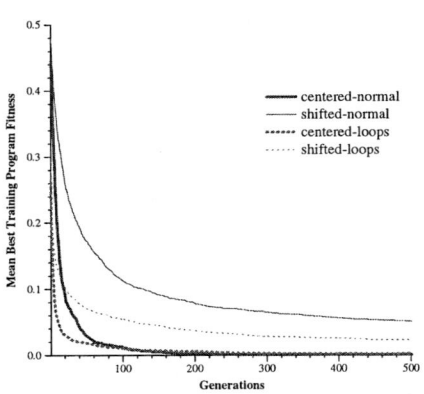

Fig. 7. Mean best training program fitness, average of 100 runs

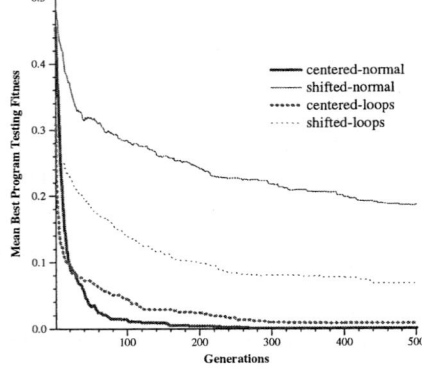

Fig. 8. Mean best program testing fitness, average of 100 runs

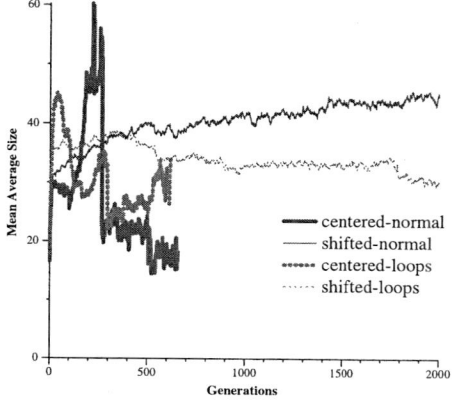

Fig. 9. Mean average program size, average of 100 runs

(d+ (d- image[37] drand0.441534) f203)

Fig. 10. One of the smallest classifiers evolved by normal method for centered images

(d- (ForLoop PosImg228 PosImg188 plus) drand9.260122)

Fig. 11. One of the smallest classifiers evolved by the loop method for centered images

Typical solutions evolved by the normal approach are not so neat. Figure 12 lists a typical program evolved by the non-loops approach and Figure 17 shows the points examined by the classifier. The program is large and the points examined are scattered all over the image. It took 13,030 evaluations to find this solution. This is much higher than the average number of evaluations (approx. 6,000) of finding a solution with loops.

Figure 11 shows one of the smallest classifiers evolved by the loop method and Figure 18 shows the points examined. The line goes from position 188 to position 288 and the program adds up all of the pixel values. By traversing this line, the program obtains enough information to distinguish the objects. This is in contrast to the random positions used by the non-loop approach.

Figure 13 shows a typical solution evolved by the loop approach and Figure 19 shows the points examined. One of the main differences between the solutions

(d+ (d- (d+ (d+ (d+ (d+ drand70.929252 image[188]) drand70.929252) (d- (d- drand22.060454 drand70.917456) (d+ drand29.415353 drand89.236116))) (d+(d- (d- image[2] image[155]) (d- image[11] image[26])) (d+ (d+ image[150] image[37]) (d- drand52.450194 drand38.299516)))) (d+ (d- (d+ (d+ image[133] drand72.779942) (d+ image[139] image[130])) (d- (d+ drand72.943129 drand86.640064) image[114])) (d+ (d- (d- image[170] image[83]) (d- image[194] image[133])) (d+ (d- image[225] image[172]) (d- drand29.415353 f205))))) (d+ (d+ (d+ (d- (d- f18 f194) (d- drand85.580583 image[209])) (d+ (d+ drand61.098601 image[60]) (d+ image[93] drand59.032376))) (d+ (d+ (d+ image[224] drand2.089882) (d- image[229] drand82.981664)) (d- (d- image[135] image[209]) (d- image[187] image[14])))) image[56]])

Fig. 12. A typical classifier evolved by the normal method for centered images

(d- (ForLoop PosImg161 PosImg228 plus) (d- (d+ (d+ drand76.701336
(ForLoop PosImg144 PosImg172 plus)) (d- (d- PosImg152
drand54.382222) PosImg157)) drand14.021874))

Fig. 13. A typical classifier evolved by the loop method for centered images

(d+ (d+ (d- (d- (d+ drand34.087990 f236) (d- f225 f221)) (d-
drand34.087990 (d- drand96.220403 (d- drand72.832995 f34)))) (d- (d-
(d+ (d+ drand38.457827 drand2.639772) drand2.639772) (d- drand96.220403
(d+ f5 f210))) (d- drand72.832995 drand93.951264))) drand7.458120)

Fig. 14. One of the two successful classifiers evolved by the normal method for shifted images

(d- (d- drand87.318493 (d- (d+ (d- (xForLoop pf87 pf45 minus) f165)
drand40.885102) (d- (xForLoop pf247 pf199 plus) drand87.318493)))
(d- f198 drand17.579794))

Fig. 15. One of the smallest classifiers evolved by the loops method for shifted images

with loops and those without is that a run using loops examines more pixels in a linear manner, therefore, covers more areas of the graph.

Figure 14 displays one of the two solutions evolved by normal method for shifted images and Figure 20 shows the points examined. They are scattered at the top and bottom to catch the information of the shifted objects. In contrast, the loop method (Figure 21) uses two lines to distinguish all of the shifted images.

In summary, the classifiers using loops examine a sequence of points to distinguish the objects. The non-loop classifiers examine a seemingly random set of points in the image.

5 Conclusion

The goal of this paper was to investigate the evolution of programs with loops for an image classification problem, that of distinguishing noisy circles and squares. In this, we have been successful. We have developed a loop syntax and semantics which leads to successful evolution of programs for the non-trivial image classification task.

The programs with loops took fewer generations to evolve. The difference was particularly evident in the more difficult shifted problem. The classifiers with loops were generally better than those without loops in that they were more accurate and easier to understand. However, there was little difference in size. The classifiers with loops were more robust in that they examined a sequence of pixels covering the areas in an image in which the circles and squares are different. In contrast, the

Using Loops in Genetic Programming 907

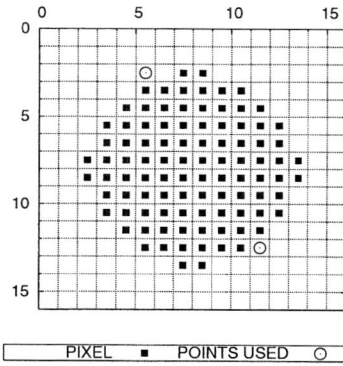

Fig. 16. Points examined for the program without loops shown in Figure 10

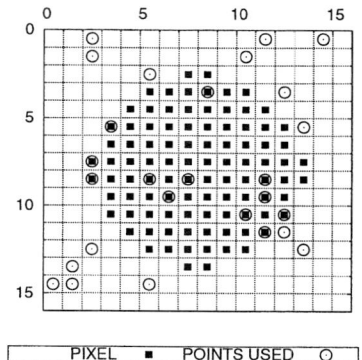

Fig. 17. Points examined for the program without loops shown in Figure 12

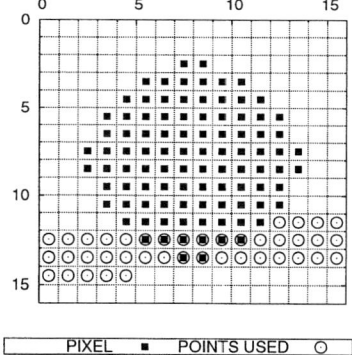

Fig. 18. Points examined for the program with loops shown in Figure 11

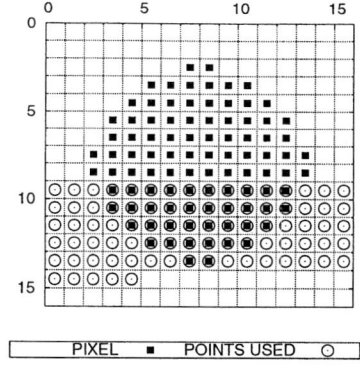

Fig. 19. Points examined for the program with loops shown in Figure 13

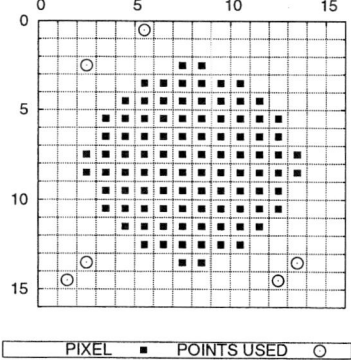

Fig. 20. Points examined for the program without loops shown in Figure 14

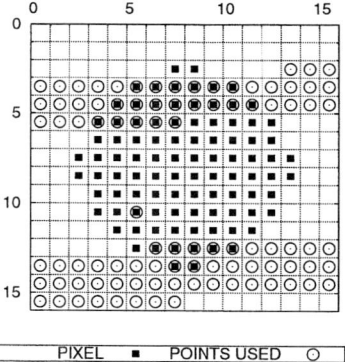

Fig. 21. Points examined for the program with loops shown in Figure 15

classifiers without loops examined points randomly scattered throughout the images. In future work we intend to examine more complex grey level object detection problems.

Acknowledgment

This work was partially supported by grant EPPNRM054 from the Victorian Partnership for Advanced Computing.

References

1. W. B. Langdon and R. Poli. Why ants are hard. In John R. Koza, Wolfgang Banzhaf, Kumar Chellapilla, Kalyanmoy Deb, Marco Dorigo, David B. Fogel, Max H. Garzon, David E. Goldberg, Hitoshi Iba, and Rick Riolo, editors, *Genetic Programming 1998: Proceedings of the Third Annual Conference*, pages 193–201, University of Wisconsin, Madison, Wisconsin, USA, 22-25 1998. Morgan Kaufmann.
2. John R. Koza, Forrest H Bennet III, David Andre, and Martin A. Keane. *Genetic Programming III; Darwinian invention and problem solving*. Morgan Kaufmann, 1999.
3. Kenneth E. Kinnear, Jr. Generality and difficulty in genetic programming: Evolving a sort. In Stephanie Forrest, editor, *Proceedings of the 5th International Conference on Genetic Algorithms, ICGA-93*, pages 287–294, University of Illinois at Urbana-Champaign, 17-21 1993. Morgan Kaufmann.
4. William B. Langdon. Data structures and genetic programming. In Peter J. Angeline and K. E. Kinnear, Jr., editors, *Advances in Genetic Programming 2*, pages 395–414. MIT Press, Cambridge, MA, USA, 1996.
5. Sidney R. Maxwell III. Experiments with a coroutine model for genetic programming. In *Proceedings of the 1998 United Kingdom Automatic Control Council International Conference on Control (UKACC International Conference on Control '98), University of Wales*, volume 455, Swansea, UK, 1-4 1998. IEEE Press.
6. Mengjie Zhang and Victor Ciesielski. Genetic programming for multiple class object detection. In Norman Foo, editor, *Proceedings of 12th Australian Joint Conference on Artificial Intelligence*, volume 1747 of *LNAI*, pages 180–192, Sydney, Australia, 6-10 December 1999. Springer-Verlag.
7. Simon C. Roberts and Daniel Howard. Genetic programming for image analysis: Orientation detection. In Darrell Whitley, David Goldberg, Erick Cantu-Paz, Lee Spector, Ian Parmee, and Hans-Georg Beyer, editors, *Proceedings of the Genetic and Evolutionary Computation Conference (GECCO-2000)*, pages 651–657, Las Vegas, Nevada, USA, 10-12 July 2000. Morgan Kaufmann.
8. Brian J. Ross, Anthony G. Gualtieri, Frank Fueten, and Paul Budkewitsch. Hyperspectral image analysis using genetic programming. In W. B. Langdon, E. Cantú-Paz, K. Mathias, R. Roy, D. Davis, R. Poli, K. Balakrishnan, V. Honavar, G. Rudolph, J. Wegener, L. Bull, M. A. Potter, A. C. Schultz, J. F. Miller, E. Burke, and N. Jonoska, editors, *GECCO 2002: Proceedings of the Genetic and Evolutionary Computation Conference*, pages 1196–1203, New York, 9-13 July 2002. Morgan Kaufmann Publishers.

9. Vic Ciesielski and Xiang Li. Experiments with explicit for-loops in genetic programming. In *Proceedings of Congress on Evolutionary Computation (CEC2004)*, pages 494–501. IEEE Press, June 2004.
10. John R. Koza. *Genetic Programming II: Automatic Discovery of Reusable Programs*. MIT Press, 1994.
11. Thomas D. Haynes, Dale A. Schoenefeld, and Roger L. Wainwright. Type inheritance in strongly typed genetic programming. In Peter J. Angeline and K. E. Kinnear, Jr., editors, *Advances in Genetic Programming 2*, pages 359–376. MIT Press, Cambridge, MA, USA, 1996.
12. W. B. Langdon and R. Poli. Fitness causes bloat: Mutation. In Wolfgang Banzhaf, Riccardo Poli, Marc Schoenauer, and Terence C. Fogarty, editors, *Proceedings of the First European Workshop on Genetic Programming*, volume 1391, pages 37–48, Paris, 14-15 1998. Springer-Verlag.

A Negotiation Agent

John Debenham

Faculty of Information Technology,
University of Technology,
Sydney, NSW, Australia
debenham@it.uts.edu.au
http://www-staff.it.uts.edu.au/~debenham/

Abstract. A negotiation agent exchanges proposals, supported by claims, with an opponent. Each proposal and claim exchanged reveals valuable information about the sender's position. A negotiation may brake down if an agent believes that its opponent is not playing fairly. The agent aims to give the impression of fair play by responding with comparable information revelation whilst playing strategically to influence its opponent's preferences with claims. It uses maximum entropy probabilistic reasoning to estimate unknown values in probability distributions including the probability that its opponent will accept any deal.

1 Introduction

A negotiation agent extends the simple, offer-exchange, bargaining agent described in [1] that evaluates and generates proposals based on information extracted from the marketplace, the World Wide Web and by observing the behavior of its opponent. In addition to exchanging proposals, an argumentation agent exchanges arguments, and so it requires mechanisms for evaluating arguments, and for generating arguments [2]. An *argument* is information that either justifies the agent's negotiation stance or attempts to influence its opponent's stance [2]. Argumentation here is approached in the *rhetorical* sense in which arguments are intended to beneficially influence the opponent's evaluation of the issues [3]. The negotiation agent, Π, attempts to fuse the negotiation with the information that is generated both by and because of it. To achieve this, it draws on ideas from information theory rather than game theory. Π makes no assumptions about the internals of its opponent, including whether she has, or is even aware of the concept of, utility functions. Π is purely concerned with its opponent's behavior — what she does — and not with assumptions about her motivations.

Π assumes that unknown probabilities can be inferred using *maximum entropy inference* [4], *ME*, which is based on random worlds [5]. The maximum entropy probability distribution is "the least biased estimate possible on the given information; i.e. it is maximally noncommittal with regard to missing information" [6]. In the absence of knowledge about the opponent's decision-making apparatus the negotiating agent assumes that the "maximally noncommittal" model is the correct model on which to base its reasoning.

2 The Negotiation Agent: Π

Π operates in an information-rich environment that includes the Internet. The integrity of Π's information, including information extracted from the Internet, will decay in time. The way in which this decay occurs will depend on the type of information, and on the source from which it is drawn. Little appears to be known about how the integrity of real information, such as news-feeds, decays, although the effect of declining integrity has been analyzed.

One source of Π's information is the signals received from Ω. These include offers from Ω to Π, the acceptance or rejection by Ω of Π's offers, and claims that Ω sends to Π. This information is augmented with sentence probabilities that represent the strength of Π's belief in its truth. If Ω rejected Π's offer of $8 two days ago then what is Π's belief now in the proposition that Ω will accept another offer of $8 now? Perhaps it is around 0.1. A linear model is used to model the integrity decay of these beliefs, and when the probability of a decaying belief approaches 0.5 the belief is discarded. The model of decay could be exponential, quadratic or what ever.

A *deal* is a pair of commitments $\delta_{\Pi:\Omega}(\pi,\omega)$ between an agent Π and an opponent agent Ω, where π is Π's commitment and ω is Ω's commitment. $\mathcal{D} = \{\delta_i\}_{i=1}^D$ is the deal set — ie: the set of all possible deals. If the discussion is from Π's point of view then the subscript "$\Pi:\Omega$" may be omitted. These commitments may involve multiple issues and not simply a single issue such as trading price. The set of *terms*, $\mathcal{T}$, is the set of all possible commitments that could occur in deals in the deal set. An agent may have a real-valued *utility* function: $\mathbf{U}: \mathcal{T} \to \Re$, that induces an ordering on $\mathcal{T}$. For such an agent, for any deal $\delta = (\pi,\omega)$ the expression $\mathbf{U}(\omega) - \mathbf{U}(\pi)$ is called the *surplus* of δ, and is denoted by $\mathbf{L}(\delta)$ where $\mathbf{L}: \mathcal{T} \times \mathcal{T} \to \Re$. For example, the values of the function $\mathbf{U}$ may expressed in units of money. It may not be possible to specify the utility function either precisely or with certainty.

The agents communicate using sentences in a first-order language $\mathcal{C}$. This includes the exchange, acceptance and rejection of offers. $\mathcal{C}$ contains the following predicates: $Offer(\delta), Accept(\delta), Reject(\delta)$ and $Quit(.)$, where $Offer(\delta)$ means "the sender is offering you a deal δ", $Accept(\delta)$ means "the sender accepts your deal δ", $Reject(\delta)$ means "the sender rejects your deal δ" and $Quit(.)$ means "the sender quits — the negotiation ends". $\mathcal{C}$ also contains predicates to support argumentation.

2.1 Agent Architecture

Π uses the language $\mathcal{C}$ for external communication, and the language $\mathcal{L}$ for internal representation. Two predicates in $\mathcal{L}$ are: $\Pi Acc(.)$ and $\Omega Acc(.)$. The proposition $(\Pi Acc(\delta) \mid \mathcal{I}_t)$ means: "Π will be comfortable accepting the deal δ given that Π knows information $\mathcal{I}_t$ at time t". The idea is that Π will accept deal δ if $\mathbf{P}(\Pi Acc(\delta) \mid \mathcal{I}_t) \geq \alpha$ for some threshold constant α. The proposition $\Omega Acc(\delta)$ means "Ω is prepared to accept deal δ". The probability distribution $\mathbf{P}(\Omega Acc(.))$ is estimated in Sec. 3.

Each incoming message M from source S received at time t is time-stamped and source-stamped, $M_{[S,t]}$, and placed in an *in box*, $\mathcal{X}$, as it arrives. Π has an *information repository* $\mathcal{I}$, a *knowledge base* $\mathcal{K}$ and a *belief set* $\mathcal{B}$. Each of these three sets contains statements in a first-order language $\mathcal{L}$. $\mathcal{I}$ contains statements in $\mathcal{L}$ together with sentence probability functions of time. $\mathcal{I}_t$ is the state of $\mathcal{I}$ at time t and may be inconsistent. At some particular time t, $\mathcal{K}_t$ contains statements that Π believes are true at time t, such as $\forall x(Accept(x) \leftrightarrow \neg Reject(x))$. The belief set $\mathcal{B}_t = \{\beta_i\}$ contains statements that are each qualified with a *given sentence probability*, $\mathbf{B}(\beta_i)$, that represents Π's belief in the truth of the statement at time t.

Π's actions are determined by its "strategy". A *strategy* is a function $\mathbf{S} : \mathcal{K} \times \mathcal{B} \to \mathcal{A}$ where $\mathcal{A}$ is the set of actions. At certain distinct times the function $\mathbf{S}$ is applied to $\mathcal{K}$ and $\mathcal{B}$ and the agent does something. The set of actions, $\mathcal{A}$, includes sending $Offer(.), Accept(.), Reject(.), Quit(.)$ messages and claims to Ω. The way in which $\mathbf{S}$ works is described in Secs. 3. Two "instants of time" before the $\mathbf{S}$ function is activated, an "import function" and a "revision function" are activated. The import function $\mathbf{I} : (\mathcal{X} \times \mathcal{I}_{t-}) \to \mathcal{I}_t$ clears the in-box, using its "import rules".

An example now illustrates the ideas in the previous paragraph. Suppose that the predicate $\Omega Acc(\delta)$ means that "deal δ is acceptable to Ω". Suppose that Π is attempting to trade a good "g" for cash. Then a deal $\delta(\pi, \omega)$ will be $\delta(g, x)$ where x is an amount of money. If Π assumes that Ω would prefer to pay less than more then $\mathcal{I}_t$ will contain: $\iota_0 : (\forall g x y)((x \geq y) \to (\Omega Acc(g, x)) \to \Omega Acc(g, y))$. Suppose Π uses a simple linear decay for its import rules: $f(M, \Omega, t_i) = trust(\Omega) + (0.5 - trust(\Omega)) \times \frac{t - t_i}{decay(\Omega)}$, where $trust(\Omega)$ is a value in $[0.5, 1]$ and $decay(\Omega) > 0$. $trust(\Omega)$ is the probability attached to S at time $t = t_i$, and $decay(\Omega)$ is the time period taken for $\mathbf{P}(S)$ to reach 0.5 when S is discarded. Suppose at time $t = 7$, Π receives the message: $Offer(g, \$20)_{[\Omega, 7]}$, and has the import rule: $\mathbf{P}(\Omega Acc(g, x) \mid Offer(g, x)_{[\Omega, t_i]}) = 0.8 - 0.025 \times (t - t_i)$, ie: *trust* is 0.8 and *decay* is 12. Then, in the absence of any other information, at time $t = 11$, $\mathcal{K}_{t_{11}}$ contains ι_0 and $\mathcal{B}_{t_{11}}$ contains $\Omega Acc(g, \$20)$ with a sentence probability of 0.7.

Π uses three things to make offers: an estimate of the likelihood that Ω will accept any offer [Sec. 3], an estimate of the likelihood that Π will, in hindsight, feel comfortable accepting any particular offer, and an estimate of when Ω may quit and leave the negotiation — see [1]. Π supports its negotiation with claims with the aim of either improving the outcome — reaching a more beneficial deal — or improving the process — reaching a deal in a more satisfactory way.

An exemplar application follows. Π is attempting to purchase of a particular second-hand motor vehicle, with some period of warranty, for cash. So the two issues in this negotiation are: the period of the warranty, and the cash consideration. A deal δ consists of this pair of issues, and the deal set has no natural ordering. Suppose that Π wishes to apply *ME* to estimate values for: $\mathbf{P}(\Omega Acc(\delta))$ for various δ. Suppose that the warranty period is simply $0, \cdots, 4$ years, and that the cash amount for this car will certainly be at least \$5,000 with no warranty, and is unlikely to be more than \$7,000 with four year's warranty. In what follows all price units are in thousands of dollars. Suppose then that the deal set in this application consists of 55 individual deals in the form of pairs of warranty periods and price intervals: { $(w, [5.0, 5.2)), (w, [5.2, 5.4)), (w, [5.4, 5.6)), (w, [5.6, 5.8)), (w, [5.8, 6.0)), (w, [6.0, 6.2)), (w, [6.2, 6.4)), (w, [6.4, 6.6)), (w, [6.6, 6.8)), (w, [6.8, 7.0)), (w, [7.0, \infty))$ }, where $w = 0, \cdots, 4$. Suppose that Π has previously received two offers from Ω. The first is to offer 6.0 with no warranty, and the second to offer 6.9 with one year's warranty. Suppose Π believes that Ω still stands by these two offers with probability 0.8. Then this leads to two beliefs: $\beta_1 : \Omega Acc(0, [6.0, 6.2))$; $\mathbf{B}(\beta_1) =$

0.8, β_2 : $\Omega Acc(1, [6.8, 7.0])$; $\mathbf{B}(\beta_2) = 0.8$. Following the discussion above, before "switching on" *ME*, Π should consider whether it believes that $\mathbf{P}(\Omega Acc(\delta))$ is uniform over δ. If it does then it includes both β_1 and β_2 in $\mathcal{B}$, and calculates $\mathcal{W}_{\{\mathcal{K},\mathcal{B}\}}$ that yields estimates for $\mathbf{P}(\Omega Acc(\delta))$ for all δ. If it does not then it should include further knowledge in $\mathcal{K}$ and $\mathcal{B}$. For example, Π may believe that Ω is more likely to bid for a greater warranty period the higher her bid price. If so, then this is a multi-issue constraint, that is represented in $\mathcal{B}$, and is qualified with a sentence probability.

3 Negotiation

Π engages in bilateral bargaining with its opponent Ω. Π and Ω each exchange offers alternately at successive discrete times. They enter into a commitment if one of them accepts a standing offer. The protocol has three stages:

1. Simultaneous, initial, binding offers from both agents;
2. A sequence of alternating offers, and
3. An agent quits and walks away from the negotiation.

In the first stage, the agents simultaneously send *Offer*(.) messages to each other that stand for the entire negotiation. These initial offers are taken as limits on the range of values that are considered possible. The exchange of initial offers "stakes out the turf" on which the subsequent negotiation will take place. In the second stage, an *Offer*(.) message is interpreted as an implicit rejection, *Reject*(.), of the opponent's offer on the table. Second stage offers stand only if accepted by return — Π interprets these offers as indications of Ω's willingness to accept — they are represented as beliefs with sentence probabilities that decay in time. The negotiation ceases *either* in the second round if one of the agents accepts a standing offer *or* in the final round if one agent quits and the negotiation breaks down.

To support the offer-exchange process, Π has do two different things. First, it must respond to offers received from Ω. Second, it must send offers, and possibly information, to Ω. This section describes machinery for estimating the probabilities $\mathbf{P}(\Omega Acc(\delta))$ where the predicate $\Omega Acc(\delta)$ means "Ω will accept Π's offer δ". In the following, Π is attempting to purchase of a particular second-hand motor vehicle, with some period of warranty, for cash from Ω. So a deal δ will be represented by the pair (w, p) where w is the period of warranty in years and $\$p$ is the price.

Π assumes the following two preference relations for Ω, and $\mathcal{K}$ contains:

κ_{11} : $\forall x, y, z((x < y) \rightarrow (\Omega Acc(y, z) \rightarrow \Omega Acc(x, z)))$
κ_{12} : $\forall x, y, z((x < y) \rightarrow (\Omega Acc(z, x) \rightarrow \Omega Acc(z, y)))$

These sentences conveniently reduce the number of possible worlds. The two preference relations κ_{11} and κ_{12} induce a partial ordering on the sentence probabilities in the $\mathbf{P}(\Omega Acc(w, p))$ array from the top-left where the probabilities are ≈ 1, to the bottom-right where the probabilities are ≈ 0. There are fifty-one possible worlds that are consistent with $\mathcal{K}$.

Suppose that the offer exchange has proceeded as follows: Ω asked for $6,900 with one year warranty and Π refused, then Π offered $5,000 with two years warranty and Ω refused, and then Ω asked for $6,500 with three years warranty and Π refused. Then at the next time step $\mathcal{B}$ contains: β_{11} : $\Omega Acc(3, [6.8, 7.0])$, β_{12} : $\Omega Acc(2, [5.0, 5.2])$

and $\beta_{13} : \Omega Acc(1, [6.4, 6.6))$, and with a 10% decay in integrity for each time step: $\mathbf{P}(\beta_{11}) = 0.7, \mathbf{P}(\beta_{12}) = 0.2$ and $\mathbf{P}(\beta_{13}) = 0.9$.

Maximum entropy inference is used to calculate the distribution $\mathbf{W}_{\{\mathcal{K},\mathcal{B}\}}$ which shows that there are just five different probabilities in it. The probability matrix for the proposition $\Omega Acc(w, p)$ is:

	$w=0$	$w=1$	$w=2$	$w=3$	$w=4$
$p = [7.0, \infty)$	0.9967	0.9607	0.8428	0.7066	0.3533
$p = [6.8, 7.0)$	0.9803	0.9476	0.8330	**0.7000**	0.3500
$p = [6.6, 6.8)$	0.9533	0.9238	0.8125	0.6828	0.3414
$p = [6.4, 6.6)$	0.9262	**0.9000**	0.7920	0.6655	0.3328
$p = [6.2, 6.4)$	0.8249	0.8019	0.7074	0.5945	0.2972
$p = [6.0, 6.2)$	0.7235	0.7039	0.6228	0.5234	0.2617
$p = [5.8, 6.0)$	0.6222	0.6058	0.5383	0.4523	0.2262
$p = [5.6, 5.8)$	0.5208	0.5077	0.4537	0.3813	0.1906
$p = [5.4, 5.6)$	0.4195	0.4096	0.3691	0.3102	0.1551
$p = [5.2, 5.4)$	0.3181	0.3116	0.2846	0.2391	0.1196
$p = [5.0, 5.2)$	0.2168	0.2135	**0.2000**	0.1681	0.0840

In this array, the derived sentence probabilities for the three sentences in $\mathcal{B}$ are shown in bold type; they are exactly their given values.

Π's *negotiation strategy* is a function $\mathbf{S} : \mathcal{K} \times \mathcal{B} \to \mathcal{A}$ where $\mathcal{A}$ is the set of actions that send $\textit{Offer}(.)$, $\textit{Accept}(.)$, $\textit{Reject}(.)$ and $\textit{Quit}(.)$ messages to Ω. If Π sends $\textit{Offer}(.)$, $\textit{Accept}(.)$ or $\textit{Reject}(.)$ messages to Ω then she is giving Ω information about herself. In an infinite-horizon bargaining game where there is no incentive to trade now rather than later, a self-interested agent will "sit and wait", and do nothing except, perhaps, to ask for information. The well known bargaining response to an approach by an interested party "Well make me an offer" illustrates how a shrewd bargainer may behave in this situation.

An agent may be motivated to act for various reasons — three are mentioned. First, if there are costs involved in the bargaining process due *either* to changes in the value of the negotiation object with time *or* to the intrinsic cost of conducting the negotiation itself. Second, if there is a risk of breakdown caused by the opponent walking away from the bargaining table. Third, if the agent is concerned with establishing a sense of trust with the opponent — this could be the case in the establishment of a business relationship. Of these three reasons the last two are addressed here. The risk of breakdown may be reduced, and a sense of trust may be established, if the agent appears to its opponent to be "approaching the negotiation in an even-handed manner". One dimension of "appearing to be even-handed" is to be equitable with the value of information given to the opponent. Various bargaining strategies, both with and without breakdown, are described in [1], but they do not address this issue. A bargaining strategy is described here that is founded on a principle of "equitable information gain". That is, Π attempts to respond to Ω's messages so that Ω's expected information gain similar to that which Π has received.

Π models Ω by observing her actions, and by representing beliefs about her future actions in the probability distribution $\mathbf{P}(\Omega Acc)$. Π measures the value of information that it receives from Ω by the change in the entropy of this distribution as a result of representing that information in $\mathbf{P}(\Omega Acc)$. More generally, Π measures the value of information received in a message, μ, by the change in the entropy in its entire representation, $\mathcal{J}_t = \mathcal{K}_t \cup \mathcal{B}_t$, as a result of the receipt of that message; this is denoted by: $\Delta_\mu |\mathcal{J}_t^\Pi|$, where $|\mathcal{J}_t^\Pi|$ denotes the value (as negative entropy) of Π's information in $\mathcal{J}$ at time t. It is "not unreasonable to suggest" that these two representations should be similar. To support its attempts to achieve "equitable information gain" Π assumes that Ω's reasoning apparatus mirrors its own, and so is able to estimate the change in Ω's entropy as a result of sending a message μ to Ω: $\Delta_\mu|\mathcal{J}_t^\Omega|$. Suppose that Π receives a message $\mu = \textit{Offer}(.)$ from Ω and observes an information gain of $\Delta_\mu|\mathcal{J}_t^\Pi|$. Suppose that Π wishes to reject this offer by sending a counter-offer, $\textit{Offer}(\delta)$, that will give Ω expected "equitable information gain". $\delta = \{\arg\max_\delta \mathbf{P}(\Pi Acc(\delta) \mid \mathcal{I}_t) \geq \alpha \mid (\Delta_{\textit{Offer}(\delta)}|\mathcal{J}_t^\Omega| \approx \Delta_\mu|\mathcal{J}_t^\Pi|)\}$. That is Π chooses the most acceptable deal to herself that gives her opponent expected "equitable information gain" provided that there is such a deal. If there is not then Π chooses the best available compromise $\delta = \{\arg\max_\delta (\Delta_{\textit{Offer}(\delta)}|\mathcal{J}_t^\Omega|) \mid \mathbf{P}(\Pi Acc(\delta) \mid \mathcal{I}_t) \geq \alpha\}$ provided there is such a deal.

The "equitable information gain" strategy generalizes the simple-minded alternating offers strategy. Suppose that Π is trying to buy something from Ω with bilateral bargaining in which all offers and responses stand — ie: there is no decay of offer integrity. Suppose that Π has offered \$1 and Ω has refused, and Ω has asked \$10 and Π has refused. If amounts are limited to whole dollars only then the deal set $\mathcal{D} = \{1, \cdots, 10\}$. Π models Ω with the distribution $\mathbf{P}(\Omega Acc(.))$, and knows that $\mathbf{P}(\Omega Acc(1)) = 0$ and $\mathbf{P}(\Omega Acc(10)) = 1$. The entropy of the resulting distribution is 2.2020. To apply the "equitable information gain" strategy Π assumes that Ω's decision-making machinery mirrors its own. In which case Ω is assumed to have constructed a mirror-image distribution to model Π that will have the same entropy. At this stage, time $t = 0$, calibrate the amount of information held by each agent at zero — ie: $|\mathcal{J}_0^\Pi| = |\mathcal{J}_0^\Omega| = 0$. Now if, at time $t = 1$, Ω asks Π for \$9 then Ω gives information to Π and $|\mathcal{J}_1^\Pi| = 0.2548$. If Π rejects this offer then she gives information to Ω and $|\mathcal{J}_1^\Omega| = 0.2548$. Suppose that Π wishes to counter with an "equitable information gain" offer. If, at time $t = 2$, Π offers Ω \$2 then $|\mathcal{J}_2^\Omega| = 0.2548 + 0.2559$. Alternatively, if Π offers Ω \$3 then $|\mathcal{J}_2^\Omega| = 0.2548 + 0.5136$. And so \$2 is a near "equitable information gain" response by Π at time $t = 2$.

References

1. J. Debenham: Bargaining with information. In Jennings, N., Sierra, C., Sonenberg, L., Tambe, M., eds.: Proceedings Third International Conference on Autonomous Agents and Multi Agent Systems AAMAS-2004, ACM (2004) 664 – 671
2. Rahwan, I., Ramchurn, S., Jennings, N., McBurney, P., Parsons, S., Sonenberg, E.: Argumentation-based negotiation. Knowledge Engineering Review (2004)
3. Ramchurn, S., Jennings, N., Sierra, C.: Persuasive negotiation for autonomous agents: A rhetorical approach. In: Proc. IJCAI Workshop on Computational Models of Natural Argument. (2003) 9–17

4. MacKay, D.: Information Theory, Inference and Learning Algorithms. Cambridge University Press (2003)
5. Halpern, J.: Reasoning about Uncertainty. MIT Press (2003)
6. Jaynes, E.: Information theory and statistical mechanics: Part I. Physical Review **106** (1957) 620–630

Agent Services-Driven Plug-and-Play in F-TRADE[1]

Longbing Cao, Jiarui Ni, Jiaqi Wang, and Chengqi Zhang

Faculty of Information Technology, University of Technology Sydney, Australia
{lbcao, jiarui, jqwang, chengqi}@it.uts.edu.au

Abstract. We have built an agent service-based enterprise infrastructure: F-TRADE. With its online connectivity to huge real stock data in global markets, it can be used for online evaluation of trading strategies and data mining algorithms. The main functions in the F-TRADE include soft plug-and-play, and back-testing, optimization, integration and evaluation of algorithms. In this paper, we'll focus on introducing the intelligent plug-and-play, which is a key system function in the F-TRADE. The basic idea for the soft plug-and-play is to build agent services which can support the online plug-in of agents, algorithms and data sources. Agent UML-based modeling, role model and agent services for the plug-and-play are discussed. With this design, algorithm providers, data source providers, and system module developers of the F-TRADE can expand system functions and resources by online plugging them into the F-TRADE.

1 Introduction

Information technology (IT) has been getting involved in finance more and more inseparably. Both IT and finance are getting more and more professional and technical. It is very hard for financial persons to devote themselves to both financial trading/research and IT for supporting their trading/research. On the other hand, powerful IT support can make financial trading and research more efficient and profitable. This is one way for IT persons to set foot in financial markets. We call it $IT_{R\&D}$-Enabled Finance. In consideration of this, we have built an agent service-based [1] infrastructure called F-TRADE [2], which can support trading and mining.

The main objective of building the F-TRADE is to provide financial traders and researchers, and miners on financial data with a practically flexible and automatic infrastructure. With this infrastructure, they can plug their algorithms into it easily, and concentrate on improving the performance of their algorithms with iterative evaluation on a large amount of real stock data from international markets. All other work, including user interface implementation, data preparation, and resulting output, etc., is maintained by this platform. For financial traders, for instance, brokers and

---

[1] F-TRADE is a web-based automated enterprise infrastructure for evaluation of trading strategies and data mining algorithms with online connection to huge amount of stock data. It has been online running for more than one year. It gets fund support from CMCRC (Capital Market CRC, www.cmcrc.com) for the Data Mining Program at CMCRC. The current version F-TRADE 2.0 can be accessed by http://datamining.it.uts.edu.au:8080/tsap, information can also be reached from http://www-staff.it.uts.edu.au/~lbcao/ftrade/ftrade.htm.

retailers, the F-TRADE presents them a real test bed, which can help them evaluate their favorite trading strategies iteratively without risk before they put money into the real markets. On the other hand, the F-TRADE presents a large amount of real stock data in multiple international markets, which can be used for both realistic back-testing of trading strategies and mining algorithms.

The F-TRADE looks also like an online service provider. As a systematic infrastructure for supporting data mining, trading evaluation, and finance-oriented applications, the F-TRADE encompasses comprehensive functions and services. They can be divided into following groups: (i) trading services support, (ii) mining services support, (iii) data services support, (iv) algorithm services support, and (v) system services support. In order to support all these services, soft plug-and-play is essential in the F-TRADE. It gets involved in plug in of data sources, data requests, trading or mining algorithms, system functional components, and the like. As a matter of fact, it has been a significant feature which supports the evolution of the F-TRADE and the application add-ons on top of the F-TRADE. In this paper, we'll focus on introducing the soft plug-and-play.

The basic idea of soft plug-and-play is as follows. The Agent service-oriented technique [1] is used for designing this flexible and complex software service. We investigate the agent services-driven approach for building a plug-and-play engine. The Agent UML is used for the modeling of the plug-and-play; role model is built for it. Service model for the plug-and-play is presented. The implementation of plug-in algorithms and system modules are illustrated as an instance of plug-and-play.

More than 20 algorithms of trading strategies have been plugged into the F-TRADE using the plug-and-play. All new-coming system modules supporting the migration of the F-TRADE from version 1.0 to 2.0 are logged on using the plug-in support. We have also tested remote plug-in from CMCRC in city of Sydney to the F-TRADE server located at Univ. of Technology Sydney (UTS). With the soft plug-and-play, both researches and applications from finance such as mining algorithms, system modules for technical analysis, fundamental analysis, investment decision support and risk management can be easily embedded into the F-TRADE.

The remainder of this paper is organized as follows. In Section 2, the modeling of the plug-and-play is discussed. Section 3 introduces agent services-driven plug-and-play from the following aspects: role model, agent services, and user interfaces. We conclude this study and discuss the future work in Section 4.

2 Plug-and-Play Modeling

As we have discussed in the above, plug-and-play gets involved in many functions and the evolutionary lifecycle of the F-TRADE. In this paper, we'll take the plug-in of an algorithm as an instance, and introduce the conceptual model, role model [3], agent services [1, 2, 4], and the generation of the user interface to plug-in an algorithm. In this section, we discuss the modeling of the proposed plug-and-play.

We use Agent Unified Modeling Language (AUML) technology [5] to model the agent service-based plug-and-play. In Agent UML, Package is one of the two techniques recommended for expressing agent interaction protocols. We use packages to describe the agent interaction protocols in plug-in support.

There are four embedded packages for supporting the process of plug-in: To Implement, To Input, To Register, and To Generate, as shown in Figure 1. They present the process of agent interactions in the plug-in activities. The package To Implement programs an algorithm in AlgoEditor by implementing the AlgoAPIAgent and ResourceAPIAgent. The To Input package types in agent ontologies of the programmed algorithm and requests to plug in the algorithm. The real registration of the algorithm is done by the package of To Register; naming, directory and class of the algorithm are stored into an algorithm base, and linkage to data resources are set at this moment. Finally, the input and output user interfaces for the algorithm are managed by package To Generate.

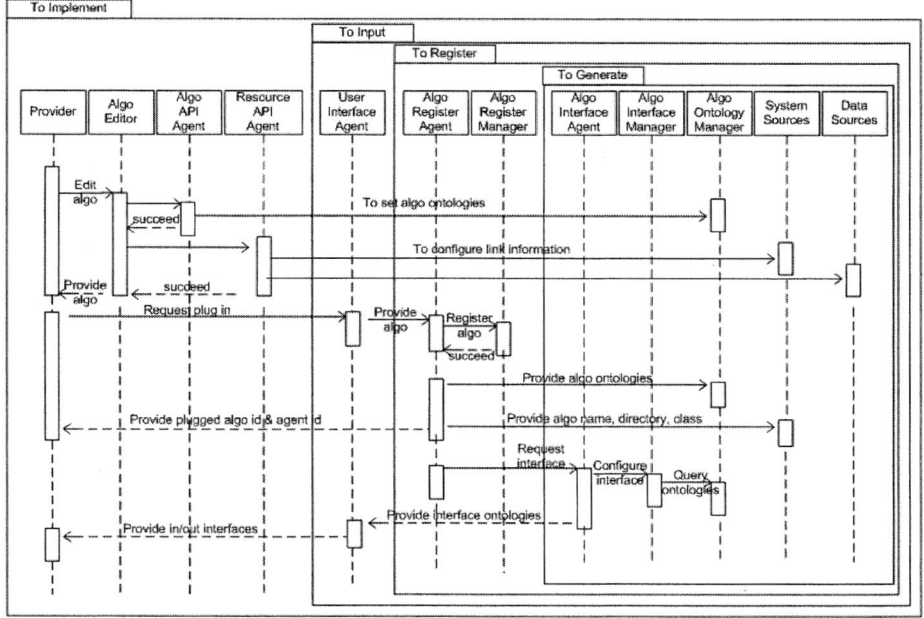

Fig. 1. Package diagram of the plug-and-play

3 Agent Services-Driven Plug-and-Play

In this section, we focus on discussing the analysis and design of the agent services-driven plug-and-play. We first introduce the role model for plug-and-play. Afterwards, the Agent service for plug-and-play is presented in details. Finally, the user interface for algorithm and system module plug-in is presented.

3.1 Role Model for the Plug-and-Play

In the agent-based F-TRADE, there is a role PLUGINPERSON which is in charge of the function of plug-and-play. Role model [2] can be built for the PLUGINPERSON, which describes attributes of permissions, responsibilities, protocols and activities of the role. Figure 2 shows the role schema of PLUGINPERSON.

Role Schema: PLUGINPERSON
Description: This preliminary role involves applying registering a nonexistent algorithm, typing in attribute items of the algorithm, and submitting plug in request to F-TRADE.
Protocols and Activities: ReadAlgorithm, <u>ApplyRegistration</u>, <u>FillinAttributeItems</u>, SubmitAlgoPluginRequest

Permissions:
        reads   Algorithms   // an *algorithm will be registered*
        changes *AlgoApplicationForms* // *algorithm registration application form*
        changes *AttributeItems*   // *all attribute items of an algorithm*

Responsibilities
Liveness:
    PLUGINPERSON = (ReadAlgorithm).(<u>ApplyRegistration</u>).
                   (<u>FillinAttributeItems</u>)+.(SubmitAlgoPluginRequest)
 	
Safety:
   • The algorithm agent has been programmed by implementing AlgoInterface agent and ResourceInterface agent, and is available for plug in.
   • This algorithm hasn't been plugged into the algorithm base.

Fig. 2. Schema for role PLUGINPERSON

The objective of this role is to plug in an algorithm into the F-TRADE, which is nonexistent in the algorithm base. The agent playing this role will execute the protocol ReadAlgorithm, followed by the activities <u>ApplyRegistration</u> and <u>FillinAttributeItems</u>, and then executes the protocol SubmitAlgoPluginRequest. The role has rights to read the algorithm from non-plug in directory, and changes the application content for the registration and the attributes of the algorithm. As preconditions, the agent is required to ensure that two constraints in safety responsibility are satisfied.

3.2 Agent Services for the Plug-and-Play

In reality, many agents and services are involved in the plug-and-play in order to make it successful. There are three directly related agent services which handle the plug-and-play. They are the *InputAlgorithm*, *RegisterAlgorithm* and *Generate AlgoInterface* services, respectively. Here, we just take one service named *RegisterAlgorithm* as an example, and introduce it in details in Figure 3. More information about agent service-oriented analysis and design and about the plug-and-play can be reached from [1].

AgentService
  RegisterAlgorithm(algoname;inputlist;inputconstraint;outputlist;outputconstraint;)
Description:
  This agent service involves accepting the registration application submitted by role PluginPerson, checking the validity of attribute items, creating the name and directory of the algorithm, and generating a universal agent identifier and a unique algorithm id.
Role: PluginPerson
Pre-conditions:
  - A request of registering an algorithm has been activated by protocol SubmitAlgoPluginRequest
  - A knowledge base storing rules for agent and service naming and directory
Type: algorithm.[datamining/tradingsignal]
Location: algo.[algorithmname]
Inputs: inputlist
InputConstraints: inputconstraint[;]
Outputs: outputlist
OutputConstraints: outputconstraint[;]
Activities: Register the algorithm
Permissions:
  - Read supplied knowledge base storing algorithm agent ontologies
  - Read supplied algorithm base storing algorithm information
Post-conditions:
  - Generate a unique agent identifier, naming, and a locator for the algorithm agent
  - Generate a unique algorithm id
Exceptions:
  - Cannot find target algorithm
  - There are invalid format existing in the input attributes

Fig. 3. Agent service RegisterAlgorithm

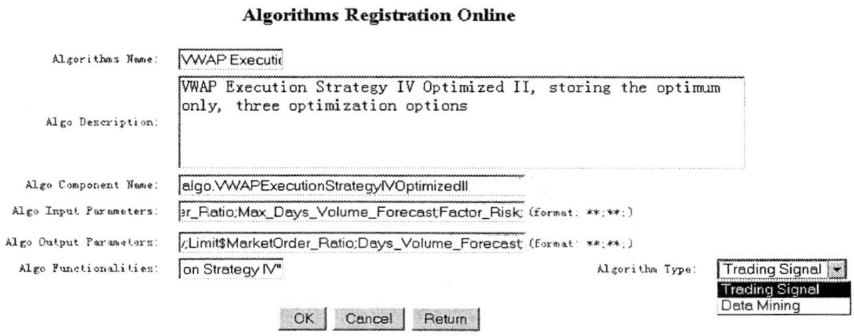

Fig. 4. User interface for an algorithm plug-in

3.3 Implementation

User interfaces must be implemented in association with the plug-and-play. Figure 4 shows the user interface for plugging an algorithm into the F-TRADE. Ontologies include all parameters of the algorithm, and specifications for and constraints on every ontology element must be defined and typed here. After submitting the registration request, the input and output interfaces for this algorithm will be generated automatically, respectively. As we discussed before, plug-and-play can be used not only for algorithms, but also for data sources and functional agents and services.

4 Conclusions and Future Work

We have built an agent services-driven infrastructure F-TRADE, which supports trading and mining in international stock markets. It can be used as a virtual service provider offering services such as stock data, trading and mining algorithms, and system modules. In this paper, we have focused on introducing a key function called soft plug-and-play provided in the F-TRADE. We have studied the agent services-driven approach to building this function. Agent UML-based conceptual model and role model for the plug-and-play have been discussed. We also have presented the agent services and user interfaces for the plug-and-play. Our experiments have shown the agent services-driven approach can support flexible and efficient plug-and-play of data sources, trading and mining algorithms, system components, and even top-up applications for the finance to the F-TRADE.

Further refinements will be performed on how to make the plug-and-play more intelligent. The first issue is to support more user-friendly human agent interaction; ontology profiles will be enhanced in the interaction with user agents. The second investigation is to develop more flexible strategies for the mediation of agents and services, which can help search and locate the target agents and services efficiently.

References

1. Cao, L.B.: Agent service-oriented analysis and design. PhD thesis, University of Technology Sydney, Australia (2005) (to appear)
2. Cao, L.B., Wang, J.Q., Lin, L., Zhang, C.Q.: Agent Services-Based Infrastructure for Online Assessment of Trading Strategies. In Proceedings of the 2004 IEEE/WIC/ACM International Conference on Intelligent Agent Technology, IEEE Computer Society Press (2004)
3. Zambonelli, F., Jennings, N. R., Wooldridge, M.: Developing multiagent systems: the Gaia Methodology. ACM Trans on Software Engineering and Methodology, 12 (3) (2003) 317-370
4. Java Community Process. Java agent services specification. 5 Mar (2002)
5. Agent UML: www.auml.org

# Applying *Multi-medians Location and Steiner Tree Methods* into Agents Distributed Blackboard Architecture Construction

Yi-Chuan Jiang and Shi-Yong Zhang

Department of Computing and Information Technology,
Fudan University, Shanghai 200433, P.R.China

Abstract. Distributed blackboard is one of the popular agent communication architectures, where the blackboards location and communication topology are two important issues. However, there are few works about the issues. To solve this problem, this paper presents a new method, which applies *Multi-Medians Location Method* to compute the sub-blackboard locations, and applies *Steinner Tree Method* to compute the communication topology among sub-blackboards. The model can construct the distributed blackboard architecture effectively according to the current underlying network topology.

Keywords: Multi Agents; Agents Communication; Distributed Blackboard; Multi-Medians Location; Steinner Tree.

1 Introduction

In the blackboard communication architecture, some sub-blackboards are set in the system and each sub-blackboard takes charge of the communications of some agents [1]. Here agents are organized into some federated systems where agents do not communicate directly with each other but through their respective sub-blackboards. The agents in a federated system surrender their communication autonomy to the sub-blackboards and the sub-blackboard takes full responsibility for their needs.

In the distributed blackboard architecture, the location of sub-blackboards and the communication path among sub-blackboards should be attached much importance. However, there are few researches on such issues and sub-blackboards are always located randomly in the underlying network of current agent systems.

To solve the above problem, the paper presents a model for constructing agent distributed blackboard communication architecture. According to the current underlying network topology, the model can uses *multi-medians location method* to compute the sub-blackboard locations, and uses *Steiner tree method* to compute the communication topology among sub-blackboards. Such constructed architecture can perform better than the initial architecture that sub-blackboards are located randomly, which is testified by our simulation experiments.

2 Multi-medians Location and Steiner Tree Problem

Problem of finding the "best" location of facilities in graph is to minimize the total sum of the distances from vertices of the graph to the nearest facility, which is generally referred to as *minisum location problem* [2]. The facility locations resulting from the solution to a minisum problem are called the *medians*.

Now we discuss the problem of finding p-median of a given graph G; that is the problem of locating a given number (p say) of facilities optimally so that the sum of the shortest distances to the vertices of G from their nearest facility is minimized [3].

Firstly, let $G = (X, E)$ be a graph with X the set of vertices and E the set of edges. Let X_p be a subset of the set X of vertices of the graph $G = (X, E)$ and let X_p contain p vertices. Now we write

$$d(X_p, x_j) = \min_{x_i \in X_p}[d(x_i, x_j)] \quad (1)$$

Where $d(x_i, x_j)$ denotes the shortest path distance between x_i and x_j.

If x_i' is the vertex of X_p which produces the minimum in (1), we will say that vertex x_j is *allocated* to x_i'. The *transmission numbers* for the set X_p of vertices are defined as (2).

$$\sigma(X_p) = \sum_{x_j \in X} d(X_p, x_j) \quad (2)$$

A set $\overline{X}_{po}$ for which

$$\sigma(\overline{X}_{po}) = \min_{X_p \subseteq X}[\sigma(X_p)] \quad (3)$$

is now called the *p-medians* of G. The aim of *multi-medians location problem* is to select p vertices to be medians and assign each of the other vertices to its closest media so as to minimize the total distance between the medians and other vertices.

The *Steiner tree problem* is to interconnect (a subset of) the nodes such that there is a path between every pair of nodes while minimizing the total cost of selected edges.

A minimum Steiner tree is defined to be the minimal cost subgraph spanning a given set of nodes in the graph [5] [6]. Formally, it can be formulated as follows: Given a weighted, undirected graph $G=(V, E, w)$, V denotes the set of nodes in the graph and E is the set of edges (or links). Let $w: E \rightarrow R$ be a positive edge weight function, and designate a non-empty set of terminal nodes M, where $\phi \subset M \subset V$.

The nodes that belong to the complementary subset $\overline{M}$, where $\overline{M} = V - M$, are called non-terminals. A Steiner tree for M in G is a tree that meets all nodes in M. The MST problem is to find a Steiner tree of minimum total edge cost. The solution to this problem is a *minimum Steiner tree T*. Non-terminal nodes that end up in a minimum Steiner tree T are called *Steiner Nodes*.

3 Compute the Sub-blackboard Locations

To construct the distributed blackboard architecture, firstly we should compute the locations of sub-blackboards, so as to minimize the total communication cost between sub-blackboards and their allocated agents. The communication cost is a function of the distance between sub-blackboards and their allocated agents, so the location of sub-blackboards should minimize the total communication distances.

Based on the approximate algorithm of multi-medias problem [2][4], we can compute the sub-blackboard locations.

The method proceeds by choosing any p nodes in the network at random to form the initial set S that is assumed to be an approximation to the sub-blackboard locations set $\overline{X}_p$. The method then tests if any node $x_j \in X - S$ could replace a node $x_i \in S$ as a sub-blackboard location node and so produce a new set $S' = S \cup \{x_j\} - \{x_i\}$ whose transmission $\sigma(S')$ is less than $\sigma(S)$. If so, the substitution of node x_i by x_j is performed thus obtaining a set S' that is a better approximation to the p-location nodes set $\overline{X}_p$. The same tests are now performed on the new set S' and so on, until a set $\overline{S}$ is finally obtained for which no substitution of a vertex in $\overline{S}$ by another vertex in $X - \overline{S}$ produces a set with transmission less than $\sigma(\overline{S})$. This final set $\overline{S}$ is then taken to be the required approximation to $\overline{X}_p$.

Algorithm1. Computing_Subblackboard Locations (int p).

Step 1. Select a set S of *p* vertices to form the initial approximation to the sub-blackboard locations. Call all vertices $x_j \notin S$ "untried".

Step 2. Select some "untried" vertex $x_j \notin S$ and for each vertex $x_i \in S$, compute the "reduction" Δ_{ij} in the set transmission if x_j is substituted for x_i, i.e. compute:

$$\Delta_{ij} = \sigma(S) - \sigma(S \cup \{x_j\} - \{x_i\}) \tag{4}$$

Step 3. Find $\Delta_{i_o j} = \max_{x_i \in S}[\Delta_{ij}]$.

I. If $\Delta_{i_o j} \leq 0$ call x_j "tried" and go to step 2.

II. If $\Delta_{i_o j} > 0$ set $S \leftarrow S \cup \{x_j\} - \{x_i\}$ call x_j "tried" and go to step 2.

Step 4. Repeat steps 2 and 3 until all vertices in $X - S$ have been tried. This is referred to as a cycle. If, during the last cycle no vertex substitution at all has been made at step 3(i), go to step 5. Otherwise, if some vertex substitution has been made, call all vertices "untried" and return to step 2.

Step 5. Stop. The current set S is the estimated sub-blackboard location nodes set $\overline{X_p}$.

4 Compute the Communication Topology Among Sub-blackboards

Since in our agent system, the communication cost is mainly influenced by communication distance among nodes, we should compute the communication topology among sub-blackboards with the least total communication distances. Therefore, we can apply Steiner tree method in the topology computation.

On the base of the KMB algorithm [6] [7], now we compute the communication topology among sub-blackboards.

Given a weighted undirected graph $G = (V, E, w)$ which denotes the underlying network topology, and a set of sub-blackboard nodes $M \subseteq V$, consider the complete undirected graph $G' = (V', E', w')$ constructed from G and M in such a way that $V' = M$, and for every edge $(i, j) \in E'$, weight $w(i, j)$ is set equal to the weight sum of the shortest path from node i to node j in graph G. For each edge in G', there corresponds a shortest path in G. Given any spanning tree in G', we can construct a subgraph G by replacing each edge in the tree by its corresponding shortest path in G.

Fig 1 shows a network G and sub-blackboard set M= {1, 3, 9, 7} (shaded nodes). We first calculate the shortest distance between every two sub-blackboards in G. They are 8, 9, 13, 7, 8, 5 respective to a<1, 9>, b<1, 3>, c<1, 7>, d<3, 9>, e<3, 7>, f<7, 9>. Let a, b, c, d, e, f form a graph G', shown as Fig 1 (b). The minimum spanning tree of G' is shown with thick lines in Fig 1 (b), and then we construct the communication topology among sub-blackboards by replacing each edge in the tree by its corresponding shortest path in the network G. The communication topology among sub-blackboards is shown as thick lines in Fig 1 (c).

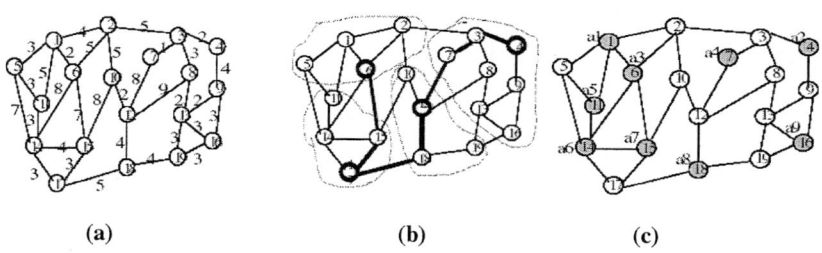

Fig. 1. An example of a Steiner tree construction in network

5   Case Studies and Simulation Experiment

To show how effectively our proposed model can work, we compare the performance of (i) the distributed blackboard architecture that sub-blackboards are randomly located and (ii) the one that applies multi-medians location & Steiner tree method.

Fig 2 illustrates a simulated network topology, and Fig 6 illustrates an agents communication relations. Let the number of sub-blackboards is 4, now we use multi-medians location & Steiner tree methods to construct the agents distributed blackboard architecture.

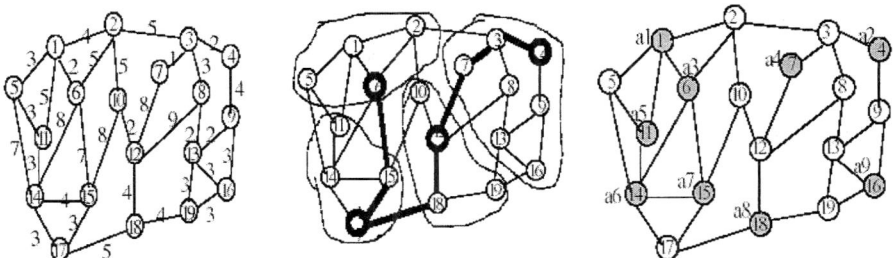

Fig. 2. Simulated network   **Fig. 3.** Constructed blackboard architecture   **Fig. 4.** Agent distribution

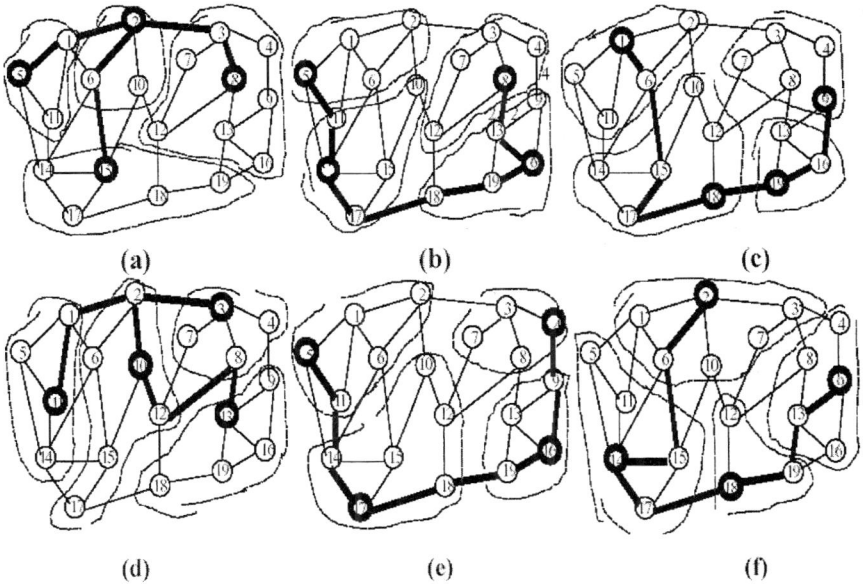

Fig. 5. Randomly constructed distributed blackboard architecture

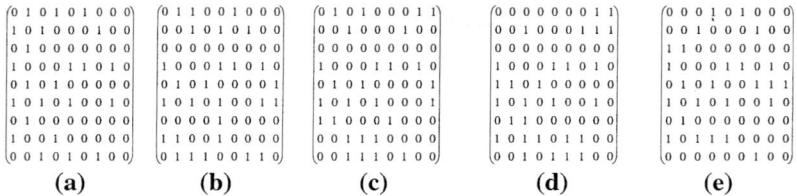

Fig. 6. Agents' communication relations

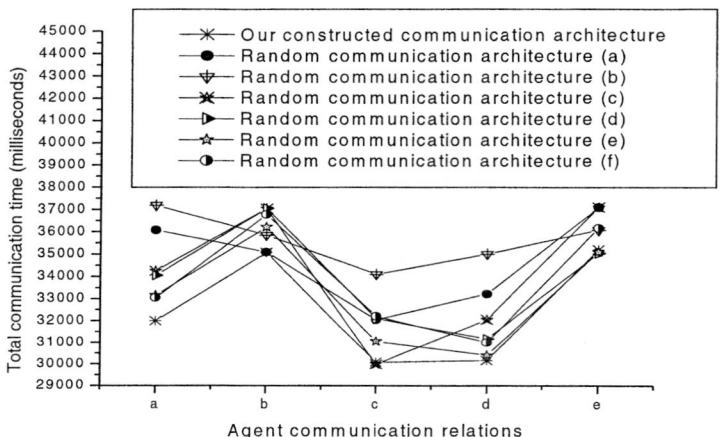

Fig. 7. Comparison of all kinds of agent communication architecture

Therefore, the final agents distriubted blackboard architecture is show as Fig. 3.

Now we have some agents locate on the network, shown as Fig 4. Let there be 6 kinds of agents communication relations, shown as Fig 6. In the matrix, if a_i communicate to a_j, then $r_{ij}=1$, else $r_{ij}=0$.

Now we make simulation for the agents communication by the archicture of Fig 3 and other architectures where sub-blackboards are randomly located of Fig 5.

Fig 7 is the simulation test results, from which we can see that the architecture in Fig 3 is the most efficient. Therefore, our model that applies multi-medians location & Steiner tree methods into agents distributed blackboard architecture construction is correct and effective.

References

[1] Cyprian Foinjong Ngolah. A Tutorial on Agent Communication and Knowledge Sharing. http://www.enel.ucalgary.ca/People/far/Lectures/SENG60922/PDF/tutorials/2002/Agent_Communication_and_Knowledge_Sharing.pdf
[2] Nicos Christofides. Graph Theory: an algorithmic approach. Academic Press, London. 1975. 79-120.

[3] Teitz, M.B. and Bart, P.(1968). Heuristic Methods for Estimating the Generalized Vertex Median of a Weighted Graph, Ops. Res., 16. P.955.
[4] Cooper, L. (1963). Location Allocation problems, Ops.Res., 11, P 331.
[5] Martini Zachariasen. Algorithms for Plane Steiner Tree Problems. Ph.d Thesis. [1998]. University of Copenhagen, Denmark.
[6] Brian Dazheng Zhou. Steiner Tree Optimization in Multicast Routing. M.S. Thesis [2002]. University of Guelph. July, 2002.
[7] L.Kou, G.Markowsky, and L.Berman. A Fast Algorithm for Steiner Trees. Acta Informatica. Vol.15, 1981.

Meta-game Equilibrium for Multi-agent Reinforcement Learning

Yang Gao[1], Joshua Zhexue Huang[2], Hongqiang Rong[2], and Zhi-Hua Zhou[1]

[1] National Laboratory for Novel Software Technology,
Nanjing University, Nanjing 210093, China
{gaoy, zhouzh}@nju.edu.cn
[2] E-Business Technology Institute,
The University of Hong Kong, Hong Kong, China
{jhuang, hrong}@eti.hku.hk

Abstract. This paper proposes a multi-agent Q-learning algorithm called meta-game-Q learning that is developed from the meta-game equilibrium concept. Different from Nash equilibrium, meta-game equilibrium can achieve the optimal joint action game through deliberating its preference and predicting others' policies in the general-sum game. A distributed negotiation algorithm is used to solve the meta-game equilibrium problem instead of using centralized linear programming algorithms. We use the repeated prisoner's dilemma example to empirically demonstrate that the algorithm converges to meta-game equilibrium.

1 Introduction

Recently there have been growing interests in extending reinforcement learning to the multi-agent domain. Based on the Markov (or stochastic) game models, many multi-agent reinforcement learning algorithms have been proposed. Littman suggested the minimax-Q learning algorithm for zero-sum stochastic games [5]. A second approach was pursued by Claus and Boutilier to deal with common-payoff stochastic games[1]. Hu et al. in 1998 made a pivotal contribution by introducing Nash-Q learning to general-sum games[3][4]. Littman replaced Nash-Q learning by Friend-and-Foe-Q learning in some special stochastic games[6]. Furthermore, Greenwald et al. introduced the correlated equilibrium concept and proposed CE-Q learning to generalize both Nash-Q and Friend-and-Foe-Q learning methods[2].

Shoham et al. have raised the question of the justification of using Nash equilibrium in multi-agent setting[7]. To answer this question, we think that Nash equilibrium is not optimal in general-sum games. In dealing with the collective rationality, new solutions can be adopted to replace the Nash equilibrium. When agents can consider their own preferences and predict actions of other agents correctly, they can reach meta-game equilibrium that is the optimal joint policy in the general-sum game. Based on this concept, we discuss the meta-game equilibrium and introduce the meta-game-Q learning algorithm in this paper.

In the next section we briefly review Markov game and multi-agent reinforcement learning. In Section 3, we introduce the meta-game equilibrium concept. Then, we present a distributed negotiation algorithm to solve the meta-game equilibrium problem in the general-sum game in Section 4. In Section 5, we discuss our experimental results. Finally, in Section 6 we draw some conclusions.

2 Multi-agent Reinforcement Learning

Game theory is one of the most important mathematical foundations to formulate a multi-agent system. When we use the games to model a multi-agent system, all discrete states in the MDP model are regarded as some distinguishing games. Therefore, the immediate rewards of one agent received from the world not only depend on its own action chosen by itself, but also depend on other actions by other agents. As a result, the single agent reinforcement learning algorithm fails in the multi-agent domain.

When the probability transitions between different games satisfy the Markov property, the MDP model for single agent can be generalized to the Markov game for the multi-agent system.

Definition 1. A Markov game is a tuple $\langle I, S, (A_i(s))_{s \in S, 1 \leq i \leq n}, T, (R_i)_{1 \leq i \leq n} \rangle$, where I is a set of n agents, S is a finite set of states of the world, $A_i(s)$ is a finite set of the ith agent's actions at state s, T is the probability function that describes state-transition conditioned on past states and joint actions, and $R_i(s, \vec{a})$ is the ith agent's reward for state $s \in S$ and joint actions $\vec{a} \in A_1(s) \times \ldots \times A_n(s)$[2].

In order to find the optimal action sequence policy $\pi : S \to \vec{a}$, a state-action value function $Q_i^\pi(s, \vec{a})$ is defined as the agent i's value of taking action $\vec{a}$ in state s under a policy π, i.e.,

$$Q_i^\pi(s, \vec{a}) = E_\pi\{\Sigma_{j=0}^\infty \gamma^j r_i(s_{j+1})\} \quad (1)$$

where γ is a discounter factor. The optimal policy Q_i^* is defined as

$$Q_i^*(s, \vec{a}) = \max_\pi Q_i^\pi(s, \vec{a}) \quad (2)$$

Because the parameters of the Markov game model are unknown, the agent can only get its experiences by trial-and-error to approximate the optimal policy through reinforcement learning. In the Markov games, the ith agent's Q-values are updated on states and the action-vector $\vec{a}$ as

$$Q_i(s, \vec{a}) = Q_i(s, \vec{a}) + \alpha[r_i(s, \vec{a}) + \gamma \max_{\vec{a'} \in A'} Q_i(s', \vec{a'}) - Q_i(s, \vec{a})] \quad (3)$$

3 Meta-game Equilibrium

Fig. 1 shows the Prisoner's Dilemma game which is an abstraction of social situations where each agent is faced with two alternative actions: *cooperation* and

Fig. 1. Prisoner's Dilemma game G

$$\text{Agent 2} \begin{array}{c|cc} & \multicolumn{2}{c}{\text{Agent 1}} \\ & d & c \\ \hline d & (r_1\text{=-9},r_1\text{=-9}) & (r_3\text{=0},r_2\text{=-10}) \\ c & (r_2\text{=-10},r_3\text{=0}) & (r_4\text{=-1},r_4\text{=-1}) \end{array}$$

Fig. 2. Meta-game 1G of Prisoner's Dilemma game G

$$\text{Agent 2} \begin{array}{c|cccc} & \multicolumn{4}{c}{\text{Agent 1}} \\ & f_1 & f_2 & f_3 & f_4 \\ \hline d & (-9,-9) & (0,-10) & (-9,-9) & (0,-10) \\ c & (-10,0) & (-1,-1) & (-1,-1) & (-10,0) \end{array}$$

defecting. Prisoners will receive different payoffs r_1, r_2, r_3, r_4 for different combinations of actions, where $r_3 > r_4 > r_1 > r_2, 2r_4 > r_2 + r_3 > 2r_1$. It is well-known that the joint policy (d,d) holds Nash equilibrium in the Prisoner's Dilemma problem. However, the optimal joint policy is (c,c) because every prisoner can get more rewards than the rewards under Nash equilibrium (d,d). From the Prisoner's Dilemma game, we can see that the combination of individual agents' optimal policies may not be the optimal joint policy of the entire multi-agent system in the general-sum game. In other words, Nash equilibrium may not be the optimal strategy if collective rationality is considered.

When the agents' payoff for different action combinations become common knowledge, one agent can get the optimal policy of the entire system by means of revising its own policy through deliberating its preference and predicting others' policies. This approach is the most important principle of the meta-game theory.

Meta-game is a hypothetical game derived from the original game situation by assuming that other agents have taken their actions first. Meta-game can be presented as an extended strategic form. When extending the ith agent's strategy to a function of other agents' strategies in game G, the meta-game K_iG is constructed, where K_i is the sign of the ith agent. Obviously, the recursive meta-game can be derived from the meta-game too. Fig. 2 presents the meta-game 1G as an extended form game in Fig. 1.

In this extended form, agent 1 has four different actions, f_1, f_2, f_3 and f_4. $f_1(*) =' d'$ means that agent 1 always chooses action $'d'$ regardless of agent 2's action. Similar to f_1, the second action of agent 1 is $f_2(*) =' c'$. The third action $f_3(*) =' *'$ means that agent 1 chooses the same action as agent 2's. If agent 1 always chooses the action opposite to the agent 2's action, it is $f_4(*) =' \neg *'$. So, the game shifts to the new stable equilibrium called meta-game equilibrium if all agents can predict other's actions correctly.

Definition 2. In a multi-agent system with n agents, the meta-game $12\ldots nG$, or $n(n-1)\ldots 21G$, or one meta-game whose prefix is any kind of permutation of $1,2,\ldots,n$ is the complete game of the origin game G.

Definition 3. A joint policy $\vec{a}_m = (a_{1,m}, a_{2,m}, \ldots, a_{n,m})$ is called meta-game equilibrium in a complete game $K_1K_2\ldots K_nG$ if every agent satisfies

$$\min_{a_{P_i}} \max_{a_i} \min_{a_{F_i}} R_i(a_{P_i}, a_i, a_{F_i}) \leq R_i(a_{P_i,m}, a_{i,m}, a_{F_i,m}) \quad (4)$$

where P_i is the set of the agents listed in front of the sign i and F_i is the set of the agents listed after the sign i in prefixes $K_1 K_2 \ldots K_n$[8].

4 Meta-game-Q Reinforcement Learning

In many multi-agent settings, the reward function and the probability-transition function are unknown in advance. We cannot find the optimal Q-value by means of linear programming directly. Every agent needs to approximate the correct Q-value through trial-and-error. As shown in Eq. 5, agents must update their current Q-values with meta-game equilibrium.

$$Q_i(s, \vec{a}) = Q_i(s, \vec{a}) + \alpha[r_i(s, \vec{a}) + \gamma Q_i(s', \vec{a}_m(s')) - Q_i(s, \vec{a})] \qquad (5)$$

We cannot use a centralized algorithm to compute any equilibrium in multi-agent learning since each agent cannot know anything about other agents' rewards in advance. Instead, we have designed a distributed negotiation algorithm for meta-game-Q learning. Assume that there are only two agents a and b in a multi-agent system. The algorithm of agent a is given Table 1, where $Q_a(s, a, b)$ is agent a's current Q-value after it chooses the joint policy (a, b) in state s.

Table 1. Negotiation algorithm for solving meta-game equilibrium

---
Initial $J_a = NULL$;
Step1: agent a chooses a joint policy $(a, b) \notin J_a$;
Step2: If $Q_a(s, a, b) \geq max_{a' \in A} Q_a(s, a', b)$, $J_a = J_a + (a, b)$, return step1; else, record (a', b), goto step3;
Step3: Agent a broadcasts the message to agent b, ask agent b to judge, $Q_b(s, a', b) \geq max_{b' \in B}(s, a', b')$.
 Step3.1: If it is satisfied, agent b returns 'SUCCESS MESSAGE' to agent a. After agent a receives the 'SUCCESS MESSAGE', $J_a = J_a + (a, b)$, return step1.
 Step3.2: If it isn't satisfied, agent b return 'FAIL MESSAGE' to agent a. After agent a receives the 'FAIL MESSAGE', record the (a', b'), goto step4.
Step4: Agent a judges whether $Q_a(s, a', b') \geq Q_a(s, a, b)$. If it is satisfied, return step1, else, return $J_a = J_a + (a, b)$ and return step1.
Step5: When all agents get their final joint action sets, the meta-game equilibrium could be obtained through computing the intersection of all joint action sets, viz. $J_a \cap J_b$.

A template for meta-game-Q reinforcement learning is presented in Table 2.

5 Experimental Results and Analysis

We used the repeated prisoner's dilemma(RPD) game to test our meta-game-Q reinforcement learning algorithm. The RPD game consists of ten independent prisoner's dilemma games. The immediate reward of each independent prisoner's

Table 2. Algorithm for meta-game-Q reinforcement learning

Step1: Initialization. $\forall s \in S, \forall i \in I, \forall \vec{a}, Q_i(s, \vec{a}) = 0; \alpha = 1, \gamma = 0.9, Pr = 0.9$;
Step2: Select action. The ith agent chooses the action $a_{i,m}$ with probability Pr, or randomly chooses any other action with probability $1 - Pr$;
Step3: Observation. The ith agent observes the reward r_i and next state s';
Step4: Negotiation to get the meta-game equilibrium $\vec{a}_m(s')$ at s';
Step5: Learning. Update the Q-value $Q_i(s, \vec{a})$ using Eq.5.
Step6: Adjust the learning rate α and selection factor Pr. And return step2 until end.

---

dilemma game is given in Fig. 1. The state transitions between each independent game is deterministic. The value of the game for one agent is defined as its accumulated reward when both agents follow their meta-game equilibrium strategies in Fig. 3.

$$\text{Agent 2} \quad \begin{array}{c|cc} & \multicolumn{2}{c}{\text{Agent 1}} \\ & d & c \\ \hline d & r_1 + \sum_{j=1}^{10-i} \gamma^j r_4, r_1 + \sum_{j=1}^{10-i} \gamma^j r_4 & r_3 + \sum_{j=1}^{10-i} \gamma^j r_4, r_2 + \sum_{j=1}^{10-i} \gamma^j r_4 \\ c & r_2 + \sum_{j=1}^{10-i} \gamma^j r_4, r_3 + \sum_{j=1}^{10-i} \gamma^j r_4 & r_4 + \sum_{j=1}^{10-i} \gamma^j r_4, r_4 + \sum_{j=1}^{10-i} \gamma^j r_4 \end{array}$$

Fig. 3. The Q-value matrix of the ith game in the repeated prisoner's dilemma game, where the sum of the game's number is 10 and $r_1 = -9, r_2 = -10, r_3 = 0, r_4 = -1$

Similar to the single prisoner's dilemma game, the joint policy (c, c) is the optimal solution in RPD because of $r_3 + \sum_{j=1}^{10-i} \gamma^j r_4 > r_4 + \sum_{j=1}^{10-i} \gamma^j r_4 > r_1 + \sum_{j=1}^{10-i} \gamma^j r_4 > r_2 + \sum_{j=1}^{10-i} \gamma^j r_4, 2r_4 + 2\sum_{j=1}^{10-i} \gamma^j r_4 > r_2 + r_3 + 2\sum_{j=1}^{10-i} \gamma^j r_4 > 2r_1 + 2\sum_{j=1}^{10-i} \gamma^j r_4$. All Q-values of the matrix of the RPD game are unknown before agents begin to learn the optimal action sequence.

We ran 10 trails and calculated the difference between the current Q-value and the optimal Q-value in Fig. 3. In our experiment, we employed a training period of 100 episodes. The performance of the test period was measured by the Q-value difference when agents followed their learned strategies, starting from the first prisoner's dilemma game to the last game. The experimental result for RPD is shown in Fig. 4. From Fig. 4, we can see that when both agents were meta-game-Q learners and followed the same meta-game updating rule, they ended up with the meta-game equilibrium 100% of the time.

6 Conclusions

In this paper, we have discussed algorithms for learning optimal Q-values in the Markov game, given the meta-game equilibrium solution concept. Different

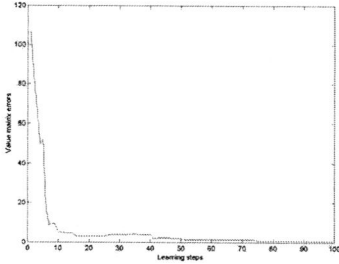

Fig. 4. On-line performance of meta-game-Q agents in RPD

from the Nash-Q learning algorithm, we have used the meta-game equilibrium instead of Nash equilibrium in the general-sum game. Specifically, we have replaced the centralized linear programming algorithms with a distributed negotiation algorithm to solve the meta-game equilibrium under incomplete common knowledge. This adaptive meta-game-Q reinforcement learning algorithm can learn the meta-game equilibrium in Markov game.

Acknowledgements

The paper is supported by the Natural Science Foundation of China (No.60103012), the National Outstanding Youth Foundation of China (No.60325207), the National Grand Fundamental Research 973 Program of China (No.2002CB312002) and the Natural Science Foundation of Jiangsu Province, China(No.BK2003409). The comments and suggestions from the anonymous reviewers greatly improved this paper.

References

1. Caroline Claus and Craig Boutilier. The dynamics of reinforcement learning in cooperative multiagent systems. In *Proceedings of the Fifteenth National Conference on Artifcail Intelligence*, pages 746–752, 1998.
2. Amy Greenwald, Keith Hall, and Roberto Serrano. Correlated-q learning. In *Proceedings of the Twentieth International Conference on*, pages 242–249, Washington DC, 2003.
3. Junling Hu and Michael P. Wellman. Multiagent reinforcement learning: theoretical framework and an algorithm. In *Proceedings of the Fifteenth International Conference on Machine Learning*, pages 242–250, 1998.
4. Junling Hu and Michael P. Wellman. Nash q-learning for general-sum stochastic games. *Journal of Machine Learning Research*, 4:1039–1069, 2003.
5. Michael L. Littman. Markov games as a framework for multi-agent reinforcement learning. In *Eleventh International Conference on Machine Learning*, pages 157–163, New Brunswick, 1994.

6. Michael L. Littman. Friend-or-foe q-learning in general-sum games. In *Proceedings of the Eighteenth International Conference on Machine Learning*, pages 322–328. Williams College, Morgan Kaufman, June 2001.
7. Yoav Shoham, Rob Powers, and Trond Grenager. Multi-agent reinforcement learning: a critical survey. Technical report, Stanford University, 2003.
8. L. C. Thomas. *Games, Theory and Applications*. Halsted Press, 1984.

A Fast Visual Search and Recognition Mechanism for Real-Time Robotics Applications

Quoc Vong Do[1], Peter Lozo[2], and Lakhmi Jain[3]

[1,3] Knowledge-Based Intelligent Engineering Systems Center, University of South Australia, Mawson Lakes, S.A. 5095, Australia
Quoc.Do@postgrads.unisa.edu.au, Lakhmi.Jain@unisa.edu.au
[2] Weapons Systems Division, Defence Science and Technology Organisation, PO Box 1500, Edinburgh, SA 5111
peter.lozo@dsto.defence.gov.au

Abstract. Robot navigation relies on a robust and real-time visual perception system to understand the surrounding environment. This paper describes a fast visual landmark search and recognition mechanism for real-time robotics applications. The mechanism models two stages of visual perception named pre-attentive and attentive stages. The pre-attentive stage provides a global guided search by identifying regions of interest, which is followed by the attentive stage for landmark recognition. The results show the mechanism validity and applicability to autonomous robot applications.

1 Introduction

Autonomous robot navigation needs a reliable and robust visual perception system to gain an understanding and awareness of the surrounding environment. Such a system could be modeled based on the effectiveness and robustness of a human visual system. Observation of the human visual system indicates that people are capable of quickly detecting a flying object and successfully avoiding collision, without the needs of object recognition. The identification of the flying object comes after the collision avoidance behaviour. This leads to a suggestion that human visual perception has two stages named pre-attentive and attentive [1]. Pre-attentive stage is a fast global process, which aims at identifying regions of interest (ROI) that are most likely to have the target object embedded within it. In comparison the attentive stage is a high level process that identifies the objects within the selected ROI regions. This is a slow computationally intensive process.

In general, when encountering a visual scene, people tend to focus on the most 'eye catching', contrasted or coloured regions. This ability can be modeled by the pre-attentive stage, where the input image is quickly analysed to determine ROI regions prior to any thorough object search. This allows the system to concentrate on ROI regions and provide a guided search mechanism for fast object recognition in the attentive stage.

Many attempts to model the pre-attentive process of visual perception have been reported in recent literature. The common methods are to detect the most 'stand out' regions based on color, features and high contrast. In [2, 3], the ROI regions are selected using a colour segmentation, prior to landmark recognition using genetic algorithms. In [4], the most highly contrastive regions are considered as ROI regions, where landmark recognition is performed using selective attention adaptive resonance theory (SAART) neural networks, starting from the highest contrastive region to the lowest region. ROI regions are larger than memory images such that a thorough landmark search and recognition is performed within each selected ROI region. This paper presents an alternative implementation of the pre-attentive stage by using knowledge from memory images to select ROI regions for landmark recognition.

2 Pre-attentive and Attentive Stages for Visual Landmark Search and Recognition

The proposed visual landmark search and recognition architecture mimics the concepts of pre-attentive and attentive stages in the human vision system for landmark recognition. Although the proposed architecture is a simpler system, with fewer functions and may be subjected to minor violations to the actual human vision system, the architecture is capable of providing fast and robust landmark search and recognition. The overall architecture shown in Figure 1 is divided into two distinct, bottom and top sections, to model the pre-attentive and attentive stages of visual perception respectively. Initially, a grey level input image of 240x320 pixels resolution is pre-processed using a 3x3-mask Sobel edge detection. The edge image is used to produce a dilated image using a 5x5 averaging window, where each pixel in the dilated edge image summons the average edge activities over a local 5x5-region in the Sobel edge image. This process is used to achieve distortion invariant landmark recognition [5], where the distorted edges are compensated by adjacent neighboring pixels. The dilated image is then passed through the pre-attentive stage, which involves the determination of ROI regions and further processes each ROI region to classify as potential regions (PR). Only PR regions are passed into the attentive stage for landmark recognition, all remaining regions are discarded.

The determination of PR regions uses the knowledge obtained from memory images to calculate two thresholds for each landmark: ROI and signature thresholds. First of all, considers three memory images of three different landmarks shown in Figure 2, a total number of significant pixels which describes a shape of each landmark is calculated by comparing each pixel against a small threshold to remove weak edges. A ROI threshold is set for each landmark, which is equal to 50% of the total number of significant pixels of the corresponding memory image. Signature thresholds on the other hand are calculated based on edge activities of internal features of each landmark, named unique region(s). These regions are fixed regions, describing physical internal appearances of each landmark and are unchanged from the camera field of views. The signature threshold is set to be equal to the number of significant pixels in the selected unique region(s) of each landmark.

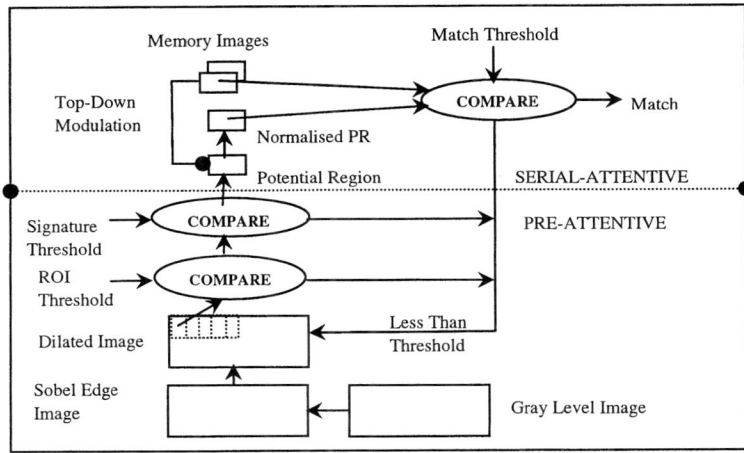

Fig. 1. The overall image processing architecture that combines the pre-attentive and the attentive stages

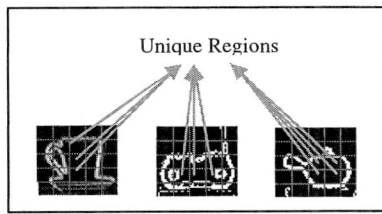

Fig. 2. Three edge detected images of selected landmarks. Regions indicated are unique regions, used for the determination of the signature threshold for each landmark

The determination of PR regions and ROI regions are based on the comparison of input regions (within the 50x50 search window) against both the ROI and signature thresholds. The input region that is greater than ROI threshold is classified as the ROI region. Then each ROI region is subjected to a further comparison with the signature threshold before being promoted into the attentive stage, where it is subjected to intensive image processing for landmark recognition.

In the attentive stage, the landmark recognition architecture is developed based on previous works [4-7], where a vision-inspired SAART neural network is proposed for landmark recognition. The SAART neural network is a derivation of adaptive resonance theories (ART) proposed by Grossberg and Carpenter [8, 9]. It incorporates an additional mechanism for top-down memory selective attention, which is achieved by pre-synaptic modulation of the input to facilitate relevant portions and inhibit irrelevant portions of input images. Thus enables the system to recognise known objects embedded in clustered images. The SAART neural network is a dynamic system and thus computationally intensive. Therefore, instead of using the whole network, the developed architecture uses only the top-down memory modulation mechanism. This mechanism uses the knowledge from memory to assist the early stage of features extraction, which increases the robustness of the landmark recognition system. Each extracted region is subjected to template matching with the corresponding memory image using the cosine rule between two 2-D images. This results in a match value range from 0-1 (where 1 represents 100% match), which is evaluated against a match threshold of 90%.

3 Results and Discussions

The performance of the developed pre-attentive stage is evaluated by measuring the time taken to completely process a series of selected scenes both with and without the pre-attentive stage. Five different scenes of different indoor environment are selected to demonstrate the effectiveness of the pre-attentive stage. The first input scene is selected with the landmark embedded in a clean background to provide an insight into the system ideal performance. The scene-2 and sense-3 are selected from office environment, and sence-4 and sence-5 are selected from a corridor environment. Figure 3 shows different image processing stages for scene-4. Initially, the system performed Sobel edge-detection on an input grey level image producing an edge image, which is blurred using a 5x5 averaging mask as shown in Figure 3(b) and Figure 3(c) respectively. The blurred image is than entered the pre-attentive stage, where a 50x50 search window is scanning across the image for PR regions determination, which is followed by landmark recognitions in the attentive stage. The results of the landmark search and recognition process are converted into a range from 0-255 and displayed as a grey level image in Figure 3(d), with the highest level of contrast represents the highest match value. The black regions are ones that have been skipped by the pre-attentive stage. The landmark is found at a location, where the match value is greater than the match threshold.

Table 1. The time taken to process each selected scene

Algorithms	Scene 1	Scene 2	Scene 3	Scene 4	Scene 5
Without Pre-Attentive	6.91s	7.12	7.02s	7.098s	6.987s
Pre-Attentive ROI Threshold	0.423s	4.051s	4.092s	3.246s	2.711s
Pre-Attentive ROI Threshold & Signature Threshold	0.276s	2.206s	3.665s	2.926s	1.328s

The time taken to process each selected scene is summarised in Table 1. The system takes 7.025s on average to process the input image without the pre-attentive stage. The system performance has improved significantly with the integration of the pre-attentive stage. For scene-1 the system is able to reduce the processing time to 0.423s using the ROI threshold and with a further reduction to 0.276s using signature threshold. This is the system ideal performance in clean background. In the office and corridor environments, scene-2 to scene-5, the processing time is reduced to approximately 2-4 seconds, with a further reduction to 1 to 2 seconds by applying the signature threshold.

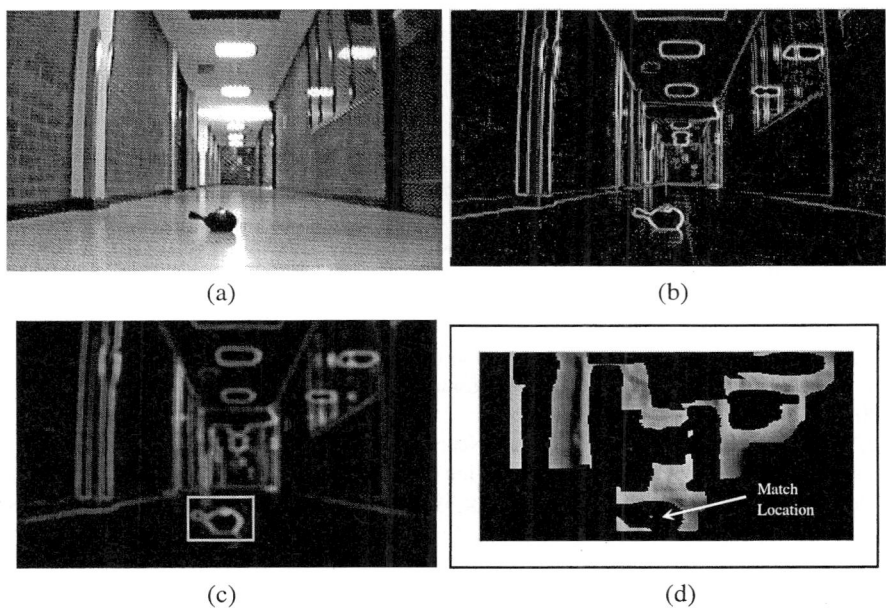

(a) (b)

(c) (d)

Fig. 3. A sample processed frame along a corridor. (a) Gray level input image, (b) Sobel edge detected image, (c) Dilated edge image, (d) Degree of match between memory and each region in the input scene, which is converted into a range from 0-255 and displayed as a grey level image

4 Conclusions

This paper has presented a fast visual search and recognition image processing architecture for real-time robotics applications. The architecture incorporates a simple implementation of pre-attentive and attentive stages for fast and robust visual landmark search and recognition. The proposed pre-attentive stage is able to reduce the recognition time from seven seconds to approximately 0.276 second depending on the amount of edge activities in the visual scene. The improvement in landmark recognition speed provides for real-time applications to autonomously navigating robots.

However, further developments to this work are required to cope with various robot navigation speeds. As the robot navigates, the size of the landmark changes constantly. This requires the robot to be capable of size invariant landmark recognition. Similarly, the appearance of the landmark depends on the approaching angle, which leads to a requirement for 2D aspect view invariant landmark recognition.

Acknowledgment

The work described in this paper was funded by Weapons Systems Division of DSTO via research contract No. 4500 177 390.

References

1. B. Juesz and J. R. Bergen, "Texons, the Fundamental elements in pre-attentive vision and perception of textures," *Bell System Technical Journal*, vol. 62, pp. 1619-1645, 1983.
2. M. Mata, J. M. Armingol, A. de la Escalera, and M. A. Salichs, "A visual landmark recognition system for topological navigation of mobile robots," presented at The IEEE International Conference on Robotics and Automation, Proceedings 2001 ICRA., pp.1124-1129, 2001.
3. M. Mata, J. M. Armingol, A. de la Escalera, and M. A. Salichs, "Using learned visual landmarks for intelligent topological navigation of mobile robots," presented at IEEE International Conference on Robotics and Automation, Proceedings. ICRA-03, pp.1324-1329, 2003.
4. E. W. Chong, C.-C. Lim, and P. Lozo, "Neural model of visual selective attention for automatic translation invariant object recognition in cluttered images," presented at Knowledge-Based Intelligent Information Engineering Systems, 1999. Third International Conference, pp.373-376, 1999.
5. J. Westmacott, P. Lozo, and L. Jain, "Distortion invariant selective attention adaptive resonance theory neural network," presented at Third International Conference on Knowledge-Based Intelligent Information Engineering Systems, USA, pp.13-16, 1999.
6. P. Lozo and C.-C. Lim, "Neural circuit for object recognition in complex and cluttered visual images," presented at The Australian and New Zealand Conference on Intelligent Information Systems, pp.254-257, 1996.
7. P. Lozo, "Neural Circuit For Self-regulated Attentional Learning In Selective Attention Adaptive Resonance Theory (saart) Neural Networks," presented at The Fourth International Symposium on Signal Processing and Its Applications, ISSPA-96, pp.545-548, 1996.
8. S. Grossberg and L. Wyse, "Invariant recognition of cluttered scenes by a self-organizing ART architecture: figure-ground separation," presented at International Joint Conference on Neural Networks, IJCNN-91-Seattle, pp.633-638, 1991.
9. G. A. Carpenter, S. Grossberg, and D. Rosen, "ART 2-A: an adaptive resonance algorithm for rapid category learning and recognition," presented at International Joint Conference on Neural Networks, IJCNN-91-Seattle, pp.151-156, 1991.

Adaptive Object Recognition with Image Feature Interpolation

Sung Wook Baik[1] and Ran Baik[2]

[1] College of Electronics and Information Engineering, Sejong University,
Seoul 143-747, Korea
sbaik@sejong.ac.kr
[2] Department of Computer Engineering, Honam University,
Gwangju 506-090, Korea
baik@honam.ac.kr

Abstract. The paper presents a novel image (feature) interpolation method to reinforce the adaptive object recognition system. The system deals with texture images in a sequence according to changing perceptual conditions. When it recognizes several classes of objects under variable conditions, a fundamental problem is that two or more classes are overlapped on the feature space. This interpolation method is useful to resolve the overlapping issue.

1 Introduction

The computer vision systems work with image sequences and manipulate models of objects represented in each image frame, in order to learn the current situation and to represent temporal changes in adapting dynamic environments [1]. In other words, the systems improve these models over time (image sequence) to detect and track the changes between an object model and reality. In applying such systems to object surface recognition, it is particularly important to discriminate objects with changes in their surface textures. These texture characteristics are highly sensitive to resolution changes and variable lighting conditions. The resolution depends on the distance between an observer and an object. If the distance varies, the resolution automatically changes when the object is registered on the image. Previous research has listed problems with the classification of texture at different but known resolutions [2]. The intensity and the light spectrum of a light source changes over time and depends on atmosphere conditions. Strong and focused light can form and cast a shadow texture on the surface of objects. Diffused light may form different shades over texture elements. Since the shading area on the object surfaces is decided by the direction of illumination, local surface orientation can be estimated through a determination of the illumination direction [3].

This paper focuses on a specific problem in which the resolutions and qualities of object surfaces change when a vision system with a lighting source approaches object scenes gradually. The experimental works presented in this paper are limited to the texture recognition problem where the texture characteristics change significantly, yet smoothly, with a change in perceptual conditions. The sequence of texture images at the image data level in Figure 1 and the sequence of texture features at the feature level illustrate the partial change of raw image resolution and of texture features, respectively. We can get the detailed and visible information over the increasing resolution in the sequence of texture images. The texture characteristics are not clear under low resolution whereas detailed and visible textures appear from high resolution images.

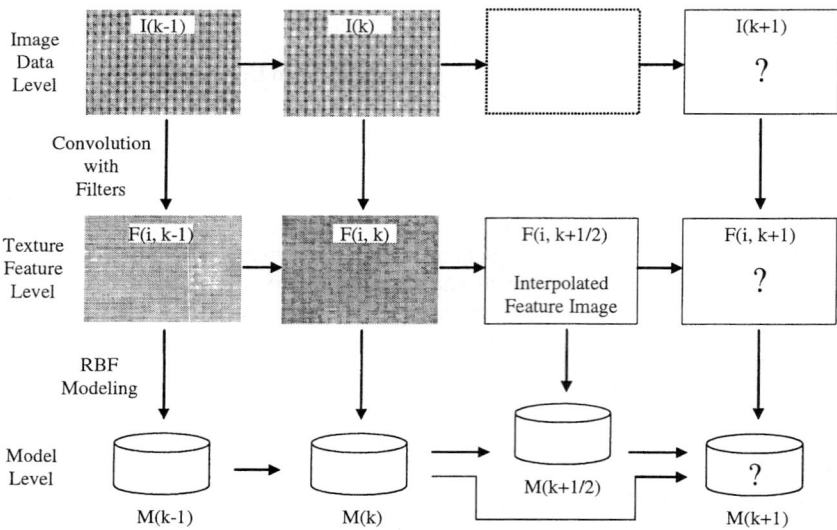

Fig. 1. The generation of interpolated feature images according to the changes of texture characteristics and their associated texture models over images in a sequence

2 Image Feature Interpolation

Image interpolation is a technique for image synthesis to obtain intermediary images between two successive images. It is mainly used to solve image analysis problems such as image compression, image coding, object tracking, and animations (motion estimation).

Image interpolation techniques are different according to image types such as still image, multi-frame images, and images in a sequence [4]. The still image interpolation considers the spatial information within a given image, whereas the image sequence interpolation deals with both spatial and temporal information available in a sequence of images. The interpolation for the multi-frame image focuses on several image frames registered from the same scene with different camera parameters.

This paper adds an image feature interpolation method to the adaptive object recognition system [1] which focused on a sequence of images acquired by a camera with a black & white option (240x320 pixels, each pixel in the 256-grayscale). Images were registered in a lab-controlled environment under smooth changes in the distance between the camera and the scene and under varying lighting conditions. The distance was gradually decreased, and the lighting source was gradually displaced across the scene.

Each image is processed to extract texture features by using the most popular texture feature extraction methods, which are 1) Gabor spectral filtering [5], 2) Laws' energy filtering [6,7], and 3) Wavelet Transformation [8-11]. Those methods have been widely used by researchers and perform very well for various classification and image segmentation tasks.

The adaptive object recognition requires a novel interpolation method that is different from general methods for interpolating between two consecutive images, (I(k) and I(k+1)), for two reasons: 1) the system does not have any information for a forthcoming image (I(k+1)) when it deals with the current image (I(k)), and 2) it is often better than the direct image interpolation to interpolate feature images obtained through texture feature extraction methods, under the situation where texture characteristics on the images are gradually changed. The interpolation method is as follows:

1. The previous images (...., I(k-2), I(k-1), I(k)) used for interpolation are selected.
2. Feature images (F(1,k-1), F(2,k-1), F(3,k-1), ...) of each image (I(k-1)) are obtained through feature extraction methods.
3. Sample feature data are obtained from each feature image (F(i,k-1)) and the mean value and the standard deviation of the sample are estimated.
4. For each feature (i), a polynomial equation is approximated according to the estimated mean values of feature images.
5. New feature images are obtained according to their polynomial equations.

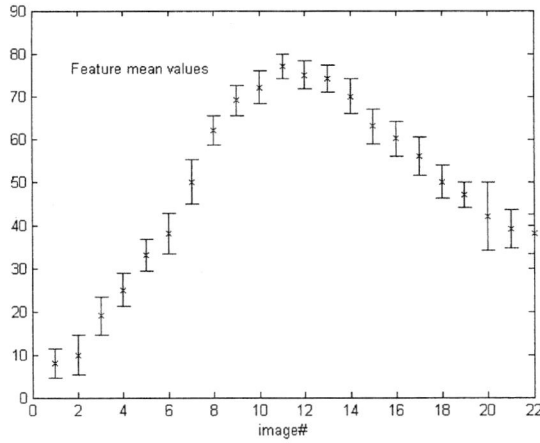

Fig. 2. The change of feature distribution over a sequence of images ('x' and the range covering it indicate the mean and standard deviation values of a class, respectively)

Figure 2 shows changes in the feature distribution of a certain class over a sequence of images when one of Gabor filters has been applied to extract texture features. Each point ('x') and range represents a mean value and a standard deviation of a feature sample distribution at each class of an image. The change of feature mean values at each class over a sequence of images can be represented by a polynomial equation approximated by the interpolation method with least square curve fitting [12].

3 Model Modification with Feature Interpolation

According to previous research [1], the adaptive object recognition can be achieved through a close-loop interaction between texture recognition and model modification systems. Texture recognition applies a RBF classifier to a current image of a sequence. The model modification of RBF classifier for adaptive object recognition is based on four behaviors such as accommodation, translation, generation, and extinction according to the change of perceptual conditions.

The accommodation behavior adjusts the shape of the corresponding RBF node in order to cover the reinforcement cluster. This behavior is mainly used when only small adjustments to an existing node are needed. The translation behavior applies more progressive modification of the RBF node than the accommodation behavior. The generation behavior is used to create a RBF node when there is a large shift in data distribution or there is an increase in distribution complexity. The extinction behavior eliminates unnecessary RBF nodes, which are not utilized by the texture recognition system over a given period of the model evolution time. The purpose of this behavior is to prevent the RBF model from increasing the number of RBF nodes through the frequent application of the generation behavior.

The most important issue in the model modification is to resolve the overlapping problem that feature data of opposite classes are confused when they are located in the feature space. The overlapping problem mainly occurs when feature data of a forthcoming image are closer to the opposite class than its associated class. The feature interpolation can often resolve the overlapping problem by bridging the gap between the forthcoming image and an object model based on the previous images of the same class. Figure 3 shows an example of the overlapping problem in the model modification for two classes. An interpolated sample shown in Figure 3 helps the recognition system to classify its corresponding forthcoming image.

The feature interpolation does not always work well. It may make the recognition system confused by deriving the model modification incorrectly. Such a mistake happens when the prediction based on the feature change of the previous images can not be applied to the next image because the feature pattern of images in a sequence begins to change in a different direction. Therefore, a verification procedure for the feature interpolation is required. The reinforcement data obtained through the feature interpolation can be used for model modification only when they pass the verification procedure. After the model parameters of these reinforcement data are combined into RBF models for the purpose of the verification, the RBF models are applied to classify new coming data. If they reject classifying the majority of new coming data due to the overlapping of the opposite classes, we have to discard the reinforcement data collected from the feature interpolation and the model modification process proceeds without regard to the feature interpolation (M(k) -> M(k+1) in the model level of Figure 1). However, if the rejection rate is less than the given threshold value, we can adopt the reinforcement data collected from the feature interpolation and the model modification process proceeds with regard to the feature interpolation (M(k) -> M(k+1/2) -> M(k+1) in the model level of Figure 1).

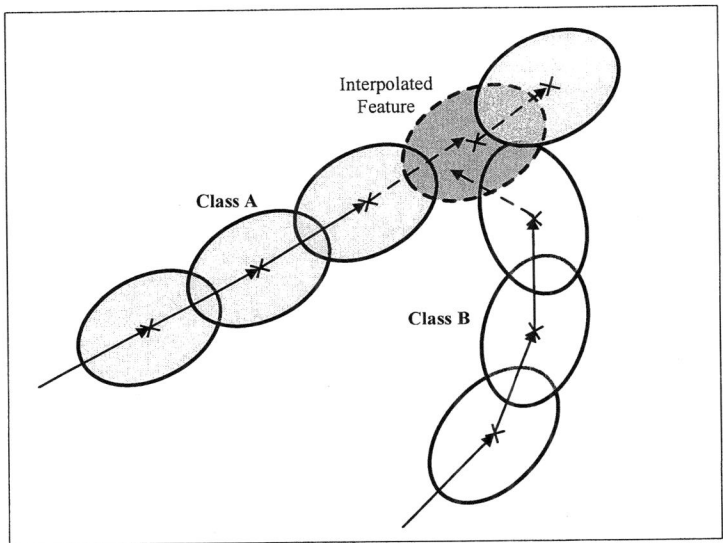

Fig. 3. An example of an overlapping problem

4 Experimental Results

This section presents an improved experimental result (Figure 4) with the texture image sequence by comparing the result shown in previous work [1]. We applied the feature interpolation to partial images (only image 7 and 8 of 22 images) on which classification error rates are relatively high, in order to improve the competence of the adaptive recognition system. Figure 4 (left side) presents classification errors registered for each new incoming image I(i+1) without the feature interpolation before the RBF models are modified. Figure 4 (right side) presents classification errors when the interpolation is applied. In Figure 4 (right side), there are 24 indices on an X-axis, which are two more than the number of total images, since image 7 and 8 take up each extra index for their associated interpolated feature images. In other words, the 7th, 8th, 9th and 10th indices indicate the 7th feature image, 7th interpolated feature image, 8th feature image, and 8th interpolated feature image, respectively. Through the feature interpolation, it can be shown that the classification error rates are reduced in the two images.

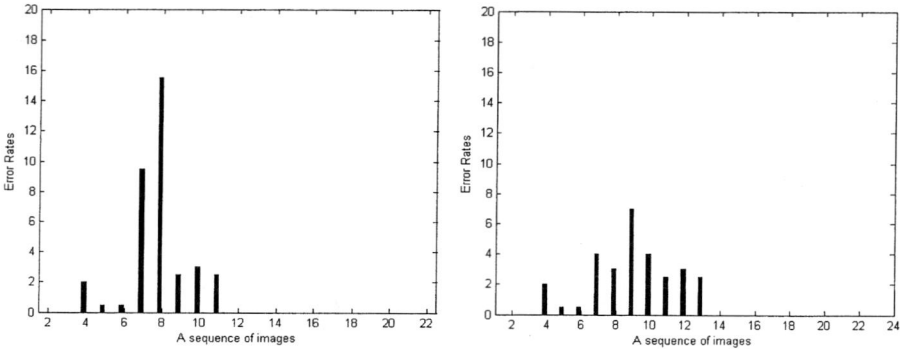

Fig. 4. Experimental results with 22 texture images in a sequence. Left and right diagrams indicate classification errors without interpolation and with interpolation for image 7 and 8 before model modification, respectively

References

1. S. W. Baik and P. Pachowicz, On-Line Model Modification Methodology for Adaptive Texture Recognition, IEEE Transactions on Systems, Man, and Cybernetics, Vol. 32, Issue. 7, 2002
2. S. J. Roan, J. K. Aggarwal,. and W. N. Martin, Multiple Resolution Imagery and Texture Analysis, Pattern Recognition, Vol. 20, No. 1, pp. 17-31, 1987.
3. Y. Choe and Kashyap, 3-D Shape from a shaded and textured surface image, IEEE Trans. on Pattern Analysis and Machine Intelligence, Vol.13, No. 9, pp. 907-919, 1991
4. C. Chuah and J. Leou, An adaptive image interpolation algorithm for image/video processing, Pattern Recognition, Vol. 34, Issue. 12, pp. 2259-2576, 2001
5. M. Farrokhnia and A. Jain, A multi-channel filtering approach to texture segmentation, Proceedings of IEEE Computer Vision and Pattern Recognition Conference, pp. 346-370, 1990.
6. M. Chantler, The effect of variation in illuminant direction on texture classification, Ph D Thesis, Dept. Computing and Electrical Engineering, Heriot-Watt University, 1994.
7. K. Laws, Textured image segmentation, Ph.D. Thesis. Dept. of Electrical Engineering, University of Southern California, Los Angeles, 1980.
8. M. Unser, Texture classification and segmentation using wavelet frames, IEEE Transactions on Image Processing, Vol. 4, No. 11, pp. 1549-1560, 1995.
9. S. Mallat, Multifrequency channel decompositions of images and wavelet models, IEEE Transactions on Acoustics, Speech and Signal Processing, Vol. 37, No. 12, pp. 2091-2110, 1989.
10. C. Chen, Filtering methods for texture discrimination, Pattern Recognition Letters, Vol. 20, pp. 783-790, 1999.
11. T. Chang and C. Kuo, A wavelet transform approach to texture analysis, Proceedings of IEEE International Conference on Acoustics, Speech, and Signal Processing, Vol. 4, pp. 661-664, 1992.
12. B. Carnahan, H.A. Luther, and J. O. Wilkes, Applied Numerical Method, John Wiley & Sons, INC

Effective Approach for Detecting Digital Image Watermarking via Independent Component Analysis

Lisha Sun[1], Weiling Xu[1], Zhancheng Li[1], M. Shen[1], and Patch Beadle[2]

[1] Key Lab. of Guangdong, Shantou University, Guangdong 515063, China
mfshen@stu.edu.cn
[2] School of System Engineering, Portsmouth University, Portsmouth, U.K.

Abstract. A basic scheme for extracting digital image watermark is proposed using independent component analysis (ICA). The algorithm in terms of fastICA is discussed and used to separate the watermark from the mixed sources. The behavior of the proposed approach with several robustness tests of the image watermark is also carried out to demonstrate that ICA technique could provide a flexible and robust system for performing digital watermark detection and extraction. The preliminary experimental results show that the proposed watermarking method is effective and robust to some possible attacks.

1 Introduction

In the past decade, there exist many methods developed for hiding digital image watermarks in various areas such as digital images, video and other multimedia for the purposes of copyright protection. The success and the effectiveness of assessing the digital watermarking methods are based on both the efficiency of the algorithms used and the abilities of resisting the possible attacks. Recently, there is a rapid growth of digital image and digital image watermark since the recent growth of network multimedia systems has met a series of problems related to the protection of intellectual property rights. Digital watermark can be regarded as a procedure of a robust and imperceptible digital code, which consists of the specified information embedded in the host signals like digital images. All types of protection systems involve the use of both encryption and authentication techniques. One of these ideas for the protection of intellectual property rights is embedding digital watermarks into multimedia data [1]. The watermark is a digital code irremovably, robustly, and imperceptibly embedded in the host data and typically contains information about origin, status, and destination of the signals. The basic principles of watermarking methods use small and pseudorandom changes to the selected coefficients in the spatial or transform domain. Most of the watermark detection schemes apply some kinds of correlating detector to verify the presence of the embedded watermarking [1].

ICA technique is a signal processing algorithm to represent a finite set of random variables as the linear combinations of independent component variables [2,3]. The ICA for digital watermarking belongs to the method of removal attack [4]. In this contribution, ICA was proposed to deal with the problem of detecting the digital image watermark and testing the robustness of the proposed scheme.

2 The Scheme of Digital Watermarking

Firstly, the procedure of watermarking embedding is provided. The basic idea is to add a watermark signal to the host data to be watermarked so that the watermark signal is unobtrusive and secure in the signal mixture but can be recovered from the signal mixture later on. Generally, three main topics were involved for designing a watermarking system, including design of the watermark W to be added to the host signal, the embedding method which incorporates the watermark to the host signal X to obtain the watermarked signal Y, and the proper extraction algorithm to recover the watermark information from the mixing signal. The watermark should be any signal related with a message. As a matter of fact, the differences of the watermark method are more or less dependent on the signal design, embedding, and recovery. Usually the correlation techniques are employed for watermark recovery [5]. We adopt the embedding procedure for our ICA scheme

$$W = X + aK + b*M \tag{1}$$

$$W = X + aK + bM \tag{2}$$

where X is the host data, K denotes key and the star symbol represents the convolution operation. Both M and K are inserted in the spatial domain of the X while a and b stand for the small weighting coefficients. The number of observed linear mixture inputs is required to at least equal to or larger than the number of independent sources so that the identification of ICA can be performed. Mostly, at least we need three linear mixtures of three independent sources for our purpose. Two more mixed images are generated to be added to the watermarked image W by using the key image and the original image I in which both c and d denote arbitrary real numbers:

$$W_1 = W, \quad W_2 = W + cK, \quad W_3 = W + dI \tag{3}$$

To apply ICA algorithm, three images above can be set as three rows in one matrix for the purpose of de-watermarking.

3 Blind Extraction

By using ICA, we desire to minimize the statistical dependence of the component of the representation [3,4]. The ICA is supposed that the time courses of activation of the sources are as statistically independent as possible. Most ICA is performed using information-theoretic unsupervised learning algorithms [4,5]. In this contribution, the fixed-point algorithm is adopted for detecting digital image watermark in two stages. First of all, the procedure of principal component analysis was used for whitening such that the whitened data matrix has the following form [6]

$$Y = \Lambda_s^{-1/2} U_s^T R \tag{4}$$

Where Λ_s denotes the diagonal matrix containing k eigenvalues of the estimated data correlation matrix, and Us is the matrix containing the respective eigenvectors in the same order. Thus from the rank of the diagonal matrix, the number of sources or independent components can be determined. Secondly, higher-order statistics (HOS) and their characteristics [7,8] were used for our problem. After finishing the procedure of whitening, the fastICA algorithm in terms of HOS can be summarized as the following three stages [9,10]: First, we need to choose an initial vector w(0) randomly which is normalized to be unit norm. The send stage is to estimate one ICA basis vector by using the following fixed-point iteration procedure:

$$w(k) = Y[Y^T w(k-1)]^3 - 3w(k-1) \qquad (5)$$

where $(\cdot)^3$ means the element-wise operation. Finally, w(k) is normalized in terms of dividing it by its norm. When w(k) is not converged, we need to go back to the second stage. If we can project a new initial basis vector w(0) onto the subspace which is orthogonal to the subspace spanned by the previously found ICA basis vectors, and follow the same procedure, other ICA basis vectors can be estimated sequentially.

4 Experimental Results

In this section, ICA is applied with some simulations to show the validity and feasibility of the proposed scheme. Both watermark detection and extraction are investigated. Fig.1 shows an example of watermark extraction. The performance of watermark extraction is evaluated by calculating the defined normalized correlation coefficient [11,12]:

$$r = \frac{\sum_{i=1}^{L} m(i)\hat{m}(i)}{\sqrt{\sum_{i=1}^{L} m(i)^2 \sum_{i=1}^{L} \hat{m}(i)^2}} \qquad (6)$$

where L denotes the total number of pixels of the image, and both m and $\hat{m}$ represent the original and the extracted watermark sequences with zero-mean values, respectively. The value range of r is between minus one and unity. The unit r means that the image extracted perfectly matched the original. The minus sign indicates that the extracted image is a reverse version of its original image. To evaluate the performance of the example in Fig.1, the normalized correlation coefficients between the original and the extracted images were estimated with the host image of 0.9991, the key image of about unity and the watermark of 0.9989, which proves that the fast ICA algorithm effectively separates the images from the mixture signal.

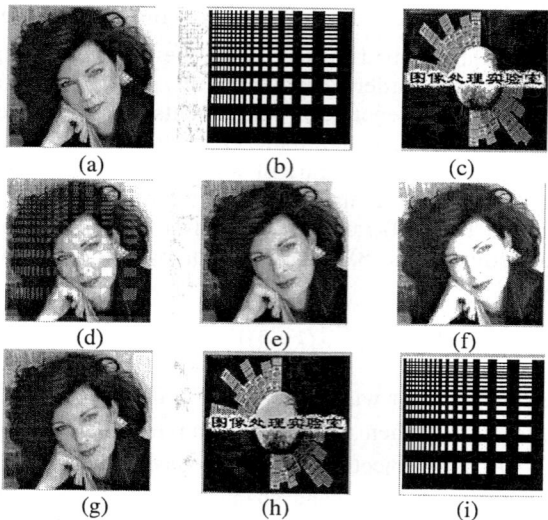

Fig. 1. (a) original Debbie image, (b) key image, (c) watermark, (d) watermarked image, (e) and (f) generated mixture images, (g) extracted Debbie image. (h) extracted watermark, (i) extracted key

5 Test of Robustness

Test of watermark attack is another important problem for assessing the performance of the proposed digital watermarking method [13]. The watermark attack is a procedure which can be used to evaluate the robustness of the presented watermarking scheme. The watermarking system should be robust against data distortions introduced through standard data processing and attacks. There are several watermark attack techniques such as simple attacks, removal attacks and detection-disabling attacks. In this section, we focus on testing the attack performances under the conditions of noise addition, the image compression and the filtering. Firstly, the test of the noise addition was investigated. The watermarked Cameraman image is corrupted by the Gaussian noise. One simulation was carried out and shown in Fig. 2. Note that the maximum acceptable noise level is limited by comparing the energy strength of the embedded watermark. When the additive noise energy level goes up to 40-50 times higher than the energy level of the text watermark, the simulation shows that the watermark become unpreventable. Next, the operation-compression is employed to test the watermarked image by using the Lenna image. The compressed format is JPEG and the compressed proportion is set with 8:1. Fig. 3 (a) and (b) show the original images. The extracted Lenna image and the watermark image in terms of the proposed algorithm are shown in Fig. 3 (c) and (d). The test results via JPEC compression demonstrate the success of the presented ICA method in extracting the watermark even after compression attacks. Finally, the attack of low pass filtering was carried out. Fig. 4 (a) and (b) give two watermarked Debbie images filtered with a 2D low-pass Gaussian and a 2D average filter of size 5x5, respectively. The text watermark was shown in Fig. 4 (c). The watermarked Debbie image filtered with a low pass average filter was demonstrated in Fig. 4 (d) while the extracted watermark image was given in Fig. 4 (e). It can be seen that the ICA scheme can well survive these types of low pass filtering attacks.

(a)   (b)   (c)

Fig. 2. Test of the strong noise attack. (a) original Cameraman image. (b) extracted Cameraman image. (c) extracted the watermark noise

(a)   (b)   (c)   (d)

Fig. 3. Illustartion of the robustness of ICA demixing ability with respect to JPEG compression. (a-b) the original images. (c-d) the extracted image from compressed mixtures of the originals

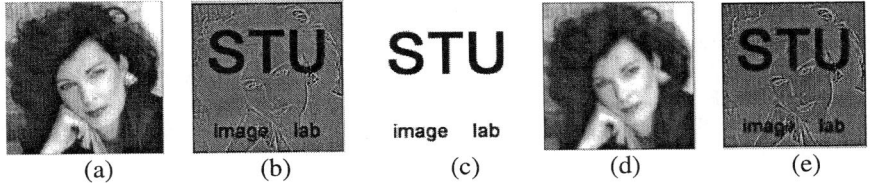

(a)   (b)   (c)   (d)   (e)

Fig. 4. The attack test with 2-D low-pass Gaussian filtering and two dimensional average filtering

6 Conclusions

We have presented a new scheme for the detection and the extraction of digital image watermarking based on independent component analysis. The fastICA algorithm was discussed and adopted to the problem of image processing. In addition, the ICA was used to investigate the robustness of the proposed procedure of digital image watermarking. Several aspects of attacks were also tested. The preliminary experimental results demonstrate the success of ICA algorithm in performing the watermark detection and extraction.

Acknowledgements

The research was supported by the Natural Science Foundation of China (60271023), the Natural Science Foundation of Guangdong (021264 and 32025), and the Key Grant of the Education Ministry of China (02110).

References

1. Hartung F. and Kutter M.: Multimedia Watermarking Techniques. Proceedings of the IEEE, Vol.87, No.7, (1999) 1079-1107
2. Comon P.: Independent Component Analysis, a New Concept? Signal Processing. Vol. 36, (1994) 287-314
3. Aapo H.: Survey on Independent Component Analysis. Neural Computing Surveys, Vol.2, (1999) 94-128
4. Cardoso J. F.: Blind Signal Separation: Statistical Principles. Proceedings of the IEEE, Vol.9, no.10, (1998) 2009-2026
5. Yu D., Sattar F., and Ma K.: Watermark Detection and Extraction Using an ICA Method. EURASIP Journal on Applied Signal Processing, (2002) 92-104
6. Petitcolas F. A. P., Anderson R. J.: Evaluation of Copyright Marking Systems. Proceedings of IEEE Multimedia Systems, Vol.1. (1999) 574-579
7. Vidal J. and et al., Causal AR Modeling Using a Linear Combination of Cumulant Slices, Signal Processing, Vol. 36. (1994) 329-340
8. Shen M, Chan F. H. Y., Sun L, and Beadle B. J.: Parametric Bispectral Estimation of EEG Signals in Different Functional States of the Brain. IEE Proceedings in Science, Measurement and Technology, Vol.147, No.6. (2000) 374-377
9. Hyvarinen A. and Oja E.: A Fast-fixed Point Algorithm for Independent Component Analysis. Neural Computation, (1997) 1483-1492
10. Hyvarinen A.: Fast and Robust Fixed-point Algorithm for Independent Component Analysis. IEEE Trans. on Neural Network, Vol. 10 (1999) 626-634
11. Kashyap R. L.: Robust Image Models and Their Applications. Advances in Electronics and Electron Physics, P. W. Hawkes, Ed., vol. 70. Academic Press (1988) 79-157
12. Juan R. and et. al.: Statistical Analysis of Watermarking Schemes for copyright Protection of Images. Proceedings of the IEEE, Vol.87, No.7. (1999) 1142-1166
13. Petitcolas F. A. P., Anderson R. J., and Kuhn M. G.: Attacks on Copyright Marking Systems. 2nd International Workshop on Information Hiding, Lecture Notes in Computer Science Vol.1525 (1998) 218-238

Extended Locally Linear Embedding with Gabor Wavelets for Face Recognition

Zhonglong Zheng, Jie Yang, and Xu Qing

Institute of image processing and pattern recognition,
Shanghai Jiao Tong University, Shanghai, China, 200030
zhonglong@sjtu.edu.cn

Abstract. Many current face recognition algorithms are based on face representations found by unsupervised statistical methods. One of the fundamental problems of face recognition is dimensionality reduction. Principal component analysis is a well-known linear method for reducing dimension. Recently, locally linear embedding (LLE) is proposed as an unsupervised procedure for mapping higher-dimensional data nonlinearly to a lower-dimensional space. This method, when combined with fisher linear discriminant models, is called extended LLE (ELLE) in this paper. Furthermore, the ELLE yields good classification results in the experiments. Also, we apply the Gabor wavelets as a pre-processing method which contributes a lot to the final results because it deals with the detailed signal of an image and is robust to light variation. Numerous experiments on ORL and AR face data sets have shown that our algorithm is more effective than the original LLE and is insensitive to light variation.

1 Introduction

Face recognition may be applied to a wide range of fields from security and virtual reality systems. One of the problems in face recognition is dimensionality reduction. Researchers up to now have proposed numerous dimensionality reduction algorithms published in the statistics, signal processing and machine learning literature. Principal component analysis and factor analysis are the two most widely used linear dimensionality reduction methods based on second-order statistics. Locally linear embedding (LLE), proposed recently by Saul and Roweis, is a conceptually simple yet powerful method for nonlinear dimensionality reduction [2][7]. When combined with fisher discriminant analysis, which is called ELLE in this paper, it shows better classification performance. Furthermore, before applying ELLE to face recognition, we use Gabor wavelets as a preprocessing procedure on the data sets due to their exhibiting desirable characteristics of spatial locality and orientation selectivity.

2 Extended Locally Linear Embedding (ELLE)

Consider a set of input data points of dimensionality D that lie on or near a smooth underlying nonlinear manifold of lower dimensionality d. Fig. 1 depicts such a situa-

tion where the C-shape 3D points map to a 2D shape like a rectangular while keeping
the topology structure.

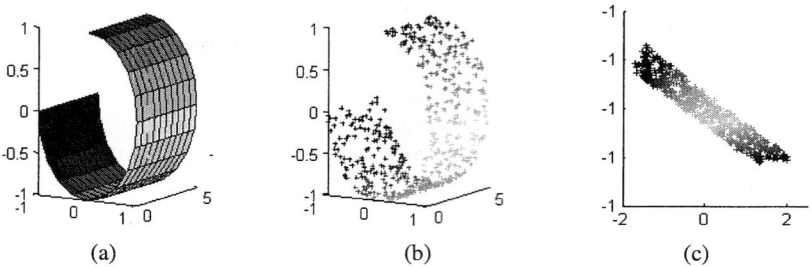

Fig. 1. (a) A two dimensional manifold. (b) Sampled from (a). (c) Neighborhood preserving mapping discovered by LLE

Just imagine that using a scissors to cut the manifold into small squares that represent locally linear patches of the nonlinear C-shape surface. And then put these squares onto a flat tabletop while preserving the angular relationship between neighboring squares. Thus, the LLE algorithm identifies the data's nonlinear structure through two linear computational steps:

In stage I, the cost function to be minimized is defined as:

$$J_1(W) = \sum_{i=1}^{N} \left| x_i - \sum_{j=1}^{K} W_{ji} x_j \right|^2 \tag{1}$$

Given $X = [x_1, x_2, ..., x_N]$, the dimension of x_i is D. For one vector x_i and weights W_{ji} that sum up to 1, this gives a contribution:

$$J_1^{(i)}(W) = \left| \sum_{j=1}^{K} W_{ji}(x_i - x_j) \right|^2 = \sum_{j=1}^{K} \sum_{m=1}^{K} W_{ji} W_{mi} C_{jm}^{(i)} \tag{2}$$

where $C^{(i)}$ is the $K \times K$ matrix:

$$C_{jm}^{(i)} = (x_i - x_j)^T (x_i - x_m) \tag{3}$$

In stage II, the weights W are fixed and new m-dimensional vectors y_i are sought which minimize another cost function:

$$J_2(Y) = \sum_{i=1}^{N} \left| y_i - \sum_{j=1}^{K} W_{ji} y_j \right|^2 \tag{4}$$

The W_{ji} can be stored in an $n \times n$ sparse matrix M, then re-writing equation (5) gives:

$$J_2(Y) = \sum_{i=1}^{N} \sum_{j=1}^{N} M_{ij} y_i^T y_i = tr(YMY^T) \tag{5}$$

To improve the LLE standalone classification performance, one needs to combine LLE with some discrimination criterion. Fisher linear discriminant (FLD) is a widely used discrimination criterion in the face recognition community [3]. The between-class and within-class scatter matrices in FLD are computed by:

$$S_B = \sum_{i=1}^{C} P(\omega_i)(M_i - M)(M_i - M)^T \tag{6}$$

$$S_w = \sum_{i=1}^{C} P(\omega_i)\varepsilon\{(y_k - M_i)(y_k - M_i)^T\} \tag{7}$$

where $P(\omega_i)$ is a priori probability, C denotes the number of classes, $\varepsilon(\cdot)$ is the expectation operator. M_i and M are the means of the classes and the grand mean. The optimal projection is given by:

$$W_{FLD} = \arg\max_{W} \frac{|W^T S_B W|}{|W^T S_w W|} = [w_1, w_2, ..., w_m] \tag{8}$$

If we depict LLE algorithm as $\Phi = LLE(X)$, when combined with FLD, each data point x_i is represented by a low dimensional feature vector computed by

$$Y = W_{FLD}\{LLE(X)\} \tag{9}$$

which we called extended locally linear embedding (ELLE).

3 Experiments

We first apply Gabor kernels on the data set to get the augmented feature vector as stated in [4]. Utilizing the ELLE algorithm proposed in section 2 to reduce dimension, we finally get the discriminanting features that will be used in recognition task. The experiments are carried out using the "leave-one-out" strategy and the nearest neighbor classifier. The similarity measures include Euclidian distance and Mahalanobis distance.

The first data set is ORL face library that consists of 400 gray level images of faces of 40 persons. Each image is cropped to the size of 64×64. The experiments of this paper are carried out on the whole data set of ORL. We implemented the PCA method [8], the LLE method, ELLE method without Gabor and tested their performance using the original face images. The comparative face recognition performance of the three methods is shown in Fig.2. The comparative result of PCA and ELLE with Gabor is shown in Fig.3. For PCA method [5], the Mahalanobis distance measure performs better than the Euclidian distance because it counteracts the fact that Euclidian distance measure weights preferentially for low frequencies in PCA space. And this is consistent with the result reported by Moghaddam and Pentland [6]. While for LLE and its related methods, Euclidian distance measure is better.

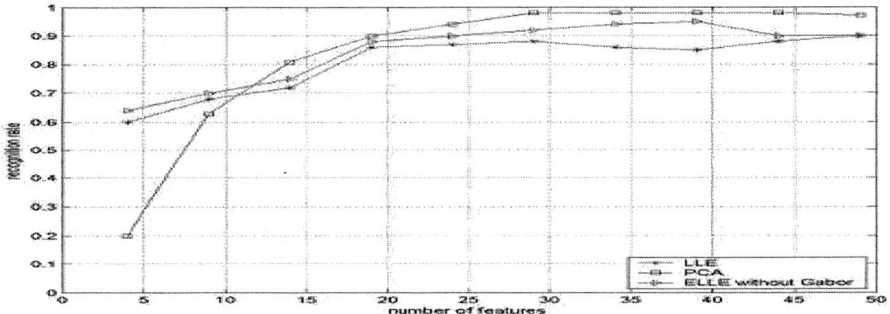

Fig. 2. Comparative recognition performance of PCA, ELLE without Gabor and LLE

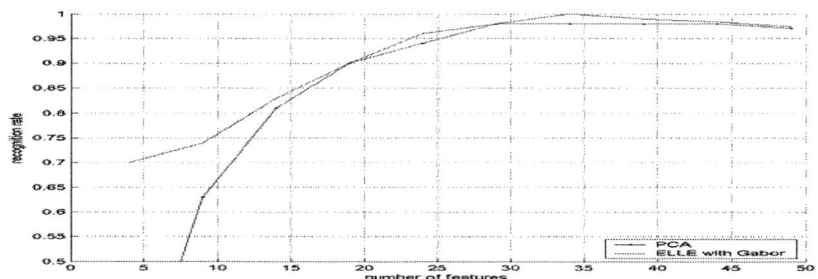

Fig. 3. PCA vs. ELLE with Gabor wavelets

The second data set is AR database that contains over 4,000 color images corresponding to 126 people's faces with different facial expressions, illumination conditions, and occlusions [1]. The experiments on AR involve 480 face images corresponding to 60 subjects. We tested both ELLE with Gabor feature extraction and PCA on these images. This time ELLE with Gabor feature extraction method is also better than PCA, but not just a little. The comparative result is shown in Fig.4.

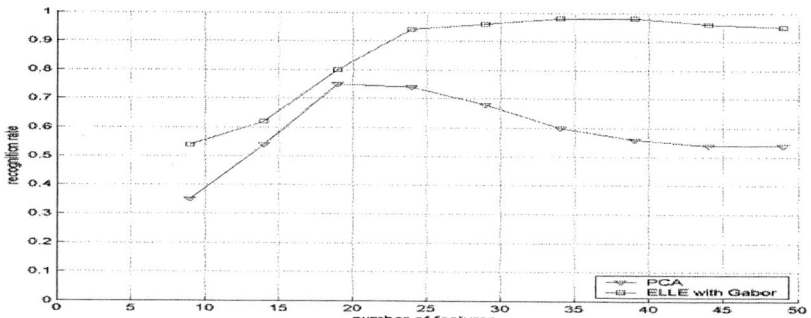

Fig. 4. Comparative recognition performance of ELLE with Gabor and PCA on AR

4 Conclusion

A novel method for face recognition, ELLE with Gabor feature extraction, is introduced in this paper. Still we implemented some other methods for the comparison purpose. The experimental results, based on both ORL and AR databases, show that our novel method performs the best especially when the variations in illumination and facial expression is large. On the one hand, the ELLE with Gabor feature extraction is capable of identifying the underlying structure of high dimensional data and discovering the embedding space nonlinearly of the same class data set. While for large data sets, they do not guarantee necessarily good embedding if the distribution of the data is not adequate. Thus a prior knowledge on the data distribution can be greatly helpful. A good illustration is that in face recognition, all images belonging to the same person should be the neighbor candidates. The experimental results also proved this.

References

1. A.M. Martinez and R. Benavente.: The AR face database. CVC Tech. Report #24, (1998).
2. J. B. Tenenbaum & al.: A global geometric framework for nonlinear dimensionality reduction. Science 290(5500), (2000) 2319-2323.
3. D. L. Swets and J. Weng.: Using discriminant eigenfeatures for image retrieval. IEEE Trans. Pattern Anal. Machine Intell., vol. 18, (1996) 831-836.
4. C. Liu, H. Wechsler.: A Gabor feature classifier for face recognition. Proc. 8th IEEE Int. Conf. Computer Vision, Vancouver, BC, Canada, July 9-12, (2001).
5. A. Martinez, A. C. Kak.: PCA versus LDA. IEEE Trans. Pattern Anal. Machine Intell.,vol.23,.(2001) 228-233.

6. B. Moghaddam, A. Pentland.: Probabilistic visual learning for object representation. IEEE Trans. Pattern Anal. Machine Intell., vol. 19, (1997) 696-710.
7. S. T. Roweis, L. K. Saul.: Nonlinear dimensionality reduction by locally linear embedding. Science, 290(5500), (2000) 2323-2326.
8. M. Turk, A. Pentland.: Eigenfaces for recognition. Journal of Cognitive neuroscience, vol. 3, (1991) 71-86.

Image Processing of Finite Size Rat Retinal Ganglion Cells Using Multifractal and Local Connected Fractal Analysis

H.F. Jelinek[1], D.J. Cornforth[2], A.J. Roberts[3], G. Landini[4], P. Bourke[5], and A. Iorio[6]

[1] School of Community Health, Charles Sturt University, Australia
hjelinek@csu.edu.au
[2] School of Environmental and Information Sciences, Charles Sturt University, Australia
dcornforth@csu.edu.au
[3] Department of Mathematics and Computing, University of Southern Queensland, Australia
aroberts@t130.aone.net.au
[4] Oral Pathology Unit, School of Dentistry, University of Birmingham, U.K.
G.Landini@bham.ac.uk
[5] Astrophysics and Supercomputing, Swinburne Univ. of Tech., Australia
pdb@swin.edu.au
[6] School of Computer Science and IT, RMIT University, Melbourne, Australia
iantony@cs.rmit.edu.au

Abstract. Automated image processing has great potential to aid in the classification of biological images. Many natural structures such as neurons exhibit fractal properties, and measures derived from fractal analysis are useful in differentiating neuron types. When fractal properties are not constant in all parts of the neuron, multifractal analysis may provide superior results. We applied three methods to elucidate the variation within 16 rat retinal ganglion cells: local connected fractal dimension (LCFD), mass-radius (MR) and maximum likelihood multifractal (MLM) analyses. The LCFD method suggested that some of the neurons studied are multifractal. The MR method was inconclusive due to the finite size of the cells. However, the MLM method was able to show the multifractal nature of all the samples, and to provide a superior multifractal spectrum. We conclude that the latter method warrants further attention as it may improve results in other application areas.

1 Introduction

The aim of this work is to collect evidence regarding the relative performance of three methods of multifractal analysis. We hope to use such measures to increase our knowledge about the structure of neurons. We were able to show that, in our application area, the third method is clearly superior. We can also conclude that the structure of these cells is multifractal. These observations indicate that the maximum likelihood multifractal (MLM) method is appropriate for this type of cells.

Fractal analysis is a useful tool in automated image processing, as it provides objective, quantitative measures that can help to characterize complex shapes.

Neurons are known to fall into several types, but distinguishing these types is a continuing problem and can be approached from an AI perspective [1, 2]. As neurons possess fractal structure, the global fractal dimension has been suggested as a useful measure [3]. Calculating the global fractal dimension of rat retinal ganglion cells (RGCs) has provided valuable additional data for classification of these cells and elucidating functional relationships [4]. Our work on rat RGCs suggests that the structure of such tissue is complex, and that there is great benefit to be obtained by applying a more sophisticated analysis than the global fractal dimension such as multifractal analysis. The presence of multifractal features has been demonstrated in the physical sciences such as ecology, but in biology and especially in neuroscience, establishing whether or not neurons are multifractal remains elusive [3, 5]. The problem is to determine if the branching pattern of neurons represents one or more developmental processes at work. The images studied in this work did not conform to the expected monofractal or multifractal attributes using traditional fractal analysis. This anomaly prompted us to apply a novel unbiased multifractal analysis method - the Maximum Likelihood Multifractal method (MLM).

2 Fractal Analysis

The fractal dimension is a measure of the complexity and self-similarity of an image, and is becoming accepted as a feature for automated classification of images having branching structures. A characteristic of fractal geometry is that the length of an object depends on the resolution or the scale at which the object is measured [3]. This dependence of the measured length on the measuring resolution is expressed as the fractal dimension (D) of the object applicable when structures have a homogeneous fractal pattern distribution (Equation 1).

$$D = \frac{\log N(r)}{\log \frac{1}{r}} \quad (1)$$

where r is the scaling factor and $N(r)$ is the number of subsets for the scaling factor.

Many biological structures such as the dendritic pattern of neurons are not homogeneous (Figure 1) with the periphery being less dense compared to the central parts near the cell body.

To ascertain the complexity of any number of components within an object, two methods can be used: 1) the local fractal dimension (D_{local}) or the local connected fractal dimension (D_{conn}) and 2) determination of the multifractal spectrum [6, 7]. D_{conn} has been extensively used in histopathology [6]. However D_{conn} does not indicate multifractality. The box-counting method has been intensely investigated for use in multifractal analysis in biology but has several limitations [7]. The main problem with this method is its sensitivity to the extent the boxes are filled and is manifested for $q < 0$ where the $D(q)$ function increases monotonically rather than decreases [8]. The determination of the spectrum using the mass-radius method has attempted to address this problem and $D(q)$ spectra decreasing monotonically with increasing q have been obtained for images other than neurons [9].

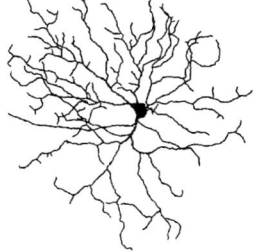

Fig. 1. Example of the dendritic pattern of a rat retinal ganglion cell

To eliminate biases such as a low number of data points and finite size effects, Roberts and Cronin have proposed a Maximum Likelihood Multifractal (MLM) analysis that compares characteristics of the data to artificially constructed multifractals based on a binary multiplicative process [10]. By maximizing the likelihood that the characteristics of the image to be analyzed are the same as a multifractal distribution, the multifractal nature of the data may be modeled by the characteristics of the artificial multifractal with the same number of data points as the data set.

In this work, we apply three multfractal methods to a set of images obtained from rat retinal ganglion cells. We compare these three techniques, showing the superiority of the latter method.

3 Methods

Drawings of 16 rat retinal ganglion cells (RGCs) were analyzed as binary images. We performed a local connected fractal dimension analysis, estimated the multifractal spectrum using the mass-radius method and performed the MLM analysis to show the superior results of this method.

3.1 Local Connected Fractal Dimension

For a particular pixel P in the set, the pixels locally connected to P within a window of set side size (the analyzing window) is computed. Next, the "mass" or number of pixels $N(\varepsilon)$ in increasingly large sub-windows of size ε (all the odd values from 1 to maximum size) always centered at P is counted. This is repeated for all possible (non-empty) locations of the image. The dependence of the number of pixels on a particular window size is a scaling relation, D_{conn} that may be estimated by the linear regression of the logarithm of the mass in a box of size ε on the logarithm of ε. Values of D_{conn} describe the local complexity of the locally connected set [6].

3.2 Mass-Radius Multifractal Analysis

The mass-radius method is a measure of mass distribution. Consider all circles of radius r that have their centre on the object. Let $M_i(r)$ be the mass within the *ith* circle and the total number of circles of radius r be $N(r)$. Then $Z(q,r)$, which is a density measure where q acts as a filter is defined as

$$Z(q,r) = \sum_{i=1}^{N(r)} \frac{[M_i(r)]^q}{N(r)}. \tag{2}$$

The multifractal dimension $D(q)$ is given by

$$qD(q) = \frac{\log(Z(q,r))}{\log(r)}. \tag{3}$$

3.3 Quaternary Maximum Likelihood Multifractal Analysis

For each image, the inter-point distances of all data points was determined to estimate the partition function $Z(q,r)$ as a function of length scale r. Plotting $log\ Z$ versus $log\ r$ a curve is fitted and any changes in the slope are identified. The kink in the slope separates the data into small and large-scale measures. Our analysis was restricted to the larger, relative coarser, length scales consisting of a few hundred data points to reduce the processing time. For the large-scale analysis Approximately 400 data points were retained from each image. For the multifractal analysis, the program fits a multiplicative quaternary multifractal to the inter-point distance information summarized in the correlation density function $Z(q,r)$. From the parameters of the best fit we determine any multifractal properties, such as the appropriate generalized dimension curves.

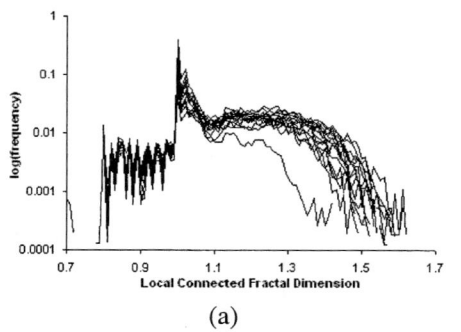
(a)

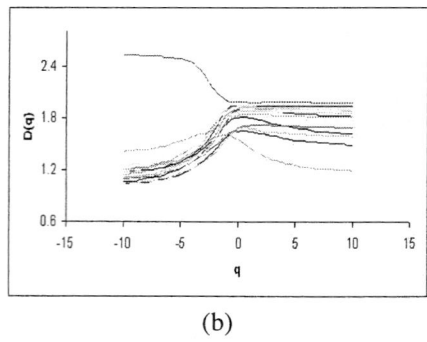
(b)

Fig. 2. The multi fractal distribution of for the 16 rat ganglion cells using a) local connected fractal dimension and b) mass-radius method

4 Results

Figure 2a depicts the distribution of the local connected fractal dimensions for all sixteen cells. Notice that one cell stands out as very different from the rest. For $D_{conn} \sim 1.35$ there is more than one order of magnitude difference in relative frequency of local connected dimension counts between this cell and the other cells. This analysis confirms that all the cells examined, with the possible exception of one, may be considered multifractal and warrant further analysis.

The results of the multifractal analysis using the mass-radius method are shown in Figure 2b. For the images studied, the $D(q)$ spectrum is monotonically increasing for negative q apart for one cell image.

Figure 3 shows the multifractal spectra for all 16 cells analyzed using the MLM analysis. Note the difference in slope between $q = -1$ and $q = 3$, clearly indicating that the majority of cells are based on a multifractal construction. Of particular interest is the cell indicated above with the LCFD analysis (Figure 2a), which in this graph stands out, with a very low value (1.5) for D(q) when q = 3. Unlike the results of the mass-radius method, the MLM Analysis has confirmed that the cell identified as different from the others by LCFD analysis is indeed multifractal.

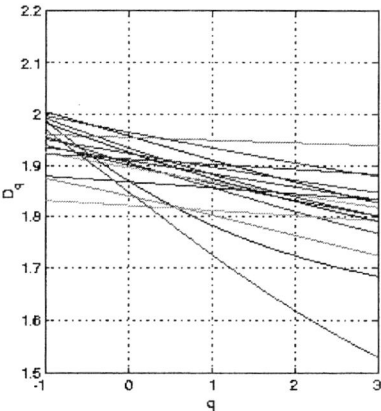

Fig. 3. Estimated generalized dimensions for the large scale branching structure of each of the cell images using the maximum likelihood multifractal analysis

5 Discussion

Applying MLM analysis provides quantitative evidence of the multifractal nature of neurons. Various approaches have been investigated that identify morphological differences at a local level. Our results clearly indicate a range of LCFDs associated with rat RGCs. Although the mass-radius method indicates some heterogeneity of the images the results are anomalous due to the increasing $D(q)$ spectrum [3]. The MLM method is ideal as it uses less processed data and allows analysis of finite-size images. In addition the number of points used in the analysis can be selected and thus the scaling region. We suggest that the MLM is an improvement on existing methods for the multifractal analysis of biological material. This is because the method depends on the image data being superimposed on the quaternary multiplicative process. The results from this method pertaining to a range of q values and combined with other morphological parameters such as circularity, density or area provide the basis for AI methods, such as automated classification, to be applied optimally for cell classification paradigms [1].

Acknowledgements

The authors like to thank Leo Peichl from the Max Plank Institute for Brain Research who provided the cell drawings and Cherryl Kolbe for technical assistance.

References

1. Jelinek, H.F., Maddalena, D.J. and Spence, I. (1994) Application of artificial neural networks to cat retinal ganglion cell categorization. Proc. 5th Australian Conference on Neural Networks, pp:177-180.
2. Jelinek, H.F., Cesar, R.M., Jr. and Leandro, J.J.G.: Exploring Wavelet Transforms for Morphological Differentiation between Functionally Different Cat Retinal Ganglion Cells.
3. Smith, J.T.G., Lange, G.D. and Marks, W.B.: Fractal Methods and Results in Cellular Morphology - Dimensions, Lacunarity and Multifractals. Journal of Neuroscience Methods.69 (1996) 123-136
4. Huxlin, K.R. and Goodchild, A.K.: Retinal Ganglion Cells in the Albino Rat: Revised Morphological Classification. The Journal of Comparative Neurology.385 (1997) 309-323
5. Fernandez, E., Bolea, J.A., Ortega, G. and Louis, E.: Are Neurons Multifractals? Journal of Neuroscience Methods.89 (1999) 151-157
6. Landini, G., Murray, P.I. and Misson, G.P.: Local Connected Fractal Dimension and Lacunarity Analysis of 60 Degree Fluorescein Angiograms. Investigative Ophthalmologi and Visual Science.36 (1995) 2749-2755
7. Kenkel, N.C. and Walker, D.J.: Fractals in the Biological Sciences. COENOSES.11 (1996) 77-100
8. Feder, J.: Fractals. Plenum Press,, New York (1988)
9. Amaral, L.A.N., Goldberger, A.L., Ivanov, P. and Stanley, H.E.: Scale-Independent Measures and Pathologic Dynamics. Physical Review Letters.81 (1998) 2388-2391
10. Roberts, A. and Cronin, A.: Unbiased Estimation of Multi-Fractal Dimensions of Finite Data Sets. Physic A.233 (1996) 867-878.

The DSC Algorithm for Edge Detection[*]

Jonghoon Oh and Chang-Sung Jeong[**]

Department of Electronics Engineering, Korea University,
Anamdong 5-ka, Sungbuk-ku, Seoul 136-701, Korea
jhoh@korea.ac.kr, csjeong@charil.korea.ac.kr

Abstract. Edge detection is one of the fundamental operations in computer vision with numerous approaches to it. In nowadays, many algorithms for edge detection have been proposed. However, most conventional techniques have assumed clear images or Gaussian noise images, thus their performance could decrease with the impulse noise. In this paper, we present an edge detection approach using Discrete Singular Convolution algorithm. The DSC algorithm efficiently detects edges not only original images but also noisy images which are added by Gaussian and impulse noise. Therefore, we evaluate that the performance of the DSC algorithm is compared with other algorithms such as the Canny, Bergholm, and Rothwell algorithm.

1 Introduction

Edge detection is a front-end processing step in most computer vision and image understanding systems such as the AI research field. The accuracy and reliability of edge detection is critical to the overall performance of these systems. Among the edge detection methods proposed so far, the Canny edge detector is the most rigorously defined operator and is widely used. We select the Canny algorithm to compare with the DSC algorithm.

In recently, a discrete singular convolution (DSC) algorithm was proposed as a potential approach for computer realization of singular integrations [1]. The mathematical foundation of the algorithm is the theory of distributions [2] and wavelet analysis. Sequences of approximations to the singular kernels of Hilbert type, Abel type and Delta type were constructed. In solving differential equations, the DSC approach exhibits the accuracy of a global method for integration and the flexibility of a local method for handling complex geometry and boundary conditions. In the context of image processing, DSC kernels were used to facilitate a new anisotropic diffusion operator for image restoration from noise [3]. Most recently, DSC kernels were used to generate a new class of wavelets, which include the Mexican hat wavelet as a special case.

The purpose of this paper is to propose a new approach based on the DSC algorithm for edge detection. We illustrate this approach by using a special

---

[*] This work was partially supported by the Brain Korea 21 Project and KIPA-Information Technology Research Center.
[**] Corresponding Author.

class of DSC kernels, the DSC kernels of delta type. In particular, DSC kernels constructed from functions of the Schwartz class are easy to use. Comparison is made between the DSC detection algorithm and the existing algorithms for edge detection such as the Canny, Bergholm, and Rothwell. Experiments indicate that the new approach is effective for image edge detection under severe Gaussian white noise and impulse noise.

2 The Overview of the Previous Algorithms

The Canny edge detection algorithm is considered a standard method used by many researchers. The Bergholm edge focusing algorithm was selected because it represented an approach that used a scale space representation to try to find edges that are significant. [4]. The last algorithm included in the experiment was unique in that it employed dynamic thresholding that varied the edge strength threshold across the image. The implementation of this algorithm was performed by combining pieces of the Canny edge detector code and pieces of C++ code obtained from the authors of the paper[5].

3 Discrete Singular Convolution

3.1 The DSC Algorithm

It is most convenient to discuss singular convolution in the context of the theory of distributions. A singular convolution is defined as equation(1). Let T be a distribution and $\eta(x)$ be an element of the space of test functions

$$F(t) = (T * \eta)(t) = \int_{-\infty}^{\infty} T(t-x)\eta(x)\,dx \qquad (1)$$

Where $T(t-x)$ is a singular kernel. Of particular relevance to the present study is the singular kernels of the delta type in equation(2)

$$T(x) = \delta^n(x), \qquad n = 0, 1, 2, \ldots \qquad (2)$$

Where δ is the delta distribution. With a sufficiently smooth approximation, it is useful to consider a discrete singular convolution (DSC)

$$F_\alpha(t) = \sum_k T_\alpha(t - x_k) f(x_k) \qquad (3)$$

Where $F_\alpha(t)$ is an approximation to $F(t)$ and x_k is an appropriate set of discrete points on which the DSC is well defined. Here, in general, $f(x)$ is not required to be a test function.

An important example of the DSC kernels is Shannon's delta kernel

$$\delta_\alpha(x) = \frac{sin(\alpha x)}{\pi x} \qquad (4)$$

3.2 The DSC Filters

From the point of view of signal processing, Shannon's delta kernel $\delta_\alpha(x)$ corresponds to a family of ideal low pass filters, each with a different bandwidth.

$$\psi_\alpha(x) = \frac{sin2\alpha x - sin\alpha x}{\pi x} \tag{5}$$

Their corresponding wavelet expressions are band pass filters. Both $\delta_\alpha(x)$ and its associated wavelet play a crucial role in information theory and theory of signal processing. However, their usefulness is limited by the fact that $\delta_\alpha(x)$ and $\psi_\alpha(x)$ are infinite impulse response (IIR) filters and their Fourier transforms $\hat{\delta}_\alpha(x)$ and $\hat{\psi}_\alpha(x)$ are not differentiable. Computationally, $\phi(x)$ and $\psi(x)$ do not have finite moments in the coordinate space; in other words, they are de-localized. This non-local feature in coordinate is related to the band limited character in the Fourier representation according to the Heisenberg uncertainty principle. To improve the asymptotic behavior of Shannon's delta kernel in the coordinate representation, a regularization procedure can be used and the resulting DSC kernel in its discretized form can be expressed as

$$\delta_{\sigma,\alpha}(x - x_k) = \frac{sin(\pi/\Delta)(x - x_k)}{(\pi/\Delta)(x - x_k)} e^{-(x-x_k)^2/2\sigma^2} \qquad \sigma > 0 \tag{6}$$

3.3 The DSC Detectors

To design the edge detectors, we consider a one dimensional, nth order DSC kernel of the delta type

$$\delta^n_{\sigma,\alpha}(x - x_k), \qquad n = 0, 1, 2... \tag{7}$$

Here $\delta^{(0)}_{\sigma,\alpha}(x - x_k) = \delta_{\sigma,\alpha}(x - x_k)$ is a DSC filter.

$$\delta^{(n)}_{\sigma,\alpha}(x_m - x_k) = \left[\left(\frac{d}{dx}\right)^n \delta_{\sigma,\alpha}(x - x_k)\right]_{x=x_m} \tag{8}$$

It is the impact of parameter σ on the filters in the time-frequency domain. The DSC parameter α can be utilized to achieve an optimal frequency selection in a practical application. For example, in many problems, the object to be processed may be corrupted by noise whose frequency distribution mainly concentrates in the high frequency region. Therefore, a small α value can be used to avoid the noise corruption.

In the present work, the nth order DSC edge detector for Noisy Image, or the nth order coarse-scale DSC edge detector, is proposed as

$$DSCNI^n(x_i, y_j) = \left| \sum_{k=-Wn}^{Wn} \sum_{l=Wo}^{Wo} \delta^{(n)}_{\sigma_n,\alpha_n}(x_i - x_k)\delta^{(0)}_{\sigma_0,\alpha_0}(y_j - y_l I(X_k, Y_l)) \right|$$

$$+ \left| \sum_{k=-Wo}^{Wo} \sum_{l=Wn}^{Wn} \delta^{((0))}_{\sigma_0,\alpha_0}(x_i - x_k)\delta^{(n)}_{\sigma_n,\alpha_n}(y_j - y_l I(X_k, Y_l)) \right| \qquad n = 1, 2, \ldots \tag{9}$$

Here I is a digital image. For simplicity, the details of this procedure are not presented in this paper.

4 Experimental Methods and Results

To demonstrate the efficiency of the proposed approach, we carry out several computer experiments on gray-level images. We select standard images, which are both real and synthetic images. Fig. 1 shows representative images. The resolution of all images is 8-bit per pixel. The size of all images is 256 × 256. The computation is carried out in a single computer. For definiteness and simplicity, we set the parameter W =3 for all experiments in this section. In the present work, the edge detection consists of two steps: edge magnitude calculation, and thresholding. For simplicity, a fixed threshold is used in the experiments.

4.1 Noisy Images

To investigate the performance of the DSC algorithm under noisy environment, we consider a number of low grade images. The Fig. 1 (a) present the noisy images, which are generated by adding I.I.D. Gaussian noise and Impulse Noise, and the peak-signal-noise-ratio (PSNR) for each image is 15 dB. Fig. 1 illustrates the resulting edge images detected from noisy environment, obtained by DSC, the Canny detector, Bergholm, and Rothwell detectors.

In general, the detected edges are blurred due to the presence of noise. The three conventional detectors, the Canny, Bergholm, and Rothwell, detect not only spatially extended edges, but also many spurious features due to noise. As a result, the contrast of their edge images is poor. Whereas, much sharper edge images are successfully attained by the DSC detector, as shown in Fig. 1(b). The difference in contrast stems from the fact that the DSC detects edges at a coarse scale, in which the high frequency noise has been remarkably smoothed out. As mentioned in the introduction, the Canny detector [6]was formulated as an optimization problem for being used under noise environment. The parameter is taken as $\sigma = 1.5$ as suggested by other researchers. Obviously, there is a visual difference between those obtained by using the DSC detector and the Canny detector. These experiments indicate the performance of the DSC based edge detector is better than that of the Canny detector.

4.2 Objective Performances

To obviously validate the DSC detector further, we present an alternative evaluation in this subsection. Edge detection systems could be compared in many ways. For synthetic images, where the exact location of edges is known, Abdou and Pratt [7] proposed a figure of merit to objectively evaluate the performance of edge detectors. It is a common practice to evaluate the performance of an edge detector for synthetic images by introducing noise in the images. A plot of F against the PSNR gives the degradation in the performance of the detector. The value of F is less than or equal to 1. The larger the value, the better the performance.

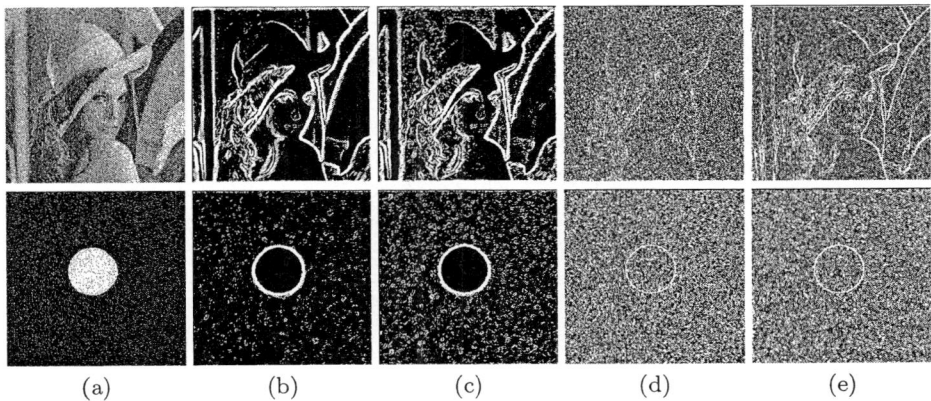

Fig. 1. Sample images(a). Edge images of the real(first row) and synthetic(second row) images with Gaussian and Impulse noise were obtained by (b) DSC detector(column1) (c) Canny detector(column2) (d) Bergholm detector(column3) (e) Rothwell detector(column4)

In Fig. 2, when the noise level is low, the F values are very close to 1 and the performances of all the four detectors are very satisfactory. With the increase of the noise level, the F value of two difference detectors which are the Bergholm and the Rothwell detectors is dramatically decreased. The F value of difference between DSC and those of two detectors is almost 0.6 when PSNR is 15 dB. In contrast, the Canny detector and the DSC detector achieve large F values over the domain of interest, suggesting their superiority to other two detectors. It is noted that the performance of an DSC is better than that of the Canny detector for small PSNR values.

4.3 Discussion

The Rothwell detector obtains better performance than the Bergholm detector because of dynamic threshold method. However, these two detectors do not carry out excellent results at noisy images. It is well-known that the performance of the Canny detector depends on the computational bandwidth W and standard deviation σ. These parameters can be utilized to obtain edges which are optimized with respect to the space of parameters for each given image. In particular, the parameter σ gives rise to excellent time-frequency localization. However, the Canny filter does not provide much freedom for frequency selection. In contrast to the Canny detector, the DSC detector has one more parameter α. Thus, DSC detector should perform at least as well as the Canny detector.

The DSC detector has an extra parameter, α_n, which controls DSC filter frequency selection . Experiments indicated that, when α_n decreases, fine details are smoothed out and main edge structures appear significant. This property can be utilized to deal with images corrupted with color noise, for which the Canny

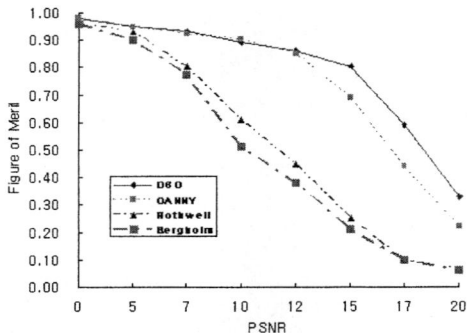

Fig. 2. The Figure of Merit of the synthetic image with noise

detector is not the best choice. The ability of frequency selection is important to many practical applications, for instance, AI research.

5 Conclusion

This paper introduces the DSC algorithm for edge detection. A number of DSC filters, low-pass filters, are proposed in the context of distribution theory. A family of regularized DSC kernels is constructed for denoising and data interpolation. The performance of the proposed algorithm is compared with other existing methods, such as the Canny, Bergholm, and Rothwell. The Canny detector can be optimized with respect to the filter length and time-frequency localization, whereas, the DSC detector can be optimized with respect to one more parameter,α, which plays the role of frequency selection. Experiments on a two kinds of images have been carried out with some selected DSC parameters, and the performance of DSC detectors is better than that of the Canny detector.

References

1. G.W. Wei:Discrete singular convolution for the solution of the Fokker-Planck equations, J. Chem. Phys. 110 (1999) 8930-8942.
2. L. Schwartz: Theore des Distributions, Hermann, Paris, (1951).
3. G.W. Wei: GeneralizedPerona-Malik equation for image restoration, IEEE Signal Process. Lett. 6 (1999) 165-168.
4. F. Bergholm: "Edge Focusing," IEEE Trans. Pattern Analysis and Machine Intelligence, vol. 9, no. 6, pp. 726-741, Nov. (1987).
5. C.A. Rothwell, J.L. Mundy, W. Hoffman,and V.-D.Nguyen:"Driving Vision by Topology,"Int'l Symp.Computer Vision, pp.395- 400, Coral Gables, Fla., Nov.(1995).
6. J. Canny.: A computational approach to edge detection, IEEE Trans. Pattern Anal. Mach. Intell. PAMI-8 (1986) 679-698.
7. I.E. Abdou, W.K. Pratt.: Quantitative design and evaluation of enhancement thresholding edge detectors, Proc. IEEE. 69 (1979) 753-763.

A Novel Statistical Method on Decision Table Analysis

Ling Wei[1,2] and Wen-xiu Zhang[2]

[1] Department of Mathematics, Northwest University, Xi'an, 710069, P.R. China
qjjwv@nwu.edu.cn
[2] Faculty of Science, Institute for Information and System Sciences,
Xi'an Jiaotong University, Xi'an, 710049, P.R. China
wxzhang@mail.xjtu.edu.cn

Abstract. Nonparametric methods in statistics is introduced to analyze decision tables. First, the raw decision table is translated to a series of corresponding contingency tables between each condition attribute and the decision attribute, and then, dependence significance testing is finished to make sure if a condition attribute is correlated with the decision. Finally, we get the reduct of decision table at a special significance level, as well as all the first-order rules. Our experiments show that the nonparametric statistical method we proposed is feasible and efficiently.

1 Introduction

A decision table is a tabular representation used to describe and analyze procedural decision situations, where the state of a number of conditions determines the execution of a set of actions [1]. Moreno Garcia A.M. et. al gave an overview of decision table literature from 1982 to 2000 in [2], which consists of about eight hundred references.

For decision tables, literature references focus on the attribute reduction and acquisition of decision rules. One effective method is the rough set theory, which is proposed by Pawlak Z. (1982) [3] to deal with imprecise or vague concepts. But rough set theory still has disadvantages. For example, there is no statistical analysis during the process of knowledge discovery using rough set theory [4]. It is well known that the databases we studied are usually samples. If there is no statistical evidence, the results obtained from these samples cannot be generalized to the population. We can also find comparison between statistical models and rough set analysis, see [4–6].

The nonparametric methods in statistics are proposed in this paper to obtain the reduct and decision rules based on the contingency tables between each condition attribute and the decision attribute in the raw decision table. Furthermore, the correlated measure of a condition attribute relative to the decision attribute can be calculated. In Sect. 4, experiments are given to describe the process. The results we acquire are the same as that of rough set theory.

2 Reduction of Decision Table Using Rough Set Theory

The correlated definitions in rough set theory are as follows.

Definition 1 ([7]). *An Information System is a triplet (U, A, F), where $U = \{x_1, \ldots, x_n\}$ is a finite set of objects $x_i (i \leq n)$, $A = \{a_1, \ldots, a_m\}$ is a finite set of attributes $a_j (j \leq m)$; $F = \{f_j : j \leq m\}$ is a set of relationship between U and A, $f_j : U \rightarrow V_j (j \leq m)$, V_j is the value set of attribute a_j. A decision table (U, C, D, F) is an information system when the attributes in A are composed by condition attribute set C and decision attribute set D, i.e. $A = C \cup D$, $C \cap D = \emptyset$.*

Definition 2 ([8]). *Let (U, C, D, F) be a decision table. Decision attribute set D is called depends on condition attribute set C in a degree k $(0 \leq k \leq 1)$, if:*

$$k = \gamma(C, D) = \frac{|\bigcup_{X \in U/D} \underline{R}(X)|}{|U|} ,$$

where $\underline{R}(X) = \{x \in U : C(x) \subseteq X\}$ is called C-lower approximation of X.

Definition 3 ([8]). *For the minimum subset C' of C, if $\gamma(C, D) = \gamma(C', D)$, we call C' a D-reduct of C, which is also called the reduct of the decision table.*

In addition, according to the rough set theory, we can get the simplest classification rule, which is such a rule that has only one condition attribute. We name it the first-order rule in the following text.

Theorem 1. *In a decision table (U, C, D, F), suppose $c \in C$, $d \in D$. We can get the first-order rule: if $c = i$, then $d = j$, when the following conditions hold:*

$$\underline{R}_c(D_j) = \{x \in U; [x]_{c=i} \subseteq D_j\} \neq \emptyset ,$$

and
$$\underline{R}_c(D_h) = \{x \in U; [x]_{c=i} \subseteq D_h\} = \emptyset \ (\text{for } h \neq j) \ .$$

Where, $[x]_{c=i} = \{y \in U; f_c(x) = f_c(y) = i\}$, $D_j = \{y \in U; f_d(y) = j\}$.

Proof. It is easy to see that the conditions of the above proposition means: when $c = i$, d has only one value j. So, we get such the first-order rule. □

3 Nonparametric Statistical Analysis on Decision Table

For an arbitary decision table with only one decision attrbute, nonparametric statistical methods based on the contingency tables are introduced to analyze the decision table. One is hypothesis testing to show if there is dependence relation between $c_l \in C$ and $d \in D$, the other is to compute their dependence degree.

All the contingency tables between each condition attribute c_l and the decision attribute d based on a decision table can be obtained as Table 1. Where,

$$\alpha_i = |\{x : f_l(x) = i, x \in U\}|, (i \leq |V_l|) ,$$

Table 1. c_l-d contingency table of a decision table

	$c_l = 1$	$c_l = 2$	...	$c_l = |V_l|$	Sum
$d = 1$	x_{11}	x_{12}	...	$x_{1,|V_l|}$	β_1
$d = 2$	x_{21}	x_{22}	...	$x_{2,|V_l|}$	β_2
...	...	...	...	...	...
$d = |V_d|$	$x_{|V_d|,1}$	$x_{|V_d|,2}$	...	$x_{|V_d|,|V_l|}$	$\beta_{|V_d|}$
Sum	α_1	α_2	...	$\alpha_{|V_l|}$	$N = |U|$

$$\beta_j = |\{x : f_d(x) = j, x \in U\}|, (j \leq |V_d|) ,$$
$$x_{ji} = |\{x : f_l(x) = i, f_d(x) = j, x \in U\}|, (i \leq |V_l|, j \leq |V_d|) .$$

Because the dependency relation between variables in samples can't show their dependency relation in population, here we choose chi-square testing to resolve the problem. The set of those condition attributes correlated with the decision attribute is the reduct of the decision table.

Theorem 2 ([9]). *For contingency table shown as Table 1, the test statistic*

$$\chi^2 = \sum_{j,i=1}^{|V_d|,|V_l|} \frac{(x_{ji} - \alpha_i \beta_j / N)^2}{\alpha_i \beta_j / N} \tag{1}$$

asymptotically follows chi-square distribution with the degree of freedom $df = (|V_d| - 1)(|V_l| - 1)$.

In addition, when the relationship we study is to forecast d using c_l, the Lambda dependence measurement used in categorical data, one of the PRE (Proportionate Reduction in Error) measurement, can express the relativity between these two attributes [10]. The Lambda coefficient is as follows:

$$\lambda_{dc_l} = \frac{\sum m_d - M_d}{N - M_d} , \tag{2}$$

where M_d is mode of variable d, m_d is mode of variable d in each column. The formula shows the reduction in error when forecasting d using c_l, and also shows the dependence degree between these two variables.

Specially, we can obtain the first-order rules of a decision table through observing the number of non-zero value in one column in each c_l-d contingency table.

Theorem 3. *In the c_l-d contingency table, if there is only one non-zero value x_{ji} in the column $c_l = i (i = 1, ..., |V_l|)$, then we get a first-order rule: if $c_l = i$, then $d = j$.*

It is evident that the theorem is equivalent to the Theorem 1 in Sect. 2, and it is also clear that the computation on contingency table is much easier than lower approximation using rough set theory.

4 Example

We consider a case database about pneumonia and tuberculosis shown as Table 2. In which, there are 20 patients, i.e. $|U|=20$.

Table 2. A case decision table

A	1	2	3	4	5	6	7	8	9	10	11	12	13	14	15	16	17	18	19	20
a	4	3	1	3	4	2	4	3	3	4	3	2	1	3	4	4	3	1	2	4
b	3	3	1	1	3	1	2	1	2	3	1	2	2	2	2	3	1	3	1	3
c	1	1	3	2	4	3	1	1	1	2	2	1	3	2	2	2	2	2	4	3
d	3	3	1	1	2	1	3	3	3	1	3	3	1	1	3	3	2	1	1	2
e	1	1	2	1	2	2	1	1	1	1	2	2	2	1	1	1	2	2	2	2

In the decision table, each patient has 4 symptoms: a—fever, b—cough, c—X-ray shadow, d—auscultate; and 1 decision: e—diagnosis result. That is, the condition attribute set $C = \{a,b,c,d\}$, and the decision attribute set $D = \{e\}$. Their values are as follows. $V_a = \{1,2,3,4\}$, where 1—no fever; 2—low fever; 3—middle fever; 4—high fever. $V_b = \{1,2,3\}$, where 1—slight cough; 2—middle cough; 3—severe cough. $V_c = \{1,2,3,4\}$, where 1—patch; 2—petechial; 3—funicular; 4—cavity. $V_d = \{1,2,3\}$, where 1—normal; 2—stridulation; 3—bubble sound. $V_e = \{1,2\}$, where 1—pneumonia; 2—tuberculosis.

4.1 Reduction Based on Rough Set Theory

Using the reduction method based on rough set theory introduced in Sect. 2, we can obtain the reduct $\{a,c,d\}$ and all the decision rules shown in Table 3. The 5 first-order rules are No. 2,4,5,9,12 rule respectively.

Table 3. Rules of the case decision table

	1	2	3	4	5	6	7	8	9	10	11	12
a	3	2	4	*	*	3	4	4	1	3	4	*
c	*	*	*	*	3	1	2	*	*	2	1	4
d	1	*	3	2	*	*	*	1	*	3	*	*
e	1	2	1	2	2	1	1	1	2	2	1	2

4.2 Reduction Based on Attributes Dependency Testing

We take the dependency testing between the condition attribute a and the decision attribute e as an example to explain the testing process. The a-e contingency table is shown in Table 4. Given the significance level $\alpha = 0.05$, and the testing troop is, H_0: a and e are independent $\leftrightarrow$ H_1: a and e are dependent.

Table 4. a-e contingency table

	$a=1$	$a=2$	$a=3$	$a=4$	Sum
$e=1$	0	0	5	5	10
$e=2$	3	3	2	2	10
Sum	3	3	7	7	20

Using (1), we compute the test statistic $\chi^2 = 8.57$. Here, the freedom degree is $df = (2-1)(4-1) = 3$. Because $\chi^2 > \chi_\alpha^2(3) = 7.82$, we refuse the null hypothesis H_0 at the significance level 5%. That is, there exists dependence relation between a and e. Then using (2), we can calculate

$$\lambda_{ea} = \frac{(3+3+5+5)-10}{20-10} = 0.6.$$

The result shows that dependence degree between the condition a (fever) and the decision e (diagnosis result) is high. It means that it will reduce 60% in error if forecast diagnosis result using fever.

Using the similar method, we find there is no dependence relation between the condition b and the decision e; and there exist dependence relations between c and e, d and e respectively at the significance level of 5%. It means that we get the reduct $\{a, c, d\}$ (at the significance level of 5%) using nonparametric testing method. The Lambda coefficient are $\lambda_{ec} = 0.6$, and $\lambda_{ed} = 0.5$, which mean it will reduce 60% and 50% in error if forecast e (diagnosis result) using c (X-ray shadow) and d (auscultate) respectively.

4.3 The First-Order Rules Based on Contingency Table

Using the rule acquisition method in Theorem 2, we get 5 first-order rules from 4 contingency tables between each condition attribute and the decision attribute.

2 rules from a-e contingency table: if $a = 1$, then $e = 2$; if $a = 2$, then $e = 2$;
2 rules from c-e contingency table: if $c = 3$, then $e = 2$; if $c = 4$, then $e = 2$;
1 rule from d-e contingency table: if $d = 2$, then $e = 2$.

There is no first-order rule in b-e contingency table. The b-e contingency table has no useful information understandable because b is a redundant attribute.

5 Conclusions

The approach we proposed in this paper introduces statistical theory into decision table analysis. Based on the contingency tables constructed by each condition attribute and the decision attribute of a decision table, we got the reduct and all the first-order rules. At the same time, the reduction in error when forecasting the decision attribute using one condition attribute can be calculated, which shows the dependence degree between the condition and the decision. This paper is our preliminary research on decision tables using statistical method, so we assume the decision table has only one binary decision for simplicity of discussion. More analysis will be done in the future.

Acknowledgements

The authors gratefully acknowledge the suggestions of the reviewers and the hard work of the AI 2004 Program Committee. The authors also gratefully acknowledge the support of the Natural Scientific Research Project of the Education Department of Shaanxi Province in China (No.04JK131), and Scientific Research Fund of Northwest University in China (No.03NW11).

References

1. Wets, G., Witlox, F., Timmermans, H.J.P. and Vanthienen, J., A Fuzzy Decision Table Approach for Business Site Selection. Proceedings of the Fifth IEEE International Conference on Fuzzy Systems, FUZZ-IEEE'96, New Orleans, Louisiana, (1996) 1605-1610.
2. Moreno Garcia A.M., Verhelle M. & Vanthienen J., An Overview of decision table literature 1982-2000, the Fifth International Conference on Artificial Intelligence and Emerging Technologies in Accounting, Finance and Tax, November 2-3, 2000, Huelva, Spain
3. Pawlak, Z., Rough Sets. International Journal of Information and Computer Science, 11 (1982) 341-356.
4. Tsumoto,S. Statistical Evidence for Rough Set Analysis, Fuzzy Systems, FUZZ-IEEE'02. Proceedings of the 2002 IEEE International Conference on fuzzy systems, Vol. 1 (2002) 757-762.
5. Tsumoto, S. Statistical Test for Rough Set Approximation Based on Fisher's Exact Test. J.J. Alpigini et al. (Eds.): RSCTC 2002, LNAI 2475, (2002) 381-388.
6. Dominik Slezak, Wojciech Ziarko: Attribute Reduction in the Bayesian Version of Variable Precision Rough Set Model. Electronic notes in theoretical computer science 82 (2003),No.4. 11 pages.
7. Pawlak, Z., Rough Sets: Theoretical Aspects of Reasoning About Data, Dordrecht: Kluwer Academic Publishers, 1991, 6-42.
8. Pawlak, Z., Rough Set Theorey and Its Applications to Data Analysis, Cybernetics and System: An International Journal, 29 (1998) 661-688.
9. Rao, C.R., Linear Statistical Inference and Its Applications, 2nd Edition, New York: John Wiley & Sons, 1973.
10. Jean D.G., Nonparametric Methods for Quantitative Analysis, 2nd Edition, American Sciences Press, Inc. 1985.

An Interaction Model for Affect Monitoring

I. Song, G. Governatori, and R. Colomb

School of Information Technology & Electrical Engineering,
The University of Queensland, Brisbane, QLD, 4072, Australia
{insu, guido, colomb}@itee.uq.edu.au

Abstract. This paper investigates how we can precisely define what process designers are ought achieve for what they have promised and more importantly in a way that satisfies human users. Toward these goals, an interaction model for processes and an Affect Monitoring Framework (AMF) are proposed based on our analysis on speech act theory and cognitive-based emotion models. The Affect Monitoring Framework is to detect and predict negative affects on users and to resolve caused or predicted causes of negative affects automatically.

1 Introduction

For any businesses, it is critical to know and predict both negative and positive affects on the users interacting with the organizations managed by business process management systems such as workflow management systems.

One of the important affects on the users interacting with processes is *emotion* since emotions are motivational processes that influence cognition and actions [3]. Emotional states of users interacting with an information system can be caused by various failures and abnormal behaviors of the system, such as delayed responses, failed operations, missed notifications, and unpleasant actions. Many of these causes result in poor usability and frustration on the users [4].

This paper investigates how we can give objective semantics to what it means by failures and abnormal behaviors of processes in the view of human users. Further we want to precisely define what process designers are ought achieve for what they have promised and more importantly in a way that satisfies human users. Toward these goals, an interaction model for processes for an Affect Monitoring Framework (AMF) is proposed based on our analysis on speech act theory and cognitive-based emotion models. The framework is to detect and predict negative affects on users and to resolve caused or predicted causes of negative affects automatically.

In the next section we give an overview of AMF. Section 3 describes an interaction model for processes which lays out objectives of this paper and conditions for satisfiable processes. Section 3 and 4 develop methods to capture necessary information for estimating emotions. Section 5 describes an example emotion generation based on a cognitive emotion model.

2 Affect Monitoring Framework

Cognitive emotion theorists [6, 1, 7] claim that events relevant to users' concerns are the main sources of emotions. If this is true, we need to know what users' goals are. We can then enumerate the events that are relevant to the goals. We then need to formulate how these events give arise to emotions on the users.

We formulate this intuition into a framework called AMF which includes the following four components: (1) *Data-mining* monitors interactions between users and processes to collect necessary information for estimating possible causes of emotions, (2) *Emotion-generation* uses the collected information (users' goals, events, and actions) to estimate users' emotions based on an emotion model, (3) *Emotion-management* monitors emotional states of users and takes appropriate actions to prevent possible causes of negative emotions and to resolve negative emotions, and (4) *Emotion-adjustment* adjusts estimated emotional states from the direct feedback from users or other observation methods such as facial expression recognition, gesture recognition, emotion recognition from email messages.

The framework includes all three types of usability evaluation automation described in the taxonomy by Ivory et al. [2]: capture (data mining), analysis (emotion generation), and critique (emotion management). However, the framework focuses only on evaluating affects on the users of processes rather than evaluating the conventional usability measures such as performance, efficiency, easy of use, and easy to learn.

3 An Interaction Model

A user with a set Q of goals comes along to use the tools provided by a process to achieve a subset $q \subset Q$ of her goals. The system provides tools (some calls them mediators or services) through a set IF of user interfaces. The user uses her own planning ability to achieve q using a subset of IF. Given IF, which defines a set M of messages that can be exchanged between the user and the process, we can drive a set G of goals that can be created through IF. In this scenario, there are three primary questions we want to address:

1. How to make sure the process is designed the way that it can achieve all the goals in G.
2. How to make sure the process achieves the goals in G in a manner that satisfies human users. (We are not considering how well IF is designed to achieve q.)
3. How to *monitor* whether processes achieve all the goals in G in a way that satisfies human users.

The designer of a process must design the database DB and a set of plans of the process in the way that the process satisfies the first two questions. Although design time tests can address the first question, it cannot address the second question because of various runtime factors. Therefore, we need to find a way to address the third question.

3.1 Process Definition

A process is defined as a structure:

$$Pr =_{def} < IF, M, G, DB, L, R, f_L(), \hbar(), PL >$$

where IF is the set of interfaces, M is the set of all messages between the process and users, G is the set of users' goals that can be created through IF, DB is the database of the process, L is the set of predicate symbols and function symbols that define the language of the process, R is a set of rules, $f_L(DB)$ is a function that maps DB to a set S of grounded atoms, $\hbar(p)$ is a function that maps a conjunction of grounded atoms to a set of records, PL is a set of plans which achieves goals in G. Let $T = S \cup R$ be the theory of the process.

A message $m \in M$ can contain several illocutionary acts α each of which is represented as $F(p)$ where F is the illocutionary force and p is the proposition of α. Then, the semantics of illocutionary acts received from users can be given with respect to the process definition as follows: (1) If F is a directive, the user wants the system to bring about p. Therefore, the goal state p is a constraint on DB that $T \vdash p$. (2) If F is an assertive or a declarative, the user wants the system to believe p. Therefore, $(\hbar(p) \subseteq DB)$ is the goal state, i.e., the database contains information p and consequently $T \vdash p$. (3) If F is a commissive, $(\hbar(I(u,p)) \subseteq DB)$ is the goal state, i.e., u is intending p and u wants the system believe it.

The semantics of commissive messages sent to users are equivalent to the directive messages from users: the goal is $T \vdash p$. Assertive and declarative messages to users are usually informing events if they are related with the goals of the users, otherwise they are actions performed by the system. Directive and expressive messages are usually actions performed by the system.

The interface consists of eight sets of grounded well formed formulas: IF_F^i for incoming messages and IF_F^o for outgoing messages where the subscripts $F \in \{d, a, c, dc\}$ stand for directive, assertive, commissive, and declarative illocutionary force, respectively. We define three types of goals for a message $(sender, receiver, F(p))$: $(T \vdash p)$, $(\hbar(p) \subseteq DB)$, and $(\hbar(I(sender, p)) \subseteq DB)$ where $p \in IF$. The set G of users' goals that this process must fulfill is defined as follows:

$$G = \{(T \vdash p) | p \in IF_d^i\} \cup \{(\hbar(p) \subseteq DB) | p \in IF_a^i \cup IF_{dc}^i\} \cup \{(\hbar(I(u,p)) | p \in IF_c^i\} \cup \{(T \vdash p) | p \in IF_c^o\}$$

Now, we impose constraints on DB and PL:
1. For all $g \in G$, there must exist a state of DB so that g is true.
2. For all $g \in G$, there must exist a plan $pl \in PL$ whose execution will lead to a state of DB that makes g true.

Those constraints are necessary conditions for a process to achieve all the goals that can be created through its interfaces. But, this does not tell us whether the process achieves the goals in a way that satisfies human users. The following sections, 4, and 5 develop a method to monitor whether the process achieves the goals in a way that satisfies human users.

Table 1. Prospective events for a goal g and their classifications

Event Names	Symbols	OCC Types	Symbols
goal failure time event	gte_g	Prospective	all
response failure time event	rte_g	Unexpected	none
confirming event	ice_g	Desirable	ice_g
disconfirming event	ide_g	Undesirable	gte_g, rte_g, ide_g
informing new time event	ite_g	Unconfirmed	rte_g, ite_g
response event	ire_g	Confirming	ice_g
		Disconfirming	ide_g

4 Events

For a process there are two types of goals concerning with its users: user requested goals and promised goals by the process. A requested goal is created when a user sends a message to the process. A promised goal is created when the process sends a message containing a commissive speech act. Given the two types of goals, we enumerate the events relevant to the goals.

When a user interacts with the system, the user is aware of all prospective events related with the messages. Therefore, the two types of goals trigger *user-side-time-events*, $TE_g = \{gte_g, rte_g\}$. The system responsible for the goals struggles to prevent the time events occurring by producing *informing-events*, $IE_g = \{ice_g, ide_g, ite_g, ire_g\}$. Table 1 lists these events and shows the classification based on Ortony, Collins and Clore (OCC) [6].

4.1 User Side Time Events

We make the following assumptions for the two types of goals. For a requested goal g, the user is expecting a response within a certain response time rt_g. The response must be either a goal achievement confirming event ice_g or a response event ire_g. If the response is not a confirming event, the user is expecting another response for a confirming event within a certain goal achievement time gt_g. The new response must be either a confirming event ice_g or an informing new time events ite_g which resets gt_g to $gt_g + \delta$ for some value $\delta > 0$. We assume that $gt_g > rt_g$ is usually the case. For a promised goal g, the user is expecting a response within a certain response time rt_g. The response must be either a confirming event ice_g or an informing new time events ite_g which resets rt_g to $rt_g + \delta$.

When the user is not informed of the achievement of the goal within gt_g, a goal failure time event gte_g fires. When neither the achievement nor an acknowledgement is informed to the user within rt_g, a response failure time event rte_g fires. When a process promises that a promised goal g will be satisfied within in a certain time rt_g and the process fails to inform the user within the time whether the goal is satisfied or a new response time rt_g is set, a response failure time event rte_g fires.

Therefore, for any goal g, $TE_g = \{gte_g, rte_g\}$ is the set of all possible time events that can cause negative effects on the user of the goal if the process does not inform appropriately the user. If g is a requested goal, the set of possible user side time events is $\{gte_g, rte_g\}$. If g is a promised goal, the set of possible events is $\{rte_g\}$.

4.2 Informing Events

The process must create appropriate informing events to prevent the user side time events occurring. We define four types of informing events: confirming events ice_g, disconfirming events, ide_g, informing new time events ite_g, and response events ire_g. These events are detected by examining the messages $F(p)$ sent to the users as follows:

$ice_g \Leftarrow requested(g) \wedge (g = (T \vdash p)) \wedge (assertive(F) \vee declaritive(F))$
$ide_g \Leftarrow requested(g) \wedge (g = (T \vdash \neg p)) \wedge (assertive(F) \vee declaritive(F))$
$ire_g \Leftarrow requested(g) \wedge (g = (T \vdash p)) \wedge (commisive(F))$
$ite_g \Leftarrow (requested(g) \vee promised(g)) \wedge (g = (T \vdash p)) \wedge (commisive(F)) \wedge ire_g$

If a confirming event ice_g or a disconfirming event ide_g occurs, no events in TE_g will fire anymore. The following two formulas summaries the event firing rules for the user side time events described in the previous subsection:

$rte_g \Leftarrow (rt_g < t) \wedge \neg ire_g \wedge \neg ite_g \wedge \neg ice_g \wedge \neg ide_g$
$gte_g \Leftarrow (gt_g < t) \wedge \neg ite_g \wedge \neg ice_g \wedge \neg ide_g.$

5 Emotion Generation

This section describes how emotional states can be deduced from the information captured in the previous sections based on the work of [5]. We only consider a subset of the OCC [6] cognitive appraisal theory of emotion: hope, satisfied, fear, fears-confirmed, disappointment, and reproach. These emotions are prospective-based emotions that are emotions in response to expected and suspected states and in response to the confirmation or disconfirmation of such states [6].

Given a set of events and a set G of goals captured for a user, we can derive the following emotions of the user for a goal $g \in G$:

$$hope(g) \Leftarrow requested(g) \wedge \neg(rte_g \vee gte_g \vee ice_g \vee ide_g) \quad (1)$$
$$fear(g) \Leftarrow requested(g) \wedge rte_g \wedge \neg(gte_g \vee ice_g \vee ide_g) \quad (2)$$
$$fear(g) \Leftarrow promised(g) \wedge rte_g \wedge \neg(ice_g \vee ide_g) \quad (3)$$
$$satisfied(g) \Leftarrow hope(g) \wedge \neg fear(g) \wedge ice_g \quad (4)$$
$$fearConf(g) \Leftarrow fear(g) \wedge request(g) \wedge (gfe_g \vee ide_g) \quad (5)$$
$$fearConf(g) \Leftarrow fear(g) \wedge promised(g) \wedge ide_g \quad (6)$$
$$disappoint(g) \Leftarrow hope(g) \wedge (gfe_g \vee ide_g) \quad (7)$$
$$relieved(g) \Leftarrow fear(g) \wedge ice_g \quad (8)$$

(Eq. 1) says that if there is a goal that is desirable to the user and no fear prospect is triggered, the user feels hope over the goal. (Eq. 2 & 3) says that if there is a goal that is desirable to the user and a fear prospect is triggered for the goal, the user might feel fear over the failure of the goal. (Eq. 4) says that if the user felt hope of an event and a confirming event occurs, the user might feel satisfied. (Eq. 5 & 6) says that if the user felt fear of an event and a disconfirming event occurs, the user might feel that the fear is confirmed. (Eq. 7) says that if the user felt hope of an event and a disconfirming event occurs, the user might be disappointed. (Eq. 8) says that if the user felt fear of an event and a disconfirming event of failure occurs for the event, the user might be relieved.

6 Conclusion

This paper proposed a human-process interaction model based on speech act theory and the cognitive-based emotion model of OCC. The model allows us to specify processes user-oriented way and observe interactions to monitor not only whether it achieves users' requests, but also in a way that satisfies human users. The model also clearly defines the requirements of the database and procedures of a process for a set of interfaces defined for the process.

We have also described how the goals of the users interacting with an information system can be captured and how such goals can be used to define events that can be used in detecting affects on the users. We believe that the framework and the model provided is independent of culture, education, and context of users. Although we have shown an emotion generation method based on the OCC model, we believe the information captured can be used with most of other cognitive-based emotion models.

References

1. Frijda, N.H.: The Emotions. Cambridge University Press (1986)
2. Ivory, M.Y., Hearst, M.A.: The state of the art in automating usability evaluation of user interfaces. ACM Computing Surveys **33** (2001) 470–516
3. Izard, C.E.: Four systems for emotion activation: Cognitive and noncognitive processes. Psychological Review **100** (1993) 68–90
4. Klein, J., Moon, Y., Picard, R.W.: This computer responds to user frustration. In: Proceedings of ACM CHI 99. Volume 2. (1999) 242–243
5. O'Rorke, P., Ortony, A.: Explaining emotions. Cognitive Science **18** (1994) 283–323
6. Ortony, A., Clore, G.L., Collins, A.: The Congnitive Structure of Emotions. Cambridge University, Cambridge (1988)
7. Roseman, I.J., Spinde, M.S., Jose, P.E.: Appraisals of emotion-eliciting events: Testing a theory of discrete emotions. Journal of Personality and Social Psychology **59** (1990) 899–915

Ontology Transformation in Multiple Domains

Longbing Cao[1], Dan Luo[2], Chao Luo[3], and Li Liu[4]

[1,4] Faculty of Information Technology, University of Technology Sydney, Australia
[2,3] Department of Electronics and Information, Liaoning Technical University, China
{1lbcao, 4liuli}@it.uts.edu.au,
{2chao.luo, 3dan.luo}@mail.ia.ac.cn

Abstract. We have proposed a new approach called *ontology services-driven integration of business intelligence* (BI) to designing an integrated BI platform. In such a BI platform, multiple ontological domains may get involved, such as domains for business, reporting, data warehouse, and multiple underlying enterprise information systems. In general, ontologies in the above multiple domains are heterogeneous. So, a key issue emerges in the process of building an integrated BI platform, that is, how to support ontology transformation and mapping between multiple ontological domains. In this paper, we present semantic aggregations of semantic relationships and ontologies in one or multiple domains, and the ontological transformation from one domain to another. Rules for the above semantic aggregation and transformation are described. This work is the foundation for supporting BI analyses crossing multiple domains.

1 Introduction

Business Intelligence (BI) [1] is getting more and more popular for scientific decision making with comprehensive analyses on top of practical Business/Operation Support Systems (BSS/OSS). The usual approach to building a BI platform is to combine all BI packages such as reporting, Data Warehouse (DW) and Data Mining (DM) engines together on top of the above mentioned Enterprise Information Systems (EIS). We have analyzed [2] that this approach cannot make its business users satisfied with some key challenges. Two main problems are (i) it can only support technology-centered but not business-oriented personalization and localization, (ii) it cannot adapt to dynamic and emergent requests on both analytical model and underlying operational systems. To figure out the above problems, we have further proposed a new approach called *ontology* [4] *services-driven integration of business intelligence* [2, 3] to building an integrated BI platform.

The basic idea for *ontology services-driven integration of business intelligence* is as follows [2, 3]. Since it is regarded as unfriendly for business persons to interact with the current technology-centered BI packages, we re-build a logic link and communication channel which links reporting, DW and DM together. This channel is isolated from the existing linkage among reporting engine, DW engine and EIS; the objective of it is to handle business-oriented rather than technology-centered interaction and integration of BI. This channel actually links the following ontological domains together [2]: a Business Ontology domain (BO) for business profiles, a DW Ontology domain (DWO) for the DW, and multiple EIS Ontology domains (EISO) for different BSS/OSS systems. Obviously, ontologies in these ontological domains are heterogeneous in an integrated BI platform.

In the above integration of BI, a key issue for its successful operations is that flexible and efficient transformation, mapping [5] and discovery of ontologies can be dealt with between the above heterogeneous ontological domains. In this paper, we discuss a foundation work about semantic aggregation and ontological transformation. The rules for the aggregation and transformation are discussed. Semantic aggregation gets involved in aggregation of semantic relationships or of ontologies in one or multiple domains. Transformation supports ontological mapping from one ontological item to another in multiple ontological domains.

The sequel of this paper is organized as follows. In Section 2, ontology semantic relationships are introduced. Section 3 presents semantic aggregation and ontological transformation in the BI platform. We conclude this study and discuss about the future work in Section 4.

2 Ontology Semantic Relationships

Before undertaking ontological mapping, two steps must be performed: (i) extraction and collection of ontological elements from the above-mentioned ontological domains, and (ii) organization and management of these ontological elements in a structured manner. With regard to (ii), the analysis of semantic relationships is quite important. Semantic relationships [6] refer to semantic dependencies between ontological elements (or called ontological items or concepts) in the same domain and between different domains.

The following summarizes seven types of semantic relationships for managing ontological items in a BI system. They are Instantiation, Aggregation, Generalization, Substitution, Disjoin, Overlap and Association, respectively. Informal definitions of them are given below; the symbol O or o refers to an ontological element.

- *Instance_of* (O, o): two ontological elements O and o, o is an instance of the ontological class O.
- *Part_of* (O_1, O_2): two ontological elements O_1 and O_2, where O_2 is part/member of O_1, or O_1 is made of O_2.
- *Is_a*(O_1, O_2): the relationship between $O2$ and $O1$ is subtype/supertype or assubsumption, i.e. O_2 is-a O_1, or O_2 is a kind of O_1. The *is_a* sometimes is also called as *subclass_of*.
- *Similar_to*(O_1, O_2): it stands for that O_1 and O_2 are identical or to a large degree similar; in this case O_2 can be substituted by O_1.
- *Disjoin_with*(O_1, O_2): it stands for that O_2 is independent of O_1.
- *Overlap_to*(O_1, O_2): it represents that there is something shared by both O_1 and O_2; but the share percentage is not high enough for one to be substituted by another.
- *Relate_to*(O_1,O_2): it is the predicate over the ontology O_1 and O_2; it represents a relationship between O_1 and O_2 which cannot be specified by any of the above six; in this case, O_1 and O_2 are associated with each other by some linkage defined by users.

3 Ontological Semantic Aggregation and Transformation

The process of a BI analysis in the integrated BI platform looks as follows. A business analyst first selects an analytical subject and relevant method according to her/his interestingness and the business requirements of the analytical problem. Then s/he specifies analytical dimensions and measures in the forms of her/his favorite business words. These arbitrary keywords are transformed to business ontologies first, and then mapped to target ontological elements in the target domain to extract/aggregate relevant data. The resulting query reports are fed back to the analyst in the predefined business terms.

Semantic aggregation and ontological transformation must be performed in the above analytical process, so that the analysis can be undertaken. There are three aspects which must be followed in order to do the semantic aggregation and ontological transformation from user-defined keywords to ontological elements in the DWO or any domain of the EISO. They are (i) semantic aggregation between semantic relationships, (ii) semantic aggregation of ontological items, and (iii) transformation of an ontology item to another one. All the above three types of transformations can be involved in either one ontological domain or multiple domains. The following three sections discuss them in details, respectively.

3.1 Semantic Aggregation of Semantic Relationships

The semantic aggregation of semantic relationships is to study whether there are transitivity, additivity and antisymmetry that can be performed between ontological semantic relationships. The aggregation of multiple semantic relationships can simplify the combination of semantic relationships, and supports to find the final reduced semantic relationship.

Let $A(a)$, $B(b)$ and $C(c)$ be arbitrary ontological items, where $A(a)$ means A or a. s, s_1, s_2 are Similarity Value defined by users. The following defines some basic specifications.

DEFINITION 1. 'AND' or 'OR' are logic connectors used to connect two ontological items which have the same grammatical function in a construction;

DEFINITION 2. The resulting output of '(A AND B)' includes both A and B, while the output of '(A OR B)' is either A or B.

DEFINITION 3. '(A AND B)' is equal to '(B AND A)'; similarly, '(A OR B)' is equal to '(B OR A)'.

DEFINITION 4. Boolean logic operators '$\wedge$' and '$\vee$' represent "and" and "or" relationships between semantic relationships or between logic formulas.

DEFINITION 5. Similarity value s measures to what degree that two ontological items are related in a semantic relationship.

This metric s usually is used with relationships *similar_to()*, *overlap_to()*, and user-defined relationship *relate_to()*. For instance, *similar_to* (A, B, s_1) means that B is similar to A in a degree of s_1.

For all the seven semantic relationships discussed in Section 2, rules will hold for semantic aggregation of combinations of the above semantic relationships. The following shows an excerpt for some cases.

Rule 1. Let $A(a)$, $B(b)$ and $C(c)$ be associated by the Instantiation relationship, then
- $\forall$ (instance_of $(A, a) \land$ instance_of $(B, A)) \Rightarrow$ instance_of (B, a)
- $\forall$ (instance_of $(A, a) \land$ instance_of $(B, a)) \Rightarrow$ instance_of $((A \text{ AND } B), a)$, which means a is an instance of both A and B

Rule 2. Let A, B and C be associated by the Aggregation relationship, then
- $\forall$ (part_of $(A, B) \land$ part_of $(B, C)) \Rightarrow$ part_of (A, C)
- $\forall$ (part_of $(A, B) \land$ part_of $(B, A)) \Rightarrow$ similar_to(A, B)
- $\forall$ (part_of $(A, B) \land$ part_of $(C, B)) \Rightarrow$ overlap_to$(A, C) \lor$ similar_to(A, C) depend on the intersection between A and C.

Rule 3. A, B and C be associated by the Generalization relationship, then
- $\forall$ (is_a$(A, B) \land$ is_a $(B, C)) \Rightarrow$ is_a(A, C)
- $\forall$ (is_a$(A, B) \land$ is_a$(A, C)) \Rightarrow$ is_a$(A, (B \text{ AND } C))$
- $\forall$ (is_a$(A, B) \land$ is_a$(B, A)) \Rightarrow$ similar_to(A, B)

Rule 4. A, B and C be associated by the Substitution relationship, then
- $\forall$ (similar_to $(A, B) \land$ similar_to $(B, C)) \Rightarrow$ similar_to (A, C)
- $\forall$ (similar_to $(A, B) \land$ similar_to $(A, C)) \Rightarrow$ similar_to (B, C)

Rule 5. A, B and C be associated by the Overlap relationship, then
- $\forall$ (overlap_to $(A, B) \land$ overlap_to $(B, C)) \Rightarrow$ overlap_to $(B, (A \text{ AND } C))$

Accordingly, we can list many other aggregation rules for reducing the combinations of the seven semantic relationships.

3.2 Semantic Aggregation of Ontological Items

Another situation for semantic aggregation is to aggregate ontological items that are linked by logic connectors associated with some semantic relationship. The objective for semantic aggregation of ontological items is to reduce items, and to generate the resulting ontological items.

To the above end, rules for aggregating ontological items can be found. The following rules hold for semantic aggregation in some cases. These rules define what the resulting logical output is for each given input logical combination with some semantic relationship inside.

Rule 6
- $\forall$ $(A \text{ AND } b)$, $\exists\, b ::= $ instance_of(B, b)
  $\Rightarrow A \text{ AND } B$, the logical resulting output is A and B
- $\forall$ $(A \text{ OR } b)$, $\exists\, b ::= $ instance_of(B, b)
  $\Rightarrow A \text{ OR } B$, the logical resulting output is A or B

Rule 7
- $\forall$ $(A \text{ AND } B)$, $\exists\, B ::= $ part_of(A, B)
  $\Rightarrow B$, the resulting output is B

Rule 8
- $\forall$ $(A \text{ AND } B)$, $\exists\, B ::= $ is_a(A, B)
  $\Rightarrow B$, the resulting output is B

Rule 9
- $\forall$ (A AND B), $\exists B ::= similar\_to(A, B)$
  $\Rightarrow$ A OR B, the resulting output is A or B

Rule 10
- $\forall$ (A AND B), $\exists B ::= disjoin\_to(A, B)$
  $\Rightarrow$ A AND B, the resulting output is A and B

Rule 11
- $\forall$ (A AND B), $\exists B ::= overlap\_to(A, B)$
  $\Rightarrow$ A AND B, the resulting output is A and B

Rule 12
- $\forall$ (A AND B), $\exists B ::= relate\_to(A, B)$
  $\Rightarrow$ (A AND B) $\vee$ (A OR B), the resulting output is A and B, or either A or B, one of the three output will hold depending on user-defined relationship

3.3 Transformation Between Ontological Items

This section discusses about the transformation of an ontological item to another one. This could be a mapping from an arbitrary keyword to its relevant items in BO domain, or from BO to another domain such as DWO or one of EISO domain. The basic idea for transformation of ontological items is as follows: given an input item, checking candidate ontological items by semantic relationships, and finding the suitable candidate as the output item.

Rules for this transformation must be built, so that the matched ontological item can be generated as output. The following lists some rules for the transformation, where C_i is an input item, O, O_1 and O_2 are candidate items in the target domain.

Rule 13
- $\forall C_i, \exists$: $(similar\_to(O, C_i) \vee is\_a(O, C_i) \vee instance\_of(O, C_i) \vee part\_of(O, C_i) \vee relate\_to(O, C_i)) \Rightarrow O$, the O is the output item

Rule 14
- $\forall C_i, \exists$: $(is\_a(O_1, C_i) \wedge is\_a(O_2, C_i)) \Rightarrow O_1$ AND O_2

Rule 15
- $\forall C_i, \exists$: $(part\_of(O_1, C_i) \wedge part\_of(O_2, C_i)) \Rightarrow O_1$ OR O_2

Rule 16
- $\forall C_i, \exists$: $(is\_a(O_1, C_i) \wedge part\_of(O_2, C_i)) \Rightarrow O_1$ AND O_2

Rule 17
- $\forall C_i, \exists$: $(similar\_to(O_1, C_i) \wedge similar\_to(O_2, C_i)) \Rightarrow O_1$ OR O_2

Rule 18
- $\forall C_i, C_j, (i \neq j), \exists$: $(part\_of(O, C_i) \wedge part\_of(O, C_j)) \Rightarrow O$

Rule 19
- $\forall C_i, C_j, (i \neq j), \exists$: $(is\_a(O, C_i) \wedge is\_a(O, C_j)) \Rightarrow O$

Rule 20
- $\forall C_i, C_j, (i \neq j), \exists$: $(relate\_to(O, C_i) \wedge relate\_to(O, C_j)) \Rightarrow O$

4 Conclusions and Future Work

There are multiple heterogeneous ontological domains existing in our proposed ontology-based integrated BI platform. In this paper, we have discussed about semantic aggregation and ontological transformation in the above multiple ontological domains. Seven types of semantic relationships of ontologies have been introduced first. Based on these relationships, semantic aggregations of semantic relationships or ontologies have been presented. The transformation of ontologies from one domain to another has also been studied. Rules for semantic aggregation and ontological transformation are given.

With this work, personalization, transformation and mapping of ontologies in multiple domains in an ontology-based BI platform become feasible. In reality, our preliminary experiments in building a practical BI system for telecom operators have shown that the above work is essential for user profiles-oriented analyses, search and query either from DW or from any EIS system dynamically and transparently.

Further work will be performed on refining rules in a real world, and designing ontology query algorithms with high performance for fast speed and accuracy; some promising work will be on supporting high dimensional discovery and transformation among multiple ontological domains.

References

[1] Whitehorn, M., et al.: Business intelligence: the IBM solution. New Springer (1999)
[2] Cao, L.B., Luo, C., Luo, D., Zhang, C.Q.: Integration of Business Intelligence Based on Three-Level Ontology Services. In Proceedings of IEEE/WIC/ACM WI'04, IEEE Computer Society Press (2004)
[3] Cao, L.B., Luo, C., Luo, D., Liu, L.: Ontology services-based information integration in mining telecom business intelligence. In Zhang, C.Q. et al. (eds) PRICAI 2004: Trends in Artificial Intelligence. LNAI 3157, Springer (2004) 85-94
[4] Gruninger, M., Lee, J.: Ontology applications and design: Introduction. Communications of the ACM, ACM Press, 45(2) (2002) 39-41
[5] Kalfoglou, Y., Schorlemmer, M.: Ontology mapping: the state of the art. The Knowledge Engineering Review, ACM Press, 18(1) (2003) 1-31
[6] Storey, V.C.: Understanding semantic relationships. The very large data bases Journal. 2(4) (1993) 455-488

A Bayesian Metric for Evaluating Machine Learning Algorithms

Lucas R. Hope and Kevin B. Korb

School of Computer Science,
and Software Engineering,
Monash University,
Clayton, VIC 3168, Australia
{lhope, korb}@csse.monash.edu.au

Abstract. How to assess the performance of machine learning algorithms is a problem of increasing interest and urgency as the data mining application of myriad algorithms grows. Rather than predictive accuracy, we propose the use of information-theoretic reward functions. The first such proposal was made by Kononenko and Bratko. Here we improve upon our alternative Bayesian metric, which provides a fair betting assessment of any machine learner. We include an empirical analysis of various Bayesian classification learners.

Keywords: Predictive accuracy, Bayesian evaluation, information reward.

1 Introduction

As interest in machine learning and data mining grows, the problem of how to assess machine learning algorithms becomes more urgent. The standard practice for supervised classification learners has been to measure predictive accuracy (or its dual, error rate) using a fixed sample divided repeatedly into training and test sets, accepting a machine learner as superior to another if its predictive accuracy passes a statistical significance test. This represents an improvement over historical practices, particularly when the statistical dependencies introduced by resampling are taken into account (cf. [1, 2]).

Nevertheless, there are a number of objections to the use of predictive accuracy, the most telling being that it fails to take into account the uncertainty of predictions. For example, a prediction of a mushroom's edibility with a probability of 0.51 counts exactly the same as a prediction of edibility with a probability of 1.0. We might rationally prefer to consume the mushroom in the second case. Predictive accuracy shows no such discernment. According to common evaluation practice, every correct prediction is as good as every other. Hence, we advocate that classification learners should be designed, or redesigned, so as to yieled probabilistic predictions rather than catagorical predictions.

We believe a cost-sensitive assessment, favouring the machine learner which maximizes expected reward is, in principle, the best way of evaluating learning algorithms. Unfortunately, finding appropriate cost functions is often difficult or impossible. Provost and Fawcett [3] use receiver operating characteristic (ROC) convex hulls for evaluation independent of cost functions. This has the useful meta-learning feature of selecting the best predictor for a given performance constraint, in the form of a selected false negative classification rate. Unfortunately, the ROC curves underlying this method again ignore the probabilistic aspect of prediction, as does predictive accuracy simpliciter.

Here we examine metrics which attend to the probability of a classification, namely information-theoretic measures and in particular, *information reward* (*IR*). We illustrate its application by comparing Naive Bayes with other classification learners, contrasting *IR* with predictive accuracy assessments.

2 Information-Theoretic Metrics

2.1 Good's Information Reward

The original information reward (*IR*) was introduced by I.J. Good [4] as *fair betting fees* — the cost of buying a bet which makes the expected value of the purchase zero. Good's *IR* positively rewarded binary classifications which were informative relative to a uniform prior. *IR* is split into two cases: that where the classification is correct, indicated by a superscripted '+', and where the classification is incorrect, indicated by a superscripted '−'.

Definition 1. *The IR of a binary classification with probability p' is*

$$I^+ = 1 + \log_2 p' \quad \text{(for correct classification)} \tag{1a}$$
$$I^- = 1 + \log_2(1 - p') \quad \text{(for misclassification)} \tag{1b}$$

IR has the range $(-\infty, 1)$. For successful classification, it increases monotonically with p', and thus is maximized as p' approaches 1; for misclassification, *IR* decreases monotonically. While the constant 1 in (1a) and (1b) is unnecessary for simply ranking machine learners, it makes sense in terms of fair fees. When the learner reports a probability of 0.5, it is not communicating any *information* (given a uniform prior), and thus receives a zero reward.

Our work generalizes Good's to multinomial classification tasks, while also relativizing the reward function to non-uniform prior probabilities.

2.2 Kononenko and Bratko's Metric

The measure introduced by Kononenko and Bratko [5] also relativizes reward to prior probabilities. Furthermore, it too is nominally based upon information theory. This foundation is seriously undermined, however, by their insistence that when a reward is applied to a correct prediction with probability 1 and an incorrect prediction also with probability 1, the correct and incorrect predictions ought precisely to counterbalance, resulting in a total reward of 0. This conflicts

with the supposed information-theoretic basis: on any account in accord with
Shannon, a reward for a certain prediction coming true can only be finite, while a
penalty for such a *certain* prediction coming false must always be infinite. Putting
these into balance guarantees there will be no proper information-theoretic interpretation of their reward function.

Kononenko and Bratko introduce the following reward function, where p' is
the estimated probability and p is the prior:

$$I_{KB}^+ = \log p' - \log p \qquad \text{(for } p' \geq p\text{)} \tag{2a}$$

$$I_{KB}^- = -\log(1-p') + \log(1-p) \qquad \text{(for } p' < p\text{)} \tag{2b}$$

This measure is assessed against the *true* class only. Since the probabilities
of other classes are not considered, in multinomial classification a miscalibrated
assessment of the alternative classes will go unpunished. For all these reasons we
do not consider the Kononenko and Bratko function to be adequate.[1]

2.3   Bayesian Information Reward

The idea behind fair fees, that you should only be paid for an *informative* prediction, is simply not adequately addressed by Good's *IR*. Suppose an expert's
job is to diagnose patients with a disease that is carried by 10% of some population. This particular expert is lazy and simply reports that each patient does
not have the disease, with 0.9 confidence. Good's expected reward per patient
for this strategy is $0.9(1+\log_2 0.9)+0.1(1+\log_2 0.1) = 0.531$, so the uninformed
strategy is rewarded substantially! The expected reward per patient we should
like is 0, which our generalization below provides. Good's *IR* breaks down in
its application to multinomial classification: any *successful* prediction with confidence less than 0.5 is penalized, even when the confidence is greater than the
prior. Good's fair fees are actually fair only when both the prior is uniform and
the task binary.

We presented a Bayesian metric similar to below in Hope and Korb [6]. Unfortunately, it failed to reward perfect calibration maximally,[2] and thus we abandoned it in favour of the following. For classification into classes $\{C_1, \ldots, C_k\}$
with estimated probabilities p'_i and priors p_i, where $i \in \{1, \ldots, k\}$:

$$IR_B = \frac{\sum_i I_i}{k} \tag{3}$$

where $I_i = I_i^+$ for the true class and $I_i = I_i^-$ otherwise, and

$$I_i^+ = \log \frac{p'_i}{p_i}$$

$$I_i^- = \log \frac{1-p'_i}{1-p_i}$$

---

[1] We did, however, include it in the empirical evaluation of [6].
[2] David Dowe pointed this out.

Clearly, when $p' = p$, the reward is 0. IR_B also retains an information-theoretic interpretation: the measure is finitely bounded in the positive direction, since prior probabilities are never zero, and misplaced certainty (i.e., when the probability for the true value is 0) warrants an infinite negative reward. Finally, correct probabilities are now rewarded maximally in the long run. The proof of this is available in [7] and [8–§10.8].

A non-uniform prior p can be obtained any number of ways, including being set subjectively (or arbitrarily). In our empirical studies we simply use the frequency in the test set given to the machine learner to compute the prior.[3] This is because we have no informed prior to work with, and because it is simple and unbiased relative to the learning algorithms under study.

Bayesian IR_B reflects the gambling metaphor more adequately than does Good's IR. Book makers are required to take bets for and against whatever events are in their books, with their earnings depending on the spread. They are, in effect, being rated on the quality of the odds they generate for all outcomes simultaneously. Bayesian IR does the same for machine learning algorithms: the odds (probabilities) they offer on all the possible classes are simultaneously assessed, extracting maximum information from each probabilistic classification.

3 Empirical Study: Bayesian Models

Our empirical evaluation focuses on machine learners that form Bayesian models, partially in response to recent work showing the power of Naive Bayes learners (e.g., [9, 10, 11]). The machine learners are Naive Bayes (NB) [12], Tree Augmented Naive Bayes (TAN) [10, 13], Averaged One Dependence Estimators (AODE) [9] and Causal MML (CaMML) [14].

For the experiment, we artificially generated data from a series of Bayesian model types. Three model types are chosen, each designed to favour a particular machine learner: Naive Bayes, TAN or AODE. Thus, we compare how the learners perform when their assumptions are broken and when they are exactly matched. To test the threshold at which a simpler model outperforms the more complex, we also systematically vary the amount of training data.

Of our machine learners, CaMML finds models of the greatest generality. Given standard convergence results, CaMML must better or equal every other machine learner in the limit. Again, AODE's and TAN's models generalize the Naive Bayes models, and given sufficient data they should perform at least on par with Naive Bayes. This suggests a converse phenomenon. At low levels of data, and *if the learner's representations include the true model*, the simpler learner should outperform the more complex, because complex machine learners converge to their optimum models slower, due to a larger search space.

Experimental Method. For statistical analysis, we regard each model type as a separate experiment. For each experiment we sample the space of appropriate

---

[3] We start the frequency counts at 0.5 to prevent overconfident probabilities.

Table 1. Table of results for the three Bayesian model experiments. The results are average information reward for each machine learner, given 50, 500 or 5000 training instances. Confidence intervals at 95% are shown

(a) Naive Bayes Models

Training samples	NBayes	AODE	TAN	CaMML
50	0.250 ± 0.053	0.238 ± 0.049	0.234 ± 0.053	0.092 ± 0.051
500	0.466 ± 0.051	0.443 ± 0.051	0.456 ± 0.053	0.459 ± 0.051
5000	0.496 ± 0.051	0.494 ± 0.051	0.495 ± 0.051	0.496 ± 0.051

(b) Tree Augmented Naive Bayes Models

50	-0.003 ± 0.039	0.124 ± 0.031	0.003 ± 0.039	-0.019 ± 0.033
500	0.214 ± 0.031	0.351 ± 0.029	0.361 ± 0.033	0.400 ± 0.033
5000	0.247 ± 0.031	0.411 ± 0.029	0.498 ± 0.035	0.504 ± 0.035

(c) Averaged One Dependence Models

50	-0.228 ± 0.041	-0.134 ± 0.025	-0.277 ± 0.041	-0.013 ± 0.014
500	0.020 ± 0.010	0.050 ± 0.012	0.000 ± 0.014	0.003 ± 0.004
5000	0.057 ± 0.008	0.113 ± 0.010	0.089 ± 0.010	0.098 ± 0.012

models. Each model has 4–8 attributes (including the target attribute), with each attribute having 2–5 values. The probabilities in each attribute are determined randomly. We sample 40 models and perform a two-factor repeated measures ANOVA, in order to provide a statistical test independent of our Bayesian assumptions. The two factors are (1) the machine learner and (2) the amount of training data (50, 500 or 5000). It is advantageous to use a repeated measure ANOVA because this design controls for the individual differences between samples (where each model is considered a sample).

We use information reward on a single test set of 1000 instances for each model to measure the 'treatment' of each machine learner at different 'doses' (amounts of training data). We don't report accuracy nor Kononenko and Bratko's measure, for the reasons given in Sections 1 and 2.2. Where we report confidence intervals, these have been adjusted by the Bonferroni method for limiting the underestimation of variance [15].

Naive Bayes Models follow the Naive Bayes assumptions: attributes are pairwise independent, given the class. This is the simplest model type we use in this evaluation, so we expect that all learners will perform reasonably.

Table 1a shows the performance of the machine learners for each amount of training data. Naive Bayes, TAN and AODE perform similarly for each level — unsurprising, since they share the correct assumption that the target class is a parent of all other attributes. For small amounts of data, CaMML performs significantly worse than the others: it cannot reliably find the correct model. As more data become available, it achieves a score similar to the others.

Tree Augmented Naive Models are formed by creating a tree-like dependency structure amongst the (non-target) attributes, with all of them directly dependent upon the target. This is more complicated than the Naive Bayes model above. Each model we generate has a random tree structure amongst the non-target attributes.

Surprisingly, Table 1b shows that TAN is not the best learner with low amounts of training data: AODE stands superior. This is likely because AODE has a richer representation than Naive Bayes (i.e., with averaged predictions), yet doesn't need to search for the tree structure. Once there are enough data both TAN and CaMML seem to find the right structure and both outperform AODE. This illustrates the additional difficulty of model selection. Although TAN assumes the correct model type, it still has to find a particular tree structure, thus TAN's performance is dependent on its search capabilities. Naive Bayes, with its inaccurate assumptions, is clearly inferior to the other learners once an adequate amount of training data is given.

Averaged One-Dependence Models are each a series of n models; in the ith model, attribute i is the parent of each other (non-target) attribute. As in Naive Bayes, each attribute is also directly dependent on the target. Thus, each AODE model is a hybrid of one-dependence models, with each model having equal chance to be selected from when sampling the model for data.

This hybrid model seems to be very difficult for the machine learners to learn, with Table 1c showing the information reward ranging from only -0.3 to 0.1. Recall that a reward of zero corresponds to a machine learner which finds no associations, returning the observed frequency of the target class as its estimate. It takes more than 50 training instances to achieve an average score higher than zero! CaMML performs slightly better with sparse data, near the level of total ignorance. The explanation of the poor performance with little data perhaps lies in each learner's assumptions: Naive Bayes, TAN and AODE assume a model where all attributes depend on the target, regardless of whether this model decreases performance. CaMML is not beholden to any particular model, and thus is free to choose no association at all. This conservatism wins out, even against Naive Bayes with small datasets. After enough training data, AODE (the only learner that can model the data properly) obtains an advantage over the other learners.

We also evaluated the learners on a set of well known datasets, including many from the UCI data repository. For this we used Dietterich's $5 \times 2cv$ evaluation method [2], modified to incorporate stratified sampling. These are reported in [7]. Briefly, we found that AODE seemed to outperform the other learners, consistent with its performance above, and also reconfirmed that accuracy and IR_B often return conflicting results.

4 Conclusion

We have reviewed a variety of metrics for the evaluation of machine learners. Accuracy is too crude, optimizing only domain knowledge while ignoring calibration. We have developed a new metric which is maximized under the combination of domain knowledge and perfect calibration. This information reward evaluates learners on their estimate of the whole class distribution rather than on a single classification. In rewarding calibration, it provides a valuable alternative to cost-sensitive metrics when costs are unavailable.

References

1. Kohavi, R.: A study of cross-validation and bootstrap for accuracy estimation and model selection. In: IJCAI. (1995) 1137–1145
2. Dietterich, T.G.: Approximate statistical tests for comparing supervised classification learning algorithms. Neural Computation **7** (1998) 1895–1924
3. Provost, F., Fawcett, T.: Robust classification for imprecise environments. Machine Learning **42** (2001) 203–231
4. Good, I.J.: Rational decisions. Journal of the Royal Statistical Society. Series B **14** (1952) 107–114
5. Kononenko, I., Bratko, I.: Information-based evaluation criterion for classifier's performance. Machine Learning **6** (1991) 67–80
6. Hope, L.R., Korb, K.B.: Bayesian information reward. In Mckay, B., Slaney, J., eds.: Lecture Notes in Artificial Intelligence. Springer (2002) 272–283
7. Hope, L.R., Korb, K.B.: A Bayesian metric for evaluating machine learners. Technical report, Monash University (2004)
8. Korb, K.B., Nicholson, A.E.: Bayesian Artificial Intelligence. Chapman & Hall/CRC (2004)
9. Webb, G.I., Boughton, J., Wang, Z.: Averaged One-Dependence Estimators: Preliminary results. In: Australasian Data Mining Workshop, ANU (2002) 65–73
10. Friedman, N., Goldszmidt, M.: Building classifiers using Bayesian networks. In: AAAI-96. (1996) 1277–1284
11. Zheng, Z., Webb, G.I.: Lazy learning of Bayesian rules. Machine Learning **41** (2000) 53–84
12. John, G.H., Langley, P.: Estimating continuous distributions in Bayesian classifiers. In: UAI 11, Morgan Kaufmann, San Mateo (1995) 338–345
13. Keogh, E., Pazzani., M.: Learning augmented Bayesian classifiers. In: AI and Statistics. (1999) 225–230
14. Wallace, C., Boulton, D.: An information measure for classification. The Computer Journal **11** (1968) 185–194
15. Keppel, G.: Design and Analysis: A Researcher's Handbook. Prentice-Hall (1991)

A Comparison of Text-Categorization Methods Applied to N-Gram Frequency Statistics

Helmut Berger[1] and Dieter Merkl[2]

[1] Faculty of Information Technology,
University of Technology, Sydney, NSW, Australia
hberger@it.uts.edu.au
[2] School of Computing and Information Technology,
University of Western Sydney, NSW, Australia
d.merkl@uws.edu.au

Abstract. This paper gives an analysis of multi-class e-mail categorization performance, comparing a character n-gram document representation against a word-frequency based representation. Furthermore the impact of using available e-mail specific meta-information on classification performance is explored and the findings are presented.

1 Introduction

The task of automatically sorting documents of a document collection into categories from a predefined set, is referred to as *Text Categorization*. Text categorization is applicable in a variety of domains: document genre identification, authorship attribution, survey coding to name but a few. One particular application is categorizing e-mail messages into legitimate and spam messages, i.e. *spam filtering*. Androutsopoulos et al. compare in [1] a *Naïve Bayes* classifier against an *Instance-Based* classifier to categorize e-mail messages into spam and legitimate messages, and conclude that these learning-based classifiers clearly outperform simple anti-spam keyword approaches. However, sometimes it is desired to classify e-mail messages in more than two categories. Consider, for example an e-mail routing application, which automatically sorts incoming messages according to their content and routes them to receivers that are responsible for a particular topic. The study presented herein compares the performance of different text classification algorithms in such a multi-class setting.

By nature, e-mail messages are short documents containing misspellings, special characters and abbreviations. This entails an additional challenge for text classifiers to cope with "noisy" input data. To classify e-mail in the presence of noise, a method used for language identification is adapted in order to statistically describe e-mail messages. Specifically, character-based n-gram frequency profiles, as proposed in [2], are used as features which represent each particular e-mail message. The comparison of the performance of categorization algorithms using character-based n-gram frequencies as elements of feature vectors with respect to multiple classes is described. The assumption is, that applying text categorization on character-based n-gram frequencies will outperform word-based frequency representations of e-mails. In [3] a related approach aims at authorship attribution and topic detection. They evaluate the performance of a *Naïve Bayes* classifier combined with n-gram language models. The authors mention, that the character-based approach has better classification results than the word-based approach for topic detection in newsgroups. Their interpretation is that the character-based approach captures regularities that the word-based approach is missing in this particular application.

Besides the content contained in the body of an e-mail message, the e-mail header holds useful data that has impact on the classification task. This study explores the influence of header information on classification performance thoroughly. Two different representations of each e-mail message were generated: one that contains *all* data of an e-mail message and a second, which consists of textual data found in the e-mail body. The impact on classification results when header information is discarded is shown.

2 Text Categorization

The task of automatically sorting documents of a document collection into categories from a predefined set, is referred to as *Text Categorization*[4]. An important task in text categorization is to prepare text in such a way, that it becomes *suitable* for text classifier, i.e. transform them into an adequate document representation. Cavnar et al. mention in [2] a statistical model for describing documents, namely *character n-gram frequency profiles*. A character n-gram is defined as an n-character long slice of a longer string. As an example for $n = 2$, the character *bi*-grams of *"topic spotting"* are {*to, op, pi, ic, c_, _s, sp, po, ot, tt, ti, in, ng*}. Note that the "space" character is represented by "_". In order to obtain such frequency profiles, for each document in the collection n-grams with different length n are generated. Then, the n-gram occurrences in every document are counted on a per document basis. One objective of this study is to determine the influence of different document representations on the performance of different text-classification approaches. To this end, a character-based n-gram document representation with $n \in \{2, 3\}$ is compared against a document representation based on *word frequencies*. In the word-frequency representation occurrences of each word in a document are counted on a per document basis.

Generally, the initial number of features extracted from text corpora is very large. Many classifiers are unable to perform their task in a reasonable amount of time, if the number of features increases dramatically. Thus, appropriate feature selection strategies must be applied to the corpus. Another problem emerges if the amount of training data in proportion to the number of features is very low. In this particular case, classifiers produce a large number of hypothesis for the training data. This might end up in *overfitting* [5]. So, it is important to reduce the number of features while retaining those that contain information that is potentially useful. The idea of feature selection is to score each potential feature according to a feature selection metric and then take the n-top-scored features.

For a recent survey on the performance of different feature selection metrics we refer to [6]. For this study the *Chi-Squared* feature selection metric is used. The Chi-Squared metric evaluates the *worth* of an attribute by computing the value of the chi-squared statistic with respect to the class.

For the task of document classification, algorithms of three different machine learning areas were selected. In particular, a *Naïve Bayes* classifier [7], partial decision trees (PART) as a rule learning approach [8] and support vector machines trained with the sequential minimal optimization algorithm [9] as a representative of kernel-based learning were applied.

3 Experiments

The major objective of these experiments is comparing the performance of different text classification approaches for multi-class categorization when applied to a "noisy" domain. By nature, e-mail messages are short documents containing misspellings, special characters and abbreviations. For that reason, e-mail messages constitute perfect candidates to evaluate this objective. Not to mention the varying length of e-mail messages which entails an additional challenge for text classification algorithms. The assumption is, that applying text categorization on a character-based n-gram frequency profile will outperform the word-frequency approach. This presumption is backed by the fact that character-based n-gram models are regarded as *more stable* with respect to noisy data. Moreover, the impact on performance is assessed when header information contained in e-mail messages is taken into account. Hence, two different corpus representations are generated to evaluate this issue. Note that all experiments were performed with *10-fold cross validation* to reduce the likelihood of overfitting to the training set. Furthermore, we gratefully acknowledge the WEKA machine learning project for their open-source software [10], which was used to perform the experiments.

3.1 Data

The document collection consists of 1,811 e-mail messages. These messages have been collected during a period of four months commencing with October 2002 until January 2003. The e-mails have been received by a single e-mail user account at the *Institut für Softwaretechnik*, Vienna University of Technology, Austria. Beside the "noisiness" of the corpus, it contains messages of different languages as well. Multi-linguality introduces yet another challenge for text classification. At first, messages containing confidential information were removed from the corpus. Next, the corpus was manually classified according to 16 categories. Note that the categorization process was performed subsequent to the collection period. Due to the manual classification of the corpus, some of the messages might have been misclassified. Some of the introduced categories deal with closely related topics in order to assess the accuracy of classifiers on similar categories.

Next, two representations of each message were generated. The first representation consists of the data contained in the e-mail message, i.e. the complete header as well as the body. However, the e-mail header was not treated in a special way. All non-Latin characters, apart from the blank character, were discarded. Thus, all HTML-tags remain part of this representation. Henceforth, we refer to this representation as *complete* set. Furthermore, a second representation retaining only the data contained in the body of the e-mail message was generated. In addition, HTML-tags were discarded, too. Henceforth, we refer to this representation as *cleaned* set. Due to the fact, that some of the e-mail messages contained no textual data in the body besides HTML-tags and other special characters, the corpus of the *cleaned* set consists of less messages than the *complete* set. To provide the total figures, the *complete* set consists of 1,811 e-mails whereas the *cleaned* set is constituted by 1,692 e-mails. Subsequently, both representations were translated to lower case characters. Starting from these two message representations, the statistical models are built. In order to test the performance of text classifiers with respect to the number of features, we subsequently selected the top-scored n features with $n \in \{100, 200, 300, 400, 500, 1000, 2000\}$ determined by the Chi-Squared feature selection metric.

3.2 Results

In Figure 1 the classification accuracy of the text classifiers (y–axis), along the number of features (x–axis), is shown. In this case, the *cleaned* set is evaluated. Note that *NBm* refers to the multi-nominal Naïve Bayes classifier, *PART* refers to the partial decision tree classifier and *SMO* refers to the Support Vector Machine using the SMO training algorithm. Figure 1(a) shows the percentage of correctly classified instances using character n-grams and Figure 1(b) depicts the results for word frequencies. Each curve corresponds to one classifier. If we consider the character n-gram representation (cf. Figure 1(a)) *NBm* shows the lowest performance. It starts with 69.2% (100 features), increases strongly for 300 features (78.0%) and arrives at 82.7% for the maximum number of features. *PART* classifies 78.3% of the instances correctly when 100 features are used, which is higher than the 76.7% achieved with the *SMO* classifier. However, as the number of features increases to 300, the *SMO* classifier gets ahead of *PART* and arrives finally at 91.0% correctly classified instances (*PART*, 86.1%). Hence, as long as the number of features is smaller than 500, either PART or SMO yield high classification results. As the number of features increases, *SMO* outperforms *NBm* and *PART* dramatically. In case of word frequencies, a similar trend can be observed but the roles have changed, cf. Figure 1(b). All classifiers start with low performances. Remarkably, *SMO* (65.7%) classifies less instances correctly than *PART* (76.0%) and *NBm* (68.6%). All three classifiers boost their classification results enormously, as the number of features increases to 200. At last, the *SMO* classifier yields 91.0% and outperforms both *NBm* (85.8%) and *PART* (88.2%).

Figure 2 shows the classification accuracy when the *complete* set is used for the classification task. Again, the left chart (cf. Figure 2(a)) represents the percentage of correctly classified instances for character n-grams and Figure 2(b) depicts the results for the word frequencies. If *NBm* is applied to character n-grams, the classification task ends up in a random sorting of instances. The best result is achieved when 100 features are used (64.8%). As the number of features

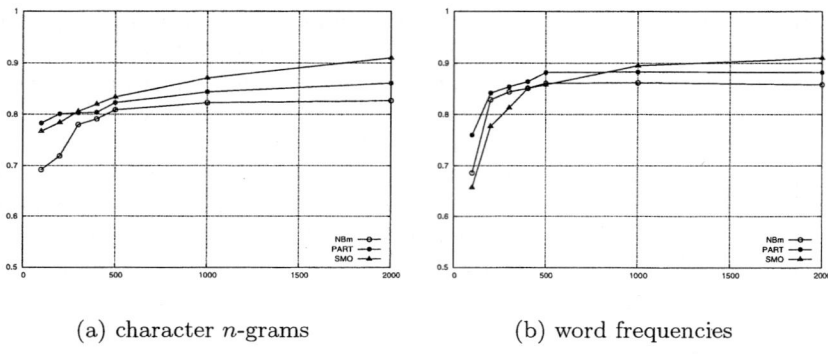

(a) character n-grams   (b) word frequencies

Fig. 1. Classification performance of individual classifiers applied to the *cleaned* set

grows, *NBm*'s performance drops to its low of 54.2% (400 features) arriving at 62.7% for 2000 features. Contrarily, *PART* classifies 84.6% of the instances correctly using 100 features. However, increasing the number of features improves the classification performance of *PART* only marginally (2000 attributes, 89.1%). *SMO* starts at 76.1%, increases significantly as 200 features are used (82.8%) and, after a continuous increase, classifies 92.9% of the instances correctly as the maximum number of features is reached.

In analogy to the results obtained with character n-grams, *NBm* shows poor performance when word frequencies are used, cf. Figure 2(b). Its top performance is 83.5% as the maximum number of features is reached. Interestingly, *PART* classifies 87.0% of instances correctly straight away – the highest of all values obtained with 100 features. However, *PART*'s performance increases only marginally for larger number of features and reaches, at last, 90.9%. *SMO* starts between *NBm* and *PART* with 80.1%. Once 400 features are used, *SMO* "jumps" into first place with 90.8% and arrives at the peak result of 93.6% correctly classified instances when 2000 features are used.

4 Conclusion

In this paper, the results of three text categorization algorithms are described in a multi-class categorization setting. The algorithms are applied to character n-gram frequency statistics and a word frequency based document representation. A corpus consisting of multi-lingual e-mail messages which were manually split into multiple classes was used. Furthermore, the impact of e-mail meta-information on classification performance was assessed.

The assumption, that a document representation based on character n-gram frequency statistics boosts categorization performance in a "noisy" domain such as e-mail filtering, could not be verified. The classifiers, especially *SMO* and *PART*, showed similar performance regardless of the chosen document representation. However, when applied to word frequencies marginally better results were

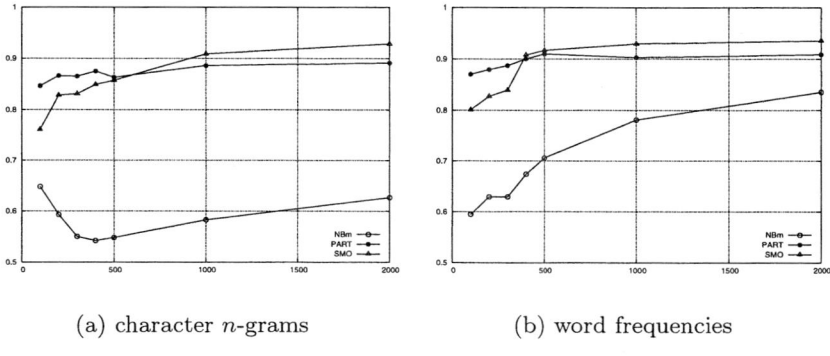

(a) character n-grams (b) word frequencies

Fig. 2. Classification performance of individual classifiers applied to the *complete* set

obtained for all categorization algorithms. Moreover, when a word-based document representation was used the percentage of correctly classified instances was higher in case of a small number of features. Using the word-frequency representation results in a minor improvement of classification accuracy. The results, especially those of *SMO*, showed that both document representations are feasible in multi-class e-mail categorization.

References

1. Androutsopoulos, I., Paliouras, G., Karkaletsis, V., Sakkis, G., Spyropoulos, C., Stamatopoulos, P.: Learning to filter spam e-mail: A comparison of a naive bayesian and a memory-based approach. In: Proc. Workshop on Machine Learning and Textual Information Access. (2000)
2. Cavnar, W.B., Trenkle, J.M.: N-gram-based text categorization. In: Proc. Int'l Symp. Document Analysis and Information Retrieval. (1994)
3. Peng, F., Schuurmans, D.: Combining naive Bayes and n-gram language models for text classification. In: Proc. European Conf. on Information Retrieval Research. (2003) 335–350
4. Sebastiani, F.: Machine learning in automated text categorization. ACM Computing Surveys **34** (2002) 1–47
5. Mitchell, T.: Machine Learning. McGraw-Hill (1997)
6. Forman, G.: An extensive empirical study of feature selection metrics for text classification. Journal of Machine Learning Research **3** (2003) 1289–1305
7. McCallum, A., Nigam, K.: A Comparison of Event Models for Naive Bayes Text Classification. In: Proc. of AAAI-98 Workshop on "Learning for Text Categorization". (1998)
8. Frank, E., Witten, I.H.: Generating accurate rule sets without global optimization. In: Proc. Int'l. Conf. on Machine Learning. (1998) 144–151
9. Platt, J.: Fast Training of Support Vector Machines using Sequential Minimal Optimization. In: Advances in Kernel Methods - Support Vector Learning. MIT Press (1999) 185–208
10. Witten, I.H., Frank, E.: Data Mining: Practical machine learning tools with Java implementations. Morgan Kaufmann, San Francisco (2000)

A Global Search Algorithm for Attributes Reduction

Songbo Tan

Software Department, Institute of Computing Technology, CAS, P. R. China
Graduate School, Chinese Academy of Sciences, P. R. China
tansongbo@software.ict.ac.cn

Abstract. Attributes reduction is a crucial problem in rough set application to data mining. In this paper, we introduce the Universal RED problem model, or *UniRED*, which transforms the discrete attributes reduction problems on Boolean space into continuous global optimization problems on real space. Based on this transformation, we develop a coordinate descent algorithm *RED2.1* for attributes reduction problems. In order to examine the efficiency of our algorithms, we conduct the comparison between our algorithm *RED2.1* and other reduction algorithms on some problems from UCI repository. The experimental results indicate the efficiency of our algorithm.

1 Introduction

The rough set approach developed by Pawlak in the early 1980's [1] provides a framework for knowledge discovery. Reduct is the most important concept in rough set-based data mining. Unfortunately, It has been shown that finding minimal reduct or all reducts are both NP-hard problems.

There has been a great interest in designing efficient algorithms to solve these problems. Traditional methods treat the reduction problem as a discrete optimization problem. Greedy algorithm is a widely used typical search algorithm, which is also adopted in the rough set literature [2].

In this paper, we show how to translate the reduction problem into a continuous, unconstrained, global optimization problem. We then show how to use a simple global optimization method, i.e., coordinate method, to solve the transformed problem. Experimental results indicate that our algorithm achieves significant performance for certain classes of reduction problems.

2 Preliminaries

Information Systems is a pair $A=(U, A)$, where U is a non-empty, finite set of objects called the *universe* and A is a non-empty finite set of *attributes*. An information system $A=(U, A \cup \{d\})$, where $d \notin A$, is usually called a ***decision table***. The elements of A we call the *conditional attributes* and d is called *decision attribute*.

The ***Discernibility Matrix*** of an information system is a symmetric $|U| \cdot |U|$ matrix with entries c_{ij} defined as $\{ a \in A / a(x_i) \neq a(x_j) \}$ if $d(x_i) \neq d(x_j)$, ϕ otherwise.

A ***Discernibility Function*** can be constructed from discernibility matrix by or-ing($\vee$) all attributes in c_{ij} and then and-ing($\wedge$) all of them together. After simplifying the discernibility function using absorption law, the set of all prime implicants determine the set of all reducts of the information system. However, simplifying discernibility function for reduct is a NP-hard problem.

If we look each attribute as one variable, look each variable of each non-empty c_{ij} as one literal, and look each non-empty c_{ij} as one clause, then obviously we can take the discernibility function as a kind of conjunctive normal form (CNF) formulas.

We take the following decision table for example. The letters a_1, a_2, a_3, a_4 denote conditional attributions and the letter d denotes decision attribute.

Table 1. The simple decision table

U	a_1	a_2	a_3	a_4	d
1	TRUE	TRUE	FALSE	FALSE	0
2	TRUE	FALSE	TRUE	FALSE	0
3	FALSE	FALSE	TRUE	TRUE	1
4	FALSE	TRUE	TRUE	FALSE	1

Then we can obtain our discernibility function f as follows:

$$f = (a_1 \vee a_2 \vee a_3 \vee a_4) \wedge (a_1 \vee a_3) \wedge (a_1 \vee a_4) \wedge (a_1 \vee a_2) . \tag{1}$$

Any reduct of A is equal to an assignment of truth values to variables (a_1, a_2, a_3, a_4) that makes the above **discernibility function satisfiable (CNF formula)**. Similarly, **a** minimal reduct of A is equal to an assignment with minimum truth-values to variables (a_1, a_2, a_3, a_4) that make the above **discernibility function (CNF formula) satisfiable**.

3   *UniRed*: The Universal Reduction Problem Model

In this section, we need to set up a special model that transforms a discrete reduction problem in Boolean space $\{0,1\}^m$ into a continuous reduction problem on real space E^m. We employ the following operations [3] to extend the well-known Boolean DeMorgan Laws into the universal DeMorgan Laws on real space E^m.

Operator Generalization: we first replace Boolean $\vee$ and $\wedge$ operators with real operators + and ×, respectively.

Variable Generalization: we extend Boolean variables x on Boolean space $\{0,1\}^m$ to real variables y on real space E^m. The correspondence between x and y is defined as follows:

$$x_i = \begin{cases} True & \text{if } 1-y_i=0 \\ False & \text{if } 1+y_i=0 \\ undefined & \text{otherwise} \end{cases} \tag{2}$$

Literal Transformation: Based on real variables, a literal function is defined for each literal as follows:

$$q_{ij}(y_j) = \begin{cases} (1-y_j)^2 & \text{if } x_i \text{ is a literal in } c_i \\ 1 & \text{if } x_j \text{ is not a literal in } c_i \end{cases} \quad (3)$$

Clause Transformation: A clause function $c_i(y)$ from E^m to E^1 is defined as a product with at most m literal functions:

$$c_i(y) = \prod_{j=1}^{m} q_{ij}(y_j) \quad (4)$$

The UniRed Model: Using literal and clause functions, a *CNF* formula $F(x)$ on Boolean space is transformed into a continuous *DNF* object function $f(y)$ on real space E^m.

$$f(y) = \sum_{i=1}^{n} c_i(y) = \sum_{i=1}^{n} \prod_{j=1}^{m} q_{ij}(y_j) \quad (5)$$

Whereas, this object function $f(y)$ can only guarantee to find a reduct of conditional attributes A. In fact our goal is to find a minimal reduct of conditional attributes A. Therefore improve above object function formula as follows:

$$f(y) = \sum_{i=1}^{n} c_i(y) = \sum_{i=1}^{n} \prod_{j=1}^{m} q_{ij}(y_j) + \sum_{j=1}^{m} (1+y_j)^2 \quad (6)$$

We take the **discernibility function of** section II as an example. Following above formulation (9), we can obtain the continuous object function $f(y)$ on real space E^m.

$$f(y) = (1-q_1)^2(1-a_2)^2(1-a_3)^2(1-a_4)^2 + (1-q_1)^2(1-a_3)^2 + (1-q_1)^2(1-a_4)^2 + (1-q_1)^2(1-a_3)^2 + (1+q_1)^2 + (1+a_2)^2 + (1+a_3)^2 + (1+q_4)^2 \quad (7)$$

But above improved object function formula still can not guarantee to find a minimal reduct of conditional attributes A. For example, given a new **discernibility function as follows**:

$$f(y) = (1-q_1)^2(1-a_2)^2(1-a_3)^2 + (1-a_2)^2(1-a_4) + (1-q_1)^2(1-a_3)^2 + (1-a_4)^2 + (1+q_1)^2 + (1+a_2)^2 + (1+a_3)^2 + (1+q_4)^2 \quad (8)$$

Obviously, we can know the minimal reduct of conditional attributes A is $\{a_2, a_4\}$ or $\{a_1, a_4\}$. That is to say the solution of the object function is (-1,1,-1,1) or (1,-1,-1,1). And the value of object function is 8 for each solution. But the solution point (-1,1,-1,-1) can also obtain the same object function value 8. Obviously, the function has three minima. Nevertheless, to our knowledge, the solution point (-1,1,-1,-1) is not the minimal reduct of conditional attributes A, for it cannot satisfy the discernibility function. Consequently, before the acceptance of a minimum of the object function, we should test the current solution point whether it satisfies the discernibility function.

4 Optimization Method

To our knowledge, the classic and popular global optimizations are gradient descent method and Newton method. But it is very time-consuming to execute, especially for large-scale problems. The coordinate method is an old, simple and efficient method for optimization. In each iteration, only one variable y_i is chosen as the descent dimension. Since variables other than y_i, i.e., y_j $(j=1,2,...,i-1,i+1,...,m)$, remain as constants. Therefore the object function was transformed into a single variable function with respect to the variable y_i:

$$f(y) = a_i(1-y_i)^2 + b_i(1+y_i)^2 + c_i \cdot \qquad (9)$$

To our knowledge, the minimum of the single variable function is the point making the derivative of $f(y)$ equal zero.

$$f'(y) = -2a_i(1-y_i) + 2b_i(1+y_i) \cdot \qquad (10)$$

We set $f(y)=0$, that is,

$$y'_i = \frac{(2a_i - 2b_i)}{(2a_i + 2b_i)} = \frac{(a_i - b_i)}{(a_i + b_i)} \qquad (11)$$

y'_i is the minimum point. As a result, in each iteration, what we need to do is compute the value a_i and b_i. Since only one term $(1+y_i)^2$ in object function with respect to y_i, consequently b_i equals 1. On the contrary, there one term or many terms $(1+y_i)^2$ in object function with respect to y_i, hereby a_i range from 0 to ∞. In practice, the value of a_i may overflow, thereby we cannot use above formula any more. When $a_i \to \infty$, in the view of mathematics, the limit of y'_i is 1. Accordingly, if a_i overflows, then we can set y'_i equal 1.

5 Proposed Algorithms

A Necessary Functions

Before giving the outline of proposed algorithm, we first introduce some necessary functions.

$y'=RoudOff(y)$: if $y \geq 0$ we return 1, else return −1. Therefore, we obtain a binary variable y' in $\{0,1\}^m$. For example, if y is (0.1, -0.4,0,0.5), we obtain $y'=(1, -1,1,1)$.

$y_i'=RoudOff\_OneVar(y_i)$: Only perform roundoff operation for one variable y_i. if $y_i \geq 0$ we return 1, else return −1.

$satflag=IsSatDisFun\_OneVar(y_i')$: Only execute satisfaction test for the clauses with respect to variable y_i'. If the binary variable y' in $\{0,1\}^m$ can satisfy the clauses with respect to the variable y_i', we return TRUE, else return FALSE.

$f_2=RealObjFun(y')$: return the sum of 1 in the binary variable y' in $\{0,1\}^m$. For example, if y' is (1, -1,1,1) then we return 3; if y' is (1, -1,1, -1), return 2.

B The *RED2.1* Algorithm

Initialization: to start, procedure *LoadData()* loads the decision table. Function gets a variable that satisfies the discernibility function. Then we save the Boolean variable after the procedure *RoundOff(y)*. By function *RealObjFun(y')* we compute the number of selected attributes. On the same time we set the max search times to *10*m*.

Global Search: in this stage, we employ the coordinate descent method to minimize the single variable function with respect to each variable y_i. Then we round off the variables, if it can reduce the number of selected attributes and satisfy the discernibility function, we save the round-off variables. And then we select next variable y_{i+1} for minimization.

Termination: in practice, it is rather hard to decide whether it is sufficient close to a global minimum. But according to our experience, if we set the max search times to *10*m*. That is to say, if we execute the *for-loop* for *10*m* times, then it is sufficient close to a global minimum in most cases.

Running Time: the running time of the *RED2.1* can be estimated as follows. Given a discernibility function with n clauses, m variables, on average l literals in each clause and on average p clauses with respect to each variable. In one iteration of the *for-loop*, minimize the single variable function with respect to one variable is $O(pl)$. The running time of *RoudOff_OneVar()* is $O(1)$ and *RealObjFun(y')* can be done in $O(m)$. *IsSatDisFun_OneVar(y_i)* takes $O(pl)$. The assignment of y' to *best_y* can be done in $O(m)$. Therefore the total running time of for is $O(m(m+pl))$.

```
Procedures RED2.1 (){
    //load the decision table data
    LoadData();
    //get a variable satisfying discernibility function
    y=Initilization();
    best_y= RoundOff(y);
    MaxSearchNum=10*m;
    best_f=RealObjFun(y');

    for(i=0; i< MaxSearchNum; i++){
        //minimizer
        i=i%m
        minimize f(y) with respect to y_i
        y_i = RoundOff_OnVar(y_i);
        if(IsSatDisFun_OneVar(y_i)){
            f= RealObjFun(y');
            if(best_f > f){
                best_f=f;
                best_y=y';
            }
        }
        else
            //ensure y satisfies the discernibility function
            y_i=- y_i;
    }
}
```

Fig. 1. The Algorithm of *RED2.1*

6 Experiment Results

In this section, we give experimental results of attributes reduction algorithm *RED2.1* on some instances from UCI repository [4]. In order to investigate the effectiveness of our algorithm, we execute the *dynamical reduct* and *genetic reduct* in ROSETTA system [5].

Table 3 indicates that *dynamical reduct* is much slower than *RED2.1*. For five datasets the time required by *dynamical reduct* is about 10 times larger than that of *RED2.1*. Among the eight datasets, for one dataset *dynamical reduct* finds smaller reduct than *RED2.1* and for three datasets dynamic reduct finds the same reduct as *RED2.1*. Therefore, we conclude that *dynamical reduct* obtains similar reducts with *RED2.1*, but costs much more time than *RED2.1*.

From table 3, we can see that, By and large, *RED2.1* is slower than *genetic reduct*, but performs better than *genetic reduct*. Therefore, we conclude that our algorithm *RED2.1* is an efficient algorithm for attributes reduction in data mining.

Table 2. Comparison between *RED2.1* and *Dynamical Reduct* on eight UCI datasets

Dataset	Instance	Original Attribute	RED2.1		Dynamic Reduct	
			Reduct	Time(Sec.)	Reduct	Time(Sec.)
Zoo	67	16	4	1.582	4	3
BreastCancerData	191	9	8	1.632	8	42
Parity5+5	100	10	5	0.46	5	6
Echocardiogram	87	7	4	0.34	6	4
Wine	118	13	4	3.685	5	14
Glass	142	9	6	2.163	9	13
Heart	180	13	9	2.744	8	39
Hungrarian	196	13	4	3.234	5	41

Table 3. Comparison between *RED2.1* and *Genetic Reduct* on eight UCI datasets

Dataset	Instance	Original Attribute	RED2.1		Genetic Reduct	
			Reduct	Time(Sec.)	Reduct	Time(Sec.)
SoybeanSmall	31	35	2	0.791	2	1.0
LungCancerData	32	56	8	1.32	4	2.0
Wine	118	13	4	3.725	5	1.0
Audiology	150	69	14	5.147	26	1.0
Pima	512	8	7	16.924	8	<1.0
hungrarian	196	13	4	3.234	8	<1.0
Glass	142	9	6	2.243	9	<1.0

7 Conclusion

In this paper, based on the Universal RED problem model and coordinate method, we develop the algorithm *RED2.1* for attributes reduction problems. We present the comparison between our algorithm *RED2.1* and other reduction algorithms on some problems from UCI repository [8]. The experimental results indicate the efficiency of our algorithms.

References

1. Pawlak, Z.: Rough sets. International Journal of Computer and Information Science. (1982)
2. Micha Gawrys, Jacek Sienkiewicz: RSL-The Rough Set Library version 2.0. Warsaw University of Technology ICS Research Report, (1994)

3. Gu, J.: Global Optimization for Satisfiability (SAT) Problem. IEEE Trans. On Knowledge and Data Engineering, (1994), Vol 6, No. 3, pp. 361-381
4. Merz, C.J., Murphy, P.: UCI repository of machine learning database. http://www.ics.uci.edu/~mlearn/MLRepository.html.
5. The ROSETTA homepage. [http://www.idi.ntnu.no/~aleks/rosetta/].

A Symbolic Hybrid Approach to Face the New User Problem in Recommender Systems

Byron Bezerra and Francisco de A. T. de Carvalho

Centro de Informatica - CIn / UFPE,
Av. Prof. Luiz Freire, s/n - Cidade Universitaria,
CEP 50740-540 Recife - PE, Brazil
{bldb, fatc}@cin.ufpe.br

Abstract. Recommender Systems seek to furnish personalized suggestions automatically based on user preferences. These preferences are usually expressed as a set of items either directly or indirectly given by the user (e.g., the set of products the user bought in a virtual store). In order to suggest new items, Recommender Systems generally use one of the following approaches: *Content Based Filtering*, *Collaborative Filtering* or *hybrid filtering methods*. In this paper we propose a strategy to improve the quality of recommendation in the first user contact with the system. Our approach includes a suitable plan to acquiring a user profile and a hybrid filtering method based on *Modal Symbolic Data*. Our proposed technique outperforms the *Modal Symbolic Content Based Filter* and the standard *kNN Collaborative Filter based on Pearson Correlation*.

1 Introduction

Recommender Systems (RS) allow E-commerce websites to suggest products to their costumers by providing relevant information to assist them in shopping tasks. This system has also increased its importance in entertainment domains [7]. In both cases, two recommendation tasks have been mainly employed by information systems: *Annotation in Context* (providing a score for an item) and *Find Good Items* (building a ranked list of items) [5]. The latter has been widely used in virtual stores.

Whatever the *RS* task is, it must collect user preferences to provide good suggestions. The more information collected, the better the provided suggestions are. The user, however, often has little time for supplying information about him/herself. It is necessary to learn about users with as little data as possible. This problem is all the more challenging during the first system usage, when there is no user information. In such cases, a suitable strategy for acquiring user preferences is quite valuable.

After acquiring user preferences, *RS* may adopt one of the following filtering approaches to build suggestions: *Content Based* (*CB*) *Filtering* (based on the correlation between the user profile and item content), *Collaborative Filtering* (based on the user profile correlation) or hybrid filtering techniques [1,3,4,5,7].

In this paper, we describe a suitable strategy for achieving better recommendation lists in first system usage based on a new hybrid information filtering method (see section 2). Basically, the idea is to ask the user to evaluate at least one item of each possible evaluation grade. The descriptions of the evaluated items are used to build a modal symbolic profile of the user. This profile is then compared with other user profiles in order to perform recommendations in a collaborative fashion. This novel strategy was experimentally tested and compared in the movie domain (see section 3), where the user can evaluate an item with a grade between 1 (worst) to 5 (best).

2 Collaborative Filtering Based on Modal Symbolic User Profiles

As described in the previous section, our strategy in the user profile acquisition phase is to request the user to evaluate at least one item of each possible evaluation grade. Regardless of the acquisition methodology, the following steps are executed to generate recommendation lists in the *CF* algorithm based on *MS* user profiles:

1. *Construction of the modal symbolic descriptions of the user profile.* This step can be done incrementally without degrading the memory usage.
2. *Weight all users based on their similarity with the active user.* Similarity between users is measured by a function which compares the *MS* descriptions of each user.
3. *Select the k closest users as neighbors of active user.* The closeness is defined by similarity between some candidate neighbor and the active user.
4. *Generation of a ranked list of items after computing predictions from a weighted combination of the selected neighbors' ratings.*

Although, the steps 2–4 are standard in *CF* algorithms, the 2nd one is done in a *CB* manner through the *MS* user profiles built in 1st step. Before detailing all phases of our algorithm we need to introduce modal symbolic data [2] (see *www.jsda.unina2.it*). Let D_j be a finite set of categories. A modal variable y_j with domain D_j defined in the set $E=\{a, b,...\}$ of objects is a multi-state variable where, for each object $a \in E$, not only is a subset of its domain D_j given, but also for each category m of this subset, a weight $w(m)$ is given that indicates how relevant m is for a. Formally, $y_j(a) = (S_j(a), q_j(a))$ where $q_j(a)$ is a weight distribution defined in $S_j(a) \subseteq D_j$ such that a weight $w(m)$ corresponds to each category $m \in S_j(a)$. $S_j(a)$ is the support of the measure $q_j(a)$ in the domain D_j. Therefore, a symbolic description of an item is a vector where there is a weight distribution in each component given by an *MS* variable.

2.1 Building the Modal Symbolic User Profile

According to [1], the construction of the *MS* descriptions of the user profile involves two steps: (a) *pre-processing* and (b) *generalization*. The general idea is (a) to build an *MS* description for each item evaluated by the user and (b) then aggregate these descriptions in some *MS* descriptions where each one represents a user interest.

The *pre-processing* step is necessary for both constructing the set of MS descriptions used to represent the user profile and comparing the user profile with a new item (in CB filtering) or with another user profile (important to step 2 of our recommendation algorithm). Let $x_i = (X_i^1,..., X_i^p, C(i))$ be the description of an item i (i=1,...,n), where $X_i^j \subseteq D_j$ (j=1,...,p) is a subset of categories of the domain D_j of the variable y_j and $C(i) \in D = \{1,...,5\}$ indicates the user evaluation (grade) for this item. For each category $m \in X_i^j$, we can associate the following weight:

$$w(m) = \frac{1}{|X_i^j|} \tag{1}$$

where $|X_i^j|$ is the number of elements belonging to X_j (its cardinality). Then, the MS description of item i is $\tilde{x}_i = (\tilde{X}_i^1,..., \tilde{X}_i^p, C(i))$, where $\tilde{X}_i^j = \tilde{X}_j(i) = (S_j(i), q_j(i))$ and $\tilde{X}_j$ is a MS variable. $S_j(i) = X_i^j$ is the support of the weighted distribution $q_j(i)$.

The *generalization* step aims to construct a suitable symbolic description of the user profile. In our approach, each user profile is formed by a set of sub-profiles. Each sub-profile is modeled by an MS description that summarizes the entire body of information taken from the set of items the user has evaluated with the same grade.

Formally, let u_g be the sub-profile of user u which is formed by the set of items that have been evaluated with grade g. Let $y_{u_g} = (Y_{u_g}^1,...,Y_{u_g}^p)$ be the MS description of the sub-profile u_g, where $Y_{u_g}^j = (S_j(u_g), q_j(u_g))$, with $S_j(u_g)$ being the support of the weighted distribution $q_j(u_g)$, $j = 1,..., p$.

If $\tilde{x}_i = (\tilde{X}_i^1,..., \tilde{X}_i^p, C(i))$, where $\tilde{X}_i^j = (S_j(i), q_j(i))$ ($j=1,...,p$), is the MS description of the item i belonging to u_g, the support $S_j(u_g)$ of $q_j(u_g)$ is defined as

$$S_j(u_g) = \bigcup_{i \in u_g} S_j(i) \tag{2}$$

Let $m \in S_j(u_g)$ be a category belonging to D_j and $|u_g|$ be the number of elements belonging to the set u_g. Then, the weight $W(m) \in q_j(u_g)$ of the category m is:

$$W(m) = \frac{1}{|u_g|} \sum_{i \in u_g} \delta(i,m), \quad \text{where} \quad \delta(i,m) = \begin{cases} w(m) \in q_j(i), & \text{if } m \in S_j(i) \\ 0, & \text{otherwise} \end{cases} \tag{3}$$

2.2 Comparing Modal Symbolic Profiles

The step compares two MS user profiles through a suitable function that measures the similarity between each MS description of user profiles. This function is then used to define the neighborhood of an active user.

Let $y_{u_g} = (Y_{u_g}^1,...,Y_{u_g}^p)$ be the MS description of the sub-profile u_g of an active user. Also, let $y_{v_g} = (Y_{v_g}^1,...,Y_{v_g}^p)$ be the MS description of the sub-profile v_g of a candidate neighbor for the active user. The comparison between the active user u and the candidate neighbor v is achieved through the following similarity function:

$$\psi(u,v) = \frac{\sum_{g \in \{1,2,3,4,5\}} h_g(y_{u_g}, y_{v_g}) * (1 - \phi(y_{u_g}, y_{v_g}))}{5} \tag{4}$$

where $h_1(y_{u_1}, y_{v_1}) = 3$, $h_2(y_{u_2}, y_{v_2}) = 2$, $h_3(y_{u_3}, y_{v_3}) = 1$, $h_4(y_{u_4}, y_{v_4}) = 4$, $h_5(y_{u_5}, y_{v_5}) = 5$ if $y_{u_5} \neq \emptyset$ and $y_{v_5} \neq \emptyset$, otherwise $h_g(y_{u_g}, y_{v_g}) = 0$. Although we have fixed the values of g due to our case study, this model may be easily adapted for other domains.

There are two hypotheses considered by function h_g. First, we agree that positive items are more useful in defining the neighbors of a user, as they may provide better suggestions than users who have similarities with the active user concerning negative preferences. Additionally, we know that items with grade 5 are preferred over items with grade 4 and, also, items with grade 1 are more disliked than items with grade 2 or 3. We take this second hypothesis into account when measuring the similarities between users through different weights for each grade.

The function $\phi(y_{u_g}, y_{v_g})$ has two components: a context free component, which compares the sets $S_j(u_g)$ and $S_j(v_g)$; and a context depend component, which compares the weight distributions $q_j(u_g)$ and $q_j(v_g)$. This function is defined as:

$$\phi(y_{u_g}, y_{v_g}) = \frac{1}{p}\sum_{j=1}^{p}\left[\frac{\phi_{cf}(S_j(u_g), S_j(v_g)) + \phi_{cd}(q_j(u_g), q_j(v_g))}{2}\right] \quad (5)$$

where ϕ_{cf} measures the difference in position in cases where sets $S_j(u_g)$ and $S_j(v_g)$ are ordered; and ϕ_{cd} measures the difference in content between y_{u_g} and y_{v_g}.

Table 1 expresses the agreement (α and β) and disagreement (γ and δ) between the weight distributions $q_j(u_g)$ and $q_j(v_g)$.

Table 1. Comparison between the weight distributions $q_j(u_g)$ and $q_j(v_g)$

		User u_g	
		+ (Agreement)	− (Disagreement)
User v_g	+	$\alpha = \sum_{m \in S_j(u_g) \cap S_j(v_g)} w(m) \bullet \beta = \sum_{m \in S_j(u_g) \cap S_j(v_g)} W(m)$	$\gamma = \sum_{m \in \overline{S_j(u_g)} \cap S_j(v_g)} w(m)$
	−	$\delta = \sum_{m \in S_j(u_g) \cap \overline{S_j(v_g)}} w(m)$	

The context dependent component ϕ_{cd} is defined as:

$$\phi_{cd}(q_j(u_g), q_j(v_g)) = \frac{1}{2}\left(\frac{\gamma + \delta}{\alpha + \gamma + \delta} + \frac{\gamma + \delta}{\beta + \gamma + \delta}\right) \quad (6)$$

If the domain D_j of the categorical variable y_j is ordered, let $m_L = min(S_j(u_g))$, $m_U = max(S_j(u_g))$, $c_L = min(S_j(v_g))$ and $c_U = max(S_j(v_g))$. The join [6] $S_j(u_g) \oplus S_j(v_g)$ is defined as:

$$S_j(u_g) \oplus S_j(v_g) = \begin{cases} S_j(u_g) \cup S_j(v_g), & \text{if the domain } D_j \text{ is non ordered} \\ \{min(m_L, c_L), max(m_U, c_U)\}, & \text{otherwise} \end{cases} \quad (7)$$

The context dependent component ϕ_{cf} is defined as:

$$\phi_{cf}(S_j(u_g), S_j(v_g)) = \begin{cases} 0, & \text{if } S_j(u_g) \cap S_j(v_g) \neq \emptyset \\ \frac{|S_j(u_g) \oplus S_j(v_g)| - |S_j(u_g)| - |S_j(v_g)|}{|S_j(u_g) \oplus S_j(v_g)|}, & \text{otherwise} \end{cases} \quad (8)$$

2.3 Generating a Ranked List of Items

Now that we are able to compute the similarity between the active user u with each user in the database, we can do the 3rd step in a straightforward manner. Based on the user neighborhood defined in the 3rd step, we can compute predictions for each unknown item in the repository, according to the following function:

$$\rho(u,i) = \bar{r}_u + \frac{\sum_{v=1}^{k}(r_{v,i} - \bar{r}_v) * \psi(u,v)}{\sum_{v=1}^{k}\psi(u,v)} \quad (9)$$

where u is the active user, i is an unknown item and k is the neighborhood size. We can present the ranked list of items according to the values produced by equation 9.

3 Experimental Evaluation

We use the Movielens (*movielens.umn.edu*) dataset joined with a content database crawled from IMDB (www.imdb.com) to perform experimental tests. This prepared dataset contains 91,190 explicit ratings between 1 to 5 from 943 different users for 1,466 movies. In this dataset, we selected all users that had evaluated at least 100 items of 1,466 available movies. These users were used in a test set to perform four different experiments concerning the type of training sets $T=\{$extratified (E), non-extratified (NE)$\}$ and the number $m=\{5,10\}$ of items provided in the training set for each user. The value of 30 was chosen for k following a recommendation of [4].

We ran an adapted version of the standard 10 fold cross-validation methodology. This adaptation consisted of arranging the training set and test set, respectively, in the proportion of 1 to 9 instead of 9 to 1 as done in the standard schema. This is compatible with the fact that the user does not furnish a sufficient amount of information in his/her first contact with the system.

The subject of our experimental analysis focused on the *Find Good Items* task, motivated by the hypothesis that this task is more useful than other available RS tasks in an E-commerce environment [5,7]. According to [5], the *half-life utility* [3] is the most appropriate metric for this type of task. Thus, it was adopted in our analysis. The following algorithms were executed in our tests:

1. (MSA) – Content-Based Information Filtering based on *MS* Data;
2. (CFA) – *kNN-CF* based on the Pearson Correlation;
3. (CMSA) - Collaborative Filtering based on Modal Symbolic User Profiles.

Table 2 displays the average ($\bar{x}$) and standard deviations (s) of *half-life utility* metric for all algorithms grouped by $T=\{E,NE\}$ and $m=\{5,10\}$.

As seen in Table 2, the proposed methodology (CMSA$_{T=E}$) achieves the best accuracy recommendation lists. Moreover, we show with a confidence level of 0.1% that by giving just one item of each class (grade), the user gets better recommendation lists than those produced by CFA or MSA algorithms, even if they use the same acquiring strategy as in our methodology. This result is very interesting, as having good recommendations with just 5 items can help systems maintain loyal customers and get new ones. Another interesting result is that the observed standard deviation of the CFA and CMSA diminishes when the size of user profile is increased to 10. The reason for this behavior is that as more items are added to the user profile, precision increases in the estimation of user neighborhood. Consequently, better recommendations can be provided by the system to users whose the profile was obscure when there was just 5 items. The most remarkable result is that CSMA reaches low standard deviations, thus implying more stable systems.

Table 2. Results of experiments grouped by T (type of training sets) and m (number of items in user profile) according to *half-life utility* metric

T	m	MSA		CFA		CMSA	
		$\bar{x}$	s	$\bar{x}$	s	$\bar{x}$	s
E	5	34,346	0,826	40,206	4,325	**63,924**	2,224
	10	31,786	1,161	58,088	1,991	63,589	2,001
NE	5	37,335	0,444	58,738	0,593	**61,482**	0,194
	10	32,467	0,657	59,731	0,333	60,000	0,157

4 Conclusions

In this paper we presented a suitable strategy for minimizing the problem of learning a user profile during first system usage. We demonstrate how our new method improves the quality of recommendation lists when there is little information on the user. As a possible future work we propose the comparison of our strategy with some *active learning* approaches. Another exciting work would be the combination of our strategy for acquiring preferences with other hybrid information filtering algorithms.

Acknowledgments. The authors would like to thank CNPq (Brazilian Agency) for its financial support.

References

1. Bezerra, B.L.D. and De Carvalho, F.A.T.: A symbolic approach for content-based information filtering. Information Processing Letters, Vol. 92 (1), 16 October 2004, 45-52.
2. Bock, H.H. and Diday, E.: Analysis of Symbolic Data. Springer, Heidelberg (2000).
3. Breese, J., Heckerman, D., and Kadie, C.: Empirical analysis of predictive algorithms for collaborative filtering. In Proceedings of the 14th Conference on Uncertainty in Artificial Intelligence (1998) 43-52.
4. Herlocker, J., Konstan, J.A., Borchers, A., and Riedl, J.: An algorithmic framework for performing collaborative filtering. Proceedings of SIGIR (1999) 230-237.
5. Herlocker, J.L., Konstan, J.A., Terveen, L.G., and Riedl, J.: Evaluating Collaborative Filtering Recommender Systems. ACM Transactions on Information Systems, Vol. 22, Issue 1 (2004) 5-53.
6. Ichino, M., Yaguchi, H.: Generalized Minkowsky Metrics for Mixed Feature Type Data Analysis. IEEE Transactions on System, Man and Cybernetics, Vol. 24 (1994) 698–708.
7. Schafer, J.B., Konstan, J.A., and Riedl, J.: E-Commerce Recommendation Applications. Data Mining and Knowledge Discovery, Vol. 5. (2001) 115-153.

A Toolbox for Learning from Relational Data with Propositional and Multi-instance Learners

Peter Reutemann[1,2], Bernhard Pfahringer[2], and Eibe Frank[2]

[1] Department of Computer Science, University of Freiburg, Freiburg, Germany
[2] Department of Computer Science, University of Waikato, Hamilton, New Zealand

Abstract. Most databases employ the relational model for data storage. To use this data in a propositional learner, a propositionalization step has to take place. Similarly, the data has to be transformed to be amenable to a multi-instance learner. The Proper Toolbox contains an extended version of RELAGGS, the Multi-Instance Learning Kit MILK, and can also combine the multi-instance data with aggregated data from RELAGGS. RELAGGS was extended to handle arbitrarily nested relations and to work with both primary keys and indices. For MILK the relational model is flattened into a single table and this data is fed into a multi-instance learner. REMILK finally combines the aggregated data produced by RELAGGS and the multi-instance data, flattened for MILK, into a single table that is once again the input for a multi-instance learner. Several well-known datasets are used for experiments which highlight the strengths and weaknesses of the different approaches.

1 Introduction

This paper describes the Proper Toolbox [4], a general framework for database-oriented propositionalization algorithms that can also create multi-instance data from relational data.[1] The paper is organized as follows: first we discuss the RELAGGS propositionalization system, which is a major component of Proper, and then the other components of Proper. After that we report on results obtained from a suite of experiments that apply Proper to some relational benchmark datasets. The final section summarizes the paper.

2 The Proper Toolbox

In this section we discuss the various components of Proper, starting with its most important building block, RELAGGS.

2.1 RELAGGS: The Propositionalization Engine

RELAGGS is a database-oriented approach based on aggregations that are performed on the tables adjacent to the table that contains the target attribute. For

---

[1] Proper is freely available from http://www.cs.waikato.ac.nz/ml/proper/.

each row in the target table the following SQL group functions are executed for all numeric columns in the adjacent tables: average, minimum, maximum, sum. Additionally standard deviation, quartile, and range are computed. For nominal columns the number of occurrences of each nominal value is counted and represented as a new attribute. RELAGGS also computes aggregations based on pairs of attributes with one nominal attribute. This nominal attribute serves as an additional `GROUP BY` condition for the aggregation process [2]. RELAGGS uses the names of primary keys to determine the relationships between the various tables in the database. Proper uses the version of RELAGGS from [3].

We modified RELAGGS to relax some of the constraints it imposes on its input. First, RELAGGS expects an integer as the primary key of a table. In some domains the primary key of the table is an alpha-numeric string. In such cases Proper generates an additional table containing the original identifiers and newly generated integer keys, which replace the original alpha-numeric keys in all other tables. Second, determining the relationship between two tables solely using primary keys proved to be problematic when the relationship between different tables is based on compound IDs. Compounds may have more than one instance and this clearly rules out the compound ID as a primary key. Therefore, instead of primary keys, indices are used to identify relationships between tables. Third, the use of indices instead of primary keys unfortunately has further consequences: joins may work differently, and care has to be taken to avoid loss of information. When importing datasets into Proper, either an additional unique index (based on table name and row-ID) is generated automatically, or some key can be specified to be the unique index. Fourth, due to the possibility of importing Prolog data, and the closed-world assumption used in Prolog-based representations, tables do not necessarily include explicit information about the absence of feature values. Hence, to prevent against potential loss of instances in joins, Proper uses the `LEFT OUTER JOIN` instead of the `NATURAL JOIN` (which is used in the original version of RELAGGS). Fifth, since the above version of RELAGGS only aggregates tables adjacent to the target table, Proper pre-flattens arbitrarily deep nested structures into temporary tables.

2.2 The Other Components of Proper

In the following we describe the Proper framework, which is depicted in Figure 1. We will explain the individual steps with suitable examples. The first step is the import of data from a file or database.

Import. Currently Proper supports two different formats for importing data into databases: Prolog (only extensional knowledge, but including ground facts with functors) and CSV-files (with or without identifiers for the columns). For both formats the types of the columns in the table are determined automatically. Supported types are `Integer`, `Double`, `Date` and `String`. CSV import is pretty straightforward, since the data is already in a column-like representation. If the file contains a header row with the names of the columns, then these are used.

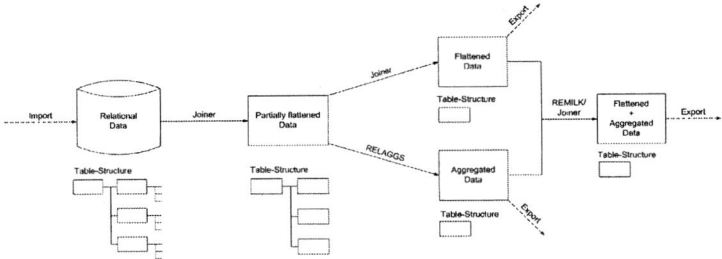

Fig. 1. Proper's program structure

Otherwise a name is constructed automatically out of both the file name and the position of each column.

```
train(east,
      [c(1,rectangle,short,not_double,none,2,l(circle,1)),
       c(2,rectangle,long,not_double,none,3,l(hexagon,1)),
       c(3,rectangle,short,not_double,peaked,2,l(triangle,1)),
       c(4,rectangle,long,not_double,none,2,l(rectangle,3))]).
```

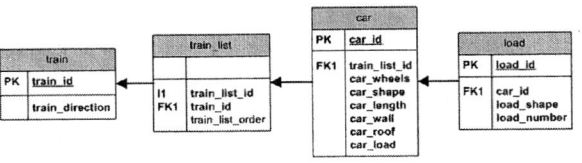

Fig. 2. East-West-Challenge Example

Prolog (or closely related formats like Progol or Golem) can be imported into databases in such a way that each functor represents a separate table. Consider the example of the East-West-Challenge in Figure 2. Since this dataset is a relational Prolog database we do not need to specify the relations between the functors explicitly. Otherwise we would have to do this by indicating which argument index functions as a key, e.g. in the well-known Alzheimer datasets the argument that contains the compound ID.

The structure of this example can easily be translated into the table structure shown in Figure 3. The `train_list` table would not actually be necessary to represent the `1..n` relationship between `train` and `car`, but this is Proper's generic approach of storing each functor in its own table. In the case of uniform lists (i.e. all lists are of same length) Proper can also turn a list directly into a table with an equal number of columns. This built-in optimization gets rid of one table thus reducing the complexity of the generated database.

Fig. 3. East-West-Challenge as a relational database

Proper also includes a few more advanced features for importing Prolog. First, if the relations cannot be determined from the Prolog database itself, it is possible to define them explicitly via *foreign key relations*. Then during import, functors will be rearranged to fit the proposed relational model. Second, for problems that are represented as flat, ground Prolog facts one also has to specify which columns are to be used for joins, as this is not necessarily obvious from the plain data. Third, depending on the representation of the data there might be more than one argument containing a key, e.g. in the Alzheimer datasets, where there are functors that define a relation between the two arguments: less_toxic(a1, b1). For a symmetric relation equally_toxic, the instance equally_toxic(a1, b1) is split into two instances equally_toxic(a1, 1) and equally_toxic(b1, 1), where the second argument is the so called split_id that links both instances together. To properly represent asymmetric relationships, new distinct functors have to be defined for each argument position and less_toxic(a1, b1). becomes less_toxic(less_toxic0(a1), less_toxic1(b1)).

Joiner. The central processing algorithm in Proper is the Joiner. As can be seen in Figure 1 the Joiner performs the flattening of arbitrarily nested structures of relations into appropriate structures for RELAGGS (maximum depth of 1), MILK (one flat table of depth 0, suitable for the multi-instance learning kit MILK) and REMILK (also one flat table). In multi-instance learning each example consists of several instances, and is also called a *bag* of instances. The data for REMILK (*RE*lational aggregation enrichment for MILK) is produced by joining the tables that have been generated for RELAGGS and MILK.

The Joiner works on tree structures. To build up such a tree structure the Joiner can either use user-specified relationships between tables or discover such relationships automatically. A GUI frontend supports specifying these tree structures. Auto-discovery of relationships determines the possible relation between tables based on column names. In order to keep the IO operations to a minimum, the joins are ordered such that smaller tables are joined first.

Left outer joins are performed in order not to lose any instances of the target table. Since classifiers normally handle missing values, the created NULL values can be interpreted as missing values. The columns over which the join is performed (i.e. the columns that are tested in the WHERE clause of the generated join-query) are determined by the intersection of the indices of the first table with all the columns of the second one. The user can specify replacement values for automatically generated NULLs on a column-basis (e.g. replacing them by "0") if they should not be treated as missing values. Such columns are updated after a join-operation.

In cases where there are additional duplicate columns beside the join columns, the duplicate columns' names are prefixed with mX_, where X is a unique number used for all columns in the current join. Without that precaution potentially essential information could be lost. A common case for this situation to arise is the handling of asymmetric relationships, where the (initially identically named) properties of both arguments have to be included in the final table.

Export. This is the last step before the classifiers can be built and evaluated. Tables generated by Proper are transformed into appropriate ARFF files for the WEKA workbench. If certain columns contain implicit knowledge like identifiers of tables (and their aggregates), it is possible to exclude them from export. In the case of multi-instance data, a bag identifier can be specified explicitly or one can be determined automatically. NULL values that were present in the data or were introduced during left outer joins are exported as missing values. If the ARFF file is too large it is possible to export only a stratified sample by specifying a sampling percentage. Finally, WEKA filters can be applied to the data before it is written to an ARFF file, e.g. nominal attributes can be turned into binary indicator attributes.

3 Experiments

We used 18 datasets in our experiments with Proper.[2] Table 1 shows the results. Note that the alzheimer_*, dd_*, and proteins datasets only have one instance per bag in the MILK and REMILK versions, so they are not "true" multi-instance datasets.

Dataset	RELAGGS	MILK	REMILK
alzheimer_amine_uptake	87.59 ± 4.31	73.35 ± 5.42	87.26 ± 4.52
alzheimer_choline	89.18 ± 2.73	79.17 ± 3.68	89.45 ± 2.68
alzheimer_scopolamine	87.84 ± 4.23	74.16 ± 5.30	87.78 ± 4.33
alzheimer_toxic	92.93 ± 2.74	88.77 ± 3.48	92.39 ± 3.00
dd_pyrimidines	92.47 ± 2.02	92.46 ± 1.94	92.46 ± 1.94
dd_triazines	74.76 ± 0.85	74.78 ± 0.85	74.78 ± 0.85
eastwest	80.00 ± 41.03	55.00 ± 51.04	75.00 ± 44.42
genes_growth	31.70 ± 1.60	34.00 ± 1.01	33.36 ± 1.25
genes_growth_bin	84.14 ± 0.42	84.33 ± 0.22	84.34 ± 0.40
genes_nucleus	76.06 ± 2.15	57.22 ± 2.19	62.55 ± 2.03
genes_nucleus_bin	87.28 ± 1.39	74.13 ± 1.67	78.49 ± 1.63
musk1_rel	80.13 ± 15.21	81.64 ± 14.68	79.50 ± 14.58
musk2_rel	72.83 ± 13.44	76.82 ± 12.61	74.40 ± 13.73
mutagenesis3_atoms	79.58 ± 8.90	81.86 ± 8.23	80.15 ± 9.24
mutagenesis3_bonds	85.38 ± 7.85	83.62 ± 7.87	86.68 ± 7.46
mutagenesis3_chains	85.31 ± 7.83	84.54 ± 7.00	84.85 ± 8.32
proteins	59.52 ± 4.08	59.12 ± 5.08	59.92 ± 3.38
suramin	45.45 ± 52.22	63.63 ± 50.45	45.45 ± 52.22

Table 1. Accuracy and standard deviation

For MILK and REMILK we used the multi-instance learner MIWrapper[3], which can be wrapped around any standard propositional learner as described in [1]. The MIWrapper approach assigns each instance of the n instances in a bag a weight of $1/n$. Therefore all the bags have the same total weight regardless of the number of instances they contain. For predicting a bag label a class probability is obtained from the propositional model for every instance of the bag. These probabilities are simply averaged to determine the resulting class label for the bag.

This approach enjoys an advantage over aggregation as performed by RE-LAGGS if the data looks like that in Figure 4, i.e. if interactions between attributes are significant for prediction. Here the aggregates generated by RE-LAGGS are identical for both classes, making discrimination impossible, but the MIWrapper algorithm would be able to create a useful classifier, for example, using a propositional decision tree learner.

---

[2] All the data used in our experiments is available from the Proper web page http://www.cs.waikato.ac.nz/ml/proper.

[3] The MIWrapper is part of MILK, the Multi-Instance Learning Kit, which is freely available from http://www.cs.waikato.ac.nz/ml/milk/.

We used unpruned decisions trees in our experiments with RELAGGS and MILK/REMILK. Only for the genes_* datasets we used boosted decision stumps instead because the trees became too large. Both learning schemes are insensitive to the relative scale of the instances' weights and that is why we used them. In all experiments we used 10 runs of stratified 10-fold cross-validation, only in case of suramin and eastwest we used Leave-One-Out. This was done because of the very small size of these datasets. Also, to imitate RELAGGS's behaviour, we binarized all nominal attributes before passing them to the MIWrapper and replaced missing values in the resulting attributes by 0.

When interpreting the results shown in Table 1, we see that RELAGGS and REMILK perform similarly (the exception being the gene_nucleus_* data, where REMILK performs worse—possibly because the RELAGGS attributes follow after the attributes from the multi-instance data in the REMILK version of the data, and the decision tree learner is thus biased towards the latter set of attributes). The results indicate that in practice one might as well run the faster and less memory-demanding RELAGGS approach instead of the combination approach REMILK.

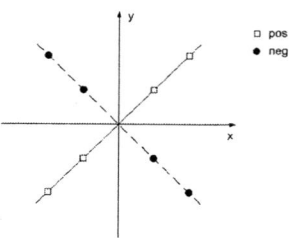

Fig. 4. Artificial dataset

MILK is performing as well as the other approaches on about two thirds of all datasets, but it does worse on the remaining datasets. Currently we do not have a good explanation for this difference, as we were actually expecting the multi-instance approach to enjoy an advantage. But this theoretical advantage (see the example discussed above) does not seem to be relevant in practice. Note that the difference on the single-instance alzheimer_* datasets is solely due to the fact that the RELAGGS approach enables the propositional learner to treat NULL effectively as a separate value rather than a missing value (because some of the aggregate functions used by RELAGGS return zero if there are no applicable records). This different treatment of missing values may be partially responsible for the differences observed in other cases as well. There are no NULL values in the musk datasets and here MILK actually has a slight edge.

4 Conclusions and Future Work

This paper presents an attempt to develop a practical database-oriented framework for different propositionalization algorithms. The flexible design allows for the future integration of other propositionalization algorithms in addition to RELAGGS. Proper makes standard propositional and multi-instance learning algorithms available for relational learning. A preliminary empirical investigation has shown the feasibility of this approach.

References

1. E. Frank and X. Xu. *Applying Propositional Learning Algorithms to Multi-instance data.* Working Paper 06/03, Computer Science, University of Waikato, 2003.
2. M.-A. Krogel and S. Wrobel. *Facets of Aggregation Approaches to Propositionalization.* In: T. Horváth and A. Yamamoto (Eds.) Proceedings of the Work-in-Progress Track at the 13th International Conference on Inductive Logic Programming, 2003.
3. M.-A. Krogel, S. Rawles, F. Železný, P. A. Flach, N. Lavrač, and S. Wrobel. *Comparative Evaluation of Approaches to Propositionalization.* In: T. Horváth and A. Yamamoto (Eds.) Proceedings of the 13th International Conference on Inductive Logic Programming. LNCS 2835, Springer-Verlag, 2003.
4. P. Reutemann. *Development of a Propositionalization Toolbox.* MSc Thesis, Computer Science, University of Freiburg, 2004.

An Improvement to Unscented Transformation*

Yuanxin Wu, Meiping Wu, Dewen Hu, and Xiaoping Hu

Department of Automatic Control, College of Mechatronics and Automation,
National University of Defense Technology, Changsha, Hunan, P. R. China 410073
yuanx_wu@hotmail.com

Abstract. This paper proposes a new sigma point selection strategy to better capture the information of a probability distribution. By doing so, the non-local sampling problem inherent in the original unscented transformation (UT) is fundamentally eliminated. It is argued that the improved UT (IUT) outperforms the original UT at the cost of increased but comparable computation burden and will be useful in constructing a nonlinear filter.

1 Introduction

The Bayesian inference provides an optimal solution framework for dynamic state estimation problems. Because the Bayesian solution requires the propagation of the full probability density, the optimal nonlinear filtering often turns out to be analytically intractable. Approximations are thus necessary. The most celebrated one is the extended Kalman filter (EKF), which is used to further approximate the nonlinearity through successive linearization at the current estimate. The EKF has been successfully applied to deal with nonlinear filtering problems in many practical systems. When employed to address significant nonlinearities, however, the EKF becomes very difficult to tune and even prone to divergence. Long-term experiences have shown that it is only reliable for systems that are almost linear in the update interval. Most of the difficulties are owed much to the local linearization at a single point without considering the given *probabilistic spread* at all [1]. This statement also applies other all Taylor series truncation based filters.

In light of the intuition that to approximate a probability distribution is easier than to approximate an arbitrary nonlinear transformation, Julier and Uhlmann [2-6] invented the unscented transformation (UT) to make probabilistic inference, i.e., 1) parameterize the mean and covariance of a probability distribution via a set of deterministically selected samples, 2) propagate them through the true nonlinear transformation, and 3) calculate the parameters of the propagated Gaussian approximation from the transformed samples. Eliminating the cumbersome derivation and evaluation of Jacobian/Hessian matrices, the UT-based unscented Kalman filter

---

* Supported in part by National Natural Science Foundation of China (60374006, 60234030 and 60171003), Distinguished Young Scholars Fund of China (60225015), and Ministry of Education of China (TRAPOYT Project).

(UKF) is much easier to implement and performs better than the EKF. Lefebvre et al. [7] interpreted the UT as a statistical linear regression (a discrete implementation of the statistical linearization [8]), which provides a very useful insight into the UT's characteristics. This insight justifies the derivative-free UKF's benefits over the linearization-based EKF.

In this paper, we propose a new sigma point selection strategy to better capture the information of a probability distribution. An outline of the paper is as follows. Section 2 sketches the principle of the UT and motivates the development of the improved UT (IUT). Section 3 develops and analyzes the IUT in the polar-to-Cartesian coordinate transformation. Summary and conclusions are given in Section 4.

2 Motivation

According to the UT's sigma point selection strategy [2, 4-6], an n-dimensional random variable $x(k)$ with mean $\hat{x}(k|k)$ and covariance $P(k|k)$ can be approximated by the following $2n$ weighted sigma points

$$\chi_i(k|k) = \hat{x}(k|k) + \left(\sqrt{nP(k|k)}\right)_i \qquad W_i = 1/2n,$$
$$\chi_{i+n}(k|k) = \hat{x}(k|k) - \left(\sqrt{nP(k|k)}\right)_i \qquad W_{i+n} = 1/2n \qquad i=1,\ldots,n. \qquad (1)$$

In order to allow information beyond the mean and covariance to be incorporated into the set of sigma points, an extra sigma points identical with the given mean is added to yield a sigma set with the same mean and covariance but different high-order moments, i.e.,

$$\chi_0(k|k) = \hat{x}(k|k) \qquad W_0 = W_0$$
$$\chi_i(k|k) = \hat{x}(k|k) + \left(\sqrt{nP(k|k)/(1-W_0)}\right)_i \qquad W_i = (1-W_0)/2n, \qquad i=1,\ldots,n. \qquad (2)$$
$$\chi_{i+n}(k|k) = \hat{x}(k|k) - \left(\sqrt{nP(k|k)/(1-W_0)}\right)_i \qquad W_{i+n} = (1-W_0)/2n$$

where $\left(\sqrt{P}\right)_i$ is the ith column or row[1] of the matrix square root of P and W_i the weight associated with the ith sigma point. The independent parameter W_0 is to be tuned to capture the most important higher order moments information. Using the analysis in Appendix II of [6], $W_0 = 1 - n/3$ is justified because it guarantees that the fourth-order moment information is mostly captured in the true Gaussian case. Then (2) becomes

---

[1] If the matrix square root is formulated as $P = S^T S$, then the rows of S are used to form sigma points. Otherwise, the columns are used.

$$\chi_0(k\mid k) = \hat{x}(k\mid k)$$
$$\chi_i(k\mid k) = \hat{x}(k\mid k) + \left(\sqrt{3P(k\mid k)}\right)_i$$
$$\chi_{i+n}(k\mid k) = \hat{x}(k\mid k) - \left(\sqrt{3P(k\mid k)}\right)_i$$

$$W_0 = 1 - n/3$$
$$W_i = 1/6 \quad , \quad i = 1,\ldots,n. \quad (3)$$
$$W_{i+n} = 1/6$$

It can be analytically shown that the sigma points are all located on the $\sqrt{3}\sigma$ contour. Under the assumption of Gaussian distribution, there is a possibility 68% for a sample occurring within the 1σ contour and a possibility 99.7% within the 3σ contour. In other words, *a satisfying sigma set should comprise of sigma points that are choicely located within the 3σ contour*. This rule takes the probabilistic spread into full consideration and can be used as a general validation rule for a sigma set. For example, the sigma set in (1) will be definitely a poor one for a random variable of dimension over nine. So would be the sigma set in (2) if the independent W_0 took a value slightly less than 1, e.g., 0.99. Under these conditions, the sigma points are indeed irrepresentative of the true probabilistic spread although some moments information has been apparently captured. The propagated statistics of course will not reflect the true posterior distribution. It is right the non-local sampling indicated in [3], where the scaled UT was adopted to address this problem, i.e., the sigma points are scaled towards the mean center by a small positive factor α (typically $\ll 1$). The scaled UT is equivalently squeezing all sigma points into a tiny sphere centered at the mean, again regardless of the true probability distribution. As a result, the non-local sampling disappears but the *non-global sampling* problem surfaces. So far, it appears that the sigma set in (3) does not get involved into any problem.

However, in view of the fact that a sample occurs outside the $\sqrt{3}\sigma$ contour with possibility 8.3%, there seems to have a margin to improve the sigma set. Motivated by the non-local and non-global sampling problems inherent in the original UT, in next section we try to seek a new sigma point selection strategy to better capture the information of a probability distribution.

3 The Improved Unscented Transformation

The IUT

The rationale of improving the UT is to determine the location of relatively a small number of sigma points and their corresponding weights so that the probabilistic spread be well represented. Ideally, the determination of a sigma point's location should take account of the characteristics of the specific nonlinear transformation. Without these prior information about the nonlinear transformation in hand, we may as well determine, first of all, a good "spread" of the sigma points and subsequently decide their weights to accomplish a "probabilistic" spread. In this case, the IUT will be hopefully less influenced by the non-global sampling problem than the original UT.

The final sigma set is composed of $6n+1$ sigma points with one point at the mean center and the other points at the 1σ, 2σ and 3σ contours, respectively, i.e.

$$\chi_0(k|k) = \hat{x}(k|k)$$
$$\chi_i(k|k) = \hat{x}(k|k) + \left(\sqrt{P(k|k)}\right)_i$$
$$\chi_{i+n}(k|k) = \hat{x}(k|k) - \left(\sqrt{P(k|k)}\right)_i$$
$$\chi_{i+2n}(k|k) = \hat{x}(k|k) + 2\left(\sqrt{P(k|k)}\right)_i$$
$$\chi_{i+3n}(k|k) = \hat{x}(k|k) - 2\left(\sqrt{P(k|k)}\right)_i$$
$$\chi_{i+4n}(k|k) = \hat{x}(k|k) + 3\left(\sqrt{P(k|k)}\right)_i$$
$$\chi_{i+5n}(k|k) = \hat{x}(k|k) - 3\left(\sqrt{P(k|k)}\right)_i$$

$$W_0 = 1 - n(1+\alpha+\beta)/(1+4\alpha+9\beta)$$
$$W_i = 1/(2+8\alpha+18\beta)$$
$$W_{i+n} = 1/(2+8\alpha+18\beta),$$
$$W_{i+2n} = \alpha/(2+8\alpha+18\beta)$$
$$W_{i+3n} = \alpha/(2+8\alpha+18\beta)$$
$$W_{i+4n} = \beta/(2+8\alpha+18\beta)$$
$$W_{i+5n} = \beta/(2+8\alpha+18\beta)$$

$i = 1,\ldots,n$. (4)

where α, β are two free parameters. It can be easily verified that the mean and covariance are completely caught. Under the assumption of a Gaussian distribution α, β are set to be

$$\alpha = \text{normpdf}(2)/\text{normpdf}(1)$$
$$\beta = \text{normpdf}(3)/\text{normpdf}(1) \quad (5)$$

where $\text{normpdf}(\cdot)$ is the standard normal probability density function.

Given a set of sigma points, the predicated mean and covariance can be calculated by

1) Each sigma point is instantiated through the process model or observation model (denoted uniformly by a nonlinear function $f(\cdot)$) to yield a set of transformed samples

$$\chi_i(k+1|k) = f(\chi_i(k|k)). \quad (6)$$

2) The predicted mean is computed as

$$\hat{x}(k+1|k) = \sum_{i=0}^{6n} W_i \chi_i(k+1|k). \quad (7)$$

3) The predicted covariance is computed as

$$P(k+1|k) = \sum_{i=0}^{6n} W_i \left(\chi_i(k+1|k) - \hat{x}(k+1|k)\right) \times \left(\chi_i(k+1|k) - \hat{x}(k+1|k)\right)^T. \quad (8)$$

The IUT allows tradeoffs between computational burden and accuracy. For example, the number of sigma points can be reduced to $4n+1$ by simply removing the last $2n$ points. The above discussions still hold true for this reduced sigma set.

Example: Polar to Cartesian Coordinate Transformation

The polar information (r, θ) returned by a sensor has to be converted to an (x, y) position in some Cartesian coordinate frame. The transformation is

$$\begin{pmatrix} x \\ y \end{pmatrix} = \begin{pmatrix} r\cos\theta \\ r\sin\theta \end{pmatrix}. \tag{9}$$

A range-optimized sonar sensor can provide fairly range measurements (2 *cm* standard deviation) but extremely poor bearing measurements (15° standard deviation) [6]. The accurate mean and covariance are calculated by Monte Carlo simulation using 10^6 samples. In order to fully evaluate the performance of the IUT against the UT in propagation of statistics, we examine those situations with much worse bearing measurements (100° standard deviation). The results are shown in Fig. 1, respectively. The UT estimates are biased and inconsistent for the standard deviation of 100°. In contrast, the IUT behaves quite well and its estimates almost coincide with the actual. It is found in fact that the IUT estimates are still valid for standard deviation as large as 110°.

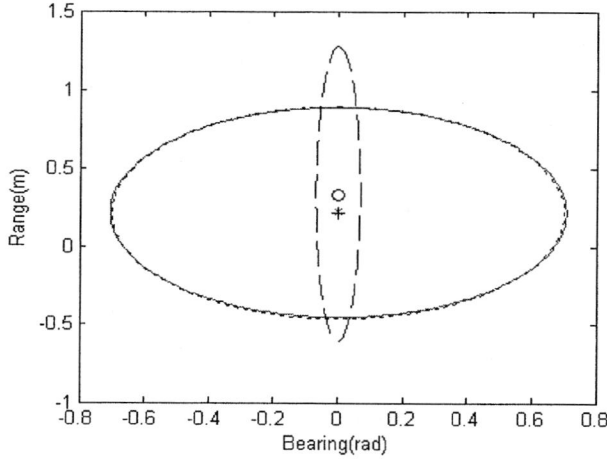

Fig. 1. The mean and standard deviation (2 cm, 100 degree) contours for the true statistics, those calculated by the UT and those calculated by the IUT. The true mean is at * and its deviation contour is solid; the UT mean is at o and its contour is slashed; and the IUT mean is at + and its contour is dotted

4 Conclusions

Motivated by the non-local and non-global sampling problems inherent in the original UT, this paper proposes a new sigma point selection strategy to better capture the information of a probability distribution. For the new IUT, the non-local problem is fundamentally eliminated while the non-global problem that has been neglected in the previous literature is also lessened. The increased but comparable computation burden incurred by the IUT can be handled by today's advanced computing power. Admittedly, it is possible to further improve the original UT through an elaborate sigma point selection strategy.

References

1. R. v. d. Merwe and E. Wan, "Sigma-point Kalman filters for probabilistic inference in dynamic state-space models," in Proceedings of the Workshop on Advances in Machine Learning. Montreal, Canada, 2003.
2. S. Julier, J. Uhlmann, and H. F. Durrant-Whyte, "A new method for the nonlinear transformation of means and covariances in filters and estimators," IEEE Transactions on Automatic Control, vol. 45, pp. 477-482, 2000.
3. S. J. Julier, "The scaled unscented transformation," in Proceedings of the 2002 American Control Conference, Vols 1-6, Proceedings of the American Control Conference, 2002, pp. 4555-4559.
4. S. J. Julier and J. K. Uhlmann, "A consistent, debiased method for converting between polar and Cartesian coordinate systems," in Acquisition, Tracking, and Pointing Xi, vol. 3086, Proceedings of the Society of Photo-Optical Instrumentation Engineers (SPIE), 1997, pp. 110-121.
5. S. J. Julier and J. K. Uhlmann, "A new extension of the Kalman filter to nonlinear systems," in Signal Processing, Sensor Fusion, and Target Recognition VI, vol. 3068, Proceedings of the Society of Photo-Optical Instrumentation Engineers (SPIE), 1997, pp. 182-193.
6. S. J. Julier and J. K. Uhlmann, "Unscented filtering and nonlinear estimation," Proceedings of the IEEE, vol. 92, pp. 401-422, 2004.
7. T. Lefebvre, H. Bruyninckx, and J. De Schutter, "Comment on "A new method for the nonlinear transformation of means and covariances in filters and estimators"," IEEE Transactions on Automatic Control, vol. 47, pp. 1406-1408, 2002.
8. A. Gelb, Applied Optimal Estimation. Cambridge, Mass.,: M.I.T. Press, 1974.

Automatic Wrapper Generation for Metasearch Using Ordered Tree Structured Patterns

Kazuhide Aikou[1], Yusuke Suzuki[1],
Takayoshi Shoudai[1], and Tetsuhiro Miyahara[2]

[1] Department of Informatics, Kyushu University, Kasuga 816-8580, Japan
{k-aikou, y-suzuki, shoudai}@i.kyushu-u.ac.jp
[2] Faculty of Information Sciences,
Hiroshima City University, Hiroshima 731-3194, Japan
miyahara@its.hiroshima-cu.ac.jp

Abstract. A wrapper is a program which extracts data from a web site and reorganizes them in a database. Wrapper generation from web sites is a key technique in realizing such a metasearch system. We present a new method of automatic wrapper generation for metasearch using our efficient learning algorithm for *term trees*. Term trees are ordered tree structured patterns with structured variables, which represent structural features common to tree structured data such as HTML files.

1 Introduction

Due to the rapid growth of HTML files at the Web space, it is important to extract useful information from the vast Web space. Since general-purpose search engines are useful but not universal, many organizations have their own search engines on their web sites, which are called *search sites* [3]. To support unified access to multiple search sites, we have developed a metasearch system for search sites. Wrapper generation from web sites has been extensively studied [1–7,9] and is a key technique in realizing such a metasearch system. However only a few automatic technique is based on theoretical foundations of learning theory. In this paper, we present a new method of automatic wrapper generation for metasearch engines for search sites. Our learning algorithm from tree structured data, called MINL algorithm [10], plays important role in this method.

Our approach of wrapper generation from web sites has the following advantages. MINL algorithm is unsupervised and needs no labeled examples which are positive and negative examples. The algorithm needs only a small number of sample HTML files of a target web site which are considered to be positive examples. Our approach has a firm theoretical foundation based on Computational Learning Theory [10]. Term trees, our representation of ordered tree structured patterns, have rich representing power and are useful to Web mining and semistructured data mining [8]. According to Object Exchange Model, we treat semistructured data as tree structured data. Since tree based wrappers are shown to be more powerful than string based wrappers [4,9], we use *term*

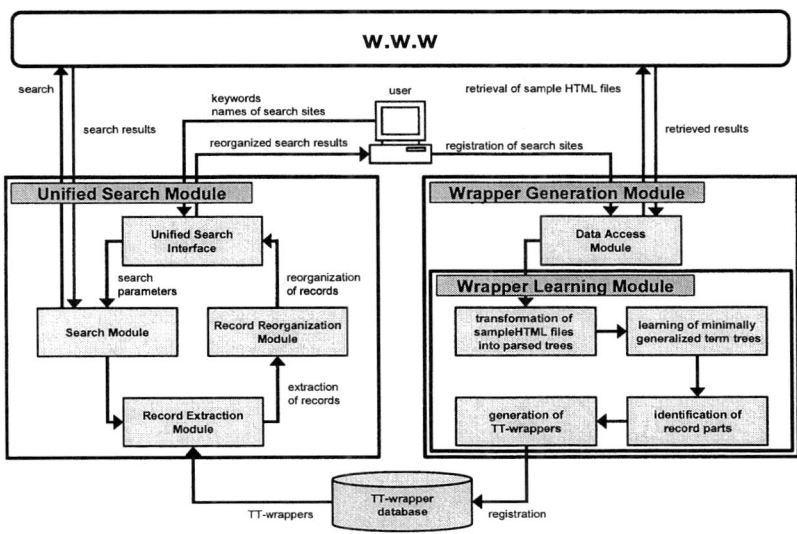

Fig. 1. Architecture of our system of metasearch from search sites

trees [10], which are ordered tree patterns with structured variables. A variable in a term tree can match an arbitrary subtree, which represents a field of a semistructured document. As a special case, a contractible variable can match an empty subtree, which represents a missing field in a semistructured document. Since semistructured documents have irregularities such as missing fields, a term tree with contractible variables is suited for representing tree structured patterns in such semistructured documents.

The key concept of our system is *minimally generalized term trees* obtained from tree structured data, which is briefly explained in Sec. 2. Let S be a set of trees each of which is transformed from an HTML file in a given HTML dataset. A *term tree wrapper generated by* S is a tuple (t, H) where t is one of minimally generalized term trees explaining S and H is a subset of variables of t. We call a term tree wrapper a **TT-wrapper**, for short. We note that search sites always output HTML files according to certain previously fixed rules. If we focus on one search site, the trees outputted by the site have no significant difference in the shapes. Thus, it is natural to guess that we can obtain a unique minimally generalized term tree for HTML files outputted by one search site. In this paper, we present a new method of automatic TT-wrapper generation for metasearch. The system provides unified access to multiple existing search sites (Fig. 1).

2 Term Trees with Contractible Variables

In this section, we give a rough definition and an example rather than give a full technical definition of a term tree. The reader is referred to [10] for details.

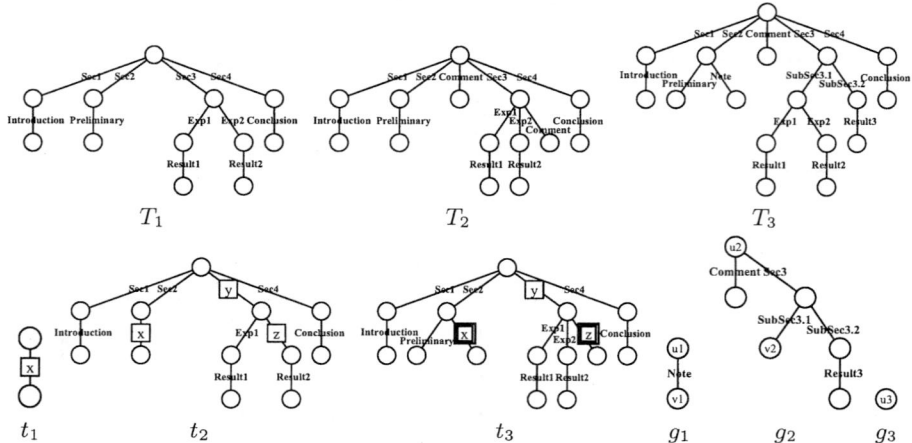

Fig. 2. Term trees t_1, t_2 and t_3 and trees T_1, T_2, T_3, g_1, g_2 and g_3. An uncontractible (resp. contractible) variable is represented by a single (resp. double) lined box with lines to its elements. The upper right tree T_3 is obtained from t_3 by replacing variables x, y, z with g_1, g_2, g_3, respectively (See [10])

Let $T = (V_T, E_T)$ be a rooted tree with ordered children, called an *ordered tree*, or a *tree* where V_T is a set of vertices and E_T is a set of edges. Let E_g and H_g be a partition of E_T, i.e., $E_g \cup H_g = E_T$ and $E_g \cap H_g = \emptyset$. And let $V_g = V_T$. A triplet $g = (V_g, E_g, H_g)$ is called an *ordered term tree*, or a *term tree* simply. And elements in V_g, E_g and H_g are called a *vertex*, an *edge* and a *variable*, respectively. We assume that every edge and variable of a term tree is labeled with some words from specified languages. There are two kind of variables, called *contractible variables* and *uncontractible variables*. A contractible variable may be considered to be an erasing variable, which must be adjacent to a leaf and can be replaced with any ordered tree including a singleton vertex. An uncontractible variable can appear anywhere in a term tree and be replaced with any ordered tree of at least 2 vertices. Variables with the same label must be replaced with the same tree. This rule often makes computational problems harder. Then we assume that all labels of variables in a term tree are mutually distinct.

Let t be a term tree. The *term tree language* of t, denoted by $L(t)$, is the set of all trees which are obtained from t by substituting trees for variables in t. We say that t *explains* a given set of trees S if $S \subseteq L(t)$. A *minimally generalized* term tree t explaining S is a term tree t which satisfies the following conditions: (i) t explains S, and (ii) $L(t)$ is minimal among all term tree languages which contain all trees in S. For example, the term tree t_3 in Fig. 2 is a minimally generalized term tree explaining T_1, T_2 and T_3. And t_2 is also minimally generalized term trees, with no contractible variable, explaining T_1, T_2 and T_3. A term tree t_1 is overgeneralized and meaningless, since t_1 explains any tree of at least 2 vertices. A term tree using contractible and uncontractible variables can express the structural feature of trees more correctly than a term tree us-

---
procedure GENTTWRAPPER(S, p, ϵ);
begin
  Let t be a minimally generalized term tree
  explaining S;
  foreach u which has at least p children **do**
  begin
    Let $c_1, \ldots, c_m$ all ordered children of u;
    Let A^u be an $m \times m$ zero matrix;
    for $i := 1$ **to** m **do**
      for $j := i + 1$ **to** m **do**
        if $t[c_i]$ and $t[c_j]$ are ϵ-equivalent **then**
          $A^u[i, j] := 1$;
    if A^u has a $q \times q$ nonzero submatrix which
    appears just $p - 1$ times horizontally **then**
    u is the parent of all records and **break**
  end;
  Let H be the set of all variables of $t[u]$;
  return (t, H)
end;

$$A^u = \begin{pmatrix} 0 & 0 & 0 & 0 & 0 & 0 & 0 & 0 & 1 & 0 & \cdots & 0 & 0 & 0 \\ 0 & 0 & 0 & 0 & 0 & 0 & 0 & 0 & 0 & 0 & \cdots & 0 & 0 & 0 \\ 0 & 0 & 0 & 0 & \boxed{1\,0} & \boxed{1\,0} & \boxed{1\,0} & \cdots & \boxed{1\,0} & 0 \\ 0 & 0 & 0 & 0 & \boxed{0\,0} & \boxed{0\,0} & \boxed{0\,0} & \cdots & \boxed{0\,0} & 0 \\ 0 & 0 & 0 & 0 & 0 & 0 & 1 & 0 & 1 & 0 & \cdots & 1 & 0 & 0 \\ 0 & 0 & 0 & 0 & 0 & 0 & 0 & 0 & 0 & 0 & \cdots & 0 & 0 & 0 \\ 0 & 0 & 0 & 0 & 0 & 0 & 0 & 0 & 1 & 0 & \cdots & 1 & 0 & 0 \\ 0 & 0 & 0 & 0 & 0 & 0 & 0 & 0 & 0 & 0 & \cdots & 0 & 0 & 0 \\ & & & & & \vdots & & & & & \end{pmatrix}$$

Fig. 3. Procedure GENTTWRAPPER outputs a TT-wrapper for search results outputted by a fixed search site. The right matrix is an image of a boolean matrix A^u after procedure GENTTWRAPPER

ing only uncontractible variables. Then we consider that t_3 is a more precious term tree than t_2. We gave an algorithm, called **MINL** algorithm, for finding a minimally generalized term tree t explaining a given set of trees S which runs in $O(N_{min}^2 N_{max}|S|)$ time where N_{max} and N_{min} be the maximum and minimum numbers of vertices of trees in S, respectively [10].

3 Automatic Wrapper Generation for Metasearch

Our system of metasearch from search sites consists of two main modules, **Wrapper Generation Module** and **Unified Search Module**. The first module generates TT-wrappers from sample HTML files from search sites. When our system receives a user query, the second module collects and reorganizes the search results from the registered search sites by using corresponding TT-wrappers, and displays the unified search results to the user (Fig. 1) .

We describe the formal algorithm in Fig. 3. Let S be a set of trees converted from search results by a certain search site. Each tree in S corresponds to one search result and each result contains a fixed number of records. We assume that all trees have exactly $p \geq 2$ records. Let $t = (V_t, E_t, H_t)$ be a minimally generalized term tree explaining S. The purpose of a TT-wrapper in metasearch is to extract all and only records from trees obtained from newly outputted search results. Thus we need to specify p groups of subtrees corresponding to each of p records. We note that all roots of these subtrees must have the unique parent. Let u be a vertex of t, which is a candidate of the parent of records, and $c_1,\ldots,c_m$ all ordered children of u. $t[v]$ denotes the term subtree of t which is induced by v and the descendants of v. First we find the candidates of the parent. Each record consists of a fixed but unknown number of subtrees. Let $q \geq 1$ be the number of subtrees corresponding to a record. For example, for some k, k' ($0 \leq k < k + q < k'$), q subtrees $t[c_{k+1}],\ldots,t[c_{k+q}]$ construct one record and other q subtrees $t[c_{k'+1}],\ldots,t[c_{k'+q}]$ construct another record and so on. In order to find such groups of subtrees, we use MINL algorithm again for testing whether or not given two term subtrees are approximately the same. For a term tree $t = (V_t, E_t, H_t)$, let $T\langle t\rangle = (V_T, E_T)$ be the tree obtained from t where $V_T = V_t$ and $E_T = E_t \cup \{\{u, v\} \mid [u, v] \in H_t\}$. All variable labels of t are thought of edge labels in $T\langle t\rangle$. For a fixed number $0 \leq \epsilon \leq 1$ and two term trees t and t', we say that t and t' are ϵ-equivalent if $||t| - |t'|| \leq \epsilon \cdot |t|$, $||\mathrm{MINL}(\{T\langle t\rangle, T\langle t'\rangle\})| - |t|| \leq \epsilon \cdot |t|$, and $||\mathrm{MINL}(\{T\langle t\rangle, T\langle t'\rangle\})| - |t'|| \leq \epsilon \cdot |t|$, where $\mathrm{MINL}(S)$ is an output term tree of our MINL algorithm. We find p groups $(c_{11},\ldots,c_{1q}),\ldots,(c_{p1},\ldots,c_{pq})$ of q children from all children $c_1,\ldots,c_m$ such that (i) $t[c_{ij}]$ and $t[c_{i'j}]$ are ϵ-equivalent for all $1 \leq i < i' \leq p$ and $1 \leq j \leq q$ and (ii) $c_{i,j+1}$ is the immediately right sibling of c_{ij} for all $1 \leq i \leq p$ and $1 \leq j < q$. The procedure GenTTwrapper (Fig. 3) generates a TT-wrapper which extracts all records of search results outputted by a fixed search site.

4 Experimental Results

We implemented our system by C on a PC with CPU Celeron 2.0 GHz and 512 MB memory. We chose total 25 search sites which output exactly 10 search results in English. The abbreviated names of these sites are given in the 1st column of Table 1. Firstly the system automatically gave two popular keywords to

Table 1. Total 17 TT-wrappers are obtained from 25 search sites by using our system

Search Sites	Page Size	Result	Search Sites	Page Size	Result
Pioneer	218	OK	TOSHIBA	454	OK
GENERAL MILLS	241	OK	BMW	472	OK
Yamanouchi	268	OK	GWF	482	OK
VOS	303	NG	HONDA	485	NG
TOYOBO	324	OK	FUJITSU	488	OK
Golden Circle	329	NG	OMRON	491	NG
Oracle	341	OK	KDDI	527	NG
MAZDA	358	OK	ASAHI_KASEI	547	NG
Microsoft	359	OK	Yahoo	552	OK
Seiko	378	OK	SONY	578	NG
DAIHATSU	383	OK	Teoma	608	NG
RRD	404	OK	Heinz	608	OK
ISUZU	441	OK			

each search site, and retrieved 2 search results for each keyword. Next the system converted the first displayed pages of these 2 results into 2 trees. The entry of the 2nd column of Table 1 shows the size of one of the trees. The mark "OK" means that the system succeeded to get a TT-wrapper of the corresponding search site. The success rate decreases in proportion to the tree size. It is natural to consider that a larger tree can contain a lot of groups of similar subtrees which might become records. Since our current system uses only knowledge of structures of search results, it often failed to generate TT-wrappers for relatively large search sites. From these observations, we are now developing new similarity measures between two subtrees with text information in order to extract records exactly.

5 Conclusions

In order to provide unified access to multiple search sites, we have presented a new method of automatic wrapper generation for metasearch for search sites, by using our learning algorithm MINL for term trees. We have reported our metasearch system for search sites. Our method uses a new type of wrappers, called TT-wrappers, which are tree structured patterns with structured variables and useful to extract information from HTML files in search sites.

References

1. V. Crescenzi, G. Mecca, and P. Merialdo. ROADRUNNER: Towards automatic data extraction from large web sites. *Proc. VLDB-2001*, pages 109–118, 2001.
2. R. Dale, C. Paris, and M. Tilbrook. Information extraction via path merging. *Proc. AI-2003,Springer-Verlag, LNAI 2903*, pages 150–160, 2003.
3. S. Hirokawa and HumanTecnoSystem Co. Research and development of the next-generation search engine by dynamic integration of search sites (in Japanese). *http://daisen.cc.kyushu-u.ac.jp/thesis/thesis.pdf*, 2002.
4. D. Ikeda, Y. Yamada, and S. Hirokawa. Expressive power of tree and string based wrappers. *Proceedings of IJCAI-2003 Workshop on Information Integration on the Web (IIWeb-2003)*, pages 21–26, 2003.
5. N. Kushmerick. Wrapper induction: efficiency and expressiveness. *Artificial Intelligence*, 118:15–68, 2000.
6. A. H. F. Laender, B. A. Ribeiro-Neto, A. S. da Silva, and J. S. Teixeira. A brief survey of web data extraction tools. *SIGMOD Record*, 31(2):84–93, 2002.
7. B. Liu, R. L. Grossman, and Y. Zhai. Mining data records in web pages. *Proc. KDD-2003, AAAI Press*, pages 601–606, 2003.
8. T. Miyahara, Y. Suzuki, T. Shoudai, T. Uchida, K. Takahashi, and H. Ueda. Discovery of maximally frequent tag tree patterns with contractible variables from semistructured documents. *Proc. PAKDD-2004, Springer-Verlag, LNAI 3056*, pages 133–134, 2004.
9. H. Sakamoto, Y. Murakami, H. Arimura, and S. Arikawa. Extracting partial structures from html documents. *Proceedings of the Fourteenth International Florida Artificial Intelligence Research Society Conference,2001*, pages 264–268, 2001.
10. Y. Suzuki, T. Shoudai, S. Matsumoto, T. Uchida, and T. Miyahara. Efficient learning of ordered and unordered tree patterns with contractible variables. *Proc. ALT-2003, Springer-Verlag, LNAI 2842*, pages 114–128, 2003.

Building a More Accurate Classifier Based on Strong Frequent Patterns

Yudho Giri Sucahyo and Raj P. Gopalan

Department of Computing, Curtin University of Technology,
Kent St, Bentley, Western Australia 6102
{sucahyoy, raj}@cs.curtin.edu.au

Abstract. The classification problem in data mining is to discover models from training data for classifying unknown instances. Associative classification builds the classifier rules using association rules and it is more accurate compared to previous methods. In this paper, a new method named CSFP that builds a classifier from strong frequent patterns without the need to generate association rules is presented. We address the rare item problem by using a partitioning method. Rules generated are stored using a compact data structure named *CP-Tree* and a series of pruning methods are employed to discard weak frequent patterns. Experimental results show that our classifier is more accurate than previous associative classification methods as well as other state-of-the-art non-associative classifiers.

1 Introduction

Classification is an important problem in data mining that involves building a model or classifier to predict the classes of unknown instances. It has been studied extensively and there are many approaches such as decision trees [1], Naïve-Bayesian (NB), *k*-nearest neighbors (*k*-NN), rule learning, case based reasoning, and neural network [2]. Associative classification is a relatively new approach that builds the classifier by taking the most effective rule(s) among all the association rules [3] mined from the dataset. Previous studies have shown that associative classification is more accurate in general [4-6]. Associative classification methods consist of three main steps: mining the frequent patterns, forming class-association rules using the frequent patterns, and building the classifier from the association rules. Our approach is different, as the classifier is built directly from the frequent patterns without the need to generate association rules. Previous associative classification methods need to generate association rules first before constructing the classifier [4].

We automatically address the *rare item problem* [7] by using partitioning to ensure that enough rules are generated for infrequent classes without over-fitting the rules for frequent classes. Our recent algorithm, CT-PRO [8], is used for mining frequent patterns. CT-PRO uses a compact data structure named *CFP-Tree* (*Compressed FP-Tree*) and frequent patterns are stored in a compact data structure named *CP-Tree* (*Classification Pattern Tree*). We then employ a series of pruning steps to discard weak frequent patterns. The frequent patterns that remain are called *strong frequent patterns* and used for constructing the classifier rules.

Our algorithm named CSFP (Classification based on Strong Frequent Patterns) is compared with previous associative classifiers including CBA [4], CMAR [5], and CPAR [6]. We also compare it with other well-known classifiers that use various other methods including: C4.5 [1], CAEP [9], DeEP [10], iCAEP [11], RIPPER [12], LB [13], NB [2], TAN [14] and k-NN [15]. The results show that CSFP generally performs better than others on accuracy.

The paper is organized as follows: In Section 2, we define relevant terms used in frequent patterns, association rule mining, and associative classification. In Section 3, we present the CFSP method. Section 4 reports the experimental results on various datasets. Section 5 contains the conclusion and pointers for further work.

2 Definition of Terms

In this section, we define terms relevant to frequent patterns, association rule mining, and associative classification.

Frequent Patterns and Association Rules. Let $I=\{i_1, i_2,..., i_n\}$ be a set of items, and D be a database consisting of a set of transactions. Each transaction T is identified by a *tid* and $T \subseteq I$. An itemset X is a subset of items ($X \subseteq I$). The *support* of X is the percentage of transactions in D that contains X. Given a *support threshold* σ, X is a *frequent pattern* if $supp(X) \geq \sigma$. An association rule is an expression of the form $R: X \rightarrow Y$, where $X \subset I$, $Y \subset I$, and $X \cap Y = \emptyset$. X and Y can consist of one or more items. X is the *body* and Y is the *head*. The *confidence* of the rule is $supp(X \cup Y)/supp(X)$. Given a *confidence threshold* γ, R is valid if $conf(R) \geq \gamma$.

Associative Classification. A training dataset D consists of a set of instances $I=\{i_1, i_2,..., i_n\}$ based on a schema $(A_1, A_2,..., A_n)$ where each A_i is an attribute with a domain of values that could be *discrete* or *continuous*. For a continuous attribute, we assume that its value range is discretized into intervals, and these intervals mapped to a set of consecutive positive integers. Then the attribute value in an instance can be treated similar to an *item* in a market basket database. Let $C=\{c_1, c_2,..., c_n\}$ be a set of *class labels*. Each instance in D has a class label $c_i \in C$. A classifier is a function F from $(A_1, A_2, ..., A_n)$ such that $F(A_1, A_2, ..., A_n)$ will return a class label. Given a pattern $P =\{p_1, p_2, ..., p_k\}$, a transaction T in D ($T \subseteq I$) is said to *match* a pattern P if and only if for ($1 \leq j \leq k$), the value of each i_j in T matches with p_j. If a pattern P is *frequent* in class c then the number of occurrences of P in c will be the *support* of rule $R: P \rightarrow c$, denoted $supp(R)$. The value of $supp(R)$ divided by the total number of occurrences of frequent pattern P in all classes is called the *confidence* of R, denoted as $conf(R)$. Note that a pattern P must be frequent in the class to be included in counting the *confidence*. This definition of *confidence* is different from that for association rules mining since we do not consider the total occurrence P in the whole dataset.

3 CSFP Method

In this section, we describe the CSFP method. It has four steps: First any continuous attribute in the dataset is discretized. The *entropy-based discretization* [16] is used for this with code from the MLC++ library [17]. Second, the dataset is *partitioned* according to its class labels. Third, *frequent patterns* are mined in each partition. In the fourth step, a series of *pruning* methods is used to discard weak frequent patterns. The remaining rules then become the classifier rules. Each step is explained below.

Partitioning Dataset and Mining Frequent Patterns in Each Partition. The dataset is partitioned according to the class labels so that each partition contains only the instances belonging to the same class. Each partition will be mined for frequent patterns using the same support level. By doing this, the *rare item problem* is naturally solved, as the support level for each partition will correspond to the class distribution. When distributing instances to their respective partitions, the frequency of each attribute value in each class is also counted. All possible values of the attribute are mapped to integers for convenience. For example, Fig. 1a shows the content of the *Golf* dataset [18] that has 14 instances, 4 attributes (*outlook-o, temperature-t, humidity-h, windy-w*) and 2 classes (*Play-P, Don't Play-D*). In CSFP, two partitions are created and the value of each attribute is mapped (see Fig. 1b).

Next, based on the support threshold given by the user, frequent patterns in each partition are mined using CT-PRO [8]. In CT-PRO, the transactions are stored in a compact data structure named *CFP-Tree*. Using a support level of 40%, Fig. 1c shows frequent items in each transaction that are selected, mapped to their index id in *HeaderTable* (Fig. 1d) and inserted into the *CFP-Tree*. Fig. 2 shows the content of *CFP-Tree* for the partition P. The frequent patterns in each partition are shown in Fig. 1e (absolute support values given in parentheses). When a frequent pattern is found, it is stored in a compact data structure named *CP-Tree*. Fig. 3 shows the *CP-Tree* for frequent patterns in P (in a simpler form). If a pattern is frequent in many classes, the one with the highest support is selected and its confidence is calculated and noted. Once a frequent pattern is found, rules concerning the pattern can be produced straight away.

Choosing Strong Frequent Patterns. The next step is pruning patterns that do not satisfy the confidence threshold. This process involves a simple tree traversal and pruning of nodes where their confidence < *confidence threshold*. The number of rules could be reduced further by using the *pessimistic error rate pruning* as in C4.5 [1]. It prunes a rule as follows: if the error rate of rule $r > r'$ (r' is obtained by deleting one condition from the conditions of r) then we can prune rule r. Furthermore, we use *subset pruning* where a rule $R_1: P \rightarrow c$ is said to be a *general rule* w.r.t rule $R_2: P' \rightarrow c$ if and only if $P \subset P'$, $supp(R_1) \geq supp(R_2)$ and $conf(R_1) \geq conf(R_2)$. The rationale of this pruning is that specific rules with lower support and confidence are not needed if they are already covered by the more general one.

At this point, we might still overfit the dataset by having too many rules to cover all cases in the dataset. Therefore, we employ the *database coverage pruning*. It is similar to that in CBA [4]. Given two rules, r_1 and r_2, $r_1 \succ r_2$ (r_1 has a higher rank than r_2) if and only if: 1) $conf(r_1) > conf(r_2)$; 2) $conf(r_1) = conf(r_2)$ but $supp(r_1) > supp(r_2)$; 3) $conf(r_1) = conf(r_2)$, $supp(r_1) = supp(r_2)$, but r_1 has fewer attributes than r_2. Rules are sorted in the rank descending order first, then for each case c in the training dataset D, we find whether there is any rule r that covers c starting from the highest ranked rule. If c is covered, *c* is removed from *D* and *r* is marked. The remaining unmarked rules are pruned and the majority class in the remaining data is chosen as the default class.

After performing all the pruning steps above, the remaining rules become the classifier rules. Both CBA [4] and CSFP generally produced more rules compared to C4.5. However, as reported later in the next section, both of them achieve a higher level of accuracy than C4.5.

(a)

o	*t*	*h*	*w*	*C*
sunny	hot	high	false	D
sunny	hot	high	true	D
overcast	hot	high	false	P
rain	mild	high	false	P
rain	cool	normal	false	P
rain	cool	normal	true	D
overcast	cool	normal	true	P
sunny	mild	high	false	D
sunny	cool	normal	false	P
rain	mild	normal	false	P
sunny	mild	normal	true	P
overcast	mild	high	true	P
overcast	hot	normal	false	P
rain	mild	high	true	D

(b)

P
2 6 7 10
3 5 7 10
3 4 8 10
2 4 8 9
1 4 8 10
3 5 8 10
1 5 8 9
2 5 7 9
2 6 8 10

D
1 6 7 10
1 6 7 9
3 4 8 9
1 5 7 10
3 5 7 9

(c)

P
2 10
5 10
8 10
2 8
8 10
5 8 10
5 8
2 5
2 8 10

D
1 6 7 10
1 6 7 9
3 9
1 5 7 10
3 5 7 9

(d)

P
2 3
2 4
1 2
1 3
1 2
1 2 4
1 4
3 4
1 2 3

D
1 2 6 7
1 2 3 6
3 4
1 2 5 7
2 3 4 5

(e)

P
(6) 8
(6) 10
(4) 2
(4) 5
(4) 8 10

D		
(3) 1	(2) 7 10	(2) 7 1 6
(2) 3	(2) 1 10	(2) 7 9
(2) 5	(2) 7 1 10	(3) 7 1
(2) 6	(2) 7 5	
(4) 7	(2) 9 3	
(3) 9	(2) 7 6	
(2) 10	(2) 1 6	

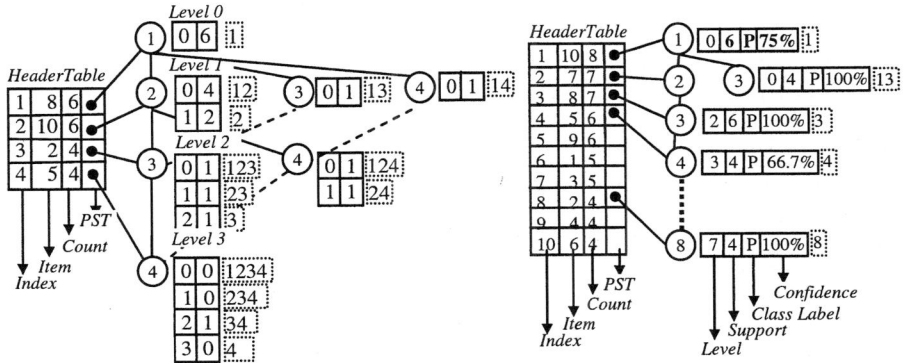

Fig. 1. Partitioning, Encoding and Frequent Patterns of the *Golf* Dataset

Fig. 2. Storing cases using *CFP-Tree*

Fig. 3. Frequent Patterns in *CP-Tree*

4 Experimental Results

In this section, CSFP is compared with other well-known classifiers including C4.5 (Rel. 8) [1], CBA [4], CMAR [5], CPAR [6], RIPPER [12], CAEP [9], DeEP [10], iCAEP [11], TAN [14], LB [13], NB [2] and *k*-NN [15] on 26 datasets from the UCI ML repository [18]. The experiments were performed on a 3 GHz Pentium 4 PC, 2

GB RAM, 110 GB HD running MS Windows 2000. CSFP was developed using MS Visual C++ 6.0. All CSFP results were obtained by *ten-fold cross validation* with *support*=1% and *confidence*=50%. Table 1 shows the accuracy comparison of CSFP with others. The best result for each dataset is indicated in bold. A blank indicates that we were not able to find previously reported results. The results where CSFP outperforms others are marked by an "*" in Table 1. Six out of 26 datasets (marked by a "+" in Table 1) are very dense datasets, which makes it infeasible to consider all frequent patterns at support of 1% and therefore we set the maximum length of the generated frequent patterns. In these experiments, we set the limit to 16.

The first part of the table shows the dataset properties and the accuracy of CSFP on each dataset. CSFP outperforms all others on 7 datasets. The average accuracy of each classifier and the average accuracy of CSFP for datasets used by others are given. We also show the accuracy improvement of CSFP over others. The second part shows the results from other associative classifiers (CBA [4], CMAR [5], CPAR [6]). The results are quoted from the respective papers. Against CBA, CMAR and CPAR, CSFP wins on 15, 13 and 12 out of 26 datasets respectively. The third part shows the results of other well-known classifiers including C4.5, RIPPER, NB, TAN, LB and *k*-NN. The results of NB, TAN, LB and *k*-NN (where k=3) are quoted from [10]. The results of C4.5 and RIPPER are quoted from [6]. CSFP wins on 15 and 18 out of 26 datasets compared to C4.5 and RIPPER respectively. CSFP also outperforms NB and LB on 8 out of 11 datasets. CSFP performs better than TAN on 5 out of 8 datasets. CSFP outperforms *k-NN* on 20 out of 25 datasets. The fourth part shows the accuracy of emerging pattern (EP)-based classifiers including CAEP, DeEP and iCAEP. The

Table 1. Comparing CSFP with other classifiers on accuracy

		1	2	3	4	5	6	7	8	9	10	11	12	13	14	15
Dataset	#inst, class, att	CSFP	CBA	CMAR	CPAR	C4.5	RIPPER	NB	TAN	LB	k-NN	CAEP	DeEP	iCAEP	#rCBA	#rCSFP
Anneal	898,6,38	97.9	96.4 *	97.3 *	98.4	94.8	95.8 *				89.7 *	85.7 *	94.4 *	95.1 *	34	41
Australian	690,2,14	86.5	86.6	86.1 *	86.2	84.7 *	87.3	85.7	85.2	85.7	66.7 *	78.6 *	84.8 *	86.1 *	148	126
Auto+	205,7,25	69.7	72.8	78.1	82	80.1	72.8				40.9 *		67.7 *		54	42
Breast-w	699,2,9	94.7	95.8	96.4	96	95	95.1	97.0		96.9	96.9	97	96.4 *	97.4	49	39
Cleve	303,2,13	84.4 *	83.3 *	82.2 *	81.5 *	78.2 *	82.2 *	82.8 *		82.2	62.6 *	83.3 *	81.2 *		78	66
Crx	690,2,15	86.9	85.9 *	84.9 *	85.7 *	84.9	84.9 *				66.6 *		84.2 *		142	124
Diabetes	768,2,8	76.9 *	74.7 *	75.8 *	75.1 *	74.2 *	74.7 *	75.1 *	76.6 *	76.7 *	69.1 *		76.8 *		57	79
German	1000,2,20	71.4	73.5	74.9	73.4	72.3	69.8 *	74.1	72.7	74.8	63.1 *	73.3	74.4	73.1	172	271
Glass	214,7,9	75.6	72.6 *	70.1 *	74.4 *	68.7 *	69.1 *				67.7 *		58.5 *		27	38
Heart	270,2,13	81.5 *	81.5 *	82.2 *	82.6 *	80.8 *	80.7 *	82.2	83.3	82.2	64.1 *	82.5 *	81.1 *	80.3 *	52	61
Hepatitis	155,2,19	87	84.9 *	80.5 *	79.4 *	80.6 *	76.7 *	83.9 *		84.5 *	70.3 *	82 *	81.2 *	83.3 *	23	32
Horse	368,2,28	80.7 *	81.3 *	82.6 *	84.2 *	82.6 *	84.8				66.3 *		84.2 *		97	93
Hypo+	3163,2,25	95	98.3	98.4	98.1	99.2	98.9				98.3	96.5	97.2	96.4	35	33
Iono+	351,2,34	89.4	91.8	91.5	92.6	90	91.2				84.0 *	87.2 *	86.2 *	90.6 *	45	41
Iris	150,3,4	94.6 *	92.9 *	94 *	94.7 *	95.3	94 *				96	94 *	96 *	93.3 *	5	12
Labor	57,2,16	95 *	83 *	89.7 *	84.7 *	79.3 *	84 *				93 *	79.3 *	87.7 *	89.7 *	12	17
Led7	3200,10,7	72.4 *	72.2 *	72.5 *	73.6	73.5	69.7 *								71	157
Lymph+	148,4,18	99.3	80.4 *	83.1 *	82.3 *	73.5 *	79 *	81.9 *	83.8 *	84.6 *	74.8 *	74.4 *	75.4 *	79.8 *	36	41
Pima	768,2,8	76.7 *	72.4 *	75.1 *	73.8 *	75.5 *	73.1 *	75.9 *	75.8 *	75.8 *	69.1 *	73.3 *	76.8 *	72.3 *	45	79
Sick+	4744,2,29	94.3	97.3	97.5	96.8	98.5	97.7				93 *		94 *		46	23
Sonar+	208,2,60	77.9 *	78.3 *	79.4 *	79.3 *	70.2 *	78.4 *				82.7 *		84.2 *		37	34
Tic-tac-toe	958,2,9	99	100	99.2	98.6	99.4	98 *				98.7	85.9 *	99.1 *	92.1 *	8	30
Vehicle	846,4,18	70	68.7 *	68.8 *	69.5 *	72.6	62.7 *	61.1 *	70.9	68.8 *	65.3 *	55.9 *	71 *	62.8 *	125	205
Waveform	5000,3,21	80.7 *	79.4 *	83.2 *	80.9 *	78.1 *	76 *	78.5 *	79.1 *	79.4 *	80.9 *	83.9 *	84.4 *	81.7 *	386	552
Wine	178,3,13	96.1 *	91.6 *	95 *	95.5 *	92.7 *	91.6 *				72.9 *	96.1 *	95.6 *	98.9 *	10	11
Zoo	101,7,16	94.2 *	94.6 *	97.1 *	95.1 *	92.2 *	88.1 *				93.9 *		97.2 *		7	9
Average		85.68	84.24	85.22	85.17	83.34	82.93	79.84	78.42	81.04	77.06	82.87	84.38	85.80	69	87
CSFP Avg for Comparison for Datasets Used by Others			85.68	85.68	85.68	85.68	85.68	82.65	80.38	82.65	86.21	88.19	86.21	88.43		
Accuracy Improvement			1.4	0.5	0.5	2.3	2.7	2.8	2.0	1.6	9.2	5.3	1.8	2.6		
Win against others	7		1	1	4	3	2	0	1	0	1	0	5	2		
CSFP Wins			15/26	13/26	12/26	15/26	18/26	8/11	5/8	8/11	20/25	12/17	14/25	10/16		

results of CAEP and iCAEP are quoted from [11]. The results of DeEP are quoted from [10] where $\alpha=12$. CSFP outperforms CAEP on 12 out of 17 datasets. Against DeEP, CSFP wins on 14 out of 25 datasets. Compared to iCAEP, CSFP outperforms on 10 out of 16 datasets. Since the average accuracy of CSFP is always better than others, we can claim that CSFP improves the accuracy with respect to previous associative classification, other EP-based classifiers, and other well-known classifiers.

The last part of the table shows average number of classifier rules for CBA and CSFP. The average number of rules produced by CSFP is somewhat more than CBA. In [4], it is mentioned that the number of rules in CBA is generally more than for C4.5. The results of CBA included in the table are quoted from [4] where CBA used single minimum support in generating the rules, and so rules from infrequent classes were not generated. As CSFP uses a partitioning method to ensure that enough rules from infrequent classes are generated, naturally more rules are produced compared to CBA.

5 Conclusion

We have presented a new classifier named CSFP. Unlike previous associative classifiers, CSFP builds the classifier based on strong frequent patterns without the need to generate association rules. CSFP is compared with other well-known classifiers on accuracy including previous associative classifiers, EP-based classifiers and other well-known classifiers on 26 test datasets from UCI ML repository. The results show that, in terms of accuracy, CSFP outperforms others.

Though CT-PRO is faster than other best-known algorithms, mining all frequent patterns with very low support threshold on very dense datasets would be infeasible. In this paper, we solved it by limiting the length of patterns generated. However, some attributes may not be considered in forming the classifiers and therefore the accuracy might be affected. Mining *maximal frequent patterns* or *closed frequent patterns* could be used as alternative ways to make CSFP feasible for dense datasets.

References

1. Quinlan, J. R.: C4.5: Program for Machine Learning. Morgan Kaufmann (1992)
2. Duda, R.O., Hart, P.E., Stork, D.G.: Pattern Classification. NY: John Wiley & Sons (2001)
3. Agrawal, R., Imielinski, T., Swami, A.: Mining Association Rules between Sets of Items in Large Databases. Proc. of ACM SIGMOD, Washington DC (1993)
4. Liu, B., Hsu, W., Ma, Y.: Integrating Classification and Association Rule Mining. Proc. of ACM SIGKDD, New York (1998)
5. Li, W., Han, J., Pei, J.: CMAR: Accurate and Efficient Classification based on Multiple Class-Association Rules. Proc. of IEEE ICDM, San Jose, CA (2001)
6. Yin, X., Han, J.: CPAR: Classification based on Predictive Association Rules. Proc. of the SIAM International Conference on Data Mining (SDM), San Fransisco, CA (2003)
7. Liu, B., Ma, Y., Wong, C.K.: Improving an Association Rule Based Classifier. Proc. of PKDD 2000, Lyon, France (2000)
8. Gopalan, R.P., Sucahyo, Y.G.: High Performance Frequent Pattern Extraction using Compressed FP-Trees. Proc. of SIAM Int. Workshop on HPDM, Orlando, USA (2004)

9. Dong, G., Zhang, X., Wong, L., Li, J.: CAEP: Classification by Aggregating Emerging Patterns. Proc. of the 2nd Int. Conf. on Discovery Science, Tokyo, Japan (1999)
10. Li, J., Dong, G., Ramamohanarao, K., Wong, L.: DeEPs: A New Instance-Based Lazy Discovery and Classification System. Machine Learning. **54** (2004) 99-124
11. Zhang, X., Dong, G., Ramamohanarao, K.: Information-based Classification by Aggregating Emerging Patterns. Proc. of IDEAL, Hong Kong (2000)
12. Cohen, W.: Fast Effective Rule Induction. Proc. of ICML, Tahoe City, CA (1995)
13. Meretakis, D., Wuthrich, B.: Extending Naive Bayes Classifiers using Long Itemsets. Proc. of ACM SIGKDD, San Diego (1999)
14. Friedman, N., Geiger, D., Goldszmidt, M.: Bayesian Network Classifiers. Machine Learning. **29** (1997) 131-163
15. Cover, T.M., Hart, P.E.: Nearest neighbor pattern classification. IEEE Transactions on Information Theory. **13** (1967) 21-27
16. Fayyad, U.M., Irani, K.B.: Multi-interval discretization of continuous-valued attributes for classification learning. Proc. of IJCAI (1993)
17. Kohavi, R., John, G., Long, R., Manley, D., Pfleger, K.: MLC++: a Machine Learning Library in C++. Tools with Artificial Intelligence. (1994) 740-743
18. Blake, C L., Merz, C.J.: UCI repository of machine learning databases. Irvine, CA: University of California, Department of Information and Computer Science (1998)

Color Texture Analysis Using Wavelet-Based Hidden Markov Model

Ding Siyi, Yang Jie, and Xu Qing

Inst. of Image Processing & Pattern Recognition, Shanghai Jiao tong Univ.,
Shanghai BOX251 1954 Huashan Road, Shanghai, P.R. China
qingxu8@hotmail.com

Abstract. Wavelet Domain Hidden Markov Model (WD HMM), in particular Hidden Markov Tree (HMT), has recently been proposed and applied to gray level image analysis. In this paper, color texture analysis using WD HMM is studied. In order to combine color and texture information to one single model, we extend WD HMM by grouping the wavelet coefficients from different color planes to one vector. The grouping way is chose according to a tradeoff between computation complexity and effectiveness. Besides, we propose Multivariate Gaussian Mixture Model (MGMM) to approximate the marginal distribution of wavelet coefficient vectors and to capture the interactions of different color planes. By employing our proposed approach, we can improve the performance of WD HMM on color texture classification. The experiment shows that our proposed WD HMM provides an 85% percentage of correct classifications (PCC) on 68 color images from an Oulu Texture Database and outperforms other methods.

Keywords: wavelet domain hidden Markov model, color texture analysis, Multivariate Gaussian Mixture Model.

1 Introduction

Texture and color are two very important attributes to describe the content of image, especially when we deal with real world images. With the advancements of the computer vision technology and applications, there has arisen a high demand for effective characterization of color texture. In this paper, we have developed an approach based on wavelet-domain hidden Markov model to characterize the color and texture jointly.

Wavelet-domain hidden Markov tree (WD HMT) model has recently been proposed by M.S.Crouse [1]. This method has been successfully applied to texture analysis [5] [6], because it can effectively characterize the joint statistics of the wavelet transforms by capturing the inter-scale dependences of the wavelet coefficients. But all applications of WD HMT are limited to gray texture. A natural extension of WD HMT for color texture is to model each color plane separately using WD HMT. This assumes different color planes are independent. However, we have observed that the regular and homogenous structures often results in certain dependencies across different color components and thus this assumption is not so sound.

In this paper, we address this problem by developing an improved version of WD HMT, which captures not only the inter-scale dependences but also the interactions between different color components. We also investigate the choice of color representation space, which have a great effect on the performance of a color analysis method. In our work, we have performed our proposed approaches in both RGB and K-L (Karhunen Loeve transform) or I1I2I3 [4] color space to evaluate the choice of the color space.

This paper is organized as follows. In section 2, we review the previous work related to the WD HMT methods. In Section 3, we develop a novel WD HMT approach to characterizing color textures accurately by involving more sophisticated graph structure. In section 4, we show how this model can be applied to color texture classification. In section 4, we compare our model with other wavelet-based methods and present the simulation results. Finally, section 5 summarizes the paper.

2 Related Works

WD HMT provides an effective approach to model both the non-Gaussian statistics and the persistence property across scales of the wavelet coefficients. The concept of WD HMT is briefly reviewed in this section.

First, to characterize non-Gaussianity of the discrete wavelet transform, WD HMT employs a Gaussian mixture model (GMM) to model the wavelet coefficients distribution density. In a 2D WD HMT model, denote $w_{j,i,k}^B$ to be the wavelet coefficient. In this presentation, B represents sub-band detail image ($B \in \{HH, HL, LH\}$). j indexes scale (1<j<J) –smaller j corresponds to higher resolution analysis. (i, k) is the spatial location of this wavelet coefficient in the j scale. The distribution of wavelet coefficient $w_{j,i,k}^B$ is determined by a discrete hidden state random variable $S_{j,i,k}^B$, whose probability mass function can be expressed as, $P(S_{j,i,k}^B = m) = p_{j,i,k}^B(m)$ (m=0....M-1). Here are M hidden states totally. Conditioning on its state $S_{j,i,k}^B = m$, $w_{j,i,k}^B$ follows a Gaussian distribution with mean $\alpha_{j,i,k,m}^B$ and variance $\sigma_{j,i,k,m}^B$. By increasing M and allowing non-zero means, we can approximate the real distributions arbitrarily close [1] and we set M=2 and $\mu_m = 0$ for simplicity here. Therefore, we can parameterize the GMM of $w_{j,i,k}^B$ by $\pi \sim \{p_{j,i,k}^B(m), \sigma_{j,i,k,m}^B \mid m \sim 0,1\}$ and the overall probability density function of $w_{j,i,k}^B$ is expressed as:
$$w_{j,i,k}^B \sim f_{j,k,i}^B(x) \sim \sum_{m \sim 0}^{M-1} p_{j,k,i}^m g(x, \sigma_{j,k,i}^m) \tag{1}$$

where $g(x, \sigma_{j,k,i}^m)$ denotes the zeros mean Gaussian distribution with variance $\sigma_{j,k,i}^m$.

Second, to capture the persistence property of the wavelet transform, a wavelet-domain hidden Markov tree model (HMT) is developed by M.S.Crouse [1]. By connecting the hidden state (parent) at a coarse scale to the four hidden states (child) at the next intermediate scale, we obtain a graph with tree-structured dependencies between state variables. Thus a state transition matrix for each parent->child link statistically quantifies the degree of persistence of wavelet coefficients. Furthermore, to obtain a robust estimation, the wavelet coefficients in the same scale are assumed to share the same statistics (the same GMM and transition matrix), which is called *tying*. Thus, when a J-scale wavelet transform is preformed on an image, its 2-D HMT (M=2, zero mean) is parameterized by

$$\theta_{HMT} = \{P_J^B(m), \varepsilon_{j,j-1}^B(m,n), \sigma_{B,j,m}^2 \mid B \in \{HH, HL, LH\}; j = 1,......J; m, n = 0, 1\}$$

Where $\varepsilon_{j,j-1}^B(m,n)$ is the transition probability of the Markov chain from scale j to scale (j-1) in sub-band B and P_J^B is the probability mass function of hidden state on J scale. θ_{HMT} can be fitted to a given W (a wavelet transform of an image) by the tree-structured EM training algorithm, which maximizes the HMT model posterior likelihood $f(W \mid \theta_{HMT})$.

3   Wavelet-Domain Hidden Markov Model for Color Image

The color image wavelet coefficients are obtained by employing discrete wavelet transform (DWT) on each color component image separately. Modeling the color wavelet coefficients using our enhanced WD HMT, we have taken into account both the interactions of different color planes and the dependences across scales. And, in order to put our emphasis on the study of the color texture characterization, we assume that the three different sub-bands are independent in our statistical model. Thus we model a color image using three independent trees (WD HMT), each of which captures the statistics of all three color components at one orientation sub-band of the wavelet transform. We will introduce this improved WD HMT in this section.

Given a color image I composed of three color component images ($I_{X_1}, I_{X_2}, I_{X_3}$) and their corresponding wavelet coefficients ($W_{X_1}, W_{X_2}, W_{X_3}$). Here $X_m, \{m \sim 1,2,3\}$ denotes one color component in a color space. To incorporate the dependencies between different color planes, wavelet coefficients at the same location, scale and sub-band, but different color planes are grouped to one vector. Specifically, denote the wavelet coefficient of A component ($A \in \{X_1, X_2, X_3\}$) at sub-band B ($B \in \{HL, HH, LH\}$), located at (k, i) in j scale as $w_{B,k,i,j}^A$. The three coefficients $w_{B,k,i,j}^{X_1}, w_{B,k,i,j}^{X_2}, w_{B,k,i,j}^{X_3}$ are grouped to produce one vector,

$$\overline{w}_{B,k,i,j} \sim \{w_{B,k,i,j}^{X_1}, w_{B,k,i,j}^{X_2}, w_{B,k,i,j}^{X_3}\}^T,$$

We assume that the distribution density of the wavelet coefficient vectors is approximated by a multivariate Gaussian mixture model (MGMM). The justification for this is that, since any marginal density from a multivariate Gaussian density is also a Gaussian density, the marginal density from a MGMM is also a Gaussian mixture model. Thus, we can expect that MGMM also captures the marginal distribution densities of the three dependent color components and the color component dependencies are captured via the non-diagonal entries in the covariance matrices of the multivariate Gaussian densities. So the wavelet vector is also associated with a hidden state. Here we also assume M=2 and zero means for MGMM. Thus the marginal distributions of the wavelet coefficient vector $\vec{w}^B_{j,k,i}$ in the j scale can be expressed as:

$$\vec{w}^B_{j,k,i} \sim f^B_j(\vec{x}) \sim \sum_{m \sim 0}^{M-1} p^m_j g(\vec{x}, C^m_j) \qquad (2)$$

where $g(\vec{x}, C^m_j)$ denotes the zero-mean 3-demension multivariate Gaussian density with covariance matrix C^m_j.

In order to capture the persistence, the color wavelet coefficient vectors are then organized into a quad-tree structure that connects each vector to its four child vectors at the next intermediate scale of the same location. State probability transition matrices are also used to describe the parent->child link relationships of these vectors. Thus, tied within scales, HMT (M=2, zero means) for color texture is parameterized as follows:

$$\theta_{HMT\_color} \sim \{p^B_j(m), \varepsilon^B_{j,j-1}(m,n), C_{B,j,m} \mid B \in \{HH, HL, LH\}; j \sim 1, 2, ..., J; m, n \sim 0, 1\}$$

where $\varepsilon^B_{j,j-1}(m,n)$ is the transition probability of the Markov chain from scale j to scale j-1 in sub-band B. P^B_J denotes the probability mass function of hidden state on J scale. Given $\overline{W}$, the θ_{HMT_color} can be estimated by employing the tree-structured EM training algorithm, which can maximize the HMT model likelihood $f(\overline{W} \mid \theta_{HMT\_color})$. The difference from EM training algorithm proposed by M.S. Crouse [1] is that GMM in the model is replaced by a MGMM in our EM algorithm. In our study, we apply this HMT for color image to color texture analysis, and obtain a superior result.

4 Experiments and Discussions

Our experiments are performed on the test suite Qutex_TC_00013 provided by Qutex texture database [2]. This database includes a collection of natural scenes. The test suite provides meaningful entity for the empirical evaluation of a candidate texture analysis algorithm. A database of 1360 color texture images (128x128) was constructed by splitting each one of 68 original texture image (746x538) into 20 sub images (128x128). Half of the sub texture databases are used as the training set, while the rest 680 images serve as a testing set. The following six experiments have been conducted: (1) We obtain the intensity images by computing the luminance of the color images, thus the color information is discarded. After a depth of 5 DWT is performed on these gray level images (here we use db-8 wavelet transform), the EM algorithm is applied to estimate the HMT parameters using the 16 training sub-images for each class. Then we use Maximum Likelihood (ML) ruler to classify the test images according to the 68 HMT models. (2) Each color component (RGB) is wavelet transformed (5-scale db8) separately and then the wavelet energy correlation signature [3] vectors are computed for each detailed sub-images, including training and test images. Here we adopt a KNN (k=15) classifier. (3) Each color component (RGB) is also wavelet transformed (5-scale db8) separately and then the EM algorithm is applied to train WD HMT for every color plane of color texture from the training set. Thus, we get three HMT model for one color texture. Since the three color plane is assumed to be independent, we obtain the total likelihood for one test texture by multiplying the three model likelihood. Finally, Maximum Likelihood (ML) ruler is used as classifier. (4) Each color component (RGB) is also wavelet transformed (5-scale db8) separately and then the EM algorithm is applied to train WD HMT vector model from training set. Finally, Maximum Likelihood (ML) ruler is used as classifier. (5) We conduct the same experiment as experiment 3, except that the RGB space is replaced by I1I2I3 (Karhunen Loeve transform) space. (6) We conduct the same experiment as experiment 4, except that the RGB space is replaced by I1I2I3 (Karhunen Loeve transform) space.

Table 1. Classification result (PCC) of 6 methods on 68 color texture images

Methods	Mean PCC	Standard deviation PCC
WDHMT for the gray image of color texture	0.4338	0.3079
wavelet energy correlation signature	0.7544	0.2707
WDHMT for modeling color planes (RGB) separately	0.7647	0.2951
WDHMT for modeling color planes (RGB) jointly	0.8515	0.2256
WDHMT for modeling color planes (I1I2I3) separately	0.7912	0.2900
WDHMT for modeling color planes (I1I2I3) jointly	0.8500	0.2483

Here we use the average percentage of correct classification (PCC) to evaluate the classification performance for each method, as shown in Table1. The PCC is computed for each class of color textures. So 68 PCCs are obtained. Our table1 just shows the average and standard deviation of 68 PCCs. Compared with method 1 (43.38% 0.3079), method 3 (75.44% 0.2707) and 5 (79.12% 0.2900), method 6 (85% 0.2483) and 4 (85.15% 0.2256) gain the better PCC over the 68 color textures, and overall better numerical stability. Method 1 fails to consider the color information, while the later four methods gain their improvement by considering color and structure information together. This proves that we can obtain a more effective characterization of color texture by combining color and structure information. Moreover, the later four methods also outperform energy signature method (75.44% 0.2707). The reason for this is that hidden Markov models can represent the statistics of wavelet coefficients more precisely than energy signature method, which only captures the mean and covariance matrix of the wavelet vector. Besides, the WD HMM methods can capture the dependences across scales.

We also observe that method 4 outperforms method 3, because method 3 ignores the correlated information of different color components. However, method 5 gains better PCC than method 3. This situation can be explained by the statistical un-correlation of different color components in I1I2I3 color space and thus the dependencies between different color planes are weaker than in RGB color space. Therefore, ignoring dependencies between color planes may cause little information loss.

6 Conclusions

In this paper, we have extended the wavelet domain hidden Markov model method to color texture analysis. And among the four wavelet-based methods, the proposed HMT for color texture provides the best classification results, because it not only captures the dependencies between scales but also take into account the interactions of the three color components. We can obtain over 85% average PCC, which has nearly much improvement over the HMT for luminance image. Besides, this approach has better numerical stability than other methods. However, we ignored the dependences across the three orientations and the computational complexity is still a big disadvantage. This would render it inappropriate for the image retrieval systems. In the future, we intend to simplify the computation by investigating K-L distance and other methods, and at the same time, modify our approach to capture the interactions of orientations and color planes together.

References

[1] M. S. Crouse, R. D. Nowak, R. G. Baraniuk. Wavelet-based statistical signal processing using hidden Markov model. IEEE Trans. Signal Proc. 46(4) 886-902. 1998.
[2] University of Oulu texture database, available at http://www.outex.oulu.fi/outex.php
[3] G. Van de Wouwer, S. Livens, P. Scheunders, D. Van Dyck. Color texture classification by wavelet energy correlation signatures. Pattern Recognition, Special issue on Color and Texture Analysis. 1998.
[4] Y. Ohta, 1985. Knowledge based interpretation of outdoor natural scenes, Pitman Publishing, London.
[5] G. Fan and X.G. Xia. Image de-noising Using Local Contextual Hidden Markov Model in the Wavelet-Domain. IEEE Signal Processing Lett. vol. 8. 125-128. 2001.
[6] G. Fan and X.G. Xia. Maximum likelihood texture analysis and classification using wavelet-domain hidden Markov models. Proc. 34th Asilomar Conf. Signals, Systems, and Computers Pacific Grove, CA, Oct. 2000.

Contributions of Domain Knowledge and Stacked Generalization in AI-Based Classification Models

Weiping Wu[1], Vincent ChengSiong Lee[1], and TingYean Tan[2]

[1] School of Business Systems,
[2] Department of Accounting and Finance,
Monash University, Wellington Road, Clayton, Victoria 3800, Australia
Tel: +61 3-9905{+5363, +2360, +2376}, Fax: +613-99055159
{weiping.wu, vincent.lee}@infotech.monash.edu.au
tingyean.tan@buseco.monash.edu.au
http://www.monash.edu.au/index.html

Abstract. We exploit the merits of C4.5 decision tree classifier with two stacking meta-learners: back-propagation multilayer perceptron neural network and naïve-Bayes respectively. The performance of these two hybrid classification schemes have been empirically tested and compared with C4.5 decision tree using two US data sets (raw data set and new data set incorporated with domain knowledge) simultaneously to predict US bank failure. Significant improvements in prediction accuracy and training efficiency have been achieved in the schemes based on new data set. The empirical test results suggest that the proposed hybrid schemes perform marginally better in term of AUC criterion.

1 Introduction

Prior research studies [2, 9, 10] on classification and clustering fields have generally concluded that the optimum solution of using classification techniques on a given problem is underpinned on the combination of multifaceted efforts. The efforts include specification of classification model structures, selection of training data, representation of input features and definition of search space.

Real-world data contain a large number of features, some of which are either redundant or irrelevant to a given task. The presence of redundant or irrelevant features can mask or obscure the distribution of truly relevant features for a target concept [6, 7]. Besides, high dimensional feature space may give rise to the feature interaction problems. Consequently, it is difficult for classification methods to learn concepts effectively and efficiently [9]. One solution is to transform original feature space into a more appropriate representation by constructing new features. Domain knowledge plays an important role in helping effective construction as well as efficient search of the input feature space [5]. In the process of feature construction, a high-dimension feature space is projected to a low-dimension space such that most information of original feature set is retained. One of the motivations of our study is to discover how domain knowledge would improve the performance of classification of bank failure.

AI research has suggested that hybridizing two or more AI techniques can enhance the classification accuracy compared with using just one individual technique. For example, decision tree algorithm has high executing efficiency and good comprehensibility with the analysis process can be checked and adequately explained [12], but its performance degrades when the data samples contain numeric attributes, missing values, and unobservable noises. By introducing the stacking meta-learner of back-propagation mulitlayer perceptron neural network (BP-MLP NN) and naïve-Bayes respectively, the resulting hybrid classifier can exploit the learning power of neural network, and the discretization ability and missing-values-immunity of naïve-Bayes with the salient characteristics of C4.5 decision tree kept intact.

The rest of the paper is organized as follows. In Section 2, the principle of stacked generalization and choice of classifiers are explained. In Section 3 we describe the data samples and their representation. Empirical test results are provided in Section 4. Section 5 concludes the paper with a summary of our main findings.

2 Stacked Generalization

Every classifier that uses different knowledge representation has different learning biases. The learning biases of various classifiers can be effectively integrated through a technique, called stacking [8] (or abbreviated as stacked generalization) to yield improved performance by the resultant hybrid classifier. When stacking is used for classification, instances is first fed into the level-0 model (base-learner), which is used to classify the instances in the training data set, and the predictions are then fed into the level-1 model (meta-learner). To allow level-1 classifier to make full use of the training data, cross-validation will be adopted for level-0 learner [11].

ROC curve is employed in identifying the appropriate learning technique to use in the level-0 and level-1. ROC curve, a plot of true positive rate against false positive rate across a series of decision thresholds, is a good visualization way for performance evaluation. A point on the curve is a measure of the prediction accuracy at a particular decision threshold. One classifier has better performance than other if its ROC point is positioned to the north-west (TP rate is higher, FP rate is lower) of the other [3]. The two measures of interests (TP- and FP-rate) can be computed as *True positive rate= TP/(TP+FN)* and *False positive rate=FP/(FP+TN)*. True Positive (TP) means a positive instance is classified as positive. False Positives (FP) means a negative instance is classified as positive. False Negative (FN) means a positive instance is classified as negative. True Negative (TN) means a negative instance is classified as negative.

The AUC (area under the ROC curve) is a single measure of performance that is invariant to the decision threshold chosen [1]. The larger AUC of a classifier means the probability that the classifier will rank a randomly chosen positive instance higher than a randomly chosen negative instance [3]. By choosing the classifier that has the best AUC as base-learner, and another one that has relative better ROC in some specific thresholds as meta-learner in a stacking scheme, a hybrid classifier that has improved AUC can be acquired.

In this study, C4.5 decision tree will be the base classifier, naïve-Bayes and back-propagation multi-layer perceptron network will serve as meta-learner respectively that combining the guesses of level-0 learner into the final prediction. WEKA (Waikato Environment for Knowledge Analysis) is employed to build the classifiers and implement stacking.

3 Data Representation and Domain Knowledge

The raw data set including 19 features (table 1) is taken from the call reports published by the Federal Deposit Insurance Corporation (www.fdic.gov).

Table 1. Input Features in Raw Data Set

Data Sources	Features	Description
Balance Sheet (Schedule RC)		
RCON0081+RCON0071	Cash_due	Cash and due from bank
RCON2145+RCON2160	Pre_oth_asset	Premises and other assets
RCON2170	Asset	Total Asset
RCON2200	Deposit	Deposits
RCON6636	Int_dep	Interest-bearing deposit
RCON6631	No_int_dep	Noninterest-bearing deposit
RCON3190	Borrow	Borrowing
RCON3210	Equity	Equity capital
Securities (Schedule RC-B)		
RCONA549+ROCNA550+RCONA551+RCONA555+ RCONA556+RCONA557+RCONA561	Short_sec	Short-term securities
RCONA552+RCONA553+RCONA554+RCONA558+ RCONA559+RCONA560+RCONA562	Long_sec	Long-term securities
Loans and Lease (Schedule RC-C)		
RCON1616	High_loans	High variable loans
RCONA570+ROCNA571+RCONA572+RCONA573+ RCONA574+RCONA575	Med_loans	Medium variable loans
RCONA564+ROCNA565+RCONA566+RCONA567+ RCONA568+RCONA569	Fix_loans	Fixed-rate loans
Income Statement (RC-I)		
RIAD4107	Int_inc	Revenues
RIAD4073	Int_exp	Interest expenses
RIAD4079	Noint_inc	No interest income
RIAD4093	Oth_exp	Other expenses
RIAD4302	Tax	Taxes
RIAD4340	Net_inc	Net Income

Data in table 1 consists of bank data of year 1990 including 127 banks failed in 1991, 122 banks failed in 1992, and 249 non-failed banks that have been matched respectively with the failed banks by states, institution class, total asset, deposit and number of offices. The matching is needed for eliminating the influence of local economic conditions and a bank's operating environment. A second data set hereafter referred to new data set (table 2) is created using the return and risk measurements based on return-on-equity model [4], which includes 10 financial ratios (features) representing domain knowledge (incorporated into the data representation).

Table 2. Input Features in New Data Set

Variable Name	Description
Return Measurements	
(Int_inc-Int_exp)/(Asset-Cash_due-Pre_oth_asset)	Interest margin=(Interest income – Interest expenses)/Earning assets
Net_inc/ Int_inc	Net margin=Net income/Revenues
Int_inc/ Asset	Asset utilization=Revenues/Assets
Net_inc/ Asset	Return on asset=Net income/Assets
Asset/ Equity	Leverage multiplier=Assets/Equity
Net_inc/ Equity	Return on capital=Net income/Equity
Risk Measurements	
Short_sec/ Deposit	Liquidity risk=Short-term securities/Deposits
(Short_sec+High_loans + Med_loans) /(Int_dep+ Borrow)	Interest rate risk=Interest-sensitive assets /Interest-sensitive liabilities
Med_loans/ Asset	Credit risk=Medium loans/Assets
Equity /(High_loans+ Med_loans+ Fix _loans+ Long_sec)	Capital risk=Capital/Risk assets

4 Empirical Test Results

Empirical tests are conducted on the two data sets using C4.5 decision tree, BP-MLP NN, naïve-Bayes and two stacking schemes with C4.5 decision tree as base-learner and the other two classifiers as meta-learner respectively. Ten-fold cross-validation is applied in this experiment because a single partition of training and test sample would not yield a reliable estimator of the true prediction accuracy of classification methods on a limited data set [10]. The averaging of ten-fold trainings yields more representative result.

Table 3 lists the evaluation indicators of the tests, including several numeric measures reflecting the aggregated prediction accuracy, TP Rate and FP rate of bank failure, and value of AUC etc. Figures 1-4 compare the ROC curves of the hybrid classifier with two single classifiers (serve as base- or meta-learner in the stacking scheme) using the two data sets respectively.

5 Conclusion

Our empirical test results suggest the following five conclusions.

- In both bank failure prediction data sets, C4.5 decision tree is the best single classifier, which justifies base-learner for the stacking schemes;
- Naïve-Bayes and BP-MLP NN have better classification accuracy than C4.5 decision tree when lower thresholds in ROC curves are adopted. ROC curves for the stacking schemes are approximately convex hull for their base-learner and meta-learner, causing AUC values of the stacking schemes to be higher than single classifiers (Figures 1-4);

Table 3. Indicators of Prediction Accuracy

	Raw Data Set					New Data Set				
	NN	NB	C4.5	NN+C4.5	NB+C4.5	NN	NB	C4.5	NN+C4.5	NB+C4.5
Correctly Classified instances(%)	68.3333	52.9167	82.7083	82.7083	82.7083	82.5	75.625	87.5	87.7083	87.7083
Incorrectly Classified Instances(%)	31.6667	47.0833	17.2917	17.2917	17.2917	17.5	24.375	12.5	12.2917	12.2917
Kappa statistic	0.3667	0.0583	0.6542	0.6542	0.6542	0.65	0.5125	0.75	0.7542	0.7542
Mean absolute error	0.4103	0.4707	0.201	0.2769	0.1938	0.2114	0.2425	0.1527	0.2	0.1324
Root mean squared error	0.4581	0.6302	0.3916	0.3764	0.3908	0.3541	0.4545	0.3236	0.3158	0.3334
Relative absolute error(%)	82.0638	94.1429	40.1984	55.3794	38.7592	42.2871	48.4977	30.5339	39.9912	26.489
Root relative squared error(%)	91.6144	126.05	78.3198	75.2795	78.1618	70.8178	90.8921	64.7238	63.1601	66.68
Time taken (seconds)	13	0.03	0.17	2.13	1.06	3.8	0.02	0.03	1.5	0.38
TP rate	0.608	0.217	0.846	0.85	0.85	0.838	0.521	0.892	0.879	0.892
FP rate	0.242	0.158	0.192	0.196	0.196	0.188	0.008	0.142	0.125	0.138
AUC	0.7344	0.5707	0.821	0.8467	0.8349	0.8983	0.8843	0.9012	0.9181	0.9272

Notes: C4.5+ NN denotes stacking scheme with C4.5 decision tree as base-learner and back-propagation multi layer perceptron network as meta-learner;
C4.5+ NB denotes stacking scheme with C4.5 decision tree as base-learner and naïve-Bayes back as meta-learner.

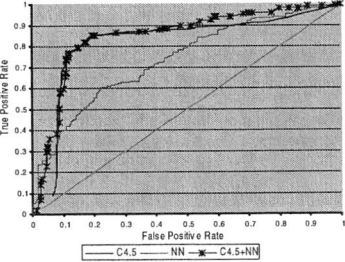

Fig. 1. C4.5+NN on Raw Data Set

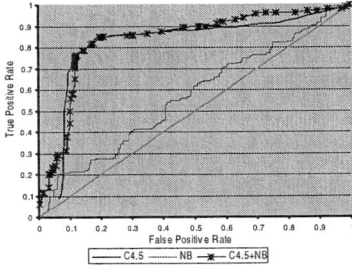

Fig. 2. C4.5+NB on Raw Data Set

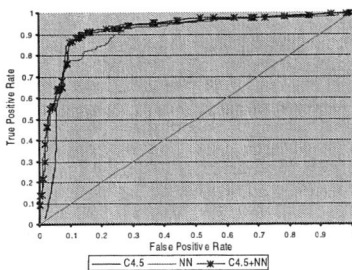

Fig. 3. C4.5+NN on New Data Set

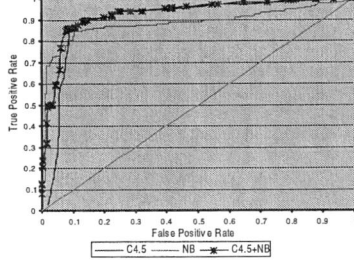

Fig. 4. C4.5+NB on New Data Set

- Two stacking schemes have slightly good performance over C4.5 decision tree in respect of AUC value, though it is hard to distinguish their advantages by referring to the four error measures. When BP-MLP NN serves as meta-learner, tradeoffs between absolute errors and squared errors (volatility) are found when adjusting the momentum value. For example, increasing the momentum constant lead to rise of root squared error and drop of absolute error, which justifies the stabilising effect of momentum constant;
- All classification methods perform better on the data incorporated domain knowledge, which is demonstrated by higher correctly classified rate, Kappa statistic, AUC value, lower error rates and time taken in the experiments; and
- Smaller data set contains one year failed bank data with 244 records has been used in previous experiments, and even ambiguous difference is found among the classifiers. It is reasonable to infer that given larger data set the distinction between the different classifiers may become more significant.

References

1. Bradley, A.P., The use of the area under the ROC curve in the evaluation of machine learning algorithms, *Pattern Recognition,* Vol. 30, 1145-1159, 1997.
2. Cherkassky, V. and Lari-Najafi, H., Data representation for diagnostic neural networks. *IEEE Expert,* Vol. 7, 43-53, 1992.
3. Fawcett, T., ROC Graphs: Notes and Practical Considerations for Researchers, http://www.hpl.hp.com/personal/Tom_Fawcett/papers/ROC101.pdf , 2004.
4. George, H.H., Donald, G.S. and Alan, B.C.: *Bank management: text and cases.* John Wiley & Sons, Inc., 1994.
5. Hirsh, H. and Noordewier, M., Using background knowledge to improve inductive learning of DAS sequences, in *Proceedings of IEEE Conference on AI for Applications,* 1994.
6. John, G., Kohavi, R. and Pfleger, K., Irrelevant features and subset selection problem, in *Proceedings of 11th International Conference on Machine Learning,* 1994.
7. Koller, D. and Sahami, M., Toward optimal feature selection, in *Proceedings of the 13th International Conference on Machine Learning,* 1996.
8. Ledezma, A., Aler, R. and Borrajo, D., Empirical study of a stacking state-space - Tools with Artificial Intelligence, in *Proceedings of the 13th International Conference. IEEE Expert,* Vol. 7-9, 210 – 217, 2001.
9. Piramuthu, S., Shaw, M.J. and Gentry, J.A., A classification approach using multi-layered neural networks, *Decision Support Systems,* Vol. 11, 509-525, 1994.
10. Radcliffe, N.J. and Surry, P.D., Fundamental limitations on search algorithms: Evolutionary computing in perspective. In: Jan Van Leeuwen (Ed.), *Computer Science Today: Recent Trends and Developments: Lecture Notes in Computer Science,* Springer-Verlag, 1995.
11. Witten, I.H. and Frank, E., *Data mining—Practical machine learning tools and techniques with Java implementation,* Morgan Kaufmann Publisher, 1999.
12. Zhou, Z.H. and Jiang, Y., NeC4.5: Neural Ensemble Based C4.5, *IEEE Transactions on knowledge and data engineering,* Vol. 16, No. 6, 770-773, 2004.

Discovering Interesting Association Rules by Clustering

Yanchang Zhao, Chengqi Zhang, and Shichao Zhang

Faculty of Information Technology, Univ. of Technology, Sydney, Australia
{yczhao, chengqi, zhangsc}@it.uts.edu.au

Abstract. There are a great many metrics available for measuring the interestingness of rules. In this paper, we design a distinct approach for identifying association rules that maximizes the interestingness in an applied context. More specifically, the interestingness of association rules is defined as the dissimilarity between corresponding clusters. In addition, the interestingness assists in filtering out those rules that may be uninteresting in applications. Experiments show the effectiveness of our algorithm.

Keywords: Interestingness, Association Rules, Clustering.

1 Introduction

Association rule mining does not discover the true correlation relationship, because high minimum support usually generates commonsense knowledge, while low minimum support generates huge number of rules, the majority of which are uninformative [8]. Therefore, many metrics for interestingness have been devised to help find interesting rules while filtering out uninteresting ones.

The interestingness is related to the properties of surprisingness, usefulness and novelty of the rule [5]. In general, the evaluation of the interestingness of discovered rules has both an objective (data-driven) and a subjective (user-driven) aspect [6]. Subjective approaches require that a domain expert work on a huge set of mined rules. Some adopted another approach to find "Optimal rules" according to some objective interestingness measure. There are various interestingness measures, such as ϕ-coefficient, Mutual Information, J-Measures, Gini indes, Conviction, collective strength, Jaccard, and so on [11].

To the best of our knowledge, for a rule $A \rightarrow B$, most existing interestingness measures are computed with $P(A)$, $P(B)$ and $P(A, B)$. In a quite different way, we devise a measure of interestingness by clustering. By clustering the items, the distances or dissimilarities between clusters are computed as the interestingness to filter discovered rules. Experiments show that many uninteresting rules can be filtered out effectively and rules of high interestingness remain. Then a domain expert can select interesting patterns from the remaining small set of rules.

The rest of the paper is organized as follows. In Section 2, we introduce the related work in studying the interestingness of association patterns. The idea of using clustering to measure the interestingness is described in detail in Section 3. Section 4 shows our experimental results. Conclusions are made in Section 5.

2 Related Work

The measures of rule interestingness fall into two categories, subjective and objective. Subjective measures focus on finding interesting patterns by matching against a given set of user beliefs. A rule is considered interesting if it conforms to or conflicts with the user's beliefs [2, 9]. On the contrary, objective ones measure the interestingness in terms of their probabilities.

Support and confidence are the most widely used to select interesting rules. With Agrawal and Srikant's itemset measures [1], those rules which exceed a predetermined minimum threshold for support and confidence are considered to be interesting.

In addition to support and confidence, many other measures are introduced in [11], which are ϕ-coefficient, Goodman-Kruskal's measure, Odds Ratio, Yule's Q, Yule's Y, Kappa, Mutual Information, J-Measure, Gini Index, Support, Confidence, Laplace, Conviction, Interest, Cosine, Piatetsky-Shapiro's measure, Certainty Factor, Added Value, Collective Strength, Jaccard and Klosgen. Among them, there is no measure that is consistently better than others in all application domains. Each measure has its own selection bias.

Three interest measures, any-confidence, all-confidence and bond, are introduced in [10]. Both all-confidence and bond are proved to be of downward closure property. Utility is used in [2] to find top-K objective-directed rules in terms of their probabilities as well as their utilities in supporting the user defined objective. UCI (Unexpected Confidence Interestingness) and II (Isolated Interestingness) are designed in [3] to evaluate the importance of an association rule by considering its unexpectedness in terms of other association rules in its neighborhood.

3 Measuring Interestingness by Clustering

3.1 Basic Idea

There are many algorithms for discovering association rules. However, usually a lot of rules are discovered and many of them are either commonsense or useless. It is difficult to select those interesting rules from so many rules. Therefore, many metrics have been devised to help filter rules, such as lift, correlation, utility, entropy, collective strength, and so on [2, 7, 11].

In a scenario of supermarket basket analysis, if two items are frequently bought together, they will make a frequent item set. Nevertheless, most frequent item set are commonsense. For example, people who buy milk at a supermarket usually buy bread at the same time, and vice versa. So "milk→bread" is a frequent pattern, which is an association rule of high support and high confidence. However, this kind of "knowledge" is useless because everyone know it.

The itemset composed of hammer and nail is another example. On the contrary, the rule "beer→diaper" is of high interestingness because beer has little relation with diaper in the commonsense and they are much dissimilar with each other.

From the above examples, we can see that the itemsets which are composed of "similar" items are uninteresting. That is to say, the frequent itemsets consisting of "dissimilar" items are interesting. Therefore, the dissimilarity between items can be used to judge the interestingness of association rules. It is difficult to judge the dissimilarity between items manually. Moreover, it is not easy to design a formula to compute the dissimilarity. Fortunately, the clustering technique can help us to do so. Since the function of clustering is grouping similar objects together, it can help us to know the dissimilarity between objects.

From this point, we devise a strategy to measure the interestingness by clustering. By taking each item as an object, the items can be clustered into a couple of groups. After clustering, the items in the same cluster are similar to each other, while two items from two different clusters are dissimilar, and the dissimilarity between them can be judged with the dissimilarity between the two clusters. When all rules have been set interestingness, those rules with high interestingness can be output if a threshold is given. An alternative way it to output the top-k rules with high interestingness, and the user can choose the number of interesting rules to output. Based on the above idea, the interestingness of rules is defined in the following.

Definition 1 (Interestingness). *For an association rule $A \rightarrow B$, the interestingness of it is defined as the distance between the two clusters, C_A and C_B, where C_A and C_B denote the clusters where A and B are in respectively. Let $Interest(A \rightarrow B)$ stand for the interestingness of $A \rightarrow B$, then the formula for interestingness is as follows.*

$$Interest(A \rightarrow B) = Dist(C_A, C_B) \tag{1}$$

where $Dist(C_A, C_B)$ denotes the distance between cluster C_A and C_B.

The above definition is for the simplest rule, where there is only one item in the antecedent. However, many rules may have several items in the left. For this kind of rules, an expanded definition is given in the following.

Definition 2 (Interestingness). *For an association rule $A_1, A_2, ..., A_n \rightarrow B$, its interestingness is defined as the minimal distances between clusters C_{A_i} and C_B, where C_{A_i} and C_B denote the clusters where A_i $(1 \leq i \leq n)$ and B are in respectively.*

$$Interest(A_1, A_2, ..., A_n \rightarrow B) = \min_{i=1}^{n}\{Dist(C_{A_i}, C_B)\} \tag{2}$$

For those kinds rule who have multiple items in the consequent, it is easy to expand the above definition for them.

INPUT: a rule set **R**, an item set **I**,
       and an interestingness threshold **T** or the number of rules (k)
OUTPUT: a set of interesting rules

Cluster the itemset **I** with an existing algorithm (e.g. k-means) for clustering;
FOR each pair of clusters C_i and C_j
    Set $Dist(C_i, C_j)$ to the distance between the centroids of C_i and C_j;
ENDFOR
FOR each rule $A_1, A_2, ..., A_n \to B$ in the rule set **R**
    $Interest(A_1, A_2, ..., A_n \to B) = \min_{i=1}^{n}\{Dist(C_{A_i}, C_B)\}$
ENDFOR
Output those rules whose interestingness is greater than the threshold **T**,
or those top-k rules with high interestingness;

Fig. 1. Algorithm for Measuring the Interestingness of Rules by Clustering

Our approach tries to measure the interestingness by clustering items, while most other measures by analyzing the transaction set. Hence, our approach complements other measures of interestingness.

3.2 Our Algorithm

Our algorithm for measuring interestingness by clustering is given in detail in Figure 1.

3.3 How to Choose the Algorithm for Clustering

There are many algorithms for clustering. Which one is suitable for a given application? It should be chosen according to the specific scenario and the requirement of users. Generally speaking, the algorithm should be capable to handle hybrid data. The reason is that most data for association analysis are of hybrid data, so the algorithm for clustering is required to be able to cluster data both of numeric attributes and categorical ones.

On the other hand, since the dissimilarity between clusters will be used as the interestingness of rules, the dissimilarity or distance should be easy to judge or compute. There are mainly four categories of algorithms for clustering, namely, partitioning, hierarchical, density-based and grid-based approaches. For density-based and grid-based ones, the clusters are generated by expanding the densely-populated regions or combining dense neighboring cells, so it is difficult to judge the dissimilarity between clusters. Fortunately, for partitioning and hierarchical algorithms, the clusters are usually compact and it is easy to compute the dissimilarity between clusters. For k-means or k-medoids algorithms, the mean or medoid is used to represent a whole cluster, so the dissimilarity can be easily computed as the distance between the means or medoids. For hierarchical approaches, single linkage, average linkage, complete linkage, and mean linkage are main measures for calculating the distances between clusters, and they can be used as the dissimilarity. Therefore, partitioning and hierarchical algorithms can be readily used in our approach, while density-based or grid-based ones are not.

In our approach, k-means is used as the algorithm for clustering. Since the k-means algorithm is only for numeric attributes, we adapt it for clustering hybrid data in the following way. The mean is used for numeric attributes, while the mode is used for categorical attributes. The distance between two clusters is defined as the weighted sum of all attributes. Actually, many other algorithms for clustering (see [4]) can be used or can be adapted for our approach.

The shortcoming of our approach is that it is only suitable for clusters of spherical shapes, not for clusters of arbitrary shapes. Therefore, the algorithms which discovers clusters of spherical shapes is needed in our approach. For algorithms which discover clusters of arbitrary shapes, an effective way to calculate the dissimilarity between clusters should be devised to be used in our approach.

4 Experimental Results

In our experiment, we will show the effectiveness of our approach to filter rules of low-interestingness. The real data from supermarket is used in our experiment. There are two datasets: an item set and a basket dataset. The item dataset are of 460 items and seven attributes, and we choose the weight, price, category, and brand as the features for clustering. An attribute of average price is derived from weight and price. In addition, the category is split into three new attributes, with each standing for a level in the hierarchy of category. The first two attributes are numeric, while the last two are categorical. K-means is used for clustering, and we adapt it for hybrid data. For numeric attributes, the representative of a cluster is set to the mean, while it is set to the mode for categorical attributes. As to the three new attributes of category, the high-level category is assigned with great weight while the low-level category with small weight.

All together 5800 association rules with both high support and high confidence are discovered with APRIORI algorithm from the transaction data. By clustering the itemset with k-means (k is set to 10), the items are partitioned into ten clusters. The dissimilarities between clusters are computed as the interestingness of corresponding rules. The top rule with highest interestingness is "#33 → #283", while item #33 is "Run Te" shampoo, and item #283 is "Hu Wang" sauce of 1000ml. Since shampoo and sauce are from totaly different categories, the rule is of high interestingness (0.909). In contrast, rule "#254 → #270" is of very low interestingness (0.231). Item #254 and #270 are respectively sausage and vinegar. The rule is uninteresting because both of them are cooking materials.

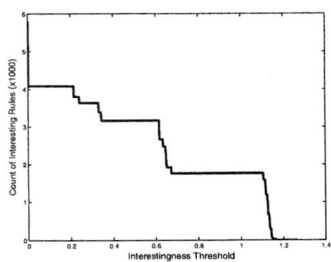

Fig. 2. Experimental Result

The count of rules remained when measuring the interestingness by clustering is shown in Figure 2. The value of interestingness ranges from 0 to 1.17. If the interestingness threshold is set to 0.5, then 3167 out of 5800 rules remain because of high interestingness. If those with interestingness less than 1.0 are filtered out, then 1763 rules remain. If the threshold is set to 1.14, only 291 rules remain while all others are filtered out. After filtering, rules of low interestingness are removed. The remaining rules of high interestingness, which are much less than the original rules, can then be judged and selected by domain experts.

5 Conclusions

In this paper, we have presented a new way to judge the interestingness of association rules by clustering. With our method, the interestingness of rules are set to be the dissimilarity of the clusters which the antecedent and the consequent are in respectively. Since the items from different clusters are dissimilar, the rules composed of items from different clusters are of high interestingness. Our method can help to filter the rules effectively, which has been shown in our experiments.

In our future research, we will try to combine existing measures of interestingness with clustering to make it more effective. In addition, subjective measures will be taken into account when clustering. For density-based and grid-based algorithms, it is not easy to judge the dissimilarity between clusters, and we will try to adapt them for measuring the interestingness of rules.

References

1. R. Agrawal, T. Imielinski and A. Swami: Mining association rules between sets of tiems in large databases. In Proc. of the ACM SIGMOD Int. Conf. on Management of Data (SIGMOD'93), Washington, D.C., USA, May 1993, pp. 207-216.
2. R. Chan, Q. Yang, and Y.-D. Shen: Mining high utility itemsets. In Proc. of the 2003 IEEE International Conference on Data Mining, Florida, USA, November 2003.
3. G. Dong and J. Li: Interestingness of discovered association rules in terms of neighborhood-based unexpectedness. In Proc. of the 2nd Pacific-Asia Conf. on Knowledge Discovery and Data Mining, Melbourne, Australia, April 1998, pp. 72-86.
4. Erica Kolatch: Clustering Algorithms for Spatial Databases: A Survey. Dept. of Computer Science, University of Maryland, College Park, 2001. http://citeseer.nj.nec.com/436843.html
5. U.M. Fayyad, G. Piatetsky-Shapiro and P. Smyth: From data mining to knowledge discovery: an overview. In Advances in Knowledge Discovery & Data Mining, pp. 1-34, AAAI/MIT, 1996.
6. Alex A. Freitas: On objective measures of rule surprisingness. In Proc. of 2nd European Symp PKDD'98, Nantes, France, 1998, pp. 1-9.
7. Robert J. Hilderman and Howard J. Hamilton: Knowledge discovery and interestingness measures: a survey. Tech. Report 99-4, Department of Computer Science, University of Regina, October 1999.

8. Won-Young Kim, Young-Koo Lee, and Jiawei Han: CCMine: efficient mining of confidence-closed correlated patterns. In Proc. of 2004 Pacific-Asia Conf. on Knowledge Discovery and Data Mining, Sydney, Australia, May 2004, pp.569-579.
9. B. Liu, W. Hsu, S. Chen, and Y. MA: Analyzing the subjective interestingness of association rules. IEEE Intelligent Systems, 15(5):47-55, 2000.
10. E. Omiecinski: Alternative interest measures for mining associations. IEEE Trans. Knowledge and Data Engineering, 15:57-69, 2003.
11. Pang-Ning Tan, Vipin Kumar, Jaideep Srivastava: Selecting the right interestingness measure for association patterns. In Proc. of the Eighth ACM SIGKDD International Conference on Knowledge Discovery and Data Mining, Edmonton, Alberta, 2002, pp. 32-41.

Exploiting Maximal Emerging Patterns for Classification

Zhou Wang, Hongjian Fan, and Kotagiri Ramamohanarao

Dept. of CSSE, The University of Melbourne, Parkville, Vic 3052, Australia
{zwang, hfan, rao}@cs.mu.oz.au

Abstract. Classification is an important data mining problem. Emerging Patterns (EPs) are itemsets whose supports change significantly from one data class to another. Previous studies have shown that classifiers based on EPs are competitive to other state-of-the-art classification systems. In this paper, we propose a new type of Emerging Patterns, called Maximal Emerging Patterns (MaxEPs), which are the longest EPs satisfying certain constraints. MaxEPs can be used to condense the vast amount of information, resulting in a significantly smaller set of high quality patterns for classification. We also develop a new "overlapping" or "intersection" based mechanism to exploit the properties of MaxEPs. Our new classifier, Classification by Maximal Emerging Patterns (CMaxEP), combines the advantages of the Bayesian approach and EP-based classifiers. The experimental results on 36 benchmark datasets from the UCI machine learning repository demonstrate that our method has better overall classification accuracy in comparison to JEP-classifier, CBA, C5.0 and NB.

Keywords: Emerging Patterns, classification, Bayesian learning, maximal Emerging Patterns.

1 Introduction

Classification is one of the fundamental tasks in data mining, and has also been studied substantially in statistics, machine learning, neural networks and expert systems over decades. Emerging Patterns (EPs) [1] are defined as multivariate features (i.e., itemsets) whose supports (or frequencies) change *significantly* from one class to another. By aggregating the differentiating power of EPs, the constructed classification systems [2,3] usually achieve high classification accuracy and demonstrate consistent effectiveness on a variety of datasets.

Previous EP mining algorithms [3,4] usually focus on finding minimal patterns satisfying the growth-rate constraint. A huge number of patterns (e.g., 10^9) may be generated, which makes efficient mining of EPs infeasible. The requirement of EPs being minimal is driven by their use in classification [3], because usually short EPs have high support and they are easy to match unknown instances. During the classification phase, the validity of any EP with respect to a test instance is determined by whether the EP is fully "contained" in the test instance. The aggregation of many minimal EPs may implicitly cause duplicate counting of individual EP's contribution, which in turn lead to decreased accuracy.

In this paper, we propose to use Maximal Emerging Patterns (MaxEPs) for classification. MaxEPs are the longest EPs, namely, supersets of MaxEPs will not be EPs any more. Using the concept of MaxEP, we are able to condense a very large number of EPs to yield a much smaller set of MaxEPs. We also turn to a new direction in terms of classification. Instead of "containment" requirement, we exploit the "intersection" relationship between a MaxEP and a test instance. The larger the overlap between them, the higher the possibility that the test belong to the class of the MaxEP. We use MaxEPs in this probabilistic approach for classification. By using the new "overlapping" mechanism to exploit strong discriminative power of Maximal Emerging Patterns, we solved the problems suffered by previous EP-based classifiers, such as low mining efficiency, duplicate contribution in classification, normalization relying on manual tuning [2]. The experiments confirm that our new classifier, called Classification by Maximal Emerging Patterns (CMaxEP), generally outperforms other state-of-the-art classification methods, such as JEP-classifier, C5.0, CBA and NB.

2 Maximal Emerging Patterns

Suppose a data object $obj = (a_1, a_2 \cdots a_n)$ follows the schema $(A_1, A_2 \cdots A_n)$, where $A_1, A_2 \cdots A_n$ are called attributes. Attributes can be categorical or continuous. For a categorical attributes, we assume that all the possible values are mapped to a set of consecutive positive integers. For a continuous attributes, we assume that its value range is discretized into intervals, and the intervals are also mapped to consecutive positive integers. We call each (attribute, integer-value) pair an *item*. Let I denote the set of all items in the encoding dataset D. A set X of items is also called an itemset, which is defined as a subset of I. We say any instance S contains an itemset X, if $X \subseteq S$. The support of an itemset X in a dataset D, $supp_D(X)$, is $count_D(X)/|D|$, where $count_D(X)$ is the number of instances in D containing X.

Given two different classes of datasets D_1 and D_2, the growth rate of an itemset X from D_1 to D_2 is defined as $GrowthRate(X) = \frac{supp_2(X)}{supp_1(X)}$ (where $\frac{0}{0} = 0$ and $\frac{\geq 0}{0} = \infty$). Given a growth rate threshold $\rho > 1$, an itemset X is said to be an ρ-*emerging pattern* (ρEP or simply EP) from D_1 to D_2 if GrowthRate(X)$\geq \rho$. An EP with high support in its home class and low support in the contrasting class can be seen as a strong signal indicating the class of a test instance containing it. The strength of an EP X is defined as $strength(X) = \frac{GR(X)}{GR(X)+1} * supp(X)$.

A Maximal Emerging Pattern (MaxEP) is the longest Emerging Pattern, i.e., it is not a subset of any other Emerging Pattern.

Definition 1 *(Maximal Emerging Pattern). Given a minimum growth-rate threshold $\rho > 1$ and a minimum support threshold ξ, an itemset X is said to be a Maximal Emerging Pattern (MaxEP) if (1) supp(X)$\geq \xi$; (2) GrowthRate(X)$\geq \rho$; (3) there exists no pattern Y such that $X \subset Y$ and GrowthRate(Y)$\geq \rho$.*

Condition 1 ensures that a MaxEP covers a certain number of training instances, hence statistically reliable for prediction. Condition 2 makes sure that each MaxEP has sharp discriminating power. Condition 3 prefers those EPs with the longest length - MaxEPs are the longest patterns that appear frequently in one class of data but not frequently (determined by high growth rates) in the other class.

The set of MaxEPs is a subset of the set of all EPs and also much smaller. Let us consider an extreme case. Suppose two classes P and N, described by k attributes. P contains one instance only and N has a number of instances. Suppose we look for MaxEPs with $\xi = 1$ (in absolute count) and $\rho = \infty$. There is only one MaxEP of class P, that is, the P instance itself, because it appears once in P and can not appear in N (assuming that the same instance can not have different class labels) and it has reached the maximum length. However, there are usually many (up to 2^k) JEPs of class P, as long as a subset does not appear in N.

From the above example, we can see that a small number of Maximal Emerging Patterns can condense the discriminating power of many individual EPs and represent a comprehensive description of essential distinguishing characteristics of the target class. Our experiments confirm that not only the number of MaxEPs is much fewer than the number of minimal EPs, but also MaxEPs are high quality predictive patterns.

A backtracking algorithm is used to efficiently generate Maximal Emerging Patterns. The detailed description of the algorithm can be found in [5].

3 Classification by Maximal Emerging Patterns

Bayes' theorem provides an optimal way to predict the class of a previously unseen instance, given a training data set. The chosen class should be the one which maximizes $P(C_i|T) = P(T, C_i)/P(T) = P(C_i)P(T|C_i)/P(T)$, where C_i is the class label, $T = \{a_1 a_2 \cdots a_n\}$ is the test case, $P(Y|X)$ denotes the conditional probability of Y given X, and probabilities are estimated from the training sample. Since classification focuses on discriminate prediction of a single class, rather than assigning explicit probabilities to each class, the denominator $P(T)$, which does not affect the relative ordering of the classes, can be omitted. So the class is chosen with the highest probability $P(T, C_i) = P(C_i)P(T|C_i)$. Because in practice it is very hard to calculate the exact probability $P(T, C_i)$, one must use approximations under some certain assumptions. The Naive Bayes (NB) classifier [6] provides the simplest and computationally efficient approach by assuming all attributes are mutually independent within each class. To improve NB's performance, there are many works on remedying violations of the assumption, such as Large Bayes (LB) [7] and our previous work BCEP [8].

Minimal (shortest) EPs and Maximal (longest) EPs represent two extreme points in the same spectrum of the discriminating characteristics. Minimal EPs are suitable to use in "containment" based mechanism, because usually many minimal EPs can be found "contained" in a test instance. However, for MaxEPs, it is very possible that they are not contained in the test. It would be very unreliable to predict a test without using any EPs. Before we describe how to use MaxEPs in the Bayesian approach for classification, we discuss a very different mechanism to use the power of maximal EPs.

3.1 Overlap/Intersection Relationship Between MaxEPs and Tests

This work changes direction in terms of classification - we exploit the "overlap" or "intersection" relationship between MaxEPs and the test instance. If a test "fully contains" a long MaxEP, it is very likely the test shares the class membership with the MaxEP, because the MaxEP is the maximal frequent combination of discriminating features (right bound of the border of EPs). When the test does not "fully contain" the MaxEP, we still can use the MaxEP by looking at the overlap or intersection between them. The larger the overlap, the higher the possibility of the test case belonging to the MaxEP's class. If there are sufficient overlap between a MaxEP and the test instance, it is highly likely that the test belongs to the class of the MaxEP. Under this new scheme, we are able to make good use of a small set of maximal patterns for classification.

Example 1. Suppose we have discovered a set of MaxEPs: $\{\{a,b,c\}, \{b,c,d\}, \{b,c,e\}\}$. These MaxEPs can represent many minimal EPs: $\{\{a,b\}, \{b,c\}, \{a,c\}, \{b,d\}, \{c,d\}, \{b,e\}, \{c,e\}\}$. To classify a test instance $T = \{a,b,c,e,f\}$, using previous "containment" mechanism, we can select many minimal EPs, but only two MaxEPs $\{a,b,c\}$ and $\{b,c,e\}$. However, by using the new "overlapping" mechanism, in addition to the above two MaxEPs, we are able to exploit the power of $\{b,c,d\}$ because there is sufficient overlap between the MaxEP and T.

3.2 Classification by Maximal Emerging Patterns (CMaxEP)

We show CMaxEP classifier in Algorithm 1. We first obtain the overlapping itemsets between T and all discovered MaxEPs (line 1). Note that the overlapping itemsets are subsets of MaxEPs. Because many subsets of MaxEPs are actually EPs, there is good chance that the overlapping itemsets are also EPs. There are some cases when overlapping itemsets do not satisfy the growth-rate threshold (non-EPs), they may be filtered by the following maximization process (line 2). We admit that there are few chances that some non-EPs still remain. Our experiments show that using few non-EPs experiences no degradation in predictive accuracy. The explanation is that these non-EPs are reliable (note that they must satisfy the support threshold) and have certain growth rates but less than the predefined threshold. From O, select only the maximal patterns from the overlapping patterns (line 2), that is, remove patterns that are subsets of other patterns. This is the final set (B) of patterns that will be used later in product approximation.

After computing the final set B, CMaxEP incrementally selects one pattern at a time into the solution according to its ranking (function next(), line 5). The selection of patterns is based on the following priorities: (1) the selected pattern must have items that have not been covered so far; (2) the selected pattern should have the least number of items that have not been covered so far; (3) prefer a longer pattern; (4) prefer a pattern with larger strength.

Algorithm 1: Classification by Maximal Emerging Patterns (CMaxEP)

---

  input : a set of MaxEPs F and a test instance T
  output: the classification of T

  /*O is the overlapping patterns between T and MaxEPs */
1 $O = \{s \cap T | s \in F\}$;
2 $B \leftarrow$ the maximal patters from O;
3 $covered = numerator = denominator = \emptyset$;
4 **while** $covered \subset T$ **do**
5 $\quad$ $e = \text{next}(covered, B)$;
6 $\quad$ $numerator = numerator \cup e$;
7 $\quad$ $denominator = denominator \cup \{e \cap covered\}$;
8 $\quad$ $covered = covered \cup e$;
  end
9 **for** *each class* **do**
10 $\quad$ $P(T, C_i) = P(C_i) \dfrac{\prod_{u \in numerator} P(u, C_i)}{\prod_{v \in denominator} P(v, C_i)}$;
  end
11 output the class with maximal $P(T, C_i)$;

---

4 Experimental Evaluation

To evaluate the accuracy and efficiency of CMaxEP, we have performed an extensive performance study on 36 datasets from the UCI Machine Learning Repository [9]. We compare CMaxEP against four popular classification methods: Naive Bayes (NB) [6], decision tree induction C5.0 [10], Classification Based on Association (CBA) [11] and JEP-C [3]. For MaxEPs, there are two important parameters, the minimum support ξ and growth rate ρ thresholds. In our experiments, $\xi = 1\%$ and $\rho = 2.5$.

For lack of space, we only present a summary of results. Our CMaxEP classifier achieves the highest average accuracy (85.93%) on the 36 datasets, compared with CBA (85.35%), JEP-C (85.01%), C5.0 (84.37%) and NB (81.28%). Among the 36 datasets, CMaxEP achieves the best accuracy on 10 datasets, while JEP-classifier wins on 7, NB wins on 8, C5.0 win on 9, CBA wins on 5. From Figure 1, The number of MaxEPs is much smaller (on average 10 times smaller) than minimal JEPs. Our method is able to use much fewer patterns to achieve higher accuracy than JEP-classifier (we beat it 19 times, draw 2 times, and lose 14 times).

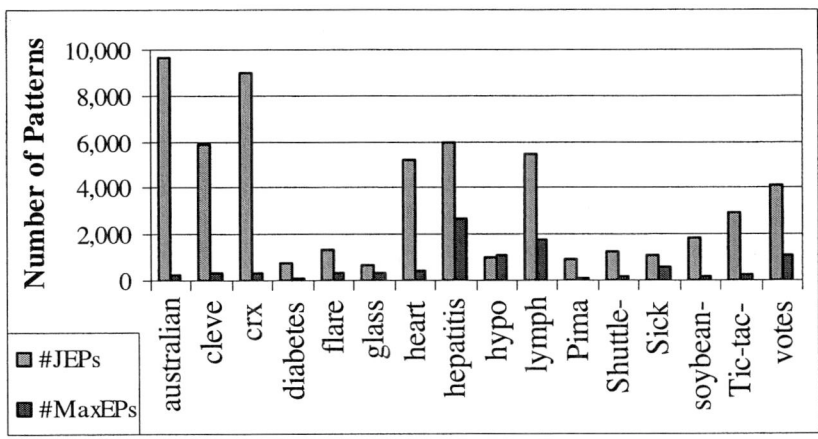

Fig. 1. Comparison of Number of JEPs and MaxEPs used in classification

5 Conclusions

We have introduced a new type of knowledge pattern called Maximal Emerging Patterns (MaxEPs). Instead of presenting a large number of fragmentary components (minimal EPs), MaxEPs represent a concise yet comprehensive description of essential discriminative knowledge between different classes of data. We use a new "overlapping" mechanism to exploit strong discriminative power of MaxEPs to build accurate and efficient classifiers, which solves common problems suffered by previous EP-based classifiers. Our experimental results on 36 benchmark datasets demonstrate that our classifier has better overall classification accuracy in comparison with JEP-Classifier, CBA, C5.0 and NB.

Acknowledgements. We would like to thank Thomas Manoukian for providing the JEP-Classifier source code and promptly answering many questions.

References

1. Dong, G., Li, J.: Efficient mining of emerging patterns: Discovering trends and differences. In: Proc. KDD'99, San Diego, CA, USA (1999) 43–52
2. Dong, G., Zhang, X., Wong, L., Li, J.: Classification by aggregating emerging patterns. In: Proc. 2nd Int'l Conf. on Discovery Science (1999) 30–42
3. Li, J., Dong, G., Ramamohanarao, K.: Making use of the most expressive jumping emerging patterns for classification. Knowledge and Information Systems **3** (2001) 131–145
4. Bailey, J., Manoukian, T., Ramamohanarao, K.: Fast algorithms for mining emerging patterns. In: Proc. PKDD'02, Helsinki, Finland (2002)
5. Wang, Z.: Classification based on maximal contrast patterns. Master's thesis, University of Melbourne (2004)

6. Domingos, P., Pazzani, M.J.: Beyond independence: Conditions for the optimality of the simple bayesian classifier. In: Proc. ICML'96. (1996) 105–112
7. Meretakis, D., Wuthrich, B.: Extending naive bayes classifiers using long itemsets. In: Proc. KDD'99. (1999) 165–174
8. Fan, H., Ramamohanarao, K.: A bayesian approach to use emerging patterns for classification. In: Proc. 14th Australasian Database Conference (ADC2003), Adelaide, Australia (2003) 39–48
9. Blake, C.L., Merz, C.J.: UCI repository of machine learning databases (1998)
10. Quinlan, J.R.: C4.5: Programs for Machine Learning. Morgan Kaufmann, San Mateo, CA (1993)
11. Liu, B., Hsu, W., Ma, Y.: Integrating classification and association rule mining. In: Proc. KDD'98, New York, USA (1998) 80–86

Feature Extraction for Learning to Classify Questions

Zhalaing Cheung, Khanh Linh Phan, Ashesh Mahidadia, and Achim Hoffmann

School of Computer Science and Engineering, The University of New South Wales,
Sydney NSW 2052, Australia
{zhalaingc, ashesh, achim}@cse.unsw.edu.au

Abstract. In this paper, we present a new approach to learning the classification of questions. Question classification received interest recently in the context of question answering systems for which categorizing a given question would be beneficial to allow improved processing of the document to identify an answer. Our approach relies on relative simple preprocessing of the question and uses standard decision tree learning. We also compared our results from decision tree learning with those obtained using Naïve Bayes. Both results compare favorably to several very recent studies using more sophisticated preprocessing and/or more sophisticated learning techniques. Furthermore, the fact that decision tree learning proved more successful than Naïve Bayes is significant in itself as decision tree learning is usually believed to be less suitable for NLP tasks.

Keywords: Question classification, feature extraction for text classification, decision tree learning, Naïve Bayes classifier.

1 Introduction

With the increase of textual information on the web, automatic processing of natural language is becoming increasingly important. Finding relevant information either in form of a complete document or in form of a single paragraph, sentence or even smaller chunks represents the major challenge in effectively utilizing the WWW. Work on automatic open-domain question answering has received new interest recently, see e.g. [8, 10]. Question answering is a more difficult task than that addressed by Internet search engines, as a concise answer to a question needs to be found instead of producing an entire, possibly very long document containing the answer. The task in the TREC question answering track is to find to a given question a short answer of no more than 50 bytes in a document library of 5 Gigabytes. A question might be *'How far can a kangaroo jump?'* or *'Which Japanese city has the largest population?'* In order to extract an answer to a question from a document it proved useful to differentiate different types of questions such that for each type one searches for different linguistic patterns surrounding the answer in the text [7]. The task of automatically classifying a question into the correct category has become known as *question classification*. Besides being useful for question answering the task of question classification can also be used to classify according to an existing list of frequently asked questions such that an automatic answer can be automatically be found. This has potential for automatic help desks applications, etc. Question classification is very different from text classification as questions are typically very short. Hence, a word frequency based classification approach is less likely to succeed. While there is a substantial body of research of learning text classification, learning the classification of questions has received very little attention so far. A notable exception is the very recent work in [4], which focussed on learning a hierarchical question classifier that was guided by a layered semantic hierarchy of answer types using Winnow, a linear threshold function learner [6].

In this paper we show how machine learning can be used effectively to develop high-quality question classifiers based on a relatively simple representation using a small number of extracted features. Our results favour decision tree learning over Naïve Bayes classifiers and achieve average classification accuracies of more than 90%. Our results also compare favourably against the work on hierarchical question classifiers in [4] as we obtain higher accuracies from comparable number of training instances using less sophisticated pre-processing and much fewer extracted features.

The paper is organized as follows: The next section describes our approach and discusses the used pre-processing in detail. In section 3 we describe our experimental set-up. Section 4 presents the results we obtained. In section 5 we present our discussion and conclusions.

2 Pre-processing Questions

Our data set was taken from the Webclopedia [2] question set, which contains hand-classified documents. We collected from Webclopedia 18,000 sample questions that have been manually tagged by the question's answer (entity) type. These questions contain 140 categories (Qtargets). Questions can also have multiple classifications and are then given multiple labels. We regrouped these classes to super-classes of similar topic area using a similar taxonomy to that used for Webclopedia. For

Table 1. 21 different question types used in the study

Question Type	Instances	Question Type	Instances
ADDRESS	283	NUMERICAL QUANTITY	1608
AGENT	264	ORGANIZATION	539
CIRCUMSTANCE MEAN	209	PROPER PERSON	3234
CONTRAST	160	PROPER PLACE	1995
DATE	420	REASON	840
DEFINITION	231	TEMPORAL QUANTITY	288
EXPRESSION ORIGIN	164	TEXT	311
INFO	1555	TRUE OR FALSE	291
METHOD	828	WHY-FAMOUS	228
MULTIPLE-CHOICE	498	YES OR NO	1112
NAME	1780		

example, PROPER PLACE can have subclasses: River, Lake, Sea, City, State, Country, Planet, Moon, and District, etc. For this study, we selected the 21 most frequent categories as listed in the Table-1.

2.1 Feature Extraction

There are many studies on how to extract features from documents. Techniques such as term weighting, co-occurrence of words for topic identification, and keyword extraction using term domain interdependence, see e.g. [5], are all statistical methods used to select keywords or phrases that may hold meaningful information about the text [3]. For the problem of question classification, statistical techniques appeared less suitable as a single question is normally rather short and, hence, does not contain enough words to allow the creation of meaningful statistics. As a consequence, we used the following sequence of steps to create a fixed-length binary feature vector for each question class: Part-of-Speech tagging, Stop word removal, Keyword extraction, Noun phrase chunking and Head phrase extraction.

This process resulted in a number of binary features to represent each question. For each class of questions, an individually tailored set of features was automatically created based on the training data set. The number of features used for an individual class ranged between about 30 and 560 depending on the question class considered. To determine the feature set for a question class C, only all the questions in the training set of that class C were selected.

Part-of-Speech Tagging: We used Brill's Part-of-Speech Tagger to tag our sentences for the following processing.

Stop Word Removal: We removed stop words, i.e. words that contribute little to the meaning of a question such as 'the', 'of'', 'it'.

Keyword Extraction: (Key)words are selected from the pre-classified question set as follows. After the removal of stop-words from all question instances in our training set, we counted the frequency of each word, noun, verb, adverb, etc, from each question class. We ignored all words that appear in more than 95% of the questions in a class, less than 0.01% of all instances or less than two times in the question set.

Noun Phrase Chunking: We used an LR-Chunker to group words in a sentence to generate more meaningful patterns (chunks). Examples include: 'car batteries', 'hard time', 'human eye', etc.

```
How/WRB far/RB can/MD [a/DT human/JJ eye/NN] see/VB
How/WRB far/RB can/MD [a/DT kangaroo/NN] jump/VB
```

Extracting Head Phrases: In our experiment, we extract the head phrase of each question sentence as a feature as it plays an important role in defining the type of the question. The head phrase is taken as the first two chunks of the sentence, since the first chunk usually contains only the single question word, such as *who, what, where*, etc. The following word appears in many cases to be an important indicator for the type of question.

3 Experimental Set-Up

In this section we evaluate the suitability of the features extracted from the training data set to learn to accurately classify questions. We used two machine learning algorithms to automatically build classifiers, namely the decision tree learner C4.5 and the Naïve Bayes classifier in their implementation within Weka [9].

Representing the Question Set: For each class we extracted the corresponding features according to the techniques described above, which include keywords, key phrases and key head phrases. Once the features were extracted for a particular class, all question instances, including the randomly selected negative instances, were represented by a corresponding binary feature vector, where each vector element indicated the presence or absence of the respective feature. As a consequence, for each class a separate binary classifier needed to be learned as different feature sets were used for each class. The following example shows how the binary feature vector of a question is created.

Question: What is the size of the earth?	Combined keys:
Keywords: [what, how, height, size]	[what, how, height, size, the dimension, the earth,
Key phrase: [the dimension, the earth]	how long, what is]
Head phrase: [how long, what is]	Binary vector: [1, 0, 0, 1, 0, 1, 0, 1]

Training Set: We took instances from the class C (positive instances) and randomly collected the same number of instances from the complete set of questions, which did not belong to class C as negative instances. We extracted keywords and phrases from the positive instances; a set of binary vectors was generated for the combined positive and negative instances based on whether the keywords/phrase exists. We generated the training set for each of the 21 classes that had more than 150 instances.

Test Set: We used 2-fold and 4-fold cross validation for evaluating the performance of the two learning algorithms on the task of question classification. The cross validation runs were repeated 10 times and averaged to reduce the bias given by the particular division of the original data set into n folds. In each case were the features selected on the basis of the training examples only. The entire set of test cases was represented as a binary vector by using the same set of features. The number of test cases varied for each question class but ranged between about 160 and 3200 for 2-fold cross validation and between 80 and 1600 for 4-fold cross validation for each fold.

4 Results

The most striking results are shown in Figure 1. Both learning techniques achieved accuracies in cross validation on unseen cases averaging at more than 86%. These were the averages across the cross validation runs as well as across all 21 classes. The two-fold cross validation results (between 86% and 88%) were weaker than those achieved using 4-fold cross validation (close to 91% for decision tree learning). The lower accuracy for the two-fold cross validation runs is due to the training set being smaller (1/2 of the total data set size) than in the 4-fold runs (3/4 of the total data set size). Probably the most interesting aspect of these results is the fact that decision tree learning clearly outperformed Naïve Bayes. Furthermore, the performance of both techniques exceeded the performance previously obtained in [4], based on another learning algorithm, generally considered to be very well suited for learning problems in NLP.

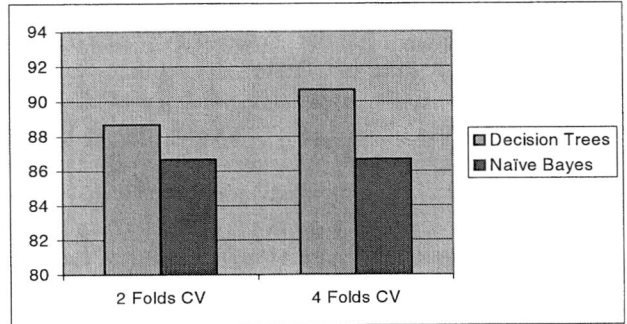

Fig. 1. Overall predictive accuracy on unseen test cases, by the two learners

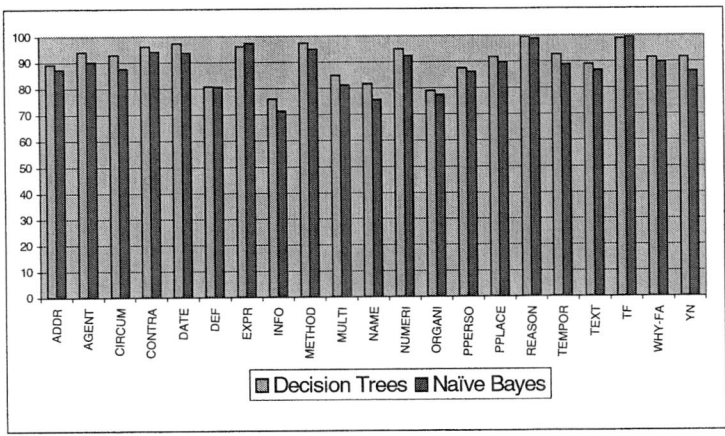

Fig. 2. Average accuracies obtained from 4-fold cross validation on unseen data for each of the 21 question classes

In Figure 2 we show the achieved accuracies for each of the 21 individual classes obtained from the 4-fold cross validation runs. In almost all the (question) classes, the Decision Tree learner outperformed the Naïve Bayes learner. It is difficult to compare our results to those presented very recently in [4], as that work used more sophisticated pre-processing resulting in up to 200,000 features being used. However, the average classification accuracy achieved in [4] was 84%, which is substantially lower than the accuracy achieved in our work. The reason for that is not quite clear at this stage. In [4] a different learning algorithm, based on Winnow [6], which learns linear threshold functions, was used.

5 Discussion and Conclusions

While there is a substantial body of work on text classification, there is very limited work on the task of question classification. Question classification attracted serious interest only recently, when the TREC series included the question answering track. In particular in the context of the use information extraction techniques it seems an important intermediate step to classify a question into one of a number of classes, where for each class a specialized information extractor can be used to obtain the answer of interest. But also for other applications, such as answering routing questions based on a catalogue of frequently asked questions, automated information services can be provided. In [1] questions were classified by using manually generated rules. In the more recent study in [4], questions were classified by an automatically generated classifier using the Winnow learning algorithm [6] and based on a vast number of attributes (in the order of magnitude of 200,000 attributes). The results in that study were inferior to our results. In [4] an average accuracy of about 84% was achieved while we obtained an accuracy of more than 90% using decision tree learning and our pre-processing of the questions. In [10] SVMs were proposed with a new type of tree kernel function which assigns weights to words occurrences depending on their location within the parse tree of the question. The results reported in [10] are again inferior to our results. Our approach produced higher accuracies (more than 90%) versus up to 87% using SVMs with the new tree kernel function. Furthermore, we used a finer-grained classification scheme (21 classes) while in [10] only 5 different question classes were used.

Overall, we demonstrated that decision tree learning in combination with our proposed preprocessing outperforms more commonly used techniques in text classification, such as Naïve Bayes. This is surprising as it is a common belief that for text classification applications, decision tree learners are not well-suited because they rely on testing a small set of features only (in each node of the tree only a single feature is tested). Furthermore, in text classification one usually has to rely on a large number of features where each feature contributes partially to justifying the classification. As a consequence of this assumption, the most commonly used learning techniques are those which take all or many features into account for making a decision. Those techniques include Naïve Bayes as well as Support Vector Machines or other Neural network type techniques, such as the Winnow algorithm used in [4], which is the study closest to our own.

However, a carefully designed pre-processing of the raw questions is necessary to allow good generalization. Our approach included Part-of-Speech tagging, Stop word removal, Keyword extraction, Noun phrase chunking followed by Head phrase extraction. This proved to be considerably more effective than the preprocessing proposed in other recent work on the problem, such as in [10].

Future work will investigate the utility of further pre-processing techniques including the extraction of proper names, synonym/hyponym relationships, and word stemming. Word suffixes could also be used to characterize semantic word groups, such as words ending with *-ate* mean some way of causing or making, e.g., liquidate, facilitate, associate, stimulate. Words ending with *-ary, -ery, -ory* relate often to place or quality, e.g. aviary, dormitory, stationery, or ordinary.

References

[1] Hermjakob, U. *Parsing and Question Classification for Question Answering*, Proceedings of the Workshop on Open-Domain Question Answering at ACL-2001.
[2] Hovy E. et al. *Question Answering in Webclopedia*. In Proceedings of the TREC-9 Conference, NIST 2001.
[3] Lewis, David. Feature Selection and Feature Extraction for Text Categorization, Proceedings of Speech and Natural Language Workshop, pp. 212—217, Morgan Kaufmann, 1992.
[4] Xin Li, Dan Roth, Learning Question Classifiers, Proceedings of COLING 2002.
[5] Suzuki, Y. Keyword Extraction using term-Domain Interdependence for Dictation of Radio News, Proceedings of COLING 1998, pp. 1272-1276.
[6] Littlestone, N.: Learning Quickly When Irrelevant Attributes Abound: A New Linear-threshold Algorithm. Machine Learning, 2(4): 285-318 (1987).
[7] Hovy, E. et al. Toward semantics-based answer pinpointing. In proceedings of the DARPA Human Language Technology conference (HLT), San Diego, CA 2001.
[8] Light, M. et al. Analyses for Elucidating Current Question Answering Technology. Journal for Natural Language Engineering, 2001.
[9] The University of Waikato. Weka 3 – Data Mining with Open Source Machine Learning Software. http://www.cs.waikato.ac.nz/~ml/weka, 1999-2000.
[10] Zhang, D. and Lee, W.S., Question classification using support vector machines, Proceedings of the 26th annual international ACM SIGIR conference on Research and development in information retrieval, pp. 26-32, 2003.

Mining Exceptions in Databases

Eduardo Corrêa Gonçalves, Ilza Maria B. Mendes, and Alexandre Plastino*

Universidade Federal Fluminense, Department of Computer Science,
Rua Passo da Pátria, 156 - Bloco E - 3° andar - Boa Viagem,
24210-240, Niterói, RJ, Brazil
{egoncalves, imendes, plastino}@ic.uff.br
http://www.ic.uff.br

Abstract. This paper addresses the problem of mining exceptions from multidimensional databases. The goal of our proposed model is to find association rules that become weaker in some specific subsets of the database. The candidates for exceptions are generated combining previously discovered multidimensional association rules with a set of significant attributes specified by the user. The exceptions are mined only if the candidates do not achieve an expected support. We describe a method to estimate these expectations and propose an algorithm that finds exceptions. Experimental results are also presented.

1 Introduction

Multidimensional association rules [4] represent combinations of attribute values that often occur together in multidimensional repositories, such as data warehouses or relational databases. An example is given by: $(Age = \text{``}30\text{--}35\text{''}) \Rightarrow (Payment = \text{``}credit\ card\text{''})$. This rule indicates that consumers who are between 30 and 35 years old, are more likely to pay for their purchases using credit card. A multidimensional association rule can be formally defined as follows:

$$A_1 = a_1, \ldots, A_n = a_n \Rightarrow B_1 = b_1, \ldots, B_m = b_m ,$$

where A_i ($1 \leq i \leq n$) and B_j ($1 \leq j \leq m$) represent distinct attributes (dimensions) from a database relation, and a_i and b_j are values from the domains of A_i and B_j, respectively. To simplify the notation, we will represent a generic rule as an expression of the form $A \Rightarrow B$, where A and B are sets of conditions over different attributes. The support of a set of conditions Z, $Sup(Z)$, in a relation D is the percentage of tuples in D that match all conditions in Z. The support of a rule $A \Rightarrow B$, $Sup(A \Rightarrow B)$, is given by $Sup(A \cup B)$. The confidence of $A \Rightarrow B$, $Conf(A \Rightarrow B)$, is the probability that a tuple matches B, given that it matches A. Typically, the problem of mining association rules consists in finding all rules that match user-provided minimum support and minimum confidence.

---

* Work sponsored by CNPq research grant 300879/00-8.

In this work we propose a human-centered approach to mine *exceptions* from multidimensional databases. An example of this kind of pattern is given by: $(Age = \text{"30–35"}) \overset{-s}{\Longrightarrow} (Payment = \text{"credit card"}) \; [Income = \text{" < 1K"}]$. This exception indicates that among the consumers who earn less than 1K, the support value of the rule $(Age = \text{"30–35"}) \Rightarrow (Payment = \text{"credit card"})$ is significantly *smaller* than what is expected.

Proposals for mining exception rules that contradict associations with high support and confidence can be found in [5, 7]. However, in our work, exceptions characterize rules that become much weaker in specific subsets of the database. Our approach was motivated by the concept of *negative association rules*, proposed in [6, 8], where a negative pattern represents a large deviation between the actual and the expected support of a rule.

This paper is organized as follows. In Sect. 2 we present the model for mining exceptions. We propose an algorithm in Sect. 3 and show experimental results in Sect. 4. Some concluding remarks are made in Sect. 5.

2 Exceptions

In order to explain our approach for mining exceptions, consider the *consumers data set* (Table 1). The data objects represent consumers of a hypothetical store. An association rule mining algorithm can obtain the following pattern from this database: "Female consumers have children" ($Sup = 40\%$ and $Conf = 66.67\%$). However, note that none of the women who earns more than 3K have children. Then, it would be interesting to infer the following *negative* pattern: "Female consumers who earn more than 3K do not have children". This negative pattern came from the positive rule "Female consumers have children" and it was obtained because the support value of "Female consumers who earn more than 3K have children" is significantly lower than what was expected. This example illustrates an *exception* associated with a positive association rule. It can be represented as:

$$(Gender = \text{"F"}) \overset{-s}{\Longrightarrow} (Children = \text{"Yes"}) \; [(Income = \text{" > 3K"})] \; .$$

Definition 1. *(Exception). Let $\mathcal{D}$ be a relation. Let $R : A \Rightarrow B$ be a multidimensional association rule defined from $\mathcal{D}$. Let $Z = \{Z_1 = z_1, \ldots, Z_k = z_k\}$ be a set of conditions defined over attributes from $\mathcal{D}$, where $Z \cap A \cap B = \emptyset$. Z is named probe set. An exception related to the positive rule R is an expression of the form $A \overset{-s}{\Longrightarrow} B \; [Z]$.*

Exceptions are extracted only if they do not achieve an expected support. This expectation is evaluated based on the support of the original rule $A \Rightarrow B$ and the support of the conditions that compose the probe set Z. The expected support for the *candidate exception* $A \Rightarrow B \; [Z]$ can be computed as:

$$ExpSup(A \Rightarrow B \; [Z]) = Sup(A \Rightarrow B) \times Sup(Z) \; . \quad (1)$$

An exception $E : A \overset{-s}{\Longrightarrow} B \; [Z]$ can be regarded as *potentially interesting* if the actual support value of the candidate exception $A \Rightarrow B \; [Z]$, given by

Table 1. Consumers data set

Gender(G)	Age(A)	Income(I)	Children(C)	Car Owner(CO)
F	<18	<1K	Yes	No
M	26-30	>3K	Yes	Yes
F	26-30	>3K	No	Yes
F	18-25	1K - 3K	Yes	Yes
F	31-40	<1K	Yes	Yes
M	18-25	>3K	Yes	No
F	26-30	1K - 3K	Yes	Yes
F	<18	>3K	No	No
M	18-25	>3K	Yes	Yes
M	<18	<1K	No	No

$Sup(A \cup B \cup Z)$, is much lower than its expected support. The IM index (*Interest Measure*) is used to calculate this deviation. This measure captures the type of dependence between Z and $A \Rightarrow B$.

$$IM(E) = 1 - \left(\frac{Sup(A \Rightarrow B \, [Z])}{ExpSup(A \Rightarrow B \, [Z])} \right). \quad (2)$$

The IM index value grows when the actual support value is lower and far from the expected support value, indicating a negative dependence. The closer the value is from 1 (which is the highest value for this measure), the more the negative dependence is. If $IM(E) \approx 0$, then Z and $A \Rightarrow B$ are independent. If $IM(E) < 0$, the actual support value is higher than the expected support value, indicating a positive dependence.

Consider the rule $R : (G = \text{``}F\text{''}) \Rightarrow (C = \text{``}Yes\text{''})$, presented at the beginning of this section. Two different values of the attribute *Income* will be used as probe sets and will be combined with this rule in an attempt to identify exceptions.

The actual support of the candidate $C_1 : (G = \text{``}F\text{''}) \Rightarrow (C = \text{``}Yes\text{''}) \, [(I = \text{``} < 1K\text{''})]$ is 20%. The support of $R$ is 40% and the support of the probe set $Z_1 = \{(I = \text{``} < 1K\text{''})\}$ is 30%. According to (1), $ExpSup(C_1) = Sup(R) \times Sup(Z_1) = 40\% \times 30\% = 12\%$. The exception $E_1 : (G = \text{``}F\text{''}) \stackrel{-s}{\Rightarrow} (C = \text{``}Yes\text{''})[(I = \text{``} < 1K\text{''})]$ is uninteresting because $IM(E_1) = 1 - (0.20 \div 0.12) = -0.67$.

The actual support of the candidate $C_2 : (G = \text{``}F\text{''}) \Rightarrow (C = \text{``}Yes\text{''}) \, [(I = \text{``} > 3K\text{''})]$ is 0%. The support of the probe set $Z_2 = \{(I = \text{``} > 3K\text{''})\}$ is 50%. The expected support for C_2 is calculated as $40\% \times 50\% = 20\%$. The exception $E_2 : (G = \text{``}F\text{''}) \stackrel{-s}{\Rightarrow} (C = \text{``}Yes\text{''})[(I = \text{``} > 3K\text{''})]$ is potentially interesting, because $IM(E_2) = 1 - (0 \div 0.20) = 1$.

In the next example, we will show that a high value for the IM index is not a guarantee of interesting information. Consider the rule "Female consumers have a car" ($Sup = 40\%$ and $Conf = 66.67\%$), obtained from the *consumers data set*. Observing Table 1, we can also notice that none of the women who are under 18 years old have a car. These information could lead us to conclude that $(G = \text{``}F\text{''}) \stackrel{-s}{\Rightarrow} (CO = \text{``}Yes\text{''}) \, [(A = \text{``} < 18\text{''})]$ is an interesting negative pattern, since the IM value for this exception is 1. However, in reality, none of the consumers who are under 18 years old have a car, *independently if they are men or women*. Suppose these consumers live in a country where only the ones who are 18 years old or above are allowed to drive. Then, the exception $(G = \text{``F''}) \stackrel{\neg s}{\Longrightarrow} (CO = \text{``Yes''})\,[(A = \text{``}< 18\text{''})]$ represents an information that is certainly obvious and useless. Therefore it should not be mined. The IM index was not able to detect the strong *negative dependence* between being under 18 years old and having a car.

Definition 2. *(Negative Dependence). Let $X = \{X_1 = x_1, \ldots, X_n = x_n\}$ and $Y = \{Y_1 = y_1, \ldots, Y_m = y_m\}$ be two sets of conditions where $X \cap Y = \emptyset$. The negative dependence between X and Y, denoted as $ND(X, Y)$, is given by:*

$$ND(X,Y) = 1 - \left(\frac{Sup(X \cup Y)}{ExpSup(X \cup Y)}\right) = 1 - \left(\frac{Sup(X \cup Y)}{Sup(X) \times Sup(Y)}\right). \qquad (3)$$

The DU index (*Degree of Unexpectedness*) is used to capture how much the negative dependence between a probe set Z and a rule $A \Rightarrow B$ is *higher* than the negative dependence between Z and either A or B.

$$DU(E) = IM(E) - \max(ND(A,Z), ND(B,Z)). \qquad (4)$$

The greater the DU value is from 0, the more interesting the exception will be. If $DU(E) \leq 0$ the exception is uninteresting. Consider, again, the rule $R: (G = \text{``F''}) \Rightarrow (C = \text{``Yes''})$ and the probe set $Z_2 = \{(I = \text{``}> 3K\text{''})\}$. First we should compute $ND(A, Z) = ND((G = \text{``F''}), (I = \text{``}> 3K\text{''})) = (1 - (0.20 \div 0.30)) = 0.33$; and $ND(B, Z) = ND((C = \text{``Yes''}), (I = \text{``}> 3K\text{''})) = (1 - (0.30 \div 35)) = 0.14$; The exception $E_2: (G = \text{``F''}) \stackrel{\neg s}{\Longrightarrow} (C = \text{``Yes''})\,[(I = \text{``}> 3K\text{''})]$ is, in fact, interesting because $DU(E_2) = 1 - max(0.33, 0.14) = 0.67$. Next, we give a formal definition for the problem of mining exceptions.

Definition 3. *(Problem Formulation). Let $MinSup \geq 0$, $I_{min} \geq 0$, and $D_{min} \geq 0$ denote minimum user-specified thresholds for Sup, IM, and DU. The problem of mining exceptions in multidimensional databases consists in finding each exception E in the form $A \stackrel{\neg s}{\Longrightarrow} B\,[Z]$, which satisfies the following conditions:*

1. (a) $Sup(A \cup Z) \geq MinSup$ and (b) $Sup(B \cup Z) \geq MinSup$;
2. $IM(E) \geq I_{min}$;
3. $DU(E) \geq D_{min}$.

3 Algorithm

An algorithm for mining exceptions is given in Fig. 1. Phase 1 (line 1) identifies all probe sets. Phase 2 (lines 2-9) generates all candidate exceptions, combining each probe set in *ProbeSets* with each positive association rule in PR (line 5). In order to compute the IM and DU indices, we need to count the actual

---

Input: $MinSup$, I_{min}, D_{min} - threshold values; PR - a set of multidimensional rules; $Atrib$ - a set of attributes; **Output:** ME - a set of mined exceptions;

procedure `FindExceptions`

1. $ProbeSets$ = generate all possible probe sets from $Atrib$;
2. $CandidateExceptions = \emptyset$; $ConditionsSet = \emptyset$; $ME = \emptyset$
3. **for** each rule $R : A \Rightarrow B$ in PR **do**
4.   **for** each probe set Z in $ProbeSets$ **do**
5. $CandidateExceptions = CandidateExceptions \cup (A \Rightarrow B\,[Z])$;
6. $X' = \{\{A\}, \{B\}, \{Z\}, \{A, B\}, \{A, Z\}, \{B, Z\}, \{A, B, Z\}\}$;
7. $ConditionsSet = ConditionsSet \cup X'$;
8.   **end for;**
9. **end for;**
10. perform a database scan to count the support of all sets in $ConditionsSet$;
11. **for** each candidate exception $E' : A \Rightarrow B\,[Z]$ in $CandidateExceptions$ **do**
12.   **if** $Sup(A \cup Z) \geq MinSup$ and $Sup(B \cup Z) \geq MinSup$ and
    $IM(E') \geq I_{min}$ and $DU(E') \geq D_{min}$ **then** $ME = ME \cup (A \stackrel{\neg s}{\Rightarrow} B\,[Z])$;
13. **end for;**

Fig. 1. Algorithm for mining exceptions in multidimensional databases

support values for the following sets: $\{A\}$, $\{B\}$, $\{Z\}$, $\{A,B\}$, $\{A,Z\}$, $\{B,Z\}$, and $\{A,B,Z\}$. The data structure $ConditionsSet$ is used to keep counters for all these sets (lines 6-7). It can be implemented as a *hash tree*, for example. In phase 3 (line 10) an algorithm such as Apriori [1] counts the support of the sets stored in $ConditionsSet$. Finally, phase 4 (lines 11-13) generates the exceptions.

4 Experimental Results

The proposed algorithm was implemented and a test was carried out on the *Mushrooms data set* [2]. This database contains 8124 tuples and 22 attributes used to describe mushrooms. A target attribute classifies each mushroom as either *edible* or *poisonous*. We use the following threshold settings on the experiment: $MinSup = 0.20\%$, $I_{min} = 0.40$, and $D_{min} = 0.10$. The evaluated rule was $(Habitat = \text{``Grasses''}) \Rightarrow (Class\,\text{``Edible''})$, with Sup = 17.33% and Conf = 65.55%. It indicates that great part of the mushrooms specimens that grow on grasses are edible. We use the remaining 20 attributes to form the probe sets. The maximum size of Z was restricted to 3.

Table 2 shows some of the mined exceptions, ranked by the DU index. The highest values for the DU measure (exceptions 1 and 3) were able to represent the best exceptions. The exception 1 shows a very interesting situation: Z is independent of both A and B. However, Z and the original positive rule are highly negative dependent ($IM = 1$). The exceptions 26 and 43 show another interesting aspect: Z and B are positively dependent. However, once again, the IM values are high. The exception 100 is less interesting due to the high negative

Table 2. Experimental results

Rank	Z (Probe Set)	IM	DU	$ND_{A,Z}$	$ND_{B,Z}$
1	($CapShape = $ "$Flat$"), ($StalkShape = $ "$Enlarging$"), ($StalkSurfBelowRing = $ "$Smooth$")	1.0000	0.9286	0.0714	0.0289
3	($GillColor = $ "$White$"), ($StalkSurfBelowRing = $ "$Ibrous$")	1.0000	0.8274	-0.0801	0.1726
26	($Bruises = $ "$True$"), ($RingNumber = $ "Two")	1.0000	0.4600	0.5400	-0.4610
43	($Population = $ "$Solitary$")	0.8382	0.4214	0.4168	-0.1986
100	($StalkColorBelowRing = $ "$Pink$")	1.0000	0.2909	0.7091	0.4060

dependence between Z and A. The adopted approach for mining exceptions was also applied to a real medical data set (the results can be found in [3]).

5 Conclusions

In this paper we addressed the problem of mining exceptions from multidimensional databases. The goal is to find rules that become much weaker in some specific subsets of the database. The exceptions are mined only if the candidates do not achieve an expected support. As a future work we intend to evaluate the interestingness of rules with large deviation between the actual and the expected confidence value. Moreover, the scalability of our algorithm should also be investigated, varying the parameters $MinSup$, I_{min} and D_{min}.

References

1. Agrawal, R., Srikant, R.: Fast Algorithms for Mining Association Rules. In 20th VLDB Intl. Conf. (1994).
2. Blake, C. L., Merz, C. J.: UCI Repository of Machine Learning Databases, http://www.ics.uci.edu/~mlearn/MLRepository.html, Dept. of Inform. and Computer Science, University of California, Irvine (1998).
3. Goncalves, E. C., Plastino, A.: Mining Strong Associations and Exceptions in the STULONG Data Set. In 6th ECML/PKDD Discovery Challenge (2004).
4. Han, J., Kamber, M.: Data Mining: Concepts and Techniques. 2nd edn. Morgan Kaufmann (2001).
5. Hussain, F., Liu, H., Suzuki, E., Lu, H.: Exception Rule Mining with a Relative Interestingness Measure. In 4th PAKDD Intl. Conf. (2000).
6. Savasere, A., Omiecinski, E., Navathe, S.: Mining for Strong Negative Associations in a Large Database of Customer Transactions. In 14th ICDE Intl. Conf. (1998).
7. Suzuki, E., Zytkow, J. M.: Unified Algorithm for Undirected Discovery of Exception Rules. In 4th PKDD Intl. Conf. (2000).
8. Wu, X., Zhang, C., Zhang, S.: Mining both Positive and Negative Association Rules. In 19th ICML Intl. Conf. (2002).

MML Inference of Oblique Decision Trees

Peter J. Tan and David L. Dowe

School of Computer Science and Software Engineering, Monash University,
Clayton, Vic 3800, Australia
ptan@bruce.csse.monash.edu.au

Abstract. We propose a multivariate decision tree inference scheme by using the minimum message length (MML) principle (Wallace and Boulton, 1968; Wallace and Dowe, 1999). The scheme uses MML coding as an objective (goodness-of-fit) function on model selection and searches with a simple evolution strategy. We test our multivariate tree inference scheme on UCI machine learning repository data sets and compare with the decision tree programs C4.5 and C5. The preliminary results show that on average and on most data-sets, MML oblique trees clearly perform better than both C4.5 and C5 on both "right"/"wrong" accuracy and probabilistic prediction - and with smaller trees, i.e., less leaf nodes.

1 Introduction

While there are a number of excellent decision tree learning algorithms such as CART [2], C4.5 and C5 [13], much research effort has been continuously directed to finding new and improved tree induction algorithms. Most decision tree algorithms only test on one attribute at internal nodes, and these are often referred to as univariate trees. One of the obvious limitations of univariate trees is that their internal nodes can only separate the data with hyperplanes perpendicular to the co-ordinate axes. Multivariate decision tree algorithms attempt to generate decision trees by employing discriminant functions at internal nodes with more than one attribute, enabling them to partition the instance space with hyperplanes of arbitrary slope - rather than only parallel to the co-ordinate axes.

We propose an oblique decision tree inference scheme by using the minimum message length (MML) principle [19, 21, 20, 17]. Test results show our new oblique decision tree inference algorithms find smaller trees with better (or near identical) accuracy compared to the standard univariate schemes, C4.5 and C5.

2 MML Inference of Multivariate Decision Trees

MML inference [19, 21, 8, 20, 17, 4, 5, 18] has been successfully implemented in [22] to infer univariate decision trees (refining [14]) and in [12, 16, 17] to infer univariate decision graphs, with the most recent decision graphs [16, 17] clearly out-performing *both* C4.5 and C5 [13] on *both* real-world and artificial data-sets on a range of test criteria - we had better "right"/"wrong" accuracy, substantially

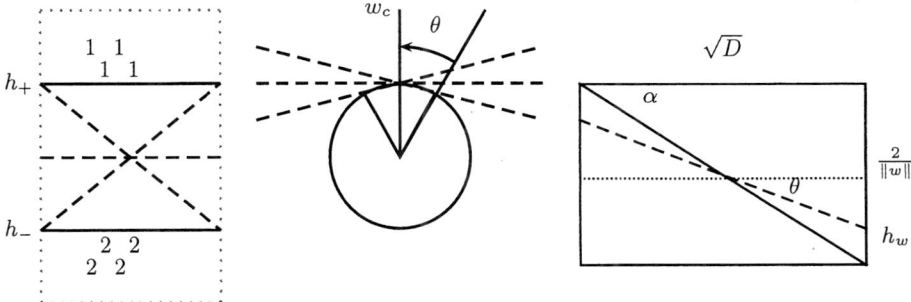

Fig. 1. The set of hyperplanes (Fig. 1a) defined by vector $w \in \Lambda(\theta)$, (Fig. 1b) a partial sphere of radius θ formed by $w \in \Lambda(\theta)$ and (Fig. 1c) the upper bound of θ

better probabilistic score and [17, Table 4] fewer leaf nodes. In this paper, we use MML to infer multivariate decision trees. The new multivariate, oblique, decision tree scheme proposed here generalizes earlier MML decision tree work and re-uses the Wallace and Patrick decision tree coding [22] as part of its coding scheme. For further implementation details, please see [16].

2.1 Encoding an Internal Split Using a Linear Discriminant Function

To infer oblique decision trees by the MML principle, we extend the Wallace and Patrick decision tree coding scheme [22]. The new MML decision tree coding scheme is able to encode an internal split using a linear discriminant function. Firstly, the data falling at an internal node is scaled and normalized so that every data item falls within a D-dimensional unit hyper-cube, where D is the number of input attributes. A linear decision function d(w, x, b)=0 is written as $(\sum_{i=1}^{D} w_i x_i) + b = w \cdot x + b = 0$ where $w, x \in R^D$, $\cdot$ denotes the dot (or scalar) product, and the scalar b is often called the bias. The data is divided into two mutually exclusive sets by the following rules:

If $d(w, x_j, b) > 0, j \in [1, N]$, then x_j is assigned to set I (denoted '1' or '+').
If $d(w, x_j, b) < 0, j \in [1, N]$, then x_j is assigned to set II (denoted '2' or '−').

To encode the hyperplane is equivalent to transmitting the vector w and the bias b. Suppose the desired value of the vector w is w_c. If we state w_c exactly (to infinite precision), it will cost infinitely many bits of information in the first part of the message. So instead, we attempt to state a set of vectors $\Lambda(\theta), \theta \in (0, \frac{\pi}{2})$, which is defined as $\Lambda(\theta) = \{w : \arccos(\frac{w \cdot w_c}{\|w\| \cdot \|w_c\|}) < \theta\}$. This is the set of vectors which form an angle less than θ with the optimal vector w_c as illustrated in Fig. 1b. The probability that a randomly picked vector falls into the set is given by $\frac{V_\theta}{V_T}$, where V_θ is the volume of a partial sphere of radius θ and V_T is the total volume of the unit sphere. The value of $\frac{V_\theta}{V_T}$ is given [15] by $(\sin\theta)^{2(D-1)}$, so the information required to specify the set of the vectors is $-\log((\sin\theta)^{2(D-1)})$.

By specifying one data point on each side of the hyperplane h_c, two hyperplanes which are parallel to the decision surface d(w,x,b)=0 are also defined. We denote these two hyperplanes as h_+ and h_-. These (h_+ and h_-) and the other boundaries of the unit cube form a hyper-rectangle as shown in Fig. 1a. We want to work out the value of θ so that the hyperplanes specified by vectors in the set $\Lambda(\theta)$ do not intersect with the hyperplanes h_+ and h_-. We can imagine a rectangle whose length of one side is the distance between h_+ and h_- and whose length of the other side is $\sqrt{D}$, which is the longest diagonal in a D-dimensional unit cube. As $\{x: kwx+kb=0\} \equiv \{x: wx+b=0\}$ for any non-zero k, we can choose w so that the margin between h_+ and h_- is equivalent to $\frac{2}{\|w\|}$. As shown in Figure 1c, given the margin $\frac{2}{\|w\|}$, if $\theta < \alpha$, where $\alpha = \arcsin(\frac{2}{\sqrt{D\|w\|^2+4}})$, one can show that the hyperplane h_w defined by the vector w does not intersect with hyperplanes h_+ and h_- within the D-dimensional hyper-cube (from Fig. 1a).

2.2 Search for the Optimal Hyperplane

In order to perform faster searches for optimal multivariate splits, we do not use the search heuristic used in OC1 [10] and SADT [9]. Instead, we implement a simple evolution strategy as the preliminary search heuristic for our scheme. A similar approach has appeared in [3], in which promising results were reported. The search process in our scheme can be summarized as follows. Assuming the linear discriminant function in our scheme takes the form $\sum_{i=1}^{d} w_i x_i < w_{d+1}$, for each leaf node L, let M(unsplit) denote the message length of the node L while the node is unsplit, and let M(T) denote the message length of the subtree when node L is split by vector w^T at round T. The algorithm searches for the best vector w via the following steps: Set T=0, input R, MaxP, M(unsplit)

1. Re-scale the coefficients of the vector w such that $\sum_{i=1}^{d} w_i^2 = 1$.
2. With $v \sim N(0,1)$, randomly pick $j \in [1, d+1]$, $w_j^{T+1} = w_j^T + v$.
3. if $M(T+1) < M(T)$, go to step 5
4. $w_j^{T+1} = w_j^T$
5. T=T+1; if $T < R$, go to step 1.
6. Randomly pick d (in this paper, d is limited to 2 or 3) attributes
7. P=P+1; if $P < MaxP$, go to step 1
8. if $M(R) < M(unsplit)$, return w, M(R), else return null and M(unsplit).

The search process (from steps 2 and 6) is non-deterministic, thus our algorithm is able to generate many different trees. As such, our algorithm can be extended to take advantage of this by choosing the best one (i.e., MML tree) among these trees or by averaging [20, p281] results from these trees.

3 Experiments

3.1 Comparing and Scoring Probabilistic Predictions

To evaluate our new oblique decision tree scheme, we run experiments on nine data sets selected from the UCI Repository [1]. The performance of our scheme is compared with those of C4.5 and C5 [13]. In addition to the traditional right/wrong accuracy, we are also keen to compare the probabilistic performance [17, sec 5.1] [7, 6, 11, 16] of the learning algorithms. In a lot of domains, like oncological and other medical data, not only the class predictions but also the probability associated with each class is essential. In some domains, like finance, (long term) strategies heavily rely on accurate probabilistic predictions. For C4.5, C5 and our approach, we ascribe class probabilities from frequency counts in leaves using "+1.0" (Laplace estimation) from [17, sec. 5.1]. To compare probabilistic prediction performances, we propose a metric called the related (test data) code length (RCL), defined as $RCL = -\frac{\sum_{i=1}^{n} \log(p_i)}{n \log(M)}$, where n is the total number of test data, M is the arity of the target attribute and p_i is the probability assigned to the real class associated with the test instance i by the model. The related test data code length (RCL) is equivalent to the code length of the test data encoded by a model divided by the code length encoded by the null theory; thus normalizing [17, Sec. 5.1] [7, 6, 11, 16] $-\sum_{i=1}^{n} \log(p_i)$. The smaller RCL, the better the model's performance on probabilistic prediction.

3.2 Data Sets

The purpose of the experiment is to have our algorithms perform on real world data, especially on oncological and medical data, such as **Bupa**, **Breast Cancer**, **Wisconsin**, **Lung Cancer**, and **Cleveland**. The nine UCI Repository [1] data-sets used are these five, **Balance**, **Credit**, **Sonar** and **Wine**. For each of the nine data sets, 100 independent tests were done by randomly sampling 90% of the data as training data and testing on the remaining 10%.

4 Discussion

We compare the MML oblique tree scheme to C4.5 and C5. The results from Table 1 clearly suggest that the MML oblique trees are much smaller (fewer leaves) than the C4.5 and C5 univariate trees. The MML oblique trees perform significantly better than C4.5 and C5 (which often have RCL scores worse than the default "random null" of 1.0) on all data-sets. MML oblique trees also have higher "right"/"wrong" accuracy than C4.5 and C5 except (for very close results) on the Bupa and Wine (and Cleveland) data, suggesting a possible need to refine the searches. As expected, none of the algorithms have good results on the Lung Cancer data - learning from a small set of data with a great number of attributes remains a great challenge for machine learning algorithms.

Table 1. Test Results

Name	Metric	C4.5	C5	MML Oblique Tree	Random NULL
Balance	Accuracy(%)	77.8 ±4.3	77.8 ± 4.5	88.5 ± 4.0	33.3
	RCL	0.93±0.12	0.92 ±0.11	0.33 ± 0.08	1.00
	Tree Size	81.6±9.7	41.7 ±4.6	10.4 ±0.9	1
Bupa	Accuracy(%)	65.5 ± 7.4	65.5 ± 7.8	65.1 ± 8.1	50.0
	RCL	1.07±0.22	1.07 ±0.21	0.96 ± 0.15	1.00
	Tree Size	49.2±9.8	27.3 ±5.4	6.7 ± 2.6	1
Breast Cancer	Accuracy(%)	71.2 ± 8.7	71.1 ± 8.4	72.8 ± 8.0	50.0
	RCL	0.88±0.17	0.88 ±0.17	0.84 ± 0.14	1.00
	Tree Size	24.2±8.3	13.1 ±4.2	3.0 ± 0.6	1
Wisconsin	Accuracy(%)	94.6 ± 2.5	94.8 ± 2.5	96.0 ± 2.3	50.0
	RCL	0.26±0.10	0.25 ±0.12	0.21 ± 0.10	1.00
	Tree Size	23.7±5.3	12.3 ±2.8	5.5 ± 0.9	1
Credit	Accuracy(%)	73.2 ± 4.3	73.3 ± 3.8	75.4 ± 4.7	50.0
	RCL	0.88±0.08	0.88 ±0.08	0.79 ± 0.09	1.00
	Tree Size	151.4±17.7	77.6 ±9.1	6.5 ± 2.4	1
Lung Cancer	Accuracy(%)	40.0 ± 23.3	40.7 ± 24.8	46.8 ± 22.4	33.3
	RCL	1.83±0.50	1.86 ±0.65	0.94 ± 0.30	1.00
	Tree Size	12.2±2.3	6.6± 1.1	2.2 ± 0.4	1
Cleveland	Accuracy(%)	77.1 ± 7.6	77.2 ± 7.9	77.2 ± 7.8	50.0
	RCL	0.80±0.24	0.81 ±0.21	0.76 ± 0.22	1.00
	Tree Size	36.7±7.2	20.0 ±4.2	7.3 ± 1.8	1
Sonar	Accuracy(%)	72.8 ± 9.2	73.9 ± 10.0	76.0 ± 9.2	50.0
	RCL	1.07±0.37	1.06 ±0.42	0.98 ± 0.33	1.00
	Tree Size	28.2±3.1	14.9 ±1.6	11.6 ± 9.3	1
Wine	Accuracy(%)	93.6 ± 5.7	93.2 ± 5.8	93.2 ± 6.1	33.3
	RCL	0.42±0.30	0.44 ±0.29	0.28 ± 0.18	1.00
	Tree Size	9.6±1.3	5.4 ±0.7	3.6 ± 0.5	1

5 Conclusion and Future Research

We have introduced a new oblique decision tree inference scheme by using the MML principle. Our preliminary algorithm produces very small trees with excellent performance on both "right"/"wrong" accuracy and probabilistic prediction. The search heuristic could be (further) improved. Also, as pointed out in section 2.2, the performance of the system may be enhanced by using multiple tree averaging. Further down the track, to use MML coding for internal nodes with SVMs or nonlinear splits is also an interesting research topic, as is generalising oblique trees to oblique graphs. We also wish to apply Dowe's notion of inverse learning [8] and its special case of generalised Bayesian networks [4, 5] to Dowe's notion of a(n inverse) decision graph model where two values of the target attribute have the same probability ratio in every leaf - e.g., the ternary target attribute has values (i) Female, (ii) Male whose height rounds to an even number of cm and (iii) Males whose height rounds to an odd number of cm.

The second author expresses great fondness and gratitude to his mother. We also thank our mentor, Chris Wallace (1933-2004), a quietly-achieving humble unsung genius and brilliant light clearly ahead of his time. Read his works (e.g., via www.csse.monash.edu.au/~dld/CSWallacePublications/).

References

1. C.L. Blake and C.J. Merz. UCI repository of machine learning databases, 1998. http://www.ics.uci.edu/~mlearn/MLRepository.html.
2. Leo Breiman, Jerome H. Friedman, Richard A. Olshen, and Charles J. Stone. *Classification And Regression Trees*. Wadsworth & Brooks, 1984.
3. Erick Cantu-Paz and Chandrika Kamath. Using evolutionary algorithms to induce oblique decision trees. In *Proc. Genetic and Evolutionary Computation Conference*, pages 1053–1060, Las Vegas, Nevada, USA, 2000. Morgan Kaufmann.
4. Joshua W. Comley and David L. Dowe. Generalised Bayesian networks and asymmetric languages. In *Proc. Hawaii International Conference on Statistics and Related Fields*, 5-8 June 2003.
5. Joshua W. Comley and David L. Dowe. Minimum message length, MDL and generalised Bayesian networks with asymmetric languages. In P. Grünwald, M. A. Pitt, and I. J. Myung, editors, *Advances in Minimum Description Length: Theory and Applications (MDL Handbook)*. M.I.T. Press, to appear.
6. D.L. Dowe, G.E. Farr, A.J. Hurst, and K.L. Lentin. Information-theoretic football tipping. In N. de Mestre, editor, *Third Australian Conference on Mathematics and Computers in Sport*, pages 233–241. Bond University, Qld, Australia, 1996. http://www.csse.monash.edu.au/~footy.
7. D.L. Dowe and N. Krusel. A decision tree model of bushfire activity. In *(Technical report 93/190) Dept. Comp. Sci., Monash Uni., Clayton, Australia*, 1993.
8. D.L. Dowe and C.S. Wallace. Kolmogorov complexity, minimum message length and inverse learning. In *14th Australian Statistical Conference (ASC-14)*, page 144, Gold Coast, Qld, Australia, 6-10 July 1998.
9. David G. Heath, Simon Kasif, and Steven Salzberg. Induction of oblique decision trees. In *International Joint Conference on AI (IJCAI)*, pages 1002–1007, 1993.
10. Sreerama K. Murthy. *On Growing Better Decision Trees from Data*. PhD thesis, The John Hopkins University, 1997.
11. S.L. Needham and D.L. Dowe. Message length as an effective Ockham's razor in decision tree induction. In *Proc. 8th International Workshop on Artificial Intelligence and Statistics*, pages 253–260, Key West, Florida, U.S.A., Jan. 2001.
12. J.J. Oliver and C.S. Wallace. Inferring Decision Graphs. In *Workshop 8 International Joint Conference on AI (IJCAI)*, Sydney, Australia, August 1991.
13. J.R. Quinlan. *C4.5 : Programs for Machine Learning*. Morgan Kaufmann,San Mateo,CA, 1992. The latest version of C5 is available from http://www.rulequest.com.
14. J.R. Quinlan and R. Rivest. Inferring Decision Trees Using the Minimum Description Length Principle. *Information and Computation*, 80:227–248, 1989.
15. R. Schack, G. M. D. Ariano, and C. M. Caves. Hypersensitivity to perturbation in the quantum kicked top. *Physical Review E.*, 50:972–987, 1994.
16. P.J. Tan and D.L. Dowe. MML inference of decision graphs with multi-way joins. In *Proc. 15th Australian Joint Conf. on AI, LNAI 2557 (Springer)*, pages 131–142, Canberra, Australia, 2-6 Dec. 2002.

17. P.J. Tan and D.L. Dowe. MML inference of decision graphs with multiway joins and dynamic attributes. In *Proc. 16th Australian Joint Conf. on AI, LNAI 2903 (Springer)*, pages 269–281, Perth, Australia, Dec. 2003. http://www.csse.monash.edu.au/~dld/Publications/2003/Tan+Dowe2003.ref.
18. Chris Wallace. *Statistical and Inductive Inference by Minimum Message Length*. Springer, to appear.
19. C.S. Wallace and D.M. Boulton. An Information Measure for Classification. *Computer Journal*, 11:185–194, 1968.
20. C.S. Wallace and D.L. Dowe. Minimum Message Length and Kolmogorov Complexity. *Computer Journal*, 42(4):270–283, 1999.
21. C.S. Wallace and P.R. Freeman. Estimation and Inference by Compact Coding. *Journal of the Royal Statistical Society. Series B*, 49(3):240–265, 1987.
22. C.S Wallace and J.D. Patrick. Coding Decision Trees. *Machine Learning*, 11:7–22, 1993.

Naive Bayes Classifiers That Perform Well with Continuous Variables

Remco R. Bouckaert

Computer Science Department, University of Waikato &
Xtal Mountain Information Technology,
New Zealand
remco@cs.waikato.ac.nz, rrb@xm.co.nz

Abstract. There are three main methods for handling continuous variables in naive Bayes classifiers, namely, the normal method (parametric approach), the kernel method (non parametric approach) and discretization. In this article, we perform a methodologically sound comparison of the three methods, which shows large mutual differences of each of the methods and no single method being universally better. This suggests that a method for selecting one of the three approaches to continuous variables could improve overall performance of the naive Bayes classifier. We present three methods that can be implemented efficiently v-fold cross validation for the normal, kernel and discretization method. Empirical evidence suggests that selection using 10 fold cross validation (especially when repeated 10 times) can largely and significantly improve over all performance of naive Bayes classifiers and consistently outperform any of the three popular methods for dealing with continuous variables on their own. This is remarkable, since selection among more classifiers does not consistently result in better accuracy.

1 Introduction

Naive Bayes classifiers perform well over a wide range of classification problems, including medical diagnosis, text categorization, collaborative and email filtering, and information retrieval (see [13] for a pointer to the literature). Compared with more sophisticated schemes, naive Bayes classifiers often perform better [5]. Furthermore, naive Bayes can deal with a large number of variables and large data sets, and it handles both discrete and continuous attribute variables.

There are three main methods for dealing with continuous variables in naive Bayes classifiers. The *normal method* is the classical method that approximates the distribution of the continuous variable using a parameterized distribution such as the Gaussian. The *kernel method* [9] uses a non-parameterized approximation. Finally, the *discretization methods* [6] first discretizes the continuous variables into discrete ones, leaving a simpler problem without any continuous variables. In recent years, much progress has been made in understanding why discretization methods work [8, 13, 14]. In general, it is acknowledged that the normal method tends to perform worse than the other two methods.

However, experimental comparisons among all three methods have not been performed. Also, comparisons among the normal with kernel methods [9] and normal with discretization methods [6] is based on single runs of cross validation, which is known to have an elevated Type I error [4] and suffers from low replicability [2]. In this article, we perform a proper comparison and show how to select the method that performs well using an efficient method.

In the extended version of this paper [3] we describe the classification problem, give a technical description of naive Bayes classifiers and the three methods for dealing with continuous variables. It also deals with selecting the correct method for a given data set and shows how to do this efficiently. In this abbreviated paper, we present experimental results and discuss our findings. We conclude with recommendations and directions for further research in Section 3.

2 Experiments

Taking 25 UCI datasets with continuous variables [1] (see [3] for properties) as distributed with Weka [11], we compared naive Bayes using normal distributions with normal kernel distributions [9] and supervised discretization [7]. All experiments were performed with Weka [11] using 10 times 10 fold cross validation since this guarantees high replicability [2]. Algorithms are pairwise compared both with uncorrected and variance corrected paired t-tests [10]. The uncorrected outcomes are presented because most papers use it, which makes our experiments comparable to others. However, uncorrected tests tend to have a Type I error an order of magnitudes larger than the desired significance level while variance corrected tests have a Type I error close to the significance level [2, 10].

Experiments on Naive Bayes Methods. We compared each of the three methods on their own (see [3] for full numeric results). Some observations that could be made: The normal method performs significantly worse for the majority of data sets than the kernel method. The exceptions are German credit and diabetes, where the normal method outperforms the kernel method significantly. These results confirm the ones in [9]. However, in [9] reported that colic and cleveland heart disease performed significantly better than the kernel method, a result not replicated in our experiment. This can be explained by the experimental method deployed in [9] having low replicability [2], unlike the 10x10 cross validation method we use here.

Likewise, the normal method performs significantly worse for the majority of data sets than the discretization method. However, there are six data sets where the normal method outperforms the discretization method significantly. On the whole, one can conclude that discretization often helps, so the claims to this effect [6, 14] are confirmed. It is noteworthy that these six data sets differ from the two where the normal method outperforms the kernel method.

Though both the kernel method and discretization method outperform the normal method for the majority of the data sets, there is a large performance difference between the two methods. For example, on balance scale the accuracy

Table 1. Average accuracies on 10x10 cross validation experiment for naive Bayes selection algorithms. Legend: b/o = better/worse than normal, v/* = better/worse than kernel, w/- = better/worse than discretization, c/n = better/worse than best on training, d/e = better/worse than best on 10 cv. Single marker indicate significant difference at 5% for uncorrected test, double markers for corrected test as well

Dataset	best on train	best on 10 cv	best on 10x10 cv	best in literature
anneal	96.0 ± 2.2 bb vv	95.9 ± 2.2 bb vv	95.9 ± 2.2 bb vv	98.2 [12]
arrhythmia	66.0 ± 5.4 b - -	72.2 ± 5.3 bb vv cc	72.2 ± 5.3 bb vv cc	n/a
autos	62.3 ±11.5 b -	63.7 ±12.3 b v - c	65.0 ±11.1 bb v c d	n/a
balance-scale	91.4 ± 1.3 b ww	91.4 ± 1.4 b ww	91.4 ± 1.3 b ww	n/a
breast-wisconsin	97.5 ± 1.7 bb w	97.5 ± 1.7 bb w	97.4 ± 1.8 bb * w n	97.5 [12]
horse-colic	79.3 ± 5.8	79.3 ± 5.9 b	79.4 ± 5.9 b	81.0±2.5[6]
credit-rating	86.2 ± 3.8 bb vv	86.2 ± 3.8 bb vv	86.2 ± 3.8 bb vv	85.9 [12]
german-credit	74.4 ± 3.9 o -	74.8 ± 3.5 o v	74.9 ± 3.6 o v c	75.6±0.9 [6]
pima-diabetes	74.8 ± 5.0 o -	74.9 ± 5.0 o	74.5 ± 5.2 o	76.2±4.8 [8]
ecoli	86.6 ± 5.1 b ww	86.3 ± 5.1 b * ww	86.5 ± 5.2 b * ww	84.0 [12]
Glass	71.9 ± 8.7 bb vv	71.9 ± 8.7 bb vv	71.9 ± 8.7 bb vv	71.5±1.9 [6]
heart-cleveland	84.1 ± 6.8 b	83.2 ± 6.9 * n	83.6 ± 7.1 * n	84.7 [12]
heart-hungarian	84.6 ± 5.9 *	84.4 ± 5.8 *	84.7 ± 5.8 b *	84.1±2.8 [5]
heart-statlog	83.5 ± 6.3 * w	82.8 ± 5.9 o * n	82.9 ± 6.0 * n	n/a
hepatitis	84.7 ± 9.4 b	84.3 ± 9.6 *	84.5 ± 9.6 * c	86.6 [12]
hypothyroid	98.2 ± 0.7 bb vv	98.2 ± 0.7 bb vv	98.2 ± 0.7 bb vv	98.6±0.4 [6]
ionosphere	91.8 ± 4.1 bb w	91.8 ± 4.1 bb w	91.8 ± 4.1 bb w	91.5 [12]
iris	95.9 ± 4.9 w	95.6 ± 5.2 * w	96 ± 4.9 w	96.0±0.3 [9]
labor	93.0 ±10.9 w	92.9 ±11.7 w	93.4 ±10.8 w	94.7 [12]
lymphography	83.3 ± 8.5 -	84.0 ± 8.2 b -	84.4 ± 8.3 b v -	81.6±5.9 [5]
segment	91.2 ± 1.7 bb	91.2 ± 1.7 bb vv	91.2 ± 1.7 bb vv	n/a
sick	97.1 ± 0.8 bb vv	97.1 ± 0.8 bb vv	97.1 ± 0.8 bb vv	95.6±0.6 [6]
sonar	76.5 ± 9.3 bb v	76.4 ± 9.4 bb v	76.4 ± 9.4 bb v	77.2 [12]
vehicle	61.0 ± 3.6 bb	60.9 ± 3.4 bb	60.8 ± 3.3 bb	62.3±2.2 [8]
vowel	70.3 ± 4.9 bb ww	70.3 ± 4.9 bb ww	70.3 ± 4.9 bb ww	64.8 [12]

for the kernel method is 91.44 (1.3) while for the discretization method it is 71.56 (4.77) which is significantly worse. The vowel data shows a similar difference. On the other hand, for the segment data, the kernel method gives 85.77 (1.82) while the discretization method gives 91.15 (1.72). So, surprisingly there are large differences between the performance of those two methods.

Experiments on Selection Methods. Table 1 shows results on a 10x10 cross validation experiment[1] for the three methods of selecting one of the methods for handling continuous variables. Markers are shown comparing these methods with the three naive Bayes methods as well. Further, markers are only added comparing algorithms in columns to the left.

One might expect a method that selects the best of the methods to produce an accuracy that is equal to one of the two methods. However, in our experiments, the accuracy of the 'best of both' methods typically differs from the methods it selects from. The reason is that the 'best of both' methods do not always consistently select the same method for different runs and folds in the 10x10

---
[1] Do not confuse the 10x10 cross validation (cv) experiment with the best on 10x10 cv selector. Note that for the best on 10x10 cv selector in this 10x10 cv experiment, each naive Bayes method is applied 10,000 times on each of the data sets.

cross validation experiment. Consequently, the reported accuracy is an average over a mix of the two methods.

Over all, the best on train selector performs remarkably better than the simple methods. It only performs significantly worse (corrected test) than the discretization method on the arrhytmia data set, but otherwise performs equal or significantly better (corrected test) than the normal, kernel and discretization method. On its own, this is already an indication that it helps to be selective about the method for handling continuous variables.

The 10 cv and 10x10 cv selectors perform not significantly worse than the simple methods on any data set but better on many data sets (corrected test). Further, they perform significantly better than the best on train on the arrhytmia data set (corrected). The 10 cv and 10x10 cv selectors perform comparably well, though there is some weak evidence in favor of 10x10, which performs better on the autos set and more often outperforms the other methods.

The last column in Table 1 shows the best results reported in the literature [5, 6, 8, 9, 12] with a wide range of methods for dealing with continuous variables for naive Bayes classifiers. Methods used are 20 times 66%/33% resampling [5], 5 fold cross validation [6, 8], 10 fold cross validation [9], and 10 times 3 fold cross validation [12]. So, mutual comparison of the accuracies should be taken with caution. For example, all but the last method are known to have low replicability [2] and given that they are the best of the reported experiments, should be interpreted as somewhat optimistic compared with our 10 times 10 fold cross validation experiment. Remarkably, all of the best results reported are worse or within the standard deviation of the selector algorithms (except anneal), but never are more than 2.3% better. This suggests that our method at least does not perform worse than the methods reported in the literature.

Summary of Experiments. Table 2 shows the ranking of the algorithms considered in this paper where the column 'wins' shows the number of data sets where a method is significantly better than an other, 'losses' where it is worse and 'total' is the difference between these two. The algorithms are ranked according to the total of the corrected tests (note that the uncorrected test gives the same ranking except that the kernel and discretization would be swapped). The repeated ten fold cross validation selector stands out considerably according to the uncorrected test and only slightly according to the corrected test. All methods that perform some form of selection perform considerably better than just the pure method. Since 10 fold cross validation can be performed in (about) the same time as best on training selection, this is the method of choice if computation is an issue. Otherwise, repeated cross validation for selecting the method for dealing with continuous variables is recommended.

We compared the naive Bayes methods with C4.5 on the 25 data sets. C4.5 performs significantly better (corrected) than any of the naive Bayes on some data, for instance, vowel and segment. However, in the ranking with corrected tests, C4.5 ended between the simple methods and the selector methods (as shown in Table 2). So, over all the the simple methods perform worse than C4.5, while selector methods perform better.

Table 2. Ranking of naive Bayes classifiers

Method	Uncorrected			Corrected		
	total	wins	losses	total	wins	losses
best on 10x10 cv	29	41	12	24	24	0
best on 10 cv	22	36	14	23	23	0
best on train	22	37	15	17	20	3
C4.5 discretization	-4	33	37	6	20	14
kernel method	1	42	41	-15	12	27
normal method	-70	15	85	-55	2	57

Furthermore, we performed experiments selecting the best out of the three naive Bayes methods with C4.5, or nearest neighbor or both. Space prevents us to present all results here, but in summary the selection methods never consistently outperformed all classifiers selected among (so sometimes got worse than selection among the naive Bayes methods without C4.5 and/or nearest neighbor). This indicates that simply adding methods to select from does not necessarily increase performance.

3 Conclusions

The contributions of this paper are the following. In this work, we compared all three methods mutually for the first time as far as we know. We used an experimental design that does not suffer from the flaws of the previous empirical comparisons. This comparison shows that all the three methods have their strengths and weaknesses, and none of the three methods systematically outperforms the others on all problems that we considered. We provided a methodology for selecting the best of the three methods. We gave empirical evidence that the method consistently performs at least as good as (according to a 10x10 cv experiment with corrected t-test) any of the other methods on its own. This is remarkable, since selection among naive Bayes together with other methods (C4.5 and nearest neighbor) does not consistently result in the best classifier. Finally, our method is over all better than C4.5 and often appears to perform better than the best naive Bayes classifier reported in the literature.

We recommend that 10 times repeated 10 fold cross validation is used to select a method for dealing with continuous variables. However, if this is computationally impractical, a 10 fold cross validation selection can give reasonable results while being able to be performed in (almost) the same time as selecting the best method on training data.

Work has been done to explain why discretization works for naive Bayes classifiers [8, 14]. This work raises a new question: why does selection of continuous variable handling methods work for naive Bayes classifiers? We suspect that cross validation works well for naive Bayes classifiers because naive Bayes is a stable classifier, that is, it is not very sensitive to leaving samples out of the data set. John and Langley [9] already showed that the learning rate of the normal method can be slightly better than that of the kernel method if the generating distribution is indeed Gaussian. Conditions under which any of the three methods excel is one of the open questions we would like to address in the future.

References

1. C.L. Blake and C.J. Merz. UCI Repository of machine learning databases. Irvine, CA: University of California, 1998.
2. R.R. Bouckaert and E. Frank. Evaluating the Replicability of Significance tests for comparing learning algorithms. PAKDD, 2004.
3. R.R. Bouckaert. Naive Bayes Classifiers that Perform Well with Continuous Variables. Technicl Report, Computer Science Department, University of Waikato
4. T.G. Dietterich. Approximate Statistical Tests for Comparing Supervised Classification Learning Algorithms. Neural Computation, 10(7) 1895–1924, 1998.
5. P. Domingos and M. Pazzani. On the optimality of the simple Bayesian classifier under zero-one loss. Machine Learning, 29, 103–130, 1997.
6. J. Dougherty, R. Kohavi and M. Sahami. Supervised and unsupervised discretization of continuous features. ICML, 194–202, 1995.
7. U.M. Fayyad and K.B. Irani. Multi-interval discretization of continuousvalued attributes for classification learning. IJCAI, 1022–1027, 1993.
8. C.N. Hsu, H.J. Huang and T.T. Wong. Why Discretization Works for Naive Bayes Classifiers. ICML, 399-406, 2000.
9. G.H. John and P. Langley. Estimating Continuous Distributions in Bayesian Classifiers. UAI, 338–345, 1995.
10. C. Nadeau and Y. Bengio. Inference for the generalization error. NIPS, 2000.
11. I.H. Witten and E. Frank. Data mining: Practical machine learning tools and techniques with Java implementations. Morgan Kaufmann, San Francisco, 2000.
12. Y. Yang and G.I. Webb. A Comparative Study of Discretization Methods for Naive-Bayes Classifiers. In Proceedings of PKAW 2002, 159-173, 2002.
13. Y. Yang and G.I. Webb. Discretization For Naive-Bayes Learning: Managing Discretization Bias And Variance. Techn Rep 2003/131, Monash University. 2003.
14. Y. Yang and G.I. Webb. On Why Discretization Works for Naive-Bayes Classifiers. In Proceedings of the 16th Australian Conference on AI (AI 03), 440-452, 2003.

On Enhancing the Performance of Spam Mail Filtering System Using Semantic Enrichment

Hyun-Jun Kim, Heung-Nam Kim, Jason J. Jung, and Geun-Sik Jo

Intelligent E-Commerce Systems Laboratory,
School of Computer and Information Engineering, Inha University,
253 YongHyun-Dong, Incheon, Korea 402-751
{dannis, nami4596, j2jung}@eslab.inha.ac.kr
gsjo@inha.ac.kr

Abstract. With the explosive growth of the Internet, e-mails are regarded as one of the most important methods to send e-mails as a substitute for traditional communications. As e-mail has become a major mean of communication in the Internet age, exponentially growing spam mails have been raised as a main problem. As a result of this problem, researchers have suggested many methodologies to solve it. Especially, Bayesian classifier-based systems show high performances to filter spam mail and many commercial products available. However, they have several problems. First, it has a cold start problem, that is, training phase has to be done before execution of the system. The system must be trained about spam and non-spam mail. Second, its cost for filtering spam mail is higher than rule-based systems. Last problem, we focus on, is that the filtering performance is decreased when E-mail has only a few terms which represent its contents. To solve this problem, we suggest spam mail filtering system using concept indexing and Semantic Enrichment. For the performance evaluation, we compare our experimental results with those of Bayesian classifier which is widely used in spam mail filtering. The experimental result shows that the proposed system has improved performance in comparison with Bayesian classifier respectively.

1 Introduction

As the Internet infrastructure has been developed, E-mail is used as one of the major methods for exchanging information. Meanwhile, exponentially growing spam mails have been raised as a main problem and its rate in users' mailbox is increasing every year [1]. Hence, mail service companies have troubles in managing their storage devices and also users have problems that consume time to delete spam mails. According to the recent research from one of the biggest Internet service companies, 84.4% of total mail was spam mail [2]. To solve the problem, there have been many studies using rule-based methods [3] and probabilistic methods such as Bayesian classifier. Especially, Bayesian classifier-based systems usually show high performances of precision and recall. However, they have several problems. First, they have a cold start problem, that is, training phase has to be done before execution of the system. Second, the cost of spam mail filtering is higher than rule-based systems [4]. Third, if a mail has only a few terms represent its contents, the filtering performance is fallen. In previous research, we focused on the last issued problem and proposed a spam mail filtering system using Semantic Enrichment with ontology that are constructed manually by a domain expert [5]. If there is an email with only a few terms those represent its content, we enriched conceptualized terms to emails for robust classification tasks through ontology or conceptualized index. However, a domain expert who constructs ontology can influence the performance of the system. To overcome this problem, in this paper, we adopt concept method, which can lead to the construction more accurate spam mail filtering, to generate conceptualized index automatically.

2 Related Work

Spam mail filtering system has been developed for recent years, and there have been lots of studies to increase the performance of the system. Rule-based system is suggested in 1996 to classify spam mails, but this system can be strongly influenced by the existence of key terms, specific terms can cause the failure of filtering [6]. Naïve Bayesian classifier is traditionally very popular method for document classification and mail filtering system [7]. It uses probabilistic method; it can compute test document d_i's possible categories, therefore, many spam mail filtering systems currently have adopted it. As we mentioned in earlier, there are several problems remained. Many researchers also suggested new systems using other methods such as Bayesian network enhancing the performance of Bayesian classification [8], and WBC (Weighted Bayesian Classifier) that gives weight on some key terms that representing the content's class by using SVM (Support Vector Machine) [9].

3 Concept Indexing for Semantic Enrichment

Originally, semantic enrichment is a process that upgrades the semantics of databases. This is usually done by remodeling database schemas in a higher data model in order to explicitly express semantics that is implicit in the data [10]. Such an approach can lead to construction of much more accurate filters for ambiguous emails containing only a few terms. In the previous system, we proposed that the classes on ontology which are constructed manually by a domain expert. And we enriched contents with terms of ontological classes [5]. In this paper, we adopt concept method to generate conceptualized index automatically.

3.1 Concept Indexing

There have been several studies using a concept method to represent a document topic. Some researcher propose conceptual search among documents by creating a representation in terms of conceptual word [14], [15]. And another research designs the recommendation system for customer email reply through integration of different concepts and classifications. The advantages of using a concept method are that it does away with the feature filtering step and can thus save on feature storage space. Moreover, computation complexity is reduced [11].

We first generate a concept set which is used on testing phase for semantic enrichment. We train the concept set derived from spam mail and nonspam mail. And then compute the importance of the terms for each concept. For example, let us say there are two classes, C_{Spam} and $C_{Nonspam}$. Each class has concepts, $C_{Spam}=\{c_1,c_2,...,c_n\}$ and $C_{NonSpam}=\{c_1,c_2,...,c_n\}$, which can be defined as a group of terms that are able to express the meanings of email. Each concept is characterized by a set of terms and computed as shown in the Eq. (1).

$$W_{ik} = \log(f_{ik}+1.0) \times \left(1 + \frac{1}{\log(N)} \sum_{j=1}^{N} \left[\frac{f_{ij}}{n_i} \log \frac{f_{ij}}{n_i}\right]\right) \quad (1)$$

where f_{ik} is the number of times that term i appears in concept k, N is the total number of concepts, and n_i is the number of concepts with term i. W_{ik} is the weight of term i for a particular concept k and indicates the importance of a term in representing the concept.

3.2 Spam Mail Filtering Using Semantic Enrichment

By using concept index constructed through training phase, the system can filter test mails. If there is a mail with few terms, the system makes it possible to understand mail in terms of the semantic content for effective filtering. When we assume E-mail as a document, document D_k contains its terms d_i, and each concept C_m of index also contains its terms c_j.

$$\text{Candidate Concept} = \text{Rank}(\text{Sim}(\vec{D}_k, \vec{C}_m)) = \frac{\vec{D}_k \cdot \vec{C}_m}{|\vec{D}_k||\vec{C}_m|} \quad (2)$$

As shown in Eq. (2), candidate concepts are calculated by cosine similarity method. Once the similarity is computed about all concepts, we use these concepts according to their rank. And then, the system builds relationships between terms in a mail and sub concepts of index. Then the system enriches conceptualized terms from candidate concepts. This helps a mail with few terms to be rich contents. According to the table 1, the result of traditional system is two - spam and nonspam. But it can be a problem for filtering performance because spam and nonspam is disjoint concept whereas traditionally trained systems try to learn a unified concept description [12].

Table 1. Frequency matrix which the system only trained spam and nonspam mail

	C_{Spam}				$C_{NonSpam}$			
Terms	a_1	a_2	a_3	a_4	a_1	a_2	a_3	a_4
Frequency	4	2	1	3	5	3	2	2

Table 2. Frequency matrix which the system trained spam and nonspam mail with concept indexing. (Candidate concept of C_{Spam} is $\{c_1\}$ and $C_{NonSpam}$ is $\{c_2, c_3, c_4\}$)

Category Terms	C_{Spam}				$C_{NonSpam}$			
	c_1	c_2	c_3	c_4	c_1	c_2	c_3	c_4
a_1	3	0	0	1	1	2	1	1
a_2	1	0	1	0	0	1	1	1
a_3	0	1	0	0	0	1	0	1
a_4	2	0	1	0	0	1	1	0
a_5	6	1	2	1	1	5	3	3

When there is a frequency matrix as shown in Table 1, and a test mail $D_k=\{a_1,a_2\}$, k=spam, we can get a candidate concept of C_{Spam}= 4+2 and $C_{NonSpam}$= 5+3. Therefore the system will classify D_k as nonspam mail, $C_{NonSpam}$.

But if there is another frequency matrix as shown in Table 2, the result can be changed. This table contains sub concepts on C_{Spam} and $C_{NonSpam}$. So we can calculate probability more precisely. The first step to classify D_k is finding candidate concepts from spam and nonspam classes. The candidate concept is simply computed by cosine-similarity method, and then we can find two of most similar sub concepts from spam and nonspam classes. The second step is the semantic enrichment. It is executed to D_k. As we can see in Fig. 1, each candidate concept is enriched (underlined terms, a_i is enriched terms). Unlike the result of Table 1 we can get the most reliable concept from candidate concepts, its result is different. In Fig. 3, the most reliable sub concept in spam class is C_2 and in nonspam is C_1. Finally, the system compares these two classes, and it will classify the document D_k as nonspam mail.

$$\text{Spam} : C_1 = \{ a_2, a_3, \underline{a_4}\} = \{3,1,2\} = 6$$
$$\text{NonSpam} : C_2 = \{ a_1, a_2, \underline{a_3}, \underline{a_4}\} = \{2,1,1,1\} = 5$$
$$C_3 = \{ a_1, a_2, \underline{a_4}\} = \{1,1,1\} = 3$$
$$C_4 = \{ a_1, a_2, \underline{a_3}\} = \{1,1,1\} = 3$$

Fig. 1. Semantic enrichment on each candidate concepts and the result

Surely, this result will affect on Bayesian classifier because terms' frequencies are directly influence probability of a class. Now we showed a simple example of semantic enrichment based on frequency table. However, since the Bayesian classifier is probabilistic model, terms' frequency has also influence directly on the result.

4 Experiment

The proposed system is implemented using Visual Basic, ASP (Active Server Page), MS-SQL Server and IIS 5.0 environments. All the experiments are performed on a 2.4GHz Pentium PC with 256M RAM, running Microsoft Window 2000 Server. We used *lingspam* mail set which introduced by Androutsopoulos [13]. For the experiment, we trained 329 of spam mails and 247 of nonspam mails. Meanwhile, we tested 148 of spam mails and 53 of nonspam mails. As shown in table 3, Experiment for evaluating the proposed system is comparing our system against Bayesian classifier which is widely used in text classification system and previous system which is using manually constructed ontology. Through the previous work [5], we found that when we enrich 5 of related terms, the performance shows the best. Meanwhile, when we enriched more than 12 terms, the performance is begun to down. This means that much of the enriched terms can lead to confusion. Therefore, we run experiments in performance comparison of semantic enrichment method with Bayesian classifier as setting enriched number of terms = 5.

Table 3. Comparison result between bayesian classifier and two types of proposed system

		Precision	Recall	F1-measure
A	Bayesian Classifier	89.21%	77.5%	82.94%
B1	Semantic Enrichment with manually constructed Ontology	93.33%	88%	90.58%
B2	Semantic Enrichment with Concept Indexing	96.4	89.1	92.6%
Improved Performance (B1 vs. B2)		3.07%	1.1%	2.02 %

Experimental result shows that precision, recall and F1-measure of our proposed method are improved 3.07%, 1.1% and 2.02% on those of using manually constructed ontology respectively. Not only the proposed system shows a better performance than previous system, but also it is independent on much kind of domains because this system constructs the concept index automatically. As we already mentioned in previous work [5], this system also showed a stable performance even when the number of terms is small. It covers one of major defect of Bayesian classifier. This result implied that the proposed system could make the system understandable and improve the performance of the classification

5 Conclusions and Future Work

In this paper, we proposed a new efficient method for spam mail filtering by using Semantic Enrichment technology with concept indexing. The major advantage of the system is that ambiguous mails can be filtered by making the system understandable. And even when a mail has only few terms, by enriching terms, the system can understand it. In previous work, we manually constructed ontology for enriching related terms to original mail context. However in this paper we proposed more intelligent method for constructing concept index. Also, through the concept indexing technique, we can make a hierarchy for semantic enrichment automatically and more precisely. The experimental results showed that the proposed method has better filtering performances compare to the semantic enrichment with manually constructed ontology.

As a future work, we will verify the performance of the concept indexing technique using different data sets which represent different domains. And we will develop the system in aspect of real world adaptation, that is, we need to enhance not only the filtering performance but also the computation speed.

References

1. National Computerization Agency. : National Informatization White Paper, (2002) 23.
2. Korean Telecom. : www.kt.co.kr (2004)
3. W. W. Cohen : Learning rules that classify e-mail, Proc. of the AAAI Spring Symp., (1996).
4. Provost, J. : Naive-Bayes vs. Rule-Learning in Classification of Email, Technical report, Dept. of Computer Sciences at the U. of Texas ay Austin, (1999).
5. H. J. Kim, H. N. Kim, J. J. Jung, G. S. Jo, : Spam mail Filtering System using Semantic Enrichment, Proc. of the 5th International Conference on Web Information Systems Engineering, (2004).
6. Ricardo, B.-Y. and Berthier, R.-N. : Modern Information Retrieval, Addison-Wesley, (1999).
7. Mitchell, T. M. : Machine Learning, Chapter 6: Bayesian Learning, McGraw-Hill, (1997).
8. Sahami, M., Dumais, S., Heckerman, D. and Horvitz, E. : A Bayesian Approach to Filtering Junk E-Mail. In Learning for Text Categorization, Proc. of the AAAI Workshop, Madison Wisconsin. AAAI Technical Report WS-98-05, (1998) 55-62.
9. Thomas, G. and Peter, A. F. : Weighted Bayesian Classification based on Support Vector Machine, Proc. of the 18th International Conference on Machine Learning, (2001) 207-209.
10. Hohenstein, U., Plesser, V. : Semantic Enrichment : A First Step to Provide Database Interoperability, Proc of the Workshop Föderierte Datenbanken, Magdeburg, (1996).
11. Weng, S. S and Liu, C. K. : Using text classification and multiple concepts to answer e-mail, Expert System with Application, (2004) 529-543.
12. Pádraig C., Niamh N., Sarah J. D., Mads H. : A Case-Based Approach to Spam Filtering that Can Track Concept Drift, Proc. of the ICCBR03 Workshop on Long-Lived CBR System, (2003)
13. Maedche, A. : Ontology Learning for the Semantic Web, Kluwer academic publishers, (2002) 29-55.
14. Androutsopoulos, I., Koutsias, J., Chandrinos, K.V., Paliouras, G., Spyropoulos, C.D., : An Evaluation of Naive Bayesian Anti-Spam Filtering, Proc. of the ECML 2000 Workshop on Machine Learning in the New Information, (2000) 9-17.
15. Aggarwal, C. C. and Yu, P. H. : On Effective Conceptual Indexing and Similarity Search in Text Data, Proc of the 2001 IEEE International Conference on Data Mining, (2001)
16. Alsaffar, A. H., Deogun, J. S., Raghavan, V. V., and Sever, H. : Enhancing Concept-Based Retrieval Based on Minimal Term sets, Journal of Intelligent Information Systems, (2000) 155-173

Parameterising Bayesian Networks

Owen Woodberry[1], Ann E. Nicholson[1], Kevin B. Korb[1], and Carmel Pollino[2]

[1]School of Computer Science and Software Engineering
[2]Water Studies Centre, School of Chemistry,
Monash University, Clayton, Victoria 3800, Australia
{owenw, annn, korb}@csse.monash.edu.au
carmel.pollino@sci.monash.edu.au

Abstract. Most documented Bayesian network (BN) applications have been built through knowledge elicitation from domain experts (DEs). The difficulties involved have led to growing interest in machine learning of BNs from data. There is a further need for combining what can be learned from the data with what can be elicited from DEs. In this paper, we propose a detailed methodology for this combination, specifically for the parameters of a BN.

1 Introduction

Bayesian networks (BNs) are graphical models for probabilistic reasoning, which are now widely accepted in the AI community as intuitively appealing and practical representations for reasoning under uncertainty. A BN is a representation of a joint probability distribution over a set of statistical variables. It has both a qualitative aspect, the graph structure, and a quantitative aspect, marginal and conditional probabilities. The structure is a directed acyclic graph and formally represents the structural assumptions of the domain, i.e., the variables comprising the domain and their direct probabilistic dependencies, which are typically given a causal interpretation. The quantitative aspect associates with each node a conditional probability table (CPT), which describes the probability of each value of the child node, conditioned on every possible combination of values of its parents. Given both the qualitative and the quantitative parts, probabilities of any query variables posterior to any evidence can be calculated [10].

Most reported BN applications to date (including medical and other diagnosis, planning, monitoring and information retrieval - see [6-Ch.5] for a recent survey) have been built through knowledge elicitation from domain experts (DEs). In general, this is difficult and time consuming [4], with problems involving incomplete knowledge of the domain, common human difficulties in specifying and combining probabilities, and DEs being unable to identify the causal direction of influences between variables. Hence, there has been increasing interest in automated methods for constructing BNs from data (e.g., [11, 5]). Thus far, a methodology and associated support tools for Knowledge Engineering Bayesian Networks (KEBN) are not well developed. Spiral, prototype-based approaches to KEBN have been proposed (e.g., [7, 6]), based on successful software development processes (e.g. [2]). However, these provide little guidance on how to integrate the knowledge engineering of the qualitative and quantitative components or again on how to combine knowledge elicitation from DEs and automated knowledge discovery methods. While there have been attempts at the latter, they remain rudimentary (e.g., [9, 8]). Here we present a more detailed methodology, based on the spiral prototype model, for knowledge engineering the quantitative component of a BN. Our methodology explicitly integrates KE processes using both DEs and machine learning, in both the parameter estimation and the evaluation phases. The methodology was developed during the knowledge engineering of an ecological risk assessment domain, described in [12].

2 Quantitative Knowledge Engineering Methodology

A possible methodology for quantitative KEBN is outlined in Figure 1. This method illustrates possible flows (indicated by arrows) through the different KE processes (rectangular boxes), which will be executed either by humans (the DE and the knowledge engineer, represented by clear boxes) or computer programs (shaded boxes). Major choice points are indicated by hexagons.

The initial stage in the development spiral is **Structural Development and Evaluation**, which on the first iteration will produce an unparameterized causal network; a network structure must exist prior to parameterization and may need to be reconsidered after evaluation We do not describe this process in any detail, however it should also proceed in an iterative fashion. Once a BN structure has been established, the next step is **parameter estimation**, involving specifying the CPTs for each node. Figure 1 shows that the parameter estimates can be elicited from DEs (1),[1] or learned from data (2) or, as proposed here, generated from a combination of both sources (an example is shown in path 3). In early prototypes the parameter estimates need not be exact, and uniform distributions can be used if neither domain knowledge nor data are readily available. A detailed description of the parameter estimation process is provided in Section 3 below.

The second major aspect of quantitative knowledge engineering is **quantitative evaluation**. Evaluative feedback can be generated using either DEs or data or both, as we have done here. When data is available, several measures can be used to evaluate BNs, including predictive accuracy, expected value computations and information reward. DE evaluation techniques include elicitation reviews and model walkthroughs (see Figure 1). Another kind of evaluation is *sensitivity analysis*. This involves analysing how sensitive the network is, in terms of changes in updated probabilities of some query nodes to changes in parameters and inputs. Measures for these can be computed automatically using BN tools (shown as **Sensitivity to Parameters** and **Sensitivity to Findings** processes, in Figure 1), but these need to be evaluated by the DE in conjunction with the KE. A detailed description of sensitivity analysis is given in Section 4.

---

[1] This can also include the domain literature as a source of parameter estimates.

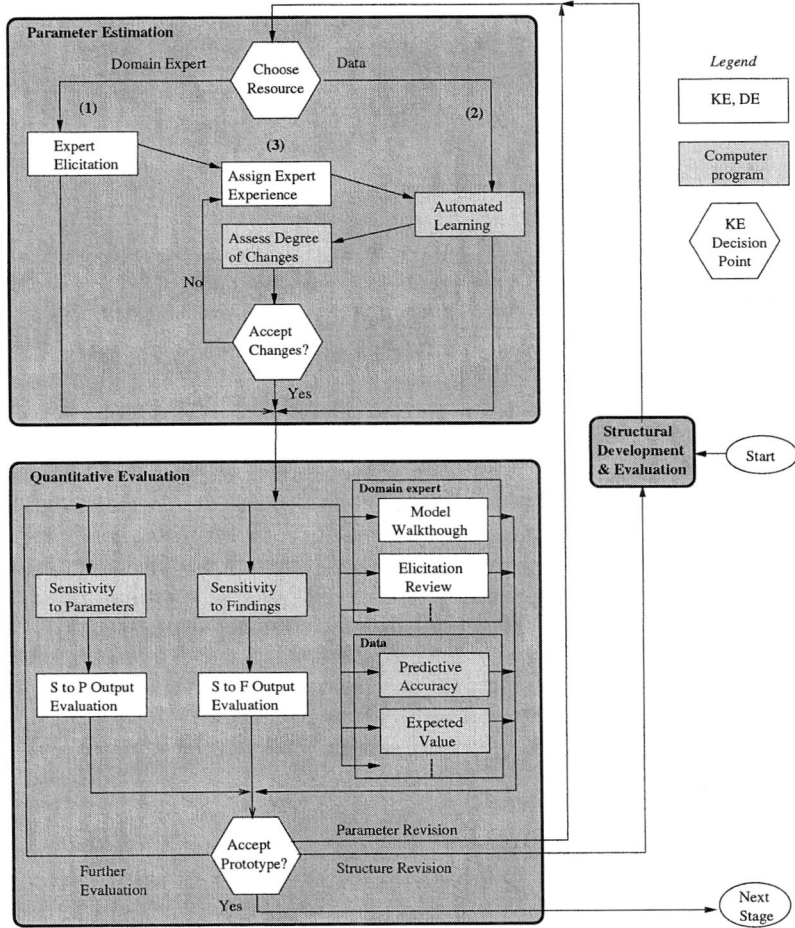

Fig. 1. Quantitative Knowledge Engineering Methodology

3 Parameter Estimation

During **expert elicitation** the DEs provide or refine estimates of the BN parameters. Direct elicitation employs such questions as *"What is the probability that variable **A** takes this state given these parent values?"* Alternatives are to use frequencies, odds, or qualitative elicitation, using terms such as 'high' or 'unlikely', with the mapping to actual probabilities calibrated separately. In addition to eliciting precise parameters, it can also be useful to elicit an acceptable range for the parameter. As many are familiar with 95% confidence intervals from statistics, DEs might be comfortable reporting intervals having a 95% chance of capturing the desired parameter, although other ways of specifying a range of values are equally legitimate. Such intervals can be used during later evaluation to identify parameters needing further attention, as we shall see.

When data is of good quality and voluminous, estimating parameters from the data is clearly preferable. Many techniques are available for this (see [6–Ch.7]). Problems with incomplete data can be ameliorated also by incorporating other sources of information for parameters, such as expert knowledge, before automated learning. The combination of elicitation and data-based parameterization requires the elicited information to be weighted relative to the data available. In Figure 1 this is done in the **Assign Expert Experience** process, where an experience weighting is assigned to the expert parameter estimates, based on the confidence in the estimates obtained during expert elicitation. These are then treated as equivalent to the size of a hypothetical initial data sample.

After incorporating the data in parameter estimation, the next step is to compare the new with the original parameterization. In Figure 1 we consider this to be an automated process, **Assess Degree of Changes**. As mentioned above, during parameter elicitation an acceptable range of values can also be elicited. Any parameters estimated from the data to be outside this range should be flagged for attention. An alternative method for comparing the parameterizations looks at the Bhattacharyya distance [1] between the two probability distributions. This distance is computed for each possible combination of parent values; higher distances between conditional distributions trigger further attention. The DE must then assess whether these flagged parameter refinements obtained after automated learning are acceptable (in the **Accept Changes** decision point in Figure 1). If not, an iterative investigation of different mappings of the expert experience into equivalent sample sizes can be undertaken.

4 Quantitative Evaluation

After parameterization, the second major aspect of quantitative knowledge engineering is evaluation, which guides further iterations of BN development. When data is available, it can be used for evaluation. Where the data is also being used to learn the structure or the CPTs, it is necessary to divide it into training data and test data, so that evaluation is not done with the very same data used for learning. The most common method of evaluation is to determine the *predictive accuracy* of the BN, which measures the frequency with which the modal node state (that with the highest probability) is observed to be the actual value.

Even when adequate data is available, it is important to involve the DE in evaluation. If expert elicitation has been performed, a structured review of the probability elicitation is important. This procedure could involve: comparing elicited values with available statistics; comparing values across different DEs and seeking explanation for discrepancies; double-checking cases where probabilities are extreme (i.e., at or close to 0 or 1), or where the DEs have indicated a low confidence in the probabilities when originally elicited.

We now review two different types of sensitivity analysis and discuss how we adapted them into algorithms suitable for our purposes. One type of sensitivity study looks at how the BN's posterior distribution changes under different observed conditions, in a "sensitivity to findings" study. The other looks at how the model's distribution changes when particular parameters are altered. Curiously, researchers thus far appear to have employed one or the other of these, but not both in any one study (e.g., [3, 7]). Both are needed for a careful investigation of the properties of a network.

Sensitivity to Findings Analysis. The properties of d-separation can be used to determine whether evidence about one variable may influence belief in a query variable. It is possible to measure this influence and rank evidence nodes by how much of an effect they have. This information can be used to provide guidance for collecting the most informative evidence or as a check on whether the model reflects the DE's intuitions.

Sensitivity to findings can be quantified using two types of measures, entropy and mutual information. **Entropy,** $H(X)$, is commonly used to evaluate the uncertainty, or randomness, of a probability distribution $H(X) = -\sum_{x \in X} P(x) \log P(x)$. We can measure the effect of one variable on another using **mutual information (MI)** $I(X|Y) = H(X) - H(X|Y)$. We have implemented this type of sensitivity to findings (see [12]). Our algorithm computes and displays both the entropy of a specified query node and the ranked mutual information values for a specified set of interest nodes, given a set of evidence for some other observed nodes. The user can subsequently investigate how changes to the evidence will affect the entropy and MI measures. This process allows the DE to identify whether a variable is either too sensitive or insensitive to other variables in particular contexts, which in turn may help identify errors in either the network structure or the CPTs.

Sensitivity to Parameters Analysis. Identifying sensitive parameters in a BN is important for focusing the knowledge engineering effort, for it will focus effort in refining parameterization on those values which have the biggest impact on the target variables. How best to identify these sensitivities remains a current research topic. Sensitivity analysis could be done using an empirical approach, by altering each of the parameters of the query node and observing the related changes in the posterior probabilities of the target node. However, this can be extremely time consuming, especially on large networks. Coupé and Van der Gaag [3] address this difficulty by first identifying a "sensitivity set" of variables given some evidence. These are those variables which can potentially change, meaning the remaining variables can be eliminated from further analysis. The sensitivity set can be found using an adapted d-separation algorithm (see [12]). Coupé and Van der Gaag also demonstrated that the posterior probability of a state given evidence under systematic changes to a parameter value can be given a functional representation, either linear or hyperbolic.

We have implemented this type of sensitivity to parameters (see [12]). When a particular evidence instantiation is set, our algorithm identifies the type of sensitivity function for the parameters by checking whether the query node has any observed descendant nodes. Once the sensitivity function is determined for a parameter, its coefficients can be computed. If the plotted sensitivity function does not behave as the DE expects (its slope, direction or range is unexpected), then this could indicate errors in the network structure or CPTs.

KE Decision: Accept Prototype. Quantitative evaluation can be used to identify problems with the BN structure and parameters. After the model has been evaluated using a particular technique, the KE and DE must determine whether the prototype is to be accepted for the next stage of development. This decision is not intended to be the end of the knowledge engineering, or even prototyping, process. If the prototype is not sufficiently validated for prototype acceptance, **Further evaluation** is one option for the KE and DE. It will often be necessary to use multiple evaluation techniques to validate the model: for example, sensitivity to findings and parameter analyses evaluate different aspects of the model with little overlap, and hence don't substitute for each other. If problems with either the structure or the parameters have been identified, it will be necessary to re-visit the relevant KE processes, **Structural Development & Evaluation** or **Parameter Estimation** respectively, via the main spiral iteration in Figure 1.

5 Conclusion

This study presents a practical approach to the knowledge engineering of Bayesian networks, specifically focusing on their parameterisation. In many real-world applications neither human expertise nor statistical data will suffice to generate parameters reliably. Our methodology incorporates both sources in an iterative prototyping approach, which is guided by quantitative evaluation techniques. We have employed this method successfully in our ecological risk assessment model, which has been accepted for use [12]. In future work we will continue to develop the methodology in application to our ERA model and in other domains.

References

1. A. Bhattacharyya. On a measure of divergence between two statistical populations defined by their probability distributions. *Bulletin of the Calcutta Mathematics Society*, 35:99–110, 1943.
2. F. Brooks. *The Mythical Man-Month: Essays on Software Engineering*. Addison-Wesley, Reading, MA, second edition, 1995.
3. V. M. H. Coupe and L. C. van der Gaag. Properties of sensitivity analysis of Bayesian belief networks. *Annals of Mathematics and Artificial Intelligence*, 36:323–356, 2002.
4. M.J. Druzdzel and L.C. van der Gaag. Building probabilistic networks: Where do the numbers come from? *IEEE Trans. on Knowledge and Data Engineering*, 12(4):481–486, 2001.
5. D. Heckerman and D. Geiger. Learning Bayesian networks. In P. Besnard and S. Hanks, editors, *Proceedings of the 11th Annual Conference on Uncertainty in Artificial Intelligence (UAI95)*, pages 274–284, San Francisco, 1995.

6. K. B. Korb and A. E. Nicholson. *Bayesian Artificial Intelligence*. Computer Science and Data Analysis. CRC, Boca Raton, 2004.
7. K.B. Laskey and S.M. Mahoney. Network engineering for agile belief network models. *IEEE: Transactions on Knowledge and Data Engineering*, 12:487–98, 2000.
8. A. Nicholson, T. Boneh, T. Wilkin, K. Stacey, L. Sonenberg, and V. Steinle. A case study in knowledge discovery and elicitation in an intelligent tutoring application. In Breese and Koller, editors, *Proceedings of the 17th Annual Conference on Uncertainty in Artificial Intelligence (UAI01)*, pages 386–394, 2001.
9. A. Onisko, M.J. Druzdzel, and H. Wasyluk. Learning Bayesian network parameters from small data sets: application of Noisy-OR gates. In *Working Notes of the Workshop on "Bayesian and Causal networks: from inference to data mining." 12th European Conference on Artificial intelligence (ECAI-2000)*, 2000.
10. J. Pearl. *Probabilistic Reasoning in Intelligent Systems*. Morgan Kaufmann, San Mateo, CA, 1988.
11. C.S. Wallace and K.B. Korb. Learning linear causal models by MML sampling. In A. Gammerman, editor, *Causal Models and Intelligent Data Management*. Springer-Verlag, 1999.
12. O. Woodberry, A. Nicholson, K. Korb, and C. Pollino. Parameterising Bayesian networks: A case study in ecological risk assessment. Technical Report 2004/159, School of Computer Science and Software Engineering, Monash University, 2004.

Radar Emitter Signal Recognition Based on Feature Selection Algorithm

Gexiang Zhang[1,2], Laizhao Hu[1], and Weidong Jin[2]

[1] National EW Laboratory, Chengdu 610036, Sichuan, China
dylan7237@sina.com
[2] School of Electrical Engineering, Southwest Jiaotong University,
Chengdu 610031, Sichuan, China

Abstract. Rough set theory (RST) was introduced into radar emitter signal (RES) recognition. A novel approach was proposed to discretize continuous interval valued features and attribute reduction method was used to select the best feature subset from original feature set. Also, rough neural network (NN) classifier was designed. Experimental results show that the proposed hybrid approach based on RST and NN achieves very high recognition rate and good efficiency. It is proved to be a valid and practical approach.

1 Introduction

Radar Support Measures (ESM) and Electronic Intelligence (ELINT) involve the search for, interception, location, analysis and identification of radiated electromagnetic energy for military purposes. ESM and ELINT hereby provide valuable information for real-time situation awareness, threat detection, threat avoidance, and for timely deployment of counter-measure. [1] Radar emitter signal (RES) recognition is a key procedure in ESM and ELINT. [1-2] Because rough set theory (RST), a new fundamental theory of soft computing, can mine useful information from a large number of data and generates decision rules without prior knowledge [3-5], it becomes an attractive and promising method in feature selection and data mining in recent years. To enhance recognition rate and efficiency, this paper combines RST with neural network to propose a novel approach to recognize RESs when signal-to-noise rate (SNR) varies in a big range. This approach includes a novel discretization method, feature selection using RST and rough neural network classifier. A large number of experiments verify the validity and practicality of the introduced approach.

2 Discretization Method and Feature Selection

Affected by multiple factors such as noise in RES recognition, features are often interval values varied in a certain range instead of fixed-point values. Existing methods

---

[1] This work was supported by the National Defence Foundation (No.51435030101ZS0502).

[6-8] cannot deal with them effectively. So a new discretization method is propose to solve the problem.

Decision system $S = \langle U, R, V, f \rangle$, where $R = C \cup \{d\}$ is attribute set, and the subsets $C(C = \{c_1, c_2, \cdots, c_m\})$ and $\{d\}$ are called as condition attribute set and decision attribute set, respectively. $U = \{x_1, x_2, \cdots, x_n\}$ is a finite object set, i.e. universe. For any $c_i (i = 1, 2, \cdots, m) \in C$, there is information mapping $U \to V_{c_i}$, where V_{c_i} is the value domain, i.e.

$$V_{c_i} = \{[v_{c_i}^{x_1^{min}}, v_{c_i}^{x_1^{max}}], [v_{c_i}^{x_2^{min}}, v_{c_i}^{x_2^{max}}], \cdots, [v_{c_i}^{x_n^{min}}, v_{c_i}^{x_n^{max}}]\} \quad (1)$$

Where $v_{c_i}^{x_j^{min}}, v_{c_i}^{x_j^{max}} \in R, (j = 1, 2, \cdots, n)$. For attribute $c_i (c_i \in A)$, all objects in universe U are partitioned using class-separability criterion function $J(V_{c_i})$ and an equivalence relation R_{c_i} is obtained, that is, a kind of categorization of universe U is got. Thus, in attribute set C, we can achieve an equivalence relation family P, ($P = \{R_{a_1}, R_{a_2}, \cdots, R_{a_m}\}$) composed of m equivalence relations $R_{c_1}, R_{c_2}, \cdots, R_{c_m}$. So the equivalence relation family P, defines a new decision system $S^P = \langle U, R, V^P, f^P \rangle$, where $f^P(x) = k, x \in U, k = \{0, 1, \cdots\}$. After discretization, the original decision system is replaced with the new one.

The core of the definition is that continuous attribute discretization is regarded as a function or a mapping that transforms continuous attribute values into discrete attribute values. The function is called as class-separability criterion function to indicate that the separability of classes is emphasized in the process of discretization. The key problem of interval valued attribute discretization is to choose a good class-sepability criterion function. When an attribute value varies in a certain range, in general, the attribute value always orders a certain law. In this paper, only the decision system in which the attributes have a certain law is discussed. To extracted features, the law is considered approximately as a kind of probability distribution. We introduce the below class-separability criterion function in feature discretization.

$$J = 1 - \frac{\int f(x)g(x)dx}{\sqrt{\int f^2(x)dx} \cdot \sqrt{\int g^2(x)dx}} \quad (2)$$

The detailed explanation of function J is given in Ref.[9]. The algorithm for interval valued attribute discretization is described as follows.

Step 1. Deciding the number n of objects in universe U and the m of attributes.
Step 2. All attributes are arrayed into a two-dimensional table in which all attribute values are represented with an interval values.

Step 3. Choosing a threshold T_h of class separability. The threshold decides the overlapping part of probability functions of two classes.
Step 4. For the attribute c_i (in the beginning, $i=1$), all attribute values are sorted by the central values from the smallest to the biggest and sorted results are $v_1, v_2, \ldots, v_n$.
Step 5. The position, where the smallest attribute value v_1 in attribute c_i is, is encoded to zero (Code=0) to be the initial value of discretization process.
Step 6. Beginning from v_1 in the attribute c_i, the class-separability criterion function value J_k of v_k and v_{k+1} ($k=1,2,\ldots,n-1$) is computed by the sorted order $v_1, v_2, \ldots, v_n$ in turn. If $J_k > T_h$, which indicates the two objects are separable completely, the discrete value of the corresponding position of attribute v_{k+1} adds 1, i.e. Code=Code+1. Otherwise, $J_k < T_h$, which indicates the two objects are unseparable, the discrete value of the corresponding position of attribute v_{k+1} keeps unchanging.
Step 7. Repeating step 6 till all attribute values in attribute c_i are discretized.
Step 8. If $i \leq m$, which indicates there are some attribute values to be discretized, $i=i+1$, the algorithm goes to step 4 and continues until $i > m$, implying all continuous attribute values are discretized.
Step 9. The original decision system is replaced with the discretized one to be used in attribute reduction.

3 Classifier Design and Experimental Result Analysis

The structure of rough neural network (RNN) is shown in Fig.1. First of all, training set samples are used to construct attribute table. Interval valued attribute discretization (IVAD) method is employed to discretize the attribute table. Then, attribute reduction method based on discernibility matrix and logical operation [10] is applied to deal with the discrete attribute table and all possible reducts can be got. Feature extraction complexity is introduced to select the final reduct with the lowest cost from multiple reudcts. According to the final reducts obtained, Naïve Scaler algorithm [10] is used to discretize the attribute table discretized by using IVAD and decide the number and position of cutting points. Thus, all cutting-point values are computed in terms of the attribute table before discretization using IVAD and the discretization rule, i.e. the preprocessing rule of NN, is generated. When NN classifiers (NNC) are tested using testing set samples, input data are firstly dealt with using preprocessing rule and then are applied to be inputs of NN. The structure of NNC adopts three-layer feed-forward network. The number of neurons in input layer is the same as the dimension of selected feature subset. 15 neurons are used and 'tansig' is chosen as the transfer function in hidden layers. The output layer has the same number of neurons as RESs to be recognized and transfer function is 'logsig'. We choose RPROP algorithm [11] as the training algorithm. Ideal outputs are "1". Output tolerance is 0.05 and training error is 0.001.

10 typical RESs are chosen to make the experiment. The 10 signals are represented with $x_1, x_2, \ldots, x_n$, respectively. The universe U is composed of the 10 signals. In our prior work [12-14], 16 features of 10 RESs have been studied. Attribute set is made up of 16 features that represented with $a_1, a_2, \ldots, a_{16}$. When SNR varies from 5 dB to 20 dB, 16 features extracted construct the attribute table shown in Table 1, in which

Radar Emitter Signal Recognition Based on Feature Selection Algorithm   1111

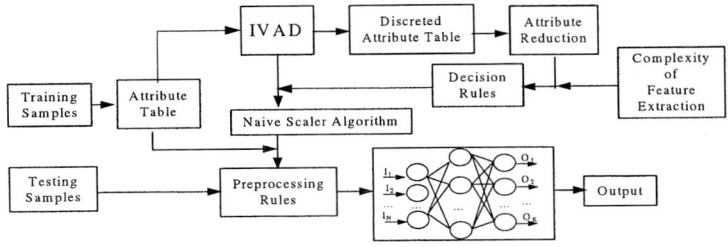

Fig. 1. Structure of rough neural network classifier

all attributes are interval values, and two terminal values of each interval value, i.e., the minimal value and the maximal value, are given. The discretized attribute table is shown in Table 2. In the process of discretization, the parameters $n=10$, $m=16$, $T_h=0.99$ and all attribute values are regarded as *Gaussian* functions. After the attributes are discretized, attribute reduction method based on discernibility matrix and logic operation [10] is used to reduce the Table 2 and the result is $a_{10}(a_3+ a_5+ a_6)$ $(a_{12}+ a_{13}+ a_{14}+ a_{16})$. There are 12 reducts of the decision table corresponding to 12 feature subsets. We introduce feature extraction complexity to select the final feature subset. After computing the complexities of all reducst, the feature subset composed of a_5, a_{10}, a_{12} has the lowest complexity.

Table 1. Attribute table before discretization. ('A' is abbreviation of 'attribute')

A	a_1	a_2	a_3	a_4	a_5	a_6	a_7	a_8
x_1	[0.690,0.707]	[1.402,1.404]	[0.122,0.125]	[0.271,0.272]	[0.435,0.436]	[1.961,2.301]	[0.952,1.021]	[0.420,0.433]
x_2	[0.671,0.682]	[1.429,1.576]	[0.115,0.162]	[0.214,0.277]	[0.362,0.428]	[1.088,2.991]	[1.115,1.261]	[0.405,0.455]
x_3	[0.546,0.598]	[1.582,1.586]	[0.292,0.304]	[0.225,0.226]	[0.374,0.375]	[0.726,1.111]	[0.691,0.755]	[0.534,0.549]
x_4	[0.893,0.896]	[1.437,1.490]	[0.373,0.652]	[0.989,1.00]	[0.856,0.867]	[11.74,20.22]	[2.157,2.960]	[0.198,0.201]
x_5	[0.897,0.909]	[1.561,1.768]	[0.200,0.223]	[0.725,0.727]	[0.330,0.337]	[6.817,7.748]	[2.899,3.130]	[0.198,0.202]
x_6	[0.419,0.453]	[1.219,1.224]	[0.562,0.585]	[0.141,0.142]	[0.243,0.244]	[2.618,2.967]	[0.195,0.309]	[0.772,0.786]
x_7	[0.396,0.413]	[1.281,1.284]	[0.080,0.082]	[0.039,0.040]	[0.000,0.001]	[6.404,6.726]	[0.257,0.326]	[0.676,0.687]
x_8	[0.657,0.684]	[1.479,1.483]	[0.066,0.067]	[0.182,0.191]	[0.115,0.129]	[2.147,3.314]	[1.423,1.664]	[0.393,0.413]
x_9	[0.521,0.562]	[1.394,1.400]	[0.078,0.081]	[0.706,0.729]	[0.584,0.612]	[17.35,19.07]	[0.921,0.977]	[0.504,0.524]
x_{10}	[0.905,0.908]	[1.384,1.458]	[0.332,0.348]	[0.625,0.630]	[0.556,0.561]	[0.345,4.67]	[3.114,3.737]	[0.202,0.211]

A	a_9	a_{10}	a_{11}	a_{12}	a_{13}	a_{14}	a_{15}	a_{16}
x_1	[41.02,41.15]	[25.51,25.87]	[15.42,15.73]	[23.01,23.37]	[2.459,2.542]	[3.681,3.775]	[11.72,11.97]	[22.52,22.88]
x_2	[41.19,50.26]	[29.27,36.34]	[10.40,15.44]	[23.64,31.04]	[0.947,5.257]	[3.139,5.668]	[7.478,9.556]	[21.54,26.25]
x_3	[109.0,110.8]	[80.45,82.09]	[28.45,28.84]	[66.86,68.40]	[13.55,13.74]	[2.009,2.292]	[7.038,7.240]	[5.718,5.867]
x_4	[1.569,1.591]	[1.567,1.575]	[0.000,0.024]	[1.555,1.577]	[0.000,0.013]	[0.000,0.012]	[0.000,0.012]	[1.546,1.576]
x_5	[1.583,1.613]	[1.585,1.591]	[0.000,0.024]	[1.574,1.589]	[0.000,0.015]	[0.000,0.012]	[0.000,0.013]	[1.562,1.584]
x_6	[462.5,478.1]	[361.2,373.9]	[101.5,104.0]	[235.5,244.8]	[125.6,129.2]	[51.88,52.89]	[49.62,51.09]	[85.06,89.04]
x_7	[273.5,275.1]	[204.1,205.5]	[69.32,69.88]	[127.4,128.5]	[76.20,77.58]	[40.94,41.37]	[28.18,28.41]	[43.69,44.42]
x_8	[38.32,40.15]	[28.34,29.58]	[9.963,10.58]	[17.69,18.28]	[10.67,11.13]	[2.333,2.516]	[7.618,8.073]	[14.35,14.66]
x_9	[117.0,119.3]	[96.44,98.11]	[20.48,21.26]	[71.09,71.98]	[25.30,26.18]	[13.29,13.86]	[7.162,7.381]	[51.58,52.14]
x_{10}	[1.769,1.877]	[1.769,1.848]	[0.000,0.030]	[1.761,1.823]	[0.022,0.119]	[0.000,0.015]	[0.000,0.016]	[1.718,1.771]

Table 2. Attribute table after discretization. ('A' is abbreviation of 'attribute')

A	a_1	a_2	a_3	a_4	a_5	a_6	a_7	A_8	a_9	a_{10}	a_{11}	a_{12}	a_{13}	a_{14}	a_{15}	a_{16}
x_1	1	2	0	0	1	0	2	1	2	2	1	3	1	2	1	3
x_2	1	2	0	0	1	0	2	1	2	3	1	3	1	2	1	3
x_3	0	2	1	0	1	0	1	1	3	4	3	4	3	1	1	6
x_4	2	2	1	1	2	1	2	0	0	0	0	0	0	0	0	0
x_5	2	2	0	1	1	1	2	0	0	0	0	0	0	0	0	0
x_6	0	0	1	0	1	0	0	3	6	7	5	7	6	5	3	7
x_7	0	1	0	0	0	1	0	2	5	6	4	6	5	4	2	4
x_8	1	2	0	0	1	0	2	1	2	3	1	2	2	1	1	2
x_9	0	2	0	1	1	1	2	1	4	5	2	5	4	3	1	5
x_{10}	2	2	1	0	1	0	2	0	1	1	0	1	0	0	0	1

Table 3. Recognition results obtained by using OFS, FSS and RNN. (%)

Types	BPSK	QPSK	MPSK	LFM	NLFM	CW	FD	FSK	IPFE	CSF
OFS	100	75.25	98.95	100	100	100	99.97	100	100	85.92
FSS	100	97.80	95.61	100	100	100	100	100	98.26	100
RNN	100	100	99.80	100	100	100	100	100	99.80	100

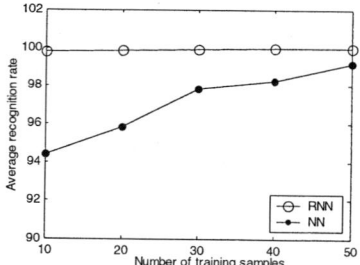

Fig. 2. Changing curves of ARR

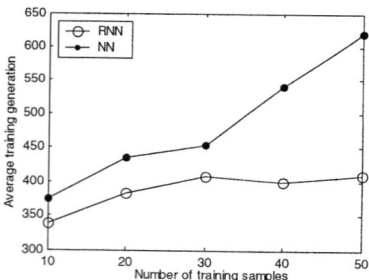

Fig. 3. Changing curves of ATG

For every RES, 150 samples are generated in each SNR point of 5dB, 10dB, 15dB and 20dB. Thus, 600 samples of each RES in total are generated. The samples are classified into two groups: training group and testing group. The training group, which consists of one third of all samples, is applied to train NNC. The testing group, represented by other two thirds of samples, is used to test trained NNC. Because the reduced result has three features, the structure of NNC is 3-15-10. To bring into comparison, original feature set (OFS) composed of 16 features is used to recognize the 10 signals. The structure of NNC is 16-25-10. After 50 experiments, average recognition rates (ARR) are shown in Table 3 in which the total ARR is 95.17%. Then, feature subset selected (FSS) is used to recognize the 10 signals. When the input data are not processed using RST, i.e. only NNC are used, the statistical results of 50 experiments are shown in Table 3. When the input data are preprocessed using RST, i.e. RNN classifiers are used, the statistical results of 50 experiments are also shown in Table 3. To compare training time, and classification and generalization capabilities of NN with those of RNN, 10, 20, 30 and 40 samples are respectively applied to train NN and RNN. Also, testing samples of 5 dB, 10 dB, 15 dB and 20 dB are respectively used to test trained NN and RNN. After 50 experiments, changing curves of ARR of NN and RNN as the number of samples are shown in Fig. 2 and changing curves of average training generations (ATG) of NN and RNN as the number of samples are shown in Fig.3.

From Table 3, feature selection using RST not only lowers the dimension of original feature set greatly, but also simplifies classifier design and enhances recognition efficiency and recognition rate. The total ARR obtained by using FSS and by using RNN are respectively 99.96% and 99.17% which are higher 4.79% and 4.00% respectively than that obtained by using OFS. From Table 3 and Fig. 3 and 4, the introduction of RST decreases the average training generation of NNC and heightens the ARR of NNC.

5 Concluding Remarks

This paper introduces RST into RES recognition for the first time and proposes a novel approach to recognize different RESs. Experimental results show that the approach is valid and feasible in improving recognition rate and recognition efficiency.

References

1. Granger, E., Rubin, M.A., Grossberg, S., et al.: A what-and-where fusion neural network for recognition and tracking of multiple radar emitters. Neural Networks. 14(3) (2001): 325-344
2. Gong, J.X., Gu, Y.P.: Electromagnetic environment of future warfare and a survey of electronic warfare technology. Proc. of intelligence research of electronic warfare. (2001) 20-36
3. Lin, T.Y.: Introduction to the special issue on rough sets. International Journal of Approximate Reasoning. 15. (1996) 287-289
4. Swiniarski, R.W., Skowron, A.: Rough set methods in feature selection and recognition. Pattern Recognition Letter. 24. (2003) 833-849
5. Wang, Y., Ding, M.Y., Zhou, C.P., and Zhang, T.X.: A hybrid method for relevance feedback in image retrieval using rough sets and neural networks. International Journal of Computational Cognition. 3(1). (2004) 78-87
6. Dai, J.H., Li, Y.X.: Study on discretization based on rough set theory. Proc. of the first Int. Conf. on Machine Learning and Cybernetics. (2002) 1371-1373
7. Tay, F.E.H., Shen, L.X.: Fault diagnosis based on rough set theory. Artificial Intelligence. 16. (2003) 39-43
8. Roy, A., Pal, S.K.: Fuzzy discretization of feature space for a rough set classifier. Pattern Recognition Letter. 24. (2003) 895-902

9. Zhang, G.X., Jin, W.D., and Hu, L.Z.: Resemblance coefficient and a quantum genetic Algorithm for feature selection. Lecture Notes in Artificial Intelligence. Vol.3245. (to appear)
10. Wang, G.Y.: Rough set theory and knowledge acquisition. Xi'an: Xi'an Jiaotong University Press, 2001
11. Riedmiller, M., Braun, H.: A direct adaptive method for faster back propagation learning: the RPROP algorithm. Proc. of IEEE Int. Conf. on Neural Networks. (1993) 586-591
12. Zhang G.X., Hu L.Z., and Jin W.D.: Intra-pulse feature analysis of radar emitter signals. Journal of Infrared and Millimeter Waves. (Accepted, to appear)
13. Zhang G.X., Hu L.Z., and Jin W.D.: Complexity Feature Extraction of Radar Emitter Signals. Proc. of 3rd Asia-Pacific Conf. on Environmental Electromagnetics. (2003) 495-498
14. Zhang, G.X., Rong, H.N., Jin, W.D., and Hu, L.Z.: Radar emitter signal recognition based on resemblance coefficient features. LNAI. 3066. (2004) 665-670

Selecting Subspace Dimensions for Kernel-Based Nonlinear Subspace Classifiers Using Intelligent Search Methods*

Sang-Woon Kim[1] and B. John Oommen[2]

[1] Senior Member, IEEE, Dept. of Computer Science and Engineering,
Myongji University, Yongin, 449-728 Korea
kimsw@mju.ac.kr
[2] Fellow of the IEEE, School of Computer Science, Carleton University,
Ottawa, ON, K1S 5B6, Canada
oommen@scs.carleton.ca

Abstract. In Kernel based Nonlinear Subspace (KNS) methods, the subspace dimensions have a strong influence on the performance of the subspace classifier. In this paper, we propose a new method of systematically and efficiently selecting optimal, or near-optimal subspace dimensions for KNS classifiers using a search strategy and a heuristic function termed as the *Overlapping* criterion. The task of selecting optimal subspace dimensions is equivalent to finding the best ones from a given problem-domain solution space. We thus employ the Overlapping criterion of the subspaces as a heuristic function, by which the search space can be pruned to find the best solution to reduce the computation significantly. Our experimental results demonstrate that the proposed mechanism selects the dimensions efficiently without sacrificing the classification accuracy. The results especially demonstrate that the computational advantage for *large* data sets is significant.

Keywords: Kernel based Nonlinear Subspace (KNS) Classifier, Subspace Dimension Selections, State-Space Search Algorithms.

1 Introduction

The subspace method of pattern recognition is a technique in which the pattern classes are not primarily defined as bounded regions or zones in a feature space, but rather given in terms of linear subspaces defined by the basis vectors, one for each class [4]. The length of a vector projected onto the subspace associated with a class is measured by the Principal Components Analysis (PCA). Since the PCA is a linear algorithm, it essentially limits the use of subspace classifiers. To overcome

---

* The work of the first author was done while visiting at Carleton University, Ottawa, Canada. The first author was partially supported by KOSEF, the Korea Science and Engineering Foundation, and the second author was partially supported by NSERC, Natural Sciences and Engineering Research Council of Canada.

this limitation, a kernel Principal Components Analysis (kPCA) was proposed in [7]. The Kernel-based Nonlinear Subspace (KNS) method is a subspace classifier, where the kPCA is employed as the specific nonlinear feature extractor [1], [3].

In KNS methods, there are three important factors to be addressed, which are: (1) The selection method of subspace dimensions, (2) The kernel function type to be employed, and (3) Parameter optimizations of the kernel function. Among these factors, the subspace dimensions have a strong influence on the performance of subspace classifiers. To obtain a high classification accuracy, a large dimension is required. However, designing the classifier with dimensions which are too large leads to a low performance due to the overlapping of the resultant subspaces. Also, since the speed of computation for the discriminant function of subspace classifiers is inversely proportional to the dimension, the latter should be kept small.

Various dimension selection methods have been reported in the literature [2], [4]. Two representative schemes are: (1) A selection method of considering the cumulative proportion, and (2) An iterative selection method using a learning modification. The details and drawbacks of these methods are omitted - they can be found in [1], [2] and [4]. Suffice it to mention that unfortunately, no formal algorithmic method for finding the most suitable dimensions (i.e., the indices of eigenvalues) from the cumulative proportion has been reported.

In this paper, we consider this problem as a *search* problem, and propose to utilize AI search methods (such as the *Breadth-First Search (BFS)* and the *Depth-First Search (DFS)* methods (descriptions of which are well known in the literature [6])) to select the most appropriate dimensions. It is well known that the choice of a heuristic function is problem dependent, and in this case, we use one which is called the *Overlapping* criterion, defined by the angle between the subspaces specified by the eigenvector columns. In other words, if the optimal subspace dimensions are used, there is no overlap between the subspaces. Thus we propose to use combinations of the Overlapping criterion, and the BFS and DFS, and enhancements of the latter schemes, to lead to dimension-selection strategies. Viewed from a computational perspective, since the optimality of our decision process is finally based on classification errors, we can say that the "Overlap Criterion" is *not* an *optimality* criterion, but, rather a pruning criterion. The rationale for the *Overlapping Criterion* is omitted here, but are in [1][1].

1.1 The Overlapping Criterion

Let $U = (U_1, \cdots, U_{p_u})$ and $V = (V_1, \cdots, V_{p_v})$ be two subspaces defined by the eigenvectors corresponding to the eigenvalues $\lambda_1 \geq \cdots \geq \lambda_{p_u}$ and $\lambda'_1 \geq \cdots \geq \lambda'_{p_v}$ respectively. First of all, observe that if U and V are column vectors of unit length, the *angle* between them is defined as $\arccos(U \cdot V)$. However, in the more

---

[1] Informally speaking, the main thrust of the theoretical result in [5] is that whenever we seek to find an heuristic solution for a problem, it is always advantageous to utilize heuristic functions that use "clues" which, in turn, lead to good solutions with *high probability*.

general case, if U and V are matrices[2], the angle between them is related to the projection of one subspace onto the second. Observe that it is not necessary that the two subspaces U and V be of the same size in order to find this projection, $Projection(U, V)$. Geometrically, this is computed in terms of the the angle between two hyper-planes embedded in a higher dimensional space, and in the case of subspaces, this projection between the two subspaces specified by the two matrices of column eigenvectors U and V, respectively, can be *computed* directly using the *subspace* function of a package like MATLAB[3], $\theta = subspace(U, V)$, and is a direct function of the projection of the first subspace on the second.

The θ gives us a measure of the amount of overlap between the two subspaces. To utilize this criterion, we *estimate* the optimal subspace dimensions as:

$$\theta(p_i, p_j) = subspace(U(p_i), U'(p_j)), \tag{1}$$

where $U(p_i) = (U_1, \cdots, U_{p_i})$ and $U'(p_j) = (U'_1, \cdots, U'_{p_j})$ are the column eigenvectors of class i and class j, computed from a characteristic equation as in [1] and p_i and p_j are the numbers of columns, respectively. To achieve this using the *Overlapping Criterion*, we define an *Overlapping Matrix* O as:

$$O = \begin{pmatrix} \theta(1,1) & \theta(1,2) & \cdots & \theta(1, p_j) \\ \theta(2,1) & \theta(2,2) & \cdots & \theta(2, p_j) \\ \cdots & \cdots & \cdots & \cdots \\ \theta(p_i, 1) & \theta(p_i, 2) & \cdots & \theta(p_i, p_j) \end{pmatrix}, \tag{2}$$

where $0 \leq O(k, l) \leq \frac{\pi}{2}$, $1 \leq k \leq p_i$ and $1 \leq l \leq p_j$.

2 Systematic Methods for Subspace Dimension Selection

2.1 A Method Based on Overlapping and Breadth-First (OBF)

The problem of selecting a subspace dimension (p_i, p_j) for a given n dimensional application (n: # of sample vectors), is a problem of selecting an integer pair (k, l) from the $n \times n$ integer space. A systematic method to achieve this is to search the whole solution space to select optimal or near-optimal subspace dimensions using a BFS or a DFS. In order to enhance the search, we propose to use the Overlapping criterion to prune the potentially useless regions of the search space. A "hybrid" procedure based on utilizing the Overlapping criterion in conjunction with a BFS (referred to here as *OBF*) can be formalized as follows, where the training set is given by T, and the p_i-dimensional subspace is given by $U(p_i)$.

1. Compute the kernel matrix[4], K, with T and a kernel function for each class i. From the K, compute the eigenvectors, $U = (U_1, \cdots, U_{p_i})$, and the eigenvalues, $\lambda_1 \geq \cdots \geq \lambda_{p_i}$;

---
[2] U and V need not be of the same size, but they must have the same number of rows.
[3] http://www.mathworks.com/
[4] In kPCA, to map the data set T into a feature space F, we have to define an $n \times n$ matrix, the so-called kernel matrix. Details for the matrix can be found in [1], [7].

2. Compute the overlapping matrix $O(k,l)$, $1 \leq k \leq p_i$, $1 \leq l \leq p_j$, for a class i and a class j with the constraint that $O(k,l) \leq \rho$. Then, set $p_m = argmax\{\max_l\{\max_k\{O(k,l)\}\}\}$;
3. Evaluate the accuracy of the subspace classifier defined by $\boldsymbol{U}(k)$ and $\boldsymbol{U}'(l)$ by traversing all values of l and k, $1 \leq k \leq p_m$, $1 \leq l \leq p_m$;
4. Report the dimensions by selecting (p_i, p_j) with the highest accuracy.

In Step 2, p_m, is determined by the parameter, ρ, which is a parameter used to prune the upper area of the search space so as to reduce the corresponding CPU-time. However, it turns out that almost all the processing CPU-time is utilized in Step 3, the evaluation step. In order to further reduce the processing time, Step 3 can be replaced by a pruning scheme (described in more detail in [1]), which limits the feasible values of ρ to lead to a lower bound value, ρ'. Thus, we can also prune off the *lower* search area, which corresponds to values of k and l which are too small. We refer to this as *Constrained OBF (COBF)*.

2.2 A Method Based on Overlapping and Depth-First (ODF)

Since the OBF is time consuming, we propose another approach in which the optimal or near-optimal subspace dimensions are selected by searching the solution space in a specified direction, namely, that is determined by using the overlapping matrix. This scheme can reduce the searching time significantly. The procedure can be formalized as follows, where the training set is given by T, and the p_i dimensional subspace is represented in $\boldsymbol{U}(p_i)$.

1. This step is the same as Step 1 in OBF.
2. This step is the same as Step 2 in OBF.
3. By increasing q from *unity* to p_m in steps of *unity* per epoch Do:
    3.1 Set (k,l), where $(k,l) = argmax\{O(q-1,q), O(q,q), O(q,q-1)\}$ or $(k,l) = (1,1)$ if $q = 1$;
    3.2 Evaluate the accuracy of the subspace classifiers defined by $\boldsymbol{U}(k)$ and $\boldsymbol{U}'(l)$ with the T, and record the evaluation results;
4. This step is the same as Step 4 in OBF.

As in the case of the OBF, almost all the processing CPU-time of ODF is utilized in executing Step 3, the evaluation step. So, again, in order to further reduce the processing time, we can prune the search space in a manner identical to the way we achieved it in devising the COBF scheme, above. We refer to this modified scheme as CODF, whose details can be found in [1].

3 Experimental Results

We tested our methods with numrous data sets. In the interest of brevity, we report here the results of two artificial data sets, "Non_normal 3" (in short, "Non_n3") and "Non_linear 3" (in short, "Non_l3"), generated with testing and training sets of cardinality 5,000, and a real-life benchmark data set, "Arrhythmia" (in short, "Arrhy"), cited from the UCI Machine Learning Repository[5].

The data set named "Non_n3" was generated from a mixture of four 8-dimensional Gaussian distributions as follows: $p_1(x) = \frac{1}{2}N(\mu_{11}, I_8) + \frac{1}{2}N(\mu_{12}, I_8)$ and $p_2(x) = \frac{1}{2}N(\mu_{21}, I_8) + \frac{1}{2}N(\mu_{22}, I_8)$, where $\mu_{11} = [0, 0, \cdots, 0]$, $\mu_{12} = [6.58, 0, \cdots, 0]$, $\mu_{21} = [3.29, 0, \cdots, 0]$ and $\mu_{22} = [9.87, 0, \cdots, 0]$. In these expressions, I_8 is the *8*-dimensional *Identity* matrix. The data set named "Non_l3", which has a strong non-linearity at its boundary, was generated artificially from a mixture of four variables as shown in [1] and [3]. The "Arrhy" data set contains 279 attributes, 206 of which are real-valued and the rest are nominal. In our case, in the interest of uniformity, we merely attempted to classify the total instances into two categories, namely, "normal" and "abnormal".

Table 1 shows the experimental results for "Non_n3", "Non_l3", and "Arrhy". In the table, each result is the averaged value of the training and the test sets, respectively[6]. Also, to be objective in this task, we compared the proposed methods and the traditional schemes[7] using three criteria, namely, the classification accuracy (%), *Acc*, the selected subspace dimensions, (p_1, p_2), and the processing CPU-times and classification times, t_1 and t_2, (in seconds), respectively.

From the results for the high-dimensional data set of "Arrhy" and from the large data sets of "Non_n 3" and "Non_l 3", we observe that the CODF is uniformly superior to the others in terms of the classification accuracy, *Acc*, while requiring a marginal additional "dimension selection" time, t_1.

4 Conclusions

In this paper we propose the first reported *algorithmic* strategy for systematically and efficiently selecting optimal or near optimal KNS classifier subspace dimensions using AI-based *search* strategies and a heuristic function termed as the *Overlapping* criterion. The proposed methods have been tested on artificial and real-life benchmark data sets, and compared with conventional schemes. The experimental results for both data sets demonstrate that one of the newly

---

[5] http://www.ics.uci.edu/mlearn/MLRepository.html

[6] For every class j, the data set for the class was randomly split into two subsets of equal size. One of them was used for training the classifiers as explained above, and the other subset was used in the validation (or testing) of the classifiers. The roles of these sets were later interchanged.

[7] In CCM (*C*onventional *C*umulative *M*ethod), we randomly selected a p_i as the subspace dimension based on the cumulative proportion [1]. In CPE (*C*umulative *P*roportion and *E*valuation method), which is one of the systematic methods based on the conventional philosophies, we selected p_i as the subspace dimension obtained by considering classification errors for candidate dimensions as suggested in [1]. Thus, the reported CCM time does not include any search in the "dimension space". In CODF, on the other hand, we select the dimensions systematically using our heuristic criterion, but without any *a priori* knowledge of the "dimension space". Indeed, the result of the CCM is presented as a reference for the classification accuracy.

Table 1. The experimental results of the proposed methods for the artificial data sets, "Non_n3" and "Non_l3", and for the real-life data set, "Arrhy". Here, Acc, (p_1, p_2), t_1, t_2, etc. are as described in the text. The final column gives the experimental *Parameters*, where $\Delta\alpha = \alpha(p_i + 1) - \alpha(p_i)$, k_0, ρ', and p_m are those of the corresponding algorithm, and Δk and ρ's for the three data sets are 0.001, 0.0001, 0.001 and 0.99, 0.999, 0.998, respectively. In the columns of (p_1, p_2) and p_m, the first one is for the training sets, and the second one is for the test sets. For the other columns such as Acc, t_1 and t_2, the results are the averaged values of the two data sets, respectively

Datasets	Methods	Acc	(p_1, p_2)	t_1	t_2	Parameters
Non_n3	CCM	94.86	(2, 2) (2, 2)	5,550.00	2,384.30	$\Delta\alpha \leq 0.001$
	CPE	94.86	(2, 2) (2, 2)	54,244.00	2,340.50	$k_0 = 0.98$;
	OBF	94.86	(2, 2) (2, 2)	44,009.50	2,324.50	$p_m = 2, 5$
	ODF	94.86	(2, 2) (2, 2)	17,127.00	2,358.50	$p_m = 2, 5$
	COBF	94.86	(2, 2) (2, 2)	28,629.40	2,380.00	$\rho' = 0.7; p_m = 2, 5$
	CODF	94.86	(2, 2) (2, 2)	14,813.00	2,377.50	$\rho' = 0.7; p_m = 2, 5$
Non_l3	CCM	89.70	(5, 5) (5, 5)	5,523.40	2,403.80	$\Delta\alpha \leq 0.001$
	CPE	85.73	(3, 3) (3, 3)	33,232.00	2,361.00	$k_0 = 0.999$;
	OBF	86.95	(5, 5) (3, 3)	430,819.50	2,413.50	$p_m = 17, 3$
	ODF	86.95	(5, 5) (3, 3)	36,999.00	2,362.00	$p_m = 17, 3$
	COBF	86.95	(5, 5) (3, 3)	1,294,357.00	2,373.50	$\rho' = 0.9; p_m = 33, 3$
	CODF	86.95	(5, 5) (3, 3)	33,366.00	2,375.00	$\rho' = 0.9; p_m = 17, 3$
Arrhy	CCM	99.56	(73,103) (75,102)	5.22	40.08	$\Delta\alpha \leq 0.0001$
	CPE	98.90	(67,66) (74,71)	827.57	23.63	$k_0 = 0.98$;
	OBF	98.46	(1, 1) (7, 7)	4,997.55	6.75	$p_m = 21, 30$
	ODF	98.46	(1, 1) (7, 7)	197.92	6.62	$p_m = 21, 30$
	COBF	97.13	(6, 9) (7, 7)	2,455.35	6.70	$\rho' = 0.9; p_m = 21, 30$
	CODF	97.13	(9, 9) (7, 7)	198.70	6.77	$\rho' = 0.9; p_m = 21, 30$

proposed schemes, a Constrained version which utilizes the Overlapping matrix and Depth-First strategy (CODF), can select subspace dimensions systematically and very efficiently without sacrificing the accuracy. However, the entire problem of analyzing the efficiency of the heuristic function remains open.

References

1. S.-W. Kim and B. J. Oommen, "On Utilizing Search Methods to Select Subspace Dimensions for Kernel-based Nonlinear Subspace Classifiers". To appear in *IEEE Trans. Pattern Anal. and Machine Intell.*, 2004.
2. J. Laaksonen and E. Oja, "Subspace dimension selection and averaged learning subspace method in handwritten digit classification", *Proceedings of ICANN*, Bochum, Germany, pp. 227 - 232, 1996.
3. E. Maeda and H. Murase, "Multi-category classification by kernel based nonlinear subspace method", in the *Proceedings of the IEEE International Conference on Acoustics, Speech, and Signal Processing (ICASSP 99)*, IEEE Press, 1999.
4. E. Oja, *Subspace Methods of Pattern Recognition*, Research Studies Press, 1983.

5. B. J. Oommen and L. Rueda, "A Formal Analysis of Why Heuristic Functions Work". To appear in *The Artificial Intelligence Journal*, 2003.
6. E. Rich and K. Knight, *Artificial Intelligence, Second Edition*, McGraw-Hill Inc., 1991.
7. B. Schölkopf, A. J. Smola, and K. -R. Müller, "Nonlinear component analysis as a kernel eigenvalue problem", *Neural Comput.*, vol. 10, pp. 1299 - 1319, 1998.

Using Machine Learning Techniques to Combine Forecasting Methods

Ricardo Prudêncio and Teresa Ludermir

Centro de Informática, Universidade Federal de Pernambuco Caixa
Postal 7851 - CEP 50732-970 - Recife (PE) - Brazil
{rbcp, tbl}@cin.ufpe.br

Abstract. We present here an original work that uses machine learning techniques to combine time series forecasts. In this proposal, a machine learning technique uses features of the series at hand to define adequate weights for the individual forecasting methods being combined. The combined forecasts are the weighted average of the forecasts provided by the individual methods. In order to evaluate this solution, we implemented a prototype that uses a MLP network to combine two widespread methods. The experiments performed revealed significantly accurate forecasts.

1 Introduction

Time series forecasting has been widely used to support decision-making. Combining forecasts from different forecasting methods is a procedure commonly used to improve forecasting accuracy [1].

An approach that uses knowledge for combining forecasts is based on expert systems, such as the Rule-Based Forecasting system [2]. This system defines a weight for each individual method according to the features of the series being forecasted. The combined forecasts are then the weighted average of the forecasts provided by the individual methods. Despite its good results, developing rules in this context may be unfeasible, since good experts are not always available [3].

In order to minimize the above difficulty, we proposed the use of machine learning techniques for combining forecasts. In the proposed solution, each training example stores the description of a series (i.e. the series features) and the combining weights that empirically obtained the best forecasting performance for the series. A machine learning technique uses a set of such examples to relate time series features and adequate combining weights.

In order to evaluate the proposed solution, we implemented a prototype that uses MLP neural networks [4] to define the weights for two widespread methods: the Random Walk and the Autoregressive model [5]. The prototype was evaluated in a large set of series and compared to benchmarking forecasting procedures. The experiments revealed that the forecasts generated by the prototype were significantly more accurate than the benchmarking forecasts.

Section 2 presents some methods for combining forecasts, followed by section 3 that describes the proposed solution. Section 4 brings the experiments and results. Finally section presents some conclusions and the future work.

2   Combining Forecasts

The combination of forecasts is a well-established procedure for improving forecasting accuracy [1]. Procedures that combine forecasts often outperform the individual methods that are used in the combination [1].

The linear combination of K methods can be described as follows. Let $Z_t(t = 1, \ldots, T)$ be the available data of a series Z and let $Z_t(t = T+1, \ldots, T+H)$ be the H future values to be forecasted. Each method k uses the available data to generate its forecasts $\widetilde{Z}_{k,t}$. The combined forecasts $\widetilde{Z}_{C,t}$ are defined as:

$$\widetilde{Z}_{C,t} = \sum_{k=1}^{K} w_k * \widetilde{Z}_{k,t} \tag{1}$$

The combining weights $w_k (k = 1, \ldots, K)$ are numerical values that indicate the contribution of each individual method in the combined forecasts. Eventually constraints are imposed on the weights in such a way that:

$$\sum_{k=1}^{K} w_k = 1 \ and \ w_k \geq 0 \tag{2}$$

Different approaches for defining combining weights can be identified [1]. An very simple approach is to define equal weights (i.e. $w_k = 1/K$), which is usually referred as the Simple Average (SA) combination method. Despite its simplicity, the SA method has shown to be robust in the forecasting of different series.

A more sophisticated approach for defining the combining weights was proposed by [6], by treating the linear combination of forecasts within the regression framework. In this context, the individual forecasts are viewed as the explanatory variables and the actual values of the series as the response variable.

An alternative approach for the combination of forecasts is based on the development of expert systems, such as the Rule-Based Forecasting system [2]. The rules deployed by the system use the time series features (such as length, basic trend,...) to modify the weight associated to each model. In the experiments performed using the system, the improvement in accuracy over the SA method has shown to be significant.

3   The Proposed Solution

As seen, expert systems have been successfully used to combine forecasts. Unfortunately, the knowledge acquisition in these systems depends on the availability of human forecasting experts. However, good forecasting experts are often scarce and expensive [3]. In order to minimize this difficulty, the use of machine learning techniques is proposed here to define the weights for combining forecasts. The proposed solution is closely related to previous works that used learning algorithms to select forecasting methods [3][7][8]. In our work, the learning algorithms are used to define the best linear combination of methods.

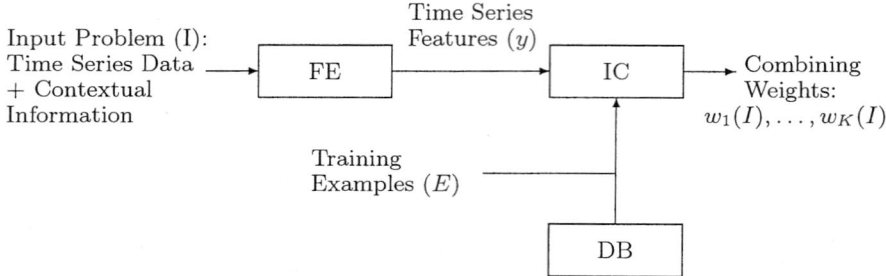

Fig. 1. System's architecture

Figure 1 presents the architecture of a system following our solution. The system has two phases: training and use. In the training phase, the Intelligent Combiner (IC) uses a supervised algorithm to acquire knowledge from a set of examples E in the Database (DB). Each example $e_i \in E$ stores the values of P features $Y_1, \ldots, Y_P$ for a particular series and the adequate combining weights $w_1, \ldots, w_K$ for K methods. Each feature $Y_j (j = 1, \ldots, P)$ is either: (1) a descriptive statistic or; (2) a contextual information. The IC module uses the set E to build a learner $\mathcal{L}$ that associates the features and the combining weights.

In the use phase, the system's user provides an input problem I (i.e. time series data and contextual information). The Feature Extractor (FE) module extracts the description $y = Y_1(I), \ldots, Y_P(I)$ (i.e. the time series features) for the input problem. The learner $\mathcal{L}$ uses these values to predict the adequate weights for the input problem: $\mathcal{L}(y) = \{w_1(I), \ldots, w_K(I)\}$.

In order to verify the viability of the proposal, we implemented a prototype which define the combining weights for $K = 2$ methods: the Random Walk (RW) and the Auto-Regressive model (AR) [5]. The prototype was applied to forecast the yearly series of the M3-Competition [9], which provides a large set of time series related to certain economic and demographic domains and represent a convenient sample for expository purposes.

3.1 The Feature Extractor

In this module, the following features were used to describe the yearly series of the M3-Competition:

1. Length of the time series (L): number of observations of the series;
2. Basic Trend (BT): slope of the linear regression model;
3. Percentage of Turning Points (TP): Z_t is a turning point if $Z_{t-1} < Z_t > Z_{t+1}$ or $Z_{t-1} > Z_t < Z_{t+1}$. This feature measures the oscillation in a series;
4. First Coefficient of Autocorrelation (AC): large values of this feature suggest that the value of the series at a point influences the value at the next point;
5. Type of the time series ($TYPE$): it is represented by 5 categories, *micro, macro, industry, finances* and *demographic*.

The first four features are directly computed using the series data and TYPE in turn is a contextual information provided by the authors of M3-Competition.

3.2 The Intelligent Combiner

The IC module uses the Multi-Layer Perceptron (MLP) network [4] (one hidden layer) as the learner. The MLP input layer has 9 units that represent the time series features. The first four input units receive the values of the numeric features (i.e. L, BT, TP, AC). The feature TYPE was represented by 5 binary attributes (either 1 or 0 value), each one associated to a different category.

The output layer has two nodes that represent the weights associated to the RW and AR models. In order to ensure that the final combining weights are non-negative and sum to one (see eq. 2), the outputs of the MLP are normalized.

The MLP training is performed by the standard BackPropagation (PB) algorithm [4] and follows the benchmark training rules provided in Proben [10]. The BP algorithm was implemented using the Neural Network Toolbox [11].

3.3 The Database

An important aspect to be considered in the prototype is the generation of the training examples. In order to construct an example using a specific series Z, the following tasks have to be performed. First, the series data is divided into two parts: the fit period $Z_t(t = 1, \ldots, T)$ and the test period $Z_t(t = T+1, \ldots, T+H)$. The test period in our prototype consists on the last $H = 6$ years of the series and the fit period consists on the remaining data. The fit data is used to calibrate the RW and AR models. The calibrated models are used to generate the individual forecasts $\widetilde{Z}_{k,t}(k = 1, 2)(t = T + 1, \ldots, T + 6)$ for the test data.

In the second task, we defined the combining weights $w_k(k = 1, 2)$ that minimize the Mean Absolute Error (MAE) of the combined forecasts $\widetilde{Z}_{C,t}(t = T + 1, \ldots, T + 6)$. This task can be formulated as an optimization problem:

Minimize:
$$MAE(\widetilde{Z}_{C,t}) = \frac{1}{6}\sum_{t=T+1}^{T+6}|Z_t - \widetilde{Z}_{C,t}| = \frac{1}{6}\sum_{t=T+1}^{T+6}|Z_t - \sum_{k=1}^{2}w_k * \widetilde{Z}_{k,t}| \quad (3)$$

Subject to:
$$\sum_{k=1}^{2} w_k = 1 \text{ and } w_k \geq 0 \quad (4)$$

This optimization problem was treated using a line search algorithm implemented in the Optimization toolbox for Matlab [12].

In the third task, the features (see section 3.1) are extracted for the fit period of the series. The features of the fit period and the weights that minimized the forecasting error in the test period are stored in the DB as a new example.

4 Experiments and Results

In this section, we initially describe the experiments performed to select the best number of hidden nodes for the MLP. In these experiments, we used the 645

Table 1. Training results

Number of Hidden Nodes	SSE Training Average	SSE Training Deviation	SSE Validation Average	SSE Validation Deviation	SSE Test Average	SSE Test Deviation
2	65.15	1.87	69.46	0.80	68.34	1.03
4	64.16	1.97	69.49	0.87	67.78	1.20
6	64.22	1.81	69.34	0.86	67.14	1.28
8	**64.13**	**2.28**	**69.29**	**0.67**	**66.74**	**1.35**
10	64.37	2.62	69.56	1.03	67.54	1.32

yearly series of the M3-Competition [9] and hence 645 training examples. The set of examples was equally divided into training, validation and test sets. We trained the MLP using 2, 4, 6, 8 and 10 nodes (30 runs for each value). The optimum number of nodes was chosen as the value that obtained the lowest average SSE error on the validation set. Table 1 summarizes the MLP training results. As it can be seen, the optimum number of nodes according to the validation error was 8 nodes. The gain obtained by this value was also observed in the test set.

We further investigated the quality of the forecasts that were generated using the weights suggested by the selected MLP. In order to evaluate the forecasting performance across all series $i \in test\ set$, we considered the Percentage Better (PB) measure [13]. Given a method Q, the PB measure is computed as follows:

$$PB_Q = 100 * \frac{1}{m} \sum_{i \in test} \sum_{t=T+1}^{T+6} \delta_{Qit} \qquad (5)$$

where

$$\delta_{Qit} = \begin{cases} 1, & \text{if } |e_{Rit}| < |e_{Qit}| \\ 0, & \text{otherwise} \end{cases} \qquad (6)$$

In the above definition, R is a reference method that serves for comparison. The e_{Qit} is the forecasting error obtained by Q in the i-th series at time t, and m is the number of times in which $|e_{Rit}| < |e_{Qit}|$. Hence, PB_Q indicates in percentage terms, the number of times that the error obtained by the method R was lower than the error obtained using the method Q. Values lower than 50 indicate that the method Q is more accurate than the reference method.

The PB measure was computed for three reference methods. The first one is merely to use RW for forecasting all series and the second is to use AR for all series. The third reference method is the Simple Average (SA) combination. The table summarizes the PB results over the 30 runs of the best MLP. As it can be seen, the average PB measure was lower than 50% for all reference methods, and the confidence intervals suggest that the obtained gain is statistically significant.

5 Conclusion

In this work, we proposed the use of machine learning techniques to define the best linear combination of forecasting methods. We can point out contributions

Table 2. Comparative forecasting performance measured by PB

Reference	PB Measure		
Method	Average	Deviation	Conf. Interv. (95%)
RW	42.20	0.26	[42.11; 42.29]
AR	40.20	0.44	[40.04; 40.36]
SA	43.24	1.45	[42.72; 43.76]

of this work to two fields: (1) in time series forecasting, since we provided a new method for that can be used to combine forecasts; (2) in machine learning, since we used its concepts and techniques in a problem which was not tackled yet.

In order to evaluate the proposal, we used MLP networks to combine two forecasting models. The experiments performed revealed encouraging results. Some modifications in the current implementation may be performed, such as augmenting the set of time series features and optimizing the MLP design.

References

1. De Menezes, L. M., Bunn, D. W. and Taylor, J. W.: . Review of guidelines for the use of combined forecasts. European Journal of Operational Research, 120 (2000) 190-204.
2. Collopy, F. and Armstrong, J. S.: Rule-based forecasting: development and validation of an expert systems approach to combining time series extrapolations. Management Science, 38(10) (1992) 1394-1414.
3. Arinze, B.: Selecting appropriate forecasting models using rule induction. Omega-International Journal of Management Science, 22(6) (1994) 647-658.
4. Rumelhart, D.E., Hinton, G.E. and Williams, R.J.: Learning representations by backpropagation errors. Nature, 323 (1986) 533-536.
5. Harvey, A.: Time Series Models. MIT Press, Cambridge, MA (1993)
6. Granger, C.W.J. and Ramanathan, R.: Improved methods of combining forecasts. Journal of Forecasting, 3 (1984) 197204.
7. Venkatachalan, A.R. and Sohl, J.E.: An intelligent model selection and forecasting system. Journal of Forecasting, 18 (1999) 167-180.
8. Prudêncio, R.B.C. and Ludermir, T.B.: Meta-Learning Approaches for Selecting Time Series Models. Neurocomputing Journal, 61(C) (2004) 121-137.
9. Makridakis, S. and Hibon, M.: The M3-competition: results, conclusions and implications. International Journal of Forecasting, 16(4) (2000) 451-476.
10. Prechelt, L.: Proben 1: a set of neural network benchmark problems and benchmarking rules, Tech. Rep. 21/94, Fakultat fur Informatik, Karlsruhe (1994).
11. Demuth, H. and Beale, M.:. Neural Network Toolbox for Use with Matlab, The Mathworks Inc, (2003).
12. The Mathworks, Optimization Toolbox User's Guide, The Mathworks Inc. (2003).
13. Flores, B.E.: Use of the sign test to supplement the percentage better statistic. International Journal of Forecasting, 2 (1986) 477-489.

Web Data Mining and Reasoning Model

Yuefeng Li[1] and Ning Zhong[2]

[1] School of Software Engineering and Data Communications,
Queensland University of Technology, Australia
y2.li@qut.edu.au
[2] Department of Systems and Information Engineering,
Maebashi Institute of Technology, Japan
zhong@maebashi-it.ac.jp

Abstract. It is indubitable that we can obtain numerous discovered patterns using a Web mining model. However, there are many meaningless patterns, and also some discovered patterns might include uncertainties as well. Therefore, the difficult problem is how to utilize and maintain the discovered patterns for the effectiveness of using the Web data. This paper presents a Web data mining and reasoning model for this problem. The objective of mining is automatic ontology extraction; whereas, the objective of reasoning is the utilization and maintenance of discovered knowledge on the ontology. The model also deals with pattern evolution.

1 Introduction

There are two fundamental issues regarding the effectiveness of using the Web data [6] [9]: *mismatch* and *overload*. The mismatch means some interesting and useful data has not been found (or missed out), whereas, the overload means some gathered data is not what users want. Currently, the application of data mining techniques to Web data, called Web mining, is used to find interesting knowledge from Web data [2] [10]. It is indubitable that we can discover knowledge in terms of discovered patterns using a Web mining model. However, there is a gap between the effectiveness of using the Web data and Web mining. One reasoning is that there exits many meaningless patterns in the set of discovered patterns [11]. Another reason is that some discovered patterns might include uncertainties when we extract them form Web data [9].

An ontology-based Web mining model has been presented for the above question, which uses ontologies to represent the discovered patterns in order to remove uncertainties from discovered patterns [6] [7] [9]. In this paper, we attempt to create a bridge between the effectiveness of using the Web data and Web mining. We extend the ontology-based Web mining model by combining data mining and data reasoning in a single umbrella. The objective of mining is automatic ontology extraction; whereas, the objective of reasoning is the utilization and maintenance of discovered knowledge on the ontology. It also deals with pattern evolution. Using this model some meaningless patterns can be removed from the set of discovered patterns. Also uncertainties in inadequate discovered patterns can be detected and removed.

2 Automatic Ontology Extraction

Let $T = \{t_1, t_2, \ldots, t_m\}$ be a set of terms, and D be a set of documents. A set of terms is referred to as a *termset*. A set of term frequency pairs, P, is referred to as a *pattern* if t denotes a term and f denotes the number of occurrences of the term in a given document for all pairs $(t, f) \in P$; and $support(P)$ is its specificity, the greater the specificity is, the more important the pattern is.

We call $termset(P)$ the termset of P, which satisfies: $termset(P) = \{t \mid (t, f) \in P\}$. In this paper, a pattern P_1 equals to a pattern P_2 if and only if $termset(P_1)=termset(P_2)$. A pattern is uniquely determined by its termset (that is why we call it as an *id* sometimes). Two patterns may be composed if they have the same termset. In this paper, we use a composition operation, $\oplus$, to generate new patterns. In general, patterns can be discovered using clustering analysis or association rule mining. The special case is that every pattern only includes a termset.

Let P_1 and P_2 are two patterns. We call $P_1 \oplus P_2$ the *composition* of P_1 and P_2 which satisfies:

$$P_1 \oplus P_2 = \{(t, f_1 + f_2) \mid (t, f_1) \in P_1, (t, f_2) \in P_2\} \cup \{(t, f) \mid t \in (termset(P_1) \cup termset(P_2)) - (termset(P_1) \cap termset(P_2)), (t, f) \in P_1 \cup P_2\} \quad (1)$$

$Support(P_1 \oplus P_2) = Support(P_1) + Support(P_2)$.

Table 1. Pattern example

Name	Pattern
P_1	{(GERMAN, 1), (VW, 1)}
P_2	{(US, 2), (ECONOM, 1), (SPY, 1)}
P_3	{(US, 1), (BILL, 1), (ECONOM, 1), (ESPIONAG, 1)}
P_4	{(US, 1), (ECONOM, 1), (ESPIONAG, 1), (BILL, 1)}
P_5	{(GERMAN, 1), (MAN, 1), (VW, 1), (ESPIONAG, 1)}
P_6	{(GERMAN, 2), (MAN, 1), (VW, 1), (SPY, 1)}

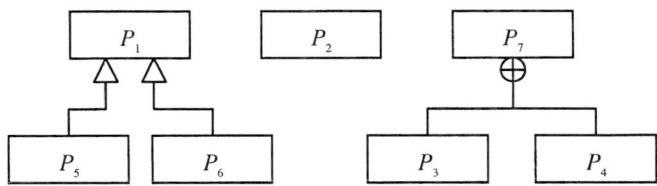

Fig. 1. Ontology example

Table 1 is an example of discovered patterns. A new pattern $P_7 = P_3 \oplus P_4$ can be generated since two patterns (P_3 and P_4) have the same termset. The composition operation is necessary to compose the two subtopics into one.

Let PN is the set of patterns, we now have $PN = \{P_1, P_2, P_3, P_4, P_5, P_6, P_7\}$, where $P_7 = \{(US, 2), (BILL, 2), (ECONOM, 2), (ESPIONAG, 2)\}$ by using Equation (1).

Figure 1 illustrates the result of automatic ontology extraction for this example, which includes seven patterns and a composition and two is-a relations since $termset(P_1) \subset termset(P_5)$ and $termset(P_1) \subset termset(P_6)$. Apart from is-a relation and composition, there exists correlation between patterns. We will discuss the correlation in next section.

3 Data Reasoning on Ontology

We should remove redundant patterns first before we use the knowledge in the ontology. The patterns used for the compositions are redundant. For example, there are two redundant subtopics in Figure 1: P_3 and P_4. After pruning we have $PN = \{P_1, P_2, P_5, P_6, P_7\}$. To illustrate the correlation between patterns, normalizations are necessary to exam patterns in a common hypothesis space. Given a pattern $P = \{(t_1, f_1), (t_2, f_2), ..., (t_r, f_r)\}$, its *normal form* can be determined using the following equation:

$$f_i = \frac{f_i}{\sum_1^r f_j} \quad \text{for all } i \leq r \text{ and } i \geq 1.$$

After normalization, we have $termset(P) = \{t \mid (t, f) \in P\}$ and $\sum_{(t,f) \in P} f = 1$. We also need to normalize *support*, which satisfies:

$$support: PN \rightarrow [0, 1], \text{ such that } support(P) = \frac{support(P)}{\sum_{P_j \in PN} support(P_j)} \quad (2)$$

for all $P \in PN$. The common hypothesis space is $= T \times [0, 1]$. According to the constraints on the patterns, there is a mapping from PN to 2^Θ, which satisfies:

$$\beta: PN \rightarrow 2^\Theta - \{\emptyset\}, \emptyset \neq \beta(P) \subseteq \Theta, \text{ and } \beta(P) \text{ is } P\text{'s normal form}.$$

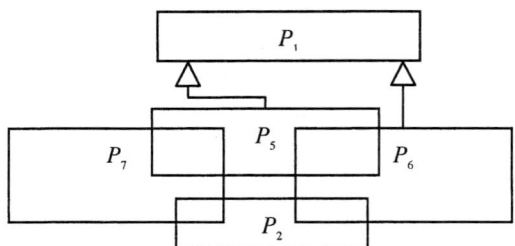

Fig. 2. The correlation between subtopics

Therefore, the correlation can be described as a pair (*support*,), which is also called an extended random set [5] [8]. Figure 2 illustrate the correlation between patterns in Figure 1.

To utilize discovered knowledge on the ontology, we transform the discovered knowledge into a computable function, for instance, a probability function in this research. Using the results from extended random sets (see [5] or [8]), we can obtain a probability function pr_β on T, the projection of the common hypothesis space, such that

$$pr_\beta(t) = \sum_{P \in PN, (t,w) \in \beta(P)} support(P) \times w \quad \text{for all } t \in T. \quad (3)$$

For an incoming document, d, we use a joint probability to evaluate its relevance, which satisfies:

$$Pr(R|T,d) = \sum_{t \in T} pr_\beta(t)\tau(t,d), \text{ where } \tau(x,y) = \begin{cases} 1 & \text{if } x \in y \\ 0 & \text{otherwise} \end{cases}$$

We also use the following formula to decide a threshold, which is complete [9]:

$$threshold = \min_{P \in NP} \{ \sum_{t \in termset(P)} pr_\beta(t) \} \quad (4)$$

4 Knowledge Evolution

Some patterns may be meaningless or may include uncertainties since there are a lot of noises in the training data. Increasing the size of the training set is not useful because of the noises. In this paper, we present a method for tracing errors made by the system. The method provides a novel solution for knowledge evolution. The ontology we constructed includes only *relevance patterns*, which come directly from the relevant data. A document is called *negative one* if it is marked in relevance by the system but it is actually non-relevant data.

To eliminate meaningless patterns and uncertainties, we use a method to trace the cause of the occurrences of negative documents. For a given negative one, nd, we check which patterns have been used to give rise to such error. We call these patterns *offenders* of nd. The set of offenders of nd can be determined by the following equation: $\Delta_{nd} = \{ P \in PN \mid termset(P) \cap termset(nd) \neq \emptyset \}$, where $termset(nd) = T \cap nd$.

There are two kinds of offenders: total conflict offenders whose *termsets* are subsets of *termset(nd)*, and partial conflict offenders whose *termsets* are not subsets of *termset(nd)* but join with *termset(nd)*. For example, we obtain the following two negative documents (Notice: using Equations (3) and (4) they are relevant):

nd_1: GERMANY FOCUS VW unveils new Passat says sales.
nd_2: SWITZERLAND Red Cross rejects US wartime spying quot charges.

Using the above definition, we also have: $\Delta_{nd_1} = \{P_1\}$ and $\Delta_{nd_2} = \{P_2, P_6, P_7\}$. According to the above definition, P_1 is a total conflict offender of nd_1, and P_2, P_6 and P_7 are partial conflict offenders of nd_2.

Figure 3 illustrates the relationship between patterns and negative documents. In this figure we only show the important relations: is-a relation and composition. This figure also indicates that pattern P_1 is a meaningless pattern since its derived concepts (e.g, nd_1) can be non-relevant.

In this research, we remove all total conflict offenders (e.g., P_1). We also need to refine partial conflict offenders (e.g., P_2, P_6 and P_7) to remove uncertainties.

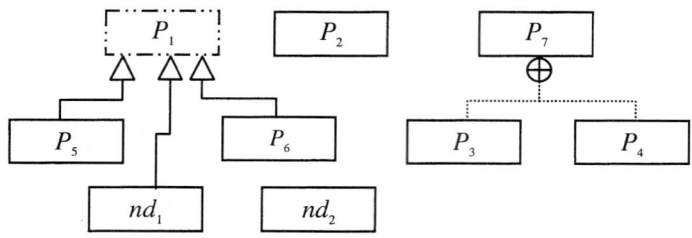

Fig. 3. The relationship between patterns and negative documents

For each partial conflict offender, we first determine the offering of the offender from the joint part of its *termset* and *termset(nd)* using the following equation:

$$\textit{offering}: \Delta_{nd} \to [0,1], \text{ such that } \textit{offering}(P) = \sum_{(t,w) \in \beta(P), t \in \textit{termset}(nd)} w$$

for all partial conflict offenders $P \in \Delta_{nd}$. We also reshuffle the partial conflict offender's frequency distribution by shifting ($1/\mu$) of the offering to the rest of part of its *termset*, where is an experimental coefficient and ≥ 2 (see [9] for more details).

5 Performance Analyses

We use TREC2002 (Text REtrieval Conference) data to evaluate the proposed model, where topics are *R101, R102* ... and *R109*. We select the most popular Rocchio classification and probabilistic model, as reference models in our testing. We use only the positive set in the training set for Rocchio method, where each document is represented as a vector of *tf*idf* weights. The probabilistic model considers both the presence of search terms in documents and their absence from documents. It also assumes

Table 2. Top precision and breakeven point

	Rocchio classification	Probabilistic model	WMR: before evolution	WMR: after evolution		
				$\mu = 2$	$\mu = 16$	$\mu = 8$
Avg top Precision	57.8%	62.2%	61.3%	65.33%	65.78%	**65.33%**
Avg break-even point	0.498	0.524	0.510	0.526	0.528	**0.536**

that the distribution of terms in relevant documents is independent and their distribution in non-relevant document is independent.

Instead of drawing many precision recall curves, we use both top 25 precision and *breakeven points* in the experiment. Table 2 illustrates the results of the experiment. It is no less impressed by the performance of the proposed model (WMR model) since it gains a significant increase in both top 25 precision and breakeven point for effectiveness while = 8.

6 Related Work and Conclusions

Association mining has been used in Web text mining, which refers to the process of searching through unstructured data on the Web and deriving meaning from it [3][4]. The main purposes of text mining were association discovery, trends discovery, and event discovery [1]. The association between a set of terms and a predefined category (e.g., a term) can be described as an association rule. The trends discovery means the discovery of phrases, a sort of sequence association rules. The event discovery is the identification of stories in continuous news streams. Usually clustering based mining techniques can be used for such a purpose. However there are two difficult problems in the effectiveness of using the Web data: meaningless patterns and uncertainties in patterns [11] [9].

This paper presents a Web data mining and reasoning model in order to build a bridge between the effectiveness of using the Web data and Web mining, which includes automatic ontology extraction, data reasoning on the ontology and pattern evolution. An experimental is conducted to test the proposed model and the result show that all objectives we expect for the model are achievable.

References

1. G. Chang, M.J. Healey, J. A. M. McHugh, and J. T. L. Wang, *Mining the World Wide Web: an information search approach*, Kluwer Academic Publishers, 2001.
2. M. Chen, J. Park, and P. Yu, Data mining for path traversal patterns in a Web environment, 16th *International Conference on Distributed Computing Systems*, 1996, Hong Kong, 385-392.
3. R. Feldman, I. Dagen, and H. Hirsh, Mining text using keywords distributions, *Journal of Intelligent Information Systems*, 1998, **10(3)**: 281-300.
4. J. D. Holt and S. M. Chung, Multipass algorithms for mining association rules in text databases, *Knowledge and Information Systems*, 2001, **3**: 168-183.
5. Y. Li, Extended random sets for knowledge discovery in information systems, 9th *International Conference on Rough Sets, Fuzzy Sets, Data Mining and Granular Computing*, China, 2003, 524-532.
6. Y. Li and N. Zhong, Web mining model and its applications on information gathering, *Knowledge-Based Systems*, 2004, **17(5-6)**: 207-217.
7. Y. Li and N. Zhong, Ontology-based Web Mining Model: representations of user profiles, *IEEE/WIC International Conference on Web Intelligence*, 2003, Canada, 96-103
8. Y. Li and N. Zhong, Interpretations of association rules by granular computing, 3rd *IEEE International Conference on Data Mining*, 2003, Florida, USA, 593-596.

9. Y. Li and N. Zhong, Capturing evolving patterns for ontology-based Web mining, *IEEE/WIC/ACM International Conference on Web Intelligence*, Beijing, China, 2004, 256–263.
10. S. K. Pal and V. Talwar, Web mining in soft computing framework: relevance, state of the art and future directions, *IEEE Transactions on Neural Networks,* 2002, **13(5):** 1163-1177.
11. S.-T. Wu, Y. Li, Y. Xu, B. Pham and P. Chen, Automatic pattern taxonomy exatraction for Web mining, *IEEE/WIC/ACM International Conference on Web Intelligence*, Beijing, China, 2004, 242–248.

A Framework for Disambiguation in Ambiguous Iconic Environments[*]

Abhishek[1] and Anupam Basu[2]

[1] Department of Mathematics, Indian Institute of Technology,
Kharagpur, 721 302, West Bengal, India
abhishek08@hotmail.com
[2] Department of Computer Science and Engineering, Indian Institute of Technology,
Kharagpur, 721 302, West Bengal, India
anupam@cse.iitkgp.ernet.in

Abstract. In this paper, we address the problem of disambiguating a sequence of semantically overloaded icons. We formulate the problem as a constraint satisfaction problem and discuss the knowledge representation required to facilitate checking of constraints. Our algorithm helps in reducing the size of vocabulary and hence makes these interfaces more usable for the disabled population.

1 Introduction and Motivation

Iconic environments are ubiquitous in communication and assistive gadgets. These are mainly used to facilitate cross language communication. In assistive systems, they are used to help cognitively and language impaired population. By being visual and unordered, they provide a method of communication, which does not require any formal education and is independent of the idiosyncrasies of the language.

However, to utilize this strength and richness, we need to interpret iconic language sentences. The generation of natural language messages from a sequence of icons is a non-trivial task. Use of simple icons makes the disambiguation easier. However, it increases the size of the vocabulary. Use of syntax directed methods presupposes the knowledge of different case-roles. Semantically overloaded icons, being polysemous, reduce the size of the vocabulary, which implies less search overhead. This is possible only if these interfaces are supplemented by robust and rich inference mechanisms to disambiguate them. The contribution of this paper is towards the specification of knowledge representation for this disambiguation. In particular, we formulate the problem of disambiguation of a sequence of random and ambiguous icons as a constraint satisfaction problem, show that ensuring the semantic consistency of sentences is equivalent to checking these constraints and specify the knowledge, which must be represented to check these constraints effectively.

We formulate the problem in the next section. In section 3, we describe how this problem reduces to checking of some constraints. We discuss the results and conclude in section 4.

---

[*] This work is supported by grants from Media Lab Asia.

2 The Problem

The problem we seek to address is to disambiguate an unordered sequence of semantically overloaded icons. For example, consider the following sample input.

Given this input, the system should output the following sentences.

- The child is playing in the room.
- The children are eating in the room.
- The child is playing on the bed.

We note that the problem of disambiguation consists of marking the following types of sentences as semantically anomalous.

1. He hid the cupboard in the cup.
2. The bird threw the elephant.
3. He slept on the bed in the playground.

While the first sentence violates our intuition about spatial consistency, the meaninglessness of the second sentence stems from our naïve knowledge about the world. The meaningfulness of the third sentence varies with different contexts. It is not impossible to conceive a situation in which a 'bed' exists in a 'playground'. However, it is common knowledge that such a situation has inherently low probability of occurrence. In this paper, we will discuss methods to deal with the above-mentioned problems.

3 Semantic Consistency as Constraint Satisfaction

The input to the inference engine is a sequence of icons with their associated senses. For example, for the first icon shown on this page, the input to the inference engine will be: 'Icon-1: Bed, Sleep, Room'. The central thesis of this paper is that the consistency of a sentence can be reduced to the problem of checking some constraints over the case-roles of the verbs. For the meaningfulness of a sentence, following types of constraints must be checked.

1. Ontological constraints, which arise because of the ontological commitments of the different case roles of the verbs.
2. Dependencies between the case roles of the verb.
3. Spatial constraints, which arise because of our world knowledge of the structure of space around us.

The verbs are represented as a collection of semantic fields and their associated selectional constraints. The nouns are represented as frames. Therefore, they have a location in ontology and are a collection of slot-value pairs. The selectional constraints of the verbs are in terms of membership in some ontological category or some condition on the slot values of the concepts. The process of generating correct sentences can be seen as finding all possible solutions of the constraint satisfaction problem, where the variables are the semantic fields of the verbs. The domains of these variables are decided by checking the selectional constraints of each of the associated semantic fields. The constraints of this constraint satisfaction problem are the dependencies between the different case-roles of the verb. These constraints are checked by comparing the slot values of the corresponding frames. The ontology, which we use, is shown in figure 1. Similar ontologies have been used in [2, 5].

```
            Entity → Physical v Abstract v Temporal v Sentient
    Physical → (Stationary v Non-Stationary) && (Living v Non-Living)
             && (Solid v Liquid v Gas) && (Natural v Artifact)
                    Sentient → Human v Organization
                Temporal → Relational v Non-Relational
                    Relational → State v Action
              Action → Physical-Action v Mental-Action
                    Living → Human v Animals v Plants
                         Human → Male v Female
         Non-Stationary → Self-Moving v Non-Self-Moving
```

Fig. 1. The Ontological Schema

A high level description of the algorithm, which essentially finds the solution of the constraint satisfaction problem of the spatial and non-spatial fields separately and takes all possible unions of these solutions, appears in figure 2.

Intuitively, steps 3-7 find all possible sentences by the verb 'v'. Step 3 finds instantiations for non-spatial semantic fields whereas step 4 does the same for spatial fields. All possible combinations of these solutions are computed in step 5. We need to retain sentences, which contain at least one concept from each icon. This is done in step 6.

We use the notion of a landmark to find the location of an object. Intuitively, these landmarks are immobile, significant entities and their locations are likely to be known to the hearer. We use the following heuristic to infer the locations of objects.

$$\text{Non-Stationary}(x), \text{Size}(x) > k \rightarrow \text{Location}(x) \tag{1}$$

Here k is a pre-determined constant. This rule has parallels in research in linguistics [3]. Formally,

$$\text{Stationary}(x), \text{Size}(x) > k, \text{Non-Stationary}(y) \rightarrow \text{At}(y, x). \tag{2}$$

Other spatial relations are more difficult to infer. Here we discuss two of the most important spatial relations, 'in' and 'on'. Our treatment of spatial relations consists of inference of relations 'in' and 'on', followed by checking their consistency by calculation of extensions.

```
Algorithm: Disambiguate
Input: A Set of icons chosen by the user and their
associated senses, I and a set of constraints on
the model of the world, C
Output: The set of conceptual representations of
all possible sentences, S.
    1. S=φ
    2. For each verb, v in I repeat steps 3-7
    3. Let A be the solution of the constraint sat-
       isfaction problem induced by the non-spatial
       semantic fields solved by the arc-consistency
       algorithm [3].
    4. B=Spatial-Scenarios(I, v, C) i.e. B is the
       solution of the constraint satisfaction prob-
       lem induced by the spatial fields of the
       verb.
    5. Let C=A x B i.e. C is the instantiations of
       all semantic fields for the verb v.
    6. For each c in C, C=C\{c} if, c does not con-
       tains concepts from each of the icon chosen.
    7. S=S U C
    8. Return S
```

Fig. 2. The Algorithm Disambiguate

We categorize physical objects as 'Objects', 'Containers' or 'Surfaces'. The inference of possible 'in' and 'on' relations is done by checking the following rules for all pair of objects.

Non-Stationary(x), Container(y), Volume(x)< Volume(y) → In(x, y).   (3)
Non-Stationary(x), Surface(y), Volume(x) < Volume(y) → On(x, y).   (4)

A high-level description of the algorithm, which finds all possible spatial combinations of the objects involved, appears in Figure 3. It takes a model of the world as input. This model is in the form of connectivity and containment constraints. For example, we might have the following constraints:

C= {Disconnected (Moon, Earth), Disconnected (Playground, Kitchen), In (Bed, Bedroom)}

For example, for the icons shown on the second page, the checking of selectional constraints for the verb 'sleep' will lead to a problem space like:

Verb: Sleep   Agent: Children, Child

Time: φ   Location: Room, Playground

```
Algorithm: Spatial-Scenario
Input: A set of icons and their associated senses, I, a
set of constraints C and a verb, v
Output: The set of all consistent spatial relations for
the spatial fields of v.
```

1. P=φ
2. For all pairs of objects infer whether In (x, y) and On (x, y) are true using rules 3 and 4.
3. Represent the concepts and relations as a directed graph where the concepts are the nodes and the arcs represent the relations.
4. Add arcs and nodes corresponding to the constraints in C.
5. Perform a topological sort over the nodes of the graph.
6. Let the set of lowest ranked nodes of Q by E and the set of remaining nodes of Q be F. Repeat steps a-c until E=φ and F=φ
    a. Find all consistent path p, from an element in E to an element in F. It can be ensured by traversing to those nodes if and only if there is no arc marked 'Disconnected' from the nodes already traversed in the path. Each such path is an extension.
    b. Add each such path to P, if all constraints in C are satisfied in it. Let V= the set of nodes on the path p.
    c. Update E=E\V and F=F\V.
7. Return P.

Fig. 3. The Algorithm Spatial-Scenario

4 Results and Conclusion

Our work is concerned with the generation of the semantically correct sentences with a random sequence of concepts. The evaluation of the above-mentioned algorithms should be based on their ability to remove a large set of semantically anomalous sentences and the usability of the interface. We have presently implemented an icon-based system, which deals with concepts from the stamp-book of Indian Institute of Cerebral Palsy. The method adopted and algorithms used are sufficient to generate all and only semantically correct sentences. The sentences generated from the system are fed to a text-to-speech system for the speech impaired. Our system has icons, which display real-world events. Due to large overloading factor, the size of the vocabulary is reduced by 67%. This is because of the fact that generally each icon represents at least three concepts. Moreover, the user is not supposed to reason with the input to benefit from the overloading. Earlier approaches of overloading ([1]) defined composition operators for overloading. Since, cognitively challenged users cannot be expected to have the knowledge of how these operators work, the utility of such systems reamins suspect. Our approach of overloading the icons and methods to disambiguate them are a novel contribution for such interfaces.

References

1. Albacete, P.L., Chang, S.K, Polese, G.: Iconic Language Design for People with Significant Speech and Multiple Impairments. In Mittal, V.O., Yanco, H.A., Aronis, J., Simpson, R.(eds): Assistive Technology and Artificial Intelligence, Applications in Robotics, user interfaces and natural language processing. Lecture Notes in Artificial Intelligence, Vol. 1458, Springer-Verlag, (1998)
2. Dahlgren, K., McDowell, J, Stabler, E.P.: Knowledge Representation for Commonsense Reasoning with Text, Computational Linguistics, 15(3), 149-170 (1989)
3. Mackworth, A.K.: Consistency in Networks of Relations, Artificial Intelligence, 8, 99-118. (1977).
4. Miller, G.A., Johnson-Laird, P.N.: Language and Perception, Cambridge University Press, (1976).
5. Nirenburg, S., Raskin, V.: The Subworld concept lexicon and the lexicon management system, Computational Linguistics, 13(3-4), 276-289 (1989)

An Intelligent Grading System for Descriptive Examination Papers Based on Probabilistic Latent Semantic Analysis

Yu-Seop Kim[1], Jung-Seok Oh[1], Jae-Young Lee[1], and Jeong-Ho Chang[2]

[1] Division of Information Engineering and Telecommunications,
Hallym University, Gangwon, Korea 200-702
{yskim01, bil78, jylee}@hallym.ac.kr
[2] School of Computer Science and Engineering,
Seoul National University, Seoul, Korea 151-744
jhchang@bi.snu.ac.kr

Abstract. In this paper, we developed an intelligent grading system, which scores descriptive examination papers automatically, based on Probabilistic Latent Semantic Analysis (PLSA). For grading, we estimated semantic similarity between a student paper and a model paper. PLSA is able to represent complex semantic structures of given contexts, like text passages, and are used for building linguistic semantic knowledge which could be used in estimating contextual semantic similarity. In this paper, we marked the real examination papers and we can acquire about 74% accuracy of a manual grading, 7% higher than that from the Simple Vector Space Model.

1 Introduction

Bang et. al. [1] developed a descriptive exam grading system running in an Internet environment. After receiving student exam papers, the system request human examiners to mark the exam paper and inform the grading results made by human examiners. In this paper, we proposed an intelligent system which makes it possible to mark exam papers automatically. We mapped the problem space into a vector space, and we constructed a semantic kernel [2] to estimate the similarity between student and model papers. In this paper, we utilized Probabilistic Latent Semantic Analysis (PLSA), which is based on a statistical model called an aspect model [3]. PLSA model could evaluate the similarity by considering the shared concepts or topics inside two documents [4].

For the construction of the PLSA-based semantic kernel, we indexed terms from a large corpus and formed vectors of documents. The vectors are constructing a matrix of a semantic kernel to transfer an input vector to a feature vector of papers. We evaluate the similarity between two papers by using the vectors and semantic kernels from PLSA algorithm, and we try to classify the paper into one of two classes, one for correct paper class and the other for incorrect class. For the experiments, we evaluate the performance of our system, comparing to that of Simple Vector Space Model (SVSM) [5] and Generalized Vector Space Model (GVSM) [6].

2 Semantic Kernel Construction Based on PLSA

In this section, we explain the Probabilistic Latent Semantic Analysis model which is used for the construction of a semantic kernel.

Probabilistic Latent Semantic Analysis (PLSA) is a statistical technique for the analysis of two-mode and co-occurrence data. PLSA is based on *aspect model* where each observation of the co-occurrence data is associated with a latent class variable $z \in Z = \{z_1, z_2, \ldots, z_K\}$ [7]. For text documents, the observation is an occurrence of a word $w \in W$ in a document $d \in D$, and each possible state z of the latent class represents one semantic topic.

A word-document co-occurrence event, (d, w), is modelled in a probabilistic way where it is parameterized as in

$$P(d,w) = \sum_z P(z)P(d,w|z)$$
$$= \sum_z P(z)P(w|z)P(d|z). \tag{1}$$

Here, w and d are assumed to be conditionally independent given a specific z. $P(w|z)$ and $P(d|z)$ are topic-specific word distribution and document distribution, respectively.

The parameters $P(z), P(w|z)$, and $P(d|z)$ are estimated by maximization of the log-likelihood function

$$L = \sum_{d \in D} \sum_{w \in W} n(d, w) \log P(d, w). \tag{2}$$

and this maximization is performed using the EM algorithm as for most latent variable models. Details on the parameter estimation are referred to [7]. To evaluate similarity between a query and a document, a learner paper and an examiner paper in this research, $P(w|z)$ is used for its semantic kernel. In equation (3), $P(w|z_i)$ are extracted and are formed as a vector like,

$$< P(w|z_0), P(w|z_1), \ldots, P(w|z_k) >. \tag{3}$$

where k is a dimension size of the latent class variables, and the vocabulary size is assumed to be n. We can construct $n \times k$ matrix with vectors for the kernel called P_k in this section. And finally the similarity between a query and a document is measured as follows.

$$sim(d, q) = cos(P_k^T d, P_k^T q) = \frac{d^T P_k P_k q}{|P^T d||P^T q|}. \tag{4}$$

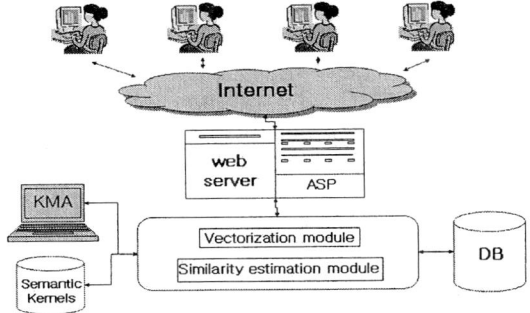

Fig. 1. The whole structure of the intelligent grading system

3 An Intelligent Grading System

Figure 1 is showing the whole structure of the intelligent grading system designed in this research. This system can be accessed through an internet by any users who want to take exams. This system has a web server which takes care of the communication with individual users. The server is composed of the two main parts, one takes charge of communication with individual users and the other for communication inside the grading system.

The server hands in questions to users and gathers the answer papers for transferring papers to the intelligent grading part. The grading part is also composed of two main parts, one is a vectorization part and the other is a similarity evaluation part. The vectorization part transforms the user-submitting exam papers to vectors with Korean Morphological Analyzer (KMA) and an indexed term dictionary. The indexed terms are selected from a very large corpora, ac-

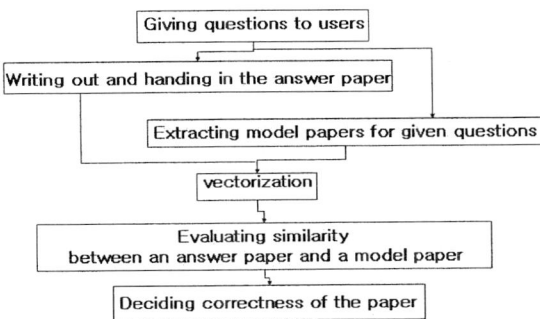

Fig. 2. Summarization of the whole process for the intelligent grading

cording to frequency in the corpus. The terms are stored in Databases. Databases manipulate two kinds of data, one is for the indexed terms and the other is for exam questions and their model papers. The vectorization part transforms the model papers to vectors, too. The similarity evaluation part estimates the similarity between two kinds of vectors transformed in the vectorization part. When evaluating the similarity, semantic kernel is used for transferring the input raw vectors, that are from user and model papers, to feature vectors representing the latent semantic structure of the papers. If the similarity value is higher than threshold, which is determined experimentally, the user paper is decided to be correct one, and otherwise that is incorrect one.

Figure 2 shows the whole process for the intelligent grading briefly.

4 Experimental results

4.1 Data and Experiment

For the experiments, we extracted 30 descriptive questions from a book named 'Proverbs' (in Korean 'Ko-Sa-Seong-Eo') [9]. 100 students were connected to the grading system and took exams and 3,000 descriptive exam answer paper examples were built for the experimental data. And we collected more than one model papers for a question in consideration of the usage of synonym words by users. We collected 38,727 Korean newspapers articles for the corpus. And we extracted 40,376 indexed terms from the corpus by using the Hangul (Korean characters) Morphological Analyzer[8]. And we decided the dimension size of PLSA to be 200 and the iteration number for the EM algorithm of the PLSA to be 50.

And we added another experiment of their simple ensemble model expressed like,

$$Ens = w_s f(sim_s) + w_g f(sim_g) + w_p f(sim_p). \tag{5}$$

where w_α means an weight value for α model, such as SVSM (s), GVSM (g), and PLSA (p) and the same as sim_α. The weight value is extracted from '$(100 - Total)/100$' in table 1. And $f(\beta)$ is a function returning 1 if $\beta \geq threshold_\alpha$, meaning that the model decided that the answer paper is correct, and 0 otherwise. Finally, if $Ens \geq threshold_{ens}$ then the paper could be decided to be correct. The value of each $threshold$ is decided empirically. A term 'Ens' appearing in tables below means the simple ensemble model constructed by an expression (5).

For the question "What is the meaning of Koo-Sa-Il-Saeng('a narrow escape from death' in English)", there may be several model answers including "to have a narrow escape after undergoing many crises to death". After taking exams, the system receives various answer papers including "to be barely brought to life" and "to overcome difficulties with troubles" from users. The first answer gets score of 0.35, 0.64, and 0.80 from SVSM, GVSM and PLSA respectively. And the second one gets 0, 0, and 0.41. Finally the system decides the first one to be correct and the second one to be incorrect because the score from PLSA is less than empirical threshold value of 0.7.

Table 1. Failure Ratio. Numbers in each cell mean the ratio of failure. In the second row('correct'), the numbers of each cell mean the failure ratio of papers decided as correct ones by models. The third row shows the same one as the second one, except that the papers are to be decided as incorrect ones. The last row means the total failure ratio of each model

	SVSM	GVSM	PLSA	Ens
correct	3.3	6.3	7.5	4.4
incorrect	54.2	60.8	46.8	46.6
total	33.47	42.67	26.8	26.4

Table 2. The number of each cell means the percentage numbers showing the proportion of each reason of failures in each model

	VSM	GVSM	PLSA	Ens
1	42.37	53.75	70.97	61.54
2	44.07	37.5	12.9	15.38
3	1.69	2.5	6.45	7.69
4	6.78	3.75	6.45	11.54
5	5.08	2.5	3.23	3.85

4.2 Evaluation of Experiments

Table 1 shows the failure ratio in marking results.

In table 1, the intelligent grading system has much failure when grading the paper to be incorrect. It tells that the intelligent algorithms have much difficulties in understanding the latent semantics in papers. However, PLSA has the best performance in finding the latent semantics. The deficiency of data needed in building semantic kernels is seemed to be the major reason of the failure.

And we analyzed the cause of grading failure generated from each model. The followings are the causes of the failure.

§1. Indexed terms were omitted in a semantic kernel.
§2. Model papers did not include various synonym terms used in students papers.
§3. No special reason to be classified.
§4. Learners' answer papers did not include keywords required by human examiners.
§5. A human examiner could not find syntactic errors in papers.

Table 2 shows the proportion of above cases in each models' failure.

In case 1, PLSA has much distinguishable result compared to other models. It says that PLSA is much affected by indexed terms. For the better accuracy, the size of indexed terms should be increased. However, PLSA has lower proportion of case 2 than other models. PLSA is more robust when the learner's paper and the examiner's paper don't have shared terms. From the result, we can infer that the performance of PLSA is less affected by the model papers directly written by examiners. And PLSA reflects the latent semantic structure in collected data better than other models.

5 Conclusion

We constructed an intelligent grading system based on a latent semantic kernel of PLSA. We found that the PLSA has similar properties to human examiners and represents the latent semantic space better than other models. For future work, we, firstly, should build corpus for a strong semantic kernel, with a larger volume and more various domain-specific characteristics. Secondly, more robust semantic kernel models are required to be designed by extending and combining the existing kernel models like PLSA. And finally, a method of combining syntactic structure of papers should be found for overcoming the limitation of bag of words methodology.

Acknowledgements

This research was supported by Korea Science and Engineering Foundation, 2004 (R05-2004-000-10376-0).

References

1. Bang, H., S. Hur, W. Kim, and J. Lee: A System to Supplement Subjectivity Test Marking on the Web-based. Proceedings of KIPS (2001) (in Korean)
2. Christianini, N., J. Shawe-Taylor, and H. Lodhi: Latent Semantic Kernels. Journal of Intelligent Information System, Vol. 18 No. 2 (2002) 127–152
3. Hofmann, T., J. Puzicha, and M. Jordan: Unsupervised learning from dyadic data. Advances in Neural Information Processing Systems, No. 11 (1999)
4. Hofmann, T.: Probabilistic latent semantic indexing. Proceedings of the 22th Annual International ACM SIGIR conference on Research and Developement in Information Retrieval (SIGIR99) (1999) 50–57
5. Salton, G., A. Wong, and C. S. Yang: A Vector Space Model for Automatic Indexing. Communication of the ACM, Vol. 19 No. 11 (1975) 613–620
6. Wong, S. K. M., W. Ziarko, and P. C. N. Wong: Generalized vector space model in information retrieval. Proceedings of ACM SIGIR Conference on Research and Development in Information Retrieval, (1985) 18–25
7. Hofmann, T.: Probabilistic latent semantic analysis. Proceedings of the Fifteenth Conference on Uncertainty in Artificial Intelligence (UAI'99) (1999)
8. Kang, S.: Hangule Morphological Analyzer. http://nlplab.kookmin.ac.kr
9. Kim, W.: Ko-Sa-Seong-Eo (Proverbs) Encyclopedia. Eu-Yu Inc. (2003)(in Korean)

Domain-Adaptive Conversational Agent with Two-Stage Dialogue Management

Jin-Hyuk Hong and Sung-Bae Cho

Dept. of Computer Science, Yonsei University,
134 Shinchon-dong, Sudaemoon-ku, Seoul 120-749, Korea
hjinh@sclab.yonsei.ac.kr, sbcho@cs.yonsei.ac.kr

Abstract. The conversational agent understands and provides users with proper information based on natural language. Conventional agents based on pattern matching have much restriction to manage various types of real dialogues and to improve the answering performance. For the effective construction of conversational agents, we propose a domain-adaptive conversational agent that infers the user's intention with two-stage inference and incrementally improves the answering performance through a learning dialogue. We can confirm the usefulness of the proposed method with examples and usability tests.

1 Introduction

Conversational agents have been studied as an effective interface to understand and respond to users. Conversations are not only convenient but also abundant and flexible for users to express what they want [1]. Pattern matching, one of popular methods for constructing the conversational agent, works favorably at a sentence, but it is not feasible to understand a dialogue in which context should be considered [2]. And the performance of conversational agents is mainly subject to the quality of dialogue management and the quantity of knowledge-base. Even with an excellent dialogue manager, the answer performance might be limited by the size of knowledge-base. Constructing knowledge-base has many difficulties encountered in knowledge engineering for expert systems. Scripts are usually designed by hand, and it costs much time and effort [3]. Furthermore, designers should be intelligent in analyzing the domain and designing scripts, since the quality of scripts affects on the answering performance.

For the construction of effective conversational agents, at first in this paper, we develop the architecture of two-stage dialogue management. Then, we propose an interactive knowledge acquisition method to construct scripts for the pattern matching of the proposed conversational agent.

2 Knowledge Acquisition from Natural Language Sources

As a basic means of the representation of information, natural language sources are obtainable in large quantities from the web and other materials. It might be successful when we utilize them to construct the knowledge base of intelligent agents instead of manual processing. If the data are static, the acquisition of information from them might be easy. In many cases, however, natural language sources are variable so that it is very difficult to extract useful information from them [4]. The knowledge acquisition from natural language sources has long been studied, and recently there are many works on extracting semantic or structural information from web pages [5].

Model-based approach is a conventional knowledge acquisition method, which employs in constructing the knowledge base of expert systems [4]. It defines the static knowledge representation of a target domain as a model, and collects necessary information from documents to complete the model. It uses templates or frames on the target domain to effectively process information, and it provides a brief process to understand [6]. Recently, the knowledge acquisition using the ontology awakes interest. Comparing with the model-based approach, it extracts rather deep semantic and structural information from documents. Especially it is now applied to acquire information by analyzing semantic structures not only within a web page but also between web pages [7].

There are some other works on the knowledge acquisition from dialogue not from simple natural language documents. Lauria *et al.*[8] tried to construct the course of the movement of a robot by natural language instructions. However, it just manages the dialogues of lower level such as simple commands, contrary to real conversation.

3 Proposed Conversational Agent

As shown in Fig. 1, the proposed conversational agent is composed of two parts: dialogue manager and knowledge manager. Dialogue manager deals with and responds to the user's query using the inference engine. If dialogue manger dose not understand a

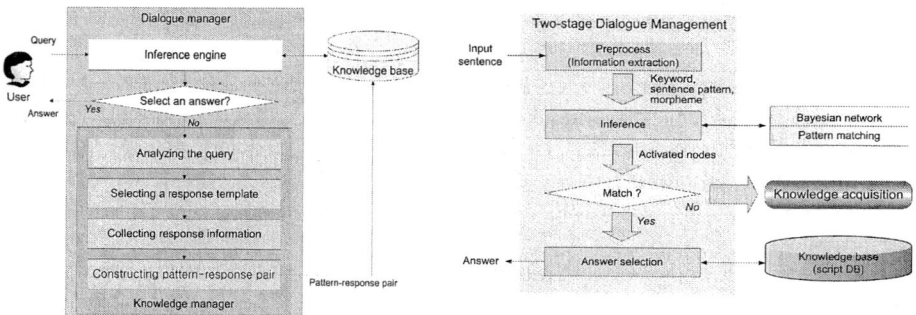

Fig. 1. The proposed conversational agent

Fig. 2. Overview of the two-stage dialogue management

query, the query is regarded as a learning dialogue and knowledge manager is executed. With a series of knowledge acquisition procedures, a script composed of patterns and responses is generated to be appended to knowledge-base. Since knowledge acquisition is conducted by conversation, it is easy to construct a domain-adaptive knowledge-base.

3.1 Two-Stage Inference for Dialogue Management

For efficient inference, useful words are extracted from the input query by preprocessing. These words are used to infer the user's intention as shown in Fig. 2. The inference process is divided into two steps: Bayesian network and pattern matching. Analyzing queries in stages makes it feasible to infer the detailed intention of the user and to model the context of conversation. Dividing knowledge-base, furthermore, improves the scalability and portability of conversational agents.

3.1.1 Topic Inference Using Bayesian Network

As a counter proposal of simple pattern matching, Bayesian network has been applied to dialogue management for the effective and accurate response. We design Bayesian network to infer the topic of conversation, which leads to define the scope of dialogue. Bayesian network is hierarchically constructed with three levels based on their functions: keyword, concept, and topic. Keyword level consists of words related to topics in the domain. Concept level is composed of the entities or attributes of the domain, while topic level represents the cases of entities whose attributes are defined. It is sometimes failed to infer the intention at one try, rather accumulating information through conversation is more efficient to infer the intention.

Words extracted from preprocessing are used as evidences in this paper. Through inference, the highest probabilistic topic node is selected if the probability is over threshold. Then pattern matching associated with a topic selected is executed to select a proper answer. If a topic is not selected, the proposed method tries mixed-initiative interaction to understand the user's intention. Since concept level contains a part of information, the agent asks the user to collect more information. After the user provides more information about his intention, the agent attempts inference again.

3.1.2 Answer Selection Using Pattern Matching

Once a topic is selected as the topic of an input query, pattern matching using knowledge-base associated with the topic is performed to select an answer. When there are

```
<SCRIPT>
<TOPIC> topic </TOPIC>
<PATTERN> words </PATTERN>
<RESPONSE> answer </RESPONSE>
</SCRIPT>
<SCRIPT>
<TOPIC> The location of school </TOPIC>
<PATTERN> where is school </PATTERN>
<PATTERN> know location school </PATTERN>
<RESPONSE> The school is located in Shinchon Dong. </RESPONSE>
<RESPONSE> It is in Shinchon Dong. </RESPONSE>
</SCRIPT>
```

Fig. 3. Definition of a script

lots of scripts, the performance declines because of the redundancy of information. In this paper, we divide scripts into several groups based on their topics so as to reduce the number of scripts compared. A script is stored as XML form, and Fig. 3 shows the definition and example of a script.

3.2 Pattern-Response Pairs Learning Through Dialogue

The pattern of a script is composed of the topic and a set of words. The topic of a query is obtained by Bayesian network, while words are extracted by preprocessing. Therefore, a pattern is simply defined by combining them and generating the pattern part of a script.

```
Definition:   (def-index template-name
                  :class        (dialogue-act)
                  :question     (question-script)
                  :requirement  (concept-of-construction)
                  :answer       (script input-position)
              )

Example:      (def-index no. 10
                  :class        (?DescriptionQuestion)
                  :question     ("What kind of location information should be provided?")
                  :requirement  (descript_value)
                  :answer("The location is %s.", descript_value)
                  :answer("It locates in %s.", descript_value)
              )
```

Fig. 4. Structure of the answer template

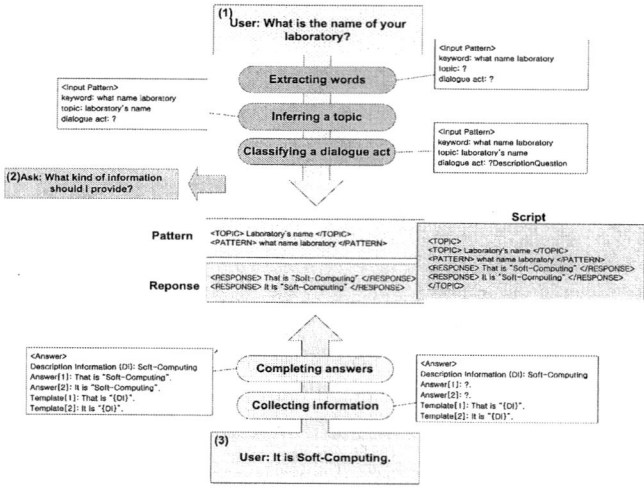

Fig. 5. Overall procedure of the knowledge manager

We consider the dialogue act of an input query to select a proper answer template for the generation of scripts. An automaton extracts a dialogue act, and 30 automata are designed for 30 dialogues. The subsumption architecture is adopted to select one dialogue act for a query. Each dialogue act has the corresponding answer template for constructing a response. An answer template is defined as shown in Fig. 4, of which "class" means the dialogue act, and "question" is a sentence to collect information. An answer script is constructed by filling "requirement (information collected from the user)" into "answer (a template)." In this paper, we define 64 templates: three templates for each question dialogue act, and six positive/negative templates for each statement dialogue act. After all, an answer is constructed by completing the template, and saved as the response part of a script.

The pattern-response pair is generated with a pattern and the responses. Fig. 5 shows the overall procedure of the generation of a pattern-response pair.

4 Experiments

4.1 Examples

The change of topics is common in real conversation, and the agent has to maintain the context of dialogue. Bayesian network of the proposed method models the context, and Dialogue 1 shows the example. Dialogue 2 shows the example of knowledge acquisition. Contrary to manual operations, a user only needs to provide what the agent requires through dialogue. It automatically performs all processes such as stemming words, defining dialogue act, and constructing answers.

User: What is your professor's telephone number? Word (what, number, telephone, professor) BN (topic: Professor's phone number) Agent: Our professor's phone number is 2123-XXXX. User: What about you? Word (what, you) High probability nodes (phone-number, professor) BN (topic: The phone number of Agent) Agent: I'm sorry, I don't have any phone. User: Hmm, so what about email address? Word (what, email, address) High probability nodes (phone-number, Agent) BN (topic: The email address of Agent) Agent: My email address is chatbot@sclab.yonsei.ac.kr.	User: Where is the laboratory? Agent: Hmm, I don't know. Change mode to Knowledge acquisition. ⇒ analyzing query Agent: Where is it? User: It locates at 529, the 3rd engineering building, 134, Yonsei university. ⇒ analyzing answer (requirement: 529, the 3rd engineering building, 134, Yonsei university) ⇒ generating the pattern-response pair <SCRIPT> <TOPIC> Laboratory's location </TOPIC> <PATTERN> where laboratory </PATTERN> <RESPONSE> It locates at 529, the 3rd engineering building, 134, Yonsei university </RESPONSE> <RESPONSE> 529, the 3rd engineering building, 134, Yonsei university </RESPONSE> <RESPONSE> It is at 529, the 3rd engineering building, 134, Yonsei university </RESPONSE> </SCRIPT> User: Where is the laboratory? Agent: It locates at 529, the 3rd engineering building, 134, Yonsei university
Dialogue 1. Context maintenance using Bayesian network	**Dialogue 2.** Knowledge acquisition by the proposed method

4.2 Usability Test

At first, we have collected a number of dialogues from 8 subjects performing 3 tasks that request to search information. 25 simple queries, 11 context-maintaining dialogues, and 11 mixed-initiative dialogues are collected. These numbers show that missing or spurious words are included in real conversation. We have compared with simple pattern matching (SPM) using these dialogues, and Table 1 shows the result. The result shows that the proposed method is superior to SPM, since it manages various types of dialogues while SPM fails to respond.

Table 1. Comparative result with simple pattern matching

Retrieval rate (RR) Average interactions (AI)		Task 1		Task 2		Task 3	
		RR	AI	RR	AI	RR	AI
SPM	Training	92.5%	1.5	95%	2.7	93.2%	4.4
	Test	87.3%	1.6	86.3%	2.7	87.7%	4.6
Proposed method	Training	100%	1.2	100%	2.1	100%	4.0
	Test	92.3%	1.4	96%	2.3	91.7%	4.5

For knowledge acquisition, we have experimented the usability test comparing with the manual construction of the knowledge base. 50 dialogues are used as training data to construct pattern-response pairs, while other 50 dialogues are used as test data. Experts and novices perform the experiment. Table 2 shows the result of the usability test for knowledge acquisition.

Table 2. Result of the usability test for knowledge acquisition

		Manual construction		Proposed method	
		Experts	Novices	Experts	Novices
Pattern-response pairs generated		50	50	44	44
File size		28 KB	30 KB	24 KB	24 KB
Construction time		20 min.	1 hour	5 min.	8 min.
Accuracy	Training	92%	84%	100%	96%
	Test	84%	82%	88%	86%
User satisfiability (0~5)		2	1	4	4

For queries having the same pattern, designers do not recognize them manually while they notice that case with the proposed method. Therefore, it reduces the size of knowledge base. In terms of construction time and the users' satisfiability, the proposed method is outstandingly superior to the manual construction.

5 Concluding Remarks

In this paper, we have constructed the conversational agent using two-stage dialogue management and its knowledge acquisition. Bayesian network used in dialogue management provides more flexible and detailed inference to manage various types of dialogues. In order to construct domain adaptive conversational agents, we have also proposed interactive knowledge acquisition. It is familiar and effective to collect useful knowledge to construct pattern-response pairs from learning dialogues. The example and the usability test have demonstrated the usefulness and power of the proposed method comparing with conventional approaches, especially for novices.

Acknowledgements

This paper was supported by Brain Science and Engineering Research Program sponsored by Korean Ministry of Science and Technology.

References

1. V. Zue and J. Class, "Conversational interfaces: Advances and challenges," Proc. of the IEEE, 88(8), pp. 1166-1180, 2000.
2. J.-H. Hong and S.-B. Cho, "A two-stage Bayesian network for effective development of conversational agent," LNCS 2690, pp. 1-8, 2003.
3. E. Horvitz, et al., "The lumiere project: Bayesian user modeling for inferring the goals and needs of software users," Proc. of the 14th Conf. on Uncertainty in Artificial Intelligence, pp. 256-265, 1998.
4. C. Schmidt and T. Wetter, "Using natural language sources in model-based knowledge acquisition," Data & Knowledge Engineering, 26(3), pp. 327-356, 1998.
5. H. Alani, et al., "Automatic ontology-based knowledge extraction from web documents," IEEE Intelligent Systems, 18(1), pp. 14-21, 2003.
6. A. Arruarte, et al., "A template-based concept mapping tool for computer-aided learning," Proc. IEEE Int. Conf. Advanced Learning Technologies, pp. 309-312, 2001.
7. R. Navigli, et al., "Ontology learning and its application to automated terminology translation," IEEE Intelligent Systems, 18(1), pp. 22-31, 2003.
8. S. Lauria, et al., "Personal robots using natural language instruction," IEEE Intelligent Systems, 16(3), pp. 38-45, 2001.

Feature Extraction Based on Wavelet Domain Hidden Markov Tree Model for Robust Speech Recognition

Sungyun Jung, Jongmok Son, and Keunsung Bae

School of Electronic and Electrical Engineering, Kyungpook National University,
1370 Sankyuk-dong, Puk-gu, Daegu, 702-701, Korea
{yunij, sjm, ksbae}@mir.knu.ac.kr
http://mir.knu.ac.kr/

Abstract. We present a new feature extraction method for robust speech recognition in the presence of additive white Gaussian noise. The proposed method is made up of two stages in cascade. The first stage is denoising process based on the wavelet domain hidden Markov tree model, and the second one is reduction of the influence of the residual noise in the filter bank analysis. To evaluate the performance of the proposed method, recognition experiments were carried out for noisy speech with signal-to-noise ratio from 25 dB to 0 dB. Experiment results demonstrate the superiority of the proposed method to the conventional ones.

1 Introduction

The performance of speech recognition systems generally degrades severely when training and testing are carried out in different environments. Even when training and testing are carried out in the same environment, improvement of recognition performance cannot be achieved for additive background noise with a signal-to-noise ratio (SNR) less than 10 dB [1]. To minimize the drop of performance for speech corrupted by background noise, various methods have been proposed [2–4] have presented a new framework for statistical signal processing based on wavelet domain hidden Markov model (HMM) that concisely models the statistical dependencies and non-Gaussian statistics encountered in real-world signals.

In this paper, we propose a new feature extraction method for robust speech recognition. It is made up of two stages in cascade. The first stage is denoising process based on the wavelet domain hidden Markov tree (HMT) model, and the second one is reduction of the influence of the residual noise in the filter bank analysis. In the first stage, the noise is estimated from the noisy signal using the HMT-based denoising method. Then, for feature parameter extraction, weighted filter bank analysis is performed with the weighting value to subtract some amount of energy proportional to the energy of estimated noise at each band. The proposed method shows remarkable performance improvement compared to the commonly used spectral subtraction method in the recognition experiments.

This paper is organized as follows. Section 2 describes the HMT-based denoising method and the residual noise remained in the enhanced speech. Then the proposed feature extraction scheme using the HTM-based denoising and weighted filter bank analysis is explained in section 3. Experimental condition and results are shown with our discussions in section 4. Finally the conclusion is given in section 5.

2 HMT Based Denoising and Residual Noise

The locality and multiresolution properties of the wavelet transform have proven very useful for removing noise components from the noisy signal [6, 7]. The HMT model represents wavelet coefficients as state variables across scale. It is a graph, as shown in Figure 1, with tree-structured dependencies between state variables. A signal denoising method based on the HMT model presented in [5] is given in Figure 2. We applied this method to removal of noise components from the noisy speech. For this an eight-scale wavelet decomposition with 'db7' mother wavelet is performed, and the number of possible states at each node was set to 2. Figure 3 shows an example of noisy and enhanced speech signals for a sentence. In this figure, it is shown that considerable amounts of noise still remain in the enhanced speech.

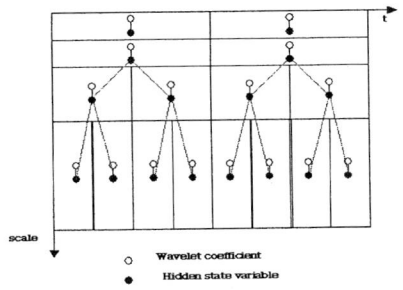

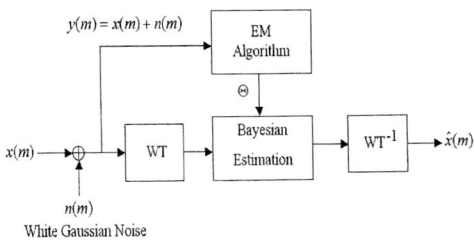

Fig. 1. Tiling of the time-frequency plane and tree structure for HMT model

Fig. 2. Block diagram for HMT-based denoising in [5]

Figure 4 shows typical temporal sequences of log filter bank energy (FBE) for clean speech, enhanced speech, estimated noise, and the residual noise. We can see that the residual noise has a great variance at initial and final silence regions, short pause intervals in the sentence while variance is small in the regions of having large speech energy, i.e., high SNR regions. The estimated noise also shows similar patterns in the silence regions of residual noise. Therefore it would be helpful for robust feature extraction if we can reduce the influence of residual

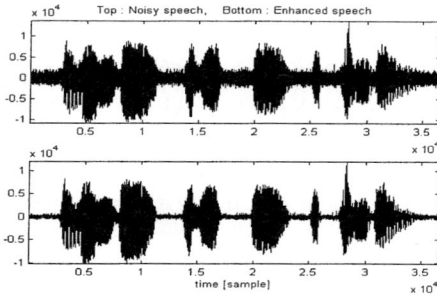
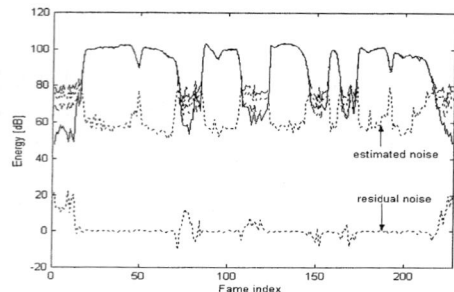

Fig. 3. An example of noisy speech (top) and enhanced speech (bottom) for SNR of 10 dB

Fig. 4. Typical temporal sequences of logFBE for clean speech(solid), enhanced speech(dashed), estimated noise(dotted), and residual noise(dotted bottom) after HMT-based denoising

noise in the filter bank analysis stage. We can do this by subtracting some amount of energy at each band depending upon the variance of residual noise. Since a priori knowledge about the residual noise is not available in real situation, however, the estimated noise obtained from the HMT-based denoising stage can be used for it.

3 Proposed Feature Extraction Scheme

In the previous section, we have shown that the residual noise in the enhanced speech has much influence on the band where signal energy is low. To reduce the influence of the residual noise in feature extraction, we propose a new feature extraction method using the HMT-based denoising and weighted filter bank analysis. Figure 5 shows the block diagram of the proposed method. First noisy speech, $y(m)$ is separated into enhanced speech, $\hat{x}(m)$ and estimated noise, $\hat{n}(m)$ using the HMT model. Through the filter bank analysis for the estimated noise, $\hat{n}(m)$, the weighting value λ_i is computed for each band. Then, mel-frequency cepstral coefficients(MFCC) are computed from the weighted filter bank analysis outputs as robust features.

Figure 6 shows the block diagram of filter bank analysis to get the weighting value in the weighted filter bank analysis from the estimated noise signal. The estimated noise frame, $\hat{n}(m)$, where $1 \leq m \leq N$, is transformed into frequency domain by applying a short-time Fourier transform (STFT), and then, power spectrum, $P_{\hat{N}}(k)$ is calculated. Once power spectrum for each frame is found, filter bank energy, e_i is calculated through ith mel-scaled bandpass filter, $\Phi_i(k)$, which is a normalized rectangular window function having the same area for all filters. After logarithm is applied to the filter bank energies, weighting value, λ_i is obtained from Equation (1).

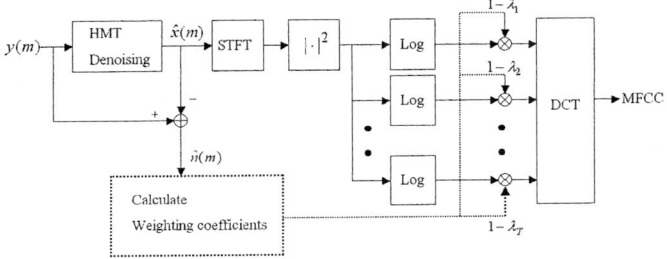

Fig. 5. Block diagram of the proposed feature extraction method

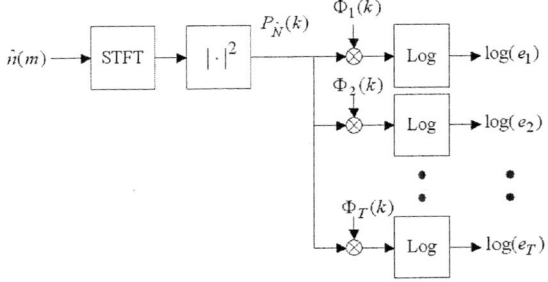

Fig. 6. Filter bank analysis with an estimated noise signal for computation of the weighting value

$$\lambda_i = \frac{\log(e_i)}{\sum_{j=1}^{T} \log(e_j)} \quad (1)$$

where T is the number of me-scaled normalized rectangular bandpass filters. Once weighting value for each band is calculated, weighted filter bank analysis is performed to reduce the influence of residual noise in log FBE domain with Equation (2).

$$Weighted\ LogFBE_i = (1 - \lambda_i)LogFBE_i \quad (2)$$

where FBE_i is ith filter bank energy of enhanced speech. Finally, a discrete cosine transform (DCT) is applied to $Weighted\ LogFBE_i$ to extract mel-frequency cepstral coefficients for robust speech recognition.

4 Experimental Results

To evaluate the performance of the proposed method, recognition experiments were carried out using Korean address database (DB). This corpus consists of phrases containing connected three words, which is "city name - district name

Table 1. Recognition results depending on SNR conditions (recognition rate of sentence and word, respectively)

SNR	Baseline	SS method	HMT-based denoising	Proposed method
25 dB	87.95	92.11	96.49	96.49
	92.73	95.28	98.37	98.37
20 dB	60.78	84.21	94.24	94.61
	75.94	91.19	97.58	97.74
15 dB	20.13	53.20	84.84	88.10
	55.30	78.29	92.69	94.86
10 dB	0.57	10.35	64.79	71.80
	34.56	54.70	82.71	86.63
5 dB	0	0.22	19.70	22.21
	12.12	30.40	54.58	55.83
0 dB	0	0	0.54	0.39
	0	15.63	23.08	23.25

- block name" in order. Here we regard a phrase as a sentence for convenience. Each sentence contains short period of silence region before and after clean speech region. All the data were digitized with sampling rate of 16 kHz, and 16 bits/sample quantization. This DB consists of 7176 training sentences from 36 male and female speakers and 800 testing sentences from 4 male and female speakers. To simulate various noisy conditions, the testing sentences were corrupted by the additive white Gaussian noise with SNR conditions from 25 dB to 0 dB.

The baseline recognition system was implemented on HTK [8] with continuous density HMM models. Triphone model was used as a basic acoustic unit. Each unit has a five-state continuous mixture HMM having a simple left-to-right structure with skipping. Each state has 5 Gaussian mixtures with a diagonal covariance matrix. Finite state network was constructed for connected 3-word strings. Using a hamming windowed analysis frame length of 20 ms, a 13th-order static cepstral coefficient vector was obtained with a set of 24 Mel-spaced rectangular filters at a frame rate of 100 Hz. The resulted 13-dimensional features plus their delta and delta-delta features, in other word, totally 39-dimensional features were used for speech recognition.

To evaluate the recognition performance of the proposed feature extraction method as well as HMT-based denoising method, they were compared with the commonly used spectral subtraction (SS) method. Table 1 shows the correct recognition rate of sentence and word, respectively, for each method as a function of the signal-to-noise ratio. It is shown that at the SNR of 25 dB both proposed method and HMT-based denoising method achieved almost the same accuracy as that of the clean speech with a baseline system. When the SNR is 15 dB, the proposed method improved the sentence recognition rate from 20.13 % to 88.10 %, and word recognition rate from 55.30 % to 94.86 % while SS method achieved 53.20 % and 78.29 % for sentence and word, respectively.

The experimental results indicate that the proposed method achieves remarkable performance improvement especially when the SNR is low. It says that the proposed method that subtracts some amount of energy proportional to the energy of estimated noise at each band is a reasonable and good approach to reduce the influence of residual noise, and to increase the robustness of the extracted features. When the SNR becomes extremely low like 5 dB or less, the recognition rate gets very poor even though the proposed method shows better performance than other ones. It is believed that this is due to the difficulty of accurate estimation of the noise from the noisy signal.

5 Conclusions

In this paper, a new feature extraction method that combines both HMT-based denoising and weighted filter bank analysis is proposed for robust speech recognition. It makes use of the estimated noise signal to obtain the weighting value that is needed for weighted filter bank analysis. Experimental results for noisy speech showed remarkable performance improvement compared to the commonly used spectral subtraction method. The proposed method showed more performance improvement especially when the SNR becomes low.

Acknowledgement

This work was supported by grant No. R01-2003-000-10242-0 from the Basic Research Program of the Korea Science & Engineering Foundation.

References

1. Acero,A.: Acoustical and environmental robustness in automatic speech recognition. Norwell, M.A Kluwer (1993)
2. Boll,S.F.: Supression of acoustic noise in speech using spectral subtraction. IEEE Trans.Acoust. Speech Signal Process., Vol.27 (1992) 113–120
3. Ephraim,Y., Malah,D.: Speech enhancement using a minimum mean-square error short-time spectral amplitude estimator. IEEE Trans. Acoust. Speech Signal Process., Vol.32, no.6 (1984) 1109–1121
4. Moreno,P.J., Raj,B., Stern,R.M.: A vector taylor series approach for environment independent speech recognition. Proc. of Int. conf.Acoust.Speech Signal Process., Atalanta, GA (1996) 733–736
5. Crouse,M.S., Nowak,R.D., Baraniuk,R.G.: Wavelet-based statistical signal processing using hidden markov models. IEEE Trans. on Signal Processing, Vol.46, no.4 (1998)
6. Donoho,D.,Johnstone,I.: Adapting to unknown smoothness via wavelet shrinkage. J. Ame. Stat. Assoc., Vol.90 (1995) 1200–1224
7. Chipmen,H., Kolaczyk,E., McCulloch,R.: Adaptive Bayesian wavelet shrinkage. J. Ame. Stat.Assoc., Vol.92 (1997)
8. Young,S.: The HTK Book (HTK Version 3.1), Cambridge (2000)

Feature Unification and Constraint Satisfaction in Parsing Korean Case Phenomena

Jong-Bok Kim[1], Jaehyung Yang[2], and Incheol Choi[3]

[1] School of English, Kyung Hee University, Seoul, Korea 130-701
[2] School of Computer Engineering, Kangnam University, Kyunggi, 449-702, Korea
[3] Language Research Institute, Kyung Hee University, Seoul, 130-701, Korea

Abstract. For a free-word order language such as Korean, case marking remains a central topic in generative grammar analyses for several reasons. Case plays a central role in argument licensing, in the signalling of grammatical functions, and has the potential to mark properties of information structure. In addition, case marking presents a theoretical test area for understanding the properties of the syntax-morphology interface. This is why it is no exaggeration to say that parsing Korean sentences starts from work on the case system of the language. This paper reports the project that develops a Korean Resource Grammar (KRG, Kim and Yang 2004), built upon the constrain-based mechanisms of feature unification and multiple inheritance type hierarchies as an extension of HPSG (Head-driven Phrase Structure Grammar), and shows that the results of its implementation in the Linguistic Knowledge Building System (cf. Copestake 2002) prove its empirical and theoretical efficiency in parsing case-related phenomena.

1 Formation of Case-Marked Elements

Nominal expressions allow various particles (including case markers) to be attached but in strict ordering relationships, as exemplified in the traditional template in (1)a and one example in (1)b (Kim 1998):

(1) a. N-base – (Hon) – (Pl) – (PostP) – (Conj) – (X-Delim) – (Z-Delim)
    b. sensayng + (nim) + (tul) + (eykey) + (man) + (i)
       teacher + Hon   + Pl   + Postp   + only + NOM
       'to the (honorable) teachers only'

As observed in (1)a, the GCASE markers such as NOM, ACC, and GEN can appear only in the final position, called Z-Delim(iter) position, whereas the SCASE markers (GOAL, LOC, etc) occupy the PostP position. We treat the particles as suffixes attached to the nominal stems in the lexicon by a step-by-step process based on the hierarchy in (2). The building process of nominal elements thus starts from the basic lexical elements of the type *nom-lxm* (nominal-lexeme), moving up to a higher type while any of these processes can be skipped and then directly be realized as (pumped up to) a *word* element in syntax.[1] Thus the attachment of the plural suffix to the *nom-lxm* will generate *nom-pl*, and that of a postposition suffix will produce a *nom-p* element.

(2)
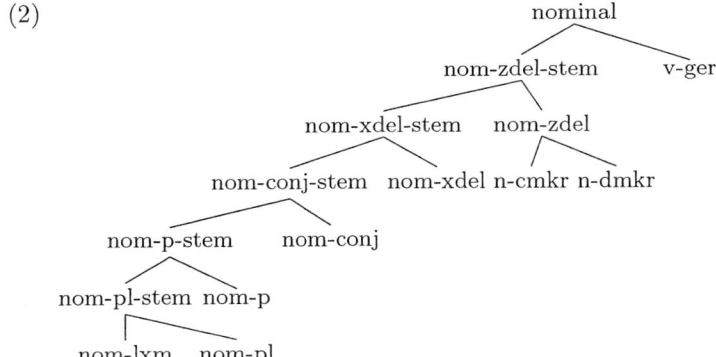

The constraints on each type place restrictions on the ordering relationship among nominal suffixes, as exemplified in (3):

(3) a. *nom-p* → [STEM *nom-pl-stem*]
    b. *nom-zdel* → [STEM *nom-xdel-stem*]

These constraints mean that the type *nom-p* requires its STEM value to be a type of *nom-pl-stem*, and the type *nom-zdel* specifies its STEM value to be *nom-xdel-stem*. These constraints explain why (4)a is well-formed, but not (4)b:

(4) a. [$_{nom-p}$ [$_{nom-pl}$ sensayngnim-tul]-eykey] 'teacher-PL-DAT'
    b. *[$_{nom-p}$ [$_{nom-zdel}$ sensayngnim-nun]-eykey] 'teacher-TOP-DAT'

The type *nom-pl* in (4)a is a subtype of *nom-pl-stem*, and this thus observes the constraint in (3)a. However, in (4)b, the type *nom-zdel* cannot serve as the STEM value of the postposition *-eykey* according to (3)a since it is not a subtype of *nom-pl-stem*.

2 Case Constraints in Syntax

Once we have the right generation of nominal elements with case information, the next issue is how argument-selecting heads and grammar rules contribute their case information to nominal elements. Phenomena such as case alternation illustrated in (5) make it hard to attribute to the case as lexical properties:

---

[1] This is one main difference from *verb-lxm*. As noted, only *v-free* elements can become a *v-word* that can appear in syntax.

(5) a. John-i   nokcha-ka/*lul   coh-ta
       John-NOM green.tea-NOM/*ACC like-DECL
       'John is fond of green tea.'
    b. John-i   nokcha-lul/*ka   coh-a   hanta
       John-NOM green.tea-ACC/*NOM like-COMP do
       'John likes green tea.'

Our analysis adopts the lexeme-based lexicon where all the verbal lexemes will minimally have the following information:

(6) $\begin{bmatrix} v\text{-}lxm \\ \text{ORTH } \langle \text{ilk-} \rangle \\ \text{ARG-ST } \langle \text{NP}\begin{bmatrix} \text{GCASE } vcase \end{bmatrix}, \text{NP}\begin{bmatrix} \text{GCASE } vcase \end{bmatrix} \rangle \end{bmatrix}$

This means that any element in the ARG-ST gets the value *vcase* as its GCASE value: the *vcase* value can be either *nom* or *acc* in syntax. The elements in the ARG-ST will, in accordance with a realization constraint, be realized as SUBJ and COMPS in syntax as indicated in the following:

(7) $\begin{bmatrix} \langle \text{ilk-ess-ta 'read-PST-DECL'} \rangle \\ \text{SYN} \begin{bmatrix} \text{HEAD} | \text{POS } verb \\ \text{VAL} \begin{bmatrix} \text{SUBJ } \langle \boxed{1} \rangle \\ \text{COMPS } \langle \boxed{2} \rangle \end{bmatrix} \end{bmatrix} \\ \text{ARG-ST } \langle \boxed{1}\text{NP}\begin{bmatrix} \text{GCASE } vcase \end{bmatrix}, \boxed{2}\text{NP}\begin{bmatrix} \text{GCASE } vcase \end{bmatrix} \rangle \end{bmatrix}$

With this declarative verb *ilk-ess-ta* 'read-PST-DECL', the SUBJ element can be *nom* whereas the COMPS can be *acc*, but not the other grammatical case value as noted in (8):

(8) John-i/*ul   chayk-ul/*i   ilk-ess-ta
    John-NOM/ACC book-ACC/NOM read-PST-DECL
    'John read a book.'

Then, the question is which part of the grammar makes sure the SUBJ is *nom* whereas COMPS is *acc*. The determination of case value in the VAL is not by a lexical process but imposed by syntactic rules. That is, we assume that Korean X' syntax includes at least the Head-Subject Rule encoded in the LKB as the following feature description:

```
head-subj-rule := hd-arg-ph &
 [ SYN.VAL [ SUBJ <>,
             COMPS #2 ],
   ARGS < #1 & [ SYN.HEAD [ CASE.GCASE nom, PRD - ] ],
          [ SYN.VAL [ SUBJ < #1 >,
                      COMPS #2 ] ] > ].
```

The rule simply says that when a head combines with the SUBJ, the SUBJ element is *nom*. As for the case value of a complement, it is a little bit more complicated since there are cases where the nonsubject argument gets NOM rather than ACC as in (5). In the language, nonagentive verbs like *coh-* assign NOM to their complements. Reflecting this type of case assignment, we adopt the head feature AGT (AGENTIVITY) and ramify the Head-Complement Rule into two as the following:[2]

(9) a. Head-Complement Rule A:

$$\left[hd\text{-}comp\text{-}ph \right] \Rightarrow \boxed{1}\left[\text{CASE} \mid \text{GCASE } acc \right], \mathbf{H}\begin{bmatrix} \text{HEAD} \mid \text{AGT } + \\ \text{COMPS} \left\langle ..., \boxed{1}, ... \right\rangle \end{bmatrix}$$

b. Head-Complement Rule B:

$$\left[hd\text{-}comp\text{-}ph \right] \Rightarrow \boxed{1}\left[\text{CASE} \mid \text{GCASE } nom \right], \mathbf{H}\begin{bmatrix} \text{HEAD} \mid \text{AGT } - \\ \text{COMPS} \left\langle ..., \boxed{1}, ... \right\rangle \end{bmatrix}$$

Within this system, we then do not need to specify *nom* to the nonsubject complement of psych verbs, diverging from the traditional literature. Just like other verbs, the complement(s) of such psych verbs like *coh-ta* 'like-DECL' will bear just *vcase*, as a general constraint on verbal elements as represented in (10)a:

(10) $$\begin{bmatrix} \text{HEAD} \begin{bmatrix} \text{POS } verb \\ \text{AGT } - \end{bmatrix} \\ \text{ARG-ST} \left\langle \text{NP}\left[\text{GCASE } vcase \right], \text{NP}\left[\text{GCASE } vcase \right] \right\rangle \end{bmatrix}$$

This lexical information would then project the following structure for (5):

(11)

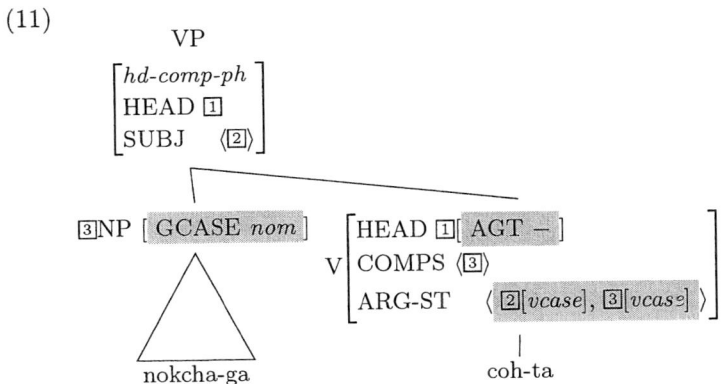

---

[2] The positive value of the AGT (AGENTIVITY), similar to STATIVITY, is assigned to the verbs that have an external argument whereas the negative value is assigned to those with no external argument.

As noted here, the verb *coh-ta* 'like' bears the head feature [AGT −]. This means that the complement of this verb will get NOM even though in the ARG-ST its case value is *vcase*. This is guaranteed by the Head-Complement Rule B in (9).

3 Some Merits of the Feature Unification

3.1 Two Nominative Cases

One tricky case pattern in the language is the double occurrence of nominative markers:

(12) sensayngnim-kkeyse-man-i   o-si-ess-ta
     teacher-HON.NOM-only-NOM came
     'Only the honorable teacher came.'

The marker *-kkeyse* here functions as a honorific subject marker and falls the same morpholoigcal slot as the postposition marker. This marker cannot mark nominative objects or adjuncts: It marks only honorable nominative subjects. This implies that the stem produced by the attachment of *kkeyse* carries at least the following information:

(13) $\begin{bmatrix} \langle \text{sensayngnim-kkeyse 'teacher-HON.NOM'} \rangle \\ \text{HEAD} \begin{bmatrix} \text{POS noun} \\ \text{HON} + \\ \text{CASE} | \text{GCASE } nom \end{bmatrix} \end{bmatrix}$

The [GCASE *nom*] value accounts for why this stem can combine only with the nominative marker. If we attach an accusative marker there will be a clash between [GCASE *acc*] and [GCASE *nom*]. This is not a possible feature unification:

(14) $*\begin{bmatrix} \langle \text{sayngkakha-kkeyse-man-ul 'teacher-HON.NOM-DEL-ACC'} \rangle \\ \text{HEAD} \begin{bmatrix} \text{POS noun} \\ \text{HON} + \\ \text{CASE} \begin{bmatrix} \text{GCASE } nom \\ \text{GCASE } acc \end{bmatrix} \end{bmatrix} \end{bmatrix}$

3.2 Case Omission and Delimiters

Another welcoming consequence of the present analysis in which the unification and subsumption operations of feature structures play key roles in the KRG comes from phenomena where case markers are not realized or replaced by delimiters. One main property of case markers is that they can be omitted or can be replaced by delimiters in proper context:

(15) haksayng-(tul) chayk-(to) ill-ess-e
    student-PL   book-even   read
    'Students even read a book.'

The basic lexical entries for the words in (15) would be something like the following:

(16) a. $\begin{bmatrix} \langle \text{ilk-ess-e 'read-PST-DECL'} \rangle \\ \text{HEAD} \mid \text{AGT } + \\ \text{ARG-ST } \langle \text{NP}[\text{GCASE } vcase], \text{NP}[\text{GCASE } vcase] \rangle \end{bmatrix}$

b. $\begin{bmatrix} \langle \text{haksayng-tul 'student-PL'} \rangle \\ \text{HEAD} \begin{bmatrix} \text{POS } noun \\ \text{CASE} [\text{GCASE } gcase] \end{bmatrix} \end{bmatrix}$ c. $\begin{bmatrix} \langle \text{chayk-to 'book-also'} \rangle \\ \text{HEAD} \begin{bmatrix} \text{POS } noun \\ \text{CASE} [\text{GCASE } gcase] \end{bmatrix} \end{bmatrix}$

Note that the nouns here, projected to NPs, are not specified with any grammatical case value even though they may have semantic information coming from the delimiters. The present analysis generates the structure (17) to the sentence (15). As represented in the tree structure, since *gcase* is supertypes of *nom* and *acc*, there is no unification failure between the case information on the lexical element and the case requirement imposed by the Head-Subject and Head-Complement Rule. For example, in accordance with the Head-Complement Rule A, the complement of the agentive head must be *acc*, but the complement itself bears *gcase*. Since *gcase* is the supertype of *acc*, there is no feature clash. The case hierarchy, together with the feature unification and subsumption, thus allows us to capture no realization of the case markers in a straightforward manner.

4 Testing the Feasibility of the System and Conclusion

The KRG we have built within the typed-feature structure system and well-defined constraints, eventually aiming at working with real-world data, has been first implemented into the LKB. In testing its performance and feasibility, we used the 231 (grammatical and ungrammatical) sentences from the literature and 292 sentences from the SERI Test Suites '97 (Sung and Jang 1997) designed to evaluate the performance of Korean syntactic parsers:

(17)
	# of Sentences	# of Words	# of Lexemes
SERI	292	1200	2679
Literature	231	1009	2168
Total	523	2209	4847

Of the 2209 words, the number of nominal elements is 1,342. These nominal elements include total 1,348 particles, which can be classified as follows:

(18)

	NOM	ACC	GEN	Delimiter	Semantic cases	Vocative	Total
Number	514	401	14	152	265	2	1,348

As the table shows, the system correctly generated all the GCASE or SCASE marked words as well as delimiter-marked elements in the literature and Test Suites. The KRG lexicon, build upon the type hierarchy with relevant constraints on each type, generate all these elements and the Case Constraints in syntax properly licensed these in the grammar. In terms of parsing sentences, the KRG correctly parsed 274 sentences out of 292 Seri Test Suites and 223 out of 231 literature sentences, failing 26 sentences (497 out of 523 sentences). Failed sentences are related to the grammar that the current system has not yet written. For example, the SERI Test Suites include examples representing phenomena such as honorification, coordination, and left dislocation of subject. It is believed that once we have a finer-grained grammar for these phenomena, the KRG will resolve these remaining sentences. Another promising indication of the test is that its mean parse (average number of parsed trees) for the parsed sentences marks 2.25, controlling spurious ambiguity at a minimum level.

As noted here, the test results provide clear evidence that the KRG, built upon typed feature structure system, offers high performance and can be extended to large scale of data. Since the test sentences here include most of the main issues in analyzing the Korean language, we believe that further tests for designated corpus will surely achieve nearly the same result of high performance too.

References

Copestake, Ann. 2002. *Implementing Typed Feature Structure Grammars.* CSLI Publications.

Kim, Jong-Bok. 1998. Interface between Morphology and Syntax: A Constraint-Based and Lexicalist Approach. *Language and Information* 2: 177-233.

Kim, Jong-Bok and Jaehyung Yang. 2004. Projections from Morphology to Syntax in the Korean Resource Grammar: Implementing Typed Feature Structures. In *Lecture Notes in Computer Science* Vol.2945: 13-24. Springer-Verlag.

Sung, Won-Kyung and Myung-Gil Jang. 1997. SERI Test Suites '95. In *Proceedings of the Conference on Hanguel and Korean Language Information Processing.*

A Comparison of BDI Based Real-Time Reasoning and HTN Based Planning

Lavindra de Silva and Lin Padgham

School of Computer Science and Information Technology,
RMIT University, Melbourne, Vic., Australia, 3000
{ldesilva, linpa}@cs.rmit.edu.au

Abstract. The *Belief-Desire-Intention* (BDI) model of agency is an architecture based on Bratman's theory of practical reasoning. Hierarchical Task Network (HTN) decomposition on the other hand is a *planning* technique which has its roots in classical planning systems such as STRIPS. Despite being used for different purposes, HTN and BDI systems appear to have a lot of similarities in the problem solving approaches they adopt. This paper presents these similarities. A systematic method for mapping between the two systems is developed, and experimental results for different kinds of environments are presented.

1 Introduction

The *Belief-Desire-Intention* (BDI) [1] agent development framework (e.g. JACK [2] and PRS [3]) appears in many ways to be very similar to the Hierarchical Task Network (HTN) approach to planning (e.g. UMCP [4], SHOP [5]), although the former arises out of the multi-agent systems community, while the latter arises out of the planning community.

Both BDI and HTN systems use a notion of decomposition, and flexible composition of parts, although BDI systems are primarily used for deciding goal directed agent actions in dynamic environments, while HTN systems are used for formulating a plan which is later executed.

Earlier research (e.g. [6,7]) mentions similarities between HTN planning and BDI style execution. The work most closely related to ours is in the *ACT* formalisms of the Cypress system [7]. Work done for Cypress is different to our work in that ACT is an *interlingua* that enables the two systems to share information, whereas we provide a mapping between HTN and BDI systems. Furthermore, the HTN planner in Cypress is a partial-order HTN planner, whereas we use a total-order (hereafter referred to simply as HTN) HTN planner.

Despite the close similarities of HTN and BDI systems, there does not appear to be any work done which systematically contrasts and compares the core approaches and algorithms developed in the two communities. This paper provides a detailed comparison between the two approaches, including a mapping from HTN to BDI representations. We also explore the efficiency of the underlying algorithms of the two kinds of systems, via experimentation in varying situations. This work provides a basis on which application developers can choose the preferred implementation platform, as well as providing some insights into how frameworks in either paradigm may be improved.

2 Similarities and Differences Between HTN and BDI

Both HTN planners and BDI agent execution systems create solutions by decomposing high level tasks (or goals) into more specific tasks and primitive actions. The tasks as well as the decomposition methods (or plans) are specified by the programmer in both cases.

However, the systems (usually) serve a different purpose in that HTN planners are used to efficiently find a plan, which can then be executed, whereas BDI systems are used to guide execution in real time. There is some work on interleaving planning and execution, using HTN planners [6], which is then very similar in style to BDI execution and is therefore suitable for guiding actions in dynamic environments. BDI systems can also be used to search for a solution before executing it, in situations where this is appropriate or desirable.

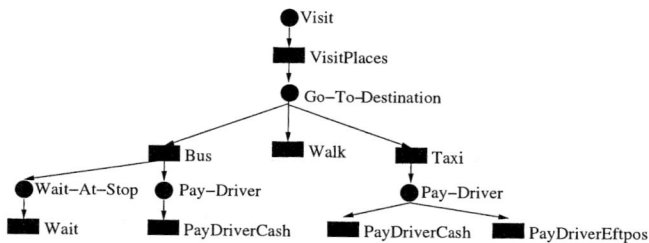

Fig. 1. Goal-plan hierarchy in BDI or Task-network in HTN

An example of a goal-plan hierarchy in BDI or a task network in HTN is shown in Figure 1[1]. In this Figure, circles represent BDI goals or HTN abstract tasks and rectangles represent BDI plans or HTN methods. The hierarchy begins by having a goal/task to make a visit which can be achieved by (decomposed into) the *VisitPlaces* plan (method). This plan (method) has a goal (task) to go to the destination which in turn can be achieved by (decomposed using) one of the three plans (methods): *Bus*, *Walk* or *Taxi*, etc.

The fact that this structure can equally well represent an HTN task network, or a BDI goal-plan tree, indicates a certain similarity between the systems. Also, the approach of returning to try an alternative path through the tree if difficulties are encountered, is similar in both cases.

However reasons for "backtracking" in this structure are subtly different. BDI systems will backtrack only if there has been some failure - usually caused by some change in the environment, or by the lack of complete predictability of actions. HTN systems backtrack when a solution that has been pursued, turns out not to work. There is no opportunity for discovering problems within the environment, during the planning process.

---

[1] This example was taken from [5] and extended.

If we are to compare execution of HTN and BDI systems we need to choose a particular HTN and BDI system to work with, and then map programs between the two systems. The HTN system we use is JSHOP which is a Java version of the SHOP planner. JSHOP is being used by the *Naval Research Laboratory for Noncombatant Evacuation Operations*[2]. SHOP2 is a generalization of SHOP/JSHOP that won one of the top four prizes in the 2002 International Planning Competition.

We have developed a systematic translation that we have used to convert JSHOP programs to JACK programs. The translation deals with the main entities of JSHOP, which are methods, operators and axioms [5], whereas the main entities of BDI according to [8], are plans, goals or events and beliefs[3].

3 Experimental Comparison

In its original form, BDI systems were designed for use in highly dynamic environments, and HTN systems were designed for use when guaranteed solutions were necessary. Some research also focussed on building hybrid systems that combine the useful (e.g. [6, 7]) properties of each system. In this section, we provide emperical foundations for past and future work, by analysing how each system performs in different environments.

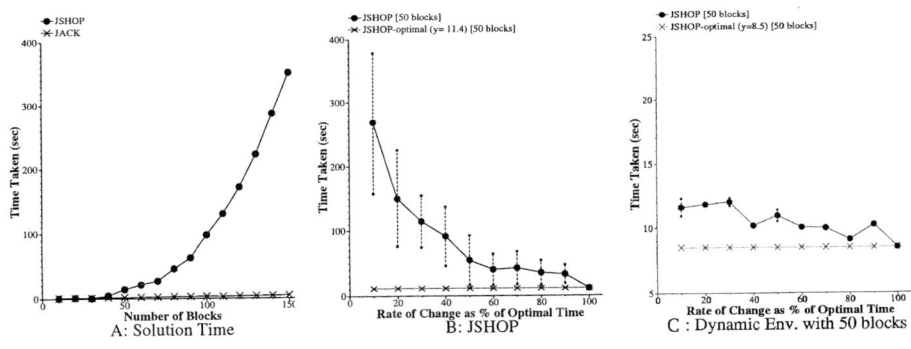

Fig. 2. A: Solution time for JACK and JSHOP with increasing number of blocks, B: and C: JSHOP and modified JSHOP (respectively) in a dynamic environment

In order to compare the performance of BDI and HTN algorithms under differing problem sizes and environmental situations, we took examples of blocks world encoding provided with JSHOP, extended these, and mapped to JACK, using the mapping mentioned previously. We then ran experiments to explore time and memory usage in static and dynamic environments. The Blocks World domain was used because it can easily be scaled to a range of problem sizes, and also because tested JSHOP encodings [5] for the problem were already provided.

---

[2] http://www.cs.umd.edu/projects/shop/description.html
[3] We leave out the details due to space restrictions. See http://www.cs.rmit.edu.au/ ldesilva for a more detailed paper.

The JSHOP blocks-world domain representation as well as sample problems from 10 blocks to 100 blocks was provided with the JSHOP planner (originally obtained from [9]). We used the problems provided and created additional problems for 110, 120, 130, 140 and 150 blocks by combining the 100 blocks problem with 10 blocks problems (including block renumbering). We randomly selected one problem of each size, for problems of size 10-100. Each problem was specified in terms of the start position of all blocks, and a goal state specifying the position of all blocks.

The program encoding consisted of one compound task *move*, with four different decompositions for achieving it, each having a different precondition. The primitive actions consisted of four operators; *pickup*, *putdown*, *stack* and *unstack*. Due to space constraints, refer to [9] for full details. An axiom was used to indicate whether a block needed to be moved. This *need-to-move(x)* axiom (where x is a block) evaluates to true or false based on whether one of a number of conditions are met. For example, *need-to-move(x)* would be true if x is on the table and there is a goal state requiring x to be on some other block. This heuristic allowed problems in this particular encoding of the blocks-world to be solved without needing HTN style lookahead, since standard BDI reasoning is not capable of such lookahead.

The mapping techniques we had developed were then used to translate from JSHOP to JACK representation for each problem.

The experiments were run on a dedicated machine, running Linux Red Hat 8.0, with an Intel Pentium IV - 2GHz CPU, and 512MB of memory. Each experiment was an average of 10 runs. Measurements taken were time[4]/memory required to create a solution. In JACK, the solution is found through execution in a simulator, whereas JSHOP produces the solution as a list of actions, which is then executed in the simulator.

The experiments performed explored: 1) *Runtime in static environments of size 10-150 blocks*, 2) *Runtime in dynamic environments of size 30 - 50 blocks*, 3) *Memory usage in environments of size 10-100 blocks*.

3.1 Runtime in Static Environment

The first experiment compared the time taken in both systems to find one solution, with an increasing number of blocks. Figure 2A shows these results.

For Figure 2A, DeltaGraph[5] showed that the time taken by JSHOP is approximately $0.03x^2$, which is quadratic, while time taken by JACK is approximately $0.02x$, which is linear. Statistical results also confirmed that these two graphs were significantly different.

Further experiments to understand JSHOP's quadratic performance revealed that JSHOP's precondition evaluation algorithm took at least 75 percent of the processing time, in particular, its *unification* algorithm used from within *theorem prover*. The unification algorithm was not complex in itself, but had a high frequency of calls. A more complete analysis of runtime in a static environment is left as future work.

Experiments for the memory usage of JSHOP and JACK using problem sizes of 10-100 blocks showed the same pattern as that of Figure 2A for unmodified JSHOP.

---

[4] Using the *time* command, the CPU + system times spent in execution.
[5] http://www.redrocksw.com/deltagraph/

3.2 Runtime in Dynamic Environment

For these experiments a dynamic Blocks World environment was used, where a random move action was introduced periodically. This simulated a situation where the environment is changing outside of the control or actions of the agent. The externally introduced move action was selected by randomly choosing (source and destination) from among the blocks that were currently clear. Differing rates of change were used, with the slowest rate being the time taken to execute the entire solution in a static environment. We call this time the *optimal time* (refer to Figure 2A). Slower change than this would of course have no effect. The dynamism was increased each time by 10 percent of the slowest rate.

For these experiments, executing the solution found by JSHOP was significant in order to determine whether it actually reached the goal, given the changing environment[6]. Failure could occur either when a planned action failed (for example due to a block to be picked up, no longer being clear), or when the whole plan had been executed, but on checking the goal had actually not been accomplished, due to environmental changes. At the point of failure, JSHOP replanned from the new environmental state.

Figure 2B shows the time taken by JSHOP to find a solution for a problem of size 50 blocks, as the dynamism in the environment decreases.[7] The horizontal dotted line crossing the y axis at y=11.4, in Figure 2B, is the optimal time. As the dynamism increases, the time taken to find a solution also increases at a rate of approximately x^3.

This is because every time the environment changes, JSHOP has to replan for the new environmental state, although usually it would have moved somewhat closer to the goal. Therefore as the dynamism increases, the number of plans generated in order to find a solution is likely to increase. The large standard deviation (dashed vertical lines) as the dynamism increases is due to the variability in how much of an effect the environmental change has on plans being created, due to whereabouts in a plan, a failure occurs.

Experiments with JACK in the same dynamic environment was linear, which showed that the behaviour of JACK does not appear to be significantly affected by the rate at which the environment changes (figure not shown due to space constraints). This is to be expected as plans are chosen in the current environment immediately prior to execution. In addition a plan choice commits only to relatively few steps, and so if it is affected by environmental change, only relatively little time is lost. Experiments also shows that there is not much standard deviation in the results, and that the standard deviation is consistent, even with an increasing rate of change.

There is an increasing amount of work in adapting HTN planners to interleave execution with planning (e.g. [6]), making them operate in some ways more like BDI agent systems. We adapted JSHOP to execute each method directly after decomposition, obtaining the experimental results shown in Figure 2C. Note that y=8.5 seconds was the optimal time for finding a solution, when the first decomposition (with at least one action) was immediately executed (as opposed to forming a complete solution).

---

[6] The changing environment here means the external environment that JSHOP finds solutions for and not changes to the initial state during planning.

[7] Results were similar for 30 and 40 blocks.

We found the degradation of the system as dynamism increases to be similar to that of JACK. Further, statistical tests showed that the behaviour of modified JSHOP is significantly different to the behaviour of the original version of Figure 2B.

4 Discussion and Future Work

On the examples tested, the growth rate of JACK of finding a solution, compared to JSHOP as problem size increases, is linear as opposed to polynomial. This has a significant impact for large applications. Future work could include an analysis of JACK's complexity, in particular, its context condition evaluation, for a comparison with JSHOP's complexity in [4]. A complexity analysis may also enable HTN systems to benefit from faster algorithms used by BDI systems (or at least by JACK).

Although our comparison used a single implementation of a BDI and total-order HTN each system, we emphasise that we considered the formalisms [8, 5] of two state of the art systems for our mapping.

Due to the similarity of the core mechanisms in the two paradigms, each can borrow some strengths from the other. Since BDI systems allow real time behaviour in quite dynamic domains, HTN systems can be made to behave like BDI systems in dynamic domains by executing methods immediately after decomposition. Alternatively, BDI agents could use HTN planning in environments when lookahead analysis is necessary to provide guaranteed solutions. In situations where the environment is not highly dynamic, BDI agents could use HTN lookahead to anticipate and avoid branches in the BDI hierarchy that would prevent the agent from achieving a goal.

We also acknowledge that both types of systems have strengths and functionality not covered in this work, which may well make them the system of choice for a particular application.

Acknowledgements

We thank Ugur Kuter, Professor Dana Nau and Fusun Yaman from the University of Maryland for providing help with the JSHOP formalisms and planner. We thank Michael Winikoff, John Thangarajah and and Gaya Jayatilleke for comments on this paper and the RMIT Agents group for constant feedback and support.

References

1. Rao, A.S., Georgeff, M.P.: BDI-agents: from theory to practice. In: Proceedings of the First International Conference on Multiagent Systems, San Francisco (1995)
2. Busetta, P., Rönnquist, R., Hodgson, A., Lucas, A.: Jack Intelligent Agents - components for intelligent agents in java. AgentLink News Letter, Agent Oriented Software Pty. Ltd, melbourne (1999)
3. Georgeff, M., Ingrand, F.: Decision making in an embedded reasoning system. In: Proceedings of the International Joint Conference on Aritificial Intelligence. (1989) 972–978
4. Erol, K., Hendler, J.A., Nau, D.S.: Complexity results for HTN planning. Annals of Mathematics and Artificial Intelligence **18** (1996) 69–93

5. Nau, D., Cao, Y., Lotem, A., Munoz-Avila, H.: SHOP: Simple Hierarchical Ordered Planner. In: Proceedings of the International Joint Conference on AI. (1999) 968–973
6. Paolucci, M., Shehory, O., Sycara, K.P., Kalp, D., Pannu, A.: A planning component for RETSINA agents. In: Agent Theories, Architectures, and Languages. (1999) 147–161
7. Wilkins, D.E., Myers, K.L., Lowrance, J.D., Wesley, L.P.: Planning and reacting in uncertain and dynamic environments. Journal of Experimental and Theoretical AI **7** (1995) 197–227
8. Winikoff, M., Padgham, L., Harland, J., Thangarajah, J.: Declarative & procedural goals in intelligent agent systems. In: Proceedings of the Eighth International Conference on Principles of Knowledge Representation and Reasoning (KR2002), Toulouse, France. (2002)
9. Gupta, N., Nau, D.S.: On the complexity of blocks-world planning. Artificial Intelligence **56** (1992) 223–254

A Formal Method Toward Reasoning About Continuous Change

Chunping Li

School of Software, Tsinghua University, Peking 100084, China
cli@tsinghua.edu.cn

Abstract. This paper presents a formal method based on the high-level semantics of processes to reason about continuous change. With a case study we show how the semantics of processes can be integrated with the situation calculus. Our aim is to overcome some limitations of the earlier works and to realize the automated reasoning about continuous change.

1 Introduction

In the real world a vast variety of applications need logical reasoning about physical properties in continuous systems, e.g., specifying and describing physical systems with continuous actions and changes. The early research work on this aspect was encouraged to address the problem of representing continuous change in a temporal reasoning formalism. The research standpoint concentrated on specialized logical formalisms, typically of the situation calculus and its extensions[7, 8, 6].

Whereas these previously described formalisms have directly focused on creating new or extending already existing specialized logical formalisms, the other research direction consists in the development of an appropriate semantic as the basis for a general theory of action and change, and applied to concrete calculi [9, 1, 10, 11, 2].

In this paper, we present a formal method of integrating the semantics of processes with the situation calculus to reason about continuous change. With a case study we show how the semantics of processes can be integrated with the situation calculus to reason about continuous change. In section 2, the semantics of processes is described briefly. In section 3, an example domain is introduced, and a conventional mathematical model is constructed. Section 4 shows the method how to represent the semantics of processes in the situation calculus. In section 5, we have the concluding remarks for this work.

2 The Semantics of Processes

In this section, we introduce the high-level semantics of processes [3] for reasoning about continuous processes, their interaction in the course of time, and their manipulation.

Definition 1. *A* process scheme *is a pair* $\langle C, F \rangle$ *where C is a finite, ordered set of symbols of size* $l > 0$ *and F is a finite set functions* $f \colon \mathbb{R}^{l+1} \to \mathbb{R}$.

Definition 2. *Let N be a set of symbols (called* names*). A* process *is a 4-tuple* $\langle n, \tau, t_0, \boldsymbol{p} \rangle$ *where*

1. $n \in N$;
2. $\tau = \langle C, F \rangle$ *is a process scheme where C is of size m;*
3. $t_0 \in \mathbb{R}$; *and*
4. $\boldsymbol{p} = (p_1, \ldots, p_m) \in \mathbb{R}^m$ *is an m-dimensional vector over* $\mathbb{R}$.

Definition 3. *A* situation *is a pair* $\langle S, t_s \rangle$ *where S is a set of processes and* t_s *is a time-point which denotes the time when S started.*

Definition 4. *An* event *is a triple* $\langle P_1, t, P_2 \rangle$ *where* P_1 *(the precondition) and* P_2 *(the effect) are finite sets of processes and* $t \in \mathbb{R}$ *is the time at which the event is expected to occur.*

Definition 5. *An event* $\langle P_1, t, P_2 \rangle$ *is* potentially applicable *in a situation* $\langle S, t_s \rangle$ *iff* $P_1 \subseteq S$ *and* $t > t_s$.

Definition 6. *Let* ε *be a set of events and* $\langle S, t_s \rangle$ *a situation, then the* successor *situation* $\Phi(\langle S, t_s \rangle)$ *is defined as follows.*

1. *If no applicable event exists in* ε *then* $\Phi(\langle S, t_s \rangle) = \langle S, \infty \rangle$;
2. *if* $\langle P_1, t, P_2 \rangle \in \varepsilon$ *is the only applicable event then* $\Phi(\langle S, t_s \rangle) = \langle S', t_s \rangle$ *where* $S' = (S \setminus P_1) \cup P_2$ *and* $t_{s'} = t$;
3. *Otherwise* $\Phi(\langle S, t_s \rangle)$ *is undefined, i.e., events here are not allowed to occur simultaneously.*

Definition 7. *An* observation *is an expression of the form* $[t] \propto (n) = r$ *where*
1. $t \in \mathbb{R}$ *is the time of the observation;*
2. $\propto$ *is either a symbol in C or the name of a function in F for some process scheme* $\langle C, F \rangle$;
3. n *is a symbol denoting a process name; and*
4. $r \in \mathbb{R}$ *is the observed value.*

Definition 8. *A* model *for a set of observations* Ψ *(under given sets of names* $\mathcal{N}$ *and events* $\mathcal{E}$ *) is a system development* $\langle S_0, t_0 \rangle, \Phi(\langle S_0, t_0 \rangle), \Phi^2(\langle S_0, t_0 \rangle), \ldots$ *which satisfies all elements of* Ψ. *Such a set* Ψ entails *an (additional) observation* ψ *iff* ψ *is true in all models of* Ψ.

3   An Example: Pendulum and Balls Scenario

We illustrate how an example, the interaction between a pendulum and balls that travel along a 1-dimension space, can be formalized. As described in Figure 1, a pendulum collides at angle $\varphi = 0$ with a ball being at position $y = y_c$ at the same time. We need to find appropriate equations describing various possible movements and interactions. Supposing the damping factor is neglected, the motion of the pendulum can be described by the following differential equation.

$$m \cdot l^2 \cdot \frac{d^2\varphi}{dt^2} = -m \cdot g \cdot l \cdot \sin\varphi - l^2 \cdot \frac{d\varphi}{dt}$$

where l is the length of the pendulum, m is the mass of the pendulum, and g is $9.8 \frac{m}{s^2}$. Solving the differential equation results in the angle of the pendulum φ, the angular velocity φ' and the angular acceleration φ''. φ_{max} denotes the maximum angle of the motion of the pendulum, T_{P0} the starting time of the motion of the pendulum, and γ the time constant of the pendulum.

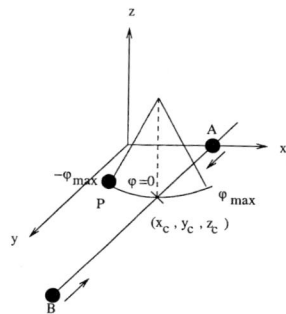

Fig. 1. Pendulum and balls A and B in positions

Here we define two different types of events. The first is the collision of two balls A and B, caused by identical locations at a certain time. The second type of event is the collision between one of the balls and the pendulum P, defined by the angle of the pendulum being zero while the ball's position is at the y-axis position of the pendulum y_c, at the same time. The pendulum is assumed to be of much larger mass than the balls, such that the collision will simply be an elastic impact with one of the balls (reflection into opposite direction) while the pendulum keeps moving continuously.

For ball A and ball B moving along the y-axis, we use the process scheme $\tau_{move} = \langle C, F \rangle$, namely, $C = \{y_0, v\}$ and $F = \{y = y_0 + v \cdot (t - t_0)\}$. As the process scheme for the motion of the pendulum we obtain $\tau_{pendulum} = \langle C', F' \rangle$ where $C' = \{\varphi_{max}, \gamma, y_c\}$ and $F' = \{\varphi, \varphi', \varphi''\}$.

4 Representing the Process Semantics in the Situation Calculus

4.1 Situation Calculus with the Branch Time

The situation calculus is the most popular formalism designed to represent theories of action and change[5]. The situation calculus does not yet provide a very rich temporal ontology. Pinto and Reiter proposed the concept of a time line to extend the original situation calculus by incorporating the basic elements of a linear temporal logic [7, 8]. For reasoning about time in the situation calculus, a predicate *actual* is incorporated. A situation is actual if it lies on the path that describes the world's real evolution.

A new sort is incorporated into the situation calculus, interpreted as a continuous time line. The sort is considered isomorphic to the non-negative real. Intuitively, each situation has a starting time and an ending time. Actions occur at the ending time of situations. This is captured by the following axioms.

$(\forall s, a)\ end(s, a) = start(do(a, s))$.
$(\forall s, a)\ start(s) < start(do(a, s))$.
$start(S_0) = 0$.

The predicate *occurs* is introduced as describing a relation between action types and situations.

$occurs(a, s) \equiv actual(do(a, s))$.

To establish the relation between actions that occur and the time at which they occur, the predicate $occurs_T$ is defined as

$occurs_T(a, t) \equiv (\exists s)\ occurs(a, s) \land start(do(a, s)) = t$.

4.2 An Axiomatization of Pendulum and Balls Scenario

In the pendulum and balls scenario, we suppose that two balls move toward each other along the y-axis. A pendulum maybe will collide at its suspension point with one of balls. The successor state axioms and action precondition axioms are suitable for formalizing the motion processes of the balls and the events. We have the following the successor state axioms:

$Poss(a, s) \rightarrow holds(moving(ball, \tau_{move}, T, (l, v)), do(a, s)) \equiv$
$\quad (a = impetus(ball, (l, v)) \land occurs_T(a, T) \land f = F(l, v, t, T)) \land$
$\quad \lor (holds(moving(ball, \tau_{move}, T, (l, v)), s) \land$
$\quad \neg(a = impetus(ball, (l, v))))$.

$Poss(a, s) \rightarrow holds(sway(Pendulum, \tau_{pendulum}, T_{P0}, (\varphi_{max}, \gamma, y_c)), do(a, s))$
$\quad \equiv (a = starting(Pendulum, (\varphi_{max}, \gamma, y_c)) \land$
$\quad occurs_T(a, T_{P0}) \land \varphi = -\varphi_{max} \cdot \cos(\frac{2\pi}{\gamma} \cdot (t - t_{P0}))) \land$
$\quad \lor (holds(sway(Pendulum, \tau_{pendulum}, T_{P0}, (\varphi_{max}, \gamma, y_c)), s)$
$\quad \land \neg(a = starting(Pendulum, (\varphi_{max}, \gamma, y_c))))$.

We formalize the actions with the action precondition axioms as follows.

$Poss(starting(ball, (l, v)), s) \equiv$
$\quad occurs_T(impetus(ball, (l, v)), T) \land start(s) < T$.
$Poss(starting(Pendulum, (\varphi_{max}, \gamma, y_c)), s) \equiv$
$\quad occurs_T(starting(Pendulum, (\varphi_{max}, \gamma, y_c)), T_{P0}) \land start(s) < T_{P0}$.

$Poss(collide((Pendulum, ball), ((\varphi_{max}, \gamma, y_c), (l_{new}, v_{new})), t), s) \equiv$
$\quad holds(sway(Pendulum, \tau_{pendulum}, T_{P0}, (\varphi_{max}, \gamma, y_c)), s) \land$
$\quad holds(moving(ball, \tau_{move}, t, (l_{old}, v_{old})), s) \land t = \frac{y_c - l_{old}}{v_{old}} + t_0$
$\quad \land l_{new} = y_c \land v_{new} = -v_{old} \land v_{old} \neq 0.$
$Poss(collision((ballA, ballB), ((l'_{A0}, v'_{A0}), (l'_{B0}, v'_{B0})), t), s) \equiv$
$\quad holds(moving(ballA, \tau_{move}, T_{A0}, (l_{A0}, v_A)), s) \land$
$\quad holds(moving(ballB, \tau_{move}, T_{B0}, (l_{B0}, v_B)), s) \land$
$\quad t = (l_{B0} - l_{A0} + v_A \cdot T_{A0} - v_B \cdot T_{B0})/(v_A + v_B) \land$
$\quad l'_{A0} = l'_{B0} = l_{A0} + v_A \cdot (t - T_{A0}) \land$
$\quad v'_{A0} = v'_{B0} = v_A + v_B \land start(s) < t.$

There are two natural actions that may occur in this scenario:

$natural(a) \equiv a = collide((Pendulum, ball), ((\varphi_{max}, \gamma, y_c), (l_{new}, v_{new})), t) \lor$
$\quad a = collision((ballA, ballB), ((l'_{A0}, v'_{A0}), (l'_{B0}, v'_{B0})), t).$

Suppose that ball A starts from position 0m at time 2sec to move with speed 0.4m/sec, while ball B starts from position 4m at time 4sec with speed -0.3m/sec. If there is no other event to occur, the two balls A and B which move toward each other along y-axis would have a collision at time 10sec. We start the pendulum with suspension point $x_c = 1$m, $y_c = 0.3$m, $z_c = 0$, time constant $\gamma = 1$ and starting angle $\varphi_{max} = 10$ at time $T_{P0} = 1$. The natural action (event) of the collision between the pendulum and ball A will occur at time $t = (y_c - y_{A0})/v_A + t_{A0} = 2.75$ sec.

This nearest event results in the pendulum moving unchanged while the ball A moves into the opposition direction, and avoids the collision possibility of the balls A and B. Here we describe the initial facts and equality constraints as follows.

$F: y = y_0 + v \cdot (t - t_0); F': \varphi = -\varphi_{max} \cdot \cos(\frac{2\pi}{\gamma} \cdot (t - t_{P0}))$

Furthermore, the occurrence axiom can be described as follows.

$occurs(starting(Pendulum, (\varphi_{max}, \gamma, y_c)), S_1) \land occurs(impetus(ballA,$
$(y_{A0}, v_A)), S_2) \land occurs(impetus(ballB, (y_{B0}, v_B)), S_3)$

where $start(S_1) = 1\sec \land start(S_2) = 2\sec \land start(S_3) = 4$sec, $S_0 < S_1 < S_2 < S_3$.

Let $AXIOMS$ be the axioms given in Subsection 4.1 with the action precondition and the successor state axioms. It is easy to see that for any model $\mathcal{M}$ of $AXIOMS$ it holds that $\mathcal{M} \models S_1 = do(starting(Pendulum, (\varphi_{max}, \gamma, y_c)), S_0)$
$\land S_2 = do(impetus(ballA, (y_{A0}, v_A)), S_1) \land S_3 = do(impetus(ballB, (l_{B0}, v_B)), S_2).$

From the occurrence axiom and the ordering statement, we infer that $\mathcal{M}$ satisfies $occurs_T(impetus(ballA, (y_{A0}, v_A)), t_{A0}) \land occurs_T(impetus(ballB, (y_{B0}, v_B)),$
$t_{B0}) \land occurs_T(starting(Pendulum, (\varphi_{max}, \gamma, y_c)), t_{P0})$ and $t_{P0} < t_{A0} < t_{B0}$.

The natural action $collide$ will occur in the time t which the equation $t = (y_c - y_{old})/v_{A0} + t_{A0} \land y_{newA} = y_c \land v_{newA} = -v_B$ will be true.

Thus, $occurs_T(collide((Pendulum, ballA), ((\varphi_{max}, \gamma, y_c), (y_{newA}, v_{newA})), t))$ will hold in the model $\mathcal{M}$. By using the successor state axiom for $sway$ and the action precondition axioms, we obtain $\mathcal{M} \models$

$S_4 = do\,(collide\,((Pendulum, ballA), ((\varphi_{max}, \gamma, y_c), (y_{newA}, v_{newA})), t), S_3) \wedge$
$holds\,(sway\,(Pendulum, \tau_{pendulum}, T_{P0}, (\varphi_{max}, \gamma, y_c))\,S_4) \wedge$
$holds\,(moving\,(ballA, \tau_{move}, T_{A0}, (y_{newA}, v_{newA})), S_4).$

5 Concluding Remarks

This paper presents a formal method based on the high-level semantics of processes to reason about continuous change. With a case study we show how to integrate the semantics of processes with the situation calculus for reasoning about continuous changes. Our method carries on some important properties of Pinto and Reiter's temporal situation calculus, and implements the automated reasoning about continuous change in the logical programming framework. The main difference is that we adopt a more general concept of the process, which is more appropriate to the semantic description in the case of continuous change. We have proved the soundness and completeness of the situation calculus with respect to the process semantics and implemented logic programs supporting the process semantics based on the situation calculus in Prolog under the environment of Eclipse. Because of space restrictions we here omit the proof of the soundness and completeness and the implementation of logic programs (for the interested reader, see [4] in detail). The current limitation of our method is not to consider events that occur simultaneously. If two or more simultaneous events involve identical objects, then the overall results might not by the combination of the results of the involved events. This requires more sophisticated means to specify suitable state transitions. Yet, this is left as future work.

References

1. Gelfond, M., Lifschitz, V.: Representing action and change by logic programs. Journal of Logic Programming **17** (1993) 301–321
2. Grosskreutz, H., Lakemeyer, G.: ccGolog: A logical language dealing with continuous change. Logical Journal of IGPL **11 (2)** (2003) 179–221
3. Herrmann, C., Thielscher, M.: Reasoning about continuous change. In Proc. of AAAI, Portland, U.S.A. (1996) 639–644.
4. Li, C.: Reasoning about processes and continuous change, Technical Report, Tsinghua University (2004), ftp://166.111.102.2/Reports/2004/reasoning.pdf
5. McCarthy, J., Hayes, P.: Some philosophical problems from the standpoint of artificial intelligence. Machine Intelligence **4**, Edinburgh University Press (1969) 463–502
6. Miller, R.: A case study in reasoning about action and continuous change. In Proc. ECAI, Budapest, Hungary (1996) 624–628.
7. Pinto, J., Reiter, R.: Reasoning about time in the situation calculus. Annals of Mathematics and Artificial Intelligence **14** (1995) 251–268
8. Reiter, R.: Natural actions, concurrency and continuous time in the situation calculus. In Proceedings of the 5th International Conference on Principles of Knowledge Representation and Reasoning. Cambridge, Massachusetts, U.S. (1996) 2–13

9. Sandewall, E.: The range of applicability and non-monotonic logics for the inertia problem. In Proc. International Joint Conference on Artificial Intelligence, France (1993) 738–743.
10. Thielscher, M.: The logic of dynamic system. In Proc. International Joint Conference on Artificial Intelligence, Montreal, Canada (1995) 639–644
11. Thielscher, M.: A Concurrent, Continuous Fluent Calculus. Studia Logica **67(3)** (2001) 315–331

A Time and Energy Optimal Controller for Mobile Robots

Sebastien Ancenay and Frederic Maire

School of SEDC, IT Faculty, Queensland University of Technology,
2 George Street, GPO Box 2434, Brisbane QLD 4001, Australia
s.ancenay@student.qut.edu.au,
f.maire@qut.edu.au

Abstract. We present a time and energy optimal controller for a two-wheeled differentially driven robot. We call a *mission* the task of bringing the robot from an initial state to a desired final state (a state is the aggregate vector of the position and velocity vectors). The proposed controller is time optimal in the sense that it can determine the minimum amount of time required to perform a mission. The controller is energy optimal in the sense that given a time constraint of n seconds, the controller can determine what is the most energy efficient sequence of accelerations to complete the mission in n seconds.

1 Introduction

The fast paced nature of robotic soccer necessitates real time sensing coupled with quick behaving and decision-making, and makes robotic soccer an excellent test-bed for innovative and novel techniques in robot control [1]. This paper concentrates on the design of a low level controller to perform elementary missions. We show how to compute off-line optimal trajectories using quadratic programming and how to use these results to build a real time controller.

The remainder of the paper is organized as follows. In Section 2, review related work. In Section 3, we describe our quadratic programming approach. In Section 4, we present some experimental results.

2 Previous Work

Many low-level robot controllers create some virtual potential to guide the motion of robots. Recent work based on repulsive potential fields by researchers from LAAS-CNRS [3] is representative of this approach. These potential methods handle well obstacle avoidance and path planning. Each obstacle produces an additive virtual potential field. The robot follows the gradient vectors to travel in the lower valleys of the potential field. The non-holonomic path deformation method [6] is a generic approach of the on-line trajectory deformation issue. It enables to deform a trajectory at execution time so that it moves away from obstacles and that the non-holonomic constraints of the system keep satisfied. Perturbations are also represented with potential fields. Potential fields can be stacked up. For robot soccer [9], a base field is built where potential values decrease towards the opponent goal to force robots to play closer to that area. A robot's position field encourages the robots to remain in their role positions to provide better robot dispersion around the playing field. Another field is used to represent obstacles and clear path to the ball. Low-level navigation controllers can be integrated in SLAM (Simultaneous Mapping and Localisation) method [4,5]. In [4], large scale non-linear optimization algorithms and extended Kalman filters were used to compute trajectories. In [10], a new path planning technique for a flexible wire robot is presented. The authors introduced a parametrization designed to represent low-energy configurations and three different techniques for minimizing energy within the self-motion manifold of the curve. In [2], a differential evolution algorithm is used to solve the path planning problem by finding the shortest path between start and goal points. This is the closest method to ours. But, the method presented in [2] does not guarantee the optimality of the returned solution (as it relies on an evolution algorithm).

3 A Quadratic Programming Approach

Energy efficient path planning can be formulated as a quadratic problem [7]. As the source of power of a mobile robot is an on-board battery, energy is a limited resource that should be consumed sparingly over a whole soccer game. By minimising the sum of the accelerations subject to some constraints, we obtain the most economical (energy-efficient) sequence of accelerations. An added benefit of this approach is that the robot trajectory is very smooth.

The dynamics of a punctual robot follow Newton's laws. A trajectory of such a robot is completely determined by the initial state of the robot (position and velocity) and subsequent sequence of accelerations. The variables P, V and A will denote respectively the position vector, velocity vector $V = \dot{P}$ and acceleration vector $A = \dot{V}$. The trajectory is discretized into n time steps of duration Δ. The derivation of P^i, the position vector at time i, and V^i the velocity vector at time i is straightforward. As $V^i = V^0 + \Delta \sum_{j=1}^{i} A^j$ and $P^i = P^0 + \Delta \sum_{j=1}^{i} V^j$, it follows that

$P^i = P^0 + \Delta i V^0 + \Delta^2 \sum_{j=1}^{i} (i-(j-1))A^j$. Treating the x and y coordinates separately presents several computational benefits including a dimension reduction. A 2D path is a linear combination of two 1D paths (Newton Laws are linear). A *mission* is the task of bringing in an energy efficient way the state of the robot from an initial state (P^0, V^0) to a desired final state (P^f, V^f) in a given number n of time steps. Two problems can be distinguished. The first problem is to find the minimum n_0 such that the mission can be completed in n_0 time steps given the physical limitations of the robots (maximum possible speed and acceleration). The second problem is, given $n \geq n_0$, find the sequence of accelerations that minimizes the energy consumption. The cost function to be optimized is $\min \sum_{k=1}^{n} \|A^k\|^2$. To solve a 2D mission, we solve two 1D missions. Considering the initial state S^0 represented by the couple of values (P^0, V^0), we want to find out the sequence of accelerations to reach the final state $S^n = (P^n, V^n)$ while minimizing the energy consumed. In order to be able to recombine the two 1D solutions, the two 1D solutions must have the same number of steps. Fig. 1 sketches the recombination process. After computing the two initial 1D solutions, we must ensure that they have the same number of steps $N_x = N_y$ in order to recombine be able to merge them. We recompute the shortest (with respect to the number of time steps) solution with the maximum of N_x and N_y. If there exists a feasible solution in N_0 time steps, then a feasible solution exists for every $N \geq N_0$. In the rest of the paper, we only consider 1D mission.

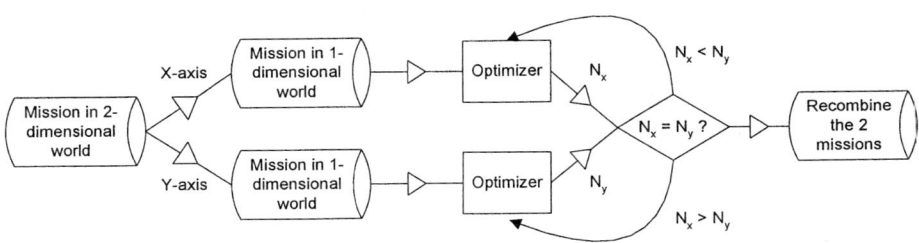

Fig. 1. 2D solution are derived from 1D solutions

There are three different constraints that must be satisfied. The final state S^f (position P^f, velocity V^f) of the robot must be reached after a given number of steps n. The norm of velocity vector must be bounded at any time to reflect the physical capabilities of the robot. This constraint is itself translated into constraints on the acceleration vectors; $\forall i \in [1;n], \|A^i\| \leq A_{\max}, \forall i \in [1;n], \|V^i\| \leq V_{\max}$, $P^n = P^f$ and $V^n = V^f$.

The first method, we investigate uses quadratic programming. We will translate the constraint that the robot must be in state S^f at time n, and the bounded velocity constraints into a system of linear inequalities. Notice, that for ease of computation, we will use the norm 1 instead of the Euclidian norm. The position constraint expressing that the robot must be in state S^f at time n yields

$$\sum_{j=1}^{n}(n-(j-1))A^j = \frac{P^f - P^0 - n\Delta V^0}{\Delta^2}.$$ This equality is of the form $MA = b$, where $M = \begin{bmatrix} n & n-1 & \ldots & 1 \end{bmatrix}$ and $b = \frac{P^f - P^0 - n\Delta V^0}{\Delta^2}$. Similarly, the final velocity constraint yields that $V^n = V^0 + \Delta \sum_{j=1}^{n} A^j = V^f$. That is,

$$\sum_{j=1}^{n} A^j = \frac{V^f - V^0}{\Delta}.$$ Again, a constraint of the form $MA = b$. The bounded velocity constraints yields another system of inequalities of the form $MA \leq b$. To estimate the minimum number of steps n_0 needed to perform the mission, a binary search is used. Starting with a small value for n, we first search an upper bound that give a feasible solution. Then, we perform a standard binary search.

In the second method we investigated, we reduce the search for an optimal sequence of accelerations to a shortest path problem in a graph. The shortest path can be computed using Dijsktra algorithm. Let discretize the state space. The vertices of the graph are the possible states of robots. Some states are not be reachable from the current state. The current velocity determines the range of states we can reach the next time step. We set the length of the arcs (when they exist) between states with the square acceleration values. The minimal number of steps required for a mission is the number of arcs of the shortest path.

4 Experiments

In the modelling, we assumed that the robot was a punctual point. However our real robot has two wheels. We have to relate the acceleration of the punctual robot and the wheel speed commands of the real robot. The optimizer provides the next acceleration vector that the centre of mass of the robot should have to follow the optimal trajectory. The wheel speeds $\dot{L}$ and $\dot{R}$ (left and right) must satisfy $\dot{L} = \|V_{i+1}\| - d \times \dot{\theta}$ and $\dot{R} = \|V_{i+1}\| + d \times \dot{\theta}$, where d is the distance between the centre of the robot and a wheel, and $\dot{\theta}$ is the angular speed. We have $|\dot{\theta}| = \cos^{-1}\left(\frac{V_{i+1} \cdot V_i}{\|V_{i+1}\| \cdot \|V_i\|}\right)$. The sign of $\dot{\theta}$ is determined with cross product between V_{i+1} and V_i. We used Matlab optimisation toolbox to implement the quadratic programming method. In the example below, the initial position is at (0; 0) with a velocity of (0; 0.4). The final state is at position (0.4; 0) with the same velocity (0; 0.4). Both methods return the same optimal number of steps although the optimal paths are slightly different due to the discretization of the graphical method.

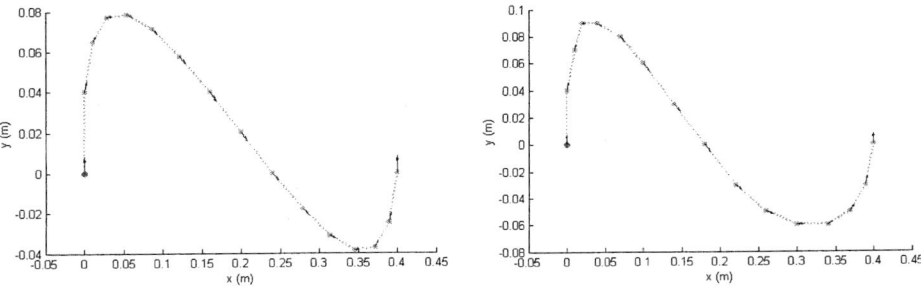

Fig. 2. $\Delta = 0.1s$, $V_{max} = 1 m.s^{-1}$, $A_{max} = 40 m.s^{-2}$. Left; quadratic programming solution. Right; dynamic programming (graph) solution

Experiments were also done on a Mirosot soccer field (dimensions set by FIRA [1]). Our experimental method requires tracking the position of the robot (with an overhead camera) at each step for a given mission. At each time step, the control system determines the closest mission amongst the one computed off-line by the optimizer and retrieves the next acceleration vector and applies it to the robot. To sort and access data, we use a fast tree indexing system that was introduced in [8]. The position and velocity estimates of the robot returned by the vision system used were noisy. But, as the mission is updated at each frame, the controller can handle inaccurate estimates. A more robust approach would be to used a Kalman filter to track the robot.

5 Conclusion and Future Work

The quadratic programming formulation for robot control was first introduced in [7] for simulated robots. At that time, we had not realized that the 2D missions could be reduced to 1D missions. The other innovation of the present paper is the resolution of the optimization problem with dynamic programming (Dijsktra algorithm). This is also the first time, that we have applied the control system to a real robot (and demonstrated that it works as well as in simulation). Our approach can be easily extended to 3D problems (for aircrafts or submarines).

An extended version of this paper is available at http://www.fit.qut.edu.au/~maire

For the future, we plan to implement the object interception behaviours that we described in [7] on a real robot.

References

[1] FIRA, Federation of International Robot-soccer Association, http://www.fira.net/ Mirosot robot-soccer competition, http://www.fira.net/soccer/mirosot/overview.html
[2] Hélder Santos, José Mendes, *Path Planning Optimization Using the Differential Evolution Algorithm*, Universidade de Tras-os-Montes e Alto Douro, Departamento de Engenharias, http://robotica2003.ist.utl.pt/main/Docs/Papers/ROB03-S1-4.pdf, 2003

[3] Florent Lamiraux, David Bonnafous, Carl Van Geem, *Path Optimization for Nonholomic Systems: Application to Reactive Obstacle Avoidance and Path Planning*, CNRS, France, 2002.
[4] P. Newman, J. Leonard, *Pure Range-Only Sub-Sea SLAM*, Massachusetts Institute of Technology, USA, 2002.
[5] Robert Sim, Gregory Dudek, Nicholas Roy, *Online Control Policy Optimization for Minimizing Map Uncertainty during Exploration*, 2003.
[6] Olivier Lefebvre, Florent Lamiraux, Cedric Pradalier, *Obstacles Avoidance for Car-Like Robots Integration And Experimentation on Two Robots*, CNRS-INRIA, France, 2002.
[7] Frederic Maire, Doug Taylor, *A Quadratic Programming Formulation of a Moving Ball Interception and Shooting Behaviour and its Application to Neural Network Control*, CITI, Faculty of IT, QUT, Australia, 2000.
[8] Sebastian Bader, Frederic Maire, *A Fast And Adaptive Indexing System For Codebooks*, ICONIP'02, November 18-22, 2002,
[9] Gordon Wyeth and Ashley Tews, *Using Centralised Control and Potential Fields for Multi-robot Cooperation in Robotic Soccer*, University of Queensland, Australia, 1998.
[10] Mark Moll, Lydia Kavraki, *Path Planning for Minimal Energy Curves of Constant Length*, Department of Computer Science, Rice University, Houston, USA, 2003.

Inheritance of Multiple Identity Conditions in Order-Sorted Logic

Nwe Ni Tun and Satoshi Tojo

Japan Advanced Institute of Science and Technology

Abstract. Guarino and Welty have developed the notion of identity condition (IC) as a subsumption constraint of ontological analysis, that is, IC must be inherited or carried among sorts. In practical cases, a sort is often regarded to carry more than one identity condition via inheritance. Thus, we provided the idea of multiple ICs in [8]. Here, we extend our idea in order-sorted logic because this logic is one of the most promising ways to treat a sort ontology. For this purpose, we reconsider the definition of identity and rigidity in terms of order-sorted language and possible world semantics. Then, we propose an inheritance mechanism of identity conditions in order to solve subsumption inconsistency among sorts. We present a practical example of knowledge management to illustrate the advantages of our formalism.

1 Introduction

The efficiency of knowledge reuse and sharing became related much to the result of ontological analysis [13]. Guarino and Welty provided a framework of ontological analysis based on some philosophical notions such as rigidity, identity, and so on in [9, 11, 12, 10]. Our contribution of multiple ICs is motivated by the subsumption ambiguity on their analysis work. There was an incompatible[1] IC between some properties even though they are satisfied by subsumption constraints defined in [9]. Unfortunately, it was not clearly solved. Thus, we provided multiple ICs and introduced a framework of subsumption consistency checking via ICs in [8].

Order-sorted logic is rigorous to support hybrid knowledge representation systems with taxonomical knowledge and assertional knowledge [5, 7]. The reasons why we employ multiple ICs in order-sorted logic are as follows:

- A subsumption declaration between two sorts ($\phi \sqsubseteq \psi$) is quite natural for taxonomy.
- A characteristic function can be defined by a function in the logic.
- A meta-property can be defined by a predicate in the logic.

Moreover, we can construct the inheritance mechanism of ICs in this logic concerning with the greatest lower sort and the least upper sort subsumption.

---

[1] There is an IC which is not relevant to a next IC in the IC set of a property.

The rest of this paper is organized as follows: Section 2 revises the definition of IC and rigidity in terms of sorted signature in possible world semantics. Section 3 presents inheritance mechanism of ICs. In Section 4, we discuss about rigid sorts and their subsumption through possible worlds by illustrating a practical example of knowledge management. Finally, we summarize our contribution.

2 Order-Sorted Logic in Possible World Semantics

Here, we extend the signature of order-sorted logic [3, 4, 6] to present a sortal taxonomy in a more algebraic formalism. In order to embed an order-sorted language in modal logic, we need to attach w to every component of signature as an index to each possible world in a given Kripke frame. A signature of an order-sorted language is a tuple $\langle N_w, X_w, S_w, \sqsubseteq_w, I_w, P_w, V_w \rangle$ ($w \in \mathcal{W}$), each of which is a set of names, a set of name variables, a set of sortal properties or sorts including the greatest element($\top$) and the least element ($\bot$), a set of subsumption or partial order relations between two sorts in S_w, a set of predicates[2], a set of characteristic functions, and a set of characteristic value symbols in $w \in \mathcal{W}$, respectively. With this signature, we present the formal syntax and semantics for a sortal taxonomy in Table 1.

Table 1. Formal Syntax and Semantics for a Sortal Taxonomy

Syntax		Semantics		
$\sqsubseteq_w$	$(\in \sqsubseteq_w)$	$\phi \sqsubseteq_w \psi$	iff	$[\![\phi]\!]_w \subseteq [\![\psi]\!]_w$
$a : \phi$	$(\phi \in S_w, a \in \mathcal{N}_w)$	$[\![a{:}\phi]\!]_w = [\![a]\!]_w$	if	$[\![a]\!]_w \in [\![\phi]\!]_w$
$sortal(a : \phi)$	$(sortal \in \mathcal{P}_w)$	$[\![sortal(x{:}\phi)]\!]_w = 1$	iff	ϕ has an IC
$\iota(a : \phi)$	$(\iota \in I_w)$	$[\![\iota(a{:}\phi)]\!]_w \in V_w$		

In the formal language, we provide the following definitions.

Definition 1 (Characteristic Function). *A function ι is a characteristic function of sort ϕ iff:*

$$\forall x, y [x = y \leftrightarrow \iota(x{:}\phi) = \iota(y{:}\phi)].$$

This means a characteristic function of a sort should provide a unique value for each of its individuals. For example, *StudentID* for student.

Definition 2 (Identity Condition). *A characteristic function ι is an identity condition of sort ϕ iff:*

$$For\ any\ w\ and\ w',\ \forall x [[\![\iota(x{:}\phi)]\!]_w = [\![\iota(x{:}\phi)]\!]_{w'}].$$

---

[2] We consider $sortal \in P_w$ is a predicate corresponding to the identity.

IC retains its value through all accessible worlds. For example, *FingerPrint* for person.

Actually, multiple ICs contribute not only to the membership problem but also to the correct position of a property in a sortal taxonomy. For that purpose, we introduce the definition of subsumption and incompatibility in terms of IC sets as follows.

Definition 3 (IC-Subsumption). *For such two sorts ϕ and ψ that $\phi \sqsubseteq_w \psi$, ϕ IC-subsumes ψ iff $\mathcal{I}_w(\psi) \subseteq \mathcal{I}_w(\phi)$.*

It said a subsumption between two sorts are consistently existed with the inclusion of their relevant ICs.

Definition 4 (Incompatible IC). *For a sort ϕ, If two ICs ι_1 and ι_2 cannot coexist, we call them* incompatible, *denoting $\iota_1 \bowtie_\phi \iota_2$.*

By the above definitions, we solve the problem of inconsistent IC between two sorts. In addition, we detect an inadequate link of subsumption by the incompatibility.

3 Sorts and ICs Inheritance

In a sortal taxonomy, every sort ϕ is defined by a set of characteristic functions, that is generally called an IC set of ϕ, $\mathcal{I}_w(\phi) \subseteq I_w$. We can distinguish the IC set of a sort by the set of own-identity and that of carrying identities, denoting $\mathcal{I}_w^{+O}(\phi)$ and $\mathcal{I}_w^{+I}(\phi)$ respectively. The meaning of each set can be interpreted as follows.

- $\mathcal{I}_w^{+O}(\phi)$: The set of own ICs of ϕ that can be supplied to its subsorts including itself.
- $\mathcal{I}_w^{+I}(\phi)$: The set of ICs that ϕ carries.

If a sort ϕ supplies an IC, that is ϕ has $+\mathbf{O}$, $\mathcal{I}_w^{+O}(\phi) = \{\iota_1, \iota_2, ...\}$ where all ι_i's are its own ICs. If ϕ has $-\mathbf{O}$, then $\mathcal{I}_w^{+O}(\phi) = \emptyset$. $\mathcal{I}_w(\phi)$ is a set of all the possible ICs for ϕ. Similarly, if ϕ has $-\mathbf{I}$, then $\mathcal{I}_w^{+I}(\phi) = \emptyset$. In general, there are the following inclusion relations for a sort ϕ:

$$\mathcal{I}_w^{+O}(\phi) \subseteq \mathcal{I}_w^{+I}(\phi) \subseteq \mathcal{I}_w(\phi) \subseteq I_w.$$

According to the above definition, the following relations would be found. For any two sorts ϕ and ψ,

$$\phi^{+O} \sqsubseteq_w \psi \quad \text{iff} \quad \mathcal{I}_w(\phi) \supseteq (\mathcal{I}_w^{+I}(\psi) \cup \mathcal{I}_w^{+O}(\phi)), \tag{1}$$

$$\phi^{+I} \sqsubseteq_w \psi \quad \text{iff} \quad \mathcal{I}_w(\phi) \supseteq (\mathcal{I}_w^{+I}(\psi) \cup \mathcal{I}_w^{+I}(\phi)), \tag{2}$$

$$\chi \sqsupseteq (\phi \sqcup_w \psi)^3 \quad \text{iff} \quad \mathcal{I}_w(\chi) \subseteq (\mathcal{I}_w^{+I}(\phi) \cap \mathcal{I}_w^{+I}(\psi)), \tag{3}$$

$$\chi \sqsubseteq (\phi \sqcap_w \psi)^4 \quad \text{iff} \quad \mathcal{I}_w(\chi) \supseteq (\mathcal{I}_w^{+I}(\phi) \cup \mathcal{I}_w^{+I}(\psi)). \tag{4}$$

We illustrate the advantages of IC inheritance represented in order-sorted signature as follows:

Example 1. *Let us consider the signature of a sortal taxonomy for a world $w \in \mathcal{W}$ such that*

$\mathcal{S}_w = \{person, student, researcher, research\_student\}$,
$\sqsubseteq_w = \{student \sqsubseteq_w person, researcher \sqsubseteq_w person, research\_student \sqsubseteq_w student, research\_student \sqsubseteq_w researcher\}$,
$\mathcal{I}_w = \{fingerprint, studentID, memberID\}$,
$\mathcal{I}_w(person) = \{fingerprint\}, \mathcal{I}_w(student) = \{fingerprint, studentID\}$,
$\mathcal{I}_w(researcher) = \{fingerprint, memberID\}$,
$\mathcal{I}_w(research\_student) = \{fingerprint, studentID, memberID\}$.

By Definition 3, we can check the consistency of given subsumption relationships concerned on their IC sets.

$student \sqsubseteq_w person$ iff $\mathcal{I}_w(person) \subseteq \mathcal{I}_w(student)$.
$researcher \sqsubseteq_w person$ iff $\mathcal{I}_w(person) \subseteq \mathcal{I}_w(researcher)$.
$research\_student \sqsubseteq_w researcher$ iff $\mathcal{I}_w(researcher) \subseteq \mathcal{I}_w(research\_student)$.
$research\_student \sqsubseteq_w student$ iff $\mathcal{I}_w(student) \subseteq \mathcal{I}_w(research\_student)$.

In the given taxonomy, *person* is *the least upper sort* of *student* and *researcher*, $student \sqcup_w researcher$, and *research student* is *the greatest lower sort* of *student* and *researcher*, $student \sqcap_w researcher$. By (1) – (4),

$\mathcal{I}_w(person) \subseteq_w (\mathcal{I}_w(student) \cap \mathcal{I}_w(researcher))$,
$\mathcal{I}_w(person) \subseteq_w (\mathcal{I}_w(student) \cup \mathcal{I}_w(researcher))$,
$student^{+\mathbf{I}} \sqsubseteq_w person$ iff $(\mathcal{I}_w^{+\mathbf{I}}(person) \cup \mathcal{I}_w^{+\mathbf{I}}(student)) \subseteq \mathcal{I}_w(student)$

According to the IC inclusion relations,

$\mathcal{I}_w^{+\mathbf{O}}(student) = \{ \}, \mathcal{I}_w^{+\mathbf{I}}(student) = \{fingerprint\}$,
$\mathcal{I}_w^{+\mathbf{O}}(student) \subseteq \mathcal{I}_w^{+\mathbf{I}}(student) \subseteq \mathcal{I}_w(student) \subseteq \mathcal{I}_w$.

It is also similar for *person, researcher* and *research_student*.

4 Rigid Sorts and Knowledge Management

In Kripke frame for predicate logic [2], it is required that for any predicate ϕ:

$$[\![\phi]\!]_w \subseteq [\![\phi]\!]_{w'} \text{ if } wRw'. \qquad (5)$$

as well as ϕ is rigid. However, we loosen this restriction for sorts, and admit that some sorts may be non-rigid or anti-rigid.

---

[3] $\phi \sqcup_w \psi$ is the least upper sort that subsumes both ϕ and ψ.
[4] $\phi \sqcap_w \psi$ is the greatest lower sort that is subsumed both by ϕ and by ψ.

Inheritance of Multiple Identity Conditions in Order-Sorted Logic   1191

Definition 5 (Rigidity). *A sort ϕ is:*

rigid iff $\models \Box\forall x[sortal(x:\phi) \rightarrow \Box sortal(x:\phi)]$ *(+R)*
non-rigid iff it is not rigid *(¬R)*
anti-rigid iff $\models \Box\forall x[sortal(x:\phi) \rightarrow \Diamond\neg sortal(x:\phi)]$ *(~R)*

A sort ϕ is rigid iff necessarily $x : \phi$ necessarily exists if $x : \phi$ exists. For example, every person should be necessarily a person in every accessible world, that is, *person* is rigid.

Definition 6 (Backbone Taxonomy). *Given a Kripke frame, the set of subsumption relations between rigid sorts, which appear in every world, is called* backbone taxonomy.

We will show a practical example with regard to this idea in Fig. 1.

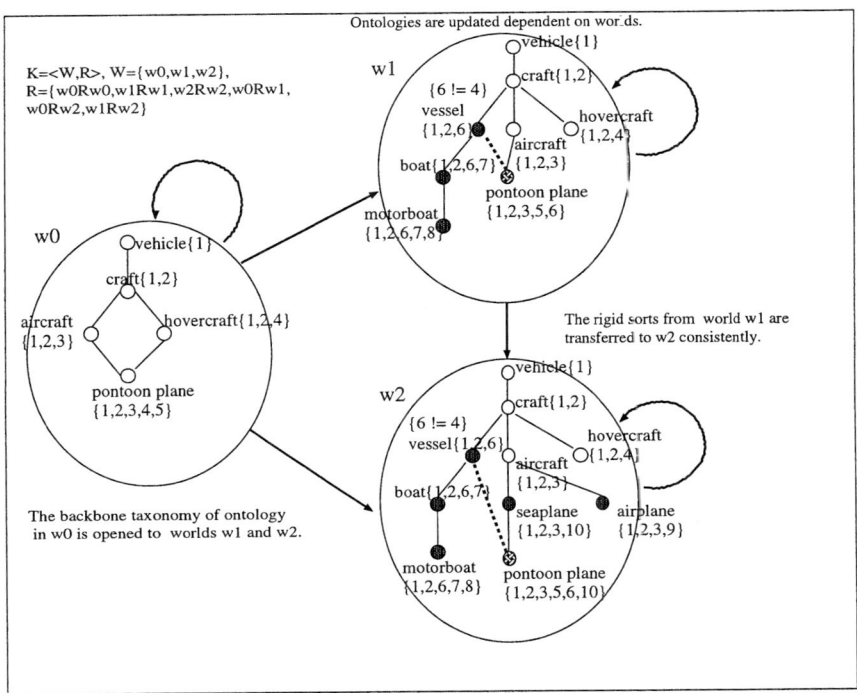

Fig. 1. Consistent Knowledge Management in Multiple Worlds

Suppose that there are multiple local knowledge bases; among them one knowledge base may consult the others but may not in the reverse directions. We can illustrate such a situation with a Kripke frame $\langle \mathcal{W}, \mathcal{R} \rangle$ where $\mathcal{W} = \{w_0, w_1, w_2\}$, $\mathcal{R} = \{w_0 R w_0, w_1 R w_1, w_2 R w_2, w_0 R w_1, w_0 R w_2, w_1 R w_2\}$. In every world, the consistency checking is performed by Definition 3 and 4 whenever a new sort or subsumption is appended to each domain ontology. The rigid sorts from world w_1 are backbone properties and they are able to be transmitted to world w_2, by $w_1 R w_2$. The ICs set and subsumption of each sort has been changed dependent on worlds. In the process of knowledge management, any subsumption with incompatible IC must be deleted. As an example, the subsumption by *hovercraft* is possible to be deleted in case of pontoon_plane. Additionally, the updating process must confirm that the parents of a sort should not be subsumed to each other. For example, *pontoon_plane* is subsumed by *aircraft* in w_1 and it is also subsumed by *seaplane* in w_2. However, *seaplane* is subsumed by aircraft in w_2. Finally, *pontoon_plane* should be subsumed by only *seaplane*. By Definition 3 and 4, the structure of taxonomy in world w_2 is updated in order to maintain consistency of subsumption among all sorts as shown in Fig. 1.

5 Conclusion

In this study, we formalized the idea of multiple ICs in order-sorted logic. The inheritance mechanism of ICs has been provided in the logic with regard to subsumption consistency. Thus, the formalization of sortal taxonomy becomes structured with their IC sets as well as conventional set-theoretical inclusion. Moreover, the logic would allow us to offer dynamic sorts [7] in a sort ontology, being coupled with the axiomatic knowledge base. That is beneficial for us to alter the positions of sorts in taxonomy dynamically. In future work, we will present a sound foundation of IC set algebra for ontological analysis.

Acknowledgements

The authors would like to thank the support by Fostering Talent in Emergent Research Fields, Special Coordination Funds for Promoting Science and Technology, Ministry of Education, Culture, Sports, Science and Technology, Japan.

References

1. A. Chagrov and M. Zakharyaschev. *Modal Logic*. Oxford Science Publications, 1997.
2. F. Landman. *Structures for Semantics*. Kluwer Academic Publishers, 1991.
3. K. Kaneiwa and S. Tojo. Event, property, and hierarchy in order-sorted logic. In Proceedings of *International Conference on Logic Programming*, 1999.
4. K. Kaneiwa and S. Tojo. An order-sorted resolution with implicit negative sorts. In Proceedings of *International Conference on Logic Programming*, 2001.
5. K. Kaneiwa and R. Mizoguchi. Ontological Knowledge Base Reasoning with Sort-Hierarchy and Rigidity. In Proceedings of *KR*, 2004.
6. M. Schmidt-Schauss. *Computational Aspects of Order-Sorted Logic with Term Declarations*. Springer Verlag, 1989.
7. C. Beierle, U. Hedtstuck, U. Pletat, P.H. Schmitt and J. Siekmann. *An Order-Sorted Logic for Knowledge Representation Systems*. Artificial Intelligence vol.55, pages 149-191, Elsevier 1992.

8. N. N. Tun and S. Tojo . Consistency Maintenance in Ontological Knowledge Updating. In Proceedings of *The 2004 IEEE International Conference on Information Reuse and Integration (IEEE IRI-2004)*, 2004.
9. C. Welty and N. Guarino. Supporting ontological analysis of taxonomic relationships. *Data & Knowledge Engineering*, vol.39, pages 51-74, Elsevier 2001.
10. C. Welty and N. Guarino. Identity and Subsumption. *LADSEB-CNR Internal Report.* 2001.
11. A. N. Kaplan. Towards a Consistent Logical Framework for Ontological Analysis. *In Proceedings of International Conference on Formal Ontology in Information Systems, 244-255. ACM Press.* 2001.
12. M. Carrara and P. Giaretta. Identity Criteria and Sortal Concepts. *In Proceedings of the International Conference on Formal Ontology in Information Systems, 234-243. ACM Press.* 2001.
13. A. Abecker and A.V. Elst. Ontologies for Knowledge Management. *International Handbooks on Information Systems: Handbook on Ontologies, 435-454. Springer.* 2003.

A Comparative Analysis of Fuzzy System Modelling Approaches: A Case in Mining Medical Diagnostic Rules

Kemal Kılıç[1], Özge Uncu[2], and I.B. Türkşen[3]

[1] FENS, Sabancı University, 34956, Istanbul, Turkey
kkilic@sabanciuniv.edu
[2] Dept. of IE, Middle East Technical University, Ankara, Turkey
uncu@ie.metu.edu.tr
[3] MIE, University of Toronto, M5S 3G8, Toronto, ON, Canada
turksen@mie.utoronto.ca

Abstract. Fuzzy system modeling approximates highly nonlinear systems by means of fuzzy if-then rules. In the literature, different approaches are proposed for mining fuzzy if-then rules from historical data. These approaches usually utilize fuzzy clustering in *structure identification* phase. In this research, we are going to analyze three possible approaches from the literature and try to compare their performances in a medical diagnosis classification problem, namely Aachen Aphasia Test. Given the fact that the comparison is conducted on a single data set; the conclusions are by no means inclusive. However, we believe that the results might provide some valuable insights.

1 Introduction

In the decision making process, one often needs to introduce soft computing techniques in order to understand the structure and the behavior of a system that is highly nonlinear. Amongst the soft computing techniques, fuzzy system modeling (FSM) provides valuable knowledge to the decision maker in terms of linguistic (and therefore easily comprehensible) fuzzy if-then rules that relate the inputs to the corresponding outputs. In earlier approaches, the fuzzy if-then rules were determined a priori from other sources such as experts' knowledge. However this methodology is highly subjective. Therefore, recent research is on modeling approaches for objective identification of the structure in the data in terms of fuzzy if-then rules [4,5,6,7,9].

Many different approaches have been proposed to date for the structure identification phase of FSM. Generally speaking, these algorithms can be classified into three broad approaches in terms of the *structure of the consequents* in the fuzzy if-then rules they generate. In this paper we will focus on the ones that have constants or fuzzy sets as the consequents. Those algorithms usually utilize fuzzy clustering in order to determine the fuzzy if then rules. The aim of this research is to compare three algorithms with three different perspectives of utilizing the fuzzy clustering.

In the following section we will first introduce the notation that will be used in this paper and later provide more details on different fuzzy if-then rule structures. In the third section we will summarize the FSM algorithms that will be used in the analysis. Section 4 will be the part where we will conduct an experimental analysis based on Aachen Aphasia Test data. Later we will present some concluding remarks.

2 Fuzzy If-Then Rules Structures

The following mathematical notation is used in the paper.

Let $X_1, X_2, ..., X_{NV}$ be NV (*number of variables*) fuzzy linguistic variables in the universe of discourse $U_1, U_2, ..., U_{NV}$ and Y be a fuzzy linguistic variable in the universe of discourse V. We will use j as the index for input variables, i.e., $j=1,..., NV$.

Let R_i be a fuzzy relation (i.e., *fuzzy rules*) in $U_1 \times U_2 \times ... \times U_{NV} \times V$. We will denote the number of rules with c. We will use i as the index for the rules, i.e., $i=1,...,c$.

Each fuzzy linguistic variable can be partitioned into fuzzy sets called fuzzy linguistic labels. We will denote these fuzzy sets with A_{ij}, the fuzzy linguistic label of the jth fuzzy input variable associated with i^{th} fuzzy rule.

Let $x_k=[x_{k,1},..., x_{k,NV}]$ denote the input vector of the kth data, where $k=1,...,ND$ and y_k is the output of the kth data.

In general the fuzzy if-then rule bases has the following structure:

$$R: \underset{i=1}{\overset{c}{ALSO}}(IF \ antecedent_i \ THEN \ consequent_i) \quad (1)$$

The antecedent part of the rules is as follows;

$$Antecedent_i = AND_{j=1}^{NV} \ x_j \in X_j \ isr \ (is \ related \ to) \ A_{ij} \quad (2)$$

Broadly speaking, there are three different rule structures based on the consequents of the rules. In Takagi-Sugeno-Kang (TSK) [8], the consequent part of fuzzy rules are represented by using a linear function of input variables. Thus, the rule base is:

$$\underset{i=1}{\overset{c}{ALSO}}(IF \ antecedent_i \ THEN \ y_i = a_i x^T + b_i) \quad (3)$$

where $x=[x_1,...,x_{NV}]$ is the input data vector, $a_i=[a_{i,1},..., a_{i,NV}]$ is the regression line coefficient vector associated with the ith rule, a_{ji} is the regression line coefficient in i^{th} rule associated with j^{th} input variable and b_i is the scalar offset in the ith rule.

On the other hand, in Mamdani type approaches the consequents are fuzzy sets [7]. Sugeno-Yasukawa (S-Y) utilized these rules and proposed a qualitative modelling algorithm [7]. A typical fuzzy rule base in S-Y like algorithms is as follows;

$$\underset{i=1}{\overset{c}{ALSO}}(IF \ antecedent_i \ THEN \ y_i \ isr \ B_i) \quad (4)$$

The third type of fuzzy rule structure is known as the simplified fuzzy rule, or Mizumoto type rules. In this rule base structure the consequent is a scalar:

$$\underset{i=1}{\overset{c}{ALSO}}(IF \ antecedent_i \ THEN \ y_i = b_i) \quad (5)$$

Note that Mizumoto type rules are actually a special version of both Mamdani type rules and TSK type rules. In a classification problem, where the consequent fuzzy sets are actually scalar, Mizumoto and Mamdani rules would have the same structure. For a TSK consequent where the regression line coefficient vector is a null vector, TSK and Mizumoto rules would be equivalent. In fuzzy control theory more interest is given to TSK type rules. However, these rules are not descriptive and the determination of the optimal regression line coefficients is costly. Therefore in data mining applications more emphasize is given to Mamdani type rules.

The analysis in this paper is based on a medical diagnosis classification problem. Hence we focus on Mamdani models (therefore Mizumoto) rather than TSK models.

3 Fuzzy System Modelling Algorithms

In FSM literature, fuzzy clustering is extensively utilized at the structure identification phase. There are three possible alternatives for incorporating the fuzzy clustering. First one, as proposed originally by Sugeno-Yasukawa [7], is based on clustering first the output space. The relation of the input variables with the output is obtained after the projection of the output clusters onto input space. A second approach is clustering the NV dimensional input space, projecting them onto each input variable and relating the output variables to each input clusters based on the degree of possibility [4]. A third possible approach is clustering the $NV+1$ dimensional space, i.e. input and output space together, and projecting the obtained clusters onto each variable in order to obtain the fuzzy if-then rules [9]. Let's provide some more details of the structure identification phase of these algorithms.

3.1 Sugeno-Yasukawa Approach and the Modified Algorithm

There are four basic steps of the Sugeno-Yasukawa (S-Y) algorithm [7]. First step is clustering the output variable. This is achieved by the well-known Fuzzy C-Means (FCM) algorithm proposed by Bezdek [3]. Next step is determining the significant input variables via a search algorithm. Third step is constructing the antecedent part of the rules. This is achieved by projecting the output membership degrees onto significant input variables. The fourth step is the fuzzy inference.

The major drawback with this approach is in the third step. While projecting the output fuzzy clusters onto input space, the natural ties among the input variables is broken and each input variable is partitioned separately. The modified algorithm (M-A) [6] addresses this problem and solves it by partitioning the input space into n-dimensional clusters. In the M-A, the output clusters are projected onto NV-dimensional input space. Hence, the $antecedent_i$ structure is as follows;

$$antecedent_i = x_k \in X_k \text{ isr } (is\ related\ to)\ A_i \qquad (6)$$

where A_i is an NV-dimensional fuzzy set. This rule structure, keeps the natural ties among the input variables. Furthermore, M-A does not assume any pre-specified shape of membership functions unlike S-Y. Note that, fitting a curve or a line to the projected data points is usually a source of misrepresentation. The unimodal and convex fuzzy set assumption of S-Y does not hold in many real life cases. Readers may find more details of the S-Y algorithm in [7] and M-A in [6].

3.2 Castellano et al. Approach

Castellano et al. [4] methodology has three major stages. The first stage is clustering the *NV*-dimensional input space where the number of multidimensional clusters is referred to as *number of prototypes (NP)*. Later the multidimensional prototypes are projected on each dimension, where they are clustered into a number of one-dimensional clusters per variable. Number of fuzzy sets (*NS*) per dimension may be chosen a value different than *NP*. Hence at the end of the first stage, there is *NP* multidimensional clusters, and *NS* single dimensional clusters per input variable.

The second stage constructs the *antecedent*s of the fuzzy rules, which are formed as a Cartesian product of one-dimensional fuzzy sets and expressed as conjunction of linguistic labels. Only those relations that represent the *prototypes* are retained, while all others are discarded, therefore *NP* is an upper bound for the number of rules.

The final step of the algorithm is obtaining the *consequent* part of the fuzzy rules. A fuzzy relation is obtained by assigning a possibility measure based on weighted occurrences of each output class. Among the set of data vectors that satisfies the *antecedent* parts of each fuzzy relation that is obtained after the second stage, the weighted occurrences of each class is obtained, and these occurrences becomes the *consequent* part of the fuzzy rules. The rule structure of this approach is as follows;

$$\underset{i=1}{\overset{c}{ALSO}}(IF \ antecedent_i \ THEN \ OR_{m=1}^{M} \ y_i = b_m \ with \ v_{i,m}) \tag{7}$$

where b_m's are possible output classes, and v_{im}'s are the possibility measures representing the weighted occurrences of the mth output class associated with the ith fuzzy rule. Further details of the algorithm are provided in [4].

3.3 Uncu and Turksen Approach

Uncu and Turksen [9] propose to cluster the *NV+1* dimensional data, i.e., augmented input variables and the output variable, by executing the FCM algorithm. Later the obtained clusters centers are projected onto *NV*-dimensional input space and the corresponding memberships are projected onto output space in order to be able to calculate the center of gravity of the induced output fuzzy sets. Thus, if we assume $v_i = (v_{i,1}, v_{i,2},..., v_{i,NV}, v_{i,NV+1})$ as the ith cluster center identified by FCM, the cluster center of the antecedent in i^{th} rule can be written as $v_i^{inp} = (v_{i,1}, v_{i,2},..., v_{i,NV})$, where v_i^{inp} is the ith input cluster (i.e., the cluster center associated with i^{th} rule). The cluster center of the consequent of the ith rule is calculated by projecting the membership values of ith *NV+1* dimensional cluster on the output space and by taking the center of gravity of the induced output fuzzy set. Hence Mizumoto type rules with scalar outputs are obtained. Note that, the number of fuzzy rules is equal to the number of clusters. Further details of the algorithm are available in [9].

4 Experimental Analysis

The performances of the three algorithms are compared with the Aachen Aphasia Test (AAT) (http://fuzzy.iau.dtu.dk/aphasia.nsf/PatLight). Aphasia is the loss or impairment of the ability to use or comprehend words – often a result of stroke or head injury. Data of 256 aphasic patients, treated in the Department of Neurology at the RWTH Aachen, were collected in a database since 1986. The database consists of the clinical diagnosis as well as the diagnosis of the aphasia type and AAT profiles. The original AAT has 30 attributes, including AAT scores, nominal values and images of the lesion profiles. The full detail of the data set is in [1].

Castellano et al. conducted some analysis in [4] for the AAT dataset. Therefore, we decided to conduct the same experimental design suggested by Castellano et al. in order to make a fair comparison of the three approaches. In [4], the data is preprocessed and only 146 cases corresponding to the four most common aphasia diagnoses were selected. These diagnoses are: Broca (motor or expressive aphasia), Wernicke (sensory or receptive aphasia), Anomic (difficulties in retrieval of words) and Global (total aphasia). The authors selected AAT scores suggested in [2] for the analysis; hence we also used the same attributes in the analysis. These attributes are the AAT scores on Articulation and prosody (melody of speech), Syntactic structure (structure of sentences), Repetition, Written Language (reading loud). To sum up, final database consisted of 146 cases, 4 attributes and the diagnoses. 20-fold stratified cross validation strategy is used in the experiments as suggested by the authors.

Castellano et al. [4] provides the results based on different even number of prototypes varying from 2 to 24. As *NP (number of protypes)* - and consequently the number of rules- increases classification error decreases. Similar analysis is conducted with varying "number of fuzzy sets per input" from 2 to 7. As number of fuzzy sets per input increases first the classification error decreases, however for higher number of fuzzy sets per input the classification error increases. The best pair of *NP* and number of fuzzy sets per input is 18 and 4, respectively, with classification error of 12%. Note that the average percentage of success is 78.4% for this algorithm.

M-A classified correctly 131 cases (misclassified only 15 cases) in the database of 146 data vectors yielding approximately 89.8% of success rate (or 10.2 % of classification error). This result is better than even the best result obtained by Castellano *at al* algorithm and Uncu-Turksen algorithm. Note that in the 20-fold cross validation strategy we conducted 20 different experiments. The number of fuzzy rules in M-A in these experiments were 2,3 and 4 in different experiments. Hence this algorithm yields the best classification error with very small fuzzy rule bases.

The Uncu-Turksen algorithm that is based on *NV+1* dimensional clustering misclassified 24 cases out of 146 data vectors. This result corresponds to 83.6 % success rate (or 16.4 % classification error). Again the number of fuzzy rules varies for each one of the 20 different experiments. Broadly speaking, 15 to 20 rules were obtained in this algorithm in different experiments.

To sum up, M-A algorithm seems to be the best performing algorithm in terms of classification error. M-A is the one that yields least number of rules among the three. However neither of the algorithms requires extensive number of rules, which could be a problem.

5 Conclusion

In this paper we analyzed three FSM algorithms that covers all possible ways of utilizing *fuzzy clustering*. These are; clustering the output data first (M-A), clustering the input data first (Castellano *et al.*), and clustering the augmented input and output data together (Uncu-Turksen).

M-A outperforms the other two in terms of classification performance in AAT data. The advantage of this approach is the fact that it keeps the natural ties among the variables. On the other hand, it is not possible to graphically represent NV-dimensional antecedents of the fuzzy rules. Therefore, lacks the descriptive rule base advantage of the FSM algorithms. This is also a problem with the Uncu-Turksen approach. One may overcome this problem by utilizing the S-Y approach (projecting onto individual dimensions) in order to represent a rule base, while carrying out the calculations in NV-dimensional space. The Castellano et al. approach assumes unimodal convex fuzzy sets, which limits the modelling capability of the algorithm in many real life cases. Finally, our experience with Uncu-Turksen suggests that, the multidimensional clusters obtained may lead to rules where the *consequents* are coinciding with each other, which result in unrealistic rule bases.

The experiments are based on a single data set; hence these results are limited and shouldn't be generalized. Yet they provide valuable insights. Future work will include utilizing other benchmark data, which might lead to more general conclusions.

References

1. Axer, H., Jantzen, J., Berks, G., Südfeld, D., v.Keyserlingk, D.G.: The Aphasia Database on the Web: Description Problems of Classification in Medicine, Proc. of ESIT 2000, Aachen, Germany, (2000) 104-111
2. Axer, H., Jantzen, J., Berks, G., Südfeld, D., v.Keyserlingk, D.G.: Aphasia Classification Using Neural Networks, Proc. of ESIT 2000, Aachen, Germany, (2000) 111-115
3. Bezdek, J.C.: Pattern Recognition with Fuzzy Objective Function Algorithms, Plenum Press, (1981)
4. Castellano, G., Fanelli, A.M., Mencar, C.: A Fuzzy Clustering Approach for Mining Diagnostic Rules, Proc. Of IEEE Conference on Systems, Man and Cybernetics, Washington, USA, (2003)
5. Delgado, M., Gomez-Skermata, A.F., Martin., F.: Rapid Prototyping of Fuzzy Models. In: Hellendoorn, H., Driankov, D. (eds.): Fuzzy Model Identification: Selected Approaches, Springer, Berlin Germany (1997) 121-161
6. Kilic, K., Sproule, B.A., Turksen, I.B., Naranjo, C.A.: Pharmacokinetic Application of Fuzzy Structure Identification and Reasoning. Information Sciences, Vol. 162, (2004) 121-137
7. Sugeno, M., Yasukawa, T.A.: A Fuzzy Logic Based Approach to Qualitative Modelling, IEEE Transactions on Fuzzy Systems, Vol. 1, (1993) 7-31.
8. Takagi, T., Sugeno, M.: Fuzzy Identification of Systems and Its Application to Modelling and Control, IEEE Transactions on Systems, Man and Cybernetics, Vol. 15, (1985) 116-132.
9. Uncu, O., Turksen, I.B., Kilic, K.: LOCALM-FSM: A New Fuzzy System Modelling Approach Using a Two-Step Fuzzy Inference Mechanism Based on Local Fuzziness Level, International Fuzzy Systems Association World Congress, IFSA, Istanbul, Turkey, (2003) 191-194

A Parallel Learning Approach for Neural Network Ensemble

Zheng-Qun Wang[1,2], Shi-Fu Chen[1], Zhao-Qian Chen[1], and Jun-Yuan Xie[1]

[1] State Key Laboratory for Novel Software Technology, Nanjing University, Nanjing, P.R. China
yzwzq@yzcn.net, {chensf, chenzq, xiejy}@netra.nju.edu.cn
[2] School of Information Engineering, Yangzhou University, Yangzhou, P.R. China

Abstract. A component neural networks parallel training algorithm PLA is proposed, which encourages component neural network to learn from expected goal and the others, so all component neural networks are trained simultaneously and interactively. In the stage of combining component neural networks, we provide a parallel weight optimal approach GASEN-e by expanding GASEN proposed by Zhou et al, which assign weight for every component neural network and bias for their ensemble. Experiment results show that a neural networks ensemble system is efficient constructed by PLA and GASEN-e.

1 Introduction

Neural network ensemble is a paradigm where a collection of a finite number of neural networks is trained for the same task[1]. In general, a neural network ensemble includes the following two steps mainly, one is how to generate the component neural networks and the other is how to combine the multiple component neural networks' predictions.

Boosting [2] and Bagging [3] are the most important techniques to generate the ensemble's individual component neural networks. When the technique of Bagging generates the ensemble's individual networks, there is no information communication among the component networks. The technique of Boosting has the information communication among the component networks through the generation of training set. The latter trained component networks absorb the previous trained component networks' information only, without transferring any information to the previous ones. Min et al. [4] presented the observation learning algorithm for neural network ensemble(OLA). The information is communicated among different component networks during their training. This method improves the individual networks' precision by increasing the training sampling points, but decreases the networks' diversity.

While the neural network is applied in the regression evaluation, the ensemble's output is usually generated according to all networks' outputs through the *simple averaging* or *weighted averaging* [5]. The key for the *weighted averaging* is to determine the component networks' weights. Zhou et al. [5] use the genetic algorithm to determine the weights of component neural network (GASEN) and achieve the wonderful neural networks ensemble result.

This paper propose a parallel training method for the ensemble's component network, meeting the requirement not only of its precision but also of its diversity with other component networks. On the component neural networks' ensemble this paper improves the parallel weights determination method (GASEN) proposed by Zhou et al. [5], and presents a new weights determination method (GASEN-e) which decreases the generalization error of network ensemble effectively.

This paper is organized as follows. Section 2 present the parallel learning algorithm (PLA) of ensemble's component networks. Section 3 presents an improved component network's weights determination method - Gasen-e. Section 4 gives the experimental results comparing several existing component network generation methods and neural network ensemble methods with the one presented in this paper. Section 5 summarizes this paper's work.

2 Parallel Learning Approach for Component Neural Network

Suppose the goal of neural network ensemble's learning is to approximate the function of $f: R^m \to R^n$. The neural network ensemble is composed of N neural networks $f_1, f_2, \cdots, f_N$, and each network is assigned the weight of $\omega_i (i=1,2,\cdots,N)$, where $\omega_i \geq 0$, $\sum_{i=1}^{N} \omega_i = 1$. The neural network ensemble's output is generated by weighted averaging all component neural network outputs.

Assume all the networks' weights are equal. After the component networks' training has been finished, the method introduced in Section 3 will be used to determine the ensemble's component networks' weights.

Suppose the training sample set of $f_i (i=1,2,\cdots,N)$ is:

$$D_i = \{(X(1), d(1)), (X(2), d(2)), \cdots, (X(L_i), d(L_i))\}$$

where $X \in R^m$, d is the target output as a scalar quantity, L_i is the training samples' number.

The ensemble's output of networks except f_i with the n th sample is written by:

$$\overline{f_{-i}}(n) = \frac{1}{N-1} \sum_{j \neq i} f_j(n). \tag{1}$$

The error function of f_i with the n th training sample is defined as Ea_i:

$$Ea_i = \frac{1}{2}\alpha(f_i(n) - d(n))^2 - \frac{1}{2}\beta(f_i(n) - \overline{f_{-i}}(n))^2 \tag{2}$$

According to (2) the derivative of Ea_i with the n th training sample output $f_i(n)$ of f_i is:

$$\frac{\partial Ea_i}{\partial f_i(n)} = \alpha(f_i(n) - d(n)) - \beta(f_i(n) - \overline{f_{-i}}(n)) \tag{3}$$

When $\alpha=2$ and $\beta=1$, the training of f_i considers both the target output and the other networks ensemble's output. In the experiments we suppose $\alpha=2$, $\beta=1$.

After the error function has been determined, the algorithm of BP is used to train all component networks simultaneously. The error function of EA_i and the algorithm of BP form the neural networks ensemble's component network parallel learning algorithm (PLA).

3 Component Network Weight Determination Method GASEN-e

Suppose $f_i' = f_i + \delta_i$ $(i = 1, 2, \cdots, N)$, δ_i is a constant to be decided. f_i' is generated by adding the bias constant δ_i to f_i and f_i' is also a neural network.

Now assume the neural network ensemble is composed of N neural networks of $f_1', f_2', \cdots, f_N'$. The neural networks ensemble's output with the input of x is

$$\hat{f}(x) = \sum_{i=1}^{N} \omega_i f_i'(x) \tag{4}$$

Suppose $\delta = \sum_{i=1}^{N} \omega_i \delta_i$ and $\overline{f}(x) = \sum_{i=1}^{N} \omega_i f_i(x)$, then it can be got from formula (4)

$$\hat{f}(x) = \sum_{i=1}^{N} \omega_i f_i(x) + \delta = \overline{f}(x) + \delta \tag{5}$$

The above formula show that the ensemble output of neural network f_i' $(i = 1, 2, \cdots, N)$ is the sum of ensemble output of f_i and δ.

Suppose the generalization of neural networks ensemble f_i' $(i = 1, 2, \cdots, N)$ is

$$\hat{E} = \int dx p(x)(\hat{f}(x) - d(x))^2 \tag{6}$$

Then it is got from Formula (5) and (6)

$$\hat{E} = \int dx p(x)(\overline{f}(x) + \delta - d(x))^2 \tag{7}$$

Making the bias derivative of $\hat{E}$ on δ results in

$$\frac{\partial \hat{E}}{\partial \delta} = 2 \int dx p(x)(\overline{f}(x) - d(x) + \delta) \tag{8}$$

Suppose $\frac{\partial \hat{E}}{\partial \delta} = 0$, then it is got

$$\delta = -\int dx p(x)(\overline{f}(x) - d(x)) \tag{9}$$

Zhou et al. [4,5] presented the method of GASEN using the genetic algorithm to optimize the component network weights. During the network weight's optimization, the reciprocal of E is used as the individual adaptive value. We also use the genetic algorithm to optimize the component network weights, and in the component network weights' evolution the reciprocal of $\hat{E}$ is used as the individual adaptive value after δ has been estimated with Formula (9). This method is the extension of GASEN, and written by GASEN-e.

4 Empirical Study

We use four data sets to perform testing. These data sets belong to the type of regression analyses including the following:

Data set 1(Friedman#1) was introduced by Friedman [3]. Every input vector contains five components and is generated according to formula (10).

$$y = 10\sin(\pi x_1 x_2) + 20(x_3 - 0.5)^2 + 10x_4 + 5x_5 + \varepsilon \qquad (10)$$

Where $x_i (i = 1,2,\cdots,5)$ obeys the uniform distribution on $[0,1]$, ε obeys the normal distribution $N(0,1)$.

Data set 2(Plane) was introduced by Ridgeway et al. [6]. Every input vector contains 2 components and is generated according to formula (11).

$$y = 0.6x_1 + 0.3x_2 + \varepsilon \qquad (11)$$

Where $x_i (i = 1,2,\cdots,5)$ obeys the uniform distribution on $[0,1]$, ε obeys the normal distribution $N(0,1)$.

Data set 3(Friedman#2) was introduced by Friedman[3]. Every input vector contains 4 components and is generated according to formula (12).

$$y = \sqrt{x_1^2 + (x_2 x_3 - (\frac{1}{x_2 x_4}))^2} \qquad (12)$$

Where x_1 obeys the uniform distribution on $[0,100]$, x_2 obeys the uniform distribution on $[40\pi, 560\pi]$, x_3 obeys the uniform on $[0,1]$, x_4 obeys the uniform on $[1,11]$.

Data set 4(Multi)was introduces by Hansen[7], used to compare several ensemble methods. Every input vector contains 5 components and is generated according to formula (13).

$$y = 0.79 + 1.27x_1 x_2 + 1.56x_1 x_4 + 3.42x_2 x_5 + 2.06x_3 x_4 x_5 . \qquad (13)$$

Where $x_i (i = 1,2,\cdots,5)$ obey s the uniform distribution on $[0,1]$.

4.1 Experimental Process and Parameters Setup

In our experiment, every data set contains 1000 samples. 5-foid method is used to test the neural network ensemble's performance. The component network's training set and the validating sets needed in the component network's training and network ensemble are all generated by bootstrap sampling the initial training sets [3].

Table 1. The initial training step and re-training step

	Data set of Friedman#1	Data set of Plane	Data set of Friedman#2	Data set of Multi
Initial training epochs	50	10	20	25
Re-training epochs	150	60	70	70
Total training epochs	200	70	90	95

The component neural network adopts the three-layer feed-forward structure and the middle layer (hidden layer) contains 10 neural cells. The size of the network ensemble is supposed to be 20.

To the component network training method proposed by us, the ensemble performance stability is the criterion to stop training. In experiments we find that this method's performance is based on that the component network has the certain accuracy. So after the initial training of component network this method is used to continue training the component network interactively. The initial training epochs of component network is set as the quarter of single neural network's training epochs. To determine the continuous training epochs of component network we perform the experimental test. The detailed assigned steps are shown in Table 1.

4.2 Experimental Result

To evaluate the generalization error of neural network ensemble, we adopt the performance comparison method for neural network ensemble proposed by Zhou et al.[5] to compare their relative generalization error. For a specific data set one neural network is trained, and the relative generalization error of network ensemble is the quotient of practical generalization error divided by this neural network's generalization error.

To the component neural network training method, the experiment compares PLA with Bagging [3] and OLA [4]. The ensemble of component neural networks adopts mostly the *simple averaging* [4] and weighted ensemble [5]. Zhou et al. [5] use the genetic algorithm to determine the weights of component neural network (GASEN) and achieve the wonderful neural networks ensemble result. We improve their method and present the new neural network ensemble method (GASEN-e). In experiment the simple averaging method of neural networks ensemble (abbr. Ave), GASEN and GASEN-e are compared. The experimental results are shown in Table 2 – 5.

It is found from experimental results that the component network generated using PLA can always achieve relatively good ensemble result, the reason for this is that PLA can guarantee the component network precision and simultaneously keep the diversity between component network and other network in the component network generation process.

Table 2. Data set of Friedman#1

	Ave	GASEN	GASEN-e
Bagigng	1.0456	0.8880	0.8428
OLA	1.0236	0.9880	0.8428
PLA	0.8234	0.8190	0.8152

Table 3. Data set of Plane

	Ave	GASEN	GASEN-e
Baging	0.8308	0.8198	0.8134
OLA	0.8289	0.8193	0.8132
CNNPLA	0.8263	0.8259	0.8122

Table 4. Data set of Friedman#2

	Ave	GASEN	GASEN-e
Bagigng	0.9946	0.8243	0.8215
OLA	0.9206	0.8333	0.8264
PLA	0.8834	0.8733	0.8261

Table 5. Data set of Multi

	Ave	GASEN	GASEN-e
Baging	0.9873	0.9876	0.9834
OLA	1.0310	0.9833	0.9340
CNNPLA	0.8892	0.8773	0.8598

The neural networks ensemble method of GASEN-e assigns a bias value to each component network generated in training, increasing the quantity of component networks selected and adjusting the generalization error of ensemble. Experiments show that GASEN-e is superior to GASEN.

5 Conclusion

This paper presents a parallel learning component network generation method of PLA. The method of PLA improves continuously the component network prediction precision in the component network training process, and simultaneously adjusts the diversity between it and other networks to decrease the generalization error of network ensemble. To the component network ensemble we improve the component neural network ensemble weights parallel determination method proposed by Zhou [5]. Assigning a bias value to the component network output can increase the quantity of component networks selected and decrease the generalization error of neural network ensemble.

Acknowledgements

The comments and suggestions from the reviewers greatly improve this paper. The National Natural Science Foundation of P.R.China(No. 60273033) and the Natural Science Foundation of Jiangsu Province, P.R.China(No. DK2002081), supported this research.

References

1. Solice P, Krogh A. Learning with ensembles: How over-Fiting can be useful. In: Touretzky D, Mozer M, Hasselmo M, eds. Advances in neural information processing systems(Vol. 7),1995,231-238.
2. Schapire R E. The Strength of weak learnability. Machine Learning, 1990, 5(2): 197-227.
3. Breiman L. Bagging predictors. Machine Learning, 1996, 24(2): 123-140.
4. Min Jang, Sungzoon Cho. Observational learning algorithm for an ensemble of neural networks, Pattern Analysis & Applications, 2002, 5: 154-167.
5. Zhou Z H, Wu J X, Tang W. Ensembling neural networks: many could be better than all. Artificial Intelligence, 2002,17(1-2): 239-263.
6. Rideway G, Madigan D., and Richardson T., Boosting methodology for regression problems, in proc. 7th Int. workshop on Artificial Intelligence and Statistics, Fort Lauderdale, FL, 1999, 152-161.
7. Hansen J H, Combining predictors: meta machine learning methods and bias/variance and ambiguity decompositions, Ph. D dissertation, Department of Computer Science, University of Aarhus, Denmark, June, 2000.

An Intelligent Gas Concentration Estimation System Using Neural Network Implemented Microcontroller

Ali Gulbag[1,2] and Fevzullah Temurtas[2]

[1] Sakarya University, Institute of Science & Technology, Adapazari, Turkey
[2] Sakarya University, Department of Computer Engineering, Adapazari, Turkey

Abstract. The use of microcontroller in neural network realizations is cheaper than those specific neural chips. In this study, an intelligent gas concentration estimation system is described. A neural network (NN) structure with tapped time delays was used for the concentration estimation of CCl_4 gas from the trend of the transient sensor responses. After training of the NN, the updated weights and biases were applied to the embedded neural network implemented on the 8051 microcontroller. The microcontroller based gas concentration estimation system performs NN based concentration estimation, the data acquisition and user interface tasks. This system can estimate the gas concentrations of CCl_4 with an average error of 1.5 % before the sensor response time. The results show that the appropriateness of the system is observed.

1 Introduction

General hardware implementations of neural networks are the application specific integrated circuits. The application specific neural chips and general purpose ones are more expensive than a microcontroller [1-3].

Usage of a microcontroller to realize a neural network has program dependent flexibility with cheapest hardware solution. However, realization of complicated mathematical operations such as sigmoid activation function is difficult via microcontrollers. A flexible and software dependent method is required to realize complicated activation functions on microcontrollers [3]. On the other hand, a neural network (NN) can be coded and trained in a high level language like C with floating point arithmetic, and then this NN structure can be embedded to a microcontroller with updated weights and biases. So the NN structures can be easily adapted to the handle systems including microcontrollers.

The volatile organic compounds in ambient air are known to be reactive photochemically, and can have harmful effects upon long-term exposure at moderate levels. These type organic compounds are widely used as a solvent in a large number of the chemical industry and in the printing plants [4]. Developing and designing sensors for the specific detection of hazardous components is important [5].

Usually, the steady state responses of the sensors are used for concentration estimations of the gases. Steady state response means no signal varying in time. But, for realizing the determination of the concentrations before the response times and decreasing the estimation time, the transient responses of the sensors must be used [6-9].

In this study, a microcontroller based gas concentration estimation system for realizing the determination of CCl_4 gas concentrations from the trend of the transient sensor responses is proposed The performance and the suitability of the method are discussed based on the experimental results.

2 Frequency Shift Measurement Circuit

The principle of the Quartz Crystal Microbalances (QCM) sensors are based on changes Δf in the fundamental oscillation frequency to upon ad/absorption of molecules from the gas phase. To a first approximation the frequency change Δf results from increase in the oscillating mass Δm [10]. A Calibrated Mass Flow Controller was used to control the flow rates of carrier gas and sample gas streams. Detailed information about QCM sensor and flow controller can be found in [6].

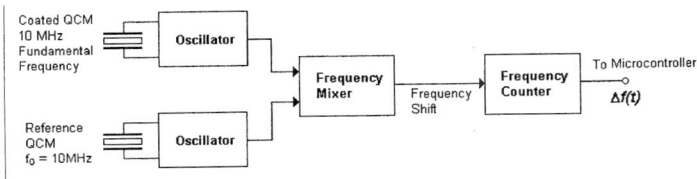

Fig. 1. Block diagram of the frequency shift measurement circuit

The transducers employed for the frequency shift measurement system were QCM with fundamental of 10 MHz. The set up consisted of two QCM, one of them as reference QCM. The other QCM was coated with a sensitive layer [6]. Figure 1 shows the block diagram of the frequency shift measurement circuit. In this study, the frequency shifts (Hz) versus concentrations (ppm) characteristics were measured for CCl_4. At the beginning of each measurement gas sensor is cleaned by pure synthetic air.

3 Training of the Neural Network for Concentration Estimation

A multi-layer feed-forward NN with tapped time delays is used for determination of the concentrations of CCl_4 from the trend of the transient sensor responses. The neural network structure is shown in Figure 2. The input, Δf is the sensor frequency shift value and the output, PPM is the estimated concentration. The networks have a single hidden layer and a single output node. The activation functions for the hidden layer nodes and the output node were sigmoid transfer functions. Data sampling rate (t_s) was equal approximately to 2 sec.

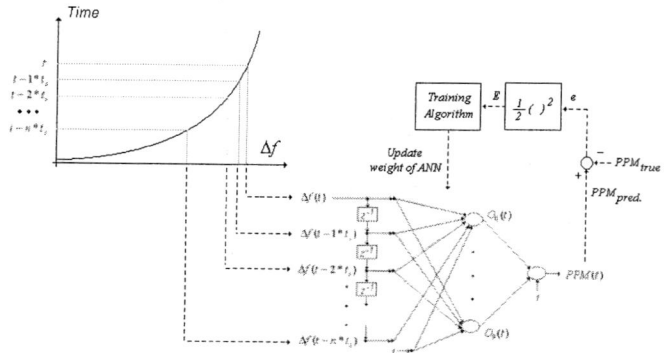

Fig. 2. The training diagram of neural network with a time delayed structure

The inputs to the networks are the frequency shift and the past values of the frequency shift. The information about the trend of the transient sensor responses can be increased by increasing the number of data. This requires additional neural network inputs. For illustrating the effect of the numbers of inputs, four different numbers of inputs to the networks are used. These are,

- the frequency shift and the two past values of the frequency shift (three inputs),
- the frequency shift and the four past values of the frequency shift (five inputs),
- the frequency shift and the seven past values of the frequency shift (eight inputs),
- the frequency shift and the nine past values of the frequency shift (ten inputs).

The three different numbers of the hidden layer nodes (five, eight and ten nodes) were used. The optimum numbers of inputs and hidden layer nodes were determined according to the training results of the NN and these values were selected for microcontroller implementation.

In this study, the BP algorithm with momentum [11] was used for updating the neural network weights and biases. The measured steady state and transient sensors responses were used for the training and test processes. Two measurements were made using same QCM sensor for this purpose. One measurement was used as training set and other measurement was used as test set. For the performance evaluation, we have used the mean relative absolute error, E(RAE) [6].

4 Microcontroller Based Concentration Estimation System

The 8051 (DS 5000 32-16) microcontroller was used as an embedded processor, based on its cost effectiveness, programming features. Microcontroller based concentration estimation system performs the frequency shift data acquisition, implements the NN to estimate the concentration and displays the result. Block diagram of the system can be seen in Figure 3.

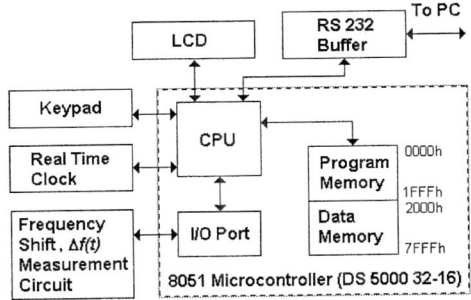

Fig. 3. Block diagram of the microcontroller based gas concentration system

The embedded neural network structure was coded in C language. Once the network has been trained to estimate gas concentration, the estimation process is a relatively straightforward operation. After training of the NN with tapped time delays to estimate gas concentration, the updated weights and biases are then applied to the embedded neural network implemented on the 8051 microcontroller. Since the embedded NN was coded in C with floating point arithmetic, four address locations were reserved for floating point number in the microcontroller memory.

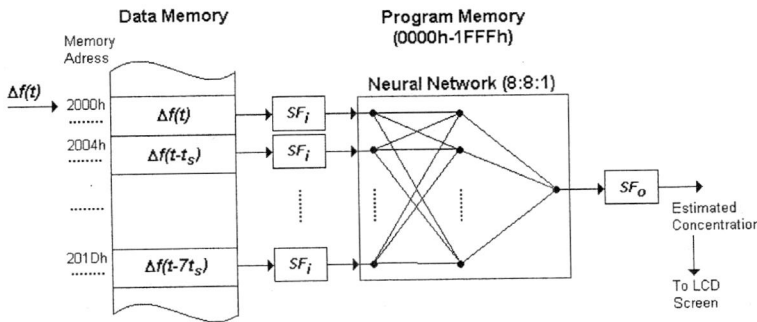

Fig. 4. The scheme of the NN based modelling of microcontroller based system

The tapped time delay structure of the used neural network (8:8:1) was implemented via data memory as seen in Figure 4. Each new Δf floating point data is stored to the 2000h memory address as four byte, while the past Δf values are moved to the next location. This process resembles the pipeline process. Once the memory locations between 2000h and 2020h (eight input values) are filled, the NN will have new inputs for each new Δf frequency shift data. The microcontroller based system makes the first estimation approximately 16 seconds after the reading of the first Δf frequency shift data. This is because of that, the first eight inputs of the NN are stored to memory approximately at this time interval ($8*t_s \approx 16$ seconds). In this NN based model, scaling factors SF_i and SF_o were used for normalization of the inputs and calculation of estimated concentration respectively. The weights, biases, activation functions and calculations of the embedded neural network were stored to program memory.

6 Results and Discussions

For determining the optimum number of the hidden layer nodes, three different values of the hidden layer nodes were used. Figure 5 shows the effects of hidden neurons on the performance of the NN. According to Figure 5, the optimum number of hidden layer nodes can be taken as eight. From the same figure, it's also shown that the increasing number of NN inputs results improving accuracy at the concentration estimations and optimum value can be taken as eight. These optimum values for the number of hidden layer nodes and number of NN inputs were used for microcontroller implementation.

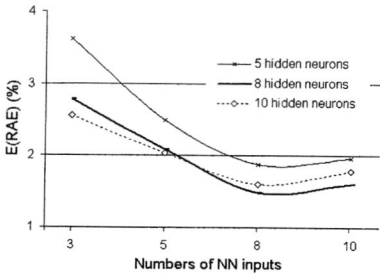

Fig. 5. Error (%) for numbers of hidden neurons versus numbers of NN inputs graph

After training of the selected neural network (8:8:1) coded in C with floating point arithmetic, C program codes of the network were converted to the 8051 assembly codes by using C51 C compiler. These 8051 assembly codes and the updated weights and biases of the NN are then stored to the program and data memories of the microcontroller respectively.

Table 1. Estimation results of the microcontroller based system for CCl_4

True concentrations (ppm)	Average concentration estimations (ppm) of the microcontroller based system	E(RAE) (%)
1000	1023	3.92
3000	2992	0.76
5000	4908	1.55
8000	8011	0.85
10000	9963	0.52
	Average E(RAE) (%) →	1.52

The performance of the microcontroller based system is summarized in Table 1. As seen in this table, acceptable good results were obtained for all the concentration values. The microcontroller based system estimates the concentration values at approximately 16 seconds, because of the tapped time delay structure of the neural network. This is because of that the frequency shift and the seven past values of the frequency shift takes approximately 16 seconds. On the other hand, the QCM sensor response time is approximately 250 seconds. This means that the determination of the concentrations of CCl_4 from the trend of the transient sensor responses is achieved before the response time using the microcontroller based system.

The microcontroller based gas concentration estimation system performs NN based concentration estimation, the data acquisition and user interface tasks. This system can estimate the gas concentrations of CCl_4 with an average error of 1.52 % before the sensor response time.

In this study, it is seen that acceptable good estimation results can be achieved for the estimation of the CCl_4 gas concentrations before the steady state response of the QCM sensor using the microcontroller based system including embedded neural network structure.

As a result, the obtained acceptable good results show that, the neural network structures can easily be realized via microcontroller for the handle gas detection systems. And the cost of this realization will be lower than that of the realization via specific neural chips. In addition to neural network based concentration estimation, this microcontroller based gas concentration estimation system performs the data acquisition and user interface tasks.

This intelligent estimation system can be easly adapted to the quantitative classification of gas compounds in their mixtures especially for the compounds developed for chemical warfare applications.

References

1. Aybay, I., Çetinkaya, S., ,Halici, U.: Classification of Neural Network Hardware, Neural Network World, IDG Co., Vol. 6, No 1, (1996) 11-29
2. Beiu, V.:, How to Build VLSI-Efficient Neural Chips, Proceedings of the International ICSC Symposium on Engineering of Intelligent Systems, EIS'98, Teneferie, Spain, (1998) 9-13
3. Avci, M., Yildirim, T.: Generation of Tangent Hyperbolic Sigmoid Function for Microcontroller Based Digital Implementations of Neural Networks, TAINN 2003, Canakkale,Turkey (2003)
4. Ho, M.H., Gullbault, G.G., Rietz, B.: Continuos Detection of Toluene in Ambient Air with a Coated Piezoelectric Crystal, Anal. Chem., 52(9), (1980)
5. Vaihinger, S., Gopel, W.: Multi - Component Analysis in Chemical Sensing in Sensors: A Comprehensive Survery Ed. W. Gopel, S. Hense, S.N. Zemel, VCH. Weinhe, New York, 2(1) (1991) 192
6. Temurtas, F., Tasaltin, C., Temurtaş, H., Yumusak, N., Ozturk, Z.Z.: Fuzzy Logic and Neural Network Applications on the Gas Sensor Data : Concentration Estimation, LECT NOTES COPMPUT SC, Vol. 2869, (2003), 178-185
7. Temurtas, F., Tasaltin, C., Temurtaş, H., Yumusak, N., Ozturk, Z.Z.: A Study on Neural Networks with Tapped Time Delays: Gas Concentration Estimation, LECT NOTES COPMPUT SC, Vol. 3046, (2004), 398-405

8. Temurtas, F., Gulbag, A., Yumusak, N.: A Study on Neural Networks using Taylor Series Expansion of Sigmoid Activation Function, LECT NOTES COPMPUT SC, Vol. 3046, (2004), 389-397
9. Temurtas, F.: A Study on Neural Networks and Fuzzy Inference Systems for Transient Data, LECT NOTES ARTIF INT, Vol. 3192, (2004), 277-284
10. King, H. W.: Piezoelectric Sorption Detector, Anal. Chem., 36 (1964) 1735-1739.
11. Haykin, S.: Neural Networks, A Comprehensive Foundation, Macmillan Publishing Company, Englewood Cliffs, N.J. (1994)

Ant Colonies Discover Knight's Tours

Philip Hingston[1] and Graham Kendall[2]

[1] Edith Cowan University, Australia
p.hingston@ecu.edu.au
[2] The University of Nottingham, UK
gkx@cs.nott.ac.uk

Abstract. In this paper we introduce an Ant Colony Optimisation (ACO) algorithm to find solutions for the well-known Knight's Tour problem. The algorithm utilizes the implicit parallelism of ACO's to simultaneously search for tours starting from all positions on the chessboard. We compare the new algorithm to a recently reported genetic algorithm, and to a depth-first backtracking search using Warnsdorff's heuristic. The new algorithm is superior in terms of search bias and also in terms of the rate of finding solutions.

1 Introduction

A *Knight's Tour* is a Hamiltonian path of a graph defined by the legal moves for a knight on a chessboard. That is, a knight must make a sequence of 63 legal moves visiting each square of an 8x8 chessboard exactly once. Murray [1] traces the earliest solutions to this problem back to an Arabic text in 840 ad. Leonhard Euler carried out the first mathematical analysis of the problem in 1759 [2]. Other well-known mathematicians to work on the problem include Taylor, de Moivre and Lagrange.

There is interest in finding both *open* and *closed* tours. A closed tour has the extra property that the 63rd move ends on a square that is a knight's move away from the start square, so that the knight could complete a Hamiltonian circuit with a 64th move. Closed tours are more difficult to find. An upper bound of the number of open tours was found to be approximately 1.305×10^{35} [3]. Löbbing and Ingo [4], calculated the number of closed tours, later corrected by McKay to be 13,267,364,410,532 tours [5]. Though there are many tours, the search space is even larger, at around 5.02×10^{58}.

A depth-first search, with backtracking, is perhaps the most obvious search method, though rather slow. A heuristic approach due to Warnsdorff in 1843, is the most widely known approach [6]. Using Warnsdorff's heuristic, at each move, the knight moves to a square that has the lowest number of next moves available. The idea is that the end of the tour will visit squares that have more move choices available.

A recent approach to finding knight's tours used a genetic algorithm [7]. This used a simple genetic algorithm [8], encoding a knight's tour as a sequence of 63x3 bits. Each triple represents a single move by the knight, with the fitness being defined by the number of legal moves (maximum = 63) before the knight jumps off the board or revisits a square. If a candidate tour leads to an illegal move, a repair operator checks the other seven possible knight's moves, replaces the illegal move with a legal move if there is one, and then attempts to continue the tour, repairing as needed. Without repair, the genetic algorithm found no complete tours. With repair, the maximum number of tours reported in a single run of 1,000,000 evaluations was 642.

2 The Ant Colony Algorithm

Ant colony optimization (ACO) algorithms are based on the observation that ants, despite being almost blind and having very simple brains, are able to find their way to a food source and back to their nest, using the shortest route. ACO's were introduced by Marco Dorigo [9], [10]. In [10] the algorithm is introduced by considering what happens when an ant comes across an obstacle and has to decide the best route to take around the obstacle. Initially, there is equal probability as to which way the ant will turn in order to negotiate the obstacle. Now consider a colony of ants making many trips around the obstacle and back to the nest. As they move, ants deposit a chemical (a *pheromone*) along their trail. If we assume that one route around the obstacle is shorter than the alternative route, then in a given period of time, a greater proportion of trips can be made over the shorter route. Thus, over time, there will be more pheromone deposited on the shorter route. Now the ants can increase their chance of finding the shorter route by preferentially choosing the one with more pheromone. This sets up a positive feedback cycle, known *stygmergy* or *autocatalytic behaviour*.

This idea has been adapted to derive various search algorithms, by augmenting pheromone trails with a problem specific heuristic. In the most famous example, ants can be used to search for solutions of the traveling salesman problem (TSP). Each ant traverses the city graph, depositing pheromone on edges between cities. High levels of pheromone indicate an edge that is in shorter tours found by previous ants. When choosing edges, ants consider the level of pheromone and a heuristic value, distance to the next city. The combination determines which city an ant moves to next.

We now present the new ACO algorithm that we use to discover knight's tours. As for the TSP, ants traverse a graph, depositing pheromones as they do so. In this case of the Knight's Tour Problem, the vertices of the graph correspond to the squares on a chessboard, and edges correspond to legal knight's moves between the squares. Each ant starts on some square and moves from square to square by choosing an edge to follow, always making sure that the destination square has not been visited before. An ant that visits all the squares on the board will have discovered a knight's tour.

We found it best to search for solutions from all starting squares simultaneously. We hypothesise that an ant starting on one square can utilize the knowledge gained by ants starting on more remote squares – knowledge that is harder to obtain from other ants starting on the same square.

We need some notation to describe the algorithm in detail. First, we define $T_{row,col,k}$ to be the amount of pheromone on the kth edge from the square in row *row* and column *col*. For squares near the edge of the chessboard, some moves would take the knight off the board and are illegal. We set $T_{row,col,k} = 0$ for those edges. We use $dest_{row,col,k}$ to denote the square reached by following edge k from square (row, col).

Initialising the Chessboard. Initially, some pheromone is laid on each edge. In our simulations we used $T_{row,col,k} = 10^{-6}$ for all edges corresponding to legal moves.

Evaporating Pheromones. Pheromones evaporate over time, preventing levels becoming unbounded, and allowing the ant colony to "forget" old information. We implemented this by reducing the amount of pheromone on each edge once per cycle, using:

$$T_{row,col,k} \to (1-\rho) \times T_{row,col,k}$$

where $0 < \rho < 1$ is the called the *evaporation rate*.

Starting an Ant. Each ant has a current square (row, col) and a tabu list, which is the set of squares that the ant has visited so far. Initially, $(row, col) = (startRow, startCol)$, and $tabu = \{(startRow, startCol)\}$. Each ant also remembers her start square, and her sequence of moves. Initially, $moves = <>$, an empty list.

Choosing the Next Move. To choose her next move, an ant computes, for each edge leading to a square not in her tabu list, the following quantity:

$$p_k = (T_{row,col,k})^\alpha$$

where $\alpha > 0$, the *strength* parameter, is a constant that determines how strongly to favour edges with more pheromone. She then chooses edge k with probability:

$$prob_k = \frac{p_k}{\sum_{j:dest_{row,col,j} \notin tabu} p_j}$$

Moving to the New Square. In some ACO algorithms, ants deposit pheromone as they traverse each edge. Another alternative, which we use in our algorithm, is for no pheromone to be deposited until the ant has finished her attempted tour. Hence, having chosen edge k, she simply moves to $dest_{row,col,k}$, and sets:

$$tabu \to tabu \cup \{dest_{row,col,k}\}, \text{ and}$$
$$moves \to moves + <k>$$

Keep Going Until Finished. Eventually, the ant will find herself on a square where all potential moves lead to a square in her tabu list. If she has visited all the squares on the chessboard, she has found a valid knight's tour, otherwise a partial tour.

Lay Pheromone. When she has finished her attempted tour, the ant retraces her steps and adds pheromone to the edges that she traverses. In order to reinforce more successful attempts, more pheromone is added for longer tours. We have found that we obtain slightly better results by reinforcing moves at the start of the tour more than those towards the end of it. Specifically, we define, for each ant a, for each row and column, and each edge k:

$$\Delta T_{a,row,col,k} = Q \times \frac{(|moves| - i)}{(63 - i)}, \text{ if ant } a\text{'s } i^{th} \text{ move used edge } k \text{ from } row, col, \text{ and}$$

$$\Delta T_{a,row,col,k} = 0 \text{, otherwise}$$

where the parameter Q is the *update rate*, and the value 63 here represents the length of a complete open tour. Thus, each ant contributes an amount of pheromone between 0 and Q. Once all ants complete their attempted tours, we update the pheromone using the formula:

$$T_{row,col,k} \rightarrow T_{row,col,k} + \sum_a \Delta T_{a,row,col,k} \, .$$

3 Experiments and Results

In this section we describe the experiments that we conducted and present the results we obtained. While the Knight's Tour is a puzzle or mathematical curiosity, it is a special case of an important NP-complete graph theoretic problem - that of finding a Hamiltonian path in a graph. In many applications, one is interested in finding Hamiltonian paths that optimize some figure of merit (such as tour length in TSP), so algorithms that generate Hamiltonian paths for evaluation are required. (Though in the case of TSP, finding paths is not the hard part, as the graph is usually well connected.) With this in mind, the aim of these experiments is to gather evidence on how well the ant colony algorithm does at generating as many knight's tours as possible. In addition, it is desirable that the algorithm achieves coverage of the complete set of knight's tours, and not be biased towards generating particular kinds of tours.

Firstly, we ran searches using a standard depth-first search with a fixed ordering of moves, and similar searches using Warnsdorff's heuristic to determine candidate moves. These experiments provide a baseline, indicating how difficult it is to locate complete tours. We then ran searches using our ant colony algorithm.

A naïve depth-first search was implemented, using the fixed move ordering given in [7]. For each possible starting square, we ran the search until 100,000,000 tours had been tried. The algorithm found an average of 308.6 complete tours for each square, all open.

We also implemented a variant of depth-first search using Warnsdorff's heuristic, in which a move is only considered valid if it obeys the heuristic. All these searches ran to completion, so we effectively enumerated all tours that obey the heuristic. The total number of "Warnsdorff tours" was found to be 7,894,584 - a tiny fraction of the total number of tours. About 15% (1,188,384) of these are closed tours. This variant is clearly very efficient in generating knight's tours, but it is also highly biased - indeed it is unable to reach most of the search space. The high proportion of closed tours found suggests that the portion of the search space that is reached is highly atypical.

For the ant colony algorithm, we first did some experimentation to discover a good set of parameters, settling on the following: evaporation rate $\rho = 0.25$; update rate $Q = 1.0$; strength $\alpha = 1.0$; in each cycle, start one ant from each start square; and greater pheromone update for moves near the end of a tour. If the evaporation rate is too low, there is not enough exploration, whilst if it is too high, there is not enough exploitation. Strength also affects this balance. Starting ants from all start squares in each cycle produces an order of magnitude more solutions compared to running the search once for each starting square. For the update rule, we also tried adding a constant amount of pheromone to each edge of a partial tour, or adding an amount proportional to the length of the partial tour. Both were inferior to the chosen formula.

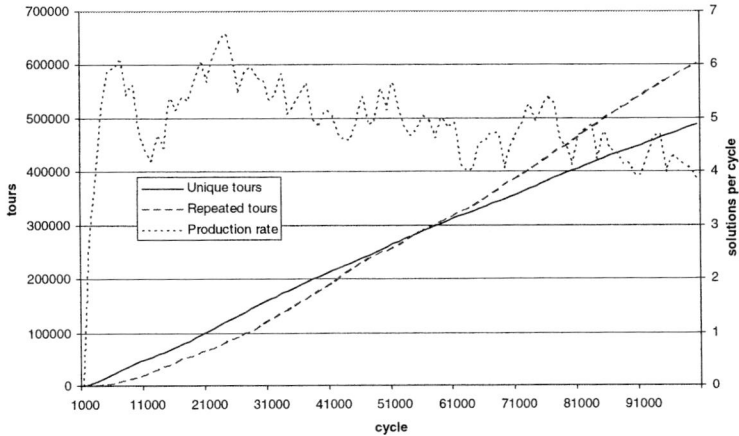

Fig. 1. Mean performance of the ant colony algorithm

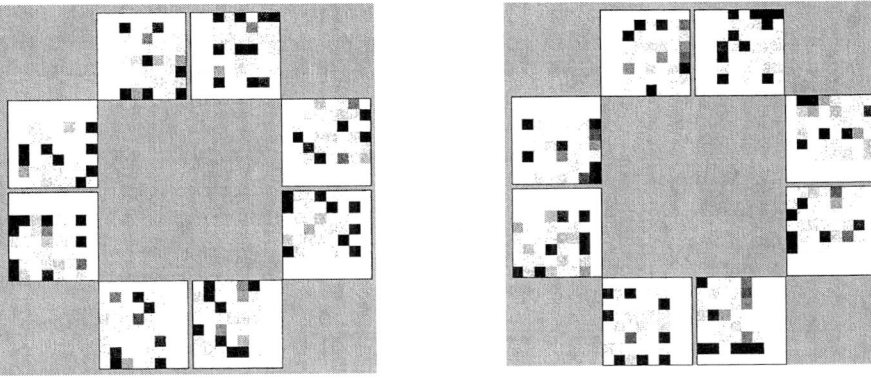

Fig. 2. Pheromone patterns at the completion of two runs of the ant colony algorithm

With these choices made, we ran the ant colony algorithm 20 times for 100,000 cycles each time. The mean number of unique complete tours found in each run was 488,245.4 (with, on average, 9,192.0 closed tours), three orders of magnitude better than the genetic algorithm. A better competitor is the heuristic depth-first search, which is more efficient than the ant colony, but only finds Warnsdorff tours.

Fig. 1 shows the mean number of unique tours discovered and the number of repeated tours for progressively more cycles. It also shows the "production rate" - the number of new tours found per cycle. Production rate increases for about the first 20,000-25,000 cycles, while the ant colony is learning a good pheromone pattern. After this, repeated tours are found, and the production rate slowly falls. A remedy might be to restart the algorithm after a few thousand cycles. We tried this idea, running the algorithm multiple times for 5,000 cycles each time. In no case were any tours discovered in more than one run. Fig. 2 shows pheromone patterns from two typical runs when the patterns have more or less converged. Each pattern has eight 8x8 grey scale rectangles. Each rectangle shows pheromone levels for one of the eight knight's moves at each square on the chessboard, darker grey indicating more pheromone. Patterns for different runs are quite different from each other.

4 Conclusion

We have introduced a new ant colony algorithm for discovering knight's tours on an 8x8 chessboard. The new algorithm is able to discover tours efficiently, without the bias of existing heuristic approaches. Just as graph theory itself was developed in the 18th century to study problems such as the Konigsberg Bridge Problem and the Knight's Tour Problem, this algorithm should be adapted easily to solve other problems involving Hamiltonian paths or cycles in other graphs.

References

[1] Murray H.J.R. (1913) History of Chess
[2] Euler L. (1766) Mémoires de l'Academie Royale des Sciences et Belles Lettres, Année 1759, vol.15, pp. 310–337, Berlin.
[3] Mordecki E. (2001) On the Number of Knight's Tours. Pre-publicaciones de Matematica de la Universidad de la Republica, Uruguay, 2001/57 (http://premat.fing.edu.uy/)
[4] Löbbing M. and Wegener I. (1996) The Number of Knight's Tours Equals 33,439,123,484,294 – Counting with Binary Decision Diagrams. Electronic Journal of Combinatorics. 3(1), R5.
[5] McKay B.D. (1997) Knight's tours of an 8x8 chessboard, Tech. Rpt. TR-CS-97-03, Dept. Computer Science, Australian National University.
[6] Warnsdorff H.C. (1823) Des Rösselsprungs einfachste und allgemeinste Lösung. Schmalkalden
[7] Gordon V.S. and Slocum T.J. (2004) The Knight's Tour – Evolutionary vs. Depth-First Search. In proceedings of the Congress of Evolutionary Computation 2004 (CEC'04), Portland, Oregon, pp. 1435-1440
[8] Goldberg D. (1989) Genetic Algorithms in Search, Optimization, and Machine Learning, Addison-Wesley
[9] Dorigo M. (1992). Optimization, Learning and Natural Algorithms. Ph.D.Thesis, Politecnico di Milano, Italy, in Italian
[10] Dorigo M., V. Maniezzo & A. Colorni (1996). The Ant System: Optimization by a Colony of Cooperating Agents. IEEE Transactions on Systems, Man, and Cybernetics-Part B, 26(1):29-41

Immune Clonal Selection Algorithm for Multiuser Detection in DS-CDMA Systems

Maoguo Gong[1], Haifeng Du[1,2], Licheng Jiao[1], and Ling Wang[1]

[1] Institute of Intelligent Information Processing and
National Key Lab of Radar Signal Processing, Xidian University
710071, Xi'an, China
[2] Industry Training Center, Xi'an Jiaotong University
710049, Xi'an, China
{Moregoodgong, lchjiao1, Haifengdu72}@163.com

Abstract. Based on the Antibody Clonal Selection Theory of immunology, we put forward a novel artificial immune system algorithm, Immune Clonal Selection Algorithm for Multiuser Detection in DS-CDMA Systems. The performance of the new detector, named by ICSMUD, is evaluated via computer simulations. When compared with Optimal Multiuser detection, ICSMUD can reduce the computational complexity significantly. When compared with detectors based on Standard Genetic Algorithm and A Novel Genetic Algorithm, ICSMUD has the best performance in eliminating multiple-access interference and "near-far" resistance and performs quite well even when the number of active users and the packet length are considerably large.

1 Introduction

In recent years, Direct-Sequence Code-division multiple-access(DS-CDMA) systems have emerged as one of prime multiple-access solutions for 3G. In the DS-CDMA framework, multiple-access interference (MAI) existing at the received signal creates "near-far" effects. Multiuser detection (MUD) techniques can efficiently suppress MAI and substantially increase the capacity of CDMA systems, so it has gained significant research interest since the Optimal MUD (OMD) was proposed by Verdu[1]. Reference [2] to [4] respective proposed their multiuser detectors based on BP Neural Network, Hopfield Neural Network and genetic algorithm. All of them can reduce the computational complexity significantly and get good performances. They provided new ideas and techniques for solving MUD. Antibody Clonal Selection Theory is very important for the immunology. Some new algorithms based on Clonal Selection Theory have been proposed successively[5][6][7].

A novel clonal selection algorithm for MUD based on Antibody Clonal Selection Theory, named by ICSMUD, is presented in this paper. The performances of ICSMUD is evaluated via computer simulations and compared with that of SGA and A Novel Genetic Algorithm based on Immunity[8] as well as with that of the OMD and Conventional Detector in asynchronous DS-CDMA systems.

2 Problem Statements

Consider a base-band digital DS-CDMA network with K active users operating with a coherent BPSK modulation format. The signal received at the output of the sensor is:

$$r(t) = \sum_{i=0}^{M-1}\sum_{k=1}^{K} A_k b_k(i) s_k(t-iT_b) + n(t) = S(t,b) + n(t) \tag{1}$$

here $n(t)$ is the additive white noise vector whose standard deviation is σ, T_b is the symbol interval, M is the packet length, A_k is the signal's amplitude of the kth user, $b_k(m)$ is the mth coded modulated symbol of the kth user and $b_k(m) \in \{\pm 1\}$, $s_k(t)$ is the kth user's signature sequence.

The matched filter output corresponding to the mth bit of the kth user is given by:

$$y_k(m) = \int_{-\infty}^{\infty} r(t) s_k(t - mT_b - \tau_k) dt \tag{2}$$

If set $y(m) = [y_1(m), y_2(m) \cdots, y_K(m)]^T$, $b(m) = [b_1(m), b_2(m), \ldots, b_K(m)]^T$, $A(m) = \text{diag}(A_1, A_2, \ldots, A_K)$, $n(m) = [n_1(m), n_2(m), \ldots, n_K(m)]^T$ and $R(q) = (\rho_{kl}(q))_{K \times K}$, where $\rho_{kl}(q) = \int_{\tau_k}^{T+\tau_k} s_k(t-\tau_k) s_l(t+qT-\tau_l) dt$ then

$$y = RAb + n \tag{3}$$

where $y = [y(m), y(m+1) \cdots, y(m+M-1)]^T$, $b = [b(m), b(m+1), \ldots, b(m+M-1)]^T$, $A = \text{diag}(A(m), A(m+1), \ldots, A(m+M-1))$ and $n = [n(m), n(m+1), \ldots, n(m+M-1)]^T$.

The OMD produces an estimate for the information vector transmitted at the discrete-time instant m. In the asynchronous systems it holds that

$$\hat{b}_{\text{optimal}} = \arg \max_{\substack{b_k(m) \in \{-1, 1\} \\ 1 \le k \le K, 1 \le m \le M}} \left\{ 2b^T Ay - b^T ARAb \right\} \tag{4}$$

Note that, if solved by Viterbi algorithm, its computational complexity will increase exponentially with the number of users and the packet length.

3 Immune Clonal Selection Algorithm for Multiuser Detection

The Antibody Clonal Selection Theory (F. M. Burnet, 1959) was proposed as the basic features of an immune response to an antigenic stimulus[9]. Inspired by the Antibody Clonal Selection Theory, we proposed a novel clonal selection algorithm for multiuser detection.

Assume that K active users share the same channel and the packet length is M, then the question (4) can be described as a combination optimization problem as

$$(P): \max\left\{ f(b) = 2b^T Ay - b^T ARAb : b \in I \right\} \tag{5}$$

where $b = \{ [b_1^{(1)}, b_2^{(1)} \cdots, b_K^{(1)}], \cdots, [b_1^{(M)}, b_2^{(M)} \cdots, b_K^{(M)}] \}$, $b_k^{(m)} \in \{-1, 1\}$ is the variants to be optimized, I denotes the antibody space. Set the antigen f as an objective function, and set I^n denotes the antibody population space as

$$I^n = \{B : B = (b_1, b_2, \cdots, b_n), \ b_k \in I, \ 1 \leq k \leq n\} \tag{6}$$

in which $B = \{b_1, b_2, \cdots, b_n\}$ is the antibody population, n is the size of the antibody population, and antibody $b_i = \{ [b_{1i}^{(1)}, b_{2i}^{(1)} \cdots, b_{Ki}^{(1)}], \cdots, [b_{1i}^{(M)}, b_{2i}^{(M)} \cdots, b_{Ki}^{(M)}] \}$. Then the novel clonal selection algorithm can be implemented as Fig 1.

Immune Clonal Selection Algorithm for Multiuser Detection (ICSMUD)
begin
    $k := 0$;
    initialize $B(k)$ and algorithm parameters;
    calculate affinity of $B(k)$: $\{f(B(k))\} = \{f(b_1(k)), f(b_2(k)), \cdots f(b_n(k))\}$;
    while not finished **do**
        $k := k + 1$;
        generate $B(k)$ from $B(k-1)$ by the Clonal Selection Operator including Clonal Operating T_c^C, Clonal Mutation Operating T_m^C, Clonal Selection Operating T_s^C and Clonal Death Operating T_d^C;
        calculate the affinity of $B(k)$, namely, evaluate $B(k)$;
    end
end

Fig. 1. The Immune Clonal Selection Algorithm for Multiuser Detection

The major elements of Clonal Selection Operator are presented as follows.

Clonal Operating T_c^C **:** Define

$$Y(k) = T_c^C(B(k)) = [T_c^C(b_1(k)) \ T_c^C(b_2(k)), \ \cdots, \ T_c^C(b_n(k))]^T \tag{7}$$

where $Y_i(k) = T_c^C(b_i(k)) = I_i \times b_i(k)$, $i = 1, 2, \cdots, n$, I_i is q_i dimension row vector and

$$q_i(k) = g(N_c, f(b_i(k))) \tag{8}$$

$N_c > n$ is a given value relating to the clone scale. After clone, the population becomes:

$$Y(k) = \{Y_1(k), Y_2(k), \cdots, Y_n(k)\} \tag{9}$$

where $Y_i(k) = \{y_{ij}(k)\} = \{y_{i1}(k), y_{i2}(k), \cdots, y_{iq_i}(k)\}$ and $y_{ij}(k) = b_i(k)$, $j = 1, 2, \cdots, q_i$.

Clonal Mutation T_m^C: According to the mutation probability p_m, the cloned antibody populations are mutated as follows:

$$Z_i(k) = \{z_{ij}(k)\} = \{T_m^C(y_{ij}(k))\} = \{(-1)^{random \leq p_m} y_{ij}(k)\} \tag{10}$$

$(-1)^{random \leq p_m} y_{ij}(k)$ means each number of the antibody $y_{ij}(k)$ multiplies -1 with probability of p_m.

Clonal Selection Operating T_s^C: $\forall i = 1,2,\cdots n$, if there are mutated antibodies $b_i'(k) = \max\{Z_i(k)\} = \{z_{ij}(k) \mid \max f(z_{ij}(k)) \ j = 1,2,\cdots,q_i\}$, the probability of $b_i'(k)$ taking place of $b_i(k) \in B(k)$ is:

$$p_s^k\left(b_i(k) = b_i'(k)\right) = \begin{cases} 1 & \text{when } f(b_i(k)) < f(b_i'(k)) \\ 0 & \text{when } f(b_i(k)) \geq f(b_i'(k)) \end{cases} \tag{11}$$

Clonal Death Operating T_d^C: After the clonal selection, the new population is:

$$B(k+1) = \{b_1(k+1), b_2(k+1), \cdots, b_i'(k+1), \cdots, b_n(k+1)\} \tag{12}$$

where $b_i'(k+1) = b_j(k+1) \in B(k+1)$ $i \neq j$ and $f(b_i'(k+1)) = f(b_j(k+1))$, in which $b_j(k+1)$ is one of the best antibodies in $B(k+1)$. Whether $b_i'(k+1)$ should be canceled or not depends on the clonal death proportion $T\%$.

We have proved that the algorithm of ICSMUD is convergent with probability of 1 based on Markov Chain.

In this contribution, we succeeded in reducing the complexity of the Optimal MUD by employing the sub-optimal ICSMUD, which performs only $O((K \times M)^2)$ search.

4 Simulation Results

In this section, we present some simulation results and comparisons that demonstrate the advantage of our algorithm. The performance of the ICSMUD is evaluated via computer simulations and compared with that of Standard Genetic Algorithm (GAMUD) and A Novel Genetic Algorithm based on Immunity [8] (IAMUD) as well as with that of Optimal Multiuser Detector (OMD) and conventional Matched Filters Detector (MFD) in asynchronous DS-CDMA systems.

It is assumed that the number of users is K and the packet length is M, Gold sequences of length 31 are used as code sequences. The signal to noise ratio of the kth user is $SNR_k = A_k^2/\sigma^2$. For ICSMUD, IAMUD and GAMUD, we will terminate the search at the Yth generation where $Y = 1.5 \times K \times M$. In GAMUD and IAMUD, the size of population is 25, the selection probability $P_r = 0.4$, the cross probability $P_c = 0.6$

and the mutation probability $p_m = 0.05$. In ICSMUD, the size of population is 5, clonal scale is 5, $T\% = 50\%$ and $P_m = 1/(K \times M)$. We take all the experiments based on 10000 bits signals. Our performance metric is the average Bit Error Ratio (BER).

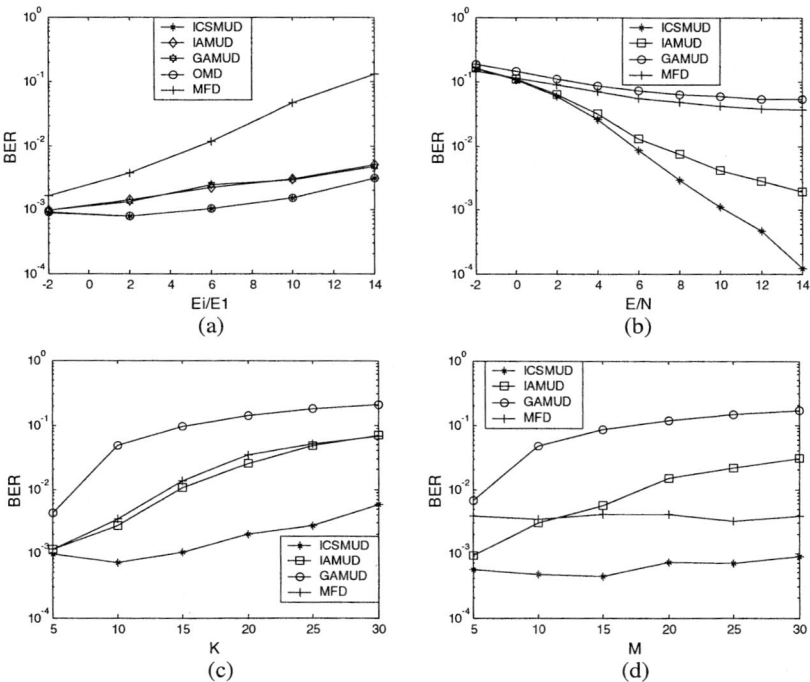

Fig. 2. The simulation results. (a) The performances in 'near-far' resistance; (b) The performances in eliminating noise's disturbing; (c) The performances in accommodating users; (d) The performances in accommodating packet length

A. In order to gain the results of the OMD, we assumed that $K=3$, $M=3$, SNR=10 dB. The first user is the desired user while other users are disturbing users and all users have the same power. The ratio of power between disturbing users and desired user denotes the ratio of 'near-far'. The performances in 'near-far' resistance of mentioned receivers are shown in Fig 2(a).

B. It is assumed that $K=10$, $M=10$. All users have the same power. Changing the value of SNR from -2 dB to 14 dB. The performances in eliminating noise's disturbing of mentioned receivers are shown in Fig 2(b).

C. It is assumed that $M=10$, SNR=10 dB, the number of users is changed from 5 to 30, all users have the same power. The performances in accommodating users of mentioned receivers are shown in Fig 2(c).

D. It is assumed that SNR=10 dB, K=10, the packet length is changed from 5 to 30, all users have the same power. The performances in accommodating packet length of mentioned receivers are shown in Fig 2(d).

As we can see from Fig 2(a), the conventional detector produces the receivable estimate only when powers of the users are close to each other. The GAMUD and IAMUD are better than conventional detector. But their performances are unacceptable either when powers of disturbing users are much larger than that of desired user. As we expect, ICSMUD exhibits the best performance and seldom fails to produce the correct estimate for the transmitted symbols, so its performance is almost the same good as the OMD. When the cumulative BER is evaluated versus the value of the SNR of all the users, from Fig 2(b) we can see that ICSMUD receiver achieves acceptable performance, whereas the performances of conventional detector, GAMUD and IAMUD are very poor. When the number of users or the transmitted packet length is relatively large, the advantage of ICSMUD can be seen in Fig 2(c) and Fig 2(d). The simulations suggest that, ICSMUD detector still performs quite well when K and M are relatively large.

5 Conclusions

In this paper, a novel multiuser detection receiver based on Immune Clonal Selection Algorithm was proposed. Monte Carlo simulations show that the new algorithm could significantly reduce the computational complexity and achieve better performance in eliminating MAI and "near-far" resistance over other algorithms such as the conventional detection, SGA and improved GA. It greatly improves the system capacity in acceptable computational cost for practical implementation in CDMA systems.

References

1. Sergio, V.: Optimum Multiuser Asymptotic Efficiency. IEEE Trans. Commun. Vol.34, No.9, (1986) 890–897
2. Aazhang, B., Paris, B.P., Orsak, G.C.: Neural Networks for Multiuser Detection in Code-division Multiple-Access Communications. IEEE Trans. Commun. Vol.40, No.7, July (1992) 1212–1222
3. Kechriotis, G., Manolakos, E.S.: Hopfield Neural Network Implementation of Optimal CDMA Mutiuser Detector. IEEE Trans. Neural Networks. Vol.7, No.1, (1996)131–141
4. Ng, S.X., Yen, K., Hanzo, L.: M-ary Coded Modulation Assisted Genetic Algorithm based Multiuser Detection for CDMA Systems. In: IEEE Communications Society (ed.): Proceedings of IEEE Wireless Communications and Networking 2003, Vol.2. IEEE, New Orleans (2003)779–783
5. Castro, L.N., Von, F.J.: The Clonal Selection Algorithm with Engineering Applications. In: Darrell, W., David, G., Erick, C. (eds.): Proceedings of Genetic and Evolutionary Computation Conference 2000, Workshop on Artificial Immune Systems and Their Applications. Las Vegas (2000)36–37

6. Kim, J., Bentley, P.J.: Towards an Artificial Immune System for Network Intrusion Detection: An Investigation of Clonal Selection with a Negative Selection Operator. In: IEEE Neural Networks Council. (ed.): Proceedings of the 2001 Congress on Evolutionary Computation, Vol. 2. IEEE, Seoul (2001)1244–1252
7. Du, H.F., Jiao, L.C., Wang, S.A.: Clonal Operator and Antibody Clone Algorithms. In: Shichao, Z., Qiang, Y., Chengqi, Z. (eds.): Proceedings of the First International Conference on Machine Learning and Cybernetics. IEEE, Beijing (2002)506–510
8. Jiao, L.C., Wang L.: A Novel Genetic Algorithm based on Immunity. IEEE Trans. Systems, Man and Cybernetics, Part A. Vol.30, No.5 (2000)552–561
9. Zhou, G.: Principles of Immunology. Shanghai Technology Literature Publishing Company, Shanghai (2000)

Intrusion Detection Based on Immune Clonal Selection Algorithms*

Liu Fang, Qu Bo, and Chen Rongsheng

School of Computer Science and Engineering, Xidian University,
Xi'an 710071, China
F63liu@163.com

Abstract. Immune clone selection algorithm is a new intelligent algorithm which can effectively overcome the prematurity and slow convergence speed of traditional evolution algorithm because of the clonal selection strategy and clonal mutation strategy. We apply the immune clonal selection algorithm to the process of modeling normal behavior. We compare our algorithm with the algorithm which applies the genetic algorithm to intrusion detection and applies the negative selection algorithm of the artificial immune system to intrusion detection in the dataset kddcup99. The experiment results have shown that the rule set obtained by our algorithm can detect unknown attack behavior effectively and have higher detection rate and lower false positive rate.

1 Introduction

With the rapid development of Internet, the computer network has been widely used and become the most important basic instrument, and Internet has brought us great economic benefits. However, the threat to information assurance is on the rise, and the network security has become a very important issue. Intrusion detection system which is a component of network security measure is more and more concerned.

Evolutionary Computation (EC) is a term covering Genetic Algorithms (GAs), Genetic Programming (GP), Evolutionary Strategies and Evolutionary Programming. Recently there has been some works within the GAs and GP communities and there have been several works that have attempted to produce classifier rules[1][2][3] using evolutionary techniques. For example, Gomez[4] and Gonzalez[5] use genetic algorithm to build classification rules for intrusion detection. Forrest[7] applies the negative selection algorithm of the human immune system to intrusion detection.

A novel intrusion detection based on Immune Clonal Selection Algorithm[6] (ICSA) is proposed in this paper. We apply the immune clonal selection algorithm to the process of modeling normal behavior. Experiment results have shown that our

---

* Supported by the National Natural Science Foundation of China under Grant Nos. 60372045, 60133010; National High Technology Development 863 Program of China under Grant No. 2002AA135080.

algorithm can detect novel attack behavior effectively and has higher detection rate and lower false positive rate in testing the rule sets obtained.

2 Intrusion Detection Based on Immune Clonal Selection Algorithm

In the rule set the if-part of each rule is a conjunction of one or more conditions to be tested and the then-part of the rule describes the class label of the rule. kim[8] uses a kind of the expression of the rule.

This kind of genotype representation allows a single attribute of each rule to have more than one value. Because each gene is comprised of nucleotides and the existing attribute values determine the number of nucleotides, the chromosome length corresponding to the presentation is too long and the search space is too large.

According to the analysis above, a rule genotype and phenotype presentation method (Figure 1) is proposed in the paper. The rule genotypes consist of a number of genes where each gene presents an attribute of the rule phenotype. Each gene is comprised of a nucleotide. Each nucleotide is an integer whose value indicates the index value of the corresponding attribute value of rule phenotype.

Gene1 Gene2 Gene3

| 4 | 1 | 3 |

⇓

Gene1 cluster table

ID	Gene Value
1	tcp
2	udp
3	icmp
4	tcp or udp
5	tcp or icmp
6	udp or icmp
7	Any Value

Gene 2 cluster table

ID	Gene Value	ID	Gene Value
1	[min...10]	9	[10...17]or[20...max]
2	[10...17]	10	[17...20]or[20...max]
3	[17...20]	11	[min...10]or[10...17]or[17...20]
4	[20...max]	12	[min...10]or[10...17]or[20...max]
5	[min...10]or[10...17]	13	[min...10]or[17...20]or[20...max]
6	[min...10]or[17...20]	14	[10...17]or[17...20]or[20...max]
7	[min...10]or[20...max]	15	Any Value
8	[10...17]or[17...20]		

Gene3 cluster table

ID	Gene Value
1	[min...324]
2	[324...max]
3	Any Value

⇓

Rule Phenotype
If(Attribute1=tcp or udp) And (Attribute2=[min...10] And (Attribute3=Any Value) Then Detector detects SELF

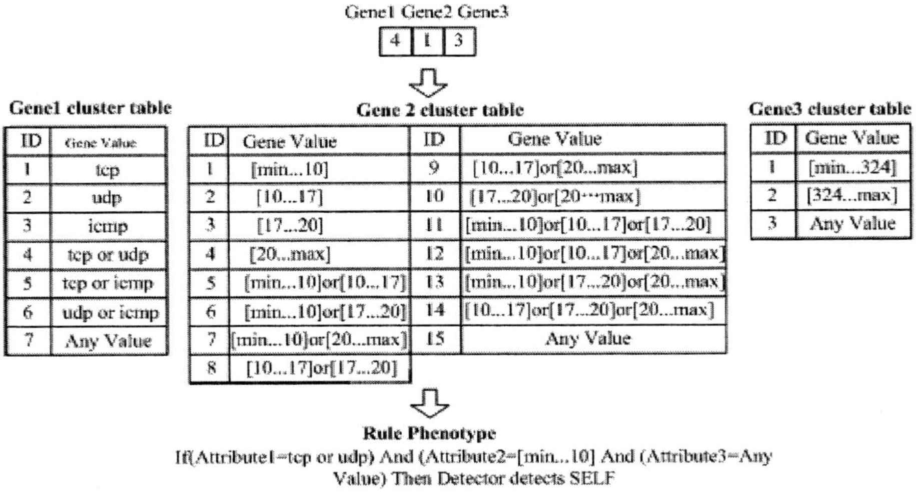

Fig. 1. Rule genotype and phenotype which this paper put forward

Each nucleotide is an integer whose value indicates the index value of the corresponding attribute value of rule phenotype. A gene is equal to the index value that the corresponding attribute of rule phenotype may be equal to any value, which means that the attribute is a redundant attribute. The rule genotype and phenotype presentation which we put forward decrease sharply the chromosome length and the search space.

The aim applying the immune clonal selection algorithm to evolve the rule sets is to extract the predicted rule set which describes the normal behavior of network traffic data, so we designed an affinity function formula (1):

$$f(Antigen) = \frac{TP}{1+FN} \quad (1)$$

where TP is true positive rate, FN is false negative rate.

The algorithms applying the immune clonal selection algorithm to evolve the rule set is presented as follows:

Step 1. All the training samples are the antigen and the initial antibody population ($C(k)$) is generated randomly;
Step 2. Initialize algorithm parameters and set k=0;
Step 3. Repeat;
Step 4. Calculate the affinity $C(k)$ of and generate $C(k+1)$ from $C(K)$ by Clonal Selection Operator including Clonal Operating T_c^C, Clonal Mutation Operating T_m^C, Clonal Selection Operating T_s^C
Step 5. k=k+1;
Step 6. Until the condition is satisfied.

The elements of Clonal Selection Operator are introduced as follows:

Clonal Operating T_c^C:

$$T_c^C(\overline{A}(k)) = [T_c^C(A_1(k)), T_c^C(A_2(k)), \cdots, T_c^C(A_n(k))]^T \quad (2)$$

After clone operating, the antibody population becomes the formula (3):

$$A' = \{A, A_1', A_2', \ldots, A_n'\} \quad (3)$$

where $A_i' = \{a_{i1}, a_{i2}, \ldots, a_{iq_i-1}\}$, $a_{ij} = a_i$ and $j=1,2,\ldots,q_i-1$

Clonal Mutation Operating T_g^C: We apply the Gauss mutation here. Mutate the population clone operated with the probability p_m

$$\overline{A}'(k) = T_g^C(\overline{A}(k)) \quad (4)$$

Clonal Selection Operating T_m^C: $\forall i = 1,2,\cdots n$ exits mutated antibody $B = \{A_{ij}'(k) | \max f(A_{ij}'), j=1,2,\ldots,q_i-1\}$, Then B replaces the antibody $A_i(k) \in \overline{A}(k)$ in the original population by the possibility p_s.

$$p_s = \begin{cases} 1 & f(A_i(k)) < f(B) \\ \exp(-\dfrac{f(A_i(K))-B(K)}{\alpha}) & f(A_i(k)) \geq f(B) \text{ and } A(K) \text{ is the best antibody} \\ 0 & f(A_i(k)) \geq f(B) \text{ and } A(K) \text{ is not the best antibody} \end{cases} \quad (5)$$

where $\alpha > 0$ is a value related to the population diversity. So the antibody population is updated, and the information exchanging among the antibody population is realized.

The detection method is presented as follows:

Step 1. A number of rules are extracted from the rules which are evolved by the immune clonal selection algorithm, so the new rule set is established;

Step 2. The rule genotypes in the new rule set is converted into the rule phenotype;

Step 3. The testing samples are tested by the rule phenotype, if a testing sample matches anyone in the new rule set, then it is recognized as normal, else it is recognized as abnormal.

3 Experiments Results and Analysis

The dataset used in the experiments is the KDD CUP 1999 data, which is a version of the 1998 DARPA intrusion detection evaluation data set prepared and managed by MIT Lincoln Labs. The raw data includes the training data and test data and consists of a great deal of normal and attack network traffic data. It is important to note that the test data is not from the same probability distribution as the training data, and it includes specific attack types not in the training data.

One hundred thousand samples are randomly selected from the 10% data set, which is composed of our training samples. Then one hundred thousand samples are randomly selected from the rest of the 10% data set, which is composed of our testing samples $test1$. The other two testing sample sets $test2$ and $test3$ are selected from the test data to examine if novel attack behavior can be detected with our algorithm effectively. Five thousand samples are selected from the novel attack types data of the test data, and ninety five hundred thousand samples are selected from the rest of the test data, which is composed of our testing samples $test2$. Similarly our testing samples $test3$ is selected from the test data.

Because the raw data has continuous and discrete value, the recursive minimal entropy discretisation algorithm proposed by Fayyad and Irani[9] is used to discretize the continuous attributes. Dougherty[10] compare several discrete algorithms, his experiments have showed that the algorithm improved the classification accuracy of c4.5 and naïve-Bayes algorithm on various data sets.

In the training phase, our algorithm is compared with the method in bibliography[7] and the method applying the genetic algorithm to evolving the rule set. The parameter setting in the experiments is showed as following: a population size of 400 was used. In our algorithm, the iterative times of 800 is used, $Nc = 600$, $=0.2$ and $p_m = 0.65$. In the genetic algorithm, the iterative times of 800 are used, the crossover probability is 0.65 and the mutation probability is 0.1. In the method in bibliography[7], the detectors of 100 is used, the activation threshold is 10 and the match length is 12.

In the training phase, the average results of 20 times which are generated by our algorithm and genetic algorithm is shown as figure 2(a). It is obvious that the convergence speed of our algorithm is faster than that of genetic algorithm and our algorithm effectively overcomes the prematurity of the genetic algorithm.

In the testing phase, our algorithm is compared with the other two methods. The predicted rule sets with the varying rule number are composed of the best rule and other unrepeated rules extracted from the evolved rule set in terms of affinity. For example, a rule in the predicted rule set is shown as following:

if duration=0 and protocol_type=tcp and ... and dst_host_rerror_rate =0 **then** normal

The average results of 50 times which are generated by the three algorithms with the testing samples *test*1 are shown in the figure2(b) and figure2(c). It is shown that when the rule number of 20 is used, the higher detection rate and the lower false positive rate are obtained. The detection rate and false positive rate are greatly influenced by the rule number of the predicted rule set generated by the method in bibliography[7]. When the rule number of 80 is used, the higher detection rate and the lower false positive rate are obtained.

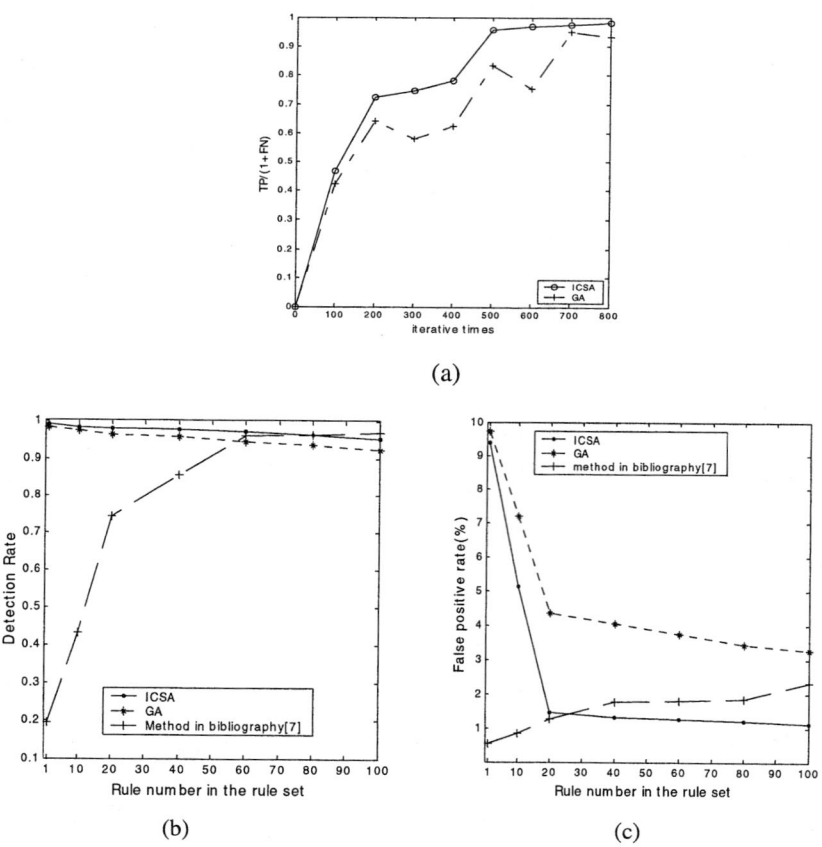

Fig. 2. The experiment results

According to the experiment results above, there are 20 rules all together extracted from the rules evolved by our algorithm and genetic algorithm and 80 rules by the method in bibliography[7]. When the parameters are set as above, the average results of 50 times are shown in table 1, which are generated to detect known attack and unknown attack by the three algorithms with the testing samples *test2* and *test3*. It is obviously that our algorithm is better than the other two algorithms and the detection rate on the novel attack behavior obtained by our algorithm is about eighty four percent, which indicates that novel attack behavior can be detected with our algorithm effectively.

Table 1. The comparison of detection rate for detecting known and novel attack behavior

Algorithms	Test2		Test3	
	Known attack (%)	Novel attack (%)	Known attack (%)	Novel attack (%)
Our algorithms	98.60	84.20	98.31	83.64
Genetic algorithms	93.54	50.63	92.42	49.10
Method in bibliography[7]	95.84	60.42	95.33	65.11

4 Conclusion

Immune clone selection algorithm overcomes the prematurity and slow convergence speed of traditional evolution algorithm. We apply the immune clonal selection algorithm to the anomaly detection. The experiment results show that novel attack behavior can be detected effectively and higher detection rate and lower false positive rate are obtained while testing our predictive rules with our algorithm.

References

1. K. De Jong and W. Spears (1991).: Learning Concept Classification Rules Using Genetic Algorithms. Proceedings of the Twelfth International Joint Conference on Artificial Intelligence:651-656
2. C.E. Bojarczuk, H.S. Lopes and A.A. Freitas (1999).: Discovering comprehensible classification rules using genetic programming: a case study in a medical domain. Proc. Genetic and Evolutionary Computation Conference GECCO99,Morgan Kaufmann:953-958
3. J. Liu and J. Kwok (2000).: An extended genetic rule induction algorithm. Proceedings of the Congress on Evolutionary Computation(CEC):458-463
4. J.Gomez and D. Dasgupta.: Evolving Fuzzy Classifiers for Intrusion Detection. In Proceedings of the 2002 IEEE Workshop on Information Assurance:68-75Appendix: Springer-Author Discount

5. F. Gonzalez, J.Gomez and D.Dasgupta.: An Evolutionary Approach to Generate Fuzzy Anomaly(Attack) Signatures . Proceedings of the 2003 IEEE Workshop on Information Assurance United States Academy, West point, NY June 2003
6. Jiao Licheng, Du Haifeng,: An Artificial Immune System: Progress and Prospect, ACTA ELECTRONICA SINICA, 2003,31(10):1540~1549
7. Hofmeyr S,Forrest S.: Architecture for an Artificial Immune System. Evolutionary Computation, 2000,7(1):45-68
8. Kim J, Bentley P.: Towards an artificial immune system for network intrusion detection an investigation of clonal selection with a negative selection operator. Proc Congress on Evolutionary Computation , Seoul, Korea, 2001. 27- 30
9. Fayyad,U.M., and Irani,K.B.: Multi-Interval Discretization of Continuous-Valued Attributes for Classification Learning. Proceeding of The Thirteenth International Joint Conference on Artificial Intelligence:1022-1027
10. J. Dougherty, R.Kohavi and M.Sahami.: Supervised and Unsupervised Discretization of Continuous Features. Proceedings of the Twelfth International Conference ,1995

Mapping Dryland Salinity Using Neural Networks

Matthew Spencer, Tim Whitfort, and John McCullagh

Department of Information Technology, La Trobe University,
PO Box 199, Bendigo, VIC, 3552, Australia
mattspencer@lexicon.net,
{t.whitfort, j.mccullagh}@latrobe.edu.au

Abstract. Salinity is a growing problem that affects millions of hectares of agricultural land. Due to the devastating effects of dryland salinity, land owners, the government and catchment groups require cost effective information in the form of salinity maps. This paper investigates the use of a backpropagation neural network to map dryland salinity in the Wimmera region of Victoria, Australia. Data used in this research includes radiometric readings from airborne geophysical measurements and satellite imagery. The results achieved were very promising and indicate the potential for further research in this area.

1 Introduction

Since European settlement, many environmental changes have occurred in Australia. Trees were cleared to promote agricultural practices, resulting in the environmental balance being broken. Shallow-rooted vegetation was unable to absorb sufficient water from rainfall, resulting in the unused water sinking to the groundwater, causing watertables to rise. As watertables rise towards the earth's surface, the salts carried within the groundwater also rise, causing non-salt tolerant plants to die. When groundwater reaches near to the surface, the land is considered unsuitable for agricultural practices due to its salinity content. These events result in dryland salinity, which is a form of man-made salinity caused by agricultural practices. The extent of the dryland salinity problem within Australia includes the loss of millions of hectares of agricultural land and loss of flora affected by rising watertables [1]. In addition, dryland salinity increases maintenance costs to infrastructure such as road and rail. Due to the devastating effects associated with this growing problem, steps have been taken to identify regions at risk of developing dryland salinity.

The three main research areas involving the problem of dryland salinity are mapping, predicting and combating salinity. Mapping salinity is used by catchment groups, land owners and the government to identify salinity-affected land. Predicting salinity trends is used to indicate areas that may be at risk of developing dryland salinity in the future. Combating the problem of dryland salinity involves developing strategies or plans in affected areas, such as salt-mining, revegetation and irrigation practices [2]. The focus of this study is the mapping of dryland salinity.

There is a growing interest in models that can produce accurate salinity maps. Traditionally, expert assessments were made on-site by reading soil measurements to represent a region of land. This process was initially achieved through the collection of soil samples and assessment of electrical conductivity (EC). These techniques are considered to be a time-consuming, expensive and incomplete exercise, promoting interest in alternative techniques.

Remotely sensed data is a cost-efficient, complete and accurate method of obtaining information about land and soil. Two sources of such data are available: satellite imagery and airborne geophysics. Satellites are able to collect data about the landform, such as elevation, curvature and slope. Airborne geophysics can take measurements of materials at or below the Earth's surface. These include measurements such as radiometrics, which have a relationship to salinity risk. This study focuses on the use of remotely sensed data to assess a neural network's ability in mapping dryland salinity.

2 Mapping Salinity

Limited research has been conducted into the problem of mapping salinity using remotely sensed data. Statistical methods were used in a study at Kakadu National Park, Australia to map soil salinity using Airborne Synthetic Aperture Radar (AirSAR) and Landsat TM satellite data [3]. Variables used in this study included Electrical Conductivity (EC), percentage ground cover, vegetation height and species and leaf litter depth. The salinity map produced classified salinity presence into 9 different classes, broken up by density of salinity and vegetation. The best level of accuracy on test data was 82%. The accuracy of this study was quite high, however several of the classes that contributed a small portion of the population were not very well classified using this model. Hocking [4] used fuzzy modelling to map dryland salinity in the Wimmera Plains, Australia. Data collected for this study included radiometrics, DEMs (Digital Elevation Models) and DEM derived data. Factors used included the slope of the land, elevation, potassium and thorium content. Assessment of salinity risk was not output to 'crisp' classifications, but rather towards estimating a degree of risk in each study example. The results from the fuzzy techniques were poor, with a correlation of 0.32 between the outputs of the fuzzy system to the expected result. Evans [5] used Conditional Probabilistic Networks to examine if probabilistic relationships could be identified for mapping dryland salinity. The focus of this study was to demonstrate that the accuracy of mapping salinity could be increased by incorporating prior knowledge of relationships between attributes and salinity. Previous years' attributes were combined with the assessed year to estimate salinity risk. The overall results of the study were poor, with many non-saline examples being classified as saline.

Due to the difficulty in mapping dryland salinity using statistical techniques, there has been growing interest in exploring a variety of other methods including Artificial

Intelligence techniques. Research was conducted to investigate the use of decision trees for mapping salinity in the Wimmera region [6]. The decision tree was developed using C4.5, a software package used for the generation of rule sets [7]. The data used was a combination of radiometrics, satellite imagery and DEMs. The variables included potassium and thorium content, curvature, elevation and slope. For a localised area of the study space, the results were 97% for training examples and 91% for testing for the classification of salinity. However, when this study space was increased to a wider area, the accuracy was reduced to 63.7%. A study was performed in Western Australia to investigate the use of decision trees and neural networks in mapping dryland salinity [5]. Data collected for this study included satellite imagery, DEMs, drainage models and ground truth data. Although the salinity maps produced using decision tree approach appeared promising, 7% of non-saline examples were recorded as saline. Neural Networks were also used to determine whether the technique was a more effective method for the mapping of dryland salinity. The technique accurately classified approximately 94% of non-saline regions and 74% of saline regions. It was believed that these results may have been influenced by data selection. Because the training set contained many non-saline examples, the results may have been biased towards non-saline classifications. Artificial Neural Networks have been studied in other salinity-based problems including the prediction of groundwater activity [8], river salinity [9][10] and dryland salinity [11].

3 Data

The data used was remotely sensed using satellite imagery and airborne geophysics. Data was collected from Landsat TM (satellite) and radiometrics in a 34km X 17km area of the Western Wimmera region in Victoria, Australia (see Figure 1). Readings were taken for each 20m X 20m cell in the study area. The variables used in the study are summarised in Table 1 below.

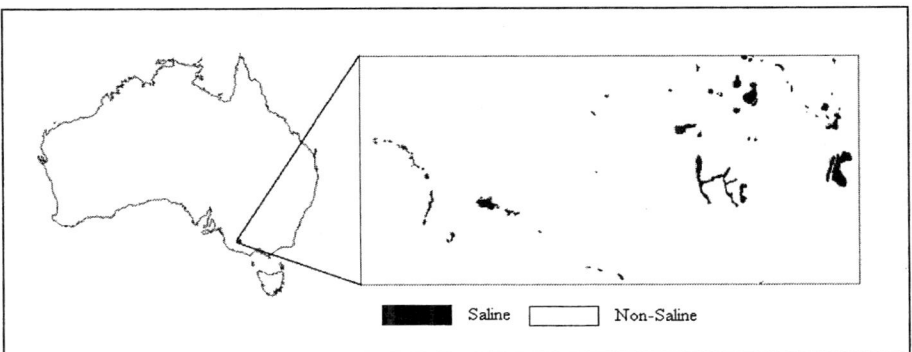

Fig. 1. Map of Australia showing region under study

Table 1. Variables available for this study

Variable	Description
aspect	Direction of the downward slope (degrees)
curvature	Curvature of the Earth
elevation	Elevation above sea level (metres)
potassium	Potassium (% by volume)
slope	Slope (%)
soil	Soil composition classification
thorium	Thorium
TWI	Topographic Wetness Index
target	Expert assessment of salinity

Training, testing and validation sets were created to find a relationship between the input variables and the target, and assess network accuracy on unseen data. A large proportion of the study area was non-saline (98.5%). To help minimise network bias towards a particular class, non-saline and saline examples were randomly selected in equal numbers for experiments.

4 Experimentation

The experimentation conducted in this research examined the potential of neural networks to map dryland salinity. This section is divided into two parts: methodology, and experimental results and discussion.

4.1 Methodology

Before being presented to a network for training, data was preprocessed to aid network performance. In addition to the original values for inputs, relative values were calculated for the following factors: curvature, elevation (x 2), potassium, slope and thorium. Relative measurements were calculated based on readings of nearby cells. These were used to indicate changes of land characteristics such as elevation. The soil type was the only discrete input, with 8 soil types. A separate input was created for each soil type. Based on the distribution of inputs, appropriate scaling techniques were applied to the data. Non-linear scaling was applied to the slope. The other continuous inputs were scaled linearly. In total, 21 inputs were supplied to the network (7 continuous, 6 continuous relative, and 8 discrete soil). The neural network architecture and parameters used in the experiments are outlined in Table 2. Assessment of training and testing accuracy was made using the percentage of samples correctly estimated.

Examples were either classified as saline or non-saline. The training, testing, and validation set each comprised 6,612 examples: with 3,306 non-saline and 3,306 saline examples randomly selected.

Table 2. Neural network parameters and architecture

Parameters	Values
No. of hidden layers	1
Hidden layer neurons	2-30
NN passes	100,000 – 1,600,000
Learning rate	0.1 – 0.9
Momentum	0.1 – 0.9
Epoch size	1 - 100
Initial weights	± 0.1

4.2 Results and Discussion

Table 3 shows the performance of the neural networks. The best network used 1,500,000 network passes, 16 hidden layer neurons, a learning rate of 0.4, momentum of 0.9 and an epoch size of 5.

Table 3. Training, Testing and Validation performance

Training Accuracy	Testing Accuracy	Validation Accuracy
81.2%	79.1%	78.4%

To assess the significance of this research, the results achieved were compared to two previously published studies. The first study was conducted in the Western Wimmera to determine if rule induction was a suitable tool for estimating the presence of salinity [6]. The second study involved the use of maximum likelihood classifiers and neural networks in the agricultural regions of Western Australia using multi-temporal data to estimate the presence of salinity [5]. The results of this comparison are presented in Table 4. They indicate that the performance for the salinity set experiments clearly outperforms the results for the other two studies. It should be noted that the results presented in this research are preliminary in nature, however they do indicate the potential for further work in this area.

Table 4. Validation performance compared to other studies

Technique	Validation
Artificial Neural Networks (Wimmera)	78.4 %
Decision Trees (Wimmera) [6]	74.0 %
Maximum Likelihood Class (West Aust) [5]	75.1 %
Neural Networks (West Aust) [5]	63.7 %

5 Conclusion

Remote sensing techniques have been used as a cost effective technique to collect data that may be associated with salinity. The data has been used to reduce the costs associated with the production of salinity maps. Mapping salinity using statistical approaches on remotely sensed data has been demonstrated to be difficult. Neural Networks were used in this study to produce salinity maps, with promising results. It is believed that, with further research, the accuracy of this technique could be improved. Potential areas for further research include: (a) finding other cost-efficient inputs that influence salinity risk; (b) modifying relative data calculations to better identify significant readings and show the difference to nearby cells; (c) investigating the right balance of saline and non-saline examples to incorporate the large proportion of non-saline cases without causing imbalance to neural network training; and (d) investigating the application of expert neural networks.

References

1. Australian Bureau of Statistics: AusStats: Land Degradation [online] Available: http://www.abs.gov.au/ausstats/abs@.nsf/0/FAEB6096CDA4D9ADCA256BDC001223FF?Open&Highlight=0,Salinity [Accessed 27 March 2003] (2002)
2. NSW Department of Land and Water Conservation: Salinity in NSW: All about salinity. [online] Available: http://www.dlwc.nsw.gov.au/care/salinity/management/dryland.html [Accessed 22 March 2003] (2000)
3. Bell, D., Menges, C.H., Bartolo, R.E., Ahmad, W. and VanZyl, J..J.: A multistaged approach to mapping soil salinity in a tropical coastal environment using airborne SAR and Landsat TM data. In: Geoscience and Remote Sensing Symposium, 3. (2001) 1309-1311
4. Hocking M.: Salinity Risk on the Wimmera Plains. In: Technical Report No. 72, Centre for land protection research, Bendigo, Dept. of Natural Resources and Environment (2001)
5. Evans, F.H.: An investigation into the use of maximum likelihood classifiers, decision trees, neural networks and conditional probabilistic networks for mapping and predicting salinity. In: MSc thesis, Department of Computer Science, Curtin University (1998)
6. Walklate, J.: Machine Learning Using AI Techniques. In: BComp(Hons) Thesis, La Trobe University, Bendigo (2002)
7. Quinlan, J.R.: C4.5: Programs for Machine Learning. Morgan Kaufmann, San Mateo, CA (1993)
8. Clarke, C.J., George, R.J., Bell, R.W. and Hatton, T.J.: Dryland salinity in south-western Australia: its origins, remedies, and future research directions. In: Australian Journal of Soil Research, 40. (2002) 93-113
9. Maier, H.R. and Dandy, G.C.: Understanding the behaviour and optimising the performance of back-propagation neural networks: an empirical study. In: Environmental Modelling & Software, 13(2). (1998) 179-91
10. Rajkumar, T. and Johnson, M.L.: Prediction of salinity in San Francisco bay delta using neural network. In: Proceedings of IEEE SMC, Arizona, USA (2001) 329-334
11. Evans, F. H. and Caccetta, P. A.: Broad-scale spatial prediction of areas at risk from dryland salinity. In: Cartography, 29(2). (2000) 33-40

Normalized RBF Neural Network for Real-Time Detection of Signal in the Noise

Minfen Shen[1], Yuzheng Zhang[1], Zhancheng Li[1], Jinyao Yang[2], and Patch Beadle[3]

[1] Key Lab. of Guangdong, Shantou University, Guangdong 515063, China
mfshen@stu.edu.cn
[2] Ultrasonic Institute of Shantou, Shantou, Guangdong, China
[3] School of System Engineering, Portsmouth University, Portsmouth, U.K.

Abstract. A new solution to real time signal detection in the noise is presented in this paper. The proposed approach uses the modified RBF neural network (RBFNN) for the purposes of enhancing the ability of signal detection with low signal-to-noise radio (SNR). The characteristics and the advantages of the normalized RBFNN are discussed. As an application, the extraction of single-trial evoked potentials (EP) is investigated. The performance of the presented method is also addressed and compared with adaptive and common RBFNN methods. Several results are included to show the applicability and the effectiveness of the new model.

1 Introduction

A significant number of schemes regarding the problem of real-time signal detection in noise have been investigated since many measured signals in practice are often contaminated with different kinds of background noise. Another problem we face is that the transient characteristics of the underlying signal. One of approaches for dealing with these problems is called ensemble averaging (EA) technique, but EA method fails to real-time track the signal in noise. As we know, evoked potentials (EPs) are very special time-varying signals which are totally corrupted by the electroencephalograph (EEG). The problem of tracking EPs changes is quite important and practical significant in neural science and other areas [1,2]. The measurement of the time-varying EPs is always buried in relatively large background noise which is the on-going electrical activity of other brain cells known as electroencephalograph (EEG). To extract the real-time EPs more effectively from the noise, advanced signal processing technique is required. Our main task is to design a real-time estimator with which the unwanted contribution of the on-going background noise can be filtered out from the observations as much as possible.

Adaptive noise canceller (ANC) has been widely used to improve the estimate result of transient noisy signals, but many of them need a meaningful reference signal for its good tracking [3,4,5]. Some researches apply radial basis function neural network (RBFNN) as the filter to detect the desired signal since RBFNN enables to deal with any nonlinear multidimensional continuous functions [6,7,8,9]. Both ANC and RBFNN were much better than EA in the case of tracking real-time response and extracting the temporal information of the measurement. However, when the SNR is very low and the response is fast transient, the methods discussed above may not provide good behaviors. To overcome this limitation, a modified RBFNN is proposed by normalizing the RBFNN to form a new structure with good performance for our purpose.

This paper is organized as follows. In section 2, the proposed modified RBF neural network structure and its advantages are discussed. In addition, the simulated results for evaluating the performance are compared and demonstrated to prove the effectiveness of the presented method in section 3. Finally, some significant results are discussed and summarized.

2 Proposed Approach

The normalized RBF neural network (NRBFNN) can be obtained in terms of dividing each radial function in RBF network by the sum of all radial functions. General RBF neural network is a multiplayer feed-forward neural network consisting of input layer, kernel layer and output layer. The units in the kernel layer provide an array of nonlinear RBF which is usually selected as Gaussian functions. Local basis functions have advantages because of the increased interpretability of the network, the ability of producing locally accurate confidence limits and the locality [10,11]. Normalization is common practice in local linear modeling. The normalization of the basis functions in such a network is proposed to obtain a partition of unity across the input space, which leads to the basis functions covering the whole of the input space to the same degree, i.e. the basis functions sum to unity at every point. Partition of unity means that the sum of the normalized basis functions equals unity at any point in the input space. Partitioning unity is an important property for basis function networks in many applications such as noisy data interpolation and regression. It often results in a structure which can be less sensitive to poor center selection and in cases where the network is used within a local model structure. Also since the basis function activations are bounded between 0 and 1, they can be interpreted as probability values. Covered the space between training vectors without excessive overlap, the RBF eventually approach either zero or one at the extremes of the input. The effect of the normalization also improves the interpolation properties and makes the network less sensitive to the choice of the widths parameters [8,10]. The NRBFNN is therefore adopted in this paper to detect the signal in the noise and compared with other two common methods: ANC and RBFNN algorithms.

3 Results

In this section, both ANC and RBFNN are computed and compared with the proposed NRBFNN method by employing the simulated data and real EEG signals. We carry out the evaluations in the following three aspects: (a) comparing the performance with relative mean square error (MSE), (b) evaluating the ability of tracking signal's variation, and (c) testing the signal detection ability with different SNR.

Firstly, we generate 50 epochs of 500 samples with input SNR of –20 dB and –40 dB, respectively, for evaluating the behaviors. All three models, ANC, RBFNN and NRBFNN, were tested with the simulated data. Fig. 1 shows the corresponding performance of real-time detection at SNR of -40dB. Though being able to track single-trial data rapidly, RBFNN can only achieve it under certain circumstance, such as a higher SNR input. In all situations, the normalized RBFNN provides the best performance in the fitting ability as well as in the convergence rate. The performance of the estimation is also evaluated based on the mean square errors (MSE) that were shown in terms of the MSE versus three different types of methods in Fig.2. The behaviors with two kinds of SNR were estimated and compared. It can be seen that the NRBFNN is the best as compared to the other models, especially at very low SNR condition. Finally, we compared the performance of the signal detection at different SNR, varying from –40 dB to 0 dB. Fig.3 illustrated the corresponding results. It is clear that the MSE of NRBFNN is the smallest at all noise levels. The NRBFNN method effectively eliminates the background noise with the best behavior.

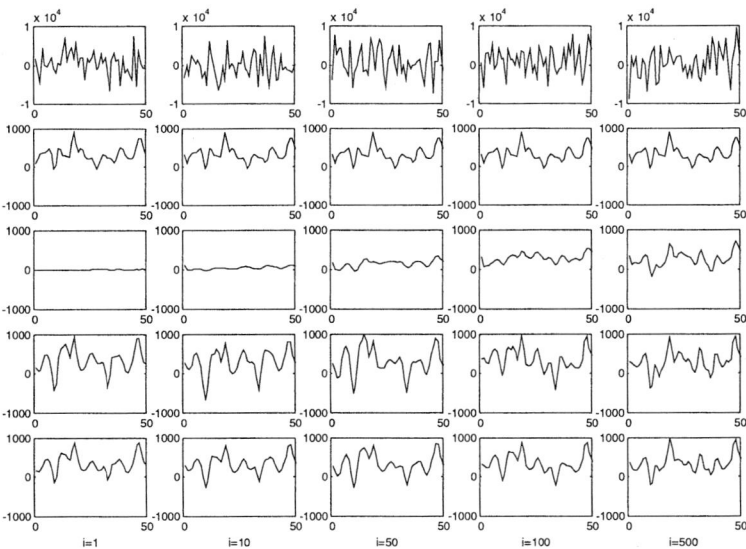

Fig. 1. Comparison of the performance of ANC, RBFNN and NRBFNN with SNR of -40dB. From top to below: raw noisy signal, true pure signal component, responses detected with ANC, RBFNN and NRBFNN. i denotes the trial number

Based on the preliminary results above, several significant conclusions can be drawn. First of all, to overcome the drawback of traditional methods, the proposed NRBFNN can obtain the preferable results for real-time signal detection under low SNR conditions. By using singular value decomposition algorithm, we investigated and optimized the normalized RBF neural network, which enables to eliminate the redundant hidden nodes of the network and to obtain a reasonable network structure. Thus the modified RBFNN technique significantly suppresses the additive noises and enhances the ability of the real-time signal detection in the noise. In addition, several performances of the proposed NRBFNN, comparing with other three different types of models, were carried out to prove that the presented algorithm has its best behaviors in different aspects such as the relative mean square error, the ability of tracking signal variation and the ability of signal detection at low SNR conditions. All simulation results show the effectiveness and the applicability of the presented NRBFNN model.

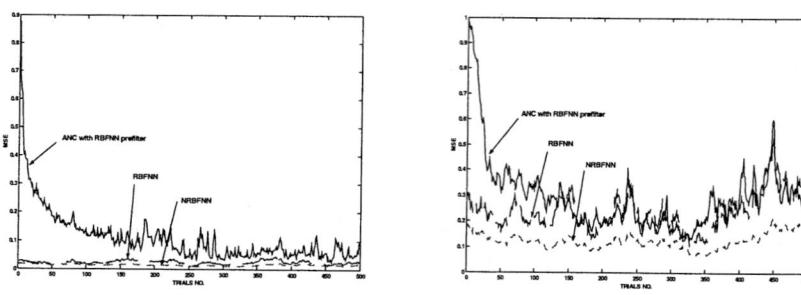

Fig. 2. Comparison of the three approaches based on MSE with SNR of –20 dB and –40 dB

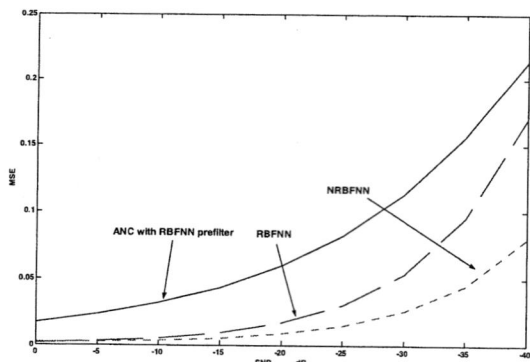

Fig. 3. Comparison of the MSE vs SNR for three different methods

Secondly, as an example in medical application, we investigated the problem of obtaining real-time EPs measurement and tracking EPs' variations across each trial.The visual event-related potentials (ERPs) during processing two kinds of visual attention tasks were collected and studied. Event-related potentials are transient change in the electroencephalogram (EEG) due to external stimuli or cognitive processes triggered by external events. Our particular interest aims at determining the temporal relationship of variations from trial to trial and measuring the response synchronously to each visual stimulus. NRBFNN is conducted to estimate visual ERPs from actual recordings and to identify how the brain gets to know the visual stimuli by providing a direct comparison of visual response from multiple cortical areas of individual. Based on the recordings from 100ms stimuli onset to 900ms post-onset of the 72th electrode, NRBFNN was used to deal with the collected raw EEG for two different kinds of visual stimuli, watching O shape and X shape on the monitor. Note that it is only one trial input by which NRBFNN can accurately detect this ERP response from the large background noises. Fig. 4 (a) and (b) show all trials detected by using NRBFNN for the stimulus of O shape with 200 trials and X shape with 50 trials, respectively. We can get the different responses in only one trial input and the trial-to-trial variations. It shows that NRBFNN significantly improve the behavior of the ERPs detection, especially under very low SNR conditions. By employing the NRBFNN, the changes of all real-time ERPs from trial to trial can be clearly obtained, which significantly help our understanding for many practical applications in neural science and cognitive study. Based on the empirical results, the NRBFNN is more efficiance to the real-time detection of signals in noise than other common schemes. The main reason for that is because the local interpolation properties of NRBFNN is greatly improved, which makes the neural network less sensitive to the choice of other parameters. The NRBFNN scheme, therefore, significantly improved the ability with respect to the responding speed and output SNR.

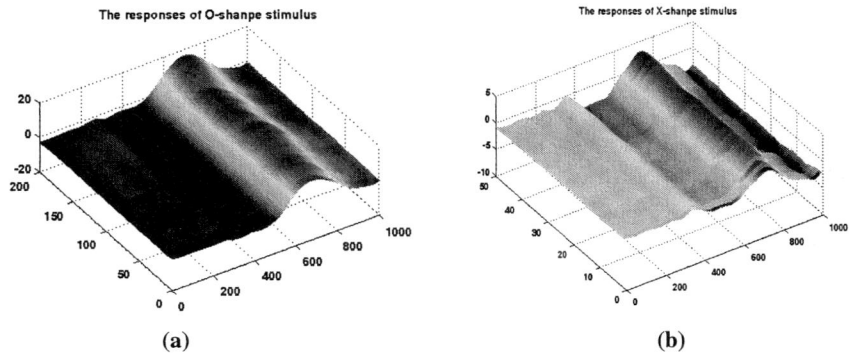

Fig. 4. All ERP variations from trial to trial induced from O-shape and X-shape visual stimuli, respectively, by using the normalized RBF neural network

4 Conclusions

A new method for signal detection in noise was proposed in this contribution in terms of the presented modified RBF neural network. The advantages of the normalized RBF neural network were discussed. With the simulations, the performances of the

NRBFNN were also evaluated and compared with two different types of common methods, ANC and RBFNN. We also focused on an application of extracting each visual ERP trial from the collected raw EEG signal. Both simulations and real ERP experiment show the success of making use of normalized RBF neural network for our problem. The NRBFNN is more applicable to the real-time detection of single-trial ERPs than other existing methods, such as the nonlinear ANC and common RBFNN. The enhancement of SNR enables us to characterize the high variations in ERP's peak amplitude and latency over trials. The NRBFNN successfully solve the problem of traditional EA and detect each ERP trial from the raw EEG, which supports the single-trial signal estimation with second unit, leading to more reliable dynamic ERP study and clinical applications. All significant results have proved the effectiveness and the advantage of the presented method.

Acknowledgements

The research was supported by the Natural Science Foundation of China (60271023), the Natural Science Foundation of Guangdong (021264 and 32025), and the Key Grant of the Education Ministry of China (02110).

References

1. Qiu W., and et. al.: Adaptive Filtering of Evoked Potentials with Radial-Basis-Function Neural Network Prefilter. IEEE Trans. Biomedical Engineering, Vol. 49, No.3, March (2002) 225-232
2. Shen M., Sun L., and Chan F. H. Y.: Method for Extracting Time-Varying Rhythms of Electroencephalography via Wavelet Packet Analysis. IEE Proceedings in Science, Measurement and Technology, Vol.148, No.1, January (2001) 23-27
3. Laguna P., Jane R., Meste O., Poon P. W., Caminal P., Rix H., and Thakor N. V.: Adaptive Filter for Event-Related Bioelectric Signals Using An Impulse Correlated Reference Input: Comparison with Signal Averaging Techniques. IEEE Trans. Biomedical Engineering, Vol.39, (1992) 1032-1244
4. Bernard W., John G. and et al.: Adaptive Noise Canceling: Principles and Applications. Proceedings of The IEEE, Vol. 63. IEEE Press, Piscataway NJ (1975) 1692-1716
5. Zhang Z.: Nonlinear ANC Based on RBF Neural Networks. Journal of Shanghai Jiaotong University Vol.32. Shanghai Jiaotong University Press, Shanghai (1998) 63-65
6. Platt J. C.: A Resource Allocating Network for Function Interpolation. Neural Computation, Vol. 3. MIT Press, Cambridge (1991) 213-225
7. Moody J. and Darken C. J.: Fast Learning in Network of Locally-tuned Processing Units. Neural Computation, Vol. 1. MIT Press, Cambridge (1989) 281-294
8. Hartman E. J., Keeler J. D. and Kowalski J. M.: Layered Neural Networks with Gaussian Hidden Units as Universal Approximation. Neural Computation, Vol. 2. MIT Press, Cambridge (1989) 210-215
9. Zhu C. F. and Hu G. S.: Estimation of Single-Trial Evoked Potential with RBFNN. International Conf. on Information Systems Analysis and Synthesis, SCI 2001/ISAS 2001

10. Murray-Smith R. and Hunt K. J.: Local Model Architectures for Nonlinear Modeling and Control. in Hunt K. J., Irwin G. W., and Warwick K., editors, Neural Network Engineering in Dynamic Control Systems, Advances in Industrial Control, Springer-Verlag (1995) 61-82
11. Xu L., Bzak A. K. and Yuille A.: On Radial Basis Function Nets and Kernel Regression: Approximation Ability, Convergence Rate and Receptive Field Size. Neural Networks, Vol.7, (1994) 609-628

Statistical Exploratory Analysis of Genetic Algorithms: The Influence of Gray Codes upon the Difficulty of a Problem

Andrew Czarn[1], Cara MacNish[1], Kaipillil Vijayan[2], and Berwin Turlach[2]

[1] School of Computer Science and Software Engineering,
The University of Western Australia,
Crawley WA 6009
[2] School of Mathematics and Statistics,
The University of Western Australia,
Crawley WA 6009

Abstract. An important issue in genetic algorithms is the relationship between the difficulty of a problem and the choice of encoding. Two questions remain unanswered: is their a statistically demonstrable relationship between the difficulty of a problem and the choice of encoding, and, if so, what it the actual mechanism by which this occurs?

In this paper we use components of a rigorous statistical methodology to demonstrate that the choice of encoding has a real effect upon the difficulty of a problem. Computer animation is then used to illustrate the actual mechanism by which this occurs.

1 Introduction

Genetic algorithm (GA) practitioners report that changing the representation which is used in GAs affect their performance [1,2]. However, two important questions remain unanswered, namely:

1. Is their a statistically demonstrable relationship between the difficulty of a problem and the choice of encoding or could any observed change in performance be simply due to the stochastic nature of the GA; and
2. If the relationship between the difficulty of a problem and the choice of encoding is a real effect, what is the actual mechanism by which this occurs?

In earlier research [3, 4] we demonstrated that for difficult problems (problems requiring greater computational resources) high mutation rates are required and that as a problem became more difficult, due to increased modality (more local optima), it is generally more likely to demonstrate statistically significant interaction between crossover and mutation. However, an unexpected result was that certain problems in our *FNn* test function series appeared more difficult to solve despite the fact that they have lower modality. Specifically, *FN3* appeared a more difficult problem to solve than *FN4*, in contrast to the trend of this test series of increasing difficulty with increasing modality.

In this paper we use components of our methodology to demonstrate that the type of encoding used can have a real affect upon the difficulty of a problem. We then use animation to illustrate the actual mechanism by which this effect occurs. An extended version of this paper can be found in [5].

2 Methods

A detailed explanation of our statistical approach can be found in [3, 4, 5]. First, we created a series of test functions, *FNn*, that increase in modality with n according to Equation 1:

$$FNn(\mathbf{x}) = \Sigma_{i=1}^{2} 0.5 \left(1 - \cos(\frac{n\pi x_i}{100}) e^{-|\frac{x_i}{1000}|}\right) \qquad (1)$$

Secondly, as the variation seen in GA runs is due to the differences in the starting population and the probabilistic implementation of mutation and crossover, which is in turn *directly* dependent on seed, it was necessary to control for the effect of seed via the implementation of a *randomized complete block* design. Seed is blocked by ensuring that the seeds used to implement items such as initialization of the starting population of chromosomes, selection, crossover and mutation are identical within each block. An increase in sample size occurs by *replicating* blocks identical except for the seeds so as to assess whether the effects of parameters are significantly different from variation due to changes in seed.

Thirdly, in order to compare performances for 2 or more parameters using a randomized complete block design we use the statistical test for the equality of means known as the analysis of variance (ANOVA). ANOVA allows for the testing of significance of individual parameters and allows for the testing of interaction between parameters. Interaction is simply the failure of one parameter to produce the same effect on the response variable at different levels of another parameter [6].

Fourthly, in performing statistical tests such as the analysis of variance (ANOVA) it is important to ensure a balanced design. This requires removing censored data. In practical terms this means identifying the regions of the GA parameters where the GA succeeds and restricting statistical analysis to those regions. An early step in our methodology is therefore to generate *dot diagrams* which show the regions of censored data. Moreover, dot diagrams provide an initial assessment of the difficulty of a problem given our previous experience that for difficult problems low mutation rates prove to be ineffective [3, 4].

Finally, in order to closely study the behaviour of *FN3* and *FN4* we implemented an animation of the GA in solving each function in their one-dimensional (one bit string) forms. We were able to visualize the behaviour of the population of chromosomes from epoch to epoch after the processes of selection, crossover and mutation. Our previous work has shown that the best rate of crossover for *FN3* and *FN4* is 100% [4]. Thus, we studied the behaviour of the chromosomes by setting crossover at 100% and varying the rates of mutation in accordance with the results from dot diagram analysis.

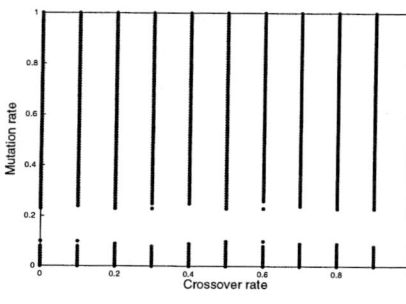

Fig. 1a. Dot Diagram: *FN3*   **Fig. 1b.** Dot Diagram: *FN4*

3 Results

3.1 Dot Diagram Analysis of *FN3* and *FN4*

Dot diagram analysis of *FN3* and *FN4* are shown in Figures 1a and 1b. For *FN3* mutation rates of 10% or less were associated with censoring. In contrast, for *FN4* low rates of mutation were not associated with censoring. This suggested that *FN3* was proving a more difficult function to solve than *FN4*.

3.2 ANOVA Analysis of *FN3* and *FN4*

The results of ANOVA analysis of *FN3* and *FN4* are described in detail in [4]. It was shown that the interaction between crossover and mutation for *FN3* was significant with a p-value of 0.011 while the interaction term for *FN4* was non-significant with a p-value of 0.933. Thus, ANOVA analysis also suggested that *FN3* was a more difficult problem to solve than *FN4*.

3.3 Dot Diagram Analysis of One Dimensional Projections

In order to explain the above anomaly we utilized computer animation. Visualization of the behaviour is simpler for a one-dimensional (one bit string) problem. Since our test function is linear separable, its optimization by a GA can be envisaged as decomposable into two independent one-dimensional (one bit string) sub-problems [7]. Providing those sub-problems exhibit the same phenomenon, we can confine our study to their one-dimensional (one bit string) forms. These are denoted as $FN3_{1D}$ and $FN4_{1D}$.

Dot diagram analysis of $FN3_{1D}$ and $FN4_{1D}$ were undertaken and are shown in Figures 2a and 2b. As can be seen, low mutation rates were associated with censoring for $FN3_{1D}$, while for $FN4_{1D}$ there was an absence of censoring. As these results paralleled those for the two-dimensional (two bit string) functions we proceeded to study the behaviour of $FN3_{1D}$ and $FN4_{1D}$ via animation.

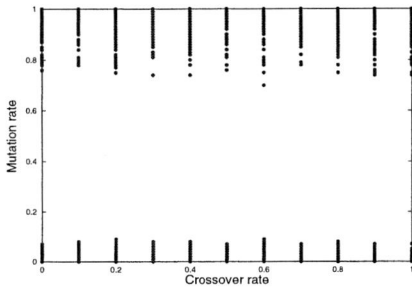 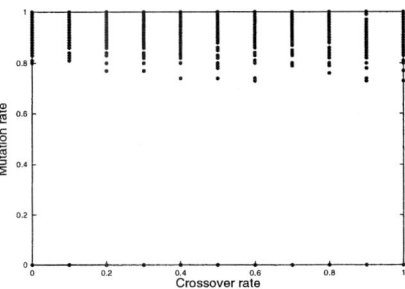

Fig. 2a. Dot Diagram: $FN3_{1D}$ **Fig. 2b.** Dot Diagram: $FN4_{1D}$

3.4 Animation Analysis of $FN3_{1D}$ and $FN4_{1D}$

We implemented a number of animations of $FN3_{1D}$ and $FN4_{1D}$. The observed behaviour revealed interesting insights into the performance of the GA. As shown in Figures 3a and 3b, for $FN3_{1D}$, starting with chromosomes outside of the global optimum, after applying a low mutation rate a number of chromosomes would lie in the upper part of the global optimum. However, after selection these chromosomes would be culled and fail to survive into the next generation. In contrast, as illustrated in Figures 4a and 4b, high mutation rates were able

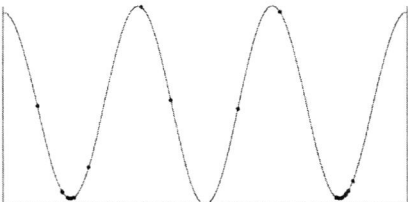 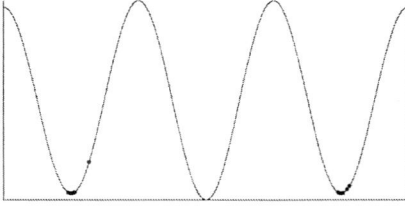

Fig. 3a. $FN3_{1D}$: Chromosome population after applying a low mutation rate

Fig. 3b. $FN3_{1D}$: Chromosome population after selection

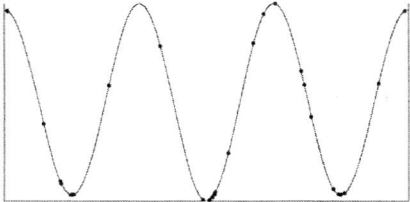 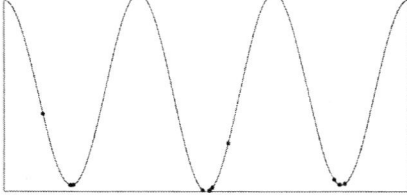

Fig. 4a. $FN3_{1D}$: Chromosome population after applying a high mutation rate

Fig. 4b. $FN3_{1D}$: Chromosome population after selection to produce chromosomes lying deep enough in the global optimum to survive culling and be selected into the next generation. Thus, it appeared for $FN3_{1D}$ that movement from the local optima to the global optimum was a difficult task that could only be achieved with the use of high mutation rates. In contrast, for $FN4_{1D}$, low mutation rates were able to produce chromosomes lying deep enough in the global optimum to survive into the next generation. Thus, this movement was not as difficult as for $FN3_{1D}$. However, an additional interesting observation from $FN4_{1D}$, as shown in Figures 5a, 5b and 5c, was that chromosomes appeared to move with greater ease again from the outer-most local optima to the local optima adjacent to the global optimum. This was in contrast to chromosomes moving from the local optima adjacent to the global optimum to the global optimum itself.

We hypothesized that the difficulty of jumping between local optima was related to the number of *coincident* mutations required to make that transition. The probability of a successful jump would therefore reduce with the product of the probabilities of each individual mutation required. To test this hypothesis we examined the Hamming Distances between local optima in $FN3_{1D}$ and $FN4_{1D}$.

3.5 Hamming Distances for $FN3_{1D}$ and $FN4_{1D}$

For $FN3_{1D}$, as illustrated in Figure 6a, the Hamming Distance between the local optima and the global optimum was 12. In contrast for $FN4_{1D}$ the Hamming Distance between the local optima adjacent to the global optimum and

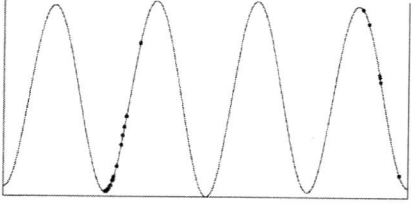

Fig. 5a. $FN4_{1D}$: Chromosome population prior to applying mutation

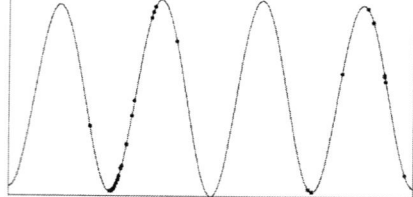

Fig. 5b. $FN4_{1D}$: Chromosome population after applying a low mutation rate

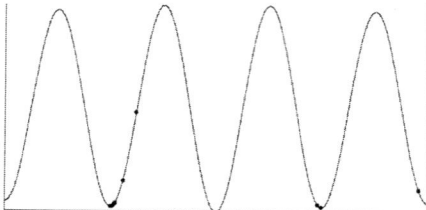

Fig. 5c. $FN4_{1D}$: Chromosome population after selection

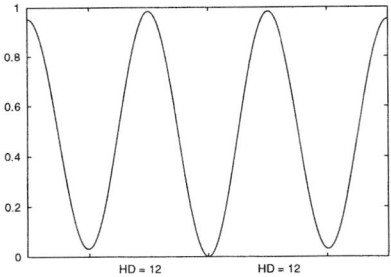
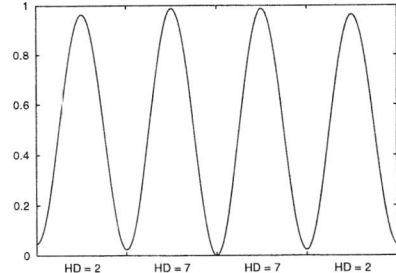

Fig. 6a. $FN3_{1D}$ (HD=Hamming Distance)

Fig. 6b. $FN4_{1D}$ (HD=Hamming Distance)

the global optimum was only 7. Since mutation probabilities are multiplicative (for example, 0.1^7 versus 0.1^{12}), there existed a much lower probability of chromosomes moving into a sufficiently fit part of the global optimum to survive selection for $FN3_{1D}$ as opposed to $FN4_{1D}$. This explained why higher mutation rates were necessary for $FN3_{1D}$. Furthermore, for $FN4_{1D}$ the Hamming Distance between the outer-most local optima and the local optima adjacent to the global optimum was only 2. Thus, it proved easy for chromosomes to move into the local optima adjacent to the global optimum. Hence, the fact that $FN4_{1D}$ was more modal than $FN3_{1D}$ was of little consequence since the Hamming Distance between these local optima was comparatively small. These data were a direct result of the relationship between the encoding and the solution space.

4 Discussion

In this paper we have showed that a lower modality problem can be significantly more difficult to solve with a Gray encoding than a higher modality problem. Specifically, dot diagram analysis and ANOVA suggested that $FN3$ was a more difficult problem than $FN4$. In addition, we have demonstrated that the ability of chromosomes to move between local optima and avoid culling in the two functions was much more difficult in $FN3_{1D}$ than for $FN4_{1D}$ because of the significantly higher Hamming Distances involved. These Hamming Distances are a direct result of the encoding.

In conclusion, we have statistically demonstrated that there is a real relationship between the difficulty of a problem and the choice of encoding. We have also illustrated the mechanism by which this occurs in relation to the different Hamming Distances occurring at particular regions of the solution space.

References

1. Rothlauf, F.: Representations for Genetic and Evolutionary Algorithms. Studies in Fuzziness and Soft Computing. 1st edition. 2nd printing 2003 edn. Volume 104. Heidelberg: Springer (2002)

2. Davis, L., ed.: Handbook of genetic algorithms. Van Nostrand Reinhold, 115 Fifth Avenue, New York, New York 10003, USA (1991)
3. Czarn, A., MacNish, C., Vijayan, K., Turlach, B., Gupta, R.: Statistical exploratory analysis of genetic algorithms. IEEE Transactions on Evolutionary Computation **8** (2004) 405–421
4. Czarn, A., MacNish, C., Vijayan, K., Turlach, B.: Statistical exploratory analysis of genetic algorithms: The importance of interaction. In: Proc. 2004 Congress on Evolutionary Computation (CEC 2004), IEEE Press (2004) 2288–2295
5. Czarn, A., MacNish, C., Vijayan, K., Turlach, B.: Statistical exploratory analysis of genetic algorithms: The influence of gray codes upon the difficulty of a problem (extended version). Technical Report UWA-CSSE-04-004, The University of Western Australia, Crawley, Western Australia, 6009 (2004)
6. Montgomery, D.C.: Design and analysis of experiments. John Wiley and Sons, Inc, New York, New York, USA (1976)
7. Salomon, R.: Re-evaluating genetic algorithm performance under coordinate rotation of benchmark functions: a survey of some theoretical and practical aspects of genetic algorithms. BioSystems **39** (1996) 263–278

The Semipublic Encryption for Visual Cryptography Using Q'tron Neural Networks

Tai-Wen Yue and Suchen Chiang

Computer Science and Engineering, Tatung University, Taiwan
twyu@mail.cse.ttu.edu.tw, suchen@ms27.url.com.tw

Abstract. The paper proposes the *semipublic encrypting scheme* for visual cryptography using the *Q'tron neural-network (Q'tron NN)* model. This encrypting scheme hides only the true secret from the public. That is, the pictorial meaning appearing in a *public share* describes the public information in a document while leaving its confidential part undisclosed. A piece of confidential information is retrievable if and only if a right *user share* is available. The method to construct the Q'tron NN to fulfill the aforementioned scheme will be investigated. An application that uses the scheme for *key distribution* in a public area will be demonstrated.

1 Introduction

This paper proposes the so-called *semipublic encrypting scheme* for visual cryptography [1,3]. This scheme includes one *public share* and one or more *user shares*. The public share displays the public information of a document only. Hence, it doesn't take a risk to divulge any confidential information even being announced in a public area. However, the right information for the right users can be retrieved if and only if a right *user share* is available.

Fig. 1, for example, shows such an application that uses the semipublic encrypting scheme for key distribution. Corresponding the figure, the origin document describes as: *there are four members who use our lab database; they are Janet, Jenny, Hsunli, and Bill; their key values to access the database are 'AB', 'CD', 'XY', and 'UV', respectively.* The topmost image in the figure is the public share, which symbolically represents the database resource in our lab. It can be published in a public area, e.g., a web page. The four images in the middle are user shares for the four lab members. The owner of each user share can be identified by viewing the context displayed in the share. Respectively stacking the public share with each user share, the key value belonging to a particular user account will appear. This key value, for example, can be used as a key for secure communication.

This paper proposes a neural-network (NN) approach to fulfill visual cryptography. The NN model to conduct the research is the Q'tron NN model [4]. Using the approach, an access scheme can be described completely using a set of gray images, e.g., see Fig. 1, and only this set of images is needed to be fed into the NN to produce the desirable shares. The shares, as a result, will be

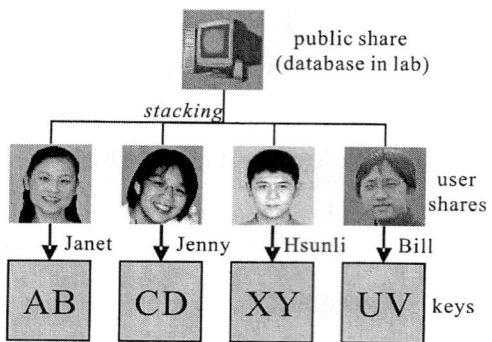

Fig. 1. The semipublic encryption for key distribution

halftone images that mimic the gray share-images, and stacking each subset of shares described in the access scheme will produce a halftone image that mimics the corresponding gray target-image. Relevant researches can be found in [5, 6].

This paper is organized as follows: Section 2 gives a brief review for the Q'tron NN model. Section 3 describes the strategy to build a Q'tron NN for visual cryptography. Section 4 describes the method to operate the Q'tron NN in a question-answering mode for semipublic encryption. Section 5 demonstrates the experimental results. Finally, we draw some conclusions in Section 6. More information, including Java applet and source code, related to this research can be found on http://www.cse.ttu.edu.tw/twyu/vc.

2 The Q'tron NN Model

In this model of NN, the basic processing elements are called Q'tron's (quantum neurons) [4]. The Q'tron NN model is a type of energy-driven NN, which is substantially extended from the Hopfield model [2]. Therefore, the NN model solves problems by minimizing energy. In the following, the noise-free version of the model will be introduced.

The Q'trons

Let μ_i denote the ith Q'tron in a Q'tron NN with n Q'trons. The input stimulus $\mathcal{H}_i$ of μ_i is

$$\mathcal{H}_i = \sum_{j=1}^{n} T_{ij}(a_j Q_j) + I_i, \tag{1}$$

where a_i is the active weight of μ_i, $Q_i \in \{0, 1, ..., q_i - 1\}$ ($q_i \geq 2$) is output-level of μ_i, T_{ij} is the connecting strength between μ_i and μ_j, and I_i is the external stimulus fed into μ_i. Furthermore, each pair of Q'trons in the NN is symmetrically connected, i.e., $T_{ij} = T_{ji}$, and T_{ii} is usually nonzero. At each time step only one Q'tron is selected for level transition subject to the following rule:

$$Q_i(t+1) = Q_i(t) + \Delta Q_i(t), \tag{2}$$

with

$$\Delta Q_i(t) = \begin{cases} +1 & \mathcal{H}_i(t) > \frac{1}{2}|T_{ii}a_i| \text{ and } Q_i(t) < q_i - 1; \\ -1 & \mathcal{H}_i(t) < -\frac{1}{2}|T_{ii}a_i| \text{ and } Q_i(t) > 0; \\ 0 & \text{otherwise,} \end{cases} \tag{3}$$

Operating Modes of Q'trons

Each Q'tron can either be operated in *clamp* mode, i.e., its output-level is clamped fixed at a particular level, or in *free* mode, i.e., its output-level is allowed to be updated according to the level transition rule specified in Eq. (2). Furthermore, we categorize Q'trons in an NN into two types: *interface Q'trons* and *hidden Q'trons*. The former provides an environment to interface with the external world, whereas the latter is functionally necessary to solve certain problems. Hidden Q'trons usually run in free-mode only. However, the NN discussed in the paper doesn't need any hidden Q'tron. Some examples that require hidden Q'trons were given in [5]. Interface Q'trons operated in clamp-mode are used to feed the available or affirmative information into the NN. The other free-mode interface Q'trons, on the other hand, are used to perform association to 'fill in' the missing or uncertain information.

System Energy — Stability

The system energy $\mathcal{E}$ embedded in a Q'tron NN is defined as:

$$\mathcal{E} = -\frac{1}{2}\sum_{i=1}^{n}\sum_{j=1}^{n}(a_iQ_i)T_{ij}(a_jQ_j) - \sum_{i=1}^{n}I_i(a_iQ_i) + K; \tag{4}$$

where n is total number of Q'trons in the NN, and K can be any suitable constant. It was shown that the energy $\mathcal{E}$ defined above will monotonically decrease with time. Therefore, if a problem can be mapped into one which minimizes the function $\mathcal{E}$ given in the above form, then the corresponding NN will autonomously solve the problem after $\mathcal{E}$ reaches a global/local minimum.

3 The Q'tron NN for Visual Cryptography — (2, 2)

In this section, we will discuss the method to build a Q'tron NN to fulfill the $(2,2)$, read as two-out-of-two access scheme, of visual cryptography.

The Q'tron NN Structure

In $(2,2)$, three informative images are involved. One is for target T, and two are for shares $S1$ and $S2$. In this approach, these images are described using gray images, denoted as GT, $GS1$, and $GS2$, respectively.

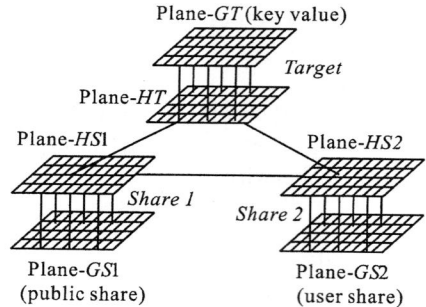

Fig. 2. The Q'tron NN architecture for (2, 2)

The Q'tron NN for $(2,2)$ to be constructed has the structure of Fig. 2. It contains three pairs of Q'tron planes, i.e., (Plane-Gx, Plane-Hx), $x \in \{T, S1, S2\}$. Plane-Gx and Plane-Hx will be used to represent the gray and halftone images of x, respectively.

The Encrypting Scenario

Clamping images GT, $GS1$, and $GS2$ onto Plane-GT, $GS1$, and $GS2$, respectively, the NN, as a result, will produce three binary images HT, $HS1$, and $HS2$ in Plane-HT, $HS1$, and $HS2$, respectively, when it settles down. Printing $HS1$ and $HS2$, which are the halftone version of $GS1$ and $GS2$, respectively, on transparencies and stacking them together will produce image HT, which is the halftone version of GT.

Image Representation

We'll use an integer value between 0 and 255 to represent the pixel value in a gray image. Unconventionally, however, we will use 0 to represent the pure white color, and 255 to represent the darkest black color. Similarly, we will use 0 and 1 to represent an white (uninked) pixel and black (inked) pixel in a halftone image, respectively.

Let μ_{ij}^{Gx} and μ_{kl}^{Hx}, where $x \in \{T, S1, S2\}$, represent the ij^{th} Q'tron in Plane-Gx and the kl^{th} Q'tron in Plane-Hx, respectively. It is natural to choose $a_{ij}^{Gx} = 1 = a^G$, $q_{ij}^{Gx} = 256 = q^G$, i.e., $Q_{ij}^{Gx} \in \{0, \ldots, 255\}$, $a_{kl}^{Hx} = 255 = a^H$ and $q_{kl}^{Hx} = 2 = q^H$, i.e., $Q_{kl}^{Hx} \in \{0, 1\}$. With these, $(a^G Q_{ij}^{Gx})$ and $(a^G Q_{ij}^{Gx})$ then represent the effective 'darknesses' for the ij^{th} pixel in image Gx and kl^{th} pixel in image Hx, respectively.

The Encryption Rules

Two rules must be satisfied to make the Q'tron NN workable in the aforementioned scenario. They are

1. *Halftone Rule:* Image in Plane-Hx is the halftone version of image in Plane-Gx for all $x \in \{T, S1, S2\}$. This implies that the pictorial meaning described in Gx is preserved in Hx.
2. *Stacking Rule:* Stacking $HS1$ and $HS2$, we hope that the resulted image equals to HT. This requires that each pixel value in Plane-HT is black if and only if none of the corresponding pixels in Plane-$HS1$ and $HS2$ is black. For clarity, Fig. 3 shows the costs for all possible stacking patterns. The cost function is defined by

$$\mathcal{C}(s_1, s_2, t) = [1.5t - (s_1 + s_2)]^2, \tag{5}$$

where $s_1, s_2 \in \{0,1\}$ represent the pixel values of two share pixels, and $t \in \{0,1\}$ represents their stacking result. One can see from the figure that if a stacking pattern is valid the corresponding cost is relatively low.

The Energy Function

Assume that the image size for the involved images in the scheme is $M \times N$. Then, the above two rules can be fulfilled by minimizing the following energy function:

$$\mathcal{E}_{(2,2)} = \mathcal{E}_{htone} + \lambda \mathcal{E}_{stack}, \tag{6}$$

$$\mathcal{E}_{htone} = \frac{1}{2} \sum_{x \in P} \sum_{\substack{1 \le i \le M \\ 1 \le j \le N}} \left\{ \sum_{(k,l) \in N^r_{ij}} a^{Hx} Q^{Hx}_{kl} - \sum_{(k,l) \in N^r_{ij}} a^{Gx} Q^{Gx}_{kl} \right\}^2, \tag{7}$$

$$\mathcal{E}_{stack} = \frac{1}{2} \sum_{i=1}^{M} \sum_{j=1}^{N} \{1.5(a^H Q^{HT}_{ij}) - (a^H Q^{HS1}_{ij} + a^H Q^{HS2}_{ij})\}^2, \tag{8}$$

where $P = \{T, S1, S2\}$, N^r_{ij} denotes the r-neighborhood of ij^{th} Q'tron in a Q'tron plane, defined by

$$N^r_{ij} = \{(k,l) : 1 \le k \le M, 1 \le l \le N, |i - k| \le r \text{ and } |j - l| \le r\}, \tag{9}$$

and $\lambda > 0$. In our experiment, we set $r = 1$ and $\lambda = 10$. The terms in the brace of Eq. (7) represent the squared-error of total darkness between a pair of small

s_1	s_2	t	C	s_1	s_2	t	C
0 □	0 □	0 □	0	0 □	0 □	1 ■	2.25
0 □	1 ■	1 ■	0.25	0 □	1 ■	0 □	1
1 ■	0 □	1 ■	0.25	1 ■	0 □	0 □	1
1 ■	1 ■	1 ■	0.25	1 ■	1 ■	0 □	4

Fig. 3. Cost function (C) for share pixels (s_1 and s_2), and their target (t)

rectangular areas located at the same place in images Gx and Hx. Therefore, the minimization the total sum of such squared errors, indeed, fulfills the goal of halftoning. Referring to Fig. 3, one than see that the minimization of $\mathcal{E}_{stack}$ is to prevent from stacking-rule violation.

The Q'tron NN Construction

The other parameters, including the connection strength between each pair of Q'trons and external stimulus fed into each Q'tron, of the Q'tron NN can be found by mapping Eq. (6) to Eq. (8) to the energy function for the two-dimensional Q'tron planes shown in Fig. 2, namely

$$\mathcal{E} = -\frac{1}{2} \sum_{x \in P} \sum_{i=1}^{M} \sum_{j=1}^{N} \sum_{y \in P} \sum_{k=1}^{M} \sum_{l=1}^{N} (a^x Q_{ij}^x) T_{ij,kl}^{xy} (a^y Q_{kl}^y) - \sum_{x \in P} \sum_{i=1}^{M} \sum_{j=1}^{N} I_{ij}^x (a^x Q_{ij}^x),$$

where $P = \{GT, HT, GS1, HS1, GS2, HS2\}$.

4 Applications

In the following subsections, we are going to describe the possible applications for the NN we constructed. We assume that the histograms for the involved graytone images in these applications have been properly reallocated [6]. We also assume that all free-mode Q'trons are randomly initialized before the NN starts running.

Application — (2, 2)

For $(2, 2)$, the input to the Q'tron NN is a set of graytone images, say GT, $GS1$ and $GS2$, which are clamped onto Plane-GT, Plane-$GS1$ and Plane-$GS2$, respectively. Therefore, all Q'trons in Plane-GT, Plane-$GS1$ and Plane-$GS2$ are operated in clamp-mode, and all of the other Q'trons are in free-mode. As the NN settles down, binary images HT, $HS1$ and $HS2$ produced in Plane-HT, Plane-$HS1$ and Plane-$HS2$ will be the halftone versions of GT, $GS1$ and $GS2$, respectively, and the superposition of $HS1$ and $HS2$ will be HT. This, hence, fulfill $(2, 2)$.

Application — Semipublic Encryption

Referring to Fig. 1, the access scheme for semipublic encryption includes three sets of graytone images. They are

1. $P^G = \{GP\}$ — describes the public share;
2. $U^G = \{GU_1, \ldots, GU_n\}$ — describes n user shares; and
3. $K^G = \{GK_1, \ldots, GK_n\}$ — describes n key values.

In definition, we require that stacking GP with each user share, say, GU_i produces GK_i. Applying the procedure described shortly, we will obtain the following halftone images. They are

4. $P^H = \{HP\}$ — the halftone version of P^G; it can be announced in public;
5. $U^H = \{HU_1, \ldots, HU_n\}$ — the halftone version of U^G. HU_i is held by the ith user; and
6. $K^H = \{HK_1, \ldots, HK_n\}$ — the halftone version of K^G; any image, say, HK_i in this set is invisible unless a right user share, say, HU_i is available to stack with public share HP.

To make life easier, we always assign Plane-$GS1$ and Plane-$HS1$ for public share, and Plane-$GS2$ and Plane-$HS2$ for user share. One convenient method to generate the public share, i.e., HP is described as follows. By letting $GT = GK_1$, $GS1 = GP$ and $GS2 = GU_1$, and applying the operation for $(2,2)$ described in the last subsection, two shares will be produced in Plane-$HS1$ and Plane-$HS2$ after the NN settles down. The administrator can then keep the image appearing in Plane-$HS1$ as the public share HP. Clearly, HP is visually similar to GP.

We now describe the most efficient method to generate user shares for each user by taking advantage of available knowledge. It is affirmative that overlapping a black pixel in one share with a pixel (black or white) in another share can only produce a black pixel. Therefore, stacking HP with any shares, the pixels at the positions where HP's pixels are black must be also black. With this knowledge, we can use the following method to produce user shares. Suppose that we now want to produce the ith user share. First, we copy GU_i and GK_i to Plane-$GS2$ and Plane-GT, respectively, and copy HP both to Plane-$HS1$ and Plane-HT. All Q'trons in Plane-$HS1$, Plane-$GS2$ and Plane-GT are set to clamp-mode. Additionally, the Q'trons in Plane-HT whose output-levels now are one, i.e., black pixels, are also set to clamp-mode. All of other Q'trons are set to free-mode. With such an initial setting, we can then get the desired user share, i.e., HU_i, from Plane-$HS2$ when the NN settles down. Note that Plane-$GS2$ plays no role in this application.

5 Experimental Results

An experimental result for semipublic encryption is shown in Fig. 4. Fig. 4(a) is the public share. Fig. 4(b) to (e) are user shares. Clearly, the image displayed in the user shares can be used for authentication purpose. Fig. 4(f) to (i) shows the superposed image obtained by staking the public share with different user shares.

6 Conclusions

In the paper, we propose a novel approach for visual cryptography using the Q'tron NN model, which is a generalized version of the Hopfield NN model [2].

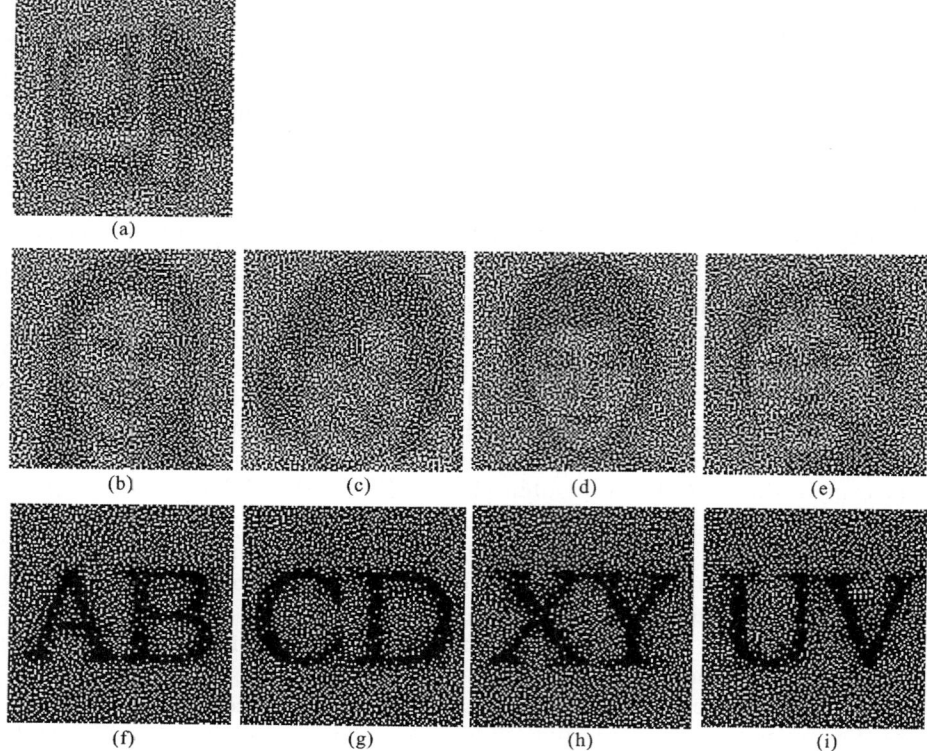

Fig. 4. An experimental result of semipublic encryption scheme, see text

Using approach, the access schemes of visual cryptography are described using gray images. This is completely different from the traditional approaches, which deal with binary images directly. Two main rules, namely, halftone rule and stacking rule, were adopted to deal with the feasibility of solutions. Each of them was reformulated as an energy term of a Q'tron NN. Initially, the Q'tron NN was constructed to fulfill the (2, 2) access scheme of visual cryptography. Effortlessly, the NN can also be used for another application by simply switching the operation modes of its Q'trons. We demonstrated such an *auto-association* capability, or called *auto-reversibility*, by applying the NN for semipublic encryption.

Acknowledgement

Financial support of this research by Tatung University, Taipei, Taiwan, under the grant B9208-I04-027 is gratefully acknowledged.

References

1. G. Ateniese, C. Blundo, A. D. Santis, D. R. Stinson, "Visual Cryptography for General Access Structures", *Information and Computation,* vol. 129, no. 2, pp. 86-106, 1996.
2. J. J. Hopfield, "Neural Networks and Physical Systems with Emergent Collective Computational Abilities," *Proc. Nat. Acad. Sci. USA,* vol. 79, pp. 2554-2558, Apr. 1982.
3. M. Naor and A. Shamir, "Visual Cryptography," *Advances Cryptology-Eurocrypt '94, Lecture Notes in Computer Science,* vol. 950, pp. 1-12, 1995.
4. T. W. Yue, *A Goal-Driven Neural Network Approach for Combinatorial Optimization and Invariant Pattern Recognition,* Phd's Thesis, Department of Computer Engineering, National Taiwan University, Taiwan, 1992.
5. T. W. Yue and S. C. Chiang, "The General Neural-Network Paradigm for Visual Cryptograph," *IWANN 2001, LNCS 2048,* pp. 196-206, 2001.
6. T. W. Yue and S. C. Chiang, "A Neural-Network Approach for Visual Cryptography and Authorization," *International Journal of Neural Systems,* vol. 14, no. 3, pp. 175-187, 2004.

The T-Detectors Maturation Algorithm Based on Genetic Algorithm

Dongyong Yang and Jungan Chen

Zhejiang University of Technology, No.6 District, Zhaohui Xincun,
Hangzhou, Zhejiang, 310032, China
yangdy@ieee.org,friendcen21@hotmail.com

Abstract. Negative selection algorithm is used to generate detector for change detection, anomaly detection. But it can not be adapted to the change of self data because the match threshold must be set at first. In this paper, inspired from T-cells maturation, a novel algorithm composed of positive and negative selection is proposed to generate T-detector. Genetic algorithm is used to evolve the detectors with lower match threshold. The proposed algorithm is tested by simulation experiment for anomaly detection and compared with negative selection algorithm. The results show that the proposed algorithm is more effective than negative selection algorithm. Match threshold is self-adapted and False Positive is controlled by parameter S.

1 Introduction

As a new area of soft computing, artificial immune system constructs the algorithms based on negative selection, immune network model, or clonal selection [1][2][3]. In negative selection of T-cells maturation, T-cells which recognize self cells are destroyed before leaving the thymus. Similarly, Negative Selection Algorithm (NSA) generates detectors randomly and eliminates detectors that detect self [1].

NSA is applied to change detection [1], detection for time series data [5]. Several extensions are made and applied to network intrusion detection [4]. Real-valued NSA is combined with classification system and used to anomaly detection [6].

Match rule is one of the most important components in NSA. There are several major types [4][7]. But no matter what kind of match rule, the match threshold (r) is needed and must be set at first, So NSA can not be adapted to the change of self data.

T-cells maturation goes through two processes, positive and negative selection [7]. Positive selection requires T-cells to recognize self cells with lower affinity, while T-cells must not recognize self cells with higher affinity in negative selection. Similarly, the minimal distance (*selfmin*) between detector and selves must be bigger than 0 and the maximal distance (*selfmax*) must be smaller than r. So the value of r is equal to *selfmax*+1, i.e., r can be adapted to the change of self data because *selfmax* is evaluated by the self data. When nonself's distance with detector is equal to or bigger than r (*selfmax*+1), nonself is detected. Based on this idea inspired from T-cells maturation, a novel algorithm which r is self-adapted is proposed to generate T-detector. Except the self-adapted character, a parameter (S) is introduced to control the number of selves in the maturation process. The bigger S means more selves to evaluate *selfmax*; fewer selves's distance with detectors is bigger than *selfmax*, so fewer selves are detected. Because False Positive (FP) is equal to (number of selves detected by detectors / number of total selves), FP is controlled by S.

2 The Novel T-Detectors Maturation Algorithm

2.1 The Model of Algorithm

In this work, T-detectors Maturation Algorithm based on Genetic Algorithm (TMA-GA) is proposed. Genetic algorithm is used to evolve detectors with lower *selfmax*.

```
1:  initialize the detector population

2:  For gen=0 to maxgen

3:         children =Reproduction (only mutation)

4:         DETECTORS ={ DETECTORS ∪ children }

5:         Fitness scoring(DETECTORS)

6:         Rank DETECTORS with fitness from big to small

7:         DETECTORS = Select(PSize) from DETECTORS

8:  End
```

Fig. 1. Algorithm of TMA-GA

The model of TMA-GA is shown in Fig.1. The variable *maxgen* is defined as maximal generation; *gen* is as current generation; *DETECTORS* is as detector population; *PSize* is as size of detector population. Only the mutation operator is applied to reproduction of detectors. Based on the affinity maturation process [3], the number of bits to be mutated is $(l- selfmin) / 2$, where l is the number of bits in detector. The selector selects the detectors with higher fitness from parents and children. The parents are selected when the fitness of parents and children is the same. Fitness scoring is shown in Fig.2. Hamming distance match rule is used [7]. S is defined as the rate to select self samples from self set; *SELF* is as self samples; $H[ij]$ is as the distance between *DETECTORS[i]* and *SELF[j]*; *selfmax[i]* is as the maximal distance between *DETECTORS[i]* and SELF; *selfmin[i]* is as the minimal distance; *Fitness[i]* is as the fitness of *DETECTORS[i]*. Steps 8 simulate the *negative selection* which requires r to be *selfmax*+1. Steps 9 simulate the *positive selection* which requires *selfmin* to be bigger than 0.

Fitness Scoring (*DETECTORS*)

```
1: Select S*(size of self set) SELF from self set
2: For each detector DETECTORS[i]
3:      For each self sample SELF[j]
4:           Compute H[ij] (the number of the same bits)
5:           If  H[ij]>selfmax[i] then selfmax[i]=H[ij]
6:           If  H[ij]<selfmin[i] then selfmin[i]=H[ij]
7:      End
8:      r of DETECTORS[i] = selfmax[i]+1
9:      If selfmin[i]=0 then Fitness[i]=0
        Else Fitness[i]=1-selfmax[i]
10:End
```

Fig. 2. Fitness Scoring of TMA-GA

2.2 Experiments for Anomaly Detection

The objective of the experiment is to:

1. Compare True Positive (TP) of TMA-GA with TP of NSA.
2. Evaluate the value of self-adapted *r* and the range between *selfmax* and *selfmin*.

Table 1. The self data set to test is shown ('*' is either 0 or 1)

Self Pattern	Self Data 1 The number of selves	Self Data 2 The number of selves
1111************	2	4
****1111********	2	4
********1111****	2	4
************1111	2	4

In this experiment, binary pattern strings is used to simulate the real selves which always have common characters. Table1 shows the self data set. TMA-GA runs for ten times. The maximal generation is 2000. Self set is Self data 1 when the program starts, and self data 2 is added to self set at 1001th generation. The number of detectors is 5. S is equal to 1. To compare TMA-GA with NSA, NSA is tested on both Self Data 1 and the union of Self Data 1, 2. It runs for 100 times with different r.

Table 2. The average True Positive of NSA running 100 times with different r

	Self Data 1 as Self				Self Data 1,2 as Self			
R	7	8	9	10	8	9	10	11
TP	0	0.868	0.841	0.692	0	0.622	0.621	0.405

Table 3. The average True Positive of TMA-GA when s=1

	Self Data 1 as Self(1000th)	Self Data 1,2 as Self(2000th)
TP	0.859	0.636

2.3 Analysis

1. The Results of TP

Table 2 shows that TP is the best when r is equal to 8 and 9 in different self set. So 8 and 9 is taken as the optimized value of r. In this experiment, self data 1 is self set before the 1000th generation; self data 1, 2 is self set after that. So TP of TMA-GA at 1000th and 2000th generation is taken as the best TP in different self set. Table 3 results show that neither of TMA-GA and NSA is better than other.

It is possible that genetic algorithm leads detectors to be more similar. So NSA is a little better than TMA-GA when self data 1 is defined as self. The results are coincided with that "similar antibodies have a small hamming distance between them and this corresponds to an overlapping coverage of antigen space [8]".

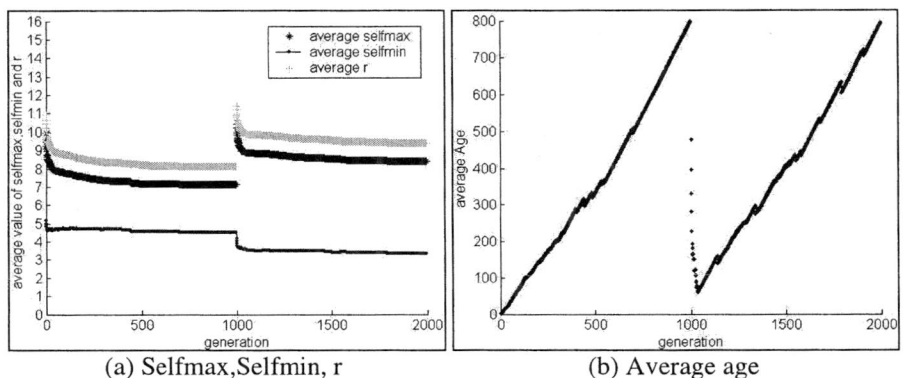

(a) Selfmax,Selfmin, r   (b) Average age

Fig. 3. Results on the self-adapted character of TMA-GA

2. The Value of Self-Adapted r and the Range Between Selfmax, Selfmin

In Fig.3 (a), the distance between detector and selves is between *selfmax* and *selfmin* because of the effect of T-cells maturation. The value of *r* converges to the optimized value 8, 9 because genetic algorithm evolves detectors with lower *r*. The results indicate that r is self-adapted because the value *(selfmax+1)* is adapted to the change of self set. Fig.3 (b) shows that detectors are adapted to the change of self set after 1000th generation.

3 Improvement of TMA-GA

The results of the experiment above show that *r* is self-adapted. But genetic algorithm sometimes leads detectors to be more similar. To avoid the similarity of detectors, an improved algorithm (I-TMA-GA) is proposed. It is known that the difference between two strings is evaluated by computing the hamming distance. So it is used to evaluate the difference of detectors (called *otherness evaluation*). The otherness evaluation shown in Fig.4 is appended after the fitness scoring.

```
1: For each detector DETECTORS[i]
2:     sum =0
3:     For each detector DETECTORS[j], j is not equal to i
4:         Compute H[ij] (the number of the same bits)
5:         sum =sum+ H[ij]
6:     End
7:     Fitness[i]= Fitness[i] +1/sum
8: End
```

Fig. 4. Otherness Evaluation

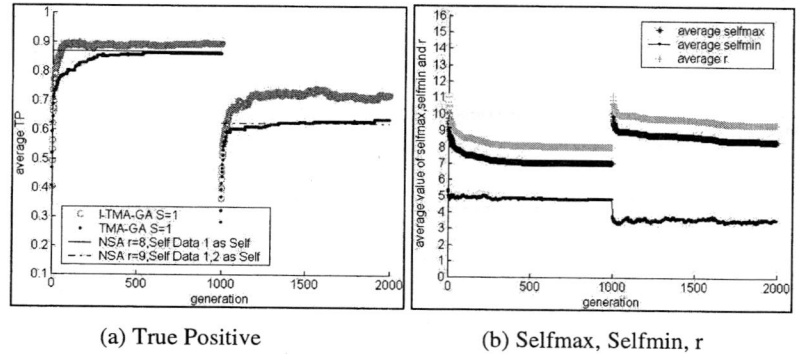

(a) True Positive (b) Selfmax, Selfmin, r

Fig. 5. Reuslts on the effect of otherness evaluation in I-TMA-GA

Experiment to test the effect of otherness evaluation is done and the data set is the same as the experiment above. In Fig.5 (a), the results show that TP of I-TMA-GA is the best whenever generation is before or after the 1000th generation. r is still self-adapted in Fig.5 (b). So the results indicate that the *otherness evaluation* is effective.

4 Conclusion

In summary, the proposed algorithm TMA-GA is effective with following characters:

1. S can control the FP. The higher S causes lower FP but less effective because the number of selves to evaluate *selfmax* is more.
2. The match threshold r converges to the optimized value through genetic algorithm. TMA-GA and NSA is almost the same when both r is equal to the optimized value.
3. The match threshold is self-adapted. So it is possible to be applied to dynamic environment where the self data changes with time.

In this work, the holes problem [4] is not considered about. But the match threshold is self-adapted, so it is possible to solve holes problem according to "the different value of r for each detector can fill the potential holes [9]". Clonal Selection Algorithm can maintain diversity in population [10]. But TMA-GA has no such character and is resorted to the *otherness evaluation* to work better. Of course, it is possible to use the fitness sharing to maintain the diversity in population. But a parameter is required to set and the self-adapted ability of TMA-GA will be less effective.

References

[1] Forrest, S., Perelson, A. S., Allen, L., and Cherukuri, R., Self-nonself Discrimination in a Computer, Proceedings of the 1994 IEEE Symposium on Research in Security and Privacy, Los Alamos, CA: IEEE Computer Society Press, 1994. Available at http://www.cs.unm.edu/~forrest/papers.html

[2] de Castro, L. N. and Von Zuben, F. J., aiNet: An Artificial Immune Network for Data Analysis, Book Chapter in Data Mining: A Heuristic Approach, H. A. Abbass, R. A. Sarker, and C. S. Newton (eds.), Idea Group Publishing, USA, Chapter XII, pp. 231-259, 2001

[3] de Castro, L. N. and Von Zuben, F. J., Learning and Optimization Using the Clonal Selection Principle, IEEE Transactions on Evolutionary Computation, Special Issue on Artificial Immune Systems, 6(3), pp. 239-251. 2002

[4] Hofmeyr, S. A., An Immunological Model of Distributed Detection and its Application to Computer Security, PhD Dissertation, University of New Mexico, 1999.

[5] Dasgupta, D., Forrest, S.,Novelty Detection in Time Series Data using Ideas from Immunology. In Proceedings of The International Conference on Intelligent Systems, 1999.

[6] González, F., and Dagupta, D., Anomaly detection using real-valued negative selection.Genetic Programming and Evolvable Machines, 4(4), pp.383-403, 2003

[7] Gonzalez, F., A Study of Artificial Immune Systems applied to Anomaly Detection, PhD Dissertation, The University of Memphis, May 2003.

[8] Hightower, R., Forrest, S., and Perelson, A. S., The Evolution of Emergent Organization in Immune System Gene Libraries, Proceeding of the Sixth International Conference. on Genetic Algorithms, L.J. Eshelman (Ed.), Morgan Kaufmann, San Francisco, CA, pp.344-350, 1995.
[9] D'haeseleer, P., Forrest, S., and Helman, P., A Distributed Approach to Anomaly Detection,1997, Available http://www.cs.unm.edu/~forrest/isa_papers.htm
[10] Smith, R. E., Forrest, S., and Perelson, A. S., Searching for diverse, cooperative populations with genetic algorithms, Evolutionary Computation, Vol. 1, No. 2, pp. 127-149 ,1993

Author Index

Abbass, Hussein A.   39, 873
Abhishek   1135
Ahn, KyoungKwan   171
Aikou, Kazuhide   1030
Albrecht, David   140
Allison, Lloyd   203
Ancenay, Sebastien   1181
Astigarraga, A.   86, 742
Auer, Jeanette   414

Bae, Keunsung   1154
Baik, Ran   132, 943
Baik, Sung Wook   132, 943
Baker, Gavin   74
Barnes, Nick   74
Basu, Anupam   1135
Beadle, Patch   949, 1239
Berger, Helmut   998
Bezerra, Byron   1011
Bo, Qu   1226
Boddhireddy, Prashanth R.   778
Bouckaert, Remco R.   1089
Bourke, P.   961
Bourne, Owen   658
Brooks, Michael J.   160, 180
Brzostowski, Jakub   694
Buchanan, Bruce   450

Calvo, Rafael   438
Cao, Longbing   917, 985
Castano, Rebecca   51
Chan, Samuel W.K.   574
Chang, C.S.   803
Chang, Jeong-Ho   1141
Chawla, Sanjay   296
Chen, Huowang   475
Chen, Jungan   1262
Chen, Shi-Fu   1200
Chen, Yuexin   475
Chen, Zhao-Qian   1200
Cheung, Zhalaing   1069
Chiang, Suchen   1253
Chien, Steve   51
Cho, Sung-Bae   1, 120, 1147

Cho, Woo-Chul   344
Choi, Incheol   1160
Chu, Tianguang   766
Cichy, Benjamin   51
Ciesielski, Vic   898
Clarke, Douglas   140
Clay, Chris   718
Colomb, Robert   979
Corbett, Dan   259
Cornforth, D.J.   961
Crescini, Vino Fernando   623
Cronin, Alex   886
Czarn, Andrew   1246

Dale, Robert   438
Davies, Ashley   51
Debenham, John   910
de Carvalho, Francisco A.T.   526, 1011
de Silva, Lavindra   1167
Dick, Anthony R.   160, 180
Dix, Trevor I.   203
Do, Quoc Vong   937
Dowe, David L.   1082
Du, Haifeng   840, 1219

Ebecken, Nelson F.F.   513
Edwards, Catherine   500
Estivill-Castro, Vladimir   284

Fan, Hongjian   1062
Fang, Liu   1226
Feng, Boqin   357
Ferreira, Valnir, Jr.   730
Foo, Norman   670
Foon, Neo Han   64, 192
Frank, Eibe   488, 538, 1017

Gao, Yang   930
Geiselbrechtinger, Franz   886
George, Sarah   587
George, Susan E.   425
GhasemZadeh, Mohammad   681
Goldberg, David   873
Gonçalves, Eduardo Corrêa   1076

Author Index

Gong, Maoguo 1219
Gopalan, Raj P. 391, 1036
Governatori, Guido 979
Gulbag, Ali 1206
Guo, Haipeng 307, 778
Guo, Songshan 636
Guo, Ying 26

Hall, Mark 538
Hall, Richard 414
Hawkins, Peter 706
Hengel, Anton van den 180
Hingston, Philip 1213
Hoffmann, Achim 1069
Holmes, Geoffrey 368, 488
Hong, Jin-Hyuk 120, 1147
Hope, Lucas R. 991
Hruschka, Eduardo R. 513
Hruschka, Estevam R., Jr. 513
Hsu, William H. 307, 778
Hu, Dewen 1024
Hu, Laizhao 1108
Hu, Xiaoping 1024
Huang, Joshua Zhexue 930

Iida, Shingo 272
Iorio, A. 961
Iorio, Antony W. 861
Ishikawa, Seiji 152
Itoh, Hidenori 272

Jain, Lakhmi 937
Je, Sung-Kwan 98
Jelinek, H.F. 961
Jeong, Chang-Sung 967
Jiang, Yi-Chuan 923
Jiao, Licheng 840, 1219
Jie, Li 319
Jie, Yang 1043
Jin, Andrew Teoh Beng 64, 192, 227
Jin, Weidong 1108
Jin, Xiaoyi 840
Jo, Geun-Sik 1095
Jung, Jason J. 1095
Jung, Sungyun 1154

Kang, Mi-young 562
Kang, Sanggil 754
Kanoh, Masayoshi 272
Kato, Shohei 272

Kazmierczak, Ed 74
Kechadi, Tahar 886
Kendall, Graham 1213
Kibriya, Ashraf M. 488
Kılıç, Kemal 1194
Kim, Cheol Ki 853
Kim, Gwang-Ha 98
Kim, Heung-Nam 1095
Kim, Hoirin 599
Kim, Hyun-Jun 1095
Kim, JongBae 171
Kim, Jong-Bok 1160
Kim, Kwang-Baek 98, 853
Kim, Sungtak 599
Kim, Sang-Woon 1115
Kim, Wonil 754
Kim, Yu-Seop 1141
Klotz, Volker 681
Ko, Hanseok 610
Kolluri, Venkateswarlu 450
Kong, Ying 636
Koprinska, Irena 296
Korb, Kevin B. 991, 1101
Kowalczyk, Pawel 550
Kowalczyk, Ryszard 694
Kukulenz, Dirk 462
Kumar, Dinesh K. 215
Kuwayama, Kiyotake 272
Kwan, C.M. 803
Kwon, Hyuk-chul 562

Lagoon, Vitaly 706
Landini, G. 961
Lazarescu, Mihai 718
Lazkano, E. 86, 742
Lee, Heungkyu 610
Lee, Jae-Young 1141
Lee, Justin 791
Lee, Keon Myung 14
Lee, Kevin 248
Lee, Kyungmi 284
Lee, Sang Ho 14
Lee, Vincent ChengSiong 1049
Ler, Daren 296
Li, Chunping 1174
Li, Jiaming 26
Li, Mi 368
Li, Xiang 898
Li, Xiaodong 861
Li, Yanrong 391

Li, Yuefeng   1128
Li, Zhancheng   949, 1239
Li, Zhoujun   475
Licheng, Jiao   319
Lim, Andrew   636
Lima Neto, Eufrasio de A.   526
Ling, David Ngo Chek   64, 192, 227
Liu, Li   985
Lozo, Peter   937
Ludermir, Teresa   1122
Luo, Chao   985
Luo, Dan   985

MacNish, Cara   1246
Mahidadia, Ashesh   1069
Maire, Frederic   646, 1181
Martínez-Otzeta, J.M.   86, 742
Mayer, Wendy   259
McCullagh, John   1233
McEnery, Orla   886
Meinel, Christoph   681
Mendes, Ilza Maria B.   1076
Merkl, Dieter   998
Metzler, Douglas   450
Meyer, Thomas   248
Min, Jun-Ki   1
Miyahara, Tetsuhiro   1030
Mutter, Stefan   538

Ni, Jiarui   917
Nicholson, Ann E.   1101
Niemann, Michael   550, 587

Oh, Jonghoon   967
Oh, Jung-Seok   1141
O'Leary, Stephen   74
Oommen, B. John   1115
Ou, Monica H.   718

Padgham, Lin   1167
Pang, Kwok Pan   402
Pang, Ying-Han   227
Park, Kang Ryoung   237
Peppas, Pavlos   670
Pfahringer, Bernhard   368, 488, 1017
Phan, Khanh Linh   1069
Phuan, Alex Tay Leng   828
Plastino, Alexandre   1076
Pollino, Carmel   1101
Poulton, Geoff   26

Powell, David R.   203
Provost, Foster   450
Prudêncio, Ricardo   1122

Qin, Zhenxing   380
Qing, Xu   332, 955, 1043

Rabideau, Gregg   51
Rahman, M. Masudur   152
Ramamohanarao, Kotagiri   1062
Rañó, I.   742
Raskutti, Bhavani   500
Rasmussen, Rune   646
Reutemann, Peter   1017
Richards, Debbie   344
Roberts, A.J.   961
Rong, Hongqiang   930
Rongsheng, Chen   1226

Sarker, Ruhul   39
Sastry, Kumara   873
Sattar, Abdul   658
Sharma, Arun   215
Shen, Chunhua   180
Shen, M.   949
Shen, Minfen   1239
Sherwood, Rob   51
Shi, Hong   766
Shoudai, Takayoshi   1030
Sierra, B.   86, 742
Sitte, Joaquin   791
Siyi, Ding   1043
Son, Jongmok   1154
Song, Insu   979
Spencer, Matthew   1233
Stuckey, Peter J.   706
Sucahyo, Yudho Giri   1036
Sun, Lisha   949
Suzuki, Yusuke   1030

Tan, Hiong Sen   425
Tan, Peter J.   1082
Tan, Songbo   1004
Tan, TingYean   1049
Tang, Yongchuan   816
Temurtas, Fevzullah   1206
Tenorio, Camilo P.   526
Thornton, John   730
Tilbrook, Marc   438
Ting, Kai Ming   402

Tischer, Peter   140
Tojo, Satoshi   1187
Tran, Daniel   51
Tun, Nwe Ni   1187
Türkşen, I.B.   1194
Turlach, Berwin   1246

Uncu, Özge   1194

Vijayan, Kaipillil   1246

Wang, Dianhui   109
Wang, Fan   636
Wang, Jiaqi   904
Wang, Kuanquan   109
Wang, Ling   1219
Wang, Long   766
Wang, Lu   109
Wang, Sun'an   840
Wang, Tao   475
Wang, Zheng-Qun   1200
Wang, Zhou   1062
Wang, Ziqiang   357
Wei, Kong   332
Wei, Ling   973
West, Geoff A.W.   718
Whitfort, Tim   1233
Woodberry, Owen   1101
Wu, Meiping   1024
Wu, Weiping   1049
Wu, Yuanxin   1024
Xiang, Yin   828

Xie, Jun-Yuan   1200
Xinbo, Gao   319
Xu, Lisheng   109
Xu, Weiling   949

Yan, Yuejin   475
Yang, Ang   39
Yang, Dongyong   1262
Yang, Jaehyung   1160
Yang, Jie   955
Yang, Jinyao   1239
Yang, Seung-Ryong   1
Yoon, Aesun   562
Yue, Tai-Wen   1253
Yue, Zhou   332
Yun, Eun-Kyung   120

Zhang, Chengqi   380, 917, 1055
Zhang, Gexiang   1108
Zhang, Lin   766
Zhang, Shichao   380, 1055
Zhang, Shi-Yong   923
Zhang, Weicun   766
Zhang, Wen-xiu   973
Zhang, Yan   623, 670
Zhang, Yuzheng   1239
Zhao, Yanchang   1055
Zheng, Jiacheng   816
Zheng, Zhonglong   955
Zhong, Ning   1128
Zhou, Zhi-Hua   930
Zhuang, Jian   840
Zukerman, Ingrid   550, 587

Lecture Notes in Artificial Intelligence (LNAI)

Vol. 3339: G.I. Webb, X. Yu (Eds.), AI 2004: Advances in Artificial Intelligence. XXII, 1272 pages. 2004.

Vol. 3315: C. Lemaître, C.A. Reyes, J.A. González (Eds.), Advances in Artificial Intelligence – IBERAMIA 2004. XX, 987 pages. 2004.

Vol. 3303: J.A. López, E. Benfenati, W. Dubitzky (Eds.), Knowledge Exploration in Life Science Informatics. X, 249 pages. 2004.

Vol. 3275: P. Perner (Ed.), Advances in Data Mining, Applications in Image Mining, Medicine and Biotechnology, Management and Environmental Control, and Telecommunications. VIII, 173 pages. 2004.

Vol. 3265: R.E. Frederking, K.B. Taylor (Eds.), Machine Translation: From Real Users to Research. XI, 392 pages. 2004.

Vol. 3264: G. Paliouras, Y. Sakakibara (Eds.), Grammatical Inference: Algorithms and Applications. XI, 291 pages. 2004.

Vol. 3259: J. Dix, J. Leite (Eds.), Computational Logic and Multi-Agent Systems. XII, 251 pages. 2004.

Vol. 3257: E. Motta, N.R. Shadbolt, A. Stutt, N. Gibbins (Eds.), Engineering Knowledge in the Age of the Semantic Web. XVII, 517 pages. 2004.

Vol. 3249: B. Buchberger, J.A. Campbell (Eds.), Artificial Intelligence and Symbolic Computation. X, 285 pages. 2004.

Vol. 3245: E. Suzuki, S. Arikawa (Eds.), Discovery Science. XIV, 430 pages. 2004.

Vol. 3244: S. Ben-David, J. Case, A. Maruoka (Eds.), Algorithmic Learning Theory. XIV, 505 pages. 2004.

Vol. 3238: S. Biundo, T. Frühwirth, G. Palm (Eds.), KI 2004: Advances in Artificial Intelligence. XI, 467 pages. 2004.

Vol. 3230: J.L. Vicedo, P. Martínez-Barco, R. Muñoz, M. Saiz Noeda (Eds.), Advances in Natural Language Processing. XII, 488 pages. 2004.

Vol. 3229: J.J. Alferes, J. Leite (Eds.), Logics in Artificial Intelligence. XIV, 744 pages. 2004.

Vol. 3215: M.G.. Negoita, R.J. Howlett, L.C. Jain (Eds.), Knowledge-Based Intelligent Information and Engineering Systems, Part III. LVII, 906 pages. 2004.

Vol. 3214: M.G.. Negoita, R.J. Howlett, L.C. Jain (Eds.), Knowledge-Based Intelligent Information and Engineering Systems, Part II. LVIII, 1302 pages. 2004.

Vol. 3213: M.G.. Negoita, R.J. Howlett, L.C. Jain (Eds.), Knowledge-Based Intelligent Information and Engineering Systems, Part I. LVIII, 1280 pages. 2004.

Vol. 3209: B. Berendt, A. Hotho, D. Mladenic, M. van Someren, M. Spiliopoulou, G. Stumme (Eds.), Web Mining: From Web to Semantic Web. IX, 201 pages. 2004.

Vol. 3206: P. Sojka, I. Kopecek, K. Pala (Eds.), Text, Speech and Dialogue. XIII, 667 pages. 2004.

Vol. 3202: J.-F. Boulicaut, F. Esposito, F. Giannotti, D. Pedreschi (Eds.), Knowledge Discovery in Databases: PKDD 2004. XIX, 560 pages. 2004.

Vol. 3201: J.-F. Boulicaut, F. Esposito, F. Giannotti, D. Pedreschi (Eds.), Machine Learning: ECML 2004. XVIII, 580 pages. 2004.

Vol. 3194: R. Camacho, R. King, A. Srinivasan (Eds.), Inductive Logic Programming. XI, 361 pages. 2004.

Vol. 3192: C. Bussler, D. Fensel (Eds.), Artificial Intelligence: Methodology, Systems, and Applications. XIII, 522 pages. 2004.

Vol. 3191: M. Klusch, S. Ossowski, V. Kashyap, R. Unland (Eds.), Cooperative Information Agents VIII. XI, 303 pages. 2004.

Vol. 3187: G. Lindemann, J. Denzinger, I.J. Timm, R. Unland (Eds.), Multiagent System Technologies. XIII, 341 pages. 2004.

Vol. 3176: O. Bousquet, U. von Luxburg, G. Rätsch (Eds.), Advanced Lectures on Machine Learning. IX, 241 pages. 2004.

Vol. 3171: A.L.C. Bazzan, S. Labidi (Eds.), Advances in Artificial Intelligence – SBIA 2004. XVII, 548 pages. 2004.

Vol. 3159: U. Visser, Intelligent Information Integration for the Semantic Web. XIV, 150 pages. 2004.

Vol. 3157: C. Zhang, H. W. Guesgen, W.K. Yeap (Eds.), PRICAI 2004: Trends in Artificial Intelligence. XX, 1023 pages. 2004.

Vol. 3155: P. Funk, P.A. González Calero (Eds.), Advances in Case-Based Reasoning. XIII, 822 pages. 2004.

Vol. 3139: F. Iida, R. Pfeifer, L. Steels, Y. Kuniyoshi (Eds.), Embodied Artificial Intelligence. IX, 331 pages. 2004.

Vol. 3131: V. Torra, Y. Narukawa (Eds.), Modeling Decisions for Artificial Intelligence. XI, 327 pages. 2004.

Vol. 3127: K.E. Wolff, H.D. Pfeiffer, H.S. Delugach (Eds.), Conceptual Structures at Work. XI, 403 pages. 2004.

Vol. 3123: A. Belz, R. Evans, P. Piwek (Eds.), Natural Language Generation. X, 219 pages. 2004.

Vol. 3120: J. Shawe-Taylor, Y. Singer (Eds.), Learning Theory. X, 648 pages. 2004.

Vol. 3097: D. Basin, M. Rusinowitch (Eds.), Automated Reasoning. XII, 493 pages. 2004.

Vol. 3071: A. Omicini, P. Petta, J. Pitt (Eds.), Engineering Societies in the Agents World. XIII, 409 pages. 2004.

Vol. 3070: L. Rutkowski, J. Siekmann, R. Tadeusiewicz, L.A. Zadeh (Eds.), Artificial Intelligence and Soft Computing - ICAISC 2004. XXV, 1208 pages. 2004.

Vol. 3068: E. André, L. Dybkjær, W. Minker, P. Heisterkamp (Eds.), Affective Dialogue Systems. XII, 324 pages. 2004.

Vol. 3067: M. Dastani, J. Dix, A. El Fallah-Seghrouchni (Eds.), Programming Multi-Agent Systems. X, 221 pages. 2004.

Vol. 3066: S. Tsumoto, R. Słowiński, J. Komorowski, J.W. Grzymała-Busse (Eds.), Rough Sets and Current Trends in Computing. XX, 853 pages. 2004.

Vol. 3065: A. Lomuscio, D. Nute (Eds.), Deontic Logic in Computer Science. X, 275 pages. 2004.

Vol. 3060: A.Y. Tawfik, S.D. Goodwin (Eds.), Advances in Artificial Intelligence. XIII, 582 pages. 2004.

Vol. 3056: H. Dai, R. Srikant, C. Zhang (Eds.), Advances in Knowledge Discovery and Data Mining. XIX, 713 pages. 2004.

Vol. 3055: H. Christiansen, M.-S. Hacid, T. Andreasen, H.L. Larsen (Eds.), Flexible Query Answering Systems. X, 500 pages. 2004.

Vol. 3048: P. Faratin, D.C. Parkes, J.A. Rodríguez-Aguilar, W.E. Walsh (Eds.), Agent-Mediated Electronic Commerce V. XI, 155 pages. 2004.

Vol. 3040: R. Conejo, M. Urretavizcaya, J.-L. Pérez-de-la-Cruz (Eds.), Current Topics in Artificial Intelligence. XIV, 689 pages. 2004.

Vol. 3035: M.A. Wimmer (Ed.), Knowledge Management in Electronic Government. XII, 326 pages. 2004.

Vol. 3034: J. Favela, E. Menasalvas, E. Chávez (Eds.), Advances in Web Intelligence. XIII, 227 pages. 2004.

Vol. 3030: P. Giorgini, B. Henderson-Sellers, M. Winikoff (Eds.), Agent-Oriented Information Systems. XIV, 207 pages. 2004.

Vol. 3029: B. Orchard, C. Yang, M. Ali (Eds.), Innovations in Applied Artificial Intelligence. XXI, 1272 pages. 2004.

Vol. 3025: G.A. Vouros, T. Panayiotopoulos (Eds.), Methods and Applications of Artificial Intelligence. XV, 546 pages. 2004.

Vol. 3020: D. Polani, B. Browning, A. Bonarini, K. Yoshida (Eds.), RoboCup 2003: Robot Soccer World Cup VII. XVI, 767 pages. 2004.

Vol. 3012: K. Kurumatani, S.-H. Chen, A. Ohuchi (Eds.), Multi-Agents for Mass User Support. X, 217 pages. 2004.

Vol. 3010: K.R. Apt, F. Fages, F. Rossi, P. Szeredi, J. Váncza (Eds.), Recent Advances in Constraints. VIII, 285 pages. 2004.

Vol. 2990: J. Leite, A. Omicini, L. Sterling, P. Torroni (Eds.), Declarative Agent Languages and Technologies. XII, 281 pages. 2004.

Vol. 2980: A. Blackwell, K. Marriott, A. Shimojima (Eds.), Diagrammatic Representation and Inference. XV, 448 pages. 2004.

Vol. 2977: G. Di Marzo Serugendo, A. Karageorgos, O.F. Rana, F. Zambonelli (Eds.), Engineering Self-Organising Systems. X, 299 pages. 2004.

Vol. 2972: R. Monroy, G. Arroyo-Figueroa, L.E. Sucar, H. Sossa (Eds.), MICAI 2004: Advances in Artificial Intelligence. XVII, 923 pages. 2004.

Vol. 2969: M. Nickles, M. Rovatsos, G. Weiss (Eds.), Agents and Computational Autonomy. X, 275 pages. 2004.

Vol. 2961: P. Eklund (Ed.), Concept Lattices. IX, 411 pages. 2004.

Vol. 2953: K. Konrad, Model Generation for Natural Language Interpretation and Analysis. XIII, 166 pages. 2004.

Vol. 2934: G. Lindemann, D. Moldt, M. Paolucci (Eds.), Regulated Agent-Based Social Systems. X, 301 pages. 2004.

Vol. 2930: F. Winkler (Ed.), Automated Deduction in Geometry. VII, 231 pages. 2004.

Vol. 2926: L. van Elst, V. Dignum, A. Abecker (Eds.), Agent-Mediated Knowledge Management. XI, 428 pages. 2004.

Vol. 2923: V. Lifschitz, I. Niemelä (Eds.), Logic Programming and Nonmonotonic Reasoning. IX, 365 pages. 2003.

Vol. 2915: A. Camurri, G. Volpe (Eds.), Gesture-Based Communication in Human-Computer Interaction. XIII, 558 pages. 2004.

Vol. 2913: T.M. Pinkston, V.K. Prasanna (Eds.), High Performance Computing - HiPC 2003. XX, 512 pages. 2003.

Vol. 2903: T.D. Gedeon, L.C.C. Fung (Eds.), AI 2003: Advances in Artificial Intelligence. XVI, 1075 pages. 2003.

Vol. 2902: F.M. Pires, S.P. Abreu (Eds.), Progress in Artificial Intelligence. XV, 504 pages. 2003.

Vol. 2892: F. Dau, The Logic System of Concept Graphs with Negation. XI, 213 pages. 2003.

Vol. 2891: J. Lee, M. Barley (Eds.), Intelligent Agents and Multi-Agent Systems. X, 215 pages. 2003.

Vol. 2882: D. Veit, Matchmaking in Electronic Markets. XV, 180 pages. 2003.

Vol. 2872: G. Moro, C. Sartori, M.P. Singh (Eds.), Agents and Peer-to-Peer Computing. XII, 205 pages. 2004.

Vol. 2871: N. Zhong, Z.W. Raś, S. Tsumoto, E. Suzuki (Eds.), Foundations of Intelligent Systems. XV, 697 pages. 2003.

Vol. 2854: J. Hoffmann, Utilizing Problem Structure in Planing. XIII, 251 pages. 2003.

Vol. 2843: G. Grieser, Y. Tanaka, A. Yamamoto (Eds.), Discovery Science. XII, 504 pages. 2003.

Vol. 2842: R. Gavaldá, K.P. Jantke, E. Takimoto (Eds.), Algorithmic Learning Theory. XI, 313 pages. 2003.

Vol. 2838: N. Lavrač, D. Gamberger, L. Todorovski, H. Blockeel (Eds.), Knowledge Discovery in Databases: PKDD 2003. XVI, 508 pages. 2003.

Vol. 2837: N. Lavrač, D. Gamberger, L. Todorovski, H. Blockeel (Eds.), Machine Learning: ECML 2003. XVI, 504 pages. 2003.

Vol. 2835: T. Horváth, A. Yamamoto (Eds.), Inductive Logic Programming. X, 401 pages. 2003.

Vol. 2821: A. Günter, R. Kruse, B. Neumann (Eds.), KI 2003: Advances in Artificial Intelligence. XII, 662 pages. 2003.

Vol. 2807: V. Matoušek, P. Mautner (Eds.), Text, Speech and Dialogue. XIII, 426 pages. 2003.